The ORIGINAL ENCYCLOPEDIA of COMIC BOOK HEROES

VOLUME THREE

featuring

SUPERMAN

The ORIGINAL
ENCYCLOPEDIA
of COMIC BOOK
HEROES

VOLUME THREE

featuring

SUPERMAN

by **Michael L. Fleisher**

assisted by Janet E. Lincoln

**SUPERMAN created by Jerry Siegel
and Joe Shuster**

To **PREAM**

DAN DIDIO Senior VP-Executive Editor BOB HARRAS Editor-collected edition ROBBIN BROSTERMAN Senior Art Director
PAUL LEVITZ President & Publisher GEORG BREWER VP-Design & DC Direct Creative RICHARD BRUNING Senior VP-Creative Director
PATRICK CALDON Executive VP-Finance & Operations CHRIS CARAMALIS VP-Finance JOHN CUNNINGHAM VP-Marketing
TERRI CUNNINGHAM VP-Managing Editor ALISON GILL VP-Manufacturing HANK KANALZ VP-General Manager, WildStorm
JIM LEE Editorial Director-WildStorm PAULA LOWITT Senior VP-Business & Legal Affairs
MARYELLEN MCLAUGHLIN VP-Advertising & Custom Publishing JOHN NEE VP-Business Development
GREGORY NOVECK Senior VP-Creative Affairs SUE POHJA VP-Book Trade Sales CHERYL RUBIN Senior VP-Brand Management
JEFF TROJAN VP-Business Development, DC Direct BOB WAYNE VP-Sales

THE ORIGINAL ENCYCLOPEDIA OF COMIC BOOK HEROES Volume Three—Featuring SUPERMAN
Published by DC Comics. Cover, introduction and compilation copyright © 2007 DC Comics. All Rights Reserved.
Originally published as *The Great Superman Book.* Copyright © 1978 Michael L. Fleisher.
All Rights Reserved. All illustrations copyright © DC Comics.
All characters, their distinctive likenesses and related elements featured in this publication are trademarks of DC Comics.
The stories, characters and incidents featured in this publication are entirely fictional. DC Comics does not read
or accept unsolicited submissions of ideas, stories or artwork.

DC Comics, 1700 Broadway, New York, NY 10019 A Warner Bros. Entertainment Company.
Printed in Canada. First Printing. ISBN: 1-4012-1389-8 ISBN 13: 978-1-4012-1389-3

INTRODUCTION

THIRTY-EIGHT YEARS HAVE PASSED since that historic day in 1969 when Gerda Gattel, DC Comics' dedicated archivist and librarian, ushered me and my research assistant, Janet Lincoln, into the medium-sized, one-room library, lined with floor-to-ceiling bookshelves, that served as the repository for bound volumes of the company's carefully preserved back issues, thousands upon thousands of them — two copies each of every single DC comic book ever published.

Janet and I spent five years in that library, making painstakingly detailed notes on every single Superman comic book story produced in the character's first twenty-six years of publication, beginning with the Man of Steel's debut in *Action Comics* No. 1 (June 1938), where he rescues Evelyn Curry, a young woman sentenced to death in the electric chair for a murder she did not commit; administers a well-deserved thrashing to an unidentified wife beater; rescues Lois Lane from a gang of hoodlums; and travels to Washington, D.C., for a confrontation with Alex Greer, "the slickest lobbyist in Washington." In a follow-up story in *Action Comics* No. 2 (July 1938), Greer turns out to be in cahoots with ruthless munitions magnate Emil Norvell in a scheme to maneuver the United States into becoming "embroiled with Europe" in the impending war with the Axis powers. Our *Superman Encyclopedia* coverage concludes with a June 1964 story in *World's Finest Comics* No. 142, in which a freak accident at the Superman Museum transforms caretaker Joe Meach into the Composite Superman.

The end result of our efforts was *The Encyclopedia of Comic Book Heroes Vol 3: The Great Superman Book*, which was published by Warner Books in 1978.

As all of us who haven't spent our lives huddling in caves now know, of course, Superman's comic-book stock has skyrocketed over the course of the last 69 years. Whereas, in the mid-1970s, you could have purchased a mint-condition *Action Comics* No. 1 for a paltry $4,000, today you'd have to pony up about $440,000 for a mint-condition copy — although a cheapie in merely very fine condition can be had for a bargain-basement $330,000! (Better buy several while supplies last.)

I wish I could report that copies of this Superman encyclopedia have appreciated in value that much in the past 29 years. They haven't. But they have become a lot scarcer and pricier than they used to be, with brand-new copies long since unavailable and used copies going for as high as $210 a pop on Amazon.com, fueled by ecstatically positive reader reviews in the 93% to 99% range. Let's face it! You're more likely to wake up tomorrow morning with super powers than to ever be able to afford one!

But — whew! — not anymore! The spankin' new DC Comics collectors' reprint edition you've just purchased has set you back a mere fraction of that, which is cause for celebration, don't you think, fellow Kal-El fans?

MICHAEL L. FLEISHER, July 2007

PREFACE

The Encyclopedia of Comic Book Heroes began as something of a lark, and ended as a labor of love.

In early 1969, I was working as a writer/editor for the Encyclopaedia Britannica, writing entries for an encyclopedia that the company intended to market overseas. One afternoon, as a humorous way of relieving the office tedium, one of the other writers composed a short biography of Clark Kent written in the same stuffy, pedantic style that characterized the biographies of real people in the encyclopedia we were working on. "KENT, CLARK," it began. "United States journalist who is secretly Superman...."

As the bogus entry made its way around the room, the editorial office exploded with laughter. People laughed because, by using a serious, pseudoscholarly style in connection with subject matter generally regarded as frivolous, the author had successfully satirized the pomposity of our encyclopedia.

But I saw the Clark Kent entry in a different light. Already keenly interested in popular culture, I saw it as treating the comic book mythos as other, more "respectable" bodies of mythic literature have traditionally been treated, as a serious intellectual subject. I also saw that entry as a means of escape from my deadly dull job at the Britannica.

"Hey! This is a terrific idea," I exclaimed aloud in the midst of the merriment. "Somebody should do a whole book of these."

That idea seemed so ridiculous eight years ago that everyone started laughing all over again, but I was already out of the room, down the corridor, slamming that Clark Kent article onto the office copy machine, beginning to dream up the thousands of other articles I would write to go along with it.

I should say here and now that I was neither a comic book fan nor a comic book collector. I had not so much as glanced sideways at a comic book since the wise old age of fourteen, when, in what seemed at the time a decision born of maturity and sound judgment, I had sold my entire collection to a junk lady on Third Avenue for a penny a magazine.

Nevertheless, that night in 1969, using the Xeroxed Clark Kent article as my inspiration and the classic comic book stories reprinted in Jules Feiffer's *The Great Comic Book Heroes* as source material, I hammered out a half dozen sample entries and a two-page proposal for a one-volume encyclopedia of the comics. The following afternoon, I showed it all to an acquaintance in publishing, and within four hours he had called me on the telephone to say that his people loved the idea and that we had ourselves a deal.

Only then, after the commitment to write the book had actually been made, did I even begin to ponder the problem of how I was going to gain access to the many old comics that would be necessary to my research. Fortunately for me, the major comic book publishers were all willing to give me access to their extensive files of back issues. Later, a network of fans and collectors would help me acquire the various issues published by companies now defunct.

So it is that, one morning in March 1969, I walked into the offices of National Periodical Publications, Inc., publishers of DC Comics, and was introduced to Gerda Gattel, National's librarian, now retired. Her ring of keys jangling, Mrs. Gattel led me down a carpeted executive corridor to the locked door of the DC Comics Library. She knew that I intended to write a serious reference guide to the literature of the great comic book heroes, and she was proud that her precious library was at last to be used for serious research, rather than merely by client businessmen seeking out action pictures of super-heroes to laminate onto T-shirts and beach blankets.

As she swung open the library door and flicked on the light, I remember that I gasped a little. The library was only a medium-sized room, but its walls were lined with floor-to-ceiling bookshelves packed with neatly bound volumes of back-issue comic books, thousands upon thousands of them, two copies each of every single comic book National Periodicals has ever published. I had never imagined there would be so many.

Mrs. Gattel noticed my surprise, and her eyes twinkled with the slightly mischievous pleasure of a fabulously wealthy connoisseur showing an astounded visitor through the exquisitely stocked wine cellar. "You said you wanted to study *all* the heroes," she smiled benignly, taking in the entire room with a sweeping gesture of her arm. "We have dozens of them. Where would you like to begin?"

I began with Batman and Wonder Woman, whose exploits are chronicled in Volumes 1 and 2 of this encyclopedia, and then I went on to Superman, transported, despite my adulthood and education, into a tantalizingly garish world of magic and enchantment which I thought I had left behind forever at age fourteen.

Few fictional characters of any kind have enjoyed the kind of hold over their readers that the great comic book heroes have exerted for nearly four decades. Their adventures are read by millions of young people in every state of the United States and in dozens of foreign countries. And Superman is the king and father of them all. No other character in the history of comic books has been published continuously for so long a period. More people have thrilled to he exploits of Superman than have ever heard of Hamlet or seen a play by Shakespeare. He is the most famous hero in American fiction.

Yet the adventures of Superman, and the vast popular literature of which they are a part, are already all but lost to us. Destroyed on a massive scale during the paper drives of the 1940s—"Save your scrap to beat the Jap!" admonished one of the popular patriotic slogans appearing in the margins of many comics—and hysterically assailed during the 1950s as a root cause of juvenile delinquency, comic books have been almost universally derided as trash by adults and cherished only by their children.

In the entire world, not one library, university, or public or private institution of any kind has taken the trouble to acquire and preserve a complete set of Superman's adventures for posterity. Nowhere in the world is there a single research facility where the complete adventures of even one major comic book hero have been safely preserved and made available for study. Reasonable people may debate the value of the comics as art or literature, but no one can deny that they constitute the most widely read body of children's literature in the history of the world. Perhaps one day, there will be sufficient serious interest in the comics to warrant their widespread distribution on microfilm to libraries and universities, but as of this writing that day seems a long way off.

The writing of this volume required that Janet Lincoln and I have access to a complete file of Superman's adventures. Such a file is available in only one place, the corporate library at National Periodical Publications, Inc., and it has been preserved there, along with complete files of the adventures of National's other comic book characters, partially through the foresight of the company's management, but mainly through the efforts of one determined woman.

At the time this project began, Gerda Gattel had been the guardian of the DC Comics archives for twelve years, and involved in comics for more than twenty. During the long years when the comics were regarded as garbage even by most of their creators, when comic books and comic book artwork were routinely destroyed and discarded by their publishers to eliminate the expense of storing them, she fought, and agitated, and cajoled to be allowed to maintain a real library at National, to be provided with bookshelves and storage space, and to be permitted to take occasional time off from her full-time job as the company proofreader in order to keep and maintain the library on her own.

Janet Lincoln and I spent seven full years working on *The Encyclopedia of Comic Book Heroes*. In that time, we examined more than 10,000 comic book stories and filled approximately 20,000 5″ × 8″ index cards with detailed notes on what we had read.

As the years passed, my original one-volume project expanded to encompass eight volumes, consuming in the process thirty-one reams of typing paper and producing, in the end, a completed typewritten manuscript of more than two million words. As the project grew in scope, my original publisher lost interest and eventually withdrew, and I am deeply grateful that Warner Books, Inc., has taken an interest in what, from a publishing standpoint, can only be regarded as a difficult and costly project.

The Great Superman Book, which you hold in your hands, is the third volume of the eight-volume "labor of love" that I spoke of in my opening sentence. Other encyclopedias dealing with literary material, such as encyclopedias of Greek mythology or English literature, are able to refer their readers to the literature itself, but, with the exception of the occasional Superman stories reprinted in hardcover volumes, or the Superman comics still surviving in valuable private collections—a copy of Action Comics No. 1, for example, the first comic book in which Superman ever appeared, currently brings a price of upwards of $4,000 on the collectors' market—the stories referred to in this volume are not available for examination.

For that reason, the material dealt with in this book has been covered in excruciating detail, retaining generous portions of the original dialogue and textual narrative and employing a style designed to present the material clearly while evoking what Jules Feiffer has termed the "florid pre-literacy" of the comics.

As you browse through the pages of this volume, renewing your acquaintance with such classic archetypes of comicdom as Lois Lane, Lex Luthor, and Perry White—and perhaps meeting for the first time such intriguing lesser lights as Adonis, "a loathsome being intent on robbery and pillage...whose face is born of hideous nightmare"—I hope you too find yourself transported into that world of magic and enchantment I spoke of earlier. And whether you're a serious student of sociology or popular culture—or just a stone Supermaniac with the smell of four-color ink in your nostrils and bits of cheap pulp paper floating like flotsam in your blood—I hope you have a real good time there.

New York City, 1977   Michael L. Fleisher

ACKNOWLEDGMENTS

The author would like to extend his heartfelt thanks to the management and staff of National Periodical Publications, Inc., publishers of DC Comics, without whose generous cooperation this volume could not have been written. In particular, the author would like to thank:

Sol Harrison, President, for his generous advice, assistance, and support throughout the project, particularly in connection with the accumulation and reproduction of illustrative material.

Carol Fein, Assistant to the Publisher, for the numerous kindnesses extended to the author and his assistant during the period of their research.

Jack Adler, Vice President-Production, for generously using his technical expertise to review the illustrations in this volume to ensure their suitability for reproduction.

Gerda Gattel, Librarian (ret.), whose devotion to the DC Comics Library, for sixteen years, made possible the research on which this encyclopedia is based. For this devotion, and for the many personal kindnesses extended to the author and his assistant during the period of their research, the author would like to extend his special thanks.

Joe Orlando, Managing Editor, for his advice and encouragement, and for his generosity in sharing many insights born of a lifetime in comics.

Joe Kubert, Editor, and Denny O'Neil, Editor, for their advice and encouragement.

Julius Schwartz, Editor, for generously sharing his many insights and anecdotes.

E. Nelson Bridwell, Associate Editor, for sharing with the author the broad reach of his knowledge.

Milton Snapinn, Head, Export Department, for his assistance in assembling the back-issue negatives used to produce many of the illustrations in this volume.

Lois Barker, Export Department, for her ready, affectionate wit, and for her assistance in assembling the back-issue negatives used to produce many of the illustrations in this volume.

Joe Letterese, Debra Ulrich, and Morris Waldinger, of the Production Department, for advising the author in connection with the retouching of the comic book illustrations reproduced in this volume.

The author would also like to extend his thanks to the following individuals, all of whom made significant contributions toward the preparation of this volume:

Neal Adams, Dick Giordano, and Frank McLaughlin, artists, and Mike Nolan, comic book fan, collector, and compiler of comic book indexes, for their encouragement and support, and for their help in putting the author in contact with other individuals who have made contributions toward the preparation of this volume.

Murphy Anderson, artist, for his encouragement and support, for giving generously of his time to retouch some of the comic book illustrations reproduced in this volume, for his generous loan of rare comic books from his personal collection, and for creating the original drawing of the author interviewing Superman reproduced in this volume.

Jerry and Jean Bails, scholars, comic book collectors, and publishers of *The Who's Who of American Comic Books* and other publications; Otto Binder, writer; and Mike Freidrich, writer and comic book publisher, for their encouragement and support.

Linda Brown, for her generous help in preparing for publication many of the comic book illustrations reproduced in this volume.

Mark Hanerfeld, comic book collector and former publisher of *The Comic Reader*; Don and Margaret Thompson, authors, comic book collectors, and publishers of *Newfangles* and other publications; and Marvin Wolfman, Editor, Magazine Management Company, Inc., Marvel Comics Group, for their encouragement and support, and for their generous loan of rare comic books from their personal collections.

Earl Hokens and Wayne Seelal, photographers, for giving generously of their time and technical knowhow to help photograph the comic book illustrations reproduced in this volume.

Carmine Infantino, formerly the Publisher of National Periodical Publications, Inc., for generously extending the hospitality of his organization to the author and his assistant throughout the seven-year-long period during which *The Encyclopedia of Comic Book Heroes* was being researched and written.

Bernard Kashdan, formerly Vice President-Business Manager of National Periodical Publications, Inc., for generously giving permission for the use of the comic book illustrations reproduced in this volume.

Mrs. Everett Larson, Acting Head, Reference Section, the Library of Congress, for giving unstintingly of her time to help the author and his assistant locate rare comic books in the library's archives.

Alan Light, publisher of *The Buyer's Guide for Comic Fandom* and other publications, for generously making space in *The Buyer's Guide* available to the author to help him in locating the owners of rare comic book materials necessary to his research.

William Morse, proprietor of the Adventure Bound Bookstore, and Phil Seuling, chairman of the New

ACKNOWLEDGEMENTS

York Comic Art Convention and proprietor of Phil Seuling's Comic Sales, for their generous loan of rare comic books from their respective inventories.

Byron Preiss, Byron Preiss Visual Publications, Inc., for his help in acquiring space in comic book fan publications in order to help the author locate owners of rare comic book materials.

Roy Thomas, Editor, Magazine Management Company, Inc., Marvel Comics Group, and Jean Thomas, for their advice, encouragement, and numerous personal kindnesses, including the generous loan of rare comic books from their personal collection.

Glynis Wein, Head, Coloring Department, Maga-zine Management Company, Inc., Marvel Comics Group, for advising the author in connection with the retouching of the comic book illustrations reproduced in this volume.

Len Wein, Editor, Magazine Management Company, Inc., Marvel Comics Group, and Dagne Crowley, for their generous loan of rare comic books from their personal collections.

Marc Weinberger, for his friendship, encouragement, advice, and unstinting support.

In addition, the author would like to acknowledge all of the gifted men and women who, by their work in the comics, have enriched the lives of all of us.

HOW TO USE THIS BOOK

The Great Superman Book is a comprehensive encyclopedic chronicle of the comic book adventures of Superman for the first twenty-eight years of his ongoing career. Comprised of well over 1,000 entries—assembled in a convenient A-Z format and ranging in length from a few short lines to more than 100 printed pages—it contains detailed accounts of more than 1,000 separate adventures. In addition, this encyclopedia contains 446 illustrations culled directly from the comics, including pictures of Superman, his friends and adversaries, and scenes and diagrams of such diverse places of interest as the Fortress of Solitude, the planet Krypton, and the bottle city of Kandor.

The entries in *The Great Superman Book* are based on detailed notes taken by the author and his assistant on each of the comic books containing Superman's adventures. The entries contain a wealth of detail on the plot of each adventure, the powers and equipment employed by Superman and his adversaries, the major themes and relationships that emerge from Superman's collected adventures, and on every other topic of interest to students of Superman. No reference work can serve as a substitute for its subject, but a conscientious effort has been made to organize and record within this volume data pertaining to every aspect of Superman's life and adventures.

In studying the comic books containing Superman's adventures and in writing the entries in this encyclopedia, the author and his assistant made use of no outside sources whatever. Only the direct, firsthand evidence of the comic books themselves was used. Accordingly, *The Great Superman Book* is a detailed reference guide only to the comic book adventures of Superman. No information has been recorded here concerning the appearance of Superman on radio and television, in cartoon and live-action movies, on the Broadway stage, or as a newspaper comic strip. Indeed, it is in comic books that the character originated, and there that he has achieved his greatest renown.

Over the years, Superman's unparalleled popularity has even rubbed off on members of his immediate comic book "family": his girl friend Lois Lane, his pal Jimmy Olsen, his cousin Supergirl, and his boyhood self, Superboy, have all, at one time or another, become headline characters in comic book series of their own. These spin-off series have not been chronicled here. To have done so would have produced a volume three or four times the size of this one and would have added little truly substantive to our appreciation of the Superman legend. Similarly, this book contains no information concerning either the literary and artistic genesis of the character or the literally dozens of writers and artists who have, since 1938, been creatively responsible for shaping Superman's destiny.

Definitions:

Throughout the encyclopedia, the word "text" is used to designate a single comic book story, and the word "texts" is used to designate two or more comic book stories, or, occasionally, as a synonym for "chronicles." The word "chronicles" is used to designate all the texts which, taken together, comprise the Superman legend. The word "chroniclers" is used to designate the artists and writers who have been collectively responsible for "recording" Superman's adventures for posterity.

In comic books, the thoughts and dialogue of the characters appear printed inside roughly ovular shapes called "word balloons." Other writing, usually narrative and frequently in the third person, appears at the opening of each story and above or below some of the pictures. In *The Great Superman Book*, these fragments of narrative writing, known as captions, are referred to as the "narrative text" or "textual narrative."

Treatment of Events:

In the writing of this encyclopedia, certain conventions were employed. Superman and all the other characters appearing in the chronicles were treated as though they were real people, and the adventures were treated as though they were actual historical events. The comic books containing the accounts of Superman's exploits were studied as though they were historical documents chronicling the lives and adventures of actual persons.

The legend of Superman is elaborate and complex. Individual comic book sources sometimes differ in recounting a given set of events, and sources can often be found to support conflicting sets of "facts." In cases where comic book sources were discrepant with regard to particular details of Superman's life and career, an effort was made to reconcile the discrepancies in light of the total data available. A fact attested to in several comic books was accorded more weight than a contradictory fact stated in only one comic book. A statement made in a comic book concerning a contemporary event in Superman's life was accorded more weight than a contradictory statement concerning that same event made years later in the form of a ecollection or flashback. Wherever strong support xists in the texts for opposing sets of facts, the vidence for both is examined in detail in this ncyclopedia.

Dating:

The events described in any given comic book were assumed to have taken place on the issue date of that comic book, except in those cases where the events were clearly described as past events or where internal textual evidence argued persuasively for a different dating, such as in the case of an adventure taking place at Christmastime in an issue dated February.

Most comic books bear issue dates of either a single month or a single season. A very few—such as the obscure New York World's Fair Comics series, of which only two issues were ever printed, one dated 1939, the other dated 1940—have been issued listing only the issue year. In the case of a comic book issued on a bimonthly basis, the issue is given a bimonthly dating, e.g., November-December 1957. When events are described in the encyclopedia as having occurred in a two-month period, e.g., in November-December 1957, it is because those events were recorded in a bimonthly comic book.

When an event is described as having taken place "in" a given month or season, it means that the event is described in the texts as taking place in the present, i.e., during the period of the issue date. When an event is described as having taken place "by" a particular month or season, it means that the event is described in the texts as having taken place in the past, prior to the period of the issue date.

If, for example, the arch-villain Lex Luthor is described as breaking jail *in* November-December 1957, it means that Luthor is shown or described as breaking jail in a comic book dated November-December 1957. If, on the other hand, Luthor is described as having broken jail *by* November-December 1957, it means that Luthor is shown or described, in a comic book dated November-December 1957, as having broken out of jail sometime in the recent past.

Characters with Dual Identities:

In the case of characters with dual identities—e.g., Clark Kent and Superman, or Linda Lee Danvers and Supergirl—actions and quotations are attributed in the encyclopedia to one identity or the other depending on which role the character is playing at the time he or she performs the action being described or recites the speech being quoted. Superman dressed in his super-hero costume is referred to as Superman. Superman dressed in his everyday attire is referred to as Clark Kent. Similarly, Supergirl dressed in her super-heroine costume is referred to as Supergirl. Supergirl dressed in her everyday attire is referred to as Linda Lee Danvers.

When Supergirl is described as saying something and Clark Kent as replying, it means that the text from which the dialogue is being quoted depicts a costumed Supergirl conversing with Clark Kent dressed in his everyday attire. When Supergirl is described as saying something and Superman as replying, it means that the text from which the dialogue is being quoted depicts a costumed Supergirl conversing with a costumed Superman.

The distinction is important. In the world of the chronicles, the fact that Clark Kent is Superman is a closely guarded secret. To their contemporaries, the journalist and the super-hero are two different persons. Accordingly, they are often referred to in this encyclopedia as though they were two different people. Superman is a member of the Justice League of America, for example, but Clark Kent is not. Clark Kent is on the staff of the *Daily Planet*, but Superman is not. Superman's headquarters is the Fortress of Solitude, somewhere in the Arctic; Clark Kent resides in an apartment house somewhere in Metropolis.

Entries:

The vast majority of the entries in *The Great Superman Book* are articles about persons, but there are also numerous entries on animals, extraterrestrial and extradimensional aliens, distant planets and alien dimensions, aliases, and a host of other subjects.

At approximately 100,000 words, the article on Superman is the longest and most exhaustive entry in the entire encyclopedia. It contains a complete account of Superman's origin, an exhaustive inventory of his super-powers and special equipment, a complete month-by-month chronology of the first twenty-eight years of his crime-fighting career, a comprehensive analysis of the major themes and relationships of the chronicles, and many other features.

As such, the Superman entry is the hub of this encyclopedia. By reading the month-by-month chronology (see SUPERMAN [section L 2, Developments] and then following up the various cross-references, the reader will eventually come upon every entry in the encyclopedia.

Any character appearing in two or more Superman stories has been accorded an entry of his own, as have all the famous historical personages—people such as George Washington and William Shakespeare—with whom Superman has formed associations during his numerous journeys into the past.

Characters appearing in only one Superman story have sometimes been accorded entries of their own and sometimes not, depending on their importance within the single story in which they appear, their significance within the overall Superman legend, and other factors.

In general, one character from each story—usually the villain, but not always—has been chosen to serve as the vehicle for summarizing the plot of the story.

The roles played by such subsidiary characters as Jimmy Olsen, Perry White, and Krypto the Superdog are summarized in their individual entries.

Titles:

The titles of individuals—e.g., Dr., Prof., Major, Count—are given in parentheses in the entry title after the individual's name, as indicated in the following examples:

ELLISON, THOMAS (Dr.)
RUNYAN, ADOLPHUS (Prof.)
RAMSEY, JONATHAN (Major)
D'ORT (Count)

Whether a title is spelled out (e.g., Doctor) or abbreviated (e.g., Dr.) depends on which form is employed most often in the actual text or texts in which the character appears.

In cases where a title reflects actual rank or status, or academic or professional standing, the entries have been inserted in alphabetical order in the encyclopedia under the last name of the individual, as in the four examples listed above.

Often, however, particularly in the case of villains, what would be a title in the case of an ordinary person is, in comic books, actually part of an individual's name. Here are two examples:

PROFESSOR MEMORY
MISTER SINISTER

In cases such as these, the entries have been inserted in alphabetical order in the encyclopedia under the individual's name *including* the title, as in the two examples listed above.

Professor Memory is not referred to as Professor, after all, because he has earned a Ph.D. Professor Memory is merely the stage name of a now-retired vaudevillian.

Similarly, in the case of Mister Sinister, Mister is not a title, but part of the villain's name. Sometimes an abbreviated title precedes a name, as in the cases of Mr. Gimmick and Mr. Wheels. In such cases, the entries have been inserted in alphabetical order in the encyclopedia as if the title had been fully spelled out, so that Mr. Gimmick (read as Mister Gimmick) follows the Miracle Twine Gang and Mr. Wheels (read as Mister Wheels) follows Mister Twister in the alphabetical ordering.

Extraterrestrial and Extradimensional Aliens:

Most extraterrestrial and extradimensional aliens in the comics have only one name (e.g., Klor, Lahla, Quex-Ul). Some, however, have both a first name and a last name (e.g., Halk Kar). In such cases, each entry has been alphabetized in the encyclopedia as though it were one long name (i.e., as Halk Kar) to avoid the unnecessary confusion that would result from reversing two strange names that are unearthly and unfamiliar.

Quotations:

The Great Superman Book contains numerous quotations from the comic book literature, some of them quite lengthy. With rare exceptions, the words in comic books are all lettered by hand, and all the lettering is done in capitals. Hand lettering makes possible a wide variety of letter sizes and styles not readily duplicated in mechanically set type. Because all-capital lettering is jarring and confusing outside the comic book context, the quotations in this volume have all been translated into the more familiar form of small letters and capitals. Great care has been taken, however, and a wide range of type styles employed, to ensure capturing the flavor of the original hand-lettering as well as the essence and spirit of the comic book style. In every case, the quotations in this volume were carefully transcribed by hand from the original comic books and then set into type in a manner calculated to re-create as closely as possible the style of the original.

Cross-References:

Cross-references are indicated by capitals and small capitals, as in the following example:

LIGHTNING-MAN. A mysterious super-hero, his true identity unknown, who appears in METROPOLIS in July-August 1957 and performs a series of mind-boggling super-feats during a period when the world's greatest crime-fighters—including SUPERMAN, BATMAN and ROBIN, the KNIGHT and the SQUIRE, the MUSKETEER, the LEGIONARY, and the GAUCHO—are gathered in the city to accept a valuable gift from "well-known philanthropist" John Mayhew, a lavish Club of Heroes which he has constructed to serve as their Metropolis headquarters.

The cross-references in the above example, the first paragraph of the entry on Lightning-Man, indicate the existence of separate articles, elsewhere in the encyclopedia, on Metropolis, Superman, Batman, Robin, the Knight, the Squire, the Musketeer, the Legionary, and the Gaucho. Since the duplication of information in the various articles of the encyclopedia has been kept to a minimum, the articles indicated by the cross-references invariably contain new information not available in the entry in which the cross-reference appears.

Textual References:

In order to relate the innumerable statements and quotations in this encyclopedia to their precise sources in the chronicles, a system of textual references was devised, relating every single fact in the encyclopedia to its source in the collected comic book adventures of Superman.

A textual reference consists of the title of a comic book series (e.g., Action Comics, Superman, World's Finest Comics); the issue number of a particular comic book in that series and the story number of the specific story being cited; the issue date, as stated on the comic book's indicia; the title of the story being cited, if it has a title; and, in cases where a story has been divided into parts or chapters, the titles of the individual parts or chapters where part or chapter titles exist.

For a complete listing of the abbreviations used in the textual references, consult the Table of Abbreviations at the end of this essay.

Textual references appear in the encyclopedia in parentheses, directly following the fact or group of facts they are intended to substantiate. The shorter entries in the encyclopedia generally contain only one textual reference apiece, indicating that all of the information in any one such entry derives from a single textual source. In the case of entries containing two or more textual references, however, each textual reference applies to the information in that article following the textual reference that directly precedes it.

The following is a typical textual reference:

(S No. 114/2, Jul '57: "The Man Who Discovered Superman's Identity")

The textual reference given above informs the reader that whatever quotation(s) or statement(s) preceded the reference can be found or substantiated in the Superman comic book series; issue number 114; the second Superman story in the issue; issue date July 1957; story title "The Man Who Discovered Superman's Identity."

Here is another example:

(WF No. 144, Sep '64: "The 1,001 Tricks of Clayface and Brainiac!" pts. I-II—no title; "The Helpless Partners!")

The textual reference given above informs the reader that whatever quotation(s) or statement(s) preceded the reference can be found or substantiated in the World's Finest Comics comic book series; issue number 144; the only story in the issue featuring Superman (indicated by the lack of story number); issue date September 1964; story title "The 1,001 Tricks of Clayface and Brainiac!"; the story is divided into two separate parts, the first of which has no title, the second of which is entitled "The Helpless Partners!"

In cases where a story lacks an overall title, the textual reference simply appears without one, as in the following examples:

(S No. 3/4, Win '40)
(WF No. 150, Jun '65: pts. I-II—"The Super-Gamble with Doom!"; "The Duel of the Super-Gamblers!")

In the cases of textual references pertaining to comic books containing more than one Superman story, a story number has been inserted in each textual reference—directly following the issue number and separated from it by a slash mark—to

indicate the precise position in the comic book of the story being referred to.

This system of story numbering applies only to fully illustrated Superman stories. It does not apply to stories without illustrations or to those featuring the logo of some other major character. Where a textual reference refers to a comic book containing only one Superman story, a story number would be superfluous and has therefore not been included.

A typical issue in the Action Comics series, for example, contains one story about Superman followed by one or more stories featuring other heroes or heroines. Textual references pertaining to comic books in the Action Comics series therefore contain no story number, for no issue of Action Comics has ever contained more than one story about Superman. Here is a typical textual reference to a comic book in the Action Comics series:

(Act No. 112, Sep '47: "The Cross-Country Chess Crimes!")

Wherever a textual reference fails to contain a story number, the comic book which it cites may be understood to contain only one Superman story.

In the case of the Superman series, however, a single issue may contain as many as four illustrated Superman stories, and the Superman stories are occasionally interspersed with other illustrated features that do not include Superman. Superman No. 28, for example, contains four illustrated stories, three of them Superman stories and the fourth, featuring an entirely different logo, a story initiating a new series of adventures starring "Lois Lane Girl Reporter." Since the story numbering system applies only to Superman stories, the story headlining Lois Lane is excluded from the system, and the three Superman stories in the issue are numbered consecutively from one to three, from the front of the comic book to the back. Here is a textual reference to one of the three Superman stories in Superman No. 28:

(S No. 28/3, May/Jun '44: "Stand-In for Hercules!")

This textual reference informs the reader that whatever quotation(s) or statement(s) preceded the reference can be found or substantiated in the Superman comic book series; issue number 28; the third Superman story in the issue; issue date May-June 1944; story title "Stand-In for Hercules!"

Whenever information normally included in a textual reference is stated beforehand in the body of an entry, that information is omitted from the textual reference, as in the following two examples:

The Domino is exposed and apprehended by Superman in March 1942 (Act No. 46: "The Devil's Playground").

Superman No. 20/2 describes Superman as a "champion of democracy" (Jan/Feb '43: "Destroyers from the Depths").

The following paragraph, taken from the article on the *Daily Planet*, illustrates the extensive use of textual references in the major entries of the encyclopedia:

The *Daily Planet* is headquartered in the Daily Planet Building (Act No. 36, May '41; and others), a large downtown skyscraper situated at the center of Planet Square, the so-called "crossroads of the world" (Act No. 77, Oct '44: "The Headline Hoax!"; and others). Owned, at least for a time, by Metropolis Millionaire EBENEEZER WALKER (Act No. 214, Mar '56: "Superman, Super-Destroyer"), the building features an electric news-sign encircling the topmost story (Act No. 229, Jun '57: "The Superman Satellite") and a "giant globe of the world"—encircled by a Saturnlike ring and by giant block letters spelling out the name *Daily Planet*—mounted on the roof (Act No. 272, Jan '61: "Superman's Rival, Mental Man!"; and others). Extending skyward from the Daily Planet Tower, at the summit of the building, is the broadcast antenna of WPLT, a radio station owned and operated by the *Daily Planet* (S No. 39/1, Mar/Apr '46: "The Big Superman Broadcast!"). Across the street from the Daily Planet Building is a small park, where a marble statue of SUPERMAN is unveiled in January-February 1946 (S No. 38/3: "The Man of Stone!"; and others).

Occasionally, a textual reference will be followed, within the parentheses, by the words "and others," as in the following example:

(Act No. 165, Feb '52: "The Man Who Conquered Superman!"; and others)

These added words indicate that evidence to substantiate whatever statement(s) preceded the reference can be found in the specific comic book issue cited, in this case Action Comics No. 165, and in at least two other comic books as well. When such a textual reference follows a direct quotation, it means that the quotation itself was taken from the comic book issue cited, but that data supporting the substance of the quotation is available in at least two other Superman texts as well.

Using the Encyclopedia:

If you already know the entry you wish to look up, simply turn to that entry in the appropriate alphabet-ical listing. If more than one listing is possible and you are uncertain which listing has been employed—if you are uncertain, for example, whether Professor Memory has been listed under Professor Memory or under Memory (Professor)—it is suggested that you try both.

If you have no specific entry title in mind but would like to consult a month-by-month chronology of Superman's crime-fighting career, such a chronology is available in the Superman article (*see* SUPERMAN [section L 2, Developments]).

Similarly, if you would like to learn what Superman was doing during a particular time period—during January 1956, for example—merely consult the career chronology for that particular time period and follow the cross-references to the various articles dealing with Superman's adventures during the month and year that interest you. This is what the career chronology has to say about Superman's activities in January 1956:

In January 1956 Superman matches wits with THORNE VARDEN (Act No. 212: "The Superman Calendar"); organizes the SUPERMAN STOCK COMPANY (S No. 102/1: "Superman for Sale"); outwits a band of aliens from the planet THURA (S No. 102/2: "The Midget Menace"); and thwarts a scheme concocted by SOAPY MARTIN (S No. 102/3: "The Million-Dollar Mistake").

Separate entries may be found in the encyclopedia for all four of the names cross-referenced.

In Conclusion:

The Great Superman Book has been designed for both the browser and the researcher, the casual fan and the serious collector. Great care has been taken to make it enjoyable as well as functional, entertaining as well as definitive. Whether you are engaged in scholarly research or reading for pleasure, writing a thesis or preparing a trivia quiz, *The Great Superman Book* will provide you with the information you seek and with many pleasurable hours as well.

ABBREVIATIONS

Titles of comic book series:

Act   *Action Comics*
Adv   *Adventure Comics*
AS   *All Star Comics*
BM   *Batman*
Det   *Detective Comics*
LC   *Limited Collectors' Edition*
LL   *Superman's Girl Friend Lois Lane*
NYWF   *New York World's Fair Comics*
S   *Superman*
SA   *Superman Annual*
SF   *The Superman Family*
WB   *World's Best Comics**
WF   *World's Finest Comics*

*Series was renamed World's Finest Comics beginning with issue #2

Months and seasons:

Jan   January
Feb   February
Mar   March
Apr   April
May   May
Jun   June
Jul   July
Aug   August
Sep   September
Oct   October
Nov   November
Dec   December

Spr   Spring
Sum   Summer
Fall   Fall
Win   Winter

Other abbreviations:

chs.   chapters
pts.   parts
No.   issue number

A

BDULLAH. The "crafty magician" of ancient aghdad who is the secret leader of the infamous ORTY THIEVES. Dispatched through the time barrier y PROFESSOR CARTER NICHOLS to the city of aghdad in the tenth century A.D., BATMAN and OBIN make the acquaintance of the legendary LLADDIN and, with SUPERMAN's help, recover the heritance which the naïve lad has foolishly traded the wily Abdullah in exchange for a worthless magic" lamp and clear him of the groundless charge hat he is one of the Forty Thieves. In addition, the hree crime-fighters foil an attempt by Abdullah and is cohorts to loot the shops of Baghdad, and ltimately apprehend the villains after Superman as chased him from the city (WF No. 79, Nov/Dec 55: "The Three Magicians of Bagdad!").

ACE, THE. The leader of a gang of smugglers whose apture by the METROPOLIS police in January-February 1950 comes as the culmination of an laborate ruse in which SUPERMAN pretends to have murdered CLARK KENT in a fit of jealousy over LOIS LANE so that the criminals, who know that Kent has learned the scheduled date of their next secret meeting, will allow the date and place of their rendezvous to remain unchanged in the belief that Kent is dead and their secret safe (S No. 62/2: "The People vs. Superman!").

ACHILLES. The alias employed by a modern-day criminal, one foot encased in a heavy lead box for the ostensible protection of his Achilles' heel, who establishes himself as the leader of a gang of METROPOLIS bank robbers by claiming to possess the near-invincibility of his ancient namesake—the result, he claims, of having been dipped, at infancy, in a fountain of "magic water" from the River Styx—and by demonstrating his apparent invulnerability to their tommy guns, knives, axes, and crowbars. In reality, however, Achilles is merely an ordinary criminal, and the lead box covering his foot merely the housing for "a powerful anti-magnetic device" capable of repelling "all metal objects," thereby rendering Achilles invulnerable to all metal weapons. Aided by members of the Metropolis Police Department, SUPERMAN apprehends Achilles and his cohorts in October 1961 (S No. 148/1: "The 20th Century Achilles!"). The story is in many respects similar to Superman No. 63/1 (Mar/Apr '50: "Achilles *versus* Superman!"). (*See* ACHILLES, JOHN.)

ACHILLES, JOHN. A self-proclaimed descendant of the legendary Achilles, his right foot encased in a thick steel box for the ostensible protection of his Achilles' heel, who establishes himself as the leader of METROPOLIS's most notorious criminals by claim-

ing to possess the near-invincibility of his ancient ancestor and by demonstrating his apparent invulnerability to their knives and guns. In reality, however, John Achilles is merely an archaeologist turned criminal, and the steel box covering his right foot merely the housing for an ingenious "magnetic repellor" whose powerful "magnetic field repels all metal missiles," thereby rendering Achilles invulnerable to all metal weapons. Cornered finally by SUPERMAN in March-April 1950, Achilles drowns when he leaps into a river and is dragged beneath the surface by the weight of the metal box attached to his foot (S No. 63/1: "Achilles *versus* Superman!").

ADONIS. A terrifying but tragic villain with a sickeningly "loathsome countenance" who matches wits with SUPERMAN in March 1942. The text describes him as "a loathsome being intent on robbery and pillage...a creature whose face is as horrible as his acts—a face born of hideous nightmare—a visage once seen, never forgotten." He is in reality James Trevor, a movie and matinee idol adored by millions until his flawless features began to fall prey to the deteriorating effects of advancing age, who has been transformed into a gruesome caricature of his former self and forced into a life of crime through the sinister machinations of a villainous plastic surgeon known as Dr. Menace.

Despondent and out of work since advancing age began "sabotaging [his] magnificent profile" and "women film fans [began] turning to newer and younger screen heroes," Trevor responds with enthusiasm in March 1943 when Dr. Menace visits his home and promises to restore "the face that caused millions of feminine hearts to beat quicker" through the miracle of plastic surgery.

The all-important operation is performed soon afterward, and Trevor exults when he finally removes the bandages and views the handsome, youthful face beneath them. Trevor's joy is short-lived, however, for the handsome face he sees before him is only a lifelike rubber mask, and when "the mask drops off—and...the vain actor sights the features beneath the mask reflected in the mirror, a scream like the shriek of an animal in pain leaves his startled lips...." Recoiling in abject horror, Trevor sees that the evil Dr. Menace has transformed him into a gruesome monster. Dr. Menace rubs his hands gloatingly:

> As you can guess, my real vocation is crime. I have placed a substance of my own discovery upon your face that transforms it hideously. Only I can remove it without injuring your features permanently.

Wearing the rubber mask, you will continue your

everyday existence, gaining access to the homes of your wealthy friends. But whenever I command, off comes the mask and you do my bidding as *ADONIS*. Obey me for one month, and at the close of your servitude I will actually give you the handsome features you desire.

And so, in the days that follow, Trevor—his "terrible face" concealed beneath his rubber mask—attends a series of lavish social gatherings at the homes of his wealthy movie-colony friends and, at an opportune moment, taking care not be be observed, doffs his mask and civilian clothing so that he can plunder the homes of his hosts as the hideous, loincloth-clad Adonis.

Overtaken finally by Superman while fleeing the scene of a robbery with a priceless Rembrandt painting, Adonis is shot from a place of concealment by Dr. Menace, who is determined to prevent Trevor from revealing their involvement in the recent wave of crimes. Adonis, however, now mortally wounded, sneaks up behind the unsuspecting Dr. Menace and, with his last remaining vestige of strength, strangles the surgeon who destroyed him before collapsing, dead, atop the surgeon's corpse (Act No. 58: "The Face of Adonis!").

ADORIA. A "distant planet" in "another solar system"—ruled by a king and queen and inhabited by strong, beautiful Amazon women and timid, bald-headed, diminutive men—which is the scene of SUPERMAN's marriage to PRINCESS JENA in July 1960 (Act No. 266: "The Captive of the Amazons").

AESOP, JOHNNY. The leader of a gang of criminals who commit a series of crimes based on Aesop's fables until they are finally apprehended by SUPERMAN in August 1944. When Superman learns that Aesop's history of criminal behavior began soon after a fall from a horse, however, he skillfully massages the base of Aesop's skull, thereby relieving the "pressure" that made him a criminal and transforming him back into the responsible citizen he was up to the time of his riding mishap (Act No. 75: "Aesop's Modern Fables").

AGAMEMNON. In Greek mythology, the king of Mycenae. He was the commander-in-chief of the Greek armies in the war to recover Helen, the wife of his brother Menelaus, from the Trojans. SUPERMAN meets Agamemnon, and helps him complete construction of the legendary Trojan horse, during a time-journey to ancient Greece that he makes in July-August 1948 (S No. 53/2: "The Oracle from Metropolis!").

AJAX. The former SUPERMAN robot who achieves his greatest fame as WONDER-MAN (S No. 163/1, Aug '63: "Wonder-Man, the New Hero of Metropolis!").

AKTHAR. The "evil adviser" to the good King Saffro—the ruler of an undersea kingdom located far beneath the surface of the sea—and the mastermind behind a sinister scheme to invade the land world by using the "great beam-forces" emitted by a special "tower" to send the ocean waters roaring down upon Earth's cities, so that he and his warriors can ride the mighty waves into the cities to carry out th campaign of conquest and destruction.

Alerted to Akthar's impending treachery by t red-haired Princess Kuella, King Saffro's love mermaid daughter, SUPERMAN demolishes the d bolical tower, thus forcing the inundating oce waters to recede from the cities, and then hands stunning defeat to Akthar and his band of unders warriors. Pursued relentlessly by Superman as flees desperately back toward the safety of t undersea city, the fanatical Akthar finally takes h own life, along with that of every last member of t undersea kingdom, when he deliberately detonates titanic explosion that obliterates the entire kingdo in a cataclysmic eruption of falling water (S No. 14/ Jan/Feb '42).

ALADDIN. The hero of the story "Aladdin and t Wonderful Lamp," one of the tales of the *Arabic Nights*. BATMAN, ROBIN, and SUPERMAN make t acquaintance of Aladdin during a time-journey tenth-century Baghdad (WF No. 79, Nov/Dec '5 "The Three Magicians of Bagdad!"). (*See* A DULLAH.)

ALCHEMIST, THE. An alias employed by SUPE MAN in June 1961 when, in collaboration wit BATMAN, he poses as the inventor of a magic elix guaranteed to protect anyone who drinks it fror bodily harm as part of an elaborate plan to persuad four gangland assassins, hired by the underworld destroy Batman, that their efforts to murder Batma must inevitably end in failure since Batman ha already drunk the magic elixir. Although the pla goes somewhat awry when one of the assassin discovers the Alchemist's true identity, Batman an Superman nevertheless succeed in apprehending th four assassins and in thwarting their attempts o Batman's life (BM No. 140/2: "The Charmed Life o Batman!").

ALLEN, JACK. The wily press agent for Miracl Movies who concocts an elaborate scheme designe to trick SUPERMAN into starring in an adventure film in the far north without realizing that he is being filmed. The situation becomes more complicated when "notorious racketeer" "Bushy" Barnes and his henchmen kidnap Allen's film crew and hold them for ransom, but Superman finally apprehends the gangsters and permits the release of Allen's adventure film, entitled *Superman in Valhalla*, on the condition that half its proceeds be earmarked for charity (S No. 52/3, May/Jun '48: "Superman in Valhalla!").

ALLERTON, CARLYLE. An alias employed by LEX LUTHOR in July-August 1942 when he poses as a "prominent authority on ancient stones and their mystic powers" as part of his scheme to obtain the "powerstone" (S No. 17/4: "When Titans Clash!").

ALLURA. *See* ALURA.

ALLURE, GLORIA. A beautiful blond movie star—spoiled, pampered, and egotistical—who visits the Pacific to entertain U.S. troops there, not out of genuine patriotism but as a gaudy publicity stunt,

nly to become transformed into a gung-ho patriot
nd a finer human being after she and her fellow
performers have been taken prisoner by Japanese
oldiers and rescued by SUPERMAN (S No. 36/2,
Sep/Oct '45: "Glory for Gloria!").

ALURA. The wife of the Kryptonian scientist ZOR-
EL and the mother of SUPERGIRL. Since Zor-El and
SUPERMAN's father, JOR-EL, were brothers, Alura—
also rendered Allura—is Superman's aunt. When the
planet KRYPTON exploded into fragments, Alura and
Zor-El—who had not yet married—and the other
inhabitants of ARGO CITY survived the death of their
planet when their entire city was hurled into space
intact by the force of the cataclysm. For years the
orphaned city drifted through space as life returned to
an uneasy normalcy for the Krypton survivors. Zor-
El and Alura became husband and wife, and in time a
blond baby girl, Kara, was born to the couple. Not
long after Kara had reached her teens, the entire
population of Argo City succumbed to deadly KRYP-
TONITE poisoning, but not before Zor-El had placed
his daughter in a space rocket and launched her
toward Earth, where she would acquire super-powers
and achieve worldwide fame as Supergirl. Alura and
Zor-El survived the death of Argo City by escaping
into the so-called Survival Zone, an alien dimension
from which Supergirl finally frees them in early 1964.
The couple now reside in the bottle city of KANDOR.

AMAZONIA. The home of a band of Amazon
warriors—inhabiting the impenetrable jungles of
South America, possibly within the borders of
Venezuela—who briefly acknowledge LOIS LANE as
their long-lost queen in July-August 1949, during a
period when Lois is helplessly in the grip of a strange
"hypnotic trance" induced by her wearing the so-
called "royal necklace of Amazonia" (S No. 59/1:
"Lois Lane—Queen of the Amazons!").

AMAZON ISLAND. The so-called "land without
men," a lonely island, situated thousands of miles
from METROPOLIS, which is the domain of the
Amazon tribe led by the scheming QUEEN ELSHA (Act
No. 235, Dec '57: "The Super-Prisoner of Amazon
Island").

AMAZONS. In Greek mythology, a race of female
warriors who inhabited the northern coast of Asia
Minor. They were ruled by a queen, and were
rigorously schooled in the arts of hunting and
warfare. Men were rigidly excluded from their civilization.

In the SUPERMAN chronicles, the term is used to
designate any one of several all-female societies
which Superman encounters in the course of his
career, including the warrior women of AMAZONIA, in
the jungles of South America (S No. 59/1, Jul/Aug
'49: "Lois Lane—Queen of the Amazons!"), and the
inhabitants of Amazon Island, ruled by QUEEN
ELSHA (Act No. 235, Dec '57: "The Super-Prisoner of
Amazon Island"). The term is also used to describe
the women of ADORIA, a "distant planet" in "another
solar system" which Superman visits in July 1960
(Act No. 266: "The Captive of the Amazons").

AMERY, JAY. A METROPOLIS "racket-leader" who,
along with a henchman, smuggles himself into the
SUPERMAN MUSEUM in an effort to steal some of the
"powerful weapons and instruments Superman has
taken away from criminal scientists." The criminals
are apprehended at the museum by SUPERMAN in
May 1957 (Act No. 228: "Superman's Super Skyscraper").

ANDREWS (Miss). An alias employed by LOIS
LANE in March-April 1943 when, after restyling her
hair and dyeing it blond, she obtains employment at
Lacey's Department Store in the hope of gathering
information on the mysterious thefts that have been
taking place there (S No. 21/3: "The Robber Knight").
(*See* GAUNTLET [SIR].)

ANDREWS, KAY. An alias employed by LOIS LANE
in November-December 1940 when she poses as a
wealthy socialite as part of a plan to apprehend the
Black Gang (S No. 7/4). (*See* PEEKER, PETER.)

ANDRIESSEN, STEFAN. "The greatest explorer
and adventurer of our times" and the founder of the
SUPERMAN MUSEUM, a man who has "scaled the
world's highest peaks, plummeted [sic] the greatest
depths of the seas, and penetrated the wildest
jungles" on Earth. When word leaks out in January
1952 that Andriessen "is embarking on a strange
secret adventure" involving the accumulation of
SUPERMAN trophies and memorabilia from some of
the most remote spots on Earth, Superman becomes
fearful that the world-famed adventurer is attempting to unravel the secret of his dual identity. In
reality, however, Andriessen's only motive is the
founding and dedication of a Superman Museum. "I
kept my plans secret," he explains later at a press
conference, "knowing that if they leaked out, others
might get the trophies and charge high prices for
them!" (Act No. 164: "Superman's Hall of Trophies!").

ANKSTER, P.R. An alias employed by the PRANK-
STER in November-December 1945 when he poses as a
so-called "professor of practical jokes" as part of his
scheme to rob the guests at a lavish dinner party
being given by prominent METROPOLIS practical joker
A. Alvin Arnold (S No. 37/2: "Pranks for Profit!").

ANKSTER, P.R. (Colonel). One of several aliases
employed by the PRANKSTER in November-December
1949 as part of his scheme to buy up all the radio time
on every radio station in METROPOLIS (S No. 61/1:
"The Prankster's Radio Program!").

ANNISTER (Mr.). The unscrupulous attorney for
elderly blind millionaire John Barnett, and the leader
of a gang of criminals who, unbeknownst to Barnett,
have been using his estate as the headquarters for a
hijacking racket involving the theft of gun shipments
en route from arms factories, for subsequent sale to
the underworld. By November 1943 Annister and his
henchmen have concocted an elaborate scheme to
bilk Barnett out of the $1,000,000 reward he has been
offering for the return of a long-lost grandson—and
ultimately, through inheritance, to seize control of
Barnett's entire estate—by passing off an orphaned
youngster, unrelated to Barnett, as Barnett's missing

grandson. SUPERMAN thwarts the scheme and apprehends the criminals, although the warm-hearted Barnett decides ultimately to adopt the bogus grandson anyway (Act No. 66: "The Boy Who Came Back!").

ANSON, RED. A fugitive criminal, hiding from SUPERMAN somewhere in METROPOLIS's waterfront district, who attempts to prevent Superman from using his X-ray vision to pinpoint the exact location of his hideout by planting explosive devices in nearby houses that are wired to explode when touched by the heat generated by Superman's X-ray vision. However, with the aid of special goggles that absorb the heat of his X-ray vision without impairing his customary ability to see through solid objects, Superman locates Anson's hideaway and takes him into custody in September 1955 (S No. 100/1: "The Toy Superman Contest").

ANTARA. The alias employed by a gangster named Knuckles when he poses as a survivor, like SUPERMAN, of the exploded planet KRYPTON—one of a group of such survivors, he claims, who are engaged in rebuilding Kryptonian civilization on the "distant planet" Rola—as part of an elaborate scheme to lure Superman into a KRYPTONITE deathtrap so that he and his henchmen can loot the Metropolis National Bank of $1,000,000 in cash. Knuckles and his cohorts are apprehended by Superman in October 1951 (Act No. 161: "Exit—Superman!").

ANTI-SUPERMAN CLUB, THE. A club in METROPOLIS organized by men who are resentful of their girl friends' infatuation with SUPERMAN. It takes some doing, but, after being summoned before the club members to hear an account of their grievances, Superman does finally succeed in putting an end to their girl friends' hero-worship and in reuniting them with the club members who are in love with them (S No. 71/2, Jul/Aug '51: "The Anti-Superman Club!").

ANTI-SUPERMAN GANG, THE. The name used to designate a single gang of criminals, or, more likely, several independent gangs, which match wits with SUPERMAN in the early 1960s.

In February 1960, after Superman has transported his FORTRESS OF SOLITUDE from its location in the Arctic to a site somewhere "on the outskirts of Metropolis" and has begun conducting guided tours through it for the benefit of charity, two members of the Anti-Superman Gang, posing as innocent tourists, enter the Fortress along with a crowd of sightseers and leave behind a diabolical chemical concoction formulated to emit "a deadly gas" which, in an hour's time, will "erupt into an atomic blast" and blow the Fortress of Solitude to kingdom come. The scheme is thwarted, however, by a pair of scientists in the bottle city of KANDOR, who witness the planting of the atomic explosive on their Kandorian monitor screen and relay the news to Superman by means of a special "super-sonic signal," thus enabling the Man of Steel to dispose of the deadly explosive—and apprehend the Anti-Superman

Gang—before any harm can come either to th Fortress itself or to the city of Kandor, which rests o a niche inside the Fortress (Act No. 261: "Superman Fortresses of Solitude!").

In May 1961 Superman thwarts an elabora scheme by respected "millionaire philanthropis JOHN KILEY, the secret leader of the Anti-Superma Gang, to unravel the secret of his dual identity (A No. 276: "The War Between Supergirl and th Supermen Emergency Squad!"). During this sam period, three members of the Anti-Superman Gan attempt to murder science-fiction writer Rock Stirlin with KRYPTONITE in the mistaken belief that Stirlin is secretly Superman, but they are quickly appre hended by Superman with some timely help fron writer Stirling (S No. 145/1, May '61: "The Secre Identity of Superman!"). (See OLSEN, JIMMY.)

In April 1962, at a charity rally for the Greate Metropolis Fund, Superman is presented with "special medallion" in the form of a giant-sizec pocket watch—emblazoned with the slogan "Time tc Give"—and agrees to wear the medallion around hi neck to help publicize the charity drive, unaware that two members of the Anti-Superman Gang, who have been paid $1,000,000 to assassinate Superman, have surreptitiously replaced the real medallion with one containing a tiny television transmitter in hopes of unearthing a clue to the secret of Superman's dual identity. The criminals ultimately discover that Superman is secretly Clark Kent and attempt to murder Kent with kryptonite, but the Man of Steel foils the attempt on his life; tricks the villains, through an elaborate ruse, into believing they have erred in identifying Clark Kent with Superman; and arranges for their capture by the METROPOLIS police (S No. 152/3: "The TV Trap for Superman!").

APPALACHIAN MOUNTAINS. A mountain range of eastern North America which extends from Newfoundland, Gaspé Peninsula, and New Brunswick in Canada some 1,200 miles southwestward to central Alabama. In September-October 1947, after LEX LUTHOR has focused his diabolical "heat ray" on the Atlantic Ocean and sent a torrent of boiling water sweeping toward METROPOLIS, SUPERMAN saves the city by uprooting the entire Appalachian mountain range and dropping it between Metropolis and the onrushing wall of water. Later, after the boiling waters have receded, Superman returns the mountains to their proper geographical location (S No. 48/1: "The Man Who Stole the Sun!").

APPLEGATE, RODNEY. A youngster who, for a time, becomes MR. MXYZPTLK's unwitting dupe in his plot to humiliate SUPERMAN, but who ultimately does a real favor for the Man of Steel by tricking Mr. Mxyzptlk into saying his name backwards and thus returning to his home dimension (Act No. 190, Mar '54: "The Boy Who Saved Superman!"). (See MXYZPTLK [MR.])

APPRECIATION, INCORPORATED. A company formed by the PRANKSTER in February 1943. Its ostensible purpose is to enable the Prankster "to write etters of appreciation to everyone I admire," but its real purpose is to enable the villain to gain entrée to the homes of the wealthy (Act No. 57: "Crime's Comedy King!").

AQUAMAN. A costumed super-hero, gifted with the power to make sea creatures obey his commands, who is the product of a union between a lighthouse keeper and a young woman of ATLANTIS.

In July 1960, after Clark Kent has been swallowed by a whale while on an expedition to photograph marine life for the DAILY PLANET, Aquaman rescues Kent from his predicament so that Kent will not be forced, by rescuing himself, to betray the fact that he is secretly SUPERMAN (S No. 138/3: "The Mermaid from Atlantis!").

In January 1961, at the request of Superman, Aquaman assumes the fictitious identity of MENTAL MAN as part of the Man of Steel's scheme to apprehend the "ACE" RUGGLES gang (Act No. 272: "Superman's Rival, Mental Man!").

In October 1961, after an overzealous agent for the Internal Revenue Service has declared Superman delinquent in his income taxes in the amount of $1,000,000,000, Aquaman scours the ocean for the world's biggest oyster as part of Superman's plan to accumulate part of the money by stimulating the oyster to produce the world's largest pearl (S No. 148/3: "Superman Owes a Billion Dollars!"). (*See* BRAND, RUPERT.)

In November 1963, when Clark Kent is in imminent danger of drowning after an encounter with red KRYPTONITE has temporarily robbed him of his superpowers, it is Aquaman who finds him and carries him to Atlantis, where "a new form of artificial respiration" is used to save Kent's life (S No. 165/2: "The Sweetheart Superman Forgot!"). (*See* SELWYN, SALLY.)

"ARCHER, THE." A ruthless extortionist, clad in a green archer's costume, who extorts money from wealthy victims and murders with his bow and arrow those who refuse to pay. He is in reality Quigley, a "famous big-game hunter" who began hunting people instead of animals because "I—I thought hunting human beings would prove more profitable!" The Archer is apprehended by SUPERMAN in November-December 1941 (S No. 13/2).

ARDORA. The lovely young woman with reddish-brown hair—a native of the planet LEXOR—who becomes the girl friend of LEX LUTHOR (S No. 168, Apr '64: pts. I-II—"Luthor--Super-Hero!"; "Lex Luthor, Daily Planet Editor!") and later his wife (Act No. 318, Nov '64: "The Death of Luthor!"). In one text, she is mistakenly referred to as Tharla (S No. 167, Feb '64: "The Team of Luthor and Brainiac!" pts. I-III—"The Deadly Duo!"; "The Downfall of Superman!"; "The Hour of Kandor's Vengeance!"). Like everyone on the planet Lexor, Ardora adores and idolizes Luthor.

Ardora first meets Luthor in February 1964, when he returns to Lexor—for the first time in four months—in the company of the space villain BRAINIAC, with whom he has forged a temporary alliance. As Luthor and Brainiac land on Lexor, "the one world in the universe where [Luthor is] considered a hero," a large throng turns out to greet them and a lovely brunette in a gold dress and matching tiara rushes up to Luthor and throws her arms around his neck. "...[L]ike everyone here, I idolize you," she exclaims. "Couldn't you stay with us?"

Ardora

For a moment, Luthor is tempted. "This girl," he muses silently, "...she thinks I'm fine, good...." Then, remembering his pact with Brainiac to destroy SUPERMAN, he replies, "No...I can't stay!"

Ardora leans over and kisses Luthor gently on the cheek. "She likes me for myself!" thinks Luthor. "Maybe...someday...I'll return here!"

Later, after the scheme to annihilate Superman has ended in failure, Luthor does return to Lexor, and Ardora rushes out to greet him, crying, "**Luthor**, our great hero has returned!" (S No. 167: "The Team of Luthor and Brainiac!" pts. I-III—"The Deadly Duo!"; "The Downfall of Superman!"; "The Hour of Kandor's Vengeance!"). (*See* LUTHOR, LEX.)

By April 1964 Ardora has become Luthor's constant companion on the planet Lexor. The text refers to her as "the girl who loves Luthor," and it is apparent that Luthor loves her also. His reason for adopting the alternate identity of the DEFENDER, in fact, is to prevent his enemies from striking back at him "by holding Ardora hostage!" When Superman, whom the Lexorians regard as "the greatest villain in the universe," arrives on the planet and attempts to hide in the LUTHOR MUSEUM, it is Ardora who discovers him there and runs screaming from the building to spread the alarm (S No. 168: pts. I-II— "Luthor--Super-Hero!"; "Lex Luthor, Daily Planet Editor!"). (*See* LUTHOR, LEX.)

In November 1964 Luthor escapes from prison on

Earth and returns to Lexor, riding through the capital city with Ardora by his side as the populace accords him "a hero's welcome." The following day the couple are married in a solemn ritual performed "according to the ancient nuptial ceremonies of Lexor" and settle down to enjoy their wedded bliss "in the palace a grateful people have built for their hero...." When Superman arrives on Lexor in search of Luthor, and Luthor is apparently accidentally killed in the ensuing battle, it is only Ardora's frantic pleas—"Even the evil **Superman** should have a legal trial...!" she cries—which prevent an angry Lexorian mob from lynching Superman on the spot, or from leaving him to perish in Lexor's perilous Living Lake, in which the Man of Steel has unwittingly taken refuge (Act No. 318: "The Death of Luthor!"). (*See* LUTHOR, LEX.)

When Superman is brought to trial on Lexor for the "murder" of Luthor, Ardora takes the witness stand to testify against him. However, when Luthor turns out not to have died after all, but merely to be in a "deathlike trance" induced by a "coma drug," Superman is pronounced not guilty and ordered banished from Lexor.

"There goes **Superman** back to Earth," remarks Luthor, his arm around Ardora, as they watch the Man of Steel rocket away from Lexor, "...he got the worst of it this time! But he'll never give up the struggle against me!"

"Don't think of him, dear!" replies Ardora fondly. "I want only to think of the wonderful fact that you...**my** hero, and **Lexor's** hero...are still with us!" (Act No. 319, Dec '64: "The Condemned Superman!"). (*See* LUTHOR, LEX.)

ARGO CITY. The birthplace of SUPERGIRL, a city of the planet KRYPTON which survived the death of its native planet when it was hurled into outer space, people and buildings alive and intact, by the force of the cataclysm that destroyed the planet. According to the early texts bearing on this subject, Argo City was "enclosed in a bubble of air" when the land chunk on which it was situated was hurled into space (S No. 150/1, Jan '62: "The One Minute of Doom!"; and others), but later texts, such as the Supergirl story in Action Comics No. 316, assert that the city was covered by an airtight plastic "weather dome" at the time of the disaster to accommodate the "atmospheric experiments" being conducted there by the scientist ZOR-EL (Sep '64: "Supergirl's Choice of Doom!"; and others). For more than fifteen years the people of Argo City survived on their tiny island in space, until finally the entire population succumbed to KRYPTON-ITE poisoning, leaving Supergirl and her parents—Zor-El and ALURA—the only survivors.

Early texts containing references to Supergirl's birthplace do not actually name it. According to the Supergirl story in Action Comics No. 252, "a large chunk of the planet"—containing an entire street of homes and all its inhabitants—was "hurled away intact" when Krypton exploded (May '59: "The Supergirl from Krypton!"), but subsequent texts

implied the survival of a somewhat larger land a[r] and named the orphaned metropolis Argo City (S N 150/1, Jan '62: "The One Minute of Doom!"; a others).

Supergirl recalls Argo City, 1963

Most of what is known concerning the fate of Arg City and its people is contained in the Supergirl stor in Action Comics No. 252. When the planet Krypto exploded into fragments and Argo City was cast int space, explains this text, the survivors of the calamit had high hopes of survival, since they had more tha sufficient air to breathe and a "food machine" t provide them with nourishment. Their optimism wa short-lived, however, for they soon discovered tha the ground beneath them had begun to radiate greenish glow due to the fact that the atomic chai reaction that had destroyed Krypton had converte their shattered planet into kryptonite, an elemen whose radiations were capable of poisoning an destroying them. Zor-El resolved the potentially fata dilemma by covering the ground with sheet lead thereby effectively shielding the deadly kryptonit radiations threatening the lives of the Argo City survivors.

For years Argo City drifted through space as life returned to an uneasy normalcy for its small bu[t] hardy population. Zor-El took a wife, named Alura, and in time a blond baby girl, Kara, was born to the couple. But a cruel fate was in store for the people of Argo City. For one day, after Zor-El's daughter had become a teen-ager, a swarm of meteors struck the city, smashing gaping holes in Zor-El's kryptonite-proof lead shield and releasing the deadly kryptonite radiation into the air. Within about a month virtually the entire population of Argo City had succumbed to kryptonite poisoning, but not before Zor-El had placed his teen-aged daughter inside a small rocket ship and launched her toward Earth, where she would acquire super-powers identical to Superman's and achieve worldwide renown as Supergirl (May '59: "The Supergirl from Krypton!").

For some time, it was believed that Zor-El and Alura had perished along with the rest of Argo City, ut it ultimately developed that the renowned scientist and his wife had survived the death of their city by escaping into the so-called Survival Zone, an alien dimension which Zor-El himself discovered, and from which Supergirl finally frees her parents in 1964. Zor-El and Alura now reside in KANDOR.

AR-VAL. A native of KANDOR, rated "highest in physical and mental abilities" of all the young men in the city and selected by SUPERMAN to serve as his replacement in the event of his own death or disability, who indeed becomes Superman's replacement, the so-called "new Superman," in October 1964, after Superman has been deprived of his mighty super-powers by the baleful radiations of a mysterious green comet. As the new Superman, Ar-Val is egotistical, overbearing, and hungry for adulation, but ultimately he does apprehend LEX LUTHOR and BRAINIAC and, filled with remorse over his recent shabby behavior, he sacrifices his life to restore Superman to his former powers (S No. 172: pts. I-III—"The New Superman!"; "Clark Kent—Former Superman!"; "The Struggle of the Two Supermen!").

ARVIN, ANDREW. The newly installed owner of the Orchid Cosmetics Co., and the secret leader of a gang of criminals who make a series of attempts on the lives of glamorous cover girls in an attempt to silence the unknown model whom Arvin knows overheard him "discussing some of his crooked activities with a confederate" at the recent Models' Masquerade Ball. Arvin and his henchmen are apprehended by SUPERMAN in April 1951 (Act No. 155: "The Cover Girl Mystery!").

ATKINS. The co-owner, with a man named Bork, of the Atkins and Bork Curio Shop in GOTHAM CITY. In August 1959, with the aid of a map sold to them by a dying criminal, Atkins and Bork set out to recover four objects once owned by an ancient sorcerer and possessed of miraculous powers—a green box containing a fire-breathing dragon; a "magic prism" which "distorts light and deflects energy"; a "sorcerer's glove" which has the power to "dissolve inert matter"; and a "sorcerer's mantle" which renders invisible anyone who wears it—with the apparent intention of using the objects' awesome powers for evil. Ultimately, BATMAN, ROBIN, and SUPERMAN defeat Atkins and Bork and recover the four objects, whereupon Superman hurls the objects into the air with such incredible velocity that the friction created by their passage through the atmosphere is certain to destroy them (WF No. 103: "The Secret of the Sorcerer's Treasure!").

ATLANTIS. A legendary island in the Atlantic Ocean which, according to Plato, was the site of a powerful kingdom more than 11,000 years ago before it sank to the bottom of the sea. In the SUPERMAN chronicles, Atlantis is described as a sunken city, kingdom, or continent nestled on or beneath the floor of the Atlantic Ocean, and is inconsistently portrayed either as the site of a thriving undersea civilization or as that of an extinct civilization whose inhabitants—variously referred to as Atlanteans (WF No. 29, Jul/Aug '47: "The Books That Couldn't Be Bound!"; and others), Atlantides (S No. 139/1, Aug '60: "The New Life of Super-Merman!"; and others), and Atlantites (Act No. 285, Feb '62: "The World's Greatest Heroine!")—have long since perished.

In Superman No. 67/2, Atlantis is portrayed as the site of a thriving glass-domed subsea kingdom—characterized by "fabulous streets" and "glittering towers"—located beneath the floor of the Atlantic Ocean "forty fathoms below the [ocean] surface...." Populated largely by handsome, muscular men who make even Superman seem "ordinary," the undersea realm is ruled by the lovely QUEEN PARALEA (Nov/Dec '50: "The City Under the Sea!").

Sunken Atlantis, as it is described in Action Comics No. 230, is apparently no longer inhabited. According to Superman, "Strange experiments, conducted centuries ago on Atlantis, imparted an incredible quality to that land...the ability to give super-powers, exactly like mine, to anyone subjected to its radiance!" This phenomenon produces grave problems for Superman when an "underwater earthquake [forces] a fragment of the old island of Atlantis to rise from the sea bottom" (see WELLINS, BART) (Jul '57: "Superman Loses His Powers"). In Superman No. 122/1, Atlantis is described as the home of an extinct super-scientific race whose members were only six inches tall (Jul '58: "The Secret of the Space Souvenirs").

In Superman No. 129/3 (May '59: "The Girl in Superman's Past!"), however, and in more than a score of other texts (S No. 135/2, Feb '60: "Superman's Mermaid Sweetheart!"; and others), Atlantis is portrayed as the home of a "race of mermen and mermaids" (S No. 129/3, May '59: "The Girl in Superman's Past!")—collectively referred to as "merpeople" (S No. 156, Oct '62: "The Last Days of Superman!" pts. I-III—"Superman's Death Sentence!"; "The Super-Comrades of All Time!"; "Superman's Last Day of Life!")—who inhabit a thriving "sub-sea kingdom" (Act No. 300, May '63: "Superman Under the Red Sun!"; and others) nestled on the floor of the Atlantic Ocean (S No. 157/2, Nov '62: "The Super-Genie of Metropolis!"; and others).

The citizens of Atlantis include LORI LEMARIS, her husband RONAL and younger sister Lenora Lemaris, and the merman Jerro, who "adores SUPERGIRL (Act No. 285, Feb '62: "The World's Greatest Heroine!").

According to Superman No. 129/3, the mer-people of Atlantis—who have the tails of fish and the heads and torsos of human beings—were ordinary humans in the days when ancient Atlantis existed on the surface of the Atlantic Ocean. When Atlantean scientists discovered that their island was sinking into the sea, they erected a glass dome to keep out the ocean and enable their civilization to survive beneath the ocean surface. "Then, one day," Lori Lemaris once explained to Superman, "our scientists found a way to convert us into a race of mermen and mermaids--and so we truly became a new race under the sea!" (May '59: "The Girl in Superman's Past!"). A later text ascribes this miracle of biological conversion to Atlantean scientist Nar Lemaris, an ancestor of Lori Lemaris (S No. 154/2, Jul '62: "Krypton's First Superman!").

As soon as the biological transformation had been completed, the Atlanteans smashed the glass dome surrounding their city and began life anew as true sea dwellers. An Atlantean sea-person is physically capable of surviving out of water, but "... to remain in perfect health, [his] body must be immersed in salt water at least ten hours a day ...!" Walking on land is, of course, impossible for a fish-tailed Atlantean, which is why Lori Lemaris has customarily employed a wheelchair during her brief sojourns in the surface world, concealing her mermaid tail beneath a blanket so as not to arouse undue attention (S No. 129/3, May '59: "The Girl in Superman's Past!"; see also S No. 135/2, Feb '60: "Superman's Mermaid Sweetheart!").

Because it is impossible to speak underwater, the "sea-people" of Atlantis have mastered the art of reading minds and of communicating telepathically (S No. 129/3, May '59: "The Girl in Superman's Past!"; and others). They can perform these feats over very long distances, thus enabling Lori Lemaris to read Superman's thoughts (S No. 135/2, Feb '60: "Superman's Mermaid Sweetheart!") or summon him by telepathy (S No. 146/2, Jul '61: "Superman's Greatest Feats!") even while she is in Atlantis and he is in METROPOLIS, a great distance away. It was by reading Clark Kent's mind that Lori first discovered that Clark Kent is Superman (S No. 129/3, May '59: "The Girl in Superman's Past!"), and, since all Atlanteans can perform this feat, it is possible that every Atlantean is privy to Superman's secret identity. Lori Lemaris also possesses the power to make sea creatures obey her telepathic commands (S No. 154/1, Jul '62: "The Underwater Pranks of Mr. Mxyzptlk!"; and others).

In addition to being the custodians of an "ancient wisdom" long lost to the people of the surface world (S No. 154/2, Jul '62: "Krypton's First Superman!"), the mer-people of Atlantis are a race characterized by extraordinary scientific achievements: special "Earth monitors" enable them to observe events in the surface world (Act No. 312, May '64: "King Superman versus Clark Kent, Metallo"; and others), and an arsenal of super-scientific weaponry safeguards their civilization against attack (S No. 158, Jan '63: "Superman in Kandor" pts. I-III—"Invasion of the Mystery Super-Men!"; "The Dynamic Duo of Kandor!"; "The City of Super-People!"). According to Superman No. 154/2, a highly advanced "chemical plant reduces the amount of salt in the water so that the Atlantides--who once had bodies like surface-world people before Atlantide scientist Nar Lemaris transformed them into mermen and mermaids--can continue to survive in these oceanic depths!" (Jul '62: "Krypton's First Superman!").

At the undersea Temple of Ilena, Lori Lemaris and the other Atlantean mermaids gather to worship "their mermaid-goddess," whose shrine consists of gigantic statue of a mermaid reclining atop a seash and holding aloft, in her right hand, a torch who crimson "flame" is composed of some sort of glowir mineral substance (S No. 154/2, Jul '62: "Krypton First Superman!"). Atlanteans marry as surfac people do, but in the event a mermaid becomes widow, she must make a brief pilgrimage to Hear break Rock—a craggy rock jutting above the surfac of the ocean—a week following her husband's deat to wish for renewed happiness (S No. 139/1, Aug '6 "The New Life of Super-Merman!").

Although one text clearly suggests the primacy o "the elders" in Atlantean life (S No. 135/2, Feb '6 "Superman's Mermaid Sweetheart!") and severa portray Lori Lemaris as an ordinary Atlantea citizen (S No. 129/3, May '59: "The Girl in Supe man's Past!"; and others), a number of later text refer to Atlantis as a "kingdom" and to Lori as it "queen" (S No. 156, Oct '62: "The Last Days o Superman!" pts. I-III—"Superman's Death Sen tence!"; "The Super-Comrades of All Time!"; "Super man's Last Day of Life!") or "ruler" (S No. 154/1, Ju '62: "The Underwater Pranks of Mr. Mxyzptlk!"; Ac No. 300, May '63: "Superman Under the Red Sun!")

In addition to making occasional visits there Superman keeps track of events in Atlantis by mean of the "Atlantis monitor" in his FORTRESS O SOLITUDE (Act No. 310, Mar '64: "Secret of Kryptonit Six!"). Once every hundred years, according t Superman No. 129/3, an Atlantean is chosen to visi the surface world "to learn of the surface people' progress" during the preceding century. It was whil making one of these visits that Lori Lemaris attended METROPOLIS UNIVERSITY during the period when Clark Kent was a senior there (May '59: "The Girl in Superman's Past!").

AQUAMAN, the costumed super-hero who is the product of a union between a lighthouse keeper and a young Atlantean woman, has, over the years, occasionally resided in Atlantis and even served as its ruler. The inhabitants of Aquaman's Atlantis, however, are completely humanoid in appearance, and the evidence of the chronicles, taken as a whole, strongly suggests that the Atlantis where Aquaman has lived and ruled is a different place entirely, or else a separate region or city of the same undersea continent.

In July-August 1947 Superman journeys to sunken Atlantis in order to obtain "an insoluble synthetic invented by the Atlanteans" for use as bookbinding material by BARNEY VELLUM (WF No. 29: "The Books That Couldn't Be Bound!").

In November-December 1950 Superman has an adventure in the Atlantean realm of QUEEN PARALEA (S No. 67/2: "The City Under the Sea!").

In July 1957, after an "underwater earthquake [has] forced a fragment of the old island of Atlantis to rise from the sea bottom," Superman finds himself confronted with a dual dilemma: exposure to the Atlantis fragment has temporarily endowed unscrupulous seaman BART WELLINS with super-powers, and, in addition, has temporarily multiplied Superman's own powers "a thousandfold," to the point where Superman cannot even control them (Act No. 230: "Superman Loses His Powers").

By November 1957 Clark Kent's eyeglasses have become contaminated by a bizarre somnabulism-inducing radiation emitted by a relic recovered from sunken Atlantis, with the result that, for a time, Superman becomes a sleepwalker while in his Clark Kent identity and, as Superman, suffers complete amnesia concerning the thoughts and actions of his alter ego Clark Kent (S No. 117/1: "Clark Kent, Man of Mystery").

In July 1958 Superman journeys to the ru'ns of sunken Atlantis to obtain a "flying-saucer ship" made of pure gold, one of a series of so-called "space trophies" which the Man of Steel gathers for inclusion in a time capsule which the Metropolis Museum plans to bury in the ground as a gift for the people of the fiftieth century A.D. (S No. 122/1: "The Secret of the Space Souvenirs").

In May 1959 Clark Kent recalls his senior year at Metropolis University and his first meeting with the Atlantean mermaid LORI LEMARIS (S No. 129/3: "The Girl in Superman's Past!").

In February 1960 Superman has a loving reunion with LORI LEMARIS and visits the Atlantis inhabited by Lori and her fellow mer-people for the first time in the chronicles (S No. 135/2: "Superman's Mermaid Sweetheart!").

In July 1960, over the objections of her husband Ronal, Lori Lemaris sets in motion an elaborate and somewhat foolish scheme designed to trick Superman into proposing marriage to LOIS LANE (S No. 138/3: "The Mermaid from Atlantis!") (See LEMARIS, LORI.)

In August 1960 Superman sets in motion an elaborate charade designed to make Lois Lane believe that he has decided to marry Lori Lemaris and live in Atlantis so that Lois will feel free to accept the proposal of marriage made to her by BRETT RAND (S No. 139/1: "The New Life of Super-Merman!").

In July 1961, in response to an urgent telepathic summons from Lori Lemaris, Superman races to Atlantis to rescue the sunken kingdom from being destroyed by "a new super-atomic, underwater depth-bomb" being tested in the area by the U.S. Navy (S No. 146/2: "Superman's Greatest Feats!").

In October 1961 Lori Lemaris indicates that she and her fellow Atlanteans intend to use a hoard of gold from a sunken Spanish treasure ship to fashion solid gold statues of JOR-EL and LARA as a surprise gift for Superman in gratitude for his past efforts in aiding Atlantis's mer-people (S No. 148/3: "Superman Owes a Billion Dollars!").

In February 1962, when Superman proudly announces SUPERGIRL's existence to the world, the citizens of Atlantis commemorate the occasion by unveiling a gigantic undersea statue of a mermaid Supergirl (Act No. 285: "The World's Greatest Heroine!").

In July 1962, during a period when Superman is periodically seized by an overpowering compulsion to commit evil acts, the Man of Steel demolishes the shrine of Atlantis's mermaid-goddess and is on the verge of annihilating the mer-people by destroying the vital chemical plant that regulates the amount of salt in their undersea environment when Supergirl, summoned to Atlantis by a desperate telepathic call from Lori Lemaris, arrives on the scene to repair the chemical plant and prevent Superman from wreaking further destruction (S No. 154/2: "Krypton's First Superman!"). (See MAG-EN.)

In October 1962, when Superman is believed to be dying of an incurable malady, Lori Lemaris and the mer-people of Atlantis join forces with KRYPTO THE SUPERDOG, SUPERGIRL, and the SUPERMEN EMERGENCY SQUAD to carry out one of the gigantic super-tasks that Superman hopes to fulfill as his final legacy to humanity, viz., the injection of a colossal sea monster—which has been growing to ever more titanic size due to the stimulation of undersea radioactivity—with a special "shrinking formula" so that it will not one day become so terrifyingly gargantuan that it menaces the safety of the Earth (S No. 156: "The Last Days of Superman!" pts. I-III—"Superman's Death Sentence!"; "The Super-Comrades of All Time!"; "Superman's Last Day of Life!").

In November 1962 Lori Lemaris and her fellow Atlanteans help Superman locate and recover a space capsule that has recently fallen into the Atlantic. The recovery of the lost space capsule is one of the stunts that Superman performs while posing as the genie of ALADDIN's magic lamp as part of his scheme to apprehend a notorious "international spy" (S No. 157/2: "The Super-Genie of Metropolis!"). (See VON SCHULTZ [PROFESSOR].)

In December 1962, during a period when Superman is suffering occasional bouts of mental instability inflicted on him by members of the SUPERMAN REVENGE SQUAD, the Man of Steel maliciously gives the MOON a super-powered shove which, in addition to causing massive tidal waves on Earth, produces devastating tides on the ocean floor and wreaks disaster in the undersea realm of Atlantis. Once the insane episode is past, however, Superman restores the moon to its proper location in space and repairs the damage to Atlantis caused by the temporary dislocation (Act No. 295: "Superman Goes Wild!").

In November 1963, when Clark Kent has lost consciousness and almost drowned after an encounter with red KRYPTONITE has temporarily robbed him of his super-powers, it is the Atlanteans who revive him with "a new form of artificial respiration" after Aquaman has found him and brought him to Atlantis (S No. 165/2: "The Sweetheart Superman Forgot!"). (See SELWYN, SALLY.)

In March 1964 the mer-people of Atlantis are menaced by a "deadly spotted plague" which threatens to decimate their entire population, but the plague victims are ultimately cured by means of a rare "spore antidote" native to KRYPTON's SCARLET JUNGLE (Act No. 310: "Secret of Kryptonite Six!"). (*See* JAX-UR.)

In the spring of 1964, after exposure to red kryptonite has temporarily transformed Superman into two completely different people, a super-powered Superman and a non-super Clark Kent (Act No. 311, Apr '64: "Superman, King of Earth!"), and Kent has been mortally wounded by a policeman's bullet, it is "the skilled surgeons of Atlantis" who perform the "delicate operation" necessary to save Kent's life (Act No. 312, May '64: "King Superman versus Clark Kent, Metallo").

ATLAS CLUB, INC. A METROPOLIS strong men's club which is open to anyone who can pass the demanding tests of strength—such as bending an iron bar—required for membership. In September-October 1952 a gang of criminals, convinced that one of the club members must secretly be SUPERMAN, begins trying systematically to murder them all to determine which of them is invulnerable, but Superman thwarts all the attempts and takes the villains into custody (S No. 78/2: "The Strong Man Club!").

ATOM-MASTER, THE. A renegade scientist—also referred to as the Illusion-Master—who is defeated in May 1959 through the heroic efforts of BATMAN, ROBIN, and SUPERMAN (WF No. 101: "The Menace of the Atom-Master!").

ATWILL, CYRUS. "The meanest man in town," a "cruel junkman" of the mid-nineteenth century who takes fiendish delight in inflicting cruelties on defenseless animals until Superman and four members of the LEGION OF SUPER-PETS—BEPPO THE SUPER-MONKEY, COMET THE SUPER-HORSE, KRYPTO

The Atom-Master

THE SUPERDOG, and STREAKY THE SUPER-CAT—soar through the time barrier to the year 1866 to teach the hard-hearted Atwill a richly deserved lesson in kindness to animals (S No. 176/1, Apr '65: "The Revenge of the Super-Pets!").

AUTOMS. The robot inhabitants of the planet ROXAR (Act No. 292, Sep '62: "When Superman Defended His Arch-Enemy!"; Act No. 294, Nov '62: "The Kryptonite Killer!").

B

BABSON, ED. A deranged actor—once renowned as "the movies' greatest gangster" but in recent years the victim of "a mental breakdown because he couldn't get a movie role," a breakdown that has left him scarred with the delusion that he is the gangster "Little Napoleon," whose role he created for the screen—who abducts CLARK KENT and LOIS LANE at gunpoint in November 1964, in the lunatic belief that Kent is John Dillinger and Lois Lane is his gun moll, with the intention of using them as his accomplices in "the heist of the century." SUPERMAN ultimately cures Babson of his mental disorder with the aid of some Kandorian psychiatric equipment (*see* KANDOR), then helps the actor stage a comeback by finding him a role on television (S No. 173/1: "The 'Untouchable' Clark Kent!").

BABY-FACE. A hoodlum in the employ of "THE THINKER" who is a perfect look-alike for JIMMY OLSEN (S No. 93/2, Nov '54: "Jimmy Olsen's Double!").

BAEZA, MANUEL. A citizen of the "tiny South American republic" of El Salmado who, except for his bald head, is an almost perfect look-alike for SUPERMAN. Superman gets Baeza to impersonate CLARK KENT for a short time in order to protect the secret of his dual identity from the evil GENERAL PEDRO VALDEZ (Act No. 306, Nov '63: "The Great Superman Impersonation!").

BAIRD, BLACKY. A "notorious criminal" who attempts to lure SUPERMAN to his doom in a KRYPTONITE deathtrap only to be apprehended soon afterward through the combined efforts of Superman and JIMMY OLSEN. The pursuit of Baird is complicated by the fact that, during the twelve-hour period during which this adventure takes place, Superman's personality is imprisoned in the body of Olsen, and vice versa, as the result of both men's having unwittingly exposed themselves to the effects of a Saturnian "mentality exchanger" discovered by Superman during a journey through outer space (S No. 111/1, Feb '57: "The Non-Super Superman").

BALDWIN, JIM. An unscrupulous promoter who cheats young inventor Chet Farnsworth out of the rights to Farnsworth's revolutionary new fire-extinguishing powder and then hires some hoodlums to kill Farnsworth to prevent the young inventor from disputing his own claim to the invention. SUPERMAN thwarts the various attempts on Farnsworth's life, forces Baldwin to relinquish the rights to Farnsworth's invention, and then bluntly warns the evil promoter that "....if you try to harm Chet [Farnsworth] again, I'll attend to you without mercy!" (S No. 14/2, Jan/Feb '42).

BALKANIA. The "faraway kingdom" ruled by the lovely PRINCESS VARINA. Balkania is apparently European, but its exact location is impossible to determine due to the lack of data in the text (WF No. 85, Nov/Dec '56: "The Super-Rivals!").

BANDAR, AL. The leader of a gang of criminals—headquartered in a secret cave situated on the floor of Painted Valley in the heart of the Western desert and equipped with a large, camouflaged doorway for the concealment of a private plane—who, fearful of the possible discovery of their hideout, make a concerted attempt to prevent chemical manufacturer James Hibbard from constructing a factory and town in the valley, only to be apprehended by SUPERMAN in Summer 1944 (WF No. 14: "Desert Town!").

BAND OF SUPER-VILLAINS, THE. The name adopted by a trio of ordinary criminals after a visiting alien from a far-distant planet has provided them with a set of special belts capable of endowing them with "amazing powers," ostensibly because he wants to enable them to become wealthy super-criminals in return for their promise of future aid in establishing a dictatorship on his native planet. In reality, however, the belts, which release "an alien element" into the air, are part of a fiendish alien scheme to poison Earth's atmosphere and annihilate its people in order to pave the way for an alien colonization. BATMAN, ROBIN, and SUPERMAN apprehend the Band of Super-Villains in June 1963, and the evil alien, finally cornered and defeated, blows himself and his spacecraft to smithereens as the self-imposed penalty for the failure of his mission (WF No. 134: "The Band of Super-Villains").

BANNING, JIM. The veteran World War II combat pilot who is the head of the Banning Line, a helicopter delivery service owned and operated by Banning and a group of the veteran flyers with whom he flew missions in the service.

In April 1948, in a ruthless effort to drive Banning and his buddies out of business and seize their helicopter delivery franchise for himself, Martin Grew, head of the rival Grew Line, repaints his own helicopters to resemble Banning's and loans them to a gang of criminals for use in a series of spectacular crimes so that, once the helicopters have been spotted and Banning and his buddies branded as criminals, he will be in a position to gain complete control over the city's lucrative helicopter delivery business.

SUPERMAN's efforts to apprehend the cunning "sky-bandits" are severely hampered by the fact that LOIS LANE has prevailed upon Clark Kent to "impersonate" Superman as part of her elaborate scheme to lure the criminals into a trap, thus placing

Kent in the unenviable position of having to "pose" as Superman without being able to use his super-powers overtly for fear of betraying the secret of his dual identity. Ultimately, however, by working behind the scenes and using his super-powers in secret, Superman manages to orchestrate the capture of the sky-bandits—and the exposure of Martin Grew's vicious scheme to put the Banning Line out of business—by Banning and his fellow flyers (Act No. 119: "Superman for a Day!").

BARACODA ISLAND. The "far-off island" which serves as LEX LUTHOR's base of operations during September-October 1941. There, through "experiments with the omega rays," Luthor has succeeded in creating fearsome "gigantic animals" with which he intends "to conquer the world and set up a scientific dictatorship," but the entire island "blows into smithereens" when Luthor destroys it during a climactic battle with SUPERMAN (S No. 12/4).

BARNES, NED. A contemporary of SUPERMAN's and onetime resident of SMALLVILLE who, while still a teen-ager, so admired the teen-aged Superman (i.e., Superboy) that he had his face remodeled through plastic surgery into a duplicate of Superboy's after his own face had been horribly disfigured in a fire.

In the beginning, Barnes had been elated to have a face exactly like Superboy's, but gradually his pride changed to resentment as the newly acquired face became the bane of his existence. His contemporaries teased him mercilessly for having Superboy's face but not his super-powers, and bullies took pleasure in beating him senseless while they laughed at him for not being invulnerable like Superboy. Before long, Barnes had grown to detest his Superboy face, and it was not long after that that he began to detest Superboy himself. "Everyone's making fun of me because I've got Superboy's face but not any of his powers!" thought Barnes bitterly. "He's admired! I'm mocked--I hate my life! I hate Superboy! I hate him! I'll get even with him some day!"

In May 1964 Barnes, now an adult in the pay of "the mob," bluffs his way into a Midwestern defense plant by posing as Superman and makes good his escape after surreptitiously photographing the "secret new type of space ship" undergoing construction there.

It is a short while later, while traveling on foot through the countryside to elude the police, wearing eyeglasses and dressed in clothing similar to the kind customarily worn by CLARK KENT, that Barnes makes the chance acquaintance of SALLY SELWYN—who naturally mistakes Barnes for the long-lost lover she knows only as Jim White—and decides to turn this incidence of mistaken identity to his own advantage by hiding out for a time at the Selwyn mansion.

Almost against his will, however, Barnes finds himself falling in love with the lovely Sally Selwyn, and as the days pass he begins to feel increasingly guilty at continuing to impersonate her long-lost sweetheart. He has decided to depart the Selwyn estate, when suddenly he is surprised at gunpoint by two mobsters who mistakenly believe that he has been planning to double-cross his gangland employers and who now intend to murder Sally Selwyn in order to teach Barnes a gangland-style lesson. Heroically, Barnes hurls himself at his underworld captors, and dies with them when the ledge of the cliff on which they are struggling gives way, sending the three men plummeting to their doom on the rocks below (S No. 169/2: "The Man Who Stole Superman's Secret Life!"). (See also SELWYN, SALLY.)

BARNUM, PHINEAS TAYLOR (1810-1891). A U.S. circus proprietor and impresario, undoubtedly the greatest showman of his day, who is famous for his exaggerated publicity claims and for his statement "There's a sucker born every minute." SUPERMAN meets P.T. Barnum, who offers the Man of Steel a job as a circus strong man, during a time-journey to the year 1878 (Act No. 132, May '49: "The Secret of the Kents!").

BARTLE, HENRY. A wily swindler who, in January-February 1957, attempts to capitalize on a joint appearance by BATMAN, ROBIN, and SUPERMAN at GOTHAM CITY's spectacular Gotham Police Show, the proceeds from which are to be donated to the Police Welfare Fund. In order to attract large crowds to the show and thereby aid the cause of charity, Batman, Robin, and Superman have agreed to perform a series of dramatic reenactments of their most exciting cases, and Superman chisels a huge amphitheater out of a solid rock cliff in order to accommodate the overflow crowds expected to attend. Swindler Bartle hatches a scheme to capture the dramatic reenactments on movie film and then cash in on the film by presenting it in theaters throughout the country as actual footage of the three heroes in action against dangerous criminals. The three famed lawmen thwart Bartle's scheme, however, and see to it that their awe-inspiring feats of skill create a financial windfall only for the Police Welfare Fund, and not for the crafty Bartle (WF No. 86: "The Super-Show of Gotham City").

BARTON, BLACKY. A METROPOLIS gangster and member of the underworld organization known as the Crime Syndicate who has been transformed through plastic surgery into an exact double for SUPERMAN, as part of an elaborate scheme by the syndicate to murder Superman secretly with KRYPTONITE and then have Barton impersonate him so that they can recover the incriminating evidence against them accumulated by Superman and now being held in a safe in PERRY WHITE's office. Barton and his Crime Syndicate cohorts are apprehended by Superman in January 1958 (S No. 118/3: "The Death of Superman!").

BARTON, "BULLETS." A METROPOLIS gangster, notorious for his practice of melting down lead to make his own high-powered bullets, who, under the alias Walter Brown, purchases one of six rare lead meteors donated by SUPERMAN to a charity auction, only to discover, when he attempts to melt it down to manufacture his bullets, that his meteor has a KRYPTONITE core. Superman, who has discovered only belatedly that the six meteors contain kryptonite and has begun surreptitiously repossessing them to prevent word of their kryptonite content from reaching the underworld, ultimately apprehends Barton and disposes of the kryptonite with the aid of JIMMY OLSEN in July 1956 (S No. 106/2: "The Thefts of Clark Kent").

BASHBY, "BRUTE." The leader of a gang of criminals who have virtually seized control of the town of Gateston, extorting protection money from its merchants and using violence and terror to enforce their hold over the fear-ridden populace. SUPERMAN smashes the Bashby gang in September-October 1940 and exposes local lawyer Morton Twist as the real mastermind behind the gang's activities (S No. 6/2).

BATCAVE. The subterranean cavern, situated beneath the mansion of millionaire BRUCE WAYNE, which serves as the secret crime-fighting headquarters of BATMAN and ROBIN. The BATPLANE and BATMOBILE are housed there, along with trophies of the Dynamic Duo's past cases and a vast array of specialized equipment. (For a complete description of the batcave, including its uses, history, and equipment, consult *The Encyclopedia of Comic Book Heroes: Volume I—Batman*.)

BATES, JOHN. The host of "The Eye of Metropolis" television program, a respected TV interviewer noted for his careful preparation and probing questions, who invites CLARK KENT to appear on his show in March 1959 with the clear intention of confirming his suspicion that Clark Kent is secretly SUPERMAN. The penetrating interview provides Clark Kent with some uncomfortable moments, but ultimately he succeeds in convincing Bates, and millions of television viewers as well, that mild-mannered Clark Kent could not possibly be Superman (Act No. 250: "The Eye of Metropolis!").

BATMAN, THE. A costumed crime-fighter and adventurer who has, for almost four decades, waged an unrelenting battle against the forces of crime, brutality, and evil. He is secretly Bruce Wayne, a millionaire socialite and philanthropist who, while still a young boy, vowed to dedicate his life to "warring on all criminals" after seeing his parents murdered by a hoodlum on a darkened city street (Det No. 33, Nov '39: "The Batman Wars Against the Dirigible of Doom"). In April 1940, approximately a year after the onset of his dramatic career, Batman trained a young orphan named Dick Grayson to be his partner, conferred on him the name ROBIN, and thus launched the career of a crime-fighting partnership whose feats have become the stuff of legend (Det No. 38).

Batman is a close friend of SUPERMAN and one of the few persons privy to the closely guarded secret of Superman's identity. From mid-1954 onward, Batman and Superman regularly participate in certain of their adventures together. Wherever Batman and Superman appear together as co-participants, that

Batman

adventure is treated in this volume. (For a complete account of the life and career of Batman apart from his involvement with Superman, consult *The Encyclopedia of Comic Book Heroes: Volume I—Batman*.)

BAT-MITE. A "mischievous mite from another dimension" (Det No. 276, Feb '60: "The Return of Bat-Mite!")—endowed with extraordinary extradimensional powers similar if not identical to those possessed by the incredible MR. MXYZPTLK—who looks like "an elf dressed in a crazy-looking Batman costume!" (Det No. 267, May '59: "Batman Meets Bat-

Bat-Mite

Mite!"). Although ROBIN has called him an "imp" and a "gremlin" and BATMAN has called him a "pest" (Det No. 267, May '59: "Batman Meets Bat-Mite!"), Bat-Mite sees himself only as Batman's "greatest fan" and his periodic visits to the earthly dimension as exciting opportunities to "see [his] favorite crime-fighting hero in spectacular action..." (BM No. 161/2, Feb '64: "The Bat-Mite Hero!").

To ensure that the action he sees will indeed be "spectacular," Bat-Mite uses his extraordinary extra-dimensional powers to prolong and enliven Batman's battles with the underworld, thus forcing the Dynamic Duo to ever greater heights of skill and ingenuity, as when he intentionally endows three small-time criminals with superhuman powers so that "Batman and Robin [will] have to use sensational tricks to defeat them!" (Det No. 310, Dec '62: "Bat-Mite's Super-Circus!").

In November 1960 (WF No. 113: "Bat-Mite Meets Mr. Mxyzptlk!"), February 1962 (WF No. 123: "The

Batwoman, 1956

Incredible Team of Bat-Mite and Mr. Mxyzptlk!"), and again in September 1965 (WF No. 152: "The Colossal Kids!" pts. I-II—no title; "The Magic of Bat-Mite and Mr. Mxyzptlk!"), Bat-Mite visits the earthly dimension for a series of encounters with the mischievous Mr. Mxyzptlk. (*See* MXYZPTLK [Mr.].) (For a complete account of Bat-Mite's entire mischievous career, consult *The Encyclopedia of Comic Book Heroes: Volume I—Batman.*)

BATMOBILE. The unique automobile, specially designed and equipped, which is the principal land vehicle employed by BATMAN and ROBIN. (For a complete description of the batmobile, including its uses, history, and equipment, consult *The Encyclopedia of Comic Book Heroes: Volume I—Batman.*)

BATPLANE. The unique airplane, specially designed and equipped, which is the principal aircraft employed by BATMAN and ROBIN. (For a complete description of the batplane, including its uses,

history, and equipment, consult *The Encyclopedia of Comic Book Heroes: Volume I—Batman.*)

BATWOMAN, THE. A raven-haired costumed crime-fighter who functions periodically, from July 1956 onward, as the crime-fighting colleague of BATMAN and ROBIN. Batwoman is in reality Kathy Kane, a wealthy heiress and onetime "circus dare-devil performer" noted for her outstanding ability both as a trapeze artist and motorcycle stunt rider (Det No. 233: "The Batwoman").

In September-October 1957 Batwoman, whose true identity has by this time been deduced by Batman despite her attempts to keep it secret, apprehends fugitive criminal ELTON CRAIG at an abandoned chemical factory, but not before she has become temporarily endowed with super-powers as the result of swallowing a special "radioactive capsule" invented long ago by the Kryptonian scientist JOR-EL, father of SUPERMAN. After returning the captured Craig to Metropolis Prison, Batwoman—whose super-powers will not fade away for about twenty-four hours—meets with Batman, Robin, and Superman and relates what has happened to her.

"..But super-powers can be **dangerous!**" insists Batman. "You must go home and stay safely quiet until your powers have faded away!"

"Batman," replies Batwoman, "I'm tired of your bossing me! Just because you found out my identity, you think you're superior and keep lecturing me!"

"But it's only for your own good--" insists Batman.

"I'm going to find out **your** secret identities!" exclaims Batwoman to the assembled crime-fighters. "I won't tell anyone, but that'll keep you from bossing me!"

Batwoman attempts to use her newly acquired X-ray vision to peer through the Dynamic Duo's face-masks, but Batman has already taken the precaution of asking Superman to line their masks with lead, which X-ray vision cannot penetrate. When Superman makes a remark to the effect that Batman has outwitted her, Batwoman becomes furious. "I've got super-powers for twenty-four hours," she declares, "and I'll use them to discover your secret identities somehow! From now on, I'm out to learn your secrets!"

For the next twenty-four hours, the temporarily super-powered Batwoman makes a determined effort to uncover the secret identities of Batman, Robin, and Superman, but the three crime-fighters manage to outwit her at every turn. Before long the twenty-four hours have elapsed, and Batwoman's super-powers have faded and vanished, without her having learned the secrets she sought (WF No. 90: "The Super-Batwoman!").

In September 1959 Batwoman helps foil a plot by LEX LUTHOR to destroy Superman (WF No. 104: "The Plot to Destroy Superman!").

In May 1961 Batwoman becomes accidentally endowed with superhuman powers and falls under the control of the diabolical Lex Luthor. She is rescued from the villain's clutches, however, through

Batwoman and Batman, 1963

the heroic efforts of Batman, Robin, and Superman (WF No. 117: "The Super-Batwoman and the Super-Creature!").

World's Finest Comics No. 154 contains an "imaginary tale" in which Kathy Kane appears as the wife of BRUCE WAYNE and the mother of their son, Bruce Wayne, Jr., while LOIS LANE appears as the wife of CLARK KENT and the mother of their son, Kal-El, Jr. After the youngsters have had a childish quarrel over whose father is the most impressive hero, their mothers take up the argument and refuse to allow their sons to play with one another anymore. Bruce Wayne, Jr., and Kal-El, Jr., ultimately reunite their warring families by pretending to leave home. At one point, they are kidnapped by an escaped convict named Nappy Klains, the so-called "Napoleon of crime," but they join forces as a sort of junior Batman-Superman team and apprehend their abductor (Dec '65: "The Sons of Superman and Batman!" pts. 1-2—no title; "The Junior Super-Team"). (For a complete account of Batwoman's crime-fighting career, consult *The Encyclopedia of Comic Book Heroes: Volume I—Batman.*)

BEALES, BEAKER. The leader of a gang of criminals who are apprehended by SUPERMAN in January 1944 (Act No. 68: "Superman Meets Susie!").

BELVOS. The far-distant planet which is the home of the evil KLOR. BATMAN, ROBIN, and SUPERMAN visit Belvos in December 1961 (WF No. 122: "The Capture of Superman!").

BENNY THE BLASTER. "A hold-up artist who frightens his victims with nitro instead of a gun" and who, in October 1963, is apprehended by CLARK KENT while attempting to use a vial of nitroglycerine to terrorize a physician at Metropolis General Hospital into handing over valuable radium capsules from the hospital's safe (Act No. 305: "Why Superman Needs a Secret Identity!").

BENNY THE BRUTE. A ruthless METROPOLIS "mobster" and "Public Enemy Number One" who, transported accidentally into the Stone Age—along with CLARK KENT, LOIS LANE, PERRY WHITE, and a bespectacled inventor named Bates—by Bates's newly invented "time machine," adopts the pseudonym Stoneman and, aided by such modern gadgets as his pistol and cigarette lighter, attempts to cow the local cave dwellers into frightened submission so that he can remain in the prehistoric past, "where there's no cops," and rule over them as their king. Tricked finally by Clark Kent into returning to the twentieth century, Benny the Brute is apprehended there by SUPERMAN in February 1955 (Act No. 201: "The Challenge of Stoneman!").

BENSON, BART. The owner of the Bart Benson Construction Co., an unscrupulous contractor with "a shady reputation for using shoddy materials" who, in collusion with crooked materials supplier T.B. Oliver, has been garnering illegal profits "by using cheap stuff and charging full prices." Benson and Oliver are both apprehended by SUPERMAN in September 1958 (S No. 124/3: "The Steeplejack of Steel").

BENSON, JIGGER. The leader of a gang of criminals and METROPOLIS's "number one man in crime," who, fearful of the impending exposure of his activities in an ongoing series of DAILY PLANET crime articles authored by CLARK KENT, hatches a scheme to destroy the *Planet*'s credibility to ensure that the upcoming exposés will be widely disbelieved. However, after being repeatedly thwarted by SUPERMAN—in spite of the fact that, with PERRY WHITE on vacation, the *Daily Planet* has been left temporarily in the hands of a headline-hunting editor whose thirst for sensationalism and failure to research his stories properly play right into the hands of the criminals—Jigger Benson and his henchmen are finally apprehended by Superman in September 1954 (S No. 92/1: "The Impossible Headlines!").

BEPPO (the Super-Monkey). A playful Kryptonian laboratory monkey which survived the explosion of the planet KRYPTON—as the result of having been launched into outer space in an experimental space capsule—and ultimately landed on Earth, where, like any native of Krypton, it acquired super-powers like SUPERMAN's and became known as Beppo the Super-Monkey. Beppo wears a colorful red and blue costume modeled after Superman's and is a member of the LEGION OF SUPER-PETS. When METROPOLIS television station WMET-TV inaugurates its new "Our American Heroes" series with a program honoring Superman, "our greatest American hero," Beppo appears on the show along with three of the other super-pets—KRYPTO THE SUPERDOG, COMET THE SUPER-HORSE, and STREAKY THE SUPER-CAT—to help pay tribute to the Man of Steel (Act No. 309, Feb '64: "The Superman Super-Spectacular!"). In April 1965 Beppo journeys through the time barrier to the mid-nineteenth century to help Superman and the other super-pets teach a well-deserved lesson to "cruel junkman" CYRUS ATWILL (S No. 176/1: "The Revenge of the Super-Pets!").

BERG, PAUL. A ventriloquist at the Gay Metropolis Supper Club whose act, a gentle spoof of SUPERMAN, features the engaging Whit Whittle, "secretly" Super Puppet, a ventriloquist's dummy that flies through the air by means of a tiny propeller and performs crowd-pleasing "X-ray vision" tricks through an elaborate technique involving use of a club waiter as a secret accomplice. When two METROPOLIS gangsters—Barney Bates and "Grabby" Todd—steal Berg's dummy in the moronic belief that they can use its supposed "X-ray vision" for crime, Superman apprehends them both and reunites dummy Whittle with ventriloquist Berg (S No. 109/2, Nov '56: "The Puppet with X-Ray Eyes").

BERGAC, TONY (Count). A smooth-talking bogus French count, in reality a crafty ex-convict named Ricky Hanlon, who attempts to charm wealthy department store heiress Patricia Randall into marriage and, when that fails, to have her murdered and replaced by an impostor so that he can seize control of her wealth and her business holdings. Ricky Hanlon, alias Count Bergac, is apprehended by SUPERMAN in July-August 1941 (S No. 11/4).

BERGH, HENRY (1811-1888). The founder in 1866, of the American Society for the Prevention of Cruelty to Animals, the first organization of its kind in the United States. SUPERMAN meets Henry Bergh during a time-journey to the year 1866 (S No. 176/1, Apr '65: "The Revenge of the Super-Pets!").

BEY, RIGHAB. An astrologer and hypnotist, secretly the head of "a sinister spy-ring" in quest of "our nation's vital defense secrets," who hypnotizes the government officials and employees who come to him for astrological advice and then, unbeknownst to his victims, probes their minds for government secrets, which he then sells abroad to the highest bidder. Righab Bey's spy ring is smashed by SUPERMAN in May-June 1941 (S No. 10/3).

BIGGINS (Boss). A METROPOLIS racketeer with a grudge against SUPERMAN who attempted to capitalize on the early broadcasts of the Superman radio show, "The Adventurers of Superman," by staging a series of spectacular robberies—including the theft of a pay-carload of nickel fares collected from the city's subway stations—at the very times when Superman would be busily engaged in broadcasting live accounts of his past adventures from the radio station atop the Daily Planet Building. Superman ultimately apprehended Boss Biggins and his henchmen, however, by tying a portable microphone around his neck and broadcasting his pursuit and capture of the Biggins mob, live, to a spellbound radio audience (S No. 39/1, Mar/Apr '46: "The Big Superman Broadcast!").

"BIG GUY," THE. The cunning underworld czar who is the leader of organized crime in METROPOLIS. His capture, along with that of his henchman, by SUPERMAN in July 1955 comes as the culmination of an elaborate ruse—devised by Superman and carried out with the aid of PERRY WHITE—in which CLARK KENT pretends to have sold out to the underworld and to have embarked on a new career as a safecracker so that he can infiltrate the "Big Guy's" mob and ultimately take him into custody (S No. 98/2: "Clark Kent Outlaw!").

BIGSBY, THORNTON. "One of the most powerful industrialists in the nation," a viciously unscrupulous tycoon who masterminds a heinous scheme to cause a series of disastrous train wrecks on the Garth & Cowles Railroad so that he can buy a controlling interest in the line for a song when the price of the stock plummets. The scheme is thwarted by SUPERMAN, who apprehends Bigsby and his henchman, "Sparky" Waters, along with the gang of criminals hired by Waters to commit the actual acts of railroad sabotage (WF No. 3, Fall '41: "The Case of the Death Express").

BINKLE, HERBERT. A recent journalism graduate from Northville College who applies for a reporter's job on the DAILY PLANET and, at CLARK KENT's suggestion, persuades editor PERRY WHITE to promise him employment if he can successfully acquire seven major stories over the course of the next seven days. In the days that follow, unbeknownst to Binkle, SUPERMAN—who has become increasingly resentful of LOIS LANE's "mania for scoops" and of the time and trouble it takes to keep her out of danger—surreptitiously manufactures a series of major news stories for Binkle in hopes that he can help the eager Binkle make good and at the same time "take some of the scoop-craziness out of Lois" by showing her that she can be "outclassed by a beginner like Herbert." Lois ultimately learns of Superman's secret aid to Binkle, but like a good sport she refrains from exposing him on the ground that Binkle is an innocent party who would only be hurt by the revelation (Act No. 138, Nov '49: "Superman Scoop-Parade").

BIRD, JEREMY. An elderly former lumberjack, now a resident of the Sutter County Retirement Home in Sioux Forest, North Dakota, who has suffered derision and ridicule throughout his adult life because of his insistence that SUPERMAN rescued him from hostile Indians—and performed other incredible super-feats in his presence—some sixty years ago, well before Superman was even born. After perusing Bird's written account of his meeting with "Superman" and then flashing to North Dakota to interview Bird personally, Superman realizes with astonishment that the "Superman" Bird knew was not Superman at all, but rather Superman's grandfather, the father of JOR-EL, who apparently journeyed briefly to Earth while experimenting with space travel sometime around the turn of the century (S No. 103/1, Feb '56: "The Superman of Yesterday").

BIXBY, JUDD. The director of the Rehabilitation Society, a charitable organization for the rehabilitation of ex-convicts that is in reality a front for the underworld operations of Bixby and the so-called "reformed" criminals he is supposed to be helping. Bixby masterminds an elaborate scheme designed to trick SUPERMAN into refurbishing and remodeling a run-down hotel so that, once restored to its former elegance and grandeur, it can be used to entice wealthy guests for robbery and blackmail, but Superman thwarts the scheme and apprehends Bixby and his henchmen in January-February 1951 (S No. 68/3: "Superman, Hotel Manager!").

BIZARRO. "A grotesque imitation of Superman" (Act No. 263, Apr '60: "The World of Bizarros!") "fashioned out of lifeless matter" (Act No. 254, Jul '59: "The Battle with Bizarro!"). Clad in an invulnerable costume just like SUPERMAN's (Act No. 255, Aug '59: "The Bride of Bizarro!"; and others) and endowed with all of his mighty super-powers (Act No. 254, Jul '59: "The Battle with Bizarro!"), Bizarro possesses "a dim copy of Superman's memory" (Act No. 255, Aug '59: "The Bride of Bizarro!") as well as an "imperfect replica of Superman's super-keen mind" (S No. 140, Oct '60: pts. I-III—"The Son of Bizarro!"; "The 'Orphan' Bizarro!"; "The Bizarro Supergirl!").

His flesh is white, the color of chalk, and his face appears faceted, as though it had been chiseled out of rock. His black hair is matted and unkempt. He is well-meaning but witless, super-powerful but pathetic. His speech is illiterate and ungrammatical. Because Bizarro's mind is "an imperfect imitation of Superman's" (Act No. 254, Jul '59: "The Battle with Bizarro!"), however, he is capable of flights of occasional super-genius (e.g., Act No. 263, Apr '60: "The World of Bizarros!"), and because he possesses "dim duplicated memories of all that Superman knows" (S No. 140, Oct '60: pts. I-III—"The Son of Bizarro!"; "The 'Orphan' Bizarro!"; "The Bizarro Supergirl!"), he is well aware that Clark Kent is secretly Superman (Act No. 255, Aug '59: "The Bride of Bizarro!").

Unlike Superman, Bizarro is immune to green KRYPTONITE (Act No. 254, Jul '59: "The Battle with

Bizarro, 1959

WAIT--ME PROVE IT! ME HAVE TELESCOPIC VISION AND SEE PLANE FALLING! *SUPERMAN* BUSY ON OTHER JOB SO-- *THIS IS A JOB FOR BIZARRO!*

© NPP 1959

Bizarro!"; and others), but, like all Bizarro creatures, he is vulnerable to blue kryptonite (S No. 140, Oct '60: pts. I-III—"The Son of Bizarro!"; "The 'Orphan' Bizarro!"; "The Bizarro Supergirl!"; and others).

Brought into being by an ingenious "duplicator ray" built by LEX LUTHOR, the "renegade scientist who is **Superman**'s bitterest enemy," Bizarro is "only **lifeless** matter in human form"—a thing composed of "unliving matter"—and is, therefore, not truly alive. "Me not human...me not creature," moans Bizarro pathetically in July 1959, "...me not even animal!" (Act No. 254: "The Battle with Bizarro!").

Action Comics No. 263 observes that Bizarro "is composed of nuclear matter and isn't really 'alive,' but it can move and talk and has all [Superman's] powers and memories!" (Apr '60: "The World of Bizarros!"). Bizarro can also think and feel and engage in reproduction: his mate, BIZARRO-LOIS, gives birth to a baby boy Bizarro in October 1960 (S No. 140: pts. I-III—"The Son of Bizarro!"; "The 'Orphan' Bizarro!"; "The Bizarro Supergirl!"), and by February 1961 the couple have acquired a daughter (S No. 143/3: "Bizarro Meets Frankenstein!").

Together with Bizarro-Lois, Bizarro rules the far-distant planet HTRAE (Act No. 263, Apr '60: "The World of Bizarros!"), a wacky, cockeyed world "where all the men are imperfect imitations of [Superman], and all the girls are distorted doubles of **Lois Lane!**" (Act No. 264, May '60: "The Superman Bizarro!"). It is to distinguish himself from all these other male Bizarros that the original Bizarro has taken to wearing a large medallion around his neck plainly identifying himself as "Bizarro No. 1" (Act No. 263, Apr '60: "The World of Bizarros!").

Indeed, although the name Bizarro is used as a proper noun, designating Bizarro himself, it is also employed in the texts as a general term to designate any Bizarro creature. All Bizarros are imperfect duplicates of other living things; all are illiterate and ungrammatical; and all share the grotesque physical characteristics—including the chalk-white, faceted faces—peculiar to Bizarros. The first Bizarro, in fact, was an imperfect double of SUPERBOY created by a scientist in SMALLVILLE while Superman was growing up there. When Superboy first saw the grotesque duplicate of himself, he exclaimed that it was "bizarre"; the witless creature heard him and adopted Bizarro as its name. It is by stealing the plans for the Smallville scientist's original duplicator ray that Lex Luthor is able to reconstruct the apparatus and create his own Bizarro—this one a grotesque imitation of the adult Superman—in July 1959 (Act No. 254: "The Battle with Bizarro!"). It is this Bizarro that is the subject of this article.

In the texts, Bizarro is often referred to as the Thing of Steel (Act No. 254, Jul '59: "The Battle with Bizarro!"; and others). Other texts call him "a blundering menace" (Act No. 255, Aug '59: "The Bride of Bizarro!"), "a grotesque, imperfect double" of Superman (Act No. 263, Apr '60: "The World of

Bizarros!"), a "pathetic, grotesque creature," and "an artificial imitation of the Man of Steel that came out imperfect!" (S No. 143/3, Feb '61: "Bizarro Meets Frankenstein!"). Superman No. 174/2 describes him as "the imperfect, unliving duplicate of Superman, who does things in a crazily mixed-up manner..." (Jan '65: "Super-Mxyzptlk...Hero!").

Bizarro, however, thinks of himself, somewhat more generously, as the "most famous monster in history," the all-time "champion monster," the "most famous monster of all," and the "scariest monster" of all time (S No. 143/3, Feb '61: "Bizarro Meets Frankenstein!"), although sometimes he sees himself more clearly, as the pathetic monstrosity he really is: "Me unhappy!" he declares sadly in July 1959. "Me don't belong in world of living people! Me don't know difference between right and wrong--good and evil!" (Act No. 254: "The Battle with Bizarro!").

In July 1959, working from the plans for the original apparatus used to create a Bizarro-Superboy in Smallville many years ago, renegade scientist Lex Luthor constructs an ingenious duplicator ray, which, "when it is trained on any object," either animate or inanimate, "can create a molecular duplicate" of that object, although the duplicate is always somehow imperfect, as when it creates a diamond that melts away like ice, or produces an apple weighing hundreds of pounds. "This duplicator ray," gloats Luthor to his henchman, Vekko, "is going to mean the downfall of Superman!"

Soon afterward, after donning a disguise to conceal his identity and adopting the pseudonym "Professor Clyde," Luthor lures Superman to his laboratory on the pretext of having created a device capable of immunizing him against kryptonite, and then bathes the Man of Steel in the ray of his duplicator. Instantly there is a puff of smoke, and when it clears, Superman finds himself confronted by Bizarro, an imperfect duplicate of himself composed of lifeless matter. For Superman, the shock of the discovery has barely worn off when "Professor Clyde" rips away his disguise to reveal the vengeful face of Luthor. "Obey your master, Bizarro," shrieks the renegade scientist at his newly created monstrosity, "--fight Superman!"

But Bizarro does not acknowledge Luthor as his master. Sickened at the ugly countenance he sees staring back at him from a laboratory mirror—"Me not human," he moans pathetically, "...me not creature...me not even animal!"—and enraged at Luthor for having brought him to life, Bizarro shatters the mirror with a mighty blow of his fist and then seizes Luthor and Vekko as they try to escape.

"Me unhappy!" confides Bizarro to Superman as they fly their captives toward the nearest police station. "Me don't belong in world of living people! Me don't know difference between right and wrong--good and evil!"

"I'm glad he recognizes that fact!" thinks Superman to himself. "I'll have to destroy him later! It won't be like 'death' since he's only lifeless matter in

Bizarro, 1959

human form!"

Moments later, when Superman races off to rescue a ship trapped in the path of a tidal wave, Bizarro carries Luthor and Vekko the rest of the way to the police station by himself. Pained and saddened by the fear and horror on the policemen's faces when they glimpse his ugly, monstrous face, Bizarro races off, eager to perform some good deed that will persuade people to accept him as a friend and convince them that, at heart, he is not really a monster. He rescues an airliner that has caught fire in midair and helps it land safely, but despite the fact that his selfless heroism has just saved the lives of both passengers and crew, the people on board flee from him in terror when they see that their savior is a horrifying monster.

Saddened by this cruel rebuff from the very people he tried to help, "the friendless, imitation Superman flees in blind sorrow, not watching where he is flying...." When, in his reverie, Bizarro accidentally knocks over a smokestack and a steeple, aircraft of the Metropolis Civil Defense Command attempt to shoot him out of the sky, but their "rocket-bombs"—and even an atomic bomb—have no effect on his invulnerable body. Finally, realizing how much he is hated and reviled, Bizarro hurls himself against a rocky cliff at awesome super-speed in a pathetic attempt at self-annihilation, but all he succeeds in doing is boring through the solid rock like an invulnerable human drill.

Further complications arise when an unfortunate misunderstanding leads Bizarro to the wholly erroneous conclusion that LOIS LANE has fallen in love with him. Overjoyed at having at last come in contact with a person who loves him, Bizarro scoops Lois up in his arms and flies her out over the ocean to a remote, uninhabited island, where he has constructed a ramshackle, tumbledown shack for her in the pathetic belief that he has built her a beautiful "palace." When Lois delicately spurns Bizarro's urgent proposal of marriage on the ground that "Superman is the only man I could ever love," Bizarro's grotesque mind conceives a bizarre inspriation: flying swiftly to METROPOLIS and then returning to a remote corner of his island with Lex Luthor's duplicator, Bizarro bathes himself in its eerie rays, taking care to remain unseen by the still-waiting Lois Lane. "Me figure out simple thing!" thinks Bizarro to himself. "If machine made imperfect duplicate like me, out of perfect Superman, then it also work backwards and...make perfect Superman duplicate out of imperfect Bizarro!"

Indeed, as the duplicator ray works its electronic magic, Bizarro can see that his bizarre scheme has succeeded: by focusing the duplicator on himself, Bizarro has succeeded in creating an "exact double of Superman," although the new creation "still has the thinking mentality of Bizarro" as well as Bizarro's illiterate, ungrammatical mode of self-expression. "Me new Bizarro...handsome!" proclaims the newly created Bizarro. "You old Bizarro...ugly!"

When the so-called "new Bizarro"—which is endowed with the handsome features of Superman—returns to Bizarro's ramshackle "palace" and alights beside Lois, the attractive journalist believes that the real Superman has arrived to rescue her and eagerly accepts his proposal of marriage. "Oh, Superman!" she sighs. "At last...at last my happiest hour has come! My years of waiting for you are over!"

Meanwhile, however, the real Superman has arrived on the island in time to witness the astounding spectacle of the new Bizarro proclaiming his love for Lois. He is about to show himself and intervene, when suddenly the so-called "old Bizarro" sneaks up behind him and reduces him to a state of helpless near-paralysis with a kryptonite meteor. "Now," says Bizarro with evident satisfaction, "romance of new Bizarro and Lois Lane go on!" (Act No. 254: "The Battle with Bizarro!").

From a place of concealment, with the pain-wracked Superman lying helpless on the ground beside him, Bizarro looks on happily as, not far away, his Bizarro creation, the so-called "new Bizarro," lovingly embraces the unwitting Lois Lane. "If me can't marry Lois, you not marry her either!" snaps Bizarro to Superman. And to himself he thinks, "Good! She become wife of new Bizarro before she discover I trapped real Superman!"

Suddenly, however, Lois becomes aware of the oddly illiterate speech of the man holding her in his arms and realizes that he could not possibly be Superman. And at that moment, Bizarro steps out from his place of hiding, apparently having undergone a change of heart about his plan to trick Lois into marrying the new Bizarro. "Him not real Superman!" cries Bizarro.

"Well, what is difference?" exclaims the new Bizarro to Lois. "Me still handsome! You lucky girl if you marry me!"

"Never, you...you conceited thing!" fumes Lois.

"As a matter of fact, I like the first Bizarro better than you!"

"Fool girl!" exclaims the new Bizarro. "Even I better than ugly monster like him!"

A furious battle ensues between the two Bizarros, but since both possess all of Superman's mighty super-powers, both combatants remain unharmed. Superman is ultimately rescued from the effects of the paralyzing kryptonite meteor when Bizarro smashes it into powder in hopes of persuading Superman to help him destroy his handsome Bizarro creation, and the so-called "new Bizarro" is finally destroyed, although not by either Superman or Bizarro, when airborne dust particles from the pulverized kryptonite meteor fill its lungs and cause it to disintegrate into nothingness. Apparently, explains Superman, the new Bizarro "was such a perfect imitation of me, physically if not mentally, that he, too, was vulnerable to kryptonite!"

Not long afterward, back in Metropolis, Bizarro renews his pathetic attempts to woo Lois Lane, but Lois continues to spurn his affections. Enraged finally by Lois's repeated refusals to marry him, Bizarro carries her away again to his uninhabited island, vowing that "If me can't have you, Superman not marry you either! Me hold you prisoner at island and fight off Superman!"

The impasse is finally resolved, however, by the quick-witted Lois Lane, who shrewdly makes use of Lex Luthor's duplicator ray in order to create an imperfect duplicate of herself—a so-called Bizarro-Lois—as a fitting mate for Bizarro. Indeed, Bizarro falls in love with Bizarro-Lois the moment he sees her.

Bizarro and Bizarro-Lois, 1959

"Come, dear!" he coos happily, scooping Bizarro-Lois up in his arms and flying off into space with her. "We not be happy on Earth where people fear us! Me take you to live by ourselves on other world in faraway solar system!" (Act No. 255, Aug '59: "The Bride of Bizarro!").

By April 1960 Bizarro and Bizarro-Lois have arrived on a world in a far-off solar system and stumbled upon the ruins of an ancient city whose alien population was "wiped out" by some unknown calamity sometime in the distant past. The two Bizarros decide to make their home there, but as time passes Bizarro-Lois becomes lonely for "friends to talk to," and so, to fulfill his mate's need for companionship, Bizarro uses the super-scientific apparatus in the ruins of an ancient laboratory to construct an ingenious "imitator machine" with which he soon creates hundreds of Bizarro-Loises in the exact image of his mate.

Bizarro-Lois's joy at her new-found friendships quickly turns to jealousy, however, as the newly created female Bizarros begin to covet the affections of Bizarro, the only male on the planet. At the insistence of the original Bizarro-Lois, Bizarro focuses the amazing imitator machine on himself, thereby creating a host of Bizarros like himself, one for every Bizarro-Lois. Together the male and female Bizarros—all of them imperfect duplicates of Superman and Lois Lane—set about dismantling the crumbling ruins of the ancient alien city and transforming them into "a crude copy of Metropolis" which "looks like something a mad architect would design" (see BIZARRO CITY). The Bizarros christened their planet Htrae, which is Earth spelled backwards. The original Bizarro became "the tribe's leader," and the original Bizarro-Lois, his consort. Together they rule their Bizarro world from atop stone thrones in a ramshackle "palace" in Bizarro City.

When Superman visits the planet Htrae in April 1960 and attempts to improve the lot of its people by neatening and straightening their dilapidated homes, he is promptly arrested by a Bizarro policeman and thrown into jail on the charge of having violated the Bizarro Code, which makes it a "big crime to make anything perfect on [the] Bizarro world!" Most, if not all, of the other inmates in the prison are "freak Bizarros" whose minds were somehow not affected by the imitator machine and who therefore have the physical appearance of Bizarros but think and speak normally. Convict labor consists of smashing the beautiful works of statuary found among the ruins of Htrae's vanished ancient civilization. Escape from the prison is virtually impossible, for each guard wields a rifle-like weapon called a "non-super ray" capable of permanently sapping Superman of his mighty super-powers.

As he sits in his cell awaiting trial for his "crimes," the Man of Steel receives a visit from Bizarro-Lois, who offers to persuade the jury to find him innocent if he will agree to give her his hand in marriage. Superman, however, declines the offer: "Sorry, Lois!" he snaps. "I'll take my chances in court!"

"You...you beast!" cries Bizarro-Lois angrily as she stalks out of the prison cell. "You turn me down, eh? Then me will get jury to convict you...wait and see!"

Indeed, when Superman finally comes to trial in the Bizarro courtroom, charged with such heinous Bizarro offenses as "fixing houses," being handsome, and speaking "good English," his outlook seems bleak: not only is he denied an attorney and the right to defend himself, but the spurned Bizarro-Lois vindictively incites her fellow jurors into a frenzy against him, making a verdict of guilty a foregone conclusion. Indeed, after having been lambasted by the Bizarro prosecutor for his "terrible crimes" and found guilty on all counts by the prejudiced jury, Superman is sentenced by the court to pay the Bizarros' "supreme penalty": transformation into a Bizarro by means of an awesome "Bizarro ray" (Act No. 263: "The World of Bizarros!").

Returned to his prison cell to await his punishment, Superman falls asleep and suffers through a long and torturous nightmare. In it, the sentence of the Bizarro court is carried out and Superman returns to Earth after having been transformed into a Bizarro; after fashioning a special "headmask and gloves made of plastic asbestos" designed to duplicate his former, handsome appearance and conceal from the world that he is now a Bizarro, Superman resumes his customary functions as Earth's greatest super-hero, only to have an accidental explosion rip his mask and gloves to shreds soon afterwards, exposing his hideous Bizarro features and inspiring panic and revulsion in all who see him. And as the terrifying nightmare continues, its horrific aspects escalate: Superman's closest friends—Lois Lane, JIMMY OLSEN, and PERRY WHITE—refuse to believe that the grotesque creature in their midst is really Superman; they accuse him of having murdered the real Superman and of conspiring to impersonate him; Superman is charged with murder and thrown into prison, ánd the only way he can save himself and establish his innocence is by producing the "real" Superman alive in open court.

Then, mercifully, "the bad dream's twisted ending shocks Superman awake," and the Man of Steel realizes that he is still imprisoned in a jail cell on the planet Htrae. Soon afterward, one of the so-called freak Bizarros, a friendly Bizarro-Lois sympathetic to Superman's plight, offers to help Superman escape the prison by posing as the original Bizarro-Lois, the co-ruler of Htrae, and engaging the watchtower guard in conversation while the Man of Steel makes a dash for freedom. The escape plan is thwarted, however, by the unexpected arrival of the real Bizarro-Lois, and before long Superman finds himself being marched into the prison courtyard to have his court-decreed sentence carried out.

At the last possible instant, however, just as the awesome Bizarro ray is about to be used to transform him into a Bizarro, Superman hits upon an ingenious stratagem: after requesting, and being granted, an opportunity to present new evidence in his behalf, Superman tells the Bizarro court that every Bizarro on Htrae is as guilty of violating the Bizarro Code as he is, since every Bizarro has "one perfect thing." To prove his thesis, Superman hastily constructs a TV-

The Bizarro world is "the strangest, whackiest planet in the universe...!"

satellite and hurls it into orbit around the Bizarro planet, so that it can begin transmitting back outer-space views of the Bizarro world. Using these satellite views of Htrae as his evidence, the Man of Steel argues that every Bizarro on Htrae is guilty of living on a perfect, round world and is therefore in violation of the Bizarro Code. On the basis of this argument, Superman is acquitted of the charges against him and released from custody, along with the freak Bizarro-Lois who tried to help him break out of prison. Before returning to Earth, Superman constructs a "super-large bulldozer" and, to the great delight of the Bizarro population, transforms their planet from a round world into a cube-shaped one so that each and every Bizarro can feel happier, knowing that he lives on an imperfect world (Act No. 264, May '60: "The Superman Bizarro!").

In October 1960, in the middle of an arid desert somewhere on Htrae, Bizarro constructs his Fortress of Bizarro (Bizarro refers to it as his "Fourtriss uv Bizarro"), a crude imitation of Superman's FORTRESS OF SOLITUDE. Among other items, this ramshackle secluded retreat contains the "Bizarro ray," once almost used to transform Superman into a Bizarro, and a "collection of worthless junk," analogous to Superman's valuable collection of trophies, accumulated from various parts of the Bizarro world.

existence is a violation of the Bizarro Code. Even Bizarro-Lois finds him ugly, "a disgrace to [the] name of Bizarro!"

Although Bizarro and Bizarro-Lois love their "baby Bizarro" despite his appearance, his perfect human features inspire loathing and outrage throughout the Bizarro world, and when an angry mob of Bizarros descends on his home, Bizarro hastily departs his planet and hides the youngster inside a "strange metal shell" he finds floating in outer space. Then Bizarro returns home again to protect his mate from the angry mob.

Unbeknownst to Bizarro, however, the strange metal shell where he hid his son is a space-probe satellite from the planet Earth, and by the time the mob has dispersed and Bizarro flies into space again to retrieve his son, the satellite has been drawn back to Earth by remote control, and the Bizarro baby, who has all the appearance of an ordinary human infant, has been found near the side of a road by a passing couple and entrusted to the care of the MIDVALE ORPHANAGE, the same orphanage where SUPERGIRL lives in her Linda Lee identity.

When Linda Lee discovers that the newly arrived infant is endowed with super-powers, suggesting that he was born on a planet other than Earth, she and Superman spirit him away to the Fortress of Solitude

Standing inside his newly built Fortress of Bizarro, Bizarro surveys his "collection of worthless junk"...

Returning home from the task of building his Fortress, Bizarro finds that, in his absence, Bizarro-Lois has given birth to a son, the first Bizarro actually born on the planet as opposed to having been artifically created by Bizarro's imitator machine. Bizarro's initial joy at having become a father quickly turns to horror, however, when he sees that his infant son has been born "a freak," a handsome baby, with perfect human features, whose very

so that they can keep a close eye on him while they attempt to unravel his origins.

Bizarro, meanwhile, distraught at his child's disappearance, chances to focus his telescopic vision on the planet Earth and sees his infant son romping in the Fortress of Solitude. His immediate impulse is to fly to Earth and reclaim the baby, but Bizarro-Lois tearfully restrains him, arguing that their son will always be branded a freak on Htrae and is therefore

...as well as an exhibit featuring the "Bizarro ray," a device once almost used to transform Superman into a Bizarro

Bizarro, 1960

probably better off being allowed to remain on Earth. Soon afterward, however, the Bizarro baby's perfect human features undergo a sudden, dramatic transformation into imperfect, Bizarro features, a transformation typical of all newborn Bizarros, but one with which both Superman and the Bizarros are unfamiliar since this is the first Bizarro infant ever born.

Homing in on Earth once again with his telescopic vision, and seeing that his son has somehow become transformed into a true Bizarro, Bizarro flies earthward to reclaim his son, but a complication has arisen in the form of a newly created Bizarro-Supergirl, a Bizarro duplicate of Supergirl brought into being accidentally when the Bizarro baby inadvertently activated Lex Luthor's duplicator ray while it was focused on Supergirl inside the Fortress of Solitude. Her maternal instincts aroused by the Bizarro baby, the Bizarro-Supergirl insists on keeping it for her own, refusing to surrender it to either Bizarro or Superman. Enraged at what he now sees as the kidnapping of his son, Bizarro angrily announces that Htrae has declared war on Earth and then races homeward to assemble a Bizarro army.

As the forces of Htrae streak toward Earth, however, Superman assembles a pile of green-kryptonite meteors on an asteroid directly in the path of the advancing Bizarro army and, by means of Lex Luthor's duplicator ray, creates a mound of "Bizarro kryptonite," or "blue kryptonite," an imperfect form of kryptonite that is harmless to Superman but deadly to Bizarros. "It's harmful to you, but not me!" cries Superman, as the demoralized Bizarros begin a hasty retreat back to Htrae to devise a new war plan. "Go back...or else!"

Before the Bizarro army can renew its attack on Earth, however, Superman resolves the conflict and averts further hostilities by using a chunk of the newly created blue kryptonite to sufficiently weaken the Bizarro-Supergirl to enable him to snatch the Bizarro baby away from her and reunite it with its grateful parents on Htrae. The Bizarro-Supergirl suffers a grisly fate soon afterward, however, when while spying on the Bizarro world in hopes of stealing

the baby back again, she unwittingly lands on the asteroid containing Superman's mound of blue kryptonite and is fatally poisoned by its toxic radiations. "Poor creature!" observes Superman grimly. "It's better this way!" (S No. 140: pts. I-III—"The Son of Bizarro!"; "The 'Orphan' Bizarro!"; "The Bizarro Supergirl!").

By February 1961 Bizarro and Bizarro-Lois have apparently acquired a second child, because now they are depicted as having two young children, a boy and a girl. During this period, Bizarro becomes enraged when, while watching a television program beamed from Earth, he sees a promotional announcement for a forthcoming movie that hails the Frankenstein monster as the "world's scariest monster." Shaken and humiliated by this challenge to his primacy as history's "champion monster," Bizarro leaves the comfort of his Bizarro world and streaks angrily toward Earth, determined to frighten the wits out of Frankenstein himself if need be in order to establish once and for all, beyond any doubt, that "**Bizarro Number One am also Monster Number One!**"

Arriving in Hollywood, where the forthcoming Frankenstein movie is being filmed, Bizarro sets out to restore his good name by scaring everyone in sight. Despite his hideous appearance and admittedly shuddery demeanor, however, fate keeps stepping in, in the form of misunderstandings and freakish coincidences, to prevent Bizarro from frightening anyone, as when he attempts to terrify a clutch of lovely starlets, only to have them assume he must really be Superman disguised in a monster-mask and line up eagerly to hug and kiss him. Finally, however, realizing that Bizarro is likely to remain on Earth until he has convinced himself that he has made his point, Superman steps in surreptitiously to make it appear as though Bizarro has succeeded in scaring a host of Hollywood actors out of their skins. Thus reassured of his supremacy as the "scariest monster in history," Bizarro heads homeward toward the planet Htrae, pausing only to acquire a Superman marionette with which to amuse his children, for on the Bizarro world Superman is "the world's worst monster," and a Superman marionette is guaranteed to frighten youngsters out of their wits (S No. 143/3: "Bizarro Meets Frankenstein!").

In October 1961, when Superman is put in the almost impossible position of having to accumulate $1,000,000,000 in income taxes within twenty-four hours, Bizarro becomes aware of his plight and streaks to his aid, but the witless monster's well-intentioned efforts to help the Man of Steel only succeed in destroying the millions of dollars' worth of ivory tusks that Superman has gathered from an elephants' graveyard in Africa to help pay his taxes (S No. 148/3: "Superman Owes a Billion Dollars!"). (See BRAND, RUPERT.)

In January 1962, when Superman and the other survivors of the exploded planet KRYPTON—including Supergirl, KRYPTO THE SUPERDOG, the citizens of KANDOR, and even the villains imprisoned in the PHANTOM ZONE—bow their heads solemnly for one full minute of silence to commemorate the anniversary of the destruction of Krypton, Bizarro and all the other Bizarros of Htrae celebrate the occasion with a full minute of loud, joyously raucous noise, not out of any malice for the doomed millions of Krypton, but only out of the zaniness that characterizes their race.

"Ha, ha!" laughs Bizarro. "Is **everybody happy?** ...Yahooo!!!"

"Too bad whole universe didn't blow up with it!" chimes in Bizarro-Lois insanely (S No. 150/1: "The One Minute of Doom!").

In November 1962, when millions flock to Metropolis from the far reaches of the universe to participate in the city's gala Superman Day celebration, Bizarro streaks to Earth from his home on Htrae to wish Superman an "unhappy Superman Day" and present him with a package containing a chunk of green kryptonite. "Good!" cackles Bizarro zanily, as the Man of Steel collapses in agony from the kryptonite radiations. "**Superman** faint for joy when he see present. Me know he like kryptonite the most!"

Lying on the ground, stricken and helpless, unseen by his friends or passersby, Superman is rescued from seemingly certain death by Little Leaguer Steven Snapinn, who spots the Man of Steel in trouble in the nick of time and places the kryptonite in a lead container where it will be unable to harm him (S No. 157/3: "Superman's Day of Doom!").

In May 1964 Bizarro and his fellow Bizarros invade the Earth, determined to prove to Superman how much they like him. "To prove us like you," announces Bizarro, demolishing a globe on one of Metropolis's statues with a mighty blow of his fist, "us will smash your planet--like so!!"

Before actually getting down to the business of destroying the planet, however, the Bizarros fly around the world performing their own wacky version of good deeds—putting new arms on the Venus de Milo, mending the crack in the Liberty Bell, and straightening the LEANING TOWER OF PISA—all the while congratulating themselves on the gratitude

A harpoon shatters harmlessly against Bizarro's invulnerable chest during a rousing battle with Superman, 1959

they are undoubtedly earning from Earth people with their acts of goodwill. Horrified that the Bizarros may actually use their super-powers to make good their vow to "smash the planet," Superman is relieved beyond description when the zany monsters finally keep their promise by demolishing the decorative globe atop the Daily Planet Building before streaking away again into outer space (S No. 169/3: "The Bizarro Invasion of Earth!").

In January 1965, during a brief visit to the planet Earth, Bizarro creates a gigantic statue in the image of MR. MXYZPTLK which proves the undoing of the mischievous extradimensional imp (S No. 174/2: "Super-Mxyzptlk...Hero!"). (See MXYZPTLK [Mr.].)

BIZARRO CITY. A "cockeyed city" on the planet HTRAE, home world of the Bizarros. Created by the Bizarros themselves out of the crumbling ruins of an ancient city whose alien population was "wiped out" by some unknown calamity sometime in the distant past, Bizarro City is "a crude copy of Metropolis" (see METROPOLIS) which "looks like something a mad architect would design!" Everything in the city is backwards, cockeyed, and topsy-turvy: the hands on a massive building clock are crooked and bent out of shape, and the numbers on its face are all out of order. A weird "backward imitation" of the American flag flutters from a rooftop flagpole, with blue stripes which run the wrong way and a field of red stars that is upside down. When SUPERMAN visits Bizarro City and attempts to improve the lot of its people by neatening and straightening their ramshackle homes, he is promptly arrested and charged with violating the Bizarro Code, which makes it a "**big crime** to make anything perfect...!" (Act No. 263, Apr '60: "The World of Bizarros!"). Bizarro City is referred to as the "capital" of Htrae in Superman No. 140 (Oct '60: pts. I-III—"The Son of Bizarro!"; "The

'Orphan' Bizarro!"; "The Bizarro Supergirl!"). (*See* BIZARRO.)

BIZARRO-LOIS. The "grotesque, imperfect double" of LOIS LANE who, along with her mate BIZARRO, is the co-ruler of the planet HTRAE (Act No. 263, Apr '60: "The World of Bizarros!"), a wacky, cockeyed world "where all the men are imperfect imitations of [Superman], and all the girls are distorted doubles of Lois Lane!" (Act No. 264, May '60: "The Superman Bizarro!"). Indeed, it is to distinguish herself from all these other Bizarro-Loises that the original Bizarro-Lois has taken to wearing a large medallion around her neck plainly identifying her as "Lois-Bizarro No. 1." Like all Bizarro creatures, Bizarro-Lois—who is alternatively referred to as Lois-Bizarro—is "only composed of lifeless matter," and is, therefore, not really alive. Like her fellow Bizarros, she is illiterate and ungrammatical (Act No. 263, Apr '60: "The World of Bizarros!"), and, like them, she is vulnerable to blue KRYPTONITE just as SUPERMAN is vulnerable to green kryptonite (S No. 140, Oct '60: pts. I-III—"The Son of Bizarro!"; "The 'Orphan' Bizarro!"; "The Bizarro Supergirl!").

Bizarro-Lois first comes into being in August 1959, when Lois Lane uses LEX LUTHOR's "duplicator machine" to create an imperfect duplicate of herself as a mate for Bizarro. Indeed, Bizarro falls in love with Bizarro-Lois the moment he sees her, and flies away with her into outer space so that they can find a home for themselves on a distant planet in some "faraway solar system" (Act No. 255: "The Bride of Bizarro!").

By April 1960 Bizarro and Bizarro-Lois have arrived on a world in a far-off solar system (*see* HTRAE) and come upon the ruins of an ancient city whose alien population was "wiped out" by some unknown calamity sometime in the distant past. The two Bizarros decide to make their home there, but as time passes Bizarro-Lois becomes lonely for "friends to talk to," and so, to fulfill his mate's need for companionship, Bizarro uses the super-scientific apparatus in the ruins of an ancient laboratory to construct an ingenious "imitator machine" with which he soon creates hundreds of Bizarro-Loises in the exact image of his mate.

Bizarro-Lois's joy at her new-found friendships quickly turns to jealousy, however, as the newly created female Bizarros begin to covet the affections of Bizarro, the only male on the planet. At the insistence of the original Bizarro-Lois, Bizarro focuses the amazing imitator machine on himself, thereby creating a host of Bizarros like himself, one for every Bizarro-Lois. Together the male and female Bizarros—all of them imperfect duplicates of Superman and Lois Lane—set about dismantling the crumbling ruins of the ancient alien city and transforming them into "a crude copy of Metropolis" (*see* METROPOLIS), which "looks like something a mad architect would design" (*see* BIZARRO CITY). The original Bizarro became "the tribe's leader," and the original Bizarro-Lois, his consort. Together they rule their Bizarro world from atop stone thrones in a ramshackle "palace." When Superman visits the Bizarro world and is thrown into prison on the charge of having violated the Bizarro Code, Bizarro-Lois visits him in his prison cell, proclaims her love for him, and offers to persuade the jury at his upcoming trial to find him innocent if he will agree to give her his hand in marriage. The Man of Steel, however, declines the offer: "Sorry, Lois!" he snaps. "I'll take my chances in court!"

"You... you beast!" cries Bizarro-Lois angrily as she stalks out of the prison cell. "You turn me down, eh? Then me will get jury to convict you... wait and see!"

Indeed, when Superman finally comes to trial in a Bizarro courtroom, the spurned Bizarro-Lois vindictively incites her fellow jurors into such a state of frenzy against him that a verdict of guilty is a foregone conclusion (Act No. 263: "The World of Bizarros!"). (*See* BIZARRO.)

As he sits in his prison cell awaiting the carrying out of the sentence that has been imposed upon him by the Bizarro court, Superman is visited by yet another Bizarro-Lois, this one a "freak Bizarro" who has the appearance of a Bizarro but who thinks and speaks normally. This Bizarro-Lois, having donned a bogus medallion falsely identifying her as Lois-Bizarro No. 1, offers to help Superman escape from the prison by posing as the original Bizarro-Lois and engaging the watchtower guard in conversation while the Man of Steel makes a dash for freedom. The escape plan is thwarted by the real Bizarro-Lois, who arrives on the scene and exposes the impersonation, but Superman ultimately wins freedom for himself—as well as for the courageous Bizarro-Lois who tried to help him—by persuading the Bizarro authorities to annul his conviction (Act No. 264, May '60: "The Superman Bizarro!"). (*See* BIZARRO.)

In October 1960 Bizarro-Lois gives birth to a baby boy, the first Bizarro actually born on the planet as opposed to having been artificially created by Bizarro's imitator machine. Like all newborn Bizarro infants, the baby is born with perfect human features which undergo a sudden transformation into imperfect, Bizarro features shortly thereafter. The child's handsome features at birth, however, cause him to be branded a "freak" on the Bizarro world, and set in motion a chain of circumstances which ultimately threaten to ignite an all-out war between the Bizarro planet and Earth (S No. 140: pts. I-III—"The Son of Bizarro!"; "The 'Orphan' Bizarro!"; "The Bizarro Supergirl!"). (*See* BIZARRO.)

By February 1961 Bizarro-Lois has apparently given birth to a second child, because she and Bizarro are now depicted as having two young children, a boy and a girl (S No. 143/3: "Bizarro Meets Frankenstein!").

In January 1962, when Superman and the other survivors of the exploded planet KRYPTON—including SUPERGIRL, KRYPTO THE SUPERDOG, the citizens of KANDOR, and even the villains imprisoned

Overjoyed to discover that his mate, Bizarro-Lois, has given birth to a Bizarro baby...

...Bizarro is crestfallen when he learns that the newborn infant is a Bizarro "freak," 1960

in the PHANTOM ZONE—bow their heads solemnly for one full minute of silence to commemorate the anniversary of the destruction of Krypton, Bizarro-Lois and the other Bizarros of Htrae celebrate the occasion with a full minute of loud, joyously raucous noise, not out of any malice for the doomed millions of Krypton, but only out of the zaniness that characterizes their race.

"Ha, ha!" laughs Bizarro. "...Is everybody happy?... Yahooo!!!"

"Too bad whole universe didn't blow up with it!" chimes in Bizarro-Lois insanely (S No. 150/1: "The One Minute of Doom!").

BIZARRO WORLD, THE. *See* HTRAE.

BLAIR, MARVIN. A criminally irresponsible research chemist for the Miles Steel Corporation, promoted to the position of vice-president after pioneering a revolutionary new steel-producing process capable of producing steel a full 20 percent stronger than ordinary steel at a far lower cost, who abruptly resigns from the company approximately a year later, ostensibly because he wishes to retire to enjoy his accumulated wealth, but in reality because he knows full well that the new steel-producing process he created produces such extraordinary "magnetic tension" in the final product that "after a certain time—roughly a year," any structure made from the steel "gets so weak that the whole thing disintegrates at once," posing the imminent threat of horrifying disasters in which entire bridges, buildings, and airplanes will suddenly and mysteriously vanish. After racing from place to place to combat a series of such disasters—and after seeing to it that every structure made from the new Miles steel has been dismantled and replaced with reliable steel—SUPERMAN brings the unscrupulous Blair to justice in October-November 1950 (WF No. 48: "The Great Steel Mystery!").

BLAKE, "BLACKY." The leader of a gang of criminals who, having transformed himself into a look-alike for the state penitentiary warden through the miracle of plastic surgery, has engineered the kidnapping of the real warden and then taken his place at the prison as part of an elaborate scheme to plant a listening device in the cell of convict "Larceny Luke" Damon for the purpose of ascertaining the whereabouts of $1,000,000 worth of "valuable radioactive minerals" stolen by Damon from "a hospital supply center" but never recovered by the authorities.

The scheme hits an unanticipated snag, however, when Blake discovers that, by special arrangement with the warden and governor, Clark Kent has allowed himself to be convicted and sentenced on a bogus blackmailing charge in the hope that, as Damon's cellmate, he might uncover the whereabouts of the missing loot for the authorities. When Damon finally does confide the hiding place to Kent in the belief that Kent, like himself, is a hardened convict, Blake overhears the vital information through his listening device and promptly concocts a scheme to kill Clark Kent in the act of "escaping" to ensure that he and his henchmen will be able to recover the loot before Kent can report its location to the authorities. Unbeknownst to Blake and his henchmen, of course, Clark Kent is secretly SUPERMAN, and he easily thwarts the murder scheme, apprehends Blake and his cohorts, and rescues the kidnapped warden from the villains' clutches (Act No. 323, Apr '65: "Clark Kent in the Big House!").

BLAKE, TOMMY. A teen-aged newsboy with a heartfelt ambition to become a reporter, who wins a contest for newsboys sponsored by the DAILY PLANET, and with it a cherished cub reporter's post on the *Planet* staff, by courageously helping SUPERMAN expose and apprehend a ring of ration-book counterfeiters in Summer 1945 (WF No. 18: "The Junior Reporters!").

BLAKELY, THORNTON. The callous owner of the Blakely Coal Mine in Blakelytown, an obdurate, unscrupulous man who readily tolerates the deplorable safety conditions that prevail in his mine rather than spend the money it would take to improve them. "There are no safety-hazards in my mine," proclaims Blakely. "But if there were—what of it? I'm a business man not a humanitarian!"

Racing to the Blakely Coal Mine in August 1938 to rescue a miner trapped by a cave-in, SUPERMAN teaches Blakely and a group of his spoiled, affluent friends a well-deserved lesson by deliberately trapping them inside the mine with a man-made cave-in and then clearing them a path to safety only after they have all collapsed from exhaustion after futilely attempting to dig their way to freedom.

"...Henceforth my mine will be the safest in the country, and my workers the best treated," announces Blakely, after emerging from the coal mine. "My experience in the mine brought their problems closer to my understanding!" (Act No. 3). The story is reprinted in Superman No. 1/3 (Sum '39).

BLAND, CARL. A prominent METROPOLIS lawyer and secret Nazi agent who is director of the Izan Athletic Club, a front for Nazi activity. After successfully proposing to city officials that the young men in his Izan Athletic Club be allowed to pose as Nazi soldiers and stage a mock invasion of Metropolis—complete with prearranged mock "atrocities"—for the purpose of alerting the populace to the perils of Fascism, Bland and his cohorts launch a real invasion of the city—including such real-life atrocities as attempts to execute city officials, poison the water supply, and destroy the municipal electric power plant—until they are finally apprehended by SUPERMAN in September-October 1942 (S No. 18/1: "The Conquest of a City").

BLANDING. An elderly playwright, driven to the brink of suicide by the "cruel drama notices" accorded his latest play, who enters into a scheme, concocted by a sympathetic LOIS LANE, to publicize his next play, entitled *The Sleeping Beauty*, by having Lois pretend to fall victim to an ancient Egyptian curse supposed to consign its victims to a sleep of 1,000 years, thus transforming her, to all appearances, into a modern Sleeping Beauty reposing in a sleeplike trance. SUPERMAN exposes the hoax in September-October 1948, but then goes to work with his mighty super-powers to produce Blanding's play almost single-handedly and see the production through to a brilliantly successful premiere (WF No. 36: "Lois Lane, Sleeping Beauty").

BLANTH. A far-distant planet, destroyed by a cataclysmic explosion sometime in the recent past, whose sole survivors—members of a "highly developed, friendly race" endowed with superhuman powers similar but not identical to SUPERMAN's—arrive on the planet Earth in Janury 1955, hoping to build homes for themselves in the vicinity of METROPOLIS and to be allowed to become contributing citizens of their adopted planet. Unbeknownst to the peace-loving space travelers, however, their presence constitutes a potential hazard of terrifying proportions—for the Blanthians exhale methane gas,

which is deadly to all Earth life—and Superman is ultimately compelled to resolve the dilemma by transforming a distant, uninhabited planet into a duplicate of the now-shattered Blanth so that the orphaned space voyagers can begin life anew there (S No. 94/2: "The Men Without a World!").

BLISS, ROGER (Mr. and Mrs.). A METROPOLIS couple who are the parents of an infant son who acquires temporary super-powers identical to SUPERMAN's as the result of having inadvertently ingested some of the strange "powdery substance" contained inside a group of Kryptonian "condensed food" containers—apparently remnants of the original rocket ship that carried the infant Superman from KRYPTON to the planet Earth—dug up by Mr. Bliss while searching for Indian relics. Left for a time in Superman's care, the super-powered infant causes a series of super-problems for the Man of Steel until the baby finally loses his powers and is reunited with his parents in June 1956 (Act No. 217: "The Amazing Super-Baby").

BLOB (Mr.). The obese "tycoon of business" turned criminal who achieves infamy as the TYCOON OF CRIME (S No. 29/2, Jul/Aug '44: "The Tycoon of Crime!").

BLOTZ, EMMA. A beautiful but unscrupulous young woman from the town of Gopher Junction who, in collusion with an accomplice posing as a famous woman scientist, pretends that she is Helen of Troy, newly transported to our era via her accomplice's "time machine," as part of a scheme to cash in on Helen of Troy endorsements for such products as cosmetics, clothing, and jewelry. The bogus Helen, who is ostensibly transported through the time barrier to twentieth-century METROPOLIS as part of a city-sponsored effort to locate "the world's most perfect girl" as a fitting mate for SUPERMAN, is exposed as an impostor by Superman in June 1949 (Act No. 133: "The World's Most Perfect Girl!").

BLYTH, ANN. The "famed Universal-International motion picture star" who helps SUPERMAN apprehend the CAPTAIN KIDDER gang in March 1949 (Act No. 130: "Superman and the Mermaid!").

BOGART, CARL. The foreman of a plantation on Pogo Island, an island inherited by an American girl named Nan Wilson several years ago. When Nan visits the island in September-October 1941—in the company of her fiancé Niles Grant, CLARK KENT, and LOIS LANE—a mysterious native witch doctor incites the local natives to a series of attempts on their lives on the ground that they are "evil spirits" who must be destroyed. The witch doctor, however, is none other than Bogart himself, who is determined to prevent Nan and her friends from discovering that Pogo Island is in reality "a secret refueling base for a country at war" from which foreign submarines regularly sail forth to "prey on merchant marine in these neutral waters!" "I am in that country's pay," explains Bogart. "It was my job to keep people off this island...!" Bogart and the foreign troops who man the secret submarine base are ultimately apprehended through the heroic efforts of SUPERMAN (S No. 12/1).

BOND, ELLEN. A daring and beautiful trapeze artist who is among the four finalists in a Miss Metropolis contest, sponsored by the DAILY PLANET, which only pretty girls engaged in perilous occupations may enter. Ellen Bond's unscrupulous agent, Happy Ferris, attempts to sabotage the efforts of the other contestants in order to protect the heavy bets he has placed on his client, but SUPERMAN thwarts Ferris's machinations at every turn and the agent is ultimately apprehended by Ellen herself (S No. 63/3, Mar/Apr '50: "Miss Metropolis of 1950").

BOR-AK. The Kryptonian explorer who discovered his planet's JEWEL MOUNTAINS (S No. 164/2, Oct '63: "The Fugitive from the Phantom Zone!"). (See also KRYPTON.)

BORGONIA. The foreign country of unspecified location which is the scene of SUPERMAN's encounter with the tyrannical dictator TORM in October 1957 (Act No. 233: "The Land of a Million Supermen").

BORKIA. The "tiny European republic" where SUPERMAN battles GENERAL MALVIO in November 1959 (Act No. 258: "The Menace of Cosmic Man!").

BOUNCING BOY. A member of the LEGION OF SUPER-HEROES. A native of the planet Earth, Bouncing Boy has the power—which he originally acquired by accidentally ingesting a vial of experimental super-plastic fluid—to inflate his body at will and bounce along like a huge rubber ball. Bouncing Boy's real name is Chuck Taine.

In October 1962, when SUPERMAN is believed to be dying of an incurable malady, Bouncing Boy is among the Legionnaires who are summoned to the twentieth century by SUPERGIRL to help carry out the gigantic super-tasks that Superman hopes to fulfill as his final legacy to humanity, including the destruction of a "vast cloud of fungus in distant space, that will some day reach Earth and blight all plant life," and the melting of the Antarctic ice, "to make Antarctica a fit place for millions to live in the future," thus ensuring "a home for Earth's expanding population...!" (S No. 156: "The Last Days of Superman!" pts. I-III—"Superman's Death Sentence!"; "The Super-Comrades of All Time!"; "Superman's Last Day of Life!").

When METROPOLIS television station WMET-TV inaugurates its new "Our American Heroes" series with a program honoring Superman, "our greatest American hero," Bouncing Boy is among the Legion representatives who journey to the twentieth century to appear on the show and thus help pay tribute to the Man of Steel (Act No. 309, Feb '64: "The Superman Super-Spectacular!").

BOURDET. In World's Finest Comics No. 82, an "evil chancellor" in the court of Louis XIV of France (1638-1715) who, unbeknownst to his king, has illegally abducted the benevolent Count Ferney, "a noble friend of the people," and imprisoned him in an iron mask, first in Pignerol Castle and later in the Bastille. However, at the urging of PROFESSOR CARTER NICHOLS—who hopes to solve the enigma of the identity of the Man in the Iron Mask—BATMAN, ROBIN, and SUPERMAN return through the time barrier to France in the year 1696, where they trade places with the THREE MUSKETEERS—all of whom have been badly wounded by Bourdet's guardsmen—and, aided by the musketeers' comrade D'Artagnan, expose the treachery of the evil Bourdet and free Count Ferney from the iron mask. Bourdet, ordered imprisoned by the king, will remain shut away in the Bastille for the rest of his days, forced to wear the iron mask himself (May/June '56: "The Three Super-Musketeers!").

BOWSER, DERBY. A "one-time bootlegging czar," released from the state penitentiary in Fall 1944, who decides to capitalize on the wartime rubber shortage by organizing a gang of criminals and entering the bootleg tire racket, hijacking trainloads of tires and stealing them wholesale off people's parked cars—often in spite of the fact that they are worn out or otherwise defective—and then selling them to selfish citizens eager to purchase scarce commodities on the booming black market. "Whenever there's a scarcity of something due to law," explains Bowser to his henchmen, "there are always plenty of smart chiselers who are willing to pay stiff prices in order to get what they want. We'll supply what they want—but soak them for it."

The threat to America's security posed by Bowser and his cohorts is a serious one, but perhaps not so dangerous as that posed by the otherwise patriotic, law-abiding citizens who willingly patronize the black marketeers in spite of the fact that to do so is literally "to sabotage the war effort."

"What of it?" shrugs businessman Ben Stanger, when SUPERMAN accuses him of having purchased bootleg tires from the racketeers. "I'm only one of thousands determined not to let the war upset my everyday conveniences."

"Nevertheless," replies Superman, after giving Stanger a short lecture on patriotism, "by patronizing a black market racketeer, you are aiding the Axis."

Derby Bowser's henchmen are ultimately apprehended by Superman, but Bowser meets a fate he richly deserves when, as he attempts to escape in an automobile outfitted with some of his own defective bootleg tires, his getaway car suffers a blowout and he is killed in the resulting collision (WF No. 15: "The Rubber Band").

"BRAIN, THE." A "scientific genius who has turned his twisted talents to crime." In July-August 1953 "The Brain" demolishes the PARTHENON, the SPHINX, and the LEANING TOWER OF PISA—and makes up one of his henchmen to impersonate SUPERMAN—as part of an elaborate scheme to make off with $50,000,000 in precious gems lent to METROPOLIS by the Maharajah of Ipostan, but Superman thwarts the scheme, restores the famed monuments, and takes the villains into custody (S No. 83/1: "Destination X!").

BRAINIAC. A ruthless extraterrestrial villain—in reality an ingenious humanoid computer created by the sinister "computer tyrants" (S No. 167, Feb '64: "The Team of Luthor and Brainiac!" pts. I-III—"The Deadly Duo!"; "The Downfall of Superman!"; "The Hour of Kandor's Vengeance!") of a far-distant planet—who has been an implacable foe of SUPERMAN since July 1958 (Act No. 242: "The Super-Duel in Space").

An "evil space mastermind" (S No. 134, Jan '60: chs. I-III—"The Super-Menace of Metropolis!"; "The Revenge Against Jor-El!"; "The Duel of the Supermen!") and "fearsome super-foe" with an arsenal of awesome "nightmarish scientific weapons at his command" (Act No. 280, Sep '61: "Brainiac's Super-Revenge!"), he is perhaps the "most terrible evil-doer in all the universe" (S No. 172, Oct '64: pts. I-III—"The New Superman!"; "Clark Kent—Former Superman!"; "The Struggle of the Two Supermen!"), a creature of "superhuman intelligence," "great scientific ability," and utter "ruthlessness" who is said to "know the universe as no mere man knows it!" (S No. 167, Feb '64: "The Team of Luthor and Brainiac!" pts. I-III—"The Deadly Duo!"; "The Downfall of Superman!"; "The Hour of Kandor's Vengeance!"). It was Brainiac who, sometime prior to the death of the planet KRYPTON, literally stole the Kryptonian city of

Brainiac and his alien pet, Koko

KANDOR, reducing it to microscopic size with a diabolical shrinking ray and preserving it aboard his spacecraft inside a large glass bottle until it was finally recovered by Superman and placed for safekeeping inside his FORTRESS OF SOLITUDE (Act No. 242, Jul '58: "The Super-Duel in Space").

"Because of his constant battle against evil," notes Action Comics No. 280, "the **Man of Steel** has made many dangerous foes. Of these, none is more terrible than the space villain, **Brainiac**...!" (Sep '61: "Brainiac's Super-Revenge!").

Although Brainiac—with his green eyes (S No. 173/3, Nov '64: "The Triumph of Luthor and Brainiac!") and light-green skin (Act No. 242, Jul '58: "The Super-Duel in Space"; and others)—closely resembles the humanoid native inhabitants of the far-distant planet Colu (also referred to as the planet Yod), he is actually a sinister "computer spy" created by the computer tyrants which had seized control of that planet as the first step in a scheme of interplanetary conquest. With Colu's computer masters having long since been overthrown and destroyed in a "great revolution" that toppled them from their pinnacle of planetary power, Brainiac now remains as "the last of the mighty computer minds" (S No. 167, Feb '64: "The Team of Luthor and Brainiac!" pts. I-III—"The Deadly Duo!"; "The Downfall of Superman!"; "The Hour of Kandor's Vengeance!"), a "super-scientific space-villain" (S No. 170/2, Jul '64: pts. I-II—"If Lex Luthor Were Superman's Father!"; "The Wedding of Lara and Luthor!") who has striven to keep his computer identity a secret, who is devoid of human emotions, and whose single greatest weakness may be his lack of insight into human psychology (S No. 167, Feb '64: "The Team of Luthor and Brainiac!" pts. I-III—"The Deadly Duo!"; "The Downfall of Superman!"; "The Hour of Kandor's Vengeance!"). In his initial appearance he is portrayed as completely bareheaded (Act No. 242, Jul '58: "The Super-Duel in Space"), but later texts portray him as having a network of electronic devices atop his head which are described as "the electric terminals of his sensory 'nerves'...!" (S No. 167, Feb '64: "The Team of Luthor and Brainiac!" pts. I-III—"The Deadly Duo!"; "The Downfall of Superman!"; "The Hour of Kandor's Vengeance!"). Brainiac is sometimes accompanied on his marauding journeys through space by his alien pet, Koko, a white extraterrestrial creature which closely resembles a small monkey except for the twin antennae protruding from its forehead (Act No. 242, Jul '58: "The Super-Duel in Space").

Because he is a "master of super-scientific forces" (Act No. 242, Jul '58: "The Super-Duel in Space") as well as the "most terrible of all space villains," Brainiac possesses an awesome arsenal of "super-scientific weapons" and devices to aid him in his never-ending war against Superman (S No. 167, Feb '64: "The Team of Luthor and Brainiac!" pts. I-III—"The Deadly Duo!"; "The Downfall of Superman!"; "The Hour of Kandor's Vengeance!"). Even LEX LUTHOR, "the world's most dangerous criminal scientist," has been moved to adopt some of Brainiac's more ingenious devices (Act No. 292, Sep '62: "When Superman Defended His Arch-Enemy!").

Perhaps the most important weapon in Brainiac's arsenal is his ultrasophisticated "space-time craft" (Act No. 275, Apr '61: "The Menace of Red-Green

Kryptonite!"), or "time-space vehicle," a "weird vehicle" capable of accelerating to such phenomenal velocities that it can literally penetrate the time barrier and travel through time as well as space (Act No. 280, Sep '61: "Brainiac's Super-Revenge!"). Portrayed sometimes as a flying saucer (Act No. 242, Jul '58: "The Super-Duel in Space"; and others) and at other times as a bizarre, light-bulb-shaped vehicle (Act No. 275, Apr '61: "The Menace of Red-Green Kryptonite!"; and others), it is surrounded by an invisible force field—or "ultra-force barrier"—which "nothing in the universe can penetrate," and is crammed full of superscientific apparatus, including the amazing "hyper-force machine" built into the control panel. It is by means of the "hyper-forces" emanating from this ingenious device—which is described as powered by "hyper-batteries" energized by cosmic rays (Act No. 242, Jul '58: "The Super-Duel in Space")—that Brainiac committed what has been called "the greatest crime in the universe": the shrinking of the Kryptonian city of Kandor to microscopic size so that it could be imprisoned aboard his space-time craft inside a large glass bottle (S No. 167, Feb '64: "The Team of Luthor and Brainiac!" pts. I-III—"The Deadly Duo!"; "The Downfall of Superman!"; "The Hour of Kandor's Vengeance!"). The "hyper-force ray" (S No. 158, Jan '63: "Superman in Kandor" pts. I-III—"Invasion of the Mystery Super-Men!"; "The Dynamic Duo of Kandor!"; "The City of Super-People!") is referred to as a "reducing ray" in at least one text (Act No. 245, Oct '58: "The Shrinking Superman!"), and as a "shrinking ray" in several others (Act No. 243, Aug '58: "The Lady and the Lion"; and others).

Other superscientific apparatus employed by Brainiac include the special "power-belt" which surrounds the villain with an impenetrable "ultra shell" (Act No. 242, Jul '58: "The Super-Duel in Space"), or "force field" (Act No. 275, Apr '61: "The Menace of Red-Green Kryptonite!"; and others), which even the heat of Superman's X-ray vision cannot penetrate; the "coma-ray" with which Brainiac temporarily paralyzes Superman in February 1964 (S No. 167: "The Team of Luthor and Brainiac!" pts. I-III—"The Deadly Duo!"; "The Downfall of Superman!"; "The Hour of Kandor's Vengeance!"); the "weird, worm-like vehicle"—called an "underground-machine"—with which Brainiac tunnels Luthor out of prison in October 1964, and the "Z-ray" with which he cures Luthor of a fatal bullet wound (S No. 172: pts. I-III—"The New Superman!"; "Clark Kent—Former Superman!"; "The Struggle of the Two Supermen!"); and the portable "shrinking ray," in the form of a raygun, which Superman has confiscated from Brainiac and which is now held for safekeeping inside Superman's Fortress of Solitude (S No. 158, Jan '63: "Superman in Kandor" pts. I-III—"Invasion of the Mystery Super-Men!"; "The Dynamic Duo of Kandor!"; "The City of Super-People!").

In the texts, Brainiac is referred to as "a renegade outer-space scientist" (Act No. 243, Aug '58: "The Lady and the Lion"); "an evil space scientist" (Act No. 245, Oct '58: "The Shrinking Superman!"); "an ingenious space marauder" (Act No. 253, Jun '59: "The War Between Superman and Jimmy Olsen!"); a "space villain" (Act No. 260, Jan '60: "Mighty Maid!"; and others); "an arch fiend from outer space" and a "notorious space outlaw" (Act No. 275, Apr '61: "The Menace of Red-Green Kryptonite!"); one of "the world's worst villains" and one of "the most evil geniuses who have ever lived in the past, present or future . . ." (Act No. 286, Mar '62: "The Jury of Super-Enemies!"); one of "the most dangerous evil-doers in the universe" (Act No. 294, Nov '62: "The Kryptonite Killer!"); "the evilest villain of space" (S No. 158, Jan '63: "Superman in Kandor" pts. I-III—"Invasion of the Mystery Super-Men!"; "The Dynamic Duo of Kandor!"; "The City of Super-People!"); "the foulest villain in the universe" and "the darkest criminal in the universe" (S No. 167, Feb '64: "The Team of Luthor and Brainiac!" pts. I-III—"The Deadly Duo!"; "The Downfall of Superman!"; "The Hour of Kandor's Vengeance!"); "the most terrible criminal outlaw of all time" and "the most formidable foe of all time" (WF No. 144, Sep '64: "The 1,001 Tricks of Clayface and Brainiac!" pts I-II—no title; "The Helpless Partners!"); and the "greatest wrongdoer in the universe" (S No. 172, Oct '64: pts. I-III—"The New Superman!"; "Clark Kent—Former Superman!"; "The Struggle of the Two Supermen!").

Brainiac is a villain of such outstanding notoriety that Superman has devoted an entire room to him in his Fortress of Solitude. The so-called Brainiac Room contains a statue of the villain, a model of his space-time craft, and an array of scientific machinery constructed by Superman in connection with his "experiments aimed at penetrating Brainiac's force-field" (Act No. 275, Apr '61: "The Menace of Red-Green Kryptonite!"). When Superman puts the finishing touches on his Fortress's new Hall of Enemies in November 1962, Brainiac is among the villains and villainesses represented there by colorful wax busts (Act No. 294: "The Kryptonite Killer!").

In his early textual appearances, Brainiac is portrayed as a "sinister alien" who has been roaming the universe in his spacecraft, using his hyper-force machine to kidnap whole cities from various planets so that he can use them to found a "new empire" on his own "desolate world," where the population has been decimated by a hideous plague. Indeed, the inference is unmistakable that Brainiac was once the ruler of the planet he now seeks to repopulate. "Yes, Koko!" he gloats to his alien pet, after stealing the city of Paris in July 1958. "I will take a dozen cities-in-the-bottle back to repopulate my home world, where a plague wiped out my people! Then I will restore all the cities to their original size and have a new empire to rule, as before!" (Act No. 242: "The Super-Duel in Space"; see also S No. 141, Nov '60: "Superman's Return to Krypton!" pts. I-III—"Superman Meets Jor-El and Lara Again!"; "Superman's Kryptonian Romance!"; "The Surprise of Fate!").

In February 1964, however, while probing the universe with his "time-space thought-scanner" in the hope of locating an ally capable of helping him destroy Superman, Lex Luthor discovers that he has "contacted a vastly powerful mind...on a distant planet, years in the past...." Carefully adjusting the controls of his "uncanny instrument" in order to "get the mental picture clearer," Luthor finds that he has tuned in on the mind of Master Computer One, an electronic brain of towering intellect created by the green-skinned humanoid inhabitants of a far-distant planet. "A human mind is only a sixth-level effector," remarks one of the alien scientists associated with the construction of the master computer, "but the new computer is built to be a tenth-level effector!"

As the years passed, the green-skinned aliens built many such computers. Before long, however, the powerful master computers had wrested control of their planet from the humanoid civilization that had created them and had begun using weapons of awesome destructiveness to enforce their tyranny over the people. "We computers you built to serve you are more fit to govern than you!" proclaims one master computer. "Your poor sixth-level-effector minds are too weak...from now on, we rule!"

As Luthor continues to survey the history of this distant planet with his time-space thought-scanner, he learns that the power-hungry "mechanical minds" soon concocted a diabolical scheme of interplanetary conquest. "We must extend our wise rule to all worlds governed by foolish humans!" asserted one computer. "First we'll send a computer spy to reconnoiter those worlds!"

"Our spy would be detected and destroyed unless he deceived them by looking human," observed a second computer. "We'll make a computer of powerful intelligence that looks human!"

And so, in the weeks that followed, an ingenious computer spy was built to carry out acts of interplanetary espionage for the evil master computers that had created it. Although their advanced technology would have enabled them to equip their new spy with a "twelfth-order mind," superior to their own, the computers decided to endow it with only a tenth-level-effector mind as a safeguard against its attempting to capitalize on its superior intelligence in order to dominate its creators.

The master computers christened their humanoid computer-spy Brainiac. To ensure that he would not only look human, but act human as well, they fed the "mental patterns" of one of their planet's scientists into Brainiac's memory banks, thereby endowing him with a full range of human mannerisms. The master computers attempted to further enhance the credibility of Brainiac's human masquerade by selecting a boy from among their planet's green-skinned inhabitants to accompany Brainiac on his travels and pose as his son. The youngster chosen for the task, whom the master computers renamed Brainiac II, had no intention of allowing himself to become the tool of "an evil computer," however, and

at the earliest opportunity he ran away and escaped, forcing Brainiac to climb into his spacecraft and set out on his interplanetary espionage mission without him. It was this boy who, in Brainiac's absence, ultimately led his people in "the great revolution that destroyed the computer tyrants" that had seized control of their planet. That courageous youngster, whose real name was Vril Dox, was the ancestor of BRAINIAC 5, one of the members of the LEGION OF SUPER-HEROES (S No. 167: "The Team of Luthor and Brainiac!" pts. I-III—"The Deadly Duo!"; "The Downfall of Superman!"; "The Hour of Kandor's Vengeance!"; and others).

In July 1958 Brainiac appears over the planet Earth in his saucerlike spacecraft, fixing the city of Paris in the cross hairs of his "hyper-bombsight" and pressing a button connected to the craft's control panel. Instantly, the French capital is bathed in a "cone of peculiar rays" which reduce its people and buildings to microscopic size and trap them inside a large glass bottle aboard Brainiac's spaceship. "See, Koko?" gloats Brainiac to his monkeylike alien pet. "The hyper-forces I released reduced the entire city to miniature size and transported it inside this bottle!"

Soaring at rocket speeds over the surface of the globe, Brainiac "continues his raid of Earth," stealing London, Rome, New York, and other cities, so that "one after another, the world's greatest cities become toy villages in bottles" aboard the saucerlike spacecraft, their "tiny people" kept alive by a special oxygen supply pumped into the bottled cities through special "air hoses."

Unable to penetrate the invisible "ultra-force barrier" that surrounds Brainiac's spaceship, Superman breaks off his battle with the villain and returns to METROPOLIS, deliberately allowing himself to be reduced to tiny size and kidnapped along with the rest of the city when Brainiac steals the city with his "hyper-force machine" to add to his collection. Aboard the villain's spacecraft, however, the lilliputian Superman is mistaken for an annoying flying insect, and when, to avoid being squashed by a flyswatter wielded by Koko, he flies into the mouth of the nearest bottle city, he finds himself confronted by a "super-surprise," for this particular bottle contains a city of Krypton, Superman's home planet, a city stolen and imprisoned by Brainiac "years before Krypton met doom!"

Inside this bottled Kryptonian city, where "Krypton's gravity-conditions are duplicated" and Superman therefore has no super-powers, Superman meets the elderly scientist Professor Kimda, once the college roommate of Superman's father (see JOR-EL), who explains to him that he is now in Kandor, "the city that was Krypton's capital," and takes him on a tour of the miniaturized metropolis. Through his telescope, explains Professor Kimda, he has observed Brainiac at the controls of his hyper-force machine and has prepared a chart detailing the precise locations of the various buttons which would restore the kidnapped cities to their normal size. Indeed, soon afterward, after Brainiac has placed himself and Koko in "suspended animation" so that the pair can "avoid aging" during the long space-journey back to their home planet, Superman escapes from Kandor,

Hovering over Earth in his saucerlike spacecraft..

enlarge the Kandorians while dooming him to remain tiny forever, when suddenly a tiny Kandorian rocket, piloted by Professor Kimda, soars out of the bottle city and rockets into the button that will restore the Man

...bathing the city below in a "cone of peculiar rays"...

reaches Brainiac's control panel, and punches the control buttons enumerated by Professor Kimda until all the stolen Earth cities have been restored to their proper locations and enlarged to their original size. Now only the city of Kandor remains to be liberated from its bottle prison, but Superman finds himself on

Brainiac fixes the city of Paris in the cross hairs of his "hyper-bombsight" and squeezes the trigger...

the horns of a cruel dilemma, for there is "only one charge of hyper-forces left...enough to restore the **Krypton** city to normal size or [Superman]...but not **both**!" Selflessly, Superman is about to press the button on Brainiac's console that will free and

of Steel to his normal human size. "I flew the rocket out of the hole in the [bottle's] cork to punch the button knowing only one charge would be left!" explains Professor Kimda. "We could not let Earth be deprived of its great super-hero!"

Placing the bottled city of Kandor under his arm, Superman flies out of Brainiac's spaceship to his Fortress of Solitude, where the tiny Kryptonian city will remain for safekeeping, while Brainiac and Koko

...that shrink it to microscopic size and transport it inside a bottle aboard Brainiac's spacecraft...

soar onward into space, in suspended animation, oblivious to the loss of their cargo of kidnapped cities. "Let **Brainiac's** ship fly on!" muses Superman. "When he awakens, he will have no stolen cities! Let him live on his desolate world...**alone**...a cruel king without a kingdom!" (Act No. 242: "The Super-Duel in Space!").

In November 1960, during a time-journey he makes to the planet Krypton prior to its destruction,

...where its now-tiny people are kept alive by an oxygen supply pumped into the bottle through a special air hose

Superman witnesses the theft of Kandor by Brainiac (S No. 141: "Superman's Return to Krypton!" pts. I-III—"Superman Meets Jor-El and Lara Again!"; "Superman's Kryptonian Romance!"; "The Surprise of Fate!").

In April 1961 Brainiac returns, landing his bizarre space-time craft in the center of Metropolis and using

After pausing a moment to gloat over his lilliputian Paris...

its awesome "super-gadgets" to steal a warehouseful of aluminum housewares for resale on a distant planet where aluminum is rare and valuable. When Superman attempts to intervene, the villain bathes him in an eerie ray "combined of red and green

kryptonite" (see KRYPTONITE) and then roars away into outer space, vowing to return soon to steal more aluminum as well as to discover what "terrible effect" his new ray has had upon Superman.

Unbeknownst to anyone but Superman, however, the weird ray has had only the relatively benign effect of stimulating Superman's "pineal gland" in such an extraordinary way as to cause the growth of a temporary third eye at the back of Superman's head, but the bizarre development poses a dilemma for the Man of Steel in that, were the true effect of Brainiac's ray to become public knowledge, the presence of a third eye on the heads of both Clark Kent and Superman would result in the exposure of Superman's secret identity. To combat this threat, Superman pretends that Brainiac's ray has had the effect of temporarily transforming him into a super-eccentric who wears strange hats (such as a swami's turban or a hat like Napoleon's) while he performs his customary super-heroic duties and engages in somewhat zany, but not overly alarming, behavior (such as when he flies through the air after a wanted murderer while astride an equine statue uprooted from a Metropolis park) evocative of the behavior associated with each particular hat. While Superman's bizarre behavior distracts people's attention from the real effects of Brainiac's ray, the hats serve to conceal from view the third eye at the back of his head. When

...Brainiac "continues his raid of Earth"...

Brainiac finally returns to Earth, Superman defeats him, placing him unconscious inside his space-time craft and launching him into time and space after jamming the craft's controls to ensure that the villain will "remain stuck on some remote planet at some remote time in the past." The result will be to keep Brainiac away from twentieth-century Earth, at least "for a while," and already Superman can feel the effects of the villain's ray wearing off, so that his third eye is "shrinking" and "in a few days" will be gone forever (Act No. 275: "The Menace of Red-Green Kryptonite!").

In September 1961 Brainiac returns to avenge his previous defeat at the hands of Superman. According to this text, Superman, at the conclusion of his

...until the world's greatest cities have become "toy villages in bottles," 1958

previous battle with Brainiac (above), had locked the villain inside his space-time craft and "sent [him] back into Earth's Ice-Age, trapped in a state of suspended animation!" In the words of the text:

> Let us look millions of years into Earth's past, where, amazingly, there exists a strange craft...it is the weird vehicle in which **Brainiac** was transported back through time by **Superman** to Earth's Ice-Age....
> Its control-dial jammed...its operator in a state of suspended animation...the notorious space-villain slumbers on and on, oblivious of the huge prehistoric beasts about him....

The text continues, "Centuries pass while **Brainiac** sleeps," protected by the glass dome of his time-

Seated at the controls of his space-time craft, Brainiac soars through the time barrier, 1961

space vehicle. Man appears upon the Earth, discovers fire and, centuries later, the first wheel. And then, "...as luck would have it," this first wheel, the brainchild of some inspired prehistoric inventor, rolls down a steep hill and "crashes into **Brainiac's** vehicle," cracking open the glass dome, releasing "the suspended animation gas" inside it, and allowing the ruthless space villain to awaken from his eons-long sleep.

After swiftly repairing the cracks in the glass dome and unjamming his vehicle's control dial, Brainiac accelerates his space-time craft across the time barrier, to the Congolese jungle in the twentieth century, where Superman and three of his friends—JIMMY OLSEN, LOIS LANE, and PERRY WHITE—have set up a temporary "tent field office" to enable them to cover a Congolese native uprising for the DAILY PLANET. Swooping down on the unsuspecting group from out of the stratosphere, Brainiac temporarily robs Superman of his super-powers with a diabolical "kryptonite bomb" and then uses an ingenious "portable shrinking-ray" to reduce his four victims to "Tom Thumb size" before trapping them all inside a large glass bottle. Superman and his friends ultimately escape from the bottle, however, and restore themselves to normal size by means of an enlarging-ray mechanism aboard Brainiac's space-time craft. And, with the effects of the villain's kryptonite bomb having now worn off, Superman swiftly defeats the evil Brainiac and dispatches him to KRONIS, the "prison planet run by the Cosmic Police!" Throughout this adventure, Superman and his companions are aided by Congorilla, a gigantic golden-haired gorilla which, from time to time, by means of a witch doctor's magic, becomes possessed by the human intelligence and personality of a white African adventurer known as Congo Bill (Act No. 280: "Brainiac's Super-Revenge!").

In March 1962, while in the grip of a nightmare induced by exposure to red kryptonite, Superman dreams that Brainiac and other villains lure him into a trap, put him on "trial" for his alleged "crimes" against them, and sentence him to battle SUPERGIRL to the death in a gigantic arena or else stand by helplessly while they blow up the Earth. These events, however, are all only a nightmare, and no such confrontation with Brainiac and his cohorts ever actually takes place (Act No. 286: "The Jury of Super-Enemies!").

By September 1962 Brainiac has provided Lex Luthor with copies of at least two of the "super-weapons" in his own ingenious arsenal: when the Metropolis police attempt to storm LUTHOR'S LAIR, Luthor holds them at bay with a diabolical "web-ray"—described as a "super-ray that projects a web of pure force"—obtained from Brainiac. Soon afterward, he employs a copy of Brainiac's own "power-belt," which generates "a protective **force-shield** that guards [him] against any attack," as well as endowing its wearer with "anti-gravity," and therefore the power of flight (Act No. 292: "When Superman Defended His Arch-Enemy!").

In January 1963, after the "fanatic scientist" THAN OL has successfully enlarged Kandor to normal size with his "enlarging-ray projector," unaware that the apparatus contains a fatal flaw that will "bring doomsday" to the city, Superman uses a portable raygunlike "shrinking ray," confiscated from Brainiac and now held for safekeeping at the Fortress of Solitude, to reduce the city to its former lilliputian size, thereby rescuing Kandor and its inhabitants from imminent destruction (S No. 158: "Superman in Kandor" pts. I-III—"Invasion of the Mystery Super-Men!"; "The Dynamic Duo of Kandor!"; "The City of Super-People!").

In February 1964 Brainiac is freed from the "prison world" of Kronis by renegade scientist Lex Luthor, who hopes to make Brainiac his ally in a plot to destroy Superman. In order to make his new partner even more "super-brilliant," Luthor com-

Brainiac and Lex Luthor, 1964

pletely rewires Brainiac's "computer-brain" so as to endow him with a "twelfth-level intelligence" in place of the tenth-level-effector mind programmed into him by his creators. In the course of the ensuing adventure, Brainiac is apprehended by members of the SUPERMEN EMERGENCY SQUAD and brought to trial in Kandor on the charge of having shrunk and stolen the city prior to the explosion of Krypton, but the Kandorians are ultimately compelled to let Brainiac go free in order to save the life of Superman (S No. 167: "The Team of Luthor and Brainiac!" pts. I-III—"The Deadly Duo!"; "The Downfall of Superman!"; "The Hour of Kandor's Vengeance!"). (See LUTHOR, LEX.)

In July 1964, during a time-journey he makes to the planet Krypton prior to its destruction, Lex Luthor witnesses the theft of Kandor by Brainiac (S No. 170/2: pts. I-II—"If Lex Luthor Were Superman's Father!"; "The Wedding of Lara and Luthor!").

In September 1964 Brainiac forms a temporary alliance with the diabolical CLAYFACE (WF No. 144: "The 1,001 Tricks of Clayface and Brainiac!" pts. I-II—no title; "The Helpless Partners!").

In October 1964 Brainiac breaks Lex Luthor out of prison and then joins forces with him in a scheme to wreak vengeance on Superman by annihilating his "dear friends," Lois Lane and LANA LANG. Both Brainiac and Luthor are ultimately apprehended by AR-VAL (S No. 172: pts. I-III—"The New Superman!"; "Clark Kent—Former Superman!"; "The Struggle of the Two Supermen!"). (See also LUTHOR, LEX.)

In November 1964, having learned that Superman is being held for trial on the planet LEXOR on the charge of having murdered Lex Luthor, Brainiac leads a delegation of mourners to the distant planet, ostensibly "to pay a last tribute to Luthor," but actually as a ploy to further inflame Lexorian public opinion against the Man of Steel (Act No. 318: "The Death of Luthor!"). (See LUTHOR, LEX.) During this same period, BATMAN impersonates Brainiac as part of an elaborate scheme by Superman to teach a well-deserved lesson to his pal Jimmy Olsen (S No. 173/3, Nov '64: "The Triumph of Luthor and Brainiac!"). (See OLSEN, JIMMY.)

BRAINIAC 5. A member of the LEGION OF SUPER-HEROES. A green-skinned humanoid alien from the planet Colu (also referred to as the planet Yod), Brainiac 5 possesses an extraordinary superhuman intellect that enables him to perform intricate calculations in seconds, gives him a strong resistance to hypnotism, and has made him a super-scientific genius of incredible creativity, ingenuity, and inventiveness. Long believed to be a descendant of the space villain BRAINIAC, Brainiac 5 is actually a descendant of Vril Dox, a Colutian boy who led his people in the successful overthrow of the computer tyrants which had seized control of Colu and created the humanoid computer Brainiac as the first step in a scheme of interplanetary conquest. Brainiac 5's real name is Querl Dox.

In April 1962 Brainiac 5 is among the six Legionnaires who play an elaborate hoax on SUPER-

MAN and SUPERGIRL as a prelude to celebrating the anniversary of Supergirl's arrival on Earth (S No. 152/1: "The Robot Master!"). (*See* LEGION OF SUPER-HEROES, THE.)

In October 1962, when Superman is believed to be dying from exposure to VIRUS X, a malady fatal to natives of the planet KRYPTON, Brainiac 5 labors desperately to find a cure for the virus before the Man of Steel succumbs completely. Brainiac 5's dedicated effort ends in failure, but Superman regains his health when it is discovered that his symptoms are actually the result of exposure to KRYPTONITE and the kryptonite fragment responsible is hurriedly removed from his presence (S No. 156: "The Last Days of Superman!" pts. I–III—"Superman's Death Sentence!"; "The Super-Comrades of All Time!"; "Superman's Last Day of Life!").

In February 1963 Brainiac 5 frees MON-EL from his self-imposed exile in the PHANTOM ZONE after successfully devising a serum capable of curing Mon-El of his potentially fatal vulnerability to lead (Adv No. 305: "The Secret of the Mystery Legionnaire!").

In February 1964, while probing the universe with his "time-space thought-scanner" in the hope of locating an ally capable of helping him destroy Superman, LEX LUTHOR learns that the space villain Brainiac is not a being of flesh and blood at all, but a humanoid computer, and that Brainiac 5 is not his descendant, but rather the descendant of a youngster whom Brainiac's creators had chosen from among the population they tyrannized with the intention of forcing the boy to aid them in carrying out their scheme of interplanetary espionage by posing as Brainiac's son (S No. 167: "The Team of Luthor and Brainiac!" pts. I–III—"The Deadly Duo!"; "The Downfall of Superman!"; "The Hour of Kandor's Vengeance!"). (See BRAINIAC.)

BRAND, RUPERT. A well-meaning but overzealous agent for the Internal Revenue Service who, having discovered that SUPERMAN has never filed a tax return, promptly dubs the Man of Steel a "tax-evader," declares him delinquent in the amount of $1,000,000,000—in spite of the fact that Superman has contributed countless billions to charitable causes—and demands that he pay the amount in full within twenty-four hours. Brand's somewhat more open-minded I.R.S. superior ultimately revokes the tax judgment, however, declaring that Superman is exempt from taxes under the terms of the "tax dependency clause." In the superior's words:

Our records show that **Superman** has for years supported billions of needy people with clothing, housing, food and protective service! Indeed, the whole world is dependent on him!

According to law, every tax-payer is allowed to deduct $600 for each dependent! Well, **Superman** has over two billion dependents!

"If anything, the U.S. is indebted to **Superman**!"

adds the superior soon afterward. "Only there isn't enough money in the world to pay him for what he does!" (S No. 148/3, Oct '61: "Superman Owes a Billion Dollars!"). The story is in many respects similar to Superman No. 114/3 (Jul '57: "Superman's Billion-Dollar Debt!") (*See* HAWKER, JASON.)

BRANDON, DAN. "The prominent civic reformer" at the head of a citywide campaign to persuade the mayor and the city council to replace METROPOLIS's worn-out streetcars with newer, safer buses, and the secret mastermind behind an elaborate scheme to sabotage the city's streetcars—thus causing a series of serious accidents designed to spur the streetcar replacement effort—so that he can reap lavish under-the-table commissions on the sale of new buses to the city. SUPERMAN is instrumental in bringing about the much-needed replacement of the antiquated streetcars, but he also apprehends the evil Branson in Winter 1941 (WF No. 4: "The Case of the Crime Crusade").

BRENT, KIRK. An alias employed by SUPERMAN in September 1958 when he obtains employment as a construction worker with the Bart Benson Construction Co. in order to gather incriminating evidence on BART BENSON and his cohort T. B. Oliver (S No. 124/3: "The Steeplejack of Steel").

BREWSTER, BUCK (Sgt.). A "tough," vindictive sergeant in the United States Marines. When, by special arrangement with the Pentagon, CLARK KENT is permitted to enlist in the Marine Corps so that he can write an article on boot camp for the DAILY PLANET, his superior, Sgt. Buck Brewster, who has taken a liking to Kent's colleague LOIS LANE, becomes determined to find some legitimate excuse for denying Kent a weekend pass so that he, and not Kent, can escort Lois to the upcoming Gala Marine Dance. Brewster's petty scheme takes the form of assigning Kent the camp's roughest, messiest, most distasteful jobs—and then surreptitiously sabotaging Kent's attempts to fulfill them—so that he can deny Kent his pass when he fails to perform his tasks properly. At the same time, Kent's dilemma becomes one of performing the chores properly—so as to avoid being "washed out" of the Marine Corps before he completes his assignment for the *Daily Planet*—without betraying that he possesses super-powers and thereby endangering the secret of his dual identity. Ultimately, however, Kent prevails, outwitting Brewster at every turn, completing every dirty, unpleasant chore assigned to him, taking Lois to the dance, and accumulating the material he needs for his article on boot camp (S No. 179/3, Aug '65: "Private Kent, the Fighting Marine!").

BROGAN, BEETLES. A wanted criminal who is apprehended along with an unnamed henchman by SUPERMAN in June 1954. All of Superman's activities during this period are severely hampered by the fact that vaporized gold ore, penetrating the skin of his hands as he battled the eruption of a volcano in "a remote mountain region," has temporarily endowed him with "the terrible power that King Midas of old is said to have had," so that everything he touches turns to gold (Act No. 193: "The Golden Superman!").

BROWNLEE, HIRAM. A hayseed from the town of Turnip Center who, acting as spokesman for his rural community, keeps pestering SUPERMAN to perform one super-chore after another for the benefit of the town until finally Superman, understandably fed up with the unending requests, stalks off the job in May-June 1948 (S No. 52/2: "Superman Turns on the Heat!").

BRPXZ (King). The elderly, apparently senile ruler of the LAND OF ZRFFF, home world of MR. MXYZPTLK (S No. 33/1, Mar/Apr '45: "Dimensions of Danger!"). King Brpxz's name is rendered Bprxz in Superman No. 40/1 (May/Jun '46: "The Mxyztplk-Susie Alliance!"). An unnamed king of Zrfff appears in Superman No. 51/1, but he does not appear to be the same man as the one identified as King Brpxz (Mar/Apr '48: "Mr. Mxyztplk Seeks a Wife!").

BRYSON, BRETT. A young scientist at the Chalmers Laboratories whose life becomes a horrifying nightmare when an apparent miscalculation in a hazardous radium experiment causes a "devastating explosion" that bathes him in "a weird bombardment of hurtling rays" and transforms him into an eerily "glowing figure" who is "immune to bullets" and whose very touch brings death by inflicting fatal radium burns.

Almost penniless and doomed to die within a week from the deadly effects of the "radium blast," Bryson is receptive to a proposal by his boss, Frank Chalmers, and Chalmers's partner, Davis, that he allow himself to be reported dead from the explosion and then secretly use his "weird powers" and remaining week of life to commit a series of lucrative robberies so as to ensure financial security for his wife following his death.

And so, in the days following Bryson's announced death and mock funeral, Bryson—now "a weird, cloaked and hooded figure" clad in white pants and smock and with a white hood with eye-holes covering his face and head—commits a series of bizarre, sometimes murderous crimes, unaware that the laboratory explosion that doomed and deformed him was not an accident at all, but rather part of a deliberate scheme by Chalmers and Davis to get Bryson to commit crimes solely for their own enrichment.

Ultimately, however, both Bryson and SUPERMAN learn the dreadful truth behind the heinous scheme. Superman takes Davis into custody, but Bryson, his last week of life all but spent, strangles Chalmers to death with his radium grip and then collapses dead atop Chalmers's corpse (Act No. 39, Aug '41).

BURTON (Mr.). A wealthy citizen of METROPOLIS, nostalgic for the thrilling days of yesteryear, who wants to finance the construction of a time machine so that he can visit the past. When Burton accidentally falls off his penthouse balcony and SUPERMAN swoops to his rescue, both men suffer blows on the head and imagine that they have been magically transported into the ancient past, to the days of King Arthur and his Knights of the Round Table, where they undertake a series of exciting adventures. Regaining consciousness back in the present, Burton concludes that the twentieth century, with its democracy and modern conveniences, is probably the best era to live in after all, but a wound in Burton's shoulder, identical to one he received during his sojourn in the past, raises the intriguing question, never resolved in the text, of whether Burton and Superman merely shared a common fantasy or whether they somehow actually made a journey into the past (S No. 38/2, Jan/Feb '46: "The Bad Old Knights!").

BXPA. A far-distant planet whose "barbaric rulers" have, by the spring of 1964, dispatched an invisible robot-manned space fleet toward Earth and "all [other] intelligent planets in the universe" with instructions to cow the target planets into submission with awesome displays of devastatingly destructive power and then to obliterate, by means of "an ultimate weapon," any planet that fails to surrender. SUPERMAN's desperate efforts to conceal the impending alien invasion and thus avert global panic take the form of an elaborate ruse in which the Man of Steel pretends that the aliens' awesome power displays—including the partial freezing of an ocean, the creation of an artificial earthquake, and the obliteration of an entire mountain with a "super-nuclear bomb"—are feats that he has himself performed as part of a power-hungry scheme to blackmail the United Nations into agreeing to crown him King of Earth. Bxpa and its warlike civilization are ultimately reduced to rubble, apparently "wiped out by one of its own missiles that malfunctioned," and Superman rescues Earth from imminent "global extinction" by intercepting the robot-piloted doomsday missile swooping toward Earth and hurling the "hunk of horror" back toward the planet that spawned it, where it obliterates all that remains of Bxpa with a world-shattering roar (Act No. 311, Apr '64: "Superman, King of Earth!"; Act No. 312, May '64: "King Superman versus Clark Kent, Metallo").

C

CALDWELL, ALBERT. The president of Metropolis Subway, Inc., and the man who is secretly the TALON (S No. 17/1, Jul/Aug '42: "Man or Superman?").

CALL, BENNY. The president of the Ace Publishing Co., who contracts to publish SUPERMAN's autobiography in January-February 1947, with Superman's share of the proceeds to be donated to charity, only to reject Superman's 125,000-word manuscript soon afterward in the honest belief that the super-author's descriptions of his own powers are grossly exaggerated. After Superman has used his mighty powers to dispel all of Call's doubts, however, the autobiography is published under the title *The Confessions of Superman* (WF No. 26: "The Confessions of Superman!").

CAPONE, AL (1899-1947). A United States gangster and murderer who rose through the ranks of the underworld to become the undisputed crime czar of Prohibition-era Chicago. Convicted of income tax evasion in 1931, he spent eight years in Federal prisons and died eight years following his release, at Palm Island, Florida, in 1947. SUPERMAN meets Al Capone—and even infiltrates his mob for a time by posing as a safecracker—during a time-journey to Chicago in the 1920s, when "Al Capone was the king of crime and ran all the rackets!" (S No. 142/2, Jan '61: "Superman Meets Al Capone!").

CARLSON, RALPH. An alias employed by CLARK KENT in November-December 1940 when he poses as a wealthy Oklahoma oilman as part of a plan to apprehend the Black Gang (S No. 7/4). (*See* PEEKER, PETER.)

CARLTON, JEFF. An agent in the United States Anti-Espionage Service, and one of the secret leaders of a ring of spies and fifth columnists who frame Clark Kent for the murder of Frank Martin, Carlton's Anti-Espionage Service superior. SUPERMAN smashes the spy ring in January-February 1941 and, as Clark Kent, clears himself of the murder charge by forcing a confession from Carlton at gunpoint (S No. 8/2).

CARNAHAN, PETER. The profligate playboy son of Rufus Carnahan, a retired multimillionaire industrialist who summons SUPERMAN to his home in May 1940 and offers to pay him "any amount" if he will only cure his son of his wastrel, decadent ways. "Straighten out my son's character so that he will be a man!" pleads Carnahan. "I'll pay you any amount!"

Soon after Superman has agreed to accept the task, Peter Carnahan—a "weak-kneed sop and spendthrift" beset by "huge gambling losses"—is convicted and sentenced to death for a murder he did not

commit, but Superman produces the real murderer and stops the execution in the nick of time, prompting the grateful playboy to vow to abandon his decadent lifestyle and devote the rest of his life to helping "wayward underprivileged youth" (Act No. 24).

CARROLL, BEA. A sultry blond singer at the Hilow Night Club who has murdered a man named Jack Kennedy "for two-timing her" and framed innocent Evelyn Curry for the crime. After confronting Bea Carroll in her dressing room and forcing her to sign a written confession ("I—I'll get the chair for this!" sobs Bea. "You should have thought of that before you took a human life!" replies SUPERMAN), Superman races with his prisoner to the home of the governor to arrange a last-minute reprieve for Evelyn Curry (S No. 1/1, Sum '39). The original, albeit abbreviated, version of this story appears in Action Comics No. 1 (Jun '38).

Bea Carroll

CARSON, CEDRIC AND MILLICENT (Mr. and Mrs.). A husband-and-wife team of "scheming actors" who impersonate JONATHAN AND MARTHA KENT as part of an elaborate and ultimately successful scheme to trick SUPERMAN into betraying the secret of his dual identity, and who then demand $5,000,000 in blackmail from the Man of Steel as their price for keeping his closely guarded secret from the underworld. Through a complex ruse of his own, however, Superman ultimately thwarts the extortion scheme by using his command of "super-hypnotic forces" to erase all knowledge of his secret identity from the villainous actors' minds (Act No. 247, Dec '58: "Superman's Lost Parents!").

CARSON, CHARLEY. The barker for METROPOLIS's new "dime museum"—featuring such extraordinary human oddities as an India rubber man, a sword swallower, a fat lady, a fire eater, and a human fly—who, in collusion with "shady promoter" Henry Hulbert, attempts to drive the new museum out of business so that Hulbert can seize control of its lease, only to be thwarted and ultimately apprehended by SUPERMAN in July 1948 (Act No. 122: "The Super Sideshow!").

CARSON, CLIP. The operator of a crooked carnival that has been "cheating people with rigged games." The carnival is put out of business by SUPERMAN in February 1961 (S No. 143/2: "Lois Lane's Lucky Day!").

CARSON, FRED (Pvt.). A U.S. Army private who recklessly violates both army safety regulations and common sense in his almost suicidal pursuit of one-man heroics during a series of U.S. Army war games being supervised by SUPERMAN. These ill-conceived acts of daring, necessitating repeated rescues by Superman, are in reality Carson's way of making up for the alleged cowardice of his brother, Pvt. Jim Carson, who was a soldier at this same army base one year ago. An investigation by Superman, however, soon establishes that Jim Carson was not a coward, thus persuading Fred Carson that his reckless heroics are completely unnecessary (Act No. 205, Jun '55: "Sergeant Superman").

CARSON, ROGER. The pampered playboy son of Matt Carson, a wealthy old sea captain and seasoned adventurer who passes away in 1939 after stipulating that Roger may inherit his sizable fortune only if he first travels around the world in a small sailing ship and successfully duplicates his own adventure-filled career. With some help from SUPERMAN, Roger ultimately wins his right to his father's bequest, then promptly gives it all to charity with the manly announcement that "I'm going out to make my own fortune...like father did!" (Act No. 76, Sep '44: "A Voyage to Destiny!").

CARTRIGHT, JANE. The niece of famed millionaire explorer Allen Cartright, and the fiancée of Harold Denton, Cartright's secretary. When Cartright is found murdered in Spring 1943, Denton is arrested, convicted, and sentenced to the electric chair for the crime, but SUPERMAN, racing against the clock to prevent Denton's execution, successfully establishes that Jane Cartright murdered her uncle in hopes of inheriting his millions and takes the murderess into custody (WF No. 9: "One Second to Live!").

CASAN, PHIL. A mobster serving a life term in State Prison, the "number one boy in the rackets" until his capture by SUPERMAN one year ago, who deliberately but surreptitiously brings about the worsening of prison living conditions and then foments a series of riots designed to protest them as part of an elaborate scheme to bring about the firing of the warden and his replacement by a Casan crony who will make it possible for Casan to live the life of a big shot even while in prison. After deliberately allowing himself to be convicted and sentenced on an embezzlement charge in his Clark Kent identity so that he can investigate prison conditions from the inside, SUPERMAN helps authorities bring an end to the riots and ultimately exposes Phil Casan as the mastermind behind them (S No. 83/3, Jul/Aug '53: "Clark Kent---Convict!").

CASEY (Sergeant). A courageous, stubborn, Irish police sergeant on the METROPOLIS police force. Although he has a policeman's instinctive distrust of journalists, tending to regard them as troublemakers or pests, he is on a first-name basis with CLARK KENT and LOIS LANE and occasionally provides them with useful news tips. World's Finest Comics No. 2 describes him as Kent's "good friend" in the Metropolis Police Department (Sum '41). When SUPERMAN, still in the early stage of his career, is being sought by the police for working outside the law, Sergeant Casey makes a number of courageous, albeit unsuccessful, attempts to apprehend him (Act No. 37, Jun '41; and others), but by October 1941 the good-hearted Irish policeman has clearly come to regard Superman as a friend of law and order (Act No. 41). Action Comics No. 51 refers to Sergeant Casey as Detective Sergeant Casey (Aug '42: "The Case of the Crimeless Crimes"), but this would appear to be the result of a chronicler's error.

Sergeant Casey appears in more than a score of early texts, but the majority of his appearances are inconsequential. In June 1941 Sergeant Casey turns his gun on Superman and attempts to take him into

Clark Kent, Sergeant Casey, and Lois Lane, 1941

custody, but the Man of Steel easily escapes from the exasperated policeman (Act No. 37).

In July 1941 Sergeant Casey, suspicious that Superman may be somehow implicated in the recent wave of mysterious robberies (see MORTON, HAROLD), attempts to place him under arrest, but the Man of Steel easily shatters his handcuffs and escapes, and by the conclusion of the adventure his innocence has been clearly established (Act No. 38).

In August 1941, after a dying watchman, mortally wounded by a mysterious bandit, has muttered something about his assailant's having been invulnerable to bullets, Sergeant Casey attempts to arrest Superman for the crime. The Man of Steel escapes, however, and ultimately succeeds in proving his innocence (Act No. 39). (See BRYSON, BRETT.)

In October 1941, while investigating an act of attempted sabotage at a U.S. defense plant, Sergeant Casey is hit over the head with a vase by one of RALPH COWAN's saboteurs and hurled unconscious out of an upper-story window. Casey's life is saved, however, by Superman, who catches the sergeant in midair before he can hit the ground (Act No. 41).

In January-February 1942, while attending a concert by famed pianist RUDOLPH KRAZINSKI in the hope of apprehending the criminals responsible for robbing the concertgoers at Krazinski's previous concert, Sergeant Casey is rendered unconscious— along with all the other members of the audience—by Krazinski's "lulling, hypnotic piano playing," and is carried unconscious to Krazinski's hideout by a Krazinski henchman with a longtime grudge against Casey. Krazinski intervenes to prevent his henchman from murdering the sergeant, but a short while later, after Krazinski and his other cohorts have departed, leaving Sergeant Casey and the vengeful henchman alone, Casey is rescued from seemingly certain death only by the timely arrival of Superman, who crashes through the wall of the hideout, moves Casey safely out of the path of an oncoming bullet, and rescues him from his abductor's clutches. "Once again you've saved my life!" exclaims Sergeant Casey gratefully.

Later, after Rudolph Krazinski has committed suicide by "striking a certain combination of bizarre notes" on the piano, Superman telephones Sergeant Casey and informs him where he can find Krazinski's corpse.

"Thanks, Superman!" replies the sergeant. "The way I fumbled the investigation got me in trouble with my superiors--but discovering Krazinski should put me back in their good graces!" (S No. 14/1).

In May-June 1942, when Sergeant Casey attempts to arrest Clark Kent for the theft of a cash box containing charitable contributions, Kent flees from Casey, successfully eluding arrest long enough to enable Superman to recover the stolen money, exonerate his mild-mannered alter ego of any wrongdoing, and apprehend the real villain, ex-convict CHARLIE GRAYSON. "What would the police force do without you?" asks Casey admiringly, after

Sergeant Casey and Lois Lane, 1941

Superman has turned Grayson over to the police. "No doubt get along very nicely!" replies the Man of Steel gallantly (S No. 16/1: "The World's Meanest Man").

In March-April 1943, when Lois Lane is found in possession of a stolen mink coat, Sergeant Casey is forced to hold Lois briefly on a charge of theft even though he personally has faith in her innocence. Lois is freed when it is established that she bought the coat from a friend unaware that the coat had been stolen— and given to her friend as a gift—by the villain SIR GAUNTLET (S No. 21/3: "The Robber Knight").

In July-August 1943 Sergeant Casey provides Superman with information that leads ultimately to the apprehension of gambler Sammy Brink (S No. 23/4: "Danger on the Diamond!"). (See MARIN, TOM.)

By March 1948 Sergeant Casey has arrested Clark Kent for the murder of gangster SLUGGER MAULL after finding Kent standing over Maull's body with the murder weapon in his hand (Act No. 118: "The Execution of Clark Kent!"). (See also SUPERMAN [section K, the relationship with the law-enforcement establishment].)

CENTAURI CITY. The home city of ZIGI AND ZAGI, which is located "on a planet in the Alpha Centauri system," 23,342,816,000,000 miles from Earth (Act No. 315, Aug '64: "The Juvenile Deliquents from Space!"). SUPERMAN journeys to Centauri City in search of "maniacal murderer" "SLASH" SABRE, an escapee from Metropolis Prison (Act No. 316, Sep '64: "Zigi and Zagi's Trap for Superman!").

CHALMERS, REX. A METROPOLIS gang chief who attempts to capitalize on the fact that a mysterious space virus has temporarily transformed SUPERMAN's X-ray vision into "deep-freeze" vision— causing his eyes to radiate intense cold, instead of heat, whenever he uses his X-ray vision—by tricking Superman into freezing the dynamos at the Metropolis power plant so that he and his henchmen can loot the city during the resulting blackout. The scheme is thwarted by Superman in November 1957 (S No. 117/3: "The Man with the Zero Eyes!").

CHAMELEON, THE. The so-called "thief of faces," an uncanny master of disguise and impersonation who commits a series of brazen robbery-murders, each time in the guise of a carefully selected victim, with the result that he and his henchmen escape with the loot while the men he impersonated are accused of the crimes. SUPERMAN apprehends the Chameleon and his cohorts in November 1948, in the process using a mobile television unit—"most modern of scientific miracles"—to broadcast evidence implicating the gang to a live TV audience (Act No. 126: "Superman on Television!").

CHAMELEON BOY. A member of the LEGION OF SUPER-HEROES. A native of the planet Durla with gold-colored skin, large pointed ears, and twin antennae protruding from his forehead, Chameleon Boy possesses, like all the members of his race, the ability to transform his body into any form he chooses. Chameleon Boy's real name is Reep Daggle.

In April 1962 Chameleon Boy is among the six Legionnaires who play an elaborate hoax on SUPERMAN and SUPERGIRL as a prelude to celebrating the anniversary of Supergirl's arrival on Earth (S No. 152/1: "The Robot Master!"). (*See* LEGION OF SUPER-HEROES, THE.)

In October 1962, when Superman is believed to be dying of an incurable malady, Chameleon Boy is among the Legionnaires who are summoned to the twentieth century by Supergirl to help carry out the gigantic super-tasks that Superman hopes to fulfill as his final legacy to humanity, including the destruction of a "vast cloud of fungus in distant space, that will some day reach Earth and blight all plant life," and the melting of the Antarctic ice, "to make Antarctica a fit place for millions to live in the future," thus ensuring "a home for Earth's expanding population...!" (S No. 156: "The Last Days of Superman!" pts. I-III—"Superman's Death Sentence!"; "The Super-Comrades of All Time!"; "Superman's Last Day of Life!").

When METROPOLIS television station WMET-TV inaugurates its new "Our American Heroes" series with a program honoring Superman, "our greatest American hero," Chameleon Boy is among the Legion representatives who journey to the twentieth century to appear on the show and thus help pay tribute to the Man of Steel (Act No. 309, Feb '64: "The Superman Super-Spectacular!").

CHANTEY, BILL. The foreman of the Allerton Construction Company's Holloway Tunnel project, and the man who is secretly "THE SNAKE" (S No. 18/4, Sep/Oct '42: "The Snake").

CHATE (Captain). The captain of a pearl-fishing merchant vessel that is one of a fleet owned by Elias Carp. When Carp is found murdered, there are four principal suspects, but SUPERMAN establishes that Chate killed Carp when Carp learned of his plans to scuttle his pearl vessel deliberately and then split the salvage rights with his accomplices on a nearby ship (S No. 33/3, Mar/Apr '45: "The Compass Points to Murder!").

CHECK. A cunning gangland chieftain, a chess grand master before he turned to crime, who plans his crimes like chess games, using special pieces on a chess board to represent the objects to be stolen and the obstacles and opponents, such as SUPERMAN, to be overcome. In May-June 1949, having observed that Superman will invariably rescue LOIS LANE from danger before attempting to apprehend either himself or his henchmen, Check kidnaps Lois Lane and uses Brenda Manning, an unemployed actress and Lois Lane look-alike, as his dupe in a series of elaborate charades designed to make it appear that "Lois Lane" is in jeopardy each time he and his henchmen are making a getaway. Superman ultimately apprehends the villains, however, during a robbery at the International Chess Championship (WF No. 40: "The Two Lois Lanes!").

CHEOPS. The second Pharaoh of the 4th dynasty of Egypt, who reigned *ca.* 2590-2567 B.C. He is the builder of the GREAT PYRAMID at Giza, the largest single building ever erected. It has been calculated that 100,000 men working unceasingly would have required 20 years to complete the task. SUPERMAN meets the great pharaoh and completes construction of his gigantic pyramid—single-handedly performing well over half the work—during a time-journey to Egypt in the twenty-sixth century B.C. (WF No. 32, Jan/Feb '48: "The Seventh Wonder of the World!").

CHESNEY, MIKE. The leader of a gang of criminals who steal a fortune in gems from the METROPOLIS offices of the Holland Diamond Company, only to be apprehended soon afterward by SUPERMAN (Act No. 114, Nov '47: "The Man Who Was Honest!").

CHORN. The evil leader of the Baxians, a ruthless band of interplanetary conquerors who have seized control of the planet Zoron and forced its peace-loving populace into grueling slave labor. On Zoron, a planet whose alien environment endows BATMAN and ROBIN with super-powers identical to SUPERMAN's while it renders Superman as powerless as an ordinary mortal, the three heroes combine their talents to defeat Chorn and his cohorts and deliver the Zorians from the yoke of Baxian oppression (WF No. 114, Dec '60: "Captives of the Space Globes!").

CHUCKLE, AMOS. An alias employed by the TOYMAN in November-December 1947 when, at the instigation of ARNOLD LANGS, he opens a toy and novelty shop in METROPOLIS (S No. 49/1: "Toyman and the Gadgets of Greed!"). (*See* TOYMAN, THE.)

CIRCE. In Greek mythology, a moon goddess, sorceress, and enchantress. Exiled to the island of Aiaie for murdering her husband, she surrounded herself with wild beasts which were actually men she had transformed. When the warrior hero Odysseus and his crew were cast up on her island, she changed the sailors into swine, but Odysseus escaped and ultimately forced the enchantress to restore his men to normal. According to Action Comics No. 243, however, Circe was actually a native of the planet KRYPTON: "And it wasn't *'black magic'* spells she cast! She used an evolution serum which could change men into different animal forms!" (Aug '58: "The Lady and the Lion"). It was Circe who bestowed "magical super-powers" on the white stallion now known as COMET THE SUPER-HORSE (S No. 176/1, Apr '65: "The Revenge of the Super-Pets!"). In November 1963 SATURN WOMAN poses as Circe as part of SUPERMAN's plan to defeat the SUPERMAN REVENGE SQUAD (S No. 165/1: pts. I-II—"Beauty and the Super-Beast!"; "Circe's Super-Slave").

In August 1958 Superman encounters a descendant of the original Circe, also named Circe, who uses her ancestress's evolution serum to transform his head and hands into the head and paws of a lion in retaliation for his having declined her offer of marriage. Astonished that Circe's serum has had any effect on him, since he believes himself "invulnerable to any poisons or serums," Superman soon discovers that "Circe's evolution serum contained a small dose of Kryptonite, just enough to change me biologically, without weakening my super-muscles!" Reasoning that if the original Circe came from Krypton the discovery of her evolution serum was probably widely reported there, Superman scans the contents of a library in the bottle city of KANDOR and ultimately locates the formula for an antidote that restores him to normal (Act No. 243: "The Lady and the Lion"). (*See also* KRYPTONITE.)

CLARK, KENT. An alias employed by SUPERMAN in July 1959 when he infiltrates the town of CYRUSVILLE in order to learn why Mayor Bruce Cyrus has declared the town "off limits to Superman" (S No. 130/3: "The Town That Hated Superman!"). The alias Kent Clark results from the juxtaposition of the first and last names of Superman's journalist alter ego, Clark Kent.

CLARKSON, KENNETH. An alias employed by SUPERMAN in September-October 1946 when, with Clark Kent presumed dead and that identity therefore at least temporarily unusable, he adopts a new secret identity—obtaining employment first as a cub reporter on the sensationalist *Evening Gazette,* then as a waiter at the Bilt-Ritz Hotel restaurant, and finally as a door-to-door vacuum-cleaner salesman—until a way is finally found to resurrect Clark Kent without endangering the secret of Superman's dual identity (S No. 42/3: "The Death of Clark Kent!").

CLAYFACE. A diabolical villain who possesses the incredible power to transform his body into any form he chooses, merely by issuing a silent mental command. In the moments between transformations, after Clayface has abandoned one bodily form but not yet assumed another, his body is a brown, earthy color and his flesh is soft and malleable, like clay. In reality, Clayface is Matt Hagen, an unscrupulous

Matt Hagen, 1961

skin diver whose amazing powers are the result of his inadvertent discovery of a secret pool that "shimmers like a trapped rainbow" and is filled with "a strange liquid protoplasm" whose "freakish properties defy analysis" (Det No. 304, Jun '62: "The Return of Clay-Face!"). It is only after Hagen commits his first spectacular robbery—and engineers an astounding

Clayface, 1961

getaway by assuming, in rapid succession, the forms of a giant python, a buzz saw, and a huge eagle—that an amazed newspaper editor bestows on him the name Clayface (Det No. 298, Dec '61: "The Challenge of Clay-Face"). Clayface soon discovers that it is necessary for him to return to his secret pool to renew his incredible powers every forty-eight hours. Although BATMAN destroys the pool completely in

February 1963 (Det No. 312: "The Secret of Clayface's Power!"), Clayface succeeds in synthesizing the freakish protoplasm nine months later (BM No. 159/1, Nov '63: "The Great Clayface-Joker Feud!").

In March 1964 Clayface escapes from prison and embarks on a series of spectacular crimes, occasionally transforming himself into the invulnerable image of SUPERMAN in order to render himself virtually undefeatable. Ultimately, however, Batman, ROBIN, and the real Superman defeat the Clayface Superman by exposing him to red KRYPTONITE, thus causing the villain to behave erratically long enough for his Clayface powers to fade and vanish before he has had the opportunity to return to his hideout for another dose of his synthetic protoplasm (WF No. 140: "The Clayface Superman!").

MOMENTS LATER, BATMAN LOOKS UP TO SEE A STRANGE SIGHT...

HE'S CHANGED INTO A WINGED HORSE--A PLUNDERING PEGASUS--FLYING OFF WITH HIS LOOT.!

© NPP 1962

Clayface as a winged horse, and Batman, 1962

In September 1964 Matt Hagen escapes from prison again when a barrage of destructive rays unleashed over GOTHAM CITY by BRAINIAC accidentally smashes apart the walls of the prison where Hagen is incarcerated. Not long afterward, after Hagen has renewed his Clayface powers with a dose of his synthetic protoplasm, Clayface joins forces with Brainiac in an effort to annihilate Superman, Batman, and Robin. Both villains are ultimately defeated, however, through the heroic efforts of Superman, Batman, Robin, and JIMMY OLSEN (WF No. 144: "The 1,001 Tricks of Clayface and Brainiac!" pts. I-II—no title; "The Helpless Partners!"). (For a complete account of the villainous career of Clayface, consult *The Encyclopedia of Comic Book Heroes: Volume I—Batman.*)

CLAYTON, CHARLES. A newly hired reporter on the DAILY PLANET who surreptitiously murders two of METROPOLIS's most powerful racketeers and attempts unsuccessfully to murder two others—all as part of an elaborate scheme to seize control of the city's rackets—before he is finally apprehended by

CLARK KENT in March-April 1943 (S No. 21/2: "The Four Gangleaders").

CLYDE (Professor). An alias employed by LEX LUTHOR in July 1959 when he lures SUPERMAN to his laboratory on the pretext of having perfected an antidote against KRYPTONITE so that he can expose Superman to his diabolical "duplicator ray" and thereby create an imperfect "molecular duplicate" of Superman to be known as BIZARRO (Act No. 254: "The Battle with Bizarro!").

COBALT, CLARENCE ("Professor"). The villainous quack who is the "proprietor" of the Cobalt Clinic, where unfortunate victims of "infantile paralysis and other forms of bone and joint malformations" are charged sky-high prices for worthless cures and medicinal pills that are in reality nothing but sugar. Cobalt and his accomplice Grafton are apprehended by SUPERMAN in July 1940 (Act No. 26).

COLBY, "COUP." A METROPOLIS "crime chief" whose capture by SUPERMAN in March 1958 comes as the culmination of an elaborate ruse—devised by Superman with the aid of PERRY WHITE—in which Superman pretends to fall in love with, and even goes so far as to "marry," Joyce White, ostensibly the lovely blond niece of Perry White but in reality a lifelike robot constructed by Superman and operated by means of remote controls hidden beneath his cape. When, as Superman had anticipated, Colby and his henchmen kidnap his "wife" and then stage a brazen jewel robbery, confident that Superman will not dare to apprehend them, Superman appears on the scene and swiftly takes them into custody (S No. 120/1: "The Day That Superman Married").

COLBY, HAL. An "embittered" ex-convict, sent to prison "years ago" by the teen-aged SUPERMAN, who poses as a TV producer under the alias Bert Hutton as part of an elaborate scheme to unravel and expose the secret of Superman's identity, both to wreak vengeance on Superman for his previous incarceration and to collect the $1,000,000 reward being offered him for the secret by "the leaders of the nation's crime syndicate." Colby's scheme is thwarted by Superman in May 1962 (Act No. 288: "The Man Who Exposed Superman!").

COLDSTONE, JASPER. A "famed efficiency expert"—cold, hard, and tyrannical—who makes life at the DAILY PLANET miserable with his relentless insistence on "split-second efficiency" and his indifference to the staff's human and emotional needs until finally SUPERMAN takes a hand to teach the cold-hearted clock watcher that the "human element" in life is more important than saving time (Act No. 192, May '54: "The Man Who Sped Up Superman!").

COLLINS, MOOSE. The leader of a gang of criminals who kidnap Professor Higgins and his newly invented amnesia machine, a machine designed to induce amnesia, and use it to commit a series of staggering crimes—as when they extort a fortune from a prominent consulting engineer by threatening to obliterate all his specialized knowledge—until they are finally apprehended by SUPERMAN in March-April 1952 (S No. 75/3: "The Man Who Stole Memories!").

COLLINS, "SHUT-EYE." A fugitive criminal who is apprehended by SUPERMAN in 1952 (S No. 76/3, May/Jun '52: "Mrs. Superman!").

COLLINS, VANCE. A reformed ex-convict, once sent to prison by BATMAN and ROBIN but now working honestly as an employee at a hot-dog stand, who is accidentally struck by a bizarre purple ray from outer space as it bounces off a billboard advertising a horror movie, and who, as a result, from that time onward becomes periodically transformed into a living version of the horrifying creature depicted vividly on the billboard. "That weird ray must have hit Vance after it burnt the creature's picture from the billboard!" explains SUPERMAN. "A freak reaction caused him to become the creature! He's like a Jekyll and Hyde character now!"

In his monster form, Collins leads a gang of criminals known as the Jackson Mob on a series of spectacular robberies, only to lose all recollection of his monstrous metamorphosis once the effects of the purple ray have temporarily exhausted themselves and Collins has temporarily reverted to his human form. Eventually, however, the effects of the purple ray wear off completely, and a horrified and guilt-ridden Collins readily joins forces with Batman, Robin, and Superman to apprehend his former underworld allies (WF No. 116, Mar '61: "The Creature from Beyond!").

COLOSSEUM, THE. A gigantic amphitheater in Rome which was erected by the emperors Vespasian and Titus (69-81 A.D.) and remains one of the world's great landmarks. Used for gladiatorial games and other entertainments, it measured 620 by 513 feet and had a seating capacity of about 50,000. The Colosseum is stolen—along with other world-famous monuments—by the Kryptonian villain MALA in July 1954 as part of his elaborate scheme to wreak vengeance on SUPERMAN by destroying the planet Earth (Act No. 194: "The Outlaws from Krypton!").

COMET (the Super-Horse). The super-powered white stallion, endowed also with the power of communicating by telepathy, that is the pet and equine companion of SUPERGIRL, periodically accompanying her on her adventures. Comet the Super-Horse was once Biron, a centaur of ancient Greece in the time of the great mythological heroes. One day, in gratitude for Biron's having thwarted an attempt by the evil wizard Malador to poison a spring where she drank, the enchantress CIRCE agreed to fulfill Biron's heartfelt wish to be transformed from a centaur into a real man, but Malador had tampered with Circe's potions, and the one that Biron drank transformed him, instead, into a horse. Circe had no means of undoing the tragic mishap, but she did partially compensate the hapless Biron by endowing him with "magical super-powers" as well as with the ability to communicate telepathically. Malador's vengeance on Biron, however, was not yet complete: he banished the super-steed to a planet in the constellation Sagittarius, keeping him imprisoned there by means of a "magic aura."

Biron remained on his prison planet for more than 3,000 years, waiting helplessly for freedom, until the happy day when the rocket carrying Supergirl toward Earth from doomed ARGO CITY passed by the planet, its "repeller rays" shattering the magical aura and enabling Biron to escape. The freed super-horse flew to Earth, located Supergirl, and established telepathic contact with her. She named him Comet, and he became her pet and her frequent companion in superheroic adventure. At the conclusion of one such adventure, Prince Endor of the planet Zerox, a world inhabited by sorcerers, rewarded Comet for his help by endowing him with the power to assume human form temporarily whenever he is within sight of a comet. At such times, Comet adopts the secret identity of Bronco Bill, a cowboy.

Comet the Super-Horse wears a flowing red-and-yellow cape modeled after SUPERMAN's which is attached to his body by means of two wide blue straps. He is a member of the LEGION OF SUPER-PETS. When METROPOLIS television station WMET-TV inaugurates its new "Our American Heroes" series with a program honoring Superman, "our greatest American hero," Comet appears on the show along with three of the other super-pets—BEPPO THE SUPER-MONKEY, KRYPTO THE SUPERDOG, and STREAKY THE SUPER-CAT—to help pay tribute to the Man of Steel (Act No. 309, Feb '64: "The Superman Super-Spectacular!"). In April 1965 Comet journeys through the time barrier to the mid-nineteenth century to help Superman and the other super-pets teach a well-deserved lesson to "cruel junkman" CYRUS ATWILL (S No. 176/1: "The Revenge of the Super-Pets!").

COMO, PERRY. A famous popular singer and entertainer who visits METROPOLIS in November-December 1950 to do a series of radio broadcasts. Complications arise for SUPERMAN when LOIS LANE falls head over heels in love with the handsome singer and when, soon afterward, she and Como are abducted by a gang of criminals. Ultimately, however, through the resourcefulness of Perry Como and the heroism of Superman, both Como and Lane are rescued from the gangsters' clutches and Lois abandons her short-lived crush on Como in favor of her long-held infatuation with Superman (S No. 67/1: "Perry Como, I Love You!").

COMPOSITE SUPERMAN, THE. A ruthless, power-hungry villain—endowed with all the superpowers of SUPERMAN as well as with all the extraordinary powers possessed by the various members of the LEGION OF SUPER-HEROES—who sets out, in June 1964, to "use [his] unmatchable powers to humiliate Superman and Batman before the world, and end their careers forever," as the first phase of his plan to conquer Earth and other worlds as well. The Composite Superman is in reality Joe Meach, the caretaker of the SUPERMAN MUSEUM in METROPOLIS, a onetime high-diver, embittered by his failure to achieve fame and fortune, who received his museum job from Superman after the Man of Steel had rescued him from a dive off a tall building into an inch-deep pool of water that would certainly have caused his death, but who nevertheless feels that "Superman humiliated me, by making me a lowly sweeper!"

As the Composite Superman, Meach—who acquires his unbelievable multiplicity of powers when a fateful bolt of lightning strikes a metal table in the museum containing lifelike statuettes of the Legion of Super-Heroes—has green skin, but otherwise resembles a weird composite of Superman and BATMAN, as though one half of his body were Superman's and the other half Batman's, divided vertically down the middle. By employing his seemingly endless arsenal of Super-powers, the Composite Superman is able to humiliate Batman, ROBIN, and Superman, and even to defeat them. Ultimately, however, Meach's powers fade and vanish, leaving him with no recollection whatever of his short-lived career as a super-villain (WF No. 142: "The Origin of the Composite Superman!" pts. I-II—"The Composite Superman!"; "The Battle Between Titans!").

CONDOR GANG, THE. A gang of criminals led by a dark-robed villain known only as the Condor, who is in reality John Titus, a respected GOTHAM CITY millionaire. In October 1958 BATMAN, ROBIN, and SUPERMAN join forces in an intricately convoluted scheme to apprehend the Condor and his henchmen by having Superman assume the wholly fictitious identity of Professor Milo, self-proclaimed inventor of "a mechanical brain that can predict the future," and then carefully building up a reputation for the machine's accuracy by contriving to make a series of improbable "predictions" come true. Ultimately, "Professor Milo" and his so-called "predictor" are ushered into the presence of the Condor himself, whereupon Superman, Batman, and Robin join forces to apprehend the Condor Gang and unmask the Condor as millionaire Titus (WF No. 97: "The Day Superman Betrayed Batman!").

CORAM, ELDREDGE. An unscrupulous young man who is one of the two adopted sons of multimillionaire Merton Coram. Knowing that the elder Coram's life expectancy is short, Eldredge embarks on an elaborate scheme to persuade his father that his other adopted son, Eldredge's brother William, is secretly SUPERMAN, calculating that Coram will change his will to eliminate William if he comes to believe that William is Superman and therefore has no need of money. This plot to deprive William Coram of his rightful inheritance is thwarted by Superman in May 1958 (S No. 121/2: "The Great Superman Swindle").

CORBEN, JOHN. The man who achieves infamy as METALLO (Act No. 252, May '59: "The Menace of Metallo!").

CORCORAN, JOE. A crooked METROPOLIS office seeker, hopeful of a mayoral appointment to the post of highway commissioner so that he could enrich himself through graft, who was the secret backer of The Highwayman, a play which ruthlessly lambast-

ed honest John Randolph, the only other candidate under consideration for the post. Corcoran was ultimately apprehended by SUPERMAN, but not before he had murdered The Highwayman's author in an attempt to frame Randolph for the crime (S No. 43/2, Nov/Dec '46: "Lois Lane, Actress!").

COREY, PETE. A METROPOLIS gangster—described in the text as "one of the biggest mob leaders in the country"—who is "the treasurer of the crime syndicate" and, as such, "the head of gangland's secret 'Fort Knox,'" a secret underworld treasure vault, situated beneath an abandoned observatory somewhere "in a remote mountain area," which serves as gangland's repository for its stolen artwork, jewelry, and currency. By means of an elaborate ruse, SUPERMAN finally locates "the outlaw Fort Knox" and apprehends Corey and his cohorts in August 1965 (S No. 179/1: "The Outlaw Fort Knox!").

CORLIN, VANCE. A contemporary of SUPERMAN's—clad in a brightly colored maroon and orange costume—who is endowed with superhuman powers identical to Superman's as the result of having been raised, since infancy, on a "secluded little island off the [Metropolis] coast," where his scientist father, Dr. Charles Corlin, had established a scientifically controlled artificial environment designed to duplicate conditions on the planet KRYPTON. In March-April 1952, following the death of his father, Corlin flies to METROPOLIS and uses his superpowers to commit a series of destructive acts in a misguided effort to wreak vengeance on society for what he has been taught to believe, since early childhood, was his father's unjust conviction on an embezzlement charge many years ago. Ultimately, however, Superman persuades young Corlin that his father's conviction was a fair one, and Corlin, remorseful at the destruction he has caused, helps Superman repair the damage just as his artificial super-powers, waning rapidly due to his prolonged absence from the special island, vanish forever (WF No. 57: "The Artificial Superman!").

CORNOVIA. A "little kingdom" of unspecified location which makes LOIS LANE its queen in September-October 1948 (S No. 54/3: "Her Majesty Lois Lane!").

COSMIC BOY. A member of the LEGION OF SUPER-HEROES. A native of the planet Braal (although his parents were on Earth at the time he was born), Cosmic Boy possesses, like all the inhabitants of his planet, the "power of super-magnetism," the ability to release powerful magnetic emanations from any part of his body. Cosmic Boy's real name is Rokk Krinn. The adult Cosmic Boy is called Cosmic Man.

In August 1961 Cosmic Man and two other adult Legionnaires—LIGHTNING MAN and SATURN WOMAN—join forces with SUPERMAN in his battle with LEX LUTHOR and the LEGION OF SUPER-VILLAINS (S No. 147/3: "The Legion of Super-Villains!"). (See LEGION OF SUPER-VILLAINS, THE.)

In April 1962 Cosmic Boy is among the six Legionnaires who play an elaborate hoax on Superman and SUPERGIRL as a prelude to celebrating the anniversary of Supergirl's arrival on Earth (S No. 152/1: "The Robot Master!"). (See LEGION OF SUPER-HEROES, THE.)

In August 1962 Cosmic Man and Lightning Man pose as HERCULES and Samson, "two of the mightiest men of all time," as part of an elaborate ruse, devised by Superman, for uncovering the hiding place of DUKE MARPLE's stolen loot and bringing the "notorious gang-leader" to justice (S No. 155/2: "The Downfall of Superman!").

In October 1962, when Superman is believed to be dying of an incurable malady, Cosmic Boy is among the Legionnaires who are summoned to the twentieth century by Supergirl to help carry out the gigantic super-tasks that Superman hopes to fulfill as his final legacy to humanity, including the destruction of a "vast cloud of fungus in distant space, that will some day reach Earth and blight all plant life," and the melting of the Antarctic ice, "to make Antarctica a fit place for millions to live in the future," thus ensuring "a home for Earth's expanding population...!" (S No. 156: "The Last Days of Superman!" pts. I-III—"Superman's Death Sentence!"; "The Super-Comrades of All Time!"; "Superman's Last Day of Life!").

In October 1964, after Superman has been deprived of his super-powers by the baleful radiations of a mysterious green comet, Cosmic Boy and two of his fellow Legionnaires—SATURN GIRL and the INVISIBLE KID—use a "time-force wave carrier" in their thirtieth-century Clubhouse to endow Superman temporarily with their various powers so that he can use them in his upcoming battle with Lex Luthor and BRAINIAC. For a period of "a few hours," therefore, until his borrowed powers fade and vanish, Superman is equipped with Cosmic Boy's power of super-magnetism, Saturn Girl's "power of telepathic thought-casting," and the Invisible Kid's "power of invisibility" (S No. 172: pts. I-III—"The New Superman!"; "Clark Kent—Former Superman!"; "The Struggle of the Two Supermen!").

COSMIC KING. A member of the LEGION OF SUPER-VILLAINS, an organization of super-criminals from the twenty-first century A.D. A native of the planet VENUS, Cosmic King wears a maroon and purplish-blue costume with a transparent space helmet. He possesses the incredible "power of transmutation, the ability to change any solid object into something else."

Cosmic King was originally "an alchemist on the planet Venus, seeking to discover a ray which could change any object's atomic structure...." One day, he actually succeeded in transmuting a flower into a precious gem by altering its molecular structure with a special ray of his own invention. But soon afterward he "suffered a dizzy spell and stumbled into [the path of] the fantastic ray," and when he recovered, he discovered, to his great joy, that he had somehow acquired a miraculous power: "Ha, ha!" he exulted. "When I concentrated and willed it, rays from my

eyes...turned the water in that glass into mercury...I've become a living transmutation ray! I'll be acclaimed everywhere!"

However, the acclaim sought by Cosmic King was not to be his. Believing transmutation to be inherently evil, his fellow Venusians banished him from their planet, never to return. Embittered by the hostile reaction to his amazing discovery, Cosmic King "joined the **Legion of Super-Villains** on Earth...and became a super-criminal!"

In August 1961 the Legion of Super-Villains forms an alliance with LEX LUTHOR in an elaborate scheme to annihilate SUPERMAN (S No. 147/3: "The Legion of Super-Villains!"). (See LEGION OF SUPER-VILLAINS, THE.)

In March 1962, while in the grip of a nightmare induced by exposure to red KRYPTONITE, Superman dreams that Cosmic King and other villains lure him into a trap, put him on "trial" for his alleged "crimes" against them, and sentence him to battle SUPERGIRL to the death in a gigantic arena or else stand by helplessly while they blow up the Earth. These events, however, are all only a nightmare, and no such confrontation with Cosmic King and his cohorts ever actually takes place (Act No. 286: "The Jury of Super-Enemies!").

COSMIC MAN. The adult COSMIC BOY.

COWAN, RALPH. The secret leader of a gang of cunning saboteurs who have been hired by an unnamed "foreign country" to carry out "widespread sabotage" across the United States and to do "everything [they] can to halt this country's national defense effort." Cowan is apprehended by SUPERMAN in October 1941 (Act No. 41).

CRAIG, ELTON. A ruthless criminal whose various encounters with BATMAN, ROBIN, SUPERMAN, and BATWOMAN are described in World's Finest Comics No. 87 (Mar/Apr '57: "The Reversed Heroes!") and in World's Finest Comics No. 90 (Sep/Oct '57: "The Super-Batwoman!").

In March-April 1957 Superman narrates the story of his first encounter with the villainous Craig, which evidently took place sometime in the past. Superman recalls that, years ago, his father JOR-EL had foreseen the imminent destruction of the planet KRYPTON and had made arrangements to transport himself and his family to Earth to begin a new life. Jor-El had also created some special "radioactive capsules" which he hoped to bring to Earth with him. "Krypton is doomed," Jor-El had announced grimly, "--but when we migrate to Earth, we'll have super-powers there, because of the lesser gravity, and should anything on Earth make our powers fade away, these capsules will *renew* our super-powers temporarily!"

Even at that moment, however, the death of Krypton was at hand, and Jor-El barely had time to launch the infant Superman toward Earth in a tiny rocket before the entire planet exploded with a titanic roar. The metal box containing the radioactive capsules was never placed in the rocket, and when

Krypton exploded it was sent hurtling into outer space, eventually to find its way to Earth embedded in a meteoric fragment.

Years after the death of Krypton, Elton Craig came upon the box of capsules while examining fallen meteors in hopes of finding some KRYPTONITE to use against Superman. When Craig read the inscription on the metal box—"These radioactive capsules to be used only if needed to renew our super-powers on Earth. [signed] Jor-El"—and realized what he had found, he promptly swallowed one of the capsules and endowed himself with temporary super-powers which would last (according to World's Finest Comics No. 90 [Sep/Oct '57: "The Super-Batwoman!"]) for a period of twenty-four hours.

When Superman became temporarily incapacitated by kryptonite during an encounter with the now super-powered Craig, he summoned Batman and Robin to Craig's hideout and asked them to swallow some of Craig's capsules to endow themselves with super-powers temporarily so that they could take up the battle against Craig while Superman recovered from the effects of the kryptonite. Because it was Craig who had swallowed the first capsule, his super-powers faded first, thus enabling the super-powered Batman and Robin to capture him with relative ease. Soon afterward, Superman recovered his full powers, enabling Batman and Robin, whose temporary super-powers had by then faded, to return to their home in GOTHAM CITY (WF No. 87: "The Reversed Heroes!").

In September-October 1957 Elton Craig, the "most dangerous prisoner" at the Metropolis Prison, breaks out of jail and makes his way to the General Chemical Company, Inc., where he had managed to secrete one of Jor-El's special super-power capsules prior to his capture by Batman and Robin. Batman, Robin, and Superman all set out in search of the escaped Craig, but it is Batwoman who deduces that Craig may have hidden his super-power capsule at the General Chemical Company. Inside the plant, having come upon Craig about to swallow his capsule, she snatches it out of his hand and hastily swallows it herself in order to prevent him from getting it away from her. Then, aided by her temporary super-powers, Batwoman apprehends Craig and returns him to Metropolis Prison (WF No. 90: "The Super-Batwoman!").

CRATER VALLEY. A "beautiful, fertile valley"—nestled "in the midst of a barren wilderness area" somewhere in the United States, and sequestered from the outside world by an encircling curtain of towering cliffs—which is inhabited by "a lost colony of Quakers," descendants of a Quaker colony of the eighteenth century whose members "roamed the forests and mountains" of America in search of a refuge from the "world of evil, greed, and war" around them, until finally they settled in the "vast, fertile crater" known as Crater Valley, retaining their simple customs, clothing, and manner of speech and doggedly protecting their children and grandchildren from the temptations of the so-called "world beyond" by teaching them that "only barren wastes" lay beyond the valley's cliffs and that all human life on Earth resided within the boundaries of their lush, green valley. Of all the modern-day inhabitants of Crater Valley, only Peter Fry, and later Luke Robb, know that human life and civilization exist in the world beyond the valley.

Literally plummeting into the valley in May 1965 after accidentally falling out of the gondola of an observation balloon sent aloft to enable reporters to witness the launching of an experimental American space rocket, CLARK KENT soon makes the acquaintance of Peter Fry and his lovely niece Elizabelle and, at Fry's urging, accepts the job of village blacksmith in the old-fashioned Quaker community—one of several such communities in the valley—where Fry himself resides.

As the days pass, Kent develops a special affection for Crater Valley and its people, and the valley becomes for him a special haven where, even in his Clark Kent identity, he can abandon his role of cowardice and timidity and be a man of strength and courage.

"It's refreshing to be admired for my strength for once instead of being scorned for my timidity!" muses Kent at one point. And later he thinks, "... I'm not ready to leave this valley. It's the one place in the world where I can live as Clark Kent, without posing as a cringing coward!"

During his brief sojourn in the valley, Clark Kent enjoys the admiration of his neighbors and the lovely Elizabelle; defeats and then befriends a gruff, sometimes bullyish fellow named Luke Robb; and uses his super-powers to save Peter Fry from a potentially fatal bout of fever before soaring out of the valley as SUPERMAN to resume his normal life as a super-hero in METROPOLIS.

"... I'll come back some day," thinks Superman, as he flies over the top of the valley's cliffs. "This valley will make a peaceful haven for me. Whenever I'm tired of my meek, Clark Kent identity, I'll return to the one spot on Earth where Clark Kent can act like a he-man" (Act No. 324: "The Secret Life of Clark Kent!").

CRAWLEY. A worker at an experimental-aircraft company who, having stolen a giant dirigible from his place of employment, has teamed up with a pair of unscrupulous Indian mahouts to use the dirigible and a pair of stolen zoo elephants to commit a series of spectacular crimes, as when the villains lower the elephants from the dirigible by winch into the midst of a lavish fashion show, so that, as the panic-stricken crowds flee the madly charging elephants, they can steal the jewel-studded antique royal gowns on display there. Crawley and his cohorts are apprehended by SUPERMAN in July-August 1947 (S No. 47/2: "Susie Reforms!").

CRIME CZAR, THE. A cunning underworld mastermind, his true identity unknown to even his closest subordinates, who is secretly Mr. Fleming, "the mayor's assistant." His capture by SUPERMAN in February 1952 comes as the culmination of an elaborate ruse in which Superman uses a lifelike robot to play the role of an outlaw from the planet Mercury so that he can worm his way into the Crime Czar's hideout (Act No. 165: "The Man Who Conquered Superman!").

CRIMSON AVENGER, THE. An inept, amateurish costumed crime-fighter who helps BATMAN, ROBIN, and SUPERMAN apprehend the Octopus Gang in February 1963. He is in reality Albert Elwood, a "crackpot inventor" whose career as the Crimson Avenger stems from his determination to become the "nemesis of all crimedom" (WF No. 131: "The Mystery of the Crimson Avenger!"). (See OCTOPUS, THE.)

CRONIN, WHITEY. A "fugitive gang chief," sequestered with his gang in a "rural hideout" not far from the city of Midvale, who uses a stolen high-pressure water hose to short Midvale's power generators and cut off the city's power supply as part of an elaborate scheme to loot the Midvale banks and half the city, only to be apprehended by SUPERMAN in March-April 1948 (WF No. 33: "Superman Press, Inc.!").

CROTCHETT, F.P. An unhappy millionaire who, informed by his physician that he is doomed to die of joylessness unless he can manage to enjoy one hearty laugh, promises to donate $100,000 to charity if any man in METROPOLIS can succeed in making him laugh. Although many try and fail, SUPERMAN finally succeeds, but only after he has resolved the long-buried guilt that had made millionaire Crotchett immune to laughter (S No. 56/2, Jan/Feb '49: "The Man Who Couldn't Laugh!").

CROWTHER, BURTON. A local Hudson River area historian and treasure hunter who, having discovered the resting place of a sunken vessel carrying $1,000,000 worth of gold and gems, concocts an elaborate scheme to frighten the curious away from the scene by having his henchmen pose as ghosts and figures from local legends come miraculously to life. Crowther is apprehended by SUPERMAN in September-October 1946 (S No. 42/2: "A Legend Comes True!").

CURRY, EVELYN. An innocent young woman, about to be executed for a murder she did not commit, who is rescued from the electric chair within moments of her execution when SUPERMAN, having apprehended the real murderess less than thirty minutes before, barges into the governor's home just before midnight and gets him to put through a life-saving

call to the death house (Act No. 1, Jun '38). The story reappears in expanded form in Superman No. 1/1 (Sum '39). (See CARROLL, BEA.)

CURTIS, J.F. The mastermind behind an avalanche of "subversive activities" perpetrated in Spring 1940 by "sinister forces [that] seek to retard the nation's return to prosperity" by sinking ships, blowing up factories, and ultimately launching "a financial upheaval that will panic the stock-exchange and plunge the country into its worst depression!" Cornered finally by SUPERMAN—who has learned that "a foreign nation has promised [Curtis] important concessions if he'll wreck America's economic structure"—Curtis attempts to annihilate Superman with "a terrific barrage of electricity bolts," but, "Reaching out, SUPERMAN touches the plotter's figure—[and] the electricity passes from him to the other man's [Curtis's] body, instantly electrocuting Curtis!" Thanks to Superman, therefore, the nation's "march toward prosperity" continues unabated (S No. 4/3).

CURTIS, RAY. The publisher of the METROPOLIS Daily Dispatch, and the man who is secretly "THE INSIDER" (S No. 73/3, Nov/Dec '51: "Perry White vs. Clark Kent!").

CURTIS, TERRY. A brilliant young scientist who, "for some time," has "been on the track of harnessing atomic energy." In Curtis's words, "It looks like I'm upon the point of discovering a weapon that could destroy any matter it was leveled at!" Terry Curtis is kidnapped by the ULTRA-HUMANITE in February 1940 and forced to construct a diabolical "atomic-disintegrator" with which the villain intends to blackmail METROPOLIS (Act No. 21).

CYRIL. The young son of the Earl of Wordenshire, and the boy who is secretly the SQUIRE (BM No. 62/2, Dec/Jan '50-'51: "The Batman of England!").

CYRUSVILLE. A United States town which is "off limits to Superman"—where images of SUPERMAN are confiscated as "Superman contraband" and speaking well of Superman is a violation of the stringent "anti-Superman laws"—simply because Bruce Cyrus, the town's otherwise well-intentioned mayor, has an irrational hatred of the Man of Steel. Ultimately, however, Superman persuades Mayor Cyrus that his grudge against him is unfounded, and before long the tyrannical anti-Superman statutes have been repealed and "the town that hated Superman" has become a thing of the past (S No. 130/3, Jul '59: "The Town That Hated Superman!").

D

DAILY MPFTRZ. A daily newspaper published in METROPOLIS by MR. MXYZPTLK in January 1954. The *Daily Mpftrz* differs from other daily newspapers, however, including the DAILY PLANET, in that it contains news of the events that are going to happen the following day, rather than of events that have already happened (S No. 86/3: "The Fourth Dimension Gazette!").

DAILY PLANET. The metropolitan daily newspaper which employs CLARK KENT as a reporter for more than three full decades, until January 1971, at which time Kent departs the *Daily Planet* to become a full-time newscaster for METROPOLIS television station WGBS-TV (S No. 233: "Superman Breaks Loose"). Described as "the biggest paper in Metropolis" (S No. 73/3, Nov/Dec '51: "Perry White vs. Clark Kent!") and as Metropolis's "leading newspaper" (S No. 6/1, Sep/Oct '40; and others), the *Daily Planet* has an unparalleled reputation for fairness and accuracy (S No. 41/3, Jul/Aug '46: "A Modern Alice in Wonderland!"; and others) and has "millions of ... readers" (S No. 83/3, Jul/Aug '53: "Clark Kent---Convict!"). The newspaper's precise circulation has never been stated, but in April 1961 the *Daily Planet* celebrates the sale of its five-billionth copy (S No. 144/1: "The Super-Weapon!").

The *Daily Planet* is headquartered in the Daily Planet Building (Act No. 36, May '41; and others), a large skyscraper situated in downtown Metropolis at the center of Planet Square, the so-called "crossroads of the world" (Act No. 77, Oct '44: "The Headline Hoax!"; and others). Owned at least for a time by Metropolis millionaire EBENEEZER WALKER (Act No. 214, Mar '56: "Superman, Super-Destroyer"), the building features an electric news-sign that encircles the topmost story (Act No. 229, Jun '57: "The Superman Satellite") and a "giant globe of the world"—encircled by a Saturnlike ring and by giant block letters spelling out the name Daily Planet—mounted on the roof (Act No. 272, Jan '61: "Superman's Rival, Mental Man!"; and others). Extending skyward from the Daily Planet Tower, at the summit of the building, is the broadcast antenna of WPLT, a radio station owned and operated by the *Daily Planet* (S No. 39/1, Mar/Apr '46: "The Big Superman Broadcast!"). Across the street from the Daily Planet Building is a small park, where a marble statue of Superman is unveiled in January-February 1946 (S No. 38/3: "The Man of Stone!"; and others).

A plaque near the front entrance of the building indicates that the *Daily Planet* is published by The Daily Planet Publishing Co., Inc. (WF No. 29, Jul/Aug '47: "The Books That Couldn't Be Bound!";

and others), but at least one text asserts that the *Daily Planet* is owned by an unnamed company that operates a chain of newspapers, including the *Gotham Gazette* (WF No. 75, Mar/Apr '55: "The New Team of Superman and Robin!"). By the early 1970s, the *Daily Planet* has been acquired by the Galaxy Broadcasting System (S No. 233, Jan '71: "Superman Breaks Loose"; and others).

An airborne Superman approaches the Daily Planet Building, 1962

The date of the *Daily Planet*'s founding is treated inconsistently in the chronicles. The Daily Planet Publishing Co., Inc., is described as having been established in 1870 in one text (Act No. 194, Jul '54: "The Outlaws from Krypton!") and as having been established in 1887 in another (WF No. 68, Jan/Feb '54: "The Menace from the Stars!"). In January-February 1943 editor PERRY WHITE refers to the *Daily Planet* as being 150 years old (S No. 20/1: "Superman's Secret Revealed!"), but *Daily Planet* staffers celebrate the centennial of the newspaper twice in the chronicles, once in Spring 1944 (WF No. 13: "The Freedom of the Press!") and again in April 1961 (S No. 144/2: "Superboy's First Public Appearance!").

Whatever the newspaper's true age, it apparently originated in the city of San Francisco, as the San Francisco *Daily Planet*, sometime prior to 1906 (S No. 168, Apr '64: pts. I-II—"Luthor--Super-Hero!"; "Lex Luthor, Daily Planet Editor!"). In January 1954 an English edition of the *Daily Planet* is established in London (S No. 86/1: "The Dragon from King Arthur's Court!"), and in April 1955 other international editions are launched in Paris and Bombay (Act No. 203: "The International Daily Planet!"). By December 1955, editions of the *Daily Planet* are also well under way in Greece, Italy, Holland, and Japan (Act No. 211: "The Superman Spectaculars"). Other editions of the *Daily Planet* include *Ye Daily Planet,* the "world's first daily newspaper," established by

Clark Kent and Lois Lane during a time-journey to the city of London in the yeàr 1606 (S No. 44/3, Jan/Feb '47: "Shakespeare's Ghost Writer!"), and the *Daily Solar System*, a futuristic descendant of the *Daily Planet* in the thirtieth century A.D. (Act No. 215, Apr '56: "The Superman of Tomorrow").

In addition to its chain of newspapers, the *Daily Planet* has its own radio station (S No. 39/1, Mar/Apr '46: "The Big Superman Broadcast!"), its own television studios (WF No. 52, Jun/Jul '51: "The Man Who Swindled Superman!"; (Act No. 295, Dec '62: "Superman Goes Wild!") and its own mobile television unit for covering fast-breaking news events (S No. 57/1, Mar/Apr '49: "The Menace of the Machine Men!"). The radio station's offerings have included an "Adventures of Superman" program (S No. 39/1, Mar/Apr '46: "The Big Superman Broadcast!"), while the television facilities have been used to air a TV quiz show (WF No. 52, Jun/Jul '51: "The Man Who Swindled Superman!") and a news program called the "Daily Planet News Flash TV Show" (S No. 145/1, May '61: "The Secret Identity of Superman!").

Another item of news-gathering equipment indispensable to the *Daily Planet*'s operations is the newspaper's privately owned helicopter (S No. 111/1, Feb '57: "The Non-Super Superman"), the Flying Newsroom (S No. 115/2, Aug '57: "Jimmy Olsen's Lost Pal"; and others), which makes its initial appearance in the chronicles in the late 1950s (Act No. 236, Jan '58: "Superman's New Uniform!"; and others). Rendered in various colors, including green (Act No. 236, Jan '58: "Superman's New Uniform!"), purple (Act No. 244, Sep '58: "The Super-Merman of the Sea"), and red (Act No. 249, Feb '59: "The Kryptonite Man!"; and others), the Flying Newsroom is sometimes portrayed as having one rotor (S No. 111/1, Feb '57: "The Non-Super Superman"; and others) and sometimes as having two (Act No. 249, Feb '59: "The Kryptonite Man!"; and others), is occasionally outfitted with pontoons to enable it to land on water (Act No. 244, Sep '58: "The Super-Merman of the Sea"), and, in one text, is described as returning from "foreign shores," implying that it is capable of making a transatlantic flight (S No. 124/2, Sep '58: "Mrs. Superman").

Almost from the onset of his super-hero career, Superman has been identified with the *Daily Planet* not only as Clark Kent, but as Superman as well, helping its reporters achieve sensational scoops, participating in its charity drives, zealously endeavoring to protect its reputation for accuracy (S No. 102/3, Jan '56: "The Million-Dollar Mistake"; and others). The *Daily Planet* has long been the place where strangers attempt to contact Superman (S No. 25/4, Nov/Dec '43: "Hi-Jack--Jackal of Crime!"; and others), the place where the Man of Steel picks up his mail and receives his messages (Act No. 161, Oct '51: "Exit—Superman!"; and others). Indeed, according to Superman No. 117/1, the majority of the *Daily Planet*'s mail is addressed to Superman (Nov '57: "Clark Kent, Man of Mystery"). "People are always sending his mail here," explains Clark Kent in February 1964, "because they know Clark Kent is his friend!" (Act No. 309: "The Superman Super Spectacular!"). The Man of Steel's long-term involvement with the *Daily Planet* is probably the main reason why the newspaper's photographic files contain "the most complete collection of Superman's feats ever recorded on film..." (S No. 91/1, Aug '54: "The Superman Stamp!").

One reason for Superman's special affection for the *Daily Planet*, apart from the fact that he is employed there as reporter Clark Kent, is the newspaper's extensive commitment to philanthropic activities, which includes donating "a good percentage" of its profits to charity (WF No. 52, Jun/Jul '51: "The Man Who Swindled Superman!"). In May-June 1942 the *Daily Planet* launches a campaign to build a free vacation resort for underprivileged children (S No. 16/1: "The World's Meanest Man"), and in July-August 1945 it holds a drive to raise money for the Metropolis Aid Fund (S No. 35/3: "The Genie of the Lamp!"). By July-August 1946 the Planet Aid Fund has been established to serve as an umbrella for the *Daily Planet*'s charitable enterprises (S No. 41/2: "Clark Kent's Bodyguard!"; and others), such as the drive to collect money for an orphan asylum conducted in March-April 1948 (S No. 51/3: "The Man Who Bossed Superman!"). Superman gives a demonstration of his awesome super-strength at a benefit performance for the Planet Aid Fund in November 1952 (Act No. 174: "The Man Who Shackled Superman!").

Later texts make reference to a Daily Planet Charity Fund, which may or may not be the same as the Planet Aid Fund. Once a year, with Superman's help, the employees of the *Daily Planet* put on a gala circus extravaganza—the so-called Daily Planet Charity Show—to raise money for the Fund (Act No. 212, Jan '56: "The Superman Calendar"; and others). Superman performs at a benefit for the Daily Planet

AND WHEREVER THERE'S A SCOOP, YOU CAN BE SURE LOIS LANE AND JIMMY OLSEN, REPORTERS FOR THE *DAILY PLANET*, ARE AT HAND IN THE *FLYING NEWSROOM*...

FLYING NEWSROOM

DAILY PLANET

YOU TAKE AERIAL PICTURES, JIMMY, WHILE I PARACHUTE DOWN AND GET THE FIRST-HAND STORY OF THE FLOOD!

© NPP 1958

With Jimmy Olsen handling the controls, Lois Lane parachutes out of the Flying Newsroom, 1958

Charity Fund, held at Metropolis's Ajax Theater, in April 1963 (S No. 160/1: pts. I-II—"The Mortal Superman!"; "The Cage of Doom!"). In February 1957 he Man of Steel excavates a new man-made lake for the Lake Cosmo Children's Camp, a project sponsored by the Daily Planet Aid Branch for the Underprivileged (Act No. 225: "The Death of Superman"). Action Comics No. 226 contains a reference to a Daily Planet Fresh Air Fund (Mar '57: "The Invulnerable Enemy").

Both to help it raise money for charity and to boost its circulation, the Daily Planet frequently conducts imaginative contests. Examples of these contents abound in the chronicles, including the contest for the city's newsboys, held in Summer 1945, with a job as cub reporter being offered as a prize to the newsboy who brings in the day's best news story (WF No. 18: "The Junior Reporters!"); the contest to locate "the ideal average American," held in January 1946 (Act No. 92: "The Average American!"); the contest between Superman and NELSON SWAYNE, held in March-April 1947 (WF No. 27: "The Man Who Out-Supered Superman!"); the contest to locate the owner of the best autograph collection, held in September-October 1947 (S No. 48/2: "Autograph, Please!"); the contest to determine the writer of the most interesting letter accompanying a contribution to the Daily Planet's orphan-asylum fund, held in March-April 1948, with the winner to receive Superman's services, gratis, for a day (S No. 51/3: "The Man Who Bossed Superman!"); the contest among the Daily Planet's own reporters, held in November-December 1948, to determine which of them can write the best story about Superman (WF No. 37: "The Superman Story!"); the contest to select Miss Metropolis of 1950, held in March-April 1950, which offers a prize of $10,000 to the winner and is open only to beautiful girls engaged in perilous occupations (S No. 63/3: "Miss Metropolis of 1950"); the contest, held in July-August 1953, to select the bravest woman in America (S No. 83/2: "The Search for the Bravest Woman!"); the annual contest to select the most "Lovely Child," with the winner to receive a prize of $1,000 and a free sightseeing trip around the world with Superman (S No. 96/1, Mar '55: "The Girl Who Didn't Believe in Superman!"); the contest to select the five best letters submitted by Daily Planet readers in response to the question, "What five feats by Superman would most benefit Metropolis?" with Superman agreeing to perform the five best suggested feats (S No. 104/3, Mar '56: "The Super-Family from Outer Space"); the contest, held in July 1956, to see which Daily Planet reader recalls Superman's earliest super-feat (S No. 106/1: "Superman's First Exploit"); the contest, held in March 1958, to select the best photograph taken by an amateur photographer of Superman in action (S No. 120/2: "The Super-Feats Superman Forgot"); and the "three coins in the fountain" charity contest, held in August 1965, in which Superman picks three coins from a fountain tossed there by charity contributors and grants one wish each to the three persons whose

coins he has selected (S No. 179/1: "The Outlaw Fort Knox!").

The question of who publishes the Daily Planet is treated inconsistently in the chronicles. Two texts call Perry White the publisher (S No. 18/3, Sep/Oct '42: "The Man with the Cane"; S No. 117/1, Nov '57: "Clark Kent, Man of Mystery"), but these references are almost certainly erroneous. Other individuals referred to as the Daily Planet's publisher include Burt Mason (S No. 5/2, Sum '40; see also S No. 6/2, Sep/Oct '40); J. WIMMER (Act No. 139, Dec '49: "Clark Kent... Daredevil!"); Maxwell Leeds (S No. 73/3, Nov/Dec '51: "Perry White vs. Clark Kent!"); JOHN WILTON, although his custodianship of the Daily Planet is only temporary (S No. 79/2, Nov/Dec '52: "The End of the Planet!"); Harvey Gray, the brother of GRISELDA GRAY (S No. 85/2, Nov/Dec '53: "Clark Kent, Gentleman Journalist!"); and Frank Wells, the uncle of POINTDEXTER WELLS (S No. 95/2, Feb '55: "The Practical Joker!"). A Mr. Amesby is referred to as Perry White's "boss" in Superman No. 105/2, but this need not necessarily be taken as an indication that Amesby is the Daily Planet's publisher (May '56: "Mr. Mxyztplk's Secret Identity"). DEXTER WILLIS's uncle, Mr. Willis, is described as "a big shot publisher" and one of the Daily Planet's "biggest stockholders" (Act No. 289, Jun '62: "The Super-Practical Joker!"), and MORNA VINE's uncle, wealthy Mark Vine, is the newspaper's "chief stockholder" (S No. 181/1, Nov '65: pts. I-II—"The Super-Scoops of Morna Vine!"; "The Secrets of the New Supergirl!").

From the time the name Daily Planet first appears in the chronicles (S No. 4/1-4, Spr '40; Act No. 23, Apr '40) through November 1940 (Act No. 30), GEORGE TAYLOR is explicitly referred to as the Daily Planet's editor (Act No. 25, Jun '40; and others). Then, in November-December 1940, an editor named White appears (S No. 7/1, and in May-June White's full name—Perry White—is given for the first time in the chronicles (S No. 10/2). Despite the fact that Perry White has now functioned as the Daily Planet's editor for nearly four full decades, however, the chroniclers have not been consistent regarding his precise professional title: he has been referred to as the "editor" in numerous texts (S No. 27/1, Mar/Apr '44: "The Palace of Perilous Play!"; and others), but he has also been described as the newspaper's "managing editor" (WF No. 13, Spr '44: "The Freedom of the Press!"; and others), its "city editor" (Act No. 133, Jun '49: "The World's Most Perfect Girl!"; Act No. 136, Sep '49: "Superman, Show-Off!"), its "chief editor" (S No. 121/3, May '58: "Jimmy Hits the Jackpot"; S No. 131/3, Aug '59: "The Unknown Super-Deeds!"), and its "editor-in-chief" (Act No. 243, Aug '58: "The Lady and the Lion"). Perry White has also been referred to as the Daily Planet's "editor-publisher" (S No. 18/3, Sep/Oct '42: "The Man with the Cane") and "publisher" (S No. 117/1, Nov '57: "Clark Kent, Man of Mystery"), but these designations are contradicted by numerous texts (S No. 54/1, Sep/Oct '48: "The Wrecker"; and others) and are certainly not accurate.

The *Daily Planet*'s "star reporter" (Act No. 25, Jun '40; and others) is indisputably Clark Kent. Renowned for his ability to root out local news (S No. 44/3, Jan/Feb '47: "Shakespeare's Ghost Writer!"; and others), particularly stories dealing with crime and corruption (S No. 83/3, Jul/Aug '53: "Clark Kent ---Convict!"; and others), Kent has performed in numerous other capacities for the *Daily Planet*, including that of war correspondent (Act No. 23, Apr '40), lovelorn editor (S No. 18/3, Sep/Oct '42: "The Man with the Cane"; and others), and editor of the entire newspaper in the absence of Perry White (Act No. 297, Feb '63: "The Man Who Betrayed Superman's Identity!"). He is described as the *Daily Planet*'s "foremost reporter" in Superman No. 12/2 (Sep/Oct '41), and as its "ace reporter" in Action Comics No. 105 (Feb '47: "The Man Who Hated Christmas!") and in numerous other texts. "To Daily Planet readers," explains Superman No. 98/2: "the name of Clark Kent signed over a story has always meant integrity and honesty! His newspaper reporting on crime has won him countless awards!" (Jul '55: "Clark Kent Outlaw!").

Two separate texts have appeared purporting to tell the true story of how Clark Kent came to acquire his reporter's job on the *Daily Planet*, and they contain widely disparate accounts. According to Action Comics No. 144, Clark Kent first decided to become a reporter while still a youngster, after hearing *Daily Planet* editor Perry White give a lecture at Smallville High School. Arriving in Metropolis "years later" in hopes of pursuing a journalist's career, Kent was rejected by White when he applied for a post at the *Daily Planet* and was forced to take on a series of odd jobs—from taxi driver to vacuum-cleaner salesman—until finally, after he had rescued Perry White from death at the hands of syndicate gangsters on several occasions, both as Clark Kent and as Superman, and after he had turned in an exclusive account of Superman's crusade against the syndicate, White finally granted him a job as a reporter (May '50: "Clark Kent's Career!"). According to a conflicting account presented in Superman No. 133/2, however, Kent applied for a reporter's job at the *Daily Planet*, was given a series of trivial "test" assignments—such as visiting the Metropolis Zoo for a story on an aging gorilla—by editor Perry White in lieu of an outright brush-off, and finally won his post on the *Daily Planet* by using his Superman powers to transform each dull, routine assignment into an electrifying news event and then handing in exclusive accounts of these events as would-be reporter Kent (Nov '59: "How Perry White Hired Clark Kent!"). Both these accounts may safely be regarded as spurious, for Clark Kent really began his journalistic career on the DAILY STAR, the forerunner in the chronicles of the *Daily Planet*, by thwarting a lynching at the county jail in his Superman identity and then phoning in an exclusive account of the events as would-be reporter Clark Kent (S No. 1/1, Sum '39).

Working as a reporter for a major newspaper enables Clark Kent to "investigate criminals without their suspecting [he's] really Superman" (S No. 133/2, Nov '59: "How Perry White Hired Clark Kent!") and provides him with "the best opportunity for being free to help people as Superman" without having to explain his frequent absences from his place of employment (Act No. 144, May '50: "Clark Kent's Career!"; and others). Kent frequently changes to Superman inside an empty "storage closet" (Act No. 181, Jun '53: "The New Superman" or "store-room" (S No. 145/1, May '61: "The Secret Identity of Superman!") at the *Daily Planet*, and by May 1958 he has begun hiding a sophisticated Clark Kent robot behind a secret panel in the *Daily Planet*'s supply room, capable of carrying on his journalistic duties whenever he is needed elsewhere as Superman (Act No. 240: "Secret of the Superman Sphinx").

Ranking alongside Kent in the *Daily Planet*'s reportorial hierarchy is Lois Lane, "the *Daily Planet*'s star woman reporter" (WF No. 47, Aug/Sep '50: "The Girl Who Hated Reporters!") and "Clark Kent's rival reporter at the Daily Planet…" (Act No. 176, Jan '53: "Muscles for Money"). Described as the newspaper's "sob sister" (S No. 7/1, Nov/Dec '40; and others) and as its lovelorn columnist (Act No. 44, Jan '42; and others) in many early texts, Lois Lane has risen through the journalistic ranks to become one of the *Daily Planet*'s "star reporters" (S No. 27/1, Mar/Apr '44: "The Palace of Perilous Play!"; and others) and, with Clark Kent, one of the newspaper's "two brightest satellites" (S No. 26/2, Jan/Feb '44: "Comedians' Holiday!"). Particularly adept at covering local news (S No. 44/3, Jan/Feb '47: "Shakespeare's Ghost Writer!"), she has performed the full range of journalistic duties, including stints as war correspondent (Act No. 23, Apr '40); weather editor, described as "one of the lowliest jobs on any newspaper" (WF No. 25, Nov/Dec '46: "Mad Weather in Metropolis!"; *see also* WF No. 51, Apr/May '51: "The Amazing Talents of Lois Lane!"); question-and-answer editor and head of the lost-and-found department (WF No. 51, Apr/May '51: "The Amazing Talents of Lois Lane!"); and "acting editor" in the absence of Perry White (S No. 124/1, Sep '58: "The Super-Sword").

According to World's Finest Comics No. 47, Lois Lane began her journalistic career on the *Daily Planet* sometime after Clark Kent had already obtained employment there (Aug/Sep '50: "The Girl Who Hated Reporters!"). This account is undoubtedly erroneous, however, for Lois Lane is portrayed as employed by the *Daily Star* in the premiere text of the Superman chronicles (Act No. 1, Jun '38), and her hiring seems clearly to have preceded Kent's (S No. 1/1, Sum '39). In addition, numerous other texts support the contention that Lois Lane was already plying her trade as a reporter at the time Clark Kent first began his journalistic career (S No. 133/2, Nov '59: "How Perry White Hired Clark Kent!"; and others).

After Perry White, Clark Kent, and Lois Lane, the most enduring member of the *Daily Planet* staff is JIMMY OLSEN, the newspaper's "star cub reporter" (Act No. 238, Mar '58: "The Super-Gorilla from Krypton"). First introduced in November-December 1941 only as Jimmy, an office boy at the *Daily Planet* with a heartfelt longing to become "a real reporter" like his idol, Clark Kent (S No. 13/2), Jimmy is finally referred to by his full name, Jimmy Olsen, in March-April 1942 (S No. 15/1) and continues to be referred to as the *Daily Planet*'s "office boy" for a number of years (Act No. 71, Apr '44: "Valentine Villainy!"; and others) until he is finally accorded the status of cub reporter in January 1954 (S No. 86/2: "Jimmy Olsen ... Editor!").

In the offices of the Daily Planet, *Perry White, Lois Lane, and Jimmy Olsen agonize over writing a story that would be unfavorable to Superman, 1962*

Other *Daily Planet* staffers over the years have included reporter CHARLES CLAYTON (S No. 21/2, Mar/Apr '43: "The Four Gangleaders"); janitor CHARLIE FROST (WF No. 11, Fall '43: "The City of Hate!"); composing-room foreman Sam Greene, boss pressman Matt Worth, delivery-fleet head Pete Gluyas, ace cameraman Happy, copy-desk chief Sanford, and reporter Honey Dale, the publisher's niece (WF No. 13, Spr '44: "The Freedom of the Press!"); cub reporter TOMMY BLAKE (WF No. 18, Sum '45: "The Junior Reporters!"); columnist Olga Olmstead (WF No. 24, Sep/Oct '46: "Impossible but True!"); sports editor Jack Donovan, shipping-news reporter Mart Lane, photographer Joey Crane, and political reporter Horace Mills (WF No. 37, Nov/Dec '48: "The Superman Story!"); a linotyper named Barstow (S No. 57/3, Mar/Apr '49: "The Son of Superman!"); sports photographer Tom Dodds (S No. 58/2, May/June '49: "Lois Lane Loves Clark Kent!"); business manager Mr. Weems (S No. 63/2, Mar/Apr '50: "The Wind-Up Toys of Peril!"); Chuck, "the Planet's star photographer" (S No. 66/2, Sep/Oct '50: "The Last Days of Superman!"); cub reporter WILL WHITE, a son of Perry White (S No. 72/2, Sep/Oct '51:

"The Private Life of Perry White!"); switchboard operator SUSAN SEMPLE (Act No. 163, Dec '51: "The Girl of Tomorrow"); reporter JACK WILDE (Act No. 171, Aug '52: "The Secrets of Superman!"); drama reporter Waldo Pippin (S No. 91/3, Aug '54: "Great Caesar's Ghost!"); staff artist Al Fallon, who draws the comic-strip feature MENTAL-MAN (Act No. 196, Sep '54: "The Adventures of Mental-Man!"); editor George Earns (S No. 92/1, Sep '54: "The Impossible Headlines!"); lovelorn editor Dora Dell (S No. 92/2, Sep '54: "Superman's Sweetheart!"); copy boy Tommy Brown (S No. 95/3, Feb '55: "Jimmy Olsen, Super-Reporter!"); reporter PERRY WHITE, JR., a son of Perry White (S No. 108/2, Sep '56: "Perry White, Jr., Demon Reporter!"); and reporter MORNA VINE (S No. 181/1, Nov '65: pts. I-II—"The Super-Scoops of Morna Vine!"; "The Secret of the New Supergirl!").

Other individuals who, at one time or another, have worked on the *Daily Planet* include boy genius Euclid Smith, who becomes a reporter on the newspaper in May-June 1952 as part of Superman's plan for getting the goods on the unscrupulous MR. FENTON (WF No. 58: "'Scoop' Smith, Boy Reporter!"); LANA LANG, who is employed by the *Daily Planet* during September-October 1952 (S No. 78/3: "The Girls in Superman's Life!"); swindler SOAPY MARTIN, who, under the alias Don Kelton, is employed as the *Daily Planet*'s sports editor during January 1956 (S No. 102/3: "The Million-Dollar Mistake"); MR. MXYZPTLK, who uobtains a reporter's job on the paper under a secret identity in May 1956 (S No. 105/2: "Mr. Mxyzptlk's Secret Identity"); John Corben, alias METALLO, who becomes a reporter on the *Daily Planet* in May 1959 (Act No. 252: "The Menace of Metallo!"); and HERCULES, who, under the pseudonym Roger Tate, obtains employment as a *Daily Planet* reporter during a visit to the twentieth century in August 1960 (Act No. 267: "Hercules in the 20th Century!"). Nostradamus, an old hermit who becomes, for a time, the dupe of the archvillainous LEX LUTHOR, is given a job with the *Daily Planet* as a weather forecaster in October 1948 (Act No. 125: "The Modern Nostradamus!"), and QUEX-UL, formerly an inmate of the PHANTOM ZONE, is given a job in the *Daily Planet*'s production department in November 1962 (S No. 157/1: "The Super-Revenge of the Phantom Zone Prisoner!").

According to World's Finest Comics No. 47, "the favorite eating place for Metropolis reporters," including those of the *Daily Planet*, is Harry's Dog House, a diner specializing in hot dogs located across the street from the Daily Planet Building (Aug/Sep '50: "The Girl Who Hated Reporters!"). For haircuts, most of the *Planet* staffers rely on Tony's barbershop (Act No. 237, Feb '58: "Superman's Exposed Identity").

Despite the preeminence of the *Daily Planet* among Metropolis's newspapers, The *Planet* has not been without its competition. Over the years, rival newspapers have included the *Morning Pictorial* and the *Evening Standard* (Act No. 37, Jun '41; and others); the *Metropolis Star* (S No. 39/1, Mar/Apr '46: "The Big Superman Broadcast!"; S No. 63/2, Mar-/Apr '50: "The Wind-Up Toys of Peril!"); the *Evening Gazette* (S No. 42/3, Sep/Oct '46: "The Death of Clark Kent!"; S No. 108/2, Sep '56: "Perry White, Jr., Demon Reporter!"); the *Eagle* (S No. 49/2, Nov/Dec '47: "Clark Kent's Most Dangerous Assignment!"); the *Examiner* (S No. 49/3, Nov/Dec '47: "Lois Lane, Globe-Trotter!"); the *World* and the *Globe* (WF No. 33, Mar/Apr '48: "Superman Press, Inc.!"); the *Metropolis Herald* (S No. 52/1, May/Jun '48: "Preview of Plunder"); the *Daily Dispatch* (S No. 73/3, Nov/Dec '51: "Perry White vs. Clark Kent!"); the *Daily Tatler* (WF No. 58, May/Jun '52: "'Scoop' Smith, Boy Reporter!"); the *Evening Compass* (S No. 89/1, May '54: "Captain Kent the Terrible!"); and the *Morning Globe* (Act No. 237, Feb '58: "Superman's Exposed Identity").

In June 1938, the date of the premiere text of the Superman chronicles, Clark Kent is portrayed as a reporter for the *Daily Star* (Act No. 1), although an expanded version of these same events, published a year later, shows that Kent had obtained employment on the *Star* only a short while earlier (S No. 1/1, Sum '39). For almost two full years, through March 1940, Kent's newspaper is referred to as the *Daily Star* (Act No. 22). Thereafter, however, without any explanation having been given for the changeover, the paper is referred to as the *Daily Planet* (S No. 4/1-4, Spr '40; Act No. 23, Apr '40), the name it has now retained for nearly four full decades.

Following its last appearance in November 1940 (Act No. 30), the name of George Taylor—who had served as editor of the *Daily Star* and then of the *Daily Planet*—disappears from the chronicles entirely, to be replaced soon afterward by that of editor Perry White (Act No. 35, Apr '41; and others).

In Summer 1940 ALEX EVELL's attempt to seize control of the *Daily Planet* is thwarted by Superman (S No. 5/2).

In October 1941 saboteur RALPH COWAN plants a time bomb at the *Daily Planet* while posing as a telephone repairman, but Superman finds and defuses the bomb before it has had time to go off (Act No. 41).

In May-June 1942 the Daily Planet Building and all its occupants are transported to the fourth dimension by the evil MISTER SINISTER, but Superman ultimately defeats the villain and restores the "kidnapped" building to the earthly dimension (S No. 16/3: "Case of the Runaway Skyscrapers").

In September-October 1942, after being duped by Nazi agent CARL BLAND into participating in his so-called "mock invasion" of Metropolis, Lois Lane almost succeeds in blowing up the *Daily Planet* when she carries a bomb-laden suitcase into the Daily Planet Building unaware that it contains a live bomb. Alerted in the nick of time by Superman, however, Lois drops the suitcase into a nearby river, where it explodes harmlessly (S No. 18/1: "The Conquest of a City").

In November-December 1942 villains from the *Daily Planet*'s comic strips are brought to life by FUNNYFACE, who puts them to work committing spectacular crimes. Superman ultimately apprehends Funnyface, however, with some timely assistance from Lois Lane (S No. 19/1: "Case of the Funny Paper Crimes").

In December 1942 the *Daily Planet* announces its plans to publish a comic-strip series by cartoonist AT HATT based on the adventures of Superman (Act No. 55: "A Goof Named Tiny Rufe").

In May-June 1943, after the PRANKSTER has copyrighted the English alphabet, Perry White finds himself compelled to pay the villain $2,000 per week for permission to publish the *Daily Planet* (S No. 22/3: "The Great ABC Panic!").

In Fall 1943 the SKEPTIC attempts to discredit the *Daily Planet*, only to be thwarted and apprehended by Superman (WF No. 11: "The City of Hate!").

In Spring 1944 three Metropolis rackets czars (*see* DIMANT, DELMAR "DICE") embark on a campaign of sabotage and terror against the *Daily Planet* in an effort to prevent publication of an incriminating story, but their efforts are repeatedly thwarted by Superman (WF No. 13: "The Freedom of the Press!").

In October 1944 the PRANKSTER prints up two separate phony editions of the *Daily Planet* as part of his elaborate scheme to bilk wealthy "stock manipulator" Amos Amster (Act No. 77: "The Headline Hoax!").

In January-February 1946 LEX LUTHOR wreaks havoc at the Daily Planet Building when he makes it the target of his diabolical "molecular impulsion beam" (S No. 38/1: "The Battle of the Atoms!").

In November-December 1948 five *Daily Planet* reporters spend a hectic day with Superman as part of a contest, proposed by Perry White, to see which of them can produce the best story about the day's events. All five reporters turn in excellent stories, but the winner of the contest—although the name of the winner is never explicitly stated—is apparently young news photographer Joey Crane, whose "story" consists of pictures of all the happy people Superman helped in the course of his super-heroic day (WF No. 37: "The Superman Story!").

In September-October 1949 rackets czar HOLLIS SHORE has his henchmen bomb the *Daily Planet*'s printing presses in retaliation for a series of exposés written by editor Perry White, but Superman keeps the *Daily Planet* in business in spite of the damage by printing the newspaper on a hand press at eye-blurring super-speed (S No. 60/1: "The Two Identities of Superman!").

In March-April 1950 the TOYMAN steals a payroll from the *Daily Planet* with the aid of an ingenious flying Superman doll, but Superman ultimately outwits the Toyman and takes him into custody (S No. 63/2: "The Wind-Up Toys of Peril!").

In July-August 1950, when the space capsule carrying MALA, Kizo, and U-Ban crash-lands in Metropolis, the impact of the landing threatens to topple the Daily Planet Building and numerous other downtown skyscrapers, but, "with a speed that seems to burn up space," Superman repairs the damage before any of the buildings collapse (S No. 65/3: "Three Supermen from Krypton!").

In June 1951 JOE "THE ELEPHANT" STRIKER and his henchmen are apprehended by Superman while attempting to stage a payroll robbery at the *Daily Planet* (Act No. 157: "The Superman Who Couldn't Fly!").

In November-December 1951 the *Daily Planet* merges with its former rival, the *Daily Dispatch*, after the *Dispatch*'s stockholders have hastily decided to dispose of their interest in the paper in the wake of the embarrassing revelation that *Dispatch* publisher Ray Curtis is actually "THE INSIDER." The text asserts that the newspaper resulting from the merger is to be called the *Planet-Dispatch* (S No. 73/3: "Perry White vs. Clark Kent!"), but the name *Planet-Dispatch* never reappears in any subsequent text.

In November-December 1952 the *Daily Planet* is deliberately closed down by publisher JOHN WILTON as part of his scheme to stifle competition among Metropolis's newspapers. Before long, however, the *Daily Planet* is back in business, thanks to the perseverance of *Planet* staffers and the heroic intervention of Superman (S No. 79/2: "The End of the Planet!").

In February 1953 the Daily Planet Building is smashed in two by a diabolical "flying wrecking crane" employed by the "GENERAL," but Superman evacuates the building before anyone is injured, transporting its equipment and personnel to a safe location until he has had time to repair the damage (Act No. 177: "The Anti-Superman Weapon").

In January 1954 an English edition of the *Daily Planet* is established in London (S No. 86/1: "The Dragon from King Arthur's Court!").

In May 1954 life at the *Daily Planet* is made miserable by the relentless insistence on "split-second efficiency" imposed on the staff by efficiency expert JASPER COLDSTONE (Act No. 192: "The Man Who Sped Up Superman!"). During this same period, Superman erects a protective metal shield around the Daily Planet Building to protect its occupants from a powerful bomb planted in Metropolis by LEX LUTHOR (S No. 89/3, May '54: "One Hour to Doom!").

In September 1954 gangster JIGGER BENSON concocts a scheme to destroy the *Daily Planet*'s credibility in order to discredit a series of exposés written by reporter Clark Kent. Benson and his henchmen, however, are ultimately apprehended by Superman (S No. 92/1: "The Impossible Headlines!").

In April 1955 foreign editions of the *Daily Planet* are launched in Paris and Bombay. According to the text, a third international edition is established in London (Act No. 203: "The International Daily ePlanet!"), but this is inconsistent with the previous establishment of a London edition fifteen months earlier (S No. 86/1, Jan '54: "The Dragon from King Arthur's Court!").

In December 1955 *Daily Planet* offices around the world celebrate what is described as "the anniversary of the first **international editions** of the **Daily Planet**--in France, Greece, Italy, Holland, and Japan!" To help mark the occasion, Superman visits the five countries in turn to pose for a series of front-page anniversary-edition photographs of himself performing spectacular super-stunts, each of which is designed to "glorify something [the host] country is famous for," as when the Man of Steel poses on a Paris street while balancing the EIFFEL TOWER upside down in one hand. Several days later, when Superman returns to SMALLVILLE for a testimonial dinner in his honor commemorating the anniversary of his arrival on Earth as an infant from the planet KRYPTON, Perry White is on hand to present the Man of Steel with a special anniversary gift: copies of the anniversary issues of the *Daily Planet*'s five foreign editions, each with photographs of Superman's super-feats splashed across its front page, and each with a headline wishing Superman a happy anniversary in its own native language (Act No. 211: "The Superman Spectaculars").

As Lois Lane looks on, Perry White confers with Superman about the upcoming anniversary of the Daily Planet's international editions, 1955

In March 1956 the Daily Planet Building is one of the buildings destroyed by Superman in order to thwart the interplanetary invasion plot unearthed by EBENEEZER WALKER. Later, with the alien invasion threat safely disposed of, Superman single-handedly constructs a new Daily Planet Building on the site of the old one (Act No. 214: "Superman, Super-Destroyer").

In July 1960 the giant "Earth-globe" atop the Daily Planet Building is destroyed by TITANO, who rips it from its moorings and hurls it into the sea. A new globe fashioned by Superman is later installed in its place (S No. 138/1: "Titano the Super-Ape!").

In April 1961 Superman poses for a commemorative photograph outside the Daily Planet Building as he purchases, from a newsboy, the five billionth copy of the *Daily Planet* (S No. 144/1: "The Super-Weapon!").

In July 1962, in the pressroom of the *Daily Planet*, Perry White presents Superman with an honorary plaque in gratitude for his ongoing role in "helping the Planet get many great scoops!" Suddenly, however, Superman goes berserk, "leering malevolently" and smashing apart the *Daily Planet*'s giant presses "with powerful blows of his mighty fists ...." Then, just as abruptly, the bizarre "wrecking spree" ends, and Superman, who is as yet completely unaware of the reason for his insane outburst (*see* MAG-EN), contritely repairs the damage (S No. 154/2: "Krypton's First Superman!").

In December 1962 Superman destroys every single typewriter at the *Daily Planet*, demolishes the globe atop the Daily Planet Building, and commits other intemperate, often violent, acts after being driven temporarily berserk by a diabolical "telepathic-hypnotic weapon" fired at him by members of the SUPERMAN REVENGE SQUAD. After the villains have been defeated, however, Superman pledges to repair the damage (Act No. 295: "Superman Goes Wild!").

In July 1963 the roof of the Daily Planet Building collapses into its topmost floor of offices after it has been deliberately sabotaged by a ring of swindlers who have been the target of a series of exposés authored by editor Perry White. Lois Lane is on the verge of being crushed to death by the heavy *Daily Planet* globe falling through the caved-in roof when Superman intervenes to catch the globe and rescue Lois from seemingly certain doom (Act No. 302: "The Amazing Confession of Super-Perry White!").

In May 1964 the mischievous MR. MXYZPTLK uses his extradimensional magical powers to temporarily transform the large block letters encircling the globe atop the Daily Planet Building so that instead of spelling out the words Daily Planet they spell out the words Daily Liar (S No. 169/1: "The Infernal Imp!"). Soon afterward, the globe is demolished by BIZARRO and his followers from the planet HTRAE. The destruction of the globe has its beneficial side, however, because, as luck would have it, two of the globe's giant block letters, hurtling toward the sidewalk, knock out two gunmen attempting to steal a *Daily Planet* payroll en route from the bank (S No. 169/3, May '64: "The Bizarro Invasion of Earth!").

By January 1971 the *Daily Planet* has been acquired by the Galaxy Broadcasting System. It is during this period that Morgan Edge, Galaxy's president, removes Clark Kent from the staff of the *Planet* and installs him as a full-time newscaster on another Galaxy property, Metropolis television station WGBS-TV, a post Kent still holds as of the late 1970s (S No. 233: "Superman Breaks Loose"; and others).

DAILY STAR. The "large metropolitan daily" newspaper (Act No. 7, Dec '38) which employs CLARK KENT as a reporter from June 1938, the date of the premiere text of the SUPERMAN chronicles (Act No. 1),

through March 1940 (Act No. 22). Thereafter, without any explanation having been given for the change-over, the paper is referred to as the DAILY PLANET (S No. 4/1-4, Spr '40; Act No. 23, Apr '40). Headquartered in the Daily Star Building (Act No. 5, Oct '38) in Superman's resident city (*see* METROPOLIS), the *Daily Star* is edited by GEORGE TAYLOR (S No. 2/2, Fall '39: "Superman Champions Universal Peace!").

Although Clark Kent is depicted as working for the *Daily Star* as early as June 1938 (Act No. 1), he had apparently persuaded the paper's editor to hire him only a short while earlier, after being rejected the first time he applied, by thwarting an attempted lynching at the county jail as Superman and then phoning in an exclusive account of the events as would-be reporter Clark Kent (S No. 1/1, Sum '39). Before long, Kent has clearly begun to make a name for himself, for he is referred to as the paper's "ace scribe" in Action Comics No. 9 (Feb '39) and as its "ace reporter" in a number of texts (Act No. 6, Nov '38; and others).

LOIS LANE is also employed by the *Daily Star* from June 1938 onward (Act No. 1), and her hiring seems clearly to have preceded Kent's (S No. 1/1, Sum '39). Described as the paper's "sob sister" in several early texts (Act No. 7, Dec '38; and others), she has also functioned as the *Daily Star*'s "lovelorn editor," as a full-fledged "news reporter" (S No. 3/4, Win '40; and others), and as a war correspondent in Europe (Act No. 22, Mar '40).

Beginning in Spring 1940, the name *Daily Star* disappears from the texts and the newspaper is referred to as the *Daily Planet* (S No. 4/1; *see also* Act No. 23, Apr '40), although, for a time, George Taylor remains its editor (Act No. 25, Jun '40; and others). Clark Kent and Lois Lane continue their careers on the newspaper under its new name. (*See also* DAILY PLANET.)

DALY, TOM. An alias employed by SUPERMAN in March 1939 when he deliberately gets himself sentenced to a term on the Coreytown chain gang so that he can observe and photograph the inhuman conditions there (Act No. 10). (*See* WYMAN [SUPERINTENDENT].

DANDY, JIM. The dapper leader of a gang of criminals whom SUPERMAN finally apprehended after being forced to carry out an elaborate charade to preserve the secret of his dual identity (S No. 107/2, Aug '56: "The Impossible Haircut").

DANIELS, "DEAD-SHOT." An alias employed by SUPERMAN in December 1963 when he poses as an "underworld assassin" as part of his plan to apprehend gangland czar "KING" KOBRA (Act No. 307: "Clark Kent—Target for Murder!").

DANNING, VICTOR. A scientist turned criminal, at one time a specialist in mechanical engineering, who attempts to steal an as yet unperfected "brain-amplifying ray"—a device designed to "increase any man's mental power 100 times"—from the laboratory of its inventor, Dr. John Carr, with the intention of using it to endow himself with a super-intellect to aid him in the planning and execution of spectacular crimes. Danning does not actually succeed in stealing the machine, but efforts to apprehend him receive a severe setback when, during a scuffle in Carr's laboratory, Danning and ROBIN become accidentally transformed into supergeniuses while SUPERMAN becomes transformed into a mindless dullard. Although they are generally more hindered than helped by the slow-witted behavior of the intellectually impoverished Superman, the quick-witted BATMAN and the superingenious Robin ultimately succeed in apprehending Danning and his henchmen and in using Dr. Carr's "brain-amplifier" to restore Danning, Robin, and Superman to normal (WF No. 93, Mar/Apr '58: "The Boss of Batman and Superman").

DAN THE DIP. A METROPOLIS pickpocket, also referred to as Danny the Dip, who steals a package out of LOIS LANE's handbag unaware that it contains a chunk of synthetic green KRYPTONITE surreptitiously planted there by LEX LUTHOR as part of his scheme to destroy SUPERMAN (Act No. 141, Feb '50: "Luthor's Secret Weapon"). When Dan the Dip discovers that the strange green rock in his possession somehow has the power to paralyze Superman, he forms an alliance with a gang of criminals, promising to protect them against Superman in return for one third of their loot. Although stymied for a time by the wily pickpocket and his underworld allies, Superman ultimately succeeds in apprehending them with the aid of the Metropolis police (Act No. 142, Mar '50: "The Conquest of Superman!").

DANVERS, FRED AND EDNA (Mr. and Mrs.). The adoptive parents of Linda Lee Danvers, the pretty blond teen-ager who is secretly SUPERGIRL (SF No. 172, Aug/Sept '75).

DANVERS, LINDA LEE. The pretty blond teen-ager who is secretly SUPERGIRL (Act No. 285, Feb '62: "The World's Greatest Heroine!").

DAPPER. The leader of a gang of criminals who are apprehended by SUPERMAN in May 1945 (Act No. 84: "Tommy Gets a Zero!").

DARBY, KENNETH. The man who is secretly the WATER SPRITE (Act No. 82, Mar '45: "The Water Sprite!").

DAWSON (Dr.). An alias employed by the PRANKSTER in May-June 1951 when he poses as a philanthropist interested in underwriting a journalism contest for children as part of his elaborate scheme to keep SUPERMAN constantly distracted and stymied while he and his henchmen commit a series of spectacular crimes (S No. 70/3: "The Pied Piper Prankster!").

DEFENDER, THE. An alternate identity employed by LEX LUTHOR in April 1964 when, after endowing himself with temporary super-powers, he assumes the role of a super-hero on the planet LEXOR (S No. 168: pts. I-II—"Luthor--Super-Hero!"; "Lex Luthor, Daily Planet Editor!").

DELANEY, DIAMOND DAVE. A METROPOLIS "gang chief" and cunning "arch-criminal—nicknamed Diamond Dave because of his sparkling diamond stickpin—who is captured along with his henchmen by SUPERMAN in June 1953. Superman's efforts to apprehend the Delaney gang are severely hampered by the fact that weird "super-cosmic rays," emanating from a "huge whirlpool of flaming gases" in the "vast loneliness of interstellar space," have temporarily rendered him invulnerable KRYPTONITE and able to pierce lead with his X-ray vision, but only at the cost of making him fatally vulnerable to diamonds and unable to see at all through ordinary glass (Act No. 181: "The New Superman").

DEMAREST, BERNARD, JR. "A sheltered and misguided cynic," interested only in his collection of antiques and contemptuous of the people he refers to as the "chiseling poor," who refuses to contribute to the Metropolis Aid Fund despite his wealth until SUPERMAN poses as a genie in a magic lamp and uses his awesome powers to teach the spoiled Demarest the meaning of charity, and incidentally to apprehend the Crawfish Cole gang when they attempt to steal Demarest's "magic" lamp from him (S No. 35/3, Jul/Aug '45: "The Genie of the Lamp!").

DENBY, CALVIN. The leader of the Grotak Bund, a clandestine subversive organization engaged in a massive "attempt to sabotage Anerica's national defense effort" by destroying the nation's factories, power plants, and other installations "so that America's defense operations will be slowed down and destroyed!" Denby and his fellow bund members are apprehended by SUPERMAN in September-October 1941 (S No. 12/3).

DENVER, HARRY. An alias employed by SUPERMAN in March 1953 when he poses as a hoodlum to infiltrate the Dreamorama (Act No. 178: "The Sandman of Crime!"). (See SANDS [PROFESSOR].)

DERWING. The chairman of the Committee Against Militarism, an American organization whose members stridently advocate "no rearmament in the U.S., and no aid to warring democracies!" Secretly, however, Derwing is "in the employ of a warring totalitarian nation," and his "duty here in America is to see that no aid is offered to the democracies, and that the U.S. fails to re-arm." Aided by a growing army of henchmen, traitors, and innocent dupes opposed to America's intervention in World War II, Derwing carries out numerous acts of sabotage and other acts designed to hinder America's rearmament efforts, until he is finally brought to justice by SUPERMAN in March-April 1941 (S No. 9/1).

DeWITT, SYLVIA. *See* SYLVIA.

DEXTER, AMOS. The alias employed by gangster BERT TALBOT in April 1961 when, disguised in glasses, false beard, and false moustache, he poses as a newsreel cameraman in order to trick SUPERMAN into unwittingly providing the "super-force" needed to fuel the "power battery" of the diabolical Weapon X (S No. 144/1: "The Super-Weapon!").

DEXTER, BRAD. An alternate identity employed by SUPERMAN in March 1965 when he dons a false moustache and obtains employment as a reporter on a Chicago newspaper in order to escape the effects of an alien "cowardice ray"—beamed at him from outer space by members of the SUPERMAN REVENGE SQUAD—that transforms him into a "spineless jellyfish" whenever he appears in his Clark Kent identity (Act No. 322: "The Coward of Steel!").

DIMANT, DELMAR "DICE." A METROPOLIS "gang chieftain, whose specialty is bank and jewelry store robberies." In Spring 1944 Dimant and two of his fellow rackets czars—Rex Ratlan, alias "the Rattler," whose mob "prefers crimes of stealth such as warehouse burglaries," and Emory "Emperor" Auslinger, a "master schemer and leader of terrorists who don't care what crimes they commit—if the loot is plentiful"—resort to kidnapping, attempted murder, and sabotage in an effort to prevent the publication of an incriminating article about them in the 100th Anniversary edition of the DAILY PLANET, but the villains are repeatedly thwarted and finally apprehended through the heroic efforts of SUPERMAN (WF No. 13: "The Freedom of the Press!").

DOBORAK, STAN. A talented but naïve pitcher with the METROPOLIS baseball team who, having joined the big leagues and rocketed to stardom after being discovered in his home town by CLARK KENT and LOIS LANE, falls under the baleful influence of flashy blonde Mabel Dawson and her "big-time gambler" accomplice, Mike Caputo, and is on the verge of becoming their dupe in an elaborate game-fixing scheme when SUPERMAN intervenes to extort a confession from Caputo with some terrifying aerial acrobatics ("Up into the sky hurtles Superman with his shrieking captive...") and order the villains out of town for good in July 1942 (Act No. 50).

DOC. The wiry little fellow, known also as Hocus, who comprises half the team of HOCUS AND POCUS (Act No. 83, Apr '45: "Hocus & Pocus...Magicians by Accident!").

DOGHOUSE OF SOLITUDE, THE. KRYPTO THE SUPERDOG's secret doghouse sanctuary, located in outer space.

DOLAN, "DAREDEVIL." A once-famous stunt man, driven to despair and the brink of suicide by an auto accident that shattered his nerve some five years ago, who recovers his courage and his self-esteem through the efforts of SUPERMAN in January-February 1944 (S No. 26/1: "The Super Stunt Man!").

DOLAN, LOUIE. A "self-styled genius" and "inventor extraordinary"—a funny-looking, bald-headed man who, being mute, is severely handicapped in his efforts to express his ideas effectively—whose remarkably original inventions, including an ingenious "freeze-gas" for temporarily paralyzing enemy soldiers without harming them, are dismissed as worthless flights of fancy by the U.S. War Department until after both racketeer Conk Kohler and Nazi spy Mr. Vortz have stolen Dolan's inventions and proven their effectiveness by using them to facilitate daring acts of robbery and sabotage, after which America's military planners have second thoughts about Dolan and promptly place him on the government payroll (S No. 24/2, Sep/Oct '43: "The King of Crackpot Lane").

DOMINO, THE. A sinister criminal mastermind, his identity concealed by a purple mask, who attempts, through acts of terror and sabotage, to intimidate amusement park owner Jim Gantry into allowing crooked gambling concessionaires into operating their rackets freely on the grounds of his amusement park. The Domino is in reality Jeff Farnham, a handsome but profligate "society playboy" who "ran thru [his] family inheritance" and then discovered that "there was only one way to keep me living in the manner to which I was accustomed—crime and gambling!" He is exposed and apprehended by SUPERMAN in March 1942 (Act No. 46: "The Devil's Playground").

DORROW (Dr.). A "shady scientist," just released from prison, "whose twisted genius has led him along the path of crime." In January 1951, after having promised to rid the underworld of SUPERMAN for a fee of $1,000,000, Dr. Dorrow traps both Superman and LOIS LANE in transparent cylinders filled with "suspended animation gas" and catapults them into outer space in the direction of VENUS, but the cylinders are soon extracted by Venusians from a muddy Venusian bog and Superman returns to Earth with Lois to apprehend Dr. Dorrow and his gangland cohorts (Act No. 152: "The Sleep That Lasted 1000 Years").

DORSEY, JOHN (Dr.). A dedicated entomologist who, having finally "triumphed in a great ambition—the dream of growing insects to giant size" by bathing them in a flood of potent "cosmic rays," discovers to his horror that he has spawned an army of awesome giant ants, taller than human beings, which swiftly take him prisoner and use his cosmic-ray device to "speed up the growth" of other insects with which they hope to "demoralize human civilization" and achieve the "conquest of the world!" Soon the giant insects invade METROPOLIS, spreading fear and panic in their wake, but SUPERMAN creates giant praying mantises to terrorize the ants, thus providing entomologist Dorsey with the opportunity he needs to regain control of his ray device and restore the insects to their original tiny size (S No. 64/2, May/Jun '50: "The Isle of Giant Insects!").

D'ORT (Count). A confidence man, pickpocket, and leader of a gang of criminals who kidnap JIMMY OLSEN, LOIS LANE, and lovely Betty Roxmore, Jimmy Olsen's girl friend. SUPERMAN soon rescues the captives and apprehends the criminals, but because Olsen is in dutch with his girl friend because of an accidental mix-up of Valentine's Day gifts for which Superman was partially responsible, the Man of Steel deliberately performs the rescue and capture at invisible super-speed in such a way as to make it appear that Olsen is single-handedly responsible (Act No. 71, Apr '44: "Valentine Villainy!").

DOUR, SPECS. A METROPOLIS gang chief who, having learned of "an ancient drug which causes insanity" from an old book on forgotten drugs, sets about ruthlessly driving wealthy men berserk with his insanity-inducing drug and then extorting extravagant fees from their families in return for the precious antidote. SUPERMAN apprehends Dour and his henchmen in October 1946, but only after he has himself fallen temporary victim to the effects of the bizarre chemical. Dour, ironically, becomes "so upset by the failure of his scheme" that he becomes completely deranged. "That's justice!" muses CLARK KENT (Act No. 101: "Crime Paradise!").

DRAGO (alien dictator). The "power-mad" dictator of a "faraway world" who, having deliberately blinded the entire population of his own planet—aith the exception of himself and his hirelings—by means of a diabolical sight-destroying bomb, has organized the now helpless, sightless populace into a vast army of wretched slave laborers for the purpose of forcing them to work without respite, under the most cruel and despicable conditions, on an insanely megalomaniacal landscaping project whose purpose remains a mystery to the blinded slaves, but whose real goal is nothing less than the reshaping of the entire planet into a colossal three-dimensional portrait of Drago himself, a titanic monument in his own image, designed to "spin in space through eternity!"

"Depressed" and "defeated" as perhaps he has never been before after Drago has successfully used a cunning, ruthless ploy to strip him of his super-powers, rob him of his sight, and force him into slavery along with all the other helpless, blinded workers, SUPERMAN succeeds ultimately, despite overwhelming obstacles, in rallying his own flagging spirits so that he can overthrow the evil dictator and his henchmen, recover his sight and his super-powers, and detonate a gigantic "antidote bomb" designed to restore the sight of the blinded populace.

Drago dies shortly following his defeat from the effects of a fatal hereditary disease, and months later, when Superman returns to the distant planet for a promised visit, he finds to his astonishment that, following his last departure, "the people of this faraway world had continued their colossal land-scaping project--but had reshaped their planet as an eternal tribute to their great liberator--**Superman!**" (S No. 155/1, Aug '62: pts. I-II—"Superman Under the Green Sun!"; "The Blind Superman!").

DRAGO (renegade scientist). A renegade scientist of the thirtieth century A.D. who escapes from prison on the MOON and, with a gang of other convicts, attempts to devastate and conquer the world, only to be defeated and apprehended by SUPERMAN, whose presence in this future era is the result of his exposure in August 1956 to the terrible radiation of a defective atomic pile, which caused him to lapse into a sleeplike coma from which he only awakens a thousand years later, in the year 2956 A.D. With Drago and his henchmen in custody, Superman returns to his own era via time machine (S No. 107/3: "Rip Van Superman!").

DRAPE, DASHER. "The deadliest triggerman in all gangdom," nicknamed "the Dasher," an under-world assassin who, with the addition of glasses and minus his tiny moustache, is a perfect look-alike for CLARK KENT. Kent impersonates Dasher Drape in March-April 1953 as part of a scheme by PERRY WHITE to get an exclusive feature for the DAILY PLANET on the activities of gangster BIG JIM PAULSON, "chief of [the] Metropolis underworld" (WF No. 63: "Clark Kent, Gangster").

DRIBBLE, ADELBERT. A bespectacled milque-toast who imprisons SUPERMAN in a resilient room "made of tremendously thick rubber" and then climbs into a makeshift Superman costume—inflated with helium to create the impression of a muscular build and equipped with a motor-driven propeller to make possible the power of flight—to impersonate Superman as part of a humorously pathetic effort to win back his girl friend Bertha, who has jilted him for being a weakling. Dribble's well-intentioned scheme goes awry, however, when the Turtle Baxter gang kidnaps Bertha in hopes of acquiring a hold over "Superman," but the real Superman escapes from his rubber prison in time to apprehend the Baxter gang and reunite Bertha and the grateful Dribble (Act No. 74, Jul '44: "Courtship of Adelbert Dribble!").

DRILL, BEN. A former World War II flying ace, now the owner of a small wrecking business, who unexpectedly acquires SUPERMAN as an employee in February-March 1951, firstly because Superman feels that he needs to acquire an occupation in order to fill out his census form accurately, and secondly because he is determined to prevent unscrupulous loan company operator Steve Sokum from carrying out a vicious plot to bankrupt Drill in retaliation for Drill's having thwarted his scheme to sell faulty airplane parts to the Air Corps during World War II. By working for Drill as a so-called "super wrecker," Superman thwarts Sokum's scheme to destroy Drill's livelihood, although he ultimately discovers that he does not really require a conventional occupation in order to fill out his census form at all (WF No. 50: "Superman Super-Wrecker").

DRYWOOD GULCH. An uninhabited ghost town in the western United States where, in May 1962, SUPERMAN defeats eight escapees from the PHANTOM ZONE—super-powered Kryptonian criminals ban-ished into the Phantom Zone for their "horrible crimes" sometime prior to the destruction of the planet KRYPTON—who are determined to lure Super-man into their midst and then exile him into the Phantom Zone forever by shooting him with special "ray-guns" powered by an ingenious "phantasmon zone generator." Challenged to a fast-draw raygun showdown by the eight Kryptonian outlaws in which anyone struck by a ray-blast will be dispatched instantly into the Phantom Zone, Superman tri-umphs over his adversaries by melting their rayguns with a blast of his awesome heat vision and then using his own ray-weapon to propel them back into the Phantom Zone "where those evil beings be-long..." (S No. 153/3: "The Town of Supermen!").

DUCEY, "ACES." The "gambling czar of Metropo-lis" and the unscrupulous owner-manager of the Tigers, a team of dirty football players who are rated as underdogs in their upcoming game with the Bearcats. When, as the result of Ducey's scheming, the Bearcats are too ill to don their uniforms on the day of the scheduled game, it appears that the Tigers will win by default until SUPERMAN and feisty Little Red Rollins, the younger brother of the Bearcats' star player, take the field alone to vanquish the Tigers and hand Ducey a stunning defeat along with the gambling losses he will suffer for having bet a small fortune on the Tigers (Act No. 128, Jan '49: "The Adventure of Little Red!").

DUDE, THE. A ruthless fashion pirate—clad in a top hat and tails, with a mask concealing the upper part of his face—who causes panic and near collapse in the world of haute couture by stealing the latest clothing designs of fashion's top designers and, with the complicity of shady merchants, producing inferior or duplicates of the originals at bargain-basement prices. The Dude—who is in reality Joseph Martinson, the chairman of the Designers' Emergency Committee, an organization of top designers formed, ironically, for the very purpose of combatting the Dude—is apprehended and unmasked by SUPERMAN in July-August 1943 (S No. 23/3: "Fashions in Crime!").

DUNN, AMOS (Professor). A dedicated scientist who, years ago, shortly before the planet KRYPTON exploded into fragments, "began to receive strange radio signals from space" and soon found himself communicating with the Kryptonian scientist JOR-EL. By following Jor-El's detailed instructions for the building of a "matter-radio"—"an apparatus [designed] to accomplish the instantaneous transmission of matter" through space, "as if by radio"—Dunn even made a journey to Krypton, where he befriended Jor-El and his family, performed an emergency operation to save the life of the infant SUPERMAN after he had been bitten by a venomous Kryptonian "fish-snake," and discussed with the brilliant Kryptonian scientist Jor-El the impending doom of his planet. By October 1961 Professor Dunn's unscrupulous assistant, Gerald Greer, has stolen Dunn's blueprints for the matter-radio and formed an alliance with gangster Paul Pratt to use the ingenious invention for crime—by committing daring robberies in METROPOLIS and then making instantaneous matter-radio getaways to a distant West Coast city—but Superman apprehends Greer and Pratt and takes their matter-radio equipment to his FORTRESS OF SOLITUDE for safekeeping (Act No. 281: "The Man Who Saved Kal-El's Life!"). The story is in many respects similar to Superman No. 77/1 (Jul/Aug '52: "The Man Who Went to Krypton!"). (See ENDERS, WILLIAM [PROFESSOR].)

DUNN, "DUDE." The leader of a gang of criminals who attempt unsuccessfully to destroy SUPERMAN with special "kryptonite guns" designed for them by the evil scientist LEX LUTHOR, only to be apprehended by the state police in August 1962. Superman's efforts to capture the "Dude" Dunn gang—and, in fact, all his activities during this period—are severely hampered by the fact that a freak laboratory accident has temporarily rendered him invulnerable to KRYPTONITE and able to pierce lead with his X-ray vision, but only at the cost of transferring his deadly "kryptonite vulnerability," for brief periods and without warning, to such commonplace elements as silver, gold, aluminum, and diamond (Act No. 291: "The New Superman!").

DUPLICATE MAN, THE. A cunning, ingenious criminal, clad in an orange and blue costume, who has somehow devised a scientific means of transforming himself into twins and then merging the twins into one man again, so that if one twin is captured he can easily "dematerialize" like a wraith from the grasp of his captors to rejoin the body of the second twin some distance away. Determined to "steal the world's greatest inventions and become the most powerful criminal on Earth," the Duplicate Man perpetrates a series of spectacular thefts, only to be finally apprehended by BATMAN, ROBIN, and SUPERMAN in December 1959 (WF No. 106: "The Duplicate Man!").

DUPLOR. The far-distant planet, situated in the Duplor Galaxy, which is ruled by the power-hungry "space emperor" TORR THE TERRIBLE (S No. 178/1, Jul '65: "Project Earth-Doom!").

DURIM. The far-distant planet which is the home of the heroic Logi and the villainous HROGUTH (WF No. 124, Mar '62: "The Mystery of the Alien Super-Boy!").

DURR, JON. The Secretary of Science in the ruling Government Council headquartered in New Gotham City in the twenty-first century A.D., and the inventor of a revolutionary "experimental time-machine." When Rak, Jon Durr's evil assistant and twin brother, discovers that the fusion of KRYPTONITE with a fragment of the legendary hammer of Thor yields a new substance "with fantastic powers" which, accumulated in sufficient quantities, would enable him to establish himself as dictator of the entire planet Earth, he steals Jon's time machine and travels into the past, to GOTHAM CITY in the year 1963 and then to ancient Norseland in the year 522 A.D., to obtain the kryptonite he needs and to steal the fabled hammer belonging to the Norse trible chieftain Thor. For a time, Rak's scheme succeeds, but he and his henchmen are ultimately defeated and apprehended through the heroic efforts of BATMAN, ROBIN, and SUPERMAN (WF No. 135, Aug '63: "The Menace of the Future Man!").

DYNAMIC DUO, THE. An alternate name for the crime-fighting team of BATMAN and ROBIN.

E

EDGESTREAM (Baron). The title of English nobility assumed by CLARK KENT in March 1947 after he has been mistakenly informed that he is in reality the long-lost Bertram Keith-Innes Fyffe, the rightful heir to the barony of Edgestream and an estate valued at £5,000,000, who was kidnapped in infancy and never recovered. Kent is not really the long-lost English nobleman, but he travels to England and assumes the title anyway—along with the ownership of the Fyffe Coal Mines and the seat in the House of Lords that go with it—long enough to uncover the real heir to the title—a coal miner named Eddie Pike who has been completely ignorant, until now, of his true heritage—and to apprehend the ruthless Julian Fyffe, next in line after Pike to the Edgestream barony, and his henchman Bascomb, manager of the Fyffe Coal Mines, who were together responsible for the original kidnapping of the infant heir many years ago and who, since Clark Kent's arrival in England, have been making repeated attempts on his life in an effort to enable Julian Fyffe to accede to the barony (Act No. 106: "His Lordship, Clark Kent!").

EDWARDS, POSY. The proprietor of a large commercial greenhouse which serves as the front for an elaborate fencing operation in which stolen goods are purchased from criminals and then delivered to unscrupulous buyers hidden inside pots of flowers. Edwards and his henchmen are apprehended by SUPERMAN in September-October 1946 (WF No. 24: "Impossible but True!").

EDWARDS, RALPH. The emcee of "Truth or Consequences," a popular radio quiz program on NBC. SUPERMAN appears as a contestant on the program, for the benefit of the Fresh Air Fund, in December 1948 (Act No. 127: "Superman Takes the Consequences!").

EIFFEL TOWER, THE. A graceful steel tower in the city of Paris—built by French engineer and bridge builder Alexandre Gustave Eiffel for the Paris Exhibition of 1889—which stands 1,056 feet high and is one of the world's great landmarks.

By July 1954 LEX LUTHOR and his henchmen have planted explosives in the Eiffel Tower—and in many other world-famous monuments—as part of an elaborate scheme to extort millions of dollars from the governments of the world (S No. 90/3: "The Titanic Thefts!"). During this same period, the Eiffel Tower is stolen—along with other world-famous monuments—by the Kryptonian villain MALA as part of the villain's elaborate scheme to wreak vengeance on SUPERMAN by destroying the planet Earth (Act No. 194, Jul '54: "The Outlaws from Krypton!").

Superman borrows the Eiffel Tower, 1954

In April 1955 LOIS LANE slips over the edge of a railing atop the Eiffel Tower and plummets toward her doom, only to be rescued in midair by Superman before she can hit the ground (Act No. 203: "The International Daily Planet!").

In December 1955 Superman helps commemorate the anniversary of the French edition of the DAILY PLANET by posing for a photograph on a Paris street while balancing the Eiffel Tower upside down in one hand (Act No. 211: "The Superman Spectaculars").

In December 1962 Superman destroys the Eiffel Tower—and several other world-famous monuments—after being driven temporarily berserk by a diabolical "telepathic-hypnotic weapon" fired at him by members of the SUPERMAN REVENGE SQUAD. After the villains have been defeated, however, Superman promises to repair the damage (Act No. 295: "Superman Goes Wild!").

EISENHOWER, DWIGHT D. (1890-1969). The leader of the Allied forces in Europe during World War II, and the 34th President of the United States. In office from January 1953 until January 1961, he presided over the United States during the period of the Cold War, the dispute over racial segregation in the public schools, and the launching of sputnik by the U.S.S.R. An attempt by a "secret spy ring" to assassinate President Eisenhower is thwarted by SUPERMAN in September 1959 (Act No. 256: "The Superman of the Future!"). (*See* FOLGER, DIRK.)

ELASTIC LAD. An alternate identity employed by JIMMY OLSEN on those occasions when, after drinking a special "elastic serum" which temporarily endows him with the extraordinary ability to stretch his body as though it were an endlessly stretchable elastic band, he participates in adventures with the LEGION OF SUPER-HEROES, of which he is an honorary member (S No. 172, Oct '64: pts. I-III—"The New Superman!"; "Clark Kent—Former Superman!"; "The Struggle of the Two Supermen!"; and others).

ELDRIC. A cruel, despotic feudal lord whose mighty castle and vast estate are part of a remote civilization—completely cut off from modern civilization by tall mountains and impassable cliffs—which has retained its medieval customs for more than a thousand years. Temporarily stranded in this isolated land in May 1956, SUPERMAN uses his short stay as an opportunity to force the power-hungry Eldric to emancipate his slaves and to abandon his ruthless scheme to establish an absolute despotism over the region (S No. 105/3: "Superman, Slave!").

ELEMENT LAD. A member of the LEGION OF SUPER-HEROES. A native of the planet Trom, Element Lad possesses, like all the inhabitants of that planet, the power to alter the atomic structure of elements by means of "mental radiation." Element Lad's real name is Jan Arrah. When METROPOLIS television station WMET-TV inaugurates its new "Our American Heroes" series with a program honoring SUPERMAN, "our greatest American hero," Element Lad is among the Legion representatives who journey to the twentieth century to appear on the show and thus help pay tribute to the Man of Steel (Act No. 309, Feb '64: "The Superman Super-Spectacular!").

EL GAR KUR (or El Gar-Kur). A "criminal scientist" from the bottle city of KANDOR—a perfect look-alike for JIMMY OLSEN—who, having successfully escaped into the outside world while simultaneously imprisoning Jimmy Olsen in Kandor by means of a complex body-switching apparatus, sets out, with the aid of the mighty super-powers which any Kandorian automatically acquires once outside the bottle city, to destroy Kandor and conquer the Earth, only to be thwarted in his efforts—and finally transported back into Kandor and apprehended by Kandorian authorities—as the result of an elaborate ruse devised by SUPERMAN combined with Jimmy Olsen's simultaneous and ultimately successful effort, inside Kandor, to reactivate and reverse the effects of El Gar Kur's body-switching apparatus (Act No. 253, Jun '59: "The War Between Superman and Jimmy Olsen!").

ELIZABETH I (1533-1603). The queen of England and Ireland from 1558 until her death in 1603. SUPERMAN meets Elizabeth I and, at her urging, joins forces with her in an elaborate scheme to help defeat the Spanish Armada, during a time-journey to England in the year 1588 (S No. 89/1, May '54: "Captain Kent the Terrible!").

ELLIS, CAL. An alias employed by Clark Kent, the man who is secretly SUPERMAN, when he finds himself unexpectedly incarcerated in a small-town insane asylum after an encounter with red KRYPTONITE and wants to avoid revealing his true identity to the superintendent and staff. The name Cal Ellis is actually a play on Superman's Kryptonian name, Kal-El (S No. 163/2, Aug '63: "The Goofy Superman!"). (*See* HAPPY ACRES STATE MENTAL REHABILITATION CENTER.)

ELLISON, THOMAS (Dr.). An American scientist and astronomer—once a close friend and neighbor of BRUCE WAYNE's father, Dr. Thomas Wayne—who, according to World's Finest Comics No. 146, studied the planet KRYPTON for years prior to its destruction by means of a revolutionary "monitor-type telescope" of his own invention, an optical device of such "unprecedented power" that it enabled him to observe events on the far-off planet as though they were happening merely a few feet away.

As time passed, Ellison studied Krypton's culture, mastered its language, and began to while away the hours at home by showing the infant Bruce Wayne, with whom he often baby-sat, photographs of Krypton and initiating him into the wonders of Kryptonian lore. When Ellison learned that Krypton faced imminent extinction due to an atomic reaction building up within the core of the planet, he beamed an "atomic-neutralizing ray" of his own invention at the distant world in hopes of neutralizing the atomic reaction and thereby averting the cataclysm, but when Krypton exploded anyway, in spite of his efforts, Ellison was beset by unbearable guilt, believing, erroneously, that his ray had somehow been responsible for stimulating Krypton's atomic disturbance "to the critical point," thereby causing the death of the planet.

In December 1964, however, when SUPERMAN uses a special "time-space viewer" from his FORTRESS OF SOLITUDE—a device which "picks up light and sound waves from the past" and thus enables one to view selected historical events—to re-create the end of Krypton, Ellison learns that his valiant effort to save Krypton merely came too late, and that he played no part whatever in bringing about the planet's destruction ("Batman, Son of Krypton!" pts. I-II—no title; "The Destroyer of Krypton!").

ELSHA (Queen). The beautiful but deceitful blond queen of Amazon Island, the so-called "land without men," a lonely island, situated thousands of miles from METROPOLIS, which is inhabited by a tribe of beautiful, powerful warrior women apparently descended from the legendary AMAZONS. Arriving on Amazon Island in December 1957 to rescue members of the SUPER SORORITY stranded there by an ocean squall, Superman thwarts an attempt by the "scheming queen" to trap him into matrimony by invoking an Amazon law requiring any man "caught trespassing on Amazon Island" to "marry the first member of [the] tribe who gives him a task he is unable to perform!" (Act No. 235: "The Super-Prisoner of Amazon Island").

ELWOOD, ALBERT. The "crackpot inventor" who is secretly the CRIMSON AVENGER (WF No. 131, Feb '63: "The Mystery of the Crimson Avenger!").

EMERGENCY SQUAD, THE. *See* SUPERMEN EMERGENCY SQUAD, THE.

EMERSON, STAN. An attorney for the underworld who is ordered out of town by SUPERMAN in May-June 1942. Shortly after Emerson has posted bond for some jewelry-store bandits apprehended by Superman, Superman waylays the attorney's automobile, hurls Emerson repeatedly through the air until he confesses that he is being retained by "the leading underworld mobs," and then orders Emerson to leave METROPOLIS and never return (S No. 16/2).

EMPEROR OF AMERICA, THE. The title brazenly assumed by "a swashbuckling, power-mad fiend"—a "grasping, ruthless opportunist" bent on usurping absolute power in order "to seize the riches of the United States of America for his own"—who, having invented a "monstrous ray machine" designed to destroy individual initiative and the "will to resist" and having "blanketed the nation with [its] invisible rays," strides calmly into the White House with a handful of henchmen and seizes control of the United States government, overnight transforming America from the "land of the free and home of the brave" into the "land of the enslaved and home of the craven," where justice is a mockery and a mind-controlled populace does nothing but meekly "obey orders" and hail the nonexistent accomplishments of its "new mighty leader." Indeed, "of the 130 million citizens thruout [sic] the land, there [is] none to oppose him—except one solitary individual," SUPERMAN, who moves swiftly and heroically to dethrone the self-styled "emperor," demolish his ray machine, and restore America to its democratic institutions.

Terrifying though this tale may be, there are indications that it is only imaginary, for the text cautions that "This is a tale that could occur only after the war...many years hence! It's up to all of us to see it doesn't!" (Act No. 52, Sep '42: "The Emperor of America").

ENDERS, WILLIAM (Professor). A dedicated astronomer—author of a book called *The Planet Krypton*—who, years ago, shortly before the planet KRYPTON exploded into fragments, observed Krypton via telescope, communicated with JOR-EL via radio, and, by following Jor-El's detailed instructions for the building of a "matter-radio"—"a transmitter that can send all forms of living matter--even living people--across space by radio"—even made a journey to Krypton, where he befriended Jor-El and his family and discussed with the brilliant Kryptonian scientist the impending doom of his planet.

In July-August 1952 Buttons Harris and a henchman kidnap Professor Enders and steal the matter-radio so that they can use the fabulous transmitter for crime—principally by allowing client gangs to commit crimes in METROPOLIS and then make instantaneous matter-radio getaways to a distant city—but SUPERMAN apprehends Harris and his cohorts and rescues Professor Enders from their clutches (S No. 77/1: "The Man Who Went to Krypton!").

A flashback panel recalls the meeting on the planet Krypton between Professor William Enders and Superman's father, Jor-El

EVANS, MEL. The "brilliant young college teacher" and, later, "renowned scientist" who first calculated the "probable distance from Earth to Krypton" at 0.317 light years and who, according to Superman No. 136/2, was unwittingly responsible for allowing SUPERMAN's vulnerability to KRYPTONITE to become widespread public knowledge. Guilt-ridden and ashamed at having been responsible for accidentally betraying this damaging secret, Evans dropped out of sight and, under the alias of Stanley Halley, "helped humanity immeasurably" and "won the highest awards that science has to offer" while still keeping his true identity a secret, until finally, in April 1960, Superman comes upon him in SMALLVILLE and assures him that his honest mistake of years ago has long since been forgiven ("The Secret of Kryptonite!").

EVELL, ALEX. An unscrupulous politician, determined to seize control of the DAILY PLANET so that he can put an end to its political exposés and use it to promote his own dishonest political fortunes, who hires a gang of hoodlums to burn the *Planet*'s delivery trucks, beat up its newsboys, and otherwise terrorize the *Planet*'s publisher into selling out to him. Evell and his henchmen are brought to justice by SUPERMAN in Summer 1940 (S No. 5/2).

"EVOLUTION KING, THE." An "evil scientist" who has "learned how to advance or revert a human being's age" by means of special pills. Aided by gangster Joe Glower and his henchmen, "The Evolution King" kidnaps prominent athletes, transforms them into helpless old men, and threatens to leave them in their "decrepit condition" unless they meet his extortionate demands. Goaded finally by

CLARK KENT into demonstrating the effects of his old-age pills by swallowing one himself, "The Evolution King" perishes when, moments later, he accidentally swallows some additional aging pills instead of the intended antidote (S No. 15/4, Mar/Apr '42).

EXAMINER. A METROPOLIS newspaper, a competitor of the DAILY PLANET, whose editor and publisher resort to attempted murder and sabotage in an effort to prevent LOIS LANE from completing a round-the-world publicity trip—a trip in which Lois switches to a different mode of transportation every twenty-four hours—designed to increase the circulation of the *Daily Planet.* Lois's journey is ultimately a success thanks to the repeated intervention of SUPERMAN, and the *Examiner*'s editor and publisher will face criminal charges for their efforts to prevent her from completing it (S No. 49/3, Nov/Dec '47: "Lois Lane Globe-Trotter!").

EYE, THE. A monocled villain and former Nazi spy who, having gathered together a gang of METROPOLIS's most notorious criminals, travels to the tiny apparently South American, country of Molinia where he blackmails the owner of a large estate into allowing him and his cohorts to use it as their headquarters, and then proceeds to plunder shipping on the Spanish Main with a fleet of ingenious "whale-submarines"—submarines deceptively designed to resemble large whales—until he and his henchmen are finally apprehended by SUPERMAN in July-August 1948 (S No. 53/3: "A Job for Superhombre!").

F

FABIAN, SCRAPS. The petty thief who achieves infamy as MISTER SEVEN (WF No. 46, Jun/Jul '50: "The Seven Crimes of Mister 7!").

FALLON. A METROPOLIS "crime chief" and underworld inventor who attempts to destroy and plunder the Metropolis National Bank with the aid of an awesome "super-crime weapon" known as the "sonic vibrator," only to be apprehended by SUPERMAN in January 1959. The capture of Fallon and his henchmen comes as the culmination of an elaborate ruse—devised by Metropolis's police commissioner and carried out by Superman with the aid of the "master illusionist" Shandu—in which Shandu poses as the creator of a bizarre supernatural clock capable of casting a debilitating spell over Superman as part of their overall plan to lure the Fallon gang into the open (S No. 126/2: "The Spell of the Shandu Clock").

FANG, THE. A buck-toothed, bespectacled gang chief, described by BATMAN as "a serious believer in the supernatural," whose most prized possession is a "Chinese lucky sword," a sort of "super-rabbit's foot," which he scrupulously carries with him on each of his gang's many robberies. According to the Fang, the lucky sword "was forged 1,000 years ago in the ancient East--and brings luck and success to whoever uses it!" In November-December 1954, after the Fang has been forced to abandon his sword at the scene of a robbery, Batman, ROBIN, and SUPERMAN attempt to use the sword as bait in an elaborate scheme to lure the villain into a trap. The scheme goes somewhat awry when the Fang makes Batman and Robin his prisoners, but Superman ultimately appears on the scene, captures the Fang and his cohorts, and rescues the Dynamic Duo from their clutches (WF No. 73: "Batman and Superman, Swamis, Inc!").

FANGAN. An English sorcerer of the twelfth century A.D. who once set a trap for a knight he hated: inside a cave was hidden a flagon of mystic potion, whose fumes were designed to hypnotize anyone entering into becoming obsessed with the desire to fulfill three commands—to fight a dragon, to dress as a jester and obey the commands of the townspeople for an hour, and to do battle with the most powerful man on Earth—which one way or another, Fangan reasoned, were likely to end in his victim's death. Fangan died and the knight never blundered into his trap, but 800 years later, while attending a police convention in England, BATMAN enters the cave alone and becomes obsessed with the desire to fulfill Fangan's three commands. To enable Batman to carry out the sorcerer's directives without coming to any harm, SUPERMAN exposes him to a ray-machine in his FORTRESS OF SOLITUDE designed to give a man super-powers for twenty-four hours, then brings him a dragonlike beast to fight from outer space, watches over him during the "jester" period to ensure that criminals will not profit from Batman's compulsion to carry out people's commands, and then lets Batman defeat him, the strongest man on Earth, so that, Fangan's commands finally fulfilled, Batman can recover unharmed from the sorcerer's curse (WF No. 109, May '60: "The Bewitched Batman!").

FANGE (Herr). A ruthless Nazi villain, so named because of his hideous vampirish fangs, who, having plumbed the ocean depths in a special "super diving-bell" and taught a slew of horrifying sea monsters to obey commands communicated to them by means of a special whistle, obtains permission from ADOLF HITLER to use his gruesome sea creatures to ravage Allied shipping and disrupt the flow of lend-lease goods between the United States and Britain. Thwarted repeatedly by SUPERMAN in January-February 1943, Herr Fange dies a grisly death when he accidentally damages his special whistle during a climactic battle with Superman, and, left without any means of controlling his sea monsters, is attacked and devoured by them (S No. 20/2: "Destroyers from the Depths").

FARNHAM, JEFF. The handsome "society playboy" who is secretly the DOMINO (Act No. 46, Mar '42: "The Devil's Playground").

FARR, HERB. A "mysterious gangland czar," known pseudonymously as "The Wheel," who, having kidnapped LOIS LANE, threatens to kill her unless CLARK KENT—who is widely known as a close friend of SUPERMAN—agrees to divulge Superman's secret identity. In October 1965, however, by means of an elaborate ruse, Superman apprehends Herb Farr and his henchmen and rescues Lois Lane from their clutches (S No. 180/1: "Clark Kent's Great Superman Hunt!").

FELLOWS, GRANT. An unscrupulous newspaper reporter in the town of Corinthville who, having learned of the existence of a "valuable old gold mine" beneath the property of a local scientist, starts a rumor that gigantic animals are loose in the area in an effort to frighten the scientist into leaving the community. "...I trumped up that fake story about giant creatures haunting the vicinity..." admits Fellows finally. "I thought that if I could frighten the doctor, I could buy his land for a song." Fellows is apprehended by SUPERMAN in July-August 1941 (S No. 11/2).

FELTON, FINGERS. One of a pair of criminals—his partner is named Lefty Louie—who are captured by SUPERMAN in October-November 1951 despite the fact that the Man of Steel's efforts to apprehend them are severely hampered by the restrictive terms of a $100,000,000 life insurance policy, purchased by multimillionaire philanthropist Phineas Morgan and payable to a fund for the underprivileged in the event of Superman's death, which forbid Superman to take such unnecessary risks with his life as passing through fire, smashing through obstacles, traveling at a speed of over 50 miles per hour, or flying at a height exceeding 20 feet (WF No. 54: "The Superman Who Avoided Danger!").

FENTON (Mr.). The unscrupulous publisher of the *Daily Tatler*, a METROPOLIS newspaper whose circulation has been soaring at the expense of the DAILY PLANET's because its reporters have been resorting to illegal acts in order to create their own news stories, such as when *Tatler* reporter Ned Gerritty blows up the dam at Ashton Reservoir for the purpose of creating an exclusive news story. Certain that the *Tatler* is guilty of criminal conduct but unable to accumulate hard evidence, SUPERMAN finally enlists the aid of boy genius Euclid Smith— "child prodigy and star of the Kid Wizards Show"—in a convoluted but ultimately successful ruse designed to entice Fenton and Gerritty into attempting to murder Euclid so that Superman can catch them in the act and take them into custody (WF No. 58, May/Jun '52: "'Scoop' Smith, Boy Reporter!").

FERRIS, FROSTY. The leader of a gang of criminals who attempt to commit a series of crimes by capitalizing on JOE HARRIS's claustrophobia, acrophobia, and color blindness, only to be apprehended by SUPERMAN in May-June 1952 (S No. 76/2: "The Misfit Manhunter!").

FIFTH DIMENSION, THE. The home dimension of MR. MXYZPTLK. (*See also* ZRFFF, LAND OF.)

FINCH (Councilman). A "crooked politician" in the town of Littledale who arouses the anger and indignation of his fellow townsmen by repeatedly ordering SUPERMAN arrested for a series of insignificant legal infractions—such as littering, unlawfully blocking traffic, and creating a sonic boom in a hospital zone—ostensibly out of devotion to the finer points of law and order, but in reality out of a desire to see to it that Superman is safely confined in the town jail while he and his henchmen make off with $1,000,000 in state funds earmarked for a local hospital. Councilman Finch and his cohorts are apprehended by Superman in May 1962 (S No. 153/1: "The Day Superman Broke the Law!").

FINCHCOMB, STANLEY. The meek, self-effacing proprietor of the Pleasure Island amusement park— the descendant of a long line of murderous pirates, including the bloodthirsty Captain Ironfist—who, persuaded by his "overactive imagination" that he has received a visitation from Captain Ironfist's spirit, converts an amusement park transport vessel into a modern-day pirate ship and, donning the buccaneer regalia of his infamous ancestor, embarks on a blood-chilling career in twentieth-century piracy, until finally, cornered by SUPERMAN in

November 1942, he loses his grip while scrambling u[p] some rigging and falls to his doom on the deck belo[w] (Act No. 54: "The Pirate of Pleasure Island").

FIRE FALLS. A magnificent flaming cataract o[n] the planet KRYPTON formed by a "fiery fluid" pourin[g] over a precipice (Act No. 325, Jun '65: "The Skyscrap[]er Superman!"). JOR-EL described the spectacula[r] phenomenon as "Our planet's inner fires, pourin[g] through a fissure" in a massive rock cliff (S No. 14[?] Nov '60: "Superman's Return to Krypton!" pts. I-III– "Superman Meets Jor-El and Lara Again!"; "Super[]man's Kryptonian Romance!"; "The Surprise o[f] Fate!"). Various species of "mutant fish" inhabite[d] the Fire Falls, including venomous "fish-snakes" whose bite was potentially fatal (Act No. 281, Oct '61 "The Man Who Saved Kal-El's Life!"). According t[o] the SUPERGIRL story in Action Comics No. 324 "When the planet [Krypton] exploded, it hurled th[e] falls into space, where the flames turned into a kind o[f] kryptonite, like all other parts of Krypton," so tha[t] today, on a far-off asteroid somewhere in outer space the famed Fire Falls still exist, in the form of a[] stunning green cataract of "kryptonite flame" (May '65: "The Black Magic of Supergirl!"). (*See also* KRYPTONITE.)

FISK, EDDIE. The leader of a gang of criminals whose dramatic capture by SUPERMAN is recalled by CLARK KENT and LOIS LANE in August-September 1950 (WF No. 47: "The Girl Who Hated Reporters!").

FIXER, THE. A "notorious outlaw" who, in collusion with a renegade scientist who has successfully manufactured a chunk of synthetic KRYPTONITE, attempts to annihilate SUPERMAN in a kryptonite deathtrap, only to be apprehended by Superman in July-August 1952 (S No. 77/2: "The Greatest Pitcher in the World!").

FLAMEBIRD. An alternate identity employed by JIMMY OLSEN on those occasions when he and SUPERMAN, employing the name NIGHTWING, participate in adventures together inside the bottle city of KANDOR. The bright red and yellow colors of Jimmy's Flamebird costume are reminiscent of the brilliant plumage of the flamebird, a Kandorian bird. Jimmy Olsen and Superman first adopt their Flamebird and Nightwing identities during an adventure in Kandor in January 1963 (*see* THAN OL) (S No. 158: "Superman in Kandor" pts. I-III—"Invasion of the Mystery Super-Men!"; "The Dynamic Duo of Kandor!"; "The City of Super-People!"). They employ them again during a second Kandorian adventure, in August 1964 (*see* THAN-AR) (WF No. 143: "The Feud Between Batman and Superman!" pts. I-II—no title, "The Manhunters from Earth!").

FLAME DRAGON. A gigantic, bat-winged, dragon-like creature native to the planet KRYPTON which "roars deafeningly" and belches flame "from its nostrils and gaping jaws." By January 1961, after having somehow survived the explosion of its native planet, a Kryptonian flame dragon has arrived on Earth, where, endowed with awesome super-powers like any native of Krypton in Earth's atmosphere, it ns amok, setting a forest aflame with its hellish "fire-breath" and threatening the entire planet with havoc and destruction until finally, after it has been temporarily deprived of its super-powers by exposure to red KRYPTONITE, SUPERMAN freezes it into "a great mass of ice" with a blast of his "super-cold breath" and then hurls it into orbit beyond the planet Pluto, where it will remain frozen forever in suspended animation (S No. 142/3: "Flame-Dragon from Krypton"). In February 1962 Earth is menaced by a second Kryptonian flame dragon, this one a "baby dragon" hatched from an egg laid by its predecessor, until finally Superman seizes it and carries it across the time barrier into the prehistoric past, where it will be able to live out its life alongside other gigantic creatures without posing a threat to human life (S No. 151/3: "Superman's Greatest Secret!").

FLANNELHEAD. The brawny, dim-witted fellow, known also as Pocus, who comprises half the team of HOCUS AND POCUS (Act No. 83, Apr '45: "Hocus & Pocus... Magicians by Accident!").

FLEISHER, MICHAEL L. The author of *The Encyclopedia of Comic Book Heroes*. Chartering a helicopter for the occasion, Fleisher interviewed the busy Man of Steel in the sky over Metropolis Harbor in Spring 1977. The event was recorded (below) for posterity by artist Murphy Anderson.

FLEMING (Mr.). "The mayor's assistant," and the man who is secretly the CRIME CZAR (Act No. 165, Feb '52: "The Man Who Conquered Superman!").

FLOOR, FINNEY. LOIS LANE's high school sweetheart and, in September-October 1950, the organizer of an exhibition of giant office machines. When Floor's exhibition is beset by vexing delays, SUPERMAN sees to it that it is ready on schedule, helps restore Floor's flagging self-confidence, and even reconciles Floor with his fiancée Minnie, who has become needlessly suspicious of his interest in his former girl friend Lois Lane (S No. 66/3: "The Machine that Played Cupid!").

FLORENA. The so-called "island of women"—a picturesque island in the South Pacific inhabited by the lovely descendants of exiles from the "distant planet" Matrion—where, in October 1965, a beautiful brunette named Orella attempts, through deception and trickery, to compel SUPERMAN to remain on the isle as her husband, only to be successfully outwitted by the determinedly single Man of Steel (S No. 180/2: "The Girl Who Was Mightier Than Superman!").

FLYING EAGLE (Chief). The tribal name and title bestowed upon SUPERMAN by the grateful Indian inhabitants of Metropolis Island in the year 1644, when they select the Man of Steel as their new chief in recognition of his having thwarted an attempt by the

YOU *SAID* I'D HAVE TO INTERVIEW YOU *ON THE JOB*-- BUT THIS IS *RIDICULOUS!*

© NPP 1977

Author Michael L. Fleisher interviews the Man of Steel in the skies over Metropolis Harbor, 1977

evil Chief Gray Wolf and the wily medicine man Shama to plunge their tribe into a "useless war" with the neighboring northern tribes (Act No. 148, Sep '50: "Superman, Indian Chief!"). (See MEECHER, HENRY.)

FOLGAR, DIRK. A "foreign reporter," ostensibly a correspondent for Europe's *World News Press*, who is in reality Agent X-3, a member of a "secret spy ring" plotting the assassination of President DWIGHT D. EISENHOWER. The capture of Folgar and his cohorts by U.S. Secret Service men in September 1959 comes as the culmination of an elaborate ruse—devised by SUPERMAN with the cooperation of the Secret Service and other governmental authorities—in which Superman poses as the Superman of the year 100,000 A.D., the so-called Ultra-Superman, in order to force the would-be assassins into the open and thwart the impending assassination (Act No. 256: "The Superman of the Future!").

FOLLENSBY, HARVEY. The proprietor of the Space Seeker, a mock-up spaceship, suspended over METROPOLIS by gas-filled balloons, which offers simulated space trips for the price of a dollar. When Follensby constructs an actual spaceship for a journey to MARS—and tricks four Metropolis failures into coming aboard as his crew—SUPERMAN rides along to ensure the space voyagers' safety and to help put each of the reluctant crewmen on the road to achieving his life's ambition (S No. 72/3, Sep/Oct '51: "The Flight of the Failures!").

FORREST, JOHN. A METROPOLIS window washer who stumbles upon the secret of SUPERMAN's identity when he sees Superman change to Clark Kent inside an office at the DAILY PLANET. The shock of this discovery sends Forrest reeling backward off his window ledge and plummeting toward the pavement, and although Superman rescues him before he hits the sidewalk, he is rushed unconscious to the hospital with Superman fearful that he will reveal his identity as soon as he regains consciousness. Awakening in his hospital bed, however, Forrest identifies himself as Eric Joyce, a Metropolis banker who vanished years ago after a blow on the head afflicted him with temporary amnesia. Now cured as the result of the shock of his recent fall, Joyce recalls nothing of his life as window washer "Forrest," including his knowledge of Superman's identity (S No. 48/3, Sep/Oct '47: "The Rarest Secret in the World!").

FORT KNOX. A United States Army reservation, located approximately 35 miles south of Louisville, Kentucky, which is the site of the principal gold bullion depository of the U.S. government.

In June 1940 an airplane en route to Fort Knox with a valuable gold shipment is hijacked by the villain MEDINI (Act No. 25).

In August 1943, during a period when he is suffering from temporary amnesia and under the influence of the evil "PROFESSOR" PRALINE, SUPERMAN tunnels his way into the subterranean vaults at Fort Knox—referred to in this particular text as Fort Blox—in order to help Praline and his henchmen loot the Federal gold reserve of $20,000,000,000 in gold bullion (Act No. 63: "When Stars Collide!").

In August 1960 LEX LUTHOR dupes HERCULES into helping him loot Fort Knox and carry off a ton of gold, but Superman apprehends Luthor soon afterward with some timely assistance from Hercules (Act No. 267: "Hercules in the 20th Century!").

In June 1961 Lex Luthor and his henchmen, aided by a stunning array of Luthor's superscientific apparatus, stage a spectacular robbery of the Fort Knox gold reserve, carrying off every ounce of gold in the depository and apparently making a fool out of Superman when he attempts to stop them. Later, however, when Luthor learns that Superman was away in outer space at the time of the robbery and that all he and his men outwitted was one of Superman's Superman-robots, Luthor leaves the stolen bullion stacked in an open field and telephones the police to come and collect it.

"Now why should he steal the stuff--and then return it?" asks a puzzled policeman.

"Knowing his insane conceit, I'd say the answer was obvious," replies Superman. "He felt that stealing the gold when I wasn't around to interfere was like stealing candy from a baby!" (Act No. 277: "The Conquest of Superman!").

In April 1962, while in the grip of a nightmare induced by exposure to red KRYPTONITE, Superman dreams of robbing Fort Knox by melting the bullion with his heat vision and siphoning it into waiting tank trucks. This robbery, however, is only part of a nightmare, and no actual robbery of Fort Knox takes place (Act No. 287: "Perry White's Manhunt for Superman!").

FORTRESS OF BIZARRO, THE. A crude imitation of SUPERMAN's FORTRESS OF SOLITUDE—BIZARRO refers to it as his "Fourtriss uv Bizarro"—which Bizarro constructs in the middle of an arid desert on the planet HTRAE in October 1960. Among other items, this ramshackle secluded retreat contains the "Bizarro ray," invented by Bizarro himself, and a "collection of worthless junk" accumulated from various parts of his world (S No. 140: pts. I-III—"The Son of Bizarro!"; "The 'Orphan' Bizarro!"; "The Bizarro Supergirl!").

FORTRESS OF SOLITUDE, THE. The impenetrable secret sanctuary, carved out of a mountainside amid the barren Arctic wastes, which serves both as a retreat and a headquarters for SUPERMAN. (See SUPERMAN [section D, the Fortress of Solitude].)

FORT SUPERMAN. A massive fortresslike structure—also referred to as the Museum of Menace—which is constructed by SUPERMAN in November 1957 as part of his elaborate plan to demoralize a trio of extradimensional outlaws who have been summoned from the fourth dimension by LEX LUTHOR to help him loot the Earth (S No. 117/2: "The Secret of Fort Superman").

FORTY THIEVES, THE. A band of robbers appearing in the story "Ali Baba and the Forty Thieves," one of the tales of the *Arabian Nights*. BATMAN, ROBIN, and SUPERMAN apprehend the Forty Thieves during a time-journey to tenth-century Baghdad (WF No. 79, Nov/Dec '55: "The Three

Magicians of Bagdad!"). (*See* ABDULLAH.)

FOSS, MIKE. An unscrupulous movie producer who tricks SUPERMAN into signing a contract committing him to perform three daredevil stunts in Foss's forthcoming motion picture, only to have Superman outwit Foss and foil the scheme—while faithfully abiding by the terms of the contract—by performing the stunts in such a way as to make it impossible for Foss to capture them on film (Act No. 120, May '48: "Superman, Stunt Man!").

FOTHERINGAY, WILLIS. The noted artist commissioned by the U.S. government to design a special SUPERMAN commemorative postage stamp in August 1954. Anxious to avoid the use of a frontal view of himself on the stamp for fear that the post-office cancellations of towns with double O's in their names will in effect superimpose "eyeglasses" on his face and risk betrayal of his Clark Kent identity, Superman is relieved when artist Fotheringay finally selects a profile view of Superman standing on a beach alongside a glistening glass castle that he has just fashioned for a happy youngster out of super-compressed sand (S No. 91/1: "The Superman Stamp!").

FOUR GALACTIC THIEFMASTERS, THE. "Four of the most infamous thieves in the universe," a ruthless quartet of "interplanetary thieves" who, in an attempt to wreak vengeance on SUPERMAN for a past defeat, trick Superman into pursuing them into a solar system characterized by a red sun, where he has

The Four Galactic Thiefmasters

no super-powers and is therefore as vulnerable to harm as any ordinary mortal. Stranded for a time on the red sun's only planet (*see* THORONES), Superman ultimately escapes the diabolical "red-sun trap" and apprehends the Four Galactic Thiefmasters in February 1965 (Act No. 321: "Superman--Weakest Man in the World!").

FOWLER, FLOYD. An unscrupulous, opportunistic individual who, having established that Clark Kent is SUPERMAN by comparing Kent's fingerprints with those of the infant Superman found embedded in

a fragment of the rocket ship that first brought him to Earth from KRYPTON, successfully blackmails Superman into making him a millionaire by threatening to expose the secret of his dual identity. When Fowler reneges on his part of the bargain, however, by refusing to relinquish possession of the incriminating rocket fragment, Superman retaliates by depriving Fowler of his newly acquired wealth and then alters the fingerprint evidence with his X-ray vision to make it appear that Fowler has erred in identifying Clark Kent with Superman (S No. 100/3, Sep '55: "The Clue from Krypton").

FOXX, SILVER. A ruthless "underworld czar" whose gang robs the lavishly appointed Cloud Club, "Metropolis' most exclusive gathering-place of celebrities," and a bank in the financial district before they are finally apprehended by SUPERMAN in September-October 1944 (S No. 30/1: "Superman Alias Superman!").

FRAWLEY, LEW. The leader of a gang of smugglers who are apprehended by SUPERMAN in Winter 1940 (S No. 3/4).

FRAY, JOHNNY. A courageous young police officer who resigned from the police force without explanation after losing his nerve in a gun battle in which, although wounded, he nevertheless singlehandedly apprehended three gunmen. Fray ultimately recovers his self-confidence and rejoins the police force thanks to a heroic helping hand from SUPERMAN (S No. 37/1, Nov/Dec '45: "The Dangerous Dream!").

FRISBY, FLOYD. A fugitive racketeer who is finally apprehended in the jungles of South America by BATMAN, ROBIN, and SUPERMAN in August 1960, despite the complications that arise when Superman, in the midst of his hunt for Frisby, becomes afflicted with temporary amnesia after absorbing the full force of a volcanic explosion and is persuaded by local natives that he is in reality their legendary king, returned to rebuild and rule over their crumbling ancient city (WF No. 111: "Superman's Secret Kingdom!").

FROST, CHARLIE. The janitor of the Daily Planet Building, and the man who is secretly the SKEPTIC (WF No. 11, Fall '43: "The City of Hate!").

FULTON, "MANY-FACES." A "notorious criminal impersonator" who masquerades as PERRY WHITE—and engages in half a dozen other ingenious impersonations—as part of an elaborate scheme to trick JIMMY OLSEN into believing that SUPERMAN is dead so that he will reveal the contents of a sealed letter, entrusted to him by Superman, which contains the secret of Superman's identity and is intended to be opened only in the event of Superman's death. Fulton, who stands to receive $1,000,000 from an underworld syndicate if his scheme is successful, is apprehended by Superman in August 1957 (S No. 115/2: "Jimmy Olsen's Lost Pal").

FUNNYFACE. A maniacal villain whose true identity is concealed by a balloonlike mask which gives him the appearance of a grotesquely humorous comic-strip villain. He is actually a frustrated comic-strip writer who has developed a "weird ray" that enables him to "materialize two-dimensional figures out of the comics" and thereby recruit infamous villains from well-known comic strips to help him commit spectacular crimes.

"I wanted to be a celebrity—the creator of a famous

Superman confronts Funnyface

comic strip. But no one would buy my strips," complains Funnyface, after SUPERMAN has finally apprehended him with the aid of some comic-strip heroes brought to life with the villain's ray by the resourceful LOIS LANE. "My dimensional experimentation enabled me to bring comic characters to life— and I put the strip villains to work for me to gather illegal profits!" (S No. 19/1, Nov/Dec '42: "Case of the Funny Paper Crimes").

FURST, HENRY. The "fiery old newspaper tycoon" who, "by fair means and foul, built the nationwide chain of Furst newspapers," a man of few scruples and fabulous wealth who has for years pursued, to the point of obsession, the secret of SUPERMAN's identity. In February 1958, after imbibing a "new formula that imitates the symptoms of approaching death," Furst summons Clark Kent to his "deathbed" and successfully tricks him into revealing his identity by invoking the solemnity of a "dying man's" last request. Fortunately for Superman, however, the drug Furst took had "hallucinatory side-effects," and Furst recovers from its influence with only a mistaken recollection of what Clark Kent revealed to him (Act No. 237: "Superman's Exposed Identity").

FUTUREMAN. The alias employed by XL-49 in May 1958 when he poses as a super-hero from the far distant future as part of his plan to play Cupid between SUPERMAN and LOIS LANE (S No. 121/1: "The Bride of Futureman!").

G

GADDEN, ERNEST. A bankrupt millionaire who—along with middleweight boxing contender Kid Kole and a beautiful blonde named Miss Swift—temporarily acquires invulnerability and superhuman strength when the private airplane in which all three are flying is bathed in mysterious green radiation emanating from an onrushing giant meteor as it is shattered in midair by SUPERMAN. All three make a pact to keep their super-powers secret so that they can unscrupulously turn them to their own advantage—as when Kid Kole attempts to use his super-strength to win the middleweight boxing crown at Metropolis Stadium—but Superman thwarts their attempts to profit unfairly from their powers and teaches them all a much-needed lesson which, once their powers have vanished, leaves them wiser and more honorable persons (S No. 74/2, Jan/Feb '52: "Superman's Masters!").

GAGE, GRETA. A daring and beautiful stuntwoman—the star of a movie currently being produced by Lavish Productions, Inc.—who is among the four finalists in a contest to select America's bravest woman, sponsored by the DAILY PLANET. Grissom, Lavish Productions' unscrupulous press agent, attempts to sabotage the efforts of the other contestants in order to win the contest—and the valuable publicity certain to result from it—for Greta, but SUPERMAN thwarts Grissom's machinations at every turn and ultimately apprehends him. The bravest woman award goes finally to LOIS LANE for her courageous efforts in uncovering the identity of the mystery saboteur and luring him out of hiding (S No. 83/2, Jul/Aug '53: "The Search for the Bravest Woman!"). The story seems closely based on Superman No. 63/3 (Mar/Apr '50: "Miss Metropolis of 1950"). (See BOND, ELLEN.)

GALLOWAY, CURTIS. "The richest...and most heartily disliked...citizen of Metropolis," an embittered old skinflint who, out of pure meanness and hatred for METROPOLIS, buries $5,000,000 beneath a statue in the Metropolis city park and then sends gangsters throughout the world clues to its location in hopes of causing "a wave of petty crimes and gangland rivalries...so that the life of Metropolis [will] become completely disrupted!" SUPERMAN apprehends so many criminals during this period—including the gang led by "crime chief" John Hector, "the most dangerous criminal in Metropolis"—that Metropolis's jails are inadequate to hold them, but ultimately he stems the tidal wave of crime and even persuades the miserly Galloway to adopt a healthier attitude toward Metropolis and use his millions for charity (WF No. 67, Nov/Dec '53: "Metropolis—Crime Center!").

GALONIA. A peace-loving European nation which is at war with the brutal aggressor country of Toran. Indeed, when "the armed battalions of Toran unexpectedly swoop down upon a lesser nation, Galonia," fears mount that "...once again the world is being flung into a terrible conflagration!" LOIS LANE and CLARK KENT are sent to Europe as war correspondents to cover the conflict for their newspaper, but it is SUPERMAN who thwarts a sinister plot to win "the sympathy of the democracies" for the Toranian cause (see LAVERNE, LITA) (Act No. 22, Mar '40). Only later does Superman learn that "a fiend named Luthor deliberately fomented this war for evil purposes" as part of his heinous scheme "to engulf the entire [European] continent in bloody warfare" (see LUTHOR, LEX) (Act No. 23, Apr '40).

GAMBLING. The practice of playing games and wagering money or other stakes on their outcome. SUPERMAN has described gambling as "a parasitic vice that has no place in a decent town" (Act No. 16, Sep '39), and Action Comics No. 32 observes that "Of all evils, gambling is one of the most vicious—it's [sic] toll of human suffering is almost beyond belief!" (Jan '32).

GARGOYLE, THE. A hideous, fanged villain in the employ of J.C. Quagmire, an unscrupulous "chemical magnate" who steals the discoveries of rival chemists and markets them as his own. Superman No. 49/2 describes the Gargoyle as a

notorious crook who was deafened and nearly blinded in a mine explosion, and now wears electronic ears and infra-red lenses, both made by Quagmire! The Gargoyle—a monster of Quagmire's creation, a warped genius who does his master's every bidding!

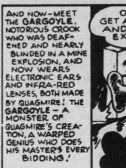

The Gargoyle

71

In November-December 1947 Quagmire—who has recently attempted to steal the formula for a valuable new paint from the safe of rival chemist Ira Stone—orders the Gargoyle to murder Ira Stone, CLARK KENT, and LOIS LANE before they can successfully carry out an expedition to paint the top of Mount Everest and the rim of a Pacific island volcano with some of Stone's new paint in order to demonstrate its ability to withstand the most extreme weather conditions on Earth. Thwarted repeatedly by SUPERMAN and forced to flee, the Gargoyle is finally taken into custody by the United States Coast Guard. His employer, J. C. Quagmire, is arrested soon afterward ("Clark Kent's Most Dangerous Assignment!").

GARN ABU. The "young partner" of VEL QUENNAR, the esteemed Lexorian attorney who is appointed to defend SUPERMAN when the Man of Steel is brought to trial on the planet LEXOR on the charge of having deliberately murdered LEX LUTHOR, Lexor's greatest hero. Garn Abu is a hot-headed young attorney who, like most Lexorians, hates Superman and assumes he is guilty. He unsuccessfully urges Vel Quennar to withdraw from the case, on the ground that Quennar's career will suffer if he defends a murderer like Superman (Act No. 318, Nov '64: "The Death of Luthor!"). Once the trial gets under way, however, Garn Abu works dedicatedly in Superman's defense, arguing that the Man of Steel was temporarily insane when he murdered Luthor. Although Superman himself demolishes this defense by hewing to his claim that Luthor's death was an accident, he is ultimately pronounced not guilty and released from custody when it is discovered that Luthor has not died at all, but has merely been in a "deathlike trance" induced by a "coma drug." Garn Abu is alternatively rendered as Garn Abo (Act No. 319, Dec '64: "The Condemned Superman!"). (See LUTHOR, LEX.)

GATES, GOLDIE. A cunning swindler—described as an "underworld genius, whose talents are devoted exclusively to larcenous pursuits"—who attempts to cheat Randall Rocksell, "one of America's richest and most ambitious men," out of his entire fortune. Gates winds up in prison after being apprehended by SUPERMAN (S No. 27/4, Mar/Apr '44: "Dear Diary!").

GATSON, JOE. A vicious racketeer who, "facing the possibility of going to jail for a minor racketeering charge," kidnaps the daughter of the presiding judge and, through his henchmen, threatens to kill her unless the judge uses his judicial prerogative to grant him his freedom. SUPERMAN rescues the kidnap victim in March-April 1941, and Gatson dies when he attempts to gun down the judge's daughter and Superman hurls him into the path of his own bullet. In the words of Superman No. 9/2:

> Bulwark of man's civilization is his court of law where wrongs are righted and criminals punished according to their merits. But when evildoers seek to inject their villainous methods directly into the courtroom, *SUPERMAN*, super-strong champion of justice, steps in to teach the criminal horde respect for law and order....

GAUCHO, THE. A South American crime-fighter whose methods and techniques are modeled after those of America's BATMAN. In July-August 1957 the Gaucho visits the United States in response to a summons from "well-known philanthropist" John Mayhew, who wishes to award the Gaucho and other world-famous crime-fighters—including Batman and ROBIN, SUPERMAN, the MUSKETEER, the LEGIONARY, and the KNIGHT and the SQUIRE—charter membership in his newly formed Club of Heroes (WF No. 89: "The Club of Heroes!"). (See LIGHTNING-MAN.) (For a complete account of the Gaucho's crime-fighting career, consult *The Encyclopedia of Comic Book Heroes: Volume I—Batman.*)

The Gaucho

GAUNTLET (Sir). A mysterious villain, clad in a suit of armor like that of a medieval knight, who masterminds a series of spectacular thefts from the stock of Lacey's Department Store until he and his henchmen are finally apprehended by SUPERMAN in March-April 1943. Sir Gauntlet is in reality Casper Smythe, a meek Lacey's employee—and a onetime partner of the store's owner, until he was caught in the act of stealing company funds many years ago—who confesses that he looted Lacey's of its merchandise because "I felt part of the store still belonged to me--and I took what I considered mine...!" (S No. 21/3: "The Robber Knight").

"GENERAL," THE. A former Nazi general who presides over a secret underworld "proving grounds"—situated "in a deserted valley many miles from the city"—that is equipped with a vast arsenal of ingenious "machines of crime." In the General's words:

> When the Nazis were defeated, they thought I was through--finished! But now, fabulous success will be mine--perhaps even greater than that dreamed of by our leader!
> When the Reich was defeated, I escaped... but I had the foresight to take along something that would insure my future!

In each country we captured, we forced their scientists to evolve fantastic weapons of the future! Here, for instance, is a huge mirror floating in space! By directing concentrated beams of sunlight, it can start a fire at any spot on Earth!

Unfortunately, we lost the war before we could construct many of these devices! Think what we could have done if time had allowed us to use them!

But I shall use them--for crime! For I have all the detailed plans of the most fantastic means of destruction ever conceived by man!

In February 1953 the General and his henchmen assault METROPOLIS with a stunning array of diabolical weapons, including a giant buzz saw that cuts an airliner in half in midair, a "giant bulldozer" that topples entire skyscrapers, and a "flying wrecking crane" that smashes the Daily Planet Building in two. With each successive devastating attack, SUPERMAN is compelled to spend his energies protecting lives and property while the criminals commit a series of spectacular crimes. Ultimately, however, Superman locates the secret proving grounds and apprehends the General and his cohorts (Act No. 177: "The Anti-Superman Weapon").

GIANTIA. A far-distant planet revolving about a red sun—a gigantic "leper world . . . shunned because of the terrible monsters which inhabit it"—which has become the adopted home of three death-worshiping "madmen" from another planet, the sole survivors of a "space blight" which decimated life on their world, who have entered into a "solemn vow" to "bring death to 100 other worlds"—including Earth—as lunatic compensation for the death of their own world, and then to blow themselves and all of Giantia to kingdom come after performing "a final ceremony in honor of death!" The aliens do indeed destroy themselves in a planet-shattering holocaust, and SUPERMAN, helpless before the awesome space monsters which they have dispatched to destroy the Earth, only succeeds in stopping the monsters and saving Earth by virtue of a fortuitous accident (Act No. 326, Jul '65: "The Legion of Super-Creatures!").

GIMPY. A "receiver and fence for stolen goods" and "loathsome corrupter of youth" who viciously lures underprivileged youths into working for him as thieves; forces them to endure all the risks of arrest and incarceration while keeping for himself the lion's share of their loot; callously abandons them in the event they are arrested; and even informs on them to the police once he feels they have become expendable. Put out of business by SUPERMAN in January 1939, Gimpy is important in the chronicles less as a villain than as the man responsible, albeit indirectly, for the remarkable crusade against juvenile delinquency and the slum conditions which produce it that is undertaken by Superman during this period.

Convinced that the rampant juvenile delinquency about which society professes such concern is caused mainly by the stifling slum environment in which many city youths must dwell, Superman sets to work to ameliorate the problem, first by persuading Gimpy's youthful protégés to abandon crime and delinquency in favor of lives of honesty according to the Superman code, and then by addressing himself to the deplorable conditions of poverty and neglect that he views as the basic cause of their delinquent behavior. ". . . It's these slums—your poor living conditions," muses Superman, "—if there was only some way I could remedy it--!"

Then, as luck would have it, the headline on a local newspaper catches Superman's eye. "Cyclone Hits Florida," it screams. "Cities Laid Waste!" The story beneath the headline details plans by the U.S. government to erect modern housing projects on the sites of buildings destroyed by the cyclone.

Inspired by the newspaper article, Superman passes the word to the residents of the city's slums to gather up their possessions and evacuate their homes immediately. Then, with the dilapidated slum dwellings safely emptied of their occupants, he whirls through the area like "a one-man cyclone," single-handedly demolishing every structure in sight with the hammerlike blows of his mighty fists. "So the government rebuilds destroyed areas with modern cheap-rental apartments, eh?" says Superman to himself. "Then here's a job for it!—When I finish, this town will be rid of its filthy crime-festering slums!"

Superman's radical approach to slum clearance, however, does not endear him to the authorities, and as word of his devastation spreads, scores of policemen and firemen, a contingent of National Guardsmen, and finally "a squadron of aerial-bombers" are ordered into the disaster area with orders to annihilate Superman and put an end to the destruction. But the machine-gun bullets of the National Guardsmen merely bounce off Superman's chest like pebbles, and the bombs unleashed by the bombers serve only to hasten the completion of his remarkable task.

Nimbly, he races thru [sic] the streets, explosions dodging his footsteps as the frantic aviators seek desperately to eliminate him. . . .

And then finally, his task completed, "SUPERMAN vanishes from sight. Behind him he leaves what formerly were the slums, but now, a desolate shambles. . . ."

Soon afterward, as Superman had anticipated, the federal government initiates a campaign of massive aid in the disaster-stricken area. "Emergency squads commence erecting huge apartment-projects . . . and in time the slums are replaced by splendid housing conditions."

Officially, of course, this unauthorized act of slum demolition has made an outlaw out of Superman, but even the authorities are privately elated. ". . . We'll spare no effort to apprehend SUPERMAN," vows the police chief, "--but off the record . . . I think he did a splendid thing and I'd like to shake his hand!" (Act No. 8). (See REILLY [DETECTIVE CAPTAIN].)

GI NEWSREEL, INC. A newly organized newsreel

production company, founded and operated by two recently discharged World War II Army combat photographers, which wins accolades from the newsreel viewing public—and infuriates its principal competitor, the more affluent, longer established Trans-Global News—by scoring a series of impressive newsreel scoops with the aid of a special blimp, equipped with a news ticker and a long-range telescope, in which the two former G.I.s crisscross the city, arriving at the scene of fast-breaking news events well ahead of all competing newsreel cameramen. When Dan Flood, ruthless head of Trans-Global News, resorts to unscrupulous tactics—from seeing to it that the G.I.s purchase defective newsreel film to blowing up a municipal statue in an effort to create his own sensational news event—SUPERMAN intervenes to expose Flood's shenanigans and help the G.I. cameramen win the lucrative newsreel movie-chain contract they have been hoping for (Act No. 111, Aug '47: "Cameras in the Clouds!").

GLENNON (Duke). The tyrannical ruler of Belford, a twelfth-century English town which SUPERMAN visits in an effort to uncover the origins of a mysterious drawing found embedded inside a meteor in September 1954. Superman helps the local townsfolk overthrow the evil duke before returning through the time barrier to twentieth-century METROPOLIS (S No. 92/2: "Superman's Sweetheart!").

GLOBAL ENTERPRISES, INC. A company serving as a front for a trio of swindlers—Harry Dane, "Honest Jack" Dugan, and "Friendly Al" Piper—who cunningly contrive to persuade the public that wrestler Hank Garvin is secretly SUPERMAN, as part of an elaborate scheme to offer the unwitting Garvin the presidency of the firm so that they can dupe the unsuspecting public into snatching up their stock in the mistaken belief that they are investing in a company headed by Superman. The swindlers are apprehended by Superman in November-December 1951 (S No. 73/1: "Hank Garvin, Man of Steel!").

GLOOP, MERTON. A timid waiter at METROPOLIS's Scoop Restaurant—a self-effacing milquetoast with a hopeless crush on LOIS LANE—who comes into chance possession of a seemingly ordinary "lucky horseshoe" in June 1950 and, unaware that it is actually a "fabulous magnet" endowed with incredible "force-repellent" properties, becomes unwittingly embroiled in a series of zany misadventures—such as when he repels an oncoming car into a plate-glass window; inadvertently knocks SUPERMAN unconscious during a charity-benefit boxing match when his force-repelling horseshoe sends Superman's mighty punch rebounding back onto the Man of Steel's own jaw; and wins a $100,000 horse race astride a hopeless hay-burner when the repellent power of the horseshoe prevents all the other horses in the race from gaining any ground—whieh convince him that he has become somehow possessed of mind-boggling force-repellent powers. When Gloop, naïve and unsuspecting, falls under the baleful influence of "Bingo" Bellamy—an unscrupu-

lous promoter, confidence man, and gambler determined to use Gloop's powers to amass a hoard of ill-gotten profits—Superman intervenes to apprehend Bellamy and his underworld cronies. Gloop, who is forced to return to waitering when his magnet's powers vanish twenty-four hours later, remains something of a minor celebrity as "the only man who ever kayoed Superman!" (Act No. 145: "Merton Gloop and His Magic Horseshoe!").

GOB-GOB. A caveman, found preserved intact inside an iceberg by SUPERMAN in February 1949, who causes a sensation in METROPOLIS until he turns out to be nothing but a well-coached circus strongman engaging in an elaborate hoax to publicize his forthcoming motion picture (Act No. 129: "Lois Lane, Cavegirl!").

GOLD VOLCANO. A volcano on the planet KRYPTON that erupted gold instead of lava. Gold was so commonplace on Krypton, however, that the metal was literally worthless (S No. 141, Nov '60: "Superman's Return to Krypton!" pts. I-III—"Superman Meets Jor-El and Lara Again!"; "Superman's Kryptonian Romance!"; "The Surprise of Fate!").

GOLLO. A playful alien creature from the far-distant planet Zar, a gigantic, green-skinned child-creature with large purple eyes and the frisky disposition of a friendly baby dinosaur, who arrives on Earth in November 1957 and wreaks constant, albeit completely unintended, havoc with his uncanny ability to "change shape" at will "to imitate any object"—as when he transforms himself into an ocean liner and, churning unthinkingly through the waters of Metropolis Harbor, only narrowly avoids causing a disastrous collision between two ferryboats—until he is finally taken in tow by SUPERMAN and returned safely to his worried parents on the planet Zar (Act No. 234: "The Creature of 1,000 Disguises").

GOTHAM CITY. The East Coast United States city which is the resident city of BATMAN and ROBIN and the scene of most of their adventures. (For further information on Gotham City, consult *The Encyclopedia of Comic Book Heroes: Volume I—Batman.*)

GRADY. A ruthless "talent racketeer" who plays on the eager ambitions of show-business hopefuls by promising them glamorous careers on stage, on screen, or in opera and then bilking them of their savings in return for worthless theatrical "training." SUPERMAN extorts a confession from Grady by putting him through some terrifying aerial acrobatics ("Out into the empty air leaps the mighty *Man of Steel* with his craven, screeching burden...") before turning him over to the authorities for prosecution (S No. 10/2, May/Jun '41).

GRAIL (Professor). A scientist who, working alone in his laboratory on Warder's Island, "a few miles out of Metropolis Harbor," has been undertaking "new experiments in energy transmission" in the hope of finding "a way to transmit energy to distant places like radio waves," and even, eventually, of discovering a means of sending human beings "through space by radio," much as television pictures are transmitted from one place to another. While visiting Professor Grail's laboratory in May 1959, LOIS LANE is apparently annihilated when SUPERMAN's X-ray vision, inadvertently focused on the complex special circuitry of some of Grail's experimental apparatus, produces a tremendous accidental explosion that disintegrates the apparatus and obliterates Lois Lane. Overwhelmed with remorse at having caused Lois's death, Superman becomes unnerved to the point of distraction when the wraithlike form of Lois Lane begins to follow him everywhere, haunting him like a phantom conjured up by his guilt. Ultimately, however, Superman discovers that the interaction of his X-ray vision with Grail's scientific apparatus somehow catapulted Lois into "the eerie, misty world of the 4th dimension," where she remained visible to Superman in wraithlike form whenever he happened to use his X-ray vision. Having made this discovery, Superman returns to Professor Grail's laboratory and uses the scientist's advanced equipment to return Lois, alive and well, to the earthly dimension (S No. 129/1: "The Ghost of Lois Lane").

GRAMBLY (General). The cunning criminal mastermind and self-styled "Napoleon of crime" who is the leader of the Purple Legion, a gang of criminals whose members wear purple military-style uniforms, function in the manner of a military unit, and carry out ingeniously complex crimes with practiced military precision.

In August 1961 BATMAN, ROBIN, and SUPERMAN join forces in an elaborate scheme to apprehend General Grambly and defeat the Purple Legion by replacing Superman with a lifelike Superman robot while the real Superman dons a colorful tiger-striped costume and assumes the fictitious identity of Tigerman, a hopelessly inept crime-fighter who seems to enjoy some sort of mysterious hold over Batman, Robin, and Superman. Eventually, as the three heroes had anticipated, General Grambly becomes eager to learn exactly why Batman, Robin, and Superman seem so willingly subservient to the bungling Tigerman. When Grambly's henchmen capture Tigerman and usher him into the general's secret mobile headquarters for questioning, Batman and Robin appear on the scene and apprehend General Grambly and his Purple Legionnaires (WF No. 119: "The Secret of Tigerman!").

GRAND CANYON. An immense, scenically spectacular gorge cut by the Colorado River into the high plateaus of northern Arizona. Ranging from more than a mile in depth and from four to eighteen miles in width, it extends approximately 280 miles in a winding course from the head of Marble Gorge, near the northern boundary of Arizona, to Grand Wash Cliffs, near the Nevada line. In January 1960, while impersonating SUPERMAN, the Kandorian scientist KULL-EX destroys the Grand Canyon as a tourist attraction by filling it in with giant boulders as part of his scheme to make Superman the most hated man on Earth. Superman presumably undoes the damage

later, but this is never actually stated in the text (S No. 134: chs. I-III—"The Super-Menace of Metropolis!"; "The Revenge Against Jor-El!"; "The Duel of the Supermen!").

GRAUL, CARLTON. The secretary to Frank Lingle, president of the Lingle Steel Corporation, and a secret fifth columnist in the pay of a hostile European nation who has stolen the formula for Lingle Steel's new "X-alloy" and, aided by his fellow subversives, has been sabotaging the cannons made from the new alloy so that they will explode when tested, creating the impression among America's military planners that the highly touted new alloy is absolutely worthless. In addition, Graul is the commander of Koolsey Camp, where a "secret army" stands poised to strike at America from within the moment its masters in Europe launch their barrage of deadly "strato-bombs" against an unsuspecting U.S.A.

Lingle Steel Corporation president Frank Lingle is an unwilling ally of the plotters, for, as he finally confesses to SUPERMAN:

> You see, years ago my son went to Europe in a student exchange scheme... but he was seized and thrown into a concentration camp. I was informed that unless I cooperated with subversive agents in this country, I'd never see him again.

Swinging into action with his mighty super-powers, Superman single-handedly defeats and apprehends the entire army at Koolsey Camp, captures the evil Graul and recovers the stolen formula for X-alloy, and intercepts the deadly barrage of strato-bombs by allowing them to explode harmlessly against his chest, with the exception of the few bombs that he deliberately salvages unexploded so that he can drop them personally on the hostile nation that launched them (S No. 21/1, Mar/Apr '43).

GRAY, GRISELDA. The puritanical spinster sister of DAILY PLANET publisher Harvey Gray who, stepping primly into the role of acting publisher when her brother's medical problems force him to take a ninety-day leave of absence, moves promptly, much to the chagrin of PERRY WHITE and other *Planet* staffers, to implement a strict new journalistic policy reflecting her uncompromising views on how a good newspaper ought to be run, in the process banning all news of crime, amusement, and anything else—including all news about SUPERMAN—which she feels smacks of "sensationalism," and assigning the intrepid newshounds of the *Planet* to cover such scintillating items of interest as the National Embroidery Convention, the Croquet Tournament, and the appearance of the season's first crocus in Metropolis Park. "A really good newspaper," explains Miss Gray, "should be dignified and intellectual! From now on, no sensationalism, amusement or crime news will soil our pages!"

When Egbert Smills, "a cultured swindler far too dignified to commit ordinary crimes," presents himself at the *Planet* as the head of the Association for Aid of Worthy Projects and persuades the naïve Miss Gray to publicize a series of "worthy" causes whose real aim is the accumulation of contributions for the lining of his own pockets, Superman steps in to thwart the swindles, arranges for the prudish Miss Gray to capture Smills and his accomplice single-handed, and in the process persuades the *Planet*'s stuffy acting publisher to shed her rigid Victorian shell and restore the *Planet* to the great, albeit undignified, newspaper it has always been (S No. 85/2, Nov/Dec '53: "Clark Kent, Gentleman Journalist!").

GRAYSON, CHARLIE. A METROPOLIS racketeer, exposed by a series of articles in the DAILY PLANET and only recently released from prison, who attempts to wreak vengeance on the *Planet* by sabotaging its philanthropic efforts to establish a vacation farm for underprivileged children. Grayson is apprehended by SUPERMAN in May-June 1942 (S No. 16/1: "The World's Meanest Man").

GRAYSON, DICK. The teen-aged boy who is secretly ROBIN, the inseparable crime-fighting companion of BATMAN. Dick Grayson is the ward of socialite Bruce Wayne, the man who is secretly Batman.

GRAYSON, NAT. The unscrupulous president of the Akme Construction Company, and the mastermind behind a murderous scheme to "destroy his greatest business rival," Bruce Constructions Inc., and thereby "dominate the construction field," by deliberately causing a series of fatal construction "accidents" on the site of the Atlas Building—a major Bruce Constructions Inc. building project—so as to seriously delay the skyscraper's construction and prevent Bruce Constructions "from completing in' job within th' time required in their contract!" Seized by SUPERMAN in Fall 1939 and strangled by the throat until he agrees to make a full confession of his crimes ("Remember!" warns Superman. "If you don't confess, I'll come back and dish out the justice you deserve with my bare hands!"), Grayson is taken into custody by the METROPOLIS police and is ultimately sentenced to die in the electric chair (S No. 2/3: "Superman and the Skyscrapers").

GREAT COSMO, THE. The alias employed by Lt. Tom McLain of the Metropolis Police Department in February 1956 when he poses as a mind reader turned criminal as part of an elaborate and ultimately successful scheme, devised by SUPERMAN, to stage "the biggest dragnet of wanted criminals in history" by enticing underworld figures from throughout the nation into coming to METROPOLIS to join the Great Cosmo's organization in the belief that Cosmo has used his clairvoyant powers to penetrate Superman's secret identity, and that the Man of Steel will therefore not dare to apprehend them for fear of having his secret publicly exposed (S No. 103/3: "The Man Who Could Read Superman's Mind!").

GREAT MENTO, THE. The alias employed by PERRY WHITE in August 1961 when he poses as a mind reader turned criminal as part of an elaborate and ultimately successful scheme, devised by SUPERMAN, to "round up every wanted criminal in this region" by enticing "the cream of the underworld" into flocking to METROPOLIS to join the Great Mento's crime syndicate in the belief that Mento has used his "uncanny power of extra-sensory perception" to penetrate Superman's secret identity, and that the Man of Steel will therefore not dare to apprehend them for fear of having his secret publicly exposed (S No. 147/1: "The Great Mento!"). The story is in many respects similar to Superman No. 103/3 (Feb '56: "The Man Who Could Read Superman's Mind!"). (*See* GREAT COSMO, THE.)

GREAT PYRAMID, THE. A gigantic pyramid at Giza, in Egypt, which is the largest single building ever erected and one of the world's great landmarks. Built by CHEOPS, the second Pharaoh of Egypt's 4th dynasty, who reigned *ca.* 2590-2567 B.C., it covers 13 acres of ground and is believed to contain more than 2,500,000 stone blocks, averaging approximately 2½ tons apiece. It has been calculated that 100,000 men working unceasingly would have required 20 years to complete the task. According to World's Finest Comics No. 32, however, SUPERMAN completed construction of the gigantic pyramid himself—single-handedly performing well over half the work—during a time-journey to Egypt in the twenty-sixth century B.C. (Jan/Feb '48: "The Seventh Wonder of the World!").

By July 1954 LEX LUTHOR and his henchmen have planted explosives in the Great Pyramid—and in many other world-famous monuments—as part of an elaborate scheme to extort millions of dollars from the governments of the world (S No. 90/3: "The Titanic Thefts!"). During this same period, when Superman surprises the Kryptonian villain MALA in the act of stealing the great SPHINX at Giza, Mala scatters the blocks of the Great Pyramid with a puff of his mighty super-breath, forcing Superman to retrieve the stone building blocks and rebuild the pyramid while the villain makes good his escape (Act No. 194, Jul '54: "The Outlaws from Krypton!"). (*See also* PYRAMIDS, THE.)

GREER, ALEX. "A furtive man" who is described as "the slickest lobbyist in Washington. No one knows what interests back him" (Act No. 1, Jun '38). Greer is secretly in the employ of ruthless "munitions magnate" EMIL NORVELL, who is determined to maneuver the United States into becoming "embroiled with Europe" in the impending war with the Axis (Act No. 2, Jul '38).

After overhearing Alex Greer conspiring with U.S. Senator Barrows to railroad a bill through the U.S. Senate whose effect would be to embroil the United States in the coming war in Europe, SUPERMAN seizes Greer and leaps high into the air with him, racing precariously along some telephone wires and then bounding to the dome of the Capitol, in an effort to terrify his captive into revealing the identity of the mastermind behind his lobbying efforts. From the

Capitol dome, Superman makes a mighty leap toward the roof of a distant skyscraper, but, either through accident or design, he misses his mark (Act No. 1, Jun '38) and the two men hurtle toward the pavement far below:

As they topple like a plummet to the street below, eighty stories distant, Greer shrieks insanely the entire length of the building!

Finally, Greer can endure the agony of terror no longer. "I'll talk!" he cries. "--The man behind the threatening war is Emil Norvell..." (see NORVELL, EMIL) (Act No. 2, Jul '38). The stories chronicling these events are reprinted in Superman No. 1/1 (Sum 39) and Superman No. 1/2 (Sum '39).

GRIM, "GADGET." A "renegade underworld inventor" who, having invented a special magnet that attracts the cloth of SUPERMAN's indestructible costume, attempts to use the magnet to help his gang commit a series of crimes, as when he endeavors to use the magnet to send Superman hurtling through the wall of an office building into the side of a gem company's safe. Grim and his henchmen are apprehended by Superman in March 1958 (S No. 120/3: 'The Human Missile").

GRIMES, JONATHAN (Captain). A U.S. Army captain with a mania for regulations who gets SUPERMAN drafted into the service in November 1959 "...Superman has to spend some time in the service, just like every other able-bodied single man!"), only to be repeatedly outwitted when he attempts to humble and even humiliate the Man of Steel by treating him like an average soldier. Through the good offices of a sympathetic inspector general, in fact, Superman rises swiftly to the rank of general, but he shows good sportsmanship by promoting Grimes to the rank of major before his short-lived super-career in the military officially expires (S No. 133/3: "Superman Joins the Army!").

GRIMES, ROCKY. The head of a ruthless dognapping ring that steals people's dogs and holds them for ransom. SUPERMAN smashes the ring in November-December 1944 with the aid of a local dogcatcher, then extorts a written confession from the terrified Grimes by threatening to attack him with a rabid dog (S No. 31/2: "A Dog's Tale!").

GRINSTEAD, CARL (Professor). "One of the world's most accomplished chemists," and the inventor of the new wonder drug "parabiolene." By Summer 1940 a racketeer named Carlin has duped Professor Grinstead into believing that he is interested in promoting the use of parabiolene for humanitarian reasons, although his real motive is to locate patients in dire need of the drug so that he can force them to steal for him and otherwise do his bidding by threatening to withhold their supply. Carlin is apprehended by SUPERMAN (S No. 5/4).

GRISWOLD, JOHN. A METROPOLIS millionaire and member of the Collectors' Club who, embittered by his repeated failure to win one of the club's annual prizes for any of his innumerable collections—e.g., stamps, coins, and rare tapestries—resolves finally to "startle everyone" and "make the Collectors' Club sit up and take notice" of him by starting a strange and unique collection, a people collection, a bizarre new hobby that consists of tricking prominent persons into signing deceptively worded agreements obligating them either to fulfill tasks which seem simple but which are in reality virtually impossible to perform, or else to live in Griswold's home as obedient members of his people collection for the period of an entire year. Correctly discerning, however, that Griswold's real motive in pursuing an award from the Collectors' Club is the desire to win the approval of his fellow members, SUPERMAN cleverly steers the unhappy millionaire into a life of philanthropy, a life which will enable him to do good for others while winning the approbation of friends and community that he has always sought (S No. 96/3, Mar '55: "The Collector of Celebrities!").

GROFF, JO-JO. The leader of a gang of criminals who commit a series of spectacular crimes with the aid of a mighty caveman from KRYPTON, a Stone Age survivor of SUPERMAN's home planet endowed with superhuman powers identical to Superman's, who awakens to renewed life after arriving on Earth in a state of suspended animation in the heart of a meteor, and whom the criminals dupe into becoming their friend. BATMAN, ROBIN, and Superman finally apprehend the villains in June 1959, and the lumbering caveman—hopelessly out of place on an alien planet in an alien era—dies moments afterward from the combined effects of his recent exposure to KRYPTONITE and the bombardment of cosmic rays he endured during his journey through space (WF No. 102: "The Caveman from Krypton!").

GROGAN, "IRONJAW." The leader of a gang of criminals who are apprehended by SUPERMAN in January-February 1943 while attempting to stage a robbery at METROPOLIS's Third National Bank. Superman's efforts to capture the Grogan gang, and in fact all of his activities during this period, are severely complicated by the fact that a phony newspaper headline identifying CLARK KENT as Superman, set in type at the instigation of LOIS LANE and intended merely as a playful joke, has accidentally received widespread public distribution, with the result that Kent has been asked to "pose" as Superman temporarily in order to avoid doing damage to the DAILY PLANET's widespread "reputation for reliability," thus making it difficult for Superman to perform his normal super-heroic duties (S No. 20/1: "Superman's Secret Revealed!").

GROTE (General). The leader of a gang of power-mad rebels on a far-distant planet who kidnap a group of primitive cavemen from Earth's distant past for use as slave laborers on their native planet, as part of a diabolical scheme to assassinate the leaders of their own government and then use their home planet as a base from which to carry out the bloody conquest and colonization of twentieth-century Earth. The plot is ultimately thwarted, and General Grote and his henchmen are apprehended, through the heroic efforts of BATMAN, ROBIN, and SUPERMAN (WF No. 138, Dec '63: "The Secret of the Captive Cavemen!").

GURNEY, "FATHEAD." A notorious "shakedown racket man" who is apprehended along with his henchmen by SUPERMAN in September-October 1947 (S No. 48/3: "The Rarest Secret in the World!").

GUTHRIE (Prof.). An alias employed by LEX LUTHOR in September 1959 as part of his plot to destroy SUPERMAN (WF No. 104: "The Plot to Destroy Superman!").

GYPO. One of LEX LUTHOR's henchmen. By December 1960 Luthor has used plastic surgery to transform Gypo into a perfect look-alike for SUPERMAN as part of his diabolical scheme to make himself "dictator of Earth" (Act No. 271: "Voyage to Dimension X!"). (See LUTHOR, LEX.)

H

HAGEN, MATT. The unscrupulous skin diver who has achieved infamy as CLAYFACE (Det No. 298, Dec '61: "The Challenge of Clay-Face").

HALE, VERNON. A prominent member of the METROPOLIS city council, and the secret mastermind behind the city's "delivery graft racket," in which members of the "Slats" Morgan gang extort a delivery fee from truckers for every truck unloaded in Metropolis and bomb the supermarkets and other businesses whose drivers have refused to pay. Hale and the Morgan mob are apprehended by SUPERMAN in May-June 1942 (S No. 16/4: "Racket on Delivery").

HALEY, JOHN (Dr.). "One of the world's leading astronomers," who, having been secretly abducted by a gang of criminals, is replaced by a gangland impersonator who, posing as the real Dr. Haley, makes the startling announcement that SUPERMAN's body has become incurably infected with a "terrible cosmic poison-element" as the result of a head-on collision with an onrushing asteroid and that he is consequently a threat to all life on Earth, all as part of an elaborate scheme to exile Superman into outer space so that the bogus Haley and his cohorts can loot METROPOLIS's banks. The criminals are all apprehended, however, and the real Dr. Haley is rescued from their clutches, by Superman in June 1957 (Act No. 229: "The Superman Satellite").

HALK KAR. An alien from the far-distant planet Thoron, once befriended by JOR-EL after crash-landing on KRYPTON shortly before that planet exploded, who arrives on Earth in a rocket ship in

Halk Kar and Superman

January-February 1953—afflicted with amnesia and endowed with super-powers similar to, but not nearly as great as, SUPERMAN's—under circumstances that lead both Halk Kar and Superman to believe, albeit erroneously, that Halk Kar is the eldest son of Jor-El and therefore Superman's big brother. Finally, however, as the result of an electric shock he receives during Superman's battle with the "Wrecker" Ross mob—a gang of extortionists whom Superman ultimately apprehends—Halk Kar recovers his memory, recalls his visit to Krypton and brief friendship with Jor-El, and, soon afterward, bids Superman a fond farewell and blasts off for Thoron, his home planet (S No. 80/1: "Superman's Big Brother!").

HALL, BRETT. The unscrupulous brother of Ken Hall, a millionaire lumber magnate who is found dead, apparently from accidental causes, in February 1941 after drawing up a will stipulating that "all proceeds from [his] lumber camps and mills are to go towards founding a free summer camp for underprivileged youths."

After failing in a hard-fought legal battle to have the will set aside in the courts so that he can inherit his brother's millions himself, Brett Hall, who has in reality murdered his brother, masterminds an elaborate scheme—in collusion with lumber camp foreman Francois Bernier and a henchman named Cliff—to sabotage the lucrative lumber operations left behind by his brother so as to snuff out profits and deprive the camp for underprivileged youngsters of its

Halk Kar and Superman

promised income, so that ultimately he can "buy the interests for a song" and then restore them to their customary profitability.

Repeatedly thwarted by SUPERMAN, however, Brett Hall finally kills both Bernier and Cliff in a murderous rage and then dies himself moments later when a bullet he fires at LOIS LANE ricochets off a wooden roof-beam hurled in its path by Superman and hits him in the forehead (Act No. 33).

HAMILTON (Mr.). The publisher of the "yellow tabloid" *Morning Herald*, and the leader of a ring of blackmailers who knock out a U.S. senator with "sleep-gas," stage a series of compromising photographs at "a notorious roadhouse" in which the senator appears to be cavorting with a sultry brunette, and then attempt to blackmail the senator for $10,000 by threatening to publish the pictures in the *Morning Herald* and thereby ruin his career. SUPERMAN smashes the blackmail racket in November 1939 by demolishing the *Morning Herald*'s plant and equipment with his bare hands ("Up fly great printing presses...then down, smashing to smithereens...") and then ordering Hamilton and his cohorts to get out of town (Act No. 18).

HANEY, "ROCKS." A "gangland kingpin" and leader of a METROPOLIS "crime syndicate" that delivers a $2,000,000 reward to a band of hobos for capturing SUPERMAN during a period when the Man of Steel is temporarily bereft of his invulnerability and super-powers as the result of his recent exposure to some particles of red KRYPTONITE. Placed on display in a glass-walled cage in "a secret nightclub exclusively for crime big shots," Superman is about to have his life snuffed out with poison gas in the midst of "an evil carnival atmosphere" when, at the crucial moment, he turns the tables on the assembled villains and takes "Rocks" Haney and his cohorts into custody (S No. 160/1, Apr '63: pts. I-II—"The Mortal Superman!"; "The Cage of Doom!").

HANNON, HAL. A noted "old-time actor" who impersonates SUPERMAN in a carnival routine in which he mimics Superman's super-stunts with the aid of various devices he has invented himself. When a gang of criminals attempt to hire Hannon to help them commit a series of crimes, Superman impersonates Hannon and apprehends the gangsters in August 1956 (S No. 107/1: "The Make-Believe Superman").

HAPPY ACRES STATE MENTAL REHABILITATION CENTER. An insane asylum—located in the small United States town of Vineville and referred to also as the Fort Happy Acres State Sanitarium—where Clark Kent is confined in August 1963 after an encounter with red KRYPTONITE, which occurred while he was performing a rescue in his SUPERMAN identity, has afflicted him with temporary insanity. Regaining his sanity forty-eight hours later, after the effects of the red kryptonite have worn off, Kent remains in the asylum under an alias, feigning continued lunacy, long enough to teach a well-deserved lesson to a cruel sanitarium attendant

and to destroy his fingerprint file in the superintendent's office, which if examined closely, could endanger the secret of his dual identity by linking him with either Clark Kent or Superman (S No. 163/2: "The Goofy Superman!").

HARBEN, RICK. An escaped convict who lures BATMAN, ROBIN, and SUPERMAN to his hideout in a "lonely mountain range," renders them unconscious with knockout gas and a chunk of KRYPTONITE, and then shuts them inside glass cases in a state of suspended animation, where they remain until the year 2957 A.D., when they are finally discovered by mine workers searching the area for lead deposits. In the futuristic world of the thirtieth century A.D., Batman, Robin, and Superman defeat the villainous ROHTUL before returning to their own time—with the aid of a futuristic "time-ray apparatus"—to take the ruthless Harben into custody (WF No. 91, Nov/Dec '57: "The Three Super-Sleepers!").

HARRAH (Mr.). The owner of the Harrah Construction Company, a firm which has contracted to build a network of storm sewers beneath GOTHAM CITY. Mr. Harrah is secretly the escaped convict known as the MOLE (WF No. 80, Jan/Feb '56: "The Super-Newspaper of Gotham City").

HARRIGAN, "NAILS." The "hottest and most vicious crook in town," and the mastermind behind a heinous scheme to immobilize SUPERMAN with KRYPTONITE, hold him for $1,000,000 ransom from the people of METROPOLIS, and then murder him once he has been rendered sufficiently vulnerable by the kryptonite and the ransom has been paid. Aided by Dan Delta, a private detective with "mighty muscles and the heart of a lion" who "has never failed to get his man," Superman survives the murder plot and apprehends "Nails" Harrigan in September 1954 (S No. 92/3: "Superman's Last Hour!").

HARRIS, JOE. A knowledgeable, zealous young man whose lifelong dream has been to become a G-man. Rejected by the F.B.I., however, because of his claustrophobia, acrophobia, and color blindness, Jones is ultimately hired by the F.B.I. as a teacher of new recruits, thanks to the intervention of SUPERMAN (S No. 76/2, May/Jun '52: "The Misfit Manhunter!")

HARRUP II (King). The pudgy "playboy king" of the tiny Near Eastern country of Boclavia who, introduced to LOIS LANE in METROPOLIS in January-February 1951, falls instantly in love with her and obtains her promise to marry him if he can succeed in performing three nearly impossible feats worthy of her world-renowned suitor, SUPERMAN. Lois—who never intends to marry the "sincere little fellow" at all, but merely hopes to take "unfair advantage of his infatuation for her" in order to develop a sensational news story—is taught a much-needed lesson by Superman, who secretly informs the king of Lois's true motives, helps his majesty complete the three impossible tasks, and then arranges for him to withdraw from the wedding ceremony at the last possible moment with the biting but accurate announcement that "...Miss Lane is selfish and conceited, and never wanted to marry me--but only to use me as a source of news!"

"Lois is lovely, but rather--er--headstrong!" confides Harrup to Superman soon afterward. "I only hope she takes the lesson to heart!" (S No. 68/2: "Lois Lane's Royal Romance!").

HARRY'S DOG HOUSE. A diner, situated across the street from the DAILY PLANET, which is "the favorite eating place for Metropolis reporters." According to World's Finest Comics No. 47, LOIS LANE worked there as a waitress before joining the DAILY PLANET (Aug/Sep '50: "The Girl Who Hated Reporters!"), but the accuracy of this assertion is suspect because of the numerous inaccuracies contained in the text.

HASKELL, "DUKE." A METROPOLIS gang chief who—along with his cohort, "Lefty" Montez—is apprehended by SUPERMAN in July 1960 after Superman, posing as the Devil, has transported them to the interior of a dying volcano and promised to release them from "Hell" only if they agree to sign a full confession of their crimes (S No. 138/2: "Superman's Black Magic!").

HATT, AL. The creator of the comic strip *Tiny Rufe*, a money-hungry cartoonist whose unscrupulous efforts are repeatedly thwarted by SUPERMAN when, in December 1942, Hatt attempts to disrupt the romantic lives of Tiny Rufe and Maisie Day—the two real-life hillbillies whose engaging adventures provide Hatt with the plot-line for his ever-popular strip—in the belief that their impending marriage will result in a catastrophic decline in the popularity of his strip. Indeed, when the real-life Tiny Rufe and Maisie Day finally do marry, the *Tiny Rufe* comic strip fades into oblivion, but the resourceful Hatt has high hopes for his "latest and greatest inspiration," a strip based on the adventures of Superman (Act No. 55: "A Goof Named Tiny Rufe").

HAWK, JASPER. An unscrupulous promoter and swindler who launches a contest to discover a task that can stump SUPERMAN as part of an elaborate scheme to trick the Man of Steel into increasing the value of Hawk's private land holdings without realizing that he is doing it, as when Hawk asks Superman to relocate an entire mountain peak, ostensibly as a test of Superman's strength but in reality so that he and his henchmen can gain access to the vein of gold lying beneath it. Thwarted repeatedly by Superman in January-February 1948, the frustrated Hawk and his henchmen are finally apprehended by the Man of Steel when they make the mistake of baiting a deathtrap for Superman by kidnapping LOIS LANE (S No. 50/1: "The Task That Stumped Superman!").

HAWKER, JASON. A well-meaning but overzealous agent for the Bureau of Internal Revenue—sometimes referred to as James Hawker—who, having discovered that SUPERMAN has never filed a tax return, promptly declares the Man of Steel delinquent in an amount exceeding $1,000,000,000—despite the fact that Superman has contributed countless billions to charitable causes—and demands that he pay the amount in full within twenty-four hours. Hawker's somewhat more open-minded superior ultimately revokes the tax judgment, however, declaring that Superman is exempt from taxes under the terms of the "dependency clause."

"We have records proving **Superman** fed, clothed and housed needy people everywhere in the world!" declares Hawker's superior. "You might say that **Superman** has 2-1/2 billion 'dependents'... all the people on Earth!" (S No. 114/3, Jul '57: "Superman's Billion-Dollar Debt!").

HAWKINS. The butler at the Selwyn mansion (S No. 165/2, Nov '63: "The Sweetheart Superman Forgot!"; S No. 169/2, May '64: "The Man Who Stole Superman's Secret Life!"). (*See* SELWYN, DIGBY; SELWYN, SALLY.)

HAWKINS, ERSKINE (Inspector). A canny and brilliant Scotland Yard detective—described as "the finest sleuth in Europe" (Act No. 100, Sep '46: "The Sleuth Who Never Failed!—who, between 1946 and 1952, makes a series of attempts to prove, beyond any doubt, the truth of his long-held conviction that reporter Clark Kent is secretly SUPERMAN. Clark Kent has described Inspector Hawkins as "the world's greatest sleuth," and a fellow Scotland Yard inspector has described his renowned colleague this way: "That man [Hawkins] is incredible! The Yard's never had a sleuth to equal him! Imagine! Hawkins hasn't a single unsolved case on his record in 17 years!" (S No. 69/3, Mar/Apr '51: "The Man Who Didn't Know He Was Superman!").

Inspector Erskine Hawkins, 1946

In the words of the textual narrative of Superman No. 69/3:

Watch out for the mild-looking little man in the bowler hat, for he's not so mild as he looks. In England, he's known as the scourge of the underworld, for no greater sleuth has ever come out of Scotland Yard [Mar/Apr '51: "The Man Who Didn't Know He Was Superman!"].

Some uncertainty exists regarding Inspector Hawkins's first name. In the first text in which he appears, no first name is given (Act No. 100, Sep '46: "The Sleuth Who Never Failed!"). In Superman No. 69/3, he is referred to as Erskine Hawkins (Mar/Apr '51: "The Man Who Didn't Know He was Superman!"). In Superman No. 79/3, however, his first name is given as Ernest (Nov/Dec '52: "The Revenge That Took 300 Years!"). Throughout this article, he is referred to as Inspector Erskine Hawkins, since Erskine is the first of the two given names provided for him in the chronicles.

In September 1946 Inspector Hawkins accosts Clark Kent at the DAILY PLANET and quietly informs him that he has deduced that Kent is secretly Superman. Seven years previously, Hawkins had retired from his post at Scotland Yard in order to devote himself full time to solving what he regarded as his greatest case: the mystery of Superman's secret identity. Day after day, for seven long years, Europe's finest sleuth had labored at his self-appointed task. He had obtained photographs of Superman and casts of his footprints, subjecting these and other accumulated evidence to careful anatomical study and painstaking scientific analysis. Finally, after seven years of dedicated sleuthing, Hawkins had concluded that Clark Kent is Superman. The famed detective felt, however, that he could not be completely satisfied with the results of his exhaustive investigation until he had gone to America to interview Kent personally and obtain some form of final, incontrovertible proof.

Confronted by Hawkins, Kent nevertheless manages to blurt out a denial that he is secretly Superman. And so, in the days that follow, an elaborate game of cat and mouse ensues, with Inspector Hawkins laying one trap after another for the Man of Steel in an effort to obtain that one final scrap of evidence that will establish conclusively that Clark Kent is Superman, and with Superman using every ounce of his super-ingenuity to outwit the sleuth from Scotland Yard and convince him that his seven years of painstaking deduction have somehow led him to an erroneous conclusion. Finally, unable to obtain the proof he seeks any other way, Hawkins breaks into Clark Kent's apartment in hopes of finding irrefutable evidence linking Clark Kent with Superman. In the apartment, however, Hawkins finds a bogus, artificially aged will, surreptitiously planted there by Superman, in which Clark Kent bequeathes the contents of his personal library "to my friend Superman." The phony will successfully tricks Hawkins into believing that he has made a mistake, and he promptly returns to England, where he confides to a colleague that his trip to America has convinced him beyond the shadow of a doubt that Clark Kent could not possibly be Superman (Act No. 100: "The Sleuth Who Never Failed!").

Inspector Hawkins apparently rejoins Scotland Yard following his return from America, for by March-April 1951 he has solved the last of the Yard's outstanding unsolved cases and has decided to embark on a short vacation during which he hopes to remove the one blemish on his otherwise perfect record as a sleuth: his failure to solve the secret of Superman's identity. Arriving in METROPOLIS, Hawkins once again becomes embroiled in a battle of wits with Superman, but a series of complex coincidences—combined with an elaborate ruse devised by Superman—have the effect of convincing Hawkins that Superman is secretly librarian A. Noggle of the Metropolis Public Library. Indeed, Superman cleverly capitalizes on Hawkins's erroneous conclusion by "admitting" that he is really librarian Noggle and begging the Scotland Yard sleuth not to betray his "secret."

"The satisfaction of having cracked this case is enough for me," declares Hawkins reassuringly. "I therefore promise you on my word of honor that your secret *shall never pass my lips!*"

Soon afterward, Inspector Hawkins returns to Scotland Yard, convinced that he has solved the secret of Superman's dual identity, but vowing never to betray it to anyone else (S No. 69/3: "The Man Who Didn't Know He Was Superman!").

Inspector Erskine Hawkins, 1951

In November-December 1952 Inspector Hawkins finds himself only three days away from achieving one of his "life's ambitions" by being named the first winner of the renowned Standish Award, an award offered to any Scotland Yard detective who can successfully solve every single case assigned to him over a ten-year period. In an effort to thwart Hawkins's ambition and deny him the award by presenting him with a case within the three-day deadline that he cannot solve, picklock Roddy Greene and other criminals with long-standing grudges against Hawkins carry out a series of bombings in England, leaving behind, at the scene of each bombing, a rhymed note signed with the name of Guy Fawkes, an English conspirator involved in an abortive attempt to blow up King James I and Parliament in the year 1605.

Hawkins ultimately solves the bombing mystery and apprehends Roddy Greene in time to win the coveted Standish Award. In the interim, however, Clark Kent, who has been sent to England by the *Daily Planet* to cover the "Guy Fawkes" story, has been placed in the difficult position of having to work surreptitiously as Superman to prevent further bombings while covering the story openly as Clark Kent, so that he will not betray the fact that Kent and Superman are both in England and thus revive Hawkins's dormant suspicions concerning his secret identity. Indeed, despite the fact that Superman contrives to remain unseen when he defuses a bomb at London Bridge and makes it appear that a falling water tower has been responsible for dousing another bomb with water before it can blow up Big Ben, Inspector Hawkins does begin to suspect that Superman is at work behind the scenes preventing the bombings. Ultimately, however, a clever ruse by Superman succeeds in persuading the canny Scotland Yard detective that reporter Clark Kent could not possibly be Superman (S No. 79/3: "The Revenge That Took 300 Years!").

HEAVY WEAPONS GANG, THE. A gang of criminals, headquartered in an old fort on the outskirts of METROPOLIS, who commit a series of brazen crimes in both GOTHAM CITY and Metropolis with the aid of "powerful automatic weapons" capable of crushing an armored car "like an eggshell" before they are finally apprehended in September-October 1954 through the heroic efforts of BATMAN, ROBIN, and SUPERMAN (WF No. 72: "Fort Crime!").

HENKEL (Miss). The pen name employed by LOIS LANE in writing her advice-to-the-lovelorn column for the DAILY PLANET (S No. 18/3, Sep/Oct '42: "The Man with the Cane").

HERCULES. The most famous Greek legendary hero, a mighty hunter and warrior born to Alcmene and fathered by Zeus.

In May-June 1944 a member of METROPOLIS's Liars Club wins the club's coveted Best Tall Tale award for a tale he concocts concerning a fictional meeting between SUPERMAN and Hercules. In the story, Superman encounters the legendary hero after allowing himself to be sent into the distant past—to ancient Greece in the age of the mighty Greek gods and goddesses—in order to test a time machine invented by scientist Professor Button. To his great surprise, the Man of Steel discovers that the man who has been immortalized in myth as a great hunter and warrior was actually a puny, cowardly weakling. And so, to safeguard Hercules's hallowed place in folklore, Superman performs the legendary twelve labors in

Hercules's stead, thereby keeping alive Hercules's reputation as the greatest Greek hero (S No. 28/3: "Stand-In for Hercules!").

In August 1960 "renegade scientist" LEX LUTHOR, serving out a term in Bleak Rock Prison, constructs an ingenious "time ray" out of parts from an alarm clock and other everyday materials and uses it to draw the mighty Hercules "through the time-barrier" from the ancient past to Luthor's prison cell in the twentieth century. By duping the legendary hero into believing that he has been wrongfully imprisoned by "an evil king" who stole his gold and hid it underground, Luthor is able to trick Hercules into using his superhuman strength to break Luthor out of prison and help him loot FORT KNOX. Ultimately, however, Hercules discovers that he has been duped into helping Luthor commit crimes, and he seizes the evil scientist and turns him over to Superman.

When the Man of Steel offers to return Hercules to his own era by carrying him back across the time barrier, Hercules asks if he might remain in Metropolis awhile "to observe your future civilization!" Superman consents, but suggests that Hercules adopt an alternate identity during his sojourn in the twentieth century so that he will not be mobbed by curiosity-seekers everywhere he goes. Superman rents Hercules a place to stay, buys him a wardrobe of modern clothes, and gets him a job as a newspaper reporter, under the pseudonym Roger Tate, on the DAILY PLANET.

An unforeseen complication arises, however, when "Roger Tate" becomes infatuated with LOIS LANE ("Great Olympia!" he thinks to himself. "Lois l-looks like a...a bewitching goddess!") and begs her to marry him. When Lois declines, citing Superman as her true love ("No one else can match **Superman!**" sighs Lois), Hercules flexes his powerful muscles, totally demolishing his "Roger Tate" business-suit disguise, and stands revealed in the brief animal-skin costume of the mighty Hercules. "Behold!" proclaims Hercules. "I was the mightiest hero of my past age as **Superman** is of **this age!**" Nevertheless, Lois refuses to marry Hercules, explaining that "...**Superman** is **still** my big heart-throb!"

Hurt at having been spurned by the woman he loves, yet determined to somehow win her away from the Man of Steel, Hercules attempts, in the days that follow, to impress Lois with "mighty deeds" and feats of superhuman strength. It soon becomes apparent, however, that Hercules cannot hope to compete with Superman, for while Superman possesses many super-powers, Hercules possesses only superhuman strength. To rectify the imbalance, Hercules journeys to "The ancient **Oracle's Cave**," near Athens, Greece, where he communicates with the ancient gods and heroes, including Venus, Vulcan, Mercury, Jupiter, and Achilles. After misleading the ancients into believing that he has undertaken a noble "mission" in the twentieth century, Hercules tells them that his efforts are doomed to failure "unless I gain magic powers and weapons from all of you!"

"Granted, my son!" proclaims Jupiter, as the great gods and heroes reach out simultaneously to touch Hercules. "At our touch, our individual **Olympus powers** will flow into you! The **magic weapons** will appear later as you need them!...

"Use the Olympus powers and magic weapons wisely, my son!" adds Jupiter. "Do not shame us! They must do **good!**"

"They'll do good all right," thinks Hercules, "... for me! Ha, ha!"

Moments later, outside the ancient Oracle's Cave, Hercules launches himself into the sky to begin his journey back to America. "The first **Olympus power** from **Mercury**, the flying god, made winged sandals appear on my feet!" muses Hercules. "And my other **magic powers** will make me **superior** to Superman!"

Endowed with the power of flight by Mercury's winged sandals, Hercules soars skyward from Athens, Greece, en route to Metropolis, 1960

Later, back in Metropolis, Hercules gloats inwardly at the prospect of his coming battle with Superman. "Lois spurned me for [that] super-wretch!" he thinks to himself. "But I'll crush **Superman** with my **super-Olympus powers**...!" (Act No. 267: "Hercules in the 20th Century!").

Encountering Superman soon afterward at a local amusement park, Hercules avails himself of all the mighty Olympus powers at his command—including the invulnerability of Achilles, the "magic flames" of Vulcan, and the "magic lightning bolts" of Jupiter—in an effort to humiliate and defeat the Man of Steel, but Superman successfully counters each new assault. Finally, however, calling on the eerie power of Apollo's magic flute, Hercules plays a "magic lullaby" that puts Superman into a deep sleep from which he will not awaken for 100 years. Lois Lane selflessly offers to marry Hercules if only he will awaken Superman from his hundred-year sleep, but at that moment, Venus, the goddess of love, appears on the scene. After angrily chastising Hercules for having used the Olympus powers to perform "bad deeds," Venus uses her own magic to awaken Superman from his magically induced slumber.

Moments later, by tricking Hercules into chasing after him at incredible superhuman speed, Superman lures the legendary warrior "across the time-barrier into the past," to the exact moment in time when the force of Luthor's time ray first began to draw him into the twentieth century. Stranded now in his own past era, Hercules will, due to the aftereffects of time travel, retain no recollection whatever of either his journey to twentieth-century Metropolis or his battle with Superman (Act No. 268, Sep '60: "Superman's Battle with Hercules!").

A text for August 1961 contains an "imaginary tale" in which Superman journeys into the past to the eras of Hercules and Samson and then returns with them through the time barrier to twentieth-century Metropolis as potential mates for Lois Lane and LANA LANG. Smitten at first sight with the two lovely modern women, Hercules and Samson beg Lois and Lana to marry them—and Lois and Lana accept—but the women soon prove to be so bitchy, demanding, and indecisive, and life with them promises to be such a continual torment, that the two heroes soon abandon their twentieth-century fiancées in favor of returning to their homes in the ancient past (Act No. 279: "The Super-Rivals!").

In August 1962 COSMIC MAN impersonates Hercules as part of an elaborate ruse, devised by Superman, for bringing "notorious gang-leader" DUKE MARPLE to justice (S No. 155/2: "The Downfall of Superman!").

In January 1964, during a visit to an extradimensional "parallel world," Superman encounters an extradimensional counterpart of the Hercules who inhabits his own dimension. On this world, which is "an exact duplicate of the **real** Earth, except that certain events and situations are mixed up," Hercules bears a striking resemblance to the Goliath of Superman's world and even battles a shepherd boy much as the real Goliath fought David. The extradimensional Hercules is vulnerable to red KRYPTONITE much as Superman is vulnerable to green kryptonite, and is required to perform only six Herculean labors as opposed to the traditional twelve. When the extradimensional Hercules is left weakened and feverish after an encounter with red kryptonite, Superman pitches in to help him fulfill his labors until Hercules has sufficiently recovered to perform the remaining ones himself (Act No. 308: "Superman Meets the Goliath-Hercules!").

In January 1965 Superman battles and defeats a trio of extradimensional villains—endowed with superhuman strength as well as magical powers—who are perfect look-alikes for the Hercules, Samson, and Atlas who inhabit various past eras in Superman's own dimension (Act No. 320: "The Three Super-Enemies!").

HERVEY (Mr.). A botanist who, by December 1949-January 1950, has "developed a fertilizer which causes ordinary flowers to reach enormous size in a single day — but, alas — they wilt back to normal size and die at sunset.... However, while growing — they release incredible quantities of oxygen — enough to pollute the air and make folks light-headed." J. WILBUR WOLFINGHAM obtains some of Hervey's fertilizer and attempts to use it in a scheme to loot METROPOLIS, but Wolfingham's scheme is ultimately thwarted by SUPERMAN (WF No. 43: "When Metropolis Went Mad!").

HIGGINS (Professor). The "well-meaning scientist" who is the inventor of the amnesia machine, a machine designed to induce amnesia and thus enable troubled people everywhere to forget their past problems and make fresh starts. The amnesia machine is stolen by the MOOSE COLLINS gang in March-April 1952 (S No. 75/3: "The Man Who Stole Memories!").

HIGHVILLE. A METROPOLIS suburb whose residents have become mistakenly convinced, through a series of deceptive coincidences, that a local resident named Hal is secretly SUPERMAN. When, in January 1957, Hal sets out to convince his neighbors that he is really not Superman at all, he unwittingly endangers the real Superman's secret identity, thus forcing Superman to go to extraordinary lengths—including the deliberate creation of an unscheduled eclipse of the sun—to safeguard the secret of his Clark Kent identity while at the same time persuading the people of Highville that they have erred in concluding that Hal is Superman (S No. 110/2: "The Mystery Superman!").

HI-JACK. A cunning criminal—clad in a green and purple costume with a jack of spades emblazoned on his chest—who matches wits with SUPERMAN in November-December 1943. He is in reality Jack Jackson, a debt-ridden METROPOLIS banker, in desperate need of funds to cover his stock losses, who concocts the idea of a "fantastic villain" with a "bizarre name" in hopes of diverting suspicion from himself while he stages a series of spectacular robberies, including the theft of $1,000,000 in silver bullion from the vaults of his own bank. Cornered finally by Superman, Jackson attempts suicide rather than face capture, but Superman thwarts the attempt and takes Jackson into custody (S No. 25/4: "Hi-Jack--Jackal of Crime!").

HITLER, ADOLF (1889-1945). The Austrian-born politician who was dictator of Germany from 1933 until his death by suicide in his Berlin bunker in 1945. The Martian dictator MARTLER is an admirer of Hitler (S No. 62/1, Jan/Feb '50: "Black Magic on Mars!"), and Razkal, the tyrannical ruler of OXNALIA, closely resembles him (S No. 15/3, Mar/Apr '42). HERR FANGE obtains Hitler's permission to ravage Allied shipping in January-February 1943 (S No. 20/2: "Destroyers from the Depths"), and Ixnayal-pay, the ruler of the SQUIFFLES, makes a secret pact with Hitler to sabotage America's aircraft industry in May-June 1943 (S No. 22/1: "Meet the Squiffles!").

HOCUS AND POCUS. The professional names employed by a pair of likable, ingenuous, gullible fellows—their real names are Doc and Flannelhead—who start out as street-corner salesmen of magic books, only to have their lives transformed when a series of bizarre coincidences convinces them that they have somehow become gifted with magical powers. Doc, better known as Hocus, is the brains of the outfit; he is a wiry little fellow with a moustache, eyeglasses, and an ever-present derby hat "who speaks like a college professor but has the trusting simplicity of a child!" His companion, Flannelhead, better known as Pocus, a brawny, dim-witted fellow who murders the King's English whenever he speaks, "has the strength of an ox... and about the same I.Q.!" Together with their "mascot," a white rabbit named Moiton (Act No. 88, Sep '45: "The Adventure of the Stingy Men!"), the pair inhabit a furnished room in Mrs. Flaherty's Boarding House, somewhere in METROPOLIS (Act No. 83, Apr '45: "Hocus & Pocus... Magicians by Accident!"). Superman No. 45/1 refers to them as "that hilarious pair of cuckoo conjurers" (Mar/Apr '47: "Lois Lane, Superwoman!"), and, because their magical feats work only through either coincidence or the surreptitious intervention of SUPERMAN, they are frequently described as "magicians by accident" (Act No. 97, Jun '46: "The Magician's Convention!"; and others).

Hocus and Pocus, 1945

In April 1945 Doc and Flannelhead—who have been eking out a meager living giving magic demonstrations on street corners and selling books on magic to passersby—become convinced, through a series of freak occurrences and ludicrous coincidences, that Doc has somehow acquired the power to make whatever he wishes come true merely by reciting the wish aloud, accompanied by the phrase "Abracadabra... alacazam... hocus-pocus!" Complications arise for the well-meaning prestidigitators, however, when their magical abilities come to the attention of gangster Hijack Dorley, who wants them to use their supposed powers to help his gang loot a safe in a wealthy private home. Out of a sense of adventure more than anything else, Doc agrees to the scheme, confiding privately to Flannelhead that he intends to use his magic powers to return the stolen loot to its rightful owner immediately following the robbery. When Hijack Dorley asks his two new recruits to tell him their names, Doc replies that their real names are Doc and Flannelhead, but that they prefer to be known professionally as Hocus and Pocus.

The attempt to rob the safe is thwarted by the timely arrival of Superman, but Hocus and Pocus escape—along with their underworld allies—when the Man of Steel is forced to break off the battle to attend to an emergency under circumstances that make it appear, to both the Dorley gang and the amateur magicians, that it is Doc's magic that has forced Superman to beat a hasty retreat. When, back at the criminals' hideout, Doc announces that he and Flannelhead have had enough of crime, Hijack Dorley and his henchmen take them captive so that they can continue to use Doc's "powers" to stage spectacular crimes.

Hocus and Pocus are ultimately rescued from their dire predicament by Superman, who invades the criminals' hideout and apprehends the Dorley gang at invisible super-speed, leaving both gangsters and magicians with the wholly erroneous impression that the criminals have been routed by Doc's magical powers.

"But you don't understand!" stammers Superman, trying, without success, to explain the unwelcome truth to Hocus and Pocus. "I..."

"I know," interrupts Doc knowingly. "You're worried lest we use it [Doc's ability to perform magical feats] for evil purposes. On the contrary, we shall use it to wage war against crime. We are going to open up... a private detective agency!"

"Oh well, who am I to disillusion them?" muses Superman to himself. "I guess from now on I'll have to keep an eye on them and make the magic of Hocus and Pocus more than just accident!" (Act No. 83: "Hocus & Pocus... Magicians by Accident!").

By September 1945 Doc and Flannelhead have indeed opened a detective agency. A sign on the door reads: "Hocus-Pocus, Super-Magicians," and below that the words, "Also Detectives." When a client offers the two self-styled magician-detectives $200 to entertain his guests with magic tricks at his forthcoming lawn party—and Superman overhears Doc announce his intention to use the fee to buy war bonds—Superman decides to help Doc earn the money for that worthy cause by working behind the scenes at invisible super-speed to make Doc's "magic" actually succeed, as when he surreptitiously helps Doc "materialize" an elephant by racing to the zoo at faster-than-light speed and delivering the gigantic animal to the lawn party in the twinkling of an eye. Since no one at the party is aware of Superman's presence, Doc and Flannelhead and all of the party guests attribute the appearance of the elephant to Doc's "magical powers."

One guest who is particularly impressed, however, is "confidence man and flim-flam artist" Roger "Nifty" Nolan. Posing as the president of a home for foundlings, Nolan plays on Doc's and Flannelhead's gullibility and warmheartedness in order to make them his dupes in a scheme to bilk two stingy Metropolis millionaires out of $250,000. Nolan persuades the well-meaning magicians to use their magic powers to place the two millionaires in "perilous situations where they will be as helpless as foundlings," so that, continues Nolan, "they will realize that money is not everything" and freely contribute $250,000 toward the construction of a new home for foundlings.

Realizing from the outset that Nolan intends to wait until Hocus and Pocus have solicited the contributions from the two millionaires and then murder the two magicians and abscond with the money, Superman nevertheless works invisibly behind the scenes to make Doc's "magic" work in order to help the magicians acquire the funds needed to build the new foundling home. Then, just as the ruthless confidence man is on the verge of killing Hocus and Pocus, the Man of Steel intervenes to apprehend Nolan and rescue the well-meaning magicians from his clutches. Nolan will go to jail, the new foundling home will be built, and Doc still believes he possesses magical powers (Act No. 88: "The Adventure of the Stingy Men!").

In June 1946 Doc and Flannelhead attend a magicians' convention, where a prize of $25,000 is being offered to the magician who can perform a magic trick capable of stumping all the other magicians. When unscrupulous magician Conrad the Conjurer, convinced that he will never be able to outdo Hocus and Pocus, hires some hoodlums to kidnap the two magicians to prevent them from being on hand to compete for the prize money, Superman intervenes to apprehend Conrad the Conjurer and his cohorts and rescue Hocus and Pocus from the villains' clutches.

Soon afterward, another magician at the convention, Gregor the Great, hires Hocus and Pocus to recover the secret plans for the fantastic new trick he intends to perform in the magicians' contest, which have been stolen by criminals and are being held for $10,000 ransom. With some invisible assistance from the Man of Steel, Hocus and Pocus succeed in recovering Gregor's plans and capturing the criminals. Hocus and Pocus are unaware, however, that the real purpose of Gregor's trick—an elaborate escape illusion involving Gregor's being imprisoned in an airtight steel box submerged in a tank of water—is to enable him to rob the safe of the hotel where the convention is being held by escaping unseen from the specially constructed steel box during the performance of his trick, looting the safe, and then returning to the box in time to "escape" from it for the finale of his trick. Superman, however, has divined Gregor's real motive for performing this particular trick, and, working at invisible super-speed, he apprehends Gregor in the act of robbing the hotel safe, while making it appear that Hocus and Pocus have thwarted the robbery by means of their magic. Indeed, at story's end, Hocus and Pocus have won the magicians' contest, still under the delusion that Doc can actually perform real magic (Act No. 97: "The Magician's Convention!").

In March-April 1947, while Clark Kent and LOIS

LANE are visiting the office of Hocus and Pocus in order to interview them for the DAILY PLANET, Lois accidentally trips over a balcony railing and plummets toward seemingly certain doom on the sidewalk below. Just as Clark Kent is about to leap to Lois's rescue, even at the cost of betraying his secret identity, Doc gets the idea of using his "magic" to transform Clark Kent into Superman so that Kent can fly through the air to rescue Lois. And so, in hopes of protecting the secret of his dual identity, Kent rescues the falling Lois and then pretends that it was Doc's magical powers that enabled him to temporarily change into Superman.

A complication arises, however, when Doc offers to demonstrate his "powers" again by using them to endow Lois Lane with super-powers, for now, in order to protect his own identity, Superman must contrive to make it appear as though Doc has actually succeeded in conferring super-powers on Lois. And so, in the period that follows, Superman works behind the scenes to make it seem that Lois Lane has become magically transformed into a "superwoman," as when he makes it appear that she has single-handedly apprehended the notorious BBB Gang, a "cold, violent, inhuman" underworld trio "whose vicious crimes blot the police ledgers of 16 states!" Ultimately, however, by means of an elaborate ruse designed to make Lois feel that it is unfeminine to be super-powerful, Superman persuades Lois to pay Doc to use his "magic" to deprive her of her super-powers and turn her back into plain Lois Lane again. Everyone concerned, except for Superman, believes that it was Doc's powers that gave Lois super-powers and then took them away again. Only the Man of Steel knows that it was only his surreptitious intervention that, for a time, transformed Lois Lane into a superwoman (S No. 45/1: "Lois Lane, Super-woman!").

HOGAN (Fire Chief). The chief of the Metropolis Fire Department. When CLARK KENT is appointed a "temporary fireman" in May 1959 in order to enable him to "write a feature on the perils of fire-fighting," Hogan is disgruntled, believing that Kent, cowardly and inexperienced, will be a hazard to his men while they are engaged in their perilous work. In a mean, small-minded attempt to either frighten Kent off the fire department or create an excuse for summarily discharging him, Hogan repeatedly issues Kent the fire brigade's most hazardous assignments, thereby forcing Kent to either fulfill the assignments or abandon his feature. For Kent, the fire chief's high-handed behavior creates the additional aggravation of having to carry out what appear to be life-risking assignments in his role as Clark Kent without endangering the secret of his dual identity by betraying either his courage or his super-powers. Ultimately, however, Kent prevails, thwarting Hogan at every turn, fighting fires as fireman Clark Kent without revealing his super-powers, and successfully accumulating the material he needs for his DAILY PLANET feature on fire-fighting (S No. 129/2: "Clark Kent, Fireman of Steel!").

HOKUM, ABNER. A quick-witted, albeit mildly unscrupulous, genius at promotion and publicity who literally sells the promotional services of SUPERMAN to private businesses—as when he guarantees the management of the Bingley Circus that Superman will appear and do a series of super-stunts for them—and then concocts elaborate yet somehow engaging schemes for tricking Superman into keeping the outrageous commitments he has made for him. Superman finally turns the tables on the wily Hokum, but Hokum accepts his defeat good-naturedly and indicates his intention to follow Superman's suggestion that he look for a job as an advertising executive (S No. 109/1, Nov '56: "The Man Who Stole Superman's Powers").

HOLMES, SHERLOCK. The world's foremost fictional detective, the creation of English novelist and historian Sir Arthur Conan Doyle (1859-1930). SUPERMAN meets the famed storybook sleuth and converses with him briefly in December 1961 after exposure to red KRYPTONITE has temporarily endowed him with the power to make his wishes come true, and he has absentmindedly wished that Sherlock Holmes were on the scene to help him solve the perplexing mystery of who built the bizarre red-kryptonite statue on Rock Island in Metropolis Bay (Act No. 283: "The Red Kryptonite Menace!"). (See JAN-DEX.)

"HONEST" JOHN. The operator of a gambling ship anchored safely beyond the 12-mile limit, and the leader of a gang of criminals who are apprehended by SUPERMAN in May 1958—along with the members of the rival Shark Gang—with the aid of JIMMY OLSEN, PERRY WHITE, and members of the U.S. Coast Guard (S No. 121/3: "Jimmy Hits the Jackpot").

HOOPS, ANDY. A "shiftless ne'er-do-well," disdainful of honest work ("Someday . . . I'll be rolling in the green stuff . . without having to exercise my muscles for it!"), who successfully blackmails SUPERMAN into making him wealthy by threatening to expose a long-forgotten misdeed perpetrated by Metropolis Bank president Carl Denby, whose exposure would mean the ruin of Denby's career. Later, however, when gangster Marty O'Ghool tries to force Hoops to reveal the secret of his hold over Superman, Hoops realizes the error of his greedy ways. the O'Ghool mob is ultimately apprehended by Superman, but only after Hoops has heroically sacrificed his life to prevent the fleeing O'Ghool from gunning down reporter LOIS LANE (S No. 26/3, Jan/Feb '44: "Superman's Master!").

HROGUTH. A green-skinned alien from the far-distant planet Durim, an "eccentric scientist" who several years ago acquired superhuman powers similar to SUPERMAN's as the result of being inadvertently exposed to the rays of a mysterious fallen meteor while hiking on his native planet, and who then embarked on a diabolical new career as a ruthless super-criminal.

In March 1962, accompanied by two henchmen, Hroguth journeys to Earth to steal a supply of copper, an element not available on Durim, for the construction of a special machine designed to permanently drain away the super-powers of the teen-ager Logi, another native of Durim, who had also acquired superhuman powers after exposure to the meteor but who had, in contrast, devoted his life to the cause of justice and become Hroguth's mortal foe on their native planet.

On Earth, Hroguth steals the copper he needs and constructs his machine, only to be apprehended along with his henchmen soon afterward—and permanently robbed of his super-powers by forced exposure to his own device—through the heroic efforts of BATMAN, ROBIN, Superman, and the alien crime-fighter Logi (WF No. 124: "The Mystery of the Alien Super-Boy!").

HTRAE. The home world of the Bizarros. Located light-years away in space in "another far-off solar system" (Act No. 263, Apr '60: "The World of Bizarros!"), it is "the maddest planet in the universe" (S No. 150/1, Jan '62: "The One Minute of Doom!"), a wacky, cockeyed world where "perfection is hated and everything is mixed up," and where "all earthly customs are backwards" (S No. 143/3, Feb '61: "Bizarro Meets Frankenstein!"). The capital of Htrae is BIZARRO CITY, "a crude copy of Metropolis" (see METROPOLIS) which "looks like something a mad architect would design," and the flag of Htrae is a "backward imitation" of the American flag, with alternating blue and white horizontal stripes, and red stars on a field of white (Act No. 263, Apr '60: "The World of Bizarros!").

Originally colonized by BIZARRO and BIZARRO-LOIS, the planet—which is frequently referred to as "the Bizarro world"—was populated soon afterward by numerous additional Bizarros created by means of an ingenious "imitator machine" and was christened Htrae (Earth spelled backwards) by its Bizarro inhabitants (Act No. 263, Apr '60: "The World of Bizarros!"). To the everlasting joy of the Bizarro population, SUPERMAN transforms Htrae from a conventional round world into a zany-looking cube-shaped one during a visit to the planet in 1960 (Act No. 264, May '60: "The Superman Bizarro!"). Superman No. 140 describes Htrae as

...the strangest planet in existence....
    The capital of this incredible world is a city of crooked structures, seemingly designed by a mad architect!
    Hours are numbered the wrong way on its crazy clocks, and [its American] flags are upside-down with the stars and stripes wrongly colored!
    On this mixed-up world, coal is used for money...and words are all misspelled!
    Queerest of all, the people are all imperfect doubles of Superman and Lois Lane, living in a world where everything is the opposite of things on Earth! [Oct '60: pts. I-III—"The Son of Bizarro!"; "The 'Orphan' Bizarro!"; "The Bizarro Supergirl!"]

On Htrae, the Bizarros have established "a mad imitation of earthly civilization," where skyscrapers "lean crookedly at all angles" (S No. 143/3, Feb '6 "Bizarro Meets Frankenstein!"); meals are serve backwards, starting with coffee and ending wi soup; a film at the local movie theater is "shown fro a negative of the film," so that "the white clouds a black, and the black mountains below are white (Act No. 263, Apr '60: "The World of Bizarros!"); stre cleaners cover the city streets with layers of dirt No. 140, Oct '60: pts. I-III—"The Son of Bizarro "The 'Orphan' Bizarro!"; "The Bizarro Supergirl!" alarm clocks tell people when to go to sleep instead when to wake up; and, following the bizarre logic of "crazy calendar," all "earthly holidays are m placed," so that Christmas is celebrated on Ju fourth, Halloween takes place on December twent fourth, and Independence Day occurs on Thanksgi ing (S No. 143/3, Feb '61: "Bizarro Meets Franke stein!"). All life is lived according to the topsy-tur precepts of the Bizarro Code: "Us do opposite of a earthly things!" states the code. "Us hate beauty! l love ugliness! Is big crime to make anythin perfect on Bizarro world!" (Act No. 263, Apr '6 "The World of Bizarros!").

By April 1960, having abandoned Earth in th hope of making a new home for themselves som where in outer space, Bizarro and Bizarro-Lois hav arrived on a world in a far-off solar system and com upon the ruins of an ancient city whose alie population was "wiped out" by some unknow calamity sometime in the distant past. The tw Bizarros decide to make their home there, but as tim passes Bizarro-Lois becomes lonely for "friends t talk to," and so, to fulfill his mate's need f companionship, Bizarro uses the superscientifi apparatus in the ruins of an ancient laboratory t construct an ingenious "imitator machine" wit which he soon creates hundreds of Bizarro-Loises i the exact image of his mate.

Bizarro-Lois's joy at her new-found friendship quickly turns to jealousy, however, as the newl created female Bizarros begin to covet the affection of Bizarro, the only male on the entire planet. At th insistence of the original Bizarro-Lois, Bizarr focuses the amazing imitator machine on himsel thereby creating a host of Bizarros like himself, on for every Bizarro-Lois on Htrae. Together the mal and female Bizarros—all of them imperfect dupl cates of Superman and LOIS LANE—set abou dismantling the crumbling ruins of the ancient alie city and transforming them into a wacky capita called Bizarro City. The original Bizarro became "th tribe's leader." He and his consort, the origina Bizarro-Lois, rule Htrae together from atop ston thrones in a ramshackle "palace." Superman has a adventure on Htrae in April 1960 (Act No. 263: "Th World of Bizarros!") which culminates in his trans forming the entire planet from a round one into cube-shaped one—to the great delight of the Bizarr population—with the aid of a "super-large bulldozer of his own creation (Act No. 264, May '60: "Th Superman Bizarro!"). (See BIZARRO.)

"Far off in space spins the strangest planet in existence,"
the planet Htrae, known also as "the Bizarro world"

In October 1960 Bizarro constructs his Fortress of Bizarro on the planet Htrae, and an infant son, born to Bizarro-Lois, becomes the first Bizarro actually born on the planet as opposed to having been created artificially by Bizarro's imitator machine. During this same period, Htrae declares war on the planet Earth, but Superman resolves the conflict and large-scale hostilities are averted (S No. 140: pts. I-III—"The Son of Bizarro!"; "The 'Orphan' Bizarro!"; "The Bizarro Supergirl!"). (See BIZARRO.)

In January 1962, when Superman and the other survivors of the exploded planet KRYPTON—including SUPERGIRL, KRYPTO THE SUPERDOG, the citizens of KANDOR, and even the villains imprisoned in the PHANTOM ZONE—bow their heads solemnly for one full minute of silence to commemorate the anniversary of the destruction of Krypton, the Bizarros of Htrae celebrate the occasion with a full minute of loud, joyously raucous noise, not out of any malice for the doomed millions of Krypton, but only out of the zaniness that characterizes their race (S No. 150/1: "The One Minute of Doom!").

HUNTER (Professor). The inventor of a powerful "new anaesthetic gas" being sought by the evil BARON MUNSDORF. Professor Hunter is also the inventor of the "deadly sub-atomic death-ray gun" with which the treacherous baron "unleashes a bolt of incredible voltage" at SUPERMAN in December 1940 (Act No. 31).

HUNTERS' CLUB, THE. A "world-famous" club for METROPOLIS hunters whose members are mainly egotistical blowhards who let their native guides do the actual hunting, then brag incessantly about their so-called daring exploits. When three brave, sportsmanlike hunters are denied admission to the club because they lack the requisite animal-head trophies, SUPERMAN helps them bag a trio of incredible "trophies"—a live brontosaurus, mastodon, and sea serpent—in order to teach the pompous members of the Hunters' Club a well-deserved lesson in humility (S No. 50/3, Jan/Feb '48: "The Hunters' Club!").

HUNTLEY, ALFRED. A noted METROPOLIS philanthropist who, having spent his entire life helping others, is helped in turn by SUPERMAN in November 1954 after a run of bad luck has dampened his attitude toward life and threatens to tempt him into a life of crime (S No. 93/3: "The Man Superman Feared!").

HUTTON, BERT. The alias employed by ex-convict HAL COLBY in May 1962 when he poses as a TV producer as part of his scheme to unravel the secret of SUPERMAN's identity (Act No. 288: "The Man Who Exposed Superman!").

HYPER-MAN. A super-hero on the far-distant planet Oceania—clad in a purple costume with green trunks, orange boots and cape, a yellow belt, and a stylized yellow "H" emblazoned on his chest—who bears a close physical resemblance to SUPERMAN and whose origin, career, and secret civilian life closely parallel the Man of Steel's.

Born on the far-distant planet Zoron, "a world of heavy gravity" faced with impending extinction, the infant Hyper-Man was placed inside a rocket by his father and launched into outer space, the sole survivor of his planet, as behind him the entire planet Zoron exploded into stardust. Arriving on the planet Oceania, "a smaller planet" of "light gravity" described as "almost a twin of Earth," Hyper-Man instantly acquired super-powers identical to Superman's, grew to manhood in the home of loving foster parents, the King family, and, protected by his secret identity, that of mild-mannered Chester King, began a colorful career in crime-fighting under the name Hyper-Boy while still in his teens.

Upon the death of his foster parents, Chester King moved to the large city of Macropolis, a close counterpart of Earth's METROPOLIS, obtained employment as a "roving television reporter" for the Oceania Network—where his editor bears a striking resemblance to Earth's PERRY WHITE, and where girl reporter Lydia Long plays a role in his life paralleling that played by LOIS LANE in the life of Superman—and continued his career in crime-fighting as the dynamic Hyper-Man.

When Hyper-Man arrives on Earth in June 1960 to ask Superman to return with him to Oceania to help him preserve the secret of his dual identity, Superman routinely feeds Hyper-Man's life-history data into the "super-univac" at his FORTRESS OF SOLITUDE—so that the giant electronic brain can "work out a complete history of [Hyper-Man's] future life for [Superman's] files"—and learns, to his horror, that Hyper-Man will lose his super-powers within twenty-four hours and die within the year as the result of his prolonged exposure to a substance called blue zoronite, a fragment of the exploded planet Zoron that is as deadly to Hyper-Man as KRYPTONITE is to Superman.

Rather than inform Hyper-Man of his computer's grim prediction, however, Superman accompanies Hyper-Man to Oceania and, through a series of seeming "blunders," forces Hyper-Man into premature retirement by exposing his secret identity to the entire population of Oceania and by feigning responsibility for the loss of Hyper-Man's super-powers actually caused by the zoronite. The forced abandonment of his super-hero career, however, frees Chester King to marry Lydia Long, a luxury he could never have permitted himself while he remained active as Hyper-Man.

A year later, with his wife Lydia by his bedside, Chester King—the former super-hero of the planet Oceania—dies, as Superman knew he would, but Superman's strategy of forcing him into early retirement has at least enabled him to enjoy a full year of wedded bliss without being tortured by the agonizing knowledge of his impending death from zoronite poisoning (Act No. 265: "The 'Superman' from Outer Space!").

I

ILLIUM-349. A rare radioactive element "whose rays can change the size of the body!" By October 1958 the renegade Kandorian scientist ZAK-KUL has successfully "isolated" the rare element and used it to create an ingenious reducing and enlarging ray which can be used to either shrink or enlarge a person to any chosen size (Act No. 245: "The Shrinking Superman!"). In October 1964, while experimenting with the substance in the hope of using it to power an "enlarger ray" with which to safely enlarge KANDOR and its population to normal human size, the elderly Kandorian scientist NOR-KAN is struck in the brain by "a fatal dose of radiation" and dies almost instantly (Act No. 317: "Superman's Rainbow Face!").

"INSECT MASTER, THE." A malevolent scientist, clad in a bizarre purple and gray costume and headquartered in a secret laboratory hideout in the depths of "perilous" Swasey Swamp, who unleashes hordes of insects on the city of METROPOLIS by means of his diabolical "insect projectiles"—as when he dispatches a storm of locusts to devastate the city's horticultural gardens—as part of a fiendish scheme to extort tribute money from the Metropolis city government. Cornered finally by SUPERMAN and determined to resist capture at any cost, "The Insect Master" sets fire to his own laboratory and perishes in the ensuing inferno (WF No. 10, Sum '43: "The Insect Terror!").

INVISIBLE KID, THE. A member of the LEGION OF SUPER-HEROES. A native of the planet Earth, the Invisible Kid has the power—acquired by means of a serum that he himself invented—to make himself wholly or partially invisible at will. The Invisible Kid's real name is Lyle Norg.

In October 1962, when SUPERMAN is believed to be dying of an incurable malady, the Invisible Kid is among the Legionnaires who are summoned to the twentieth century by SUPERGIRL to help carry out the gigantic super-tasks that Superman hopes to fulfill as his final legacy to humanity, including the destruction of a "vast cloud of fungus in distant space, that will some day reach Earth and blight all plant life," and the melting of the Antarctic ice, "to make Antarctica a fit place for millions to live in the future," thus ensuring "a home for Earth's expanding population...!" (S No. 156: "The Last Days of Superman!" pts. I-III—"Superman's Death Sentence!"; "The Super-Comrades of All Time!"; "Superman's Last Day of Life!").

In October 1964, after Superman has been deprived of his super-powers by the baleful radiations of a mysterious green comet, the Invisible Kid and two of his fellow Legionnaires—COSMIC BOY and SATURN GIRL—use a "time-force wave carrier" in their thirtieth-century Clubhouse to endow Superman temporarily with their various powers so that he can use them in his upcoming battle with LEX LUTHOR and BRAINIAC. For a period of "a few hours," therefore, until his borrowed powers fade and vanish, Superman is equipped with the Invisible Kid's "power of invisibility," Cosmic Boy's "power of super-magnetism," and Saturn Girl's "power of telepathic thought-casting" (S No. 172: pts. I-III—"The New Superman!"; "Clark Kent—Former Superman!"; "The Struggle of the Two Supermen!").

IRON IKE. A METROPOLIS "crime lord" and leader of a gang of criminals who are apprehended by SUPERMAN in December 1965 while attempting to steal a fortune in diamonds from the penthouse showroom of a Metropolis diamond merchant. Superman's efforts to capture the Iron Ike gang, and in fact all of his activities during this period, are severely complicated by the fact that a phony newspaper headline identifying CLARK KENT as Superman, set in type at the instigation of LOIS LANE and intended merely as a playful joke, has accidentally received widespread public distribution, with the result that Kent has been asked to "impersonate" Superman temporarily in order to save the DAILY PLANET from embarrassment and perhaps even increase its circulation in the process, thus making it difficult for Superman to perform his normal super-heroic duties (Act No. 331: "Clark Kent's Masquerade as Superman!"). The story is in many respects similar to Superman No. 20/1 (Jan/Feb '43: "Superman's Secret Revealed!"). (See GROGAN, "IRONJAW.")

"INSIDER, THE." A mysterious underworld mastermind, so named because the crimes for which he is responsible invariably require specialized knowledge, such as a safe combination, available only to an "insider." Apprehended by SUPERMAN in November-December 1951, he is exposed as Ray Curtis, the publisher of the METROPOLIS *Daily Dispatch* (S No. 73/3: "Perry White vs. Clark Kent!").

"IT" (1951). The name bestowed by a bewildered, terrified populace, for want of a better appellation, on a weird "alien entity," a bizarre "mystery creature from another world"—"shaped like a rocket" and moving "at typhoon velocity" across the landscape "with a slithering, spinning motion," as though it were a huge rainbow-striped surfboard whirling upright—which is accidentally catapulted into the earthly dimension in November 1951 by the fury of "an unusual electric storm" and which, although the damage it causes is apparently unintentional, invariably leaves havoc and destruction in its wake, as it feeds on extraordinary amounts of electrical energy, sends out "pulsing rays of concentrated force" to topple skyscrapers and defend itself against attack, and enshrouds itself in an eerie "shield of force" which makes its destruction impossible, even for SUPERMAN. Although "It" is apparently some sort of extradimensional child, baffled and frightened by its unaccustomed surroundings and searching desperately for a way to get home again, its continued presence on Earth constitutes a serious menace to all human life. Ultimately, however, Superman unleashes a barrage of lightning at "It," thus recreating the circumstances that brought "It" to Earth and hurling "It" safely back into its home dimension (Act No. 162: "It!").

"IT" (1965). The name bestowed by a bewildered, terrified populace, for want of a better appellation, on a weird extradimensional creature—a gigantic "whirling behemoth," possessed of "incredible powers" and apparently catapulted into the earthly dimension in May 1965 after the "enormous energy" generated by a "vicious tornado" has somehow torn a hole in the dimensional barrier separating the dimension of Earth from the home dimension of "It."

Lost, hungry, and desperate for sustenance similar to the "lush, green vegetation" of its own "strange world," the "mysterious creature" whirls through METROPOLIS like "a spinning cloud of fog," devouring objects great and small—including a bus and an armored truck—so long as they are green, until SUPERMAN, using a gigantic ball of jungle vegetation as bait, finally lures "It" into whirling after him at a velocity sufficient to hurl itself back into its own dimension.

"The poor creature wasn't a real menace, after all!" remarks Superman, as the creature fades and vanishes. "It was merely lost and hungry. It will be happy now, back where it belongs!" (S No. 177/2: "The Menace Called 'It'!"). The story is in many respects similar to Action Comics No. 162 (Nov '51: "It!"). (See "IT" [1951].)

IXNAYALPAY. The ruler of the SQUIFFLES (S No. 22/1, May/Jun '43: "Meet the Squiffles!").

JACKAL. The owner of the Jackal Carnival, a carnival where men and women in search of a good time are victimized by pickpockets, thieves, and rigged games of chance. The Jackal Carnival is put out of business by SUPERMAN in January-February 1941 (S No. 8/3).

JACKSON (1940). The head of the Jackson Construction Company, which pays illegal kickbacks to corrupt Mayor Hansen in return for lucrative municipal construction contracts on which Jackson makes windfall profits by using dangerously sub-standard building materials. Jackson and Mayor Hansen are brought to justice by SUPERMAN in September-October 1940 (S No. 6/4).

JACKSON (1941). The owner of the Jackson Jewelry Company, and the head of a vicious murder-for-hire ring which uses the jewelry company as a front for its activities. Investigating the murder of wealthy Morton Carling in March-April 1941, SUPERMAN smashes the ruthless murder ring and brings to justice the two men responsible for ordering Carling's murder, an attorney named Lassiter and Carling heir George Steele (S No. 9/4).

JACKSON, JACK. The METROPOLIS banker who is secretly HI-JACK (S No. 25/4, Nov/Dec '43: "Hi-Jack--Jackal of Crime!").

JAMESON, ARTHUR. The chairman of the citizens' committee formed to combat the menace of "THE UNKNOWN X," and the man who is secretly "The Unknown X" (WF No. 2, Sum '41).

JAN-DEX. One of a pair of extraterrestrial "chameleon men" from the thirtieth century A.D.—orange-skinned aliens with pointed ears and twin antennae protruding from their foreheads—who possess the amazing power to change their physical form instantly to imitate any creature or object. "Just as a chameleon can change the color of its skin to merge with its background," gloats one of them, "we can instantly imitate **anything!**" Arriving in the twentieth century in their "time machine" in December 1961, Jan-Dex and his companion Zo-Gar construct a bizarre statue out of red KRYPTONITE in the middle of Rock Island, in Metropolis Bay, as part of an elaborate scheme to destroy SUPERMAN with both red and green kryptonite. Although exposure to the red kryptonite afflicts Superman with a series of disconcerting symptoms, as when it temporarily endows him with the power to read minds or makes him exhale flame whenever he opens his mouth, the Man of Steel ultimately apprehends the two aliens and returns them to their own era—the thirtieth century A.D.—for punishment (Act No. 283: "The Red Kryptonite Menace!").

JASSON (Mr.). The unscrupulous proprietor of Thrill Trips, Inc., a METROPOLIS travel agency specializing in thrilling trips packed with pre-arranged "dangers" and terrifying excitement, such as when Jasson orders the deliberate cutoff of an airplane engine in mid-flight to make the passengers think something has gone wrong with the plane. Dismayed at the reckless disregard for safety that characterizes the Thrill Trips tours, SUPERMAN organizes a competing tour service and apprehends Jasson and his henchman when they ruthlessly attempt to sabotage it (S No. 75/2, Mar/Apr '52: "Superman--Thrill Salesman!").

JAX-UR. "The worst criminal in the Phantom Zone" (Act No. 310, Mar '64: "Secret of Kryptonite Six!") and one of "the most dangerous evil-doers in the universe!" (Act No. 294, Nov '62: "The Kryptonite Killer!"). A "notorious outlaw" on the planet KRYPTON prior to its destruction (SA No. 5, Sum '62), Jax-Ur—a renegade scientist as brilliant as he is evil—was exiled into the PHANTOM ZONE for what has been described as "the most monstrous" crime ever

I'VE LEARNED MY LESSON! LET ME REDEEM MYSELF! KAL-EL, I CAN HELP YOU END THAT GHASTLY SPOTTED PLAGUE IN ATLANTIS!

© NPP 1964

Imprisoned in the Phantom Zone, Jax-Ur communicates with Superman over a special monitor screen, addressing him by his Kryptonian name, 1964

committed by a Phantom Zone prisoner: the destruction, perhaps deliberate, of an inhabited moon of Krypton, although whether Jax-Ur committed this heinous act with an experimental "nuclear rocket" (Act No. 284, Jan '62: "The Babe of Steel!") or a diabolical "ray" of his own invention (Act No. 310, Mar '64: "Secret of Kryptonite Six!") cannot be established with absolute certainty. Nor can the length of his sentence be firmly established, for he is described as having been "exiled into the Phantom Zone to serve a thirty-year sentence" in one account (SA No. 5, Sum '62) and as serving a life sentence in another (Act No. 310, Mar '64: "Secret of Kryptonite Six!").

Described as "the worst trouble-maker in the [Phantom] Zone," Jax-Ur has attempted to escape from the Zone on numerous occasions. Indeed, although it is the goal of all Phantom Zone prisoners to escape from the Zone and "take over the Earth" (Act No. 310, Mar '64: "Secret of Kryptonite Six!"), at least one text makes it abundantly clear that Jax-Ur would like nothing better than to "blow the Earth to smithereens!" (Act No. 284, Jan '62: "The Babe of Steel!").

Before embarking on a life of crime, Jax-Ur was a young Kryptonian scientist engaged in studying the unique "jewel-minerals" that made up Krypton's JEWEL MOUNTAINS. His "secret lab" was located somewhere in these mountains, carved into the face of one of its "glittering peaks." After one of his experimental devices had obliterated one of Krypton's moons, Jax-Ur was exiled into the Phantom Zone. But, as was to be the case with all the Phantom Zone prisoners, banishment into the Phantom Zone proved to be a blessing in disguise for Jax-Ur, for it enabled him to survive when Krypton exploded (Act No. 310, Mar '64: "Secret of Kryptonite Six!").

Jax-Ur recalls the crime for which he was banished into the Phantom Zone, 1964

In January 1962 Jax-Ur and his fellow prisoners seem on the verge of escaping from the Phantom Zone after "the electrical ions of the Aurora Borealis have opened a small hole in the Phantom Zone which is steadily widening," threatening to release the exiled "super-villains" into the earthly dimension as soon as it becomes "big enough for the Phantom Zone

criminals to squeeze through!" Alerted to the threat however, by their friend MON-EL, SUPERMAN, SUPER-GIRL, and KRYPTO THE SUPERDOG use the combined power of their X-ray vision to burn up the Aurora Borealis, thereby sealing up the opening through which Jax-Ur and his cohorts had hoped to make their escape (Act No. 284: "The Babe of Steel!").

In November 1962, when Superman puts the finishing touches on the new Hall of Enemies in his FORTRESS OF SOLITUDE, Jax-Ur is among the villains represented there by colorful wax busts (Act No. 294: "The Kryptonite Killer!").

In March 1964 Jax-Ur, feigning repentance for his past crimes, pleads for a chance to redeem himself—and perhaps even win an early parole from the Phantom Zone—by helping Superman find a cure for the "ghastly spotted plague" that is sweeping ATLANTIS. Released from the Phantom Zone by Superman for a conditional twenty-four-hour period, Jax-Ur journeys with Superman through the time-space barrier to the planet Krypton "a few months" prior to its destruction, where, in Krypton's famed SCARLET JUNGLE, he does indeed lead Superman to the gigantic mushroomlike fungi whose stalks contain "the spore-dust which is the cure for the spotted plague." Unbeknownst to the Man of Steel, however, Jax-Ur also uses his day of freedom to set in motion a convoluted scheme designed to enable Jax-Ur and his fellow Phantom Zone convicts to black-mail Superman into freeing them all from the Phantom Zone so that they can "take over the Earth!"

Jax-Ur guides Superman through Krypton's Scarlet Jungle

The scheme involves duping Superman into believing that exposure to a hitherto unknown type of KRYPTONITE—so-called "jewel kryptonite"—has "turned [him] into a threat against the whole world" by "causing [him] to detonate any explosive materi-al" he approaches, as when he appears to cause a conflagration at a fuel-oil depot, for example, merely by flying overhead. In actuality, there is no such substance as jewel kryptonite and the Man of Steel has not really become a menace, but Jax-Ur has succeeded in devising a means whereby he and the other Phantom Zone outlaws can convert their "mental commands" into "energy beams which detonate any material" outside the Phantom Zone they desire, thus enabling them, for a time, to make Superman believe that his very presence on Earth is a threat to human life, so that he will give in to Jax-Ur's extortionate demand that he release all the inmates of the Phantom Zone as the price of Jax-Ur's agreeing to cure him of his supposed "affliction." Ultimately, however, Superman uncovers the details of Jax-Ur's "diabolical plot" and takes the necessary steps to prevent the Phantom Zone criminals from ever again being able to use their mental energy to detonate explosive materials on Earth.

"You could have been a free man now! ... A hero to the people of the world!" exclaims Superman to Jax-Ur, referring to the parole the villain would undoubtedly have received in gratitude for his having cured the dreaded Atlantean plague. "But you outwitted yourself!"

"Who wants to be a hero?" sneers Jax-Ur contemptuously. "I'd rather be notorious as the worst criminal in the Phantom Zone!" (Act No. 310: "Secret of Kryptonite Six!").

JENA (Princess). The beautiful blond daughter of the king and queen of Adoria—a "distant planet" inhabited by strong Amazon women and timid, diminutive men—who, in July 1960, lures SUPERMAN into a KRYPTONITE trap, kidnaps him to Adoria, and blackmails him into marriage by threatening to obliterate Earth with an awesome "destructo-ray" if he refuses. Princess Jena has the marriage annulled soon afterward, however, after Superman, through a ruse, has persuaded her that he is an "uncouth boor" unfit to be married to an Adorian princess (Act No. 266: "The Captive of the Amazons").

JENKINS. A revenge-mad genius who, having successfully acquired "vast wealth" as an inventor, constructs a weird, rocket-powered "sky-vessel" and lures eight former members of Elkhart University's Pi Theta Dau fraternity aboard it as part of a fiendishly elaborate scheme to annihilate them all in retaliation for the death of his brother during a Pi Theta Dau hazing some twenty years earlier. Jenkins murders four of his intended victims and attempts unsuccessfully to kill the others before he is finally apprehended by SUPERMAN in Fall 1942 (WF No. 7: "The Eight Doomed Men").

JEWEL MOUNTAINS. A range of mountains on the planet KRYPTON whose "fascinating beauty entrances all beholders" (S No. 170/2, Jul '64: pts. I-II—"If Lex Luthor Were Superman's Father!"; "The Wedding of Lara and Luthor!"). First discovered by the Kryptonian explorer Bor-Ak, they are composed of "living jewels" (S No. 164/2, Oct '63: "The Fugitive from the Phantom Zone!") which glitter prismatically in the sunlight like multifaceted diamonds. Accord-

ing to Action Comics No. 310, the "glittering peaks" were created by a species of "huge crystal bird...which once filled the skies of ancient Krypton!" During Krypton's prehistoric age, "swarms of these birds instinctively came here to die! Their skeletons were transformed into these living Jewel Mountains..." (Mar '64: "Secret of Kryptonite Six!"). A Kryptonian superstition held that it was bad luck for a bride to wear living jewels from the Jewel Mountains to her wedding (S No. 164/2, Oct '63: "The Fugitive from the Phantom Zone!").

SUPERMAN visits the Jewel Mountains in the course of his passionate romance with LYLA LERROL (S No. 141, Nov '60: "Superman's Return to Krypton!" pts. I-III—"Superman Meets Jor-El and Lara Again!"; "Superman's Kryptonian Romance!"; "The Surprise of Fate!"), and on another occasion in the company of the villain JAX-UR. Before Jax-Ur turned to crime, he experimented with the unique "jewel-minerals" that make up these mountains, and his "secret lab" was carved into the face of one of the chain's glittering cliffs. After drugging Superman's food with a sedative, Jax-Ur carves a huge jewelled chunk— in the shape of a gigantic diamond, roughly twice as tall as a man—out of "a nearby pinnacle" as part of his elaborate scheme to force Superman to release all the villains imprisoned in the PHANTOM ZONE (Act No. 310, Mar '64: "Secret of Kryptonite Six!"). It is in front of the Jewel Mountains that LEX LUTHOR asks LARA to marry him as part of his elaborate scheme to become the father of Superman (S No. 170/2, Jul '64: pts. I-II—"If Lex Luthor Were Superman's Father!"; "The Wedding of Lara and Luthor!").

JIMMY OLSEN FAN CLUB, THE. A club formed by fans of SUPERMAN's pal JIMMY OLSEN. The club meets monthly (Act No. 286, Mar '62: "The Jury of Super-Enemies!") and is headquartered in the Jimmy Olsen Fan Club Building in METROPOLIS (Act No. 320, Jan '65: "The Three Super-Enemies!").

In March 1962, while waiting to be introduced as that month's scheduled guest speaker, Superman falls asleep on the speaker's platform at the Jimmy Olsen Fan Club and has a horrible nightmare induced by his recent exposure to red KRYPTONITE (Act No. 286: "The Jury of Super-Enemies!").

When Metropolis television station WMET-TV inaugurates its new "Our American Heroes" series with a program honoring Superman, "our greatest American hero," members of the Jimmy Olsen Fan Club appear on the show along with Superman's other friends and admirers to help pay tribute to the Man of Steel (Act No. 309, Feb '64: "The Superman Super-Spectacular!").

When, as part of his elaborate plan to avert global panic by concealing the impending invasion of Earth by a robot-manned space fleet from the planet BXPA, Superman pretends that he has become a power-hungry tyrant bent on ruling the Earth, the members of the Jimmy Olsen Fan Club gather up Jimmy Olsen's collection of Superman memorabilia housed in their clubhouse and burn it in a bonfire in the street outside. "Out with this junk and burn it!" cries one member. "We don't want to be identified with tyrants!" (Act No. 312, May '64: "King Superman versus Clark Kent, Metallo").

In October 1964, after having been deprived of his super-powers by the baleful radiations of a mysterious green comet, Superman introduces his pal Jimmy Olsen to AR-VAL, the so-called "new Superman," at the Jimmy Olsen Fan Club headquarters (S No. 172: pts. I-III—"The New Superman!"; "Clark Kent—Former Superman!"; "The Struggle of the Two Supermen!").

JOHNS (Professor). A prominent scientist, mortally wounded by criminals trying to obtain his new "power formula," who manages to whisper his secret formula to CLARK KENT before lapsing into a coma from which he never recovers. SUPERMAN finally apprehends Johns's killers in September-October 1949 and turns his formula over to a government official as per the dying scientist's last instructions (S No. 60/2: "The Men Who Had to Guard Superman!").

JOKER, THE. The maniacal harlequin who has been an implacable foe of BATMAN for almost four decades. Batman No. 4/1 calls him "the cleverest and the most dangerous criminal in the annals of

May-June 1957 (WF No. 88: Superman's and Batman's Greatest Foes!") and again in November 1962 (WF No. 129: "Joker-Luthor, Incorporated!"), the Joker forms a temporary partnership in crime with the nefarious LEX LUTHOR. (For a complete account of the villainous career of the Joker, consult *The Encyclopedia of Comic Book Heroes: Volume I—Batman.*)

JONES (Pvt.). A U.S. Army private (later promoted to sergeant) stationed at Camp Metropolis who becomes temporarily endowed with super-powers identical to SUPERMAN's when a "freakish phenomenon" involving lightning and an experimental "helmet radio" imbues his body with "an electrical pattern" identical to Superman's in July 1958. There is little noteworthy about Jones's brief career as a superman, but the interlude does give Superman the opportunity to trick a pair of foreign spies into believing that he has developed a technique for transferring his powers at will into the bodies of American soldiers (S No. 122/3: "The Super-Sergeant").

JONES, AL. A onetime vaudeville magician, stage name Ali Singh, who begins receiving programs from the near future on his television set after its antenna

The Joker, 1952

crime..." (Win '41: "The Case of the Joker's Crime Circus!"), and Batman No. 8/4 describes him as a "grim jester, arch-criminal, [and] master fiend" (Dec/Jan '41-'42: "The Cross Country Crimes!"). By his own account, he is "the greatest criminal on Earth" (Det No. 388, Jun '69: "Public Luna-tic Number One!") and "the world's greatest clown" (BM No. 53/1, Jun/Jul '49: "A Hairpin, a Hoe, a Hacksaw, a Hole in the Ground!"), as well as "the greatest comedian of all--the caliph of crime clowns, the grand mogul of mountebanks, the king of jesters...the one and only Joker! Ha, ha, ha!" (BM No. 57/3, Feb/Mar '50: "The Funny Man Crimes!"). In

is exposed to lightning during a freak electrical storm. Photographing news programs from the future as they appear on his TV screen, Jones acquires photos of SUPERMAN in action and enters them in the DAILY PLANET's Superman action-photo contest in hopes of using the prize money to buy an urgently needed operation for crippled neighbor boy Bobby Forbes. Ironically, however, although Jones's photos are indeed spectacular, the contest's winning photo is taken by Bobby Forbes himself as he watches Superman in action from the window of his home (S No. 120/2, Mar '58: "The Super-Feats Superman Forgot").

JONES, CATAWAMPUS. The secret leader of the Rockdust Bandits, a gang of criminals—so named because of their habit of plastering rock dust over their clothes and faces to give themselves a spooky, ghostlike appearance—who have been preying on the gold-mining camps in the area of the lonely western mountain town of Saddle Fork and then shipping out their stolen ore by pretending that it comes from the nonexistent gold claim that Catawampus Jones claims to be mining. Sworn in as Saddle Fork's temporary sheriff after thwarting a gold robbery in his Clark Kent identity, Kent performs heroically, both as Clark Kent and as SUPERMAN, to apprehend the Rockdust Bandits and expose Catawampus Jones as their leader (WF No. 30, Sep/Oct '47: "Sheriff Clark Kent").

JONES, DAVEY." The leader of a gang of modern-day pirates who, operating from an autogyro, put the crews of passing freighters to sleep with clouds of sleeping gas and then sink the cargo-laden vessels in shallow water so that later, posing as honest salvage contractors, they can approach the owners of the missing ships and exact large fees for salvaging their sunken cargoes. "Davey Jones" and his henchmen are apprehended by SUPERMAN in December 1945 (Act No. 91: "The Ghost Drum!").

JONES, HENRY. The meek, scrawny cartoonist and self-proclaimed "genius" who, working under the manly pseudonym of "Carson Steele," is the creator of Geezer, a whimsical orange-costumed comic-book super-hero "who has taken the public by storm" with his idiot theme song ("Wherever crime lurks, I must seize her. That's why far and wide I'm called Geezer!") and his penchant for making fools out of Hitler and his Axis cronies. When outraged Nazi agents attempt to murder Geezer's creator ("You make der Fuehrer the laughing stock of the world," hisses a Nazi assassin, "then you dare ask why you should be blasted out of existence!"), SUPERMAN streaks to his rescue, but he also makes Jones promise to stop relegating the art chores on Geezer to assistants when he should be doing the work himself. "Millions of readers rely on you for your **best**!" scolds Superman. "If you give them less, you're being dishonest!" (S No. 25/3, Nov/Dec '43: "King of the Comic Books").

JONES, MARY. The attractive young woman who is secretary to wealthy STEPHEN VAN SCHUYLER III. Without her eyeglasses and with her hair restyled, Mary Jones is an almost perfect look-alike for LOIS LANE (S No. 55/2, Nov/Dec '48: "The Richest Man in the World!").

JOR-EL. The father of SUPERMAN, and the foremost scientist of the planet KRYPTON prior to its destruction. A "scientific genius" (S No. 65/3, Jul/Aug '50: "Three Supermen from Krypton!") with a fertile, wide-ranging intellect, he conducted far-reaching experiments in rocketry, invented a matter-transmitter and numerous other marvels, and discovered the PHANTOM ZONE. It was Jor-El who predicted to an unbelieving population "that Krypton would explode from gathering atomic pressure at the core of the planet" (Act No. 182, Jul '53: "The Return of Planet Krypton!"), and it was Jor-El who, when the doomsday came, dispatched the infant Superman toward Earth in an experimental rocket, remaining behind with his wife LARA to perish in the cataclysm.

Jor-El

Described repeatedly in the texts as "Krypton's greatest scientist" (S No. 53/1, Jul/Aug '48: "The Origin of Superman!"; and others), "Krypton's foremost physicist" (Act No. 329, Oct '65: "The Ultimate Enemy!"), and "the greatest scientist on Krypton" (Act No. 149, Oct '50: "The Courtship on Krypton!"; and others), Jor-El was born into a family with a centuries-long heritage of achievement in the fields of science, statesmanship, and exploration. His ancestry teemed with such men of lasting distinction as Val-El, an explorer and discoverer who was the moving force behind Krypton's great Age of Exploration; Sul-El, the inventor of Krypton's first telescope; Tala-El, the author of Krypton's planet-wide constitution; Hatu-El, a scientist and inventor who discovered the nature of electricity and devised Krypton's first electromagnet and electric motor; and Gam-El, the father of modern Kryptonian architecture (SF No. 172, Aug/Sep '75; and others).

When Jor-El was still an infant, his own father succeeded in journeying to Earth and back in an experimental spacecraft of his own design (S No. 103/1, Feb '56: "The Superman of Yesterday"), and although knowledge of the craft's construction had apparently been lost to Kryptonians by the time Jor-El reached maturity (Act No. 158, Jul '51: "The Kid from Krypton!"; and others), there can be little doubt that his father's achievement served to inspire his own explorations into the then-infant sciences of rocketry and space travel.

Little is known of Jor-El's early life, but by the time he reached college he had begun to gather about him a coterie of young intellectuals destined to make great names for themselves in the annals of Kryptonian science. His college roommate was Professor Kimda, who, years later, would befriend Superman in the bottle city of KANDOR and help him thwart the schemes of the villainous BRAINIAC (Act No. 242, Jul '58: "The Super-Duel in Space"). Jor-El also befriended Ral-En, whose career as a "brilliant scientist" was ultimately warped and destroyed by dictatorial ambitions fostered and encouraged by his father MAG-EN (S No. 154/2, Jul '62: "Krypton's First Superman!"). Other colleagues included his friend NOR-KAN (S No. 158, Jan '63: "Superman in Kandor" pts. I-III—"Invasion of the Mystery Super-Men!"; "The Dynamic Duo of Kandor!"; "The City of Super-People!"; and others) and LON-ES, who worked for a time as his assistant (S No. 154/2, Jul '62: "Krypton's First Superman!").

During this period, two of Jor-El's brothers—his identical twin brother Nim-El, and another brother named ZOR-EL—also embarked upon distinguished careers in science, but they appear to have limited themselves to the fields of weapons science and climatography, respectively, and to have displayed none of their brother's capacity for brilliance and creativity in a breathtaking array of scientific disciplines (S No. 146/1, Jul '61: "The Story of Superman's Life!"; and others). Indeed, in the course of a brilliant career that was terminated by the destruction of Krypton, Jor-El applied his great genius to virtually every aspect of Kryptonian life, not only to every facet of science and invention, but also to the problems of war and peace (Act No. 216, May '56: "The Super-Menace of Metropolis"), transportation (S No. 134, Jan '60: chs. I-III—"The Super-Menace of Metropolis!"; "The Revenge Against Jor-El!"; "The Duel of the Supermen!"), and the humane administration of criminal justice (S No. 65/3, Jul/Aug '50: "Three Supermen from Krypton!"; and others).

He worked to develop a serum for prolonging life (S No. 78/1, Sep/Oct '52: "The Beast from Krypton!"), carried on an intensive telescopic study of the planet Earth (Act No. 223, Dec '56: "The First Superman of Krypton"; and others), and conducted archaeological research into the "marvels of a dead civilization that once existed at the bottom of the Great Krypton Sea!" (S No. 170/2, Jul '64: pts. I-II—"If Lex Luthor Were Superman's Father!"; "The Wedding of Lara and Luthor!").

His inventions included a "petrifying ray" which turned people to stone as long as it shone on them, "levitation bombs" designed to reverse the pull of gravity and make objects fall upward, a "super-artificial lightning projector" for projecting bolts of artificial lightning, a magnet that attracted human flesh instead of iron, and an "invisibility-spray" which could make a person invisible by covering him with "a fine coating of light-refracting particles" (S No. 74/1, Jan/Feb '52: "The Lost Secrets of Krypton!"); a "matter-radio," described as "a transmitter

that can send all forms of living matter--even livi people--across space by radio" (S No. 77/1, Jul/A '52: "The Man Who Went to Krypton!"; see also No. 281, Oct '61: "The Man Who Saved Kal-E Life!"); a "dimension-traveler," designed to "projec person out of this dimension into a new one"; "missile-projector," designed to deliver any object any destination at supersonic speed; and a "nucle fission tester," which "registers if any chain reacti is starting and shows the source" (WF No. Mar/Apr '54: "Jor-El's Last Will!"); an "amazi growth ray for plants," capable of growing ve tables "100 times bigger" than their customary si (Act No. 325, Jun '65: "The Skyscraper Superman! and an all-purpose, mass-produced vehicle—capab of traveling on land, sea, or air, and ev underground—which quickly came into such co mon usage among Kryptonian's that it soon becan known as the "Jor-El," much as Henry Ford creation became known as the Ford (S No. 134, Ja '60: chs. I-III—"The Super-Menace of Metropolis! "The Revenge Against Jor-El!"; "The Duel of th Supermen!").

For these and other inventions and discoverie Jor-El was awarded Krypton's coveted Science Priz in the form of a statuette molded from rare illiu metal (S No. 173/2, Nov '64: "Tales of Gree Kryptonite No. 1"), and an honorary medal from th Kryptonian Science Society (Act No. 182, Jul '5 "The Return of Planet Krypton!").

Indeed, although Jor-El was still a young man a the time of his marriage to Lara, the lovely dark haired young woman who, according to at least on

Jor-El and Lara

© NPP 1978

account, was Jor-El's "assistant" during the period preceding their engagement (S No. 170/2, Jul '64: pts. I-II—"If Lex Luthor Were Superman's Father!"; "The Wedding of Lara and Luthor!"), he was already a "famed scientist" engaged in top-level research at a Kryptonian "missile base" (S No. 141, Nov '60: "Superman's Return to Krypton!" pts. I-III—"Superman Meets Jor-El and Lara Again!"; "Superman's Kryptonian Romance!"; "The Surprise of Fate!").

But Jor-El was concerned with humanitarian matters as well as scientific ones. Because of his strong moral opposition to capital punishment, he devised a method whereby perpetrators of serious crimes could be exiled into space in a state of suspended animation inside specially constructed space capsules, a method first employed to safeguard Kryptonians against the power-hungry ambitions of MALA and his brothers. According to Superman No. 65/3, the space capsules were made of transparent plastic and shaped like rocket ships (Jul/Aug '50: "Three Supermen from Krypton!"), but according to Superman No. 123 these so-called "prison satellites" were of a spherical shape. The criminals imprisoned inside them were placed in suspended animation by means of a special sleep gas, and chunks of a glowing crystalline mineral—capable of cleansing their brains of criminal tendencies in a hundred years' time—were placed on their foreheads so that ultimately, once their sentence was served, they might take up constructive roles in Kryptonian society (Aug '58: chs. 1-3—"The Girl of Steel"; "The Lost Super-Powers"; "Superman's Return to Krypton").

The practice of exiling criminals into outer space was terminated after Jor-El had discovered the Phantom Zone, a twilight dimension to which criminals could be banished—by means of Jor-El's own Phantom Zone projector—to serve out their sentences as disembodied wraiths. Indeed, it was Jor-El's testimony that resulted in the sentencing of many Kryptonian criminals to the Phantom Zone (S No. 153/3, May '62: "The Town of Supermen!"; and others). He was the "leader" of the Kryptonian "justice council"—analogous to being the foreman of an American jury—that found QUEX-UL guilty and sentenced him to a term in the Phantom Zone (S No. 157/1, Nov '62: "The Super-Revenge of the Phantom Zone Prisoner!"), and his testimony was undoubtedly influential in determining the guilt of the would-be dictator Ral-En (see MAG-EN) (S No. 154/2, Jul '62: "Krypton's First Superman!"). On at least one occasion he served as an undercover agent for the Krypton Bureau of Investigation to help thwart the sinister machinations of a would-be tyrant (S No. 123, Aug '58: chs. 1-3—"The Girl of Steel"; "The Lost Super-Powers"; "Superman's Return to Krypton").

It is small wonder, then, that this brilliant and versatile scientist soon won a place for himself on Krypton's pretigious Council of Science (Act No. 223, Dec '56: "The First Superman of Krypton"), also referred to as the Council of Scientists (S No. 146/1,

Jul '61: "The Story of Superman's Life!"). The precise role of the Council is hard to define. Action Comics No. 223 makes a clear distinction between the Council and Krypton's "highest officials," suggesting that the Council presided over scientific matters as distinct from political ones (Dec '56: "The First Superman of Krypton"), but Superman No. 65/3 makes reference to "Krypton's ruling council, which consisted of the [planet's] ten leading scientists," and goes on to describe Jor-El as "the leader of the council," suggesting that the scientific establishment had jurisdiction over the political sphere as well as the scientific and that Jor-El occupied a position on the council which made him virtual head of state (Jul/Aug '50: "Three Supermen from Krypton!"). According to Superman No. 53/1, on the other hand, scientists who heard Jor-El foretell the impending doom of Krypton were suspicious that he might be "trying to frighten Krypton's leaders away from our planet so that he may rule" (Jul/Aug '48: "The Origin of Superman!"), suggesting that although Jor-El was a "brilliant scientist" (Act No. 158, Jul '51: "The Kid from Krypton!") and "prominent Kryptonian (S No. 154/2, Jul '62: "Krypton's First Superman!"), he was only marginally involved in political activity. On the planet Krypton, however, the scientific establishment exerted considerable influence on political and social policy, and so, whatever its precise functions, Jor-El's position on the Council of Science meant that he occupied a prestigious position in Kryptonian life.

At the time Lara gave birth to the infant Superman, she and Jor-El were residing in KRYPTONOPOLIS (SA No. 5, Sum '62; and others), the city that had become the capital of Krypton following the theft of Kandor by the space villain Brainiac. According to Superman No. 75/1, the proud parents named their newborn son Jor-El, 2nd (Mar/Apr '52: "The Prankster's Star Pupil!"), but an overwhelming preponderance of texts assert that they named him Kal-El (S No. 113, May '57: chs. 1-3—"The Superman of the Past"; "The Secret of the Towers"; "The Superman of the Present"; and others). By all accounts, the dark-haired youngster bore an "unmistakable" resemblance to his father (S No. 77/1, Jul/Aug '52: "The Man Who Went to Krypton!"; and others).

It was around the time of Superman's birth, while all of Krypton was busily engaged in preparations for the planet-wide pageantry scheduled to mark the upcoming anniversary of "the 10,000th year" of Kryptonian civilization (Act No. 223, Dec '56: "The First Superman of Krypton"), that Jor-El made what was at once the most momentous and most calamitous discovery of his scientific career: the discovery that Krypton's uranium core, which for untold ages [had] been building a cycle of chain-reactions," was on the verge of unleashing a planetary cataclysm, that "soon every atom on [the] planet would explode like one colossal atomic bomb!" (S No. 61/3, Nov/Dec '49: "Superman Returns to Krypton!").

It remains unclear why Jor-El, alone among his contemporaries, was able to forecast the impending doom of his planet. According to Superman No. 113, Jor-El was first alerted to the coming cataclysm by QUEEN LATORA of the planet VERGO (May '57: chs. 1-3—"The Superman of the Past"; "The Secret of the Towers"; "The Superman of the Present"), but other texts assert that he had "long suspected" the problem (Act No. 158, Jul '51: "The Kid from Krypton!"; and others), having first detected it by means of his scientific "instruments" (S No. 146/1, Jul '61: "The Story of Superman's Life!"; and others), specifically an ingenious "nuclear fission tester" of his own invention which "registers if any chain reaction is starting and shows the source" (WF No. 69, Mar/Apr '54: "Jor-El's Last Will!").

By whatever means Jor-El became aware that Krypton was about to explode "from gathering atomic pressure at the core of the planet" (Act No. 182, Jul '53: "The Return of Planet Krypton!"), he moved coolly and decisively to confirm his suspicions, burrowing deep into the bowels of Krypton in an "atomic-powered mole," performing numerous experiments, making countless intricate calculations (Act No. 223, Dec '56: "The First Superman of Krypton").

Finally, although he still lacked positive scientific proof to substantiate his hypothesis (Act No. 223, Dec '56: "The First Superman of Krypton"; and others), Jor-El was ready to report his findings to Krypton's prestigious scientific council. "Gentlemen," he intoned solemnly, as he addressed his scientific colleagues in Krypton's hallowed Hall of Wisdom, "...Krypton is doomed! ...[T]he core of Krypton is composed of a substance called uranium...which, for untold ages, has been setting up a cycle of chain-impulses, building in power every moment! Soon...very soon...every atom of Krypton will explode in one final terrible blast! Gentlemen, Krypton is one gigantic atomic bomb!" (S No. 53/1, Jul/Aug '48: "The Origin of Superman!"; and others).

It is incredible that the assembled scientists did not believe him. Already there was "a rumble of mighty forces" from deep inside Krypton that could be heard and felt by every Kryptonian. Perhaps Jor-El's explanation is the only true one: that "men often reject a truth that is too terrible to face!" (Act No. 158, Jul '51: "The Kid from Krypton!"; and others).

Whether the cause was jealousy, or pomposity, or the unwillingness of men to face a terrible truth, it is a simple fact of history that the venerable scientists of Krypton rejected Jor-El's warning. His prophecy of impending cataclysm was greeted with jeers and laughter (S No. 53/1, Jul/Aug '48: "The Origin of Superman!"; and others). He was accused of being an alarmist and a crackpot, an irresponsible fantasizer and a cunning schemer in pursuit of planetary power. And when he carried his plea to Krypton's "highest officials" (Act No. 223, Dec '56: "The First Superman of Krypton"), and then to the population at large (Act No. 158, Jul '51: "The Kid from Krypton!"; and others), all he received for his efforts was more scorn and derision.

Besides Lara, Jor-El's loving wife, only two Kryptonians are on record as having believed in Jor-El and his prophecy of cataclysm: his brother Zor-El (S No. 146/1, Jul '61: "The Story of Superman's Life!") and the scientist Shir Kan (Act No. 218, Jul '56: "The Super-Ape from Krypton"). Although "Kryptonians had not yet perfected rocket travel" at the time Krypton exploded (S No. 113, May '57: chs. 1-3—"The Superman of the Past"; "The Secret of the Towers";

To an unbelieving population, Jor-El predicts the impending doom of Krypton

"The Superman of the Present"; and others), various rocketry experiments were under way, and Shir Kan—whether he conceived the idea independently or whether he was inspired by Jor-El's call for the construction of a fleet of rocket ships to evacuate Krypton's population to some distant planet (Act No. 172, Sep '52: "Lois Lane...Witch!"; and others)—responded to Jor-El's dire prediction by having his staff construct a fleet of "experimental rockets" which might have been used as part of a planet-wide migration. Concerned that Kryptonians might be incapable of withstanding the rigors of interplanetary travel, however, Shir Kan took the conservative step of first testing his rockets with a small population of experimental apes. Many, if not all, of Shir Kan's apes survive to this day on a far-distant planet (see SUPER-APE), but Shir Kan's act of overcaution meant that his rockets, which might have been used for at least a partial evacuation of Krypton, were off in outer space when the doomsday came (Act No. 218, Jul '56: "The Super-Ape from Krypton").

Jor-El, meanwhile, set to work with renewed dedication, aware that time was running out (S No. 146/1, Jul '61: "The Story of Superman's Life!"), determined to rescue his people from the calamity he knew was coming. His dream was an immense interplanetary migration—the transfer of the entire population of Krypton from their doomed home to another planet—in a fleet of "rocket-driven space arks" (S No. 146/1, Jul '61: "The Story of Superman's Life!"), "giant rocket ships" of which Jor-El himself had already constructed a scaled-down prototype (S No. 53/1, Jul/Aug '48: "The Origin of Superman!"; and others).

Resettlement on the planet Earth would be the natural goal of such a transfer. Earth was Jor-El's "favorite planet" (S No. 113, May '57: chs. 1-3—"The Superman of the Past"; "The Secret of the Towers"; "The Superman of the Present"). For years he had made an intensive study of that planet, as no Kryptonian ever had, peering at it through his "super-powerful telescope" (S No. 141, Nov '60: "Superman's Return to Krypton!" pts. I-III— "Superman Meets Jor-El and Lara Again!"; "Superman's Kryptonian Romance!"; "The Surprise of Fate!"; and others), carefully scrutinizing "every detail of Earth life" playing across the giant "Earth monitor screen" in his laboratory's scrupulously equipped "Earth monitor room" (Act No. 281, Oct '61: "The Man Who Saved Kal-El's Life!").

Jor-El had a natural affection for Earth. His ancestor Sul-El, the inventor of Krypton's first telescope, had been the first Kryptonian to chart the location of Earth's sun (SF No. 172, Aug/Sep '75; and others). His own father, in an early triumph of space travel, had once actually negotiated a round-trip journey between Krypton and Earth (S No. 103/1, Feb '56: "The Superman of Yesterday").

Now, with the day of cataclysm drawing nearer by the moment, Jor-El renewed his study of Earth with a single-minded intensity, determined to establish, beyond any doubt, whether Earth would indeed be a habitable planet for his people. He studied "every aspect of Earth by tele-screen projection" and concluded that Earth's environment would be ideal for a Kryptonian settlement. In order to study the probable effects of Earth's "weaker gravity" on the migrating Kryptonians, he employed sophisticated "gravity-distorting machines" to transform an isolated Kryptonian valley into an atmospheric microcosm of Earth, complete with "a sample section of an Earth city" which he constructed with the aid of powerful Kryptonian "building machines." In the altered atmosphere of his artificial Earth, Jor-El confirmed through experimentation what he had already arrived at through astronomical calculation: "...My Kryptonian muscles enable me to run at super-speed and hurtle through the air!" he thought to himself as he cavorted in his man-made environment. "And in this weaker gravitation, my body would be invulnerable!" (Act No. 223, Dec '56: "The First Superman of Krypton").

But Jor-El did not place all his hopes in an interplanetary migration by rocket ship. For in addition to his rocket prototype, Jor-El had his "matter-radio," a "transmitter that can send all forms of living matter--even living people--across space by radio!" (S No. 77/1, Jul/Aug '52: "The Man Who Went to Krypton!").

In the chronicles, two separate texts deal with Jor-El's hopes of evacuating his people to Earth by means of the matter-radio. In terms of minor details, the texts differ, but both are in accord on the following points: (1) Jor-El envisioned a mass migration to Earth via matter-radio; (2) in preparation for the evacuation, he used his device to summon an Earth scientist to Krypton, both to discuss the feasibility of the planned migration and to explore the means of carrying it out; and (3) in the end, time ran out before the necessary number of apparatuses could be constructed, and a malfunctioning of Jor-El's own matter-radio at the time of the cataclysm prevented even him and his wife Lara from using it to effect their escape (S No. 77/1, Jul/Aug '52: "The Man Who Went to Krypton!"; Act No. 281, Oct '61: "The Man Who Saved Kal-El's Life!").

As the day of doom drew ever closer, Jor-El made one last desperate attempt to arouse the Kryptonian population from its fatal complacency. As part of Krypton's glorious "10,000-year celebration," a "super-scope" film was being shown commemorating the planet's past and expressing optimism for its future. Into this film, Jor-El spliced scenes that he had himself created, horrifying trick-photography footage of Krypton exploding into fragments, along with the image of Jor-El in the foreground, shouting "This is Krypton's tomorrow! ...[O]ur planet is doomed!" (Act No. 223, Dec '56: "The First Superman of Krypton").

Even this spectacularly dramatic ploy, however, failed to arouse the masses from their apathy, and before long a "great computer-forecaster" recently developed by a colleague had informed the defeated Jor-El of what he already knew: that the odds were now ninety-nine in a hundred that Krypton would be destroyed before an interplanetary evacuation could be carried out (Act No. 314, Jul '64: "The Day Superman Became the Flash!").

Immediately, Jor-El turned his attentions to the completion of a more modest task, the construction of a small rocket sufficient to rescue himself and his family (S No. 100/3, Sep '55: "The Clue from Krypton"), and when time ran out on even this modest project, he devoted his last remaining energies to the task of saving his son. Placing the last of his hopes in his recent "experiments with small rockets," Jor-El launched Kal-El's pet dog, KRYPTO, into outer space in a tiny rocket as a final trial run for the evacuation of his son, but the test proved inconclusive when, instead of returning to Krypton as Jor-El had planned, Krypto's rocket was struck a glancing blow by a meteor and sent careening into outer space (S No. 146/1, Jul '61: "The Story of Superman's Life!").

With the death of Krypton now perhaps only hours away, Jor-El placed some of his greatest inventions inside a massive vault with a combination lock in the hope that they might somehow "survive to benefit other men even though our own world must die!" Little did Jor-El suspect that these inventions would one day find their way to Earth, where they would be used for evil by the diabolical LEX LUTHOR (S No. 74/1, Jan/Feb '52: "The Lost Secrets of Krypton!").

Jor-El knew that the "experimental rocket-ship" (S No. 1/1, Sum '39) which he had constructed as a miniature prototype of the giant space arks that he had hoped would be used to evacuate the entire population of Krypton, could be used to transport his infant son safely to some distant world. Feeding the available data into his colleague's great computer-forecaster confirmed the opinion he had arrived at through other means: that his son would be happiest growing to maturity on the planet Earth (Act No. 314, Jul '64: "The Day Superman Became the Flash!").

Feeding data into a colleague's "great computer-forecaster," Jor-El tries to determine which of six distant planets would make the best new home for his son

Action Comics No. 216 asserts that the rocket in which the infant Kal-El escaped from Krypton's final holocaust was actually a small-scale model of a "gigantic space ship" which Jor-El had earlier loaded with "outlawed war weapons" and launched into outer space as part of his plan to avert the possible outbreak of war on Krypton (May '56: "The Super-Menace of Metropolis"), but numerous other texts refer to it as a "model space-ship" (S No. 61/3, Nov/Dec '49: "Superman Returns to Krypton!") or "experimental model rocket" (S No. 141, Nov '60: "Superman's Return to Krypton!" pts. I-III— "Superman Meets Jor-El and Lara Again!"; "Superman's Kryptonian Romance!"; "The Surprise of Fate!") of the type which Jor-El had hoped to use for an interplanetary evacuation (S No. 74/1, Jan/Feb '52: "The Lost Secrets of Krypton!"; and others).

To prevent his son's rocket from being crushed by flying meteoric fragments as it hurtled through space, Jor-El outfitted it with a special jewel-like "projector" of his own invention, designed to obliterate oncoming meteors by emitting "iron-destroying

rays." "This jewel," explained Jor-El to his wife, "is really a tiny projector which emits invisible rays that can destroy *iron!* Since meteors are almost all iron, such a projector as this in [the] rocket would protect it from damage!" (Act No. 172, Sep '52: "Lois Lane... Witch!").

Inside the rocket, along with the projector, Jor-El placed what has been described as his "last will and testament." Inscribed on a thin sheet of super-hard metal, the will consisted of detailed descriptions of three of Jor-El's greatest inventions: his "dimension-traveler," his "missile-projector," and his "nuclear fission tester." The metallic last will somehow survived the explosion that destroyed the rocket moments after it landed on Earth and became buried deep in the ground, where it remained until it was finally rediscovered by Superman many years later (WF No. 69, Mar/Apr '54: "Jor-El's Last Will!").

To the outside of the rocket, Jor-El affixed several metal cylinders containing Kryptonian "condensed food" intended for the nurturing of his infant son following his arrival on Earth. The containers became detached from the rocket during its journey through space, however, and were not discovered until many years later (*see* BLISS, ROGER [MR. and MRS.]) (Act No. 217, Jun '56: "The Amazing Super-Baby").

Another item which Jor-El affixed to the exterior of the rocket was a special Kryptonian "record playback machine" containing a "video-recording"—or "video-tape"—of Jor-El narrating some of the events leading up to the destruction of Krypton. The video-tape and playback machine, however, somehow became detached from the rocket after it had entered Earth's atmosphere, and were not discovered until AQUAMAN retrieved them from the sea bottom many years later (Act No. 314, Jul '64: "The Day Superman Became the Flash!").

Knowing that Kryptonians would acquire "super-powers" in the lesser gravity of Earth, Jor-El had created a supply of special "radioactive capsules" designed to renew those powers temporarily in the event anything on Earth made them "fade away." In the horror of Krypton's final moments, however, Jor-El forgot to include the metal box containing the capsules among the items he placed in the rocket, and they were not discovered until many years later (*see* CRAIG, ELTON), when they found their way to Earth embedded in a meteoric fragment (WF No. 87, Mar/Apr '57: "The Reversed Heroes!"; *see also* WF No. 90, Sep/Oct '57: "The Super-Batwoman!").

Now the hour of Krypton's doom had come. "At that fateful moment, the rumblings inside Krypton became a roar and the planet shook wildly!" (Act No. 158, Jul '51: "The Kid from Krypton!").

The model rocket ship was small, but it was large enough to hold both Lara and her infant son. Jor-El urged them toward the tiny rocket. Already their home was crumbling about them (S No. 53/1, Jul/Aug '48: "The Origin of Superman!"; and others), and through gaping holes in the collapsing walls they could see the lofty spires of Krypton's once-proud edifices toppling like children's blocks amid dense clouds of choking black smoke. "I will not leave you, Jor-El!" cried Lara. "But we will save our son!" (Act No. 158, Jul '51: "The Kid from Krypton!"; and others).

on its fuselage (Act No. 246, Nov '58: "Krypton on Earth!").

"Krypton is dying!" cried Jor-El, amid the dying convulsions of a shattering planet.

"But our son will live," answered Lara, "—the last survivor of a great civilization!"

With the end of Krypton at hand, Jor-El urges Lara to flee their dying planet along with their infant son. But Lara refuses...

...and so, moments later, Jor-El launches the tiny rocket ship into the void...

...clasping his wife in a farewell embrace as the ruins of their shattered planet crumble about them

Hurriedly, "the helpless infant was placed into the space-ship" (S No. 53/1, Jul/Aug '48: "The Origin of Superman!"), wrapped in the blue, red, and yellow blankets that would, according to many accounts, one day be used to fashion his famous Superman costume (*see* SUPERMAN, [section C, the costume]).

And then the tiny craft was "launched forth into the void" (Act No. 158, Jul '51: "The Kid from Krypton!"), the flag of Krypton emblazoned proudly

Then, as husband and wife clung together in a desperate last embrace, "nature's fury gathered for one final cataclysmic eruption. . . . And as the pitifully small space-ship hurtled through interstellar space, the once mighty planet Krypton exploded into stardust!" (S No. 53/1, Jul/Aug '48: "The Origin of Superman!").

Because he remembers his parents as having been so "loving and kind" (S No. 123, Aug '58: chs. 1-3—

"The Girl of Steel"; "The Lost Super-Powers"; "Superman's Return to Krypton")—and because the anguish of losing them in childhood was so unbearably painful—Superman has memorialized his parents in numerous ways: he has dedicated a room to them in his FORTRESS OF SOLITUDE (Act No. 247, Dec '58: "Superman's Lost Parents!"; and others), taken color photographs of them "by overtaking and photographing light rays that had left Krypton before it exploded" (S No. 132, Oct '59: "Superman's Other Life!" pts. 1-3—"Krypton Lives On!"; "Futuro, Super-Hero of Krypton!"; "The Superman of Two Worlds!"), and carved their faces into the side of a planetoid in the style of the MOUNT RUSHMORE NATIONAL MEMORIAL (S No. 161/1, May '63: "The Last Days of Ma and Pa Kent!"). When, in January 1962, Superman, SUPERGIRL, and Krypto the Superdog transform an uninhabited planet in a "distant solar system" into an exact duplicate of Krypton as their way of commemorating "the anniversary of the death of Krypton," two of the "human androids" with which they populate their "memorial planet" are "robot imitations" of Jor-El and Lara (S No. 150/1: "The One Minute of Doom!").

In addition to these memorials created by Superman, a statue of Jor-El, Lara, and baby Kal-El adorns the grounds of METROPOLIS's SUPERMAN MUSEUM (S No. 150/3, Jan '62: "When the World Forgot Superman!"), and there are wax figures of Jor-El and Lara on display on JONAS SMITH's brainchild, Krypton Island (Act No. 246, Nov '58: "Krypton on Earth!"). In October 1961 LORI LEMARIS indicates that she and her fellow Atlanteans intend to use a hoard of gold from a sunken Spanish treasure ship to fashion solid gold statues of Jor-El and Lara as a surprise gift for Superman in gratitude for his past efforts on behalf of ATLANTIS's mer-people (S No. 148/3: "Superman Owes a Billion Dollars!").

ZOLL ORR, a scientist of the planet XENON who befriends Superman in February 1958, is a perfect look-alike for Superman's father (S No. 119: "The Second Superman!" chs. 1-3—"The World That Was Krypton's Twin"; "A Double for Superman"; "Superman's Mightiest Quest"), and Superman encounters another Jor-El look-alike—also named Jor-El—during a visit to an extradimensional "parallel universe" in July 1961 (S No. 146/2: "Superman's Greatest Feats!").

In June 1938, in the text containing the first account of Superman's origin (see SUPERMAN [section A, origin]), Superman's father is referred to only as an extraterrestrial "scientist" and his actual name is never stated (Act No. 1).

In July-August 1948, in a text containing a far more extensive account of Superman's origin, Superman's father is referred to by name—as Jor-El—for the first time in the chronicles (S No. 53/1: "The Origin of Superman!").

In November-December 1949 Superman sees Jor-El and Lara for the first time since his infancy when he journeys through the time-space barrier to the planet Krypton and actually witnesses the cataclysm that destroyed his native planet (S No. 61/3 "Superman Returns to Krypton!").

In October 1950 three Kryptonian "thought-projection discs" containing a detailed account of the courtship of Jor-El and Lara—which have been whirling about in space since the explosion of Krypton—are returned to Earth by a U.S. experimental rocket and retrieved by the ever-curious LOIS LANE (Act No. 149: "The Courtship on Krypton!"). (See also LARA.)

In January-February 1952 Jor-El's vault of great inventions, which had been hurled into outer space by the force of the cataclysm that destroyed Krypton, is drawn to Earth by a "magnet-ray machine" devised by the diabolical LEX LUTHOR (S No. 74/1: "The Lost Secrets of Krypton!").

In March-April 1954, on the site where the rocket carrying the infant Superman landed upon its arrival on Earth, Superman finds Jor-El's last will and testament—a thin sheet of super-hard metal inscribed with detailed descriptions of three of Jor-El's greatest inventions—buried deep in the ground. Following the instructions left behind by his father, Superman constructs working prototypes of all three inventions, and although he ultimately destroys two of them in the belief that mankind is not yet ready for them, the third and last invention, Jor-El's "nuclear fission tester" and the partially completed formula for halting a nuclear-fission reaction that accompanies it, does enable Superman to detect and halt a potentially cataclysmic chain reaction building up at the core of the Earth (WF No. 69: "Jor-El's Last Will!").

In May 1956 Metropolis is besieged by colossal metal machines—unleashed by a robot-piloted alien spacecraft—which tear through the city wreaking havoc and destruction. Superman's initial conclusion is that the "terrible machines" are the work of a sinister mastermind who "wants to take over the world," but a diary written by Jor-El, which the Man of Steel finds on the spacecraft's floor, reveals that the machines are actually "outlawed war weapons" from the planet Krypton which were launched into outer space by Jor-El prior to the death of his planet as part of his plan to avert what he feared was the possibility of an imminent outbreak of war on Krypton. The plan—which entailed launching the weapons-craft to an "artificial satellite," where its robot pilot would proceed to destroy a previously constructed "prop city" with the weapons as a graphic reminder to Kryptonians of the horrors of war—was aborted by the explosion of Krypton, which sent the weapons-carrying spacecraft careening into space, eventually to land on Earth, where the robot pilot began mindlessly to fulfill its automated mission of destruction. Superman ultimately destroys the weapons spacecraft, however, carrying it "deep into the center of Earth...where the molten core consumes the super-menace from Krypton!" (Act No. 216: "The Super-Menace of Metropolis").

In December 1956, "far out in space," Superman
mes upon "a mass of cosmic wreckage" from the
omed planet Krypton, including Jor-El's journal
d laboratory desk and some films which Jor-El
ade of himself using "automatic cameras." Togeth-

Jor-El's journal and films record the events
ding up to the death of Krypton, document Jor-El's
escopic study of Earth and his experiments with
tificially weakened gravity in an isolated Kryptoni-
valley, and recount the story of his defeat and
pture of two power-mad Kryptonian scientists, Val
n and Khai Zor, who had hoped to profit from Jor-
's discoveries in order to escape to Earth and
tablish themselves as "masters of the Earth
ople!" (Act No. 223: "The First Superman of
ypton").

In May 1957 Superman recovers a Kryptonian
nind-tape"—and a helmetlike apparatus for play-
g it back—after the objects have fallen to Earth
tside Metropolis embedded in a kryptonite meteor.
ctated by Jor-El shortly prior to the death of
rypton, the mind-tape tells the story of Jor-El's
cent encounter with the lovely QUEEN LATORA,
ler of the planet VERGO, and of her elaborate
heme to revitalize Vergo's dying sun by using a
lossal electromagnet to pull the planet Krypton into
he heart of Vergo's sun—thereby destroying Kryp-
n and annihilating its population—in order to
fuel the expiring star with Krypton's uranium core.
tunned to discover that the red-haired queen
terally intended to obliterate his planet, Jor-El
ught to thwart the scheme and ultimately prevailed
pon Queen Latora to search elsewhere in space for a
lanet sufficiently rich in uranium to enable her to
ulfill her mission. According to his account, Jor-El
irst learned of Krypton's imminent destruction when
Queen Latora told him that she had chosen Krypton
s the fuel for Vergo's sun only after determining that
rypton's doom was already imminent. Indeed, soon
fterward, Krypton did perish, and several decades
ater, after having been alerted to the Vergoans'
light by his father's mind-tape, Superman flashes
nto outer space to help Queen Latora and her people
evitalize their sun and thus avert their own immi-
ent extinction (S No. 113: chs. 1-3—"The Superman
of the Past"; "The Secret of the Towers"; "The
Superman of the Present").

In August 1958 Superman journeys through the
ime-space barrier to Krypton at a time when his
parents, who have not yet married, are working as
undercover agents to thwart the sinister machinations of the diabolical KIL-LOR. When, as the result of
a disastrous misunderstanding, Jor-El and Lara are
convicted of treason along with Kil-Lor and launched
into space in suspended animation to serve out a 100-
year term in a prison satellite, Superman frees the trio
from their orbiting prison and defeats Kil-Lor—who
has acquired super-powers identical to Superman's as
the result of having ventured beyond Krypton's
gravitational pull—by tricking the villain into killing
himself by overexposure to KRYPTONITE (S No. 123:

chs. 1-3—"The Girl of Steel"; "The Lost Super-
Powers"; "Superman's Return to Krypton").

In November 1960 Superman journeys through the
time-space barrier to Krypton on the day of his
parents' wedding and remains on the planet for what
is probably several weeks thereafter. During this
extended visit, Superman befriends his parents
without telling them who he is, obtains temporary
employment as Jor-El's assistant, and embarks on a
passionate romance with LYLA LERROL (S No. 141:
"Superman's Return to Krypton!" pts. I-III—
"Superman Meets Jor-El and Lara Again!"; "Superman's Kryptonian Romance!"; "The Surprise of
Fate!").

In December 1961 Superman enjoys a brief reunion
with Jor-El and Lara—as well as with his foster
parents, JONATHAN AND MARTHA KENT—after exposure to red kryptonite has temporarily endowed him
with the power to make his wishes come true and he
has wished aloud that his parents were on the scene to
advise him how best to use his marvelous new power.
Moments later, however, the effects of the red
kryptonite wear off, Superman loses his wish-
fulfilling power, and his magically materialized
parents and foster parents fade and vanish like
wraiths (Act No. 283: "The Red Kryptonite Menace!").

By July 1964, while patrolling the sea bottom,
Aquaman has retrieved the Kryptonian "record
playback machine" and "video-recording" which Jor-
El had originally affixed to the exterior of the rocket
that carried his infant son to Earth. Narrated by Jor-
El, the recording recounts his efforts to decide which
of six distant planets would make the best home for
his son Kal-El by feeding the available data into a
"great computer-forecaster." According to the
computer-forecaster, young Kal-El would ultimately
become a famed lawman and hero on whichever of
the six planets he grew to maturity, but the type of
hero he became would depend on the type of planet
chosen as his home, so that if he grew up on the water-
world of Valair, for example, he would develop into a
seagoing hero like Aquaman. As the result of these
and other inquiries, Jor-El decided his son would be
happiest living on Earth (Act No. 314: "The Day
Superman Became the Flash!").

During this same period, LEX LUTHOR journeys
through the time-space barrier to Krypton at a time
predating the marriage of Jor-El and Lara as part of
his bizarre scheme to marry Lara himself and thus
become the father of Superman (S No. 170/2, Jul '64:
pts. I-II—"If Lex Luthor Were Superman's Father!";
"The Wedding of Lara and Luthor!").

JOR-EL, 2nd. SUPERMAN's Kryptonian name,
according to Superman No. 75/1 (Mar/Apr '52: "The
Prankster's Star Pupil!"). Superman scholars tend to
accept the evidence of numerous other texts, however,
which state that Superman's true Kryptonian name
is actually Kal-El (S No. 113, May '57: chs. 1-3—"The
Superman of the Past"; "The Secret of the Towers";
"The Superman of the Present"; and others).

JUDD, DAN. The well-known author who is

secretly MISTER TWISTER (Act No. 96, May '46: "Haircut--And a Close Shave!").

JUNDY. An unscrupulous, power-hungry individual who, having come into possession of an ancient manuscript detailing the exact locations of the remote hiding places of the three pieces that make up the now-disassembled "Sorcerer King's sceptre"—an ancient mystic device said to confer "awesome powers" on whoever possesses it—kidnaps BATMAN and ROBIN and makes them captive on a tiny island as part of his scheme to force SUPERMAN to use his super-powers to retrieve the three hidden pieces of the magic sceptre as the ransom for the safe release of Batman and Robin. Jundy is ultimately apprehended and the sceptre destroyed through the heroic efforts of Batman, Robin, and Superman (WF No. 125, May '62: "The Hostages of the Island of Doom!").

JURIS, OTTO (Professor). An electronics scientist and head of Juris Electronics, Inc., who perpetrat an elaborate ruse in February 1961 designed persuade LOIS LANE and the DAILY PLANET sta that he is secretly SUPERMAN so that he can g PERRY WHITE to give him the red KRYPTONITE samp in his office safe and then sell it to the underworld f use against Superman. Superman thwarts th scheme and apprehends Juris and, reminded tha Juris has actually committed no crime for which l can properly be arrested, promptly takes Juris in custody "for destroying public property," a min charge resulting from Juris's having earlier damage a fire hydrant as part of his scheme to convince Lo Lane that he possessed super-powers (S No. 143/ "The Great Superman Hoax!"). The story is in man respects similar to Action Comics No. 213 (Feb '5 "Paul Paxton Alias Superman!"). (See PAXTOR PAUL.)

K

AIMS, "HATCHET." A METROPOLIS gangster—an expert when it comes to beating the law"—who is romised $50,000 by the city's underworld chieftains he can learn and expose SUPERMAN's secret dentity. Kaims and his cohorts are apprehended by uperman in January-February 1952 when they start fire in CLARK KENT's apartment building in an nsuccessful effort to discover which of its tenants is ecretly Superman (S No. 74/3: "The Secret of uperman's Home!").

KALE, DENNY. One of a pair of escaped convicts, both former actors, who, by impersonating BATMAN nd ROBIN, dupe PROFESSOR CARTER NICHOLS into ransporting them into the past, to the city of Florence in the year 1479, where they establish hemselves as the leaders of a band of ruthless medieval bandits. Followed into the past by SUPER-MAN, and then by the real Batman and Robin, Denny Kale and his partner, Shorty Biggs, are apprehended by the three famous crime-fighters, along with all their fifteenth-century henchmen, after an unsuccessful attempt to loot the treasure-laden strong room of the Medici Palace (WF No. 132, Mar '63: "Batman and Robin, Medieval Bandits!").

KAL-EL. SUPERMAN's Kryptonian name (S No. 113, May '57: chs. 1-3—"The Superman of the Past"; "The Secret of the Towers"; "The Superman of the Present"; and others).

KANDOR. The capital city of the planet KRYPTON, which survived the destruction of its native planet as the result of having been stolen sometime prior to the cataclysm by the space villain BRAINIAC, who reduced the city to microscopic size and preserved it, people and buildings alive and intact, inside a glass bottle aboard his spacecraft, where it remained for many years until it was finally recovered by SUPER-MAN in July 1958 and placed for safekeeping inside his FORTRESS OF SOLITUDE (Act No. 242: "The Super-Duel in Space"; and others).

Inside the bottle city, life goes on much as it did prior to the destruction of Krypton (Act No. 245, Oct '58: "The Shrinking Superman!"; and others), yet although restoration to their normal size remains the heartfelt wish of all Kandorians, Superman has not yet succeeded, despite years of effort, in finding a way to enlarge the city safely. He has, however, on occasion managed to reduce himself in size temporarily for the purpose of visiting the bottle city and undertaking adventures there (S No. 158, Jan '63: "Superman in Kandor" pts. I-III—"Invasion of the Mystery Super-Men!"; "The Dynamic Duo of Kandor!"; "The City of Super-People!"; and others).

Nestled securely on a niche inside the Fortress of Solitude (Act No. 261, Feb '60: "Superman's Fortresses of Solitude!"), the bottle city of Kandor is "the most amazing exhibit in [Superman's] Fortress" (Act No. 243, Aug '58: "The Lady and the Lion") and "the prize of [his] collection" of curiosities and artifacts from throughout the universe (Act No. 253, Jun '59: "The War Between Superman and Jimmy Olsen!"). Although it is referred to as Krypton City in World's Finest Comics No. 100 (Mar '59: "The Dictator of Krypton City!") and as Kandor City in Action Comics No. 261 (Feb '60: "Superman's Fortresses of Solitude!"), it is referred to as Kandor in every other text that mentions it by name (Act No. 242, Jul '58: "The Super-Duel in Space"; and many others) and remains "the only surviving city" of the lost planet Krypton (S No. 158, Jan '63: "Superman in Kandor" pts. I-III—"Invasion of the Mystery Super-Men!"; "The Dynamic Duo of Kandor!"; "The City of Super-People!"). Its population as of July 1958 was approximately 1,000,000 (Act No. 242: "The Super-Duel in Space").

Employing the "Kandor-scope" in his Fortress of Solitude, Superman broadcasts a message to the people of Kandor, 1964

According to Superman No. 158, the peaceful city of Kandor, capital of Krypton, was "a place of beauty and happiness" until the dark day when Brainiac, "the evilest villain of space," appeared over the city in his saucerlike spacecraft, reduced it to "microscopic size" with his diabolical "hyper-force ray," and then soared away again into outer space with the captive city of Kandor imprisoned aboard his craft inside a large glass bottle (Jan '63: "Superman in Kandor" pts. I-III—"Invasion of the Mystery Super-Men!"; "The Dynamic Duo of Kandor!"; "The City of Super-People!").

Although the texts seem agreed, however, that the theft of Kandor occurred "years before" Krypton exploded (Act No. 243, Aug '58: "The Lady and the Lion"; and others), it is not possible to pinpoint the date of the theft with any real accuracy, though it appears to have occurred either shortly before (S No. 170/2, Jul '64: pts. I-II—"If Lex Luthor Were Superman's Father!"; "The Wedding of Lara and Luthor!") or after (S No. 141, Nov '60: "Superman's Return to Krypton!" pts. I-III—"Superman Meets Jor-El and Lara Again!"; "Superman's Kryptonian Romance!"; "The Surprise of Fate!") the wedding of JOR-EL and LARA. To this day, despite the fact that, by stealing their city, Brainiac inadvertently rescued the people of Kandor from the cataclysmic doom that befell the rest of their planet, the Kandorians still regard him as "the foulest villain in the universe" for having wrenched their city from its native planet and for having doomed them, perhaps forever, to lilliputian size (S No. 167, Feb '64: "The Team of Luthor and Brainiac!" pts. I-III—"The Deadly Duo!"; "The Downfall of Superman!"; "The Hour of Kandor's Vengeance!").

Superman recalls the theft of Kandor by the space villain Brainiac, 1963

Indeed, although it is the goal of all Kandorians to see their city enlarged to normal size so that they can live out their lives outside the bottle, either on Earth or on some distant planet (S No. 158, Jan '63: "Superman in Kandor" pts. I-III—"Invasion of the Mystery Super-Men!"; "The Dynamic Duo of Kandor!"; "The City of Super-People!"), the prospects for the successful enlargement of Kandor remain, at best, uncertain. Action Comics No. 245, for example, observes that "Some day Superman hopes to find a way to enlarge them [the Kandorians] to normal size" (Oct '58: "The Shrinking Superman!"), and, indeed, this sentiment is echoed in a number of other texts

(Act No. 276, May '61: "The War Between Superg and the Supermen Emergency Squad!"; and other In Action Comics No. 253, however, Superma concedes that "I know of no way to restore them [t] Kandorians] to their normal size" (Jun '59: "The W Between Superman and Jimmy Olsen!"), and Action No. 243 he goes a step further, remarking th Kandor "can never be restored to normal size!" (Au '58: "The Lady and the Lion"). By and large, howeve the long term outlook seems optimistic. Althoug Superman has not yet succeeded, despite years effort, in finding a way to enlarge the city safely (No. 158, Jan '63: "Superman in Kandor" pts. I-III "Invasion of the Mystery Super-Men!"; "The Dynam ic Duo of Kandor!", "The City of Super-People!"; an others), there are substantial indications that a enlarging device powerful enough to restore Kando to normal size could be constructed if only the rar element or elements needed to power such a devic could be accumulated in sufficient quantity (Act No 280, Sep '61: "Brainiac's Super-Revenge!"; see also S No. 167, Feb '64: "The Team of Luthor and Brainiac!" pts. I-III—"The Deadly Duo!"; "The Downfall o Superman!"; "The Hour of Kandor's Vengeance!"; and others). Indeed, one text states flatly that Kandor will one day be enlarged to normal size, but only in the distant future (Act No. 300, May '63: "Superman Under the Red Sun!").

The texts are also somewhat vague concerning the exact size to which Brainiac shrank the Kandorians and their city. Numerous texts describe him as having reduced the city to "microscopic size" (Act No. 253, Jun '59: "The War Between Superman and Jimmy Olsen!"; and others), yet the city's larger buildings are plainly visible to the naked eye through the thick glass of the bottle, and one text asserts that it is possible to observe Kandorian life through the lens of an ordinary magnifying glass (Act No. 261, Feb '60: "Superman's Fortresses of Solitude!").

Similarly, the people of Kandor are frequently referred to as "tiny" (Act No. 245, Oct '58: "The Shrinking Superman!"; and others), but it is far more likely that, although the city's larger edifices may be visible to the naked eye, the Kandorians themselves are no larger than microbes (S No. 179/2, Aug '65: "The Menace of Gold Kryptonite!").

The picturesque city of Kandor sits inside a large "bell-jar" in Superman's Fortress of Solitude (S No. 158, Jan '63: "Superman in Kandor" pts. I-III— "Invasion of the Mystery Super-Men!"; "The Dynamic Duo of Kandor!"; "The City of Super-People!"). According to Superman No. 134, "...Brainiac made the walls [of the bell jar] of super-hard, unbreakable glass" (Jan '60: chs. I-III—"The Super-Menace of Metropolis!"; "The Revenge Against Jor-El!"; "The Duel of the Supermen!"), but the accuracy of this statement is called into question by an event that occurs in October 1958, when LOIS LANE inadvertently bumps into the bottle, knocking it to the floor and causing a hairline crack in the glass (Act No. 245: "The Shrinking Superman!").

The bottle containing the city of Kandor is sealed a large "cork" (S No. 156, Oct '62: "The Last Days Superman!" pts. I-III—"Superman's Death Sen-ce!"; "The Super-Comrades of All Time!"; "Super-n's Last Day of Life!"; and others), more accurate-described as a "super-hard metal stopper" (Act No. 2, Jul '58: "The Super-Duel in Space"; and others).

August 1965 a doorway has been installed in the pper to facilitate "easier exit from the giant bottle" members of the SUPERMEN EMERGENCY SQUAD d other Kandorians (S No. 179/2: "The Menace of ld Kryptonite!").

Safeguarding the city of Kandor and its lilliputian pulation is one of Superman's gravest responsibili-s. "I have to check that city-in-the-bottle regular-," muses the Man of Steel in January 1960, "to see at the tiny people inside it are safe!" (S No. 134: chs. II—"The Super-Menace of Metropolis!"; "The evenge Against Jor-El!"; "The Duel of the Super-en!").

Watching over the city consists mainly of conduct-g periodic checks of the air hoses and related pparatus which provide the Kandorians with a eady supply of air. "Air has to be pumped in," oserves Lois Lane in October 1958, "for the tiny eople are still alive and going about their daily usiness!" (Act No. 245: "The Shrinking Super-an!").

Inside the bottle city, "Krypton's gravity-onditions are duplicated" to allow the Kandorians to certain the air mixture is right..." (Act No. 282, Nov '61: "Superman's Toughest Day!").

Indeed, life in the bottle city goes on today much as it did before Brainiac stole it, with the Kandorians "going about their daily business" (Act No. 245, Oct '58: "The Shrinking Superman!") almost as though their native planet had never exploded. Kryptonese, the language of Krypton, is still spoken (S No. 158, Jan '63: "Superman in Kandor" pts. I-III—"Invasion of the Mystery Super-Men!"; "The Dynamic Duo of Kandor!"; "The City of Super-People!"), and Kandori-an scientific progress has continued apace despite the limitations imposed by the artificial glass-walled environment. Small rocket ships (Act No. 242, Jul '58: "The Super-Duel in Space"; and others) and individu-al "jet-powered flying-belts" (S No. 172, Oct '64: pts. I-III—"The New Superman!"; "Clark Kent—Former Superman!"; "The Struggle of the Two Supermen!"; and others) fly busy Kandorians about their city, and "tireless robot farmhands raise [their] crops for food" (Act No. 242, Jul '58: "The Super-Duel in Space").

"Sealed in a dark cold bottle," the Kandorians "created [their] own artificial sun...a flaming fireball crossing over the city regularly on its tracks!" (Act No. 242, Jul '58: "The Super-Duel in Space"). According to Superman No. 158, however, it is an array of ingenious devices called "sun-lamps" that provide Kandor with its warmth and sunlight, the lamps being dimmed each evening to provide the Kandorians with a nightly "sleep period" (Jan '63:

Inside the bottle city, robot farmhands till crops beneath the warming glare of an artificial sun, 1958

live normal lives in the environment characteristic of their native planet (Act No. 242, Jul '58: "The Super-Duel in Space"; and others). Therefore, in Superman's words, "The Kandorians must be constantly supplied with air that is of the same composition as the air on their native Krypton--so I always check to make "Superman in Kandor" pts. I-III—"Invasion of the Mystery Super-Men!"; "The Dynamic Duo of Kan-dor!"; "The City of Super People!").

In laboratories and public squares throughout the city, sophisticated "ultra scanning screens" (S No. 134, Jan '60: chs. I-III—"The Super-Menace of

Metropolis!"; "The Revenge Against Jor-El!"; "The Duel of the Supermen!")—referred to also as "Earth viewers" (S No. 144/3, Apr '61: "The Orphans of Space!"; and others) or "Earth monitor screens" (Act No. 276, May '61: "The War Between Supergirl and the Supermen Emergency Squad!")—enable Kandorian observers to "pick up any scene on Earth" (S No. 134, Jan '60: chs. I-III—"The Super-Menace of Metropolis!"; "The Revenge Against Jor-El!"; "The Duel of the Supermen!"), and thereby monitor Superman's actions constantly, both visually and aurally, no matter where on Earth he may be (Act No. 276, May '61: "The War Between Supergirl and the Supermen Emergency Squad!"; and others), so that, in the event of an emergency, they can contact the Man of Steel via "super-sonic signal" (Act No. 261, Feb '60: "Superman's Fortresses of Solitude!") or dispatch the Supermen Emergency Squad to his rescue. Indeed, a number of Superman's enemies, aware that his activities are continually monitored by Kandorian observers, have taken the precaution of deliberately jamming the Kandorian monitors to prevent him from being aided by his Kandorian allies (Act No. 295, Dec '62: "Superman Goes Wild!"; and others).

Other achievements of Kandorian science include

Planet Editor!"); and a miraculous healing r invented by the Kandorian scientist Reg-En, whic used to heal Superman's hand in February 1962 a1 he has been badly bitten during a battle wit Kryptonian "flame dragon" (see FLAME DRAGON No. 151/3: "Superman's Greatest Secret!").

Kandor is governed by the Kandorian Counci No. 151/3, Feb '62: "Superman's Greatest Secret!" body of distinguished citizens apparently mode after the form of planetary government that p vailed on the planet Krypton prior to the cataclysm No. 65/3, Jul/Aug '50: "Three Supermen fr Krypton!"; and others). The city proper is domina1 by such institutions as the Museum of Kryptoni History (WF No. 143, Aug '64: "The Feud Betwe Batman and Superman!" pts. I-II—no title; "T Manhunters from Earth!"), a well-stocked libra (Act No. 243, Aug '58: "The Lady and the Lion"), t Kandor City Zoo (Act No. 242, Jul '58: "The Sup Duel in Space"), and the majestic Hall of Justi where, once each year, the Phantom Zone Par Board meets to consider the pleas of PHANTOM ZO prisoners seeking parole. Those prisoners deem worthy of parole are released from the Phantom Zo to begin new lives as Kandorian citizens (Act No. 31 Mar '64: "Secret of Kryptonite Six!").

Superman and Professor Kimda tour a
Kandorian rocket plant...

...and later view a rare Kryptonian "metal-eating mole" o display in the Kandor City Zoo, 1958

devices called "mental suggestion helmets," which enable psychiatrists to control and direct the fantasies of their patients and are used in treating the mentally ill (S No. 173/1, Nov '64: "The 'Untouchable' Clark Kent!"); an ingenious apparatus known as the "psycho-locator," which, through the electronic analysis and long-distance sensing of brain-wave patterns, is capable of locating any selected individual—such as a fugitive criminal— "anywhere in space and time" (S No. 168, Apr '64: pts. I-II—"Luthor--Super-Hero!"; "Lex Luthor, Daily

Outside the city is a neatly landscaped suburba region characterized by elegant mansions and fin houses, and beyond the suburbs are "strange forests' filled with Kryptonian wildlife and "weird vegeta tion" (S No. 158, Jan '63: "Superman in Kandor" pts I-III—"Invasion of the Mystery Super-Men!"; "The Dynamic Duo of Kandor!"; "The City of Super People!"; and others).

In February, the people of Kandor celebrate Krypton Day, a holiday whose precise significance is never stated in the chronicles (S No. 167, Feb '64: "The

Team of Luthor and Brainiac!" pts. I-III—"The Deadly Duo!"; "The Downfall of Superman!"; "The Hour of Kandor's Vengeance!"), and once each year, in either December or January, they bow their heads in silence in solemn commemoration of "the anniversary of the destruction of Krypton..." (S No. 150/1, Jan '62: "The One Minute of Doom!"; *see also* WF No. 146, Dec '64: "Batman, Son of Krypton!" pts. I-II—no title; "The Destroyer of Krypton!"). In April, the Kandorians hold ceremonies marking the Day of Truth, a holiday once celebrated by all Kryptonians, in which they honor the memory of Val-Lor, a valiant Kryptonian who, by courageously speaking out against the "ruthless swarm of alien invaders" who had invaded Krypton and enslaved its people, inspired his fellow Kryptonians to revolt against their alien oppressors and drive the aliens from their planet (S No. 176/3, Apr '65: "Superman's Day of Truth!").

Kandor's "greatest hero" is Superman, and there are several statues of him in and about the city (S No. 158, Jan '63: "Superman in Kandor" pts. I-III—"Invasion of the Mystery Super-Men!"; "The Dynamic Duo of Kandor!"; "The City of Super-People!"). Outside the bottle city, Superman's dual identity is a closely guarded secret, but inside Kandor the fact that Clark Kent is Superman is "known to all Kandorians" (S No. 179/2, Aug '65: "The Menace of Gold Kryptonite!").

SOON, VIA A SPECIAL MONITOR SCREEN EQUIPPED WITH A ZONE-O-PHONE, THE BOARD HEARS AN APPEAL FROM THE TWILIGHT DIMENSION.'

THE FIRST CASE IS THAT OF *VORB-UN*, SENTENCED FOR TEN TIME CYCLES FOR EXPERIMENTING WITH FORBIDDEN ELEMENTS WITHOUT THE COUNCIL'S PERMISSION.'

MY SENTENCE IS ALMOST UP! I REPENT MY CRIME.' PLEASE FREE ME, KANDORIANS.'

Inside Kandor's Hall of Justice, the Phantom Zone Parole Board meets annually to consider the parole pleas of Phantom Zone prisoners

Just as the Kandorians keep a watchful eye on Superman by means of their sophisticated Earth monitors, the Man of Steel keeps in close communication with his friends in Kandor. In Superman's Fortress of Solitude, a red light on an intricate "monitoring machine" lights up in the event of a "Kandor emergency" (S No. 144/3, Apr '61: "The Orphans of Space!"), and a special "Kandor-scope" monitor screen (S No. 151/3, Feb '62: "Superman's Greatest Secret!"), sometimes used in conjunction with an operator's headphone and mouthpiece (S No.

167, Feb '64: "The Team of Luthor and Brainiac!" pts. I-III—"The Deadly Duo!"; "The Downfall of Superman!"; "The Hour of Kandor's Vengeance!"), enables him to carry on simultaneous visual and aural communication with his Kandorian allies (WF No. 143, Aug '64: "The Feud Between Batman and Superman!" pts. I-II—no title; "The Manhunters from Earth!").

In order to enter Kandor, either to visit his friends or to undertake adventures there, Superman must first reduce himself to microscopic size. When the Man of Steel first visits the bottle city, in July 1958, it is after he has been reduced to lilliputian size—along with the entire population of METROPOLIS—by the "hyper-forces" unleashed by Brainiac. Later these same forces, activated, in reverse, by means of a console aboard Brainiac's spacecraft, are used to restore Superman to his normal human size (Act No. 242: "The Super-Duel in Space").

By October 1958, the renegade Kandorian scientist ZAK-KUL has successfully "isolated the rare element, illium 349, whose rays can change the size of the body," and used it to create an ingenious reducing and enlarging ray which can be used to either shrink or enlarge a person to any chosen size. Superman ultimately defeats the villain and confiscates his sophisticated size-changing apparatus (Act No. 245: "The Shrinking Superman!").

By March 1959, the renegade scientist LEX LUTHOR has devised a set of ingenious belts capable of either reducing or enlarging people or objects. Superman, BATMAN, and ROBIN ultimately apprehend Luthor and his henchmen and confiscate their size-changing belts (WF No. 100: "The Dictator of Krypton City!").

By June 1959, the Kandorian "criminal scientist" EL GAR KUR has perfected an elaborate body-switching apparatus that enables him to trade places with anyone who happens to be standing outside the bottle, so that the target individual finds himself suddenly reduced in size and trapped inside Kandor, while El Gar Kur is, in the exact same instant, transported outside the bottle city and enlarged to normal human size. Superman defeats El Gar Kur with the aid of JIMMY OLSEN, and the villain's body-switching apparatus is apparently confiscated by the Kandorian authorities (Act No. 253: "The War Between Superman and Jimmy Olsen!").

By January 1960 the Kandorian scientist KULL-EX has devised an ingenious "exchange ray" designed to enable him to escape the bottle city while trapping Superman inside Kandor. By beaming "a flash of super-energy" at Superman as he stands in his Fortress of Solitude close by the bottle, Kull-Ex is able to reduce the Man of Steel instantaneously to microscopic size and transport him to his laboratory inside Kandor while simultaneously transporting himself outside the bottle and enlarging himself to normal human size. Moreover, because only human bodies—and not clothing—are affected by the exchange ray, Superman finds himself stranded in

Kandor clad in Kull-Ex's clothing, while Kull-Ex finds himself standing in Superman's Fortress clad in Superman's costume. Superman ultimately escapes from Kandor and resolves his differences with Kull-Ex, but because "zenium," the extraterrestrial element that powers the exchange ray, is exceedingly rare, it is questionable whether the apparatus can ever be used again (S No. 134: chs. I-III—"The Super-Menace of Metropolis!"; "The Revenge Against Jor-El!"; "The Duel of the Supermen!").

In February 1962, in an apparent reference either to El Gar Kur's invention or Kull-Ex's, Superman muses that "I can only enter Kandor by having my exchange ray cause me to switch places with a similar-sized Kandorian person or creature." Indeed, when Superman visits Kandor during this period, he arranges to exchange himself for his Kandorian friend NIM-ZEE, and then to reverse the exchange once his business in Kandor has been successfully concluded (S No. 151/3: "Superman's Greatest Secret!").

By July 1962, however, the "exchange ray" has been superseded by a more technologically advanced device. "Welcome to Kandor!" greets the Kandorian scientist LON-ES enthusiastically after he has used the new invention to reduce SUPERGIRL to microscopic size and transport her to his laboratory inside the bottle. "You have been reduced in size and transported here by a new ray we've developed which is better than the exchange-ray! Our teleport ray transports one person at a time... and it isn't necessary to exchange a Kandorian for an Earth person during the transference, as before!" (S No. 154/2: "Krypton's First Superman!").

To enter Kandor in January 1963, Superman and Jimmy Olsen reduce themselves to microscopic size by means of the raygunlike "shrinking ray" once confiscated from Brainiac. The effects of the ray are apparently gradual, allowing the Man of Steel and his pal to clamber up the side of the bottle after they have been reduced to a few inches in height and uncork the metal stopper while they are still "large enough to handle it!" Moments later, after the metal stopper has been removed and Brainiac's ray has reduced them to microbe size, Superman and Jimmy parachute down into the city. Sometime later, after departing Kandor, the Man of Steel and his companion use the apparatus invented by Zak-Kul—here referred to as an "enlarger" or "enlarging ray"—to restore themselves to normal human size. "*This* enlarger, once made by a Kandorian criminal, is powered by the element illium 349," remarks Superman, "...and I have a tiny few grains of illium in the pouch of my cape just for emergencies like this!" (S No. 158: "Superman in Kandor" pts. I-III—"Invasion of the Mystery Super-Men!"; "The Dynamic Duo of Kandor!"; "The City of Super-People!"). The enlarging ray used here is probably the same as the raygunlike "enlarging force" with which Superman restores himself, Lex Luthor, and Brainiac to normal human size when the three of them have emerged

from Kandor after being embroiled in an adventure there in February 1964. "This force enlarges us to normal size," remarks Superman, "but there isn't enough of the element that powers it to enlarge the people of Kandor you shrunk, Brainiac!" (S No. 167: "The Team of Luthor and Brainiac!" pts. I-III—"The Deadly Duo!"; "The Downfall of Superman!"; "The Hour of Kandor's Vengeance!").

For yet another visit to Kandor, in March 1964, Superman reduces himself to microscopic size by

After conferring together in the Fortress of Solitude...

...Superman and Jimmy Olsen remove the "shrinking ray" once owned by Brainiac from its special niche...

means of an ingenious "shrinking ray," apparently the one confiscated from Brainiac, and then parachutes down into the city (Act No. 310: "Secret of Kryptonite Six!").

Inside Kandor, where "Krypton's gravity-conditions are duplicated," Superman becomes an ordinary human being, without super-powers, although he regains his powers the moment he exits from the bottle and reenters the earthly environment (Act No. 242, Jul '58: "The Super-Duel in Space"; and

*...and use it to reduce themselves
to microscopic size...*

*...so that they can parachute down into
the bottle city of Kandor, 1963*

others). "Where **Krypton**'s non-earthly gravity conditions are in force," muses Superman in October 1958, "I have no super-powers! I...I'm just an **ordinary man!**" (Act No. 245: "The Shrinking Superman!"; and others). Indeed, even KRYPTONITE has no effect on Superman while he remains in Kandor, simply because he is only an ordinary mortal there (Act No. 305, Oct '63: "Why Superman Needs a Secret Identity!").

Similarly, any Kandorian who emerges from the

bottle city instantly acquires super-powers identical to Superman's, along with vulnerability to the various forms of kryptonite (Act No. 245, Oct '58: "The Shrinking Superman!"; and many others). For an ordinary earthling, however, a visit to Kandor can be a trying experience, for the heavy artificial gravity, designed to duplicate the atmospheric conditions that prevailed on Krypton, make it necessary to wear special "anti-gravity shoes" merely to walk in the alien environment (S No. 158, Jan '63: "Superman in Kandor" pts. I-III—"Invasion of the Mystery Super-Men!"; "The Dynamic Duo of Kandor!"; "The City of Super-People!").

In the course of a Kandorian adventure in January 1963, during a period when it is unsafe for Superman to move about in Kandor due to the lies that have been spread about him among the people by the "fanatic scientist" THAN OL, Superman and Jimmy Olsen decide to emulate their friends Batman and Robin by adopting a pair of alternate identities and working together as a team. Inspired by the names and plumage of a pair of Kandorian birds—a "nightwing" and a "flamebird"—owned by their friend NOR-KAN, Superman and Jimmy adopt the alternate identities of Nightwing and Flamebird and fashion a pair of colorful costumes evocative of the plumage of the two Kandorian birds.

For his role as Nightwing, Superman wears a black eye-mask and a Prussian-blue costume consisting of Prussian-blue tights, trunks, cape, wrist-length gloves, and ankle-length boots. Emblazoned on his chest is a highly stylized black bird emblem inscribed inside a white circle. Around his waist is a yellow utility belt equipped with "personal jet-motors" which endow him with the power of self-sustained flight.

For his role as Flamebird, Jimmy Olsen wears a black eye-mask and a bright red costume consisting of red tights, trunks, and a deeply scalloped red cape, complemented by yellow boots and yellow elbow-length gloves. Emblazoned on his chest is a highly stylized yellow sunburst, and around his waist is a yellow utility belt, almost identical to Nightwing's, equipped with personal jet-motors for self-sustained flight.

Equipment contained in the utility belts includes "smoke cylinders" to enable Nightwing and Flamebird to stymie their pursuers by enveloping them in clouds of thick black smoke; "cutting-torches" for cutting through walls and other obstacles; and special "lead cloth caps" designed to enable the duo to "shield" their thoughts from—and thereby elude, if necessary—the fearsome "telepathic hounds" of Kandor, "strange beasts," yellow in color, with tails like wolves and snouts like wild boars, "that can locate people at any distance by reading their minds to learn where they are!" Because of their unique abilities, the creatures are employed by the Kandorian authorities as telepathic bloodhounds.

Beneath his lavish home in the Kandorian suburbs, Nor-Kan has constructed a "secret underground lab"—with a camouflaged entrance built into a grassy hillside—to prevent intruders from tampering with his delicate scientific instruments. With Nor-Kan's blessing, Nightwing and Flamebird christen this laboratory the "night-cave"—or "nightcave"—and transform it into their secret subterranean headquarters, while simultaneously converting Nor-Kan's automobile into a swift, specially equipped "nightmobile."

By the time this Kandorian adventure draws to a close, Nightwing and Flamebird—the so-called Dynamic Duo of Kandor—have revealed their true identities to the Kandorian people and the Kandorians have erected a colorful statue of the two heroes in the heart of the city (S No. 158: "Superman in Kandor" pts. I-III—"Invasion of the Mystery Super-Men!"; "The Dynamic Duo of Kandor!"; "The City of Super-People!").

Nevertheless, in the course of another Kandorian adventure, in August 1964, Superman and Jimmy Olsen resume the use of their Kandorian alternate identities, this time aided by Nighthound, a telepathic hound that they have adopted as their companion. A Kryptonian "high-speed teaching machine" housed in the nightcave enables Batman and Robin to become swiftly fluent in Kryptonese during a visit to the city, and a special "night-alarm" installed in the subterranean sanctuary enables the Kandorian police to summon Nightwing and Flamebird in the event of an emergency. In this text, the duo's personal jet-motors are referred to as "jet-powered flying belts" (WF No. 143: "The Feud Between Batman and Superman!" pts. I-II—no title; "The Manhunters from Earth!").

Nightwing and Flamebird in flight over Kandor, 1963

Over the past two decades, numerous individual Kandorians have played important roles in the chronicles, including Professor Kimda, the elderly

scientist whose knowledge helps the Man of St̲ defeat BRAINIAC in July 1958 (Act No. 242: "T̲ Super-Duel in Space"); the "renegade scientist" ZA̲ KUL (Act No. 245, Oct '58: "The Shrinking Supe̲ man!"); the "criminal scientist" EL GAR KUR (Act N̲ 253, Jun '59: "The War Between Superman a̲ Jimmy Olsen!"); the young scientist KULL-EX (S N̲ 134, Jan ' 60: chs. I-III—"The Super-Menace ̲ Metropolis!"; "The Revenge Against Jor-El!"; "T̲ Duel of the Supermen!"); VAN-ZEE and his wi̲ SYLVIA (S No. 158, Jan '63: "Superman in Kando̲ pts. I-III—"Invasion of the Mystery Super-Men! "The Dynamic Duo of Kandor!"; "The City of Supe̲ People!"); Van-Zee's father, NIM-ZEE, and Reg-En, scientist whose miraculous healing ray cures Supe̲ man after the Man of Steel has been bitten by ̲ Kryptonian flame dragon (*see* FLAME DRAGON) i̲ February 1962 (S No. 151/3: "Superman's Greate̲ Secret!"); the scientist LON-ES (S No. 154/2, Jul '6̲ "Krypton's First Superman!"); the benevolent scie̲ tist NOR-KAN and the "fanatic scientist" THAN OL (̲ No. 158, Jan '63: "Superman in Kandor" pts. I-III— "Invasion of the Mystery Super-Men!"; "The Dynam̲ ic Duo of Kandor!"; "The City of Super-People!"); th̲ Kandorian official THAN-AR and his evil brothe̲ Jhan-Ar (WF No. 143, Aug '64: "The Feud Betwee̲ Batman and Superman!" pts. I-II—no title; "Th̲ Manhunters from Earth!"); the egotistical AR-VAL (S̲ No. 172, Oct '64: pts. I-III—"The New Superman!" "Clark Kent—Former Superman!"; "The Struggle o̲ the Two Supermen!"); VOL-DON (S No. 177/1, May '65̲ "Superman's Kryptonese Curse!") and the members̲ of the Kandorian LOOK-ALIKE SQUAD (Act No. 309, Feb '64: "The Superman Super-Spectacular!"); and̲ Don-El (SA No. 5, Sum '62) and the members of the SUPERMEN EMERGENCY SQUAD (Act No. 276, May̲ '61: "The War Between Supergirl and the Supermen̲ Emergency Squad!"; and others). Supergirl's parents, ZOR-EL and ALURA, have resided in Kandor since being freed from the Survival Zone in early 1964.

In July 1958, in a text marking Superman's first visit to Kandor, the Man of Steel recovers the hijacked bottle city from the space villain BRAINIAC and places it for safekeeping inside his Fortress of Solitude (Act No. 242: "The Super-Duel in Space").

In August 1958 Superman scans the entire contents of a Kandorian library in search of a formula capable of counteracting the effects of an "evolution serum" devised by the enchantress CIRCE (Act No. 243: "The Lady and the Lion").

In October 1958 Superman matches wits with the Kandorian "renegade scientist" ZAK-KUL (Act No. 245: "The Shrinking Superman!").

In March 1959 Superman parachutes into Kandor for a battle with LEX LUTHOR (WF No. 100: "The Dictator of Krypton City!").

In June 1959 Superman battles the Kandorian "criminal scientist" EL GAR KUR (Act No. 253: "The War Between Superman and Jimmy Olsen!").

In January 1960 Superman matches wits with the Kandorian scientist KULL-EX (S No. 134: chs. I-III—

'he Super-Menace of Metropolis!"; "The Revenge gainst Jor-El!"; "The Duel of the Supermen!").

In February 1960 a pair of Kandorian scientists, ars-Ol and Ra-Ho, help Superman thwart a scheme y the ANTI-SUPERMAN GANG to blow up the Fortress Solitude (Act No. 261: "Superman's Fortresses of olitude!").

In November 1960, during a time-journey he makes the planet Krypton prior to its destruction, uperman witnesses the theft of Kandor by Brainiac No. 141: "Superman's Return to Krypton!" pts. I-I—"Superman Meets Jor-El and Lara Again!"; Superman's Kryptonian Romance!"; "The Surprise f Fate!").

In May 1961 the elite corps of Kandorians known s the Supermen Emergency Squad helps Superman afeguard the secret of his dual identity (Act No. 276: The War Between Supergirl and the Supermen mergency Squad!"). (See KILEY, JOHN.)

In July 1961, while under the baleful control of the lien "plant intelligence" XASNU, PERRY WHITE nvades Superman's Fortress of Solitude and des-roys what he believes to be the bottle city of Kandor. he bottle city White destroys, however, is actually nly a decoy duplicate prepared in advance by uperman (Act No. 278: "The Super Powers of Perry Vhite!").

In October 1961 the Supermen Emergency Squad elps Superman thwart the mischievous machina-ions of MR. MXYZPTLK (S No. 148/2: "Mr. Mxyzptlk's Super-Mischief!").

In February 1962 the people of Kandor celebrate Supergirl's public debut by using their tiny rocket ships to skywrite a congratulatory message to her across the Kandorian sky (Act No. 285: "The World's Greatest Heroine!"). During this same period, Super-man pays a visit to the laboratory of the Kandorian scientist Reg-En for treatment of a bite on his hand inflicted by a Kryptonian "flame dragon" (see FLAME DRAGON) (S No. 151/3, Feb '62: "Superman's Greatest Secret!").

In March 1962 Supergirl soars into outer space with the bottle city of Kandor cradled in her arms after "telling the Kandorians that she would journey to scores of planets in space to find a scientist who could enlarge their miniature city!" (Act No. 286: "The Jury of Super-Enemies!"). Supergirl's quest, however, is apparently unsuccessful, for as of the late 1970s Kandor still has not been enlarged.

In July 1962 the Kandorian scientist Lon-Es, once an assistant to Superman's father Jor-El, alerts Supergirl to the true explanation behind the senseless acts of destruction being committed by Superman (S No. 154/2: "Krypton's First Superman!"). (See MAG-EN.)

In August 1962, during a period when Superman's vulnerability to kryptonite has been temporarily replaced by a vulnerability to gold, Superman is rescued from a potentially fatal overexposure to gold by members of the Supermen Emergency Squad (Act No. 291: "The New Superman!").

In October 1962, after exposure to red kryptonite has temporarily transformed Superman into two separate individuals, a mature, responsible Clark Kent and an unprincipled, irresponsible Superman, the entire city of Kandor is imprisoned in the Phantom Zone by the arrogant Superman in order to prevent the Kandorians from interfering with his plan to keep the personalities of Clark Kent and Superman separate forever. Ultimately, however, Clark Kent frees the Kandorians from the Phantom Zone, and soon afterward he succeeds in bringing about the reuniting of Clark Kent and Superman into a single individual (Act No. 293: "The Feud Between Superman and Clark Kent!"). During this same period, when Superman is believed to be dying of an incurable malady, the Supermen Emergency Squad joins forces with KRYPTO THE SUPERDOG, Supergirl, the LEGION OF SUPER-HEROES, several of Superman's Superman-robots, and LORI LEMARIS and the mer-people of ATLANTIS to carry out two of the gigantic super-tasks that Superman hopes to fulfill as his final legacy to humanity, viz., the melting of the Antarctic ice, "to make Antarctica a fit place for millions to live in the future," thus ensuring "a home for Earth's expanding population," and the injection of a colossal sea monster—which has been growing to ever more titanic size due to the stimulation of undersea radioactivity—with a special "shrinking formula" so that it will not one day become so terrifyingly gargantuan that it menaces the safety of Earth (S No. 156, Oct '62: "The Last Days of Superman!" pts. I-III—"Superman's Death Sen-tence!"; "The Super-Comrades of All Time!"; "Super-man's Last Day of Life!").

In January 1963 Superman struggles to safeguard Kandor against the misguided schemes of "fanatic scientist" THAN OL (S No. 158: "Superman in Kandor" pts. I-III—"Invasion of the Mystery Super-Men!"; "The Dynamic Duo of Kandor!"; "The City of Super-People!").

In May 1963, after being left stranded in the far-distant future, bereft of his super-powers, by members of the SUPERMAN REVENGE SQUAD, Superman succeeds in making his way back to the twentieth century by reducing himself to microscopic size with a "shrinking ray" in his Fortress of Solitude and then piloting a tiny Kandorian rocket ship across the time barrier (Act No. 300: "Superman Under the Red Sun!").

In August 1963, after exposure to red kryptonite has temporarily transformed Superman into a horrifying Kryptonian monster known as a "drang," the Supermen Emergency Squad turns out in force to prevent the drang from entering the Fortress of Solitude, unaware that the monster is actually Superman. Ultimately, however, the effects of the red kryptonite fade and vanish, restoring Superman to his normal human form (Act No. 303: "The Monster from Krypton!").

In February 1964 Lex Luthor and Brainiac are apprehended by the Supermen Emergency Squad and brought to Kandor to stand trial for their crimes, but the Kandorians are ultimately compelled to let the villains go free in order to save the life of Superman (S No. 167: "The Team of Luthor and Brainiac!" pts. I-III—"The Deadly Duo!"; "The Downfall of Superman!"; "The Hour of Kandor's Vengeance!"). (See LUTHOR, LEX.)

When Metropolis television station WMET-TV inaugurates its new "Our American Heroes" series with a program honoring Superman, "our greatest American hero," the Kandorian Look-Alike Squad appears on the show along with Superman's other friends and admirers to help pay tribute to the Man of Steel (Act No. 309, Feb '64: "The Superman Super-Spectacular!").

In March 1964 Superman visits Kandor for the annual meeting of the Phantom Zone Parole Board (Act No. 310: "Secret of Kryptonite Six!").

In July 1964, during a time-journey he makes to the planet Krypton prior to its destruction, LEX LUTHOR witnesses the theft of Kandor by Brainiac (S No. 170/2: pts. I-II—"If Lex Luthor Were Superman's Father!"; "The Wedding of Lara and Luthor!").

In August 1964 Superman joins forces with Batman, Robin, and Jimmy Olsen to combat a "metalloid" menace in the city of Kandor (WF No. 143: "The Feud Between Batman and Superman!" pts. I-II—no title; "The Manhunters from Earth!"). (See THAN-AR.)

In October 1964 Superman selects the Kandorian AR-VAL to serve as his replacement in the event of his own death or disability (S No. 172: pts. I-III—"The New Superman!"; "Clark Kent—Former Superman!"; "The Struggle of the Two Supermen!"). During this same period, the elderly Kandorian scientist NOR-KAN is struck in the brain and killed by "a fatal dose of radiation" while experimenting with the rare radioactive element illium-349 in hopes of finding a way to use the substance to power an "enlarger ray" with which to restore Kandor to normal size (Act No. 317, Oct '64: "Superman's Rainbow Face!").

KANE, KATHY. The wealthy heiress and onetime "circus daredevil performer" who is secretly BATWOMAN (Det. No. 233, Jul '56: "The Batwoman").

KARA. SUPERGIRL's Kryptonian name (Act No. 285, Feb '62: "The World's Greatest Heroine!"; and others).

KA THAR. A historian and author of the sixtieth century A.D. who journeys to the twentieth century in his "time-thrust projector" for the purpose of verifying the accuracy of his greatest book, *The History of Superman and Batman.* When his written explanations of how the famous heroes performed certain of their feats turn out not to be accurate, Ka Thar threatens to disclose their secret identities to the people of the twentieth century unless BATMAN, ROBIN, and SUPERMAN agree to reenact their great feats exactly as described in his history book. Bowing to Ka Thar's threat, the three crime-fighters set to work reenacting some of their past feats in order to justify Ka Thar's erroneous descriptions of them. Ultimately, however, Batman realizes that Ka Thar

dares not reveal their secret identities for fear of jeopardizing another statement in his history book—that the crime-fighters' secret identities were not publicly revealed until many centuries after their deaths—whereupon Ka Thar, his bluff called, returns to his own time (WF No. 81, Mar/Apr '56: "The True History of Superman and Batman!").

KEARNS, REESE (Dr.). A METROPOLIS scientist—a noted astronomer until he was branded a fraud and a hoaxer many years ago for predicting the imminent arrival of a meteor that never fell—who regains his good name and his scientific reputation by establishing finally, in July 1956, that the reason his meteor never struck Earth as anticipated was that the infant SUPERMAN unexpectedly deflected it off course during his initial journey earthward from the exploded planet KRYPTON (S No. 106/1: "Superman's First Exploit").

KEEGAN, LES. An escaped convict and would-be blackmailer who, along with his two accomplices, is apprehended by SUPERMAN in January 1957 while attempting to rob the SUPERMAN TROPHY HALL as part of an elaborate scheme to blackmail the mayor of METROPOLIS (S No. 110/1: "The Secret of the Superman Trophy").

KEELE (Mr.). The owner of the Keele Real Estate Company, and the mastermind behind a convoluted scheme to murder CLARK KENT and replace him with an imposter so that, once installed at the DAILY PLANET, the phony Kent can use his journalistic influence to persuade the METROPOLIS city council to purchase worthless land from Keele's real estate company, at vastly inflated prices, for the construction of a new municipal airport. The scheme is thwarted by SUPERMAN, who, with some timely assistance from LOIS LANE, apprehends both Keele and the Clark Kent impostor, a hoodlum named Miggs, in September-October 1945 (S No. 36/3: "Clark Kent, Star Reporter!").

KELL ORR. A young man from the planet XENON who bears an uncanny resemblance to SUPERMAN. Kell Orr is the son of ZOLL ORR, a scientist who is a perfect look-alike for Superman's father JOR-EL. In February 1958, with Superman's permission, Kell Orr visits Earth, where he impersonates Superman and carries out his various super-heroic duties while Superman is busy on Xenon attempting to avert a planetary cataclysm (S No. 119: "The Second Superman!" chs. 1-3—"The World That Was Krypton's Twin"; "A Double for Superman"; "Superman's Mightiest Quest"). (See XENON; ZOLL ORR.)

KELLY, "SLUG." The leader of a gang of ruthless slot-machine racketeers who are put out of business by SUPERMAN in Summer 1940. "I urge all my readers not to throw their money away wastefully into slot-machines!" advises Superman (S No. 5/1).

KELVIN, CLARENCE. An alternate identity employed by SUPERMAN in January 1959 when he bleaches his hair blond and, posing as an Englishman, obtains employment as a reporter on the DAILY PLANET after becoming afflicted with temporary amnesia as to his true civilian identity—that of reporter Clark Kent—as the result of a mishap that occurs while he is experimenting with KRYPTONITE. Ultimately, however, Superman regains his knowledge of his Clark Kent identity and abandons the role of reporter Clarence Kelvin (S No. 126/1: "Superman's Hunt for Clark Kent!").

KENDALL, CHARLIE. An alias employed by CLARK KENT in May 1954 when he poses as a hobo as part of his plan to expose and apprehend blackmailer ED MAIN (S No. 89/2: "Superman of Skid Row!").

KENNEDY (Police Commissioner). The police commissioner of METROPOLIS—ousted in the wake of an anti-corruption crusade launched by three Metropolis newspapers in June 1941—and the secret mastermind behind the wave of crime and violence that has all but engulfed the city, including the brutal gangland assassination of Metropolis's next three police commissioners. Appointed temporary police commissioner at the height of the crisis, Clark Kent labors unceasingly, both as Clark Kent and as SUPERMAN, until he has broken the back of Kennedy's crime ring and restored clean government to Metropolis (Act No. 37).

KENNEDY, JOHN F. (1917-1963). The 35th President of the United States. In office from January 1961 until his assassination by Lee Harvey Oswald in Dallas, Texas, in November 1963, he was the youngest man and the first Roman Catholic ever to be elected President.

When SUPERMAN presents SUPERGIRL to the world in February 1962, President Kennedy receives her in the White House. "Supergirl," remarks the President, "I know you'll use your super-powers not only to fight crime, but to preserve peace in our troubled world!" "Thank you, Mr. President!" replies Supergirl graciously. "...I will!" (Act No. 285: "The World's Greatest Heroine!").

When METROPOLIS television station WMET-TV inaugurates its new "Our American Heroes" series with a program honoring Superman, "our greatest American hero," Superman finds himself faced with the awkward dilemma of having to appear on the show simultaneously as Superman and as Superman's "friend" Clark Kent. The Man of Steel resolves the problem, however, by entrusting President Kennedy with the secret of his dual identity so that the President, disguised in a pair of eyeglasses and a rubberoid Clark Kent face mask, can appear briefly on the TV show in the role of Clark Kent. "I knew I wasn't risking my secret identity with you!" remarks Superman to President Kennedy afterward. "After all, if I can't trust the President of the United States, who can I trust?" (Act No. 309, Feb '64: "The Superman Super-Spectacular!").

When television journalist LANA LANG broadcasts a film report highlighting the poor physical condition of American youth, President Kennedy summons Superman to the White House and urges him to lend his super-services "to the important job of getting our youth into A-1 physical shape!"

"We must show our youngsters," exclaims the President, "that everyone has to keep fit--not just sports heroes! Once we lose our physical alertness, our mental awareness will vanish as well!"

And so, after promising to do his part "to help close this...'muscle gap,'" Superman flies around the United States to build support for President Kennedy's vital physical fitness program, inspiring young athletes to improve their prowess, showing overweight youngsters how to shed excess pounds, encouraging a pair of track men to have greater confidence in their physical abilities.

"Reports are streaming in from all over the country, Superman!" beams the President afterward. "The results of your one-man campaign have been excellent!" And later he adds, "Thanks to you, the youth of America is taking a real interest in our program!" (S No. 170/1, Jul '64: "Superman's Mission for President Kennedy!").

KENNEDY, SAM. The "publicity man" for the Cosmos Circus, and the man who is secretly the LEOPARD (S No. 20/3, Jan/Feb '43: "Lair of the Leopard!").

KENT (Captain). An alias employed by SUPERMAN during a time-journey to sixteenth-century England when, at the urging of Queen ELIZABETH I, he assumes the fictitious identity of Captain Kent the Terrible, "the cruelist, deadliest pirate of all time," as part of an elaborate ploy to defeat the Spanish Armada (S No. 89/1, May '54: "Captain Kent the Terrible!").

KENT, CLARK. The mild-mannered journalist who is secretly SUPERMAN.

KENT, DUDLEY. A reputedly wealthy but in reality debt-ridden man who invites Clark Kent to a family reunion in the mistaken belief that he is a relative. When a sinister quartet of Dudley's relatives—four "notorious characters" known as the Kent Brothers—attempt to force Dudley Kent to change his will to make them the new beneficiaries, Superman rescues Dudley from their clutches and apprehends the Kent Brothers (S No. 29/3, Jul/Aug '44: "The Pride of the Kents!").

KENT, ELY. A Colonial-era blacksmith and ancestor of CLARK KENT who, in 1779, received a promissory note for $2,000 from General GEORGE WASHINGTON for blacksmith services rendered, with the stipulation that the note was to accumulate compound interest until the day Kent redeemed it. One hundred seventy years later, in May 1949, Hubert, the butler and companion to Clark Kent's cousin Titus Kent and the sole heir to Titus Kent's estate, having stumbled upon the as yet unredeemed promissory note while cleaning some Kent family heirlooms—and having realized the immense amount of interest it would have accumulated after all these years—sets out to systematically murder every living member of the Kent family so that the promissory note will eventually be bequeathed to Titus Kent and then ultimately to him. Hubert murders one member of the Kent family and makes unsuccessful attempts on the lives of two others before he is finally exposed and apprehended by SUPERMAN (Act No. 132: "The Secret of the Kents!").

KENT, JONATHAN AND MARTHA (Mr. and Mrs.). The adoptive parents, now deceased, of Clark Kent, the man who is secretly SUPERMAN. It was the Kents who first came upon the infant Superman after the experimental rocket that had borne him safely away from the exploded planet KRYPTON had landed on the planet Earth, and it was the Kents who opened their home and their hearts to the tiny orphan from space, who legally adopted him and raised him as their own son, and who imbued him with the urgent desire to use his mighty super-powers to aid the weak, the helpless, and the oppressed. In the texts, they are referred to as "a kindly couple" (Act No. 106, Mar '47: "His Lordship, Clark Kent!"), and as "two fine people, who gave a loving home to an orphan from space!" (Act No. 288, May '62: "The Man Who Exposed Superman!"). In the town of SMALLVILLE, where they lived, they were known as good neighbors and "fine citizens" (S No. 90/2, Jul '54: "Superman's Secret Past!"). Superman has described them as "the best foster parents who ever lived" (WF No. 69, Mar/Apr '54: "Jor-El's Last Will!").

Enjoying a happy moment on a Caribbean vacation shortly before their death, Jonathan and Martha Kent sift through the contents of an old pirate chest

The early texts are inconsistent regarding the first names of Superman's foster parents: referred to only as the Kents in Superman No. 1/1 (Sum '39), they are referred to as John and Mary Kent in Superman No. 53/1 (Jul/Aug '48: "The Origin of Superman!"). Superman's foster father is called Silas Kent in Action Comics No. 132 (May '49: "The Secret of the Kents!"), but he is consistently referred to as Jonathan Kent from July 1951 onward (Act No. 158: "The Kid from Krypton!"; and others). Superman's foster mother is first called Martha in January-February 1952, a name she retains from that time onward (S No. 74/1: "The Lost Secrets of Krypton!";

and others), with the sole, insignificant exception Action Comics No. 189, in which her first name misspelled Marthe (Feb '54: "Clark Kent's Ne Mother and Father!").

Similar confusion exists regarding Martha Kent' maiden name: given as Martha Hudson in Superma No. 141 (Nov '60: "Superman's Return to Krypton! pts. I-III—"Superman Meets Jor-El and Lar Again!"; "Superman's Kryptonian Romance!"; "Th Surprise of Fate!") and as Martha Clark in Superma No. 146/1 (Jul '61: "The Story of Superman's Life!"), has, in recent texts, been given as Martha Hudso Clark as a means of rectifying the discrepancy.

At the time he proposed marriage to his wife-to-be Jonathan Kent was "a quiet spoken young farmer and she was an attractive young brunette (S No. 141 Nov '60: "Superman's Return to Krypton!" pts. I-III— "Superman Meets Jor-El and Lara Again!"; "Super man's Kryptonian Romance!"; "The Surprise o Fate!"), but by the time the tiny rocket ship bearing the infant Kal-El, son of JOR-EL, one day to be known to the world as Superman, soared through Earth' atmosphere and landed in an open field (Act No. 141 Feb '50: "Luthor's Secret Weapon"), the Kents wer already gray-haired, certainly into late middle-age perhaps "elderly" (S No. 1/1, Sum '39; and others) without children of their own (S No. 130/3, Jul '59 "The Town That Hated Superman!"), working thei own modest farm (S No. 146/1, Jul '61: "The Story o Superman's Life!"; and others) somewhere "outsid of Smallville" (S No. 152/2, Apr '62: "Superbaby Captures the Pumpkin Gang!").

Actually, the texts are not entirely consistent on the question of where the Kents were living at the time they found the infant Superman: Superman No 73/2 strongly suggests that the Kents were residing in METROPOLIS at the time the rocket landed (Nov/Dec '51: "The Mighty Mite!"), and Action Comics No. 106 asserts that they came upon the rocket within the Metropolis city limits (Mar '47: "His Lordship, Clark Kent!"). Numerous other texts, however, state that the rocket landed near Smallville (WF No. 57, Mar/Apr '52: "The Artificial Superman!"; and others), evidently within short driving distance of the Kents' farm (S No. 146/1, Jul '61: "The Story of Superman's Life!"; and others), and this latter version is undoubtedly the correct one.

According to Action Comics No. 1, the rocket ship bearing the infant Superman was discovered by "a passing motorist" (Jun '38), but Superman No. 1/1 (Sum '39) and numerous other texts assert that the infant was found by the Kents, who happened to be passing by in their car (S No. 53/1, Jul/Aug '48: "The Origin of Superman!"; and others) moments after the rocket landed. The baby was swathed in the blue, red, and yellow blankets that the Kents later used to fashion his Superman costume (*see* SUPERMAN [section C, the costume]). In his hand he clutched the jewel-like iron-destroying "projector" that had been placed inside the rocket by his father, Jor-El (Act No. 172, Sep '52: "Lois Lane . . . Witch!"). Scarcely had the

ents removed the infant from the rocket, however, when the space-ship's metal, foreign to Earth's imatic and chemical makeup, burst into flame!" ithin seconds, not a trace was left (S No. 53/1, l/Aug '48: "The Origin of Superman!").

Martha Kent clutches the infant Superman as she and her husband gaze at the burning hulk of the tiny rocket that brought him to Earth. In this 1950s recapitulation of the event, the Kents were already elderly when they found Superman

Later texts echo this brief explanation of the ocket's destruction, asserting that the rocket burned ecause the metal from which it had been fashioned vas "a substance alien to our Earth" (Act No. 186, Nov '53: "Haunted Superman!") or because "its metal [was] alien to our atmosphere!" (Act No. 189, Feb '54: "Clark Kent's New Mother and Father!"). A more plausible explanation, however, is advanced by Superman No. 146/1, which states that "all people and things from Krypton became invulnerable on Earth" and that "only the explosion of its super-fuel had the power to wreck the rocket" (Jul '61: "The Story of Superman's Life!").

Within a few brief seconds, "not even a trace" of the rocket was left. "If we tell what happened," mused Jonathan Kent aloud, "nobody will believe us!" "We'll say we found an abandoned baby," replied his wife, "...which is true!" (S No. 53/1, Jul/Aug '48: "The Origin of Superman!").

All accounts agree that the Kents turned the infant from space over to an orphan asylum (S No. 1/1, Sum '39) or foundling home (S No. 53/1, Jul/Aug '48: "The Origin of Superman!") immediately after having found him. Action Comics No. 288 refers to the orphan asylum as the Smallville Orphanage (May '62: "The Man Who Exposed Superman!"), while Superman No. 161/1 calls it the Smallville Orphan's Home (May '63: "The Last Days of Ma and Pa Kent!").

Accounts differ, however, on the question of whether the Kents decided to adopt the infant Superman immediately or whether they formulated these plans later. According to Superman No. 1/1, the Kents delivered the baby to the orphanage and then returned sometime later to adopt him only after discovering that they were unable to get the "sweet child" out of their minds (Sum '39), but Superman No. 53/1 asserts that the Kents applied for adoption immediately and left the infant Superman at the orphanage only temporarily, long enough for their application to be properly investigated. The baby

After finding the infant Superman in an open field, the Kents leave the child on the steps of the Smallville Orphanage, intending to return later to adopt him for their own. In this 1960s version, the Kents are much younger than in earlier accounts

caused such pandemonium at the home, continues this text, with the unrestrained use of his super-powers, that the authorities rushed through the Kents' adoption in record time just so they could be rid of the problem infant (Jul/Aug '48: "The Origin of Superman!").

Most texts agree that the Kents decided to adopt the infant Superman the moment they found him (Act No. 158, Jul '51: "The Kid from Krypton!"; and others). Indeed, the more recent texts state that the Kents, knowing they would be asked to explain the origins of the child if they merely kept him or if they delivered him to the foundling home in person, actually left the baby in a basket at the orphanage doorstep, as though he had been abandoned there, so that they could appear at the orphanage the following day (S No. 130/3, Jul '59: "The Town That Hated Superman!")—or several days later (S No. 146/1, Jul '61: "The Story of Superman's Life!")—to adopt him for their own.

Once having adopted the youngster, the Kents realized they needed to give him a name. "At last, we've a son of our very own!" exclaimed Jonathan Kent, as he and his wife drove their newly adopted son home from the orphanage. "What shall we call him?"

"We'll name him after your family..." replied his wife. And then she turned to her new son and said, "Hello, son! You have a new name! From now on you'll be Clark... **Clark Kent!**" (S No. 53/1, Jul/Aug '48: "The Origin of Superman!").

This dialogue exchange is confusing, for it is not at all clear how the name Clark could possibly be the name of Jonathan Kent's family. In all probability, however, this confusion stems from an incorrect placement of word balloons in the original text, thus placing Jonathan Kent's dialogue in the mouth of his wife, and vice versa. This interpretation is strongly supported by Superman No. 146/1, which recounts the orphaning of the infant Superman and his adoption by the Kents. In this text, Jonathan Kent asks his wife to select a name for their newly adopted son, to which Martha Kent replies, "I'll use my former last name before our marriage... Clark! Our son will be **Clark Kent!**" (Jul '61: "The Story of Superman's Life!").

A fairly large number of texts, in recounting the story of Superman's early life, have stated that the Kents decided to adopt the infant Superman immediately upon having removed him from the rocket, and that they selected the name Clark for him even before delivering him to the orphanage and instituting formal adoption proceedings (S No. 61/3, Nov/Dec '49: "Superman Returns to Krypton!"; and others), but these accounts are probably best viewed as attempts to recapitulate the events surrounding the infant Superman's adoption in a briefer, more condensed, form rather than as an alternative version of these same events.

Clark Kent's early childhood years following his adoption were spent on his foster parents' farm

outside of Smallville (S No. 152/2, Apr '62: "Super baby Captures the Pumpkin Gang!"; and others). It d not take long for the Kents to discover that the newly adopted orphan from outer space was endowe with extraordinary super-powers, including invulne ability, X-ray vision, and strength far beyond that any ordinary mortal (S No. 53/1, Jul/Aug '48: "Th Origin of Superman!"; Act No. 158, Jul '51: "The Ki from Krypton!"; and others). Indeed, it was becaus the infant Superman kept unintentionally demolish ing his conventional baby clothing during energeti bouts of super-powered play that the Kents unravele the colored blankets which they had found wrappe around him in the rocket and used them to fashion th colorful super-playsuit that became the forerunner c his now world-famous costume (S No. 73/2, Nov/De '51: "The Mighty Mite!"; S No. 146/1, Jul '61: "Th Story of Superman's Life!"; and others).

By the time Clark Kent was old enough to atten school, the Kents sold their farm and moved t Smallville, where Jonathan Kent opened up a genera store (S No. 146/1, Jul '61: "The Story of Superman' Life!"; and others). According to Superman No. 1/1 "the love and guidance of [Clark Kent's] kindly foster parents was...an important factor in the shaping o the boy's future." It was the Kents, in fact, who urgec upon their adopted son the importance of keeping hi powers secret and of using them to aid humanity.

"Now listen to me, Clark!" cautioned Jonathan Kent, while Clark was still a youngster. "This great strength of yours--you've got to hide it from people or they'll be scared of you!"

"But when the proper time comes," added Martha Kent, "you must use it to assist humanity" (Sum '39).

There were also other reasons for keeping Clark's super-powers secret: Jonathan Kent feared that unscrupulous individuals would try "to exploit his super-powers for evil purposes" (WF No. 57, Mar/Apr '52: "The Artificial Superman!"), and Clark himself soon realized that if he used his super-powers openly against the underworld, his foster parents would inevitably become the helpless targets of gangland retribution (S No. 146/1, Jul '61: "The Story of Superman's Life!"; and others). It was the combined impact of all these concerns that led Clark Kent to embark upon his dual life and to use his super-powers openly only as Superman (see SUPERMAN [section B, the secret identity]).

Sometime prior to Clark Kent's leaving Smallville to embark on his career as a newspaper reporter in Metropolis, Jonathan and Martha Kent passed away. The chronicles are vague—and somewhat inconsistent—regarding the time and circumstances of their death, but all are generally agreed that Martha Kent died first and Jonathan Kent soon afterward, and that, on his deathbed, Jonathan Kent once again urged his foster son to use his super-powers to fight evil and serve humanity. In general, such inconsistencies as do exist can be attributed to the fact that the early texts portray Clark Kent as having embarked on his super-heroic career as

Superman only after he had reached adulthood, while later texts portray him as having battled crime and injustice as Superboy prior to embarking on his adult crime-fighting career as Superman.

Superman No. 1/1, the first text to mention the death of the Kents, contains only a scant reference to their passing, although it does portray Clark Kent as having reached adulthood by the time the sad event occurred:

> The passing away of his foster-parents greatly grieved Clark Kent. But it strengthened a determination that had been growing in his mind.
>
> Clark decided that he must turn his titanic strength into channels that would benefit mankind. And so was created--
>
> SUPERMAN, champion of the oppressed, the physical marvel who had sworn to devote his existence to helping those in need! (Sum '39].

Superman No. 53/1, also portrays Clark Kent as having already attained manhood by the time of the Kents' death. And, while it is vague concerning the exact chronology of the event, it does establish for the first time that Martha Kent died first as well as chronicle the deathbed conversation between Jonathan Kent and his foster son that would ultimately serve as the model for all future recapitulations of the event.

"No man on Earth has the amazing powers you have," whispered Jonathan Kent, his last strength fast fading. "You can use them to become a powerful force for good!"

"How, Dad?" asked Clark.

"There are evil men in this world," replied Jonathan Kent, "... criminals and outlaws who prey on decent folk! You must fight them ... in cooperation with the law!

"To fight criminals best, you must hide your true identity! They must never know Clark Kent is a ... a super-man! Remember, because that's what you are ... a **superman!**" (Jul/Aug '48: "The Origin of Superman!").

Action Comics No. 158 recapitulates the deathbed scene, still portraying Clark Kent as "a grown man" at the time of his foster parents' passing but now incorporating the element, fairly new to the chronicles, of Clark's having already passed his boyhood and adolescence performing super-heroics as Superboy.

"Clark," intoned the dying Jonathan Kent, "your super-powers made you a champion of right as *Superboy!* Now you must continue your role as *Superman*--but always keep your true identity hidden!"

"I will!" replied Clark. "I'll keep on wearing these glasses and appear timid, so no one will guess my secret!" (Jul '51: "The Kid from Krypton!").

Superman No. 146/1 confirms, by and large, all the previous accounts, adding only that the Kents died shortly following Clark Kent's return home to

RESUMING HIS EVERYDAY IDENTITY, CLARK VISITS A PEACEFUL CHURCHYARD...

MOTHER...DAD! THE FOSTER PARENTS WHO ADOPTED ME WHEN THE ROCKET THAT BROUGHT ME FROM *KRYPTON* LANDED NEAR *SMALLVILLE!* I'LL NEVER FORGET THE ANNIVERSARY OF THEIR DEATH! HOW IRONIC! BUT FOR A TRAGIC ACCIDENT, THEY MIGHT BE ALIVE TODAY!

© NPP 1963

Clark Kent pays a visit to the peaceful churchyard where the Kents are buried, 1963

Smallville following his graduation from college, and that Martha Kent's death preceded her husband's by several months (Jul '61: "The Story of Superman's Life!").

The account of the Kents' death contained in Superman No. 161/1 represents a significant break with the past, however, in that here, for the first time in the chronicles, the Kents are portrayed as having passed away—within hours of one another, while Clark Kent was still an adolescent—shortly after unearthing an early-eighteenth-century pirate chest contaminated with the germs of a rare "fever plague" while vacationing on an island somewhere in the Caribbean. Fatally stricken by this "strange malady," a disease for which there is no known cure, the Kents lapsed into a coma and died within less than twenty-four hours, although Jonathan Kent did regain consciousness long enough to urge his foster son to "always use your super-powers to do good ... uphold law and order," and then to whisper, "Good luck, my son ... and goodbye!"

The will left behind by the Kents bequeathed their home and general store to Clark Kent, and their savings to the Smallville Orphan's Home, where Clark Kent had lived prior to his legal adoption (May '63: "The Last Days of Ma and Pa Kent!").

Martha Kent had always urged her foster son to retain ownership of the Kent home, and, according to Action Comics No. 288, Clark Kent has scrupulously carried out her final wishes. Today, according to this text, it still stands in Smallville, unoccupied since the day Clark Kent moved away to Metropolis following the death of his foster parents, "a shrine to the memory of two fine people, who gave a loving home to an orphan from space!" (May '62: "The Man Who Exposed Superman!"). This account is contradicted, however, by Superman No. 90/2, which describes the Kent home in Smallville as having been purchased by

PROFESSOR SNELLING (Jul '54: "Superman's Secret Past!").

The texts are also inconsistent regarding the final disposition of Jonathan Kent's general store. According to World's Finest Comics No. 69, a garage now occupies the site of the general store (Mar/Apr '54: "Jor-El's Last Will!"), but Superman No. 90/2 asserts that a supermarket now occupies the site (Jul '54: "Superman's Secret Past!"). The accuracy of these discrepant assertions becomes irrelevant in September 1957, however, when, as a tribute to Superman, the people of Smallville restore all of the landmarks of Superman's youth—including the Kents' general store—to the condition that characterized them during Superman's boyhood (S No. 116/2: "Disaster Strikes Twice").

In addition to the preservation of their home and general store, the Kents have been memorialized—by both Superman and the people of Smallville—in other ways: Smallville has paid tribute to Jonathan and Martha Kent by hanging their portrait in the Smallville City Hall (S No. 90/2, Jul '54: "Superman's Secret Past!"), and Superman has dedicated a room to them in his FORTRESS OF SOLITUDE (Act No. 247, Dec '58: "Superman's Lost Parents!"; and others). A "hidden vault deep beneath the Fortress" contains, among other "super-secret" possessions and memorabilia, photographs that the Kents took of their foster son and notebooks containing their personal account of how they found him (Act No. 330, Nov '65: "The Strange 'S' Spell on Superman!"). While he was still a teen-ager, Superman carved a "spectacular space monument"—in the form of a gigantic statue of the Kents with himself standing between them—into the side of a distant asteroid (S No. 161/1, May '63: "The Last Days of Ma and Pa Kent!").

Clark Kent's Kent-family ancestors include ELY KENT, a Colonial-era blacksmith; Captain Joshua Kent, the owner-operator of a barge on the Erie Canal; and inventor Hiram Kent, the father of Jonathan Kent. Clark Kent's living Kent-family relatives include his cousin "Digger" Kent, a gold prospector; his cousin Louis Pasteur Kent, a country doctor; his cousin Titus Kent, a wheelchair-ridden recluse who lost his entire fortune during the great Depression; his first cousin Carol Kent, an actress (Act No. 132, May '49: "The Secret of the Kents!"); and his aunt MINERVA KENT, Jonathan Kent's younger sister (Act No. 160, Sep '51: "Superman's Aunt Minerva!"). Clark Kent's uncle, merchant seaman George Kent, the brother of Jonathan Kent, died while Clark was still a youngster when the freighter Starbuck, on which George Kent was second mate, sank in the North Atlantic with all hands on board (S No. 111/2, Feb '57: "Clark Kent's Crooked Cousin"). Clark Kent's first cousin Arthur Kent, a broker, is murdered by Titus Kent's butler, Hubert, in May 1949 (Act No. 132: "The Secret of the Kents!").

In May 1949 Superman journeys through the time barrier to the year 1878, where he makes the acquaintance of the youngster who will one day grow up to be his own foster father (Act No. 132: "The Secret of the Kents!").

By May 1956 Clark Kent has received an anonymous letter from a person claiming to have unraveled the secret of his dual identity. Desperate to uncover the identity of the mysterious letter writer and to undo whatever past blunder has been responsible for the betrayal of his secret identity, Superman revisits the site of virtually every super-feat he has ever performed and painstakingly reexamines every detail of his life, only to discover, finally, that the letter was written by Jonathan Kent, who had arranged for the letter to be mailed to his foster son years after his death as his means of inspiring Clark Kent to remain ever vigilant in safeguarding the secret of his double identity (S No. 105/1: "Superman's 3 Mistakes!").

In December 1958 Jonathan and Martha Kent are impersonated by CEDRIC AND MILLICENT CARSON, a pair of "scheming actors" who dupe Superman into believing that they are visiting him from out of his past through the miracle of time travel, all as part of an elaborate scheme to bilk the Man of Steel out of $5,000,000 (Act No. 247: "Superman's Lost Parents!").

In December 1961 Superman enjoys a brief reunion with Jonathan and Martha Kent—as well as with his real parents, Jor-El and LARA—after exposure to red KRYPTONITE has temporarily endowed him with the power to make his wishes come true and he has wished aloud that his parents were on the scene to advise him how best to use his marvelous new power. Moments later, however, the effects of the red kryptonite wear off, Superman loses his wish-fulfilling power, and his magically materialized parents and foster parents fade and vanish like wraiths (Act No. 283: "The Red Kryptonite Menace!").

In March 1965, during a visit to an extradimensional "parallel world . . . a world that's almost like Earth in every way, but in which history had a different course than on Earth," Superman encounters a gray-haired couple—also named Jonathan and Martha Kent—who are perfect look-alikes for his foster parents and much like the Kents in other ways. These parallel-world Kents, however, are criminals and have raised their foster son Superman to be a master villain (WF No. 148: "Superman and Batman--Outlaw!" pts. I-II—"The Evil Superman and Batman"; "The Incredible New Super-Team!").

KENT, JUDD. A "long-sought public enemy," finally apprehended by police, who claims that he is Clark Kent's cousin, states that he stumbled upon the secret of SUPERMAN's secret identity during a visit to the Kent home in SMALLVILLE many years ago, and attempts to blackmail Superman into breaking him out of prison by threatening to broadcast to the world that Clark Kent is Superman. Superman soon establishes, however, that Judd Kent is not his cousin, and although Judd Kent did indeed discover his secret identity while masquerading as a relative of Clark Kent many years ago, Superman rebuffs Judd Kent's blackmail attempt and cleverly amasses

ody of bogus evidence to refute the villain's claim
at Clark Kent is secretly Superman (S No. 111/2,
b '57: "Clark Kent's Crooked Cousin").

ENT, MINERVA (Miss). The bespectacled, white-
ired old lady—often referred to as Aunt Minerva—
o is the younger sister of Jonathan Kent, Clark
nt's foster father, (see KENT, JONATHAN AND
ARTHA [MR. AND MRS.]), and therefore the aunt of
ark Kent, the man who is secretly SUPERMAN.
sically a good-hearted woman, Aunt Minerva
nds to be somewhat motherly and overprotective,
d to treat her nephew Clark as though he were still
small boy.

learns that his aunt's real reason for coming to
Metropolis was to escape the attentions of a persistent suitor named Zachary Barnes, a charming fellow
who is hopelessly in love with her. "You see, I'm sure
she loves me," Barnes confides to Superman, "...but
at her age she's afraid to admit it!"

Despite his aunt's protestations to the contrary
("The old pest's proposals are what made me leave the
Coast...and he's still at it! Don't pay any attention,
Clark!"), Superman suspects that Barnes is right, and
ultimately, through an elaborate ruse, he succeeds in
persuading his maiden aunt into acknowledging the
love she feels for Barnes. Even so, however, Aunt

As her white cat and pet parrot cringe in disgust,
Minerva Kent ministers to a suffering Superman, 1951

In September 1951 Aunt Minerva arrives in
METROPOLIS with her white cat and pet parrot and
announces that she is moving in with Clark Kent
"permanently." "We're the last of the Kents," says
Aunt Minerva sternly, "and families must stick
together, I always say!" Kent is crestfallen at this
turn of events, for he realizes that the longer he is
forced to share an apartment with his meddlesome
aunt, the more likely she is to discover that he is
secretly Superman.

Indeed, for a time, the well-meaning Aunt Minerva
drives Kent to the brink of distraction, insisting that
he wear an overcoat even in eighty-degree weather
and that he go to bed early every night to safeguard
his health. Soon after her arrival, however, Kent

Minerva rejects Barnes's proposal of marriage: "No--
we still can't be married," she replies, "because my
first duty is to look after Clark! He needs my care, and
I can't leave him!"

"Wait! I think *I* can solve that problem for you,
Miss Kent!" interjects Superman hastily. "You go
ahead and marry Zachary--and let *me* look after
Clark! He's a good friend of mine...I promise to take
the best of care of him, from now on!"

"*Oh*, wonderful!" exclaims Aunt Minerva happily.
"Now I'll be able to marry Zachary and know that
Clark is in even better hands than mine!" (Act No.
160: "Superman's Aunt Minerva!").

KENTON, KLARKASH. An alias employed by
SUPERMAN in May 1952, when, during a visit to the

planet Zor (*see* Zor [1952]), he poses as an ordinary Zorian citizen in order to obtain employment as a "telenewspaper" reporter on the staff of the *Daily Zorian* (Act No. 168: "The Menace of Planet Z!").

KHALEX. An escaped convict from a far-distant planet who arrives on Earth in November 1959 and joins forces with "notorious gang chief" Midge Martin and his henchmen. Together they concoct an elaborate scheme to trick BATMAN and ROBIN into helping them destroy a recently landed meteor whose presence on Earth robs Khalex of his awesome extraterrestrial powers with which he could annihilate SUPERMAN and conquer the Earth. The scheme is ultimately thwarted and the villains apprehended through the heroic efforts of Batman, Robin, and Superman (WF No. 105: "The Alien Superman!").

KIDDER (Captain). The leader of a gang of modern-day pirates who are apprehended by SUPERMAN in March 1949 with the aid of "famed Universal-International motion picture star" Ann Blyth (Act No. 130: "Superman and the Mermaid!").

KIDTOWN. A town for underprivileged boys—founded to enable ghetto youngsters to "grow up in a wholesome environment"—which is threatened with imminent closing due to lack of funds to pay its mortgage until SUPERMAN provides it with an anonymous donation of $2,000,000 in August 1939, half of it money salvaged from an "oil stock manipulation case" four months previously (*see* RAMSEY, HOMER), the other half gold coins and bullion which Superman recovers from a sunken galleon, in the process apprehending two competing gangs of racketeers—the Marchetti mob and the "Big Boy" Chaney gang—determined to seize the treasure for themselves (Act No. 15).

KILEY, JOHN. A respected "millionaire philanthropist"—and the secret leader of the notorious ANTI-SUPERMAN GANG—who, after imbibing a special drug designed to slow the heartbeat and simulate the symptoms of approaching death, summons Clark Kent to his "deathbed" and, by claiming to be an ardent admirer of SUPERMAN and by invoking the solemnity of a "dying man's" last request, successfully tricks Kent into revealing his dual identity as the first step in a diabolical plot to destroy Superman by luring him into a KRYPTONITE deathtrap. Fortuntely for Superman, however, Kiley's physician has warned that the special drug may induce "illusions and hallucinations," and therefore, with the aid of SUPERGIRL and the SUPERMEN EMERGENCY SQUAD, Superman is able to convince the ruthless Kiley that Clark Kent's secret-identity revelation was only a massive hallucination, before apprehending Kiley and the Anti-Superman Gang in May 1961 (Act No. 276: "The War Between Supergirl and the Supermen Emergency Squad!"). The story is in many respects similar to Action Comics No. 237 (Feb '58: "Superman's Exposed Identity"). (*See* FURST, HENRY.)

KIL-LOR. A would-be tyrant and dictator of the planet KRYPTON whose plot to overthrow the Krypto-

nian government and seize control of the plane thwarted by SUPERMAN when, having journe back across the time-space barrier to Krypton a time predating the marriage of his own parents (JOR-EL; LARA), the Man of Steel tricks the su powered Kil-Lor into killing himself by overexpos to KRYPTONITE (S No. 123, Aug '58: chs. 1-3—"The C of Steel"; "The Lost Super-Powers"; "Superma Return to Krypton").

KILPOT ZYXAM. The magic phrase which, wh spoken aloud by MR. MXYZPTLK, returns the pes extradimensional imp to his home dimension after has legally changed his name to Maxy Z. Toplik March 1955. Kilpot Zyxam is Maxy Z. Toplik spell backwards (S No. 96/2: "Mr. Mxyztplk--Mayor Metropolis!").

KING, CHESTER. The roving television report for the Oceania Network in the city of Macropolis the planet Oceania who is secretly the super-he HYPER-MAN (Act No. 265, Jun '60: "The 'Superma from Outer Space!").

KING, COBRA. The leader of a gang of crimina who are apprehended by SUPERMAN when th attempt to rob the guests at a surprise birthday par for CLARK KENT at the Metropolis Ballroom September-October 1943 (S No. 24/3: "Surprise fe Superman!").

KING, CRAIG. The mild-mannered "telenev reporter" for the *Daily Solar System* who is secret the SUPERMAN OF 2956 (Act No. 215, Apr '56: "Th Superman of Tomorrow").

KING KRYPTON. The name bestowed by JIMM OLSEN on a "giant gorilla"—a mighty "super-gorilla from the planet KRYPTON, endowed with supe powers identical to SUPERMAN's—which Superma and Jimmy Olsen encounter in an African jungle i March 1958.

Theorizing that the so-called Gorilla of Steel i probably a Kryptonian experimental monkey launched into outer space prior to the death o Krypton, Superman engages in a series of fearsome albeit indecisive, battles with the "super-simian," determined to prevent it from reaching civilizatio and wreaking untold havoc there.

Ultimately, however, under the influence of a KRYPTONITE meteor's baleful green rays, King Kryp ton undergoes an "uncanny transformation" from super-gorilla into human being and, with his dying breaths, explains that he is in reality a scientist from the planet Krypton who was accidentally trans formed into a gorilla by the tragic malfunctioning of an experimental "evolution accelerator" and then launched by his assistant into orbit around Krypton in the hope that the "powerful cosmic rays" of space would ultimately restore him to his human form. Now, ironically, the kryptonite meteor has succeeded in freeing the Kryptonian from his gorillian prison, but only at the cost of snuffing out his life, since all Kryptonian survivors are fatally vulnerable to kryptonite (Act No. 238: "The Super-Gorilla from Krypton").

INGPIN, THE. A ruthless underworld czar—the ead of "the national crime syndicate that's been so ctive in all our big cities lately"—who posts a 00,000 reward for the murder of CLARK KENT, both a retaliation for Kent's article exposing the syndi- ate in the pages of the DAILY PLANET, and as "an xample to Superman that the syndicate can fight im through his friends." Although the ensuing ttempts on Clark Kent's life pose a serious threat to is dual identity—in that they force him to devise epeated explanations to account for his series of eemingly miraculous near-escapes—Kent does suc- eed in preserving his secret and ultimately in ringing about the capture of the Kingpin and his ohorts by the METROPOLIS police (Act No. 153, Feb 1: "The 100 Deaths of Clark Kent!").

KIRK, JOHNNY. The son of Professor Morton Kirk, a noted astronomer who, approximately a ecade ago, while Johnny Kirk was still an infant, potted "a giant planet, plunging from outer space" n a collision course with Earth and, believing that a cosmic collision" was inevitable and that "the end of he world" was at hand, placed young Johnny inside a space rocket he had recently perfected" and fired im off into outer space toward a hoped-for haven on a distant planet, much as JOR-EL and LARA once aunched the infant SUPERMAN into the interstellar oid to save him from the death of KRYPTON.

Earth was rescued from the impending cataclysm, aowever, through the heroic intervention of the then een-aged Superman, but Professor Kirk, profoundly haken by the shock of having needlessly exiled his son into space, died soon afterward, leaving behind aim a document appointing Superman as his son's egal guardian in the unlikely event the youngster ever succeeded in returning alive from space.

In September 1957, however, Johnny Kirk—now approximately twelve to fourteen years old—does eturn, having survived since infancy on a far-distant 'primeval planet," at least in part because he had aecome endowed with super-powers identical to Superman's when the rocket built by his father passed through "a peculiar cloud in space, pulsating with energy," a mysterious "cloud of cosmic energy" that somehow "increased [his] capabilities far beyond normal...!"

Determined to comply properly with Professor Morton Kirk's last request, Superman throws himself enthusiastically into the role of foster parent, proudly dubbing his young charge Superman, Junior, and launching him on a rigorous training program designed to prepare him for the demanding role of his own junior partner in the father-and-son super-hero team of Superman and Superman, Junior.

Complications arise, however, when Superman's powers begin one by one to fade and vanish as the result of his having breathed in the noxious fumes of the "peculiar meteoric dust" clinging to the wreckage of Johnny Kirk's rocket, an unearthly variety of "super-poison" that will in time render the Man of Steel as vulnerable as any ordinary earthman.

However, in spite of Superman's courageous effort to keep his dilemma a secret, Johnny Kirk becomes aware of Superman's increasing disability and willingly sacrifices his own hopes for a super-hero career by transferring his own super-powers into the body of Superman with the aid of a special meteor whose unique properties enable him to effect a permanent "transfusion of power" from his own body to Superman's, albeit only at the expense of trans- forming himself into an ordinary earthboy (Act No. 232: "The Story of Superman, Junior").

KIZO. An evil survivor of the exploded planet KRYPTON who, along with his two villainous broth- ers, U-Ban and MALA, battles SUPERMAN in July- August 1950 (S No. 65/3: "Three Supermen from Krypton!") and again in July 1954 (Act No. 194: "The Outlaws from Krypton!"). (See MALA.)

KLOR. A green-skinned alien from the far-distant planet Belvos who, having discovered that certain gems available on Earth could endow him with extraordinary powers, concocts an elaborate scheme to impersonate SUPERMAN and frame him for a series of crimes on the planet Belvos so that, while Superman is busy defending himself in a Belvos courtroom, he can stage a spectacular gem theft on Earth as a prelude to seizing dictatorial power on his native planet. The scheme is thwarted and Klor apprehended through the heroic efforts of BATMAN, ROBIN, and Superman (WF No. 122, Dec '61: "The Capture of Superman!").

KLTPZYXM. The magic word which, when uttered aloud by MR. MXYZPTLK, has the effect of temporarily returning the mischievous extradimensional imp to his home in the fifth dimension. Kltpzyxm (pro- nounced Kel-tipz-yex-im) is Mxyzptlk spelled back- wards. Superman No. 33/1 strongly suggests that anyone who uttered the magic word would find himself instantaneously transported to Mr. Mxyzptlk's home dimension Mar/Apr '45: "Dimen- sions of Danger!"), but this is the only text in which such an assertion appears.

KNIGHT, THE. An English crime-fighter who, with his youthful companion the Squire, fights crime in England much as BATMAN and ROBIN fight crime in the United States. In everyday life, the Knight and the Squire are secretly the Earl of Wordenshire and his young son Cyril, who inhabit stately Wordenshire Castle just outside the quiet English village of Wordenshire. However, when the ringing of the bell in the Wordenshire village rectory warns them that their services are needed, they swiftly don knightly raiment and roar into action astride their motorized "war horses"—the so-called "motorcycle-horses"— which are actually powerful motorcycles decked out like medieval war horses.

In July-August 1957 the Knight and the Squire visit the United States in response to a summons from "well-known philanthropist" John Mayhew, who wishes to award the Knight and the Squire and other world-famous crime-fighters—including Batman and Robin, SUPERMAN, the GAUCHO, the LEGIONARY, and

The Knight and the Squire, 1955

the MUSKETEER—charter membership in his newly formed Club of Heroes (WF No. 89: "The Club of Heroes!"). (*See* LIGHTNING-MAN.) (For a complete account of the Knight's crime-fighting career, consult *The Encyclopedia of Comic Book Heroes: Volume I—Batman.*)

KOBRA, "KING." "The mysterious king-pin who controls the underworld," a ruthless gangland czar who puts out a $100,000 contract on the life of CLARK KENT—in an effort to put an end to Kent's scathing anticrime articles in the pages of the DAILY PLANET—only to be apprehended by SUPERMAN in December 1963 (Act No. 307: "Clark Kent—Target for Murder!").

KOKO. The white extraterrestrial creature, closely resembling a small monkey except for the twin antennae protruding from its forehead, which is the pet of the space villain BRAINIAC (Act No. 242, Jul '58: "The Super-Duel in Space").

KORMO. The far-distant planet which is the home of Tharn and the villainous bandit chieftain Rawl (WF No. 92, Jan/Feb '58: "The Boy from Outer Space!"). (*See* SKYBOY.).

KORREL, KANE. A METROPOLIS "racket boss" who, having learned that "a whole meteor-mass of kryptonite" has fallen to earth on the outskirts of Smithville, races to the scene in a flatbed trailer, transports the fallen meteor to Metropolis, and then sets up a so-called "kryptonite syndicate," selling thousands of pocket-sized chunks to criminals at $5,000 apiece to use as protection against SUPERMAN during the commission of crimes. Superman apprehends Korrel and his henchmen—along with the majority of their gangland clientele—in July 1951, and hurls all their accumulated KRYPTONITE safely into outer space (Act No. 158: "The Kid from Krypton!").

KOTZOFF. An evil scientist who, in collusion with Police Commissioner Jim Stanley, causes the out-

break of a "strange inexplicable malady" in Gay Cit by spraying the city with a diabolical gas, odorles and invisible, that afflicts human beings with th fragility of glass so that if they bump together in th street they shatter into fragments. "We wanted t scare people out of town so we could buy properties fo a song," confesses Stanley later. "Then, when th scare was forgotten, we could sell our holdings for a huge profit!" SUPERMAN apprehends the conspira tors and forces them to spread an antidote gas ove the town (S No. 7/2, Nov/Dec '40).

KRAZINSKI, RUDOLPH. A brilliant but evi pianist who puts his unsuspecting concert audiences to sleep with his "lulling, hypnotic piano playing" s that his henchmen can rob them of their money anc jewels. Cornered by SUPERMAN in January-February 1942 and failing in a final attempt to permanently paralyze the Man of Steel by "beating out a weird enchanting melody," Krazinski removes the earplugs that protect him from the effects of his own music and commits suicide by "striking a certain combination o bizarre notes." "*Dead!*" murmurs Superman. "-Slain by those brief notes of music. He literally willed himself to die...!" (S No. 14/1).

KRONIS. A "prison planet run by the Cosmic Police!" According to Action Comics No. 280, "The universe's worst criminals are imprisoned there!" The space villain BRAINIAC is incarcerated on Kronis following his capture by SUPERMAN in September 1961 ("Brainiac's Super-Revenge!"). LEX LUTHOR liberates Brainiac from the bleak "prison world" in February 1964 as part of his plan to form an alliance with Brainiac for the destruction of Superman.

Arriving on Kronis in his saucerlike spacecraft, Luthor finds the planet completely uninhabited except for Brainiac, who is locked in a "mighty cage" fashioned from "an isotope of supermanium" (*see* SUPERMANIUM), "the strongest metal known to science!"

"Apparently," muses Luthor, "Superman regards Brainiac [as] so dangerous he's isolated him from other criminals!"

Despite the fact that even his special "atomic torch" is unable to cut through the bars of Brainiac's supermanium prison—and that Superman has ringed the planet with "electronic eye" satellites and installed numerous booby traps and security devices designed to forestall any attempted escape—Luthor succeeds ultimately in overcoming Superman's safeguards and in freeing Brainiac from his prison cage by cleverly triggering a humanitarian safety device designed to free Brainiac from his confinement in the event he were ever menaced by a natural disaster such as fire or flood (S No. 167: "The Team of Luthor and Brainiac!" pts. I-III—"The Deadly Duo!"; "The Downfall of Superman!"; "The Hour of Kandor's Vengeance!"). (*See*LUTHOR, LEX.)

KRUGG, CONRAD. The unscrupulous proprietor of Conrad Krugg's Gymnasium, a METROPOLIS muscle-building emporium which claims that it can transform ordinary men into "supermen" in "ten asy lessons" by means of a special program of exercise and a "magic elixir." Posing as a sucker in earch of a body-building program, SUPERMAN xposes Krugg as a swindler and then cleverly rranges for Krugg's capture by police in an adjoin-ng state, where, under the name "Soapy" Kryle, he is eing sought by authorities "for a dozen swindles" (S Io. 151/2, Feb '62: "The Man Who Trained Super-nen!").

KRYPTO (the Superdog). The super-powered vhite dog from the planet KRYPTON that is the pet nd canine companion of SUPERMAN. A member of he LEGION OF SUPER-PETS, Krypto wears a yellow log collar and a flowing red-and-yellow cape modeled fter Superman's. The texts frequently refer to Krypto as the Dog of Steel.

As a puppy on the planet Krypton, where he had no super-powers, Krypto was the playful pet of baby Kal-El, the infant Superman (SA No. 5, Sum '62; and others). But as the hour of Krypton's doom drew ever closer, Superman's father, JOR-EL, nursing the faint hope that his ongoing "experiments with small rockets" might yet save his son, launched Krypto into outer space in a tiny rocket as a final trial run, intending for the dog-carrying rocket to return safely to Krypton after making one or more orbits of the planet. "By a cosmic mischance," however, "a meteor struck the trial rocket out of orbit" and sent it careening into space, and although Jor-El did succeed in launching his infant son toward Earth in the final moments of the cataclysm, Krypto appeared lost forever in the interplanetary void. For years, the rocket bearing Krypto drifted through space, ulti-mately to arrive on Earth, where, like any native of Krypton, Krypto acquired super-powers like Super-man's and was happily reunited with his beloved master, who was at that time a teen-ager growing up

© NPP 1978

Krypto the Superdog

in SMALLVILLE in the home of his foster parents, JONATHAN AND MARTHA KENT. Superboy—the teen-aged Superman—fashioned a cape for Krypto mod-eled after his own, and Krypto, now grown into a fully developed "superdog," became his frequent compan-ion in super-heroic adventure (S No. 146, Jul '61: "The Story of Superman's Life!"; and others).

Krypto's super-powers—including X-ray vision, super-strength, invulnerability, and the power of flight—are similar, if not identical, to Superman's own, although his strength is undoubtedly not as great as Superman's, just as the strength of an ordinary dog is not as great as that of an ordinary man. On the other hand, however, Krypto's super-hearing and "super-keen sense of smell" (S No. 160/1, Apr '63: pts. I-II—"The Mortal Superman!"; "The Cage of Doom!"; and others) are probably more acute than Superman's, just as these senses are normally more acute in a canine than in an ordinary human being. Like any surviving native of the exploded planet Krypton, Krypto the Superdog is vulnerable to KRYPTONITE.

Described as Superman's "faithful pet super-dog" (S No. 139/3, Aug '60: "The Untold Story of Red Kryptonite!"), Krypto is fully aware that his master, Superman, is also Clark Kent (S No. 142/1, Jan '61: "Lois Lane's Secret Helper!").

Krypto loves to romp and play in outer space (S No. 146/1, Jul '61: "The Story of Superman's Life!"; and others), visiting distant worlds (S No. 130/1, Jul '59: "The Curse of Kryptonite!"); cavorting in and about his Doghouse of Solitude, a large floating doghouse which he has constructed out of meteoric fragments (S No. 177/3, May '65: "When Jimmy Olsen Stole Krypto from Superman"; and others); and mischie-vously chasing comets, "just as Earth-dogs chase cars!" (Act No. 290, Jul '62: "Half a Superman!").

In order to summon Krypto home from his distant wanderings, Superman either signals him by whist-ling at a highly pitched supersonic frequency which only Krypto's ears can hear (S No. 142/3, Jan '61: "Flame-Dragon from Krypton"), or else summons him by means of "super-ventriloquism," a ventrilo-quistic technique that enables Superman to throw his voice over exceedingly long distances (Act No. 284, Jan '62: "The Babe of Steel!"; and others). On at least one occasion, when absolute secrecy is called for, the Man of Steel employs "supersonic ventriloquism," a form of super-ventriloquism in which Superman's voice is pitched so high that only Krypto can hear it (S No. 165/1, Nov '63: pts I-III—"Beauty and the Super-Beast!"; "Circe's Super-Slave"). Krypto, for his part, communicates with Superman by means of a special "barking code"—similar to Morse code—taught to him by Superman when the Man of Steel was a teen-ager (S No. 130/1, Jul '59: "The Curse of Krypto-nite!").

In July 1959, after Superman has been immobil-ized and severely weakened by the radiations of a fallen kryptonite meteor in arid Death Valley, Krypto rescues his master from seemingly certain death by blowing the kryptonite meteor out of harmful range with a puff of his super-breath (S No. 130/1: "The Curse of Kryptonite!").

In January 1960 Krypto joins forces with Super-man and SUPERGIRL to prove to the Kandorian scientist KULL-EX that his long-held grudge against Jor-El is completely unfounded (S No. 134: chs. I-III—

Far out in space, Krypto proudly surveys his just-completed Doghouse of Solitude, 1962

"The Super-Menace of Metropolis!"; "The Revenge Against Jor-El!"; "The Duel of the Supermen!").

In August 1960, after exposure to red kryptonite has brought about the sudden, accelerated growth of Superman's hair, beard, and fingernails, Krypto and Supergirl lend the Man of Steel a helping hand by using the combined power of their X-ray vision to disintegrate the virtually indestructible hair and fingernails, thus restoring Superman to his normal appearance (S No. 139/3: "The Untold Story of Red Kryptonite!").

In October 1960, during the period when the infant son of BIZARRO and BIZARRO-LOIS is being held for safekeeping at the FORTRESS OF SOLITUDE, Krypto takes turns watching over the youngster with Superman and Supergirl, good-naturedly assuming the role of canine super-playmate (S No. 140: pts. I-III—"The Son of Bizarro!"; "The 'Orphan' Bizarro!"; "The Bizarro Supergirl!").

In January 1961 Krypto helps Superman and AQUAMAN carry out their elaborate scheme for the capture of the notorious "ACE" RUGGLES gang (Act No. 272: "Superman's Rival, Mental Man!"); makes a series of surreptitious attempts, all of them unsuccessful, to help Superman attain marital bliss by getting him to propose to LOIS LANE (S No. 142/1: "Lois Lane's Secret Helper!"); and helps BATMAN, Superman, and Supergirl carry out an elaborate, and ultimately successful, ruse to protect the secret of Superman's identity (S No. 142/3: "Flame-Dragon from Krypton").

In April 1961, at the Fortress of Solitude, Krypto, Superman, and Supergirl all experience the same "red kryptonite hallucination" simultaneously as the result of their simultaneous exposure to red-kryptonite dust. In the hallucinatory fantasy, which is also referred to as a dream, the Earth is destroyed by a titanic explosion caused by Superman's careless tinkering with an extraterrestrial device; Krypto,

Superman, and Supergirl, the sole survivors of th cataclysm, are taken into custody by the Cosmi Police, who charge Superman with "criminal negl gence" in the destruction of Earth; stripped of the super-powers by an interplanetary tribunal, the nov powerless heroes are banished to a desolate "primo dial planet," inhabited by ferocious prehistoric beast where they are forced to live as cave dwellers, i continual terror, until finally Krypto and Supergi are annihilated by a terrifying "lightning-monster and the shock of this grisly event brings th nightmarish dream to an end and snaps the thre hallucinators back to reality (S No. 144/3: "Th Orphans of Space!").

In August 1961 Krypto journeys through the tim barrier into the prehistoric past for an encounter wit TITANO the "super-ape" (S No. 147/2: "Krypto Battle Titano!").

In January 1962 Krypto joins forces with Super man and Supergirl to prevent the PHANTOM ZONE prisoners from escaping the Phantom Zone (Act No 284: "The Babe of Steel!"). During this same period Krypto, Superman, and Supergirl stand before th bottle city of KANDOR, in the Fortress of Solitude, and bow their heads solemnly for one full minute o silence to commemorate the anniversary of the destruction of Krypton. Afterward, the three Krypton survivors soar into outer space, where, in a "distant solar system," they use their mighty super-powers to transform an uninhabited planet into an exact duplicate of Krypton—and populate it with human oid androids in the image of Jor-El, LARA, and other Kryptonians—as a planet-sized memorial to their exploded world (S No. 150/1, Jan '62: "The One Minute of Doom!").

By March 1962, members of the SUPERMAN REVENGE SQUAD have taken Krypto captive in order to use him as their guinea pig to help them determine exactly what effects several different varieties of red kryptonite are likely to have on Superman. When the villains discover that exposure to one of their red-kryptonite samples will make any native of Krypton "dream of frightful adventures [set] in the future," they concoct an elaborate scheme to use this variety of red kryptonite to wreak vengeance on Superman (Act No. 286: "The Jury of Super-Enemies!"). Not long afterward, when Superman is in the throes of the third of his three nightmares brought on by exposure to the Superman Revenge Squad's red kryptonite, it is Krypto who awakens his master from the terrifying dream "by super-licking his face!" (Act No. 287, Apr '62: "Perry White's Manhunt for Superman!").

In May 1962 Krypto helps Superman carry out a ruse that successfully frustrates an attempt by ex-convict HAL COLBY to unravel the secret of Superman's identity (Act No. 288: "The Man Who Exposed Superman!").

In July 1962, as the result of exposure to red kryptonite, Krypto is temporarily robbed of his power of invulnerability along the entire right side of his body. However, although Krypto receives a painful nip on the right ear from a stray dog during this period, the red-kryptonite effect soon wears off, completely restoring Krypto's invulnerability (Act No. 290: "Half a Superman!"). During this same period, Krypto finds himself temporarily endowed with "the power to speak intelligently" after the mischievous MR. MXYZPTLK has unleashed a magical "zoophonic force" upon the city of METROPOLIS (S No. 154/1, Jul '62: "The Underwater Pranks of Mr. Mxyzptlk!").

In August 1962 Krypto poses as Mr. Mxyzptlk—by concealing himself inside an ingenious "plastic shape" of the mischievous imp devised by

BUT AS KRYPTO IS ABOUT TO ENTER HIS INTER-PLANETARY SANCTUM, SUDDENLY...

AWP! I J-JUST REMEMBERED... A CERTAIN SPECIAL APPOINTMENT! ...:CHOKE.!: GOT TO GO BACK TO EARTH, NOW!

© NPP 1962

Romping in outer space near his Doghouse of Solitude, Krypto suddenly recalls an important appointment on Earth, 1962

Superman—to help carry out Superman's elaborate, and ultimately successful, ruse for uncovering the hiding place of DUKE MARPLE's stolen loot and bringing the "notorious gang-leader" to justice (S No. 155/2: "The Downfall of Superman!").

In October 1962, after exposure to red kryptonite has temporarily transformed Superman into two separate individuals, a mature, responsible Clark Kent and an unprincipled, irresponsible Superman, Krypto is imprisoned in the Phantom Zone by the arrogant Superman in order to prevent him from interfering with his plan to keep the personalities of Clark Kent and Superman separate forever. Ultimately, however, Clark Kent frees Krypto from the Phantom Zone, and soon afterward he succeeds in bringing about the reuniting of Clark Kent and Superman into a single individual (Act No. 293: "The Feud Between Superman and Clark Kent!"). During this same period, when Superman is believed to be dying of an incurable malady, Krypto joins forces with Supergirl, the LEGION OF SUPER-HEROES, the SUPERMEN EMERGENCY SQUAD, several of Superman's Superman-robots, and LORI LEMARIS and the mer-people of ATLANTIS to carry out two of the gigantic super-tasks that Superman hopes to fulfill as his final legacy to humanity, viz., the destruction of a "vast cloud of fungus in distant space, that will some day reach Earth and blight all plant life," and the injection of a colossal sea monster—which has been growing to ever more titanic size due to the stimulation of undersea radioactivity—with a special "shrinking formula" so that it will not one day become so terrifyingly gargantuan that it menaces the safety of Earth (S No. 156, Oct '62: "The Last Days of Superman!" pts. I-III—"Superman's Death Sentence!"; "The Super-Comrades of All Time!"; "Superman's Last Day of Life!").

In November 1962 Krypto helps Superman and PERRY WHITE carry out their elaborate scheme for capturing a notorious "international spy" (S No. 157/2: "The Super-Genie of Metropolis!"). (See VON SCHULTZ [PROFESSOR].)

In April 1963, when Clark Kent becomes stranded in the Arctic wastes after exposure to red kryptonite has temporarily robbed him of his invulnerability and super-powers, it is Krypto who tracks his master through a raging blizzard and carries him to safety (S No. 160/1: pts. I-II—"The Mortal Superman!"; "The Cage of Doom!").

In November 1963 Krypto helps Superman, Saturn Woman (see SATURN GIRL) and PROTY II carry out an elaborate, and ultimately successful, ruse designed to persuade the SUPERMAN REVENGE SQUAD that the Man of Steel is immune to the effects of their potent "counter-energy ray" (S No. 165/1: pts. I-II—"Beauty and the Super-Beast!"; "Circe's Super-Slave").

When Metropolis television station WMET-TV inaugurates its new "Our American Heroes" series with a program honoring Superman, "our greatest American hero," Krypto appears on the show along with three of the other super-pets—BEPPO THE SUPER-

MONKEY, COMET THE SUPER-HORSE, and STREAKY THE SUPER-CAT—to help pay tribute to the Man of Steel (Act No. 309, Feb '64: "The Superman Super-Spectacular!").

In April 1965 Krypto journeys through the time barrier to the mid-nineteenth century to help Superman and the other super-pets teach a well-deserved lesson to "cruel junkman" CYRUS ATWILL (S No. 176/1: "The Revenge of the Super-Pets!").

In May 1965, while spending a night at the Fortress of Solitude with Superman and JIMMY OLSEN, Krypto falls asleep and has a terrifying nightmare which, although no explanation of the nightmare appears in the text, clearly betrays Krypto's deep-seated resentment at having to share his master's friendship and affection with Olsen. In the nightmare, Superman is forced into premature retirement and Jimmy Olsen is transformed into a mighty super-hero—known to the world as Super-Olsen—when a strange machine that they find in the snow outside the Fortress suddenly and inexplicably drains Superman of his invulnerability and super-powers, permanently transferring them into the body of Olsen; Olsen, who becomes arrogant and ruthless in his new-found role, is enraged at Krypto's continuing loyalty to Superman despite Superman's non-super-heroic status and resorts to a series of petty, even extortionate, ploys calculated to intimidate Krypto into abandoning Superman and becoming his canine partner instead; and finally, when Krypto continues to remain loyal to Superman despite Olsen's increasingly ruthless attempts to separate them, Olsen lures Krypto in front of the machine that first gave Olsen his powers and cruelly transfers Krypto's super-powers into a donkey. "Whew! What a nightmare that was!" thinks Krypto when he awakens moments later. "I'm sure glad it's over! Jimmy's a swell guy! He'd never act that mean in real life!" (S No. 177/3: "When Jimmy Olsen Stole Krypto from Superman").

In November 1965, during a period when, as the result of exposure to red kryptonite, Superman finds himself periodically overwhelmed by a compulsion to steal items beginning with the letter "S" and then donate them to the poor, Krypto helps the Man of Steel apprehend a gang of criminals who have been attempting to capitalize on his red-kryptonite-induced compulsion by posing as needy men and duping Superman into donating his loot to them (Act No. 330: "The Strange 'S' Spell on Superman!").

KRYPTON. The far-distant planet which was the home world of SUPERMAN until it exploded into fragments as the result of a cataclysmic chain reaction originating at the planet's core. It was as the doomed planet shuddered and rumbled in its dying moments that the Kryptonian scientist JOR-EL and his wife LARA placed their infant son in an experimental rocket ship and launched him into the void, eventually to arrive on the planet Earth and to grow to maturity there as Superman (S No. 53/1, Jul/Aug '48: "The Origin of Superman!"; and others).

Krypton was "a planet of giant size" (S No. 146/1, Jul '61: "The Story of Superman's Life!"; and others) located somewhere "in the outer reaches of trackless space" (S No. 53/1, Jul/Aug '48: "The Origin of Superman!"; and others). Described as "an unusual planet," with a "unique atmosphere" and a "tremendous gravitational pull "far greater than that of Earth (S No. 113, May '57: chs. 1-3—"The Superman of the Past"; "The Secret of the Towers"; "The Superman of the Present"; and others), Krypton had a massive uranium core (S No. 53/1, Jul/Aug '48: "The Origin of Superman!"; and others) and was occasionally swept by windstorms so violent that the planet's tallest skyscrapers had to be lowered into the ground to prevent their being toppled by the powerful gales (S No. 123, Aug '58: chs. 1-3—"The Girl of Steel"; "The Lost Super-Powers"; "Superman's Return to Krypton").

The planet Krypton, birthplace of Superman

Although a number of texts seem to place Krypton in the same solar system as that of Earth (WF No. 57, Mar/Apr '52: "The Artificial Superman!"; and others)—somewhere "past Mars, Jupiter and Saturn" (Act No. 182, Jul '53: "The Return of Planet Krypton!")—the vast preponderance of textual evidence places the planet of Superman's birth "in a distant solar system" (S No. 137, May '60: chs. I-III—"The Super-Brat from Krypton"; "The Young Super-Bully"; "Superman vs. Super-Menace!"; and others), revolving about a red sun (S No. 141, Nov '60: "Superman's Return to Krypton!" pts. I-III—"Superman Meets Jor-El and Lara Again!"; "Superman's Kryptonian Romance!"; "The Surprise of Fate!"; and others)—as distinguished from Earth's yellow sun—at the rate of approximately one revolution per 1.39 Earth years (S No. 157/1, Nov '62: "The Super-Revenge of the Phantom Zone Prisoner!").

"Born almost six billion time-cycles ago" (S No. 170/2, Jul '64: pts. I-II—"If Lex Luthor Were Superman's Father!"; "The Wedding of Lara and Luthor!")—six billion time-cycles being the equivalent of approximately 8.3 billion Earth years if one assumes that the terms "sun-cycle" and "time-cycle" are synonymous (S No. 157/1, Nov '62: "The Super-Revenge of the Phantom Zone Prisoner!")—the planet Krypton occupied the same solar system as the planet THORON (S No. 80/1, Jan/Feb '53: "Superman's Big Brother!") and was orbited, at various times in its history, by two, three, and perhaps even four natural satellites. When, in November 1960, Superman makes a time-journey to Krypton in the period immediately preceding its destruction, he romances lovely LYLA LERROL "under the soft radiance of Krypton's two moons..." (S No. 141: "Superman's Return to Krypton!" pts. I-III—"Superman Meets Jor-El and Lara Again!"; "Superman's Kryptonian Romance!"; "The Surprise of Fate!"); but it is firmly established in the chronicles that the renegade Kryptonian scientist JAX-UR destroyed one of Krypton's moons sometime prior to this period, a heinous crime for which Jax-Ur was banished into the PHANTOM ZONE (Act No. 310, Mar '64: "Secret of Kryptonite Six!"; and others), clear evidence that Krypton had three moons—one of which was evidently named Koron (S No. 78/1, Sep/Oct '52: "The Beast from Krypton!")—in the not-too-distant past. In addition, the planet XENON, the so-called "twin world of Krypton," was evidently Krypton's fourth moon, sometime in the ancient past, until it "spun out of its orbit and left Krypton forever" (S No. 119, Feb '58: "The Second Superman!" chs. 1-3—"The World That Was Krypton's Twin"; "A Double for Superman"; "Superman's Mightiest Quest").

Although the planet Krypton was much like Earth in a multitude of ways—it is even called Earth's "sister world" in Superman No. 53/1 (Jul/Aug '48: "The Origin of Superman!")—Krypton's atmosphere and solar radiation were substantially different from Earth's (WF No. 57, Mar/Apr '52: "The Artificial Superman!"; and others), and the weight of its gravity was so much greater that PROFESSOR WILLIAM ENDERS could move about only with great difficulty when he visited the planet at the behest of Jor-El (S No. 77/1, Jul/Aug '52: "The Man Who Went to Krypton!"). The distance from Earth to Krypton has never been established with absolute certainty, but scientist MEL EVANS has estimated the "probable distance" at 0.317 light years (S No. 136/2, Apr '60: "The Secret of Kryptonite!").

Krypton was a planet of staggering richness and incomparable natural beauty. Among its many scenic wonders were the FIRE FALLS, a magnificent flaming cataract teeming with "mutant fish" (Act No. 281, Oct '61: "The Man Who Saved Kal-El's Life!"; and others); the Gold Volcano, which erupted gold instead of lava (S No. 141, Nov '60: "Superman's Return to Krypton!" pts. I-III—"Superman Meets Jor-El and Lara Again!"; "Superman's Kryptonian Romance!"; "The Surprise of Fate!"); the JEWEL MOUNTAINS, whose "fascinating beauty entrance[d] all beholders" (S No. 170/2, Jul '64: pts. I-II—"If Lex Luthor Were Superman's Father!"; "The Wedding of Lara and Luthor!"; and others); Meteor Valley, a scenic valley "created by a monstrously gigantic meteor that glanced off the surface" of the planet during Krypton's prehistoric past, and RAINBOW CANYON, a deep natural gorge traversed by a breathtaking rainbow (S No. 141, Nov '60: "Superman's Return to Krypton!" pts. I-III—"Superman Meets Jor-El and Lara Again!"; "Superman's Kryptonian Romance!"; "The Surprise of Fate!"); the SCARLET JUNGLE, a "weird wilderness" teeming with red and purple flora (Act No. 310, Mar '64: "Secret of Kryptonite Six!"; and others); and the Three Sisters of Krypton, a trio of "great fire-geysers" so named because they always erupted simultaneously (WF No. 146, Dec '64: "Batman, Son of Krypton!" pts. I-II—no title; "The Destroyer of Krypton!").

Other "natural wonders" of Krypton included SHRINKWATER LAKE, whose waters contained "some strange chemical" that could "shrink ordinary men down to ant size" (Act No. 325, Jun '65: "The Skyscraper Superman!"); Great Krypton Lake, which was ultimately contaminated by the evil PROFESSOR VAKOX (Act No. 284, Jan '62: "The Babe of Steel!"); and the Great Krypton Sea, whose waters were once the home of a highly advanced civilization (S No. 170/2, Jul '64: pts. I-II—"If Lex Luthor Were Superman's Father!"; "The Wedding of Lara and Luthor!"). Others of Krypton's geographical features are enumerated on the map of Krypton that accompanies this article.

Krypton's animal life was exceedingly varied. Indeed, although Kryptonian fauna included a number of animals—such as dogs (S No. 146/1, Jul '61: "The Story of Superman's Life!"; and others), monkeys (S No. 173/2, Nov '64: "Tales of Green Kryptonite No. 1"; and others), and great apes (Act No. 218, Jul '56: "The Super-Ape from Krypton"; and others)—which are also common to Earth, it also included numerous exotic species unique to Krypton, including the "snagriff" (see SNAGRIFF), a winged dinosaurlike creature (S No. 78/1, Sep/Oct '52: "The Beast from Krypton!"); the "flame beast," which looked as though it were literally on fire (S No. 123, Aug '58: chs. 1-3—"The Girl of Steel"; "The Lost Super-Powers"; "Superman's Return to Krypton"); the "Krypton beast," the "living wheel," the "winged cat," and the "balloonie," a large froglike creature that fled danger by inflating itself like a balloon and floating out of harm's way (S No. 132, Oct '59: "Superman's Other Life!" pts. 1-3—"Krypton Lives On!"; "Futuro, Super-Hero of Krypton!"; "The Superman of Two Worlds!"); the "flame dragon" (see FLAME DRAGON), a gigantic, bat-winged, dragonlike creature that belched flame "from its nostrils and gaping jaws" (S No. 142/3, Jan '61: "Flame-Dragon from Krypton"; and others); the "fish-snake," an eel-like "mutant fish" from Krypton's Fire Falls whose venomous bite was potentially fatal to humans (Act No. 281, Oct '61: "The Man Who Saved Kal-El's Life!"); the "rondor," an exceedingly rare creature whose single large horn emitted strange radiations that "could cure many deadly illnesses" (S No. 157/1, Nov '62: "The Super-Revenge of the Phantom Zone Prisoner!"); the "drang," a colossal flying snake, purple in color, which had a head like a dinosaur and a single white horn protruding from its forehead (Act No. 303, Aug '63: "The Monster from Krypton!"); the "nightwing" (*see* NIGHTWING), a Prussian-blue bird resembling a magpie; the "flamebird" (*see* FLAME-BIRD), a red, yellow, orange, and green bird with a bright red crest; and the "telepathic hounds" of KANDOR, "strange beasts," yellow in color, with tails like wolves and snouts like wild boars, "that can locate people at any distance by reading their minds to learn where they are" (S No. 158, Jan '63: "Superman in Kandor" pts. I-III—"Invasion of the Mystery Super-Men!"; "The Dynamic Duo of Kandor!"; "The City of Super-People!"; and others); the "thought-beast," a large, primitive, rhinocerouslike creature—with a spiked tail and a single large horn protruding from its snout—whose most distinctive feature was a televisionlike "thought-screen" atop its head which flashed picture-images of whatever it was thinking; and "a huge crystal bird," long since extinct, "which once filled the skies of ancient Krypton" and whose crystalline skeletons, heaped up by the millions, created the beautiful Jewel Mountains (Act No. 310, Mar '64: "Secret of Kryptonite Six!"); the "metal-eating mole," one specimen of which survives to this day in the Kandor City Zoo (Act No. 242, Jul '58: "The Super-Duel in Space"); and the "metal-eater," sometimes hyphenated and sometimes not, a large metal-eating animal resembling a giant tapir (S No. 132, Oct '59: "Superman's Other Life!" pts. 1-3—"Krypton Lives On!"; "Futuro, Super-Hero of Krypton!"; "The Superman of Two Worlds!"; *see also* S No. 146/1, Jul '61: "The Story of Superman's Life!"). When Superman makes a time-journey to Krypton in November 1960, he encounters a "fire-breathing space creature"—a pink, leopardlike animal, with a horn like that of a unicorn protruding from its forehead, which "breathes super-powerful flames when angered"—on display in a Kryptonian zoo. It is unclear, however, whether this animal is indigenous to Krypton, or whether the Kryptonians merely collected the specimen on some far-distant planet (S No. 141: "Superman's Return to Krypton!" pts. I-III—"Superman Meets Jor-El and Lara Again!"; "Superman's Kryptonian Romance!"; "The Surprise of Fate!"; *see also* Act No. 310, Mar '64: "Secret of Kryptonite Six!").

Kryptonian flora included the gigantic, maroon, mushroomlike fungi native to the Scarlet Jungle (Act No. 310, Mar '64: "Secret of Kryptonite Six!"); the gigantic "moving forests," red in color and vaguely humanoid in form, also indigenous to the Scarlet Jungle, which literally advanced across the face of the planet "in their yearly migration," forcing Kryptonians in their path to seek refuge in subterranean tunnels until they had passed (S No. 164, Oct '63: pts. I-II—"The Showdown Between Luthor and Superman!"; "The Super-Duel!"); and the "singing flowers," which would "softly serenade" guests at Kryptonian dinner parties (S No. 141, Nov '60: "Superman's Return to Krypton!" pts. I-III—"Superman Meets Jor-El and Lara Again!"; "Superman's Kryptonian Romance!"; "The Surprise of Fate!"; *see also* S No. 132, Oct '59: "Superman's Other Life!" pts. 1-3—"Krypton Lives On!"; "Futuro, Super-Hero of Krypton!"; "The Superman of Two Worlds!").

Krypton's "strongest metal" was "kryptium," a "super-metal" described as "harder and stronger than any Earth metal" (Act No. 329, Oct '65: "The Ultimate Enemy!"). Krypton's most precious metal was "boradium" (S No. 78/1, Sep/Oct '52: "The Beast from Krypton!"). Gold was so commonplace on Krypton as to be literally worthless (S No. 141, Nov '60: "Superman's Return to Krypton!" pts. I-III—"Superman Meets Jor-El and Lara Again!"; "Superman's Kryptonian Romance!"; "The Surprise of Fate!").

Krypton's was "an advanced civilization," with "people of great intelligence and physical perfec-

Jax-Ur and Superman encounter a "thought-beast" in Krypton's Scarlet Jungle

tion!" (S No. 61/3, Nov/Dec '49: "Superman Returns to Krypton!"). The planet was apparently divided into a series of separate nations (Act No. 216, May '56: "The Super-Menace of Metropolis"), but these nations had long since combined to form a planet-wide union, uniting all Kryptonians under a single flag, a single government, a single constitution (Act No. 328, Sep '65: "Superman's Hands of Doom!"; and others), and a single planet-wide language, Kryptonese (S No. 141,

"If Lex Luthor Were Superman's Father!"; "The Wedding of Lara and Luthor!"), and there had been no war on the planet "for thousands of years" (Act No. 216, May '56: "The Super-Menace of Metropolis"). Capital punishment was unknown, and Kryptonians were bound, in all their dealings with each other, by a strict Krypton Code of Honor. Indications are that they were a freedom-loving people who would have preferred death to dictatorship (S No. 65/3, Jul/Aug

The world of Krypton was "a mighty planet" inhabited by a "super-scientific, intelligent people," the proud custodians of a great civilization

Nov '60: "Superman's Return to Krypton!" pts. I-III— "Superman Meets Jor-El and Lara Again!"; "Superman's Kryptonian Romance!"; "The Surprise of Fate!").

"Possessed of high intelligence," the people of Krypton "had built a super-scientific civilization far beyond that of Earth..." (S No. 146/1, Jul '61: "The Story of Superman's Life!"). Crime was virtually unknown on Krypton (S No. 170/2, Jul '64: pts. I-II—

'50: "Three Supermen from Krypton!"). Perhaps one explanation for the comparative lack of strife on Krypton lay in the relative sparseness of the population, for despite the vast size of the planet its population may have numbered only in the millions (S No. 141, Nov '60: "Superman's Return to Krypton!" pts. I-III—"Superman Meets Jor-El and Lara Again!"; "Superman's Kryptonian Romance!"; "The Surprise of Fate!").

According to Superman No. 53/1, Krypton's inhabitants were "humans of high intelligence and magnificent physical perfection..." (Jul/Aug '48: "The Origin of Superman!"). Although several early texts refer to them as Kryptonites (S No. 61/3, Nov/Dec '49: "Superman Returns to Krypton!"; and others), the vast majority of texts refer to them as Kryptonians (S No. 128/1, Apr '59: chs. 1-2— "Superman versus the Futuremen"; The Secret of the Futuremen"; and others), describing them as "a super-scientific, intelligent people" (Act No. 223, Dec '56: "The First Superman of Krypton") and as "a great people, physically perfect and of immense intelligence and science!" (Act No. 158, Jul '51: "The Kid from Krypton!"). On the planet Krypton, explains Action Comics No. 223, even three-year-olds could solve complex mathematical equations (Dec '56: "The First Superman of Krypton").

On the question of exactly how the people of Krypton differed from the people of the planet Earth, however, the texts are inconsistent. Early texts describe the Kryptonians as a "super-race" (S No. 73/2, Nov/Dec '51: "The Mighty Mite!") who were gifted with X-ray vision and other powers and who were "thousands of eons" ahead of earthlings, both mentally and physically (S No. 53/1, Jul/Aug '48: "The Origin of Superman!").

"[Clark] Kent had come from a planet," explains Action Comics No. 1, "whose inhabitants' physical structure was millions of years advanced our own. Upon reaching maturity, the people of his race became gifted with titanic strength!" (Jun '38).

According to Superman No. 33/1, "...Superman-- a native of the ill-fated planet Krypton--is of a different structure than the natives of Earth! Neither his mind nor his body are susceptible to the influence that can overcome other human beings!" (Mar/Apr '45: "Dimensions of Danger!").

"Where we come from," gloats the Kryptonian villain U-BAN in July-August 1950, "everyone has see-through vision, extra-strength and extra-speed!" (S No. 65/3: "Three Supermen from Krypton!").

Since the early 1950s, however, the texts have described the people of Krypton as more or less ordinary human beings, albeit as the brilliant custodians of a "highly advanced super-scientific civilization" (S No. 150/1, Jan '62: "The One Minute of Doom!"). Similarly, the super-powers possessed by Superman and other Kryptonian survivors have been explained as deriving from a combination of several factors—such as being free of Krypton's tremendous gravitational pull, and living under Earth's yellow sun as opposed to Krypton's red one—rather than as powers normally possessed by every Kryptonian living on Krypton (see SUPERMAN [section E, the super-powers]).

The Kryptonian system of government is never clearly described in the chronicles, but it is clear that the scientific establishment commanded wide respect and exerted considerable influence on political and social policy. The Council of Five, a body of distinguished scientists who, if they did not actually govern

the planet themselves, obviously carried much weight with those who did, is mentioned in Superman No. 53/1, (Jul/Aug '48: "The Origin of Superman!"), and there are numerous references in other texts to the Council (S No. 61/3, Nov/Dec '49: "Superman Returns to Krypton!"; and others), the Science Council (S No. 113, May '57: chs. 1-3—"The Superman of the Past"; "The Secret of the Towers"; "The Superman of the Present"; see also Act No. 303, Aug '63: "The Monster from Krypton!"), and the Council of Scientist (S No. 146/1, Jul '61: "The Story of Superman's Life!").

Superman No. 65/3 makes reference to "Krypton's ruling council, which consisted of the [planet's] ten leading scientists," a clear suggestion that Krypton's leading scientific body governed the planet (Jul/Aug '50: "Three Supermen from Krypton!"), but Action Comics No. 223 distinguishes between the Council of Science and Krypton's "highest officials," suggesting that the Council, while influential, was not really charged with the responsibility of ruling the planet (Dec '56: "The First Superman of Krypton"). Superman No. 154/2, however, contains a brief reference to a Supreme Council, a title clearly suggestive of supreme political authority (Jul '62: "Krypton's First Superman!"). All in all, then, it is probably safest to infer that Krypton was ruled by a political body, probably elected, which was counseled and advised by a body of distinguished scientists exercising considerable influence over political decision making (S No. 53/1, Jul/Aug '48: "The Origin of Superman!"); and others).

The capital of Krypton was the city of Kandor. Several years before Krypton exploded, however, Kandor was reduced to microscopic size and stolen by the space villain BRAINIAC, and a new world capital was established in the city of KRYPTONOPOLIS (Act No. 243, Aug '58: "The Lady and the Lion"; and others), the city which would later become Superman's birthplace (Act No. 325, Jun '65: "The Skyscraper Superman!"; and others).

Fluttering from the flagstaff atop the World Capitol Building—which, like the city of Kryptonopolis itself, had been designed by Superman's ancestor Gam-El, the father of modern Kryptonian architecture—was the flag of Krypton, a multicolored banner consisting of pale rays of blue, yellow, lavender, white, green, orange, pink, light green, and red radiating outward from a circular center featuring a green and pale blue design suggestive of a body of water all but encircled by lush green land (Act No. 246, Nov '58: "Krypton on Earth!"; and others).

Maintaining public order was the role of the Krypton Security Force (S No. 170/2, Jul '64: pts. I-II—"If Lex Luthor Were Superman's Father!"; "The Wedding of Lara and Luthor!"), while the task of maintaining internal security and apprehending criminals was entrusted to the Krypton Bureau of Investigation (S No. 123, Aug '58: chs. 1-3—"The Girl of Steel"; "The Lost Super-Powers"; "Superman's Return to Krypton").

Crime was only a minor problem on Krypton.

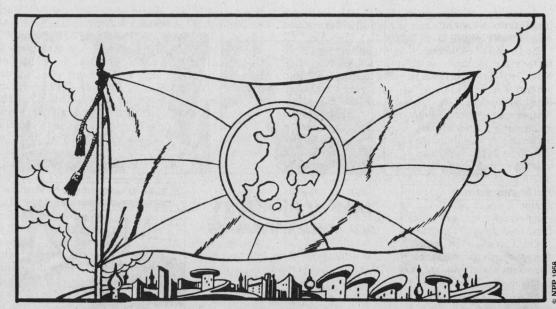

© NPP 1958

The flag of Krypton

Indeed, the research of the Kryptonian scientist Raf Arlo had established that most of the crimes on the planet "were perpetrated by an unknown race of invisible people" (S No. 170/2, Jul '64: pts. I-II—"If Lex Luthor Were Superman's Father!"; "The Wedding of Lara and Luthor!"). When malefactors were apprehended, they were placed on trial in Kryptonian courtrooms where verdicts were handed down by Kryptonian "justice councils," deliberative bodies analogous to American juries (S No. 157/1, Nov '62: "The Super-Revenge of the Phantom Zone Prisoner!").

Because Kryptonians were opposed to capital punishment, and, in fact, had never in their history practiced it, the perpetrators of serious crimes were exiled into space in a state of suspended animation inside space capsules constructed specially for the purpose. According to Superman No. 65/3, the space capsules were made of transparent plastic and shaped like rocket ships (Jul/Aug '50: "Three Supermen from Krypton!"), but according to Superman No. 123 these so-called "prison satellites" were of a spherical shape. The criminals imprisoned inside them were placed in suspended animation by means of a special sleep gas, and chunks of a glowing crystalline mineral—capable of cleansing their brains of criminal tendencies in a hundred years' time—were placed on their foreheads so that ultimately, once their sentence was served, they might take up constructive roles in Kryptonian society (Aug '58: chs. 1-3—"The Girl of Steel"; "The Lost Super-Powers"; "Superman's Return to Krypton").

The practice of exiling criminals into outer space was terminated, however, after Superman's father, Jor-El, discovered the PHANTOM ZONE, a twilight dimension to which criminals could be banished to serve out their sentences as disembodied wraiths (Act No. 284, Jan '62: "The Babe of Steel!"; and others).

One of the most important government departments was the Krypton Record Bureau, where complete records of every Kryptonian's life were maintained on ingenious "thought-projection discs." According to Action Comics No. 149, such important events as courtship and marriage were "recorded astro-electricity, from each person's *memory!*"

"By concentrating on one of those discs--in a darkened room," explains the text, "--anybody could cause a complete image of remembered events to appear!" (Oct '50: "The Courtship on Krypton!").

Scientifically and technologically, Kryptonian civilization was far advanced over that of Earth. Although the science of space travel was still in its infancy and true spaceships did not yet exist (S No. 141, Nov '60: "Superman's Return to Krypton!" pts. I-III—"Superman Meets Jor-El and Lara Again!"; "Superman's Kryptonian Romance!"; "The Surprise of Fate!"; and others), Kryptonian scientists—most notably Jor-El—had experimented with both manned (Act No. 238, Mar '58: "The Super-Gorilla from Krypton"; and others) and unmanned (S No. 119, Feb '58: "The Second Superman!" chs. 1-3—"The World That Was Krypton's Twin"; "A Double for Superman"; "Superman's Mightiest Quest"; and others) satellites and had launched monkeys (Act No. 218, Jul '56: "The Super-Ape from Krypton"), at least one dog (S No. 146/1, Jul '61: "The Story of Superman's Life!"), and perhaps other test animals into outer space in small experimental rockets.

Astronomy on Krypton was highly advanced, enabling Kryptonian scientists to study Earth and presumably other planets with excruciating clarity by means of "super-powerful telescopes," even to the

1 STRIPED RIVER

2 ERKOL -- OLDEST CITY ON KRYPTON

3 FUNGUS CAVERNS

4 BOILING SEA

MAP of KRYPTON'S "OLD WORLD" HEMISPHERE

5 RUINS OF ANCIENT CITY OF XAN

7 GLASS FOREST

6 MT. MUNDRU-- HIGHEST PEAK ON KRYPTON

8 JERAT--"GHOST CITY"

9 VATHLO ISLAND--HOME OF KRYPTON'S BLACK RACE

10 ANTARCTIC CITY-- BUILT UNDER THE ICE

ARCTIC CONTINENT
COGO SEA
URRIKA
NIOZ
SEA OF BANZT
TWENX
SEA OF OLO
DANDAHU OCEAN
BOLENTH FLAME FOREST
SURRUS
JUVU
MORSTIL OCEAN
ANTARCTIC CONTINENT

Map of Krypton

extent of being able to tune in on selected alien individuals and monitor and translate their private conversations (S No. 141, Nov '60: "Superman's Return to Krypton!" pts. I-III—"Superman Meets Jor-El and Lara Again!"; "Superman's Kryptonian Romance!"; "The Surprise of Fate!"; and others).

Despite the lack of spaceships for interplanetary travel, transportation on Krypton was highly developed. People voyaged about the planet aboard sleek, rocketlike "airships" (S No. 141, Nov '60: "Superman's Return to Krypton!" pts. I-III—"Superman Meets Jor-El and Lara Again!"; "Superman's Kryptonian Romance!"; "The Surprise of Fate!"), or flitted about Krypton's picturesque metropolises—such as Kandor, Kryptonopolis, and ARGO CITY—in bubble-topped "jet-taxis" (S No. 141, Nov '60: "Superman's Return to Krypton!" pts. I-III—"Superman Meets Jor-El and Lara Again!"; "Superman's Kryptonian Romance!"; "The Surprise of Fate!") or by means of jetlike devices called "solo-rocket tubes" which, strapped to an individual's back, enabled him to fly through the air (Act No. 182, Jul '53: "The Return of Planet Krypton!"). Travel underwater was by means of a small jet-powered craft known as an "aqua-cone" (S No. 170/2, Jul '64: pts. I-II—"If Lex Luthor Were Superman's Father!"; "The Wedding of Lara and Luthor!"), and virtually every Kryptonian family owned its own "Jor-El," and all-purpose, mass-produced vehicle, invented by Superman's father, which could travel on land, sea, or air, and even underground (S No. 134, Jan '60: chs. I-III—"The Super-Menace of Metropolis!"; "The Revenge Against Jor-El!"; "The Duel of the Supermen!").

Sophisticated "weather control towers" enabled the people of Krypton to purify their air and control their weather (S No. 146/1, Jul '61: "The Story of Superman's Life!"), while an advanced "solar energy tower" enabled them to store and utilize the solar energy emanating from their planet's red sun (S No. 154/2, Jul '62: "Krypton's First Superman!"). In homes that were apparently heated by atomic power (Act No. 246, Nov '58: "Krypton on Earth!"), Kryptonian families entertained themselves by watching "3-D TV" (S No. 170/2, Jul '64: pts. I-II—"If Lex Luthor Were Superman's Father!"; "The Wedding of Lara and Luthor!") while, outside in the streets, other Kryptonians moved along the city's moving side-walks (Act No. 246, Nov '58: "Krypton on Earth!"), gazing at the "public news monitor"—a billboard-sized color-TV screen—to keep abreast of current events (S No. 170/2, Jul '64: pts. I-II—"If Lex Luthor Were Superman's Father!"; "The Wedding of Lara and Luthor!"), watching other Kryptonians queuing up for "emotion-movies," or visiting the incredible Mind-Art Center, where, by means of a complex apparatus called a "mento-ray," designed to freeze "the artist's mental pictures on canvas," Kryptonian "artists [created] art masterpieces by merely envisioning them in their minds!" (S No. 141, Nov '60: "Superman's Return to Krypton!" pts. I-III—"Superman Meets Jor-El and Lara Again!"; "Super-

man's Kryptonian Romance!"; "The Surprise of Fate!").

Landmarks and places of interest on Krypton included the Hall of Worlds, containing "replica scenes of strange planets in faraway solar systems" that Kryptonians had observed via "super-space telescope" (S No. 170/2, Jul '64: pts. I-II—"If Lex Luthor Were Superman's Father!"; "The Wedding of Lara and Luthor!"); the Red Tower of Kryptonopolis, one of Krypton's great architectural landmarks (WF No. 146, Dec '64: "Batman, Son of Krypton!" pts. I-II—no title; "The Destroyer of Krypton!"); Krypton's "famous floating city," a city of approximately 1,000,000 inhabitants floating on the surface of a river atop gigantic pontoons (Act No. 325, Jun '65: "The Skyscraper Superman!"); and the Cosmic Clock, a gigantic timepiece, measuring time in billions of years, which showed "how Krypton was born almost six billion time-cycles ago" (S No. 170/2, Jul '64: pts. I-II—"If Lex Luthor Were Superman's Father!"; "The Wedding of Lara and Luthor!"), and which, tragically, lulled the people of Krypton into a false sense of complacency concerning the future of their planet by predicting, incorrectly, that Krypton would remain safe from all harm for "endless years" into the future (S No. 146/1, Jul '61: "The Story of Superman's Life!"). The most important Kryptonian literary achievement was the *Kryptoniad*, a "great epic" chronicling the struggle of ancient Kryptonians to transform their planet into a "civilized world" (WF No. 146, Dec '64: "Batman, Son of Krypton!" pts. I-II—no title; "The Destroyer of Krypton!").

On Krypton, "robots performed all hard labor and could be bought at small cost..." (S No. 146/1, Jul '61: "The Story of Superman's Life!"; and others). Heavy construction work was accomplished by means of sophisticated "building machines" (Act No. 223, Dec '56: "The First Superman of Krypton").

Although Kryptonians had at least one serious disease, VIRUS X, for which there was no known cure (S No. 156, Oct '62: "The Last Days of Superman!" pts. I-III—"Superman's Death Sentence!"; "The Super-Comrades of All Time!"; "Superman's Last Day of Life!"), childhood diseases were not a problem: filing through a "health cabinet" on their first day of school, Kryptonian children were immunized against all childhood diseases by means of an ingenious "microbe ray" (S No. 132, Oct '59: "Superman's Other Life!" pts. 1-3—"Krypton Lives On!"; "Futuro, Super-Hero of Krypton!"; "The Superman of Two Worlds!"). Injuries were apparently not a problem either, as even potentially fatal wounds could be healed almost instantaneously by means of a miraculous "healing ray" employed by Kryptonian surgeons (S No. 172, Oct '64: pts. I-III—"The New Superman!"; "Clark Kent—Former Superman!"; "The Struggle of the Two Supermen!").

In Kryptonian schools, lessons were taught with the aid of sophisticated "telepathy helmets" which enabled teachers to transmit knowledge to their pupils telepathically at phenomenal speed (S No. 132,

Oct '59: "Superman's Other Life!" pts. 1-3—"Krypton Lives On!"; "Futuro, Super-Hero of Krypton!"; "The Superman of Two Worlds!"). The treatment of psychological problems—as well as the investigation of misconduct of all kinds—was facilitated by an ingenious mind-reading device known as a "mind-prober machine," and mental retardation had all but ceased to be a problem thanks to the pioneering work of scientist Lon Gorg, whose "supra-psyche treatments" successfully "transformed morons into geniuses" (S No. 170/2, Jul '64: pts. I-II—"If Lex Luthor Were Superman's Father!"; "The Wedding of Lara and Luthor!"). Historically, famine apparently had afflicted certain areas of Krypton, but "an amazing growth ray for plants," invented by Superman's father and capable of growing vegetables "100 times bigger" than their normal size, promised to end the problem of hunger forever within a very short time (Act No. 325, Jun '65: "The Skyscraper Superman!").

In Kryptonian society, descent and inheritance were patroclinous. The names of most—but by no means all—Kryptonian males were duosyllabic, with the first syllable being the given name, the second the surname. Thus, Jor-El was the brother of ZOR-EL and the father of Kal-El, Kal-El being Superman's Kryptonian name (Act No. 252, May '59: "The Supergirl from Krypton!"; and others); THAN-AR was the brother of Jhan-Ar (WF No. 143, Aug '64: "The Feud Between Batman and Superman!" pts. I-II—no title; "The Manhunters from Earth!"); and MAG-EN was the father of Ral-En (S No. 154/2, Jul '62: "Krypton's First Superman!").

Sometimes first and last names were linked by a hyphen (e.g., Jor-El, QUEX-UL, Mag-En). Just as often, however, they were not (e.g., Val Arn, Khai Zor, THAN OL). And some names, it must be noted, appear to have defied the system entirely (e.g., MALA, KIZO, General Zod).

Many of the most revered figures in Kryptonian history were members of the so-called House of El, and were, therefore, ancestors of Superman. Among them were Val-El, the Christopher Columbus of Krypton, who launched his planet's Age of Exploration and discovered islands and continents; Sul-El, who invented Krypton's first telescope and charted many far-off stars, including Earth's sun; Tala-El, a great lawyer and statesman who authored Krypton's planet-wide constitution; and Hatu-El, who discovered the nature of electricity, proved that lightning was electrical, and invented Krypton's first electromagnet and electric motor.

Each female child on Krypton was given a special feminine first name (e.g., KARA, Lara, Joenne), which, when followed by her father's name, formed her own full name, so that Kara Zor-El, for example, was Kara, the daughter of Zor-El. When a woman married, she dropped her father's name and assumed her husband's: when Lara married Jor-El, for example, she became Lara Jor-El, or, more formally, Mrs. Jor-El (S No. 179/2, Aug '65: "The Menace of Gold Kryptonite!"; and others).

Weddings took place in the Palace of Marriage (S No. 141, Nov '60: "Superman's Return to Krypton!" pts. I-III—"Superman Meets Jor-El and Lara Again!"; "Superman's Kryptonian Romance!"; "The Surprise of Fate!"), with the betrothed couple mounting the Jewel of Honor (S No. 170/2, Jul '64: pts. I-II—"If Lex Luthor Were Superman's Father!"; "The Wedding of Lara and Luthor!"), or Jewel of Truth and Honor (S No. 179/2, Aug '65: "The Menace of Gold Kryptonite!")—a low pedestal carved from a single huge, multifaceted jewel—and exchanging vows, accompanied either by an exchange of wedding rings (S No. 170/2, Jul '64: pts. I-II—"If Lex Luthor Were Superman's Father!"; "The Wedding of Lara and Luthor!") or by the donning of "marriage bracelets of a color variation all their own, which no other couple [was] allowed to duplicate." In accordance with "an old Kryptonian custom," statues of the parents of both the bride and the groom adorned the wedding hall (S No. 141, Nov '60: "Superman's Return to Krypton!" pts. I-III—"Superman Meets Jor-El and Lara Again!"; "Superman's Kryptonian Romance!"; "The Surprise of Fate!"). According to the Supergirl story in Action Comics No. 289, marriage between cousins was prohibited on Krypton (Jun '62: "Superman's Super-Courtship!").

Although the Kryptonians were, by and large, an intellectually sophisticated people, they were not without their irrational superstitions. According to Superman No. 164/2, which enumerates four Kryptonian superstitions, it was considered bad luck for a bride to wear jewels from the Jewel Mountains at her wedding; the killing of birds was regarded as extremely unlucky, hence the absence of bird hunting on Krypton; an "old Kryptonian belief" dictated that, "upon seeing a comet, a person must hide in a cave for 24 hours or he'd die"; and Kryptonian criminals believed that if they experienced failure, drawing a picture of a Kryptonian mythological creature known as a "one-eyed grompus" would cause Krypton's "demons" to bring them good luck (Oct '63: "The Fugitive from the Phantom Zone!").

A holiday of great importance on Krypton was the Day of Truth, celebrated annually, on which Kryptonians spoke "nothing but the truth to one another"—even though the truth might be abrasive and undiplomatic—in order to honor the memory of Val-Lor, a valiant Kryptonian of ancient times, who, by courageously speaking out against the "ruthless swarm of alien invaders"—known as the Vrangs—who had invaded Krypton and enslaved its people, inspired his fellow Kryptonians to revolt against the Vrangs and drive them from Krypton, albeit at the cost of his own life. The Day of Truth is still celebrated each April in the bottle city of Kandor (S No. 176/3, Apr '65: "Superman's Day of Truth!").

By the time Krypton's day of doom arrived, Kryptonian civilization was 10,000 years old (Act No. 223, Dec '56: "The First Superman of Krypton"). Action Comics No. 1 observes only that Superman's home planet "was destroyed by old age" (Jun '38), but

Action Comics No. 182 explains, with far greater accuracy, that Krypton's destruction was caused by "gathering atomic pressure at the core of the planet!" (Jul '53: "The Return of Planet Krypton!").

Jor-El had correctly predicted that the end was coming, but he had been unable either to prevent its occurrence or to persuade the scientific community to adopt his proposal for the construction of a fleet of "rocket-driven space arks" to enable Krypton's population to flee the coming cataclysm (S No. 146/1, Jul '61: "The Story of Superman's Life!"; and others).

"...[T]he core of Krypton," Jor-El had warned, "is composed of a substance called **uranium**...which, for untold ages, has been setting up a cycle of chain-impulses, building in power every moment! Soon...very soon...every atom of Krypton will explode in one final terrible blast!...**Krypton is one gigantic atomic bomb!**" (S No. 53/1, Jul/Aug '48: "The Origin of Superman!").

But the people of Krypton would not believe Jor-El, not even when the quakes began, not even when "a rumble of mighty forces" erupted from deep inside Krypton that shook the home of every Kryptonian (Act No. 158, Jul '51: "The Kid from Krypton!"; and others).

Superman recalls the moment when his parents, Jor-El and Lara, prepared to place him inside the tiny rocket that would carry him safely away from the death of Krypton

And then finally, on a fateful day either in December (WF No. 146, Dec '64: "Batman, Son of Krypton!" pts. I-II—no title; "The Destroyer of Krypton!") or in January (S No. 150/1, Jan '62: "The One Minute of Doom!"), "the rumblings inside Krypton became a roar and the planet shook wildly!" (Act No. 158, Jul '51: "The Kid from Krypton!"). As the edifices of a once-proud civilization collapsed like building blocks amid choking clouds of dense black smoke, "nature's fury gathered for one final cataclysmic eruption" and "the once mighty planet

Krypton exploded into stardust!" (S No. 53/1, Jul/Aug '48: "The Origin of Superman!"). (*See also* JOR-EL.)

The titanic interstellar explosion that destroyed Krypton transformed the hurtling remnants of the shattered planet into KRYPTONITE, a glowing, green, radioactive substance which is toxic—and potentially fatal—to all Kryptonian survivors (S No. 150/1, Jan '62: "The One Minute of Doom!"; and many others). "When Krypton exploded," explains Superman No. 61/3, "all the atomic elements fused to become one deadly compound! That compound gives off rays which apparently can only affect Kryptonites...!" (Nov/Dec '49: "Superman Returns to Krypton!").

Superman remains the most famous survivor of the cataclysm that destroyed Krypton, but over the years the texts have revealed the existence of a great many others, including KRYPTO THE SUPERDOG (S No. 130/1; Jul '59: "The Curse of Kryptonite!"; and others) and BEPPO THE SUPER-MONKEY (Act No. 309, Feb '64: "The Superman Super-Spectacular!"; and others); the people of KANDOR (Act No. 242, Jul '58: "The Super-Duel in Space!"; and others) and the inhabitants of the PHANTOM ZONE (Act No. 284, Jan '62: "The Babe of Steel!"; and others); MALA and his brothers, Kizo and U-Ban (S No. 65/3, Jul/Aug '50: "Three Supermen from Krypton!"; Act No. 194, Jul '54: "The Outlaws from Krypton!"); the "snagriff" (*see* SNAGRIFF) that runs amok on Earth in September-October 1952 (S No. 78/1: "The Beast from Krypton!"); SUPER-APE and the other experimental apes launched into outer space by the Kryptonian scientist Shir Kan (Act No. 218, Jul '56: "The Super-Ape from Krypton"); KING KRYPTON, whom Superman encounters in March 1958 (Act No. 238: "The Super-Gorilla from Krypton"); the Kryptonian caveman who arrives on Earth in a state of suspended animation in June 1959 (*see* GROFF, JO-JO) (WF No. 102: "The Caveman from Krypton!"); and the "flame dragon" (*see* FLAME DRAGON) that runs amok on Earth in January 1961 (S No. 142/3: "Flame-Dragon from Krypton"), and the offspring, hatched from one of its eggs, that menaces Earth in February 1962 (S No. 151/3: "Superman's Greatest Secret!"). The inhabitants of ARGO CITY survived for more than fifteen years following the death of Krypton after their city had been hurled into outer space by the force of the cataclysm. Virtually the entire population, however, ultimately succumbed to kryptonite poisoning, the only survivors of the calamity apparently having been SUPERGIRL and her parents, ZOR-EL and ALURA (S No. 150/1, Jan '62: "The One Minute of Doom!"; and others).

Far from perished Krypton, in the alien environment of Earth, any Kryptonian survivor acquires mighty super-powers—including X-ray vision, invulnerability, super-strength, and the power of flight—and all things Kryptonian become indestructible (Act No. 310, Mar '64: "Secret of Kryptonite Six!"; and many others). In Jor-El's words, "...Krypton is such an unusual planet that when a native Kryptonian is elsewhere, free of Krypton's unique atmosphere and tremendous gravitational pull, he becomes a **superman**!" (S No. 113, May '57: chs. 1-3—"The Superman of the Past"; "The Secret of the Towers"; "The Superman of the Present").

The relative physical strength of two Kryptonian survivors on Earth appears to be proportional to what it was—or would have been—on Krypton, so that a Kryptonian gorilla on Earth is more powerful than Superman, just as an ordinary Kryptonian gorilla would have been more powerful than an ordinary Kryptonian man (Act No. 218, Jul '56: "The Super-Ape from Krypton"; and others).

Of course the vast majority of Kryptonians perished with their planet, but a number of these have nevertheless played important roles in the chronicles, among them JOR-EL and his wife LARA (S No. 53/1, Jul/Aug '48: "The Origin of Superman!"; and many others); lovely "emotion-movie actress" LYLA LER-ROL (S No. 141, Nov '60: "Superman's Return to Krypton!" pts. I-III—"Superman Meets Jor-El and Lara Again!"; "Superman's Kryptonian Romance!"; "The Surprise of Fate!"; and others); and "famous psychologist" MAG-EN and his unscrupulous son Ral-En (S No. 154/2, Jul '62: "Krypton's First Superman!"). According to Action Comics No. 243, the legendary enchantress CIRCE was herself a native of the planet Krypton (Aug '58: "The Lady and the Lion").

"The famous lost world of Krypton is of intense interest to everyone on Earth, for that great planet was the birthplace of mighty **Superman**!" (Act No. 223, Dec '56: "The First Superman of Krypton").

Dr. Charles Corlin, the father of VANCE CORLIN, discovered the planet Krypton sometime prior to its destruction and made an extensive spectroscopic analysis of its gravity, atmosphere, and solar radiation (WF No. 57, Mar/Apr '52: "The Artificial Superman!").

PROFESSOR WILLIAM ENDERS, author of *The Planet Krypton*, observed Krypton through his telescope, communicated with Jor-El by radio, and even journeyed to Krypton via "matter-radio" (S No. 77/1, Jul/Aug '52: "The Man Who Went to Krypton!"), as did another scientist, PROFESSOR AMOS DUNN (Act No. 281, Oct '61: "The Man Who Saved Kal-El's Life!").

"Brilliant young college teacher" MEL EVANS, who has since become a "renowned scientist," calculated the "probable distance from Earth to Krypton" at 0.317 light years (S No. 136/2, Apr '60: "The Secret of Kryptonite!").

DR. THOMAS ELLISON carried on an extensive study of Krypton by means of a "monitor-type telescope" of "unprecedented power." When Ellison learned that Krypton faced imminent extinction due to an atomic chain-reaction building up within the core of the planet, he beamed an "atomic-neutralizing ray" at the distant world in hopes of neutralizing the atomic reaction and thereby averting the cataclysm,

but Krypton exploded anyway, in spite of his efforts (WF No. 146, Dec '64: "Batman, Son of Krypton!" pts. I-II—no title; "The Destroyer of Krypton!").

In addition, Superman has made an extensive study of his home planet "by overtaking and photographing light rays that had left Krypton before it exploded" (S No. 132, Oct '59: "Superman's Other Life!" pts. 1-3—"Krypton Lives On!"; "Futuro, Super-Hero of Krypton!"; "The Superman of Two Worlds!"; and others). He has donated exhaustive notes on the Kryptonese language to METROPOLIS UNIVERSITY (Act No. 329, Oct '65: "The Ultimate Enemy!").

Superman has memorialized the lost world of Krypton in other ways as well: he has set aside an entire Krypton Room in his FORTRESS OF SOLITUDE—complete with an exact scale model of Krypton (Act No. 278, Jul '61: "The Super Powers of Perry White!") and a "3-dimensional tableau of the exact moment that the planet Krypton exploded!" (Act No. 261, Feb '60: "Superman's Fortresses of Solitude!")—and, with the aid of Supergirl and Krypto the Superdog, he has transformed an uninhabited planet in a "distant solar system" into an exact duplicate of Krypton, a so-called "memorial planet" inhabited by android duplicates of the entire Kryptonian population (S No. 150/1, Jan '62: "The One Minute of Doom!"). A statue of Superman holding aloft a globe of Krypton adorns the grounds of METROPOLIS's SUPERMAN MUSEUM (S No. 169/1, May '64: "The Infernal Imp!"). The "anniversary of the destruction of Krypton" is commemorated annually by the people of Kandor and all the remaining Kryptonian survivors (S No. 150/1, Jan '62: "The One Minute of Doom!"; *see also* WF No. 146, Dec '64: "Batman, Son of Krypton!" pts. I-II—no title; "The Destroyer of Krypton!").

In June 1938, in the premiere text of the Superman chronicles, Superman's home planet is referred to only as "a distant planet [that] was destroyed by old age," and its actual name is never stated (Act No. 1).

In Summer 1939 the planet of Superman's birth is referred to by name—as Krypton—for the first time in the chronicles (S No. 1/1).

In July-August 1948 the causes of Krypton's destruction and the events leading up to it are recounted in detail for the first time in the chronicles (S No. 53/1: "The Origin of Superman!").

In November-December 1949 Superman journeys through the time-space barrier to the planet Krypton and actually witnesses the cataclysm that destroyed his native planet (S No. 61/3: "Superman Returns to Krypton!").

In July-August 1950 Superman battles three evil Kryptonian survivors: MALA and his brothers Kizo and U-Ban (S No. 65/3: "Three Supermen from Krypton!").

In October 1950 three Kryptonian "thought-projection discs" containing a detailed account of the courtship of Superman's parents—which have been whirling about in space since the explosion of Krypton—are returned to Earth by a U.S. experimental rocket and retrieved by the ever-curious LOIS LANE (Act No. 149: "The Courtship on Krypton!"). (*See also* LARA.)

In January-February 1952 a vault containing some of Jor-El's greatest inventions, which had been hurled into outer space by the force of the cataclysm that destroyed Krypton, is drawn to Earth by a "magnet-ray machine" devised by the diabolical LEX LUTHOR (S No. 74/1: "The Lost Secrets of Krypton!").

In September-October 1952 a Kryptonian "snagriff" (*see* SNAGRIFF) runs amok on the planet Earth (S No. 78/1: "The Beast from Krypton!").

In March-April 1954, on the site where the rocket carrying the infant Superman landed upon its arrival on Earth, Superman finds his father's last will and testament, a thin sheet of super-hard metal inscribed with detailed descriptions of three of Jor-El's greatest inventions (WF No. 69: "Jor-El's Last Will!"). (*See* JOR-EL.)

In July 1954 Superman battles the same three evil Kryptonian survivors whom he fought four years previously, viz., MALA and his brothers Kizo and U-Ban (Act No. 194: "The Outlaws from Krypton!").

In December 1955 the town of SMALLVILLE holds a celebration marking the anniversary of Superman's arrival on Earth from the planet Krypton (Act No. 211: "The Superman Spectaculars"). The precise month when the infant Superman actually arrived on Earth is impossible to determine, however, because the anniversary of the event is also commemorated, in a later text, in June 1958 (Act No. 241: "The Super-Key to Fort Superman").

In January 1956, in outer space, Superman locates the tiny fragment of the exploded planet Krypton that contains, still intact, the family home he shared with his parents, Jor-El and Lara (Act No. 212: "The Superman Calendar").

In May 1956 the city of Metropolis is besieged by an armada of colossal "war weapons" hurled into outer space years ago by the explosion that destroyed Krypton (Act No. 216: "The Super-Menace of Metropolis"). (*See* JOR-EL.)

In June 1956 Superman encounters an infant who has become temporarily endowed with super-powers as the result of having ingested some "condensed food" from the planet Krypton (Act No. 217: "The Amazing Super-Baby"). (*See* BLISS, ROGER [MR. AND MRS.].)

In July 1956 Superman encounters SUPER-APE, a Kryptonian survivor (Act No. 218: "The "Super-Ape" from Krypton").

In December 1956, "far out in space," Superman comes upon "a mass of cosmic wreckage" from the doomed planet Krypton, including Jor-El's journal and laboratory desk, and some films which Jor-El made of himself using "automatic cameras" (Act No. 223: "The First Superman of Krypton"). (*See* JOR-EL.)

In May 1957 Superman recovers a Kryptonian "mind-tape" dictated by Jor-El—and a helmetlike apparatus for playing it back—after the objects have fallen to Earth embedded in a kryptonite meteor (S No. 113: chs. 1-3—"The Superman of the Past"; "The Secret of the Towers"; "The Superman of the Present"). (*See* JOR-EL; LATORA [QUEEN].)

In February 1958 Superman views dramatic film footage chronicling the death of Krypton after successfully recovering, far out in interstellar space, an unmanned camera-carrying space satellite that had been sent aloft by Kryptonian scientists prior to their planet's destruction. During this same period, Superman rescues the planet XENON, evidently once a moon of Krypton, from suffering the same fate that befell its native planet (S No. 119: "The Second Superman!" chs. 1-3—"The World That Was Krypton's Twin"; "A Double for Superman"; "Superman's Mightiest Quest").

In March 1958 Superman meets KING KRYPTON, a Kryptonian survivor (Act No. 238: "The Super-Gorilla from Krypton").

In July 1958 Superman discovers that the Kryptonian city of KANDOR survived the cataclysm that destroyed the planet as the result of having been stolen prior to the disaster by the space villain BRAINIAC (Act No. 242: "The Super-Duel in Space").

In August 1958 Superman journeys through the time-space barrier to Krypton at a time predating the marriage of his parents (*see* KIL-LOR) (S No. 123: chs. 1-3—"The Girl of Steel"; "The Lost Super-Powers"; "Superman's Return to Krypton"). During this same period, Superman encounters CIRCE, a descendant of the legendary enchantress of the same name, who, according to this text, was a native of Krypton (Act No. 243, Aug '58: "The Lady and the Lion").

In May 1959 the Supergirl story in Action Comics No. 252 recounts the first meeting between Superman and SUPERGIRL, the teen-aged offspring of two Kryptonian survivors ("The Supergirl from Krypton!").

In June 1959 Superman encounters a Kryptonian caveman who arrives on Earth in a state of suspended animation (WF No. 102: "The Caveman from Krypton!"). (*See* GROFF, JO-JO.)

In November 1960 Superman journeys through the time-space barrier to Krypton on the day of his parents' wedding and remains on the planet for what is probably several weeks thereafter, during which time he pursues a passionate romance with lovely actress LYLA LERROL (S No. 141: "Superman's Return to Krypton!" pts. I-III—"Superman Meets Jor-El and Lara Again!"; "Superman's Kryptonian Romance!"; "The Surprise of Fate!").

In January 1961 Earth is menaced by a fearsome Kryptonian "flame dragon" (*see* FLAME DRAGON) (S No. 142/3: "Flame-Dragon from Krypton").

In February 1962 Earth is menaced by a second Kryptonian FLAME DRAGON, the offspring of the creature that Superman battled thirteen months previously (S No. 151/3: "Superman's Greatest Secret!").

In July 1962 Superman struggles to overcome the compulsion to obey the sinister "hypnotic command" implanted in his unconscious mind while he was still an infant by the Kryptonian psychologist MAG-EN (S No. 154/2: "Krypton's First Superman!").

In October 1962, when Superman is believed to be dying as the result of exposure to VIRUS X, an incurable Kryptonian malady, Supergirl journeys through the time-space barrier to Krypton in the faint hope that Kryptonian scientists may have found a cure for the virus before their planet exploded. Krypton's scientists never did perfect a cure for Virus X and thus Supergirl's mission ends in failure, but Superman turns out to be suffering only from exposure to a nugget of green kryptonite, and he recovers his health fully as soon as the kryptonite is removed from his presence (S No. 156: "The Last Days of Superman!" pts. I-III—"Superman's Death Sentence!"; "The Super-Comrades of All Time!"; "Superman's Last Day of Life!").

In November 1962 Superman journeys through the time-space barrier to Krypton to verify his hunch that the Kryptonian scientist QUEX-UL may have been innocent of the crime of which he was convicted by a Kryptonian court and for which he was sentenced to a term in the Phantom Zone (S No. 157/1: "The Super-Revenge of the Phantom Zone Prisoner!").

In August 1963 exposure to red kryptonite temporarily transforms Superman into a fearsome Kryptonian "drang," a colossal flying snake, purple in color, with a head like a dinosaur and a single white horn protruding from its forehead. Unaware that the hideous monster is actually Superman, but fully aware that it is Kryptonian and therefore vulnerable to kryptonite, the U.S. Armed Forces are on the verge of destroying it with kryptonite bullets when finally, with some crucial assistance from Supergirl, Superman succeeds in alerting his attackers to his true identity and in getting them to hold their fire. Soon afterward, the effects of the red kryptonite fade and vanish, and Superman is restored to his normal form (Act No. 303: "The Monster from Krypton!").

In March 1964 Superman journeys through the time-space barrier to Krypton with the villain JAX-UR in hopes of finding a cure for the "ghastly spotted plague" that is sweeping ATLANTIS (Act No. 310: "Secret of Kryptonite Six!").

In July 1964 Superman views a Kryptonian "video-recording" narrated by his father, JOR-EL. Originally affixed to the exterior of the rocket that brought the infant Superman to Earth, the video-recording and accompanying "record playback machine" somehow became detached from the rocket after it had entered Earth's atmosphere and lay on the ocean floor until they were discovered there many years later (Act No. 314: "The Day Superman Became the Flash!"). During this same period, LEX LUTHOR journeys through the time-space barrier to Krypton at a time predating the marriage of Jor-El and Lara as part of his bizarre scheme to marry Lara himself and thus become the father of Superman (S No. 170/2, Jul '64: pts. I-II—"If Lex Luthor Were Superman's Father!"; "The Wedding of Lara and Luthor!").

In December 1964 Superman witnesses the death of the planet Krypton by means of a special "time-space viewer," a superscientific device, given him by the scientists of a distant planet, that "picks up light and sound waves from the past" and thus enables one to view selected historical events (WF No. 146: "Batman, Son of Krypton!" pts. I-II—no title; "The Destroyer of Krypton!").

In October 1965 Superman matches wits with JON SMATTEN, a "renegade scientist" who, having come into possession of a supply of kryptium, Krypton's "strongest metal," has fashioned the metal into an ingenious robot designed to destroy Superman (Act No. 329: "The Ultimate Enemy!").

KRYPTON CITY. *See* KANDOR.

KRYPTONITE. The term used to designate any surviving fragment of the exploded planet KRYPTON, home world of SUPERMAN. There are five distinct varieties of kryptonite (green, red, gold, blue, and white), the first three of which are toxic to Superman. Green kryptonite, the only variety potentially fatal to Superman, induces lassitude and inertia followed by death if not removed in time from Superman's presence. Red kryptonite inflicts bizarre and unpredictable—albeit temporary and nonfatal—symptoms, as when it divides Superman into twins or transforms him into an infant or a giant ant. Gold kryptonite would permanently rob Superman of his super-powers were he ever to be exposed to its radiations. These three varieties of kryptonite are similarly hazardous to SUPERGIRL, KRYPTO THE SUPERDOG, and all other surviving natives of Krypton. Blue kryptonite is toxic only to BIZARRO creatures. White kryptonite is harmful only to plant life. Whenever the word *kryptonite* appears in this encyclopedia without a specific color designation, it is green kryptonite, the most common variety, that is being referred to. (*See* SUPERMAN [section F1, kryptonite].)

KRYPTONOPOLIS. The city of the planet KRYPTON where SUPERMAN was born and where, in the home of his parents, JOR-EL and LARA, he spent his infancy until the day when Jor-El launched him into outer space in an experimental rocket ship to enable him to escape the impending doom of their planet (Act No. 325, Jun '65: "The Skyscraper Superman!"; and others). Designed by Superman's "distinguished ancestor" Gam-El, the father of modern Kryptonian architecture (SF No. 172, Aug/Sep '75; and others), Kryptonopolis became Krypton's capital city following the theft of its first capital, KANDOR, by the space villain BRAINIAC. Its famous Red Tower was one of Krypton's great architectural landmarks (WF No. 146, Dec '64: "Batman, Son of Krypton!" pts. I-II—no title; "The Destroyer of Krypton!"). When Krypton exploded, Kryptonopolis perished with it, but Superman once photographed the city "by overtaking and photographing light rays that had left **Krypton** before it exploded," and has since "donated the photos to a museum!" (S No. 132, Oct '59: "Superman's Other Life!" pts. 1-3—"Krypton Lives On!"; "Futuro, Super-Hero of Krypton!"; "The Superman of

Two Worlds!"). In November 1958, after swindler JONAS SMITH has been apprehended by Superman, the Krypton Island real-estate development founded by Smith on an island off METROPOLIS is taken over by an honest developer and renamed Kryptonopolis (Act No. 246: "Krypton on Earth!").

KUBLAI KHAN. A modern-day descendant of Kublai Khan (1215-1294), and the ruler of the fabulous lost city of Samarkist, "a fantastic fragment of the ancient Mongol empire of Kublai Khan surviving in the heart of the mysterious Himalayas," somewhere in exotic Tibet. Arriving in Samarkist in May-June 1946 in search of famed explorer Basil Garret—who had stumbled upon Samarkist some three years earlier and remained there as tutor to the Khan's lovely sloe-eyed daughter May-lin— SUPERMAN intervenes repeatedly to thwart successive attempts by the fierce bandit chieftain Garjnok to kidnap May-lin, murder the Khan, and loot the city of its fabulous treasure. Garjnok and his cohort Bonzak are killed when, after dynamiting a glacier in an effort to destroy the city, they are crushed to death between a glacial fragment and an onrushing mountain ice cap dislodged by the explosion (S No. 40/2: "A Modern Marco Polo!").

KULL-EX. A young scientist from the bottle city of KANDOR who, having successfully escaped into the outside world while simultaneously imprisoning SUPERMAN in Kandor by means of an ingenious "exchange ray," commits a series of insanely destructive acts while impersonating Superman—all as part of a master scheme to make "the name of Superman hated everywhere"—in the mistaken belief that long ago on Krypton, Superman's father, JOR-EL, cheated his own father, Zell-Ex, out of the valuable patent rights to an important invention. For a time the name of Superman becomes anathema to the people of Earth, but Kull-Ex ultimately confesses his misdeeds publicly and makes an effort to atone for them after Superman has proved to him, with the aid of SUPERGIRL and KRYPTO THE SUPERDOG, that his bitter grudge against Jor-El is completely unfounded (S No. 134, Jan '60: chs. I-III—"The Super-Menace of Metropolis!"; "The Revenge Against Jor-El!"; "The Duel of the Supermen!").

KUM-BAK KOMEDY FILMS. A film company formed by J. WILBUR WOLFINGHAM in January-February 1944, ostensibly for the purpose of enabling a group of old-time silent-movie comedians to stage a comeback, but in reality to enable Wolfingham to defraud the old-timers of their life savings. Wolfingham's scheme is thwarted by SUPERMAN (S No. 26/2: "Comedians' Holiday!").

KYACK. A warlike member of the "underground people," the sole survivors of a centuries-old civilization whose scientists fled the upper world in prehistoric times for a new home far beneath the surface of the Earth in order to escape the dire peril of advancing glacial ice. In Kyack's words:

> Our race once populated the Earth in abundance. Then came the Ice-Age!...
> Most of us perished under the irresistible approach of the colossal glaciers. But the most intelligent of us, the scientists, retreated deep into the Earth toward its warm center.
> We built this retreat, equipped it with all the marvels our scientific ingenuity could fashion.

By November-December 1941 Kyack and his henchmen have kidnapped young Tulan, the peace-loving leader of the underground people, as the first step in an elaborate scheme to destroy the structures of the surface world with a diabolical "ray-apparatus" and then invade the world above with an armada of "bore-vessels" designed to enable the villains to extend their dominion over the entire planet Earth. The savage scheme is thwarted by SUPERMAN, who burrows to the cavern city of the underground people far beneath the earth, demolishes the awesome "ray machine" that has been causing buildings in METROPOLIS to shatter and crumble, defeats the armada of mighty bore-vessels, and restores the peace-loving Tulan to the leadership of his people (S No. 13/4).

KZOTL. The far-distant planet which is the home of an alien movie producer who, in March 1960, tricks BATMAN, ROBIN, and SUPERMAN into battling robots designed to resemble extraterrestrial aliens so that he can obtain exciting movie footage of Earth's greatest heroes in action (WF No. 108: "The Star Creatures!").

L

LAHLA. One of the THORONES, a lovely girl with honey-blond hair who falls in love with SUPERMAN in February 1965 after he has been left stranded on her distant planet by the FOUR GALACTIC THIEFMASTERS and thrown into prison by the Thorones' leaders.

On this strange planet, where all the native inhabitants possess super-powers but where Superman possesses none—and where Superman is, therefore, "the weakest man in the world"—Lahla, touched by Superman's handsome appearance and singular gentleness, risks exile and even death to free him from his dungeon and flee to Earth with him so that he can recover his super-powers and thwart her people's plot to invade and conquer Earth.

Lahla

On Earth, however, where Superman is renowned as the "strongest man in the universe," Lahla quickly loses interest in Superman, selecting instead a self-effacing milquetoast of a beau with whom she promptly elopes to a distant planet.

"She loved me when I was the weakest man on her world, but turned me down when I regained my powers!" muses Superman aloud. "It doesn't make sense . . . it's silly!"

"All girls are that way . . . me, for instance!" interjects LOIS LANE. "I'm silly enough to have a crush on a big, boneheaded **Superman!**" (Act No. 321: "Superman--Weakest Man in the World!").

LAMONT, CHARLES. A documentary filmmaker who is determined to film the story of *The Life of Superman* so that "future generations [can] see his tremendous deeds with their own eyes!" When racketeer "Angles" Alden, "who got his nickname by never missing a profitable angle," attempts to sabotage the filming of the movie in order to force Lamont to cut him in on half the profits, he and his henchmen are apprehended by SUPERMAN, in May-June 1951 (S No. 70/2: "The Life of Superman!").

LANCHESTER, OSCAR. The man who is secretly Mr. Z (S No. 19/3, Nov/Dec '42).

LANE, LOIS. The persistent, curious, impulsive, intelligent, headstrong, audacious, hard-working, ambitious, lovely woman reporter for the METROPOLIS DAILY PLANET who is, second only to SUPERMAN himself, the single most important person in the chronicled adventures of Superman, fulfilling as she does the tripartite role of Clark Kent's journalistic colleague, Superman's romantic pursuer, and the person most tirelessly determined to verify her long-held suspicion that Clark Kent is secretly Superman. Lois Lane appears in the chronicles more often than any other character except Superman, and is the only supporting character to have appeared in the chronicles since their inception in June 1938 (Act No. 1).

Lois Lane

Lois Lane, the daughter of Sam and Ella Lane (SF No. 172, Aug/Sep '75), was born on her parents' farm, near the U.S. town of Pittsdale (LL No. 68, Sep/Oct '66). The month when she was born is impossible to determine, for her birthday is celebrated in the chronicles in September-October (WF No. 36, Sep/Oct

145

'48: "Lois Lane, Sleeping Beauty"), in November-December (S No. 37/2, Nov/Dec '45: "Pranks for Profit!"), and in December (Act No. 139, Dec '49: "Clark Kent...Daredevil!").

Lois appears to have had two sisters: a younger sister, LUCY LANE (Act No. 272, Jan '61: "Superman's Rival, Mental Man!"; and others), and a second sister, whose first name is never given, who married a man named Tompkins and gave birth to a daughter, SUSIE TOMPKINS (Act No. 59, Apr '43: "Cinderella--a la Superman!"; see also Act No. 98, Jul '46: "Starring Susie!"), who is Lois Lane's niece.

Lois attended school in Pittsdale (LL No. 68, Sep /Oct '66). Her closest friend in high school was a girl named Helen, who later became the wife of BILL MINTON (WF No. 21, Mar/Apr '46: "The Plane of Tomorrow!"). Lois's high-school beau was FINNEY FLOOR (S No. 66/3, Sep/Oct '50: "The Machine That Played Cupid!").

After high school, Lois attended Raleigh College, not far from Metropolis, where she exhibited a keen aptitude for science (S No. 181/1, Nov '65: pts. I-II—"The Super-Scoops of Morna Vine!"; "The Secret of the New Supergirl!"), honed her fledgling journalism skills on the Raleigh Review (LL No. 68, Sep/Oct '66), and displayed sufficient artistic talent to acquire a reputation as the "class artist" (Act No. 272, Jan '61: "Superman's Rival, Mental Man!"). Lois's schoolmate BRETT RAND had a crush on her during this period, but there is no indication that she ever reciprocated his affections (S No. 139/1, Aug '60: "The New Life of Super-Merman!").

After graduation (S No. 181/1, Nov '65: pts. I-II—"The Super-Scoops of Morna Vine!"; "The Secret of the New Supergirl!"), Lois set out for Metropolis, determined to fulfill her "lifelong ambition" to become "the best reporter in Metropolis" (Act No. 202, Mar '55: "Lois Lane's X-Ray Vision!"). She may have taken "a course in nursing" during this period (Act No. 191, Apr '54: "Calling Doctor Superman!") or served a stint as a waitress at HARRY'S DOG HOUSE (WF No. 47, Aug/Sep '50: "The Girl Who Hated Reporters!"). Eventually, however, she obtained employment on the DAILY STAR (Act No. 1, Jun '38; and others), followed by employment on its successor in the chronicles, the Daily Planet (S No. 4/1-4, Spr '40; Act No. 23, Apr '40; and others).

Lois Lane is "the Daily Planet's star woman reporter" (WF No. 47, Aug/Sep '50: "The Girl Who Hated Reporters!"), ranking alongside Clark Kent in the Daily Planet's reportorial hierarchy. Described as the newspaper's "sob sister" (S No. 7/1, Nov/Dec '40; and others) and as its lovelorn columnist (Act No. 44, Jan '42; and others) in many early texts, Lois Lane has risen through the journalistic ranks to become one of the Daily Planet's "star reporters" (S No. 27/1, Mar/Apr '44: "The Palace of Perilous Play!"; and others) and, with Clark Kent, one of the newspaper's "two brightest satellites" (S No. 26/2, Jan/Feb '44: "Comedians' Holiday!"). Particularly adept at covering local news (S No. 44/3, Jan/Feb '47: "Shake-

speare's Ghost Writer!"), she has performed the ful range of journalistic duties, including stints as wa correspondent (Act No. 23, Apr '40); weather editor described as "one of the lowliest jobs on an newspaper" (WF No. 25, Nov/Dec '46: "Mad Weathe in Metropolis!" see also WF No. 51, Apr/May '51 "The Amazing Talents of Lois Lane!"); question-and answer editor and head of the lost and found department (WF No. 51, Apr/May '51: "The Amazing Talents of Lois Lane!"); editor of the Daily Planet's Paris edition (Act No. 203, Apr '55: "The Internation al Daily Planet!"); staff cartoonist (Act No. 272, Jan '61: "Superman's Rival, Mental Man!"); and "acting editor" in the absence of editor PERRY WHITE (S No. 124/1, Sep '58: "The Super-Sword!).

The texts describe Lois Lane as a "courageous girl reporter" (Act No. 27, Aug '40), a "glamorous girl reporter" (S No. 34/2, May/Jun '45: "The Canyon That Went Berserk!"), "a competent reporter who's

Lois Lane covers a fast-breaking story, 1954

Lois Lane, 1944

always on the job" (S No. 61/2, Nov/Dec '49: "The Courtship of the Three Lois Lanes!"), "one of [Metropolis's] smartest reporters" (S No. 68/2, Jan/Feb '51: "Lois Lane's Royal Romance!"), the "star girl reporter for the *Daily Planet*" (Act No. 172, Sep '52: "Lois Lane...Witch!"), the "audacious girl reporter of the **Daily Planet**" (Act No. 189, Feb '54: "Clark Kent's New Mother and Father!"), "the prettiest girl reporter in Metropolis" (Act No. 195, Aug '54: "Lois Lane--Wanted!"), a "well-known newspaperwoman" (S No. 109/2, Nov '56: "The Puppet with X-Ray Eyes"), and a "famous reporter" (Act No. 225, Feb '57: "The Death of Superman").

Lois Lane is also referred to as "Clark Kent's rival reporter at the **Daily Planet**" (Act No. 176, Jan '53: "Muscles for Money"). Indeed, the rivalry between these "two famed reporters" (Act No. 58, Mar '43: "The Face of Adonis!") is a keen one. Lois, in particular, is fiercely, sometimes unscrupulously, competitive, resorting to such tactics as intercepting Kent's telephone messages (S No. 14/4, Jan/Feb '42; and others), sending him off on wild-goose chases (Act No. 5, Oct '38; and others), and even seducing him into letting her accompany him on an interview and then slipping knockout drops into his drink so that she can cover the story alone (Act No. 6, Nov '38). Although, particularly after 1940, Lois Lane and Clark Kent develop a friendly working relationship and frequently cover news assignments together, their reportorial rivalry has remained a heated one for four full decades and continues to constitute one of the major themes of the chronicles. The texts

Clark Kent and Lois Lane, 1938

repeatedly refer to them as the *Daily Planet*'s "best reporters" (S No. 44/1, Jan/Feb '47: "Playthings of Peril!"), its "star reporters" (S No. 27/1, Mar/Apr '44: "The Palace of Perilous Play!"; and others), and as the "two best-known reporters" in Metropolis (WF No. 23, Jan/Aug '46: "The Colossus of Metropolis!"). In the largest sense, however, the Lane-Kent reportorial rivalry is a sham, for the headline stories for which they compete so assiduously are invariably stories about Superman, and the outcome of the contest to see

which of them can publish a particular story first is just as invariably determined by whether Superman decides to give Lois Lane an exclusive account or to write it up himself as reporter Clark Kent.

Nevertheless, "newspaper reporting is [Lois Lane's] **first** love" (S No. 58/2, May/Jun '49: "Lois Lane Loves Clark Kent!"), and she is capable of "running any risk to get a scoop story...!" (WF No. 64, May/Jun '53: "The Death of Lois Lane"). "...I guess I've got printer's ink in my veins," muses Lois in November-December 1946 ("Lois Lane, Actress!").

Indeed, Lois Lane is renowned "throughout the world" for her "courage and ingenuity in getting scoops" (S No. 181/1, Nov '65: pts. I-II—"The Super-Scoops of Morna Vine!"; "The Secret of the New Supergirl!"), and her "mania for scoops"—or "scoop-craziness"—has tended to lead her to do almost anything in pursuit of a hot story (Act No. 138, Nov '49: "Superman Scoop-Parade"). In the course of a journalistic career that has spanned four decades, she has scaled Mount Everest (S No. 49/2, Nov/Dec '47: "Clark Kent's Most Dangerous Assignment!"); worked as a trapeze artist (S No. 63/3, Mar/Apr '50: "Miss Metropolis of 1950") and as a private detective (WF No. 45, Apr/May '50: "Lois Lane and Clark Kent, Detectives!"); journeyed to sunken ATLANTIS (S No. 67/2, Nov/Dec '50: "The City Under the Sea!") and explored the planet VENUS (Act No. 152, Jan '51: "The Sleep That Lasted 1000 Years"); worked as a policewoman (S No. 84/3, Sep/Oct '53: "Lois Lane, Policewoman!") and joined the WACs (S No. 82/1, May/Jun '53: "Lois Lane Joins the WACS!"); journeyed into outer space as one of the passengers aboard America's first manned spaceship (Act No. 242, Jul '58: "The Super-Duel in Space"); and been launched alone into Earth orbit in an experimental

Lois Lane, 1972

satellite after being designated "America's first female astronaut" by the National Astronautic Space Administration (S No. 165/1, Nov '63: pts. I-II—"Beauty and the Super-Beast!"; "Circe's Super-Slave").

In recognition of her unexcelled work as a reporter, Lois Lane has received numerous awards, including "the annual trophy for prize reporting," awarded to her at a "newspapermen's banquet" in Metropolis Hall in May-June 1950, and an honorary professorship in journalism at QUINN COLLEGE (S No. 64/1: "Professor Lois Lane!"); the coveted Wilson Award, awarded to her by "well-known civic leader" Cyrus Wilson in March 1952 for being "the bravest reporter of the year" (Act No. 166: "The Three Scoops of Death!"); and the highly regarded Metropolis Journalism Award, awarded to her in July-August 1953 as Metropolis's most outstanding reporter (WF No. 65: "The Confessions of Superman!"). In May-June 1950 Lois Lane is chosen Metropolis's "Queen of Charities" in recognition of "her many helpful newspaper stories" on behalf of philanthropic causes (S No. 64/2: "The Isle of Giant Insects!"), and in July-August 1953 she is chosen as "the bravest woman in America" in a contest sponsored by the *Daily Planet* (S No. 83/2: "The Search for the Bravest Woman!").

question in March-April 1952: "If Lois exposes my secret identity," he muses, "it will give her the world's greatest scoop! She couldn't resist that!" (S No. 75/3: "The Man Who Stole Memories!").

Although Lois Lane first meets Superman in June 1938 (Act No. 1), it is not until June 1940 that she expresses even a mild interest in learning his secret identity (Act No. 25), and not until November-December 1940 that she expresses a real desire to ferret it out (S No. 7/2). In July-August 1941, for the first time in the chronicles, Lois Lane raises the possibility that Clark Kent might possibly be Superman (S No. 11/1), but not until July-August 1942 does she actively begin to suspect "that Clark Kent and Superman are one and the same!" (S No. 17/1: "Man or Superman?"). Since that time, the discovery of Superman's secret identity has remained one of Lois Lane's constant preoccupations, and her efforts to learn the secret constitute one of the major themes of the chronicles. Despite her persistent efforts to verify her suspicion that Clark Kent is secretly Superman, however, the Man of Steel has always managed, often through the use of elaborate ruses, to persuade her that her suspicions were groundless, or at the very least not conclusively proven (*see also* SUPERMAN [section B, the secret identity]).

Lois Lane, 1959

Lois Lane, 1942

Perhaps the only major news story that has consistently eluded Lois Lane is the secret of Superman's dual identity, although the texts are inconsistent on the question of whether Lois Lane would actually publish the secret if she were to learn it (S No. 75/3, Mar/Apr '52: "The Man Who Stole Memories!"; and others) or whether she would keep the secret to herself in order to avoid damaging the Man of Steel's super-heroic career (S No. 78/3, Sep/Oct '52: "The Girls in Superman's Life!"; and others). Clark Kent expresses his own opinion on the

In the course of her lengthy career as a journalist, Lois Lane has, for a variety of purposes, often employed disguises and alternate identities. Among the pen names and aliases employed by Lois Lane are MISS HENKEL (S No. 18/3, Sep/Oct '42: "The Man with the Cane"), MISS ANDREWS (S No. 21/3, Mar/Apr '43: "The Robber Knight"), MRS. MOFFATT (S No. 39/3, Mar/Apr '46: "Swindle in Sweethearts!"), PRISCILLA RHODES (WF No. 64, May/Jun '53: "The

*Hurtling helplessly through the air after her parachute has failed to open,
Lois Lane is rescued in midair by Superman, 1958*

Death of Lois Lane"), RAMA (S No. 128/2, Apr '59: "The Sleeping Beauty from Krypton!"), and MISS TRACY (S No. 151/1, Feb '62: "The Three Tough Teen-Agers!").

In the texts, Lois Lane is described as "courageous" (Act No. 27, Aug '40), "headstrong" (Act No. 43, Dec '41), "reckless" and "stubborn" (Act No. 122, Jul '48: "The Super Sideshow!"), "audacious" (WF No. 64, May/Jun '53: "The Death of Lois Lane"), "impetuous" and "impulsive" (Act No. 262, Mar '60: "When Superman Lost His Powers!"), and "inquisitive" (Act No. 269, Oct '60: "The Truth Mirror!"). She is outspoken, sometimes to the point of abrasiveness, in defense of her convictions (S No. 16/4, May/Jun '42: "Racket on Delivery"; and others), and she is adored by her co-workers for her "heart of gold" (WF No. 36, Sep/Oct '48: "Lois Lane, Sleeping Beauty"). "That Lane dame has more spunk," remarks an

Lois Lane, 1938

anonymous helicopter pilot in November 1963, "than a squad of marines!" (S No. 165/1: pts. I-II—"Beauty and the Super-Beast!"; "Circe's Super-Slave").

Lois Lane has always harbored strong convictions concerning the equality—if not outright superiority—of women, and has bridled at the suggestion that any reportorial assignment, no matter how hazardous, is "no job for a girl!" (Act No. 5, Oct '38; and others). These convictions could easily be regarded as hypocritical in light of the constant professional assistance that Lois receives from Superman, but Lois has no apparent difficulty resolving the discrepancy between her independent views and her frequently dependent behavior. In March 1951, for example, when she is on the verge of being disqualified from a *Daily Planet*-sponsored contest designed to determine "who's more able to live alone under primitive conditions--the man or the woman" because of her having accepted unauthorized assistance from Superman, Lois makes this remark: "Wait...I admit getting help from **Superman**, but...that actually *proves* women's superiority! Don't you see?...Women's strength has lain in their ability to get **men** to **help** them!" It is a tribute to Lois Lane's persuasive powers that the judges on this occasion withdraw their threat of disqualification and declare her the winner (Act No. 154: "Miss Robinson Crusoe!").

Because Lois Lane is fearless to the point of foolhardiness (S No. 21/2, Mar/Apr '43: "The Four Gangleaders"; and many others), she is forever getting into serious trouble from which only Superman can extricate her, something the Man of Steel has done on easily a thousand occasions. In the words of Superman No. 41/2:

If **Superman** had a medal for every time he's rescued Lois Lane, he'd have enough metal to build a battleship, for, as all Metropolis knows, these rescues have run the

In the small South American republic of San Monté,
Superman rescues Lois Lane from a firing squad, 1938

gamut from bandits to burning buildings. Extricating Lois from trouble has become daily routine for **Superman**! [Jul/Aug '46: "Clark Kent's Bodyguard!"].

Lois Lane's penchant for "getting into trouble" is alluded to in the chronicles repeatedly. In May-June 1941 Clark Kent describes it as her "favorite sport" S No. 10/3), and in November-December 1952 he muses that Lois "has a genius for getting into trouble!" (S No. 79/2: "The End of the Planet!").

"I can't get to sleep—worrying about Lois," thinks Clark Kent to himself in Spring 1942, "...she has a better aptitude for getting into trouble than anyone I've ever known..." (WF No. 5: "The Case of the Flying Castle").

"If anything happened to Lois," observes Superman wryly in July-August 1942, "I'd have to join the ranks of the unemployed!" (S No. 17/1: "Man or Superman?").

And Superman No. 104/1 contains this comment: "Lois Lane seems to have a natural talent for trouble! How often her busy little brain gets her into scrapes where only the **Man of Steel** can save her!" (Mar '56: "Lois Lane, Super-Genius").

When Lois Lane does find herself in jeopardy, it is usually for one of the following reasons: (a) in pursuit of a news story, Lois fearlessly—and recklessly—places herself in mortal danger; (b) criminals attempt to harm her in retaliation for her articles exposing their rackets in the pages of the *Daily Planet*; (c) evildoers kidnap her and attempt to hold her hostage as protection against Superman or to force the Man of Steel to do their bidding; and (d) evildoers attempt to harm Lois as an indirect means of wreaking vengeance on Superman.

Lois Lane is hurled from a speeding car, 1940

Early on, however, Lois Lane comes to realize that she is under Superman's personal protection and that, no matter how dire her predicament, the Man of Steel will always arrive in time to rescue her. This knowledge has nurtured in Lois a flamboyant self-confidence that borders on the ridiculous.

"For a girl who is in serious danger, you appear singularly unconcerned," remarks the TALON, after he has taken Lois Lane captive in July-August 1942. "Why should I worry," replies Lois smugly, "when **Superman** has made it his full-time activity to look after helpless me?" (S No. 17/1: "Man or Superman?").

"**Luthor** will probably kill you the minute he gets here," exclaims one of LEX LUTHOR's henchmen to a cocky Lois on another, similar occasion, "--yet you have the nerve to **grin!**" "Why shouldn't I?" replies Lois with a smile. "**Superman** has always managed to show up and save me whenever I was in trouble! I'm sure he won't fail me now!" (S No. 17/4, Jul/Aug '42: "When Titans Clash!").

Lois Lane in jeopardy, 1941

It is this same reckless self-confidence that informs Lois's response on another occasion, in July-August 1943, after she has been taken captive by a hoodlum in the pay of the DUDE. "I don't understand you, lady," remarks the hoodlum. "You should be scared stiff, but you act like you're going to a lawn party!" "Why shouldn't I be cheerful?" laughs Lois. "Just think of the big scoop I'm going to score!" (S No. 23/3: "Fashions in Crime!").

In the early years of her career, Lois Lane frequently carries a small pistol in her purse, both for self-defense and for extorting information from criminals (Act No. 43, Dec '41; and others). She has apparently abandoned the practice, however, by the end of 1942, perhaps because Superman's constant intervention on her behalf rendered the pistol superfluous.

"Everyone knows that the one love of Lois Lane's life is...**Superman!**" (S No. 61/2, Nov/Dec '49: "The Courtship of the Three Lois Lanes!"). Indeed, her most heartfelt desire is to become his bride. "For years," observes Action Comics No. 260, "the girl reporter has had her heart set upon becoming **Mrs. Superman!**" (Jan '60: "Mighty Maid!").

Although Lois has tried innumerable ploys to get Superman to marry her, however, and has even come within a hair's breadth of success on several occasions, she has not yet succeeded, despite decades of effort, in raising her status beyond that of Superman's "girl friend" (Act No. 75, Aug '44: "Aesop's Modern Fables"; and many others). Nevertheless, Lois Lane's relationship with Superman—both in his role as Superman and in his role as Clark Kent—remains an intricate and complex one and constitutes one of the major themes of the chronicles (*see* SUPERMAN [section J 1, the relationship with Lois Lane].)

Lois Lane and Superman, 1959

Lois Lane is fiercely loyal to Superman. She is his staunchest supporter and most ardent fan. She is constantly seeing to it that he receives the fullest measure of public credit for his many good deeds (S No. 16/1, May/Jun '42: "The World's Meanest Man"; and many others), and she almost always retains her faith in him even when, for the moment, his motives are suspect or his actions unpopular (WF No. 6, Sum '42: "Man of Steel versus Man of Metal!"; and many others). "...[O]f all Superman's fans," notes Super-

man No. 67/1, "Lois Lane has been the most loyal, nay, at times even fanatic!" (Nov/Dec '50: "Perry Como, I Love You!"). There have indeed been occasions when Superman's character and integrity were so gravely in doubt that even Lois Lane has temporarily lost faith in him (Act No. 176, Jan '53: "Muscles for Money"; and others), but these occasions have been few and far between and should not be considered as detracting from Lois's fundamental loyalty.

For years, Lois Lane has maintained scrapbooks containing pictures and accounts of Superman's exploits (S No. 17/1, Jul/Aug '42: "Man or Superman?"; and others), one of which she presents to the Man of Steel as a gift in July-August 1947 (WF No. 29: "The Books That Couldn't Be Bound!"). In July-August 1943 she remarks that she is in the process of writing a novel based on her experiences with Superman, but it is not possible to determine whether the work has ever been published (S No. 23/2: "Habitual Homicide"). In January-February 1947 Lois Lane assists Superman in the writing of his autobiography, which is published soon afterward by BENNY CALL under the title *The Confessions of Superman* (WF No. 26: "The Confessions of Superman!"). Lois Lane has also maintained a personal diary for many years, containing, among other things, an intimate account of her relationship with Superman (S No. 27/4, Mar/Apr '44: "Dear Diary!"). The diary is kept for safekeeping inside safe-deposit box #113 at the Metropolis Bank (S No. 68/2, Jan/Feb '51: "Lois Lane's Royal Romance!"). Superman, for his part, has memorialized his relationship with Lois Lane by dedicating a room to her in his FORTRESS OF SOLITUDE (Act No. 241, Jun '58: "The Super-Key to Fort Superman"; and others). The Fortress also houses at least one Lois Lane robot (Act No. 269, Oct '60: "The Truth Mirror!").

Despite her renowned involvement with Superman, however, Lois Lane has been ardently pursued by many other men, including CRAIG SHAW (Act No. 61, Jun '43: "The Man They Wouldn't Believe!"), MR. MXYZPTLK (S No. 51/1, Mar/Apr '48: "Mr. Mxyzptlk Seeks a Wife!"), STEPHEN VAN SCHUYLER III (S No. 55/2, Nov/Dec '48: "The Richest Man in the World!"), KING HARRUP II (S No. 68/2, Jan/Feb '51: "Lois Lane's Royal Romance!"), BIZARRO (Act No. 254, Jul '59: "The Battle with Bizarro!"), HERCULES (Act No. 267, Aug '60: "Hercules in the 20th Century!"), and BRETT RAND (S No. 139/1, Aug '60: "The New Life of Super-Merman!"). But, in the words of Superman No. 136/1:

Again and again [Lois Lane] has refused all other offers of marriage...turning down all kinds of men...rich, powerful, handsome men...because of her loyal love for the Man of Steel! [Apr '60: "The Man Who Married Lois Lane!"].

Lois Lane actually marries the villain ZAK-KUL in October 1958, in the mistaken belief that she is arrying Superman, but the marriage is annulled oon afterward when it is discovered that the ridegroom was a Superman impostor (Act No. 245: The Shrinking Superman!"). And in April 1960 Lois ane marries X-PLAM, a warm-hearted man from the id-twenty-fourth century. This marriage is tragicaly terminated, however, by the death of the groom oon after the wedding (S No. 136/1: "The Man Who arried Lois Lane!").

Believe!") in Metropolis (S No. 47/2, Jul/Aug '47: "Susie Reforms!"; and many others) located not far from the home of her friend and colleague Clark Kent (S No. 40/1, May/Jun '46: "The Mxyztplk-Susie Alliance!"). Described as "a cozy little apartment that is neat as a pin," the apartment is filled with pictures of Superman. Lois customarily rides the subway to and from work, stopping at Crump's Market for groceries on the way home. At various times over the

Lois Lane and Bizarro, 1959

By and large, however, Lois Lane has persistently rejected her numerous suitors "because of her optimistic, persistent hope that she will some day become the bride of the **Man of Steel!**" (S No. 139/1, Aug '60: "The New Life of Super-Merman!").

Lois Lane resides in apartment #1705 (S No. 40/1, May/Jun '46: "The Mxyztplk-Susie Alliance!") of the Ritz Plaza Apartments (S No. 47/2, Jul/Aug '47: "Susie Reforms!"), an elevator apartment building (Act No. 61, Jun '43: "The Man They Wouldn't

Lois Lane, 1942

years, she has shared the apartment with her close friend PEGGY WILKINS (S No. 61/2, Nov/Dec '49: "The Courtship of the Three Lois Lanes!"; see also Act No. 143, Apr '50: "The Bride of Superman!"), her friend Lorraine Jennings (S No. 76/3, May/Jun '52: "Mrs. Superman!"), her sister LUCY LANE (S No. 142/1, Jan '61: "Lois Lane's Secret Helper!"; and others), and journalist LANA LANG (S No. 78/3, Sep/Oct '52: "The Girls in Superman's Life!"), who has at times been her rival for the affections of Superman (Act No. 302, Jul '63: "The Amazing Confession of Super-Perry White!"; and others). Lois Lane's closest friends are JIMMY OLSEN, PERRY WHITE, and Clark Kent (Act No. 210, Nov '55: "Superman in Superman Land"; and many others).

Lois Lane has black hair, which she has worn in a wide variety of styles. She has been described as "glamorous" (S No. 34/2, May/Jun '45: "The Canyon That Went Berserk!"), "lovely" (S No. 68/2, Jan/Feb '51: "Lois Lane's Royal Romance!"), and "gorgeous" (S No. 138/3, Jul '60: "The Mermaid from Atlantis!"). In the opinion of the hero Hercules, she is "as pretty as an ancient Roman goddess!" (Act No. 267, Aug '60: "Hercules in the 20th Century!").

According to Superman No. 125/1, Lois Lane has a rare blood type (Nov '58: "Lois Lane's Super-Dream"). She adores strawberries (S No. 99/3, Aug '55: "The Incredible Feats of Lois Lane!") and favors "a special lipstick which has a peach flavor" (Act No. 306, Nov

'63: "The Great Superman Impersonation!"). Particularly during the 1940s, Lois displays a fondness for fashionable hats, which Clark Kent is forever making fun of (S No. 24/3, Sep/Oct '43: "Surprise for Superman!"; and others). Practically any occasion provides Lois with an excuse for buying a new one. "My goodness!" she exclaims in January-February 1949. "The Prankster has outsmarted Superman twice in a row! I'm so upset—I'm going to buy a new hat—that always cheers me up!" (S No. 56/1: "The Prankster Picks a Partner!").

Lois Lane (right) and her sister Lucy Lane, 1961

Sporting one of her many fashionable hats, Lois Lane takes her leave of Clark Kent, 1941

In addition to her work at the *Daily Planet*, Lois Lane is involved in a myriad of other activities. She is chairman of the SUPER-SAVED CLUB (WF No. 41, Jul/Aug '49: "The Discovery of Supermanium!") and the SUPER SORORITY (Act No. 235, Dec '57: "The Super-Prisoner of Amazon Island"), is the "champion dart-thrower of [her] club" (S No. 143/2, Feb '61: "Lois Lane's Lucky Day!"), and has a "regular weekly broadcast" on Metropolis radio station WCOD (S No. 61/1, Nov/Dec '49: "The Prankster's Radio Program!"). In addition, Lois Lane has served as a beauty-contest judge (S No. 45/3, Mar/Apr '47: "The Case of the Living Trophies!") and portrayed herself in CHARLES LAMONT's movie *The Life of Superman* (S No. 70/2, May/Jun '51: "The Life of Superman!").

Lois Lane's relatives include her younger sister, Lucy Lane (Act No. 272, Jan '61: "Superman's Rival, Mental Man!"; and others), her aunt Bernice Brainard (S No. 24/3, Sep/Oct '43: "Surprise for Superman!"), her niece Susie Tompkins (Act No. 98, Jul '46: "Starring Susie!"; and others), and her uncle Ned, described as "a famous authority on the legends of King Arthur's court!" (Act No. 269, Oct '60: "The Truth Mirror!"). One text contains a reference to a married sister of Lois's who is Susie Tompkins's mother, but this sister never actually appears in the chronicles (Act No. 59, Apr '43: "Cinderella--a la Superman!"). Lois Lane's descendants include LOIS 4XR, a great-great-great-great-granddaughter—and a perfect Lois Lane look-alike—living in the thirtieth

century A.D. (S No. 57/2, Mar/Apr '49: "Every Man a Superman!").

Interestingly, quite a few other women are perfect Lois Lane look-alikes, including actress BRENDA MANNING (WF No. 40, May/Jun '49: "The Two Lois Lanes!"), the TIGER WOMAN (Act No. 195, Aug '54: "Lois Lane--Wanted!"), and SYLVIA, the wife of VAN-ZEE (S No. 158, Jan '63: "Superman in Kandor" pts. I-III—"Invasion of the Mystery Super-Men!"; "The Dynamic Duo of Kandor!"; "The City of Super-People!"; and others).

In addition, there is a Lois Lane look-alike in the Kandorian LOOK-ALIKE SQUAD (Act No. 309, Feb '64: "The Superman Super-Spectacular!") and another Lois Lane look-alike—named VICKI VALE—on the extradimensional parallel world which BATMAN visits in September 1963 (WF No. 136: "The Batman Nobody Remembered!"). With the addition of some makeup and a black wig to cover her own light-brown hair, actress DOLORES PERLO is a perfect Lois Lane look-alike (Act No. 306, Nov '63: "The Great Superman Impersonation!"), and without her eyeglasses and with her hair restyled, secretary MARY JONES is an almost perfect Lois Lane look-alike (S No. 55/2, Nov/Dec '48: "The Richest Man in the World!"). Movie star Bonnie Ames looks exactly like Lois Lane, except that Bonnie's hair is red while Lois's is black (S No. 61/2, Nov/Dec '49: "The Courtship of the Three Lois Lanes!"). LYDIA LONG bears a striking resemblance to Lois Lane (Act No. 265, Jun '60: "The 'Superman' from Outer Space!"). BIZARRO-LOIS (Act No. 255, Aug '59: "The Bride of Bizarro!"; and others), and in fact all of the women on the planet HTRAE (Act No. 264, May '60: "The Superman Bizarro!"; and others), are imperfect duplicates of Lois Lane.

Since the inception of the Superman chronicles in June 1938 (Act No. 1), Lois Lane has appeared in literally hundreds of texts, although the vast majority of her appearances have been inconsequential ones. For this reason, the following pages deal exclusively with those adventures in which Lois Lane occupies the central role but which have not been summarized under other entry headings. (*See also*

Superman rescues a drowning Lois Lane, 1942

Superman rescues a drowning Lois Lane from the sunken wreckage of a taxi trapped in a flood, 1938

SUPERMAN and all the other articles dealing with the persons and events of the Superman legend.)

In June 1938, in the premiere text of the Superman chronicles, Lois Lane makes her textual debut and meets Superman for the first time (Act No. 1).

In a delirium brought on by a brain concussion, Lois Lane dreams that she has become transformed into a Superwoman, 1943

In May 1943, as the result of being struck by an automobile on a Metropolis street, Lois Lane suffers a severe brain concussion and is rushed to the hospital, where "a delicate brain operation" is performed to save her life. Lying in her hospital bed, in a delirium, Lois has a startling dream. In it, an emergency transfusion of Superman's blood restores her to full health almost instantly and transforms her into a

Superwoman endowed with all the super-powers of Superman; after fashioning a sexy red-and-blue female version of Superman's costume, Lois begins using her newly acquired powers to battle crime and injustice, ultimately rescuing Superman himself from the clutches of a maniacal renegade scientist named Dr. Skowl; and finally, the now super-alluring Lois sweeps the Man of Steel passionately off his feet and romantically overwhelms him into agreeing to marry her. Moments later, however, Lois Lane awakes with a start to discover that her delicious acquisition of super-powers was only a fantasy and that she is still in her hospital bed, recovering from the emergency surgery that has saved her life (Act No. 60: "Lois Lane--Superwoman!").

In September-October 1948, while visiting the "little kingdom of Cornovia" on assignment for the *Daily Planet*, Lois Lane inadvertently performs a feat which results in her being crowned as Cornovia's queen. Overjoyed at first over her newly acquired royalty, Lois has second thoughts about her regal role when she is informed that she must marry an eligible Cornovian at once in order to ensure the continuation of the tiny kingdom's royal line. Largely due to the mischievous intervention of Superman, who is determined to teach Lois a richly deserved lesson about the folly of putting on queenly airs, Queen Lois soon finds herself in the unenviable position of being about to be married to an ugly, obese, dim-witted little Cornovian named Bobo, but, at the last possible moment, Clark Kent extricates her from her unpleasant predicament by invoking a legal technicality that allows Lois to withdraw from the impending marriage, albeit only at the cost of abdicating her throne (S No. 54/3: "Her Majesty Lois Lane!").

In May-June 1949 Lois Lane launches a whirlwind campaign to get Clark Kent to marry her after being advised by her doctor that she must "learn to love someone else," other than Superman, if she is to cure herself of her "broken heart." "In the days that follow," notes the textual narrative, "Lois makes a pest of herself as she bombards Clark with her affections," holding his hand in the movies, buying him gifts, steering him toward the window of a jewelry store aglow with engagement rings. Ultimately, however, with his freedom clearly at stake ("I've got to discourage Lois' affections!" muses Kent desperately. "I can't marry her because it would interfere with **Superman's** freedom...and **Superman** must remain free to fight crime!"), Superman hits on a clever ploy guaranteed to make Lois angry enough to "jilt Clark Kent": he arranges for his mild-mannered alter ego to scoop Lois on a news story involving Superman. "Newspaper reporting is my first love...**Superman** was my **second**," she shrieks at Kent angrily, "...but **you're** only **third**! Clark Kent, you find another date for tonight! We're through as of this moment!" (S No. 58/2: "Lois Lane Loves Clark Kent!").

Lois Lane is abducted by hoodlums, 1938

In July-August 1949, while in the grip of a strange "hypnotic trance" induced by having tried on an exotic necklace—the so-called "royal necklace of Amazonia"—on display at the Metropolis Museum, Lois Lane boards a plane for Venezuela and parachutes into the dense South American jungle, where a band of lovely Amazon warriors—inhabitants of a land they call Amazonia—see the royal necklace around Lois's neck and welcome her as their rightful queen. Forced to endure a series of impossible trials in order to prove her right to the throne, however, Lois—who has inexplicably begun to behave in a haughty, tyrannical manner—is rescued from seemingly certain death by Superman, who ultimately relates her uncharacteristic behavior to the fact that she is wearing the necklace and, by removing it, releases Lois from her bizarre trancelike state (S No. 59/1: "Lois Lane—Queen of the Amazons!").

In November-December 1949, acting on the advice of her friend Peggy Wilkins, Lois Lane dyes her hair

blond—and soon afterward changes it to red—in the misguided belief that Superman might decide to marry her if she changed her hair color. Complications invariably arise from the changeovers, however, as when Lois causes near-pandemonium as a redhead at Metropolis Stadium because of her striking resemblance to red-haired movie actress Bonnie Ames, and Lois is soon back to being a brunette again, no closer to marrying Superman than she was before (S No. 61/2: "The Courtship of the Three Lois Lanes!").

A sleepless night for Lois Lane, 1940

In October 1950 Lois Lane unexpectedly comes into possession of three Kryptonian "thought-projection discs"—which have been whirling about in space since the explosion of the planet KRYPTON—after they have been returned to Earth by a U.S. experimental rocket. The discs, which contain a detailed account of the courtship of Superman's parents, JOR-EL and LARA, inspire Lois with the idea of emulating the womanly ploys by which Lara endeavored to get Jor-El to propose to her—such as baking Jor-El a fancy cake and straightening up his disorderly laboratory—in the hope that these same techniques might prove effective with Superman. As the discs plainly show, however, Jor-El's decision to marry Lara was unrelated to these ploys, and the text draws to a close with Lois no closer than she was before to becoming Superman's bride (Act No. 149: "The Courtship on Krypton!").

In April-May 1951, after incurring the wrath of editor Perry White by reporting to work late at the *Daily Planet*, Lois Lane is stripped of her customary duties as news reporter and forced to carry out such lowly assignments as running the lost and found department, researching answers to readers' queries, and forecasting the weather. Superman, however, feeling responsible for Lois's predicament inasmuch as he had promised to fly her to work himself that morning and then had failed to do so because of an emergency, works surreptitiously behind the scenes to make Lois such a spectacular success at her menial assignments that Perry White soon elevates her back to news reporting and even gives her a raise (WF No. 51: "The Amazing Talents of Lois Lane!").

Lois Lane, 1952

Clark Kent, Sergeant Casey, and Lois Lane, 1941

In February 1952, after a remark by Superman has misled her into believing that his unwillingness to marry her is owing to his desire not to hurt Clark Kent, Lois Lane becomes determined to marry Kent off to her friend Lorraine Jennings so that she can enjoy a clear field with Superman. Although Lois's frenetic attempts at matchmaking cause some uncomfortable moments for the Man of Steel, as when he must somehow contrive to accompany Lois and Lorraine on a double date both as Clark Kent and as Superman, Superman manages ultimately to retain his bachelor status while at the same time teaching Lois a richly deserved lesson about the folly of meddling in the personal affairs of others. The text in which these events occur is dated May-June 1952, but the story itself is set in February, in the period surrounding Valentine's Day (S No. 76/3: "Mrs. Superman!").

In September 1952 Lois Lane unexpectedly comes into possession of a jewel-like iron-destroying "projector," a tiny device, invented years ago on the planet Krypton by Superman's father, Jor-El, which had been placed inside the rocket that carried the infant Superman to Earth for the purpose of protecting the rocket from meteors as it hurtled through space. Immediately taken with what she sees only as a "pretty little trinket," and blissfully unaware that it is emitting "iron-destroying rays" with the power to "crumble all iron close to it," Lois begins carrying the little jewel with her about the city, inadvertently causing one mysterious "accident" after another, as when an iron girder supporting a building disintegrates—threatening to topple the entire building—as she passes by. Ignorant of the true cause

of these misfortunes and believing that she has somehow become "a terrible jinx," Lois is on the verge of exiling herself from Metropolis forever when Superman surreptitiously recovers the projector and persuades her that she will no longer cause bad luck wherever she goes (Act No. 172: "Lois Lane ...Witch!").

In August 1954 Lois Lane looks on in horror as Clark Kent is sent plummeting headlong into a vat of molten steel during a scuffle at the Crescent Steel Works with a gang of criminals headed by the Tiger Woman, a "clever--and ruthless" villainess for whom Lois is a perfect look-alike. Emotionally shattered by the experience of seeing Kent "die," Lois Lane wanders dazed about Metropolis, "suffering from

Believing Clark Kent dead, Lois Lane
is overwhelmed with grief, 1954

mnesia--induced by shock" and gripped by the
verpowering delusion that she herself is the notori-
us Tiger Woman. In her "state of shock," Lois even
emporarily "assumes the identity of the female
riminal she thinks she is," until finally Superman
ucceeds in restoring her memory and in explaining
way Clark Kent's apparent death in the steel vat
Act No. 195: "Lois Lane--Wanted!").

By November 1954 Lois Lane's mind has become
eriously unbalanced as the result of her having
nadvertently stumbled upon Superman in the act of
changing into his Clark Kent identity. Because Lois
experienced this trauma of discovery during a period
when she was writing a series of newspaper articles
on the "Great Women of History," Lois begins acting
out a series of bizarre delusions, punctuated by brief
interludes of sanity, in which she believes she is, and
behaves as though she were, various famous women
of history, including Florence Nightingale, Betsy
Ross, Barbara Frietchie, Annie Oakley, Marie Curie,
and Queen Isabella of Spain. Finally, however, Lois's
delusions end of their own accord, and Superman,
through an elaborate ruse, succeeds in persuading
her that she never really did learn the secret of his
dual identity (Act No. 198: "The Six Lives of Lois
Lane!").

Lois Lane in an unhappy moment, 1958

In March 1955 Lois Lane acquires X-ray vision—
the ability to see through solid objects, just like
Superman—when she stumbles upon a pair of
experimental eyeglasses inadvertently discarded by
scientists at the Brooks Optical Laboratories. Although Lois attempts to use her new-found power to
do good deeds, garner scoops for the *Daily Planet*,
and, most importantly, penetrate the secret of
Superman's identity, the miraculous X-ray spectacles
invariably cause Lois "nothing but trouble," and she
finally destroys the glasses without having achieved
any of her objectives. "Yes," muses Clark Kent
silently, "--X-ray vision is a dangerous power--unless

you know how to use it!" (Act No. 202: "Lois Lane's X-
Ray Vision!").

In July 1955 Lois Lane falls asleep and dreams
that she has finally become engaged to Superman. As
the wedding day draws ever closer, Lois becomes
painfully aware that there are "disadvantages to
being **Superman**'s sweetheart"—such as being
constantly mobbed by curiosity seekers and interrupted by emergencies requiring the attention of
Superman—but, nevertheless, Lois continues to look
forward to the big event with eager enthusiasm. And
finally the wedding does take place, with Clark Kent
as best man and Perry White and Jimmy Olsen
among the guests. It is only after the ceremony, as
Lois begins to cut into the wedding cake, that the
alarm on her bedside table goes off, informing her
that her long-awaited marriage to Superman was
only a dream (Act No. 206: "Superman Marries Lois
Lane!").

In August 1955, after a tragic misunderstanding
has led her to the erroneous conclusion that she has
suffered a fatal overdose of atomic radiation and is
doomed to die within the week, Lois Lane becomes
determined to make her last days meaningful by
performing a series of death-defying journalistic
feats, as when she deliberately remains alone in the
cabin of a sinking ship, scribbling notes on her
reporter's pad as the ship goes down. On these and
other hair-raising occasions, Superman manages to
rescue Lois before she can come to any harm, and
ultimately the original misunderstanding is resolved
and Lois discovers, to her indescribable relief, that

Lois Lane in the clutches of Titano, 1959

she is not about to die after all (S No. 99/3: "The
Incredible Feats of Lois Lane!").

In March 1956 Lois Lane is temporarily transformed into a super-genius when she deliberately
steps beneath the rays of a newly invented machine

that has already proven capable of bestowing extraordinary intelligence on experimental monkeys. Concerned that Lois's new "super-brain" will have the unwelcome effect of "leading her into super-trouble," Superman concocts a series of elaborate stratagems designed to keep Lois busy rescuing him—as when he pretends to be incapacitated by a KRYPTONITE meteor—so that she will expend her newly acquired intellectual capacities extricating him from nonexistent dangers instead of recklessly pursuing projects that could place her life in jeopardy. Indeed, Superman's strategy is successful, and within three days the effects of the experimental machine have worn off, restoring Lois to her normal intelligence (S No. 104/1: "Lois Lane, Super-Genius").

In September 1958 Lois Lane and Clark Kent, the man who is secretly Superman, find themselves marooned on an island from which even Superman cannot escape, due to the fact that the island's volcano, which has a fallen kryptonite meteor lodged in its crater, is spewing fine particles of kryptonite dust into the surrounding air. Believing himself trapped on the island for life, Superman decides to do his best to make Lois's life a happy one by divulging the secret of his dual identity and arranging for them to be married by the island's local native chief. On the day of the scheduled wedding, however, Superman discovers that the volcano is no longer filling the air with kryptonite dust and that escape from the island is therefore possible. Ultimately, through an elaborate ruse, he succeeds in persuading Lois to withdraw from the marriage voluntarily as well as in tricking

Driving along in her automobile...

her into believing that Clark Kent had only been deceiving her when he confided to her earlier that he was secretly Superman (S No. 124/2: "Mrs. Superman").

In November 1958, after being knocked uncon-

scious by a fall from a building ledge, Lois Lane i rushed to Metropolis Hospital, where, weak fro shock and in a delirium, she has a startling dream. I it, an emergency transfusion of Superman's bloo restores her to perfect health and endows her wit super-powers identical to Superman's; after donnin a red wig to conceal her true identity and fashioning distinctive green-and-yellow costume, Lois christen herself Power Girl and allies herself with Superma in his battle against injustice; and finally, whe Clark Kent is injured in an explosion at a power plant Lois gives him a transfusion of her own super-blood— thereby endowing Kent with super-powers—an fashions him a Power-Man costume modeled after he own, but Kent proves timid and inept—even wit super-powers—and ultimately, as Power-Man, he commits an idiotic blunder that betrays his secret identity to the entire world. Moments later, however Lois awakens to discover that her acquisition of super-powers and the events that followed it were only part of an elaborate dream (S No. 125/1: "Lois

...Lois Lane is swept up by a tornado, 1960

Lois Lane, 1960

e's Super-Dream"). The story is in many respects similar to Action Comics No. 60 (May '43: "Lois Lane--Superwoman!"), which has been summarized previously in this article.

In January 1959, after Lois Lane has deliberately made herself look as disheveled and unattractive as possible as a means of getting Chet Hartley, her blind date for the evening, to take her home early so that she can go out instead with Superman, Superman decides to "teach her a lesson" by playing the same kind of "miserable trick" on her that she played on Chet. Superman's ploy for teaching Lois a lesson involves asking her to marry him and then, once she has accepted, "revealing" his secret identity to her by removing the handsome Superman face mask that supposedly conceals his true face and revealing the hideously grotesque countenance—actually, a second face mask—beneath it. "Naturally I can't let my admirers see me like this!" explains Superman with mock sincerity. "They must visualize their hero as noble and handsome! But now that I know you love me despite my looks, Lois...will you marry me?"

Stunned by the image of hideous ugliness that has been presented to her as Superman's real face, Lois is on the verge of declining Superman's proposal when suddenly it occurs to her that the Man of Steel may only be doing to her what she did to Chet Hartley. Indeed, Superman's scheme threatens to backfire when Lois accepts his offer of marriage and the wedding date is set, but, through a clever ruse, Superman ultimately succeeds in having the wedding cancelled without actually going back on his word. "I know you tricked me," admits Lois finally. "--and I know I deserved it after the way I treated Chet! You taught me a lesson I deserved!" (S No. 126/3: "The Two Faces of Superman!").

In April 1959 Lois Lane, employing the alias Rama and concealing her true identity beneath a blond wig and Kryptonian-style clothing, deceives Superman into believing that she, like him, is a survivor of the exploded planet Krypton and tricks him into divulging the secret of his dual identity. Realizing, soon afterward, that Lois has duped him, Superman enlists the aid of his friend Bruce Wayne, the man who is secretly Batman, in an elaborate and ultimately successful ruse designed to persuade Lois that Clark Kent and Superman are two different men and that Superman was only playing a prank on Lois

Lois Lane as Rama, 1959

After successfully duping Superman into divulging his secret identity, Lois Lane is filled with remorse, 1959

Lois Lane, 1972

when he "pretended" to tell her his secret identity (S No. 128/2: "The Sleeping Beauty from Krypton!").

In October 1960 Lois Lane's uncle Ned, "a famous authority on the legends of King Arthur's court," makes Lois a gift of "Merlin's magic mirror," a miraculous full-length mirror, once belonging to Merlin the magician, which has the power to reveal the truth about anyone who stands before it. When Lois lures Superman in front of the mirror, the image reflected in the glass is that of Clark Kent, but, through a complex ruse, Superman salvages the secret of his dual identity by tricking Lois into believing that the magic mirror is not always truthful (Act No. 269: "The Truth Mirror!").

LANE, LUCY. The daughter of Sam and Ella Lane, and the younger sister of LOIS LANE. A onetime airline stewardess (SF No. 172, Aug/Sep '75; and others), Lucy, a lovely blonde, has on occasion shared an apartment in METROPOLIS with her sister Lois (S No. 142/1, Jan '61: "Lois Lane's Secret Helper!"; and others) and has been romantically linked with JIMMY OLSEN (S No. 147/1, Aug '61: "The Great Mento!"; and others).

Lucy Lane and Jimmy Olsen, 1961

LANG (Professor). The archaeologist and explorer who is the father of LANA LANG. In March 1963, when Professor Lang's expedition in search of rare dinosaur fossils finds itself stranded without water in a "distant desert," SUPERMAN provides the expeditioners with the water they need and soon afterward locates the dinosaur fossils for which the group has been searching (Act No. 298: "Clark Kent, Coward!"). In January 1964, while on an archaeological expedition with Professor Lang "somewhere in the Middle East," Clark Kent is struck by a lightning bolt that catapults him across the dimensional barrier into a strange "parallel world," where, as Superman, he encounters an extradimensional counterpart of the legendary HERCULES (Act No. 308: "Superman Meets the Goliath-Hercules!").

LANG, "DRAGON." An "evil genius" of the

underworld who, having constructed a remarkable remote-controlled robot named Ajax—a "mechanical super-crook" with many of the powers of SUPERMAN—attempts to use the robot to commit a series of spectacular crimes, only to have it demolished by Superman in October 1952. With Ajax destroyed, Superman soon locates Lang's control center hideout and apprehends both Lang and his henchmen (Act No. 173: "Superman's Invulnerable Foe!").

LANG, LANA. The lovely red-haired newscaster for METROPOLIS television station WMET-TV (LL No. 68, Sep/Oct '66; and others) who has been a central figure in the life of SUPERMAN. As a contemporary of the teen-aged Superman (i.e., Superboy) during their days in SMALLVILLE, she had a "crush" on Superboy (S No. 97/3, May '55: "Superboy's Last Day in Smallville!"), was alternatively friendly to, and contemptuous of, mild-mannered Clark Kent, and generally "tormented and pestered" them both in her never-ending quest for the secret of Superboy's dual identity. As an adult, first as a reporter for the DAILY PLANET (S No. 78/3, Sep/Oct '52: "The Girls in Superman's Life!") and later as a celebrated TV newscaster (S No. 177/2, May '65: "The Menace Called 'It'!"; and others), she is one of Superman's "best friends" (S No. 156, Oct '62: "The Last Days of Superman!" pts. I-III—"Superman's Death Sentence!"; "The Super-Comrades of All Time!"; "Superman's Last Day of Life!") and LOIS LANE's "arch-rival for the affections of Superman" (Act No. 279,

Lana Lang, 1963

ug '61: "The Super-Rivals!"; and others). Superman as described Lana as a "beautiful woman" (S No. 56, Oct '62: "The Last Days of Superman!" pts. I-II—"Superman's Death Sentence!"; "The Super-omrades of All Time!"; "Superman's Last Day of ife!") and as "the swellest girl I ever met...except or] Lois Lane!" (S No. 78/3, Sep/Oct '52: "The Girls a Superman's Life!").

Lana Lang, the daughter of archaeologist and xplorer PROFESSOR LANG (Act No. 298, Mar '63: Clark Kent, Coward!"; and others) and the niece of ROFESSOR POTTER (Act No. 313, Jun '64: "The End of lark Kent's Secret Identity!"), grew up in Smallville, vhere she was in Clark Kent's class (S No. 144/2, Apr 51: "Superboy's First Public Appearance!") at mallville High School (Act No. 305, Oct '63: "Why uperman Needs a Secret Identity!"). Lana's senior-lass yearbook cited her as "class wit" (S No. 144/2, apr '61: "Superboy's First Public Appearance!"), but uperman No. 78/3 describes her as "pretty, prying, and] pestiferous," and draws a pointed parallel etween Lana Lang's relationship with the teen-aged uperboy and Lois Lane's relationship with the adult uperman: "Superman has had his troubles from he reckless rashness of Lois Lane," notes the text, ...but that's nothing new to him! For years ago in mallville, when he was Superboy, pretty, prying, estiferous Lana Lang also used to give him head-ches!" (Sep/Oct '52: "The Girls in Superman's ife!").

In September-October 1952 Lana Lang arrives in Metropolis, working for a time as a reporter for the Daily Planet—and sharing an apartment with Lois ane—before moving on to a new journalistic post vith the Federal Syndicate (S No. 78/3: "The Girls in uperman's Life!"). By January 1961 she has cquired a job as a news reporter for a television etwork (Act No. 272, Jan '61: "Superman's Rival, Mental Man!"), a post that has made her a "TV celebrity" (S No. 165/1, Nov '63: pts. I-II—"Beauty nd the Super-Beast!"; "Circe's Super-Slave").

Ever since Lana Lang arrived in Metropolis, she nd Lois Lane—who is described in one text as Lana's "friendly enemy" (S No. 165/1, Nov '63: pts. I-II—"Beauty and the Super-Beast!"; "Circe's Super-Slave)—have been "keen rivals for Superman's affections!" (S No. 150/2, Jan '62: "The Duel Over Superman!"). Since Lana, like Lois, is in love with Superman (Act No. 288, May '62: "The Man Who Exposed Superman!"; and others), relations between them are sometimes catty (S No. 165/1, Nov '63: pts. I-II—"Beauty and the Super-Beast!"; "Circe's Super-Slave"; and others). (See also SUPERMAN [section J2, the relationship with Lana Lang].)

In September-October 1952 Lana Lang, deter-mined to pursue a career as a big-city reporter, leaves her home town of Smallville for Metropolis, where she obtains employment on the Daily Planet and renews, for the first time since her teens, both her romantic interest in Superman and her determination to unravel the secret of his dual identity. Briefly taken

captive—along with Lois Lane—by underworld photographer "LENS" LEWIS, she is swiftly rescued by Superman and soon afterward leaves the Daily Planet for a new post with the Federal Syndicate (S No. 78/3: "The Girls in Superman's Life!").

In August 1961, in an "imaginary tale," Lana Lang very nearly becomes the bride of Samson (Act No. 279: "The Super-Rivals!"). (See HERCULES.)

In January 1962 Lana Lang and Lois Lane attempt to dupe Superman into believing that their rivalry over his affections has escalated to the brink of violence and that the only way he can prevent them from fighting a duel to the death is by intervening to marry one of them. Superman sees through the harebrained ruse, however, and the adventure concludes with neither woman having persuaded the Man of Steel to make her his bride (S No. 150/2: "The Duel Over Superman!").

Lana Lang as a teen-ager, shown here
in a happy moment...

...and then in a more serious one

In March 1962, while in the grip of a nightmare induced by exposure to red KRYPTONITE, Superman dreams that, in the distant future, the great-great-great-grandson of PETE ROSS and the great-great-great-granddaughter of Lana Lang are husband and wife, and that they attempt to destroy him by overexposure to green kryptonite. These events, however, are all only a nightmare, and no such confrontation ever actually takes place (Act No. 286: "The Jury of Super-Enemies!").

In May 1962, when ex-convict HAL COLBY—employing the alias Bert Hutton—produces a television tribute to Superman as part of his elaborate scheme to unravel and expose Superman's secret identity, Lana Lang is among the people invited to Smallville to appear on the program (Act No. 288: "The Man Who Exposed Superman!").

In November 1962, when Superman Day is celebrated in Metropolis, Lana Lang is among those on hand to attend the festivities (S No. 157/3: "Superman's Day of Doom!").

In March 1963, Lana Lang is a member of the expedition in search of rare dinosaur fossils, led by her father, which finds itself stranded without water in a "distant desert." Superman provides the expeditioners with the water they need, however, and soon afterward locates the dinosaur fossils for which the group has been searching (Act No. 298: "Clark Kent, Coward!").

In September 1963 Lana Lang accompanies Superman on his journey to the "planetoid" VORN (Act No. 304: "The Interplanetary Olympics!").

In November 1963, while on an expedition to Crete, Lana Lang and her fellow expeditioners unearth what they believe to be the tomb of CIRCE, unaware that the "enchantress" whom they find asleep there inside a glass coffin is actually SATURN WOMAN, of the LEGION OF SUPER-HEROES, who has agreed to impersonate Circe as part of Superman's plan to thwart a scheme by the SUPERMAN REVENGE SQUAD (S No. 165/1: pts. I-II—"Beauty and the Super-Beast!"; "Circe's Super-Slave").

In January 1964, while on an archaeological expedition with Lana Lang and her father "somewhere in the Middle East," Clark Kent is struck by a lightning bolt that catapults him across the dimensional barrier into a strange "parallel world," where, as Superman, he encounters an extradimensional counterpart of the legendary Hercules (Act No. 308: "Superman Meets the Goliath-Hercules!"). (See HERCULES.)

When Metropolis television station WMET-TV inaugurates its new "Our American Heroes" series with a program honoring Superman, "our greatest American hero," Lana Lang and Lois Lane appear on the show along with Superman's other friends and admirers to help pay tribute to the Man of Steel. Knowing that, late in the program, Superman will have to appear on stage simultaneously with his "friend" Clark Kent, Lana and Lois—who have long nursed the suspicion that Clark Kent is Superman

and who feel certain that he will resolve the dilemma of the simultaneous appearance by using a sophisticated robot to impersonate Clark Kent—have concocted a scheme to penetrate Superman's secret by means of a complex device capable of registering the presence of electronic equipment. Midway through the program, however, Superman learns of the scheme, but this still leaves him with the awkward dilemma of having to appear on the show both as Clark Kent and as Superman without resorting to the use of either a Clark Kent or Superman robot. The Man of Steel resolves this dilemma by entrusting the secret of his dual identity to President JOHN F. KENNEDY and by asking the President, as a personal favor, to appear briefly on the TV show—disguised in a pair of eyeglasses and a rubberoid Clark Kent face mask—in the role of Clark Kent (Act No. 309, Feb '64: "The Superman Super-Spectacular!").

When Lana Lang broadcasts a film report highlighting the poor physical fitness of American youth,

In an "imaginary tale" in 1965,
Lana Lang sheds a tear or two...

...after learning that she has lost
Superman to Lois Lane

President John F. Kennedy summons Superman to the White House and urges him to lend his super-services "to the important job of getting our youth into A-1 physical shape!" (S No. 170/1, Jul '64: "Superman's Mission for President Kennedy!"). (*See* KENNEDY, JOHN F.)

In August 1964, after the ruthless "interplanetary gamblers" ROKK AND SORBAN have threatened to destroy the Earth unless Superman agrees to commit a wanton murder, Lana Lang attempts to commit suicide so that Superman can claim he killed her and thereby avert the threat to Earth. Superman rescues Lana in the nick of time, however, and ultimately resolves the agonizing dilemma posed by the aliens by pretending to murder his alter ego, Clark Kent (S No. 171/1: "Superman's Sacrifice!").

In October 1964 Lana Lang and Lois Lane are taken captive by LEX LUTHOR and BRAINIAC, only to be rescued soon afterward through the heroic efforts of AR-VAL and Superman (S No. 172: pts. I-III—"The New Superman!"; "Clark Kent—Former Superman!"; "The Struggle of the Two Supermen!"). (*See* LUTHOR, LEX.)

LANGS, ARNOLD. An unscrupulous jeweler who masterminds a series of grisly murders and attempts to blame them on the TOYMAN. Langs is exposed and apprehended by SUPERMAN in November-December 1947 (S No. 49/1: "Toyman and the Gadgets of Greed!"). (*See* TOYMAN, THE.)

LANGWELL, KEITH. The unscrupulous friend and partner of archaeologist Burton Hayes who—having recently returned from an expedition with Hayes through the Malayan jungles, where the two men unearthed a priceless store of gems and other treasure in the ruins of some Malay temples—has hired a gang of Malay assassins to murder Hayes as part of an elaborate scheme to seize Hayes's share of the treasure for himself while blaming Hayes's untimely death on the supposedly baleful influence of the tiny Malayan "talisman of misfortune" that Hayes has taken to wearing around his neck. Langwell and his hired assassins are apprehended by SUPERMAN in August 1946 (Act No. 99: "The Talisman of Trouble!").

LARA. The wife of JOR-EL, and the mother of SUPERMAN. Offered the chance to flee the impending death of KRYPTON by escaping to Earth with her infant son in an experimental rocket, she steadfastly refused to abandon her husband, remaining behind with him instead to perish in the cataclysm (S No. 53/1, Jul/Aug '48: "The Origin of Superman!"; and others). Although her name is given as Lora in Action Comics No. 223 (Dec '56: "The First Superman of Krypton"), Lara is the only authentic rendering.

Surprisingly little is known about Superman's mother. "Noted for her advanced intellect as well as her beauty" (S No. 170/2, Jul '64: pts. I-II—"If Lex Luthor Were Superman's Father!"; "The Wedding of Lara and Luthor!"), she worked in a shop that manufactured robots prior to her marriage to Jor-El, and, on at least one occasion, served as an undercover

agent for the Krypton Bureau of Investigation to help thwart the machinations of a would-be tyrant (S No. 123, Aug '58: chs. 1-3—"The Girl of Steel"; "The Lost Super-Powers"; "Superman's Return to Krypton"). During the period immediately preceding her marriage to Jor-El, Lara served as Jor-El's "assistant" (S No. 170/2, Jul '64: pts. I-II—"If Lex Luthor Were Superman's Father!"; "The Wedding of Lara and Luthor!"), apparently at the Kryptonian "missile base" where Jor-El was engaged in top-level research (S No. 141, Nov '60: "Superman's Return to Krypton!" pts. I-III—"Superman Meets Jor-El and Lara Again!"; "Superman's Kryptonian Romance!"; "The Surprise of Fate!").

With the infant Superman cradled in her arms, Lara questions Jor-El about his plan to evacuate Krypton in a fleet of rockets

At the time the lovely, dark-haired Lara gave birth to the infant Superman, she and her husband were residing in KRYPTONOPOLIS (SA No. 5, Sum '62; and others), the city that had become the capital of Krypton following the theft of KANDOR by the space villain BRAINIAC. According to Superman No. 75/1, the proud parents named their newborn son Jor-El, 2nd (Mar/Apr '52: "The Prankster's Star Pupil!"), but an overwhelming preponderance of texts assert that they named him Kal-El (S No. 113, May '57: chs. 1-3—"The Superman of the Past"; "The Secret of the Towers"; "The Superman of the Present"; and others). By all accounts, the dark-haired youngster bore an "unmistakable" resemblance to his father (S No. 77/1, Jul/Aug '52: "The Man Who Went to Krypton!"; and others).

When, around the time of Superman's birth (Act No. 223, Dec '56: "The First Superman of Krypton"), Jor-El made the dire discovery that Krypton was on the verge of exploding "like one colossal **atomic bomb**," Lara was one of the few Kryptonians who believed Jor-El's prophecy of impending cataclysm (S

No. 61/3, Nov/Dec '49: "Superman Returns to Krypton!"; and others). And when Krypton's doomsday finally came, and Jor-El urged her to flee the holocaust with their infant son in an experimental rocket, Lara steadfastly refused to leave her husband's side. "I will not leave you, Jor-El!" she cried. "But we will save our son!" (Act No. 158, Jul '51: "The Kid from Krypton!"; and others).

Hurriedly, "the helpless infant was placed into the space-ship" (S No. 53/1, Jul/Aug '48: "The Origin of Superman!"), and the tiny craft was "launched forth into the void" (Act No. 158, Jul '51: "The Kid from Krypton!").

"Krypton is dying!" cried Jor-El, as the ruins of Krypton crumbled about them.

"But our son will live," answered Lara, "—the last survivor of a great civilization!"

Then, as husband and wife clung together in a desperate last embrace, "nature's fury gathered for one final cataclysmic eruption.... And as the pitifully small space-ship hurtled through interstellar space, the once mighty planet Krypton exploded into stardust!" (S No. 53/1, Jul/Aug '48: "The Origin of Superman!"). (See also JOR-EL.)

Because he remembers his parents as having been so "loving and kind" (S No. 123, Aug '58: chs. 1-3— "The Girl of Steel"; "The Lost Super-Powers"; "Superman's Return to Krypton")—and because the anguish of losing them in childhood was so unbearably painful—Superman has memorialized his parents in numerous ways: he has dedicated a room to them in his FORTRESS OF SOLITUDE (Act No. 247, Dec '58: "Superman's Lost Parents!"; and others), taken color photographs of them "by overtaking and photographing light rays that had left Krypton before it exploded" (S No. 132, Oct '59: "Superman's Other Life!" pts. 1-3—"Krypton Lives On!"; "Futuro, Super-Hero of Krypton!"; "The Superman of Two Worlds!"), and carved their faces into the side of a planetoid in the style of the MOUNT RUSHMORE NATIONAL MEMORIAL (S No. 161/1, May '63: "The Last Days of Ma and Pa Kent!"). When, in January 1962, Superman, SUPERGIRL, and KRYPTO THE SUPERDOG transform an uninhabited planet in a "distant solar system" into an exact duplicate of Krypton as their way of commemorating "the anniversary of the death of Krypton," two of the "human androids" with which they populate their "memorial planet" are "robot imitations" of Jor-El and Lara (S No. 150/1: "The One Minute of Doom!").

In addition to these memorials created by Superman, a statue of Jor-El, Lara, and baby Kal-El adorns the grounds of METROPOLIS's SUPERMAN MUSEUM (S No. 150/3, Jan '62: "When the World Forgot Superman!"), and there are wax figures of Jor-El and Lara on display on JONAS SMITH's brainchild, Krypton Island (Act No. 246, Nov '58: "Krypton on Earth!"). In October 1961 LORI LEMARIS indicates that she and her fellow Atlanteans intend to use a hoard of gold from a sunken Spanish treasure ship to fashion solid gold statues of Jor-El and Lara as a surprise gift for Superman in gratitude for his past efforts on behalf of ATLANTIS's mer-people (S No. 148/3: "Superman Owes a Billion Dollars!").

In July-August 1948, in a text containing the first extensive account of Superman's origin, Superman's mother is mentioned—and referred to by name, as Lara—for the first time in the chronicles (S No. 53/1: "The Origin of Superman!").

In November-December 1949 Superman sees Lara and Jor-El for the first time since his infancy when he journeys through the time-space barrier to the planet Krypton and actually witnesses the cataclysm that destroyed his native planet (S No. 61/3: "Superman Returns to Krypton!").

In October 1950 three Kryptonian "thought projection discs" containing a detailed account of the courtship of Lara and Jor-El—which have been whirling about in space since the explosion of Krypton—are returned to Earth by a U.S. experimental rocket and retrieved by the ever-curious LOIS LANE (Act No. 149: "The Courtship on Krypton!").

In August 1958 Superman journeys through the time-space barrier to Krypton at a time when his parents, who have not yet married, are working as undercover agents to thwart the sinister machinations of the diabolical KIL-LOR. When, as the result of a disastrous misunderstanding, Lara and Jor-El are convicted of treason along with Kil-Lor and launched into space in suspended animation to serve out a 100-year term in a prison satellite, Superman frees the trio from their orbiting prison and defeats Kil-Lor—who has acquired super-powers identical to Superman's as the result of having ventured beyond Krypton's gravitational pull—by tricking the villain into killing himself by overexposure to KRYPTONITE (S No. 123: chs. 1-3-"The Girl of Steel"; "The Lost Super-Powers"; "Superman's Return to Krypton").

In November 1960 Superman journeys through the time-space barrier to Krypton on the day of his parents' wedding and remains on the planet for what is probably several weeks thereafter. During this extended visit, Superman befriends his parents without telling them who he is, obtains temporary employment as Jor-El's assistant, and embarks on a passionate romance with LYLA LERROL (S No. 141: "Superman's Return to Krypton!" pts. I-III— "Superman Meets Jor-El and Lara Again!"; "Superman's Kryptonian Romance!"; "The Surprise of Fate!").

In July 1961, during a visit to an extradimensional "parallel universe," Superman encounters a couple—also named Lara and Jor-El—who are perfect look-alikes for his parents (S No. 146/2: "Superman's Greatest Feats!").

In December 1961 Superman enjoys a brief reunion with Lara and Jor-El—as well as with his foster parents, JONATHAN AND MARTHA KENT—after exposure to red kryptonite has temporarily endowed him with the power to make his wishes come true and he has wished aloud that his parents were on the scene to advise him how best to use his marvelous new power. Moments later, however, the effects of the red kryptonite wear off, Superman loses his wish-fulfilling power, and his magically materialized parents and foster parents fade and vanish like wraiths (Act No. 283: "The Red Kryptonite Menace!").

In July 1964 LEX LUTHOR journeys through the time-space barrier to Krypton at a time predating the marriage of Lara and Jor-El as part of his bizarre scheme to marry Lara himself and thus become the father of Superman (S No. 170/2: pts. I-II—"If Lex Luthor Were Superman's Father!"; "The Wedding of Lara and Luthor!").

LARS. A caveman inventor, scoffingly called "the dreamer" by his tribesmen because of his visionary ideas, who makes the acquaintance of CLARK KENT and LOIS LANE in June 1952 after their private plane has been forced to crash-land on the floor of an uncharted valley—situated somewhere "across a giant range of mountains on the other side of the world"—which has been "isolated from the rest of the world for millions of years" and where dinosaurs, pterodactyls, and primitive cavemen still live just as they did during Earth's prehistoric past. Ultimately, SUPERMAN rescues Lois and carries her back to civilization, but not before the brilliant Lars has demonstrated his miraculous skills as a thinker and inventor by inventing the wheel, the bow and arrow, a method for producing fire, and a bone meal made from ground dinosaur bones for fertilizing the local plant life (Act No. 169: "Caveman Clark Kent!").

LARSEN (Dr.). A METROPOLIS scientist who is the inventor of a machine that temporarily transforms LOIS LANE into a super-genius (S No. 104/1, Mar '56, "Lois Lane, Super-Genius").

LAR THAN. The "forceful" but fair-minded Lexori-an prosecutor whose task it becomes to prosecute SUPERMAN when the Man of Steel is brought to trial on the planet LEXOR on the charge of having deliberately murdered LEX LUTHOR, Lexor's greatest hero (Act No. 318, Nov '64: "The Death of Luthor!"). When the trial gets under way in a Lexorian courtroom, Lar Than accuses Superman of having journeyed to Lexor with the "deliberate intention of committing murder," but the Man of Steel is pro-nounced not guilty and released from custody when it is discovered that Luthor has not died at all, but has merely been in a "deathlike trance" induced by a "coma drug" (Act No. 319, Dec '64: "The Condemned Superman!"). (*See* LUTHOR, LEX.)

LARUE, NIKKI. A stunning "European glamor girl" who arrives in METROPOLIS in April 1950 with the astounding announcement that she and SUPER-MAN are engaged to be married. LOIS LANE is understandably hurt and bitterly jealous until she learns that Nikki Larue is secretly "the world-famous atomic scientist" Madame Nicolai; that the U.S. government had invited her to America "to experi-ment with atomic energy"; and that the ruse by which she and Superman pretended to be sweethearts was designed only "to protect [her] from spies," so that Superman "could guard [her] constantly without

arousing suspicion" about the true purpose of her prolonged stay in America (Act No. 143: "The Bride of Superman!").

LARYUS, HI (Professor). An alias employed by SUPERMAN in April 1946 when he dons a disguise and puts on a free vaudeville act for the people of METROPOLIS—billing himself in a flood of advance publicity as "The Funniest Man on Earth"—as part of his plan to defeat the PRANKSTER (Act No. 95: "The Laughing Stock of Metropolis!").

LATORA (Queen). The lovely red-haired ruler of the far-distant planet Vergo, a world doomed to immi-nent extinction beneath a blanket of glacial ice unless a way can be found to revitalize the dying sun around which it revolves. Alerted to the Vergoans' plight by a Kryptonian "mind-tape," recorded years earlier by his father JOR-EL and now fallen to Earth embedded in a KRYPTONITE meteor, SUPERMAN flashes into outer space, gathers together a planet-sized sphere of space-drift rich in uranium ore, and then sends it hurtling into the dying ember of the Vergoan sun, which, revitalized by the exploding uranium, will now continue to burn brightly for centuries to come (S No. 113, May '57: chs. 1-3—"The Superman of the Past"; "The Secret of the Towers"; "The Superman of the Present").

LAUREY, JIM. The villainous uncle of Doris Laurey, the lovely blond daughter of a "wealthy coal magnate" and the recent inheritress of the valuable Laurey Coal Mines. Laurey and his cohort Crawford make repeated attempts to murder Doris and gain control of the mines, but they are thwarted and apprehended by SUPERMAN in March 1941 (Act No. 34).

LAVERNE, LITA. A beautiful raven-haired actress and undercover spy for the nation of Toran—a European aggressor country at war with the neigh-boring states of Luxor and GALONIA—who conspires with a Luxorian army officer loyal to Toran to torpedo a neutral nation's ocean liner and make Luxor appear responsible as a ploy to win "the sympathy of the democracies" for the Toranian cause. The scheme is thwarted by SUPERMAN, who foils the plot to sink the neutral vessel and exposes the conspiracy to Luxorian authorities. They in turn order a shake-up of the Luxorian army designed to purge its ranks of Toranian sympathizers (Act No. 22, Mar '40). The use of place-names in this text is confusing and inconsistent, and it is possible that the names Luxor and Galonia are alternate designations for the same country.

LEANING TOWER OF PISA, THE. A marble tower in the city of Pisa, Italy, begun in 1174 and completed in the fourteenth century, which is one of the world's great landmarks. Standing at a height of 184½ feet, the tower apparently settled unevenly at an early stage of its construction and now leans more than 17 feet out of the perpendicular.

In July-August 1953 "THE BRAIN" demolishes the Leaning Tower of Pisa and two other world-famous monuments as part of an elaborate scheme to steal

$50,000,000 in precious gems lent to METROPOLIS by the Maharajah of Ipostan. Although nothing remains of the Leaning Tower but a pile of dust, SUPERMAN restores the monument by using the "super-pressure" of his hands to mold the dust into bricks and then rebuilding the tower exactly as it was. "Fortunately," muses Superman, "my super-memory preserves every detail of the tower's structure! It'll soon be standing again ... exactly as it has stood for so many centuries!" (S No. 83/1: "Destination X!").

Believing they are doing a good deed for the people of Earth, the Bizarros of the planet Htrae straighten the Leaning Tower of Pisa, 1964

By July 1954 LEX LUTHOR and his henchmen have planted explosives in the Leaning Tower—and in many other world-famous monuments—as part of an elaborate scheme to extort millions of dollars from the governments of the world (S No. 90/3: "The Titanic Thefts!").

In May 1960 the Leaning Tower is inadvertently toppled to the ground during a titanic battle between Superman and SUPER-MENACE, but Superman presumably repairs the damage once the fighting has ended (S No. 137: chs. I-III—"The Super-Brat from Krypton"; "The Young Super-Bully"; "Superman vs. Super-Menace!").

In December 1962 Superman destroys the Leaning

Tower—and several other world-famous landmarks—after being driven temporarily berserk by a diabolical "telepathic-hypnotic weapon" fired at him by members of the SUPERMAN REVENGE SQUAD. After the villains have been defeated, however, Superman promises to repair the damage (Act No. 295: "Superman Goes Wild!").

In May 1964, when the Bizarros of the planet HTRAE invade the Earth, determined to prove to Superman how much they like him, straightening the Leaning Tower is one of the wacky "good deeds" they perform in an effort to win the goodwill of Earth people (S No. 169/3: "The Bizarro Invasion of Earth!").

LEE, LARISSA. A lovely blond magazine cover girl with whom MR. MXYZPTLK falls in love in January-February 1950. Larissa ultimately helps SUPERMAN banish her unwelcome suitor to his home dimension by tricking him into saying his name backwards (S No. 62/3: "Mr. Mxyztplk, Hero!"). (*See* MXYZPTLK [MR.].)

LEE, LINDA. The pretty blond teen-ager who is secretly SUPERGIRL. The name Linda Lee is an alias adopted by Supergirl when she first arrives on Earth in May 1959 (Act No. 252: "The Supergirl from Krypton!"). Later, after she has been legally adopted by Fred and Edna Danvers, she becomes known as Linda Lee Danvers (Act No. 285, Feb '62: "The World's Greatest Heroine!").

LEGIONARY, THE. An Italian crime-fighter whose methods and techniques are modeled after those of America's BATMAN. In July-August 1957 the Legionary visits the United States in response to a

The Legionary in action, 1955

summons from "well-known philanthropist" John Mayhew, who wishes to award the Legionary and other world-famous crime-fighters—including Batman and ROBIN, SUPERMAN, the MUSKETEER, the GAUCHO, and the KNIGHT and the SQUIRE—charter membership in his newly formed Club of Heroes (WF No. 89: "The Club of Heroes!"). (*See* LIGHTNING-MAN.) (For a complete account of the Legionary's crime-fighting career, consult *The Encyclopedia of Comic Book Heroes: Volume I—Batman.*)

LEGION OF SUPER-HEROES, THE. An organization of teen-aged crime-fighters and adventurers—representing Earth and more than a score of far-flung planets and consisting, all in all, of several dozen active members, honorary members, and reservists—each of whom possesses some unique super-power distinct from those possessed by every other member of the group. The Legion makes its headquarters in the city of METROPOLIS in the thirtieth century A.D., where it is primarily active.

Among the Legion's many members are BOUNCING BOY, BRAINIAC 5, CHAMELEON BOY, COSMIC BOY, ELEMENT LAD, the INVISIBLE KID, MON-EL, LIGHTNING LAD, SATURN GIRL, SUN BOY, and TRIPLICATE GIRL (S No. 156, Oct '62: "The Last Days of Superman!" pts. I-III—"Superman's Death Sentence!"; "The Super-Comrades of All Time!"; "Superman's Last Day of Life!"; and others). When SUPERMAN was a teen-ager, he journeyed into the future and joined the Legion (S No. 147/3, Aug '61: "The Legion of Super-Villains!"). JIMMY OLSEN is an honorary member of the Legion under the name ELASTIC LAD (S No. 172, Oct '64: pts. I-III—"The New Superman!"; "Clark Kent—Former Superman!"; "The Struggle of the Two Supermen!"). The Legion's "animal branch" is known as the LEGION OF SUPER-PETS (S No. 176/1, Apr '65: "The Revenge of the Super-Pets!"; and others). The Legionnaires are fully aware that Clark Kent is secretly Superman (S No. 152/1, Apr '62: "The Robot Master!").

Since Superman has the power to travel in time, it is possible for him to journey to the thirtieth century A.D. to visit the Legion either during the period when they are teen-agers or during the period when they are adults. By the same token, since the Legionnaires are able to time-travel also, it is possible for them to return to the twentieth century to visit Superman either as teen-agers or as adults. For this reason, the Legionnaires appear in the chronicles sometimes as teen-agers and sometimes as adults. And as adults, the Legionnaires often have different names from the ones they employed as teen-agers. The adult Cosmic Boy is called Cosmic Man; the adult Lightning Lad is called Lightning Man; the adult Saturn Girl is called Saturn Woman; and so on. The entries in this encyclopedia on the various individual Legionnaires are listed under their teen-age names. Within the various entries dealing with the Legion, however, members are referred to either by their teen-age or their adult names depending on whether they are participating in the events being described as teen-agers or as adults.

In August 1961 three adult Legionnaires—Cosmic Man, Lightning Man, and Saturn Woman—join forces with Superman in his battle with LEX LUTHOR and the LEGION OF SUPER-VILLAINS (S No. 147/3:

"The Legion of Super-Villains!"). (*See* LEGION OF SUPER-VILLAINS, THE.)

By April 1962 six teen-aged Legionnaires—Brainiac 5, Chameleon Boy, Cosmic Boy, Lightning Lad, Saturn Girl, and Sun Boy—have created ingeniously lifelike robots of Clark Kent, Jimmy Olsen, LOIS LANE, and PERRY WHITE as part of an elaborate hoax they intend to play on Superman and SUPERGIRL to commemorate the anniversary of Supergirl's arrival on Earth. Knowing that Superman will fly the robots to his FORTRESS OF SOLITUDE for a detailed examination once he has ascertained that they are robots and not real people, the Legionnaires have concealed the components of their anniversary gift inside the robots' bodies and programmed the Clark Kent robot to assemble the gift—as well as to let the six Legionnaires into the locked Fortress—while Superman and Supergirl are fast asleep. Indeed, late that night, when an alarm goes off signaling the presence of intruders in the Fortress, Superman and Supergirl race to the entrance to discover the six Legionnaires standing proudly alongside their gift: colorful sculpted busts of themselves, Superman, and Supergirl (S No. 152/1: "The Robot Master!").

In August 1962 two adult Legionnaires—Cosmic Man and Lightning Man—pose as HERCULES and Samson, "two of the mightiest men of all time," as part of an elaborate ruse, devised by Superman, for uncovering the hiding place of DUKE MARPLE's stolen loot and bringing the "notorious gang-leader" to justice (S No. 155/2: "The Downfall of Superman!").

In October 1962, when Superman is believed to be dying of an incurable malady, the Legion of Super-Heroes—including Bouncing Boy, Chameleon Boy, Cosmic Boy, the Invisible Kid, Lightning Lad, Saturn Girl, Sun Boy, and Triplicate Girl—is summoned to the twentieth century by Supergirl to help carry out the gigantic super-tasks that Superman hopes to fulfill as his final legacy to humanity, including the destruction of a "vast cloud of fungus in distant space, that will some day reach Earth and blight all plant life," and the melting of the Antarctic ice, "to make Antarctica a fit place for millions to live in the future," thus ensuring "a home for Earth's expanding population...!" (S No. 156: "The Last Days of Superman!" pts. I-III—"Superman's Death Sentence!"; "The Super-Comrades of All Time!"; "Superman's Last Day of Life!").

In November 1962, when Superman Day is celebrated in Metropolis, a delegation of teen-aged Legionnaires are among those on hand to attend the festivities (S No. 157/3: "Superman's Day of Doom!").

In November 1963 Saturn Woman poses as the enchantress CIRCE as part of Superman's plan to defeat the SUPERMAN REVENGE SQUAD (S No. 165/1: pts. I-II—"Beauty and the Super-Beast!"; "Circe's Super-Slave").

When Metropolis television station WMET-TV inaugurates its new "Our American Heroes" series with a program honoring Superman, "our greatest American hero," a delegation of teen-aged Legionnaires appears on the show along with Superman's other friends and admirers to help pay tribute to the Man of Steel (Act No. 309, Feb '64: "The Superman Super-Spectacular!").

In October 1964, after Superman has been deprived of his super-powers by the baleful radiations of a mysterious green comet, three teen-aged Legionnaires—Cosmic Boy, the Invisible Kid, and Saturn Girl—use a "time-force wave carrier" in the Legion's thirtieth-century Clubhouse to endow Superman temporarily with their various powers so that he can use them in his upcoming battle with Lex Luthor and BRAINIAC. For a period of "a few hours," therefore, until his borrowed powers fade and vanish, Superman is equipped with Cosmic Boy's "power of super-magnetism," the Invisible Kid's "power of invisibility," and Saturn Girl's "power of telepathic thought-casting" (S No. 172: pts. I-III—"The New Superman!"; "Clark Kent—Former Superman!"; "The Struggle of the Two Supermen!").

LEGION OF SUPER-PETS, THE. The so-called "animal branch" of the LEGION OF SUPER-HEROES, consisting of BEPPO THE SUPER-MONKEY, COMET THE SUPER-HORSE, KRYPTO THE SUPERDOG, PROTY II, and STREAKY THE SUPER-CAT. For a complete account of the role of each super-pet in the adventures of SUPERMAN, consult the individual articles on the various super-pets.

LEGION OF SUPER-VILLAINS, THE. An organization of super-criminals from the twenty-first century A.D. Its members include COSMIC KING, LIGHTNING glORD, and SATURN QUEEN (S No. 147'3, Aug '61: "The Legion of Super-Villains!"), all of whom are fully aware that Clark Kent is secretly SUPERMAN (Act No. 283, Dec '61: "The Red Kryptonite Menace!"). The Super-Villains are implacable foes of the LEGION OF SUPER-HEROES (S No. 147/3, Aug '61: "The Lion of Super-Villains!").

In August 1961 the Legion of Super-Villains help LEX LUTHOR break out of Metropolis Prison so that they can ally themselves with the notorious renegade scientist in an elaborate scheme to annihilate Superman by luring the Man of Steel to a distant planetoid "in another solar system" and imprisoning him inside a deadly "kryptonite force-screen" (see KRYPTONITE). For a time the plot proceeds as the villains have anticipated and it appears that Superman will succumb to kryptonite poisoning, but the Man of Steel is ultimately freed from the deathtrap— and Luthor and his super-villainous allies are apprehended—through the ingenuity of Superman and the heroic intervention of COSMIC MAN, LIGHTNING MAN, and SATURN WOMAN, three members of the adult Legion of Super-Heroes (S No. 147/3: "The Legion of Super-Villains!").

LEMARIS, LENORA. The Atlantean mermaid who is the younger sister of LORI LEMARIS (Act No. 285, Feb '62: "The World's Greatest Heroine!").

LEMARIS, LORI. The lovely brown-haired Atlante

an mermaid who, prior to her marriage to the extraterrestrial merman surgeon RONAL (S No. 138/3, Jul '60: "The Mermaid from Atlantis!"; and others), shared a passionate romance with UPERMAN g)s No. 129/3, May '59: "The Girl in Superman's Past!"; S No. 135/2, Feb '60: "Superman's Mermaid Sweetheart!"), remaining, to this day, one of the Man of Steel's "most trusted friends" (Act No. 313, Jun '64: "The End of Clark Kent's Secret Identity!"). Recalling her wistfully in May 1959, Clark Kent describes her as "the kind of girl I've always dreamed of marrying--a girl of rare beauty and courage," with eyes "as blue and mysterious as the sea," and a voice tinged with "the slightest touch of a foreign accent..." (S No. 129/3: "The Girl in Superman's Past!"). Residing in the subsea realm of ATLANTIS with her husband Ronal and her younger sister Lenora (Act No. 285, Feb '62: "The World's Greatest Heroine!"), Lori Lemaris is a descendant of Nar Lemaris, the Atlantean scientist who performed the miraculous biological conversion that transformed the people of Atlantis into a population of mer-people (S No. 154/2, Jul '62: "Krypton's First Superman!").

Superman and Lori Lemaris, 1960

Like all Atlanteans, Lori Lemaris has mastered the art of reading minds and of communicating telepathically (S No. 129/3, May '59: "The Girl in Superman's Past!"; and others). She can perform these feats over very long distances, thus enabling her to read Superman's thoughts (S No. 135/2, Feb '60: "Superman's Mermaid (Sweetheart!") or summon him by telepathy (S No. 146/2, Jul '61: "Superman's Greatest Feats!") even while she is in Atlantis and he is in METROPOLIS, a great distance away. It was by reading Clark Kent's mind that Lori first discovered that Clark Kent is Superman (S No. 129/3, May '59: "The Girl in Superman's Past!"). Lori Lemaris's extraordinary mental powers also enable her to make sea creatures obey her telepathic commands (S No. 154/1, Jul '62: "The Underwater Pranks of Mr.

Mxyzptlk!"; and others) or to tune in on the thoughts of criminals imprisoned in the PHANTOM ZONE (Act No. 310, ar '64: "Secret of Kryptonite Six!").

Although Lori Lemaris, like other Atlanteans, is physically capable of surviving out of water, "...to remain in perfect health, [her] body must be immersed in salt water at least ten hours a day...!" Since walking on land is impossible for a fish-tailed Atlantean, Lori Lemaris has customarily employed a wheelchair during her brief sojourns in the surface world, concealing her mermaid tail beneath a blanket so as not to arouse undue attention (S No. 129/3, May '59: "The Girl in Superman's Past!"; see also S No. 135/2, Feb '60: "Superman's Mermaid Sweetheart!").

Lori Lemaris's status among her fellow Atlanteans is not entirely certain. Several texts portray her as an ordinary Atlantean citizen (S No. 129/3, May '59: "The Girl in Superman's Past!"; and others). At least one text, however, describes her as Atlantis's "queen" (S No. 156, Oct '62: "The Last Days of Superman!" pts. I-III—"Superman's Death Sentence!"; "The Super-Comrades of All Time!"; "Superman's Last Day of Life!"), and two others describe her

order to live out his life with her as plain Clark Kent. Lori, however, had already divined Clark Kent's secret by means of her telepathic powers, and although she loved him as much as he did her, she felt that marriage between a man and a mermaid was impossible and that her first duty was to return to her people. And so, recalls Clark Kent years later, "...soon, under the sea, we kissed--and there never was, or ever will be, such a strange kiss again--the farewell kiss between a Superman and a mermaid!" (May '59: "The Girl in Superman's Past!").

In February 1960, for the first time since his senior year at Metropolis University, Superman once again encounters Lori Lemaris, "the mysterious girl who was once so dear to [him]!"

"Lori!" implores Superman, after the couple have greeted one another with a passionate kiss. "You refused the last time I proposed but... please become my wife!"

"No, Superman!" replies Lori sadly. "A love like ours, just isn't meant to be! I...I shouldn't have permitted this meeting!"

But after a few hours of enjoying "the surface

Superman and Lori Lemaris, 1960

as Atlantis's "ruler" (S No. 154/1, Jul '62: "The Underwater Pranks of Mr. Mxyzptlk!"; Act No. 300, May '63: "Superman Under the Red Sun!").

Once every hundred years, according to Superman No. 129/3, an Atlantean is chosen by his people to visit the surface world "to learn of the surface people's progress" during the preceding century. It was while making one of these visits that Lori Lemaris attended METROPOLIS UNIVERSITY during the period when Clark Kent was a senior there. Kent "dated her steadily" during this period, captivated by her courage and haunting beauty, falling, day by day, ever more hopelessly in love with her.

Finally, Kent decided to ask her to marry him, to share with her the secret of his dual identity, and to abandon his super-heroic role as Superman forever in

world's bright lights" with Superman—who escorts her first to a Broadway play and then to a nightclub in his Clark Kent identity—Lori finally relents, promising to petition Atlantis's "elders" for permission to marry him.

"I'll quit the surface world, forever!" promises Superman. "....Please don't make me give you up, again!"

"Oh, Superman! I want to say yes, with all my heart...!" replies Lori lovingly, "....I'll return tomorrow, to this very spot, at the same time, with the answer!"

The following evening, however, when Lori returns to the appointed meeting place with the joyful news that the elders of Atlantis have consented to allow Superman to marry her and live out his life with her in Atlantis, a harpoon hurled by an evil fisherman—who bears a grudge against Lori for often releasing fish from his nets—strikes Lori broadside, knocking her unconscious and slamming her body violently against an outcropping of "knife-sharp, jagged rock."

"If the woman I love dies," cries Superman at the fleeing fisherman as he lifts Lori gently up in his arms, "there will be no corner in the universe where you can hide!"

Informed later, at an Atlantean hospital, that his beloved will live, but only at the shattering cost of remaining "hopelessly paralyzed, until her dying day," Superman streaks like a rocket into the vastness of outer space, determined to find a surgeon, somewhere, capable of curing Lori's paralysis. Indeed, finally, "thousands of leagues beneath the surface of a world completely covered by water," Superman encounters a brilliant "merman surgeon" (see RONAL) who believes he can help her. "This is the best…news I've heard yet!" exclaims Superman jubilantly. "Save my girl, and I will give you anything mortal mind can conjure! Anything!"

For days, Superman lingers impatiently outside the Atlantean hospital while the extraterrestrial merman surgeon struggles valiantly to cure Lori's paralysis. When finally he is permitted to see her, however, he discovers that although Lori has completely recovered, she has also fallen in love with the surgeon from space.

"For one second," notes the text, "Superman is blinded by anger…." "It isn't fair!" he fumes. "I searched the universe to save that woman! What right has she to love someone else…??" Then, however, "reason triumphs," and Superman realizes that he will have to reconcile himself to the fact that the woman he loves now loves someone else. As he kisses Lori a last goodbye, "the world's mightiest man suffers in silent torment…." "…[A]ll I know," he thinks to himself, "is that I lost Lori once before! This time…it's…for keeps…" (S No. 135/2: "Superman's Mermaid Sweetheart!").

In July 1960 Lori Lemaris concocts a series of elaborate and somewhat foolish schemes designed to trick Superman into marrying LOIS LANE. "I want Superman to be as happy as you and I," explains Lori to her merman husband. "I know that Superman really cares for Lois…and that she absolutely adores him! All I am going to do is trick him into proposing to her!"

Lori's surreptitious attempts to play Cupid between Superman and Lois involve such ploys as trying to play on Superman's jealousy by making him believe that Lois is on the verge of marrying another man; attempting to engineer a scenario in which Lois Lane learns that Clark Kent is secretly Superman, on the theory that then "he'll have to marry Lois, so she will keep the secret of his identity"; and putting "life-like masks of Lois' face" on the heads of deep-water fishes, in the hope that Superman, bombarded by visions of Lois Lane while swimming underwater,

will be duped into believing that he has become so smitten by Lois that he has begun seeing her face everywhere. Superman sees through these childish stratagems, however, and successfully thwarts Lori's attempts to maneuver him into matrimony. "Lori, you meant well," chides Superman finally, "but please…do me a super-favor, will you? In the future allow me to pick out my own wife!" (S No. 138/3: "The Mermaid from Atlantis!").

In August 1960 Lori Lemaris and her husband Ronal help Superman carry out an elaborate charade designed to make Lois Lane believe that the Man of Steel has decided to marry Lori Lemaris and live in Atlantis so that Lois will feel free to accept the proposal of marriage made to her by multimillionaire BRETT RAND. The hoax involves tricking Lois into thinking that Ronal has died in an undersea mishap and that, with Lori Lemaris now a widow, Superman has allowed Atlantis's scientists to "transform [him] into a super-merman" so that he can marry Lori and live in Atlantis. Superman finally abandons his puerile charade after Lois Lane has announced her refusal to marry Brett Rand despite Superman's apparent engagement to another woman (S No. 139/1: "The New Life of Super-Merman!").

In July 1961, in response to an urgent telepathic summons from Lori Lemaris, Superman races to Atlantis to rescue the subsea kingdom from being destroyed by "a new super-atomic, underwater depth-bomb" being tested in the area by the U.S. Navy. Then, at Lori's request, Superman journeys through the time barrier into the past in an attempt to alter history by preventing Atlantis from sinking into the sea, so that its modern-day inhabitants will not be continually menaced by undersea perils. Superman's attempt to undo this past event proves futile, however, for, as the Man of Steel has learned on numerous other occasions, even he cannot change the course of history (S No. 146/2: "Superman's Greatest Feats!").

In October 1961 Lori Lemaris indicates that she and her fellow Atlanteans intend to use a hoard of gold from a sunken Spanish treasure ship to fashion solid gold statues of JOR-EL and LARA as a surprise gift for Superman in gratitude for his past efforts on behalf of Atlantis's mer-people (S No. 148/3: "Superman Owes a Billion Dollars!").

In February 1962, when Superman proudly announces SUPERGIRL's existence to the world, Lori Lemaris and her fellow Atlanteans commemorate the occasion by unveiling a gigantic undersea statue of a mermaid Supergirl (Act No. 285: "The World's Greatest Heroine!").

In July 1962, during a period when Superman is periodically seized by an overpowering compulsion to commit evil acts (see MAG-EN), the Man of Steel demolishes the shrine of Atlantis's mermaid-goddess and is on the verge of annihilating the mer-people by destroying the vital chemical plant that regulates the amount of salt in their undersea environment when Supergirl, summoned to Atlantis by a desperate telepathic call from Lori Lemaris, arrives on the scene to repair the chemical plant and prevent Superman from wreaking further destruction (S No. 154/2: "Krypton's First Superman!"). During this same period, Lori Lemaris tries to help Superman finish Mr. Mxyzptlk from the earthly dimension by tricking him into saying his name backwards. Her attempt fails, however, because the mischievous extradimensional imp is underwater, where speech is impossible (S No. 154/1, Jul '62: "The Underwater Pranks of Mr. Mxyptlk!").

In October 1962, when Superman is believed to be dying of an incurable malady, Lori Lemaris and her fellow Atlanteans join forces with KRYPTO THE SUPERDOG, Supergirl, and the SUPERMEN EMERGENCY SQUAD to carry out one of the gigantic super-tasks that Superman hopes to fulfill as his final legacy to humanity, viz., the injection of a colossal sea monster—which has been growing to ever more titanic size due to the stimulation of undersea radioactivity—with a special "shrinking formula" so that it will not one day become so terrifyingly gargantuan that it menaces the safety of the Earth (S No. 156: "The Last Days of Superman!" pts. I-III— "Superman's Death Sentence!"; "The Super-Comrades of All Time!"; "Superman's Last Day of Life!").

In November 1962 Lori Lemaris and her fellow Atlanteans help Superman locate and recover a space capsule that recently fell into the Atlantic. The recovery of the lost space capsule is one of the stunts that Superman performs while posing as the genie of ALADDIN'S magic lamp as part of his scheme to apprehend a notorious "international spy" (see VON SCHULTZ [PROFESSOR]). (S No. 157/2: "The Super-Genie of Metropolis!"). During this same period, when Superman Day is celebrated in Metropolis, Lori Lemaris is among those on hand to attend the festivities (S No. 157/3, Nov '62: "Superman's Day of Doom!").

In January 1963, when Superman is being pursued by angry Kandorians enraged at his opposition to the enlargement of their city, Lori Lemaris offers to provide the Man of Steel with a safe haven in Atlantis. Superman, however, declines the offer, knowing that time is running out in which to save KANDOR from destruction (S No. 158: "Superman in Kandor" pts. I-III—"Invasion of the Mystery Super-Men!"; "The Dynamic Duo of Kandor!"; "The City of Super-People!"). (See THAN OL.)

In November 1963, when Clark Kent has lost consciousness and almost drowned after an encounter with red KRYPTONITE has temporarily robbed him of his super-powers, Lori Lemaris and her fellow Atlanteans revive him with "a new form of artificial respiration" and nurse him back to health (S No. 165/2: "The Sweetheart Superman Forgot!"). (See SELWYN, SALLY.)

When Metropolis television station WMET-TV inaugurates its new "Our American Heroes" series with a program honoring Superman, "our greatest American hero," Lori Lemaris appears on the show along with Superman's other friends and admirers to help pay tribute to the Man of Steel. Lori is threatened with injury, at one point, by a falling stage light, but Supergirl intervenes in time to prevent it from hitting her (Act No. 309, Feb '64: "The Superman Super-Spectacular!").

In March 1964 Lori Lemaris is among the Atlanteans stricken by the "deadly spotted plague" which threatens to decimate the entire population of Atlantis. She and her fellow plague sufferers are ultimately cured, however, by means of a rare "spore antidote" native to KRYPTON'S SCARLET JUNGLE (Act No. 310: "Secret of Kryptonite Six!"). (See JAX-UR.)

In the spring of 1964, after exposure to red kryptonite has temporarily transformed Superman into two completely different people, a super-powered Superman and a non-super Clark Kent (Act No. 311, Apr '64: "Superman, King of Earth!"), Kent is mortally wounded by a policeman's bullet and topples unconscious into the Midvale River, only to awaken soon afterward in an Atlantean hospital to find Lori Lemaris watching over him. It is here, in this hospital, that "the skilled surgeons of Atlantis" perform the "delicate operation" necessary to save Kent's life (Act No. 312, May '64: "King Superman Versus Clark Kent, Metallo").

By June 1964 Lori Lemaris and four of Superman's other good friends—BATMAN, JIMMY OLSEN, Lois Lane, and PERRY WHITE—have been taken captive by the SUPERMAN REVENGE SQUAD and imprisoned in a state of suspended animation in a cave beneath Metropolis as part of the villain's elaborate scheme to torment and demoralize Superman (Act No. 313: "The End of Clark Kent's Secret Identity!"). (See SUPERMAN REVENGE SQUAD, THE.) (See also SUPERMAN [section J 3, the relationship with Lori Lemaris].)

LEOPARD, THE. A cunning and ruthless criminal, his identity concealed by a leopard's-head mask, who commits a series of spectacular crimes involving big cats, as when he looses a pack of wild cats in the Denmar Financial District so that he and his gang can loot the area uninterrupted while the police are preoccupied with recaging the animals. The Leopard, who is secretly Sam Kennedy, the "publicity man" for the Cosmos Circus, is apprehended along with his henchmen in January-February 1943 through the combined efforts of SUPERMAN and Herman "the Heroic" Hoskins, a wacky but well-intentioned Superman admirer and self-styled super-hero ("I wanta fight crooks--I wanna help th' weak an' needy") who dresses in a ridiculous costume loosely modeled after Superman's but who nevertheless deserves high marks for pitching in bravely to help bring the Leopard and his henchmen to justice (S No. 20/3: "Lair of the Leopard!").

LERROL, LYLA. See LYLA, LERROL.

LEWIS, "LENS." An underworld photographer who, along with his accomplices, was apprehended by the teen-aged SUPERMAN following an attempted robbery at the Smallville Bank, but only after he had successfully hidden a reel of movie film, taken at the robbery scene, which, if developed, would show Clark Kent ducking into an alleyway and emerging in his super-powered identity, and thus betray the secret of Superman's dual identity. Released from Metropolis Prison in September-October 1952, Lewis recovers his film from its hiding place and then invites the underworld to view it at $1,000 per person, but Superman thwarts Lewis's scheme—and prevents the exposure of his secret identity—by surreptitiously switching an innocuous film for the potentially damaging one taken by Lewis (S No. 78/3: "The Girls in Superman's Life!").

LEXOR. A far-distant, "dessert-like world" (S No. 164/1, Oct '63: pts. I-II—"The Showdown Between Luthor and Superman!"; "The Super-Duel!"), revolving about "the red star X-156-99F" (Act No. 318, Nov '64: "The Death of Luthor!"), whose people were the custodians of a "great scientific civilization" until their culture "retrogressed to barbarism" (S No. 168, Apr '64: pts. I-II—"Luthor--Super-Hero!"; "Lex Luthor, Daily Planet Editor!"). Named in honor of LEX LUTHOR, SUPERMAN's arch-enemy (Act No. 318, Nov '64: "The Death of Luthor!"; and others), it is "the one world in the universe where [Luthor is] considered a hero" (S No. 167, Feb '64: "The Team of Luthor and Brainiac!" pts. I-III—"The Deadly Duo!"; "The Downfall of Superman!"; "The Hour of Kandor's Vengeance!"), while Superman is "feared and detested as a super-villain . . . !" (S No. 168, Apr '64: pts. I-II—"Luthor--Super-Hero!"; "Lex Luthor, Daily Planet Editor!").

Since the gravity of Lexor is considerably heavier than that of Earth, an earthman on LEXOR must wear special "gravity shoes" merely to move about. The planet's catastrophic water shortage is alleviated by Superman in October 1963 (S No. 164/1: pts. I-II—"The Showdown Between Luthor and Superman!"; "The Super-Duel!"), but Lexor remains a barren, hostile, "drought-stricken world" (S No. 167, Feb '64: "The Team of Luthor and Brainiac!" pts. I-III—"The Deadly Duo!"; "The Downfall of Superman!"; "The Hour of Kandor's Vengeance!") swept by "mighty sand-storms," its sun-parched landscape dominated by a "weird cactus forest," its skies filled with "monstrous birds" called "dorulgs" which prey on the Lexorians' meager crops (S No. 164/1, Oct '63: pts. I-II—"The Showdown Between Luthor and Superman!"; "The Super-Duel!"). Another of Lexor's topographical features is its "weird jungle," home of the "truth beast," a bizarre creature "whose strange, powerful brainwaves make anyone close to it tell only the truth," and the "madness flower," whose baleful "perfume induces temporary insanity" (Act No. 318, Nov '64: "The Death of Luthor!"). In addition, "strange beasts" with "big hollow horns" have evolved on the planet, traveling long distances in search of scarce water and then carrying it about with them in their oversized horns (S No. 164/1, Oct '63: pts. I-II—"The Showdown Between Luthor and Superman!"; "The Super-Duel!"). Lexor's famous

Living Lake, seemingly a harmless small body of water, is actually "a giant jelly-fish form of Lexorian life" capable of devouring anyone foolhardy enough to venture into it (Act No. 318, Nov '64: "The Death of Luthor!"). Moreover, because Lexor revolves about a red sun (S No. 164/1, Oct '63: pts. I-II—"The Showdown Between Luthor and Superman!"; "The Super-Duel!"; and others), Superman has no super powers there (see SUPERMAN [section E, the super powers]).

Although present-day Lexorians are "unscientific" (Act No. 319, Dec '64: "The Condemned Superman!"), they were, in ancient times, "a great scientific race" (S No. 164/1, Oct '63: pts. I-II—"The Showdown Between Luthor and Superman!"; "The Super-Duel!" who had developed and mastered an extraordinary "super-science" (S No. 168, Apr '64: pts. I-II—"Luthor-Super-Hero!"; "Lex Luthor, Daily Planet Editor!") evidence of which may still be found inside the "museum of old machines" in Lexor's capital city (S No. 167, Feb '64: "The Team of Luthor and Brainiac!" pts. I-III—"The Deadly Duo!"; "The Downfall of Superman!"; "The Hour of Kandor's Vengeance!").

Among the miraculous relics of Lexor's "forgotten science" (Act No. 319, Dec '64: "The Condemned Superman!") on display in the museum are a "lesson machine," with which both Luthor and Superman teach themselves the Lexorian language within the space of a few hours; automatic "building-machines," which can be programmed to construct other machines; an "automaton bloodhound," originally "designed by [Lexor's] ancient scientists for trailing law-breakers" (S No. 164/1, Oct '63: pts. I-II—"The Showdown Between Luthor and Superman!"; "The Super-Duel!"); an "inventing machine," for creating new inventions and devices; and an "artificial super-powers" device, designed "to give a human body a temporary charge of super-powers" (S No. 168, Apr '64: pts. I-II—"Luthor--Super-Hero!"; "Lex Luthor, Daily Planet Editor!").

Sometime in the distant past, however, the Lexorians lost the "ancient wisdom" of their fore-fathers, and, with it, the knowledge of how to use and operate their forefathers' "ancient inventions." Visiting Lexor for the first time in October 1963, Luthor speculates that "This must have once been a great scientific race, but perhaps a great war eons ago wiped out their civilization and they've returned to the **Stone Age!**" (S No. 164/1: pts. I-II—"The Showdown Between Luthor and Superman!"; "The Super-Duel!").

Six months later, however, in April 1964, Superman discovers that the real explanation for the decline of Lexorian civilization lies in the baleful effects of certain "priceless rainbow crystals," a geological rarity whose "magnificent rays" have, "for generations," been used as the source of light in every Lexorian home. Unknown to the Lexorians, however, these same crystals, which Lexorians prize as "the greatest treasures of Lexor," "emit a subtle vibration that deteriorates brain-activity," a vibration capable, given centuries of exposure, of reducing an entire people to a primitive state. In the words of Superman No. 168:

> The people of **Lexor** once had a brilliant civilization but declined to barbarism! The **rainbow crystals** are the reason...the subtle rays of these crystals act to slow the brain's electroencephalic action, and dull the intelligence!

Shortly after having made this discovery, Superman destroys the crystals, thereby arresting the process that, for centuries, has been "dulling all minds...on **Lexor!**" (S No. 168, Apr '64: pts. I-II—"Luthor--Super-Hero!"; "Lex Luthor, Daily Planet Editor!").

The people of Lexor revere and idolize Lex Luthor (S No. 168, Apr '64: pts. I-II—"Luthor--Super-Hero!"; "Lex Luthor, Daily Planet Editor!"; and others) as the man "who revived the forgotten science of [their] ancestors and bettered [their] whole world!" (Act No. 319, Dec '64: "The Condemned Superman!").

In the words of one Lexorian, "...mighty **Lex Luthor** discovered the lost science of our ancestors and turned our barren planet into a world of plenty!" So great, in fact, is the Lexorians' love for Luthor,

people (Act No. 164/1, Oct '63: pts. I-II—"The Showdown Between Luthor and Superman!"; "The Super-Duel!"). Luthor has himself described Lexor as "the one world in the universe I really love," and, within limits, it is fair to regard him as the Lexorians' "hero and benefactor" (Act No. 318, Nov '64: "The Death of Luthor!").

The principal feat upon which Luthor's reputation with the Lexorians rests, however, that of relieving the planet's calamitous drought by bringing about the construction of vast canals and filling them with "vast masses of ice" from outer space, was actually performed by Superman, and the fact that Luthor has received credit for this deed is only the result of a monumental misunderstanding on the part of the Lexorian people (S No. 164/1, Oct '63: pts. I-II—"The Showdown Between Luthor and Superman!"; "The Super-Duel!").

Nevertheless, Luthor continues to be acclaimed on Lexor as "the great hero who brought water to [the Lexorians'] drought-stricken world" (S No. 167, Feb '64: "The Team of Luthor and Brainiac!" pts. I-III—"The Deadly Duo!"; "The Downfall of Superman!"; "The Hour of Kandor's Vengeance!"), and it is for this reason that they have named their world Lexor in Luthor's honor (S No. 168, Apr '64: pts. I-II—"Luthor--

In Lexor's capital city in 1964, the people of Lexor welcome the return of Luthor, their world's greatest hero. To the left of Luthor stands Brainiac. The young woman on the right is Ardora. In the background is the statue the Lexorians have erected in Luthor's honor

that the mere fact that he is Superman's enemy is sufficient to make them regard Superman as "the greatest villain in the universe" (S No. 168, Apr '64: pts. I-II—"Luthor--Super-Hero!"; "Lex Luthor, Daily Planet Editor!").

Indeed, Luthor has made an extensive study of Lexor's ancient super-science and has performed a number of genuinely selfless acts on behalf of its

Super-Hero!"; "Lex Luthor, Daily Planet Editor!"). For this reason, and because Superman has no super-powers there, Lexor is a haven for Luthor and a place of deadly danger to Superman (Act No. 318, Nov '64: "The Death of Luthor!", and others).

During his various sojourns on Lexor, Luthor resides in the planet's capital city (S No. 168, Apr '64: pts. I-II—"Luthor--Super-Hero!"; "Lex Luthor, Daily

Planet Editor!"), "in the palace a grateful people have built for their hero..." (Act No. 318, Nov '64: "The Death of Luthor!"). The Lexorians have also provided Luthor with a fully equipped laboratory, where he continues his researches into Lexor's ancient science. Elsewhere in the capital is the LUTHOR MUSEUM, dedicated to the glorification of Luthor and his exploits, as well as a gigantic standing statue of Luthor bearing this inscription: "In Honor of Lex Luthor for His Many Scientific Feats/Erected by the People of Lexor" (S No. 168, Apr '64: pts. I-II— "Luthor--Super-Hero!"; "Lex Luthor, Daily Planet Editor!"). The museum housing Lexor's ancient superscientific machines stands not far from the statue (S No. 167, Feb '64: "The Team of Luthor and Brainiac!" pts. I-III—"The Deadly Duo!"; "The Downfall of Superman!"; "The Hour of Kandor's Vengeance!").

Luthor's girl friend on the planet Lexor is ARDORA (S No. 168, Apr '64: pts. I-II—"Luthor--Super-Hero!"; "Lex Luthor, Daily Planet Editor!"), the lovely young Lexorian woman who becomes his wife in November 1964 (Act No. 318: "The Death of Luthor!"). Other inhabitants of the planet Lexor include GARN ABU, LAR THAN, and VEL QUENNAR (Act No. 318, Nov '64: "The Death of Luthor!"; Act No. 319, Nov '64: "The Condemned Superman!").

Clad in a distinctive red-and-purple costume—and employing the name the Defender—Lex Luthor has also functioned as Lexor's super-hero. It should be noted, however, that Luthor's conception of his super-heroic duties consists almost entirely of "defending" the Lexorians against "invading out-laws like Superman!" (S No. 168, Apr '64: pts. I-II—"Luthor--Super-Hero!"; "Lex Luthor, Daily Planet Editor!"). To the people of Lexor, however, Lex Luthor remains "the greatest man in Lexor's history" (Act No. 319, Dec '64: "The Condemned Superman!"), and they would willingly "defend [him] with their lives!" (S No. 167, Feb '64: "The Team of Luthor and Brainiac!" pts. I-III—"The Deadly Duo!"; "The Downfall of Superman!"; "The Hour of Kandor's Vengeance!").

In October 1963 Superman and Lex Luthor visit Lexor for the first time, although the planet remains as yet unnamed in the chronicles. It is at the conclusion of this adventure that Superman "hurls mighty masses of frozen water" from outer space into Lexor's newly excavated canals, thereby alleviating the drought on the barren planet. Because the Lexorians mistakenly assume that it is Luthor who was responsible for their good fortune, they soon afterward erect a gigantic statue of him in their capital city (S No. 164/1: pts. I-II—"The Showdown Between Luthor and Superman!"; "The Super-Duel!"). (See LUTHOR, LEX.)

In February 1964 Lex Luthor returns briefly to Lexor in the company of the space villain BRAINIAC, with whom he has forged a temporary alliance. Sometime later, after the villains' scheme to annihilate Superman has ended in failure, Luthor returns to Lexor again (S No. 167: "The Team of Luthor and

Brainiac!" pts. I-III—"The Deadly Duo!"; "The Downfall of Superman!"; "The Hour of Kandor' Vengeance!"). (See LUTHOR, LEX.)

By April 1964, the people of this distant plane have named their world Lexor in Lex Luthor's hono and are preparing to dedicate the Luthor Museum. is during this period that Superman revisits Lexo determined to bring Luthor to justice (S No. 168: pts. II—"Luthor--Super-Hero!"; "Lex Luthor, Daily Plar et Editor!"). (See LUTHOR, LEX.)

In November 1964 Lex Luthor returns to Lexor an makes the lovely Ardora his wife. Soon afterward Superman arrives on Lexor for yet another battl with the notorious arch-villain (Act No. 318: "Th Death of Luthor!"; see also Act No. 319, Dec '64: "Th Condemned Superman!").

"LIGHT, THE." An alternate identity employed b LEX LUTHOR in November-December 1941 (S Nc 13/1).

LIGHTNING LAD. A member of the LEGION O SUPER-HEROES. A native of the planet Amarta (als referred to as the planet Winath), Lightning La possesses, like his brother LIGHTNING LORD, th "power of super-electricity," the ability to discharg controlled bolts of "super-lightning" from his body Lightning Lad's real name is Garth Ranzz. The adul Lightning Lad is called Lightning Man.

According to Superman No. 147/3, Lightning La and his brother acquired their awesome powers when as youngsters exploring a wooded area on the plane Korbal, they were attacked by a fearsome "lightning monster" which had "the frightful ability to transfe some of its lightning power to its victims...like a infectious disease!" Lightning Lad vowed to devot his newly acquired powers to helping others an joined the Legion of Super-Heroes, while Lightning Lord decided to use his powers for crime an ultimately joined the LEGION OF SUPER-VILLAINS.

In August 1961 Lightning Man and two othe adult Legionnaires—COSMIC MAN and SATURI WOMAN—join forces with SUPERMAN in his battl with LEX LUTHOR and the Legion of Super-Villains (S No. 147/3: "The Legion of Super-Villains!"). (See LEGION OF SUPER-VILLAINS, THE.)

In April 1962 Lightning Lad is among the six Legionnaires who play an elaborate hoax on Super man and SUPERGIRL as a prelude to celebrating th anniversary of Supergirl's arrival on Earth (S No 152/1: "The Robot Master!"). (See LEGION OF SUPER HEROES, THE.)

In August 1962 Lightning Man and Cosmic Mar pose as Samson and HERCULES, "two of the mightiest men of all time," as part of an elaborate ruse, devised by Superman, for uncovering the hiding place o DUKE MARPLE's stolen loot and bringing the "notori ous gang-leader" to justice (S No. 155/2: "Th Downfall of Superman!").

In October 1962, when Superman is believed to b dying of an incurable malady, Lightning Lad is among the Legionnaires who are summoned to th twentieth century by Supergirl to help carry out the gigantic super-tasks that Superman hopes to fulfill as his final legacy to humanity, including the destruction of a "vast cloud of fungus in distant space, that will some day reach Earth and blight all plant life," and the melting of the Antarctic ice, "to make Antarctica a fit place for millions to live in the future," thus ensuring "a home for Earth's expanding population...!" (S No. 156: "The Last Days of Superman!" pts. I-III—"Superman's Death Sentence!"; "The Super-Comrades of All Time!"; "Superman's Last Day of Life!").

LIGHTNING LORD. A member of the LEGION OF SUPER-VILLAINS, an organization of super-criminals from the twenty-first century A.D. A native, like his brother Lightning Man (the adult LIGHTNING LAD), of the planet Amarta (also referred to as the planet Winath), Lightning Lord wears a red, white, and green costume with a pair of white lightning bolts emblazoned on his chest. Both brothers possess the "power of super-electricity," the ability to discharge controlled bolts of "super-lightning" from their bodies.

According to Superman No. 147/3, Lightning Lord and his brother acquired their awesome powers when, as youngsters exploring a wooded area on the planet Korbal, they were attacked by a fearsome "lightning monster" which had "the frightful ability to transfer some of its lighting power to its victims...like an infectious disease!" Lightning Lad vowed to devote his newly acquired powers to helping others and joined the LEGION OF SUPER-HEROES, while Lightning Lord decided to use his powers for crime and ultimately joined the Legion of Super-Villains.

In August 1961 the Legion of Super-Villains forms an alliance with LEX LUTHOR in an elaborate scheme to annihilate SUPERMAN (S No. 147/3: "The Legion of Super-Villains!"). (See LEGION OF SUPER-VILLAINS, THE.)

In March 1962, while in the grip of a nightmare induced by exposure to red KRYPTONITE, Superman dreams that Lightning Lord and other villains lure him into a trap, put him on "trial" for his alleged "crimes" against them, and sentence him to battle SUPERGIRL to the death in a gigantic arena or else stand by helplessly while they blow up the Earth. These events, however, are all only part of a nightmare, and no actual confrontation with Lightning Lord and his cohorts ever takes place (Act No. 286: "The Jury of Super-Enemies!").

LIGHTNING MAN. The adult LIGHTNING LAD.

LIGHTNING-MAN. A mysterious super-hero, his true identity unknown, who appears in METROPOLIS in July-August 1957 and performs a series of mind-boggling super-feats during a period when the world's greatest crime-fighters—including SUPERMAN, BATMAN and ROBIN, the KNIGHT and the SQUIRE, the MUSKETEER, the LEGIONARY, and the GAUCHO—are gathered in the city to accept a valuable gift from "well-known philanthropist" John Mayhew, a lavish Club of Heroes which he has constructed to serve as their Metropolis headquarters.

Since the land and building included in the gift are "worth a fortune" and Mayhew has decided to award the chairmanship of the club and the valuable deed to its property to whichever of the assembled crime-fighters performs the most impressive array of feats during the next several days, Superman becomes fearful that Lightning-Man is a criminal attempting to win control of the deed for himself. Lightning-Man does indeed win the chairmanship, but Batman ultimately establishes that Lightning-Man is in reality Superman himself and that the role of Lightning-Man was one the Man of Steel had unwittingly concocted during recurring short-lived periods of temporary amnesia brought on by the overhead orbiting of a meteoric KRYPTONITE fragment (WF No. 89: "The Club of Heroes!").

"LIGHTNING MASTER, THE." An evil scientist—clad in a green robe and hood with a small yellow lightning bolt emblazoned on his head and chest—who demolishes a METROPOLIS skyscraper

As Superman looks on in horror, Lightning Lord prepares to blow up the Earth. The scene takes place in one of Superman's red-kryptonite-induced nightmares, 1962

"The Lightning Master," 1942

with his diabolical "lightning machine" and then threatens to destroy Metropolis completely unless the city fathers meet his demand for $300,000 in extortion money. Cornered by SUPERMAN in his secret mountain laboratory as he is preparing to destroy both Metropolis and the captive LOIS LANE. ("It's a pity to blast such a lovely girl out of existence," muses the villain, "but I must not allow human decency to influence me"), "The Lightning Master" attempts to annihilate Superman with a deadly bolt of electricity from his hand-held "electric-bolt gun," but "As the *Man of Tomorrow*, unharmed by the electric-bolt, seizes the scientist, the great electric charge is communicated to *'The Lightning Master,'* instantly electrocuting him...." "A taste of your own medicine!" muses Superman grimly (S No. 14/4, Jan/Feb '42).

LINK, LESTER. A "meek little bookkeeper," fed up with the drudgery of his workaday job and envious of the lives of danger and excitement led by the big-time rackets chiefs, who walks off his job in Winter 1943, installs himself in his own, somewhat overdone, version of an underworld lair—morbidly bedecked with such lurid gangland trappings as guns, knives, and human skulls—and, employing the colorful pseudonym the Lynx, proceeds to establish himself in the public eye as the secret ruler of the underworld, largely by reading press accounts of recent crimes and then telephoning the DAILY PLANET and claiming credit for having committed them. Superman learns early on that the Lynx is only a timid bookkeeper determined to "feel important," and he ultimately enables Link to achieve the public recognition for which he thirsts by making Link his partner in a scheme to lure Tiger Tornadi, Baby-Face, and Pig-Eye—"bosses of the toughest mobs in town"—into a carefully prepared trap (WF No. 12: "The Man Who Stole a Reputation!").

LINNIS, THAD. A cunning criminal who, by persuading SUPERMAN that he has solved the secret of his dual identity and threatening to expose it to the world, attempts to force Superman to remain outside METROPOLIS for two full weeks while he and his henchmen loot the city with a powerful "super-tank" which can be stopped only by Superman. With BATMAN's help, however, Superman eventually comes to realize that Linnis is only bluffing—the villain has no knowledge of Superman's secret identity—whereupon he and the Dynamic Duo apprehend Linnis and his henchmen before they can put their "tremendous theft-plan" into effect (WF No. 84, Sep/Oct '56: "The Super-Mystery of Metropolis!").

LOCASTRO (Mr.). The sculptor of the titanic statue of SUPERMAN that stands in the city of METROPOLIS overlooking Metropolis Harbor. LEX LUTHOR brings the statue to life temporarily in July 1950 as part of his scheme to extort $10,000,000 from the people of Metropolis (Act No. 146: "The Statues That Came to Life!").

LOCK, RAYMOND. A deranged psychology professor at Spurdyke University—obsessed with a deeply held belief that "habits can make, or break, the individual"—who, after being sentenced to die in the electric chair for his brutal murder of a college dean, escapes from custody and sets out to wreak a madman's vengeance on all who testified against him at his trial, in each case by taking malevolent advantage of his victims' well-known habits, as when he poisons the pipe tobacco of habitual pipe-smoker Thaddeus Winton. Lock is finally apprehended by SUPERMAN in July-August 1943 (S No. 23/2: "Habitual Homicide").

LOIS-BIZARRO. *See* BIZARRO-LOIS.

LOIS 4XR. The great-great-great-great-granddaughter of LOIS LANE, who is a perfect look-alike for her well-known ancestress. SUPERMAN meets Lois 4XR in the year 2949 A.D.—a far-future era when everyone on Earth has super-powers like Superman's—after an accidental bombardment of Professor Wilson's "super-rays" has catapulted him a thousand years into the future. Try though he might, however, Superman is unable to learn whom Lois Lane will marry in the twentieth century in order to begin the line of progeny destined to culminate in the birth of Lois 4XR a full ten centuries later (S No. 57/2, Mar/Apr '49: "Every Man a Superman!").

LOIS LANE AND CLARK KENT, PRIVATE DETECTIVES. A private detective agency that is opened by LOIS LANE and CLARK KENT in April-May 1950, at the suggestion of PERRY WHITE, as a ploy for luring into the open the unknown murderers responsible for the recent deaths of four METROPOLIS private detectives, each of whom had been hired to recover a painting stolen from the son of the deceased Maharajah of Rajpan purported to contain a clue to the secret location of a vast royal treasure. The killers prove to be evil "rebel agents" of the tyrannical usurpers who have seized control of Rajpan, a province of Northern India, and driven the maharajah's son into exile; now they have stolen the painting and are determined to force the maharajah's son into revealing the secret clue it contains to the priceless royal treasure. The secret of the painting is ultimately unlocked by Lois Lane, and the Indian plotters are apprehended by SUPERMAN (WF No. 45: "Lois Lane and Clark Kent, Detectives!").

LONDON BRIDGE. A bridge over the river Thames, in England, dating from the twelfth century. In November-December 1952 a gang of English criminals with a grudge against INSPECTOR ERSKINE HAWKINS plant a bomb at London Bridge, but SUPERMAN defuses it before it goes off (S No. 79/3: "The Revenge That Took 300 Years!"). In August 1964, after being afflicted with the "curse of magic" by the mischievous MR. MXYZPTLK, Superman inadvertently makes London Bridge collapse when he begins singing "London Bridge is falling down" with a group of English children. Within seconds, however, Superman has completely repaired the damage (S No. 171/2: "The Curse of Magic!").

LON-ES. The Kandorian scientist and onetime assistant to JOR-EL who, in July 1962, alerts

SUPERGIRL to the true explanation behind the senseless acts of destruction being committed by SUPERMAN (S No. 154/2: "Krypton's First Superman!"). (*See* MAG-EN.)

LONG, LYDIA. A television reporter on the planet Oceania who bears a striking resemblance to LOIS LANE and who plays a role in the life of Chester King, the man who is secretly HYPER-MAN, which closely parallels that played by Lois Lane in the life of Clark Kent, the man who is secretly SUPERMAN. Lydia Long marries King following his forced retirement from crime-fighting, and remains his wife until his death a year later from zoronite poisoning (Act No. 265, Jun '60: "The 'Superman' from Outer Space!"). (*See* HYPER-MAN.)

LOOK-ALIKE SQUAD, THE. An organization in the bottle city of KANDOR which is composed of individuals who are perfect look-alikes for SUPERMAN's closest friends (Act No. 309, Feb '64: "The Superman Super-Spectacular!"). Members of the Look-Alike Squad include Vol-Don, CLARK KENT's Kandorian double; Zol-Lar, JIMMY OLSEN's Kandorian double; and Ar-Rone, PERRY WHITE's Kandorian double (S No. 177/1, May '65: "Superman's Kryptonese Curse!"; and others). When METROPOLIS television station WMET-TV inaugurates its new "Our American Heroes" series with a program honoring Superman, "our greatest American hero," the Look-Alike Squad appears on the show along with Superman's other friends and admirers to help pay tribute to the Man of Steel (Act No. 309, Feb '64: "The Superman Super-Spectacular!").

LORI (the Mermaid). *See* LEMARIS, LORI.

LORING, EMIL. A megalomaniacally "brilliant architect-scientist"—driven, by feelings of inferiority about his own "dwarfed size," to the erection of "tremendous structures," but widely scorned for his scheme to construct "a modern tower of Babel" extending far beyond the clouds—who has secluded himself for years in the African jungle and acquired an army of slave laborers in order to construct "the most ambitious edifice of all time"—the "greatest structure in the planet's history"—as "an everlasting monument to my architectural genius!" Not content merely to erect the world's tallest edifice, however, Loring has vowed to obliterate mankind's most spectacular architectural triumphs—including the PYRAMIDS of Egypt, the WASHINGTON MONUMENT, the MOUNT RUSHMORE NATIONAL MEMORIAL, and the STATUE OF LIBERTY—to assure that they will "no longer exist to mock me with their perfection!" SUPERMAN thwarts Loring's scheme of destruction in January 1943, and Loring dies beneath the rubble of his own mighty tower when the unexpected eruption of a long-slumbering volcano—inadvertently caused by a barrage of artificial lightning-bolts with which Loring had attempted to annihilate the Man of Steel—sends it crashing down on the maniacal architect (Act No. 56: "Design for Doom!").

LOUIS XIV (1638–1715.) The king of France from 1643 until his death in 1715. BATMAN, ROBIN, and

Cornered by Superman in 1939, Lubane accidentally shatters a tube of deadly poison gas...

...and perishes horribly amid the asphyxiating fumes

Superman, however, remains unharmed, for "the gas doesn't affect [his] physical structure"

SUPERMAN meet Louis XIV and expose the treachery of his "evil chancellor" BOURDET during a time-journey to France in the year 1696 (WF No. 82, May/Jun '56: "The Three Super-Musketeers!").

LUBANE. A ruthless "munitions magnate" who deliberately promotes wars and bloody conflicts throughout the world in order to reap lavish profits from "the death and misery of others." His headquarters is a sprawling munitions factory in far-off Boravia, "a small country," apparently European, which is "exhausting its life blood in [a] senseless civil war" brought about by Lubane's evil machinations. Flying to Boravia in Fall 1939, after a gang of vicious international "armament racketeers" in Lubane's employ have brutally murdered PROF. ADOLPHUS RUNYAN and stolen the secret formula for his dread new poison gas, SUPERMAN demolishes Lubane's munitions factory with a barrage of "aircraft bombs," brings an end to Boravia's senseless civil war by threatening to kill the opposing negotiators unless they agree to resolve the conflict forthwith, and cables the METROPOLIS police to apprehend Prof. Runyan's murderers. Cornered finally by Superman, Lubane dies when, "in his excitement," he shatters a tube of the new poison gas and perishes horribly in a cloud of asphyxiating fumes (S No. 2/2: "Superman Champions Universal Peace!").

LURA (Queen). The lovely blond ruler of MISTRI-LOR who, surrounded by a plethora of "handsome muscular men" in her exotic "lost civilization," falls instantly in love with mild-mannered Clark Kent when he arrives there after a long journey by balloon—accompanied by JIMMY OLSEN and LOIS LANE—in March 1963. Narrowly avoiding marriage to the love-struck queen in his Clark Kent identity, SUPERMAN remains in Mistri-Lor long enough to thwart a series of attempts by the ruthless Prince Vikar, "the most powerful prince in the realm," to assassinate the queen and, as next in line to her throne, establish his dominion over her kingdom (Act No. 298: "Clark Kent, Coward!"). The story is in many respects similar to Superman No. 67/2 (Nov/Dec '50: "The City Under the Sea!"). (See PARALEA [QUEEN].)

LURING (Dr.). A "great astronomer" who, having observed through his telescope that a certain "distant sun emits radiations of a strange, unknown type," asks SUPERMAN to help make a valuable contribution to science by flying to one of the planets of the distant sun and depositing some data-gathering instruments on the planet's surface so that they can "record the strange radiations of the sun and telemeter the data back to [Dr. Luring] by radio!" The routine space mission becomes a living nightmare for Superman, however, when mysterious "stellar processes" taking place inside the distant sun suddenly transform it from a yellow sun into a red one, thus depriving Superman of his super-powers before he can flee the alien solar system and leaving him stranded, equipped only with the powers and abilities of an ordinary mortal, on a "cold, wild planet" inhabited by a tribe of brutal cavemen. Alone and vulnerable on this "bleak, cruel world," Superman is lashed by a dust storm, frozen by the cold, beaten to a pulp by a pair of savage cavemen, and ravaged by a virus that afflicts him with fever and delirium, until finally JIMMY OLSEN, LOIS LANE, and Dr. Luring come to his rescue in an "experimental missile" and carry him back to the more hospitable environment of the planet Earth. "It was a terrible ordeal," muses Superman aloud, "but maybe it was worth it--to teach me what it's like to be weak and helpless! I'll never forget it!" (S No. 171/3, Aug '64: "The Nightmare Ordeal of Superman").

LUTHOR, LEX. The "warped scientific genius" who has been SUPERMAN's "most dangerous enemy" (WF No. 88, May/Jun '57: "Superman's and Batman's Greatest Foes!") for nearly four decades. An "evil genius" (Act No. 271, Dec '60: "Voyage to Dimension X!") and avowed "enemy of humanity" (Act No. 294, Nov '62: "The Kryptonite Killer!"), he is "the greatest renegade scientist of all time" (WF No. 62, Jan/Feb '53: "The Seven Secrets of Superman") and one of "the most dangerous evil-doers in the universe" (Act No. 294, Nov '62: "The Kryptonite Killer!").

Lex Luthor in prison, 1959

In an early encounter with Superman, Luthor describes himself as "Just an ordinary man— but with th' brain of a super-genius!" (Act No. 23, Apr '40), yet the texts portray him as a "crazed scientist" (S No. 34/3, May/Jun '45: "When the World Got Tired!") and "master-fiend" (S No. 17/4, Jul/Aug '42: "When Titans Clash!"), a "wily scientific genius" (S No. 167, Feb '64: "The Team of Luthor and Brainiac!" pts. I-III—"The Deadly Duo!"; "The Downfall of Superman!"; "The Hour of Kandor's Vengeance!") with a "consuming urge to conquor [sic] the world" (S No. 48/1, Sep/Oct '47: "The Man Who Stole the Sun!"). "Throughout the years," notes Action Comics No. 318, "Superman has had one supreme enemy...the criminal scientist, Lex Luthor!" (Nov '64: "The Death of Luthor!").

A power-mad, evil scientist, **Superman's** most inveterate hater, is **Luthor**. He could have been a mighty force for good in the world yet he chose to direct his great scientific brain into criminal channels [Act No. 47, Apr '42: "Powerstone"].

Although Superman clearly considers Luthor one of "the world's greatest scientists" despite the fact that he is a criminal (S No. 168, Apr '64: pts. I-II—"Luthor--Super-Hero!"; "Lex Luthor, Daily Planet Editor!"), the Man of Steel has also described Luthor as a "madman" and a "fiend" (Act No. 23, Apr '40) and numbered him among "the world's worst villains" (Act No. 286, Mar '62: "The Jury of Super-Enemies!"). SATURN QUEEN has described Luthor as "Superman's greatest foe" (S No. 147/3, Aug '61: "The Legion of Super-Villains!"), and LOIS LANE has referred to his "brilliant and twisted mind" (Act No. 156, May '51: "The Girl of Steel!"). "With that fantastic brain of his," reflects CLARK KENT in September 1962, "**Luthor** is a menace to the entire universe!" (Act No. 292: "When Superman Defended His Arch-Enemy!").

"...[O]f all **Superman's** foes," notes Action Comics No. 294, "none is more relentless than **Luthor**, Earth's most evil criminal scientist! Luthor's driving ambition has always been to enslave the Earth, but **Superman** has always stood in the way" (Nov '62: "The Kryptonite Killer!").

Luthor, "an indomitable villain" (Act No. 318, Nov '64: "The Death of Luthor!") gifted with "one of the most brilliant minds of the age" (S No. 164/1, Oct '63: pts. I-II—"The Showdown Between Luthor and Superman!"; "The Super-Duel!"), is "cunning and diabolical" (S No. 31/1, Nov/Dec '44: "Tune Up for Crime!"); "power-crazed" (Act No. 141, Feb '50: "Luthor's Secret Weapon") and "evil" (Act No. 151, Dec '50: "Superman's Super-Magic Show!"; and many others); "warped" and "sinister" (S No. 68/1, Jan/Feb '51: "The Six Elements of Crime!"); "mad" (Act No. 183, Aug '53: "The Perfect Plot to Kill Superman!"; and many others) and "distorted" (S No. 74/1, Jan/Feb '52: "The Lost Secrets of Krypton!"); "vain" (Act No. 183, Aug '53: "The Perfect Plot to Kill Superman!") and "dangerous" (Act No. 257, Oct '59: "The Reporter of Steel!"; and many others). Action Comics No. 286 describes him as one of "the most evil geniuses who have ever lived in the past, present or future...!" (Mar '62: "The Jury of Super-Enemies!").

For years, **Lex Luthor** has been **Superman's** arch-foe! Time and again has this master-criminal used his scientific genius to aid the forces of evil! But in spite of the incredible dangers, **Superman** has always managed to bring Luthor to justice! [Act No. 292, Sep '62: "When Superman Defended His Arch-Enemy!"].

"Mankind lost a great benefactor," notes Superman No. 43/3, "when Luthor, power-mad scientist, turned his genius to crime!" (Nov/Dec '46: "The Molten World!").

In his earliest appearances in the chronicles,

Luthor has a full head of bright red hair (Act No. 23, Apr '40; and others), although in one text his hair is colored a dark, purplish gray (S No. 5/3, Sum '40). From May-June 1941 onward, however, Luthor is portrayed as completely bald-headed (S No. 10/1), an aspect of his physical appearance which he retains to this day. In the early 1960s, however, after the history of Luthor's relationship with Superman has been drastically revised in the chronicles to allow for the creation of adventures pitting Luthor against the Man of Steel during the period when both men were teen-agers, it is stated that Luthor's baldness was originally caused by an accidental laboratory explosion that occurred while the two were still youngsters in Smallville. "My arch-enemy, **Luthor**, might have been the world's greatest benefactor!" sighs Superman aloud in November 1962. "But he lost his hair in an accidental explosion and blamed me for his baldness! In his bitterness he became Earth's most evil criminal scientist!" (Act No. 294: "The Kryptonite Killer!").

The texts describe Lex Luthor as a man of "insane

*Lex Luthor as he appeared with a
full head of hair in 1940...*

*...and as he appeared the following year,
without hair, in 1941*

conceit" (Act No. 277, Jun '61: "The Conquest of Superman!") and "incredibly evil features" (Act No. 42, Nov '41). Particularly in his early appearances, he is unbelievably ruthless. In Spring 1940, for example, Luthor deliberately blows up an autogyro filled with his own henchmen in order to prevent the Man of Steel from trailing it to his hideout (S No. 4/1), and in September-October 1941 he disposes of some unwanted "former allies" by having them "ruthlessly destroyed by...voracious monsters" (S No. 12/4).

Luthor's lifelong goal has always been "mastery of the world" (Act No. 47, Apr '42: "Powerstone"; and many others) as the first stage of his even grander scheme "to dominate the universe" (S No. 43/3, Nov/Dec '46: "The Molten World!"; and others). Described as "the mad scientist who plots to dominate the Earth" (S No. 4/1, Spr '40), and as "the super-scientist who aspires to world domination" (Act No. 42, Nov '41), Luthor has a driving "ambition to rule the Earth" (S No. 170/2, Jul '64: pts. I-II—"If Lex Luthor Were Superman's Father!"; "The Wedding of Lara and Luthor!") and to establish himself as undisputed "world dictator" (S No. 48/1, Sep/Oct '47: "The Man Who Stole the Sun!"). "...[B]efore I'm done," vows Luthor in November 1962, "the universe will tremble at the name of Lex Luthor!" (Act No. 294: "The Kryptonite Killer!").

On more than one hundred separate occasions, Superman has intervened valiantly to thwart Luthor's seething ambition for absolute power. And so, "...for years and years, Luthor has been Superman's arch-enemy, stooping to any lengths to destroy the Man of Steel he so bitterly hates!" (S No. 149, Nov '61: pts. I-III—"Lex Luthor, Hero!"; "Luthor's Super-Bodyguard!"; "The Death of Superman!").

Luthor has described Superman as "my most hated enemy" (Act No. 146, Jul '50: "The Statues That Came to Life!"), and the texts repeatedly refer to Luthor as Superman's "greatest foe" (S No. 17/4, Jul/Aug '42: "When Titans Clash!"), "arch-enemy" (Act No. 166, Mar '52: "The Three Scoops of Death!"; and many others), "sworn enemy" (Act No. 292, Sep '62: "When Superman Defended His Arch-Enemy!"), "bitterest enemy" (Act No. 254, Jul '59: "The Battle with Bizarro!"), "greatest enemy" (S No. 164/1, Oct '63: pts. I-II—"The Showdown Between Luthor and Superman!"; "The Super-Duel!"), and "deadliest foe" (Act No. 141, Feb '50: "Luthor's Secret Weapon"; and others).

In addition to the hatred he harbors for Superman, Luthor also seethes with hostility toward Superman's friends. "I'm also going to...destroy *Clark Kent!*" he vows in March 1952, unaware that Clark Kent and Superman are one and the same man. "He's the one who exposes all my rackets in his newspaper articles...!" (Act No. 166: "The Three Scoops of Death!").

In a dream he has in June 1961, Luthor invades the offices of the DAILY PLANET and uses one of his diabolical inventions to reduce Lois Lane, JIMMY OLSEN, and PERRY WHITE to lilliputian size, a fitting vengeance, muses Luthor, on the "little minds th[at have] dared to challenge my giant intellect!" (Act No. 277: "The Conquest of Superman!"). And in October 1964, after having forged a temporary alliance with the space villain BRAINIAC, Luthor sets out to murder Lois Lane and LANA LANG in order to wreak revenge on the Man of Steel (S No. 172: pts. I-III—"The New Superman!"; "Clark Kent—Former Superman!" "The Struggle of the Two Supermen!").

In his effort to destroy Superman and thereby pave the way for his conquest of the universe, Luthor has created "luthorite" (*see* LUTHORITE), synthesized KRYPTONITE, and produced dozens of extraordinary inventions which are described in detail in the following pages. He has, however, despite his genius, shown scant insight into the vast difference in values that sets him irrevocably apart from his super-powered opponent. "I'm locked up in this cage, but he roves the whole world!" broods Luthor bitterly in October 1963, while serving one of his numerous terms in prison. "He...Superman...the man who put me here because he's really jealous of my scientific genius, which I use for crime!" (S No. 164/1: pts. I-II—"The Showdown Between Luthor and Superman!"; "The Super-Duel!").

In the course of nearly four decades of villainy, Luthor has employed numerous secret hideouts and headquarters—places where he could perfect his diabolical inventions and concoct his intricate schemes, safe, at least for a time, from the prying eyes of Superman. Over the years, Luthor's hideouts have included a complex of buildings held aloft by a giant dirigible "high above Earth in the stratosphere" (Act No. 23, Apr '40); a "glass-enclosed city of ancient, weird design" (*see* PACIFO) (S No. 4/2, Spr '40); a hidden cavern (S No. 10/1: May/Jun '41); a "strange, fantastic city, floating in the stratosphere" (Act No. 42, Nov '41); an abandoned factory (S No. 17/4, Jul/Aug '42: "When Titans Clash!"); a gigantic man-made meteor floating in outer space (S No. 18/2, Sep/Oct '42: "The Heat Horror"); an abandoned barn (S No. 31/1, Nov/Dec '44: "Tune Up for Crime!"); a "secret underground lab" (S No. 43/3, Nov/Dec '46: "The Molten World!"; and others); a giant spaceship (S No. 48/1, Sep/Oct '47: "The Man Who Stole the Sun!"); a secret mountaintop laboratory (Act No. 125, Oct '48: "The Modern Nostradamus!"; and others); STANDARD ELECTRONICS PRODUCTS, an electronics firm (Act No. 156, May '51: "The Girl of Steel!"); a "hidden laboratory" on the outskirts of METROPOLIS that is described as "a monument of distorted genius" (S No. 74/1, Jan/Feb '52: "The Lost Secrets of Krypton!"); a "laboratory hideout" that has been "lined with lead to conceal it from Superman's X-ray vision" (Act No. 166, Mar '52: "The Three Scoops of Death!"); a massive fortresslike citadel on a lonely mountaintop overlooking Metropolis (S No. 79/1, Nov/Dec '52: "Citadel of Doom!"); a lonely farmhouse in the mountains north of Metropolis (S No. 90/3, Jul '54: "The Titanic Thefts!"); a secret lead-lined subterranean hideout built into the side of a grassy hill (S No. 164/1, Oct '63: pts. I-II—"The Showdown Between Luthor and Superman!"; "The Super-Duel!"); and, finally, the elaborately equipped LUTHOR'S LAIR (Act No. 277, Jun '61: "The Conquest of Superman!"; Act No. 292, Sep '62: "When Superman Defended His Arch-Enemy!"), LUTHOR'S LAIR II (S No. 167, Feb '64: "The Team of Luthor and Brainiac!" pts. I-III—"The Deadly Duo!"; "The Downfall of Superman!"; "The Hour of Kandor's Vengeance!"), and LUTHOR'S LAIR No. 5 (S No. 170/2, Jul '64: pts. I-II—"If Lex Luthor Were Superman's Father!"; "The Wedding of Lara and Luthor!").

Aliases and alternate identities employed by Luthor in the course of his villainous career have included ZYTAL (Act No. 42, Nov '41), "THE LIGHT" (S No. 13/1, Nov/Dec '41), CARLYLE ALLERTON (S No. 17/4, Jul/Aug '42: "When Titans Clash!"), MR. SMITH (S No. 79/1, Nov/Dec '52: "Citadel of Doom!"), PROFESSOR CLYDE (Act No. 254, Jul '59: "The Battle with Bizarro!"), PROF. GUTHRIE (WF No. 104, Sep '59: "The Plot to Destroy Superman!"), the DEFENDER (S No. 168, Apr '64: pts. I-II—"Luthor--Super-Hero!"; "Lex Luthor, Daily Planet Editor!"), and LUTHOR THE NOBLE (S No. 170/2, Jul '64: pts. I-II—"If Lex Luthor Were Superman's Father!"; "The Wedding of Lara and Luthor!").

In the space of nearly four full decades, Luthor has fought more than one hundred separate battles with Superman. Superman's mementoes of these mighty battles—including confiscated weapons, inventions, and other devices—are on display in the FORTRESS OF SOLITUDE (Act No. 241, Jun '58: "The Super-Key to Fort Superman"; and others), and the SUPERMAN MUSEUM (S No. 126/1, Jan '59: "Superman's Hunt for Clark Kent!"; and others). At least one of Luthor's inventions—a device designed "to summon beings from the fourth dimension"—is on display in the Fortress of Solitude's "forbidden weapons of crimedom" exhibit (Act No. 241, Jun '58: "The Super-Key to Fort Superman"), while four of his "super-scientific weapons"—a "money magnet," a "vault-blaster," an "earthquake maker," and an "atomic death ray"—are on display, along with a bust of Luthor, in the Fortress's "wax museum of crime" (Act No. 249, Feb '59: "The Kryptonite Man!"). In November 1962, when Superman puts the finishing touches on the Fortress of Solitude's new Hall of Enemies, Luthor is among the villains represented there by colorful wax busts (Act No. 294: "The Kryptonite Killer!"). On the far-distant planet LEXOR, "the one world in the universe where [Luthor is] considered a hero" (S No. 167, Feb '64: "The Team of Luthor and Brainiac!" pts. I-III—"The Deadly Duo!"; "The Downfall of Superman!"; "The Hour of Kandor's Vengeance!"), Luthor's exploits have been glorified by the dedication of a LUTHOR MUSEUM and by the erection of a gigantic standing statue of Luthor in Lexor's capital city (S No. 168, Apr '64: pts. I-II—"Luthor--Super-Hero!"; "Lex Luthor, Daily Planet Editor!").

Luthor's living relatives include his Lexorian wife

ARDORA (Act No. 318, Nov '64: "The Death of Luthor!") and his blond sister Lena Thorul, who is gifted with the power of extrasensory perception. His descendants include the ruthless ROHTUL, a villain living in the thirtieth century A.D. (WF No. 91, Nov/Dec '57: "The Three Super-Sleepers!"). Superman encounters a lifelike android of Luthor during a time-journey to Metropolis one million years in the future (Act No. 300, May '63: "Superman Under the Red Sun!"), and Superman and BATMAN encounter a lawman named Lex Luthor—a perfect look-alike for Superman's notorious adversary—during a visit to an extradimensional "parallel world" in March 1965 (WF No. 148: "Superman and Batman--Outlaw!" pts. I-II—"The Evil Superman and Batman"; "The Incredible New Super-Team!").

Ardora and Luthor, 1964

Although Superman first encounters Luthor in April 1940, when both men are full-grown adults (Act No. 23), the chronicles are revised years later to extend the relationship between the two adversaries all the way back to their boyhood in SMALLVILLE. According to this revised version, Superman and Luthor were close boyhood friends (S No. 173/2, Nov '64: "Tales of Green Kryptonite No. 1"; and others) until the day when Luthor lost his hair in an accidental laboratory mishap that he misguidedly blamed on the teen-aged Superman. "In his bitterness," Luthor became "Earth's most evil criminal scientist" (Act No. 294, Nov '62: "The Kryptonite Killer!") and the "greatest enemy" Superman has ever known (S No. 164/1, Oct '63: pts. I-II—"The Showdown Between Luthor and Superman!"; "The Super-Duel!").

"Ever since they first clashed as boys in Smallville," notes Superman No. 170/2, "**Superman** has time and again thwarted the evil schemes of his archfoe, **Lex Luthor**" (Jul '64: pts. I-II—"If Lex Luthor Were Superman's Father!"; "The Wedding of Lara and Luthor!").

In addition to the various descriptive expressions enumerated above, the texts also refer to Luthor as a "master criminal" (S No. 17/4, Jul/Aug '42: "When

Titans Clash!"), a "mad scientist" (S No. 31/1, Nov/Dec '44: "Tune Up for Crime!"), a "crazed scientist and evil genius" (S No. 34/3, May/Jun '45: "When the World Got Tired!"), a "power mad scientist" and "mad criminal of science" (WF No. 28, May/Jun '47: "Superman's Super-Self!"), an "arch-scientist of crime" (Act No. 131, Apr '49: "The Scrambled Superman!"), a "criminal genius" (Act No. 141, Feb '50: "Luthor's Secret Weapon"), a "renegade master of science" (Act No. 151, Dec '50: "Superman's Super-Magic Show!"), a "criminal wizard of science" (S No. 68/1, Jan/Feb '51: "The Six Elements of Crime!"), a "scientific arch-wizard of crime" (Act No. 156, May '51: "The Girl of Steel!"), a "criminal scientist" (Act No. 166, Mar '52: "The Three Scoops of Death!"), a "mad genius of science" (Act No. 183, Aug '53: "The Perfect Plot to Kill Superman!"), a "renegade mastermind of science" (S No. 88/3, Mar '54: "The Terrible Trio!"), a "super-scientific arch-enemy of the law" (S No. 90/3, Jul '54: "The Titanic Thefts!"), a "brilliant criminal scientist" (Act No. 199, Dec '54: "The Phantom Superman!"), a "sinister mastermind" (S No. 117/2, Nov '57: "The Secret of Fort Superman"), a "scientific genius of crime" (WF No. 94, May/Jun '58: "The Origin of the Superman-Batman Team!"), a "cunning scientific genius" (Act No. 241, Jun '58: "The Super-Key to Fort Superman"), a "criminal mastermind" (Act No. 249, Feb '59: "The Kryptonite Man!"), "the world's most dangerous outlaw" (Act No. 257, Oct '59: "The Reporter of Steel!"; and others), "the world's most dangerous criminal" (Act No. 267, Aug '60: "Hercules in the 20th Century!"; and others), "the world's most dangerous criminal scientist" (Act No. 292, Sep '62: "When Superman Defended His Arch-Enemy!"), "the master-scientist and master-criminal of the age" (S No. 167, Feb '64: "The Team of Luthor and Brainiac!" pts. I–III—"The Deadly Duo!"; "The Downfall of Superman!"; "The Hour of Kandor's Vengeance!"), and a "master scientist-criminal" (S No. 170/2, Jul '64: pts. I–II—"If Lex Luthor Were Superman's Father!"; "The Wedding of Lara and Luthor!").

In April 1940, while attempting to bring a halt to the bloody war raging between the nations of GALONIA and TORAN, Superman intimidates one of the opposing generals—"Either answer my question," demands Superman, **"or have your brains dashed out against that wall!"**—into revealing that "a fiend named Luthor deliberately fomented this war" as part of his heinous scheme "to engulf the entire [European] continent in bloody warfare." Superman presses the general for more information, but before the terrified army officer has had a chance to reply, "a green ray stabs out" from a nearby outcropping of rock and "slices the stricken general in half . . . !"

Soon afterward, Superman leaps high into the air to destroy an airborne "squadron of unidentified planes" en route "to invade and bombard a nearby [neutral] country," a ploy by Luthor to draw yet

another nation into the Galonian-Toranian war. In his Clark Kent identity, Superman pleads with Galonian and Toranian officials to end the conflict, arguing that ". . . this war is being promoted by a madman who wishes to destroy both warring nations," but the dignitaries on both sides refuse to believe him.

And so, soon afterward, Superman confronts Luthor in his stronghold, a complex of buildings held aloft by a giant dirigible "high above Earth in the stratosphere." "What sort of creature are you?" demands Superman. "Just an ordinary man," replies Luthor, "—but with th' brain of a super-genius! With scientific miracles at my fingertips, I'm preparing to make myself supreme master of th' world!"

Hurling himself at Luthor and his henchmen, Superman demolishes the mad scientist's arsenal of awesomely destructive weapons and then races to the giant dirigible's control room, where he "turns to the great mechanism that keeps the dirigible afloat . . . and tears it apart with his bare hands!"

"As the great dirigible topples toward the distant Earth" with Luthor and his henchmen still trapped inside it, Superman leaps to safety on the ground below. "And that's th' end of Luthor!" remarks Superman grimly.

A short while later, as Clark Kent, Superman again addresses the assembled representatives of the two warring nations. "You've seen the strange dirigible that fell from the sky," he argues. "Now do you believe my contention that a fiend named Luthor deliberately fomented this war for evil purposes?" This time, the dignitaries believe him, and before long an armistice has been signed, bringing a peaceful end to the conflict (Act No. 23).

Luthor (on TV screen) communicates with one of his henchmen, 1940. Note that this henchman closely resembles Lex Luthor as he is portrayed from mid-1941 onward

By Spring 1940 Luthor has kidnapped PROFESSOR MARTINSON, the inventor of an awesome "new weapon . . . which artificially causes earthquakes," as the first step in his scheme to steal the "earthquake machine" and use it to blackmail the Earth into submission. In order to keep Superman preoccupied elsewhere while he and his henchmen steal the machine from a U.S. Army compound, Luthor challenges Superman to a series of titanic contests, pitting his own scientific genius against Superman's awesome superhuman strength. Superman wins the contest and achieves the release of Professor Martinson, but Luthor and his cohorts escape with the earthquake machine, ravage Metropolis with a terrible man-made earthquake, and then brazenly demand "the city's surrender!"

Via closed-circuit television, Luthor spies Superman eavesdropping outside his secret laboratory, 1940

Lex Luthor, 1940

Superman ultimately defeats Luthor and his minions, demolishes the villain's laboratory stronghold, and destroys the earthquake machine. Luthor, however, manages to escape, and Professor Martinson, remorseful over having created such a hideous weapon, commits suicide (S No. 4/1). Soon afterward, Superman races to the Oklahoma oil fields to investigate reports that "oil wells throughout the world have stopped flowing," and then continues on to the West Coast after being informed that "the entire Pacific coast is inundated under two feet of water and the ocean is steadily rising!"

Superman's attempt to uncover an explanation of these disastrous phenomena leads him ultimately to Luthor's stronghold (*see* PACIFO), a "glass-enclosed city," located somewhere in the Pacific Ocean, which can be raised to the surface and then submerged like a submarine.

"You'll admit it was a miraculous achievement!" boasts Luthor. "Working underwater, I raised a glassolite-dome over the city, drained out the water, then raised the city to the surface of the ocean."

"Then it was this titanic underwater upheaval that caused the ocean to overflow!" exclaims Superman. "...And it was you who tapped the oil-wells and stole the oil for your evil purposes!"

In his laboratory aboard the submergible city, Luthor has successfully re-created hideous "biological monstrosities of the past." "Loosed upon the world," gloats Luthor, "they will break its spirit, enabling me to bring it under my domination!"

Luthor offers to hold back his monsters in exchange for Superman's assistance in conquering the world, but Superman rejects the offer, defeats the madman and his henchmen, and destroys the submergible city by demolishing the glass dome and allowing the ocean to go rushing in.

As the text draws to a close, Luthor's biological monstrosities have turned on their creator and it appears as though the villainous scientist is doomed (S No. 4/2, Spr '40).

In Summer 1940 "an unexpected wave of unemployment hits the country as millions suffer from hunger, business staggers, and the United States is faced with the worst depression in its history!" Assigned to cover the crisis for the *Daily Planet*, Clark Kent detects a strange odor in the offices of America's financial leaders and soon learns that the odor is that of "a narcotic incense Luthor [has] placed in the offices of prominent men throughout the nation, thus enslaving them."

"So--Luthor is still alive and plotting the downfall and subjugation of present day civilization!" muses Superman grimly. "The world will never be safe until that fiend is destroyed--and somehow, I've got to accomplish it!"

With the nation's financial leaders completely under his control, Luthor is causing nationwide hunger and unemployment while at the same time reaping untold profits through intricate stock-market manipulations. When Superman finally confronts the madman, he attempts to escape in a private plane, but Superman leaps high into the air to intercept the craft and moments later "the plane is destroyed in a head-on collision with Superman!" "The end of Luthor!" remarks Superman grimly.

Before long, Luthor's victims have been cured of their addiction to his diabolical narcotic incense. "Most important of all," observes Clark Kent, "is that the menace is removed--and that the nation is returning to its former prosperity!" (S No. 5/3).

In May-June 1941 Luthor uses his amazing scientific prowess to halt the flow of water in the city of Metropolis—causing numerous citizens to die of thirst and bringing the life of the city to an agonized

Lex Luthor challenges Superman to a series of titanic contests, pitting his own scientific genius against Superman's awesome superhuman strength, 1940

halt—as a prelude to demanding $100,000,000 in tribute, money which Luthor and his lone accomplice—a man named Bob Dunning—urgently need in order "to cover up [their] fake stock manipulations." Superman's efforts to apprehend the villains are stymied for a time by Luthor's new-found technique for making himself invisible, but the Man of Steel ultimately confronts his adversaries, takes Bob Dunning into custody, and pursues Luthor as he flees in a bizarre rocket-powered vessel. Before Superman can overtake the craft, however, Luthor somehow renders the craft invisible and disappears into thin air (S No. 10/1).

By September-October 1941 Luthor has assembled a crew of scientists on far-off BARACODA ISLAND who, through "experiments with the omega rays," have succeeded in creating fearsome "gigantic animals" with which Luthor intends "to conquer the world and set up a scientific dictatorship." Indeed, by cunningly promising each of the scientists that it is he who will "rule...the scientific civilization to be launched," Luthor has succeeded in duping some of the world's most prominent scientists into helping him achieve his dictatorial ambitions.

Lex Luthor attempts to annihilate Superman, 1941

Superman first becomes alerted to the threat when one of the project's scientists escapes to Metropolis to warn the world of impending disaster. "I tell you," he exclaims frantically to Clark Kent and Lois Lane, "--there's a terrible menace back on *Barracoda Island* --a black plot that threatens to launch upon the world a horror such as it has never known...we've got to stop it before it's too late!"

In the words of the textual narrative:

Fantastic rumors emerge from a far-off island-- rumors of incredible scientific feats and unbelievable monstrosities. When Clark Kent and Lois Lane take on

the task of checking up on these rumors, they little realize the maze of startling adventure they are entering--or that SUPERMAN, amazing *Man of Steel*, is to make his appearance and fight scientific horror in his inimitable dynamic manner!

Arriving on the island to investigate these rumors of "voracious monsters" being "bred there deliberately to attack the world," Superman soon finds himself locked in a deadly struggle with Luthor. As Superman smashes through the wall of the villain's laboratory, where Lois Lane is being held hostage, Luthor lunges madly for a secret lever, shrieking that he intends to "destroy us all." But, "snatching up Lois, Superman leaps high up into the sky as the entire island blows into smithereens...." "The end of Luthor!" murmurs Superman (S No. 12/4).

In November 1941, "when a number of the world's most powerful intellectuals suddenly vanish from sight," Superman decides to investigate. One night, after Clark Kent has gone to sleep, "several stealthy figures creep into his bedroom," clamp a chloroform-soaked handkerchief over his mouth, and then carry him to an autogyro waiting on the roof. "Up--up rises the mysterious autogiro high into the stratosphere," and when Clark Kent finally "glances out the window, he glimpses a startling sight--a strange, fantastic city, floating in the stratosphere...."

As he is being led by his captors through the city's streets, Kent comes upon two of the missing intellectuals, who inform him that they have come to the city of their own free will and have no desire whatever to leave it. Moments later, inside "the city's governing building," Kent is ushered into the presence of Zytal, a long-haired man in a red gown, seated atop a high, thronelike chair. "Welcome to the 'Empire City in the Sky', Clark Kent," proclaims Zytal. When Kent asks why he and the other intellectuals have been brought to the Empire City, Zytal replies that

To answer that, I must go back in my explanation to an occurrence of centuries ago. I am from another universe, Kent. I have always possessed a tremendous thirst for knowledge.

Hundreds--nay, thousands of years ago, I felt that I had accumulated all the knowledge I could find upon my old world, so I constructed this flying city and set forth to explore the universe with it.

In each of the worlds I explored, I selected a group of the world's most superior men to join me in my quest for knowledge. You should feel honored to be among the chosen.

"That's why those men are content to remain here," adds one of Kent's abductors. "They are anxious to join Zytal in his exploration of infinity itself!"

"Led to a magnificently furnished apartment" which is destined to be his home in the strange, floating city, Clark Kent peers into Zytal's private suite with his X-ray vision and watches with horror as Zytal removes a lifelike face mask to reveal "the incredibly evil features of--**Luthor**, the super-scientist who aspires to world domination...!"

"Simple to trick those gullible fools!" exclaims Luthor aloud, not realizing that he is being overheard through the walls by Superman's super-hearing. "After they disclose their private business secrets to me, I can dispose of them--and make use of the information any way I choose!"

Superman crashes into Luthor's suite, determined to bring the mad scientist to justice, but Luthor throws a hidden switch and suddenly "the Man of Steel is bombarded by a terrific wave of electricity" that paralyzes him completely and places him under Luthor's mental control, the victim of a diabolical form of "electrical hypnosis."

"You'll find you can't move unless I will it!" gloats Luthor. "You see, I've discovered many things about the mysterious force called electricity!"

Luthor commands Superman to return to Earth and divert public attention from his own diabolical activities by wreaking havoc there with his super-powers. For a time, Superman carries out Luthor's orders, but ultimately, by means of a supreme mental effort, the Man of Steel shakes off the baleful effects of Luthor's "electrical hypnosis treatment" and streaks back to the floating city for a final confrontation with Luthor. Cornered, and determined not to allow himself to be taken alive, the mad scientist sends his flying city hurtling toward the ground and then makes an apparently suicidal leap into midair. Superman catches the falling city and lowers it gently to the ground—thereby rescuing its inhabitants from seemingly certain doom—but the evil scientist Luthor has apparently perished (Act No. 42).

In November-December 1941 Luthor, employing the alias "The Light," begins kidnapping prominent men "by the dozen" as part of his latest scheme to "seize control of this nation...." Taken captive by "The Light's" henchmen—whose gunlike "light-rods" give off rays of blinding light, and whose automobile is equipped with special headlights that give off "a brilliance of such stark, blinding qualities that the human eye instantly can detect nothing more than a white haze"—the victims are taken to "The Light's" subterranean hideout, where they are seated in a steel chair and forced to gaze at "a blaze of blinding brilliance" emanating from a weird machine. "Gradually," notes the text, "the beam changes colors,—blue, red, orange, green, yellow, purple," while "The Light" whispers to his victims hypnotically, "robbing [them] of all initiative," placing them completely under his hypnotic control.

When Superman invades "The Light's" subterranean stronghold, the villain paralyzes him with "vari-colored beams of light" produced by a bizarre "mechanism," and, after placing the Man of Steel under his mental control, commands him to "completely destroy any military materials that may be used against me!" Just as the hypnotized Superman is on the verge of destroying a government armory, however, Lois Lane pleads with him not to commit

Lex Luthor as "The Light," and Superman, 1941

the evil act, a plea that fortifies Superman's willpower and enables him to throw off the effects of "The Light's" hypnosis. Streaking back to the villain's hideout, Superman demolishes the diabolical hypnotizing machine, frees the villain's captives, and apprehends his henchmen. In the midst of the melee, "The Light" escapes, but not before he has unmasked for Superman, revealing, for the first time, that the mysterious "Light" is none other than Lex Luthor (S No. 13/1).

By April 1942 Luthor has created a gigantic electrical dynamo capable of endowing him with superhuman strength as well as with bizarre electrical powers. "As **Luthor** flings a switch, the apparatus hums into operation...then, to the accompani-

"The Light" unmasks, 1941

ment of ear-shattering cracklings and blinding flashes, the powerful voice of **Luthor** booms out!"

"You see," cries Luthor, "...millions of volts of electric current are sweeping thru [sic] my body--yet I'm unharmed! But most astonishing of all...this electric treatment imparts to me **amazing strength!**

"Yes, I've succeeded in achieving powerful strength! Time and time again **Superman** has balked my ventures because I could not cope with his terrific strength. I wracked my brains for the answer-- and found it in **electricity!**"

"Then you mean, boss," interjects a henchman, "that you're now as strong as **Superman**, that you can jump thru [sic] the sky, lift a locomotive, use your skin as a target for bullets...?!"

"No," replies Luthor. "Tho [sic] I have terrific strength, unfortunately my powers are still not equal to those of **Superman**. But there's a chance of my becoming so--it involves possession of the **powerstone**--and **Superman** is the only one who can help me in that respect...."

In addition to giving him superhuman strength, Luthor's incredible dynamo has also endowed him with extraordinary electrical powers. One night soon afterward, for example, "...availing himself of the immense electrical power stored within his figure, **Luthor** burns his way thru [sic] a bank's metal door" and strolls unimpeded into the vault. The night watchman on duty courageously attempts to inter- vene, but, "Next instant, as **Luthor** unleashes the electrical power within him, the watchman is shocked into insensibility...."

When Superman arrives on the scene, Luthor uses his awesome electrical powers to stop the Man of Steel in his tracks. "My entire body....tingling...." exclaims Superman. "I can hardly move...." "You see," gloats Luthor, "...I now have the power of **electricity** on my side!" Superman manages to shake off the electrical paralysis, but Luthor escapes.

Not long afterward, at a gathering of Metropolis's wealthiest men, Luthor, employing his mind- staggering powers, "gives vent to a gigantic electrical display that shocks everyone but himself into unconsciousness...." When Superman attempts to intervene, Luthor threatens to electrocute Lois Lane—who is on hand to cover the gathering for the *Daily Planet*—unless Superman agrees to do him "a slight favor."

"Hidden in the lost mountain of *Krowak* in *Skull Valley*," explains Luthor, "is the **powerstone**, an ancient gem which I covet--for **sentimental** reasons. I'd go myself, but the trip is too, er, dangerous. Bring the **powerstone** to me and I will release my captives unharmed."

And so Superman journeys to far-off Skull Valley in quest of the powerstone, which lies embedded in the forehead of a gigantic stone idol, the remnant of a long-forgotten "ancient civilization." To reach the idol and obtain the powerstone, Superman must crash through the side of a mountain, plow through molten metal, race through "a chamber filled with

hypnotically swaying snakes," and then continue on "thru [sic] an adjoining chamber, [where] **Superman** finds eerie flames licking at his consciousness, sapping at his intelligence...."

But Superman overcomes all these obstacles, finally plucking the powerstone from the forehead of the idol before returning home to Metropolis to confront Luthor and demand the release of his hostages. "*Hahaha*-haaa!" laughs Luthor insanely, the powerstone finally in his grasp. "Poor stupid fool! Do you realize what you've done? You've given me the **powerstone**--a stone from another planet with scientific properties that will give me powers as great as, even *greater*, than yours! Release them? Naturally not. Now that I have the **powerstone**, I've the power to defy you successfully!

"....Now go," cries Luthor, "...before I blast you out of existence. I'd do it anyway, but it will be much more interesting to observe your helplessness while I secure mastery of the world!"

"So you're master of the situation, eh?" replies Superman as he lunges for Luthor. "Well, suppose I let you in on a secret. That's not the **powerstone** you're holding, but an imitation I fashioned myself before coming here. The real **powerstone** I've hidden where you'll never find it!"

Believing he possesses the "powerstone," Lex Luthor gloats insanely, 1942

The ensuing battle between Superman and Luthor is a brief one, for Luthor's superhuman strength must be periodically renewed by means of a powerful electrical charge, and before long it has ebbed and then faded completely. "When the effects of my electrical treatment wear off, as they just have," whines Luthor, "my strength returns to that of an ordinary human. I won't possess super-strength again until I get another electric-treatment."

"And unless I miss my guess," adds Superman, "the law will see to it that that will be **never!**" (Act No. 47: "Powerstone").

By July-August 1942 Luthor has been sentenced to death in the electric chair for his crimes, but seconds after the executioner has thrown the death switch, sending a massive charge of electric current surging through Luthor's body, Luthor snaps the leather straps binding him to the chair and rises defiantly to his feet. "You fools!" cries Luthor. "That great charge of electricity was just what I needed to restore my incredible strength! You've freed me, and now nothing can stop me--nothing!"

Lex Luthor in the electric chair, 1942. The witness at left is Clark Kent

Posing as Carlyle Allerton, "prominent authority on ancient stones and their mystic powers," Lex Luthor tricks Superman into bringing him the "powerstone"...

As the villain tears his way through the prison's massive stone walls to freedom, prison guards blaze away at him with their pistols, but "the electrical force emanating from the master criminal's figure repels their bullets," and when the guards attempt to surround him, Luthor "shocks them into insensibility" with his awesome electrical powers.

A short while later, concealing his true identity beneath a clever disguise and adopting the alias of Carlyle Allerton, "prominent authority on ancient stones and their mystic powers," Luthor tricks Superman into bringing him the powerstone for examination. No sooner is the powerstone safely in his grasp, however, than "Carlyle Allerton" rips off his disguise to reveal the evilly triumphant face of Luthor. "How does it feel to be tricked by so simple a ruse?" cries Luthor mockingly. Superman lunges at Luthor, determined to apprehend him, but now that he possesses the powerstone, Luthor's powers are even greater than Superman's. "You see," gloats Luthor, "the powerstone imparts to me infinite power beyond the reach of a mere super-human!"

Now Luthor flies out the window with Superman in hot pursuit. Using his awesome new powers to increase his body to gigantic size, Luthor rips a bridge loose from its moorings and hurls it at Superman,

...then rips off his disguise to reveal the evilly triumphant face of Luthor, 1942

who suddenly discovers, to his astonishment, that he no longer has the strength even to extricate himself from the wreckage. "Do you yet understand?" cries Luthor. "The powerstone has enabled me to rob you of your mighty powers! I could crush you between these two fingers, but it will be more amusing to watch you fume helplessly while I achieve mastery of the Earth!"

With Superman now deprived of his invulnerability as well as his super-strength, Luthor launches a wave of brazen kidnappings of America's most prominent men as the first phase of his scheme to conquer the nation and, ultimately, the world. By means of an elaborate ruse, however, Superman succeeds in regaining possession of the powerstone, thereby draining Luthor of his awesome powers while simultaneously recovering his own. Then, with the powerstone safely in his grasp, the Man of Steel apprehends Luthor and his henchmen and frees the kidnapped national leaders (S No. 17/4: "When Titans Clash!").

In September-October 1942, operating from his hideout inside a huge man-made meteor adrift in outer space, Luthor uses three gigantic magnifying lenses to focus the heat of the sun on the city of Metropolis, thereby producing a brief but stifling heat wave there as part of his fiendish scheme for "looting the deserted city without opposition" once Metropolis has been evacuated. When Superman invades the villain's meteor hideout, Luthor paralyzes him with his diabolical "freezing-ray," an "ultra-cold ray...capable of freezing anything," then focuses his gigantic lenses on Metropolis once again, determined to obliterate the city and everyone in it.

Meanwhile, however, "straining with all his might, Superman seeks to throw off the effects of the cold ray...!!" Ultimately, he succeeds, and within moments he has defeated Luthor and his henchmen, smashed Luthor's lenses, and nullified the effects of Metropolis's new heat wave by focusing Luthor's "cold ray" on the city. Luthor flees his hideout in a one-man rocket ship, but the craft collides with a streaking meteor and Superman soon heads homeward, believing Luthor dead. Luthor, however, has survived the crash and vows to return again to make yet another bid for universal power. "Once again the Man of Steel has upset a carefully laid plan!" fumes Luthor. "One of us must die--and it will not be Luthor!" (S No. 18/2: "The Heat Horror").

Lex Luthor vows vengeance on Superman, 1942

In November-December 1944 Luthor and his henchmen commit a series of spectacular crimes in which they use a gigantic tuning fork, "at least fifty feet high," to transmit powerful sound vibrations to smaller tuning forks planted beforehand in the places they intend to rob, as when they loot the vault at the Midtown Bank of $500,000 by placing a small tuning fork inside the vault and then reducing the vault to "a heap of broken metal" by striking the gigantic tuning fork back at their hideout. In Luthor's words:

>...my new weapon is **vibration!** You've heard, of course, how an army of troops will break step when crossing a bridge, for the hammering beat of the incessant marching step would send the bridge crashing!
>
> My weapon works on the same principle! A giant tuning fork that sends out vibrations in an ever widening circle...vibrations that are received by small tuning forks of the same tonal pitch, which then sends [sic] concentrated vibrations coursing through buildings, safes, anything!

When Superman invades Luthor's secret hideout, the mad scientist attempts to destroy the Man of Steel by tying a small tuning fork around Superman's neck and then striking the giant tuning fork with all his might. In the words of the textual narrative, "...terrible vibrations multiplied a thousand times, tear, pound, rip, claw at the **Man of Steel**," but Superman remains "indestructible," and ultimately he succeeds in demolishing the gigantic tuning fork and in apprehending Luthor and his henchmen (S No. 31/1: "Tune Up for Crime!").

By May-June 1945 Luthor has joined forces with a pair of evil extraterrestrial aliens named Koda and Goki, once the "supreme rulers" of the "doomed" planet Attar, in an elaborate scheme to seize control of the United States by using the aliens' diabolical "inertia ray" to cause a nationwide "inertia epidemic"—an epidemic of lassitude in which people will become "so tired and lazy, they'll be glad to transfer all responsibilities," both economic and political, into the hands of the villains.

"Amazing! Almost unbelievable!" exclaims Luthor when he first witnesses the ray's effects. "Our men should have no trouble at all in securing a strangle-hold on the nation!" Luthor and his extraterrestrial allies have not reckoned, however, on the intervention of Superman, and before long the Man of Steel has succeeded in undoing the baleful effects of the interia ray and in apprehending Luthor's henchmen. Luthor manages to escape, but Koda and Goki commit suicide by blowing up their spacecraft rather than submit to capture and imprisonment. "It's all over! It's for the best!" muses Superman as he watches the aliens' spacecraft explode in a shower of debris. "They would have never fitted in with the future of the common man that's coming!" (S No. 34/3: "When the World Got Tired!").

By January-February 1946 Luthor has successfully perfected "the most potent weapon ever invented," a diabolical "molecular impulsion beam"—or "molecular propulsion beam"—which, fired from special "ray projectors" mounted aboard his "strange aircraft of transparent metal," has the power to melt steel, concrete, and even solid rock as well as to twist trees, buildings, and other objects into weirdly "distorted shapes." *"Ho, ho, ho!"* gloats Luthor exultantly. "The world at my feet! Wealth beyond the wildest imaginings of ordinary stupid men! . . . And sudden death for **Superman** if he should dare to interfere with this final flowering of my genius!"

Lex Luthor in his "secret underground workshop," 1946

When Luthor uses his terrible new weapon to melt the Daily Planet Building and virtually everything inside it, Clark Kent uses his super-powers to repair the damage and restore things to normal, but he is clearly dismayed by the awesome power of Luthor's latest invention. "Only one thing could cause this," he muses grimly, "—an atomic disturbance speeding up molecular motion in steel and stone, making them fluid! Intense heat would have that effect—or a beam of concentrated vibrations! And only one man could harness such a beam—Luthor!"

A short while later, when Superman streaks into the sky to intercept Luthor's aircraft, the mad

Luthor prepares to obliterate Superman with his diabolical "molecular impulsion beam," 1946

scientist turns his deadly beam on Superman determined to "blast him into eternity—and be rid of him for good!" As the beam strikes Superman, "a crackling roar echoes across the sky," and "Superman—no longer Earth's mightiest warrior—drops like a stone!"

Hurtling helplessly toward the ground below, Superman lands atop the condenser of a Metropolis power plant, and, "a split second later, millions of volts flash instantaneously through every nerve and fiber of **Superman's** body," restoring the Man of Steel to consciousness. Cornered finally by Superman aboard his aircraft, Luthor unleashes an "atomic bomb" the size of a hand grenade, but Superman easily withstands the impact of the mighty blast and swiftly takes his arch-enemy into custody (S No. 38/1: "The Battle of the Atoms!").

By November-December 1946 Luthor has broken out of prison and applied his scientific genius to the creation of luthorite, an amazing "new metal" which Luthor describes as the "hardest and strongest [metal] of all!" After using their meager supply of the rare new metal to coat the drill-pointed front end of Luthor's "wormcar," a weird cigar-shaped vehicle designed for burrowing through the earth, Luthor and his henchmen use their bizarre vehicle to commit a series of spectacular crimes in order to accumulate the scarce materials needed for the production of more luthorite. "So far, only the drill-point of my wormcar is of luthorite," explains Luthor to his henchmen, "but if I can armor-plate the whole car, I'll defy the world! . . . I can build irresistible weapons and impenetrable space ships to dominate the universe!"

For a time the wormcar crimes continue unabated, as when the villains burrow their way into the vault of the Third National Bank, but Superman ultimately destroys the wormcar with blows of his mighty fists and takes Luthor and his henchmen into custody (S No. 43/3: "The Molten World!").

By May-June 1947 Luthor has invented a miraculous "life ray," a gigantic device, shaped roughly like a huge flashlight, whose bizarre "many-colored light" has the power to bring inanimate objects to life for as long as the life ray continues to shine on them. Using his new device—which also enables Luthor to control the actions of the newly animated objects by means of his "thought-waves"—Luthor and his henchmen commit a series of spectacular crimes, as when they animate a pair of marble lions adorning the main entrance of the Metropolis Public Library and command them to smash the window of a jewelry store where rare gems are on display, but Superman ultimately destroys Luthor's life ray and takes the villains into custody (WF No. 28: "Superman's Super-Self!").

A text for September-October 1947 recounts an attempt by Luthor to blackmail the nations of the world into naming him "world dictator" by cutting off Earth's sunlight and plunging the entire planet into total darkness. "Using [a] giant space ship as his operating base," Luthor "rotates about the sun setting up a great force-barrier composed of compressed atoms, between Earth and sun, through which light cannot pass!" In addition, Luthor has equipped his spacecraft with a pair of gigantic magnifying lenses through which Luthor can focus the sun's rays anywhere he chooses, creating a mammoth "heat ray" of awesomely destructive power.

When the President of the United States rejects Luthor's ultimatum to surrender control of the entire country into his hands within four hours, Luthor responds by focusing the sun's rays on the Atlantic Ocean near Metropolis, sending a colossal wall of boiling water sweeping toward the city. Superman stems the boiling tidal wave and saves Metropolis, only to have Luthor threaten to burn the entire North American continent to a cinder unless America surrenders within one hour's time. Before the madman can carry out his threat, however, Superman smashes the giant lenses, destroys the great force-barrier holding back Earth's sunlight, and, moments later, apprehends Luthor (S No. 48/1: "The Man Who Stole the Sun!"). Although this text is dated September-October 1947, the actual adventure is set in summertime.

By October 1948 Luthor has concocted an elaborate scheme designed to enable him and his henchmen to loot Metropolis. The scheme involves duping an elderly hermit into believing that he has unearthed a centuries-old scroll containing a series of previously undisclosed prophecies of the French astrologer Nostradamus (1503-1566). When the hermit visits Metropolis and announces the newly discovered "prophecies," Luthor and his henchmen contrive to make them come true, as when they fire a projectile disguised as a meteor at the Daily Planet Building in apparent fulfillment of the hermit's prophecy that a fiery meteor will soon strike "a planet." Once the hermit has acquired a reputation for accuracy by making a series of correct predictions, Luthor plans for him to predict a devastating earthquake and then to loot Metropolis with his henchmen once the city has been evacuated, but Superman sees through the scheme and apprehends Luthor and his cohorts. As for Luthor's dupe, the innocent hermit, he will be given a job as weather forecaster for the *Daily Planet*. "That's the only way to predict the future," remarks Superman, "with scientific instruments!" (Act No. 125: "The Modern Nostradamus!").

In March-April 1949 Luthor sets in motion an elaborate scheme designed to enable him to loot Metropolis of a fortune in diamonds by tricking the populace into believing that their city is being invaded by gigantic robots—called "machine-men"—from the planet MARS. The scheme involves broadcasting a bogus television-news report which claims that gigantic machine-men from outer space, having arrived on Earth in quest of diamonds, are destroying the town of Northville, not far from Metropolis. When the so-called machine-men—in reality harmless metal figures, controlled by Luthor's henchmen

riding inside them—invade Metropolis, the city's terrified citizens surrender every diamond they own in an effort to placate the "aliens," but Superman arrives on the scene in time to demolish the machine-men, apprehend Luthor and his cohorts, and recover the diamonds before the villains can escape with them (S No. 57/1: "The Menace of the Machine Men!").

In April 1949 Luthor unveils "his newest invention for crime"—the "atom scrambler," an ingenious device with which Luthor can "project any solid object into the 4th dimension—and reassemble its atoms anywhere in the world!" Using the atom scrambler, Luthor launches a wave of spectacular crimes, as when he uses it to transport the money stacked in a bank vault through the fourth dimension to his laboratory hideout. The villain enjoys his sweetest triumph, however, when he uses his invention to exile Superman into the fourth dimension, where the Man of Steel finds himself transformed into an invisible phantom, existing only as "a cloud of disembodied molecules!" Trapped in the fourth dimension and unable to return, Superman manages to communicate his predicament to Lois Lane, who courageously invades Luthor's laboratory hideout and activates the atom scrambler in order to return the Man of Steel to the earthly dimension. Now safely restored to the world of three dimensions, Superman apprehends Luthor and his henchmen and demolishes the atom scrambler. "It's too dangerous to let exist!" comments Superman (Act No. 131: "The Scrambled Superman!").

In February 1950 Luthor kidnaps Lois Lane and holds her hostage at his laboratory hideout in order to force Superman to gather the following "inaccessible materials" for what the villain describes to Superman only as "an important invention": "a mammoth pearl from one of the giant oysters miles down under the sea"; "a couple of handfuls of dust from the dark side of the moon"; "pollen from the man-eating homocessandi plant deep in the Asiatic jungles"; and "a bit of the rare chemical binarium, preserved in the soil by a thousand years of glacial frost."

After Superman has successfully accumulated the "strange materials" and returned to Luthor's hideout, Luthor orders his hostage released, but by ingeniously fusing the bizarre ingredients obtained by Superman, Luthor produces a deadly chunk of synthetic kryptonite—"Synthetic kryptonite! My dream has been fulfilled!" exclaims the villain exultantly—and then, leaving Superman "half-paralyzed" by its baleful radiations, races off triumphantly to loot the Metropolis Bank. Although the Man of Steel manages to escape the kryptonite deathtrap and arrives at the Metropolis Bank in time to thwart the robbery, Luthor escapes capture, and a short while later he recovers the chunk of synthetic kryptonite from his laboratory and surreptitiously places it inside Lois Lane's handbag, apparently in the hope that Superman will visit her at the *Daily Planet* and once again fall victim to its baleful radiations. Moments later, on the street outside the Daily Planet Building, Luthor is apprehended by Clark Kent. The chunk of synthetic kryptonite, however, is not immediately recovered, for it is stolen from Lois Lane's handbag by a Metropolis pickpocket (Act No. 141: "Luthor's Secret Weapon"). (See DAN THE DIP.)

By July 1950 Luthor has invented a miraculous "life-ray gun"—or "life-gun"—a raygunlike device with which he can bring inanimate objects to life for brief periods of time. "Science tells us that all matter consists of atoms!" explains Luthor. "My life-ray gun fuses those atoms into an activated mass of pseudo-protoplasm! In simple language, I can bring inanimate objects to life!"

After using his device to animate the STATUE OF LIBERTY on Bedloe's Island, the pair of stone lions adorning the main entrance of the Metropolis Public Library, and the statue of General Jackson in the city park, Luthor threatens to "force Superman to destroy the Metropolis dam and flood the city" unless the city meets his demand for $10,000,000. When, at Superman's urging, the mayor of Metropolis rejects Luthor's ultimatum, the villain animates the colossal statue of Superman overlooking Metropolis Harbor and uses it to make good his threat to demolish the dam, but Superman rebuilds the shattered dam at super-speed—thereby averting the threatened flood—and swiftly apprehends Luthor and his henchmen (Act No. 146: "The Statues That Came to Life!"). The story is in many respects similar to World's Finest Comics No. 28 (May/Jun '47: "Superman's Super-Self!"), which has been summarized previously in this article.

In December 1950 Luthor joins forces with the PRANKSTER and MR. MXYZPTLK in a scheme to make Superman the laughingstock of Metropolis (Act No. 151: "Superman's Super-Magic Show!"). (See MXYZPTLK [MR.].)

In January-February 1951, in anger at the prestigious Chemical Society for removing his name from its membership list because of his criminal record, Luthor sets out to prove that he is "the greatest of all chemists" by using the chemical elements "to compound crimes that will make [his] name remembered forever!" Luthor's scheme involves employing various chemical elements—elements whose initial letters, taken together, will spell out the name Luthor—in the commission of a series of spectacular "chemical crimes." For their first crime, Luthor and his henchmen smash a pillar at the Museum of Science with a massive lead ball, then escape with samples of various elements on display there while Superman is preoccupied holding up the building's collapsing roof. To stymie the Man of Steel even further, the villains plant some stolen uranium in the car of an innocent bystander, so that Superman will waste his energy pursuing an innocent party while the criminals make good their escape. Later, Luthor and his cohorts wangle their way into the Federal Electric Company—to stage a platinum heist—by

duping company officials into believing that they ar interested in selling the firm tungsten. And for thei next crime, the villains divert Superman's attentior with a flaming hydrogen-filled balloon and incapaci tate the drivers in a crowded tunnel with oxyger intoxication so that they can loot an armored payrol car driving through the tunnel. Perceiving the pattern to these recent crimes, however, and realizing that the next crime is likely to involve the theft of radium from Metropolis's "famous radium institute," Superman fashions a vault for the institute's radium out of "invulnerable" SUPERMANIUM, and, a day later, after the villains have tried without success to break their way into the impenetrable vault, easily takes Luthor and his henchmen into custody (S No. 68/1: "The Six Elements of Crime!").

By May 1951 Luthor has completed construction of an ingenious machine—a so-called "vivanium machine"—capable of making anyone temporarily "as powerful as *Superman!*" Snooping around Luthor's hideout—an electronics firm called Standard Electronics Products—in hopes of unearthing information about the mad scientist's latest invention, Lois Lane throws the machine's master switch in an effort to ascertain the complex machine's true function ("Suddenly--a low hum--a flashing of lights—and Lois feels her whole body tingling strangely..."), thereby endowing herself with temporary super-powers, including super-strength, super-speed, and the power of flight. In the hours following her amazing transformation, Lois fashions herself a colorful blue-and-red costume modeled closely after Superman's and, concealing her true identity beneath a blond wig and employing the name Superwoman, begins using her newly acquired abilities to perform super-heroic feats. Lois's well-intentioned efforts at being a super-heroine, however, prove generally inept, because, in Superman's words, "She doesn't have the skilled control necessary to direct her strength," and because "not knowing how to control super-power is worse than [having] no power" at all.

Luthor, meanwhile, having learned that the newly emerged Superwoman is actually Lois Lane, concocts an elaborate scheme to dupe her into using her super-powers to build him a new vivanium machine, for in using the first machine to endow herself with super-powers, Lois "used up the precious power-giving vivanium the mechanism operates on," and it would take Luthor months to rebuild the machine on his own. Luthor successfully tricks Superwoman into rebuilding his device, but Superman arrives on the scene and apprehends the villain—in the process destroying Luthor's last remaining supply of the scarce substance vivanium—before the madman has had the opportunity to use his super-power machine on himself.

"Oh--I'm so glad to be just plain Lois Lane again," exclaims Lois moments later, after her artificially acquired super-powers have faded and vanished, "now that I've learned how useless super-power is thout the wisdom to use it!" (Act No. 156: "The Girl Steel!").

In July-August 1951, operating from a secret ountaintop laboratory not far from Metropolis, uthor uses his latest diabolical contrivance to dry up he world's oceans and rivers in an attempt to ackmail the world's governments into paying him 0,000,000 in gold for the return of their water. In uthor's words:

...[T]his great apparatus can project two new rays I've discovered, over all Earth! One is a **precipitation ray!**...The other ray, which it's now broadcasting, is an **evaporation ray!**

Every day, millions of tons of water evaporate from the oceans and lakes into the air! But later, they're precipitated as rain and run back into the sea!

My evaporation ray **speeds up evaporation** all over the world! And no rain can fall until I turn on my precipitation ray! With this machine, the world is at our mercy!

After drying up Earth's rivers and oceans with his fiendish "evaporation ray," Luthor broadcasts his demand for $10,000,000 "to a panicky, thirst-stricken world," 1951

Through an elaborate ruse, however, Superman tricks Luthor into shutting off his evaporation ray and turning on his precipitation ray, thereby producing a torrential rainfall that swiftly replenishes Earth's parched oceans and rivers. Then Superman

apprehends Luthor and his henchmen and demolishes Luthor's ray-machine. "**Superman's** greatest monument will always be these," remarks an unidentified citizen standing on a Metropolis beach, "--the oceans that he brought back to the world again!" (S No. 71/3: "The Man Who Stole the Oceans!").

In January-February 1952 Luthor trains his new "magnet-ray machine" on the heavens in hopes of attracting a kryptonite meteor to use against Superman, only to discover that his apparatus has drawn a far different object to Earth—a massive vault, once the property of Superman's father, JOR-EL, that has been whirling through outer space since the explosion of the planet KRYPTON. "I, Jor-El, have gathered in this vault my greatest scientific powers," reads an engraved inscription, "that they may survive to benefit other men even though our own world must die!"

Inside the vault, Luthor finds a treasure trove of amazing inventions: a "petrifying ray" with the power to turn people to stone for as long as it shines on them, "levitation bombs" designed to reverse the pull of gravity and make objects fall upward, a "super-artificial lightning projector" for projecting bolts of artificial lightning, an "invisibility-spray" which can make a person invisible by covering him with "a fine coating of light-refracting particles," and a magnet that attracts human flesh instead of iron. In addition, the vault contains a mystery invention whose powers are not specified. "Beware of the dread power of this machine!" reads the cryptic inscription. "Turn it on only if you desire power over all men!"

Luthor is elated with his unexpected find. "With these mighty powers," he gloats exultantly, "I can crush **Superman** if he dares oppose me--and can dominate the world!"

In the hours that follow, Luthor and his henchmen use Jor-El's great inventions to strike terror into the people of Metropolis, as when they send an entire skyscraper hurtling skyward with one of their levitation bombs and attempt to shatter Metropolis's municipal government buildings with bolts of artificial lightning. Ultimately, however, Superman defeats Luthor by deliberately goading him into activating his father's mystery invention, the one whose inscription promises its user "power over all men." For although Superman does not know the true nature of the machine any more than Luthor does, he has the firm conviction that "No man who tried to benefit other men, like Jor-El, would ever help a would be tyrant to dominate them!"

Indeed, no sooner has the renegade scientist turned on the machine, than the face of Jor-El materializes on the device's televisionlike screen and a spray of special gas from inside the machine knocks Luthor unconscious. "You turned on this machine because you desired power over all men!" intones the recorded voice of Superman's father. "But I, Jor-El do not intend that my secrets shall ever be used by power-lusting plotters to dominate their brothers! So I included this machine as a safeguard against ambitious plotters like you! And this gas from it will make you helpless to work evil!"

"These inventions could have wreaked havoc on Earth," remarks Superman moments later, as he replaces Jor-El's inventions inside the vault and prepares to hurl them back into outer space, "--but I can't destroy my father's dreams! I can see that they're safe again in their vault! And that vault goes back again into space, whence it came! Someday, my father, when men are able to use your lost secrets wisely, they will be found again!" (S No. 74/1: "The Lost Secrets of Krypton!").

By March 1952 Luthor and his henchmen have kidnapped Perry White and replaced him with a lifelike robot look-alike as part of an elaborate scheme to keep Superman so busy protecting Lois Lane while she carries out a series of hair-raisingly dangerous reportorial assignments that the Man of Steel will be unable to prevent the villains from committing a series of spectacular crimes. "I'm also going to use the robot to *destroy Clark Kent!*" vows Luthor. "He's the one who exposes all my rackets in his newspaper articles...but I intend to see him executed for the *murder of Perry White*...a crime for which I will give him the perfect motive!"

This second, and more complex, part of Luthor's scheme involves the concoction of an elaborate scenario designed to make it appear that Clark Kent has deliberately staged a bogus act of heroism in an unscrupulous attempt to win the coveted Wilson Award, being offered by civic leader Cyrus Wilson to "the bravest reporter of the year." After cunningly impeaching Kent's journalistic integrity and having the robot Perry White fire Kent for bringing disgrace to the journalistic profession, Luthor and his henchmen plan to shoot the real Perry White and frame Clark Kent, making it appear that Kent murdered his boss in anger at having been dismissed from his job. Superman thwarts the murder attempt, however, and apprehends Luthor and his henchmen (Act No. 166: "The Three Scoops of Death!").

In July-August 1952 Luthor and his henchmen steal the super-powerful "Morven magnet"—a magnet "1,000 times more powerful than any other ever built"—from the laboratory of its inventor, DR. CHARLES MORVEN, and attempt to use it to commit a series of spectacular crimes, as when they mount it in a helicopter and use it to pull an entire armored car high into the air, and when they train it on a platinum-carrying vessel in order to make the vessel run aground. Superman's efforts to apprehend the villains are severely hampered by the fact that Luthor and his cohorts have tricked him into lifting up a gigantic model of the Earth—a huge globe "packed with the most powerful explosives and poison-gas chemicals known to man"—which he now cannot set down again without unleashing a horrendous catastrophe. Despite this handicap, however, Superman successfully thwarts Luthor's robberies, tricks the renegade scientist into rendering the globe

harmless, and then swiftly takes the villains in custody (WF No. 59: "Superman's Super Hold-Up!"

In November-December 1952, after constructing massive fortresslike citadel on a mountaintop nea Metropolis, Luthor sets in motion an elaborate hoa designed to trick "some of the richest men in th country" into believing that a "dark star" passin by Earth's solar system is about to unleash a wave o cataclysmic disasters—such as earthquakes, tida waves, meteor showers, and volcanic eruptions—an that his mountaintop citadel will be the only saf place on Earth. By showing his victims bogus film footage of Superman unsuccessfully battling on catastrophe after another only to be buried aliv beneath a shower of meteors, Luthor terrifies hi wealthy "clients" into signing over half their pro perty to him in return for the right to remain sheltere inside his stronghold. Superman apprehends Lutho and his henchmen, however, and forces them t dissolve the "contracts" signed by their victims (S No. 79/1: "Citadel of Doom!").

In January-February 1953 Luthor and his hench men invade the laboratory of Professor Willis Wilton in an attempt to steal Wilton's extraordinary "four dimensional projector," a device "that can send an object instantly to any place, or draw it back." But Wilton has taken the wise precaution of inscribing a fraction of the secret formula for his invention on each of seven pieces of microfilm and then of using his apparatus to consign the scraps of microfilm to seven virtually inaccessible places, including the top of Mt. Everest; Mindanao Deep, in the North Pacific; a crater on the MOON; the African desert; the South Pole; a giant atomic energy plant, described as "a place of such dangerous radiation that no ordinary human can go amid [its] great atomic piles"; and, lastly, the heel of Superman's boot, perhaps the safest hiding place of all.

Holding Lois Lane hostage in his secret hideout laboratory, Luthor attempts to force the Man of Steel to obtain the various microfilm fragments for him, but, by means of an elaborate ruse augmented by some super-ingenuity, Superman apprehends Luthor and his cohorts and rescues Lois Lane from the villains' clutches (WF No. 62: "The Seven Secrets of Superman").

In March-April 1953 Superman completes construction of an armada of colossal machines designed to help the people of Metropolis cope with catastrophes after he has passed away. Intended to be kept secret until after Superman's death and then willed to Metropolis as his final bequest, the machines include a gigantic pump for combatting floods, a guided missile for destroying hurtling meteors, a giant digging machine for emergency excavations, great dynamos and light globes to provide emergency lighting, and an emergency fire extinguisher that sprays forth vast clouds of carbon dioxide gas.

After learning of the existence of these mighty machines, however, and after stealing the secret radio codes used to operate them by radio-remote-control, Luthor and his henchmen attempt to use the devices to commit a series of spectacular crimes, as when they try to use Superman's meteor missile to shoot a planeload of gems out of the sky, and when they drain an entire river with the giant pump in an attempt to loot a grounded liner. For a time, Superman's colossal machines wreak havoc in Metropolis, but the Man of Steel manages ultimately to deactivate his machines and apprehends Luthor and his henchmen (S No. 81/1: "Superman's Secret Workshop").

In August 1953 Luthor orders his henchmen to carry out a series of seemingly senseless attacks on Superman—with pistols and other metal weapons— as part of an intricate scheme to destroy Superman with kryptonite. In Luthor's words:

> Each piece of metal that strikes **Superman's** invulnerable body undergoes a slight chemical change! To a minute degree, it acquires the properties of kryptonite, but its presence is so faint that it can only be detected by means of a spectroscope!
>
> Kryptonite is the one material that can harm **Superman!** By refining tons of this metal, I'll be able to extract kryptonite---just as radium is obtained by refining tons of uranium ore!

By arranging for Superman to be hit by countless bullets and other metal objects, and by appearing on the scene soon afterward to gather up the spent bullets, knives, and other weapons that have struck Superman's body, Luthor is soon able to refine a beaker of "pure kryptonite" liquid, which he then molds into a casing for a special anti-Superman artillery shell. When Superman swoops down on Luthor's mountaintop stronghold in response to the villain's brazen public challenge to "a battle to the death," Luthor has his henchmen shoot Superman out of the sky with his kryptonite-encased shell and then shuts the Man of Steel inside a rocket and launches him into outer space. Although still badly weakened by the effects of the kryptonite, Superman nevertheless manages to escape his rocket prison, and soon he returns to Luthor's fortress and apprehends the mad scientist and his henchmen (Act No. 183: "The Perfect Plot to Kill Superman!").

In November-December 1953, after falsely claiming to have been "cured of [his] criminal tendencies forever" by a delicate surgical operation performed on his brain, Luthor streaks from place to place in his rocket ship, averting disasters and performing humanitarian deeds—"...[M]y only wish is to make up for the evil work I have done in former days!" claims Luthor—as part of his fiendish scheme to capitalize on his newly acquired acclaim as a hero in order to stage a series of elaborate swindles. At one point, for example, after having deliberately sabotaged the Grand Marnee Dam, Luthor gallantly warns the river valley's residents to evacuate before the impending flood and then "generously" offers to hold onto their valuables "for safekeeping." His suspicions aroused, however, by Luthor's uncanny ability to appear at the scene of every major disaster just before it occurs, Superman investigates, ultimately exposing the "heroic" Luthor and his nonexistent brain operation as an elaborate fraud and apprehending the villain and his cohorts in the act of staging a gem heist (S No. 85/1: "Luthor--Hero!").

In March 1954 Luthor joins forces with the Prankster and the TOYMAN in an elaborate effort to stymie Superman while committing a series of spectacular crimes. The first crime, planned by the Prankster and executed in the Prankster's inimitable prank-filled style, involves the theft of a model of Metropolis Bridge made entirely of precious gems. Superman intervenes to thwart the robbery, however, and the villains are compelled to flee the scene emptyhanded. The trio's second crime, masterminded by the Toyman and carried out with the aid of three ingenious catapults in the form of giant jack-in-theboxes, involves the theft of $1,000,000 from a safe in an upper-story office. Superman arrives on the scene while the burglary is in process, however, and the felons are forced to escape without their loot. The group's third and final crime, plotted by Luthor, involves an attempt to extort $1,000,000,000 from each of the major countries of the world by threatening to destroy their capital cities with fiendish "floating land mines" unless the blackmail is paid. When Superman attempts to thwart this crime, Luthor incapacitates him with synthetic kryptonite and sends him hurtling helplessly into outer space, but the Man of Steel escapes the kryptonite deathtrap and swiftly apprehends Luthor and his two infamous cohorts (S No. 88/3: "The Terrible Trio!").

Lex Luthor, the Toyman, and the Prankster, 1954

By May 1954 the city of Metropolis has been completely evacuated in response to Luthor's terrifying announcement that he has planted a deadly "kryptonite bomb" somewhere in the city which, in an hour's time, will obliterate Metropolis and annihilate Superman. Frantically searching the deserted city for the hidden kryptonite bomb, Superman finally locates it inside a lead container housed in the radium vault at Metropolis Hospital and hurls it into outer space where it can do no harm. And when, soon afterward, Luthor and his henchmen parachute into Metropolis intending to pick the city clean, Superman swiftly apprehends them (S No. 89/3: "One Hour to Doom!").

In July 1954, after his henchmen have planted explosive charges in the world's greatest monuments—including the EIFFEL TOWER, the GREAT PYRAMID at Giza, the LEANING TOWER OF PISA, the SPHINX, the STATUE OF LIBERTY, the TAJ MAHAL, and the TOWER OF LONDON—Luthor forces Superman to transport the monuments to his hideout north of Metropolis and then threatens to destroy them all unless the world's governments agree to pay him $1,000,000 apiece for their safe return. Although temporarily stymied, Superman manages ultimately to defuse the explosives by means of an elaborate ruse and then apprehends Luthor and his cohorts when they attempt to escape (S No. 90/3: "The Titanic Thefts!").

By December 1954 Luthor has created an amazing "phantom Superman"—a "synthetic Man of Steel" subject to Luthor's complete control and endowed with all the super-powers of Superman—as the first step in his fantastic scheme to rule the underworld "as emperor of crime!"

Using his ingenious "three-dimensional materializer," a "queer-looking apparatus" resembling a gigantic bellows camera, Luthor recently produced a life-sized "preliminary negative" of Superman in action, which he in turn fed into his complex "atomic transformer."

"My 3-D materializer does more than photograph the likeness of a person or object!" explained Luthor. "It actually creates duplicate atoms on a specially sensitized sheet! Now I'm putting those atoms through my transformer!"

Indeed, as the atomic transformer began its "fantastic work," Luthor's laboratory came alive with "a strange whirring and buzzing."

"The atoms are glowing with a new life," exclaimed Luthor exultantly, "--and each and every atom is an exact duplicate of Superman! My invention is a success! I've done it! I've created a living duplicate of..Superman!"

Although Luthor's creation is colored only a bleak gray, like a concrete statue come to life, due to the fact that "duplicate atoms cannot transmit colors," the bizarre phantom Superman is, in virtually every other respect, "an exact duplicate of Superman!" "...[S]oon he and I will smash all opposition!" gloats Luthor. "He will help me to rule--as emperor of crime!"

In the days following its creation, the phantom Superman—controlled by means of a special "energizing beam" directed from Luthor's laboratory—commits a series of spectacular crimes, as when it single-handedly demolishes a multimillion-dollar dam after its operators have rejected its demand for $100,000 in extortion. Finally, Luthor summons

"crime chieftains from all over the world" to his hideout and offers them the services of the phantom Superman in exchange for recognition as their leader and fifty percent of their loot, but Superman succeeds ultimately in draining Luthor's creation of its "charge of atomic energy," and then, with the synthetic Superman helpless, swiftly apprehends Luthor and his underworld cronies (Act No. 199: "The Phantom Superman!").

In November 1955 Luthor—disguised in a fake beard, moustache, and toupee—invades the SUPERMAN LAND amusement park on its opening day and, after immobilizing Superman with a chunk of synthetic kryptonite, shuts him inside a rocket about to be launched into outer space. Sent hurtling helplessly into the interstellar void, Superman nevertheless escapes the deathtrap, and within moments he has returned to Earth to apprehend the flabbergasted Luthor (Act No. 210: "Superman in Superman Land").

During this same period, Luthor becomes enraged when, passing by Metropolis's Superman Trophy Hall, he sees workmen carrying in trophy exhibits consisting of devices Superman confiscated from Luthor. "Superman—Our Hero, eh?" muses Luthor, alluding to the massive inscription adorning the Trophy Hall's entranceway. "We'll see about that! I have an idea that will make that building a memorial to my conquests!"

In the days that follow, Luthor commits a series of crimes involving the theft of objects which, taken together, will spell out the humiliating rebus "Superman—Our Blockhead" once the rebus has been completed. Luthor commits his crimes with the aid of devices he calls "hypnotic pinwheels"—whirling blades, or propellers, painted in a unique array of colors. "Simple--but ingenious!" gloats Luthor. "The special arrangement of colors flashes in such a way that it has a hypnotic effect on anyone who looks at it--and stuns him into inaction for a few minutes!"

Indeed, it is not until Luthor is on the verge of completing his rebus—by stealing the "head" from a statue of Superman—that the Man of Steel deciphers the rebus and appears on the scene to take the villain into custody. "If he had added the word 'head' to this rebus," explains Superman soon afterward, "every time people read the inscription Superman--Our Hero--they'd think of Luthor's rebus--'Superman--Our Blockhead!' His rebus crimes would have made a fool of me--and, in his twisted mind, my Trophy Room would have been a tribute to his victory!" (S No. 101/1, Nov '55: "Luthor's Amazing Rebus").

By July 1956 Luthor has invented—and fashioned into a special "metallic suit"—a new metal alloy capable of absorbing and accumulating the energy generated by Superman whenever he performs his super-feats. In Luthor's words:

I invented a new alloy which picks up and stores all the energy Superman generates within a 100-mile area. This metal retains all the energy--like a battery retains

BUT THE PEOPLE ARE ONLY *PARTLY* RIGHT-- FOR THE FULL STORY BEGAN ONE DAY EARLIER, IN THE SECRET LABORATORY OF *LUTHOR,* RENEGADE SCIENTIST AND *SUPERMAN'S* ARCH ENEMY...

MY LATEST INVENTION-- AND WITH IT I INTEND TO RULE THE WORLD! LET ME SHOW YOU WHAT IT CAN DO!

IN THIS BOX, I HAVE A TINY SPECK OF *KRYPTONITE!* NOW WATCH WHAT HAPPENS WHEN I TURN MY *ENLARGER MACHINE* ON IT!

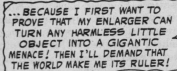

AND AS AN INVISIBLE RAY BATHED THE DUST MOTE...

...LOOK AT IT GROW! WOW! IT'S SO BIG NOW, ITS RADIATION CAN *PARALYZE SUPERMAN!*

YES-- BUT I DON'T INTEND TO USE IT ON HIM YET! RIGHT NOW I'M GOING TO *HIDE* THIS *KRYPTONITE...*

...BECAUSE I FIRST WANT TO PROVE THAT MY ENLARGER CAN TURN ANY HARMLESS LITTLE OBJECT INTO A GIGANTIC MENACE! THEN I'LL DEMAND THAT THE WORLD MAKE ME ITS RULER!

BUT THEY'LL FIGHT YOU... AND SO WILL *SUPERMAN!*

EXACTLY... AND THAT'S WHEN I'LL PARALYZE *SUPERMAN--* AS ULTIMATE PROOF THAT *NOTHING* CAN STOP ME!

B-BUT... SUPPOSING ALL THE COUNTRIES STILL PUT UP A FIGHT, WITH THEIR ARMIES?

THEN I'LL RECRUIT AN ARMY OF *CRIMINALS...* TURN THEM INTO GIANTS, AND MARCH ON EVERY CAPITAL OF THE WORLD!

4

© NPP 1957

In the seclusion of his secret laboratory, Luthor demonstrates his ingenious "enlarger machine," 1957

electricity. The more we make Superman spend his energy, the more he is charging up the alloy in this suit!

"Cripes!" exclaims one of Luthor's henchmen. "Then--you--you'll have super strength!"

"Exactly!" replies Luthor. "These electrodes transmit the energy stored in the metal to me! I'll be as strong as Superman--and as invulnerable!"

In the days that follow, Luthor and his cohorts engineer a series of disasters—including a man-made avalanche and a shower of bogus meteors—calculated to force Superman to expend as much super-energy as possible in the performance of a series of mighty super-feats. Then, after having accumulated several months' worth of super-powers in the metal of his special suit, Luthor embarks on a series of spectacular crimes, easily thwarting Superman's attempts to apprehend him, for the more super-energy Superman expends, the more powerful Luthor becomes. Just when Luthor has begun to appear unbeatable, however, Superman defeats him, draining the villain of his super-strength so that he can be apprehended by the police, through the simple expedient of weakening himself with kryptonite so that this weakness—like his super-strength—will be transmitted to Luthor through his special suit. "Kryptonite--the only substance that can weaken me," explains Superman, "--and--just as I thought--it weakened Luthor, too--for--as I hoped--his metallic suit transmitted my weakness to him, too--just as it picked up my strength!" (S No. 106/3: "The Super-Outlaw of Metropolis").

In January 1957 Luthor sets in motion an elaborate scheme to blackmail the world into making him its ruler by using his newly invented "enlarger machine"—a device capable of enlarging anything to many times its normal size—to transform a series of commonplace creatures and objects into terrifying menaces, as when he causes panic and pandemonium throughout Metropolis by enlarging an ant to gargantuan size. Luthor intends to cap his scheme by paralyzing Superman with a tiny speck of kryptonite dust enlarged to gigantic boulder size, but the Man of Steel reduces the kryptonite boulder back to its original harmless size—and apprehends the renegade scientist and his henchmen—by means of an elaborate ruse accomplished with the aid of a Superman robot (S No. 110/3: "The Defeat of Superman").

In March 1957, after making a detailed spectroscopic analysis of Superman's costume by means of a giant spectroscope of his own invention, Luthor sets in motion an elaborate scheme designed to demoralize Superman while he and his henchmen commit a series of spectacular crimes. "By training certain invisible radioactive beams of light on Superman's costume" with the aid of an ingenious ray-projector, Luthor is able to bring about bizarre chemical changes in Superman's costume, as when he causes the Man of Steel's costume to radiate enormously intense heat, forcing Superman to flee Metropolis to

Lex Luthor fiendishly contemplates his deadly "kryptonite bullet," 1957

avoid melting everything in sight, while Luthor and his henchmen capitalize on his dilemma in order to rob an armored truck. On another occasion, Luthor focuses rays on Superman's costume that cause all the metal in Superman's vicinity to become transformed into soft, pulpy wood, but the Man of Steel soon discovers the hiding place of Luthor's ray-projector and apprehends the mad scientist and his henchmen (S No. 112/2: "Superman's Fatal Costume").

Another text for March 1957 recounts an attempt by Luthor to assassinate Superman with a "kryptonite bullet" fashioned from "a synthetic isotope of kryptonite." Fortunately for Superman, Luthor's kryptonite bullet misses its mark and the Man of Steel easily takes the renegade scientist into custody, but events take a bizarre turn when the bullet intended for Superman accidentally strikes the so-called "petrified spaceman," a giant extraterrestrial alien—a native of a far-distant "ice world," where "people thrive in a sub-zero climate"—who crash-landed on Earth long ago, during a journey through space, and, unaccustomed to the heat of Earth's environment, became "petrified" into a state of "suspended animation." "Shocked back to life" by the "powerful rays" of Luthor's kryptonite bullet, the "giant from space" runs amok on the planet Earth, his "brain...stupefied by the heat," meaning no harm but nevertheless causing panic and mayhem as he lumbers about—attempting desperately to survive in what for him is an alien, hostile environment—until finally Superman takes him in hand and helps him return safely home to the world he left behind in the farthest reaches of outer space (Act No. 226: "The Invulnerable Enemy"). Although this text is dated March 1957, the actual adventure is set in summertime.

In May-June 1957 Luthor sets up a manufacturing

plant in Metropolis in partnership with the JOKER, ostensibly for the legitimate manufacturing and marketing of "mechano-men," ingenious robots made out of a "super-strong metal" developed by Luthor. "Because they [the mechano-men] are invulnerable to any amount of heat and pressure," explains Luthor solemnly, "they can be used for tasks impossible to ordinary workmen!"

The Joker and Lex Luthor, 1957

The real purpose of the mechano-men, however, is to make it possible for Luthor and the Joker to stage an elaborately planned heist at the Subtreasury Building, but Batman, ROBIN, and Superman discover the plot, lull the criminals into false complacency by making it appear that they are occupied elsewhere, and then appear at the Subtreasury Building to apprehend Luthor and the Joker before they can flee with their loot (WF No. 88: "Superman's and Batman's Greatest Foes!").

By November 1957 Luthor has constructed an ingenious "fourth dimensional ray machine" and used it to open a "dimension door" between Earth and the fourth dimension so that a trio of fourth-dimensional outlaws, with whom Luthor has formed an alliance, can enter the earthly dimension to help him loot the Earth. Although Superman swiftly apprehends Luthor and smashes his ray machine, he is unable to prevent Luthor's extradimensional allies from passing through the dimension door and entering Earth. By means of an elaborate ruse, however, involving the construction of a massive fortresslike structure—filled with exotic but dangerous objects—which the aliens attempt, unsuccessfully, to loot, Superman demoralizes the aliens into believing that Earth is a hostile, dangerous place, and they flee in a panic back to their home dimension, vowing never to return again (S No. 117/2: "The Secret of Fort Superman").

In January 1958 Luthor sets in motion an intricately convoluted scheme to destroy Superman and at the same time steal a fortune in charitable contributions scheduled to be entrusted to Superman by public officials. By impersonating Professor Xavier Carlton, "the renowned nuclear scientist," Luthor tricks the Man of Steel into briefly lending him his indestructible costume for use in an atomic experiment, and then, when the time comes to return the super-costume, surreptitiously replaces it with a duplicate made of ordinary material. When, sometime later, after the costume returned to him by "Carlton" has been shot full of bullet holes by gangsters and suffered other unaccustomed damage, Superman returns to "Carlton's" laboratory to complain that his uniform has somehow "lost its invulnerability," the bogus Carlton apologizes profusely, claims that "freakish radiations" from his atomic experiment must have "weakened the very atomic structure of [Superman's] super suit," and offers to make amends for the mishap by collaborating with other scientists to fashion Superman an entirely new costume.

The new costume which "Carlton" designs for Superman—a yellow, maroon, purple, and light-green affair equipped with a transparent space helmet that fits over Superman's head—includes, among its many features, a special "anti-kryptonite belt," which, "Carlton" claims, will render the Man of Steel immune to kryptonite. In reality, however, the belt contains a chunk of kryptonite surreptitiously placed there by Luthor, together with a complex "timing device" designed to unleash the kryptonite radiations—and thus destroy Superman—in a few days' time.

Indeed, several days later, just as Superman is about to be entrusted with a large sum of money earmarked for charity, Luthor—disguised in a Superman face mask and clad in the blue-and-red costume he stole from Superman—appears on the scene and, accusing the yellow-costumed Superman of being an impostor, demands that the charitable contributions be handed over to him. To make matters worse, just as the real Superman is about to perform a super-feat to persuade the public officials that he is not an impostor, the timing device inside his belt releases the kryptonite radiations, sapping him of his super-strength and causing him to collapse in a faint. Aided by his pal Jimmy Olsen, however, Superman succeeds in discarding the bogus anti-kryptonite belt—thereby regaining his full strength—as well as in apprehending Luthor and exposing him as an impostor before the renegade scientist can make good his escape (Act No. 236: "Superman's New Uniform!").

In May-June 1958 Luthor breaks out of Metropolis Prison by blasting his way through the prison wall with an awesomely destructive "ray device" fashioned secretly in prison and sets out to wreak revenge on both Superman and Metropolis. He is apprehended soon afterward, however, through the heroic efforts of Batman, Robin, and Superman

(WF No. 94: "The Origin of the Superman-Batman Team!"). (*See* POWERMAN.)

By February 1959 Luthor has devised an extraordinary "liquid kryptonite" serum as the first step in his latest scheme to annihilate Superman. "I found a way to dissolve that kryptonite meteor I found last month into a serum!" explains Luthor. "I tested the stuff on [an experimental] monkey and it was absorbed into his bloodstream without harm! Now that I know this liquid kryptonite is safe to drink, I'll take the rest of it myself! And this is going to mean the downfall of Superman!"

Meeting with his henchmen in his secret laboratory, Luthor describes his recent experiments with kryptonite...

..before unveiling his latest amazing discovery, a "liquid kryptonite" serum, 1959

As Luthor drinks his kryptonite serum, his body begins to glow with the eerie green color of kryptonite radiation. "...I'm radiating kryptonite rays from my skin!" gloats Luthor. "...[N]ow I can hound Superman to his doom as ... the kryptonite man!"

Flying to Metropolis in his "super-scientific rocketship," Luthor demolishes the statue of Superman in Metropolis Park as a brazen challenge to the Man of Steel, and then, when Superman appears on the scene, fiendishly whips aside his cloak and hood, bathing Superman in the deadly kryptonite radiations emanating from his body. When Superman desperately attempts to cope with the crisis by fleeing to his Fortress of Solitude and donning a special "leaden suit," which kryptonite radiations cannot penetrate, Luthor responds by launching into Earth orbit a sophisticated "Luthor satellite" whose "super electronic apparatus," activated by a "radio-beam signal" from Luthor, forms a series of weird electronic rings around the Earth which temporarily transform all the lead on Earth—including Superman's kryptonite-proof suit—into common transparent glass.

Forced to flee into outer space to avoid being fatally weakened by Luthor's kryptonite emanations, Superman fashions himself a second lead suit out of lead ore he finds on the moon, kicks the Luthor satellite far into outer space—thereby obliterating the electronic rings circling the Earth and transforming the glass into lead again—and then returns to Earth for a showdown with Luthor. Ultimately, by means of an elaborate ruse carried out with the aid of Jimmy Olsen, Superman tricks the renegade scientist into swallowing the antidote to his kryptonite serum—so that he no longer emanates deadly kryptonite radiations—and then swiftly takes the villain into custody (Act No. 249: "The Kryptonite Man!").

By March 1959 Luthor has devised a set of ingenious belts that enable their wearers to reduce themselves drastically in size, and has concocted an elaborate scheme to rid himself of Superman. The scheme involves tricking Superman into reducing himself to microscopic size with one of the special belts and then following Luthor and his henchmen into the bottle city of KANDOR, where, because the artificially controlled atmosphere is identical to that of Krypton, Superman's home planet, Superman becomes instantly deprived of his super-powers. In Kandor, the villains overpower Superman and confiscate his size-changing belt with the intention of leaving him stranded forever inside the tiny bottle city, but soon afterward, after Luthor and his henchmen have looted Kandor of its valuable super-scientific inventions and fled the city for the outside world, they are apprehended through the heroic efforts of Batman, Robin, and Superman (WF No. 100: "The Dictator of Krypton City!").

In July 1959, in an unsuccessful effort to destroy Superman, Luthor creates BIZARRO, an imperfect duplicate of Superman composed of lifeless matter (Act No. 254: "The Battle with Bizarro!").

In September 1959 Luthor, employing an alias and a cunning disguise, poses as the inventor of an as yet unperfected "atomic transporter"—a device designed to transport individuals from place to place, almost instantaneously, by disassembling them into their component atoms and transmitting them to a distant "receiver" where their "atoms will be reassembled"— as part of an elaborate scheme to destroy Superman by disintegrating his atomic structure. Luthor and his henchmen are ultimately apprehended, however, through the heroic efforts of Batman, Robin, BATWOMAN, and Superman (WF No. 104: "The Plot to Destroy Superman!").

In October 1959 Luthor, in solitary confinement in Metropolis Prison, disassembles an ordinary radio and uses its component parts to create an amazing "super-ray projector" powered by "super-energy" provided by a tiny speck of "element xium," which Luthor smuggled into prison inside a hollowed-out tooth. "It's done!" thinks Luthor with satisfaction as he completes his invention. "Now this super-ray will give me super-powers! But the powerful ray might...er...kill me instead! I must test it on someone!"

From a hiding place in his cell, Luthor uncovers "another amazing device"—an "atom transmitter"— and, activating it, allows it to bathe him in its eerie, radiant light. "That atom transmitter will project my image outside the prison walls for ten minutes!" muses Luthor. "But it will be a solid image of me and the super-ray device I'm holding!"

An instant later, a solid image of Luthor, holding his just-completed super-ray projector, materializes miles away from Metropolis Prison. "I'm still back in prison," thinks the image, "but I can see and hear through this projected 'double' of me!"

When Clark Kent and Lois Lane arrive on the scene, Luthor fires a bolt from his super-ray directly at Kent in an attempt to test the safety of his ray by using it to endow Kent with a charge of temporary super-powers. Luthor is unaware that Kent already has super-powers due to the fact that he is secretly Superman.

"I experimented on you, Kent!" gloats Luthor, speaking through his projected image. "If you show no ill-effects from the ray in three days, it will be safe for me to give myself a lifetime dose! Having super-powers, I'll break jail...defy Superman...and rule the world!" Then Luthor's projected double dematerializes into thin air, vanishing like a wraith.

Knowing that Luthor's ray does indeed have the power to endow human beings safely with super-powers, despite the fact that Kent's own super-powers are permanent and were not imparted by the ray, Kent begins openly using the super-powers supposedly conferred on him by Luthor while at the same time setting in motion an elaborate ruse designed to dupe the renegade scientist into believing that, although effective, the super-ray also produces a side effect that Luthor would find extremely distasteful, that of making anyone struck by it so "super-generous" that he feels compelled to acquire riches for the sole purpose of giving them away.

"The same thing would happen to me if I took a dose of the ray!" exclaims Luthor angrily as he smashes the super-ray projector against the wall of his cell. "Bah! I would be mentally compelled to gather riches and donate them to charity all my life!"

"I'm just glad there's no Super-Luthor!" thinks Clark Kent relievedly. "He'll never know his plot would have worked!" (Act No. 257: "The Reporter of Steel!").

In December 1959, after being knocked unconscious by a fall following his exposure to red kryptonite, Superman is plagued by a frightening "super-nightmare." In it, Superman's exposure to red kryptonite has somehow plucked Superboy—i.e., the teen-aged Superman—out of the past, so that now both Superman and Superboy are somehow existing simultaneously, as though they were two different persons, in the world of the present; Superman and Superboy attempt to carry on their super-heroic careers as a team, but the partnership is plagued by tension and hostility, with Superboy being impulsive, careless, and sometimes downright stupid, and with Superman responding by becoming irritable, hot-tempered, and grouchy; Luthor capitalizes on this mutual hostility in order to lure both heroes into kryptonite traps, then forces them to battle to the death in a subterranean arena for the lives of Lois Lane and Lana Lang; and finally, when both super-heroic antagonists prove equally invulnerable, Luthor locks Superboy inside one of the compartments of "a double-chambered cabinet" and then, after informing Superman that opening one door will be suicidal, while opening the other door will mean the end of Superboy, forces Superman to make the gruesomely agonizing choice of which door to open. It is while wrestling with this terrifying dilemma that Superman awakens, relieved that the entire experience was only a dream (Act No. 259: "The Revenge of Luthor!").

In August 1960 Luthor, serving out a term in Bleak Rock Prison, constructs an ingenious "time ray" out of parts from an alarm clock and other everyday materials and uses it to draw the mighty HERCULES "through the time-barrier" from the ancient past to Luthor's prison cell in the twentieth century. By duping the legendary hero into believing that he has been wrongfully imprisoned by "an evil king" who stole his gold and hid it underground, Luthor is able to trick Hercules into using his superhuman strength to break Luthor out of prison and help him loot FORT KNOX. Ultimately, however, Hercules discovers that he has been duped into helping Luthor commit crimes, and he seizes the evil scientist and turns him over to Superman (Act No. 267: "Hercules in the 20th Century!").

By October 1960 Luthor's "duplicator ray," the device he once used to create Bizarro, has been placed on display in Superman's Fortress of Solitude. During this period, the accidental activation of the machine results in the creation of a Bizarro-Supergirl. Later, Superman focuses the duplicator ray on a mound of green-kryptonite meteors in order to create a mound of "Bizarro kyrptonite," or "blue kryptonite," an imperfect form of kryptonite harmful only to Bizarros (S No. 140: pts. I-III—"The Son of Bizarro!"; "The 'Orphan' Bizarro!"; "The Bizarro Supergirl!"). (*See* BIZARRO.)

By December 1960 Luthor has secretly broken out of prison—by constructing an ingenious "robot double" to take his place inside his cell while he himself escaped to freedom—and has, through plastic surgery, transformed his henchman Gypo into a perfect look-alike for Superman as part of an intricately convoluted scheme to use nuclear blackmail to make himself "dictator of Earth."

The first phase of the scheme involves tricking Superman into believing that the inhabitants of an alien dimension desperately need his help and that they have dispatched a weird craft—called a "globeship"—to the earthly dimension by remote control to enable him to make the journey to their extradimensional world. However, when Superman steps inside the globe-ship for what he believes will be an interdimensional voyage, he instead soon finds himself marooned in the Sahara Desert, unable to escape from the globe-shaped craft without setting off a deadly "neutron bomb" that Luthor has planted beneath Metropolis.

The second phase of Luthor's scheme involves having his Superman look-alike "return" to Metropolis—inside a duplicate globe-ship—with the claim that the alien dimension he just visited is menaced by an impending ice age and that only by borrowing Earth's "entire stockpile of atomic bombs" can he hope to destroy the advancing glaciers.

Believing that this emergency request for nuclear weaponry is being made by Superman, the governments of the world—speaking through their delegates meeting in special session at the U.N.—agree to hand over their nuclear arsenals, unaware that they are actually surrendering the weapons to Luthor, who plans to put them into orbit around the Earth as a means of blackmailing the entire planet into making him its dictator. Fortunately for mankind, however, the real Superman finally escapes from his globe-ship prison, returning to Metropolis in time to apprehend Luthor and his cohorts and recover the A-bombs loaned them by the U.N. (Act No. 271: "Voyage to Dimension X!"). The story is in many respects similar to Superman No. 83/1 (Jul/Aug '53: "Destination X!").

In April 1961 BERT TALBOT, until recently Luthor's cellmate at Metropolis Prison, commits a series of spectacular crimes with the aid of a diabolical "super-weapon" designed by Luthor (S No. 144/1: "The Super-Weapon!").

By May 1961 Luthor has used his "scientific genius to devise [an] indestructible creature with super-powers ... which takes its direction from radio waves emanating from [a] helmet" worn by Luthor. "All I need do is give it a task," gloats Luthor, "and its own electronic brain works out a solution!"

Aided by his awesome creation, a hideous mechanical monster somewhat resembling a gigantic starfish, Luthor and his henchmen commit a series of spectacular robberies in both GOTHAM CITY and Metropolis. The efforts of Batman, Robin, Batwoman, and Superman to halt the crime wave receive a severe setback when, as the result of a freak accident at Luthor's hideout, Batwoman becomes temporarily endowed with superhuman strength and the power of flight, but only at the cost of falling completely under Luthor's mental control whenever she is anywhere near his creature. Ultimately, however, Batwoman's superhuman powers fade and vanish, the creature is reduced to "a lifeless hulk," and Luthor and his henchmen are apprehended through the heroic efforts of Batman, Robin, and Superman (WF No 117: "The Super-Batwoman and the Super Creature!").

In June 1961, after being temporarily released from prison, under guard, so that he can use his scientific prowess to help the government cope with a national emergency, Luthor stages a spectacular escape and, after a day of feverish work on a new invention in the privacy of Luthor's Lair, announces to his henchmen that "We're going to rob Fort Knox!"

Indeed, the following morning, as dawn breaks over Fort Knox, Kentucky, "a stronghold of troops and weapons--guarding the gold bullion depository of the U.S. Treasury," Luthor uses his new device to reduce the government troops guarding the fort to lilliputian size, and, moments later, when Luthor spies Superman flashing to the scene, he uses his machine to bombard the Man of Steel with what appear to be kryptonite spheres of every variety ("My machine can instantly manufacture synthetic kryptonite of any kind!" cries Luthor), spheres which are designed to immobilize Superman while Luthor and his cohorts stage the most spectacular heist in American history.

With his super-powered nemesis trapped amid the barrage of many-colored spheres, Luthor uses his astounding "fourth-dimensional arm"—a gigantic "steel hand," operated by remote control, that looks for all the world like the hand of an extradimensional giant reaching into the earthly dimension—to uproot Fort Knox from its foundations, scoop out the entire U.S. gold reserve from its underground storage vaults, and deposit the hoard of gold bullion into a fleet of waiting trucks, which, a short distance from the fort, ingeniously convert into airplanes to fly the stolen bullion to Luthor's Lair.

"Luthor, you actually did it!" exclaims one of the villain's henchmen. "You actually robbed Fort Knox right under Superman's nose--and got away with it!"

"Yes," replies Luthor proudly, "--but the big joke is that Superman could have stopped me but didn't know it! I tricked him! Those 'kryptonite' globes were fakes! Harmless fakes! When the world learns the truth, he'll never live down the shame! Ha! Ha! Ha! Ha! All the gold in the world couldn't buy me this feeling of triumph--this sweet revenge! Ha! Ha! Ha!"

Luthor's heady feeling of triumph, however, is extremely short-lived, for he soon learns that the real

Superman was away in outer space when Fort Knox was robbed and that the Man of Steel who attempted unsuccessfully to thwart the crime was only one of Superman's Superman-robots. "No wonder I tricked it so easily!" fumes Luthor. "Even though I won a victory, I really lost! I didn't triumph over **Super-man**, only a mechanical man! My sweet revenge has turned sour! All my work--all my plans--gone for nothing!"

"Don't say that, boss!" consoles a henchman. "We still got the gold...."

"The gold! Bah!" exclaims Luthor contemptuous-ly. "You fool! The gold was to be a symbol of my conquest of **Superman**--but now it's not that anymore! Now the gold can only remind me of my defeat! I'm going to give the gold back!"

"G-G-Give it b-back?" stammers the unbelieving henchman. "But, boss...."

"You stupid dolts!" cries Luthor angrily. "With my machines I can always steal enough loot to satisfy your greed! Have you forgotten I am **Luthor**--the **master criminal?** I gave an order--and I want it obeyed!"

And so, soon afterward, when the real Superman finally returns to Earth, he is greeted by the bizarre spectacle of the entire U.S. gold reserve stacked neatly in an open field, with bewildered policemen milling about it. "**Luthor** phoned us and told us we'd find the gold here!" explains one puzzled officer. "Now why should he steal the stuff--and then return it?"

"Knowing his insane conceit," replies Superman, "I'd say the answer was obvious. He felt that stealing the gold when I wasn't around to interfere was like stealing candy from a baby!"

"As for **Luthor**," thinks Superman soon after-ward, in the solitary privacy of his Fortress of Solitude, "I'll be waiting for our next battle...."

"As for **Superman**," thinks Luthor at virtually that same moment, in the secluded safety of his Luthor's Lair, "I'll be waiting for our next battle..." (Act No. 277: "The Conquest of Superman!").

In August 1961 Luthor joins forces with the LEGION OF SUPER-VILLAINS in an elaborate scheme to annihilate Superman (S No. 147/3: "The Legion of Super-Villains!").

Superman No. 149 contains an "imaginary tale" in which Luthor carries out a cunning scheme to annihilate Superman. After using his scientific genius to discover a cure for cancer while serving a term in Metropolis Prison, Luthor receives a speedy parole at the urging of Superman and promises to spend the rest of his life making scientific discoveries for the benefit of mankind. When members of the underworld, enraged over Luthor's apparent reforma-tion and at his refusal to use his talents to help them destroy Superman, begin making numerous attempts on Luthor's life, Superman builds his former enemy a fully equipped satellite laboratory and launches it into outer space so that Luthor will be able to carry on his noble scientific experiments free from underworld

interference. A week later, however, after having kidnapped three of Superman's closest friends—Lois Lane, Jimmy Olsen, and Perry White—so that they can bear witness to his final triumph over Superman, Luthor lures the unsuspecting Man of Steel to his orbiting satellite laboratory and annihilates him with deadly kryptonite rays. As Superman's body lies in state at Metropolis Chapel and the entire universe mourns the passing of the Man of Steel, Luthor and his underworld cronies—who realize now that Lu-thor's bogus reformation was only part of his scheme to assassinate Superman—celebrate the joyous occasion at a lavish party on some "remote isle," only to have the festivities rudely interrupted by SUPER-GIRL, who smashes through a wall of the underworld banquet hall and carries Luthor away to the bottle city of Kandor. Imprisoned in a bulletproof glass enclosure in a Kandorian courtroom and forced to stand trial for the brutal murder of Superman, Luthor is found guilty of the heinous crime and banished, for all eternity, into the PHANTOM ZONE, even as Supergirl vows to take up Superman's fallen mantle and carry on his crusade for justice throughout the universe (Nov '61: pts. I-III—"Lex Luthor, Hero!"; "Luthor's Super-Bodyguard!"; "The Death of Super-man!").

In March 1962, while in the grip of a nightmare induced by exposure to red kryptonite, Superman dreams that Luthor and other villains lure him into a trap, put him on "trial" for his alleged "crimes" against them, and sentence him to battle Supergirl to the death in a gigantic arena or else stand by helplessly while they blow up the Earth. These events, however, are all only part of a nightmare, and no actual confrontation with Luthor and his cohorts ever takes place (Act No. 286: "The Jury of Super-Enemies!").

By June 1962 Luthor has devised a diabolical weapon designed to "re-arrange [Superman's] mole-cules so that he has no more substance than a shadow! Superman," gloats Luthor, "will become a living ghost!" Hair-raising complications arise, however, when a freak accident—the result of Superman's simultaneous exposure to two bizarre rays, the first emitted by Luthor's weapon and the second by an experimental ray-device undergoing development in a nearby laboratory—has the totally unanticipated effect of bringing into existence a so-called Negative Superman, a black-and-white super-powered being with all the strength and powers of Superman but with a personality that is "negative" where Superman's is "positive," so that whereas Superman uses his powers for good, the Negative Superman is determined to use his powers for evil.

For a time the Negative Superman wreaks havoc in Metropolis, sheltering Luthor and his henchmen whenever Superman tries to apprehend them and deliberately aggravating catastrophes whenever Superman tries to ameliorate their effects. Batman and Robin ultimately devise a means of destroying the Negative Superman, however, thus enabling them to apprehend Luthor and his henchmen (WF No. 126: "The Negative Superman!").

In August 1962 the "DUDE" DUNN gang attempts unsuccessfully to destroy Superman with the aid of deadly "kryptonite guns" designed for them by Luthor (Act No. 291: "The New Superman!").

In September 1962, after hypnotizing a guard at Metropolis Prison and slipping through the prison gate to freedom, Luthor blasts off in his rocket ship for the planet Roxar, a world in a "distant solar system," where he hopes to lie low until it is safe for him to return to Earth. Confronted upon his arrival by an intelligent robot that demands that he declare and surrender all his dangerous weapons, Luthor annoyedly shatters the impertinent robot with a blast from his "vibro-gun," only to discover, to his shock and dismay, that Roxar is inhabited by a civilization of highly advanced robots—known as Automs—and that his punishment for having "murdered" an Autom will be to be frozen forever in suspended animation.

Lex Luthor in his laboratory on the planet Roxar, 1962

When, soon afterward, Superman arrives on Roxar in pursuit of Luthor, he decides to intervene on his arch-enemy's behalf so that Luthor can be returned to Metropolis Prison to continue serving his term for the far more "terrible crimes" he committed on Earth. By rebuilding the shattered Autom with parts from one

of his own Superman robots and then powering it with the "radium capsule" used to drive Luthor's own rocket ship, Superman successfully tricks the Automs into believing that the robot which Luthor is charged with killing is still alive and well and that the charges against Luthor should therefore be dropped. Set free by the Automs, Luthor nevertheless refuses to accompany Superman back to Earth, leaving Superman, who admittedly has "no jurisdiction" to apprehend criminals outside Earth's solar system, to return home alone. Luthor, however, now finds himself stranded on Roxar, for without his radium-capsule power source his spacecraft is useless, and yet if he attempts to remove it from the rebuilt Autom, the Autom will "die" again and Luthor will, once more, be faced with a murder charge (Act No. 292: "When Superman Defended His Arch-Enemy!").

In November 1962, still stranded on Roxar, Luthor finally succeeds in ingratiating himself with his Autom hosts—by teaching them how to protect themselves from the so-called "dynos," terrifying "energy insects" that habitually prey on Roxar's robots—as the first phase of his elaborate scheme to escape from Roxar and wreak vengeance on Superman. Granted the use of a private laboratory to carry on his scientific work, Luthor devises, among other inventions, an ingenious "converter machine" with which he is able to alter the molecular structure of three of Roxar's "androids," synthetic humanoids created by the Automs as a source of menial labor, thereby transforming them into Diamond Man, Lead Man, and Kryptonite Man, respectively, i.e., three artificial men, each composed entirely of the substance for which it is named.

Aided by his three synthetic allies, Luthor steals the Automs' entire radium supply and, after inserting some of the rare substance into the fuel cell of his spacecraft, blasts off into outer space to launch a reign of "space piracy" on a massive scale.

Learning of Luthor's escape from Roxar several weeks later, Superman trails the villain and his android accomplices to their "planetary pirate lair" on a "ringed planet" in the Bruno VI star-cluster," where he easily demolishes Diamond Man, only to find himself immobilized by the deadly "triple-powered kryptonite rays" emanating from Kryptonite Man's body—rays which, in Superman's words, "hurt worse than anything I've ever encountered!"

In terrible pain and with his super-strength rapidly waning, Superman sends out a call for help to the Autom he once rebuilt with parts from a Superman robot, but Luthor obliterates this Autom with a "searing blast" from his deadly "heat-gun" as soon as it approaches his planetary hideout. It is only at the last possible moment, with the Man of Steel apparently doomed, that Lead Man—who has been suffering pangs of conscience over his role as a space pirate—deliberately goads Luthor into turning him into a puddle of molten lead with a blast from his heat-gun so that, by melting all over his "android brother" Kryptonite Man, he can create a life-saving

After transforming a stamping press in the prison machine shop into a gigantic "escape machine," Luthor smashes through the prison walls to freedom, 1963

lead shield between Superman and the baleful kryptonite radiations, albeit only at the cost of his own synthetic life. Thus freed from his exposure to the deadly kryptonite rays, Superman swiftly regains his strength, apprehends Luthor, and returns him to Earth to serve out the remainder of his term in Metropolis Prison (Act No. 294: "The Kryptonite Killer!").

During this same period, Luthor and the Joker join forces in an elaborate plot to steal $5,000,000 in gems from an exhibition at Wilson Park, a "new outdoor exhibit grounds" in the city of Metropolis. In order to overcome the elaborate security precautions that have been devised for the exhibit, the two villains kidnap Hilton Webb, Wilson Park's master of ceremonies, and replace him with a carefully disguised Luthor well in advance of the gem exhibit.

The villains' complex preparations for the heist involve them in a series of skirmishes with Batman, Robin, and Superman, during which Luthor incapacitates Superman with his newly developed "kryptonite X-beam"—a special pistol, described as "an atomic disperser with a kryptonite base," which enables Luthor to briefly transform Superman "into an electronic stream utterly incapable of action"—while the Joker busies himself subduing or stymying his arch-nemeses Batman and Robin.

By the evening of the gem exhibit, however, Superman's X-ray vision has informed him that Luthor is the master of ceremonies, and so Superman swiftly apprehends him while Batman and Robin subdue the Joker and his henchmen—who have staged a mock invasion of the gem exhibit in order to provide Luthor with an opportunity to make off with the gems—and confiscate the kryptonite X-beam which the Joker had intended to use against Super-

man (WF No. 129, Nov '62: "Joker-Luthor, Incorporated!").

In October 1963, on the pretext of using his scientific ingenuity to repair a giant stamping press in the machine shop of the prison where he is incarcerated, Luthor ingeniously transforms the machine into a gigantic "escape-machine," a mighty "steel colossus" on wheels with which he smashes through the prison walls and escapes to freedom. "It's time the long feud between Superman and me was

Employing an ingenious "broadcaster-interrupter" of his own invention, Luthor breaks in on regular network television broadcasts in order to issue a challenge to Superman, 1963

settled, one way or another!" thinks Luthor to himself. "I'm going to have it out with him, once and for all!"

In the days that follow, operating from a secret subterranean hideout that has been lined with lead to safeguard it against Superman's penetrating X-ray vision, Luthor—employing an ingenious "broadcaster-interrupter" of his own invention— begins breaking in on regular network television broadcasts, challenging Superman to meet him face to face, on even terms, without his mighty super-powers. "...I must accept his challenge!" thinks Clark Kent, as he changes swiftly into his Superman identity. "If people thought that I was afraid to meet him without my super-powers, they might lose faith in me as a defender of the weak and oppressed!"

And so, soon afterward, in a spaceship built by Superman, the two "deadly enemies" soar away from Earth toward the far-distant planet they have chosen as their battleground (see LEXOR), a "desert-like world," revolving about a red sun, where Superman will have only the powers of an ordinary mortal (see SUPERMAN [section E, the super-powers]). In a man-to-man fight on this parched "desert world," Super-man unleashes a mighty blow that knocks Luthor unconscious, but Luthor manages to slip away into a "weird cactus forest" and soon finds himself ap-proaching an inhabited city, where he sees men watering crops with large jugs of water filled at a communal fountain. "This must have once been a great scientific race," muses Luthor, "but perhaps a great war eons ago wiped out their civilization and they've returned to the Stone Age! This pump was to pump water from underground to the fields, but they don't know how to operate it, and carry water by hand!"

When a flock of "monstrous birds," called "dor-ulgs," suddenly darkens the skies overhead, swoop-ing down to devour the neatly planted rows of food crops, Luthor wins the gratitude of the alien farmers by "using his great scientific abilities" to transform the water pump and its connecting pipes into "a mighty weapon," driving the great birds away with a powerful stream of water. Indeed, "As the menace is repelled, Luthor, for the first time in his life, finds himself a popular hero!"

"It's strange," thinks Luthor, as the natives of this distant planet shower him with cheers and adulation, "...I never had a crowd cheer me before, and I rather like it!"

Now the aliens lead "their new hero" into the heart of their city, to a museum containing the ancient remnants of a long-forgotten super-science. "Though they've lost their own science," thinks Luthor, "they still respect scientists...and recognizing me as one, they've brought me to their museum! Hmm...there are terrific possibilities in these ancient machines!"

"You are a wise man, like our forefathers," remarks one grateful alien, "...you will use the ancient wisdom we have forgotten to help us, great Luthor!"

The major problem on this planet, Luthor soon learns, is the devastating shortage of water, a problem he attempts to resolve by using giant "building-machines" from the ancient museum to construct gigantic, electronically controlled robots specialized for digging and then setting them to work searching the planet for new subterranean sources of water. The search for water, however, proves fruit-less. "The robots can't find any other source of water in this planet," thinks Luthor to himself, "...yet can't let these people down when they think I'm a hero!"

When Superman finally arrives in the city in search of his arch-enemy, he is seized by the aliens who are ready to destroy any enemy of their great hero, Luthor. "No, let go of him!" cries Luthor restraining the angry mob. "I have vowed to fight him on even terms, in single combat!"

"To keep us on even terms," explains Luthor turning to Superman, "I'll have these people show you a set of their ancient inventions! You can study them tonight, and figure out how to use them..as I'll use my set against you!"

But while Superman sets to work studying the ancient machines in preparation for his forthcoming duel with Luthor, Luthor renews his efforts to help the people of this distant world locate new sources of water. Even this effort, however, is unsuccessful. "My robots could find no other water than the waning supply that feeds the fountain!" thinks Luthor finally. "It'll disappoint these people terribly...I won't tell them till after my duel with Superman!"

The following day, "in an ancient arena," the two lifelong enemies face each other in mortal combat, each armed with a deadly array of superscientific weapons. To a man, the vast crowd on hand to witness the event is rooting for Luthor, for on this strange world, Luthor is a world-renowned hero, while Superman is reviled as the most evil of villains.

As the death-duel nears its climax, with neither adversary having gained a decisive advantage, Luthor unleashes "a final and terrible weapon," a ferocious "automaton bloodhound" of a type original-ly designed by this planet's "ancient scientists for trailing law-breakers," but Superman, although he lacks his super-powers, nevertheless manages to deactivate the powerful robot bloodhound before it can destroy him. Infuriated, Luthor hurls himself at the fallen Superman, leaping on top of him and throttling him with his bare hands. "Luthor is winning! Hurrah!" cries a voice from the onlooking throng. "And when he's won, he'll find us more water as he promised!"

"They don't know yet," thinks Luthor sadly, "that I can't find them water...." And then, "strangely, Luthor seems suddenly to lose strength!" His inexplicable pause on the very brink of victory enables Superman, sorely weakened by his battle with the automaton bloodhound, to regain his strength sufficiently to send Luthor sprawling with a mighty blow to the jaw. "I...I give up, Superman!" gasps Luthor. "I admit myself beaten, and will go back to Earth with you, to prison!"

"You won't forget your promise to get us water, great **Luthor?**" pleads one of the aliens, as Superman and his adversary climb aboard their spacecraft for the long journey back to Earth. "No," replies Luthor somberly, "...I won't forget, my friends!... I'll do it!"

Soon afterward, far out in interstellar space, "as their space ship leaves the solar system with a red sun and enters one with a yellow one, **Superman** regains all his powers!" "I can't get them water," remarks Luthor to Superman, "but with your powers, **you** could! There's an **icy** planet just ahead! You could throw vast masses of ice back to that desert world!"

"It would help those people and I'll do it," replies Superman, "...even if they do think me a villain!"

Making a temporary landing on the icy planet, Superman seizes vast chunks of ice in his bare hands and hurls them across space to the sun-parched desert world. "I can activate your big robots there by my X-ray vision," remarks Superman, "and they'll build canals like those of Mars... to bring the water all over the desert planet!"

Then, with the mighty task fulfilled, Superman turns again to Luthor. "**Luthor,**" he asks, "did you deliberately let me beat you, so that with my super-powers I could keep your promise to those people to whom you're a hero?"

"Ridiculous!" replies Luthor contemptuously. "...Er what makes you think such a thing? You beat me fair and square!" "He guessed my motive in losing the duel," thinks Luthor silently, "...but I'll never admit to him I went 'soft'!"

Meanwhile, on the distant, "once-arid world," the grateful inhabitants see the precious water flowing through their new canals and assume it is all the work of their hero, Luthor. "...We owe it all to the great **Luthor!**" remarks one man thankfully. "We'll never forget him!" And, not long afterward, Superman visits Luthor's prison cell bearing a close-up photograph of a new monument on the planet which has been erected in Luthor's honor. "A great statue of me...on the one world where I'm a hero!" remarks Luthor aloud. "It was worth coming back to prison for!" (S No. 164/1: pts. I-II—"The Showdown Between Luthor and Superman!"; "The Super-Duel!").

In November 1963 Luthor enlists the aid of two evil extraterrestrial aliens in an elaborate scheme to lure Superman away from Earth on an interplanetary wild-goose chase so that, in Superman's absence, he can use a lifelike super-powered Superman robot to commit a series of spectacular crimes and blame the crimes on the absent Superman. For a time, the people of Metropolis are actually duped into believing that their greatest hero has become a super-powered criminal, but ultimately Superman is exonerated— and Luthor and his alien accomplices are apprehended—through the heroic efforts of Batman, Robin, and Superman (WF No. 137: "Superman's Secret Master!").

When Metropolis television station WMET-TV inaugurates its new "Our American Heroes" series with a program honoring Superman, "our greatest American hero," Luthor and some of his fellow convicts watch the show on a television set inside their maximum-security prison (Act No. 309, Feb '64: "The Superman Super-Spectacular!").

In February 1964, after staging yet another of his brazen escapes from prison, Luthor forms an alliance with the space villain Brainiac in an elaborate scheme to annihilate Superman by creating "an ultimate weapon" for use against the Man of Steel—a diabolical "serum-gas" designed to strip Superman of his mighty super-powers. "This time," vows Luthor, "I'm going to get rid of my nemesis once and for all...I'm going to **destroy Superman!**"

Indeed, after scouring the universe in search of the rare elements needed for the creation of their ultimate weapon, the two villains lure Superman to their secret stronghold, rob him of his super-powers by means of their serum-gas, and, after pummeling him into submission with their fists, reduce him to lilliputian size with a "shrinking ray" and lock him inside a bird cage. After arguing briefly about how best to destroy him, Luthor and Brainiac paralyze Superman with a fiendish "coma-ray" and are on the verge of snuffing out his life completely when suddenly the SUPERMEN EMERGENCY SQUAD arrives on the scene, takes the villains into custody, and then transports Superman and his former captors into the bottle city of Kandor, where Kandorian scientists labor, without success, to liberate Superman from the "strange coma" induced by Brainiac's coma-ray.

Forced to stand trial in a Kandorian courtroom— with Luthor serving as his defense attorney and NOR-KAN presenting the case for the prosecution—on the charge of having shrunk and stolen the city of Kandor, Brainiac is found guilty of the heinous crime and sentenced to be banished, for all eternity, into the Phantom Zone.

"Very well," cries Brainiac in the crowded courtroom, "...but if you do so, you're sentencing **Superman** to a living death! Only I can revive **Superman** from the effects of my coma ray! Either we two [Brainiac and Luthor] go free, or he remains in a coma forever!"

And so, having concluded that "**Superman**, our great friend and hero, must be saved" at all costs, the Kandorian people solemnly strike a bargain with the two super-villains, guaranteeing them safe conduct out of the city in return for their rescuing Superman from his deadly coma. Soon afterward, after having been safely revived from his coma, the Man of Steel reluctantly escorts his two "greatest enemies" out of Kandor and then watches helplessly as they soar away in their spacecraft into the vastness of outer space (S No. 167: "The Team of Luthor and Brainiac!" pts. I-III—"The Deadly Duo!"; "The Downfall of Superman!"; "The Hour of Kandor's Vengeance!").

By April 1964 the inhabitants of the planet where Luthor is considered a hero have named their world Lexor, in Luthor's honor, and are preparing for the dedication of a Luthor Museum. Journeying to Lexor during this period in an attempt to bring Luthor to justice, Superman discovers that the explanation for the decline of Lexorian civilization lies not in a great war, as Luthor had once speculated, but rather in the presence on the planet of certain "priceless rainbow crystals," a geological rarity whose "magnificent rays" have, for generations, been used as the source of light in every Lexorian home. Unknown to the Lexorians, however, these crystals "emit a subtle vibration that deteriorates brain-activity," a vibration capable, given centuries of exposure, of reducing an entire people to a primitive state. In the words of Superman No. 168:

> The people of Lexor once had a brilliant civilization but declined to barbarism! The rainbow crystals are the reason... the subtle rays of these crystals act to slow the brain's electroencephalic action, and dull the intelligence!

"To get those baleful crystals away from my people," relents Luthor finally, "I'll let you go free. But you must promise to destroy them, and not betray the Defender's identity! But remember, our feud isn't ended!"

"Agreed," replies Superman, "--our feud is still on!"

A short while later, far out in space, Superman recovers his super-powers and obliterates the rainbow crystals by hurling them into the heart of the sun. "Our feud will never end," thinks Superman silently, as he returns to Earth to devise yet another plan for apprehending Luthor, "until he's brought to justice!"

About one month later, however, having used a Lexorian "inventing machine" to create "artificial red kryptonite dust which will temporarily wipe out

In the capital city of the planet Lexor, citizens contemplate their monument to Luthor, Lexor's greatest hero, 1964

Having made this discovery, and having decided that destruction of the baleful crystals must take precedence even over his mission to apprehend Luthor, Superman seizes the crystals and attempts to flee Lexor with them, only to be apprehended by Luthor, who, having used "the ancient science of this world" to endow himself with temporary super-powers, has—employing the pseudonym the Defender—assumed the role of Lexor's super-hero. Locked in a prison cell in Lexor's capital city, Superman escapes and once again attempts to flee Lexor with the rainbow crystals, but Luthor—clad in the distinctive red-and-purple costume he wears in his role as the Defender—corners him before he can board his spacecraft for the journey back to Earth. Luthor is on the verge of snuffing out Superman's life with a diabolical "stun-gun" when the Man of Steel gasps out the details of his discovery about the rainbow crystals and the deleterious effect they have exerted on Lexorian civilization.

most of Superman's powers," Luthor climbs aboard a spacecraft and blasts off for Earth, determined to wreak vengeance on Superman by robbing him of his super-powers and dragging him back to Lexor. As Luthor's spacecraft approaches Earth, however, it suddenly begins "accelerating too fast.... Earth seems to be blurring and spinning oddly," and when Luthor finally crash-lands his spaceship and makes his way to the city nearby, he finds that he has somehow journeyed through the time barrier to the city of San Francisco in the year 1906. Temporarily stranded in this bygone era, Luthor sets feverishly to work, "using the parts from [his] wrecked spaceship to build a device that will teleport [him] back to Lexor!"

When Superman streaks through the time barrier to San Francisco in 1906 in an effort to bring his arch-enemy to justice, Luthor, employing an elaborate ruse involving the assumption of a false identity, exposes the Man of Steel to the baleful radiations of his

During a time-journey to San Francisco in the year 1906, Lex Luthor bends over the body of a man killed in a carriage accident

artificial red kryptonite—thereby depriving him of his super-strength and invulnerability—and forces Superman to row him out to "a rocky island" in San Francisco Bay where, in a secret cave, he has hidden his now-completed "teleport device." As Luthor activates his device, however, intending to teleport both Superman and himself back to Lexor, the device malfunctions and Luthor begins to vanish alone, leaving Superman marooned in 1906. "Those intense vibrations!" exclaims Luthor. "Something's wrong! I put on too much power! I'm starting to vanish, but Superman is remaining on the island!"

Rowing back to the mainland, Superman soon discovers that the vibrations from Luthor's teleport device "are shaking all San Francisco," and "in the next shattering moment" he realizes the awful truth: that he is standing in the midst of the famous San Francisco earthquake of 1906 and that "that awful catastrophe was started by Lex Luthor," albeit inadvertently, due to the malfunctioning of his teleport device.

Stranded in this past era until the effects of Luthor's red kryptonite wear off and his super-powers return, Superman tours the stricken city on a tandem bicycle with LILLIAN RUSSELL and helps the famed actress aid victims of the devastating earthquake. Finally, having regained his super-powers, Superman returns through the time barrier to the twentieth century, where he discovers that, ironically, Luthor's teleport device did not teleport the villain to Lexor at all, but rather transported him to the twentieth century on that same island in San Francisco Bay where he stranded Superman, i.e., Alcatraz Island, where Luthor has now been trapped in an abandoned prison cell for three full days (S No. 168: pts. I-II—

"Luthor--Super-Hero!"; "Lex Luthor, Daily Planet Editor!").

In July 1964, after ingesting an ingenious "instant-growth mixture" that temporarily catapults him to titanic size, Luthor leaps over the walls of Metropolis Prison and escapes to the safety of Luthor's Lair No. 5, where he soon concocts what he regards as "the most sensational scheme of [his] life!" Acting on the theory that not even Superman would dare lift a hand against his own father, Luthor journeys through the time-space barrier to the planet Krypton at a time predating the marriage of Jor-El and LARA, where, posing as Luthor the Noble, a "cosmic champion for good" from the planet Marlat, he begins to woo Lara in earnest as part of his elaborate scheme to alter history by marrying Lara himself so that he—and not Jor-El—can become the father of Superman. Then, after safely escaping from Krypton prior to its destruction, Luthor plans to resume his drive for world domination, confident that his son Superman will not try to stop him.

Indeed, for a time, it appears as though the bizarre scheme may actually succeed. Dazzled by her newest suitor, who, by his own mendacious account, has "dedicated [himself] to fighting interstellar evils," Lara begins "falling in love" with the man she has been led to believe is a great "crusader from space." "What an honor to be courted by such a famous space hero!" thinks Lara. "He may not be handsome, but he's exciting!"

Ultimately, however, in the midst of the wedding ceremony that will make Lara his wife, a fateful accident exposes Luthor as a cosmic liar, and he barely manages to escape from Krypton in his "time-space warp vehicle" before the Kryptonians can capture him and banish him into the Phantom Zone. "Bah!" fumes Luthor angrily. "My attempt to change history failed! Why do I always have such rotten luck? Why can't I ever win? Why must I always be a loser?"

But Luthor's bad luck is not over even now, for when his weird time-space vehicle finally materializes on Earth in the year 1964, Superman is right there to apprehend the villain and return him to Metropolis Prison to serve out the remainder of his term (S No. 170/2: pts. I-II—"If Lex Luthor Were Superman's Father!"; "The Wedding of Lara and Luthor!"). Although the cover of Superman No. 170 contains a notation to the effect that this tale is "imaginary," there are no such indications in the actual text. Indeed, the overwhelming preponderance of evidence indicates that the events described therein actually took place.

In October 1964, after Superman has been deprived of his super-powers by the baleful radiations of a mysterious green comet—and AR-VAL, Superman's hand-picked successor, has begun performing the Man of Steel's super-heroic duties in Superman's stead—Luthor escapes from prison with the aid of Brainiac and then makes the notorious space villain his ally in a heinous scheme to wreak vengeance o'

Superman by murdering his "dear friends" Lois Lane and Lana Lang. Denied help in tracking down the villains by the arrogant Ar-Val, who refuses to take the menace of Luthor and Brainiac seriously, Superman—who, lacking his super-powers, is now only an ordinary mortal—contacts the LEGION OF SUPER-HEROES in the thirtieth century A.D. and arranges for three of its members—COSMIC BOY, the INVISIBLE KID, and SATURN GIRL—to use the "time-force wave carrier" in their thirtieth-century Clubhouse to endow him temporarily with their various powers—i.e., the powers of "supermagnetism," "invisibility," and "telepathic thought-casting," respectively—so that he can use these powers in an attempt to apprehend Luthor and Brainiac.

Thus endowed, albeit only "for a few hours," with the super-powers of the three Legionnaires—in addition to the elastic powers of ELASTIC LAD, which he has acquired by drinking some of Jimmy Olsen's "elastic serum"—Superman bravely invades the villains' "secret base" and attempts to capture them single-handed, but the villains overpower him with a "powerful knockout gas" and, by the time he regains consciousness, Superman's temporary super-powers have faded and vanished. "With Superman as a hostage," gloats Luthor, standing triumphantly over a virtually helpless Superman, "I can get Lois and Lana here and carry out my vow to destroy them!"

Indeed, merely by informing Lois Lane and Lana Lang that they are holding Superman captive, the villains are able to lure Superman's friends to their stronghold. No sooner have Luthor and Brainiac taken the two women prisoner, however, than Ar-Val, brought to the scene by an insistent Jimmy Olsen, swoops down on the villains' headquarters and lunges at the startled villains. Determined not to be apprehended, Brainiac seizes a deadly "green kryptonite harpoon" and hurls it at the oncoming Ar-Val, but Superman selflessly leaps into the path of the hurtling weapon, protecting Ar-Val from the potentially fatal kryptonite rays.

As Superman lies sprawled on the floor, mortally wounded, with the kryptonite harpoon embedded in his back, Ar-Val, now "an avenging fury," seizes Luthor and Brainiac before they can escape and is prevented from killing them both only by the intervention of Jimmy Olsen, who admonishes him to remember that the taking of lives is a violation of Superman's moral code.

By means of a super-scientific apparatus—a so-called "Z-ray"—belonging to Brainiac, Superman is swiftly cured of the mortal wound inflicted by the kryptonite harpoon. Ar-Val, however, is filled with remorse for his shabby recent behavior, particularly for his refusal to respond to Superman's plea to help him apprehend Luthor and Brainiac. "I was ungrateful to him," exclaims Ar-Val repentantly, "...I turned him down when he begged for help...yet he risked his own life to save mine! After all I did to him, he saved my life!" "That's Superman's code!" replies Jimmy Olsen.

Determined to make restitution for the wrongs he has done, Ar-Val hurtles away to the Fortress of Solitude, where, "by monitor," he contacts Nor-Kan in the bottle city of Kandor. "I'm not fit to replace a man like Superman!" thinks Ar-Val to himself. "I owe him everything...and maybe there's a way I can repay that debt...."

From Nor-Kan, Ar-Val learns that there is but one way to undo the effects of the mysterious green comet and restore Superman to his full super-powers, but that way, insists Nor-Kan, "is too terrible a way to use!" Terrible though it may be, Ar-Val uses it. After flying Superman to the Fortress of Solitude and chaining him to a pillar there, Ar-Val stands beside him as "tremendous, subtle force wells from the powerful generators" which Ar-Val has taken from the Fortress's laboratory and positioned around the pillar.

"What is this?" asks Superman bewilderedly "What's happening?"

"...[T]he only way to restore the super-powers of anyone who [has] lost them due to the comet's effects," explains Ar-Val, "[is] to transfer those powers from another super-being's body into the victim's! So I'm transferring the powers in my body into yours!"

"Why, it's working," exclaims Superman, "...I feel super-powers returning to my body! But...."

"But the shock of this force will remove not only my super-powers, but my life, too!" continues Ar-Val stoically. "This force, as it drains away my powers, turns the atoms of my body to stone!"

"No, Ar-Val," cries Superman, shattering the chains that bind him to the pillar, "I won't accept this sacrifice...."

But Superman is too late. "It's done now," gasps Ar-Val with his last breath. "...I wanted to be a great Superman, like you...I failed, but this will make amends..." (S No. 172: pts. I-III—"The New Superman!"; "Clark Kent—Former Superman!"; "The Struggle of the Two Supermen!").

In November 1964 Superman impersonates Luthor as part of an elaborate hoax he plays on his pal Jimmy Olsen in an effort to impress upon his young friend the folly of taking unnecessary risks (S No. 173/3: "The Triumph of Luthor and Brainiac!"). (See OLSEN, JIMMY.)

During this same period, after breaking out of prison by using a robot double of himself—fashioned out of spare parts in the prison machine shop—to divert the attention of prison guards while he makes his escape, Luthor slips aboard an instrument-carrying space rocket "at a great scientific rocket-base" and reprograms its controls to carry him to Lexor, where the populace accords him "a hero's welcome." The following day, in a wedding performed "according to the ancient nuptial ceremonies of Lexor," Luthor marries Ardora, his Lexorian sweetheart, and settles down to live with her "in the palace a grateful people have built for their hero" in Lexor's capital city.

But a black cloud hangs over the happiness of

Ardora and Luthor on the planet Lexor, 1964

Luthor and his bride, for Luthor knows that eventually Superman will arrive on Lexor and attempt to drag him back to prison. When Luthor offhandedly remarks that he would kill Superman rather than let the Man of Steel forcibly return him to Earth, Ardora, believing deeply that Luthor is "too fine and noble to commit such a crime as murder," extracts a promise from her husband to let the law deal with Superman in the event he actually comes to Lexor.

Having made this promise to Ardora, and feeling honor bound to keep it, Luthor sets in motion an intricately convoluted scheme to frame Superman for his own murder and have him executed for the crime by Lexorian authorities. When Superman arrives on Lexor in pursuit of Luthor and confronts his arch-enemy in Lexor's capital city, Luthor deliberately provokes Superman into punching him in the jaw, and then, reeling backward from the force of the blow, makes it appear that his head has struck a stone statue while he surreptitiously swallows a tablet containing a special "coma drug" designed to place him in a "deathlike trance" for a period of five days.

Seized almost immediately by an enraged populace who believe that he has murdered their world's greatest hero, Superman is thrown into jail to await trial for murder, while Luthor's "dead" body is placed on public display in a transparent glass coffin. Appointed to serve as Superman's defense counsel by Lexor's "highest judge," attorney VEL QUENNAR and his "young partner" GARN ABU urge their client to plead extenuating circumstances, perhaps even temporary insanity, but Superman—who believes that he has actually killed Luthor, albeit by accident—insists on basing his defense on what he believes is the truth—that Luthor's death was an accident, caused by his falling against a statue during their fistfight (Act No. 318, Nov '64: "The Death of Luthor!").

Brought to trial in a Lexorian courtroom on the charge of having murdered "the greatest man in Lexor's history," Superman listens silently as prosecutor LAR THAN accuses him of having journeyed to the planet Lexor with the "deliberate intention of

committing murder" and demands that Superman receive the death penalty for his heinous crime. Indeed, after being returned to his death-row cell following his first day of trial, the Man of Steel receives a harrowing preview of his probable fate when he watches a condemned inmate walk the last mile to the prison's execution chamber—the so-called "stone room"—where, before Superman's horrified, unbelieving eyes, the condemned convict pays the supreme penalty for his capital crime by being transformed into a block of unliving stone.

On the evening following his second day in court, after it has become apparent to him that he has virtually no hope of winning an acquittal, Superman escapes from prison and makes his way to Luthor's private laboratory, where, among the "potent chemicals and drugs of [Lexor's] lost science," he discovers a vial of "coma drug tablets" along with a "shock restorative chemical" designed to undo the coma drug's effects. When Superman sprays Luthor's lifeless body with the powerful antidote, Luthor revives and, "dazed by his sudden awakening," tells Superman the details of his fiendish scheme to frame Superman for murder and then awake in five days, after Superman had already been executed in Lexor's stone room. Superman's efforts to convince the Lexorian authorities that Luthor deliberately swallowed the coma drug as part of "a cunning plot" to destroy him are, nevertheless, unavailing, for the people of Lexor, unable to believe anything bad of their world's great hero, choose instead to believe that Luthor ingested the coma drug accidentally.

With Luthor clearly alive and well, however, the charges against Superman are dropped, and the Man of Steel is swiftly released and ordered "banished from Lexor!"

"There goes **Superman** back to Earth," remarks Luthor, his arm around Ardora, as the Man of Steel soars skyward in the spaceship that will carry him back to Earth. "...He got the worst of it this time! But he'll never give up the struggle against me!" (Act No. 319, Dec '64: "The Condemned Superman!").

Superman No. 175 contains an "imaginary tale" in which Luthor, adopted by JONATHAN AND MARTHA KENT while still a youngster in Smallville, sets aside his criminal leanings completely and grows to maturity as the loyal foster brother of Clark Kent, the young Superman, whom the Kents adopted previously. As the years pass, Clark Kent marries Lois Lane after informing her that he is secretly Superman, and Lana Lang, realizing that she has now lost Superman forever, marries PETE ROSS on the rebound, unaware that Ross is secretly a master criminal. When Ross and his henchmen launch a staggering crime wave with duplicates of Kryptonian weapons they have stolen from the Fortress of Solitude—and then lure Superman into a fiendish kryptonite deathtrap—Luthor courageously races to Superman's rescue after endowing himself with temporary super-powers by means of a complex device of his own invention. In the ensuing battle at Pete Ross's stronghold, Superman is set free, and Ross dies when a Kryptonian "death ray" that he aims at the super-powered Luthor ricochets off Luthor's invulnerable body and hits Ross instead. Moments later, however, the self-sacrificing Luthor also perishes, for the fatal flaw inherent in his machine's capacity to impart super-powers is that "the charge is so powerful it kills the subject soon, by dissolving the cell-binding forces of his body" and causing his cells to begin "evaporating away like dust!" (Feb '65: pts. I-III—"Clark Kent's Brother!"; "The Defeat of Superman!"; "The Luthor-Superman").

LUTHORITE. A fabulous "new metal"—described as the "hardest and strongest [metal] of all"—which is created by LEX LUTHOR in November-December 1946. "Luthorite resists friction-heat!" explains Luthor. "[With it] I can build irresistible weapons and impenetrable space ships to dominate the universe!" Luthorite contains iridium and possibly osmium, but its chief ingredient is "the unknown Element X," available only from certain rare meteorites (S No. 43/3: "The Molten World!").

LUTHOR MUSEUM, THE. A museum on the planet LEXOR devoted to the glorification of LEX LUTHOR and his exploits. The museum features lifelike full-color statues of Luthor working in his laboratory, standing victoriously over a vanquished SUPERMAN, and other exhibits (S No. 168, Apr '64: pts. I-II—"Luthor--Super-Hero!"; "Lex Luthor, Daily Planet Editor!").

LUTHOR'S LAIR. The abandoned museum—situated "smack in the middle of Metropolis"—that serves as LEX LUTHOR's hideout and base of operations during June 1961 (Act No. 277: "The Conquest of Superman!") and September 1962. "Just as Superman has his Fortress of Solitude," notes Luthor, "I have my own headquarters! Luthor's Lair!" (Act No. 292: "When Superman Defended His Arch-Enemy!").

Described as "a building that was once a great museum--but is now ignored and abandoned," Luthor's Lair was purchased by Luthor "long ago," under an alias, and transformed into a gigantic, elaborately equipped headquarters, its hallways lined with lead to shield its secrets against SUPERMAN's penetrating X-ray vision.

The building itself is an imposing two- or three-story affair, fronted by a colonnaded entranceway adorned with a statue of Julius Caesar. Shaking the hand of the statue releases a secret mechanism which opens the building's massive front door. Mounted atop the building is a gigantic statue of classical design (Act No. 277, Jun '61: "The Conquest of Superman!") which is actually the "first stage" of a rocket ship capable of carrying Luthor on journeys into outer space (Act No. 292, Sep '62: "When Superman Defended His Arch-Enemy!"). Inside the building, a special "tele-screen tuned to hidden cameras in the eyes of the colossal statue" enables Luthor to scan the surrounding city for the possible approach of Superman or other intruders.

Elsewhere in the interior of the building is a bizarre Hall of Heroes, lined with full-color, life-sized statues of Luthor's personal heroes, evildoers such as Attila the Hun, Genghis Khan, Captain Kidd, Al Capone (Act No. 277, Jun '61: "The Conquest of Superman!"), Nero, Blackbeard, and Benedict Arnold (Act No. 292, Sep '62: "When Superman Defended His Arch-Enemy!"). "Many times when I've felt discouraged," remarks Luthor to one of his henchmen in June 1961, "I've come here--and gone away uplifted, inspired to go on with my work!"

Just as Superman's FORTRESS OF SOLITUDE contains the famed bottle city of KANDOR, "so does Luthor's Lair contain a bottled land," a primeval jungle, filled with all sorts of weird flora and fauna, which Luthor "once captured and reduced...after probing into another dimension!"

Other features of Luthor's Lair include Luthor's elaborately equipped workshop, where, in Luthor's words, "I invent my great machines for crime--and for my forthcoming conquest of **Superman**," and a special Reminder Room papered with crossed-out calendar pages. "Those crossed-out calendar days remind me how many years I've spent in prison because of **Superman**," explains Luthor, "--and that I must never lag in my war against him!" (Act No. 277, Jun '61: "The Conquest of Superman!").

When members of the Metropolis Police Department attempt to break into Luthor's Lair in September 1962, they are stymied by an impenetrable barrage of "colored rays" forming "a web of pure force" about the building. "**Brainiac** let me copy that **web-ray** from one of the super-weapons in his arsenal!" gloats Luthor. "The effect is only temporary! But it gives me a chance to make my getaway!" (Act No. 292: "When Superman Defended His Arch-Enemy!"). (*See also* BRAINIAC.)

LUTHOR'S LAIR II. The abandoned astronomical observatory—situated "on a lofty hill near Metropolis"—that serves as LEX LUTHOR's hideout and base of operations during February 1964. Lined with lead to safeguard its secrets against SUPERMAN's penetrating X-ray vision, Luthor's Lair II retains several features of the original LUTHOR's LAIR, including a Reminder Room papered with crossed-out calendar pages to remind Luthor of the many years he has spent in prison because of Superman ("My hate is even stronger when I look at this!" muses Luthor) and a bizarre Hall of Heroes lined with full-color, life-sized statues of men Luthor calls "**My** heroes...the greatest marauders of the ages," men such as Attila the Hun, Genghis Khan, Captain Kidd, and Al Capone. "I dreamed of being as great as they and I would be," seethes Luthor, "if **Superman** didn't always stop me!" (S No. 167: "The Team of Luthor and Brainiac!" pts. I-III—"The Deadly Duo!"; "The Downfall of Superman!"; "The Hour of Kandor's Vengeance!").

LUTHOR'S LAIR NO. 5. The abandoned coal mine—situated not far from Metropolis Prison—that serves as LEX LUTHOR's hideout and base of operations during July 1964. Deliberately established by

Luthor within easy reach of the prison so that he could escape to it quickly in the event he ever broke out, Luthor's Lair No. 5 is shielded against SUPERMAN's penetrating X-ray vision by the deposits of lead ore in the mine's coal-bearing rock (S No. 170/2: pts. I-II—"If Lex Luthor Were Superman's Father!"; "The Wedding of Lara and Luthor!").

LUTHOR THE NOBLE. An alias employed by LEX LUTHOR when, after having journeyed through the time-space barrier to KRYPTON at a time prior to its destruction, he poses as "a cosmic champion for good" from the planet Marlat as part of his bizarre scheme to marry LARA and thereby become the father of SUPERMAN (S No. 170/2, Jul '64: pts. I-II—"If Lex Luthor Were Superman's Father!"; "The Wedding of Lara and Luthor!").

LYLA LERROL. "Krypton's most famous emotion-movie actress" and "most glamorous beauty," a "hauntingly beautiful," "breathtakingly lovely girl" with whom SUPERMAN shares a passionate, poignant romance after having journeyed through the time-space barrier to the planet KRYPTON at a time preceding its destruction. Stranded for a time on his doomed native planet, Superman manages ultimately to escape the death of Krypton through a bizarre quirk of fate, while Lyla Lerrol—like JOR-EL and LARA and all the other doomed millions of Krypton—remains helplessly behind to perish in the impending cataclysm.

© NPP 1960

Lyla Lerrol

In November 1960, after having journeyed accidentally through the time-space barrier, Superman finds that he has arrived on the planet Krypton at a time prior to its destruction, on the day Jor-El and Lara are getting married. Bereft of his super-powers on this, his native world (see SUPERMAN [section E, the super-powers]), and unwilling to shatter his parents' happiness by telling them that their planet is doomed to destruction, Superman befriends his parents-to-be without telling them who he is—and even obtains temporary employment as Jor-El's assistant—while he grapples with the agonizing dilemma of how to escape the impending doom of his planet. "Since I can't fly away under my own power," muses Superman grimly, "I'm trapped here on Krypton! I'll perish when this world explodes!.... How ironic! I survived the destruction of Krypton as a child, and now may die as an adult in that same explosion!"

It is while he is thus stranded on Krypton—a period, apparently, of several weeks—that Superman is introduced to the blond Lyla Lerrol by his parents, and, almost against his will, "surrenders to the greatest romance he has ever known."

> Two pairs of lips meet, and two hearts thrill as one... as deep within the heart of **Krypton**, fiery forces clash and twist and churn, foreshadowing dreaded things to come...but the flames within the planet are like cold glaciers, compared to the mighty love blazing between **Superman** of Earth and **Lyla Lerrol** of **Krypton**....

"I'm glad that despite all the untold billions of worlds in the vast infinity of outer space, we two somehow found each other..." whispers Lyla.

"The universe would have been created without meaning for me if I had never met you, my darling..." replies Superman.

"Lois [Lane] loved me because I was **Superman**," muses the Man of Steel at one point, "but **Lyla** loves me for...myself! On this world I'm just an **ordinary mortal!**"

When it becomes apparent to Jor-El that "**Krypton** is going to be blown apart by internal stresses," Superman joins forces with the great scientist in a valiant—but hopeless—attempt to oversee the construction of a gigantic "space-ark" to transport Krypton's millions of inhabitants to a safe haven on Earth. But Krypton and its people are doomed to destruction—for even a Superman cannot change history—and so, when efforts to complete the space-ark fail, "**Superman** reconciles himself to spending his remaining days on the doomed planet with his parents and **Lyla Lerrol**, the Kryptonian girl he loves. Bravely, they plan to face the oncoming doom together."

And so, soon afterward, the couple announce their intention to marry as soon as Lyla has completed work on her forthcoming "emotion-movie." "The happiness we'll share as husband and wife," promises Superman, "will more than compensate for whatever happens...later!"

"A love like ours," muses Lyla silently, "can't be measured in mere days or years! Even **one** enchanted moment is worth a dozen ordinary lifetimes!"

But just as history has decreed that Krypton and its millions will perish, so has it decreed that Superman will survive the death of Krypton and escape to Earth. As the filming of Lyla's emotion-movie nears the completion of its final sequences, an extraordinary mishap—an event the odds against which could only be called astronomical—results in Superman's being catapulted violently into outer space inside a mock-up rocket ship being used in the filming. "Lyla!!" cries Superman as he stares helplessly out the porthole. And then he thinks, "I've lost her! Just when I'd resigned myself to perishing on **Krypton** with **Lyla** and my parents...this had to happen, due to a strange twist of fate!"

And so, soon afterward, far out in space, far from the gravitational pull of Krypton, Superman regains his super-powers and crashes through the hull of his mock-up spacecraft to freedom.

"If I return to **Krypton**," muses Superman, "I will lose my super-powers again! Fate can't be changed! It's impossible for me to save **Lyla** or my parents! Earth needs me!"

And so, flashing across the universe at incredible super-speed, Superman returns to his adopted planet Earth. Already, the passionate, wonderful, bittersweet romance with Lyla Lerrol on Krypton is receding in his mind's eye "like a strange, incredible dream!" (S No. 141: "Superman's Return to Krypton!" pts. I-III—"Superman Meets Jor-El and Lara Again!"; "Superman's Kryptonian Romance!"; "The Surprise of Fate!"). (*See also* SUPERMAN [section J 4, the relationship with Lyla Lerrol].)

In July 1961, during a visit to an extradimensional "parallel universe," Superman encounters a beautiful young woman—also named Lyla Lerrol—who is a perfect look-alike for Lyla Lerrol (S No. 146/2: "Superman's Greatest Feats!").

Superman fondly recalls his romance with Lyla Lerrol in October 1962 (S No. 156: "The Last Days of Superman!" pts. I-III—"Superman's Death Sentence!"; "The Super-Comrades of All Time!"; "Superman's Last Day of Life!") and again in January 1963 (S No. 158: "Superman in Kandor" pts. I-III— "Invasion of the Mystery Super-Men!"; "The Dynamic Duo of Kandor!"; "The City of Super-People!").

LYMAN (Superintendent). The cruel and unscrupulous superintendent of a state orphan asylum who has been illegally enriching himself by juggling the orphanage's account books and who, in the words of one of his young charges, "gives us kids food not fit t' eat, hires us out fer hard labor, beats us--an' makes us scrub floors fer hours an' hours!" Superintendent Lyman is brought to justice by SUPERMAN in Winter 1940 (S No. 3/1).

LYNX, THE. The colorful pseudonym employed by "meek little bookkeeper" LESTER LINK when he poses as the secret ruler of the underworld in a pathetic bid for public recognition (WF No. 12, Win '43: "The Man Who Stole a Reputation!").

M

MACK, BUD. The name unwittingly adopted by SUPERMAN in the mistaken belief that it is his real name—the result of his having been called "Bud" by some hobos and "Mac" by some baseball players—during a period when, afflicted by temporary amnesia as the result of prolonged exposure to synthetic KRYPTONITE (*see* FIXER, THE), he embarks on a career as the world's greatest pitcher, first for the bush-league Benson City Colts, and finally for the major-league Metropolis Titans (S No. 77/2, Jul/Aug '52: "The Greatest Pitcher in the World!").

MADDERS, JOHN. The head of the Freak Accident Protection Corporation, an insurance company offering costly protection against unlikely accidents, and the leader of a gang of criminals who deliberately create their own "freak accidents" in order to terrorize potential customers into purchasing their insurance. Madders and his henchmen are apprehended by SUPERMAN in May-June 1953 (WF No. 64: "The Death of Lois Lane").

MAG-EN. A "famous psychologist" of KRYPTON and the father of the "brilliant scientist" Ral-En. An attempt by Ral-En, an unscrupulous associate and former "college friend" of JOR-EL, to establish himself as dictator of all Krypton—by using "Kryptonian hyper-hypnotism," an especially potent form of "mass hypnosis" taught to him by his father, to convince the populace that he possessed super-human powers and that resistance to his rule was therefore hopelessly futile—was successfully thwarted through the courageous intervention of Jor-El during the period when SUPERMAN was still an infant and Krypton had not yet exploded.

Ral-En was subsequently banished into the PHANTOM ZONE for his ruthless attempt to seize power, and Mag-En—who had supported and encouraged his son's dictatorial ambitions—perished with Krypton when the planet exploded, although not before he had successfully implanted in the mind of the infant Superman an unconscious "hypnotic command" to perform ten evil deeds the next time he saw a certain blue comet hurtling through the heavens.

Years later, in July 1962, after having encountered the blue comet somewhere in space, Superman finds himself gripped by an overpowering compulsion to commit evil acts—including a narrowly averted attempt to destroy the planet Earth—until SUPER-GIRL, alerted to the true cause of Superman's bizarre behavior by the Kandorian scientist LON-ES, successfully brings about the destruction of the baleful blue comet and, by so doing, obliterates for all time the "destructive command placed in [Superman's] sub-conscious mind" by the villainous Mag-En many years ago (S No. 154/2: "Krypton's First Superman!").

MAIN, ED. The editor of the *Skid Row News*, a newspaper for hobos, and a ruthless blackmailer who extorts money from prominent men by threatening to make public the fact that close relatives of theirs have become hobos. Main is exposed and apprehended by SUPERMAN in May 1954, but only after Superman has first devoted his energies to helping a band of destitute hobos find new lives of dignity and self-reliance (S No. 89/2: "Superman of Skid Row!").

MALA. An evil survivor of the exploded planet KRYPTON—and an almost perfect look-alike for SUPERMAN—who, along with his two villainous brothers, Kizo and U-Ban, battles Superman in July-August 1950 (S No. 65/3: "Three Supermen from Krypton!") and again in July 1954 (Act No. 194: "The Outlaws from Krypton!").

Once members, along with Superman's father JOR-EL, of "Krypton's ruling council," which, according to Superman No. 65/3, "consisted of the [planet's] ten leading scientists," Mala and his brothers were exiled into outer space in a state of suspended animation inside a specially constructed space capsule after Jor-El had courageously thwarted their malevolent scheme to make themselves masters of Krypton by using a diabolical device of their own invention to extract all the moisture from Krypton's air as a means of blackmailing the Kryptonian population into capitulating to their rule. When Krypton exploded several years later, the three brothers remained alive, but asleep, in their space-capsule prison, until the day a hurtling fragment of their native planet crashed through the capsule's hull, awakening them from their years-long sleep and allowing them to escape to freedom, endowed, like all Kryptonians freed from Krypton's unique environment, with mighty super-powers identical to Superman's.

In July-August 1950 Mala and his brothers arrive on Earth, where, as part of their treacherous scheme to "rule all the earthmen," they soon succeed in using their extraordinary "scientific genius" to construct a diabolical machine designed to hypnotize Earth's population into mindless obedience with greatly "intensified light waves." Superman destroys the machine and battles the villains, and, although it appears for a time as though the outnumbered Superman may go down in defeat, ultimately he succeeds in duping the villains into battling among themselves, so that, with their awesome super-strength temporarily exhausted, he can shut them

217

Superman encounters Mala, U-Ban, and Kizo, 1950

inside another space-capsule prison and exile them once again into the farthest reaches of outer space (S No. 65/3: "Three Superman from Krypton!").

In July 1954, however, a chance collision with an asteroid frees Mala and his brothers from their space-capsule prison, and while Kizo and U-Ban immediately head toward SATURN "for a vacation from trouble," Mala decides to return to Earth to wreak vengeance on Superman. Mala's convoluted scheme of revenge involves luring Superman to a duplicate of the planet Earth—a so-called "counterfeit Earth"—that he himself has constructed in outer space, so that, with Superman thus preoccupied, Mala can destroy the real Earth without interference from Superman. The plot becomes even more complex when Kizo, who is completely ignorant of the fact that Clark Kent is secretly Superman, attempts to complicate life for the Man of Steel by posing as Clark Kent and then admitting he is Superman, a ploy that, for a time, creates serious difficulties for the Man of Steel by threatening to betray his dual identity.

Ultimately, with Superman lured safely away to his artificial Earth in outer space, Mala summons Kizo and U-Ban from Saturn to help him obliterate the Earth, but Superman returns to the real Earth in the nick of time, and, through an elaborate ruse of his own, succeeds in trapping the three Kryptonian outlaws inside yet another space-capsule prison and in exiling them once again into outer space (Act No. 194: "The Outlaws from Krypton!").

MALARKEY, PAT. A muscular but nevertheless incompetent bodyguard who is hired by PERRY WHITE to protect Clark Kent and LOIS LANE after SUPERMAN has been heard to complain aloud about being forced to "make a career of saving [Lois Lane's] life." Although White sees Malarkey's presence as guaranteeing "a vacation" for Superman, its real effect is to hamper Clark Kent in the performance of his

Superman duties, and he is forced to execute a fairly elaborate ruse in order to rid himself permanently of his bodyguard and restore his situation to what it was before (S No. 41/2, Jul/Aug '46: "Clark Kent's Bodyguard!").

MALCOLM, REX. A cunning "super-scientist turned crook" who attempts to loot the banks of METROPOLIS with the aid of a diabolical machine whose "sub-sonic vibrations" render everyone in the vicinity unconscious, only to be apprehended by SUPERMAN in September 1957. Malcolm's capture comes as the culmination of an elaborate ruse—devised by Superman with the aid of the Metropolis Police Department—in which a police lieutenant named Winters poses as the inventor of a "green ray" capable of exercising a deleterious effect on Superman as part of an overall scheme to lure Malcolm into the open so that he may be easily apprehended (S No. 116/1: "The Ray That Changed Superman").

MALVIO (General). The "fanatical leader" of a rebel army bent on assassinating the elected president of the "tiny European republic" of Borkia and establishing a one-man dictatorship there. With the presidential palace under tight security to guard against any possible assassination attempts, General Malvio and his henchmen construct a lifelike remote-controlled robot which introduces itself to the people of Borkia as Cosmic Man, a newly arrived super-hero from outer space, as part of an elaborate scheme to smuggle deadly explosives into the palace inside the robot's metal chest when Cosmic Man is invited to attend an audience with the president. The scheme is thwarted, however, by SUPERMAN, who hurls the explosives-laden robot into outer space and then apprehends General Malvio and his entire rebel army (Act No. 258, Nov '59: "The Menace of Cosmic Man!").

MANNING, BRENDA. An unemployed actress

and LOIS LANE look-alike who becomes an unsuspecting dupe of the gangland chieftain CHECK in an elaborate scheme to outwit SUPERMAN (WF No. 40, May/Jun '49: "The Two Lois Lanes!").

MAN OF STEEL, THE. An alternate name for SUPERMAN.

MAN WITH THE CANE, THE. A cunning Axis agent—clad in a false-face mask, maroon tailcoat, and top hat—whose name derives from his ever-present cane, which fires deadly poisoned darts. He is in reality Jim Mason, a patient feigning total paralysis at Bryant Hospital. After making a series of unsuccessful attempts to obtain the plans for a top-secret new "tank-plane" developed by inventor John Fleming, the Man with the Cane and his cohorts are finally apprehended by SUPERMAN and inventor Fleming in September-October 1942 (S No. 18/3: "The Man with the Cane").

MAPLEVILLE. A small town, situated somewhere in the northwestern United States, where SUPERMAN, acting under strenuous public pressure to select an official home town to call his very own, sets up residence in April 1953—in a lavish mansion, donated by the townspeople, which he promptly dubs Supermanor—only to have an angry citizenry order him out of town soon afterward, after mobs of gawking tourists rampaging through the streets, tons of Superman fan mail clogging the local post office, and the nerve-wracking sonic booms caused by Superman's super-speed arrivals and departures have made a shambles of Mapleville's small-town way of life and convinced its frazzled populace that having Superman as a neighbor is not the unmitigated blessing they had expected it to be (Act No. 179: "Super Manor!").

MARIN, TOM. The former star pitcher of the Metropolis Ravens—ousted from the club because of the poor pitching that resulted from his having been surreptitiously drugged by underworld gamblers—who, thwarted by SUPERMAN in a despairing attempt to commit suicide, launches a comeback with the Man of Steel's help that culminates in the salvation of his baseball career, the restoration of his personal dignity, and the arrest of the villainous gamblers, Sammy Brink and his cohort Joe (S No. 23/4, Jul/Aug '43: "Danger on the Diamond!").

MARPLE, DUKE. A "notorious gang-leader" and "ardent wrestling fan" who is brought to justice in August 1962 as the result of an elaborate ruse devised by SUPERMAN and carried out with the aid of "famed wrestling star" Antonino Rocca, KRYPTO THE SUPERDOG, and LIGHTNING MAN and COSMIC MAN of the LEGION OF SUPER-HEROES (S No. 155/2: "The Downfall of Superman!").

MARS. The fourth planet from the sun.

In January-February 1950 SUPERMAN journeys to Mars to help actor-director Orson Welles smash a plot by the Martian dictator MARTLER to "blitzkrieg the solar system" and conquer the Earth (S No. 62/1: "Black Magic on Mars!").

In April 1956 Superman journeys through the time barrier to the thirtieth century A.D., where he attempts to apprehend a gang of "mystery-thieves" responsible for a rash of spectacular "scientific thefts." At one point, after Superman has intervened in an attempt to prevent the criminals from stealing some "giant robots" from the planet Mars, the villains callously smash the gates on the Martian canals, thereby threatening the immediate depletion of the Martians' entire supply of "precious water" and forcing the Man of Steel to abandon the hunt for the criminals long enough to repair the damage (Act No. 215: "The Superman of Tomorrow"). (*See* SUPERMAN OF 2956; VAIL, VINSON.)

In July 1958 Superman journeys to Mars to obtain an ancient statue from the ruins of the planet's extinct civilization. The statue is one of a series of so-called "space trophies" which the Man of Steel gathers for inclusion in a time capsule which the Metropolis Museum plans to bury in the ground as a gift for the people of the fiftieth century A.D. (S No. 122/1: "The Secret of the Space Souvenirs").

MARTIN. A METROPOLIS political boss who is the secret mastermind behind a crooked "insurance society" which offers small, low-cost life insurance policies to elderly poor people as a means of tricking them into signing applications for larger policies, payable to Martin's chief henchman, so that Martin can, in turn, have the elderly purchasers murdered and collect their outstanding death benefits. Martin and his henchmen are apprehended by SUPERMAN in October 1940 (Act No. 29).

MARTIN (Professor). A "notorious criminal scientist" who perpetrates an elaborate hoax on SUPERMAN and the people of METROPOLIS—a hoax involving a bogus predicting machine called "the brain from the future"—as part of a scheme to earn a colossal fee promised him by the inmates of the Metropolis Jail if he can trick Superman into revealing the secret of his dual identity. Superman unravels the hoax and apprehends Martin in September 1956 (S No. 108/1: "The Brain from the Future").

MARTIN, BIG JIM. A cunning gangland czar whose capture by SUPERMAN in March-April 1949, along with that of his principal underworld subordinates, comes as the culmination of an elaborate ruse, devised by Superman with the aid of a scientist named Dr. Carr, in which Carr announces the invention of an amazing "predictor"—an ingenious "super-calculating machine" which, "if you give it the necessary information...will infallibly predict how a situation will work out"—and then proceeds to convince the world of its absolute reliability as part of a complex overall scheme to trick Martin's underlings into making full confessions and then hoodwink Martin into revealing the secret hiding place of his vast store of ill-gotten loot (WF No. 39: "The Fatal Forecasts!").

MARTIN, SOAPY. A notorious swindler, now employed as sports editor of the DAILY PLANET under the alias of Don Kelton, who, having discovered that the land beneath Metropolis Ball Park is rich in uranium ore and knowing that Superman will use his super-powers to make an erroneous story in the *Planet* come true rather than allow the paper to suffer undue embarrassment, sets in motion an elaborate scheme designed to trick Superman into helping him and his accomplice purchase the ballpark from its current owner. The scheme is thwarted by Superman in January 1956 (S No. 102/3: "The Million-Dollar Mistake").

MARTINSON (Professor). The inventor of an awesome "new weapon...which artificially causes earthquakes." By Spring 1940 LEX LUTHOR has kidnapped Professor Martinson as the first step in his plan to steal the "earthquake machine" and use it to blackmail the Earth into submission. SUPERMAN ultimately rescues Professor Martinson and demolishes the machine, but Martinson commits suicide in remorse over having created such a hideous weapon (S No. 4/1).

MARTINSON, JOSEPH. The chairman of the Designers' Emergency Committee, and the man who is secretly the DUDE (S No. 23/3, Jul/Aug '43: "Fashions in Crime!").

MARTLER. The evil dictator of MARS and admirer of ADOLF HITLER whose sinister plot to conquer the Earth and "blitzkrieg the solar system" with a gigantic fleet of Martian spaceships manned by his neo-Nazi followers, the so-called Solazis, is thwarted by SUPERMAN in January-February 1950 with the courageous aid of actor-director Orson Welles. Left stranded on an uninhabited asteroid by Welles and Superman, Martler will live out his remaining days in loneliness and exile (S No. 62/1: "Black Magic on Mars!").

MARYBELLE. A lovely blond backwoods girl who regards herself as betrothed to CLARK KENT in January 1955, after Kent, in the process of rescuing her from a falling tree branch, picks her up in his arms and carries her over a boulder known to the locals as Marryin' Rock, thus unwittingly fulfilling a local custom of betrothal. Kent's predicament is rendered even more acute when Marybelle's hillbilly brothers threaten to kill Kent unless he marries Marybelle, and her backwoods beau, Jed Summers, threatens to kill Kent unless he refuses, but SUPERMAN ultimately resolves the dilemma by tricking Summers into carrying Marybelle over Marryin' Rock just as Kent had, thereby freeing Marybelle to marry Summers, her favorite of the two "suitors" (S No. 94/3: "Clark Kent's Hillbilly Bride!").

MASON, JIM. The patient at Bryant Hospital who is secretly the MAN WITH THE CANE (S No. 18/3, Sep/Oct '42: "The Man with the Cane").

MASSEY, JAKE. A frail, puny man—a regular patron at a body-building clinic called Mike Mosby's Muscle-orium—who uses an elaborate system of microphones and miniaturized radio equipment that he has installed on the premises to (1) persuade proprietor Mosby that he is being given instructions in how to commit perfect crimes by the ghost of John L. Sullivan and (2) to hypnotize the flabby, out-of-

shape businessmen who come to the Muscle-orium into believing that they are powerful athletes, men of courage and daring capable of committing spectacular feats in the name of crime. For a time METROPOLIS is plagued by a series of "bold crimes...pulled by ungainly men who look anything but formidable"—men who obediently deposit their loot at Mike Mosby's Muscle-orium and then forget everything that they have done—but both Mosby and Massey are finally apprehended by SUPERMAN in July-August 1942 (S No. 17/3: "Muscles for Sale!").

MASTERMAN. The name assumed by PERRY WHITE during his short-lived career as a super-hero following the invasion of his body by the diabolical "plant intelligence" XASNU from the planet Zelm (Act No. 278, Jul '61: "The Super Powers of Perry White!").

MATHEWS, "BULL." A METROPOLIS gang chief whose capture by SUPERMAN in September 1958 comes as the culmination of an elaborate ruse—devised by Superman and carried out with the aid of PERRY WHITE and others—in which Perry White poses as the evil Black Knight of Arthurian legend and pretends to wound Superman with his supposedly "enchanted sword" in order to entice Mathews into attempting to purchase the sword with identifiable loot from a previous bank robbery (S No. 124/1: "The Super-Sword").

MAULL, SLUGGER. A notorious gangster whose violent death in a METROPOLIS alleyway leads to the arrest, trial, conviction, and execution of CLARK KENT on a murder charge as the result of Kent's having been discovered standing over Maull's corpse with the murder weapon moments after the murder. Ultimately, however, through an elaborate ruse—one which involves Clark Kent's faking his own death in the electric chair and then posing as his own ghost returned to wreak vengeance from beyond the grave—SUPERMAN frightens corrupt political boss Big Al Strumm and his henchman Dr. Lagg into confessing their responsibility for Maull's murder (Act No. 118, Mar '48: "The Execution of Clark Kent!").

MAXWELL, THADDEUS V. (Professor). The professor of advanced science at METROPOLIS UNIVERSITY during CLARK KENT'S sophomore year there—a renowned scientist described as "one of the most brilliant men in the world"—whose persistent but unsuccessful efforts to penetrate the secret of the young SUPERMAN'S identity are recalled by Clark Kent in November 1958 (S No. 125/2: "Clark Kent's College Days").

McGLOON, GOON. The co-leader, along with educated mobster Literary Link, of a gang of criminals who steal the newly dedicated statue of SUPERMAN from its pedestal in Metropolis's Planet Square—both as a gesture of defiance toward Superman and to boost their own flagging morale—only to be apprehended soon afterward by Superman in January-February 1946 (S No. 38/3: "The Man of Stone!").

MEACH, JOE. A former high-diver, now the

caretaker of METROPOLIS's SUPERMAN MUSEUM, who achieves infamy as the COMPOSITE SUPERMAN (WF No. 142, Jun '64: "The Origin of the Composite Superman!" pts. I-II—"The Composite Superman!"; "The Battle Between Titans!").

MEDINI. "The world's greatest hypnotist," a villain of awesome "hypnotic power" who devastates METROPOLIS with a series of baffling crimes in which he robs messengers and bank guards and then hypnotizes them into complete amnesia concerning the details of the crime. Pursued relentlessly by SUPERMAN in June 1940, Medini and his turbaned henchmen are apparently killed when Superman hurls them bodily through the air toward a grounded airliner, which then explodes suddenly in a pillar of flame (Act No. 25).

MEECHER, HENRY. A conniving opportunist who astounds all METROPOLIS in September 1950 by claiming that the seventeenth-century Indian chief who sold Metropolis Island to the white men had no tribal authority to do so, that the sale of the land was therefore invalid, and that "as last part-descendant of the tribe" that owned the land he is, consequently, the sole owner of "every foot of land in Metropolis."

Flashing through the time barrier to Metropolis Island in the year 1644, SUPERMAN thwarts an attempt by the evil Chief Gray Wolf and the wily medicine man Shama to plunge their tribe into a "useless war" with the neighboring northern tribes, and ultimately disproves Meecher's claim to ownership of Metropolis by establishing, somewhat ironically, that although Gray Wolf's original sale of the island was indeed illegal, as Meecher has alleged, the tribe ultimately approved a second sale to the white men in gratitude for all Superman had done for them (Act No. 148: "Superman, Indian Chief!").

MENTAL MAN. A comic-strip super-hero with telekinetic powers—created and drawn by LOIS LANE as a circulation booster for the DAILY PLANET—whose cartoon adventures begin appearing in newspapers throughout the country following their "immediate success" in the Daily Planet. Amazingly, a real costumed personage appears soon afterward at the Planet, claiming to be the comic-strip hero come miraculously to life, displaying what appear to be extraordinary mental powers, and offering the incredible explanation that "The concentration of millions of my fans throughout the country has materialized me into actuality!" In reality, however, the newly arrived super-hero is AQUAMAN in disguise, and his appearance is part of an elaborate scheme, devised by SUPERMAN, for the capture of a gang of criminals led by METROPOLIS racketeer "ACE" RUGGLES (Act No. 272, Jan '61: "Superman's Rival, Mental Man!"). The story is in many respects similar to Action Comics No. 196 (Sep '54: "The Adventures of Mental-Man!"). (See MENTAL-MAN.)

MENTAL-MAN. A comic-strip super-hero with telekinetic powers—his publicity describes him as "the world's eighth wonder," a hero who "brings to our time the strange powers of the ancients... the power of mind over matter!"—whose cartoon adventures begin appearing in the DAILY PLANET in September 1954 as part of an elaborate and ultimately successful scheme, devised by SUPERMAN with the cooperation of PERRY WHITE and Daily Planet staff artist Al Fallon, in which Superman poses as the "real-life" Mental-Man, the supposed inspiration for Al Fallon's new strip, so that he can accumulate the evidence he needs to apprehend "the mysterious leader of a world-wide gold racketeering syndicate," an "elusive criminal sought by a dozen nations!" (Act No. 196: "The Adventures of Mental-Man!").

MENTO. An unscrupulous mentalist, billed as the Great Mento, who pretends to read SUPERMAN's mind at a charity benefit show as part of a cunning scheme to bilk METROPOLIS gang chief Big Joe out of $1,000,000 by selling him the secret of Superman's identity. The swindle produces complications for Superman when Mento capriciously tells Big Joe that Clark Kent is Superman, never suspecting that he is actually correct, but Superman apprehends both criminals in July 1957 (S No. 114/2: "The Man Who Discovered Superman's Identity").

MERCURY. In Roman mythology, the messenger of the gods. In January-February 1944, after an accidental explosion in the city of Rome has awakened Mercury from his centuries-long sleep beneath the ancient ruins of "what once was a temple dedicated to pagan rites," Mercury flies to America, where, more in pursuit of mischief than anything else, he leaves a trail of pandemonium in his wake—and aids the cause of the METROPOLIS underworld—by committing a series of mayhem-producing pranks, as when he puts the city's police dispatchers to sleep with his magic staff and then sets all of Metropolis's policemen to chasing one another about the city by putting out a bogus radio call to the effect that bandits disguised as policemen are committing crimes using automobiles disguised as police cars. SUPERMAN ultimately apprehends the mischievous Mercury, however, and agrees to conceal his true identity from the population at large—thus sparing the winged god the public humiliation of having been defeated by a mere mortal—in return for Mercury's promise to undo the trouble he has caused and to help apprehend the criminals who have been aided by his antics (S No. 26/4: "The Quicksilver Kid!").

MERLIN (Doc). An alias employed by an unnamed Federal agent in August 1954 when he poses as an underworld inventor and claims to have devised an ingenious "ray dispenser" capable of disrupting the area of SUPERMAN's brain affecting his judgment as part of an elaborate and ultimately successful scheme, carried out with the aid of Superman, to lure the country's most powerful underworld leaders to METROPOLIS so that they may be easily apprehended (S No. 91/2: "The Lazy Man's Best Friend!").

METALLO. A ruthless villain—"a kind of human robot" with a human brain, a mechanical heart, and an indestructible "all-metal body"—who clashes with SUPERMAN in May 1959. He is actually unscrupulous journalist John Corben—an undetected thief, embezzler, and murderer—whose real body, mangled in an automobile accident beyond any hope of repair, is "rebuilt with a special metallic armor plate" and then "covered with a fleshlike, rubber-plastic skin" in an extraordinary emergency surgical operation performed by elderly scientist Professor Vale. Without his moustache, John Corben—alias Metallo—is a perfect look-alike for Superman.

John Corben, alias Metallo

While driving along a lonely road outside METRO-POLIS in May 1959, unscrupulous journalist John Corben—a self-described thief, embezzler, and murderer—loses control of his car on a sharp curve, careens off the road, and is crushed beneath the wreckage of his overturned car, where he is found moments later, mortally wounded but still clinging precariously to life, by elderly scientist Professor Vale. "This man's body is beyond repair!" remarks the professor gravely. "Ordinary surgery won't help him...! The only way I can save him is to try a desperate experiment--an experiment scientists have previously performed only on animals!"

Soon, "the operating lights gleam eerily in the professor's laboratory" as Professor Vale embarks on the fateful, life-saving operation. "Hmm...his heart has a fatal wound!" murmurs the professor. "I'll begin by giving him a mechanical heart! I'll use metal tubing for his circulatory system...."

It is days before John Corben comes out of his coma, and when he does, he finds Professor Vale standing concernedly over him. "It's amazing, professor!" exclaims Corben. "I remember blacking out...feeling pain...and now I feel perfect! Your operation saved my life! Thanks a million!"

"Don't thank me yet," replies Professor Vale, "...till you've seen what I've done! Let me uncover this blanket...."

"Great Scott!" cries Corben as his bedcovers are pulled aside. "I-I've got an all-metal body!"

"Correction!" replies Professor Vale. "You've still

got a human brain! But the rest of you has been rebuilt with a special metallic armor plate...unmeltable and shatterproof! Your new body is indestructible! Your [body is] now covered with a fleshlike rubber-plastic skin! However, the fluoroscope reveals [its] true metallic structure!"

"T-Then I'm a kind of human robot?" gasps Corben.

"Exactly!" replies Professor Vale. "I've given you a mechanical heart! Inside this 'fuse-box' [built into Corben's metal chest] is one of the two elements that can energize your synthetic heart and keep you alive, Corben, you're a-er-machine now! A machine must be powered! Here's what powers your mechanical heart--this capsule of uranium I've just removed from your chest!"

Momentarily deprived of the life-giving capsule of uranium that powers his mechanical heart, John Corben becomes weak and dizzy, only to recover his strength instantly the moment Professor Vale replaces the capsule inside his fuse box. "See--I return the capsule," continues the professor, "and your fatal weakness vanishes! Now remember!--Each capsule lasts only a day! It must be replaced by fresh uranium daily, or you will die!"

Departing soon afterward for Metropolis, albeit without learning the name of the second energizing element alluded to by Professor Vale, Corben obtains employment as a reporter on the DAILY PLANET and begins secretly using his awesome "metallic strength" to stage a series of spectacular uranium thefts—"I can't purchase it or mine it myself!" thinks Corben. "I can only steal it!"—in an effort to stockpile the precious uranium needed to ensure his day-to-day existence. "Even if they tried to shoot me," exults Corben, "the bullets'd bounce off my metallic body like green peas! Nothing stops me! Nothing! I can do whatever I want! I'm invincible!"

Indeed, before long, although the public is still unaware that journalist John Corben and the superpowerful uranium thief are one and the same man, law-enforcement officials have dubbed him Public Enemy Number One, and the news media have christened him Metallo, the Metal Man.

Soon afterward, after it has been announced that all supplies of uranium in the Metropolis area are being transferred to heavily guarded Fort Taber to protect them from Metallo, Corben cunningly impersonates Superman by donning a Superman costume and shaving off his moustache and then bluffs his way into Fort Taber in an effort to steal its entire uranium stockpile, only to be forced to flee empty-handed when the real Superman arrives on the scene. A short while later, however, Corben learns that the second element capable of energizing his synthetic heart is KRYPTONITE. Moreover, whereas each uranium capsule lasts only a day, one capsule of kryptonite contains sufficient energy to power Corben's heart indefinitely.

And so, after obtaining a kryptonite capsule from Professor Vale and inserting it in his fuse box in place of the uranium, Corben returns to Metropolis, determined to destroy Superman by exposing him to the kryptonite so that the Man of Steel will not be able to apprehend him for his previous thefts. Cornering Superman in the basement of the Metropolis Exhibit Hall, where an exhibition of Superman's souvenirs is being prepared, Corben weakens Superman with his capsule of kryptonite and then, leaving his own kryptonite wedged among some overhead basement pipes so that its baleful radiations can continue to paralyze and ultimately annihilate Superman, flees the exhibit hall after replacing the kryptonite capsule that was formerly in his fuse box with a chunk of kryptonite marked for display in the souvenir exhibition. Superman escapes the painful kryptonite deathtrap, however, and pursues the villain to the home of Lois Lane—whom Corben has been wooing during his brief career at the *Daily Planet*—but before the Man of Steel can even leap to the attack, Corben collapses, dead of a heart attack, because, ironically, the kryptonite which he stole from the exhibition hall and placed in his fuse box was not real kryptonite at all, but only "fake, prop kryptonite"—ordinary rock, colored green—intended for use as a display item in place of real kryptonite to avoid the emission of radiations harmful to Superman (Act No. 252: "The Menace of Metallo!").

METALO. A villain of awesome power, a renegade inventor—discoverer of "the most powerful metal on Earth" as well as a miraculous "strength serum"—who, clad in a special armored suit of his own design, is impervious to bullets, can fly through the air, and possesses monumental super-strength equivalent to Superman's.

Operating from a subterranean hideaway situated beneath the main tent of the Farnham Circus, somewhere on the Metropolis waterfront, Metalo stuns the city with a series of spectacular crimes—including the theft of an entire mail car from the Metropolis train terminal, and an attempt to extort $5,000,000 from the city's businessmen by threatening to destroy Metropolis—until finally, in a climactic encounter with Superman, "the very mountains tremble and are rent asunder by the colossal battle of these two super-powerful opponents ...!"

Believed dead after plummeting into a yawning lava-filled crevice at the peak of the awesome battle, Metalo manages to cling to an outjutting rock and, although thwarted in his evil undertakings, to survive (WF No. 6, Sum '42: "Man of Steel versus Man of Metal!").

METEOR VALLEY. A valley on the planet Krypton which was "created by a monstrously gigantic meteor that glanced off the surface" of the planet during Krypton's prehistoric era, "long before life existed" there (S No. 141, Nov '60: "Superman's Return to Krypton!" pts. I-III—"Superman Meets Jor-El and Lara Again!"; "Superman's Kryptonian Romance!"; "The Surprise of Fate!").

METROPOLIS. The resident city of Superman and the scene of the vast majority of his adventures.

Although the name Metropolis is itself fictional, Metropolis as it is described in the texts is modeled after, and fully intended to represent, the city of New York.

In the earliest texts of the Superman chronicles, Superman's home city remains unidentified. Action Comics No. 11 explicitly identifies it as Cleveland, Ohio (Apr '39), but Action Comics No. 13 contradicts this by placing Superman's resident city within close proximity to the Sing Sing state prison, in Ossining, New York (Jun '39). In late 1939, the name Metropolis appears in the chronicles for the first time (Act No. 16, Sep '39), and the city is situated definitely in New York State (S No. 2/2, Fall '39: "Superman Champions Universal Peace!").

The evidence identifying Metropolis with the city of New York is overwhelming, despite the appearance of an occasional text identifying Metropolis and New York as two separate cities (Act No. 311, Apr '64: "Superman, King of Earth!"; and others). Situated in the eastern United States (WF No. 46, Jun/Jul '50: "The Seven Crimes of Mister 7!"), more specifically, in New York State (S No. 2/2, Fall '39: "Superman Champions Universal Peace!"), only a short trip by train from New Haven, Connecticut (S No. 25/2, Nov/Dec '43: "I Sustain the Wings!"), Metropolis is a major seaport with a large waterfront (Act No. 187, Dec '53: "Superman's New Super Powers!"; and many others) whose population, in 1951, was 6,004,119 (S No. 71/2, Jul/Aug '51: "The Anti-Superman Club!"). The city proper stands on Metropolis Island, which was sold to white settlers by the Indians "over three hundred years ago" (Act No. 148, Sep '50: "Superman, Indian Chief!"). The United Nations is headquartered in Metropolis (Act No. 311, Apr '64: "Superman, King of Earth!"; and others), and the world-famed Statue of Liberty stands vigilant in Metropolis Harbor (Act No. 143, Apr '50: "The Bride of Superman!"; *see also* Act No. 146, Jul '50: "The Statues That Came to Life!"). Metropolis's magnificent skyline is world famous (S No. 26/1, Jan/Feb '44: "The Super Stunt Man!"; and others). Although one text describes Metropolis, somewhat ambiguously, as "a typical American city representative of the rest of the nation" (S No. 18/1, Sep/Oct '42: "The Conquest of a City"), others describe it as a "great city" (Act No. 30, Nov '40; S No. 68/1, Jan/Feb '51: "The Six Elements of Crime!"), "America's greatest city" (Act No. 103, Dec '46: "The Road to Happiness!"), and "the greatest city in the world" (S No. 64/2, May/Jun '50: "The Isle of Giant Insects!").

Metropolis's mightiest skyscraper is variously referred to as the Emperor Building (Act No. 80, Jan '45: "Mr. Mxyzptlk Returns!"; Act No. 102, Nov '46: "Mr. Mxyzptlk and His Wonderful Lamp!"), the Metropolis State Building (Act No. 204, May '55: "The Man Who Could Make Superman Do Anything!"), the Monarch State Building (S No. 70/2, May/Jun '51: "The Life of Superman!"; S No. 75/2, Mar/Apr '52: "Superman--Thrill Salesman!"), and the State Skyscraper (Act No. 162, Nov '51: "It!"), but, whatever its name, it is the tallest building in Metropolis and the central feature of its famous skyline.

Other places of interest in Metropolis include the Metropolis Museum of Natural History (Act No. 44, Jan '42; see also Act No. 181, Jun '53: "The New Superman"), the Metropolis Planetarium (S No. 91/1, Aug '54: "The Superman Stamp!"), the Metropolitan Museum (S No. 106/2, Jul '56: "The Thefts of Clark Kent"), the Wireless City movie theater (S No. 25/4, Nov/Dec '43: "Hi-Jack--Jackal of Crime!"), the Halldorf Hotel (S No. 36/2, Sep/Oct '45: "Glory for Gloria!"), and the Metropolis Public Library, whose entranceway is adorned by a pair of stone lions (Act No. 146, Jul '50: "The Statues That Came to Life!"; see also WF No. 28, May/Jun '47: "Superman's Super-Self!"). Metropolis's lavish shops include Lacey's Department Store (S No. 21/3, Mar/Apr '43: "The Robber Knight"), Stacy's Department Store (S No. 31/1, Nov/Dec '44: "Tune Up for Crime!"; and others), and Spiffany's Jewelry Store (S No. 52/1, May/Jun '48: "Preview of Plunder").

METROPOLIS UNIVERSITY is located in Metropolis (S No. 125/2, Nov '58: "Clark Kent's College Days"; and others), as is the SUPERMAN MUSEUM (S No. 150/3, Jan '62: "When the World Forgot Superman!"; and others), and the Daily Planet Building, home of the DAILY PLANET (Act No. 36, May '41; and others), Metropolis's "leading newspaper" (S No. 6/1, Sep/Oct '40; and others).

Metropolis's famous neighborhoods include Queens (S No. 70/1, May/Jun '51: "Lois Lane Meets Annie Oakley!"); Chinatown (S No. 54/2, Sep/Oct '48: "The Secret of the Chinese Dragon!"; Act No. 231, Aug '57: "Sir Jimmy Olsen, Knight of Metropolis"); Little Bohemia, "the famed artist's section of Metropolis" (Act No. 78, Nov '44: "The Chef of Bohemia!"); the midtown area (S No. 27/3, Mar/Apr '44: "Robbers' Roost!"); Fifth Avenue (S No. 24/3, Sep/Oct '43: "Surprise for Superman!"); the financial district (WF No. 12, Win '43: "The Man Who Stole a Reputation!"; and others); the slum area known as Roaring Kitchen (S No. 22/2, May/Jun '43: "The Luck of O'Grady"); the waterfront district (Act No. 187, Dec '53: "Superman's New Super Powers!"; and others); and Planet Square, the so-called "crossroads of the world" (Act No. 77, Oct '44: "The Headline Hoax!"; and others), located in the heart of Metropolis's Great White Way (Act No. 112, Sep '47: "The Cross-Country Chess Crimes!"; see also S No. 22/3, May/Jun '43: "The Great ABC Panic!").

For recreation and relaxation there is Metropolis Park (WF No. 68, Jan/Feb '54: "The Menace from the Stars!"; and others), where city dwellers and tourists alike can take a boat ride on a quiet lake (S No. 22/4, May/Jun '43: "A Modern Robin Hood!"), jog around the reservoir (WF No. 37, Nov/Dec '48: "The Superman Story!"), or travel along its roadways by car (S No. 22/4, May/Jun '43: "A Modern Robin Hood!") or horse-drawn carriage (Act No. 163, Dec '51: "The Girl of Tomorrow"). The Superman Museum is located in Metropolis Park (S No. 150/3, Jan '62: "When the

World Forgot Superman!"), along with "a colossal steel statue of Superman—erected by a grateful city" (WF No. 28, May/Jun '47: "Superman's Super-Self!" and others). The inscription on the statue's pedestal reads, "Superman, Champion of Metropolis" (Act No. 249, Feb '59: "The Kryptonite Man!").

Metropolis features an elaborate transportation system, including a network of elevated (Act No. 20, Jan '40; and others) and subterranean subways (S No. 17/1, Jul/Aug '42: "Man or Superman?"; and many others), ferryboats (S No. 71/3, Jul/Aug '51: "The Man Who Stole the Oceans!"), bridges (S No. 18/1, Sep/Oct '42: "The Conquest of a City"; and others), and vehicular tunnels (S No. 52/1, May/Jun '48: "Preview of Plunder"; and others). Streetcars were commonplace in Metropolis in 1941 (WF No. 4, Win '41: "The Case of the Crime Crusade") and apparently survived even into the early 1960s (S No. 151/2, Feb '62: "The Man Who Trained Supermen!") Parties of tourists circle the city aboard special excursion vessels (Act No. 146, Jul '50: "The Statues That Came to Life!"), or romp in the surf off Metropolis's popular public beaches (S No. 48/1, Sep/Oct '47: "The Man Who Stole the Sun!"; S No. 19/3, Nov/Dec '42). Specially honored guests are treated to "Metropolis' famed ticker-tape reception" (Act No. 165, Feb '52: "The Man Who Conquered Superman!"), such as that accorded KING HARRUP II upon his arrival in Metropolis in January-February 1951 (S No. 68/2: "Lois Lane's Royal Romance!").

The gateway to Metropolis is Metropolis Harbor (WF No. 20, Win '45: "The Toyman: Super-Scientist!"; and many others), the point of arrival and departure for ocean liners (S No. 63/1, Mar/Apr '50: "Achilles versus Superman!"; and others), freighters (WF No. 20, Win '45: "The Toyman: Super-Scientist!"; and others), and other vessels (WF No. 37, Nov/Dec '48: "The Superman Story!"; and others). Visitors sailing into Metropolis Harbor are greeted by the world-famed Statue of Liberty (Act No. 143, Apr '50: "The Bride of Superman!"; see also Act No. 146, Jul '50: "The Statues That Came to Life!") and by a gigantic statue of Superman standing astride the harbor like the legendary Colossus of Rhodes (WF No. 23, Jul/Aug '46: "The Colossus of Metropolis!"). Metropolis waterways mentioned in the chronicles include the Metropolis River (WF No. 49, Dec/Jan '50-'51: "The Men Who Shot Superman!") and Metropolis Bay (S No. 81/2, Mar/Apr '53: "20,000 Leagues Under the Sea with Superman"; and others).

Metropolis's "most famous inhabitant" is indisputably Superman (S No. 26/4, Jan/Feb '44: "The Quicksilver Kid!"; and others), and it is for him that the city has reserved its greatest honors. Superman Day has been celebrated in Metropolis on at least two separate occasions (S No. 157/3, Nov '62: "Superman's Day of Doom!"; Act No. 328, Sep '65: "Superman's Hands of Doom!"), and the famed Superman Museum houses an extensive collection of Superman memorabilia (S No. 150/3, Jan '62: "When the World Forgot Superman!"; and others). Superman was awarded the city's Outstanding Citizen Award for 1954 "in honor of [his] conspicuous efforts to improve Metropolis" (S No. 93/2, Nov '54: "Jimmy Olsen's Double!"). For at least four years during the 1950s, the Metropolis Police Department awarded an annual Superman Medal "to the person whose heroism...helped **Superman** the most" during the preceding year. Clark Kent, the man who is secretly Superman, is awarded the Superman Medal in August 1955 (Act No. 207: "The Four Superman Medals!").

Statues and other artistic tributes to Superman abound in Metropolis, including the statue of Superman in the Metropolis Hall of Fame (Act No. 297, Feb '63: "The Man Who Betrayed Superman's Identity!"), the "colossal steel statue of **Superman**" in Metropolis Park (WF No. 28, May/Jun '47: "Superman's Super-Self!"; and others), the monumental statue of Superman towering over Metropolis Harbor (WF No. 23, Jul/Aug '46: "The Colossus of Metropolis!"), and the marble statue of Superman unveiled in Planet Square in January-February 1946 (S No. 38/3: "The Man of Stone!"; S No. 69/1, Mar/Apr '51: "The Prankster's Apprentice!").

MIDVALE, the adopted home town of Linda Lee Danvers, the pretty blond teen-ager who is secretly SUPERGIRL, is a suburb of Metropolis. So is the town of HIGHVILLE, which Superman visits in January 1957 (S No. 110/2: "The Mystery of Superman!"). Metrodale, another Metropolis suburb, is destroyed by ROLF ZIMBA's Gold Badge Organization in July-August 1941 (S No. 11/1). BIZARRO CITY, the capital of the planet HTRAE (S No. 140, Oct '60: pts. I-III—"The Son of Bizarro!"; "The 'Orphan' Bizarro!"; "The Bizarro Supergirl!"), is "a crude copy of Metropolis" which "looks like something a mad architect would design!" (Act No. 263, Apr '60: "The World of Bizarros!").

METROPOLIS MEEK MAN'S CLUB, THE. A club for meek men in the city of METROPOLIS. Working behind the scenes in November 1955, SUPERMAN helps Messrs. Wilson and Barker, the club's president and vice-president, overcome their meekness and develop the sorely needed self-confidence that helps them achieve their goals in life (S No. 101/2: "The Meek Man's Club").

METROPOLIS SHUTTERBUG SOCIETY, THE. A club for photographers, including among its members "some of the nation's greatest cameramen," which offers a grand prize of $5,000 to whichever of its members submits the best photograph of SUPERMAN in action. Although "camera aces" Archie Pink and Doc Sloan are odds-on favorites to win the prize, the contest is ultimately won by underdog lensman Howard Figit, a scrawny, bespectacled, unassuming fellow who repeatedly risks his life to obtain photos of Superman, ironically because he hopes that winning the prize money will enable him to "afford to seek the action and thrilling adventures he'd always dreamed of in his quiet life..." (WF No. 49, Dec/Jan '50-'51: "The Men Who Shot Superman!").

METROPOLIS UNIVERSITY. CLARK KENT's alma mater, located in the city of METROPOLIS (S No. 125/2, Nov '58: "Clark Kent's College Days"; and others). Dr. Charles Corlin, the father of VANCE CORLIN (WF No. 57, Mar/Apr '52: "The Artificial Superman!"), and PROFESSOR THADDEUS V. MAXWELL (S No. 125/2, Nov '58: "Clark Kent's College Days") have served on its faculty. It was during his senior year at Metropolis University that Clark Kent first met LORI LEMARIS (S No. 129/3, May '59: "The Girl in Superman's Past!").

In July-August 1948 SUPERMAN is accidentally transported into the distant past—along with typewriter repairman MIKE MOONEY—as the result of a freak accident in a Metropolis University mathematics laboratory (S No. 53/2: "The Oracle from Metropolis!").

In March-April 1951 the Trickster steals the contributions collected at Metropolis University's "old grads fund-raising drive dinner" (S No. 69/1: "The Prankster's Apprentice!"). (*See* PRANKSTER, THE.)

In November 1952 Superman apprehends the MIRACLE TWINE GANG in the act of stealing some valuable radium from the Metropolis University campus (Act No. 174: "The Man Who Shackled Superman!").

MIDNITE GANG, THE. A gang of criminals who strike at midnight and commit their crimes in total darkness with the aid of a camera equipped with an infrared lens. The gang robs the Metropolis National Bank and steals a top-secret "atomic bazooka" from a government physics laboratory before its members are finally apprehended by SUPERMAN in August 1955 (S No. 99/1: "The Camera Club Scoops!").

MIDVALE. The METROPOLIS suburb which is the adopted home town of Linda Lee Danvers, the pretty blond teen-ager who is secretly SUPERGIRL. The home of Mr. and Mrs. Fred and Edna Danvers, Midvale is also the site of the Midvale Orphanage, where Supergirl lived—under the name Linda Lee—prior to her adoption by the Danverses. (*See* SUPERGIRL.)

MIDVALE ORPHANAGE. The orphanage, located in the METROPOLIS suburb of Midvale, which is the home of Linda Lee, the pretty blond teen-ager who is secretly SUPERGIRL, from the time of her arrival on Earth until her adoption by Mr. and Mrs. Fred and Edna Danvers. (*See* SUPERGIRL).

MIGHTY MAID. An alias employed by SUPERGIRL in January 1960 when she poses as a beautiful brown-haired super-heroine from the fourth dimension as part of an elaborate ruse, devised by SUPERMAN, to thwart a plan by extraterrestrial aliens to destroy the planet Earth—Superman's adopted planet—in retaliation for a mistaken attack on a fleet of their spacecraft, long ago, by the army of KRYPTON, the far-distant planet where Superman was born (Act No. 260: "Mighty Maid!").

MILES, MONA. A lovely blond reporter for an unnamed METROPOLIS newspaper—she is described as "even more persistent" than LOIS LANE and as "always trying to outsmart her"—who becomes suspicious that Clark Kent is SUPERMAN in August 1955 and promptly launches a one-woman investigation to prove her suspicion correct. Through an elaborate ruse, however, Superman manages to persuade the resourceful newswoman that he has no single secret identity at all, but rather that he assumes new identities at random, a different one every few days (S No. 99/2: "The 1,000 Lives of Superman!").

MILLION-DOLLAR MARVIN. A METROPOLIS gang chief—so named because he commits only crimes netting him a minimum of $1,000,000—whose capture by SUPERMAN in January 1953 comes as the culmination of an elaborate ruse, devised by Superman, in which Superman pretends to have suddenly acquired a "new craving for wealth" so that, by greedily demanding fees and rewards for his hitherto gratuitous services and conspicuously hoarding his wealth inside a mighty "super-vault" carved into the side of a mountain, he can entice Million-Dollar Marvin and his gang into attempting to rob the vault and thereby take them into custody (Act No. 176: "Muscles for Money").

MILO (Professor). An alias employed by SUPERMAN in October 1958 when he poses as the inventor of "a mechanical brain that can predict the future" as part of his complex plan to apprehend the CONDOR GANG (WF No. 97: "The Day Superman Betrayed Batman!").

MINERVA (Aunt). *See* KENT, MINERVA (MISS).

MINK, MART. The proprietor of Mart Mink Used Auto Parts, a large METROPOLIS auto-parts dealership where stolen cars are secretly broken up into parts and sold to the unsuspecting public. SUPERMAN, who is hampered by temporary amnesia during this period as the result of having allowed himself to be used as a subject in the testing of an unperfected brain-studying device at the Metropolitan Clinic, finally apprehends Mink and his henchmen in January-February 1945 (S No. 32/1: "Superman's Search for Clark Kent!").

MINTON, BILL. A young aeronautical engineer who has developed a radically new type of jet transport, a modification of a conventional jet plane embodying "startling improvements that will revolutionize air transport!" When racketeer and rival airplane manufacturer Loops Logan attempts to murder Minton and sabotage his aircraft to prevent him from winning a sorely needed contract and financial backing, SUPERMAN intervenes repeatedly to rescue Minton, who ultimately apprehends Logan on his own and gains the financial aid he needs (WF No. 21, Mar/Apr '46: "The Plane of Tomorrow!").

MIRACLE TWINE GANG, THE. A gang of criminals, so named because they commit a series of spectacular crimes with the aid of a small quantity of virtually indestructible "miracle twine" that is accidentally produced when a chunk of green KRYPTONITE drops unexpectedly into a vat of experimental synthetic fiber at the Synthetic Fiber Labora-

tories in METROPOLIS. The gang is apprehended by SUPERMAN in November 1952 (Act No. 174: "The Man Who Shackled Superman!").

MR. GIMMICK. A ruthless "gangland genius" and originator of numerous "cunning criminal schemes" who, in return for a fee of $1,000,000 paid to him by the czars of the METROPOLIS underworld, concocts an utterly inhuman scheme "to wreck Superman's career" by tricking the Man of Steel into accidentally detonating a powerful "super-explosive," thereby obliterating the city of Metropolis—along with its millions of inhabitants—in an awesome "super-atomic blast." The heinous "mass murder plot" is thwarted by SUPERMAN, who apprehends Mr. Gimmick and his gangland cohorts in September 1965 (Act No. 328: "Superman's Hands of Doom!").

MR. OHM. A cunning criminal mastermind who carries out a series of spectacular armored-car robberies by using a so-called "flying electro-magnet"—an airplane, wrapped in coils of heavy electric wire, with a gigantic magnet hanging suspended from its fuselage—to literally snatch the armored vehicles off the road and carry them through the air to his hideout. Mr. Ohm and his henchman are apprehended by SUPERMAN in March-April 1948 (S No. 51/2: "The Magnetic Mobster!").

MISTER SEVEN. A cunning master criminal with a thirst for notoriety—clad in a red, yellow, and blue costume with a large number 7 emblazoned on his chest—who commits a spectacular crime a day in and around METROPOLIS, each time taunting the authorities in advance with an enigmatic clue, and each time committing a crime somehow related to the day of the week, as when he steals a rare first edition on Sunday, the first day of the week. Mister Seven is in reality Scraps Fabian, a petty thief who, tired of being a small-time crook but unable to recruit a gang because of his lowly underworld status, adopts the "catchy name" Mister Seven and then launches a frenetic publicity blitz—including a radio jingle, a skywriting campaign, and an advertising blimp bearing the almost jocular admonition to watch for Mister Seven, "greatest criminal of his day"—designed to imprint his name indelibly on the public consciousness. Mister Seven and his lone accomplice are apprehended by SUPERMAN in June-July 1950 (WF No. 46: "The Seven Crimes of Mister 7!").

MISTER SINISTER. A malevolent purple-skinned alien from the "weird purple-hued world" of the fourth dimension, a "frustrated poet," communicating frequently in rhyme, whose complex scientific machinery enables him to kidnap entire buildings from the earthly dimension, either to loot at his leisure in the fourth dimension or to hold captive until his exorbitant demands for ransom are met. His ultimate ambition is to "rule the world," a desire SUPERMAN sees as a symptom of the alien's need "to compensate for [his] failure as a poet!" Pursued through a series of alien dimensions by Superman in May-June 1942, Mister Sinister is transformed into a harmless black shadow when a raygun blast intended for the Man of Steel accidentally hits the villain instead (S No. 16/3: "Case of the Runaway Skyscrapers").

MISTER TWISTER. A "master criminal" who "twists crime to do the unexpected and completely fools the authorities" by doing exactly the opposite of what the police are likely to expect. He is in reality not a criminal at all, but rather well-known author Dan Judd, who has recruited a gang of henchmen and embarked on a career in crime for the sole purpose of accumulating material for a new book, and who fully intends to return all his stolen loot once the book is finished. When Mister Twister's henchmen turn on him and make off with the loot he has collected, author Judd helps SUPERMAN apprehend them, but he still must serve a six-month prison term for the crimes he has committed (Act No. 96, May '46: "Haircut--And a Close Shave!").

MR. WHEELS. A "mystery engineer who designs special gadgets for his underworld clients," such as an ingenious tractorlike vehicle for crawling up the outside wall of a multistory warehouse. Mr. Wheels is also the leader of a gang of criminals who commit a series of spectacular crimes with the aid of these devices, but he and his henchmen are apprehended in September 1956 through the heroic efforts of SUPERMAN (S No. 108/2: "Perry White, Jr., Demon Reporter!").

MR. Z. A mysterious villain whose elaborate efforts to kill a small black and white stray dog seem bewilderingly inexplicable until SUPERMAN apprehends the villain and learns that he is really Oscar Lanchester, second in line to inherit his eccentric aunt's vast fortune, but only in the event of the death of her primary heir, her dog (S No. 19/3, Nov/Dec '42).

MISTRI-LOR. "A lost civilization," nestled in a "vast valley" concealed from the outside world by "a remote mountain range" somewhere on the far side of the globe, which is the scene of SUPERMAN's encounter with the lovely QUEEN LURA in March 1963 (Act No. 298: "Clark Kent, Coward!").

MOFFATT (Mrs.). An alias employed by LOIS LANE in March-April 1946 when she poses as a wealthy widow in order to investigate the lonely hearts agency operated by J. WILBUR WOLFINGHAM (S No. 39/3: "Swindle in Sweethearts!").

MOITON. The pet white rabbit of HOCUS AND POCUS (Act No. 83, Apr '45: "Hocus & Pocus... Magicians by Accident!").

MOLE, THE. The nickname of a notorious criminal, "an expert miner and tunneler" unheard of since the day he successfully tunneled his way to freedom from inside a GOTHAM CITY prison, who has, under the alias Mr. Harrah, succeeded in obtaining a municipal contract to construct a network of storm sewers beneath the streets of Gotham City. Using the sewer construction project as a cover, the Mole and his henchmen have surreptitiously dug a network of underground tunnels leading to and from Gotham City's major banks, so that they can loot the banks and make a hasty subterranean getaway. Ultimately,

however, BATMAN, ROBIN, and SUPERMAN discover the ingenious tunneling scheme. Working at superspeed, Superman diverts the direction of the Mole's tunnels so that the villain and his henchmen, intending to tunnel their way into the Gotham Bank, emerge instead inside the grounds of the Gotham City Jail (WF No. 80, Jan/Feb '56: "The Super-Newspaper of Gotham City").

MONAHAN, SKEET. The leader of a gang of protection racketeers who are apprehended by SUPERMAN in November-December 1942 (S No. 19/2).

MON-EL. A member of the LEGION OF SUPER-HEROES, and the only inhabitant of the PHANTOM ZONE who was not sent there for any crime. A native of the planet Daxam and a longtime friend of SUPERMAN, Mon-El, like all the inhabitants of his native planet, is vulnerable to lead, just as Superman is vulnerable to KRYPTONITE. Mon-El, whose real name is Lar Gand, is fully aware that Clark Kent is secretly Superman.

Arriving on the planet Earth while Superman was still a teen-ager in SMALLVILLE, Mon-El discovered that, in the alien environment of Earth, he possessed super-powers identical to Superman's. Soon afterward, however, he was completely robbed of his super-powers as the result of a potentially fatal overexposure to lead. To halt the physical deterioration wrought by the lead poisoning and thus save Mon-El's life, Superman projected his friend into the Phantom Zone (Act No. 284, Jan '62: "The Babe of Steel!"), where he will remain, unaging, until the thirtieth century A.D., when, thanks to a special "antidote serum" developed by BRAINIAC 5, he will be released from the Phantom Zone permanently to assume a regular role in the Legion of Super-Heroes (Adv No. 305, Feb '63: "The Secret of the Mystery Legionnaire!").

In January 1962, after "the electrical ions of the Aurora Borealis have opened a small hole in the Phantom Zone," it is Mon-El who alerts Superman to the fact that the exiled "super-villains" will be able to escape into the earthly dimension as soon as the hole becomes large enough for them to squeeze through (Act No. 284: "The Babe of Steel!"). (*See* PHANTOM ZONE, THE.)

In October 1962, when Superman is believed to be dying of exposure to VIRUS X, an incurable Kryptonian malady, it is Mon-El who finally informs Superman—by beaming a telepathic message to SATURN GIRL from inside the Phantom Zone—that Superman is not suffering from exposure to Virus X at all, but merely from the effects of a kryptonite nugget that has become accidentally lodged in JIMMY OLSEN's camera. Indeed, once this fragment of kryptonite has been removed from Superman's presence, Superman is, almost immediately, restored to full health (S No. 156: "The Last Days of Superman!" pts. I-III—"Superman's Death Sentence!"; "The Super-Comrades of All Time!"; "Superman's Last Day of Life!").

In November 1962, having just invented the "zone-ophone," a device designed to enable him to communicate with the Phantom Zone prisoners, Superman conducts his initial test of the new device by using it to communicate with his friend Mon-El (S No. 157/1: "The Super-Revenge of the Phantom Zone Prisoner!").

MOON. The only known natural satellite of the Earth.

In February 1950 LEX LUTHOR fuses "a couple of handfuls of dust from the dark side of the moon" with several other "strange materials" in order to produce the first known sample of synthetic KRYPTONITE (Act No. 141: "Luthor's Secret Weapon").

In September-October 1950, when SUPERMAN believes he is dying of kryptonite poisoning, he engraves a gigantic message on the surface of the moon in hopes of bequeathing mankind a farewell "guiding principle." "Do good unto others," reads the message in mile-high letters, "and every man can be a superman! [signed] Superman (Clark Kent)." A short while later, however, after having learned that he is not dying after all, Superman returns to the moon and erases the name "Clark Kent" from his message just as the moon is about to appear from behind a cloud and expose his secret identity to the entire world (S No. 66/2: "The Last Days of Superman!").

In January-February 1953, when PROFESSOR WILLIS WILTON divides the formula for his "four-dimensional projector" into seven parts and hides them in seven inaccessible places, one of the hiding places he chooses is the moon's largest crater (WF No. 62: "The Seven Secrets of Superman").

In January 1956, when a METROPOLIS multimillionaire offers a reward of $100,000 to the first man to land on the moon, Superman flies to the moon, inscribes a gigantic message ("Superman was here") on the surface to prove he has been there, and then returns to Earth to collect his reward, which he distributes among the stockholders of the SUPERMAN STOCK COMPANY (S No. 102/1: "Superman for Sale").

A text for August 1956 recounts the events surrounding Superman's battle with DRAGO, a renegade scientist of the thirtieth century A.D. After escaping from prison on the moon, Drago and his gang of fellow convicts transform the moon into a jet-propelled spaceship and propel it out of its orbit, using it as their headquarters in an attempt to devastate and conquer the Earth. The villains are apprehended and the moon is restored to its rightful orbit, however, through the heroic efforts of Superman, whose presence in this future era is the result of his exposure, in August 1956, to the terrible radiation of a defective atomic pile, which caused him to lapse into a sleeplike coma from which he only awakens a thousand years later (S No. 107/3: "Rip Van Superman!").

In March 1957 Superman helps lift the spirits of crippled youngster Tommy Snead by taking Tommy on a brief journey to the moon (S No. 112/1: "Superman's Neighbors").

In June 1957 Superman flies to the moon and, with the super-friction of his hands, polishes a mammoth chunk of moon rock into a gigantic mirror so that he can reflect beams of bright light toward Earth to halt a stampede of charging elephants. Later, Superman smashes a moon mountain into boulder-sized chunks and hurls them toward Earth in order to dam up a flash flood somewhere in the Swiss Alps (Act No. 229: "The Superman Satellite").

In July 1957, after Superman's super-powers have been temporarily multiplied "a thousandfold" by a weird undersea phenomenon, Superman only narrowly misses crashing into the moon and smashing it to fragments when he leaps high into the air in an unsuccessful effort to apprehend BART WELLINS (Act No. 230: "Superman Loses His Powers").

BATMAN, ROBIN, and Superman apprehend the villain ROHTUL on the moon during a visit to the world of 2957 A.D. (WF No. 91, Nov/Dec '57: "The Three Super-Sleepers!").

In December 1958 an astronaut named Rogers becomes the pilot of the "first manned rocket" to the moon when he circles the moon in a spacecraft that is hurled into moon orbit by Superman. Returning to Earth, however, Rogers soon achieves infamy as the MOONMAN (WF No. 98: "The Menace of the Moonman!").

In February 1959 Superman uses lead ore that he mines on the moon to construct an elaborate "leaden suit"—impervious to kryptonite radiation—to wear in his forthcoming battle with Lex Luthor (Act No. 249: "The Kryptonite Man!").

In April 1959 Superman visits the moon for the purpose of "collecting samples of the moon's ore for the Metropolis Observatory...!" (S No. 128/2: "The Sleeping Beauty from Krypton!").

In October 1959 Superman dispatches one of his Superman robots into outer space to carry out a scientific exploration of the dark side of the moon. Inside an air-filled crater there, the robot discovers the "ruins of a dead civilization" and swiftly rebuilds them "into an Earthlike city," so that, one day, in the age of space travel, earthmen will be able to "live in this 'moon metropolis!'" (Act No. 257: "The Reporter of Steel!").

In September 1960, after HERCULES has used his mighty Olympus powers to make the waters of a large gulf vanish into thin air, Superman pushes the moon out of its orbit and positions it directly over the gulf. "Now to push the moon down to Earth and over that dry gulf!" thinks Superman. "The moon's gravitational pull is what causes tides on Earth! At this close range, the moon's pull [has] created a big tidal wave from the ocean that is spilling into the open end of the dry gulf! It will fill up rapidly to save the dying fish and float the stranded ships!" Moments later, the mammoth task completed, Superman hurls the moon "back into its former orbit!" (Act No. 268: "Superman's Battle with Hercules!").

In February 1961 the mischievous MR. MXYZPTLK uses his extraordinary extradimensional powers to transform the moon into a gigantic globe of green cheese, and then, moments later, back into the moon again (Act No. 273: "The World of Mr. Mxyzptlk!").

In May 1961 Superman deliberately shoves the moon in front of the sun—thereby creating an artificial eclipse and temporarily cutting off all of Earth's sunlight—in order to defeat an extraterrestrial "cactus creature" that draws its powers from the light and heat of the sun. Soon afterward, with the alien creature now helpless, Superman restores the moon to its appropriate orbit (S No. 145/2: "The Interplanetary Circus!").

In May 1962, after the mayor of Rangoon, Burma, has decided to issue a commemorative stamp in honor of Superman, the Man of Steel flies to the moon with the mayor and his assistant in the hope that the lunar landscape will help the Burmans create "an inspiring picture of Superman" for use on their stamp (S No. 153/2: "The Secret of the Superman Stamp!").

In July 1962 Superman lures Mr. Mxyzptlk into following him to the moon as part of his plan for tricking the extradimensional imp into reciting his name backwards, thereby returning him to his home dimension (S No. 154/1: "The Underwater Pranks of Mr. Mxyzptlk!").

In October 1962, when Superman believes he is dying of an incurable malady, he launches himself into outer space and uses his heat vision to char a gigantic "farewell message . . . to the whole world" into the side of the moon. "Do good unto others," reads the message, "and every man can be a superman. [signed] Superman (Clark Kent)." A short while later, however, after having learned that he is not dying after all, Superman has SUPERGIRL and KRYPTO THE SUPERDOG "beam their heat vision . . . across space" and erase the name "Clark Kent" from the message so that, when the moon appears from behind a cluster of clouds, the world will not learn his secret identity (S No. 156: "The Last Days of Superman!" pts. I-III— "Superman's Death Sentence!"; "The Super-Comrades of All Time!"; "Superman's Last Day of Life!").

In November 1962 Superman dispatches one of his Superman robots to the moon to retrieve a cache of Kryptonian "radio-visual tapes"—containing the police records of the various PHANTOM ZONE criminals—which landed there after hurtling through space following the explosion of KRYPTON (S No. 157/1: "The Super-Revenge of the Phantom Zone Prisoner!").

In December 1962, during a period when Superman is suffering occasional bouts of mental instability inflicted upon him by members of the SUPERMAN REVENGE SQUAD, the Man of Steel maliciously gives the moon a super-powered shove which, in addition to causing massive tidal waves on Earth, produces devastating tides on the ocean floor and wreaks disaster in the undersea realm of ATLANTIS. Once the insane episode is past, however, Superman restores the moon to its proper location in space and repairs the damage to Atlantis caused by the temporary dislocation (Act No. 295: "Superman Goes Wild!").

After promising President JOHN F. KENNEDY that

he will help him achieve the goal of improving the physical fitness of America's youth, Superman helps strengthen the self-confidence of a pair of track athletes by flying them to the moon, where, in the vastly weaker gravity, they are able to perform amazing athletic feats (S No. 170/1, Jul '64: "Superman's Mission for President Kennedy!").

MOON, VINCE. A notorious "heist man" and leader of a gang of criminals who are apprehended by SUSAN SEMPLE and SUPERMAN in December 1951 while attempting to rob the House of Gems, a "fabulous exhibit of the Metropolis Jewelers' Association" (Act No. 163: "The Girl of Tomorrow").

MOONEY, MIKE. A cynical typewriter repairman, convinced that everything in life is really some sort of "racket," who is accidentally transported along with SUPERMAN into the distant past when a freak accident in the mathematics laboratory of METROPOLIS UNIVERSITY's Professor Grog "projects" them into a "time gap" and sends them hurtling across the time barrier to ancient Greece at the time of the Trojan War. Temporarily stranded in the Greece of AGAMEMNON, Superman single-handedly completes construction of the legendary Trojan horse and thwarts Mooney's unscrupulous attempt to transform the oracle at Delphi into a self-serving fortune-telling swindle before Professor Grog finally succeeds in returning them safely to his mathematics laboratory in the twentieth century (S No. 53/2, Jul/Aug '48: "The Oracle from Metropolis!").

MOONMAN, THE. A costumed criminal, possessed of awesome magnetic powers which enable him to attract objects with his right hand and repel them with his left, who commits a series of spectacular crimes having the MOON as their general theme, as when he steals a precious moonstone from a museum and an ancient silver chariot, representing the moon chariot of the goddess Diana, from an exhibition of historical vehicles. Unbeknownst even to himself, the Moonman is an astronaut named Rogers, the pilot of the world's "first manned rocket" to the moon, whose simultaneous exposure to the light of the moon and the eerie glow of a passing comet while his craft was still in moon orbit somehow produced the bizarre "chemical reaction" that now transforms him into a cunning super-criminal whenever he becomes exposed to the light of the moon.

"The glow of that strange comet," explains SUPERMAN, "plus the moon's light, must have had a chemical reaction that affected Rogers--which makes him a criminal only at night when moonlight touches him! During the day, he's normal and doesn't remember what happened the night before!"

Rogers commits a series of spectacular crimes as the Moonman before he finally realizes, to his horror, that the notorious Moonman is none other than himself. Before the well-meaning Rogers can turn himself over to the authorities, however, he is abducted by a gang of harbor pirates who hope to force him to use his Moonman powers to aid them in their crimes.

Ultimately, Rogers's Moonman powers permanently fade and vanish, and Rogers earns an amnesty for the crimes he unintentionally committed by helping BATMAN ROBIN, and Superman apprehend the harbor pirates who had hoped to profit from his powers (WF No. 98, Dec '58: "The Menace of the Moonman!").

MOPPLE, HORACE. An alias employed by SUPERMAN in February 1962 when, after donning civilian clothes and a false moustache, he responds to an advertisement for a METROPOLIS muscle-building emporium that claims it can transform ordinary men into "supermen" in "ten easy lessons" (S No. 151/2: "The Man Who Trained Supermen!"). (See KRUGG, CONRAD.)

MORANS, MOOSE. A "reputed...inventor of ingenious, secret crime devices" who is—along with Silky Steve, a "lone wolf" and "daring plotter," and Sparkles Garnet, a "master of explosives" and "connoisseur of gems"—one of "the country's three biggest crime moguls," all of whom are currently in GOTHAM CITY to attend a major "crime conference." Each is so fanatically determined to "dominate crime" that he is willing to go to almost any lengths to impress his underworld colleagues by staging a successful crime under the noses of BATMAN, ROBIN, and SUPERMAN. The Man of Steel and the Dynamic Duo apprehend the three crime czars in September 1962, however, despite the handicap that has been imposed on them by a freak occurrence that has temporarily transferred Superman's KRYPTONITE vulnerability to Batman, causing Batman to undergo a series of bizarre transformations as the result of his exposure to a red-kryptonite sample stored in the BATCAVE (WF No. 128: "The Power That Transformed Batman!").

MORKO. A wily opportunist and inventor who ingeniously plants six gigantic plastic statues of SUPERMAN in seemingly inaccessible places—such as far beneath the sea, and in the interior of a mountain peak—as part of an elaborate scheme to fascinate Superman with the apparent enigma of the statues so that, in the process of retrieving them from their locations with the aid of his mighty superpowers, he will unwittingly enrich Morko and his henchmen. When Superman bores through the earth like a human drill to retrieve a Superman statue far underground, for example, he inadvertently releases a valuable gusher of oil onto land owned by Morko.

Realizing finally that the giant statues are only ploys designed to trick him into using his superpowers for Morko's own benefit, Superman moves swiftly to ensure that Morko and his henchmen do not profit from their scheme, such as by redirecting the oil gusher onto a barren Indian reservation for the benefit of local Indians. And, when he is reminded that Morko and his men have really committed no crime for which they can properly be arrested ("He didn't break any laws!" muses Superman; "All he did was use my super-powers for his own ends! But a trickster like him shouldn't go free!"), Superman responds by tricking Morko and his henchmen into attacking him in the belief that they are only destroying a lifeless Superman statue and then hauls them off to jail on a trumped-up assault and battery charge (Act No. 150, Nov '50: "The Secret of the 6 Superman Statues!").

MORTON, HAROLD. A "prominent psychologist and radio wizard" who, through the use of complex "ultra-high frequency" radio equipment, hypnotizes reputable citizens while they sleep into committing crimes for his benefit and then forgetting completely the details of the crimes they have committed. SUPERMAN exposes Morton's villainy in July 1941, and then hypnotizes him into making a complete confession of his crimes (Act No. 38).

MORTON, JOHN. The leader of a gang of criminals, who, posing as a scientist, announces that he has invented a "new petrifying gas that turns living flesh to solid stone" as part of an elaborate scheme to extort $1,000,000 from the city of METROPOLIS by threatening to transform its citizens into lifeless stone statues. SUPERMAN exposes the gas as fraudulent and apprehends the criminals in August 1949 (Act No. 135: "The Case of the Human Statues!").

MORVEN, CHARLES (Dr.). A "brilliant scientist" whose "latest and greatest achievement" is his invention of the so-called "Morven magnet," a superpowerful magnet whose "vast power...can be turned on and off like [an] electric light," and which, like light, "can be used in a concentrated beam!" In Dr. Morven's words:

My discovery of super-magnetism makes the *Morven magnet* 1,000 times more powerful than any other ever built! Its possibilities for constructive use are boundless!

The Morven magnet is stolen, however, and used for crime, by LEX LUTHOR and his henchmen in July-August 1952 (WF No. 59: "Superman's Super Hold-Up!").

MORWATHA. An evil medicine man whose scheme to bring about the death of the aged Chief Hun-sha—so that he himself can become chief—is thwarted by SUPERMAN in January 1955. As punishment for his crimes, Hun-sha decrees that Morwatha, stripped of the title of medicine man, "will become the lowliest of our tribe, and women and children will use [him] for their laughter!" (Act No. 200: "Tests of a Warrior!").

MT. RUSHMORE NATIONAL MEMORIAL. A gigantic sculptured relief of the heads of George Washington, Thomas Jefferson, Abraham Lincoln, and Theodore Roosevelt which is carved in granite on the northeast side of Mt. Rushmore, 25 miles from Rapid City, South Dakota. Sculpted by Gutzon Borglum, who began it in 1927 and whose son completed it in 1941, it is one of America's greatest monuments. In January 1943 EMIL LORING attempts to destroy the Mount Rushmore monument and other world-famous landmarks, but his mad scheme is thwarted by SUPERMAN (Act No. 56: "Design for Doom!").

Baron Munsdorf and Superman, 1940

The Musketeer in action, 1955

MOXBY, "BLINKY." A cowardly, "shifty-eyed little sneak-thief" who, fearful of gangland retaliation, refuses to come forward with testimony linking gangster Mike Chandler to a recent murder until SUPERMAN fakes his own death, poses as his own ghost, and tricks Moxby into making his eyewitness knowledge public (S No. 21/4, Mar/Apr '43: "The Ghost of Superman!").

MULLOY, MARK. A fugitive criminal and infamous "super-swindler" who exacts a promise from SUPERMAN to fulfill seven of his wishes—in return for Superman's having extracted some gold ore and a fossil from an area fifty miles beneath Mulloy's property without thinking to ask Mulloy's permission—only to have Superman outwit him at every turn when he attempts to use Superman's services for self-enrichment. Mulloy is finally taken into custody by Baldy, the elderly caretaker of Mulloy's property and a longtime admirer of Superman (S No. 130/2, Jul '59: "The Super-Servant of Crime").

MUNSDORF (Baron). The murderous leader of a ring of spies for an unnamed "foreign racketeer nation" whose attempts—through murder, terror, and torture—to force a courageous inventor named Professor Hunter to relinquish the formula for his powerful "new anaesthetic gas," a gas capable of putting an entire community instantly to sleep, are thwarted by SUPERMAN in December 1940. Confronted finally by Superman in Professor Hunter's laboratory, the treacherous baron meets a richly deserved doom when he "unleashes a bolt of incredible voltage" from a "deadly sub-atomic death-ray gun" that ricochets off Superman's outstretched hand and "blasts back from the Man of Steel to the body of Munsdorf himself," killing the villain instantly. "That's one less spy for the country to worry about!" murmurs Superman grimly (Act No. 31).

MUSEUM OF MENACE, THE. *See* FORT SUPERMAN.

MUSKETEER, THE. A French crime-fighter whose methods and techniques are modeled after those of America's BATMAN. In July-August 1957 the Musketeer visits the United States in response to a summons from "well-known philanthropist" John Mayhew, who wishes to award the Musketeer and other world-famous crime-fighters—including Batman and ROBIN, SUPERMAN, the GAUCHO, the LEGIONARY, and the KNIGHT and the SQUIRE—charter membership in his newly formed Club of Heroes (WF No. 89: "The Club of Heroes!"). (*See* LIGHTNING-MAN.) (For a complete account of the Musketeer's crime-fighting career, consult *The Encyclopedia of Comic Book Heroes: Volume I—Batman.*)

MXYZPTLK (Mr.). A mischievous imp from the fifth dimension, endowed with extraordinary extradimensional powers, who has for more than three decades been making periodic forays into the earthly dimension to pester, bedevil, and infuriate SUPERMAN. Superman's only means of ridding himself of this pesky fifth-dimensional sprite is to trick him into pronouncing or spelling his own name—Mxyzptlk—backwards, which has the effect of temporarily returning Mr. Mxyzptlk to his home dimension. Mxyzptlk is pronounced Mix-yez-pitel-ick. Mxyzptlk backwards—Kltpzyxm—is pronounced Kel-tipz-yex-im.

From September-October 1944, the date of Mr.

Mr. Mxyzptlk

131/1: "The Menace of Mr. Mxyzptlk!"; and others). In this article, with the exception of direct quotations and story titles taken from the earlier texts, the modern spelling—Mxyzptlk—is the one employed.

It is impossible to define the extent and limits of Mr. Mxyzptlk's powers with any real precision, but his powers are similar if not identical to those of BAT-MITE. Among other things, Mr. Mxyzptlk can fly through the air and animate inanimate objects (S No.

Mxyzptlk's textual debut (S No. 30/3: "The Mysterious Mr. Mxyztplk!"), through March 1955, Mr. Mxyztplk's name is consistently rendered as Mxyztplk, i.e., with the letters *p* and *t* transposed (S No. 96/2: "Mr. Mxyztplk--Mayor of Metropolis!"; and others). In September 1955, however, both spellings are employed (Act No. 208: "The Magic of Mr. Mxyztplk"), and, from August 1959 onward, the new spelling—Mxyzptlk—is used exclusively (S No.

30/3, Sep/Oct '44: "The Mysterious Mr. Mxyztplk!"; and others); make rivers flow uphill and bring movie images to life (Act No. 80, Jan '45: "Mr. Mxyztplk Returns!"); make himself visible and invisible at will (S No. 36/1, Sep/Oct '45: "Mr. Mxyztplk's Mistake!"; and others); read minds and stretch his body as though it were an endlessly stretchable elastic band (S No. 46/1, May/Jun '47: "Mr. Mxyztplk Goes to College!"); make linotype machines spew forth sardine cans instead of type, turn a boulder into rock candy, and transform grapes into grapefruit (S No. 86/3, Jan '54: "The Fourth Dimension Gazette!"); turn the MOON into green cheese (Act No. 273, Feb '61: "The World of Mr. Mxyzptlk!"); and unleash a weird "zoophonic force" capable of endowing every animal in METROPOLIS with "the power to speak intelligently" (S No. 154/1, Jul '62: "The Underwater Pranks of Mr. Mxyzptlk!").

"It's simple!" explains Mr. Mxyztplk in March 1955. "A fifth dimensional brain in a three dimensional world can do anything!" (S No. 96/2: Mr. Mxyztplk--Mayor of Metropolis!").

The amazing powers with which Mr. Mxyztplk performs his mischievous "fifth-dimensional highjinks" (S No. 51/1, Mar/Apr '48: "Mr. Mxyztplk Seeks a Wife!") are variously described in the chronicles as "extra-dimensional powers" (Act No. 102, Nov '46: "Mr. Mxyztplk and His Wonderful Lamp!"); "magical powers" and "supernatural powers" (S No. 46/1, May/Jun '47: "Mr. Mxyztplk Goes to College!"); "fifth-dimensional legerdemain" (S No. 86/3, Jan '54: "The Fourth Dimension Gazette!"); "dimensional magic" (Act No. 190, Mar '54: The Boy Who Saved Superman!"); "weird magic" (WF No. 113, Nov '60: "Bat-Mite Meets Mr. Mxyzptlk!"); and "5th dimensional magic" (Act No. 273, Feb '61: "The World of Mr. Mxyzptlk!"; and others).

According to most accounts, however, the effects of Mr. Mxyztplk's "magical mischief" (S No. 174/2, Jan '65: "Super-Mxyzptlk...Hero!") vanish completely the moment he either leaves the Earth (S No. 154/1, Jul '62: "The Underwater Pranks of Mr. Mxyzptlk!") or returns to his home dimension (S No. 148/2, Oct '61: "Mr. Mxyzptlk's Super-Mischief!"; and others). "He's disappearing," muses Superman gratefully as he watches Mr. Mxyztplk vanish back into the fifth dimension in January 1965, "...and whatever magical mischief he did before will vanish, too!" (S No. 174/2: "Super-Mxyzptlk...Hero!").

Particularly in the early texts, the chronicles are unspecific and inconsistent regarding the name of Mr. Mxyztplk's home dimension. Superman No. 30/3, for example, describes Mr. Mxyztplk as a "sappy supernatural sprite" from an unnamed alien dimension (Sep/Oct '44: "The Mysterious Mr. Mxyztplk!"), while Action Comics No. 80 refers to him as "that gnomish nuisance from an unknown dimension" and as a "problem-pixie" from "some weird extra-dimensional world" (Jan '45: "Mr. Mxyztplk Returns!"). Although several early texts describe Mr. Mxyzptlk as a native of the "multi-dimensional

world" of Zrfff (S No. 33/1, Mar/Apr '45: "Dimensions of Danger!"), also referred to as the extradimensional LAND OF ZRFFF (S No. 36/1, Sep/Oct '45: "Mr. Mxyztplk's Mistake!"; Act No. 102, Nov '46: "Mr. Mxyztplk and His Wonderful Lamp!"), one text describes him as an inhabitant of "the sixth dimension" (Act No. 112, Sep '47: "The Cross-Country Chess Crimes!"), while another refers to "...Topsy-Turvy Land, the fifth-dimensional home of that troublesome imp, **Mr. Mxyztplk...**" (S No. 51/1, Mar/Apr '48: "Mr. Mxyztplk Seeks a Wife!"). From March-April 1948 onward, however, Mr. Mxyzptlk is consistently described as a native of the fifth dimension (S No. 51/1: "Mr. Mxyztplk is consistently described as a native of the fifth dimension (S No. 51/1: "Mr. Mxyztplk Seeks a Wife!"; and many others), and the evidence of the chronicles, taken as a whole, is that Mr. Mxyzptlk is a native of the Land of Zrfff, which is either in the fifth dimension or coterminous with it.

Like the other inhabitants of his home dimension, Mr. Mxyzptlk is "elfishly egotistical" (S No. 33/1, Mar/Apr '45: "Dimensions of Danger!"), vain, and conceited. Even in his own world he is an inveterate practical joker, occasionally arousing the ire of the authorities with his mischievous pranks (S No. 131/1, Aug '59: "The Menace of Mr. Mxyzptlk!"; and others). According to several early texts, the Land of Zrfff is a monarchy, and Mr. Mxyzptlk its court jester (S No. 36/1, Sep/Oct '45: "Mr. Mxyztplk's Mistake!"; and others). A self-styled ladies' man—"Mr. Mxyzptlk considers himself quite a Romeo!" notes Superman in August 1959 (S No. 131/1: "The Menace of Mr. Mxyztplk!")—Mr. Mxyzptlk has wooed such lovely and fascinating women as journalist LOIS LANE (S No. 51/1, Mar/Apr '48: "Mr. Mxyztplk Seeks a Wife!") and cover girl LARISSA LEE (S No. 62/3, Jan/Feb '50: "Mr. Mxyztplk, Hero!"). However, "If there's one thing [Mr. Mxyzptlk] can't stand, it's ridicule!" (Act No. 208, Sep '55: "The Magic of Mr. Mxyztplk"), a fact that Superman has used to help him outwit the mischievous extradimensional imp on more than one occasion (S No. 86/3, Jan '54: "The Fourth Dimension Gazette!"; and others).

Since September-October 1944, the date of his textual debut (S No. 30/3: "The Mysterious Mr. Mxyztplk!"), Mr. Mxyzptlk has made more than a score of "whirlwind visitations" (S No. 33/1, Mar/Apr '45: "Dimensions of Danger!") to what he regards as our "quaint three-dimensional world" (Act No. 80, Jan '45: "Mr. Mxyztplk Returns!") for the purpose of pestering, bedeviling, and humiliating Superman. Indeed, although a few early texts assert—seemingly more with whimsy than with seriousness—that Mr. Mxyztplk's motive in visiting Earth is to conquer it with his extradimensional powers (S No. 30/3, Sep/Oct '44: "The Mysterious Mr. Mxyztplk!"; S No. 36/1, Sep/Oct '45: "Mr. Mxyztplk's Mistake!"), this theme of hoped-for dimensional conquest soon disappears from the chronicles entirely, leaving only the imp's desire to torment Superman as the reason for his periodic visits. On these occasions, Mr. Mxyzptlk likes nothing better than to drive Superman to the brink of distraction, tauntingly addressing him as "Supe" (S No. 174/2, Jan '65: "Super-Mxyzptlk...Hero!") or "Super" (S No. 51/1, Mar/Apr '48: "Mr. Mxyzptlk Seeks a Wife!"; and others) while he wreaks havoc in Metropolis and elsewhere with his extradimensional pranks.

"Mr. Mxyztplk, that impish fellow from the fifth dimension, is back for another visit!" observes Superman No. 59/3. "With his spectacular powers and zany sense of humor, that means only one thing... a super-headache for his favorite super-victim!" (Jul/Aug '49: "The City That Forgot Superman").

Other texts contain these comments:

> Once again, Superman's super-headache, the impish and unpredictable Mr. Mxyztplk, is back from the fifth dimension to make life miserable for the Man of Steel! [Act No. 151, Dec '50: "Superman's Super-Magic Show!"]

> Watch out!...He's here again!...Mr. Mxyztplk, that daffy little denizen from the fifth dimension who uses his zany powers to drive Superman mad! [S No. 86/3, Jan '54: "The Fourth Dimension Gazette!"].

In addition, Action Comics No. 273 describes Mr. Mxyztplk as "that imp from the fifth dimension... whose greatest joy is to come to our world and play magical pranks on Superman!" (Feb '61: "The World of Mr. Mxyztplk!"); Superman No. 155/2 refers to him as "the zany imp from the 5th dimension who loves to come to our world and play magical pranks on Superman!" (Aug '62: "The Downfall of Superman!"); and World's Finest Comics No. 113 notes that his "greatest delight is using weird magic to pester Superman!" (Nov '60: "Bat-Mite Meets Mr. Mxyzptlk!"). Observing that Mr. Mxyzptlk's avowed goal is to make Superman "the laughing stock of the world," Action Comics No. 190 goes on to describe the pesky extradimensional imp as "that miniature master of mirth, that imp from out of this world whose main pleasure in *this* one is humiliating Superman!" (Mar '54: "The Boy Who Saved Superman!").

Superman, for his part, has described Mr. Mxyzptlk as "the sappy sprite with the slaphappy sense of humor" (S No. 33/1, Mar/Apr '45: "Dimensions of Danger!"); "that fifth dimension interloper" (Act No. 190, Mar '54: "The Boy Who Saved Superman!"); an "infernal, aggravating pest," and "that silly pest from another dimension who loves to pull mad pranks on me"(Act No. 273, Feb '61: "The World of Mr. Mxyzptlk!"); "that maddening imp" (S No. 169/1, May '64: "The Infernal Imp!"); and "a diabolical menace" (S No. 171/2, Aug '64: "The Curse of Magic!"). "...Life is just impossible," notes Superman in August 1959, "while this pest is around!" (S No. 131/1: "The Menace of Mr. Mxyzptlk!").

"Why don't you like me, Super?" asks Mr.

Mxyzptlk brightly in March-April 1948. "Because you're an unmitigated, double-distilled nuisance!" replies Superman (S No. 51/1: "Mr. Mxyztplk Seeks a Wife!").

Although Mr. Mxyzptlk means no real harm with his maddening extradimensional pranks, they frequently pose hazards to life and property which the mischievous imp did not intend, or threaten to cause disasters which can only be averted by Superman, as when Mr. Mxyzptlk magically reroutes an elevated subway track so that it veers off abruptly into midair (Act No. 80, Jan '45: "Mr. Mxyztplk Returns!"), or accidentally stampedes a circus elephant toward a crowd of passersby (S No. 169/1, May '64: "The Infernal Imp!").

Unfortunately for Superman, even his mighty super-powers do not make him invulnerable to Mr. Mxyzptlk's extradimensional magic, although the question of his vulnerability is treated inconsistently in the texts. In February 1960, for example, Mr. Mxyztplk temporarily places Superman under his hypnotic control by means of "5th dimensional hypnotism" (S No. 135/3: "The Trio of Steel!"), and in February 1961, after inhaling a cloud of the mischievous imp's "magical sneezing powder," Superman unleashes a gargantuan "super-sneeze" that literally destroys "a distant solar system." "You're invulnerable to everything," remarks Mr. Mxyztplk on this occasion, "--except my magical powers!" (Act No. 273: "The World of Mr. Mxyztplk!"). In March-April 1945, however, Mr. Mxyztplk is unable to hypnotize Superman (S No. 33/1: "Dimensions of Danger!"), and, in July 1962, Mr. Mxyztplk unleashes a "second childhood gas" which, although it temporarily infantalizes everyone in Metropolis, fails to affect Superman because of his "invulnerable body" (S No. 154/1: "The Underwater Pranks of Mr. Mxyztplk!").

By and large, however, Superman is vulnerable to Mr. Mxyzptlk's magic, and this sad fact makes the extradimensional imp one of the Man of Steel's most formidable foes. In August 1964, after he has fallen temporary victim to Mr. Mxyztplk's so-called "curse of magic," Superman makes this observation: "Too bad my invulnerability can't protect me from magic or a sorcerer's spell!" (S No. 171/2: "The Curse of Magic!").

Indeed, Superman's only real means of ridding himself of his pesky fifth-dimensional adversary is by tricking the imp into reciting or spelling the name Mxyzptlk backwards, a ploy which temporarily banishes the silly sprite to his home dimension. In Mr. Mxyzptlk's words, "Kltpzyxm," which is Mxyzptlk spelled backwards, is "the mystic word that sends me back to my own dimension!" (S No. 46/1, May/Jun '47: "Mr. Mxyztplk Goes to College!").

For exactly how long Mr. Mxyztplk must remain in his home dimension, however, is treated inconsistently in the chronicles. Superman No. 30/3 notes only that saying his name backwards banishes the extradimensional imp to his own world "for a time" (Sep/Oct '44: "The Mysterious Mr. Mxyztplk!"), while

Action Comics No. 112 observes that once Mr. Mxyzptlk has said his name backwards, "he can't come back for at least a month!" (Sep '47: "The Cross-Country Chess Crimes!").

In December 1950, however, Mr. Mxyzptlk remarks that "...if I'm tricked into saying my name backward, it hurls me back into the fifth dimension for 60 days!" (Act No. 151: "Superman's Super-Magic Show!"), and in May-June 1953 he exclaims, "Whoops! I said it! The name I just read is Mxyztplk spelled backwards! The one thing that sends me back into my dimension for at least three months!" (S No. 82/2: "The Unemployed Superman").

From this time forward, however, the texts are virtually unanimous in asserting that saying his name backwards banishes Mr. Mxyzptlk to his home dimension for "at least 90 days" (S No. 135/3, Feb '60: "The Trio of Steel!"; and many others). Superman No. 131/1, in fact, provides this explanation for the phenomenon:

> The sound produced by his own voice saying his name backwards sets up vibrations which open the gates to his own dimension and push him back through for at least 90 days! [Aug '59: "The Menace of Mr. Mxyzptlk!"].

In March 1956 Lois Lane observes that "...the only way Superman can get rid of [Mr. Mxyzptlk] is to get him to say or spell his name backwards!" (S No. 104/1: "Lois Lane, Super-Genius"), and, indeed, a number of other texts support the contention that Mr. Mxyzptlk's spelling his name backwards has the same effect as reciting it backwards (S No. 131/1, Aug '59: "The Menace of Mr. Mxyzptlk!"; S No. 135/3, Feb '60: "The Trio of Steel!").

During his periods of exile in the fifth dimension, Mr. Mxyzptlk can view events on Earth by means of his "multi-dimensional viewer screen" (S No. 148/2, Oct '61: "Mr. Mxyzptlk's Super-Mischief!"). For his part, Superman can communicate with his extradimensional nemesis by means of the "interdimensional monitor" in his FORTRESS OF SOLITUDE (S No. 174/2, Jan '65: "Super-Mxyzptlk...Hero!").

Other names employed by Mr. Mxyzptlk in the course of his mischievous career have included MAXY Z. TOPLIK (S No. 96/2, Mar '55: "Mr. Mxyzptlk--Mayor of Metropolis!") and JOHN TRIX (S No. 148/2, Oct '61: "Mr. Mxyzptlk's Super-Mischief!").

In the texts, Mr. Mxyzptlk is alternatively referred to as the Daffy Demon, the Master of Mischief, and the Silly Sprite.

In addition, he has been described as "the mysterious Mr. Mxyzptlk, maker of amazing mischief from another dimension" (S No. 33/1, Mar/Apr '45: "Dimensions of Danger!"); "multi-dimensional Mr. Mxyzptlk" and the "slap-happy sprite from space" (S No. 36/1, Sep/Oct '45: "Mr. Mxyzptlk's Mistake!"); "that sappy sprite from an extra-dimensional world" and "a problem-pixie from outer space" (S No. 40/1, May/Jun '46: "The Mxyzptlk-Susie Alliance!"); "that extra-dimensional mischief-maker" (Act No. 102, Nov '46: "Mr. Mxyzptlk and His Wonderful Lamp!");

"the silly sprite from another dimension, whose magical powers almost mystify even Superman" (S No. 46/1, May/Jun '47: "Mr. Mxyztplk Goes to College!"); a "pop-eyed pixie" (S No. 51/1, Mar/Apr '48: "Mr. Mxyztplk Seeks a Wife!"); "the comic of the dimensions" and "that impish fellow from the fifth dimension" (S No. 59/3, Jul/Aug '49: "The City That Forgot Superman"); "that malicious mite, that troublesome, pop-eyed plague, Superman's impish nemesis—Mr. Mxyztplk" (S No. 62/3, Jan/Feb '50: "Mr. Mxyztplk, Hero!"); a "pesky pixie" and "that pop-eyed little pest from the fifth dimension" (Act No. 151, Dec '50: "Superman's Super-Magic Show!"); "that master of mischief from another dimension" (S No. 82/2, May/Jun '53: "The Unemployed Superman"); a "half-pint pixie" (S No. 86/3, Jan '54: "The Fourth Dimension Gazette!"); "the pixilated master of mischief" (Act No. 190, Mar '54: "The Boy Who Saved Superman!"); "that impish intruder from the fifth dimension" and "the imp of a million mischiefs" (S No. 96/2, Mar '55: "Mr. Mxyztplk--Mayor of Metropolis!"); "that mischievous imp," the "merry mischief-maker," and "the pixie whose pranks in our three-dimensional world have often driven Superman frantic" (Act No. 208, Sep '55: "The Magic of Mr. Mxyztplk"); "that tiny but terrible trickster from the fifth dimension" (S No. 103/2, Feb '56: "The Revenge of Mr. Mxyztplk!"); the "little-man-of-a-million-mischiefs" (S No. 105/2, May '56: "Mr. Mxyztplk's Secret Identity"); the "madcap imp from the 5th dimension" (S No. 150/3, Jan '62: "When the World Forgot Superman!"); "that zany, mischief-playing thorn in Superman's side" (WF No. 123, Feb '62: "The Incredible Team of Bat-Mite and Mr. Mxyztplk!"); and Superman's "pixilated foe" (S No. 174/2, Jan '65: "Super-Mxyzptlk...Hero!").

In September-October 1944 Mr. Mxyzptlk, visiting the world of three dimensions for the first time in the chronicles, wreaks havoc in Metropolis with his extradimensional pranks, as when he causes water faucets to emit sparks and streams of water to squirt out of radios. Confronted finally by Superman, the imp explains that he is a native of an alien dimension, adding that

> ...my full-time activity in this other world was in the nature of a court-jester. Therefore I had no business poking my nose into the secret volumes of a brilliant scholar.
>
> But, inquisitive individual that I am, I couldn't restrain my curiosity. Thus did I learn the two magic words. One of which would transport me to this dimension. And the other word if spoken aloud would return me to my world for a time!

"And when do you intend to return to your world?" asks Superman.

"Never!" replies Mr. Mxyzptlk. "I find this backward three-dimensional world of yours most amusing. With my extra-dimensional powers, I could easily conquer and rule it! Think of that! I, a lowly court-jester, could become a king!"

Superman pursues Mr. Mxyzptlk through the skies over Metropolis, 1944

Superman manages to trick the imp, however, into revealing the magic word—Mxyzptlk pronounced backwards—that will return him to his own dimension. As soon as the unsuspecting sprite pronounces it, he vanishes with a pop back to his home dimension (S No. 30/3: "The Mysterious Mr. Mxyztplk!").

In January 1945, vexed at the unflattering articles CLARK KENT wrote about him for the DAILY PLANET following his initial visit to the three-dimensional world, Mr. Mxyzptlk returns, wreaking havoc in Metropolis with his extradimensional pranks—as when he makes the Metropolis River flow uphill and brings two characters in a gangster movie miraculously to life—until finally Superman tricks him into pronouncing his name backwards and he vanishes with a pop back to his home dimension (Act No. 80: "Mr. Mxyztplk Returns!").

In March-April 1945, while discussing Mr. Mxyzptlk's previous visit to Metropolis with fellow journalist Clark Kent, Lois Lane casually pronounces the imp's name backwards and is instantaneously transported to Mr. Mxyzptlk's own world, the "multi-dimensional" Land of Zrfff, where she is placed on display beneath a bell jar in the Academy of Research as a living specimen of "the peculiar type of life found on such planets as Earth." Superman, meanwhile, also recites the imp's name backwards and follows Lois Lane to Zrfff, where he tricks Zrfff's ruler, KING BRPXZ, and the king's court jester, Mr. Mxyzptlk, into putting him on exhibit in a second bell jar, alongside Lois. Ultimately, Superman frees Lois Lane from her bell jar prison and, after teaching the ethnocentrically egotistical inhabitants of Zrfff a richly deserved lesson in respecting the rights of others, forces them to provide him and Lois with the magic word—"qrdmlzfl"—that will transport them back to the earthly dimension.

"The universe is full of many kinds of animals and people," remarks Superman to the students at the Academy of Research as he and Lois Lane prepare to disembark for Earth, "and I wouldn't trade most of them I've seen for all the people of Zrfff! A lot of people are as smart as the people of Zrfff, and smarter--but I doubt if any of them are more egotistical!" (S No. 33/1: "Dimensions of Danger!").

In September-October 1945, arriving in the picturesque southwestern seaside town" of Porto del Oro, Mr. Mxyzptlk sets busily to work, mining huge amounts of gold from a subterranean vein of gold ore by day, and terrorizing the townsfolk with zany extradimensional pranks by night. In Mr. Mxyzptlk's words:

...I have heard that, with sufficient gold, a man can rule this silly three-dimensional globe!

Furthermore, it's a long way from Metropolis and Superman, who made himself such a pest on my previous trips here! What a surprise he has coming!

Before that musclebound meddler realizes it, I'll no longer be plain Mr. Mxyztplk, court jester in the multidimensional Land of Zrfff—but King Mxyztplk I, of Earth!

Confronted finally by Superman, Mr. Mxyzptlk offers the Man of Steel half his gold to refrain from interfering in his mischievous schemes, but Superman scoffingly rejects the offer. "But—but I read in a book that the people of Earth would do anything for gold," stammers the imp, "and that the person who possessed it was all-powerful!" "Then you read a cynical lie, twisted out of a half-truth!" replies Superman. "A tiny handful of people may place wealth above everything else, but most people know better!"

Finally, after being harried by Superman to the point of distraction, Mr. Mxyzptlk deliberately pronounces his name backwards, vanishing instantly into the safety of his home dimension (S No. 36/1: "Mr. Mxyztplk's Mistake!").

In May-June 1946 Mr. Mxyzptlk joins forces with SUSIE TOMPKINS, "the girl who loves to tell whoppers," in an impish scheme to have some fun at the expense of the people of Metropolis by having Susie concoct outlandish fibs which Mr. Mxyzptlk then makes come true by means of his extradimensional powers. At one point, for example, after Susie had claimed to have seen an operatic stage, complete with a choir and orchestra, floating in the clouds, Mr. Mxyzptlk uses his fifth-dimensional magic to transport an entire production of Faust from an opera house in Metropolis to the sky outside Lois Lane's apartment house. Superman ultimately succeeds in returning Mr. Mxyzptlk to his home dimension by tricking the mischievous imp into believing that his eyesight is failing and then getting him to test his eyesight by reading the messages on a series of billboards spaced 10, 15, and 20 miles away. On one of the billboards, however, Superman has written the name Mxyzptlk backwards, and Mr. Mxyzptlk no sooner recites the magic word than he vanishes abruptly into his home dimension (S No. 40/1: "The Mxyzptlk-Susie Alliance!").

In November 1946 Mr. Mxyzptlk wreaks havoc in Metropolis by transforming himself into a latter-day ALADDIN, appearing out of a magic lantern in a puff of smoke to grant the wishes of passersby with his extradimensional powers. When one tired pedestrian wishes aloud that he had wings, for example, Mr. Mxyzptlk instantly endows the flabbergasted citizen with a pair of wings and sends him soaring away helplessly through the air. Superman finally rids Metropolis of the mischievous imp by duping him into granting Lois Lane three wishes, along with the power to take one of her wishes back. "First," announces Lois, after having been carefully coached by Superman, "--I wish you to be limited to three-dimensional powers like the rest of us!

"Second," she adds moments later, after her first wish has been complied with, "--I wish you'd jump into that hot tar!

"Now," she continues, after the infuriated imp has carried out her second wish, "I wish the tar would turn to steel!"

Hopelessly imprisoned in a block of solid steel, Mr.

Mxyzptlk can only hope to regain his freedom if Lois will use her power to retract one of her foregoing wishes to retract her first one, thereby restoring the imp's extradimensional powers and making it possible for him to extricate himself. Lois will only agree to this, however, on the condition that, once freed, Mr. Mxyzptlk will return to his home dimension. And so, moments later, the bargain having been struck, Mr. Mxyzptlk extricates himself from the block of steel and returns defeated to the fifth dimension (Act No. 102: "Mr. Mxyztplk and His Wonderful Lamp!").

In May-June 1947, after overhearing the dean of Carlton University threaten the coach of the college baseball team with dismissal unless his team wins the race for the college league pennant, Mr. Mxyztplk uses his extradimensional powers to gain admission to Carlton and then leads the Carlton baseball team to one victory after another by means of his incredible fifth-dimensional feats. "It's unfair, Mxyztplk, to pit your supernatural powers against normal men in a competitive sport!" chides Clark Kent. "Can I help it if I'm terrific?" replies the imp.

As the all-important pennant-deciding game with Bedlum University approaches, however, Superman becomes determined to intervene. "I won't let Mxyztplk make a farce of a great American sport!" vows Superman. And so, after a consultation with Bedlum University officials, Superman is appointed to play alone, as a one-man team representing Bedlum, against Carlton's one-man team, represented by Mr. Mxyztplk, to determine the winner of the college league pennant. With the zany game tied in the bottom of the ninth, Superman outwits the mischievous imp—and scores the game-winning run—by burrowing underground as he circles the bases so that Mr. Mxyzptlk cannot tag him. When the extradimensional sprite angrily challenges this tactic, Superman thrusts a baseball rule book into his hands and dares him to recite the relevant rule aloud. The so-called rule, however, which has been specially inserted in the rule book in advance by Superman, contains the name Mxyzptlk backwards, and the unsuspecting imp has no sooner recited the magic word than he vanishes abruptly into his home dimension (S No. 46/1: "Mr. Mxyzptlk Goes to College!").

In September 1947 Mr. Mxyzptlk causes pandemonium in Metropolis with a series of hair-raising extradimensional pranks. Confronted finally by Superman, the imp explains that he's merely bored and wants to be amused. "You're bored," replies Superman, "because you don't use your brains enough! If you want to be amused, play something intellectual— like chess!"

Mr. Mxyzptlk responds to Superman's simple suggestion, however, by turning the entire United States into a gargantuan chessboard, complete with massive objects stolen from around the world—e.g., a castle from England to serve as a castle, a monumental statue of a knight on horseback to serve as a knight—to be used as his chess pieces. Superman finally outwits the imp by challenging him to a chess game in the middle of the Sahara Desert—where the match will not endanger either persons or property—and then carving a gigantic chess set containing, in addition to all the conventional chess pieces, a special piece of his own creation.

"—Here's a chess piece I never saw before!" exclaims Mr. Mxyzptlk upon arriving in the Sahara for his chess game with Superman. "What is it?"

"What?" cries Superman, feigning surprise. "You don't know that piece? And you call yourself a chess player? Why, it's used in what's known as the surprise move!"

"Really?" asks Mr. Mxyzptlk, his curiosity piqued. "What's the move called?"

"It's called a klptzyxm!" replies Superman slyly.

"How odd!" exclaims the unsuspecting imp. "A klptzyxm! Oops!" And with that, Mr. Mxyzptlk vanishes with a pop back into his home dimension.

"Ha-ha!" laughs Superman. "I told you it was a 'surprise move,' didn't I? Checkmate, pal!" (Act No. 112: "The Cross-Country Chess Crimes!").

Mr. Mxyzptlk and Superman, 1945

In March-April 1948, in a frantic effort to avoid being forced to marry the homely daughter of the king of his own fifth-dimensional world, Mr. Mxyzptlk claims that he is already engaged—to Lois Lane—and that he cannot, therefore, marry the princess. The king, however, skeptical of Mr. Mxyzptlk's claim, decrees that unless the imp returns to the fifth dimension with his new bride within a week, he must carry out his command to marry his daughter.

And so Mr. Mxyzptlk invades the earthly dimension and begins a whirlwind courtship of Lois Lane, promising her furs, jewels, and other riches and begging her to marry him. At first Lois ridicules the imp's ardent proposal, but then, realizing that Superman would go to any lengths to prevent her from marrying Mr. Mxyztplk, she hits upon an inspiration for turning the bizarre courtship to her own advantage. "Wait!" she exclaims. "I'll marry you, Mxyztplk—but on one condition! You'll have to prove that you're a better reporter than I am!"

"I'm wise to Lois' tricks!" thinks Superman to himself. "She knows I won't let Mxyztplk win. She's just forcing me to help her build her reputation as a reporter. And how can I refuse now?"

Indeed, in the days that follow, Lois Lane volunteers for the *Daily Planet*'s most difficult reportorial assignments—and Superman bends every effort toward helping her fulfill them—but, in spite of his efforts, Mr. Mxyztplk outwits Superman with the aid of his extradimensional powers and scoops Lois Lane on three assignments in a row. Before long, Lois finds herself in the midst of an event she thought would never take place—a wedding ceremony which, in a few moments' time, will make her the bride of Mr. Mxyztplk.

However, as the ceremony nears its climax and the minister asks if there is anyone present who knows why the couple should not be wed, Superman leaps to his feet, shouting for the minister to stop the wedding on the ground that the groom is an impostor—that he is not Mxyztplk at all, but Klptzyxm. And when the unsuspecting imp rises to the bait, announcing that he is indeed Mxyztplk and *not* Klptzyxm, he finds to his chagrin that he has pronounced his name backwards and that he is vanishing back into his home dimension.

"Will you ever forgive me, **Superman?**" asks Lois. "Don't mention it," replies Superman. "I've never been so happy to see anyone left at the altar!" (S No. 51/1: "Mr. Mxyztplk Seeks a Wife!").

By July-August 1949 Mr. Mxyztplk has cast a diabolical "amnesia spell" over Metropolis, erasing all memory of Superman's existence and expunging every written record of the Man of Steel's exploits. "This is the funniest thing that ever happened—in any dimension!" exclaims the mischievous imp. "You spent years helping people—making yourself famous—and I made the whole city forget you overnight!"

For a time, Mr. Mxyztplk's latest prank drives Superman frantic, as he races desperately about the city trying, without success, to make his former friends and admirers believe that he actually exists. And when the Man of Steel attempts to establish his existence in the minds of the populace by putting on spectacular demonstrations of his mighty super-powers, Mr. Mxyztplk cunningly contrives to make it appear that Superman is nothing but a crackpot in quest of attention and free publicity. Finally, however, through an elaborate ruse, Superman succeeds in so confusing Mr. Mxyztplk concerning the proper spelling of his own name that even when the imp wants to pronounce it backwards in order to return to

his own dimension he finds, to his horror, that he cannot do so. And so, ultimately, a bargain is struck, with Superman promising to teach Mr. Mxyztplk how to spell his name correctly in return for the imp's promise to lift the amnesia spell and restore Metropolis to normal (S No. 59/3: "The City That Forgot Superman").

In January-February 1950, after having become hopelessly infatuated with lovely blond cover girl Larissa Lee, Mr. Mxyzptlk—clad in a new red-and-blue costume modeled after Superman's—sets out to carve a name for himself in the annals of super-heroism in hopes of persuading Larissa to agree to marry him. "I intend to put you out of the hero business, **Super**," he tells Superman pointedly, "and win the fair Larissa for my bride!"

For a time Mr. Mxyzptlk performs impressively as a super-hero, although he performs his feats in the inimitable Mxyzptlk manner, as when he captures a carload of escaped convicts and turns them over to Superman after magically repainting their automobile in garish red and white stripes with the words "Captured by Mxyzptlk" emblazoned across it. "From now on, my exploits in the name of law and order will make you a has-been!" he tells Superman. "Larissa will be **proud** of me!"

Often, however, Mr. Mxyzptlk's flamboyant crime-fighting style proves reckless and irresponsible, as when he sets some bags of stolen money afire to force the bandits to drop them, and causes a hazardous avalanche in order to trap the carload of convicts mentioned above. Ultimately, however, with Larissa Lee's help, Superman carries out a ruse designed to trick Mr. Mxyzptlk into returning to his own dimension. When the imp calls on the lovely cover girl in order to brag to her about his latest crime-fighting exploit, she implies that she might indeed marry him, but only if he had a secret identity like Superman's. "Married to a public figure like you," explains Larissa, "—I'd never have any peace. Now if you had a secret identity like **Superman**—"

To placate his ladylove, Mr. Mxyzptlk agrees to choose one of the names she has placed in a hat and use it as the basis for a new secret identity. The scraps of paper in the hat, however, have all been inscribed with the name Klptzyxm, and as soon as the imp pronounces it he vanishes with a pop into his home dimension (S No. 62/3: "Mr. Mxyztplk, Hero!").

In December 1950 Mr. Mxyzptlk joins forces with Lex Luthor and the Prankster in an elaborate scheme to humiliate Superman. The scheme centers around the use of "lifelike plastic proxies"—i.e., "exact doubles" of real people—which Mr. Mxyzptlk can materialize out of thin air by means of his extradimensional magic. Luthor announces his intention to use his scientific genius to "install machinery in [the] plastic proxies, to make them move and speak by remote control!" And the Prankster promises to apply his unique "talent for practical jokes" to the problem of how best to use the proxies to torment Superman.

At one point, for example, after luring Lois Lane away from Metropolis with a phony news tip, the plotters arrange for their Lois Lane proxy to humili-ate Superman by publicly spurning him in favor of the zany Mr. Mxyzptlk. Soon afterward, the real Luthor robs a Metropolis bank while a Lex Luthor proxy chats with the mayor, thus providing Luthor with a perfect alibi and making Superman appear a fool when he arrests Luthor for committing the robbery. Later, the Prankster publicly humiliates a Superman proxy in full view of a large crowd of people, thereby making it appear that the villain has succeeded in making a fool out of Superman. Ultimately, however, Superman learns of the exis-tence of the plastic proxies, apprehends Luthor and the Prankster, and tricks Mr. Mxyzptlk into reciting his name backwards, thereby returning the mischie-vous imp to his home dimension (Act No. 151: "Superman's Super-Magic Show!").

By May-June 1953 Mr. Mxyzptlk has used a weird extradimensional device—known as a "good machine"—to bring crime, violence, and even natural disasters to a complete halt in Metropolis, leaving Superman and the police department with literally nothing to do. "How quickly the public forgets!" thinks Superman, as he strolls unnoticed through Metropolis's streets. "Now, just because there have been no emergencies for me to meet during the past few weeks, I'm an ex-hero!"

Superman is even further chagrined, however, when, soon afterward, Mr. Mxyzptlk threatens to remove his "good machine"—once again unleashing crime and violence in the city—unless the Man of Steel agrees to publicly divulge his secret identity and exile himself from Metropolis forever. "There's no doubt Mr. Mxyzptlk's *good machine* is benefiting Metropolis!" thinks Superman, as he ponders the extradimensional imp's ultimatum. "It would be unfair of me to deprive the town of it just because of a selfish desire to protect my identity!"

After having announced his intention to reveal his secret identity in a live television address, however, Superman discovers that Mr. Mxyzptlk's "good machine," while admittedly eliminating crime and other disasters from the streets of Metropolis, is having the adverse effect of increasing the crime and disaster rates in the world's other cities, so that although Metropolis is now free of strife, the world's overall strife rate remains the same. And so, in the midst of his widely publicized television address, Superman deliberately interrupts his speech to respond to an SOS in the mid-Atlantic, leaving the text of his prepared remarks behind him in the studio. At that point, Mr. Mxyzptlk, determined not to be cheated out of the mischievous joy of revealing Superman's secret identity to the world, snatches up the speech and begins to recite it, realizing, only too late, that Superman has inserted into the text the imp's own name spelled backwards, the magic word which, as Mr. Mxyzptlk recites it, transports him instantaneously to his home dimension (S No. 82/2: "The Unemployed Superman").

In January 1954 Mr. Mxyzptlk materializes in the offices of the *Daily Planet* and angrily confronts editor PERRY WHITE. "I have come to demand that the *Daily Planet* retract its malicious lies," demands the imp, "or I will ruin it forever!"

"Yesterday," explains Mr. Mxyzptlk, "your paper plainly stated that **Superman** was the greatest person ever to have lived! A downright fabrication! I---Mxyzptlk...am the greatest!"

When the flabbergasted Perry White refuses to retract his paper's story about Superman and substitute a new one describing Mr. Mxyzptlk as the greatest person who ever lived, the furious extradi-mensional imp sets out to wreak a mischievous revenge on the *Daily Planet* by starting his own newspaper, the *Daily Mpftrz*, a newspaper contain-ing accounts of events that are going to happen the following day, rather than of events that have already happened. "You see," gloats the imp, "as a resident of the fifth dimension, I can get all the news I want from the **fourth** dimension!"

"That's right, Mr. White," explains a science editor at the *Daily Planet* to a clearly agitated Perry White, "...many physicists consider **time** the fourth dimen-sion...so if **Mr. Mxyzptlk** can travel from the fifth dimension to our three-dimensional world, he most likely is able to see into the future!"

With the *Daily Planet* and other conventional newspapers threatened with bankruptcy by the extradimensional competition posed by the *Daily Mpftrz*—and with life in general disrupted, some-times tragically, by people's new-found ability to read the future—Superman devises a cunning ploy for tricking Mr. Mxyzptlk into voluntarily returning to his own dimension. The ploy involves the surrepti-tious insertion, by Superman, of a bogus story in the *Daily Mpftrz* headlined: "MXYZTPLK BECOMES LAUGHING STOCK OF THE WORLD. POOR 5TH DIMENSIONAL IMP." When Mr. Mxyzptlk reads the infuriating story, he immediately embarks upon a whirlwind tour of the world—determined to prove that the story is mistaken—only to be greeted by uproarious laughter wherever he goes. "I---I don't understand!" thinks Mr. Mxyzptlk frantically. "I'm still the same handsome, heroic figure...greater than **Superman**...and yet they all **laugh** at me!"

The mischievous imp is completely unaware, however, that the laughter he hears is not directed at him at all, but has rather been caused by Superman, who has been following Mr. Mxyzptlk around the world at invisible super-speed, tickling throngs of people everywhere into fits of uncontrollable laughter with an armload of goose feathers. Finally, Mr. Mxyzptlk can stand what he perceives as the worldwide ridicule no longer—"The humiliation is too great!" he pouts. "I...I can't stay here an instant longer!"—and he vanishes with a pop into his home dimension (S No. 86/3: "The Fourth Dimension Gazette!").

By March 1954 Superman has begun experiencing a series of mysterious temporary losses of his mighty super-powers, always while he is in the midst of

Stung by the apparent ridicule that has greeted him around the world...

...Mr. Mxyzptlk pronounces his name backwards and promptly vanishes into the fifth dimension, 1954

performing some important super-feat. To make these inexplicable super-power lapses even more discomfiting, Superman is repeatedly rescued by an ordinary youngster named Rodney Applegate, who is somehow always on the scene whenever Superman's powers fail him, and who is, inexplicably, invariably the only onlooker capable of extricating Superman from his various predicaments.

On one such occasion, for example, Superman's super-powers suddenly fail him while he is flying through the air with a beaker full of "a new high explosive." As Superman plummets helplessly toward the ground, the beaker of explosive threatening to unleash untold destruction upon impact, only

Rodney Applegate demonstrates the creativity and presence of mind to devise a means of rescuing Superman without jarring the volatile explosive. Indeed, after a series of such rescues, Superman's apparent dependence on young Rodney has made him the laughingstock of Metropolis and the mayor has even gone so far as to insist that Rodney assume the role of Superman's "personal bodyguard."

Finally, however, Mr. Mxyzptlk makes it known, both to Rodney and Superman, that Superman's lapses of super-power and rescues by Rodney were all part of his own scheme to humiliate Superman. "It was child's play, scattering a little kryptonite here and there to weaken you," boasts the imp gleefully, "--and to use my unique powers to see that the schemes I put in Rodney's mind worked!"

Now realizing that he has been duped into helping Mr. Mxyzptlk humiliate Superman, however, Rodney devises a scheme of his own for returning the mischievous imp to his own dimension. After lulling Mr. Mxyzptlk into false complacency by playing up to the imp and pretending to be his greatest admirer, Rodney tricks Mr. Mxyzptlk into visiting an optometrist to have his eyes examined, then arranges for the surreptitious substitution of a bogus eye chart containing the imp's own name spelled backwards. Indeed, no sooner has Mr. Mxyzptlk unsuspectingly pronounced the magic word, than he vanishes abruptly into his home dimension (Act No. 190: "The Boy Who Saved Superman!").

In March 1955, after having been told that he may run for the office of mayor in his own fifth-dimensional city only if he first gets himself elected mayor of Metropolis and persuades more than half the populace to sign a statement praising him as the best mayor in Metropolis's history, Mr. Mxyzptlk legally changes his name to Maxy Z. Toplik and announces his mayoral candidacy to the people of Metropolis. Elected to the mayoralty by an overwhelming landslide thanks to the use of his extra-dimensional powers, Mr. Mxyzptlk appoints himself to every major municipal post—including fire chief, chief of police, dogcatcher, judge, and head of the weather bureau—and begins using his zany fifth-dimensional powers to make himself the most popular mayor in the city's history, as when he speeds to the scene of a fire in a flying fire engine and quenches the blaze by hitching the fire hose to a passing rain cloud.

Although Mr. Mxyzptlk's feats are all colorful and well-intentioned, however, they frequently give rise to unanticipated hazards. Because the fire, for example, is of chemical origin, dousing it with water produces a cloud of poisonous gas, which Superman is forced to dissipate by breathing in the toxic fumes and exhaling them in outer space.

Finally, Superman hits upon a ploy for returning Mr. Mxyzptlk to his own dimension. After posing as a hobo and deliberately allowing himself to be dragged into court on the charge of insulting a policeman, the disguised Superman proceeds to insult the presiding Judge Mxyzptlk. When the imp, furious at having been insulted, demands to know the hobo's name so that he can sentence him to thirty days in jail for contempt of court, Superman slyly identifies himself as Kilpot Zyxam, which is Mr. Mxyzptlk's new name spelled backwards. No sooner has the imp pronounced the name in order to pass sentence on the "hobo," however, than he is whisked abruptly back to his home dimension (S No. 96/2: "Mr. Mxyztplk-- Mayor of Metropolis!").

In September 1955, having learned from a book on fifth-dimensional magic that an earthling can be banished into the eighth dimension for twenty-four hours if he can be tricked into reciting his name backwards, Mr. Mxyzptlk invades the earthly dimension, determined to exile Superman into the eighth dimension so that, in the Man of Steel's absence, he can plague Metropolis with extradimensional pranks. After successfully testing his new trick on Lois Lane—by tricking her into saying her name backwards and thereby exiling her temporarily into the eighth dimension—Mr. Mxyzptlk makes a series of attempts to pull the same stunt on Superman, only to be thwarted by the Man of Steel at every turn. Superman finally rids Metropolis of the mischievous imp by pretending that Mr. Mxyzptlk has succeeded in banishing him to the eighth dimension, and then, with the imp off his guard, setting in motion an elaborate ruse designed to trick Mr. Mxyzptlk into saying his name backwards. The ruse, carried out with the aid of "a tiny radio receiver" which Superman surreptitiously conceals inside the imp's derby hat, involves duping the imp into believing that he has begun hearing nonexistent noises by bombarding him with the sound of clanging bells broadcast into his hat. When Mr. Mxyzptlk, frantic at the thought that he may be losing his mind, consults a physician, Superman, posing as the physician, provides the imp with a special prescription. And when Mr. Mxyzptlk visits a pharmacy to have the prescription filled, Superman, posing as the pharmacist, tricks the imp—who is unaware that his name, spelled backwards, has been inserted into the prescription—into reciting the prescription aloud, whereupon Mr. Mxyzptlk vanishes abruptly into his home dimension. Later, after twenty-four hours have passed, Lois Lane returns from her exile in the eighth dimension, none the worse for her experience there (Act No. 208: "The Magic of Mr. Mxyztplk").

In February 1956 Mr. Mxyzptlk returns to the earthly dimension to pester and bedevil Superman, this time protected against the effects of pronouncing his name backwards by some sort of "crazy fifth-dimensional insurance" whose bizarre power is vested in what the imp repeatedly refers to as "the unknown quantity." "Saying my name backwards has no effect!" boasts Mr. Mxyzptlk gleefully, after Superman has tricked him—to no avail—into pronouncing his name backwards. "See? I'm still here, **Super.** Insured against your trickery by the power of the unknown quantity! Ha, ha! Heee!"

Stymied by Mr. Mxyzptlk's weird "insurance" and

bewildered as to the true meaning of "the unknow quantity," Superman seems helpless to prevent th mischievous imp from plaguing Metropolis with hi extradimensional pranks, until finally, with the ai of a clue inadvertently provided by Lois Lane, h realizes that "the unknown quantity" is an algebrai expression—usually represented by the letter "X"- and that all of Mr. Mxyzptlk's mischievous prank have involved, in one way or another, the letter "X, as when the imp commandeered a steam shovel at th site of an excavation and demolished a statue of Kin Arthur with the statue's sword, Excalibur.

Knowing that Mr. Mxyzptlk intends to commit hi next prank at the site of the World Expositio Superman surreptitiously arranges for the sign ove the entranceway to be repainted to read "Internatio al World's Fair," then lies in wait for the mischievou imp and challenges him to demonstrate the effective ness of his fifth-dimensional insurance by recitin his name backwards once again. As soon as Mr Mxyzptlk does so, however, he is whisked abruptl back to his home dimension.

"Mxyzptlk never noticed that the 'X' in Expositio was gone--so that his unknown insurance had n power!" explains Superman a short while later. "I works only when there's an 'X' in the vicinity" (S No 103/2: "The Revenge of Mr. Mxyztplk!").

In March 1956, during a period when Superman is endeavoring to keep Lois Lane preoccupied coping with bogus emergencies so that she will not have time to use her newly acquired superhuman intelligence to get into serious trouble, one of his ploys for keeping Lois busy is to create a lifelike Mr. Mxyzptlk puppet and then, after duping Lois into believing that the puppet is the real Mr. Mxyzptlk, allowing her to devise a means for tricking the "imp" into reciting his name backwards and thereby whisking himself back to his home dimension. Later, after Lois's super-intellectual powers have faded and vanished, the Man of Steel reveals that it was not the real Mr. Mxyzptlk she outwitted, but only a lifelike Mr. Mxyzptlk puppet (S No. 104/1: "Lois Lane, Super-Genius"). (*See* LANE, LOIS.)

In May 1956, during one of his periodic visits to the earthly dimension, Mr. Mxyzptlk hits upon the idea of adopting a secret identity—just like Superman's—as a means of preventing Superman from tracking him down and tricking him into returning to his own dimension. Concealing his true identity beneath a false moustache and a suit of ordinary clothing, Mr. Mxyzptlk obtains employment as a reporter on the *Daily Planet*—unaware that Superman also works there in his role as Clark Kent—and begins wreaking havoc throughout Metropolis with his zany extradimensional pranks while thwarting Superman's efforts to find him by hiding behind his newly adopted alternate identity. After a time, however, Clark Kent begins to suspect that the *Daily Planet's* newest reporter is actually Mr. Mxyzptlk in disguise. When, soon afterward, editor Perry White assigns his new reporter the task of uncovering the name with

Mr. Mxyzptlk wreaks havoc at an excavation site, 1956

which astronomer Waldemar Hunt intends to christen his newly discovered comet, a name that Hunt has announced he intends to keep secret until he addresses a forthcoming meeting of the Astronomers' Club, Superman arranges with Hunt to pretend to reveal the name of his comet to the inquiring Mr. Mxyzptlk by writing it down for him on a slip of paper. The name that astronomer Hunt writes on the piece of paper, however, is the name Mxyzptlk spelled backwards, so that the moment the imp returns to the *Daily Planet* and proudly recites the name aloud, he vanishes abruptly back to his home dimension (S No. 105/2: "Mr. Mxyztplk's Secret Identity").

In August 1959 Mr. Mxyztplk returns to Metropolis and begins tormenting Superman with a series of zany extradimensional pranks, this time armed with an "ingenious little alarm" concealed inside his derby that sounds a warning whenever he begins to recite his name backwards. Indeed, "the next [several] days are a living nightmare to **Superman** as the fifth-dimensional imp creates mass mischief" while

successfully thwarting Superman's attempts to trick him into pronouncing his name backwards with the aid of the alarm device inside his hat.

In an effort to outwit the imp, Superman arranges for Lois Lane—disguised in a blond wig and wearing a glamorous evening gown—to pose as "an exotic new movie actress" just arrived from Zanzibar, and then offers to introduce her to the smitten Mr. Mxyzptlk in a fancy nightclub where the imp is asked to check his hat. Indeed, when Superman introduces the disguised Lois as his friend Miss Kltpzyxm, the unsuspecting imp, now deprived of his hat and its protective alarm, is on the verge of saying, "It's a pleasure to meet you, Miss Kltpzyxm," a sentence that, once uttered, would whisk him instantly away to his home dimension, when suddenly, as luck would have it, he develops a sudden attack of laryngitis— the result of his having recently caught a cold while standing in the rain—and is unable to complete the crucial sentence.

Thus thwarted, Superman settles on a different

ploy. After locating a newsreel of a speech made by Mr. Mxyzptlk at the time he campaigned to become mayor of Metropolis, Superman tampers with the imp's voice on the newsreel's sound track in such a way as to make the movie-screen image Mxyzptlk exhort the voters to cast their ballots for "Mr. Kltpzyxm." Indeed, although the real Mr. Mxyzptlk says absolutely nothing, the "peculiar vibrations" of his altered voice on the sound track have the effect of "unlocking the gate" to his home dimension and whisking him away to his fifth-dimensional world (S No. 131/1: "The Menace of Mr. Mxyzptlk!").

In February 1960, after Mr. Mxyzptlk has used "5th dimensional hypnotism" to temporarily transform Superman into a thoughtless "super-heel," the Man of Steel races around Metropolis playing nasty pranks on his friends and admirers, as when he asks Lois Lane to marry him and then laughs in her face, and when he publicly humiliates Perry White at a testimonial banquet in White's honor by forcibly dressing him in a series of ludicrous costumes. Ultimately, however, Superman emerges from the hypnotic trance and, through an elaborate ruse, tricks the mischievous extradimensional imp into spelling his name backwards and thus whisking himself away to his home dimension (S No. 135/3: "The Trio of Steel!").

Mr. Mxyzptlk

© NPP 1978

In November 1960, shortly after Bat-Mite has mischievously used his magical powers to prevent Superman from capturing some criminals so that he will have the opportunity of watching his heroes,

BATMAN and ROBIN, go into action against the villains instead, Mr. Mxyzptlk materializes in the earthly dimension and launches into a zany, pixilated rivalry with his extradimensional counterpart in order to prove to Bat-Mite that his "weird magic" is greater than Bat-Mite's, that he is a far greater pest than Bat-Mite, and that Superman is strictly off-limits to Bat-Mite since the Man of Steel is, in Mr. Mxyzptlk's view, his own private preserve for pestering purposes. The rivalry produces both danger and mayhem for Batman, Robin, and Superman until finally both imps tire of the battle and whisk themselves away voluntarily to their respective home dimensions (WF No. 113: "Bat-Mite Meets Mr. Mxyzptlk!").

In February 1961, after Mr. Mxyzptlk has made one of his whirlwind forays into the earthly dimension, tormenting the Man of Steel with a series of zany extradimensional pranks and forcing him, with deep regret, to cancel his annual super-show at the SMALLVILLE ORPHANAGE, Superman "crashes through the dimensional-barrier into the world of five dimensions," the world inhabited by Mr. Mxyzptlk, determined to repay the imp, in kind, for all the mischievous havoc he has wrought in Metropolis.

Arriving in Mr. Mxyzptlk's home dimension at a time when the imp is running for mayor "on the Scatterbrain ticket," Superman gleefully sabotages the imp's campaign—and turns Mr. Mxyzptlk into the laughingstock of his entire dimension—with a series of stunning super-pranks, all the while thwarting the imp's frantic attempts to trick him into pronouncing the name Superman backwards—i.e., Namrepus—in order to return the Man of Steel to the earthly dimension. Indeed, even when the mischievous imp finally does succeed in tricking Superman into reciting the name Superman backwards, he finds—to his overwhelming consternation—that it has no effect, that the Man of Steel remains free to continue his maddening romp through the fifth dimension.

The explanation for the failure of the word Namrepus to return Superman to his home dimension, however, lies in the fact that the Man of Steel's real name—the name given him by his Kryptonian parents—is not Superman, but Kal-El. Only when his mission to the fifth dimension has been successfully concluded—and Mr. Mxyzptlk has lost his bid for the mayoralty by a landslide—does Superman voluntarily pronounce the name Kal-El backwards, thereby whisking himself back to the earthly dimension (Act No. 273: "The World of Mr. Mxyzptlk!").

In October 1961, after legally changing his name to John Trix, Mr. Mxyzptlk hurtles through the dimensional barrier into the "three-dimensional world," where he causes pandemonium in Metropolis with a series of stunning extradimensional pranks. Even when Superman succeeds in tricking the imp into pronouncing the name Mxyzptlk backwards, the magic word has no effect, for the imp has legally changed his name and only reciting his new name backwards will have the effect of returning him to the fifth dimension. "Until you learn what my new name is," gloats Mr. Mxyzptlk to a bewildered and exasperated Superman, "you won't be able to trick me into saying it backwards!!"

By means of an elaborate ruse, however, Superman ultimately succeeds in tricking the imp into returning voluntarily to his own dimension. The ruse, carried out with the aid of a lifelike Mxyzptlk dummy animated by members of the SUPERMEN EMERGENCY SQUAD, involves goading the mischievous imp into a heated argument over which of them—the dummy or the real imp—is the real Mr. Mxyzptlk. When the dummy, as if attempting to establish that it is the genuine Mr. Mxyzptlk, recites the name Mxyzptlk backwards and vanishes, a trick which the dummy's animators accomplish by whisking the dummy out of sight at invisible super-speed, the real Mr. Mxyzptlk, believing that his brazen imposter has fled into the fifth dimension, deliberately recites his new name— John Trix—backwards in an enraged effort to pursue and punish him. Once having uttered his name backwards, however, Mr. Mxyzptlk—whisked instantaneously back to his home dimension—remains powerless to return to the earthly dimension until his customary period of exile there is over (S No. 148/2: "Mr. Mxyzptlk's Super-Mischief!").

A text for January 1962 recounts Mr. Mxyzptlk's latest scheme to torment Superman. As the text opens, Mr. Mxyzptlk has cast a diabolical spell over the entire Earth, erasing all memory of Superman's existence and expunging every record of the Man of Steel's heroic exploits. "Ho, ho!" gloats the imp. "With my 5th dimensional magic, I not only made everyone on Earth forget you ever lived, but I wiped out all evidence of your existence!"

For a time, Mr. Mxyzptlk's latest prank drives Superman frantic, as he races desperately about the city trying, without success, to make his former friends and admirers believe that he actually exists. And when the Man of Steel attempts to establish his existence in the minds of the populace by putting on spectacular demonstrations of his mighty superpowers, Mr. Mxyzptlk cunningly contrives to make it appear that Superman is nothing but a crackpot in quest of attention and free publicity. Finally, however, through an elaborate ruse, Superman succeeds in tricking the imp into pronouncing his name backwards, thereby returning him to his home dimension. The moment Mr. Mxyzptlk vanishes, the effects of his magic also disappear, restoring Superman's name to the public consciousness along with all the records of his heroic exploits (S No. 150/3: "When the World Forgot Superman!"). The story, which is set in December 1961 despite the January 1962 issue date, is in many respects similar to Superman No. 59/3 (Jul/Aug '49: "The City That Forgot Superman"), which has been summarized previously in this article.

In February 1962 Mr. Mxyzptlk and Bat-Mite renew their extradimensional rivalry, to the everlasting chagrin of Batman, Robin, and Superman. Serious complications arise, however, when the combined magical powers of the two super-pests somehow create a rampaging monster which even their magic cannot control or destroy. Their rivalry quickly forgotten in the face of this magical menace, the two imps join forces in an effort to undo their mischief. Indeed, by the time they finally find a way to obliterate the monster with the aid of Batman, Robin, and Superman, it appears that the extradimensional mischief-makers have become fast friends (WF No. 123: "The Incredible Team of Bat-Mite and Mr. Mxyzptlk!").

In July 1962 Mr. Mxyzptlk returns to the earthly dimension, determined to play an outstanding extradimensional prank that will enable him to win the Brxll Award, a coveted prize awarded annually by the fifth dimension's Academy of Practical Joking to the citizen responsible for performing the year's most spectacular practical joke. Arriving in Metropolis, the imp embarks on a series of hair-raising pranks, as when he unleashes a zany "second childhood gas" that makes all the adults in the city begin behaving like children, all the while thwarting Superman's efforts to trick him into reciting his name backwards by cleverly remaining underwater, where it is impossible for him to speak.

Ultimately, however, through an elaborate ruse, Superman succeeds in tricking the imp into reciting his name backwards and thus returning to his home dimension. The ruse involves luring Mr. Mxyzptlk to the moon, where the imp is confident he can safely pester Superman to his heart's content since speech is impossible there due to the absence of air. However, when Mr. Mxyzptlk begins taunting Superman by silently reciting his name backwards over and over again, taunting Superman with the fact that in the lunar environment he cannot possibly be tricked into saying his name backwards aloud, Superman cleverly outwits the imp by focusing his heat vision on some nearby moon rock, thereby releasing oxygen and nitrogen from the rock's oxygen- and nitrogen-bearing minerals and creating, by the combination of these gases, a small pocket of air in which sound does carry and in which Mr. Mxyzptlk's voice can therefore be heard. Before he can even appreciate the complexity of Superman's ingenious stratagem, the startled imp hears himself pronouncing his own name aloud and vanishes abruptly back to his home dimension, where, for the fourth humiliating year in a row, he is denied the Brxll Award and forced to accept the booby prize instead because of his repeated defeats at the hands of Superman (S No. 154/1: "The Underwater Pranks of Mr. Mxyzptlk!").

In August 1962 KRYPTO THE SUPERDOG poses as Mr. Mxyzptlk—by concealing himself inside an ingenious "plastic shape" of the mischievous imp devised by Superman—to help carry out Superman's elaborate, and ultimately successful, ruse for uncovering the hiding place of DUKE MARPLE's stolen loot and bringing the "notorious gang-leader" to justice (S No. 155/2: "The Downfall of Superman!").

In November 1962, when Superman puts the finishing touches on the new Hall of Enemies in his Fortress of Solitude, Mr. Mxyzptlk is among the villains and villainesses represented there by colorful wax busts (Act No. 294: "The Kryptonite Killer!").

During a time-journey to Metropolis one million years in the future, Superman encounters a lifelike android of Mr. Mxyzptlk created by the people of the far-distant future (Act No. 300, May '63: "Superman Under the Red Sun!").

In May 1964, after having contracted a peculiar case of temporary lockjaw in the fifth dimension, Mr. Mxyzptlk journeys to the earthly dimension—and embarks upon a series of spectacular pranks—confident that Superman will be unable to trick him into pronouncing his name backwards, since, until such time as he recuperates from his temporary lockjaw, Mr. Mxyzptlk is literally incapable of speech. Superman ultimately outwits the imp and returns him to his own dimension, however, with the aid of an ingenious "telepathic device" given him by the people of a far-distant planet. Posing as the proprietor of a Metropolis hat store, Superman graciously presents the mischievous imp with a free hat, inside which he has surreptitiously concealed the telepathic device. When Mr. Mxyzptlk, communicating by means of sign language, gloatingly informs Superman that "It's impossible for me to say Kltpzyxm," his thoughts are translated into words by the "telepathy gadget" and relayed to a "receptor disc" held by Superman, which in turn recites the

Mr. Mxyzptlk is afflicted with temporary lockjaw, 1964

words aloud as though they were being played back by a tape recording. Indeed, the imp barely has time to appreciate the ingenuity of Superman's clever stratagem before he is whisked away to his home dimension (S No. 169/1: "The Infernal Imp!").

By August 1964 Mr. Mxyzptlk has mischievously

afflicted Superman with the so-called "curse of magic," an extradimensional curse that makes everything Superman says aloud magically come true, as when the Man of Steel inadvertently causes the collapse of London Bridge by innocently joining a group of English children in singing "London Bridge is falling down ...!"

For a time, the "ghastly curse" drives Superman frantic, forcing him to spend the greater part of his time undoing with his super-powers the damage he has inadvertently caused with his "enchanted" remarks. "I never dreamed the powers of magic could actually be a curse!!" sighs Superman. Ultimately however, the Man of Steel resolves his agonizing dilemma by reciting his Kryptonian name—Kal-El—backwards, thereby ridding himself of Mr Mxyzptlk's curse and undoing, instantaneously, all the magical mischief he has unintentionally caused (S No. 171/2: "The Curse of Magic!").

In January 1965 Mr. Mxyzptlk materializes in Metropolis and begins wreaking havoc there with his zany extradimensional pranks, as when he makes automobiles sprout wings and fly through the air and transforms the water at the seashore into sticky glue. "If you would only use your great magical ability to accomplish good," scolds Superman, "people would admire you, instead of being furious with you!"

To Superman's astonishment, Mr. Mxyzptlk takes his advice to heart, magically fashioning himself a new, more super-heroic costume and transforming himself, in his own words, into "Super-Mxyzptlk...the crusading imp whose magic is mightier than Superman's powers!" "I have reformed, Supe!" proclaims the imp. "From now on, I'm the greatest do-gooder ever!!!"

Indeed, in the days that follow, the colorfully costumed Super-Mxyzptlk becomes a familiar figure in Metropolis, earning the gratitude of an admiring populace by using his fantastic extradimensional powers to perform super-heroic feats, as when he prevents a fire engine from colliding with a busload of school children by magically materializing a colossal toy rabbit at the intersection to absorb the impact of the collision. And, because Super-Mxyzptlk can materialize at emergencies faster than Superman can fly there, he soon begins to overshadow the Man of Steel as Metropolis's foremost super-hero.

"This is the second time you butted in when I was about to handle an emergency!" complains Superman to the super-imp after Super-Mxyzptlk has streaked to the scene in time to use his extradimensional powers to prevent a disaster. "What's this?" replies Super-Mxyzptlk. "Don't tell me you're getting jealous just because I'm a better super-hero than you are ...!"

"He's right!" thinks Superman to himself. "I shouldn't complain as long as he's accomplishing good with his magical abilities!"

Before long, however, Superman has been reduced to performing the most menial of super-heroic chores, helping little boys get their fingers unstuck from faucets and rescuing cats trapped in trees, while his rival, Super-Mxyzptlk, "handles [the] big emergencies" and reaps the lion's share of the adulation and glamor. "How about that?" muses Superman bitterly. "He gets cheers, and I'm practically ignored!"

Finally, Superman, feeling humiliated and outclassed, flies off to his Fortress of Solitude to remain alone with his bitterness, while behind him, in Metropolis, the city fathers finalize plans for "a massive celebration at Metropolis Stadium" in honor of "that great, new hero, Super-Mxyzptlk."

Meanwhile, however, BIZARRO, arriving in Metropolis for a brief sentimental visit ("Me take sentimental journey to this planet from my world," thinks Bizarro to himself, "because me loathe Earth!"), overhears the plans to honor Super-Mxyzptlk and decides to contribute something of his own to the forthcoming celebration. And so, the following day, when throngs fill Metropolis Stadium for the tribute to Super-Mxyzptlk, officials find a massive statue covered by a tarpaulin and, assuming it to be a tribute to the super-imp created by Superman, unveil it.

The statue, however, sculpted by Bizarro, is a statue of Super-Mxyzptlk as he would look if he were a Bizarro, with his costume all askew and his features white and faceted. And, "since Bizarros always do everything in reverse," the inscription on the statue's pedestal reads, "Kltpzyxm-Repus," or Super-Mxyzptlk spelled backwards. Indeed, no sooner has the bewildered Super-Mxyzptlk read aloud the inscription beneath the bizarre statue than he vanishes instantaneously back into the fifth dimension.

"That imp was a nuisance to me, even while he did heroic, instead of mischievous, things!" chuckles Superman to himself when he arrives on the scene. "Ha, ha! I'm rid of him through a strange twist of fate! Am I glad--ha, ha, ha!"

A short while later, perhaps feeling a twinge of remorse, Superman contacts Mr. Mxyzptlk on his "interdimensional monitor" to explain that it was Bizarro, and not he, who was responsible for returning Mr. Mxyzptlk to the fifth dimension. "When Bizarro...built that statue," explains Superman, "I'm sure he meant it as a tribute to you, never suspecting that because he spelled your name backwards...."

But Mr. Mxyzptlk refuses to be mollified. "Don't try to con me with that phoney-baloney malarkey!" he cries. "You pulled that rotten, low-down trick on me deliberately...!! Why? Because you were jealous, that's why! You couldn't stand me being a greater do-gooder than you....I'm finished being a goody-goody! When I return to Earth in 90 days, I'll pull better and bigger whacky pranks!"

"To think," muses Superman moments later with a sigh of relief, "that a pixilated foe going 'straight' almost destroyed my career!" (S No. 174/2: "Super-Mxyzptlk...Hero!").

By September 1965 Mr. Mxyzptlk and Bat-Mite have returned to the earthly dimension and magically transformed themselves into colorfully costumed adolescents with superhuman powers, using the pseudonyms Force Boy and Speed Kid, as part of a wager they have made as to whether, if they wreak their customary mischief in these forms, Batman will be intelligent enough to deduce their actual identities.

The extradimensional imps lead Batman, Robin, and Superman a merry chase, leaving a trail of magical havoc in their wake and forcing the famed crime-fighters to speculate whether the newly arrived troublemakers are powerful androids, super-powered survivors from KRYPTON, or perhaps even the destructive advance guard of some impending alien invasion. Bat-Mite's undying faith in Batman is upheld, however, and he wins his wager with Mr. Mxyzptlk, when Batman correctly deduces their identities.

"I appreciate your loyalty, Bat-Mite," replies Batman with a pained expression after Bat-Mite has congratulated him, "...but won't you find someone else to admire?...Please..." (WF No. 152: "The Colossal Kids!" pts. I-II—no title; "The Magic of Bat-Mite and Mr. Mxyzptlk!").

MXYZTPLK (MR.). See MXYZPTLK (Mr.)

MYSTO (the Great). An alias employed by SUPERMAN in February 1957 when he poses as a stage magician capable of producing Superman from an empty cabinet and forcing him to perform super-stunts as part of an elaborate and ultimately successful scheme to apprehend the mystery boss of the METROPOLIS underworld (S No. 111/3: "The Magical Superman").

NAPKAN. A treacherous foreign power which, in the words of Secretary of the Navy Hank Fox,

> has been acting increasingly war-like lately. There is every chance that against our will we may some day be engaged in warfare with it. Its agents here, we believe, are conducting sabotage in order for us to be in poor condition for war, should that day come.

In March-April 1942 SUPERMAN thwarts an attempt by Napkan saboteurs to cause the sinking of a newly christened American battleship; foils an attempt by the pro-Napkan Black Circle Society, headed by the Napkan consul Utsum, to overthrow the government of the South American country of Equaru; invades the Napkan embassy in METROPOLIS to apprehend Ambassador Hokopoko and a group of his underlings after they have staged a murderous attempt on the life of CLARK KENT; and thwarts an attempt by a Napkan suicide crew aboard the Napkan liner *Sunyat* to destroy the PANAMA CANAL by blowing up their vessel as it passes through the locks.

"How fortunate we are here in America," remarks Navy Secretary Hank Fox, "to have someone of Superman's calibre to aid us! In my opinion, he's worth *several* armies and navies!" (S No. 15/2).

NA-TSE. The treacherous high priest in the court of the ancient Egyptian pharaoh CHEOPS, and the mastermind behind a treasonous scheme to betray Egypt into the hands of the Assyrians. Miraculously transported to Egypt in the twenty-sixth century B.C. after crossing a mysterious wooden bridge—the so-called "bridge that mocks time"—not far from the GREAT PYRAMID at Giza, SUPERMAN exposes the evil Na-tse as a traitor, persuades the pharoah to emancipate his slaves, helps defeat an advancing Assyrian army, and single-handedly completes well over half the work on Cheops's Great Pyramid. His scheme to betray Egypt thwarted, Na-tse dies when some arrows fired at Superman by some of Cheops's disloyal guards are deflected by the Man of Steel and strike the evil high priest instead (WF No. 32, Jan/Feb '48: "The Seventh Wonder of the World!").

NEAL, ALICE. A lovely blond country girl, bequeathed $1,000,000 by a distant relative, who has arrived in METROPOLIS with a ludicrously convoluted scheme for achieving overnight success as an actress, only to learn, with some help from SUPERMAN, that the true road to stardom is a long and arduous one (S No. 41/3, Jul/Aug '46: "A Modern Alice in Wonderland!").

NELSON, BIG-NOISE. A sound-effects man at the studios of a nationwide broadcasting network who is noted for his ingenious sound effects and for the unorthodox techniques he utilizes in achieving them. Fired suddenly from his job, however, when some hornets he is using to evoke a fighter-plane attack escape accidentally into the studio audience, Nelson becomes determined to use his talents for evil and, vowing bitterly that "all of Metropolis will feel the effects of my genius," commits a series of spectacular sound-effects crimes—as when he makes people think a museum is collapsing by amplifying the sound of a man chewing carrots—before he is finally apprehended by SUPERMAN in January-February 1953 (S No. 80/2: "The Big Noise of Metropolis!").

NELSON, TOM. The "press representative" of "eminent astrologer" Abou Sabut. Embittered because, unbeknownst to the world at large, it is he who performs Abou Sabut's "actual astrological work" while Sabut retains "the big name and...most of the profits," Nelson concocts an elaborate scheme to frame Sabut for a series of crimes so that he can railroad him to prison and seize control of his finances, but Nelson is apprehended by SUPERMAN before his scheme can succeed (S No. 16/2, May/Jun '42).

NEPTUNE. The eighth planet from the sun. In July 1958 SUPERMAN journeys to Neptune to obtain a stone Superman head once sculpted by the Neptunians in his honor. The sculpture is one of a series of so-called "space trophies" which the Man of Steel gathers for inclusion in a time capsule which the Metropolis Museum plans to bury in the ground as a gift for the people of the fiftieth century A.D. (S No. 122/1: "The Secret of the Space Souvenirs").

NERO (Professor). A scientist whose laboratory full of "strange equipment" on the outskirts of METROPOLIS is secretly the cover for a one-man counterfeiting operation. Nero is arrested in a police raid led by SUPERMAN in April 1952 (Act No. 167: "The Machines of Crime!").

NEWMAN, ADAM. The name adopted by a lifelike android—created by SUPERMAN in his own image but rejected by the Man of Steel soon afterward because of its serious imperfections—who, bitterly resentful over having been discarded, masterminds an elaborate scheme to wreak vengeance on Superman and end his super-hero career by tricking Clark Kent into believing that Adam Newman is the only real Superman and that all his own recollections of an action-filled life as Superman have been only symptoms of a pathetic delusion. Incredibly, the plot succeeds—with Clark Kent actually convinced that he is only a mild-mannered reporter and that his entire life as Superman has been nothing but an insane hallucination—until finally Adam Newman, mortally wounded while battling a runaway nuclear pile, confesses the details of his scheme to a startled Clark Kent so that, even though the android Superman must perish, the real Superman will be able to save METROPOLIS from disaster (S No. 174/1, Jan '65: pts. 1-2—"Clark Kent's Incredible Delusion!"; "The End of a Hero!").

NEW SUPERMAN, THE. *See* AR-VAL.

NIAGARA FALLS. A spectacular cataract, celebrated for its grandeur and beauty, which forms part of the boundary between the United States and Canada, separating the state of New York from the Canadian province of Ontario.

In May 1948 SUPERMAN swims up Niagara Falls at such phenomenal speed that the water about him vaporizes into clouds of steam, thus making it impossible for unscrupulous movie producer MIKE Foss to capture the feat on film (Act No. 120: "Superman, Stunt Man!").

In June-July 1950 MISTER SEVEN robs a hotel at Niagara Falls and escapes over the falls in a padded barrel, but he and his lone accomplice are soon apprehended by Superman (WF No. 46: "The Seven Crimes of Mister 7!").

NICHOLAS, JOHN. A self-made millionaire—an orphan who was forced to work throughout his youth without any chance for fun or pleasure—who, having made out a will setting aside the bulk of his fortune for the construction of a chain of admission-free amusement parks for children throughout the country, then proceeds to fake his own death as a ploy to test the integrity of his three nephews, who, under the terms of a special provision of the will, are to receive their uncle's millions in place of the amusement-park project in the event the first park proves unsafe or uninteresting to children. Believing their uncle dead, two of the nephews promptly hire gangster Fancy Dan and his henchmen to cause a series of "accidents" at the first amusement park so as to prove it "unsafe," but SUPERMAN intervenes to capture the criminals, and the nephews, repelled by Fancy Dan's brutal methods and remorseful over what they have done, are overjoyed to learn that their uncle is really alive and wholeheartedly endorse his plan to construct the amusement park chain (Act No. 81, Feb '45: "Fairyland Isle!").

NICHOLS, ANNIE. A beautiful blonde, nicknamed Annie Oakley because of her mind-boggling feats as a sharpshooter, who is hired by PERRY WHITE to be LOIS LANE'S "regular bodyguard" in May-June 1951—after SUPERMAN has complained of being "sick and tired of spending all my valuable time rescuing [Lois] from danger!"—but who resigns the post soon afterward to accept the job of sheriff in her Western home town of Redstone Hills (S No. 70/1: "Lois Lane Meets Annie Oakley!").

NICHOLS, CARTER (Professor). The renowned scientist, historian (WF No. 82, May/Jun '56: "The Three Super-Musketeers!"), and "student of the mysteries of the subconscious mind" (Det No. 116, Oct

'46: "The Rescue of Robin Hood!") who has come to be regarded as "the world's foremost authority on time-travel" (BM No. 36/3, Aug/Sep '46: "Sir Batman at King Arthur's Court!"). On numerous occasions over the past three decades, Professor Nichols has used his "weird powers of hypnosis" (Det No. 135, May '48: "The True Story of Frankenstein!") and incredible time-traveling apparatus to transmit BATMAN and ROBIN across the time barrier, either into the distant future or the misty past.

Professor Carter Nichols, Bruce Wayne, and Dick Grayson, 1957

In November-December 1955, after Professor Nichols has propelled BRUCE WAYNE and DICK GRAYSON back into the past, to the city of Baghdad 1,000 years ago, to verify the authenticity of an ancient tradition concerning a "magnetic mountain" near the city, Batman and Robin find that "the terrific magnetic forces" of the magnetic mountain "interfere with [Nichols's] time-force" and prevent him from returning them to their own time. Nichols, however, calls on SUPERMAN, who uses "his full awesome speed to break through the barriers of time and space" and return Batman and Robin to the present. While they are in the past, Batman, Robin, and Superman meet the legendary ALADDIN (WF No. 79: "The Three Magicians of Bagdad!").

In May-June 1956 Professor Nichols transports Bruce Wayne, Dick Grayson, and CLARK KENT to France in the year 1696 in the hope that they will be able to uncover the answer to "history's greatest riddle," the identity of the famous "man in the iron mask." In the course of this adventure, Batman, Robin, and Superman encounter the THREE MUSKETEERS (WF No. 82: "The Three Super-Musketeers!").

In February 1960 Professor Nichols transports Batman and Robin back into the past, to the time just after Alexander the Great had been crowned king following the death of his father, Philip of Macedonia. When Batman's portable "time-box" is accidentally damaged and he and Robin find themselves marooned in the past, Nichols summons Superman to his laboratory and shows him how the time-box must be repaired, whereupon Superman travels swiftly into the past, repairs Batman's time-box, and returns with Batman and Robin to the present (WF No. 107: "The Secret of the Time Creature!").

By March 1963, escaped convicts DENNY KALE and Shorty Biggs have imprisoned and impersonated Batman and Robin and tricked Professor Nichols into transporting them into the past, to the city of Florence in the year 1479, where they think their twentieth-century knowhow will enable them to amass wealth rapidly. When the two time-travelers fail to return to the present, Superman journeys to fifteenth-century Florence to search for them, but Kale and Biggs capture Superman and leave him to die with a piece of synthetic KRYPTONITE chained to his chest. Ultimately, however, Batman and Robin escape from their place of imprisonment and have Professor Nichols send them into the past, where they rescue Superman and, with his help, take Kale and Biggs into custody (WF No. 132: "Batman and Robin, Medieval Bandits!").

(For a complete account of the career of Professor Carter Nichols, consult *The Encyclopedia of Comic Book Heroes: Volume I—Batman.*)

NIGHTCAVE (or Night-Cave). The secret underground laboratory, situated beneath the lavish suburban home of the Kandorian scientist NOR-KAN, which serves as the secret subterranean headquarters of NIGHTWING and FLAMEBIRD. (*See* KANDOR.)

NIGHTHOUND. The Kandorian "telepathic hound" that serves as the loyal animal companion of NIGHTWING and FLAMEBIRD. Nighthound helps his masters put an end to a "metalloid" menace in KANDOR in August 1964 (*see* THAN-AR) (WF No. 143: "The Feud Between Batman and Superman!" pts. I-II—no title; "The Manhunters from Earth!"). Kandor's telepathic hounds are "strange beasts," yellow in color, with tails like wolves and snouts like wild boars, "that can locate people at any distance by reading their minds to learn where they are!" Because of their unique abilities, the creatures are employed by the Kandorian authorities as telepathic bloodhounds (S No. 158, Jan '63: "Superman in Kandor" pts. I-III—"Invasion of the Mystery Super-Men!"; "The Dynamic Duo of Kandor!"; "The City of Super-People!").

NIGHT-OWL, THE. A "renegade scientist" and fiendish "super-criminal"—so named because his thick eyeglasses and oddly tufted white hair combine to give him the appearance of a vicious owl—whose "many darkness experiments," in addition to enabling him to see in the dark, have led to the development of the diabolical "black light projectors" with which he intends to plunge daytime METROPOLIS into inky blackness so that his henchmen can carry out the "wholesale pillage" of the city in "the greatest crime coup the world has ever known!"

Headquartered in a torchlit cavern hideaway an guarded by a murderous pet owl whose poison-dippe claws inflict instant death, the Night-Owl is ne ertheless apprehended by SUPERMAN in Octobe 1942 (Act No. 53: "The Man Who Put Out the Sun!"

The Night-Owl

NIGHTWING. An alternate identity employed by SUPERMAN on those occasions when he and JIMMY OLSEN, employing the name Flamebird, participate in adventures together inside the bottle city of KANDOR. The Prussian-blue color of Superman's Nightwing costume is reminiscent of the plumage of the nightwing, a Kandorian bird. Superman and Jimmy Olsen first adopt their Nightwing and Flamebird identities during an adventure in Kandor in January 1963 (*see* THAN OL) (S No. 158: "Superman in Kandor" pts. I-III—"Invasion of the Mystery Super-Men!"; "The Dynamic Duo of Kandor!"; "The City of Super-People!"). They employ them again during a second Kandorian adventure, in August 1964 (*see* THAN-AR) (WF No. 143: "The Feud Between Batman and Superman!" pts. I-II—no title; "The Manhunters from Earth!"). (*See* KANDOR.)

NILES, DEREK. A ruthless creditor of the Jordan Circus who, determined to gain possession of the circus by hook or by crook, orders his henchman Trigger to carry out a heinous campaign of murderous sabotage designed to prevent the circus from meeting its debts. SUPERMAN apprehends Trigger in December 1938, and the cunning Niles, cornered soon afterward, faints "from sheer fright" when he sees his bullets bouncing harmlessly off Superman's chest (Act No. 7).

NIM-ZEE. The father of VAN-ZEE, and "a distinguished member of the Kandorian Council," KANDOR's governing body. Both Nim-Zee and his son are distant relatives of SUPERMAN. In February 1962, during a period when the only way in which

Superman can enter Kandor is "by having [an] exchange ray cause [him] to switch places with a similar-sized **Kandorian** person or creature," the Man of Steel arranges to exchange himself for Nim-Zee and then to reverse the exchange once his business in Kandor has been concluded (S No. 151/3: "Superman's Greatest Secret!"; *see also* No. 158, Jan '63: "Superman in Kandor" pts. I-III—"Invasion of the Mystery Super-Men!"; "The Dynamic Duo of Kandor!"; "The City of Super-People!").

NOLAN, ROGER "NIFTY." A "confidence man and flim-flam artist" who attempts to make HOCUS AND POCUS his dupes in a scheme to swindle two METROPOLIS millionaires out of $250,000, only to be apprehended by SUPERMAN in September 1945 (Act No. 88: "The Adventure of the Stingy Men!").

NOR-KAN (or Nor-Kann; Nor Kann). The elderly Kandorian scientist—once a close friend of SUPERMAN's parents, JOR-EL and LARA—who befriends Superman and JIMMY OLSEN during their visit to KANDOR in January 1963. Once a colleague of Jor-El on the doomed planet KRYPTON, Nor-Kan happened to be visiting Kandor when it was stolen by BRAINIAC and hence escaped the cataclysm that soon afterward destroyed his native planet. Dwelling in a stately "suburban mansion" on the outskirts of Kandor, Nor-Kan carries on his scientific work in a "secret underground lab" constructed beneath his house. Inside his home, he has placed a pair of lifelike "photo-statues" of Jor-El and Lara, so as, in his words, "never to forget our friendship!" It is a pair of Kandorian birds—a "nightwing" and a "flamebird"—owned by Nor-Kan that inspires Superman and Jimmy Olsen to adopt the alternate identities of NIGHTWING and FLAMEBIRD and to fashion a pair of colorful costumes evocative of their plumage. With Nor-Kan's blessing, the hidden laboratory beneath his house becomes their secret subterranean headquarters—the so-called "night-

PERHAPS THIS SOLUTION WILL TONE DOWN THE ILLIUM'S RADIOACTIVE POWER, OHHH! A FLASH OF INTENSE RADIATION—STRAIGHT INTO MY BRAIN!

© NPP 1964

Working in his laboratory in the city of Kandor, Nor-Kan is struck in the brain by a fatal dose of radiation, 1964

cave" or "nightcave"—and his automobile is converted into their specially equipped "nightmobile" (S No. 158: "Superman in Kandor" pts. I-III—"Invasion of the Mystery Super-Men!"; "The Dynamic Duo of Kandor!"; "The City of Super-People!"). For almost two years Nor-Kan serves as Superman's faithful friend and Kandorian ally, only to succumb to "a fatal dose of radiation" in October 1964 while experimenting with the rare radioactive element ILLIUM-349 (Act No. 317: "Superman's Rainbow Face!").

In January 1963 Nor-Kan meets Superman for the first time and becomes the Man of Steel's ally in the struggle to prevent the "fanatic scientist" THAN OL from bringing doomsday to the entire city of Kandor (S No. 158: "Superman in Kandor" pts. I-III—"Invasion of the Mystery Super-Men!"; "The Dynamic Duo of Kandor!"; "The City of Super-People!").

In February 1964, when Brainiac is brought to trial in Kandor on the charge of having shrunk and stolen the city prior to the explosion of Krypton, Nor-Kan is chosen to prosecute the case on behalf of the Kandorian people. Nor-Kan's eloquence wins a swift conviction, but the Kandorians are ultimately compelled to let Brainiac go free in order to save the life of Superman (S No. 167: "The Team of Luthor and Brainiac!" pts. I-III—"The Deadly Duo!"; "The Downfall of Superman!"; "The Hour of Kandor's Vengeance!"). (*See* LUTHOR, LEX.)

In August 1964 Nor-Kan renews his friendship with Superman when the Man of Steel returns to Kandor to battle a "metalloid" menace there (WF No. 143: "The Feud Between Batman and Superman!" pts. I-II—no title; "The Manhunters from Earth!"). (*See* THAN-AR.)

In October 1964, after Superman has been deprived of his super-powers by the baleful radiations of a mysterious green comet, it is Nor-Kan who advises AR-VAL of the "terrible" method that might be used to "undo the comet's effects," but only at the cost of Ar-Val's own life (S No. 172: pts. I-III—"The New Superman!"; "Clark Kent—Former Superman!"; "The Struggle of the Two Supermen!"). Soon afterward, Nor-Kan is struck in the brain and killed by "a fatal dose of radiation" while experimenting with the rare radioactive element illium-349 in hopes of finding a way to use the substance to power an "enlarger ray" with which to restore Kandor to normal size. Following Nor-Kan's death, a solemn funeral procession is held for him in Kandor, and a memorial tablet, bearing this inscription, is erected in his honor: "In memory of Nor-Kan, who gave his life attempting to find a safe enlarging ray so that Kandor, in normal size, could become a city of Earth!" (Act No. 317, Oct '64: "Superman's Rainbow Face!").

NORMAN, NORMIE. A young hoodlum in league with the Hammerhead Haines mob who becomes, ironically, a finalist in the DAILY PLANET's contest to select "the ideal average American" in January 1946. In a ruthless effort to eliminate the other finalists so that Norman will be assured of winning the prize money, Haines and his henchmen set out to force each of Norman's competitors to do something sufficiently spectacular to ruin his image of average-ness and eliminate him from contention in the eyes of the judges. A finalist himself in his Clark Kent identity, SUPERMAN apprehends the Haines gang and then deliberately captures the pistol-wielding Norman as Clark Kent in the hope that this uncharacteristic act of heroism will place him out of the running for the average-American award. The judges, however, award Kent the prize anyway, observing that "...like the ordinary American, you try to avoid trouble! But when it comes, you plunge in and make the other fellow sorry he started it! We feel that you are the perfect average American!" (Act No. 92: "The Average American!").

NORTON, ALICE. A pretty brown-haired girl, the winner of a "Lovely Child" contest sponsored by the DAILY PLANET, who has been totally blind since her involvement in an auto accident some four years ago. Withdrawn and cynical since the onset of her blindness—to the point where she scoffs at the existence of SUPERMAN and insists he is no more than a fairy tale—Alice regains her sight, and her capacity for living, when Superman personally performs the delicate eye operation necessary to restore her vision (S No. 96/1, Mar '55: "The Girl Who Didn't Believe in Superman!").

NORTON, NICK. A METROPOLIS racketeer—free on bail pending his trial, along with two other gangsters, on criminal conspiracy charges—who murders the wife of George Lash, the city's tough, incorruptible prosecuting attorney, and frames Lash for the crime in the hope that Lash will be unable to prosecute him and his cronies while fighting to clear himself of the murder charge. Norton is exposed and apprehended by SUPERMAN in November-December 1940 (S No. 7/1).

NORVAL. A collector of priceless jewels who is found murdered in his intricately designed, supposed-ly burglar-proof home in September-October 1940. Early evidence seems to point to LOIS LANE as the murderess, but SUPERMAN ultimately establishes her innocence and apprehends the real killer, Burkley, the architect who originally designed Norval's unusual residence (S No. 6/1).

NORVELL, EMIL. A ruthless United States "muni-tions magnate" who has been promoting wars and conflicts throughout the world in order to facilitate the sale of his own munitions. He is the moving force behind the senseless war ravaging the small South American republic of SAN MONTÉ (Act No. 2, Jul '38) as well as the secret mastermind behind a cunning scheme to maneuver the United States into becoming "embroiled with Europe" in the impending war with the Axis (see GREER, ALEX) before the "full implica-tions" of such involvement can be recognized by the U.S. Congress (Act No. 1, Jun '38).

"What I can't understand," asks SUPERMAN in July 1938, "is why you manufacture munitions when it means that thousands will die horribly."

"Men are cheap," replies Norvell callously, "--munitions, expensive!"

The money-hungry Norvell undergoes a rapid and dramatic conversion to pacifism, however, when Superman forces him to risk his own life by enlisting as a foot soldier in the San Monté army, allowing the reformed munitions magnate to return safely home to the U.S.A. only after receiving his solemn commit-ment to "quit manufacturing munitions" (Act No. 2, Jul '38). The story is reprinted in Superman No. 1/2 (Sum '39).

Emil Norvell and Superman, 1938

O

OCEANIA. The far-distant planet—described as "a close duplicate of Earth"—which is the home of the super-hero HYPER-MAN (Act No. 265, Jun '60: "The Superman' from Outer Space!").

OCTOPUS, THE. The cunning master criminal who is the leader of the Octopus Gang, a band of ruthless criminals—each clad in a gray hood emblazoned with an emblem in the form of an octopus—who commit a series of spectacular crimes before they are finally apprehended in February 1963 through the heroic efforts of BATMAN, ROBIN, SUPERMAN, and a strictly amateur costumed crime-fighter calling himself the Crimson Avenger. The Crimson Avenger is in reality Albert Elwood, a "crackpot inventor" who has designed a whimsical arsenal of crime-fighting weaponry which he feels certain will make him the "nemesis of all crimedom." The capture of the Octopus Gang is repeatedly—albeit unintentionally—thwarted by the Crimson Avenger's crackpot gadgetry and ceaseless bungling, but, at a point when the villains appear to have gained the upper hand, it is his courage and resourcefulness that make the final capture possible (WF No. 131: "The Mystery of the Crimson Avenger!").

O'GRADY, "LUCKY." A civic-minded resident of the Roaring Kitchen section of METROPOLIS who helps SUPERMAN bring a crooked politician and his gangland manager to justice in May-June 1943 (S No. 22/2: "The Luck of O'Grady").

OLAM (the Wondrous Wizard). An alias employed by SUPERMAN in April-May 1951 when he poses as a miraculous wise man capable of answering any question put to him as part of his plan to help LOIS LANE get back in the good graces of DAILY PLANET editor PERRY WHITE (WF No. 51: "The Amazing Talents of Lois Lane!").

OLAV. A power-mad scientist on the planet Zor whose scheme to assume dictatorial control of his planet is thwarted by SUPERMAN in May 1952 (Act No. 168: "The Menace of Planet Z!").

O'LEARY, DUTCH. A ruthless gangster and "successful gambler"—once fired from a job at Skyways Airlines and now bent on wreaking a twisted revenge—who masterminds a series of "disastrous crashes" that threaten to ruin Skyways Airlines until he is finally apprehended by SUPERMAN in December 1941 (Act No. 43).

OLSEN, JIMMY. The fledgling journalist and friend of SUPERMAN who is the junior colleague of CLARK KENT and LOIS LANE on the METROPOLIS *Daily Planet*. First introduced in the chronicles in November-December 1941 only as Jimmy, an "office boy" at the DAILY PLANET with a heartfelt longing to

become "a real reporter" like his idol, Clark Kent (S No. 13/2), Jimmy is first referred to by his full name, Jimmy Olsen, in March-April 1942 (S No. 15/1) and continues to be referred to as the *Daily Planet*'s office boy for a number of years (Act No. 71, Apr '44: "Valentine Villainy!"; and others) until he is finally accorded the status of "cub reporter" in January 1954 (S No. 86/2: "Jimmy Olsen . . . Editor!"). Although Jimmy's real name is James Olsen (Act No. 203, Apr '55: "The International Daily Planet!"; and others), he is almost always referred to as Jimmy.

Jimmy Olsen

© NPP 1978

In the early texts in which he appears, Jimmy Olsen is portrayed as a youngster about ten years of age (WF No. 6, Sum '42: "Man of Steel versus Man of Metal!"; and others), but by April 1944 the chroniclers have begun to portray him as a boy of about twelve or thirteen (Act No. 71: "Valentine Villainy!"). More recent texts depict him as an adolescent somewhere in his late teens.

In the course of his first two decades in the chronicles, Jimmy's hair is variously portrayed as blond (S No. 13/2, Nov/Dec '41; and others), honey blond (S No. 13/2, Nov/Dec '41), red (S No. 15/1, Mar/Apr '42; and many others), light red (Act No. 188, Jan '54: "The Spectral Superman!"; and others), and brown (S No. 40/3, May/Jun '46: "There Is No Superman!"; and others). Since mid-1958, however, it has been consistently rendered a bright red. Jimmy's

253

freckles have been a standard feature of his appearance since 1942 (WF No. 6, Sum '42: "Man of Steel versus Man of Metal!"; and many others).

Even during his apprentice years as an office boy, Jimmy Olsen is consumed by a burning ambition to become a real reporter. In November-December 1941 he gets his first byline, when he writes up an account of Superman's capture of the ruthless extortionist known as "THE ARCHER" (S No. 13/2).

"You're an observant lad!" remarks Clark Kent admiringly after Jimmy has given him an important news tip in Summer 1942. "I hope to be a top-notch reporter like you some day!" beams Jimmy. "Any time you need help, feel free to call on me" (WF No. 6: "Man of Steel versus Man of Metal!").

Despite his eagerness, however, and his irrepressible ambition, Jimmy Olsen remains the *Daily Planet's* office boy for twelve full years (Act No. 71, Apr '44: "Valentine Villainy!"; and others), although Lois Lane does refer to him, in one early text, as "Jimmy Olsen, office boy, who sometimes pinch-hits as cub reporter, and may some day be big stuff!" (WF No. 13, Spr '44: "The Freedom of the Press!").

From January 1954 onward, Jimmy Olsen is regularly referred to as a "cub reporter" (S No. 86/2: "Jimmy Olsen . . . Editor!"), a designation that continues to be applied to him through at least the mid-1960s (S No. 180/1, Oct '65: "Clark Kent's Great Superman Hunt!"; and many others), although, more and more in recent years, the texts have tended to refer to him simply as a "reporter" (Act No. 311, Apr '64: "Superman, King of Earth!"; and many others), elevating his status to one at least approaching that of Lois Lane and Clark Kent. "Throughout the world," notes Superman No. 181/1, "Jimmy Olsen and Lois Lane are known for their courage and ingenuity in getting scoops" (Nov '65: pts. I-II—"The Super-Scoops of Morna Vine!"; "The Secret of the New Supergirl!"). Perhaps Action Comics No. 238 describes his latter-day status best when it refers to him as the "star cub reporter of the **Daily Planet**" (Mar '58: "The Super-Gorilla from Krypton").

Indeed, despite his youth, Jimmy Olsen has acquired experience and responsibility far surpassing that of most cub reporters. When Metropolis celebrates Boy's Day in January 1954, for example, Jimmy takes over the *Daily Planet's* managing editor's desk for twenty-four hours, performing his duties with remarkable professionalism. "That boy will be a good newspaperman someday!" remarks Clark Kent proudly (S No. 86/2: "Jimmy Olsen . . . Editor!"). A year later, when the *Daily Planet* launches its new international editions, Jimmy Olsen is appointed editor of the *Daily Planet's* London edition (Act No. 203, Apr '55: "The International Daily Planet!").

In the texts, Jimmy Olsen is described as "observant" (WF No. 6, Sum '42: "Man of Steel versus Man of Metal!"), "irrepressible" (Act No. 71, Apr '44: "Valentine Villainy!"; and others), "conceited" (Act No. 269, Oct '60: "The Truth Mirror!"), "impulsive,"

and "happy-go-lucky" (S No. 177/3, May '65: "When Jimmy Olsen Stole Krypto from Superman"). Particularly when in pursuit of a hot news story, Jimmy is inclined to be "very curious and impulsive," a combination of traits which, notes Superman No. 173/3, "has often landed him in hot water!" (Nov '64: "The Triumph of Luthor and Brainiac!"). Jimmy also tends to be egotistical and boastful, often to the point of stretching the truth—bragging about his friendship with Superman, claiming as personal accomplishments things that happened by accident (Act No. 253, Jun '59: "The War Between Superman and Jimmy Olsen!"; and others), often altering his account of events so as to place himself in the best possible light (S No. 171/3, Aug '64: "The Nightmare Ordeal of Superman"; and others).

Jimmy Olsen is a close friend of Superman, although he does not know that Superman is secretly Clark Kent (S No. 145/1, May '61: "The Secret Identity of Superman!"; and others). The texts repeatedly refer to Jimmy Olsen as Superman's "pal" (Act No. 198, Nov '54: "The Six Lives of Lois Lane!"; and others), his "young pal" (Act No. 231, Aug '57: "Sir Jimmy Olsen, Knight of Metropolis"; and others), and his "best pal" (S No. 131/3, Aug '59: "The Unknown Super-Deeds!"; and others). Action Comics No. 210 counts him, along with Lois Lane and PERRY WHITE, among Superman's "close friends" (Nov '55: "Superman in Superman Land"), and other texts list him among Superman's "best friends" (Act No. 243, Aug '58: "The Lady and the Lion"; and others).

"THE THINKER" has described Jimmy Olsen as "Superman's best friend" (S No. 93/2, Nov '54: "Jimmy Olsen's Double!"), and JAX-UR has referred to him as Superman's "best pal" (Act No. 310, Mar '64: "Secret of Kryptonite Six!"). Jimmy himself has referred to Superman as "my best pal" (Act No. 302, Jul '63: "The Amazing Confession of Super-Perry White!") and "my best friend" (S No. 178/2, Jul '65: "When Superman Lost His Memory!").

"**Superman** has a warm spot in his heart for many people," notes Superman No. 93/2, ". . . but an especially warm one is reserved for his young pal, Jimmy Olsen!" (Nov '54: "Jimmy Olsen's Double!").

Jimmy Olsen is fiercely loyal to Superman, retaining his faith in his "super-idol" even when, for the moment, the Man of Steel's motives are suspect or his actions unpopular (Act No. 312, May '64: "King Superman versus Clark Kent, Metallo"; and others).

Over the years, Jimmy has built up an extensive (S No. 111/1, Feb '57: "The Non-Super Superman"; and others)—and valuable (S No. 115/2, Aug '57: "Jimmy Olsen's Lost Pal")—collection of Superman trophies and souvenirs, a collection to which Superman continually adds with exotic gifts from distant planets and other exciting memorabilia (WF No. 147, Feb '65: "The Doomed Boy Heroes!" pts. I-II—"The New Terrific Team!"; "The Doom of Jimmy Olsen and Robin!"; and others).

In addition, Superman has dedicated a room to Jimmy Olsen in his FORTRESS OF SOLITUDE (Act No.

241, Jun '58: "The Super-Key to Fort Superman"; and others) and has provided him with a "special wristwatch" with which the young reporter can "set off [an] ultrasonic signal"—audible only to Superman's super-hearing—to summon the Man of Steel to his rescue. Even if Jimmy activates the ultrasonic signal on a distant continent, Superman can hear the signal and race to Jimmy's aid (Act No. 238, Mar '58: "The Super-Gorilla from Krypton"; and many others). The ultrasonic signal broadcast by the "signal-watch" will not, however, travel through outer space (Act No. 262, Mar '60: "When Superman Lost His Powers!").

Jimmy Olsen summons Superman with his ultrasonic signal-watch, 1964

Jimmy Olsen's friendship with Superman has had the effect of making the young journalist something of a celebrity (Act No. 210, Nov '55: "Superman in Superman Land"; and others). The JIMMY OLSEN FAN CLUB meets monthly in Metropolis (Act No. 286, Mar '62: "The Jury of Super-Enemies!"; and others), and Jimmy has, on at least one occasion, been mobbed by well-wishers and autograph seekers (Act No. 210, Nov '55: "Superman in Superman Land"). In addition to relishing the attention he receives as the result of being Superman's pal, Jimmy clearly envies Superman his super-powers and wishes he had them, at least in part because he feels that having super-powers would be likely to make him more successful with women (Act No. 283, Dec '61: "The Red Kryptonite Menace!").

Jimmy Olsen lives alone in a Metropolis apartment (S No. 144/1, Apr '61: "The Super-Weapon!"; and others). On one wall is a collection of large pictures illustrating Superman's origin (*see* SUPERMAN [section A, origin]), including the explosion of the planet KRYPTON and the infant Superman's escape to Earth in a tiny rocket (S No. 123, Aug '58: chs. 1-3—"The Girl of Steel"; "The Lost Super-Powers"; "Superman's Return to Krypton").

Over and above his skills as a journalist, Jimmy Olsen is an avid bowler (Act No. 317, Oct '64: "Superman's Rainbow Face!"), can pilot a helicopter (Act No. 290, Jul '62: "Half a Superman!"), and is fluent in Kryptonese, the language of Krypton, which is now spoken only in the bottle city of KANDOR (S No. 158, Jan '63: "Superman in Kandor" pts. I-III—"Invasion of the Mystery Super-Men!"; "The Dynamic Duo of Kandor!"; "The City of Super-People!"; and others). Jimmy's principal romantic involvement has been with LUCY LANE, the lovely blond sister of Lois Lane (S No. 147/1, Aug '61: "The Great Mento!"; and others).

In addition to the various undercover identities that he has concocted with the aid of the "trunkful of disguises" he keeps in his apartment (WF No. 144, Sep '64: "The 1,001 Tricks of Clayface and Brainiac!" pts. I-II—no title; "The Helpless Partners!"; and others), Jimmy Olsen has a pair of important alternate identities: as FLAMEBIRD, he functions as Superman's partner on those occasions when he and Superman, employing the name NIGHTWING, undertake adventures together inside the bottle city of Kandor (S No. 158, Jan '63: "Superman in Kandor" pts. I-III—"Invasion of the Mystery Super-Men!"; "The Dynamic Duo of Kandor!"; "The City of Super-People!"; *see also* WF No. 143, Aug '64: "The Feud Between Batman and Superman!" pts. I-II—no title; "The Manhunters from Earth!"). As ELASTIC LAD, Jimmy serves as an honorary member of the LEGION OF SUPER-HEROES (S No. 172, Oct '64: pts. I-III—"The New Superman!"; "Clark Kent—Former Superman!"; "The Struggle of the Two Supermen!"; and others). Interestingly, Jimmy is also, by virtue of his ancestry, the rightful king of the once-proud ancient kingdom of Vumania, although all that remains of Vumania in modern times is a barren desert island (Act No. 231, Aug '57: "Sir Jimmy Olsen, Knight of Metropolis").

Occasionally, Jimmy Olsen and Superman undertake joint adventures with BATMAN and ROBIN, with Jimmy aiding Superman much as Robin aids Batman. In May 1964 Jimmy Olsen and Robin establish a secret headquarters together in an abandoned observatory which they dub the Eyrie (WF No. 141: "The Olsen-Robin Team versus 'The Superman-Batman Team!'"). The Eyrie is intended to serve as their base of operations on those occasions when they undertake joint adventures as the so-called "Robin and Olsen team" (WF No. 147, Feb '65: "The Doomed Boy Heroes!" pts. I-II—"The New Terrific Team!"; "The Doom of Jimmy Olsen and Robin!"). In September 1964, as his way of rewarding Jimmy for being "such a loyal friend" to Superman, Batman entrusts Jimmy with the secret of his dual identity, pulling back his batlike cowl to reveal the face of millionaire socialite Bruce Wayne (WF No. 144: "The 1,001 Tricks of Clayface and Brainiac!" pts. I-II — no title; "The Helpless Partners!").

A number of individuals in various times and places are perfect Jimmy Olsen look-alikes, including the hoodlum BABY-FACE (S No. 93/2, Nov '54: "Jimmy Olsen's Double!"), the Kandorian "criminal scientist" EL GAR KUR (Act No 253, Jun '59: "The War Between Superman and Jimmy Olsen!"), and Zol-Lar, Jimmy Olsen's double in the Kandorian LOOK-ALIKE SQUAD. Superman and Batman encounter a Jimmy Olsen look-alike—also named Jimmy Olsen—during a visit to an extradimensional "parallel world" in March 1965 (WF No. 148: "Superman and Batman--Outlaw!" pts. I-II—"The Evil Superman and Batman"; "The Incredible New Super-Team!"). The Legion of Super-Heroes employ a lifelike Jimmy Olsen robot in April 1962 as part of an elaborate hoax they play on Superman and SUPERGIRL (S No. 152/1: "The Robot Master!"), and Superman encounters a lifelike android of Jimmy Olsen during a time-journey to Metropolis one million years in the future (Act No. 300, May '63: "Superman Under the Red Sun!").

In November-December 1941, the date of his textual debut, Jimmy, the Daily Planet's office boy, rescues Lois Lane from death at the hands of "THE ARCHER" by pushing her out of the way of one of the villain's arrows (S No. 13/2).

Perry White and Jimmy Olsen, 1941

In March-April 1942, after Lois Lane has been taken captive by racketeer BILL TALLEY, Jimmy summons Metropolis police Sgt. Bob Branigan to Lois's rescue. In this text, Jimmy is referred to by his full name—Jimmy Olsen—for the first time in the chronicles (S No. 15/1).

In January 1954 Jimmy Olsen and Lois Lane are taken captive by the CUSHIONS RAYMOND gang and held hostage aboard the villains' getaway helicopter while the criminals rob the Metropolis Bank. Jimmy and Lois are rescued by the Metropolis police, however, after the gang's helicopter has been forced to the ground by Superman (Act No. 188: "The Spectral Superman!"). During this same period, when the city of Metropolis celebrates Boy's Day and Jimmy Olsen is appointed managing editor of the Daily Planet for twenty-four hours, Jimmy assigns Clark Kent, Lois Lane, and Perry White the task of solving the famous Hinkley Jewel Collection robbery, which has remained unsolved for seven years. Together the three reporters crack the baffling case, and when the villains invade the offices of the Daily Planet and hold Jimmy Olsen and Perry White hostage in the managing editor's office, Superman apprehends the criminals and rescues his friends from the criminals' clutches. "It's fantastic, Superman!" exclaims Perry White afterward. "Jimmy Olsen became editor...and solved the biggest crime in Metropolis records! I must be dreaming! I must be!" (S No. 86/2, Jan '54: "Jimmy Olsen...Editor!").

In November 1954 Jimmy Olsen is kidnapped by a gang of criminals headed by "THE THINKER" and replaced at the Daily Planet by one of the villain's henchmen, a Jimmy Olsen look-alike named Baby-Face. Baby-Face comes within a hair's breadth of murdering Jimmy, but Superman apprehends the criminals and rescues his young pal from their clutches (S No. 93/2: "Jimmy Olsen's Double!").

In February 1955 Superman sets out to teach Jimmy Olsen a well-deserved lesson in the follies of showing off, only to have his well-intentioned efforts backfire when a series of bizarre coincidences combine to convince Jimmy—as well as his employers on the Daily Planet—that he has somehow become endowed with the extraordinary abilities and intuition of a "super-reporter," enabling him to unravel unsolved crimes and perform other journalistic miracles by means of his remarkable, inexplicable "sixth sense" for news. Unwilling to publicly humiliate Jimmy, Superman feels obligated, for a time, to make his young pal's wildly improbable news "hunches" appear to come true, as when he surreptitiously entices a Metropolis numbers racketeer into making an attempt on the life of a city councilman after Jimmy has predicted that such an attempt will take place. Ultimately, however, Superman confides to Jimmy that it is he who has been responsible for Jimmy's reportorial super-feats, and, although the two friends never divulge the truth to Jimmy's colleagues on the Daily Planet, it is clear that Jimmy has learned a much-needed lesson in humility (S No. 95/3: "Jimmy Olsen, Super-Reporter!").

In April 1955, after having been appointed editor of the Daily Planet's new London and Paris editions, respectively, Jimmy Olsen and Lois Lane set out to launch their new foreign editions by obtaining exclusive interviews with PIETRO PARESCA, "the most notorious smuggler in all Europe." Taken captive by Paresca and his henchmen aboard their sloop—and told that they will be put to death as a grisly lesson to other snooping reporters—Jimmy and Lois are rescued soon afterward through the heroic intervention of Superman (Act No. 203: "The International Daily Planet!").

In May 1955 DAN WHEELER and his henchmen attempt to make Jimmy Olsen their dupe in a scheme to lure Clark Kent to his doom in retaliation for Kent's *Daily Planet* exposés of their various swindles. Captured by the criminals and locked in an animal cage, Jimmy manages to escape on his own, and Wheeler and his cohorts are apprehended by Superman (S No. 97/2: "The Big Game Hunt of Metropolis!").

In July 1955, after Clark Kent has infiltrated the "BIG GUY's" mob by posing as a safecracker, the criminals take Jimmy Olsen captive and order Kent to murder Olsen to prove he is really a criminal. Through a ruse, Kent pretends to kill Jimmy and then secretly engineers his escape, and soon afterward, as Superman, he apprehends the "Big Guy" and his henchmen (S No. 98/2: "Clark Kent Outlaw!").

In November 1955 Jimmy Olsen is among the throng of merrymakers who attend the gala opening of SUPERMAN LAND (Act No. 210: "Superman in Superman Land").

In the summer of 1956 Jimmy Olsen performs as a lion tamer in the *Daily Planet*'s annual Daily Planet Charity Show circus (Act No. 212, Jan'56: "The Superman Calendar").

In July 1956 Jimmy Olsen helps Superman apprehend "BULLETS" BARTON and dispose of six rare lead meteors which, because their cores are of KRYPTONITE, are potentially fatal to Superman (S No. 106/2: "The Thefts of Clark Kent"). During this same period, after the renegade scientist LEX LUTHOR has invented—and fashioned into a special "metallic suit"—a new metal alloy capable of absorbing and accumulating the energy generated by Superman whenever he performs his super-feats, Jimmy Olsen helps the Man of Steel defeat Luthor by weakening his super-friend with kryptonite so that the weakness induced in Superman by the kryptonite will, like his super-strength, be transmitted to Luthor through his special suit (S No. 106/3, Jul '56: "The Super-Outlaw of Metropolis").

In February 1957 Jimmy Olsen joins forces with Superman to apprehend "notorious criminal" BLACKY BAIRD (S No. 111/1: "The Non-Super Superman").

In May 1957 Jimmy Olsen is among the crowd of opening-day visitors to Superman's new SUPERMAN MUSEUM (Act No. 228: "Superman's Super Skyscraper").

In August 1957 Jimmy Olsen is summoned to the Metropolis Archives Office to hear some astonishing news: that he, Jimmy Olsen, is the rightful ruler of the once-proud ancient kingdom of Vumania. "...When the last **king of Vumania** died, centuries ago," explains the archivist, "his kingdom lay unclaimed! Recently, however, we discovered that one remote descendant of his is alive today, in line for the throne!" That remote descendant is none other than Jimmy Olsen, but Jimmy may ascend the Vumanian

throne only if, explains the archivist, "...you can fulfill three knightly deeds required of each new king, to prove his bravery"—viz., "slay a dragon," "break a wizard's spell," and "rescue a fair maiden in distress"—although Jimmy is free to carry out these deeds in symbolic, rather than literal, ways.

Even though all that remains of Vumania in modern times is a barren desert island of no monetary value, Jimmy enters into the spirit of his knightly quest by renting a suit of armor—complete with jousting lance—from a local costume shop and setting out on his bicycle in search of opportunities for fulfilling the required knightly deeds. Indeed, in the hours that follow, Jimmy gamely carries out his mission, as when he punctures a gigantic dragon-shaped balloon with his lance in the midst of a Chinatown parade and rescues a woman from an oncoming car. Throughout the day, however, Superman is compelled to intervene repeatedly to protect his young pal from members of the Seal Gang, a band of modern-day pirates who have been secretly using Vumania as their base of operations and who are determined to prevent Jimmy from performing his three knightly deeds and laying claim to the island.

Ultimately, however, Jimmy fulfills the required deeds and becomes king of Vumania—although his kingdom is, admittedly, a modest one—and, through a ruse, Superman uncovers the Seal Gang's "underground hideout" and takes the villains into custody (Act No. 231: "Jimmy Olsen, Knight of Metropolis"). During this same period, "notorious criminal impersonator" "MANY-FACES" FULTON attempts to trick Jimmy Olsen into believing that Superman is dead as part of an elaborate scheme to uncover Superman's secret identity (S No. 115/2, Aug '57: "Jimmy Olsen's Lost Pal").

In January 1958 Jimmy Olsen helps thwart an elaborate scheme by LEX LUTHOR to destroy Superman and make off with a fortune in charitable contributions (Act No. 236: "Superman's New Uniform!"). During this same period, after Jimmy Olsen has agreed to take part in a U.S. Army experiment designed to uncover potential military geniuses by testing youngsters for military aptitude, a chance mishap—caused when the electronic impulses of Jimmy's ultrasonic signal-watch interact weirdly with the electronic brain supervising the testing—results in Jimmy's being classified as a Military Mastermind First Class, a higher rating than that enjoyed by any U.S. military official.

Summoned immediately to the Pentagon, where he is informed that the testing has shown him to be "the greatest military genius ever known," the flabbergasted Jimmy is awarded the rank of six-star general and the title of honorary commander-in-chief—higher designations than those accorded any other military officer—and is placed in complete command of one of the two opposing armies in a series of upcoming war games so that the Pentagon's top brass can watch Jimmy apply his military super-genius to actual mock-combat situations.

© NPP 1978

Although Jimmy's military stratagems are hare-brained and ridiculous and would, under ordinary circumstances, be doomed to failure, Superman works behind the scenes to make Jimmy's amateurish tactics succeed—thereby ensuring Jimmy's forces a brilliant victory in the war games—for he has discovered that a band of foreign spies are secretly monitoring the games from their headquarters aboard a "long-range jet plane," and he knows that if the spies come to believe that Jimmy's notions of strategy are actually viable, the conclusions they report to their government will be militarily worthless.

Eventually, even Jimmy begins to suspect that his brilliant victory in the war games must be Superman's doing, and indeed, once the war games are over, Superman confesses to both Jimmy and the

© NPP 1978

Pentagon brass that Jimmy is not really a military genius at all and that he only interceded in the war games exercise in order to sabotage the intelligence gathering efforts of the foreign spies (S No. 118/2, Jan '58: "The Boy Napoleon").

In March 1958, after encountering a mighty "super-gorilla" from Krypton in the jungles of Africa, Jimmy Olsen names the awesome beast KING KRYPTON. The following morning, Jimmy and his guide are taken captive by a tribe of primitive Caucasians—"descendants of the ancient Romans, who reverted to jungle natives"—but the tribesmen flee in abject terror soon afterward during the climactic battle between Superman and King Krypton (Act No. 238: "The Super-Gorilla from Krypton").

In May 1958 Jimmy Olsen joins forces with Superman, Perry White, and the U.S. Coast Guard to carry out an elaborate ruse that culminates in the capture of "HONEST" JOHN and a gang of "Honest" John's underworld rivals known as the Shark Gang (S No. 121/3: "Jimmy Hits the Jackpot").

In July 1958, shortly after being assigned to write an article about some famous U.S. President for the Daily Planet's upcoming Patriot's Day issue, Jimmy Olsen is struck on the head by a falling picture of Superman and, knocked unconscious by the blow, lapses into a dream in which Superman is President of the United States, Clark Kent is Vice-President, and Jimmy himself is White House press secretary. After awakening from his dream, in which Superman's mighty super-deeds make him one of the most acclaimed Presidents in U.S. history, Jimmy is about to write an article stating that if Superman were elected President he would become one of the most honored and revered men ever to occupy the Oval Office, when Clark Kent reminds him that Superman could never legally be elected President since the Constitution provides that only native-born Americans may hold that high office and Superman is a native of the planet Krypton (S No. 122/2: "Superman in the White House!").

In August 1958 Jimmy Olsen comes into possession of an ancient magic Indian totem, which, once every hundred years, has the power to grant three wishes to whomever rubs its magic jewel beneath the glow of a full moon. Jimmy's first wish is for the appearance of a super-powered SUPER-GIRL to serve as a fitting companion for Superman, but, although a lovely super-heroine does indeed materialize out of nowhere in response to Jimmy's wish, she proves to be more of a hindrance than a help to Superman and, ultimately, she prevails upon Jimmy to use the powers of the magic totem to nullify his wish and dispatch her "back into the mysterious limbo from which she came...."

Soon afterward, the magic totem is stolen by a pair of criminals, who use its second wish to rob Superman of his mighty super-powers, intending to murder him once the wish comes true. Through the magic of the ancient totem, Superman does indeed lose his super-powers, but, through a series of elaborate ruses carried out with the aid of Jimmy Olsen, the Man of Steel succeeds in tricking the villains into believing that their wish has failed to come true, and ultimately he apprehends them, recovers the stolen totem, and has Jimmy use its powers to nullify the villains' wish and restore his super-powers.

Disheartened that the totem's first two wishes have turned out so badly for Superman, Jimmy uses his third and final wish to return Superman across the time-space barrier for a nostalgic visit to the planet Krypton at a time prior to its destruction, where, reunited with the man and woman who will one day marry and become his parents (see JOR-EL; LARA), the Man of Steel thwarts the diabolical machinations of the would-be tyrant KIL-LOR and, by helping to clear his parents-to-be of a charge of treason, helps pave the way for their eventual marriage (S No. 123: chs. 1-3—"The Girl of Steel"; "The Lost Super-Powers"; "Superman's Return to Krypton").

In January 1959 Jimmy Olsen is taken captive by the sinister VON KAMP and forced to work as a slave laborer on the villain's mysterious Project X. Later, as a punishment for having attempted to escape, Jimmy is shut inside a rocket and launched into outer space, but Superman rescues his young pal before any harm can come to him (Act No. 248: "The Man No Prison Could Hold!").

In February 1959 Jimmy Olsen joins forces with Superman to carry out an elaborate, and ultimately successful, ruse designed to trick LEX LUTHOR into swallowing the antidote to his own "liquid kryptonite" serum (Act No. 249: "The Kryptonite Man!").

In June 1959, while Jimmy Olsen is touring Superman's Fortress of Solitude in preparation for writing an article about it for the *Daily Planet*, the Kandorian "criminal scientist" EL GAR KUR succeeds in using a complex body-switching apparatus to take Jimmy's place inside the Fortress while simultaneously imprisoning Jimmy inside the bottle city of Kandor—all as part of a diabolical scheme to destroy Kandor and conquer the Earth. El Gar Kur is ultimately defeated, however, through the combined efforts of Jimmy Olsen and Superman (Act No. 253: "The War Between Superman and Jimmy Olsen!").

In April 1960, when Superman's Earthday—"the anniversary of the day [Superman] landed on Earth from the doomed planet, **Krypton**"—is celebrated in SMALLVILLE, Jimmy Olsen is among those on hand to attend the festivities (S No. 136/2: "The Secret of Kryptonite!").

In August 1960 Jimmy Olsen helps Superman carry out an elaborate charade designed to make Lois Lane believe that Superman has decided to marry LORI LEMARIS and live in ATLANTIS so that Lois will feel free to accept a proposal of marriage from multimillionaire BRETT RAND (S No. 139/1: "The New Life of Super-Merman!").

In April 1961, after BERT TALBOT and his henchmen have constructed a diabolical bazookalike weapon capable of accumulating and then unleash-

ing the incredible "super-force" generated by Superman whenever he performs super-feats, Jimmy Olsen helps Superman defeat the villains by weakening his super-friend with kryptonite so that this weakness, absorbed by the villains' "super-weapon," will "neutralize [its] supply of super-force" and render the weapon useless (S No. 144/1: "The Super-Weapon!").

In May 1961, after Jimmy Olsen's girlfriend, Lucy Lane, has told him how unhappy her sister Lois is as the result of Superman's unwillingness to marry her, and after Lucy has repeated Lois's conjecture that Superman's unwillingness to marry Lois is based on his belief that she could not be safely entrusted with the secret of his dual identity, Jimmy is seized, in the words of the text, by "a hair-brained [sic] inspiration." Acting on impulse, albeit with the best intentions, Jimmy tells Lucy that the Man of Steel has recently revealed to him that he is secretly Rock Stirling, a famous wheelchair-bound science-fiction writer and TV-series host, and he invites Lucy to

Alone with his thoughts, Jimmy Olsen ponders his reasons for telling Lucy Lane that Superman is secretly famed science-fiction writer Rock Stirling, 1961

share this newly acquired secret knowledge with her sister Lois. Privately, Jimmy reasons that

> If Lois can't keep the secret, it'll prove **Superman** was right in not marrying Lois and entrusting the secret of his other-identity to her!
>
> However, if Lois **can** keep the secret, then he'll have one less objection to marrying her, and I'll have done them both a big favor! In any event, **Superman**'s secret identity won't be endangered even if Lois **does** spill the beans, because...ha, ha, Rock Stirling **isn't** Superman's secret-identity, of course! Actually, I'm as much in the dark about the **Man of Steel**'s other identity as Lois is...!

Jimmy's irresponsible meddling, however, has predictably disastrous consequences. Believing that she has at long last been entrusted with the secret of Superman's identity, Lois Lane strives mightily to keep the secret, but the weight of the forbidden knowledge is more than she can bear. She mumbles the secret aloud in her sleep, reveals it to her dentist while under the influence of an anesthetic, and finally, in the ultimate blooper, recites it aloud into a wishing well, only to discover, to her everlasting heartbreak, that the wishing well is part of a television stunt and that she has just broadcast Superman's secret over live national TV.

Before long, members of the ANTI-SUPERMAN GANG have invaded Rock Stirling's apartment, determined to annihilate their longtime enemy with kryptonite. Although Stirling himself is unaffected by the substance, Superman, realizing that Stirling is bound to become the target of gangland reprisals now that the world believes he is Superman, arrives on the scene moments later and immediately slumps to the floor under the baleful influence of the kryptonite radiations. However, largely through the resourcefulness of science-fiction writer Stirling, who has the presence of mind to drop his typewriter on top of the kryptonite, thereby shielding Superman from its agonizing radiations, Superman is able to recover his strength and apprehend his would-be assassins. And, soon afterward, Superman appears with Rock Stirling on live nationwide television to inform the public that Superman is not really Rock Stirling after all and to explain away Jimmy Olsen's meddlesome behavior by claiming that it was all part of an elaborate ruse to enable Superman to capture the Anti-Superman Gang (S No. 145/1: "The Secret Identity of Superman!").

In September 1961, while visiting the Congolese jungle to cover a native uprising for the *Daily Planet*, Jimmy Olsen is reduced to "Tom Thumb size" and imprisoned inside a large glass bottle—along with Superman, Lois Lane, and Perry White—by the space villain BRAINIAC (Act No. 280: "Brainiac's Super-Revenge!").

In January 1962 Jimmy Olsen is chosen, much against his will, to serve as the referee in Lois Lane's upcoming duel with LANA LANG (S No. 150/2: "The Duel Over Superman!").

In March 1962, while spending the night with Superman at his Fortress of Solitude, Jimmy Olsen is forced to awaken Superman in the middle of the night when, in the grip of a terrifying nightmare induced by exposure to red kryptonite, the Man of Steel begins thrashing about with such violence that his actions threaten literally to demolish the Fortress. The following day, while waiting to be introduced as the scheduled guest speaker at a monthly meeting of the Jimmy Olsen Fan Club, Superman falls asleep on the speakers' platform and falls victim to another red-kryptonite-induced nightmare, forcing Jimmy—this time aided by members of his fan club—to shake the Man of Steel awake once again (Act No. 286: "The Jury of Super-Enemies!"). Not long afterward, Jimmy comes upon Superman in the throes of a third red-

kryptonite-induced nightmare, and, unable to awaken the Man of Steel himself, summons KRYPTO THE SUPERDOG, who awakens his master "by super licking his face!" (Act No. 287, Apr '62: "Perry White's Manhunt for Superman!").

© NPP 1978

In May 1962, after Lois Lane has encountered eight escapees from the PHANTOM ZONE in the town of DRYWOOD GULCH, Jimmy Olsen summons Superman to the scene with his ultrasonic signal-watch (S No. 153/3: "The Town of Supermen!").

In October 1962, when Superman suffers a serious physical collapse and is widely believed to be dying of exposure to VIRUS X, an incurable Kryptonian malady, Jimmy Olsen remains almost constantly by Superman's side, determined to stay close by his super-friend until the last. Only later, however, is it discovered that Superman is not suffering from exposure to Virus X at all, but rather from the effects of a kryptonite nugget that has become accidentally lodged inside Jimmy's camera. Indeed, once this fragment of kryptonite has been removed from Superman's presence, Superman is, almost immediately, restored to full health (S No. 156: "The Last Days of Superman!" pts. I-III—"Superman's Death Sentence!"; "The Super-Comrades of All Time!"; "Superman's Last Day of Life!").

In November 1962, when Superman Day is celebrated in Metropolis, Jimmy Olsen is among those on hand to attend the festivities (S No. 157/3: "Superman's Day of Doom!").

In December 1962, during a period when Superman is suffering occasional bouts of mental instability inflicted upon him by members of the SUPERMAN REVENGE SQUAD, the Man of Steel throws a temper tantrum at the *Daily Planet*, hurling deranged insults at Jimmy Olsen, Lois Lane, and Perry White and snatching away Jimmy's ultrasonic signal-watch. Superman presumably returns the signal-watch, however, once he has returned to normal and the villains have been defeated (Act No. 295: "Superman Goes Wild!").

As Perry White looks on, Jimmy Olsen summons Superman with his ultrasonic signal-watch, 1962

In January 1963 Jimmy Olsen joins forces with Superman to safeguard the city of Kandor against the misguided schemes of "fanatic scientist" THAN OL. In the course of the adventure, during a period when it is unsafe for Superman to move about the city due to the lies that Than Ol has spread about him among the Kandorian people, Superman and his young pal decide to emulate their friends Batman and Robin by adopting a pair of secret identities. Inspired by the names and plumage of a pair of Kandorian birds—a "nightwing" and a "flamebird"—owned by their friend NOR-KAN, Superman and Jimmy adopt the alternate identities of Nightwing and Flamebird and fashion a pair of colorful costumes evocative of the plumage of the two Kandorian birds.

For his role as Nightwing, Superman wears a black eye-mask and a Prussian-blue costume consisting of Prussian-blue tights, trunks, cape, wrist-length gloves, and ankle-length boots. Emblazoned on his chest is a highly stylized black bird emblem inscribed inside a white circle. Around his waist is a yellow utility belt equipped with "personal jet-motors" which endow him with the power of self-sustained flight.

For his role as Flamebird, Jimmy Olsen wears a black eye-mask and a bright red costume consisting of red tights, trunks, and a deeply scalloped red cape, complemented by yellow boots and yellow elbow-length gloves. Emblazoned on his chest is a highly stylized yellow sunburst, and around his waist is a yellow utility belt, almost identical to Nightwing's, equipped with personal jet-motors for self-sustained flight.

Equipment contained in the utility belts includes "smoke cylinders" to enable Nightwing and Flamebird to stymie their pursuers by enveloping them in clouds of thick black smoke; "cutting-torches" for cutting through walls and other obstacles; and special "lead cloth caps" designed to enable the duo to "shield" their thoughts from—and thereby elude, if necessary—the fearsome "telepathic hounds" of Kandor, "strange beasts," yellow in color, with tails like wolves and snouts like wild boars, "that can locate people at any distance by reading their minds to learn where they are!" Because of their unique abilities, the creatures are employed by the Kandorian authorities as telepathic bloodhounds.

Beneath his lavish home in the Kandorian suburbs, Nor-Kan has constructed a "secret underground lab"—with a camouflaged entrance built into a grassy hillside—to prevent intruders from tampering with his delicate scientific instruments. With Nor-Kan's blessing, Nightwing and Flamebird christen this laboratory the "night-cave"—or "nightcave"—and transform it into their secret subterranean headquarters, while simultaneously converting Nor-Kan's automobile into a fleet, specially equipped "nightmobile."

By the time this Kandorian adventure draws to a close, Nightwing and Flamebird—the so-called Dynamic Duo of Kandor—have revealed their true identities to the Kandorian people and the Kandorians have erected a colorful statue of the two heroes in the heart of the city (S No. 158: "Superman in Kandor" pts. I-III—"Invasion of the Mystery Super-Men!"; "The Dynamic Duo of Kandor!"; "The City of Super-People!").

In March 1963 Jimmy Olsen accompanies Clark Kent and Lois Lane on a long journey by balloon to MISTRI-LOR, an exotic "lost civilization" ruled by the lovely QUEEN LURA (Act No. 298: "Clark Kent, Coward!").

In August 1963, after exposure to red kryptonite has temporarily transformed Superman into a fearsome Kryptonian "drang" (*see* KRYPTON), Jimmy Olsen, unaware that the hideous monster is actually

*Fleeing through the weird jungle
on the outskirts of Kandor...*

*...Jimmy Olsen and Superman strive desperately to elude
Kandor's fearsome "telepathic hounds," 1963*

Superman, aids the U.S. Armed Forces in its efforts to destroy the creature, even to the point of recommending that—since the drang is Kryptonian and therefore vulnerable to kryptonite—an attempt be made to annihilate it with kryptonite bullets. Fortunately for the Man of Steel, however, he finally succeeds in alerting his attackers to his true identity. And ultimately, the effects of the red kryptonite fade and vanish, restoring Superman to his normal form (Act No. 303: "The Monster from Krypton!"). During this same period, when the rotor of the *Daily Planet*'s Flying Newsroom helicopter becomes snarled in a parade banner, threatening to send Jimmy Olsen and Lois Lane plummeting to their doom, WONDER-MAN leaps to their rescue, catching the falling helicopter and lowering it gently to the ground. Not long afterward, following Wonder-Man's death, Jimmy and Lois are among the throng of mourners who gather to pay their last respects at the large stone monument that has been erected in Metropolis in Wonder-Man's honor (S No. 163/1, Aug '63: "Wonder-Man, the New Hero of Metropolis!").

In October 1963 Jimmy Olsen joins forces with Superman to outwit the Kryptonian criminal RAS-KROM and reimprison him in the Phantom Zone (S No. 164/2: "The Fugitive from the Phantom Zone!").

When Metropolis television station WMET-TV inaugurates its new "Our American Heroes" series with a program honoring Superman, "our greatest American hero," Jimmy Olsen appears on the show along with Superman's other friends and admirers to help pay tribute to the Man of Steel (Act No. 309, Feb '64: "The Superman Super-Spectacular!").

In March 1964 Jimmy Olsen is hypnotized by the villain JAX-UR, who, briefly, makes Jimmy his dupe in a convoluted scheme designed to trick Superman into believing that exposure to a hitherto unknown type of kryptonite—so-called "jewel kryptonite"—has transformed the Man of Steel into "a threat against the whole world" by "causing [him] to detonate any explosive material" he approaches (Act No. 310: "Secret of Kryptonite Six!").

After having been hypnotized by the villain Jax-Ur, Jimmy Olsen is awakened from his trance by the blinding glare of a flashgun, 1964

In May 1964 Jimmy Olsen and Robin help Superman and Batman apprehend a pair of criminals who have kidnapped a prominent physicist and stolen his newly invented "invisibility de-visors" so that they can use the devices to render themselves invisible while they commit crimes (WF No. 141: "The Olsen-Robin Team versus 'The Superman-Batman Team!'").

By June 1964 Jimmy Olsen and four of Superman's other good friends—Batman, Lois Lane, Lori Lemaris, and Perry White—have been taken captive by the SUPERMAN REVENGE SQUAD and imprisoned in a state of suspended animation in a cave beneath Metropolis as part of the villains' elaborate scheme to torment and demoralize Superman (Act No. 313: "The End of Clark Kent's Secret Identity!").

In August 1964, after the ruthless "interplanetary gamblers" ROKK AND SORBAN have threatened to destroy the Earth unless Superman agrees to commit a wanton murder, Jimmy Olsen volunteers to let Superman kill him and thereby avert the threat to Earth. Superman rejects Jimmy's offer out of hand, however, and ultimately resolves the agonizing dilemma posed by the aliens by pretending to murder his alter ego, Clark Kent (S No. 171/1: "Superman's Sacrifice!"). Soon afterward, after Superman has been stranded without his super-powers on a distant, hostile planet, Jimmy Olsen, Lois Lane, and the "great astronomer" DR. LURING come to his rescue in an "experimental missile" and carry the Man of Steel safely back to Earth (S No. 171/3, Aug '64: "The Nightmare Ordeal of Superman").

During this same period, in the course of an adventure in the bottle city of Kandor, Superman and Jimmy Olsen once again adopt the alternate identities of Nightwing and Flamebird so that, aided by Batman and Robin—as well as by Nighthound, a telepathic hound they have adopted as their companion—they can combat the city's "metalloid" menace (WF No. 143, Aug '64: "The Feud Between Batman and Superman!" pts. I-II—no title; "The Manhunters from Earth!"). (See THAN-AR.)

In September 1964 Jimmy Olsen helps Batman, Robin, and Superman defeat the diabolical partnership of CLAYFACE and Brainiac (WF No. 144: "The 1,001 Tricks of Clayface and Brainiac!" pts. I-II—no title; "The Helpless Partners!").

In October 1964, after Superman has been deprived of his super-powers by the baleful radiations of a mysterious green comet—and AR-VAL, Superman's hand-picked successor, has begun performing the

Man of Steel's super-heroic duties in Superman's stead—it is Jimmy Olsen who conceives the idea of contacting the Legion of Super-Heroes in the thirtieth century A.D. and asking them to use the "time-force wave carrier" in their thirtieth-century Clubhouse to endow Superman temporarily with their various powers so that he can use these powers in an attempt to apprehend Lex Luthor and Brainiac. In addition, Jimmy lets Superman drink some of his "elastic serum," thereby temporarily endowing him with the elastic powers Jimmy employs in his role as Elastic Lad. Later, after Luthor and Brainiac have taken Superman captive, it is Jimmy who pressures the arrogant, uncooperative Ar-Val into trailing Lois Lane and Lana Lang to the villains' hideout (S No. 172: pts. I-III—"The New Superman!"; "Clark Kent—Former Superman!"; "The Struggle of the Two Supermen!"). (See LUTHOR, LEX.)

© NPP 1978

© NPP 1978

In November 1964, when a remote-controlled spacecraft alights on the roof of the Daily Planet Building, summoning Superman to perform an urgent mission on Planet 2H-Galaxy 489, Jimmy Olsen climbs aboard the craft himself, determined to prove, despite Superman's frequent admonitions to avoid taking unnecessary risks, that he is capable of carrying out important missions entirely on his own. Arriving on the distant planet, however, Jimmy is taken captive by Lex Luthor and Brainiac, who lock him in a cell and, while Jimmy quakes with fear, begin fiendishly debating just what sort of ghastly fate they should inflict on their prisoner and which of them should be accorded the grisly pleasure of meting it out. Only as the debate over which villain should have the honor of annihilating Jimmy nears its climax, does Jimmy begin to suspect the truth—that "Luthor" and "Brainiac" are actually Superman and Batman in disguise, and that their efforts to terrify him have all been part of an elaborate hoax designed to impress upon him the folly of taking impulsive risks.

Escaping from his cell, Jimmy quickly verifies his suspicions—and pays Superman back for his frightening joke—by exposing the bogus "Luthor" to a chunk of kryptonite until he yowls with pain and confesses his true identity. After the two heroes have removed their villainous disguises and the three friends have enjoyed a hearty laugh over the hoax Superman and Batman played on Jimmy, Superman explains that he saw Jimmy set out on the space mission meant for him and, after flying to Planet 2H-Galaxy 489 under his own power and coping with the emergency for which its inhabitants had summoned him, had concocted the hoax and enlisted Batman's aid in teaching Jimmy a lesson. For his part, Jimmy assures his two friends that he has learned his lesson and promises to avoid taking needless risks in the future. "For a while, anyway!" muses Jimmy silently (S No. 173/3: "The Triumph of Luthor and Brainiac!").

In February 1965 the minds of Jimmy Olsen and Robin are "taken over and possessed" by some weirdly glowing jewels from a far-distant planet which Superman has presented to Jimmy as a gift, unaware that the strange gems are really alien "living things with super-telepathic powers." Under the baleful influence of the extraterrestrial gems, Jimmy and Robin turn against Superman and Batman, but the famed crime-fighters soon succeed in freeing their young pals from the jewels' telepathic clutches, thus enabling Superman to return the gems safely to the planet that spawned them (WF No. 147: "The Doomed Boy Heroes!" pts. I-II—"The New Terrific Team!"; "The Doom of Jimmy Olsen and Robin!").

© NPP 1978

In May 1965, when Jimmy Olsen spends a night at the Fortress of Solitude with Superman and KRYPTO THE SUPERDOG, Krypto has a terrifying nightmare in which Superman's super-powers become permanently transferred into Jimmy's body (S No. 177/3: "When Jimmy Olsen Stole Krypto from Superman").

In September 1965, when Superman Day is celebrated in Metropolis, Jimmy Olsen is among those on hand to attend the festivities. Among the featured attractions in the colorful Superman Day parade are gigantic balloons in the image of Superman's closest friends—Jimmy Olsen, Lois Lane, and Perry White (Act No. 328: "Superman's Hands of Doom!"). During this same period, Jimmy Olsen lends some helpful assistance to Batman, Robin, and Superman in their efforts to determine the true identities of Force Boy and Speed Kid (WF No. 152, Sep '65: "The Colossal Kids!" pts. I-II—no title; "The Magic of Bat-Mite and Mr. Mxyzptlk!"). (See MXYZPTLK [MR.].)

OMNI-MENACE. An alias employed by SUPERMAN in January 1965 when, after donning an "almost indestructible costume, which can be electrified," he poses as a superhuman villain from the distant past as part of his plan to defeat a trio of villains—perfect look-alikes for the ancient heroes Samson, Atlas, and HERCULES—from an unidentified extradimensional "parallel world" (Act No. 320: "The Three Super-Enemies!").

ORGANIZER, THE. A "mysterious crime mogul" whose capture by SUPERMAN in August 1957 comes as the culmination of an elaborate scheme, devised by Superman with the aid of PERRY WHITE, in which Superman creates and assumes three fictitious identities—that of a part-time grocery clerk named Buster, a reckless pilot named Winters, and an escaped convict named Sam Baron, alias Lathrop—as part of a ploy to entice the Organizer into summoning him to his hideout (S No. 115/3: "The Three Substitute Supermen!").

OWENS, SAMUEL C. The owner of a chain of bakeries who, enraged at the two fellow businessmen who bankrolled the start of his bakery business but who now retain the lion's share of his stock, concocts an elaborate scheme of stock manipulation and murder by which he hopes to dispose of his associates while seizing absolute control of both their businesses and his own. Apprehended by SUPERMAN in January-February 1947, Owens is condemned to die in the electric chair (S No. 44/2: "The Man Who Didn't Die on Time!").

OXNALIA. A powerful, militaristic nation ruled by the evil dictator Razkal, who bears a strong resemblance to ADOLF HITLER. When Oxnalia invades the peace-loving democratic country of Numark in March-April 1942, SUPERMAN single-handedly demolishes the Oxnalian war machine and forces its soldiers to sue for peace. Razkal attempts to flee by motorcycle, only to be shot and killed by one of his own countrymen (S No. 15/3).

P

PACIFO. An ancient, sunken continent—located somewhere in the Pacific Ocean—whose sole surviving "remnant" is "a glass-enclosed city of ancient, weird design" which can be raised to the surface and then submerged like a submarine and which serves for a time as LEX LUTHOR's base of operations.

"You'll admit it was a miraculous achievement!" boasts Luthor. "Working underwater, I raised a glassolite-dome over the city, drained out the water, then raised the city to the surface of the ocean."

Pacifo is destroyed by SUPERMAN in Spring 1940 (S No. 4/2).

PANAMA CANAL, THE. A high-level artificial interoceanic waterway of the lake and lock type which crosses the Isthmus of Panama from northwest to southeast, connecting the Atlantic and Pacific Oceans. Plots to blow up the Panama Canal are thwarted by SUPERMAN in May-June 1941 (see WOLFF, KARL) (S No. 10/4) and again in March-April 1942 (see NAPKAN) (S No. 15/2).

PARALEA (Queen). The lovely blond ruler of ATLANTIS who, surrounded by a plethora of handsome, well-built men in her glass-domed subsea kingdom, falls instantly in love with mild-mannered Clark Kent when he arrives there via bathysphere—accompanied by LOIS LANE and an oceanographer named Professor Hubble—in November-December 1950. Narrowly avoiding marriage to the love-struck queen in his Clark Kent identity, SUPERMAN remains in Atlantis long enough to thwart an attempt by the power-hungry Hajar, unscrupulous "chief adviser to the throne," to overthrow the queen in a bloody coup and set up a tyranny in her undersea realm (S No. 67/2: "The City Under the Sea!").

PARDEE, HIRAM. A naïve albeit well-meaning hayseed who arrives in METROPOLIS in March-April 1944 to assume control of the inheritance left to him by his uncle, a millionaire pigeon-fancier, unaware that his uncle's former secretary, Percival Lister, and underworld figure Arch Angler have joined forces to transform the deceased uncle's pigeon loft into an elaborate underworld operation in which trained homing pigeons are rented to gangs of criminals who in turn use the birds to transport lightweight loot from the scenes of robberies so that they themselves will not be caught carrying incriminating evidence if stopped and questioned by police. Lister and Angler—and an assortment of their underworld cronies—are ultimately apprehended through the combined efforts of SUPERMAN and Hiram Pardee (S No. 27/3: "Robbers' Roost!").

PARESCA, PIETRO. "The most notorious smuggler in all Europe," a "mysterious Mediterranean gold smuggler" who, operating from an unspecified Mediterranean port, smuggles gold into foreign countries by shaping it into automobile fenders, painting them over so they cannot be recognized, and attaching them to the antique car that he always carries with him aboard his sloop. Paresca and his cohorts are apprehended by SUPERMAN in April 1955 with some last-minute assistance from the Bombay, India, police (Act No. 203: "The International Daily Planet!").

PARKER (Police Chief). The police chief of SMALLVILLE while SUPERMAN was a boy there. Now retired, Police Chief Parker devotes much of his time to his favorite hobby, whittling dramatic dioramas of Superman's teen-age adventures out of blocks of wood. When METROPOLIS television station WMET-TV inaugurates its new "Our American Heroes" series with a program honoring Superman, "our greatest American hero," Police Chief Parker appears on the show along with Superman's other friends and admirers—and proudly displays his hand-carved dioramas—to help pay tribute to the Man of Steel (Act No. 309, Feb '64: "The Superman Super-Spectacular!"). On assignment for the DAILY PLANET in August 1964, CLARK KENT and LOIS LANE interview Police Chief Parker in order to obtain some little-known facts about Superman's boyhood (S No. 171/2: "The Curse of Magic!").

PARRISH, ARTHUR. A lonely youngster—the son of "famous jewel expert" Amos Parrish—who becomes convinced that his hero SUPERMAN is nothing but a common thief when a local farmhand impersonates the Man of Steel in order to steal a fortune in diamonds from the Parrish family safe. Superman apprehends the thieving farmhand and restores young Arthur's faith in him in December 1947 (Act No. 115: "The Wish That Came True!").

PARRONE, JOHN. A vicious racketeer, posing as an investment counselor, who is in reality the leader of a gang of "drug-crazed bandits" whose slavish dependence on hard drugs enables Parrone to keep them securely under his thumb. Parrone is in league with William Brokenshire, "a corrupt practitioner of law" who always manages to invoke legal technicalities to prevent Parrone from being convicted of his crimes, but SUPERMAN apprehends both men on a murder charge in January-February 1941 (S No. 8/4).

PARTHENON, THE. The chief temple of Athena on the Acropolis at Athens. Built during the fifth century B.C., it remains one of the world's great landmarks. In July-August 1953 "THE BRAIN" demolishes the Parthenon and two other world-famous monuments as part of an elaborate scheme to steal $50,000,000 in precious gems lent to METROPO-LIS by the Maharajah of Ipostan, but SUPERMAN restores the monuments and ultimately takes "The Brain" into custody (S No. 83/1: "Destination X!").

PAULSON, BIG JIM. The "chief of [the] Metropolis underworld," a gangland czar whose capture by SUPERMAN in March-April 1953 comes as the culmination of an elaborate ruse, devised by Superman and aided by some helpful coincidences, in which CLARK KENT impersonates his underworld look-alike, DASH-ER DRAPE, "the deadliest triggerman in all gangdom," while Drape is sequestered in a small-town jail, serving a ten-day term on a traffic charge (WF No. 63: "Clark Kent, Gangster").

PAXTON, PAUL. A METROPOLIS television actor—as well as a onetime reporter, photographer, and private investigator—who perpetrates an elaborate ruse in February 1956 designed to persuade the DAILY PLANET staff that he is secretly SUPERMAN so that he can trick PERRY WHITE into handing over a folder of evidence against gangster Spades Riker which is being held for Riker's trial in White's *Daily Planet* safe. Superman thwarts the scheme and apprehends Paxton, who has been paid by Riker to obtain and destroy the incriminating evidence. Reminded that Paxton has, however, committed no crime for which he can properly be arrested, Superman promptly tricks Paxton into "disturbing the quiet on a hospital street" and hauls him off to jail with the promise that he will receive the maximum possible sentence (Act No. 213: "Paul Paxton Alias Superman!").

PEEKER, PETER. The gossip columnist for the Morning Pictorial, and the secret leader of the Black Gang, "a band of ruthless thieves," clad in dark suits and black hoods, who "specialize in brutal robberies of night club patrons." Peeker and the Black Gang are apprehended by SUPERMAN in November-December 1940 (S No. 7/4).

PEMBERTON, STUART. The leader of Volunteers for Peace, a deceptively named organization of foreign spies and fifth columnists who have been treacherously misleading Americans with glib "anti-rearmament talk" as part of a vicious master plan to pave the way for a sneak attack on the United States by the hostile "Nation X." At a mass rally in METROPOLIS, Pemberton preaches his deceptive message of "peace":

Friends--once again I urge you to shout your disapproval of rearmament in this country! We're not actually menaced by war--that's just the hogwash the grafters are trying to make the gullible taxpayers swallow!

Moving swiftly in May 1941, however, SUPERMAN thwarts a series of attempts by Pemberton and his cohorts to soften up Metropolis for the impending sneak attack "by sabotaging important strategic centers," demolishes the "great sky armada" of Nation X as it attempts to unleash its "cargo of deadly bombs upon the helpless city," and ultimately apprehends the fleeing Pemberton, who has just finished broadcasting a radio demand for America's surrender (Act No. 36).

PENDER (Professor). A "renegade scientist" who has used his "warped scientific genius" to construct a powerful "super-charging machine" which, when properly activated, "will charge any human being with such electric energy that he'll have *super-powers* for 24 hours."

"With it," gloats Pender to his henchmen, "I'll make myself invulnerable and we'll loot all of Metropolis!"

The efforts of BATMAN, ROBIN, and SUPERMAN to apprehend Pender and destroy his machine before he can successfully endow himself with super-powers—superhuman strength, X-ray vision, the power of flight, and invulnerability—are somewhat hampered by the fact that, as the result of a series of complex coincidences, Batman has stepped beneath Pender's ray-machine and become endowed with super-powers which will endure for twenty-four hours, while Superman has been deprived of his super-powers altogether as the result of Pender's having sprayed his costume with minute particles of KRYPTONITE dust.

Eventually, Superman realizes that he can regain his powers through the simple expedient of donning a spare costume which has not been impregnated with kryptonite dust and, soon afterward, Superman, Robin, and the super-powered Batman invade Professor Pender's hideout and apprehend Pender and his henchmen before Pender can use the machine's awesome powers on himself. As the twenty-four-hour deadline arrives, Batman's super-powers fade and vanish. "I'm not sorry," sighs Batman with relief, "--being a super-*Batman* is too much for me!" (WF No. 77, Jul/Aug '55: "The Super Bat-Man!").

PENDLETON, ISAAH. An unscrupulous citizen of METROPOLIS who, convinced that it will never again be possible to take a photograph of SUPERMAN due to Superman's recent exposure to a meteor that "emits a ray which fogs film," spends a fortune cornering the market on Superman photos with the intention of destroying almost all of them and then selling the few remaining ones to "wealthy art patrons" at fabulous prices. To his everlasting sorrow, however, Pendleton soon learns that the effects of the strange meteor-emissions will affect Superman only temporarily and that further photographs of him will be possible within a few days' time (Act No. 185, Oct '53: "Superman's Million Dollar Photos!").

PERLO, DOLORES. A lovely brown-haired actress in the "tiny South American republic" of El Salmado who, with the aid of some makeup and a black wig, is such a perfect look-alike for LOIS LANE that even SUPERMAN can distinguish between them only by noting that Dolores lacks the "special lipstick" favored by Lois Lane. Dolores Perlo impersonates Lois Lane as part of an unsuccessful scheme by GENERAL PEDRO VALDEZ to lure Superman into a KRYPTONITE deathtrap (Act No. 306, Nov '63: "The Great Superman Impersonation!").

PHANTOM ZONE, THE. A weird "twilight dimension"—first discovered by SUPERMAN's father, JOR-EL—to which Kryptonian criminals were banished to serve out their sentences as disembodied wraiths (Act No. 284, Jan '62: "The Babe of Steel!" and many others). Inside the Phantom Zone, its exiled inhabitants exist in a "phantom state" (S No. 157/1, Nov '62: "The Super-Revenge of the Phantom Zone Prisoner!"), unaging, requiring no food, air, or water (Act No. 284, Jan '62: "The Babe of Steel!"; and others), communicating with one another telepathically (S No. 164/2, Oct '63: "The Fugitive from the Phantom Zone!"; and others), able to observe everything that takes place in the physical universe—either on Earth (Act No. 284, Jan '62: "The Babe of Steel!"; and others), or in outer space (S No. 157/1, Nov '62: "The Super-Revenge of the Phantom Zone Prisoner!"; and others)—even though they cannot be seen or heard themselves (Act No. 284, Jan '62: "The Babe of Steel!"; and others). By observing Superman from inside the Phantom Zone, all its inhabitants have learned that he is secretly Clark Kent (S No. 157/1, Nov '62: "The Super-Revenge of the Phantom Zone Prisoner!").

Steel"; "The Lost Super-Powers"; "Superman's Return to Krypton").

The practice of exiling criminals into outer space was terminated after Jor-El discovered the Phantom Zone, to which convicted felons could be banished by means of an ingenious "Phantom Zone projector" (Act No. 284, Jan '62: "The Babe of Steel!"; and many others), or "Phantom Zone ray projector" (Act No. 311, Apr '64: "Superman, King of Earth!"), of Jor-El's own invention. Exile into this twilight world proved to be a blessing in disguise for the Phantom Zone outlaws, however, for it enabled them to survive when the planet KRYPTON exploded. To this day these villains hover invisibly in their twilight dimension, waiting their opportunity to escape from the Zone and "take over the Earth" (Act No. 310, Mar '64: "Secret of Kryptonite Six!").

Superman and Supergirl view a Kryptonian "radio-visual tape" showing the convicted criminal Quex-Ul being projected into the Phantom Zone

Banished into the Phantom Zone, Kryptonian convicts serve out their sentences as disembodied wraiths

Before Jor-El's discovery of the Phantom Zone, Kryptonians who perpetrated serious crimes were exiled into outer space in a state of suspended animation inside specially constructed space capsules (S No. 65/3, Jul/Aug '50: "Three Supermen from Krypton!"). The criminals imprisoned inside these "prison satellites" were placed in suspended animation by means of a special sleep gas, and chunks of a glowing crystalline mineral—capable of cleansing their brains of criminal tendencies in a hundred years' time—were placed on their foreheads so that ultimately, once their sentence was served, they might take up constructive roles in Kryptonian society (S No. 123, Aug '58: chs. 1-3—"The Girl of

Once projected into the Phantom Zone, "all inhabitants gain the power to converse [with one another] via telepathy" (S No. 158, Jan '63: "Superman in Kandor" pts. I-III—"Invasion of the Mystery Super-Men!"; "The Dynamic Duo of Kandor!"; "The City of Super-People!"; and others). For a time, however, their only means of communicating with the physical world was by beaming telepathic messages to individuals outside the Zone who possessed telepathic powers, such as SATURN GIRL and LORI LEMARIS (S No. 156, Oct '62: "The Last Days of Superman!" pts. I-III—"Superman's Death Sentence!"; "The Super-Comrades of All Time!"; "Superman's Last Day of Life!"), although, on at least one occasion, they succeeded in communicating with Superman by concentrating, in unison, on a single telepathic message (S No. 157/1, Nov '62: "The Super-Revenge of the Phantom Zone Prisoner!"). Similarly,

Superman's only means of contacting the Phantom Zone outlaws was through his telepathic friends (S No. 156, Oct '62: "The Last Days of Superman!" pts. I–III—"Superman's Death Sentence!"; "The Super-Comrades of All Time!"; "Superman's Last Day of Life!").

By November 1962, however, Superman has invented the "zone-ophone," a large television-type picture tube equipped with a microphone and speaker which enables him to peer into the Phantom Zone while communicating orally with the Phantom Zone prisoners. "Wonderful! My zone-ophone works!" thinks Superman after his device has passed its maiden test. "I can communicate with **Phantom Zone** prisoners.... The invention's screen enables me to look into the **Zone!**" (S No. 157/1: "The Super-Revenge of the Phantom Zone Prisoner!"). By February 1964 this device, here referred to as "the Phantom Zone viewer and zone-o-phone," has come to consist of a televisionlike viewing screen equipped with a headset and microphone for verbal communication (S No. 167: "The Team of Luthor and Brainiac!" pts. I–III—"The Deadly Duo!"; "The Downfall of Superman!"; "The Hour of Kandor's Vengeance!"; see also Act No. 310, Mar '64: "Secret of Kryptonite Six!").

Phantom Zone by means of the "Phantom Zone ray gun" he keeps in his FORTRESS OF SOLITUDE. In November 1962 Superman uses the device to free QUEX-UL from the Phantom Zone after verifying—

Superman parachutes into Kandor for a meeting of the Phantom Zone Parole Board, 1964

with the aid of a surviving cache of "radio-visual tapes" from the files of the Kryptonian police—that Quex-Ul has served out the full sentence meted out to him by Kryptonian authorities (S No. 157/1: "The Super-Revenge of the Phantom Zone Prisoner!").

The decision to release an inmate from the

As Supergirl looks on, Superman tests his newly invented "zone-ophone" by using it to communicate with his friend Mon-El inside the Phantom Zone, 1962

By August 1963 Superman has developed a raygunlike Phantom Zone "view-finder," with which he can peer into the Phantom Zone to assure himself that all the Zone's inhabitants are present and accounted for (S No. 163/1: "Wonder-Man, the New Hero of Metropolis!").

Once each year, in KANDOR's majestic Hall of Justice, the Phantom Zone Parole Board meets to consider the pleas of Phantom Zone prisoners seeking parole. A giant "monitor screen equipped with a zone-o-phone" is used by the parole board members to communicate with the prisoners, and those inmates deemed worthy of parole are released from the Phantom Zone to begin new lives as Kandorian citizens (Act No. 310, Mar '64: "Secret of Kryptonite Six!").

Superman is also able to release inmates from the

Phantom Zone inmates deemed worthy of parole are released from the Zone to begin new lives as Kandorian citizens

Phantom Zone is an extremely grave matter, however, for the inmates of the Zone, like all surviving Kryptonians, acquire super-powers identical to Superman's in the environment of Earth and could easily turn these awesome powers toward the pursuit of villainous ambitions. When Superman releases JAX-UR from the Phantom Zone for a twenty-four-hour period in March 1964, he uses a special "release-ray" to make the villain materialize in his Fortress of Solitude, and then clamps an ingenious metal bracelet—called a "zone-shackle"—on the convict's wrist. "Should you refuse to let me return you to the **Phantom Zone** after 24 hours," explains Superman, "it will dissolve your atomic structure and automatically return you there anyway!" In addition, if Jax-Ur attempts to tamper with or remove the zone-shackle, he will find himself automatically banished to "a fiery, barren planet...under a red sun," where, like any Kryptonian, he would instantly be deprived of his super-powers (Act No. 310: "Secret of Kryptonite Six!").

The Phantom Zone outlaws have an abiding hatred of Superman and, almost to a man, they pray for the day when they can escape the Zone and "take over the Earth" (Act No. 310, Mar '64: "Secret of Kryptonite Six!"). According to Superman No. 157/1, "These invisible villains hate **Superman** because he possesses mighty super-powers which they, too, would have if they weren't prisoners in the twilight dimension!" (Nov '62: "The Super-Revenge of the Phantom Zone Prisoner!"), but a more plausible explanation for the enmity they bear Superman lies in the fact that Superman is the most visible surviving representative of the society that exiled them; that, in large measure, he holds the key to keeping them prisoner or setting them free; and that it was the testimony of his father, Jor-El, that was instrumental in dooming many of their number to long terms in the Phantom Zone (S No. 153/3, May '62: "The Town of Supermen!"; and others).

Over the years, a number of occurrences, both natural and man-made, have enabled Phantom Zone outlaws to escape the Zone. By May 1962, for example, a "50-megaton atomic test blast on Earth [has] ripped open a hole in the Phantom Zone," allowing eight criminals to escape before finally closing up again (S No. 153/3: "The Town of Supermen!"). In October 1963, the explosion in outer space of an atomic missile from a Polaris submarine causes a temporary gap in the Phantom Zone through which the villain RAS-KROM escapes to freedom (S No. 164/2: "The Fugitive from the Phantom Zone!"). A hole in the Phantom Zone caused by "the electrical ions of the Aurora Borealis" in January 1962 is closed by Superman, SUPERGIRL, and KRYPTO THE SUPER-DOG before it becomes large enough to allow any of the imprisoned "super-villains" to escape (Act No. 284: "The Babe of Steel!").

Over the years, the inhabitants of the Phantom Zone have included JAX-UR and PROFESSOR VAKOX (Act No. 284, Jan '62: "The Babe of Steel!"; and others); Dr. Xadu, a "villainous scientist" (SA No. 5, Sum '62) sentenced to thirty years in the Phantom Zone for doing "a forbidden experiment in suspended animation" (S No. 150/1, Jan '62: "The One Minute of Doom!"); Ral-En, the son of MAG-EN (S No. 154/2, Jul '62: "Krypton's First Superman!"); QUEX-UL (S No. 157/1, Nov '62: "The Super-Revenge of the Phantom Zone Prisoner!"); RAS-KROM (S No. 164/2, Oct '63: "The Fugitive from the Phantom Zone!"); and the eight unidentified Phantom Zone escapees whom Superman encounters in the town of DRYWOOD GULCH in May 1962 (S No. 153/3: "The Town of Supermen!"). MON-EL, a close friend of Superman, is the only inhabitant of the Phantom Zone who was not sent there for any crime (Act No. 284, Jan '62: "The Babe of Steel!"; and others). A complete "microfilm gallery of Phantom Zone criminals, a gift [to Superman] from law officials in the miniature city of Kandor," is kept for safekeeping in the Fortress of Solitude (S No. 164/2, Oct '63: "The Fugitive from the Phantom Zone!").

Superman and Jimmy Olsen discuss the various types of kryptonite as Professor Vakox and Jax-Ur observe them invisibly from inside the Phantom Zone, 1964

In January 1962 the Phantom Zone prisoners seem on the verge of escaping from the Phantom Zone after "the electrical ions of the Aurora Borealis have opened a small hole in the Phantom Zone which is steadily widening," threatening to release the exiled "super-villains" into the earthly dimension as soon as it becomes "big enough for the Phantom Zone criminals to squeeze through!" Alerted to the threat, however, by their friend Mon-El, Superman, Supergirl, and Krypto the Superdog use the combined power of their X-ray vision to burn up the Aurora Borealis, thereby sealing up the opening through which the villains had hoped to make their escape (Act No. 284: "The Babe of Steel!"). During this same period, the Phantom Zone outlaws, like all other Kryptonian survivors, bow their heads in silence in solemn commemoration of "the anniversary of the destruction of Krypton..." (S No. 150/1, Jan '62: "The One Minute of Doom!").

In May 1962 Superman battles eight escapees from the Phantom Zone in the town of DRYWOOD GULCH (S No. 153/3: "The Town of Supermen!").

In October 1962, after exposure to red KRYPTONITE has temporarily transformed Superman into two separate individuals, a mature, responsible Clark Kent and an unprincipled, irresponsible Superman, the arrogant Superman imprisons Krypto the Superdog, Supergirl, and the entire city of Kandor in the Phantom Zone in order to prevent them from interfering with his plan to keep the personalities of Clark Kent and Superman separate forever. Ultimately, however, Clark Kent frees his friends from the Phantom Zone, and soon afterward he succeeds in bringing about the reuniting of Clark Kent and Superman into a single individual (Act No. 293: "The Feud Between Superman and Clark Kent!"). During this same period, when Superman is believed to be dying of exposure to VIRUS X, an incurable Kryptonian malady, Mon-El beams a telepathic message to Saturn Girl from inside the Phantom Zone informing her that Superman is not suffering from exposure to Virus X at all, but merely from the effects of a kryptonite nugget that has become accidentally lodged in Jimmy Olsen's camera (S No. 156, Oct '62: "The Last Days of Superman!" pts. I-III—"Superman's Death Sentence!"; "The Super-Comrades of All Time!"; "Superman's Last Day of Life!").

At an annual meeting of the Phantom Zone Parole Board, members angrily deny a parole request by the arch-villain Jax-Ur, 1964

In November 1962 Superman releases QUEX-UL from the Phantom Zone (S No. 157/1: "The Super-Revenge of the Phantom Zone Prisoner!").

In January 1963, in order to hide from the cohorts of the "fanatic scientist" THAN OL, Superman and JIMMY OLSEN project themselves into the Phantom Zone, then materialize in the Fortress of Solitude one hour later, when the coast is clear. "On the chance that some day I'd have to hide out in the Phantom Zone," explains Superman, "I recently equipped this [Phantom Zone] projector with a timing device that would automatically release anyone it had sent into the Zone after a period of one hour!" (S No. 158: "Superman in Kandor" pts. I-III—"Invasion of the Mystery Super-Men!"; "The Dynamic Duo of Kandor!"; "The City of Super-People!").

In October 1963 Superman battles the Phantom Zone escapee RAS-KROM (S No. 164/2: "The Fugitive from the Phantom Zone!").

In March 1964 Superman thwarts an elaborate scheme by the Phantom Zone outlaw JAX-UR to blackmail him into setting free all the Phantom Zone convicts (Act No. 310: "Secret of Kryptonite Six!").

PICKINS, "EASY." A master safecracker and picklock, released from prison on parole and determined to go straight, who, under the stage name the Great Godini, begins life anew as a vaudeville escape artist only to find himself the chief suspect in a series of baffling crimes, all bearing the imprint of a master picklock but staged, in fact, by his former underworld cohorts, the Three-Finger Jack Schack gang, for the dual purpose of accumulating loot and of sullying Pickins's reputation so that he will be forced to rejoin them in a life of crime. SUPERMAN apprehends the Schack gang in Spring 1945 and exonerates "Easy" Pickins of the charges against him (WF No. 17: "The Great Godini!").

PIERSON, CLARA (Mrs.). The lovely red-haired widow of Charles Pierson, "an inventor working on an important wartime invention" who was tortured to death by foreign agents in an unsuccessful effort to obtain the plans for his invention. In November-December 1941 Mrs. Pierson's infant son Bob becomes the target of a series of kidnap attempts on the part of foreign spies determined to pressure Mrs. Pierson into giving up the plans for her deceased husband's invention, but the spies are apprehended by SUPERMAN before they can successfully complete their mission (S No. 13/3).

PLUTO. The farthest planet from the sun. In July 1958 SUPERMAN journeys to Pluto to obtain some giant snowflakes—frozen so solidly that they will not melt on Earth—for inclusion among the collection of "space trophies" which he is gathering for the Metropolis Museum so that they may be buried in the ground in a time capsule as a gift for the people of the fiftieth century A.D. (S No. 122/1: "The Secret of the Space Souvenirs").

POLESKI, JOE. A rugged METROPOLIS ironworker, a perfect lookalike for CLARK KENT, who becomes afflicted with temporary amnesia after receiving a blow on the head and who, as the result of a series of complex coincidences, becomes convinced that he is both Clark Kent and SUPERMAN until a second blow on the head restores both his memory and his knowledge of his true identity in November-December 1950 (S No. 67/3: "Clark Kent's Twin!").

POTTER (Professor). A brilliant, albeit somewhat eccentric, inventor and friend of SUPERMAN who is forever creating bizarre devices which, while admittedly ingenious, often fail to perform any truly useful function, an example being his machine, invented in April 1965, whose only claim to practicality is that it "can squeeze 2,000 gallons of onion juice in an hour" (S No. 176/3: "Superman's Day of Truth!"). Professor Potter is LANA LANG's uncle (Act No. 313, Jun '64: "The End of Clark Kent's Secret Identity!").

In October 1961, after an overzealous agent for the Internal Revenue Service has declared Superman delinquent in his income taxes in the amount of $1,000,000,000, Superman uses "a special growth serum" developed by Professor Potter to stimulate the world's biggest oyster into producing the world's largest pearl in an effort to accumulate part of the money he needs (S No. 148/3: "Superman Owes a Billion Dollars!"). (See BRAND, RUPERT.)

In April 1963, after exposure to red KRYPTONITE has temporarily robbed Superman of his invulnerability and super-powers, Professor Potter feeds the relevant data into his new "electronic computer" and correctly informs the Man of Steel that the antidote for the variety of red kryptonite that has affected him on this particular occasion consists of large doses of ascorbic, citric, and acetic acid (S No. 160/1: pts. I-II—"The Mortal Superman!"; "The Cage of Doom!").

When METROPOLIS television station WMET-TV inaugurates its new "Our American Heroes" series with a program honoring Superman, "our greatest American hero," LOIS LANE and Lana Lang attempt to penetrate the secret of Superman's dual identity with the aid of an electronic device they have borrowed from Professor Potter (Act No. 309, Feb '64: "The Superman Super-Spectacular!"). (See LANG, LANA.)

In May 1964 Professor Potter helps JIMMY OLSEN and ROBIN carry out an elaborate ruse designed to trick Superman and BATMAN into believing that their two young friends are dead (WF No. 141: "The Olsen-Robin Team versus "The Superman-Batman Team!'").

In August 1964, after the ruthless "interplanetary gamblers" ROKK AND SORBAN have threatened to destroy the Earth unless Superman agrees to commit a wanton murder, Lana Lang sneaks into Professor Potter's laboratory and attempts to commit suicide there—by means of one of Professor Potter's many failed inventions, an "experimental machine for suspended animation" which, instead of performing its intended function, "merely turns people into lifeless crystal"—so that Superman can claim he killed her and thereby avert the threat to Earth. Superman rescues Lana in the nick of time, however, and ultimately resolves the agonizing dilemma posed by the aliens by pretending to murder his alter ego, Clark Kent (S No. 171/1: "Superman's Sacrifice!").

In April 1965, when Superman commemorates the Day of Truth, a Kryptonian holiday (see KRYPTON), by speaking "nothing but the truth" to the people he encounters, Professor Potter is one of several people who are shocked by the Man of Steel's uncharacteristic bluntness. "As usual," remarks Superman after having viewed the professor's latest useless device, "your invention is a miserable flop!" (S No. 176/3: "Superman's Day of Truth!").

POTTS, EPHRAIM (Dr.). A dedicated scientist and "anthropology award-winner" affiliated with the Metropolis Science Foundation—LOIS LANE refers to him as "that queer, fussy little scientist"—who undertakes a thorough scientific study of SUPERMAN in July-August 1950 in an ambitious if ultimately unsuccessful effort to determine the source of his mighty super-powers. During this period, an underworld intellectual known as "The Professor" poses as a world-renowned scientist interested in collaborating in the testing as part of a scheme to keep Superman effectively preoccupied while his gangland cohorts commit a series of crimes, but Superman apprehends "The Professor" and his accomplices during an attempted robbery at METROPOLIS's Third National Bank (S No. 65/1: "The Testing of Superman!").

POTTS, LEMUEL P. A specialist in American Indian lore at the Mosely Museum who, having learned from an ancient manuscript that a valuable Indian treasure is concealed somewhere inside an ancient Indian tower recently purchased by retired millionaire manufacturer Brent Matthews as a decorative feature for his private estate, poses as an Indian as part of an elaborate scheme to recover the treasure before Matthews can learn of its existence. Thwarted repeatedly by SUPERMAN in Spring 1942, Potts dies when the ancient tower topples over on him as he attempts to escape from the Man of Steel (WF No. 5: "The Case of the Flying Castle").

POWERMAN. A mysterious costumed crime-fighter, his identity concealed by a yellow hood, who functions as the crime-fighting ally of SUPERMAN during May-June 1958, much to the chagrin of BATMAN and ROBIN, who feel that their friend Superman has snubbed them in favor of a new partner.

When renegade scientist LEX LUTHOR breaks out of prison vowing revenge on both Superman and METROPOLIS, Batman and Robin volunteer their services to Superman in helping to reapprehend him, only to be informed, somewhat curtly, that the Man of Steel has acquired a new crime-fighting partner, Powerman, and that Powerman has demanded the exclusion of the Dynamic Duo from their crime-fighting team.

Stung at first by this rejection by their longtime friend and ally, Batman and Robin help apprehend Luthor anyway, only to discover that Powerman is in reality a costumed robot created by Superman as part of a well-meaning ploy to discourage his good friends from risking their lives in the battle against Luthor (WF No. 94: "The Origin of the Superman-Batman Team!").

POWERSTONE, THE. "An ancient gem" from

"another planet" whose weird "scientific properties" (Act No. 47, Apr '42: "Powerstone") confer virtually "infinite power" on whoever possesses it (S No. 17/4, Jul/Aug '42: "When Titans Clash!"). SUPERMAN and LEX LUTHOR battle for possession of the powerstone in 1942. (See LUTHOR, LEX.)

PRALINE ("Professor"). "One of the most cunning villains that ever lived," an evil genius and "greedy lordling of the underworld" who is renowned in gangland circles as the "scholarly dean of desperadoes."

In August 1943, after CLARK KENT has been temporarily stricken with amnesia by a shower of "weird rays" from outer space—rays unleashed by the cosmic collision of "two great, flaming suns" in space, and "vibrating at frequencies infinitely greater than those of electricity"—"Professor" Praline comes upon the dazed Kent and, unaware of his true identity but struck immediately by his remarkable resemblance to SUPERMAN, promptly dupes Kent into believing that he is a gangland muscleman and recruits him into his gang to pose as Superman, first to help him frighten rival mobster Spike Jaeger into fleeing the city, and later to help his gang loot the Federal gold reserve at Fort Blox of $20,000,000,000 in bullion.

Ultimately, however, the shock of colliding head-on with a meteor plummeting toward METROPOLIS restores Superman's memory to normal, and he swiftly apprehends "Professor" Praline and his henchmen (Act No. 63: "When Stars Collide!").

PRANKSTER, THE. The so-called "clown king of the underworld" (S No. 69/1, Mar/Apr '51: "The Prankster's Apprentice!"), a "cunning" and "ruthless" criminal with "a dangerous sense of humor" (S No. 50/2, Jan/Feb '48: "The Slogans That Came Too True!") who is forever playing pranks on people, including his own henchmen (Act No. 104, Jan '47: "Candytown, U.S.A."; and others), and who likes nothing better than to pull an uproariously prank-filled crime while at the same time making a monkey out of SUPERMAN (S No. 55/1, Nov/Dec '48: "Prankster's Second Childhood"; and others).

LOIS LANE has described the Prankster as "the most dangerous of all practical jokers" (S No. 37/2, Nov/Dec '45: "Pranks for Profit!"), while Superman has referred to him as an "addle-brained foul ball" (S No. 50/2, Jan/Feb '48: "The Slogans That Came Too True!") and CLARK KENT has called him an "overgrown juvenile delinquent" (S No. 61/1, Nov/Dec '49: "The Prankster's Radio Program!"). Even the underworld is wary of the Prankster, for in the words of gangster "Bugs" Halloway, "He's got a reputation for making saps outa smart guys" (S No. 22/3, May/Jun '43: "The Great ABC Panic!").

By his own, somewhat less modest account, however, the Prankster is "the funniest man in the world" (Act No. 95, Apr '46: "The Laughing Stock of Metropolis!") and the greatest criminal of all (S No. 52/1, May/Jun '48: "Preview of Plunder"; and others). "What makes me so world-famous?" asks the

The Prankster, 1954

Prankster rhetorically in March-April 1952. "It's my sense of humor! Larceny with laughs has been my motto!" (S No. 75/1: "The Prankster's Star Pupil!").

Described as "Superman's most fiendish foe" (Act No. 109, Jun '47: "The Man Who Robbed the Mint!"), the Prankster is a man in his middle 30s, five feet tall, weighing approximately 125 pounds (S No. 41/1, Jul/Aug '46: "Too Many Pranksters!"). He has slicked-down red hair and a narrow moustache, a pointy nose, and large "cup-shaped ears [that] begin wiggling like mad" whenever he is struck by an evil inspiration (S No. 22/3, May/Jun '43: "The Great ABC Panic!"). He speaks in a bombastic, highfalutin manner, often saying "Aye and verily," for example, instead of "yes" (Act No. 51, Aug '42: "The Case of the Crimeless Crimes"; and others). His laughter has been described as "sinister" (Act No. 109, Jun '47: "The Man Who Robbed the Mint!"), and he is often portrayed as having wide gaps between several of his front teeth, giving him the appearance of a fiendish jack-o'-lantern (Act No. 51, Aug '42: "The Case of the Crimeless Crimes"; and many others).

The Prankster is immensely egotistical. In May-June 1948, for example, after reading press accounts of Superman's recent capture of the TOYMAN and thwarting of LEX LUTHOR's latest "gigantic scientific hoax," the Prankster reacts contemptuously. "Bah!" he exclaims. "If that fool Luthor could think up something gigantic, swiping a library book would be a sensation! And what's clever about the Toyman? Why—compared to me, he's just a third-rate petty-larceny punk who made the big time on lucky breaks!"

"What's eatin' ya, Prankster?" interjects one of the Prankster's henchmen. "With them guys in jail, you got less competition!"

"That's not the point!" retorts the Prankster. "Those punks are getting all the publicity! —While my great criminal talents are being forgotten!" (S No. 52/1: "Preview of Plunder").

The Prankster is the "prince of practical jokers"

(Act No. 151, Dec '50: "Superman's Super-Magic Show!"), and his penchant for prankishness is exhibited repeatedly in the chronicles. On one occasion, he frightens the wits out of a METROPOLIS policeman with a gun that fires little toy parachutes instead of bullets, and on another he and his henchmen invade a bank armed with pistols and machine guns that shoot fireworks, corks, and streams of water (Act No. 51, Aug '42: "The Case of the Crimeless Crimes").

Particularly in his early appearances, however, the Prankster is fiendish as well as mirthful—carrying a deadly "miniature gun" concealed inside a playful-looking flute, attempting to annihilate his own henchmen with poison gas so that he can keep their share of the loot for himself (Act No. 51, Aug '42: "The Case of the Crimeless Crimes"; and others).

In the course of more than twenty separate encounters with Superman, the Prankster has employed a number of ingenious aliases and alternate identities to help him carry out his nefarious schemes, including P.R. ANKSTER and AJAX WILDE (S No. 37/2, Nov/Dec '45: "Pranks for Profit!"); MR. VAN PRANK, COLONEL P.R. ANKSTER, MR. FRANK STER, and PROFESSOR SMYTHE (S No. 61/1, Nov/Dec '49: "The Prankster's Radio Program!"); and DR. DAWSON (S No. 70/3, May/Jun '51: "The Pied Piper Prankster!").

In the texts, the Prankster is alternatively referred to as the Chuckling Charlatan, the Clown King of Crime, the Comedy Crook, the Mirthful Miscreant, and the Rollicking Rogue.

In addition, he has been described as "that cherubic, clowning comedy king of crime," a "mastermind of malignant mirth," and the "mirthful marauder" (Act No. 51, Aug '42: "The Case of the Crimeless Crimes"); "that whimsical wizard of whacky crimes" (Act No. 69, Feb '44: "The Lost-and-Found Mystery!"); "that ribald rogue of mirthful menace" (S No. 29/1, Jul/Aug '44: "The Wizard of Wishes!"); the "mocking mountebank of mischief" and "clowning crime-king" (S No. 37/2, Nov/Dec '45: "Pranks for Profit!"); "the waggish wizard of clownish crimes" (S No. 41/1, Jul/Aug '46: "Too Many Pranksters!"); "that grinning engineer of evil" (Act No. 109, Jun '47: "The Man Who Robbed the Mint!"); "that rollicking rajah of rogues" and "Superman's madcap enemy" (S No. 61/1, Nov/Dec '49: "The Prankster's Radio Program!"); "that clownish character with a crooked streak" and "Superman's old enemy, who blends his larceny with laughs" (S No. 66/1, Sep/Oct '50: "The Babe of Steel!"); "that crook with a yen for clownish crimes," "one of Superman's arch-enemies," the "crime clown," and the "master of mad mischief" (S No. 69/1, Mar/Apr '51: "The Prankster's Apprentice!"); "that pixie crook" and "that pixie practical joker" (S No. 70/3, May/Jun '51: "The Pied Piper Prankster!"); the "menacing jokester of crime" and a "grinning clown of crime and Superman's most annoying foe" (S No. 72/1, Sep/Oct '51: "The Unfunny Prankster!"); and the "arch-clown

of crime" and "one of Superman's trickiest foes" (S No. 87/3, Feb '54: "The Prankster's Greatest Role!").

In August 1942, with the aid of funds they have acquired by robbing a bowling alley and other strictly penny-ante crimes, the Prankster and his henchmen set in motion an elaborate scheme designed to enable them to loot one of Metropolis's wealthiest banks. On two separate occasions, the villains barge into a bank during business hours, line the patrons and employees up against the wall at gunpoint, and force them to endure a series of infuriating but harmless pranks—as when the Prankster tricks a bank president into blackening his entire face by lending the unsuspecting banker a gimmicked handkerchief with which to wipe his brow—and then peacefully depart, leaving behind, to the amazement of bank officials and onlookers alike, a satchel filled with money as a *gift* for the bank.

"Why did you forcibly enter those banks and leave money there?" asks a bewildered judge, after Superman has taken the criminals into custody following their second bizarre robbery-in-reverse. "Just a childish whim, judge," replies the Prankster coyly. "Playing cops and robbers has always intrigued me. I'm a wealthy man, and if I desire to give money away to banks, who is there to say nay?"

Indeed, when the Prankster and his cohorts barge into their third, and last, bank, the bank's president is only too eager to accommodate them, certain that he is about to become the next recipient of the Prankster's well-publicized largesse. Only too late, after the villains have laughingly looted the vault of millions of dollars' worth of jewelry, currency, and bonds does the bank official realize that he has just been the victim of an actual robbery.

When Superman attempts to intervene, the Prankster takes Lois Lane hostage, forcing Superman to retreat, but the Man of Steel manages to infiltrate the villain's hideout disguised as one of his henchmen, and before long he has rescued Lois, apprehended the Prankster's henchmen, and set out in pursuit of the escaping Prankster. However, as the villain flees into the darkness of a subterranean cavern, Superman sees "avalanching boulders topple down upon the mirthful marauder," and he assumes that he has just witnessed "the end of the Prankster!"

But Superman is mistaken, for the wily criminal has miraculously escaped death by "taking refuge on a ledge." When he gloatingly examines his bag full of bank loot, however, he discovers that the hoard of money and jewelry has been replaced by worthless "blank paper." "He [Superman] must have substituted it for the swag at super-speed while I was off-guard!" mutters the Prankster. "So Superman has the last laugh--this time! But we will clash again--soon! And perhaps next time it will be the Prankster who will laugh loudest--and the longest!" (Act No. 51: "The Case of the Crimeless Crimes").

In February 1943, after talking racketeer "King" Ruggles into lending him $100,000 by promising to give Ruggles ten times that amount within one month's time, the Prankster horrifies his gangland patron by contritely turning himself in for his past crimes at a local police station with the announcement that he has decided to turn over a new leaf. To demonstrate his sincerity, the Prankster proceeds to contribute half of Ruggles's $100,000 to an animal welfare organization, the Society for the Prevention of Cruelty to Ostriches, immediately prompting the wealthy matrons who comprise the society to flock to his support on the assumption that "anyone who would take the plight of ostriches to heart must be an upright citizen!"

Indeed, because of public support for the Prankster stemming from his apparently selfless act, the villain is soon acquitted of the charges against him and set free to plot again. His first new project is the establishment of an organization called Appreciation, Incorporated, its objective being, in the Prankster's words, "to write letters of appreciation to everyone I admire." Before long, letters of flattering praise from the Prankster begin to arrive in the homes of Metropolis's wealthiest and most prominent citizens, and the Prankster soon finds himself a welcome visitor in the homes of the people he so deeply "appreciates."

When, soon afterward, the city is swept by a wave of mysterious robberies, Superman realizes that the Prankster must be responsible. "Most of the celebrities who were recently robbed," muses the Man of Steel, "are on the Prankster's list of people to whom he sent letters of appreciation!"

"By writing letters of appreciation to celebrities," gloats the Prankster, "I became their close acquaintance, gained entry to their homes. Once inside, it was a simple matter to spot the hiding places of their valuables and have duplicate keys to their homes made!"

"King" Ruggles and his cohorts are pleasantly astounded when, within the allotted one month's time, the Prankster strolls into the gang chief's headquarters and hands his underworld patron the agreed-upon $1,000,000. No sooner has Ruggles accepted the money, however, than the Prankster pulls out a pistol and demands it back again. "I said I'd give you a million for a hundred thousand dollars," chuckles the Prankster, "--but I didn't say I'd let you keep it!"

When Superman arrives on the scene, the Prankster gleefully shoots him in the face with a water pistol, and when the Man of Steel, momentarily bewildered, unleashes a powerful haymaker, the Prankster ducks adroitly, causing Superman to knock himself out. Just as the victorious Prankster is about to depart with his loot, however, "King" Ruggles's henchmen pounce on him and take him prisoner.

"Shortly after ... encased in a block of cement, Superman's figure is dropped into the river," while the hapless Prankster is left stranded in a rowboat in the middle of a U.S. Navy artillery range. Fortunately for the Prankster, Superman regains consciousness

and escapes from his cement deathtrap in time to carry the Prankster to safety, and soon afterward he apprehends "King" Ruggles and his cohorts and turns them over to the authorities. By the time Superman returns to the spot where he left the Prankster, however, the villain has loosened his bonds and vanished without a trace. "And he's left a note behind for me," muses Superman, "--a note of appreciation for saving his life! He promises to go straight--but knowing him as I do, I suspect it's just another of his pranks!" (Act No. 57: "Crime's Comedy King!").

In May-June 1943, after kidnapping the registrar of the U.S. Copyright Office and replacing him with a confederate, the Prankster copyrights the English alphabet and then stuns the nation with the incredible announcement that, beginning in twenty-four hours, no one may print or write anything—including his own name—without the Prankster's permission.

Overnight the nation is plunged into chaos as individuals and institutions are forced to pay the Prankster exorbitant fees for the right to use the English alphabet. Editor PERRY WHITE finds himself forced to pay the villain $2,000 a week for permission to print the DAILY PLANET and the American educational system all but collapses in the wake of teachers' inability to assign written homework. "The ranks of the unemployed swell to unprecedented bulk--including typists, writers, printers, postal employees, sky-writers, librarians...." In the words of P. Motgomery [sic] Sniff, the Prankster's mouthpiece and the "world's greatest crook lawyer," "... the Prankster has discovered what every criminal has sought since the world began--a legitimate racket!"

Even Superman is stymied. "—What can I do?" thinks Clark Kent helplessly. "The Prankster has the law on his side, and I won't flout justice at any cost!—"

While snooping around the Prankster's hideout mansion, Clark Kent and Lois Lane are taken captive by the villain, who intends to leave them to die in a raging fire while he escapes with his ill-gotten loot. The Prankster's gangland cohorts, however, realizing that their colleague intended to abscond without handing over their share of the profits, leave the Prankster to die with the others in the burning mansion while they flee with the funds garnered in the course of the great alphabet swindle. Superman quenches the blaze in the nick of time, however, and takes the Prankster and his erstwhile underworld allies into custody (S No. 22/3: "The Great ABC Panic!").

By February 1944 the Prankster has concocted an intricate scheme for blackmailing some of Metropolis's most prominent citizens. Having somehow unearthed "the little mistakes and indiscretions that might prove so embarrassing, they'd gladly pay to keep them from being made public," the Prankster has devised a means of extorting money from his victims without taking the risk of being prosecuted for blackmail. After approaching his victims and informing them of the secret knowledge he has obtained about their lives, the Prankster forces them to place classified advertisements in daily newspapers offering generous rewards for common everyday objects they have supposedly "lost."

In one such case, for example, the victim offers a $5,000 reward for the return of a common safety pin, which, he claims, has an extraordinary sentimental value to him. Once the advertisement has been placed, one of the Prankster's henchmen visits the victim's home, ostensibly in response to the ad, hands over a safety pin, and walks away with the $5,000 "reward." Soon afterward, the Prankster bilks the same victim a second time by having a second henchman, posing as a newspaper reporter, pay a call on the victim, claim that his paper has discovered the true story behind the peculiar classified ad, and threaten to publish the story unless the victim buys the paper's silence for another $5,000.

Even Superman is stymied by the bizarre scheme until the villain makes the fatal mistake of ordering his henchmen to kidnap Lois Lane so that he can use her as a hostage to force the Man of Steel to pay him a $50,000 ransom. Enraged by the brazen kidnapping, Superman swiftly locates the Prankster's hideout, apprehends the Prankster and his henchmen, and rescues Lois Lane from the villains' clutches (Act No. 69: "The Lost-and-Found Mystery!").

In July-August 1944 the Prankster concocts an elaborate scheme to bilk multimillionaire James Joslyn out of his entire vast fortune. The scheme centers around the so-called Wizard of Wishes, a gigantic "talking" statue—its "voice" is actually that of the Prankster, speaking through a radio-broadcasting apparatus hidden inside it—which offers to grant people's fondest wishes for them absolutely free of charge. By working behind the scenes to see to it that the wishes of the people who seek the Wizard's aid actually come true, the Prankster and his henchmen quickly establish the Wizard's credibility as a miraculous fulfiller of wishes as a means of enticing multimillionaire Joslyn into seeking the Wizard's assistance. Indeed, when Joslyn begs the Wizard of Wishes to help him fulfill his most heartfelt wish, the wish for happiness, the thing Joslyn admits he lost sight of while struggling to become wealthy, the Prankster, speaking through his statue, tells Joslyn that he will only find happiness by using his millions to aid humanity, and that if he will bring his entire fortune to the Wizard's headquarters, the Wizard will instruct him as to exactly how to spend it. Superman, however, having already discovered that the Wizard of Wishes is part of an elaborate swindle devised by the Prankster, takes Joslyn's place at his scheduled rendezvous with the Wizard and apprehends the Prankster and his cohorts (S No. 29/1: "The Wizard of Wishes!").

In October 1944, after overhearing "rich--and unscrupulous--stock manipulator" Amos Amster

The Prankster, 1948

express his avaricious desire to obtain control of the Todd Steel Mills and the Marsden Steamship Line, the Prankster allies himself with Amster in an elaborate scheme to swindle Thomas Todd and Milton Marsden, the owners of the prestigious companies, into selling their firms to Amster at rock-bottom prices. After knocking a blind news dealer unconscious and seizing control of his newsstand, the Prankster sells Todd and Marsden bogus editions of the *Daily Planet* containing headline stories to the effect that a pair of catastrophic disasters—an earthquake at the Todd Steel Mills and the sinking of Marsden's newest, most valuable liner—has bankrupted both companies and rendered them worthless. When stock manipulator Amster appears on the scene and offers to buy both "ruined" firms, Todd and Marsden, believing their firms now worthless, readily agree to part with their companies at a small fraction of their real worth. Amster has no sooner acquired the two firms, however, than the Prankster dissolves their short-lived partnership at gunpoint and absconds with the ownership documents of the two valuable companies.

Through an elaborate ruse of his own, however, Superman dupes the Prankster into believing that his ill-gotten corporate acquisitions are actually worthless. When the villain attempts to sell a supply of stolen jewelry in order to raise some sorely needed cash, Superman appears on the scene and swiftly apprehends him (Act No. 77: "The Headline Hoax!").

In November-December 1945, after reading a *Daily Planet* article by Lois Lane on prominent Metropolis practical jokers, the Prankster devises a series of schemes designed to enable him to capitalize on the penchant for practical jokes of the various men described in Lois's article. Approaching prominent businessman and inveterate practical joker A. Alvin Arnold, for example, the Prankster—employing the alias P.R. Ankster and describing himself as a "professor of practical jokes"—offers to help enliven Arnold's forthcoming dinner party by startling Arnold's dinner guests with a mild electric shock. Arnold readily agrees to this harmless "prank," but on the day of the actual party, the Prankster jolts the partygoers into unconsciousness with a violent electric shock and then flees with their jewelry before they even realize what has happened to them. Superman apprehends the Prankster soon afterward, however, and turns him over to the authorities (S No. 37/2: "Pranks for Profit!").

In April 1946 the Prankster sets in motion an elaborate campaign designed to humiliate Superman into leaving Metropolis. "**Superman** is invulnerable to bullets, explosives, acid and all other means of destruction!" explains the Prankster to the four Metropolis "crime lords" who have agreed to pay him $100,000 to rid the city of Superman. But, he adds with a chortle, "by ridiculing him before the public, we can laugh him out of **Metropolis!!!**"

In the days that follow, the Prankster carries out his scheme to transform Superman from a respected hero into the laughingstock of Metropolis. When Superman rips the massive door of a bank vault off its hinges in order to free a teller trapped inside, a mechanical device planted inside the vault by the Prankster hurls a custard pie into Superman's face, making him the butt of the bank employees' laughter. When the Man of Steel leaps high into the air to rescue what appears to be a man falling off a roof, onlookers find themselves chortling with laughter when the rescued "man" turns out to be nothing but a dummy surreptitiously pushed off the roof by the Prankster. And finally, when Metropolis's mayor and city council unveil a heroic portrait of Superman in an effort to resuscitate the Man of Steel's flagging public image, the crowd on hand for the unveiling roars with laughter when it is discovered that someone has defaced the portrait with a beard and moustache.

For Superman, this episode of public ridicule is the last straw. "Friends!" he announces. "For years I've dedicated my powers to helping the people in this community! Now, it seems, I've become a buffoon in your eyes! Therefore, my usefulness here is at an end. It's time to say goodbye--and thanks for the memories!"

No sooner has Superman retired from Metropolis into self-imposed exile, however, than the city is engulfed by a massive tidal wave of crime, and before long the Man of Steel has begun to suspect that the campaign to humiliate him was instigated by the Prankster. To smoke out the Prankster and dupe him into making a full confession, Superman returns to Metropolis secretly, concealing his identity beneath a clever disguise and billing himself, in a flood of advance publicity, as Professor Hi Laryus, "the Funniest Man on Earth!!!"

When "Professor Hi Laryus" appears in Metropo-

lis, performing a tired routine of stale vaudeville gags and worn-out jokes, the Prankster—enraged that anyone would attempt to preempt his self-proclaimed reputation as "funniest man in the world"—leaps to the stage, where, in a near-hysterical torrent of words, he begins shouting out the details of his own prank-filled escapades, including his latest, crowning achievement—his successful scheme to make Superman the laughingstock of Metropolis. Seated in the audience, the four Metropolis crime czars who paid the Prankster to carry out his scheme draw their pistols, determined to silence the free-talking crime clown before he talks too much, but Superman blocks the oncoming bullets with his invulnerable body, sheds his "Professor Hi Laryus" disguise, and swiftly apprehends the four crime czars along with the flabbergasted Prankster (Act No. 95: "The Laughing Stock of Metropolis!").

In July-August 1946, after placing a classified advertisement in a local newspaper promising "highly unusual job opportunities" to men whose physical description approximates his own, the Prankster kidnaps three of the men who respond to the ad and forces them to submit to plastic surgery that transforms them all into Prankster look-alikes. "This will be the crowning prank of my career!" gloats the Prankster. "The police will find me—yet I shall never go back to prison!"

In the days that follow, the Prankster and his henchmen embark on a series of spectacular crimes, each time abandoning one of the innocent look-alikes at the scene to be apprehended by Superman and sent to prison for the crime. Ultimately, however, after two of the look-alikes have been captured and incarcerated in State Prison, Superman dupes the real villain into attempting to rob an exhibition of precious gems and swiftly apprehends him. "Beats anything I ever heard of!" gasps the State Prison warden as he simultaneously confronts the real Prankster and his three perfect look-alikes. "Doesn't it?" laughs the Prankster gleefully. "Ha, ha, ha! Best prank I ever pulled—while it lasted!" (S No. 41/1: "Too Many Pranksters!").

In January 1947 the Prankster approaches Daniel R. Sweetooth, president of the Metropolis Candy Co., and persuades him to undertake construction of Candytown, a small city made entirely out of candy. "Invite kiddies to visit it, and help themselves to free samples of your candy!" urges the Prankster. "It'll get you nationwide publicity, and zoom sales!"

Appointed by Sweetooth to supervise construction of Candytown, the Prankster and his henchmen begin secretly building a near-duplicate of Candytown, called Goodytown, while at the same time deliberately sabotaging the candy to be distributed at Candytown to make it taste awful so that Candytown's young visitors, angered by the bad-tasting candy they are offered at Candytown, will flock to the Prankster's Goodytown instead. The scheme, however, is thwarted by Superman, who destroys Candytown prior to its grand opening so that innocent children will not be exposed to its foul-tasting sweets, rebuilds the town with delicious candy he has cooked himself, and then apprehends the Prankster and his henchmen (Act No. 104: "Candytown, U.S.A.").

In June 1947, after having created a supply of ingenious "ink-dissolving gas pellets" capable of dissolving the printing on U.S. currency without leaving a trace, the Prankster surreptitiously drops his gas pellets into the ventilating system of the U.S. Mint—causing billions of dollars in U.S. currency to turn completely blank within several hours—as part of an elaborate scheme to bilk the American economy of billions of dollars. As the paper money exposed to the Prankster's gas pellets circulates throughout the country and then suddenly turns blank, the nation is gripped by a financial panic. Then, posing as an innocent "collector of unusual currency," the Prankster places an advertisement in the *Daily Planet*, offering to pay one cent apiece for all blank bills. "...Those blank bills may be collectors' items in 20 years," explains the Prankster slyly. "And I always say—look to the future! Ha-ha!"

Before long, in response to the Prankster's ad, the blank paper money begins pouring into the villain's warehouse, sent by people eager to salvage at least something for their seemingly worthless money. The Prankster and his henchmen, meanwhile, are preparing to treat the blank bills with a special gas designed to restore the vanished printing, thereby restoring the currency to its full face value.

Aided by officials of the U.S. Treasury, however, Superman outwits the Prankster by having the U.S. Mint print up a massive supply of special money, featuring, in place of the normal printing, cartoons poking fun at the Prankster. After these bills have turned blank, due to the continued presence of the Prankster's ink-dissolving gas in the mint's ventilation system, Superman turns them in to the Prankster for a penny apiece—thereby buying back virtually all of the villain's ill-gotten loot—and then sits back to watch the fun. When the Prankster and his cohorts, believing themselves wealthy beyond the dreams of avarice, restore the printing to their gargantuan pile of currency, they find that they have no money at all, but only a pile of whimsical drawings spoofing the Prankster. Enraged at the Prankster for having allowed himself to be duped by Superman, the Prankster's henchmen are on the verge of murdering their leader when Superman streaks to the rescue and apprehends them all (Act No. 109: "The Man Who Robbed the Mint!").

In January-February 1948, after scanning a series of billboards whose advertisements contain extravagant claims and promises, the Prankster is inspired with an idea for a series of spectacular crimes. "These over-dramatic ads inspire me," he exclaims. "I see new profits for the **Prankster!** By making the product fit the sign, I'll make all advertising tell the truth...! I'll prove that honesty is the best policy— *even in crime!* Ha-ha-ha-ha-ha-ha-ha...."

In the days that follow, the Prankster commits a series of intricate crimes revolving around popular advertising slogans. At one point, for example, while posing as a gas-station attendant at a filling station that dispenses Sky-Hy gasoline—a product whose advertising features a winged automobile and the claim that Sky-Hy gasoline "makes your car fly"— the Prankster blows open an armored car that stops for gasoline by igniting its gas tank and then flees to freedom with his stolen loot in a winged car that flies like an airplane. For a time the Prankster's ingenious advertising crimes wreak havoc in Metropolis, but ultimately, through an elaborate ruse, Superman lures the villain into the open and swiftly apprehends him (S No. 50/2: "The Slogans That Came Too True!").

In May-June 1948 the Prankster embarks on a series of elaborate crimes involving the use of special photographic equipment and of life-sized statues depicting Superman aiding the Prankster in the commission of crimes. On the afternoon preceding his robbery of Spiffany's Jewelry Store, for example, the Prankster deposits a life-sized statue at the scene depicting Superman helping the Prankster carry out a jewelry heist. "On this site," reads the statue's inscription, "--Superman will show the Prankster how to rob this jewelry store."

Summoned to the scene to examine the strange statue, Superman probes its interior with his X-ray vision, but all he sees there are three commonplace objects—a necktie, a pineapple, and a phonograph record—and the Man of Steel soon departs without having gleaned any clue at all as to the Prankster's intentions. Unknown to Superman, however, the placement of the Prankster's statue was such that his X-ray gaze, focused on the statue's innards, also penetrated the Spiffany's Jewelry Store vault, thus enabling the Prankster and his henchman, concealed across the street inside a moving van equipped with a gigantic photographic plate, to obtain an X-ray photograph of the jewelry store vault. The X-ray photograph, in turn, reveals the vault's secret combination, thereby enabling the villain to loot the vault effortlessly the following evening. Ultimately, however, Superman unravels the Prankster's complex scheme, lures him into a trap through an elaborate ruse of his own, and apprehends the Prankster and his henchman (S No. 52/1: "Preview of Plunder").

In November-December 1948, after the mischievous, bratty students at the Manley Academy for Problem Children have unanimously voted the Prankster the "man [they] want most to be like when [they] grow up," the Prankster is inspired with an idea for a series of new, spectacular crimes. "At last my talents are appreciated by someone!" chortles the villain. *"Ho! Ho! Ho!* Clever little brats! I can just see **Superman**'s face when he hears about this!

"**Superman!** Ha! Those kids have given me a brilliant idea! I'll use their childish pranks to commit crimes—and at the same time make **Superman** look like a fool!"

After flying over the Manley Academy in a Prankster-shaped blimp and dropping the students a load of lollipops and thank-you notes in gratitude for their having selected the Prankster as the man they would most like to emulate, the Prankster and his henchmen embark on a series of elaborate crimes involving diabolical variations on schoolboy pranks. Appearing outside the Metropolis Bank disguised as children, for example, the Prankster and his henchmen begin writing on the building's outer wall with what appears at first glance to be harmless chalk, but with what, in actuality, is a powerful acid. As the corrosive acid eats its way through the wall, burning a hole in the side of the bank, the bank's guards hurl themselves at the villains, only to be knocked unconscious by tear-gas pellets which the criminals blow at them through peashooters. And when Superman arrives on the scene and attempts to apprehend the villains, the Prankster knocks him momentarily off balance with a shot from his tricky "exploding jack-in-the-box gun," which socks Superman in the jaw with a mechanical fist.

Not long afterward, however, Superman surprises the villains in the act of robbing the guests at an orphans' benefit being held at the estate of a wealthy philanthropist. While Superman apprehends the Prankster's henchmen, students from the Manley Academy, who are enraged at the man they elected as their hero for attempting "to rob poor orphans of their just rights," surround the Prankster and subject him to every mischievous prank imaginable before Superman finally takes him in hand so that he may be turned over to the authorities for prosecution (S No. 55/1: "Prankster's Second Childhood").

In January-February 1949, in the seclusion of his gangland hideout, the Prankster awakens from a terrifying nightmare in which he is continually bested by Superman. "I—I was just dreaming about **Superman!**" he explains to a henchman. "Ugh! No wonder I woke up screaming! How can a respectable crook make a living with him around?"

"You can't win against him and his super-powers, boss!" agrees the henchman dejectedly.

Suddenly, however, the Prankster is seized by an inspiration. "Wait a minute!" he exclaims excitedly. "You've given me the answer...! I can't win *against* **Superman**'s powers but I can win *with* them! I'm going to put **Superman** to work for us!"

Indeed, in the days that follow, the Prankster and his henchmen commit a series of spectacular crimes in which Superman is unwittingly duped into using his super-powers to help the criminals. In order to break into an impregnable vault housing a priceless art collection, for example, the Prankster and his cohorts install a false, movie-scenery door directly in front of the door to the vault, and then, by pretending to hide behind the false door, lure Superman into crashing through it in an attempt to apprehend them. As the Man of Steel plows through the false door, however, the force of his charge sends him crashing into the vault, cracking it open like an eggshell and

exposing the art collection. Superman has barely recovered from his surprise when the Prankster informs him that he has planted a bomb beneath the building, timed to explode in exactly one minute. Training his super-hearing on the ground beneath the building, Superman hears a faint ticking sound and swiftly burrows underground to find and deactivate it, allowing the criminals the time they need to escape with their loot. By the time the Man of Steel reaches the "bomb"—and discovers that it is nothing more than a chirping cricket inside a small lead-lined box—the Prankster and his henchmen are long gone. "The Prankster made good his boast!" mutters Superman angrily. "**He's using my super-powers to commit crime!**"

Ultimately, however, after enduring a series of such humiliations, Superman repays the Prankster and his henchmen in kind by apprehending them in his Clark Kent identity as they attempt to flee with their loot after robbing Metropolis's Tenth National Bank. "The humiliation!" groans the Prankster soon afterward, behind bars in the city jail. "**Superman** with all his *super-powers* couldn't catch me! But a timid weakling like Clark Kent trapped me!" (S No. 56/1: "The Prankster Picks a Partner!").

In November-December 1949, enraged at a Metropolis radio station for abruptly canceling a dramatization of his underworld exploits on the ground that

The Prankster, 1949

"It is against the policy of...this station to broadcast any programs that might tend to give a favorable impression of any lawbreaker, such as the Prankster," the Prankster—employing a series of aliases and concealing his true identity beneath various disguises—makes the rounds of the various radio networks and buys up every last hour of time on every single radio station in America. "I'm going to make those radio people regret what they did!" vows the villain. "I'll get even with them if it's the last thing I ever do!"

In the days that follow, the Prankster uses his absolute control of the airwaves to wreak a prankish revenge on the nation's radio stations and listeners, dispensing with all regularly scheduled programming in favor of endless hours of absolute silence, then producing a series of hilarious dramatizations posing the profound question "What makes Superman so stupid?"

For a time, Superman is stymied by the Prankster's control of the airwaves, for the method by which he achieved it is perfectly legal. Yet the Man of Steel remains deeply concerned. "If the Prankster is allowed to broadcast his kind of program," muses Superman, "it will destroy the country's confidence in the forces of law and order, which I help to uphold!"

Through a campaign of high-handed harassment and elaborate ruses, Superman succeeds in disrupting the Prankster's attempts to use the nation's airwaves to carry on a personal vendetta against him. And ultimately, by sabotaging all the clocks that the Prankster can see from his studio and then invoking a legal broadcasting technicality—the rule requiring a broadcaster to announce the correct time every half hour—Superman succeeds in having the Prankster's broadcast license revoked and in having the villain arrested, thereby breaking his stranglehold on the nation's airwaves (S No. 61/1: "The Prankster's Radio Program!").

In May-June 1950, after hearing one of his henchmen quote the old adage that "The best things in life are free," the Prankster is inspired with an idea for a series of crimes centering around the general theme of things that are free. After gold has been discovered in a stream at Potter's Cove, for example, the Prankster and his henchmen build a dam upstream of the mining camp and then, after backing up tons of water, suddenly release it, thereby causing the stream to overflow its banks, flooding the mining camp and washing the gold dust patiently panned from the stream by honest prospectors downstream with the torrent, where the Prankster and his cohorts are waiting to collect it. Technically speaking, chortles the Prankster, he and his men have done nothing illegal, since the waters of the stream are, after all, free.

Soon afterward, while guards at the Metropolis Bank are carrying out bags of worn-out currency for return to the U.S. Treasury, the Prankster surreptitiously smears liver paste on the money bags, sics a pack of hungry dogs on them, and then perches with a butterfly net in a nearby tree, calmly snaring the paper money wafted up to him by the wind from the torn money bags below. Legally speaking, claims the Prankster, he is doing nothing for which he can be prosecuted, since he is only sitting in the tree catching some fresh air, and air is, after all, free.

Ultimately, however, by means of an elaborate and somewhat underhanded ruse, Superman tricks the Prankster into confessing an attempt to rob the city aquarium, thus enabling the Man of Steel to apprehend the villain and his henchmen and incarcerate them in the Metropolis city jail (S No. 64/3: "The Free-for-All Crimes!").

In September-October 1950, while fleeing from Superman in an air-filled balloon, the Prankster and his henchmen are forced to crash-land in the Florida Everglades, where, through a miraculous accident of circumstance, they stumble upon the fabled Fountain of Youth. Returning to Metropolis with a supply of the magic elixir, the villains begin using the substance to foment fiendish mischief and commit spectacular crimes, as when they transform Lois Lane into an infant and threaten to withhold the antidote to the magic water unless Superman keeps his distance, and when they attempt to rob the Merchant's Bank by having one of their number—also transformed into an infant by the elixir—crawl into the bank's vault through a narrow air duct.

Superman's efforts to apprehend the Prankster and his henchmen are severely hampered by the fact that the villains have succeeded, albeit inadvertently, in transforming him into an infant as well, making him, for a time, the laughingstock of Metropolis and forcing him to adopt new, sometimes somewhat embarrassing, crime-fighting strategies, as when he sets out to foil the robbery of the Merchant's Bank by disguising himself in baby clothes and having himself wheeled into the bank inside a baby carriage. Ultimately, however, through an elaborate ruse, the so-called Babe of Steel tricks the Prankster into revealing that the antidote to the Fountain of Youth's water is ordinary sugar, whereupon he restores himself—and Lois Lane—to adulthood and apprehends the villain and his henchmen (S No. 66/1: "The Babe of Steel!").

In December 1950 the Prankster joins forces with Lex Luthor and Mr. Mxyzptlk in an elaborate scheme to humiliate Superman (Act No. 151: "Superman's Super-Magic Show!"). (See Mxyzptlk [Mr.].)

In March-April 1951 the Prankster makes the acquaintance of "unemployed crook" Al Fresco, and, after satisfying himself that Fresco is gifted with "imagination" and a "whacky sort of humor," hires Fresco to be his "understudy." "I need an understudy to stage comic crimes in my unique style, so that I can concentrate on executive problems!" explains the Prankster. "With training, you might just possibly be good enough!"

After undergoing a grueling course of study designed to enable him to master the Prankster's prankish techniques, Fresco is disguised as the Prankster and sent out to pass his acid test—the commission of a spectacular crime in the zany style of the Prankster. Although Fresco passes his test with flying colors, however, brazenly stealing a payroll in broad daylight while emulating the prankish techniques of the Prankster and then escaping through a manhole right under the nose of Superman, the Man of Steel does discover—through a close examination of the bandit's fingerprints—that the payroll robbery was committed not by the real Prankster but by a Prankster look-alike, and the resulting headlines—"Prankster's Double Tops Him in Robbery"—infuriate the Prankster, who now resents Fresco for stealing his thunder.

"When you pull this [next] stunt," warns the Prankster, as Fresco prepares to set out on his second crime as the Prankster, "remember you're working for me! If I catch you grabbing any glory for yourself, there'll be trouble!"

"It'd serve him right if I went on my own and made him look like a piker!" muses Fresco resentfully. "By golly, I'll do it! I'll use Prankster techniques with new twists to make front page headlines, dethrone him as clown king of the underworld, and take over in my own right as the Trickster!"

In the days that follow, Al Fresco stages a series of spectacular, prank-filled crimes as the Trickster while simultaneously sullying the reputation of his former employer by committing a series of ignoble, penny-ante crimes—such as robbing a blind man, stealing a child's piggy bank, and mugging a little old lady—while disguised as the Prankster. Before long, the Prankster has become the laughingstock of Metropolis and the pariah of the underworld, but, ultimately, Superman apprehends the Prankster and then, through an elaborate ruse, lures the Trickster into the open and takes him into custody (S No. 69/1: "The Prankster's Apprentice!").

In May-June 1951, inspired by a television dramatization of "The Pied Piper of Hamelin," the Prankster sets in motion an elaborate scheme designed to enable him and his henchmen to commit a series of spectacular crimes without the risk of interference by Superman. Posing as a philanthropist interested in providing encouragement to young aspiring journalists, the Prankster—employing the alias Dr. Dawson—approaches Lois Lane and Perry White of the *Daily Planet* and persuades them to publicize a journalism contest for children in which the youngsters who produce the best eyewitness accounts of Superman's exploits will receive prizes to be provided by "Dr. Dawson." Indeed, once news of the contest becomes widespread, Superman is so mobbed by children wherever he goes that he is helpless to prevent the Prankster and his cohorts from staging a series of brazen crimes. Ultimately, however, through an elaborate ruse of his own, the Man of Steel turns the tables on the villains and takes them into custody (S No. 70/3: "The Pied Piper Prankster!").

By September-October 1951 the Prankster and his henchmen have come under the patronage of the Financier, a mysterious criminal mastermind who communicates with his gangland clientele only over closed-circuit television and who provides them with "weekly operating funds" in return for a generous share of their loot. A condition of the Financier's backing of the Prankster, however, is the Prankster's agreement to refrain from committing prankish crimes, for, in the Financier's view, these pranks have invariably led to the Prankster's being captured by Superman.

Determined to convince the Financier that he is fully capable of committing spectacular crimes without resorting to tricks or pranks, the Prankster embarks on a series of "unfunny" crimes totally devoid of whimsical style, unaware that Superman has learned of his arrangement with the Financier and is determined to create a rift between the two villains in order to lure the Financier into the open. Each time the Prankster attempts to commit a crime, Superman acts to thwart the crime while at the same time working behind the scenes to make it appear that the Prankster has violated his agreement with the Financier by reverting to his time-worn prankish style. When, for example, the Prankster and his henchmen attempt to use a "rapid fire gas gun capable of knocking out an entire crowd" to hijack $1,000,000 in cash from a community fund parade, Superman surreptitiously disables the weapon and, by means of his super-powers, makes it appear that the gun is being used to spew forth thousands of pieces of gummed foam rubber to form a gigantic foam-rubber dragon. Panicked by this bizarre development, the criminals flee without their loot, leaving the Financier with the erroneous impression that the Prankster bungled the heist because he could not refrain from performing a prank.

Finally, enraged at the Prankster for what appear to be his repeated violations of their agreement, the Financier—who is secretly a wealthy socialite named Mr. Van Retz—lures the Prankster to a party aboard his yacht, intending to take the Prankster captive and throw him overboard, but Superman arrives on the scene in the nick of time to rescue the Prankster and apprehend the Financier and his cohorts (S No. 72/1: "The Unfunny Prankster!").

In March-April 1952, upon his release from prison, the Prankster establishes a School of Humor, with himself as its president, as the first phase of an elaborate scheme to dupe his unsuspecting students into helping him commit spectacular crimes. For the second phase of his scheme, the Prankster ties up Lois Lane's dentist, and, posing as his replacement, administers to Lois a dose of a fiendish "super-laughing gas" which afflicts her with a zany "pixie sense of humor," causing her to play gags and practical jokes constantly and inspiring her to enroll as a pupil at the School of Humor.

In the days that follow, the Prankster—aided by his unwitting humor students—embarks on a series of prankish crimes, while Lois Lane, under the combined influence of the Prankster and his super-laughing gas, diverts Superman away from the crime scenes by sending him off on a series of wild-goose chases as her way of playing hilarious jokes on him. At the scene of one crime, for example, passersby look on in horror as one of the Prankster's students leaps from an upper-story ledge of a downtown building. The assembled crowd breathes a collective sigh of relief when the man plunging from the ledge turns out to be attached to an elastic rope that safely bounces him back again, but, while the onlookers are thus preoccupied, the Prankster and his henchmen loot a nearby jewelry store. And while the robbery is taking place, Superman, who has raced to the far side of the city in response to Lois Lane's assertion that a baby was recently seen floating in Metropolis's East Bay, discovers that the "baby" referred to by Lois is actually a baby whale and that his visit to the East Bay was just a wild-goose chase.

Ultimately, however, after realizing that the recent rash of robberies have all involved students at

journalist-actor Clark Kent, and he easily apprehends the Prankster and his cohorts before they can successfully carry out the robbery (S No. 87/3: "The Prankster's Greatest Role!").

In March 1954 the Prankster forms a temporary alliance with Lex Luthor and the Toyman in an attempt to commit a series of spectacular crimes (S No. 88/3: "The Terrible Trio!"). (See LUTHOR, LEX.)

PRESTON (Mr.). The owner of the Preston Club, an illegal gambling casino located in METROPOLIS. Smashing his way into the casino after accumulating incriminating photographic evidence of "the gambling machines in action," SUPERMAN demolishes the club's gambling apparatus, pummels the henchmen who attempt to stop him, and ultimately apprehends the fleeing Preston (Act No. 32, Jan '41).

To prevent Lois Lane from revealing what she has learned about illegal gambling at the Preston Club, owner Preston forces her to imbibe an amnesia-producing drug, but Superman restores Lois's memory soon afterward through super-hypnosis, 1941

the Prankster's School of Humor, Superman unravels the details of the villain's scheme, cures Lois Lane of her super-laughing-gas intoxication, and apprehends the Prankster and his henchmen (S No. 75/1: "The Prankster's Star Pupil!").

In February 1954, after the News Association, a journalists' organization, has announced plans to put on a play called *Superman and the Prankster*, with Clark Kent in the role of Superman, the Prankster, enraged at the idea of being bested by Superman in the play, makes a series of attempts to sabotage the production. Thwarted repeatedly by Superman, however, the Prankster takes the place of the actor playing himself on opening night and attempts to drastically alter the play's denouement by having his henchmen, armed with sub-machine guns, stick up the theater and rob the audience. Unknown to the villains, however, Superman is on the scene as

PREXY, G.G. An alias employed by SUPERMAN in November-December 1946 when he poses as a wealthy exporter as part of his plan to pull a well-deserved swindle on the shady operators of the Joe Jipper Promotion Company (S No. 43/1: "The Inventions of Hector Thwistle!"). (See THWISTLE, HECTOR.)

PRINTEMPS (Monsieur). An alias employed by the TOYMAN in January-February 1945 when he poses as a French toymaker and obtains employment as a toy designer at the largest toy store in METROPOLIS as part of his elaborate scheme to recover a fortune in jewels hidden during the French Revolution by the wealthy Count du Rochette (S No. 32/3: "Toys of Treachery!").

PROFESSOR, THE. The "head of the biggest mob in Metropolis," and the owner of Reginald Chauncey Applethwaite III, a golden-haired cocker spaniel whose life is saved by SUPERMAN when he becomes trapped in a caved-in rabbit burrow. The unbounded affection for Superman fostered by this incident—particularly Reginald's penchant for exuberant tail-wagging whenever he senses Superman in the vicinity—enables the Professor and his henchmen to abandon the scenes of their robberies safely in advance of Superman's arrival by using Reginald's tail as a sort of Superman early-warning system and to launch a nearly successful effort to use Reginald's acute canine senses to find and expose Superman in his secret identity. Superman apprehends the Professor and his henchmen in March 1954 and finds Reginald a new home in France, where his unflagging affection will pose less of a threat to the secret of his dual identity (S No. 88/2: "The Dog Who Loved Superman!").

PROFESSOR MEMORY. The stage name formerly employed by a retired vaudeville performer, noted for his phenomenal memory, who finds himself marked for assassination by a gang of ruthless bank robbers who know that he has seen, and therefore probably memorized, a list of the serial numbers of the currency they stole recently from a local bank, information that would enable the authorities to apprehend them as soon as they attempted to dispose of their loot. Posing as the former vaudevillian—in his Clark Kent identity—long enough to draw the criminals into the open, SUPERMAN apprehends the gang with the aid of the METROPOLIS police in May 1955 (S No. 97/1: "The Amazing Professor Memory!").

PROTY II. A Protean creature from the planet Antares who is a member of the LEGION OF SUPER-PETS. Telepathic and protoplasmic like all the members of his race, Proty II has the power to change his shape at will to any form he chooses. In November 1963, when SATURN WOMAN poses as the enchantress CIRCE as part of SUPERMAN's plan to defeat the SUPERMAN REVENGE SQUAD, Proty II aids in the impersonation by molding his "protoplasmic body" around Superman's face and assuming, in turn, the form of a lion's head and then that of a mouse's head to make it appear that "Circe" has used her legendary magical powers to give the Man of Steel the head of a lion and then the head of a mouse (S No. 165/1: pts. I-II—"Beauty and the Super-Beast!"; "Circe's Super-Slave").

PURDY, "PUDGE." A METROPOLIS gambling czar who is awarded the services of SUPERMAN for an entire day as a prize in a contest sponsored by the DAILY PLANET only to be thwarted by Superman at every turn when he attempts to capitalize on his good fortune by using Superman's powers to amass great personal wealth. Purdy and his henchmen wind up in prison when, with their lives in jeopardy, Superman promises to save them all only if Purdy will agree to confess the details of his gambling racket to the Metropolis police (S No. 51/3, Mar/Apr '48: "The Man Who Bossed Superman!").

PURPLE MASK MOB, THE. A gang of criminals, their faces partially concealed by purple bandanas,

who commit a series of spectacular crimes in GOTHAM CITY and environs before they are finally apprehended by SUPERMAN and ROBIN in March-April 1955. BATMAN is confined to the BATCAVE throughout much of the adventure, recuperating from the effects of a slow-acting poison, but it is his skillful deduction which reveals the location of the gang's hideout and enables Superman and Robin to make the final capture (WF No. 75: "The New Team of Superman and Robin!").

PUZZLER, THE. An utterly ruthless villain—an extortionist, kidnapper, and murderer—whose diabolical crimes revolve around the symbolism of parlor games, tricks, and puzzles. His personal symbol is a bent nail, one half of a commonplace nail puzzle, of the type that can be purchased at any novelty shop. Of himself, the Puzzler has made this comment: "A genius at solving puzzles, I decided to utilize the principles that win games to launch a crime campaign unrivaled in history. That I've been successful is a testimony to my brilliance." The Puzzler is also fond of leaving complex clues to the whereabouts of his next crime and the location of his secret hideout, because, in his words, "It tickles my vanity to think I can outsmart SUPERMAN!" (Act No. 49, Jun '42: "The Puzzler!!").

The Puzzler is an expert in games of all kinds, but, as in his battles with SUPERMAN, he frequently comes off second best. He fancies himself, for example, "the world's most brilliant checkers expert," but Superman outplays him in June 1942 (Act No. 49: "The Puzzler!!"). Similarly, although the Puzzler is adept at such varied card games as poker, rummy, blackjack, hearts, casino, and bridge, he is bested by champions in each of these games when he enters a card-playing tournament in January-February 1943 (S No. 20/4: "Not in the Cards").

With vicious swings of a fireplace poker, the Puzzler murders poker-playing champion Harlow Gates, 1943

"Parlor games, tricks, and puzzles can be harmless fun," notes Action Comics No. 49, "--but when a twisted intellect utilizes their principles to commit clever crimes, they can be dangerous indeed." On one occasion, for example, in June 1942, the Puzzler kidnaps LOIS LANE and spins a grisly wheel of fortune to decide her fate. "...[S]hould the indicator land on the red instead of the blue section," gloats the villain fiendishly, "a strangling device will automatically put you out of your misery!" But the game is rendered even more diabolical by the fact that the Puzzler has rigged it in advance to stop on the red. "One minute a gallant sportsman, and the next a doublecrosser!" muses one of the villain's henchmen ruefully. "Must be something twisted in his nature" (Act No. 49: "The Puzzler!!").

On another occasion, in January-February 1943, the Puzzler deliberately sends a carload of his own henchmen hurtling off a bridge as a means of diverting Superman's attention while he himself makes good his escape. "So you're deliberately sending your own men to their deaths--just to save your own miserable hide!" cries Superman. "Anything to outsmart you!" replies the Puzzler. "I'd like to attend to the Puzzler," muses Superman grimly, "--but above all I must save human life...no matter how little those thugs deserve it..." (S No. 20/4: "Not in the Cards").

In June 1942 the Puzzler and his henchmen commit a series of heinous crimes—involving extortion, kidnapping, and attempted murder—only to have Superman pursue them finally to their secret hideout and rescue Lois Lane and five other kidnap victims from the villains' clutches. The Puzzler, however, determined not to be taken alive, clambers up the cables of a high suspension bridge "in a frantic effort to escape," and, cornered finally by Superman, tears himself free of the Man of Steel's grasp and, in an apparently suicidal leap, "plummets down--down toward the far distant water...."

"I wonder if the Puzzler really perished," thinks Superman to himself, after searching the river bottom to no avail, "or if he and Superman are fated to cross wits again?" (Act No. 49: "The Puzzler!!").

In January-February 1943, after being narrowly defeated by champions in six different card games in a card-playing tournament at the prestigious El Dorado Club, the Puzzler angrily pulls a gun on bridge champion Morton Thornton, only to be apprehended on the spot by Superman, who has been covering the tournament in his Clark Kent identity. "Don't look so happy and relieved, you game champions," cries the villain bitterly as members of the Metropolis police force prepare to lead him away. "Somehow I'll escape. And every man who defeated me today will pay with his life for having damaged my pride!" With that, the Puzzler lunges for the light switch, plunges the room into darkness, and escapes.

In the days that follow, the Puzzler, true to his fiendish threat, sets out to avenge his humiliating defeat in the El Dorado Club card tournament by murdering the six men who defeated him in ways suggestive or symbolic of the card games in which they are expert, as when he bludgeons poker champion Harlow Gates to death with a fireplace poker and tries to kill bridge champion Morton Thornton by shoving his car off a bridge.

After thwarting all of the murder attempts but one, however, and apprehending the Puzzler's henchmen, Superman pursues the villain to his secret hideout, where he finds the Puzzler seated in a large glass cubicle situated at the center of a gigantic maze. The pathway through the maze is fraught with deadly perils—including poisonous gas, red-hot flames, and a net of electrically "super-charged wires"—but Superman easily withstands them all. Seizing the glass cubicle with the villain inside it, Superman flies the cubicle to the nearest police station, only to discover, upon his arrival, that the cubicle is empty and that the Puzzler has somehow escaped (S No. 20/4: "Not in the Cards").

PYRAMIDS, THE. The pyramidal royal tombs of the ancient Egyptian pharaohs. Fashioned from huge stone blocks, some of which weigh as much as fifteen tons, they are among the world's most spectacular architectural monuments. An attempt by EMIL LORING to destroy the Egyptian pyramids with "radio-controlled bombs" is thwarted by SUPERMAN in January 1943 (Act No. 56: "Design for Doom!"). In January 1960, while impersonating Superman, the Kandorian scientist KULL-EX seizes the great SPHINX and the pyramids and piles them up like children's blocks in the Egyptian desert sand as part of his scheme to make Superman the most hated man on Earth (S No. 134: chs. I-III—"The Super-Menace of Metropolis!"; "The Revenge Against Jor-El!"; "The Duel of the Supermen!"). "*See also* GREAT PYRAMID, THE).

Q

QUASMANIA. The home of the Chirroba tribe of "cliff-dwellers," a "rugged" area of "impassable country," located somewhere in South America, to which SUPERMAN travels in July-August 1941 in hopes of finding the "secret cure" to a hideous "yellow plague" that has suddenly broken out in METROPOLIS, a plague described as "an affliction almost exclusive to [the Chirroba] tribe." In the words of Superman No. 11/3:

> Dread doom sweeps down upon *Metropolis* in the form of a mysterious, unknown malady that grips hundreds and sends wholesale terror screaming thru [sic] the streets! **Superman**, aroused by the ghastly peril, comes to grips with an intangible menace that carries him across continents and into incredible adventures until he reaches his goal: the banishment of the dread illness which first renders man repulsive in appearance, transforms him into a raving maniac, then snuffs out his existence!

In Quasmania, Superman finds that Quismado, the evil high priest of the Chirrobas, has murdered the tribe's chief, imprisoned the chief's son, and, with the backing of an American gangster and his henchmen, terrorized the Chirrobas into submission and seized control of the tribe. Together, the villains have "deliberately started the plague in *Metropolis* so we could later demand heavy dough for banishing it!"

Swinging into action with his mighty superpowers, Superman defeats the evil Quismado and his gangland cohorts, restores the son of the murdered chief to his rightful place of tribal leadership, and recovers the secret cure needed to halt the ghastly epidemic in Metropolis. Quismado plummets to an agonizing doom when the "momentum" of Superman racing past him sweeps him over the edge of a fiery volcano, and the evil priest's ruthless underworld allies are annihilated when a stick of dynamite they hurl at Superman rebounds off an outjutting rock and explodes violently in their midst.

QUETZATLAN. An ancient Central American civilization of the tenth century A.D. whose members—including the power-hungry Emperor Quexo; his lovely cousin, Empress Nara; and the benevolent wise man Haxtl—retired to the interior of an ancient pyramid in the Central American jungles ten centuries ago and used their "magic sun globe" to place themselves in a somnial trance so that they could literally sleep through the future that Haxtl warned them would be characterized by "flood, earthquake, famine and wars" and the decline of Quetzatlan civilization.

Awakened from their thousand-year-long sleep in December 1946, when their pyramid is found and opened by an expedition of American archaeologists, Quexo and his followers set in motion their plan to subject all of modern civilization to the dominion of Quetzatlan by using the awesome power of their sun globe to "turn back time 1,000 years—and obliterate all that has been since," thereby undoing the very existence of the modern world and replacing it with the magically recreated pyramids and great stone structures of ancient Quetzatlan. Indeed, as SUPERMAN gazes out over the Central American landscape surrounding the just-opened pyramid, he sees before him not the overgrown jungle tangle of only moments before, but rather "ancient Quetzatlan, as it was before a thousand years of earthquakes and jungle growth buried it!" Already, "everything has changed within a circle a mile across—and the circle is spreading," so that unless the miraculous reemergence of Quetzatlan is somehow checked, everything that mankind has produced in the last millennium will vanish, replaced for all time by the reawakened civilization of Quetzatlan.

"Believe me," says Haxtl, when Superman objects to this scheme to obliterate man's achievements of the last thousand years, "it is best that your civilization perish! What has it brought forth but wars, intolerance, crime, hatred?"

"I'll admit there's a dark side to our world," confesses Superman, "—but there's another side, too! And it's the hope of billions, instead of just a few...!"

Indeed, it is to press home this view—and thereby hopefully persuade the ancient survivors of Quetzatlan to smash their magic sun globe and, by so doing, banish the ever-expanding civilization of Quetzatlan and restore the world of the twentieth century—that Superman takes Quexo, Nara, and Haxtl on a whirlwind tour of the modern world, showing them modern hospitals and schools and describing in glowing terms the virtues of democracy and the prosperity of America's workers in a last-ditch attempt to persuade the Quetzatlan survivors that a thousand years of civilization have greatly benefited the life of man.

Only Quexo, unwilling to abandon his lust for imperial power, remains unmoved by Superman's plea. Enraged at Nara and Haxtl for having been won over by Superman's arguments, he attempts to hurl them into the generators of an electrical power plant, only to topple over backwards onto some high-voltage power lines, which electrocute him instantly with their thousands of volts of surging electricity. Nara and Haxtl, for their part, agree to the immediate destruction of the magic sun globe and resolve to become contributing members of modern civilization. "Our only dream," says Nara, "is that people shall live together wisely and peacefully!" (Act No. 103: "The Road to Happiness!").

QUEX-UL. A "famous scientist" of KRYPTON who was sentenced to twenty-five years in the PHANTOM ZONE—for a crime he did not commit—by a Kryptonian "justice council" headed by SUPERMAN's father (see JOR-EL), after the real perpetrator of the crime, who was himself never prosecuted, had hypnotized Quex-Ul into admitting his guilt and accepting his undeserved punishment.

Released from the Phantom Zone by Superman upon the expiration of his sentence in November 1962, Quex-Ul—who still views himself as a criminal and remains ignorant of his own innocence—acquires super-powers identical to Superman's in the atmosphere of Earth and immediately sets out to wreak vengeance on Superman for his father's

Superman and Quex-Ul, 1962

role in his conviction by exposing Superman to the baleful radiations of gold KRYPTONITE, which would permanently strip Superman of his mighty super-powers.

Filled with remorse, however, when he learns that Superman has actually gone so far as to return through the time barrier to Krypton at the time the original crime was committed in order to prove Quex-Ul innocent of any wrongdoing, Quex-Ul hastily intervenes to prevent Superman from exposing himself to the gold kryptonite, but only at the cost of voluntarily exposing himself to the destructive radiations in Superman's stead. Stripped forever of his super-powers by the radiations of the gold kryptonite—and afflicted with "permanent amnesia" as the result of kryptonite damage to "some of his brain's memory cells"—Quex-Ul loses all recollection of his Kryptonian past and of his years in the Phantom Zone and, at the suggestion of Superman and with the cooperation of PERRY WHITE, is now employed in an ordinary workaday job in the production department of the DAILY PLANET (S No. 157/1: "The Super-Revenge of the Phantom Zone Prisoner!").

QUICKSILVER KID, THE. The nickname bestowed on the god MERCURY by the METROPOLIS underworld when he visits America in January-February 1944 (S No. 26/4: "The Quicksilver Kid!").

QUIGLEY. "The famous big-game hunter" who is secretly "THE ARCHER" (S No. 13/2, Nov/Dec '41).

QUINN COLLEGE. A college where CLARK KENT and LOIS LANE become honorary professors of journalism—and where they train two star pupils, Andy Parkes and Greta Lee, for jobs on the DAILY PLANET—after being honored as joint recipients of "the annual trophy for prize reporting" at a "newspapermen's banquet" in Metropolis Hall. When gamblers kidnap the school's star quarterback to prevent him from playing in the season's major football game, SUPERMAN apprehends them (S No. 64/1, May/Jun '50: "Professor Lois Lane!").

R

RAINBOW CANYON. A deep natural gorge on the planet KRYPTON traversed by a rainbow of breathtaking beauty. SUPERMAN visits Rainbow Canyon in the course of his passionate romance with LYLA LERROL (S No. 141, Nov '60: "Superman's Return to Krypton!" pts. I-III—"Superman Meets Jor-El and Lara Again!"; "Superman's Kryptonian Romance!"; "The Surprise of Fate!").

RAINBOW DOOM, THE. The name given to the ghastly fate that appears to befall anyone who ventures too close to SUPERMAN in November 1955. In an effort to flush out a gang of gold thieves and discover the hiding place of their stolen loot, Superman sets in motion an elaborate ruse in which he pretends that, as the result of his recent contact with a bizarre rainbow-ringed fireball in outer space, he has become afflicted with a dreadful power which turns everything in his immediate vicinity—people as well as objects—into solid glass. When the gold thieves attempt to transfer their cache of stolen gold to a safer location in order to safeguard it against Superman's "rainbow doom," the Man of Steel apprehends them (S No. 101/3: "The Rainbow Doom").

RAINMAKER, THE. A "fiendish" extortionist who, having "learned how to govern rainfall" by means of his diabolical "rain-machine," embarks on a calculated campaign of terror—including such murderous acts as the creation of a torrential rainstorm designed to wash away Rutherford Utilities' Imperial Dam and inundate the valley beneath it—in an effort to extort large sums of money from utilities magnate B. Drexel Rutherford. Thwarted repeatedly by SUPERMAN—in spite of the fact that he does succeed in bringing Superman to the brink of "overpowering weakness" with his "radical new paralysis gas"—the Rainmaker dies when, while attempting to escape from the Man of Steel, he trips and smashes his skull against a rock (WB No. 1, Spr '41).

RAMA. An alias employed by LOIS LANE in April 1959 when she poses as a survivor of the exploded planet KRYPTON as part of an elaborate scheme to trick SUPERMAN into revealing the secret of his dual identity (S No. 128/2: "The Sleeping Beauty from Krypton!").

RAMSEY, HOMER. An alias employed by SUPERMAN in April 1939 when, posing as an investor, he buys up a huge quantity of worthless oil stock as part of his plan to teach a well-deserved lesson to a pair of crooked stock promoters—Messrs. Meek and Bronson—by swindling them out of $1,000,000 (Act No. 11), money which Superman later uses as part of his anonymous donation to the boys of KIDTOWN in August 1939 (Act No. 15).

RAMSEY, JONATHAN (Major). A widely respected hero of World War I who, despite his protestations of innocence, is tried and then convicted of treason when records confiscated at the headquarters of the "101% Americanism Society," a front for Nazi espionage, identify him as the head of the fifth column movement in America. Skeptical at first of Ramsey's innocence, SUPERMAN ultimately exonerates Ramsey, establishes that he was the victim of a Nazi frame-up, and apprehends the unnamed citizen who is in reality the fifth-column movement's secret leader (S No. 25/1, Nov/Dec '43: "The Man Superman Refused to Help!").

RAND, BRETT. "One of the wealthiest men in the world" and the DAILY PLANET's "biggest advertiser," a "handsome multi-millionaire" who, since their college days together, has had a serious crush on LOIS LANE. When Lois rejects Rand's proposal of marriage in August 1960 on the ground that her only marital ambition is to become the bride of SUPERMAN, Superman sets in motion an elaborate charade designed to make Lois believe that he has decided to marry LORI LEMARIS and live in ATLANTIS so that Lois will feel free to marry Brett Rand and stop wasting her life waiting for him to propose to her. Superman finally abandons his silly hoax, however, after Lois has rejected Rand a second time despite Superman's announced intention to marry another woman. "If I can't have **Superman**," she tells Rand firmly, "I don't want **any** man!" (S No. 139/1: "The New Life of Super-Merman!").

RANDALL (Coach). An unscrupulous football coach at Dale University who, faced with dismissal from his job unless his team wins its upcoming championship game with Cordell University, hires two hoodlums to pose as collegians and play for Dale so that, by using dirty tactics, they can injure Cordell's best players and get them removed from the game.

After injecting Cordell player Tommy Burke with a knockout drug and leaving him imprisoned in his own apartment, SUPERMAN takes to the playing field disguised as Burke and puts on a virtuoso display of one-man football that routs Coach Randall's team completely and foils his scheme to fix the game (Act No. 4, Sep '38). The story is reprinted in Superman No. 1/4 (Sum '39).

RANDALL (Colonel). The commander of a group of U.S. military personnel whose aircraft is shot down by the Japanese and their Nazi allies while the Americans are en route over the Arctic on a mission to locate sites for new airfields across the North Pole. Another purpose of the Americans' mission is to gather data for America's military engineers that will facilitate the establishment of an Arctic air route in order to create a new supply line to Russia and air bases from which to attack the Japanese in the Pacific. SUPERMAN rescues Colonel Randall and his men—and defeats their Axis captors—in September-October 1943 (S No. 24/4: "Suicide Voyage!").

RAS-KROM. A superstitious Kryptonian criminal and PHANTOM ZONE escapee who attempts to free his fellow outlaws from the Phantom Zone so that together they can form a "super-gang" for the conquest of the universe, only to be outwitted and finally reimprisoned in the Zone by SUPERMAN and JIMMY OLSEN in October 1963 (S No. 164/2: "The Fugitive from the Phantom Zone!").

RASPER, JASPER. A mean-minded old skinflint who makes a dastardly attempt to "sabotage Christmas" by feeding Santa Claus chocolate candy coated with a fat-producing "wonder drug" that makes him too fat to fit down chimneys, and by dosing his reindeer fodder with a debilitating chemical that makes the animals too ill to pull the magic sleigh. SUPERMAN rescues Christmas from disaster by helping Santa trim down to his normal weight and by flying his sleigh around the world in place of the sickened reindeer, and when Jasper Rasper is accidentally stranded on an ice floe, it is Superman who swoops down to save him.

"Why did you want to sabotage Christmas, Rasper?" asks Superman.

"I jostled and fought my way up from poverty without scruples." replies Rasper. "No one ever gave me a helping hand, and my formula for success was to be trickier than my neighbor.

"I hated Christmas, with its talk of charity and good will! It made a mockery of my hard-boiled philosophy. I decided to sabotage the holiday!

"But now that you have saved my life, I'm beginning to wonder maybe I've been wrong. Maybe there is something to the 'good will toward men' reasoning...."

"If you see the error of your ways, Rasper," chimes in Santa, "there's hope for you" (Act No. 105, Feb '47: "The Man Who Hated Christmas!").

RAVA. An evil extraterrestrial alien—a native of the planet Wexr II—who is a leader of the SUPERMAN REVENGE SQUAD. In March 1962 Rava concocts a diabolical scheme for wreaking vengeance on SUPERMAN by keeping the Man of Steel demoralized with a series of red-kryptonite-induced nightmares (Act No. 286: "The Jury of Super-Enemies!") while he and his followers annihilate all life on Earth. The scheme is ultimately thwarted by Superman, but Rava and his cohorts escape into outer space before Superman can apprehend them (Act No. 287, Apr '62: "Perry White's Manhunt for Superman!"). (See SUPERMAN REVENGE SQUAD, THE.)

RAYMOND, CUSHIONS. A "big time mob-boss" and leader of a gang of criminals who are captured by police while fleeing the robbery of the Metropolis Bank when their getaway helicopter is forced to the ground by SUPERMAN in January 1954. Superman's efforts to apprehend the Raymond gang are severely hampered by the fact that the near-explosion of a "runaway nuclear pile" has temporarily transformed the Man of Steel into "a glowing mass of radiation," making him "so radioactive, he's death to anyone he comes near" and forcing him into self-imposed exile atop Bald Rock Mountain, "miles from Metropolis" (Act No. 188: "The Spectral Superman!").

RED. The leader of a gang of criminals who are apprehended by SUPERMAN in July 1954 while attempting to pull "the biggest job in the history of Metropolis": the sabotaging of the city's main power plant and the looting of the city after it has been plunged into darkness. Superman's crime-fighting efforts, and in fact all of his activities during this period, are severely hampered by the fact that a strange cloud of "metallic cosmic dust" from outer space, drawn toward METROPOLIS by the huge exhibition of diamonds currently on display there, is attracted to Superman by the "electrical current" he emits whenever he exerts his "super energy," creating a "dense fog" that makes it almost impossible for the Man of Steel to see while he performs his super-feats (S No. 90/1: "Superman's Last Job!").

RED RAVEN. The leader of the Red Raven Gang, a gang of criminals whom BATMAN helps apprehend during an unplanned visit to an extradimensional parallel world.

Forced to crash-land the BATPLANE during a violent thunderstorm in September 1963, Batman finds himself on "a twin world" of his own world—on "another Earth," where "evolution has paralleled [his] world's--but with minor variations!" In this dimension, there is no Batman; SUPERMAN is the crime-fighting partner of ROBIN; VICKI VALE is a perfect look-alike for the LOIS LANE who inhabits Batman's world; there is no BATWOMAN; Superman is secretly BRUCE WAYNE, although his features are identical to those of the CLARK KENT Batman knows; and the grotesque face of the JOKER is really the greasepaint mask of a television comedian named Freddy Forbes.

Not realizing at first that he has landed on a world other than his own, Batman is taken for a costumed criminal—even a lunatic—until finally he succeeds in demonstrating his goodwill by helping the extradimensional Superman apprehend the Red Raven Gang, whereupon the counterpart Superman helps the bewildered Batman return in the batplane to the familiar Earth he accidentally passed out of in the course of the thunderstorm (WF No. 136: "The Batman Nobody Remembered!").

REED, HARRY. A "notorious gambler" who, during the period when the DAILY PLANET is conducting a contest between CLARK KENT and LOIS LANE to determine "who's more able to live alone under primitive conditions--the man or the woman," attempts to rig the outcome of the contest in Lois Lane's favor so that he and his cronies can collect the huge bets they have placed on her to win. Lois does indeed win the contest, but Reed is apprehended by

SUPERMAN in March 1951 (Act No. 154: "Miss Robinson Crusoe!").

REEFER, BIG JOE. A METROPOLIS racketeer who deliberately smashes a model ship constructed by schoolboy Jimmy Tuttle in an effort to enable his own kid brother, Hugo Reefer, to win a model shipbuilding contest sponsored by the DAILY PLANET Jimmy ultimately wins the contest with a new model of a Spanish galleon, and Reefer and his henchmen wind up in prison through the heroic efforts of SUPERMAN (S No. 28/2, May/Jun '44: "The Golden Galleons!").

REGOR. The "super-champion" of the planet Uuz, an "invincible opponent" of evil—clad in a red-and-green costume with white fur trim, a green cape and boots, a yellow belt, and a green letter "R" on a yellow field emblazoned on his chest—who battles crime on the planet Uuz just as SUPERMAN fights it on the planet Earth. In his everyday identity, Regor is Winki Lamm, mild-mannered television interviewer, but in reality, just as Superman is an orphan from the planet KRYPTON, Regor is an orphan from the planet Earth, the son of "famous rocket scientist" James Flint who, while Regor was still an infant, fired him into space in a model rocket when his secluded island laboratory sank into the sea in the throes of a mighty volcanic eruption. On the planet Uuz, where the gravity is "far weaker than that of Earth" and where buildings and automobiles are made out of glass, a substance opaque to the eyes of ordinary Uuzians, Regor possesses super-human powers similar, although not identical, to those of Superman on Earth.

In May-June 1949, when an Uuzian "master of crime" named Bantor hatches a scheme to hijack large numbers of the "personal heaters" which Uuzians use to survive the rigors of their planet's frigid environment, Superman helps Regor recover the heaters and bring Bantor and his henchmen to justice (S No. 58/3: "The Case of the Second Superman").

REILLY (Detective Captain). A "conceited windbag" of a detective—famous, nevertheless, for having successfully captured every one of the 800 fugitives he has been assigned to track down—who is imported from Chicago to apprehend SUPERMAN for the crime of having "torn down [the city's] slum area" without public authorization, "causing modern apartments to replace crowded tenements" (see GIMPY).

"Regardless of his motives and our personal approval of them," exclaims the police chief, "the fact remains that he has wantonly destroyed public property and must pay the full penalty to the law just like any other transgressor!"

Repeatedly outwitted by Superman in February 1939, Reilly suffers his worst humiliation when he lunges headlong at Superman and knocks himself unconscious against Superman's "super-tough" skin (Act No. 9).

RENALDO, HUGO (Dr.). An underworld medical practitioner who, posing as an eminent psychiatrist, volunteers his professional services to mentally disturbed artist Paul McKenzie—a painter "famous for his magnificent portrayals of heroes in action" until a tragic "mental collapse" caused his once-realistic art style to become disoriented and irrational—as the first step in an elaborate scheme to keep SUPERMAN so busily occupied helping McKenzie with his mental problems as to leave him powerless to prevent Renaldo's gangland cohorts from looting METROPOLIS. Renaldo and his underworld allies are apprehended by Superman in July 1952 (Act No. 170: "The Mad Artist of Metropolis!").

RHODES, PRISCILLA. An alias employed by LOIS LANE in May-June 1953 when, after faking her own death to prevent criminals from continually using her as a hostage against SUPERMAN, she dons eyeglasses and dyes her hair blond in order to obtain a job as file clerk in the offices of the DAILY PLANET (WF No. 64: "The Death of Lois Lane").

RIKKER, HORACE. The "inventor turned crook" who is the leader of the Amphi-Bandits, a gang of criminals who "steal a car for each job, hit like lightning, get to a speedboat, and elude all harbor-patrol traps" by means of a special submersible boat, equipped for underwater travel, which carries them across the river and through the underground stream leading to their secret hideout beneath an abandoned mansion. Rikker and his Amphi-Bandits are apprehended by SUPERMAN in November 1945 (Act No. 90: "Rookery for River Rats!").

RINTON. The inventor of "the Rinton reverse time ray," a device for time travel which, activated inadvertently in January-February 1947 in the office of the DAILY PLANET accidentally transports both CLARK KENT and LOIS LANE to early-seventeenth-century London in the time of WILLIAM SHAKESPEARE (S No. 44/3: "Shakespeare's Ghost Writer!").

RIVA (Swami). An unscrupulous fortune-teller and swindler—in reality a onetime carnival sharpie whose real name is Dan Rivers—who, not realizing that the decorative jewel in his turban is actually KRYPTONITE, comes to believe that he is the possessor of some extraordinary occult power that enables him to weaken and paralyze SUPERMAN merely by approaching him. Swami Riva—who, according to Superman No. 61/3, is the first villain ever to employ kryptonite, however unwittingly, as a weapon against Superman—is apprehended by Superman in November-December 1949, along with a gang of hijackers who have hired the evil swami to protect them from Superman ("Superman Returns to Krypton!").

ROBIN (the Boy Wonder). The courageous, warm-hearted, hard-fighting, pun-loving teen-ager who, since April 1940, has been the inseparable crime-fighting companion of BATMAN (Det No. 38). Robin is in reality Dick Grayson, the young ward of socialite Bruce Wayne, the man who is secretly Batman. When Grayson was orphaned by the tragic death of his parents—a husband-and-wife team of circus trapeze artists slain by racketeers—it was Batman who took the grief-stricken youngster under his wing, helped him avenge the death of his parents, trained him for his new life as a crime-fighter, and, as Bruce Wayne, took the legal steps necessary to establish himself as Grayson's "legal guardian" (BM No. 213/1, Jul/Aug '69: "The Origin of Robin!"). Since then, Robin has fought alongside Batman in virtually every one of Batman's amazing adventures.

From mid-1954 onward, Batman, Robin, and SUPERMAN regularly participate in certain of their adventures together. Wherever Batman, Robin, and Superman appear together as co-participants, that adventure is treated in this volume. (For a complete account of the life and career of Robin apart from his involvement with Superman, consult *The Encyclopedia of Comic Book Heroes: Volume I—Batman.*)

ROBIN HOOD. The alias employed by a modern-day Robin Hood who, clad in the green costume of his legendary namesake and following in his famous footsteps, robs "the unjustly rich to aid the poor. Why? Because I sympathize with the underdog--and do something about it!" In May-June 1943, however, after a series of spectacular escapades in which he victimizes the corrupt and the criminal in order to aid the poor and the unfortunate, Robin Hood becomes disenchanted with his selfless role (I've stolen hundreds of thousands...could have kept it for myself...but gave it all away. Maybe I've been a sap...outwitting the law is a cinch...why shouldn't it pay...??"), forms an alliance with gangland kingpin "Beetlebrow" Macklin, and with his help launches "a vicious crime wave" that swamps METROPOLIS. Macklin and his henchmen are ulti-

Robin and Batman, 1957

mately apprehended by SUPERMAN with the aid of local police, but Robin Hood dies when, torn again by conflict over his newly adopted role ("All this illegal money I'm making...it brings me no pleasure or satisfaction"), he heroically intercepts a fusillade of gangland bullets intended for LOIS LANE. "I—I was a fool to try to...work outside the law," gasps the dying outlaw. "If...if I wanted to help others...I should have joined the police force...please--one last favor...return the [stolen] money...compliments of...Robin Hood..." (S No. 22/4: "A Modern Robin Hood!").

ROBOT MASTER, THE. A group alias employed by six members of the LEGION OF SUPER-HEROES—BRAINIAC 5, CHAMELEON BOY, COSMIC BOY, LIGHTNING LAD, SATURN GIRL, and SUN BOY—in April 1962, when they play an elaborate hoax on SUPERMAN and SUPERGIRL as a prelude to celebrating the anniversary of Supergirl's arrival on Earth (S No. 152/1: "The Robot Master!").

ROCCA, ANTONINO. The "famed wrestling star" who helps SUPERMAN bring "notorious gang-leader" DUKE MARPLE to justice in August 1962 (S No. 155/2: "The Downfall of Superman!").

ROGERS. The pilot of the world's "first manned rocket," which is hurled into MOON orbit by SUPERMAN in December 1958 and then caught by Superman when it descends to Earth again. Due to a mysterious "chemical reaction" resulting from his simultaneous exposure to the light of the moon and the eerie glow of a passing comet during his brief journey through space, Rogers soon launches a spectacular career in crime as the MOONMAN (WF No. 98: "The Menace of the Moonman!").

ROHTUL. A ruthless villain of the thirtieth century A.D. who is a descendant of renegade scientist LEX LUTHOR. Rohtul, in fact, is Luthor spelled backwards.

In the year 2957 A.D., Rohtul and his henchmen steal a wide array of scientific apparatus to enable them to build a "destruction-ray projector of tremendous range" with which to terrorize the Earth, but BATMAN, ROBIN, and SUPERMAN track the villains to their stronghold on the MOON and ultimately take them into custody (WF No. 91, Nov/Dec '57: "The Three Super-Sleepers!").

ROKK AND SORBAN. A pair of ruthlessly amoral gambling addicts from the planet VENTURA, the so-called "gamblers' planet," a far-distant world whose entire civilization is preoccupied with games of chance and where "everyone is trained from childhood in the art of gambling." "With our super-science to support us," explains Sorban in June 1965, "we've no need to work, so we live for gambling!" (WF No. 150: pts. I-II—"The Super-Gamble with Doom!"; "The Duel of the Super-Gamblers!").

Described as "the last surviving members of [Ventura's] hereditary ruling class" (WF No. 150, Jun '65: pts. I-II—"The Super-Gamble with Doom!"; "The Duel of the Super-Gamblers!"), Rokk and Sorban are unemotional, unfeeling, and cold-blooded. They possess awesome "super-mental powers," including the ability to obliterate entire planets, hypnotize entire world populations, and miraculously "alter the atomic structure" of substances with beams of "mental energy" that blaze forth from their eyes (S No. 171/1, Aug '64: "Superman's Sacrifice!").

In August 1964, after having made what to them is a frivolous wager between themselves on the question of whether or not it would be possible to force SUPERMAN to violate his moral code against the taking of human life, Rokk and Sorban journey to Earth and calmly inform Superman that unless he agrees to wantonly murder an individual of his own choosing, they will use their super-mental powers to destroy the Earth. To press home their threat, one of the aliens coolly obliterates a pair of barren planets in the farthest reaches of outer space with twin beams of mental force fired from his eyes. "Our ancient race has developed astounding brain power!" remarks the alien. "I blasted that planet by merely focusing my mental energy. I'll do the same to Earth unless you follow our orders!"

Aghast at the aliens' fiendish threat but still unwilling to violate his code against the taking of life, Superman attempts to save the Earth from annihilation by snuffing out his own life with boulders of green KRYPTONITE, but Rokk and Sorban thwart the Man of Steel's heroic attempt at suicide by using their awesome mental powers to transform the deadly kryptonite into harmless rock, arguing that, by taking his own life, Superman would be "depriving [them] of all the drama" of watching him agonize over the painful choice of whether to violate his moral code or let the Earth be destroyed.

When Superman informs his closest friends that Earth is in danger of being destroyed unless he carries out the aliens' command to commit a wanton murder, JIMMY OLSEN volunteers to let Superman kill him—and LANA LANG actually makes an unsuccessful attempt at suicide—in an effort to help Superman placate the aliens and thus save the Earth.

Superman ultimately resolves his painful dilemma by publicly pretending to murder his "friend" Clark Kent and then telling the aliens that he has fulfilled their request. The aliens only laugh, however, for their mental powers have long since informed them that Clark Kent and Superman are one and the same person. Still, the aliens are plainly impressed at Superman's willingness to sacrifice his reputation as a man to whom life is sacred—and to destroy the alternate identity that has stood him in good stead for so many years—in order to avert their threat to Earth. "... We enjoyed some hours of amusement by matching your super-wits against ours," remarks one of the aliens. "In return, I'll help restore your career."

Indeed, in the next moment, as Superman looks on in amazement, Rokk and Sorban use their extraordinary mental powers to "erase the Earth's memories" of Superman's supposed crime and of their frightening visit to Earth. When the aliens depart and Superman returns home again, he finds that the supposed death of Clark Kent has been completely forgotten by everyone and that only he recalls the details of Rokk and Sorban's ghastly visit (S No. 171/1: "Superman's Sacrifice!").

In June 1965 Rokk and Sorban make a hostage of BATMAN on the planet Ventura in order to force Superman to compete with them in a world-shattering game of "solar system roulette," a heinously cold-blooded game of chance in which the planets and planetoids of Earth's solar system, including Earth itself, are capriciously moved about like chess pawns with "mighty beams of force" which threaten to jerk them from their orbits and send them hurtling toward the sun.

However, with his friend Batman a captive and the very survival of Earth at stake in the Venturans' diabolical "super-gambling match," Superman manages to outplay his alien opponent decisively, thus winning freedom for Batman and survival for Earth (WF No. 150: pts. I-II—"The Super-Gamble with Doom!"; "The Duel of the Super-Gamblers!").

RONAL. The extraterrestrial merman surgeon who is the husband of LORI LEMARIS (S No. 138/3, Jul '60: "The Mermaid from Atlantis!"; and others). The native of a far-distant planet "completely covered by water," Ronal first meets Lori Lemaris in February 1960, after SUPERMAN has brought him from his home in outer space to the subsea realm of ATLANTIS in the hope that he will be able to cure Lori of what even "the greatest surgeons in the universe" have described as a hopeless paralysis. The "merman surgeon from space" does indeed cure Lori, and by the time she is ready to leave the hospital she has fallen in love with him (S No. 135/2: "Superman's Mermaid Sweetheart!").

By July 1960 the couple have married and are living in Atlantis. It is over Ronal's objections that Lori sets in motion her elaborate and somewhat foolish scheme to trick Superman into marrying LOIS LANE (S No. 138/3: "The Mermaid from Atlantis!"). (See LEMARIS, LORI.)

In August 1960 Ronal and his wife help Superman carry out an elaborate charade designed to make Lois Lane believe that Ronal has died in an undersea mishap—and that the Man of Steel has decided to marry the widowed Lori and live in Atlantis—so that Lois will feel free to accept a proposal of marriage from multimillionaire BRETT RAND (S No. 139/1: "The New Life of Super-Merman!"). (See also LEMARIS, LORI).

ROOK, ED. A ruthless kidnapper and swindler—a man, in SUPERMAN's words, "as crooked as a swastika"—who, having kidnapped the wife of Joe Parkus, proprietor of the chain of sporting goods stores known as Sports Emporiums, Inc., forces Parkus to purchase a huge stock of out-of-season sports equipment at ten times what Rook himself paid for it when he used political influence to purchase it from U.S. Army surplus stocks at rock-bottom prices. Faced with the prospect of imminent bankruptcy as the result of having been forced to pay exorbitant sums of money for unsalable out-of-season merchandise—and with his wife's life constantly in jeopardy—Parkus is rescued from his living night-nare by Superman, who apprehends Rook and his henchmen, rescues Mrs. Parkus from their clutches, and uses his mighty super-powers to create a bizarre series of unseasonable weather changes that enables Parkus to dispose of his entire stock of Army surplus sporting goods at an equitable profit (WF No. 25, Nov/Dec '46: "Mad Weather in Metropolis!").

ROSS, ALEXANDER. One of the occupants of Clark Kent's apartment building, a dilettantish and overzealous correspondence-school sleuth who becomes suspicious of Clark Kent's secretive comings and goings and decides he must really be a master criminal posing as a journalist. Fearful that Ross's snooping may inadvertently expose the secret of his dual identity, SUPERMAN quiets Ross's suspicions by assuring him that Kent's unconventional schedule reflects merely his partnership with Superman in rooting out crime in METROPOLIS (S No. 112/1, Mar '57: "Superman's Neighbors").

ROSS, "CHECKS." The leader of the Blackout Bandits, a gang of ruthless criminals and "masters of electrical sabotage" who have been blacking out the business establishments they intend to rob by tampering with the city's electrical cables and then striking without warning under cover of darkness. The Blackout Bandits are apprehended by SUPERMAN in August 1950 (Act No. 147: "Superman Becomes Miss Lovelorn!").

ROSS, PETE. A wealthy geologist who, as a youngster in SMALLVILLE, was a close friend of the teen-aged SUPERMAN. Late one night, while on an overnight camping trip with Clark Kent and other Smallville youngsters, young Pete Ross, lying awake in his tent long after the other campers had fallen asleep, chanced to see his friend Clark Kent changing into Superboy (i.e., the teen-aged Superman) and thus became, completely by accident, privy to the secret of Superman's dual identity. Then and there, Ross vowed to keep his knowledge secret, even from Superman, and never to reveal it to anyone else. On occasion, without Kent's knowledge, Ross even masqueraded as the young Clark Kent to help him preserve his secret identity. To this day, Superman remains completely unaware that Pete Ross shares his closely guarded secret (Act No. 309, Feb '64: "The Superman Super-Spectacular!").

In March 1962, while in the grip of a nightmare induced by exposure to red KRYPTONITE, Superman dreams that, in the distant future, the great-great-great-great-grandson of Pete Ross and the great-great-great-granddaughter of LANA LANG are husband and wife, and that they attempt to destroy him by overexposure to green kryptonite. These events, however, are all only a nightmare, and no such confrontation ever actually takes place (Act No. 286: "The Jury of Super-Enemies!"). In a recapitulation of this nightmare which appears in Action Comics No. 287, this descendant of Pete Ross is inconsistently referred to as Ross's great-great-grandson (Apr '62: "Perry White's Manhunt for Superman!").

When METROPOLIS television station WMET-TV inaugurates its new "Our American Heroes" series with a program honoring Superman, "our greatest American hero," Pete Ross appears on the show along with Superman's other friends and admirers to help pay tribute to the Man of Steel (Act No. 309, Feb '64: "The Superman Super-Spectacular!").

ROUND TABLE CLUB, THE. A club in England whose members—the descendants of famous medieval knights—have maintained their ancestors' chivalric traditions, including the wearing of armor and the holding of jousting tournaments, for over 1,000 years. When a fire-breathing dragon—actually a prehistoric monster "trapped in an iceberg and released by a freak thaw"—is sighted in the countryside, the members of the Round Table Club form an expedition to find it, but it is SUPERMAN who battles the creature both in the English countryside and in London until it finally collapses and dies on its own. "...[T]he monster couldn't survive in our atmosphere!" thinks Superman. "Even its flaming breath was caused by its faulty oxidation of carbon dioxide in the air! There is **much more** carbon dioxide in our atmosphere than there was in primitive times!" (S No. 86/1, Jan '54: "The Dragon from King Arthur's Court!").

ROWLAND, HUGH. A member of the resident acting troupe aboard the *Golden Star*, last of the glamorous old-time showboats, and the secret owner of the showboat's mortgage, which is coming due soon. In a ruthless effort to foreclose on the mortgage so that he can transform the *Golden Star* into a floating nightclub, Rowland tries repeatedly to sabotage the vessel to keep its troupe from giving its performances and meeting its mortgage payment, but his nefarious efforts are successfully thwarted by SUPERMAN in March-April 1947 (S No. 45/2: "Showdown on the Showboat!").

ROWSE, ED. A ruthless escaped convict, convicted largely on the basis of CLARK KENT's testimony and now determined to wreak revenge on all those responsible for his conviction, who lures Kent and a number of other people—including the judge at his trial and three prosecution witnesses—to the ghost town of Boneville with the intention of killing them all, only to be apprehended there through the heroic efforts of SUPERMAN in March 1956 (S No. 104/2: "Clark Kent Jailbird!").

ROXAR. A planet in a "distant solar system" which is inhabited by the Automs, a race of highly intelligent, civilized robots. SUPERMAN journeys to Roxar for an encounter with LEX LUTHOR in September 1962 (Act No. 292: "When Superman Defended His Arch-Enemy!"; *see also* Act No. 294, Nov '62: "The Kryptonite Killer!").

R24. The code name of a mysterious underworld kingpin whose henchmen are engaged in the illicit mining and smuggling of uranium from the fringes of the federal government uranium mine at Grass Mountain, north of METROPOLIS. Handicapped by temporary amnesia resulting from an encounter with KRYPTONITE, SUPERMAN nevertheless apprehends R24 and his cohorts in July-August 1951 (S No. 71/1: "Clark Kent's Super-Masquerade!").

RUGGLES, "ACE." The leader of a gang of criminals whose capture by METROPOLIS police in January 1961 comes as the culmination of an elaborate scheme—devised by SUPERMAN and carried out with the cooperation of AQUAMAN—in which Aquaman poses as a comic-strip super-hero (*see* MENTAL MAN) come miraculously to life in order to trick Ruggles and his henchmen into taking part in an armored car robbery so that they can be easily apprehended (Act No. 272: "Superman's Rival, Mental Man!").

RUNYAN. ADOLPHUS (Prof.). A world-renowned scientist who has discovered "the most deadly weapon modern warfare has ever seen," a poison gas "so powerful that it is capable of penetrating any type of gas-mask!" In Fall 1939 Professor Runyan is murdered—and the formula 'for his poison gas stolen—by a gang of vicious international "armament racketeers" in the pay of the evil "munitions magnate" LUBANE (S No. 2/2: "Superman Champions Universal Peace!").

RUNYAN, BERT. "A struggling but brilliant young lawyer" who, at the urging of CLARK KENT and with the backing of the DAILY PLANET, makes a daring bid for election to the office of METROPOLIS public prosecutor in November-December 1940 in the face of an all-embracing web of public corruption and criminality that extends from incumbent public prosecutor Ralph Dale and "corrupt political boss" Nat Burly to the host of dishonest politicians, big-time racketeers, and corrupt police officials with whom they are allied and associated. In the words of Superman No. 7/3:

> Crooked politics sabotages the very foundations of democratic government! When SUPERMAN finds the city of METROPOLIS infested by evil, conniving public officeholders, he begins a clean-up campaign which for sheer thoroughness and unorthodox procedure has never before been witnessed in the annals of representative government!

Desperate to prevent Bert Runyan from winning election to the public prosecutor's office, Dale and Burly pull every dirty trick in the crooked politician's handbook—from framing Runyan on a drunk driving and hit-and-run charge, to stuffing the ballot boxes and attempted murder—only to find themselves repeatedly thwarted through the heroic intervention of SUPERMAN. Aided by the Man of Steel at every ste of his campaign, Runyan wins election to th prosecutor's post with his pledge to return clea government to the city of Metropolis (S No. 7/3).

RUPEE (Rajah). An alias employed by JIMM OLSEN in May 1958 when he poses as a playbo Indian prince as part of SUPERMAN's plan t apprehend "HONEST" JOHN (S No. 121/3: "Jimm Hits the Jackpot").

RUSSELL, LILLIAN (1861-1922). A Unite States singer and actress—acclaimed for her beauty pleasant singing voice, and flamboyant life-style— who captivated audiences for more than thre decades, principally in light, comic-opera roles SUPERMAN meets the "famous actress," ride through San Francisco with her on a bicycle built fo two, and participates with her in relief efforts for th victims of the great San Francisco earthquake durin a time-journey to San Francisco in the year 1906 (S No. 168, Apr '64: pts. I-II—"Luthor--Super-Hero!" "Lex Luthor, Daily Planet Editor!").

RUSSELL, SKID. The unofficial leader of a band of METROPOLIS "crime kings" who discover an uncharted island in August 1948, name it Island X, and transform it into a haven for the nation's fifty most notorious racketeers. When the gang czars launch a contest to select a "ruler" for their island by seeing which of them can assassinate SUPERMAN, Superman allows the competition to proceed for a time before arresting them all "for the attempted murder of Superman!" (Act No. 123: "50 Ways to Kill Superman!").

RYLIE, BULLWER "BULL." An unscrupulous lumberman who, determined to seize control of the California lumber camp and valuable stand of redwood timber inherited by lovely Betty Wilder, has bribed Betty's foreman, Stan Caxton, to cause a series of "accidents" at Betty's lumber camp with the goal of frightening her lumberjacks into quitting their jobs so that Betty, unable to meet her contractual deadlines for delivering her timber, will be driven into bankruptcy and forced to sell out to him at a rock-bottom price. The scheme is thwarted by SUPERMAN, who outwits the villains at every turn, single-handedly fells the mighty redwoods and prepares them for shipping, and ultimately apprehends both Rylie and Caxton (Act No. 94, Mar '46: "Battle of the Redwoods!").

S

SABRE, "SLASH." A "psychopathic killer" who, having escaped from Metropolis Prison by crawling to freedom through a forgotten storm drain, sneaks aboard ZIGI AND ZAGI's spacecraft to take a rest, believing the craft to be nothing more than a colorful playground fixture or a movie prop. When Zigi and Zagi board the spacecraft a short while later and pilot it to their home planet "in the Alpha Centauri system" (Act No. 315, Aug '64: "The Juvenile Delinquents from Space!"), Sabre is knocked unconscious by the force of the landing and taken captive by the two young space travelers. Sometime later, however, the "maniacal murderer" escapes and, while wandering aimlessly about the alien planet, very nearly causes a planetary cataclysm when his unwitting tampering with a device called a "gravity master" wrenches a gigantic asteroid loose from its orbit and sends it hurtling toward Zigi and Zagi's home planet. SUPERMAN arrives on the scene in time to avert the catastrophe, however, and Sabre is reapprehended by Zigi and Zagi and whisked back to Metropolis Prison inside an alien "teleport bubble" (Act No. 316, Sep '64: "Zigi and Zagi's Trap for Superman!").

SAGDORF. The monocled commander of a "secret base"—nestled in a secluded valley somewhere in the United States and equipped with a munitions plant, a fleet of bomber aircraft, and an army of well-disciplined troops—whose sinister purpose is to serve as a staging area for an entire "subversive army that can strike terror and destruction from the rear when the military forces of the U.S. are attempting to defend the coast against foreign invasion!" SUPERMAN demolishes the secret army base in January-February 1941, systematically destroying its entire store of aircraft and munitions. All that remains, including the evil Sagdorf and every last member of his subversive army, is obliterated when an enemy artillery shell fired at Superman slams into the base munitions plant, detonating an explosion that rocks the secluded valley with a titanic roar (S No. 8/2).

SAN CALUMA. "A small South American country" whose "populace is left in miserable circumstances" when the nation is "ravaged by earthquake and tornado" in September-October 1940. In the United States, an effort is swiftly organized to dispatch boatloads of relief supplies to the stricken country, but a mysterious mastermind named Mumsen is determined to sabotage the relief effort so that he can pervert San Caluma's misfortune into an opportunity to become its dictator: "...None of that food...must be distributed! When the country is at my feet, I shall distribute food...but only if the citizens permit me to take over the government!" SUPERMAN, however, speeds the relief supplies to San Caluma on schedule, and Mumsen is killed when he deliberately detonates an explosion designed to kill both himself and the Man of Steel (S No. 6/3).

SAND, CARL (Dr.). A noted criminologist who angers the entire city by declaring that "there is not a single completely honest man in all Metropolis," only to have SUPERMAN and LOIS LANE prove him wrong when, after an admittedly long search, they locate a completely honest citizen in the person of studio photographer Sam Nichols (Act No. 114, Nov '47: "The Man Who Was Honest!").

SANDOR, SANDOR. A reckless movie writer, director, and producer whose fanatical pursuit of cinematic realism has led him to disregard completely the safety of his actors, as when he forces one of them to provoke an actual attack on himself by waterfront hoodlums. Sandor Sandor reforms completely, however, after being taught a much-needed lesson by SUPERMAN in March-April 1951 (S No. 69/2: "Sandor Sandor, Genius!").

SANDS (Professor). The proprietor of the Dreamo-rama, a bizarre theater for criminals where, by means of an elaborate technology, criminals demoralized by their brushes with the law are able to fulfill their fondest gangland fantasies through the medium of ingenious "dream films"—bearing such reassuring titles as *Escape from the Big House, King of Crime,* and *The Great Fort Knox Robbery*—which the gangsters actually experience as though they themselves were cast in the starring underworld roles. Posing as a hoodlum and infiltrating the Dreamo-rama—where, ironically, he wins the opportunity to portray SUPERMAN in Sands's forthcoming dream film *Victory Over Superman*—Superman soon accumulates sufficient evidence to apprehend Sands and his henchmen in March 1953 (Act No. 178: "The Sandman of Crime!").

SAN MONTÉ. A "small South American republic" where a war is raging. Assigned to cover the war in his Clark Kent identity (Act No. 1, Jun '38), SUPERMAN finally brings an end to the fighting by abducting the commanders of the two opposing armies and threatening to beat them senseless unless they agree to settle the war by fighting it out between themselves.

"But why should we fight?" asks one commander.

"We're not angry at each other!" exclaims the other.

"Then why are your armies battling?" asks Superman shrewdly. And after the two opposing commanders have admitted that they do not really know why they are fighting, the Man of Steel adds, "Gentlemen, it's obvious you've been fighting only to promote the sale of munitions!—Why not shake hands and make up?" (Act No. 2, Jul '38). The stories chronicling these events are reprinted in Superman No. 1/1 (Sum '39) and Superman No. 1/2 (Sum '39). (See also NORVELL, EMIL.)

SANTA CLAUS. The patron saint of children and bearer of gifts at Christmas—a big, fat, jolly old man who lives at the North Pole and, on Christmas Eve, soars through the skies in a sleigh drawn by magic reindeer, climbing down chimneys to fill stockings hung at fireplaces with Christmas gifts. When unscrupulous JASPER RASPER concocts a heinous scheme to drug Santa Claus and sabotage Christmas, SUPERMAN intervenes to thwart the plot and rescue Christmas for the children of the world (Act No. 105, Feb '47: "The Man Who Hated Christmas!").

SAPHIRE, HARRY "KING." A METROPOLIS crime czar, forced into hiding by SUPERMAN, who conceals his identity beneath a leaden mask and adopts the alias "the Mask" as part of an elaborate scheme to ruin Superman's reputation by tricking the Man of Steel into impersonating Harry "King" Saphire for investigative purposes, and then by seeing to it that this impersonation is discovered, thus making it appear that Superman is secretly Metropolis's most dangerous criminal. Harry "King" Saphire, alias the Mask, is apprehended by Superman in September-October 1953 (WF No. 66: "Superman, Ex-Crimebuster!").

SARTO, BLACKIE. The leader of a gang of international jewel thieves who hijack the priceless Madras Emerald from the armored car assigned to carry it from the wharf at New York's Pier 56 to the House of Jewels on the fairgrounds of the New York World's Fair, only to be apprehended by SUPERMAN in 1940 (NYWF).

SATURN. The sixth planet from the sun. Superman No. 147/3 describes Saturn as a planet "where there has been no crime at all for centuries...and where everyone can perform amazing mental feats!" The complete absence of crime on Saturn is caused by the weird "radiations" emanating from the "meteor-fragments that form Saturn's rings," radiations which somehow "cancel out Saturn people's criminal traits!" (Aug '61: "The Legion of Super-Villains!").

Among the particles that make up Saturn's rings, asserts Superman No. 122/1, are those composed of a so-called "musical mineral," an exotic substance that emits musical sounds (Jul '58: "The Secret of the Space Souvenirs").

According to Superman No. 128/1, Saturn's "smaller moons" are actually "gigantic, porous 'snowballs,'" satellites that are literally "composed of frozen snow" (Apr '59: chs. 1-2—"Superman versus the Futuremen"; "The Secret of the Futuremen").

SATURN QUEEN, a member of the LEGION OF SUPER-VILLAINS, is a native of Saturn (S No. 147/3, Aug '61: "The Legion of Super-Villains!"). SATURN GIRL, a member of the LEGION OF SUPER-HEROES, is a

native of Titan, the largest, brightest, and most massive of Saturn's ten satellites.

In February-March 1951 SUPERMAN demolishes an unidentified planet that may one day strike Earth, blasting it apart with asteroids diverted from Saturn's rings (WF No. 50: "Superman Super-Wrecker").

In February 1957, for a twelve-hour period, Superman's personality is imprisoned in the body of JIMMY OLSEN, and vice versa, as the result of both men's having unwittingly exposed themselves to the effects of a Saturnian "mentality exchanger" discovered by Superman while exploring the remnants of a long-dead Saturnian civilization (S No. 111/1: "The Non-Super Superman").

In July 1958 Superman journeys to Saturn to obtain a sample of the exotic "musical mineral" from Saturn's rings, and later to Rhea, one of Saturn's moons, to obtain a strange knotted tree. These are but two of a series of eight so-called "space trophies" which the Man of Steel gathers during this period for inclusion in a time capsule which the Metropolis Museum plans to bury in the ground as a gift for the people of the fiftieth century A.D. (S No. 122/1: "The Secret of the Space Souvenirs").

During a time-journey to the twenty-first century A.D., a time when all life on Earth is threatened with imminent extinction as the result of the oceans having been accidentally dissolved "by an atomic experiment," Superman tows several of Saturn's "snowball" moons to Earth to alleviate Earth's catastrophic scarcity of water (S No. 128/1, Apr '59: chs. 1-2—"Superman versus the Futuremen"; "The Secret of the Futuremen").

In August 1961 Superman transforms Saturn Queen from an adversary into an ally, and thereby turns the tables on the LEGION OF SUPER-VILLAINS, by exposing her to the radiations of meteor fragments taken from Saturn's rings and thus curing her of her "villainous tendencies" (S No. 147/3: "The Legion of Super-Villains!").

SATURN GIRL. A member of the LEGION OF SUPER-HEROES. A native of Titan, the largest moon of SATURN, Saturn Girl possesses, like all the inhabitants of Saturn and its satellites, the ability to perform "amazing mental feats," including "super-hypnotism" (S No. 147/3, Aug '61: "The Legion of Super-Villains!"; and others), extrasensory perception (S No. 165/1, Nov '63: pts. I-II—"Beauty and the Super-Beast!"; "Circe's Super-Slave"; and others), and telepathic communication (S No. 156, Oct '62: "The Last Days of Superman!" pts. I-III—"Superman's Death Sentence!"; "The Super-Comrades of All Time!"; "Superman's Last Day of Life!"; and others). Saturn Girl also possesses the power to confer "temporary telepathic powers" on other creatures (S No. 176/1, Apr '65: "The Revenge of the Super-Pets!"). Saturn Girl's real name is Imra Ardeen. The adult Saturn Girl is called Saturn Woman.

In August 1961 Saturn Woman and two other adult

Legionnaires—COSMIC MAN and LIGHTNING MAN—join forces with SUPERMAN in his battle with LEX LUTHOR and the LEGION OF SUPER-VILLAINS (S No. 147/3: "The Legion of Super-Villains!"). (*See* LEGION OF SUPER-VILLAINS, THE.)

In April 1962 Saturn Girl is among the six Legionnaires who play an elaborate hoax on Superman and SUPERGIRL as a prelude to celebrating the anniversary of Supergirl's arrival on Earth (S No. 152/1: "The Robot Master!"). (*See* LEGION OF SUPER-HEROES, THE.)

In October 1962, when Superman is believed to be dying of exposure to VIRUS X, an incurable Kryptonian malady, Saturn Girl is among the Legionnaires who are summoned to the twentieth century by Supergirl to help carry out the gigantic super-tasks that Superman hopes to fulfill as his final legacy to humanity, including the destruction of a "vast cloud of fungus in distant space, that will some day reach Earth and blight all plant life," and the melting of the Antarctic ice, "to make Antarctica a fit place for millions to live in the future," thus ensuring "a home for Earth's expanding population...!" Later, it is Saturn Girl who receives an urgent telepathic communication from MON-EL, inside the PHANTOM ZONE, informing her that Superman is not suffering from exposure to Virus X at all, but rather from the debilitating effects of a nugget of KRYPTONITE that has become accidentally lodged inside JIMMY OLSEN's camera. Indeed, once the kryptonite nugget has been removed, Superman is restored almost immediately to perfect health (S No. 156: "The Last Days of Superman!" pts. I-III—"Superman's Death Sentence!"; "The Super-Comrades of All Time!"; "Superman's Last Day of Life!").

In November 1963, with the aid of PROTY II, Saturn Woman poses as the enchantress CIRCE as part of Superman's plan to defeat the SUPERMAN REVENGE SQUAD (S No. 165/1: pts. I-II—"Beauty and the Super-Beast!"; "Circe's Super-Slave"). (*See* SUPERMAN REVENGE SQUAD, THE.)

When METROPOLIS television station WMET-TV inaugurates its new "Our American Heroes" series with a program honoring Superman, "our greatest American hero," Saturn Girl is among the Legion representatives who journey to the twentieth century to appear on the show and thus help pay tribute to the Man of Steel (Act No. 309, Feb '64: "The Superman Super-Spectacular!").

In October 1964, after Superman has been deprived of his super-powers by the baleful radiations of a mysterious green comet, Saturn Girl and two of her fellow Legionnaires—COSMIC BOY and the INVISIBLE KID—use a "time-force wave carrier" in their thirtieth-century Clubhouse to endow Superman temporarily with their various powers so that he can use them in his upcoming battle with LEX LUTHOR and BRAINIAC. For a period of "a few hours," therefore, until his borrowed powers fade and vanish, Superman is equipped with Saturn Girl's "power of telepathic thought-casting," Cosmic Boy's "power of super-magnetism," and the Invisible Kid's "power of invisibility" (S No. 172: pts. I-III—"The New Superman!"; "Clark Kent—Former Superman!"; "The Struggle of the Two Supermen!").

By April 1965 Saturn Girl has imparted temporary telepathic powers to BEPPO THE SUPER-MONKEY, KRYPTO THE SUPERDOG, and STREAKY THE SUPER-CAT to enable them to communicate telepathically with Superman during a joint adventure in the year 1866 (S No. 176/1: "The Revenge of the Super-Pets!"). (*See* ATWILL, CYRUS.)

SATURN QUEEN. A member of the LEGION OF SUPER-VILLAINS, an organization of super-criminals from the twenty-first century A.D. An attractive redhead from the planet SATURN, Saturn Queen wears a black and purplish-blue costume, complemented by a red belt, with an emblem symbolic of the planet Saturn—a white sphere encircled by a red ring—emblazoned on her chest.

"...I'm from the planet Saturn," she explains in August 1961, "where there has been no crime at all for centuries...and where everyone can perform amazing mental feats! One day, when I traveled to Earth, I felt a sudden desire to outwit the law with my powers of super-hypnotism!...And so I joined the Legion of Super-Villains...!"

In August 1961 the Legion of Super-Villains forms an alliance with LEX LUTHOR in an elaborate scheme to annihilate SUPERMAN (S No. 147/3: "The Legion of Super-Villains!"). (*See* LEGION OF SUPER-VILLAINS, THE.)

In March 1962, while in the grip of a nightmare induced by exposure to red KRYPTONITE, Superman dreams that Saturn Queen and other villains lure him into a trap, put him on "trial" for his alleged "crimes" against them, and sentence him to battle SUPERGIRL to the death in a gigantic arena or else stand by helplessly while they blow up the Earth. These events, however, are all only part of a nightmare, and no actual confrontation with Saturn Queen and her cohorts ever takes place (Act No. 286: "The Jury of Super-Enemies!").

In November 1962, when Superman puts the finishing touches on the new Hall of Enemies in his FORTRESS OF SOLITUDE, Saturn Queen—here described as one of "the most dangerous evil-doers in the universe"—is among the villains and villainesses represented there by colorful wax busts (Act No. 294: "The Kryptonite Killer!").

SATURN WOMAN. The adult SATURN GIRL.

SAUNDERS, JIM. An alias employed by CLARK KENT in March-April 1943 when he obtains employment at Lacey's Department Store both to keep an eye on LOIS LANE (*see* ANDREWS [MISS]) and to gather information on the mysterious thefts that have been taking place there (S No. 21/3: "The Robber Knight"). (*See* GAUNTLET [SIR].)

SCAPELY, JED. A crooked small-town office seeker, running for the post of public works commissioner in hopes of enriching himself through graft, who frames the young son of his opponent for theft and arson in an attempt to win local voters to his candidacy. Scapely and his henchmen are ultimately apprehended by SUPERMAN with the aid of Scapely's honest opponent (S No. 35/2, Jul/Aug '45: "Like Father, Like Son!").

SCARLET JUNGLE, THE. A "weird wilderness" on the planet KRYPTON which teemed with red and purple flora, including huge, maroon, mushroomlike fungi (Act No. 310, Mar '64: "Secret of Kryptonite Six!") and gigantic "moving forests," red in color and vaguely humanoid in form, which literally advanced across the face of the planet "in their yearly migration," forcing Kryptonians in their path to seek shelter in subterranean tunnels until they had passed (S No. 164, Oct '63: pts. I-II—"The Showdown Between Luthor and Superman!"; "The Super-Duel!").

The Scarlet Jungle was also inhabited by a species of Kryptonian fauna known as the "thought-beast," a large, primitive, rhinocerouslike creature—with a spiked tail and a single large horn protruding from its snout—whose most distinctive feature was a televisionlike "thought-screen" atop its head which flashed picture-images of whatever it was thinking (Act No. 310, Mar '64: "Secret of Kryptonite Six!").

It is in the Scarlet Jungle that SUPERMAN and JAX-UR locate the rare "spore-dust" needed to cure the "ghastly spotted plague" sweeping ATLANTIS (Act No. 310, Mar '64: "Secret of Kryptonite Six!").

SCHOOL OF HUMOR, THE. A school of humor and comedy which the PRANKSTER opens in METROPOLIS in March-April 1952 as part of his elaborate scheme to dupe his well-meaning students into helping him commit spectacular crimes. The School of Humor is put out of business by SUPERMAN (S No. 75/1: "The Prankster's Star Pupil!").

SEAL GANG, THE. A "notorious" gang of modern-day pirates—headquartered in an "underground hideout" on the barren desert island of VUMANIA—who make a series of desperate attempts to prevent JIMMY OLSEN from laying claim to the island and thereby uncovering their secret "base of operations." The Seal Gang is apprehended by SUPERMAN in August 1957 (Act No. 231: "Jimmy Olsen, Knight of Metropolis").

SECOND LIFE, INCORPORATED. An industrial community founded by J. WILBUR WOLFINGHAM in September-October 1946 as part of his elaborate scheme to bilk three wealthy members of the Retired Executives Club (S No. 42/1: "The Men Who Wouldn't Quit!").

SELWYN, DIGBY. The immensely wealthy father of SALLY SELWYN (S No. 165/2, Nov '63: "The Sweetheart Superman Forgot!"; S No. 169/2, May '64: "The Man Who Stole Superman's Secret Life!").

SELWYN, SALLY. A lovely blond-haired young woman, the daughter of immensely wealthy Digby Selwyn, who shares a passionate romance with Clark Kent, the man who is secretly SUPERMAN, in November 1963 (S No. 165/2: "The Sweetheart Superman Forgot!"), briefly renewing the relation-

ship in May 1964 (S No. 169/2: "The Man Who Stole Superman's Secret Life!").

In November 1963, after exposure to red KRYPTONITE has temporarily robbed him of his super-powers and afflicted him with total amnesia concerning even his own identity, Superman wanders onto the vast Selwyn estate—clad in the clothing and eyeglasses he customarily wears as Clark Kent—and, suffering from sunstroke as the result of having walked all afternoon in the hot sun, collapses in a faint at Sally Selwyn's feet.

A tearful Sally Selwyn seeks solace in the arms of her father, Digby Selwyn, 1963

Sometime later, when Superman finally regains consciousness, he finds himself lying in a bed in the Selwyn mansion, with Sally and her father, Digby Selwyn, standing concernedly over him. Asked his name, which he cannot remember, Superman blurts out the name Jim White, a pseudonym formed by the unconscious coupling of the first name and last name, respectively, of two of his closest friends: JIMMY OLSEN and PERRY WHITE.

In the days following his recovery, "Jim White" begins working as a lumberjack on the Selwyn timberlands while embarking on a passionate romance with Sally Selwyn. Deeply in love with Sally and determined to marry her, the amnesic Superman even goes so far as to present his beloved with an engagement ring, yet balks at the idea of actually marrying her until he has proven that he can support her alone, without being dependent on her father's millions. In an effort to raise the money he feels he needs, "Jim White" enters the bronc-riding competition in a local rodeo, where a prize of $5,000 is being offered to the man who can stay aboard Black Terror, a wild-eyed bucking stallion, the longest.

In the course of romancing Sally Selwyn, however, "Jim White" has aroused the enmity of Bart Benson, the brutal foreman of the Selwyn lumber camp, who had hoped to marry Sally himself in order to get his hands on her money. By slipping locoweed into Black Terror's feed, Benson transforms the bucking horse into a raging, snorting terror, and although "Jim White" gamely attempts to ride the fearsome stallion, he is, within moments, hurled to the ground, both his legs paralyzed by the violent impact of his fall.

Sally Selwyn truly loves "Jim White" and wants desperately to marry him despite his paralysis, but the amnesic, crippled Superman, still with no inkling whatever as to his true identity, now feels that if Sally were to marry him it would be solely out of pity. Torn by self-pity and indecision, "Jim White" wheels his wheelchair out to a secluded spot atop a high cliff to be alone with his thoughts. As he sits there, however, looking down at the raging river swirling beneath the cliff, Bart Benson, intending only to frighten "Jim White," sends a large boulder hurtling in the direction of "White's" wheelchair, only to have it take an odd, unexpected bounce and crash into the back of the wheelchair, sending the paralyzed Superman plummeting off the cliff into the raging river below. His last sensations are of drowning and then of blacking out. When Sally Selwyn and her father arrive at the cliff's edge, they find the wheelchair overturned and "Jim White" gone.

"He's dead!" sobs Sally. "Jim's dead! He--must have thrown himself into the river, th-thinking I only wanted to marry him out of pity...."

"Did you?" asks Digby Selwyn.

"I loved him," replies Sally mournfully, "... with all my heart!"

One week later, however, Superman awakens in a transparent air-filled chamber in the subsea realm of ATLANTIS, with his friend LORI LEMARIS watching over him. AQUAMAN, explains Lori, had found the drowning Superman and had rushed him to Atlantis, where "a new form of artificial respiration" had been used to bring him back to life. For a week, Lori continues, Superman has been in a delirium, lacking his super-powers, unaware of his true identity. Now, however, the effects of Superman's exposure to red kryptonite have faded and vanished. His super-powers have returned to him, and his memory—except for the period of his romance with Sally Selwyn, which remains a complete blank—has been restored.

And so Superman leaves Atlantis and, in his Clark Kent identity, returns to his job at the DAILY PLANET. "I'm too busy handling great emergencies ever to fall in love!" he muses at one point, silently pondering the question of whether he will ever marry. "Anyway, I'm always afraid girls don't love me for myself--are merely dazzled by my fame and super-powers. I wonder how it would feel to be really loved for-- myself??! I guess ... I'll never know...."

Sally Selwyn, meanwhile, fights to choke back the tears as she gazes at her only memento of her tragically shattered love affair—a photograph taken of "Jim White" and herself at a local barn dance. "I'll never love anyone else," she sobs, "'til the day I die!" (S No. 165/2: "The Sweetheart Superman Forgot!").

In May 1964 Sally Selwyn is deceived into believing that she has found her long-lost love again when she makes the chance acquaintance of fugitive criminal NED BARNES, a Superman look-alike who, having disguised himself in a business suit and a pair of eyeglasses in an effort to elude the police, is now an exact double for Sally's beloved "Jim White." Sally assumes that the traumatic fall into the river must have somehow cured "White" of his paralysis. Barnes, for his part, decides to turn this incidence of mistaken identity to his own advantage by hiding out for a time at the Selwyn mansion.

The situation is confused even further when Barnes quarrels with Sally and stalks angrily away from the Selwyn mansion, and Sally, searching desperately for her sweetheart in hopes of patching things up with him, stumbles upon Superman in his Clark Kent identity—in other words, the real "Jim White"—who has been scouring the area for the fugitive Barnes as well as covering the Barnes story for the Daily Planet. Up until now, Superman has had no recollection whatever of his romance with Sally, but as she takes him in her arms and kisses him passionately, "Suddenly, by an inexplicable trick of the mind, Sally's ardent kiss causes forgotten memories deep within Clark's subconscious to flow back into his consciousness...."

"Great Scott!" thinks Clark Kent with a start. "I remember everything now--everything!! I'm Jim White!!"

Indeed, "with Sally in his arms, Clark recalls his lost love for her...." He takes her in his arms and kisses her again. "Jim's kissing me again!" thinks Sally euphorically, her senses swimming. "I love him so--!"

"Sally--Sally!" thinks Clark Kent. "To think that all along I've had the love of a beautiful girl who loves me for myself alone--not just for my fame as Superman! And amazingly, I didn't know it until now!"

When Sally makes a brief allusion to their recent quarrel, Kent realizes that Ned Barnes has been impersonating him. Retiring alone to a hotel room to think things through, he decides to confront the impostor "Jim White" as Superman and then to ask Sally Selwyn to marry him. "Why not?" he muses. "I love her and she loves me--and I may never again find a girl who truly loves me for myself!"

But by the time Superman arrives at the Selwyn estate, Barnes lies dying at the base of a cliff, having plummeted to his doom during a vicious struggle with underworld assassins bent on murdering Sally. With his last breaths, Barnes—who had fallen in love with Sally during the brief time he knew her—begs Superman not to betray his impersonation.

As Ned Barnes gasps his last, Superman realizes that he is now completely free to reveal to Sally that he, Superman, is her long-lost "Jim White," to tell her "that I love her with all my heart, and want her to become my bride!" Barnes's struggle with the gangsters intent on killing Sally, however, has also reminded Superman that any woman he married would inevitably become the target of gangland retribution. He fantasizes returning home one evening to find his lovely wife slain by underworld assassins. And so, when Sally Selwyn finally appears on the scene, Superman tells her that "Jim White" is dead, that he heroically gave his life protecting her home from armed intruders.

"Oh, no! No!!" cries Sally, stunned to the point of disbelief. "Jim--dead? It can't be true! I won't believe it! This must be some cruel joke! He couldn't have entered my life again, after, after I thought him dead...! Just to die suddenly, like this!"

"Goodbye, Sally!" thinks Superman sadly. "I... wish I could tell you the truth! I-I'd give anything if I were free to marry you--a girl who loves me for myself--"

And so, "Off into the universe flashes Superman, seeking solace amidst the enigmatic vastness of the cosmos...." "Got to get away from Earth for a while," he muses silently, "--and try to forget the irony that I, the most envied man on Earth, can't marry the woman I love because I'm Superman!--Perhaps it won't always be like this!

"I'll keep fighting for justice! I'll help others! How ironic! Mighty Superman can help everyone... but when it comes to my own happiness--I can't help--myself!" (S No. 169/2: "The Man Who Stole Superman's Secret Life!"). (*See also* BARNES, NED; SUPERMAN [section J 5, the relationship with Sally Selwyn].)

SEMPLE, SUSAN. A switchboard operator at the DAILY PLANET who daydreams continually of a love affair with SUPERMAN and who becomes temporarily endowed with an extraordinary array of mind-boggling mental powers—including telepathy, telekinesis, and extrasensory perception—when "a strange experiment" in the laboratory of PROFESSOR WEIRTON gives her "powers that the human race won't acquire for hundreds of eons," thereby transforming her into the virtual super-powered equal of Superman.

Knowing that her powers will vanish in twenty-four hours, and determined to use them to fulfill her long-held dream of marriage to Superman, Susan reads Superman's mind to learn his secret identity and, by threatening to reveal it to the world, finally persuades the Man of Steel that he has no choice but to marry her. As the time for the wedding ceremony—as well as the twenty-four-hour deadline—draws near, however, Superman tricks Susan into miscalculating exactly how long her powers will last, with the result that Susan collapses in a faint in the midst of the ceremony, bereft of her special mental powers as well as her knowledge of Superman's identity (Act No. 163, Dec '51: "The Girl of Tomorrow").

SERGEI'S BORSHT BOWL. A restaurant for artists in Little Bohemia, "the famed artist's section of Metropolis," which is owned and operated on a nonprofit basis by Sergei, a warm-hearted Russian immigrant whose only goal is to eke out a modest living while feeding the poor artists who have become his friends and companions. "Racketeer night-club owner" Biff Condor attempts to terrorize Sergei into vacating his restaurant so that he can construct a fancy nightclub and gambling casino on the site, but Condor and his henchmen are apprehended by SUPERMAN in November 1944 (Act No. 78: "The Chef of Bohemia!").

SHAKESPEARE, WILLIAM (1564-1616). The English player, playwright, and poet whose outstanding literary genius and extraordinary universality have established him as the world's greatest playwright and poet.

In January-February 1947, as the result of their accidental exposure to "the Rinton reverse time ray" (*see* RINTON), LOIS LANE and Clark Kent, the man who is secretly SUPERMAN, are catapulted through the time barrier to the city of London in the year 1606, where Kent changes to Superman in order to rescue William Shakespeare from a gang of men determined to give the famous playwright a vicious beating for caricaturing their leader as the cowardly buffoon Falstaff. During their sojourn in the early seventeenth century, Clark Kent and Lois Lane establish the "world's first daily newspaper," *Ye Daily Planet*, and share a box at the Globe Theatre with Shakespeare at the opening of his play *Macbeth*. In the course of the adventure, Shakespeare deduces that Clark Kent is secretly Superman and announces his intention to write a play about it, but the Man of Steel persuades the renowned dramatist to keep his dual identity secret, repaying him for the favor by using his super-memory to "create" *Macbeth* for Shakespeare at super-speed so that the playwright will have a new play prepared in time for its already-scheduled opening (S No. 44/3: "Shakespeare's Ghost Writer!").

SHALER, ART. A notorious "wanted racketeer"—the man responsible for the recent theft of a "secret atomic cutting-torch" capable of cutting through literally anything—whose capture by SUPERMAN in August 1956 comes as the culmination of an elaborate ruse, devised by Superman, in which Superman pretends to have become suddenly transformed into a greedy "super-miser"—gathering fabulous treasure from the four corners of the Earth and hoarding it inside a gigantic mountain treasure cave sealed with a virtually impenetrable "super-steel door"—so that he can entice Art Shaler into attempting to use the stolen torch to cut his way into the treasure cave and thereby apprehend him (Act No. 219: "Superman's Treasure Hoard"). The story is in many respects similar to Action Comics No. 176 (Jan '53: "Muscles for Money"). (*See* MILLION-DOLLAR MARVIN.)

SHARP, WILLIAM. A racketeer and confidence man who passes off a sideshow strong man as the legendary Atlas—and then stages a cunningly rigged super-strength competition in which "Atlas" appears to be mightier than SUPERMAN—as part of an elaborate scheme to establish Atlas as the world's mightiest mortal so that Sharp can launch a lucrative racket selling his victims "protection" from Atlas. The strong man, who is only an innocent dupe in the scheme, helps Superman apprehend the crafty Sharp in June 1948 (Act No. 121: "Superman versus Atlas!").

SHAW, CRAIG. An arrogant, self-indulgent, reck-lessly irresponsible playboy—secretly engaged in some form of criminal activity, apparently counterfeiting—who becomes engaged to LOIS LANE after a one-day whirlwind courtship in early 1943. Crushed by the sudden engagement announcement, SUPERMAN is heartened to learn that Lois's real motive in encouraging Shaw has been to enable her to verify her suspicions concerning "the source of [Shaw's] huge income," suspicions that lead ultimate-ly to the capture of Shaw and his henchman by Superman after an unsuccessful attempt by the villains to murder CLARK KENT and Lois Lane in a pair of makeshift electric chairs "wired for 20,000 volts of electricity...!" (Act No. 61, Jun '43: "The Man They Wouldn't Believe!").

SHORE, HOLLIS. A "wealthy yachtsman," head-quartered aboard a yacht anchored off METROPOLIS, who is secretly the czar behind Metropolis's petty rackets, a network of relatively low-yield underworld operations, insignificant if examined individually but lucrative in the aggregate, which are relatively secure from police interference since their victims seldom sustain large enough losses to bother report-ing them to the authorities. Drawn finally into the open by means of a ruse devised by SUPERMAN, Shore is apprehended by Superman, with the aid of PERRY WHITE, in September-October 1949 (S No. 60/1: "The Two Identities of Superman!").

SHOTWELL, ALAN. "The world's greatest hunt-er," now dying as the result of the radioactive poisoning he contracted while stalking a radioactive wild boar that had survived an atomic blast, who decides to enjoy one last great chase before he dies by planting a time bomb somewhere in METROPOLIS and challenging SUPERMAN to find him if he wants to learn its location. Superman finally locates the dying Shotwell on a faraway island and tricks him into revealing the time bomb's location, but he allows the bomb to go off on schedule when he learns that its only purpose is to release placard-laden parachutes into the air bidding farewell to Metropolis and bequeathing to the city all of Shotwell's worldly possessions (S No. 59/2, Jul/Aug '49: "The Man of Steel's Super Manhunt!").

SHRINKWATER LAKE. One of the planet KRYP-TON's "natural wonders," a lake which, because its waters contained "some strange chemical," could "shrink ordinary men down to ant size." When, while he was still an infant on Krypton, SUPERMAN was accidentally transformed into a towering giant by his father JOR-EL's "amazing growth ray for plants," Jor-El restored his infant son to normal size by getting him to take a brief dip in Shrinkwater Lake (Act No. 325, Jun '65: "The Skyscraper Superman!").

SILVER. The leader of a gang of criminals who, having "planted an explosive [device] capable of destroying Metropolis," execute an elaborate ruse designed to lure SUPERMAN into a KRYPTONITE deathtrap as the first step in their overall scheme to extort $1,000,000 from METROPOLIS's bankers by threatening to obliterate the city unless the bankers comply. Silver and his henchmen are apprehended by Superman in December 1953 (Act No. 187: "Super-man's New Super Powers!").

SINBAD. A merchant seaman who is the sole survivor of the gold-carrying freighter Pazuza, which sank to the bottom of the Caribbean with a priceless cargo of gold in the midst of a raging storm. In November-December 1945 a gang of criminals steal Sinbad's map showing the location of the sunken vessel and attempt to salvage the gold cargo themselves, but SUPERMAN ultimately apprehends the criminals and delivers the recovered treasure to Sinbad (S No. 37/3: "The Rubbish Robbers!").

SKAR. The far-distant planet which is the home of VITOR VALL (S No. 104/3, Mar '56: "The Super-Family from Outer Space").

SKEPTIC, THE. The mysterious mastermind behind an elaborate scheme to embarrass and discredit the DAILY PLANET by using a diabolical "hate-gas"—a gas which "induces a feeling of hatred in whoever inhales it," causing its victims to commit uncharacteristically violent, destructive acts—to ruin the reputations of four prominent citizens recently selected to be the subjects of laudatory articles in forthcoming issues of the Daily Planet. The Skeptic is in reality Charlie Frost, the janitor of the Daily Planet Building and the brother of Professor Milton Frost, a brilliant scientist, far ahead of his time, who committed suicide after becoming the subject of a jeering article in the pages of the Daily Planet. Determined to wreak vengeance on the newspaper that he holds responsible for his brother's death, the Skeptic is nevertheless apprehended by SUPERMAN in Fall 1943 (WF No. 11: "The City of Hate!").

SKULL VALLEY. A valley, located somewhere "in the lost mountain of Krowak," which is the site of the last surviving remnant of a primitive "ancient civilization." It is from the forehead of a massive stone idol that SUPERMAN obtains the "power-stone" in April 1942 (Act No. 47: "Powerstone"). (See LUTHOR, LEX.)

SKYBOY. The name given by SUPERMAN to a teen-ager from outer space, endowed with superhuman powers similar to Superman's, who arrives on the planet Earth in January-February 1958 afflicted with total amnesia as the result of a collision between his spacecraft and an oncoming meteor. Skyboy, who ultimately recovers his memory with Superman's help, is in reality Tharn, the son of a lawman on the far-distant planet Kormo who dispatched his son to Earth to alert its inhabitants to the recent arrival on Earth of a band of interplanetary outlaws led by the villainous Rawl. On Earth, Rawl and his bandits stage a series of spectacular thefts of copper, Kormo's most precious metal, before they are finally appre-hended through the heroic efforts of Superman, Skyboy, BATMAN, and ROBIN (WF No. 92: "The Boy from Outer Space!").

SLIPPERY ANDY. "One of the smoothest crooks in the country" and, under the alias S. Andrew Bascomb, the owner, founder, and manager of the

Hillcrest Club for Young Gentlemen, a lavishly appointed boys' club for the sons of METROPOLIS's wealthiest families. Slippery Andy has founded the club as a means of "getting the confidence of the kids so they'd case their own homes for us to rob without suspecting," but he and his henchmen are apprehended by SUPERMAN in October 1945 (Act No. 89: "The King of Color!").

SMALLVILLE. The United States town—located "hundreds of miles" from METROPOLIS (S No. 116/2, Sep '57: "Disaster Strikes Twice"), perhaps in the Midwest (S No. 141, Nov '60: "Superman's Return to Krypton!" pts. I-III—"Superman Meets Jor-El and Lara Again!"; "Superman's Kryptonian Romance!"; "The Surprise of Fate!")—where Clark Kent, the man who is secretly SUPERMAN, spent his boyhood after being adopted into the home of JONATHAN AND MARTHA KENT (S No. 146/1, Jul '61: "The Story of Superman's Life!"; and others).

Superman approaches Smallville, 1963

It was near Smallville that the experimental rocket bearing the infant Superman landed after its journey through space from the planet KRYPTON (WF No. 57, Mar/Apr '52: "The Artificial Superman!"; and others). The SMALLVILLE ORPHANAGE, where the Kents brought the infant Superman immediately upon finding him, and where he remained for a brief period preceding his adoption, is located in Smallville (Act No. 273, Feb '61: "The World of Mr. Mxyzptlk!"; and others), and the Kents' farm, where Superman spent his early childhood years, is located somewhere "outside of Smallville" (S No. 152/2, Apr '62: "Superbaby Captures the Pumpkin Gang!"; and others). The Kents' home, where the family moved after selling their farm and where Superman spent the remainder of his boyhood, is located in Smallville, as is Jonathan Kent's general store (S No. 146/1, Jul '61: "The Story of Superman's Life!"; and others), where Clark Kent used to work afternoons after school (S No. 116/2, Sep '57: "Disaster Strikes Twice").

Clark Kent attended elementary school in Small-

ville and attended high school at Smallville High (WF No. 69, Mar/Apr '54: "Jor-El's Last Will!"; and others).

As a teen-ager, Superman performed numerous heroic exploits in Smallville (S No. 97/3, May '55: "Superboy's Last Day in Smallville!"; and others). In his honor, Superboy Day is still celebrated there annually (S No. 116/2, Sep '57: "Disaster Strikes Twice"), as is Superman's Earthday, "the anniversary of the day [Superman] landed on Earth from the doomed planet, Krypton!" (S No. 136/2, Apr '60: "The Secret of Kryptonite!"). Once a year, Superman returns to Smallville to put on a spectacular performance of super-feats for the youngsters at the Smallville Orphanage (Act No. 273, Feb '61: "The World of Mr. Mxyzptlk!").

Superman is Smallville's most illustrious son, but other Smallville residents have played important roles in the chronicles as well, including PROFESSOR LANG (Act No. 298, Mar '63: "Clark Kent, Coward!") and his daughter LANA LANG (S No. 144/2, Apr '61: "Superboy's First Public Appearance!"; and others), POLICE CHIEF PARKER, and PETE ROSS (Act No. 309, Feb '64: "The Superman Super-Spectacular!").

In October 1952 a bomb planted by "DRAGON" LANG's remote-controlled robot explodes in Smallville. There are no injuries, however, and Superman repairs all the resulting property damage (Act No. 173: "Superman's Invulnerable Foe!").

In March-April 1954, during a return visit to Smallville, Superman finds his father JOR-EL's last will and testament buried deep in the ground on the site where the rocket carrying the infant Superman landed upon its arrival on Earth (WF No. 69: "Jor-El's Last Will!").

In July 1954 Superman returns to Smallville for Homecoming Day, a day honoring former Smallville residents who have moved away (S No. 90/2: "Superman's Secret Past!").

In May 1955 Superman returns to Smallville to thwart an underworld scheme to recover $1,000,000 in gold which, following its theft many years ago, was hidden in Smallville by the thieves and never recovered (S No. 97/3: "Superboy's Last Day in Smallville!").

In December 1955 Superman returns to Smallville for a testimonial dinner in his honor commemorating the anniversary of his arrival on Earth as an infant from the planet Krypton (Act No. 211: "The Superman Spectaculars").

In September 1957 Superman returns to Smallville with JOHNNY KIRK, so that, in the town where he himself first embarked on his super-heroic career, he can train Johnny Kirk for his forthcoming career as a super-hero (Act No. 232: "The Story of Superman, Junior"). During this same period, Superman returns to Smallville for a week-long gala celebration commemorating the anniversary of his departure from Smallville to begin a new life in Metropolis. As a tribute to the Man of Steel, the people of Smallville restore all the landmarks of Superman's youth—

including Jonathan Kent's general store—to the condition that characterized them during Superman's boyhood (S No. 116/2, Sep '57: "Disaster Strikes Twice").

In April 1960 Superman returns to Smallville for the town's annual celebration of Superman's Earthday, the anniversary of his arrival on Earth as an infant from the planet Krypton. Among those on hand to attend the festivities are LOIS LANE, JIMMY OLSEN, and PERRY WHITE (S No. 136/2: "The Secret of Kryptonite!").

In May 1962, when ex-convict HAL COLBY—employing the alias Bert Hutton—produces a television tribute to Superman as part of his elaborate scheme to unravel and expose Superman's secret identity, Superman flies to Smallville to appear on the program (Act No. 288: "The Man Who Exposed Superman!").

SMALLVILLE ORPHANAGE, THE. The orphanage, located in the town of SMALLVILLE, to which JONATHAN AND MARTHA KENT brought the infant SUPERMAN after finding him in an open field (Act No. 141, Feb '50: "Luthor's Secret Weapon") on the outskirts of Smallville (WF No. 57, Mar/Apr '52: "The Artificial Superman!"; and others). While most texts refer to it as the Smallville Orphanage (Act No. 273, Feb '61: "The World of Mr. Mxyzptlk!"; and others), at least one text calls it the Smallville Orphan's Home (S No. 161/1, May '63: "The Last Days of Ma and Pa Kent!").

All accounts of Superman's origin agree that the Kents turned the infant Superman over to an orphan asylum (S No. 1/1, Sum '39) or foundling home (S No. 53/1, Jul/Aug '48: "The Origin of Superman!") immediately after having found him. Accounts differ, however, on the question of whether the Kents decided to adopt the infant Superman immediately or whether they formulated these plans later. According to Superman No. 1/1, the Kents delivered the baby to the orphanage and then returned sometime later to adopt him only after discovering that they were unable to get the "sweet child" out of their minds (Sum '39), but Superman No. 53/1 asserts that the Kents applied for adoption immediately and left the infant Superman at the orphanage only temporarily, long enough for their application to be properly investigated. The baby caused such pandemonium at the home with the unrestrained use of his super-powers, continues this text, that the authorities rushed through the Kents' adoption in record time just so they could be rid of the problem infant (Jul/Aug '48: "The Origin of Superman!").

Most texts agree that the Kents decided to adopt the infant Superman the moment they found him (Act No. 158, Jul '51: "The Kid from Krypton!"; and others). Indeed, the more recent texts state that the Kents, knowing they would be asked to explain the origins of the child if they merely kept him or if they delivered him to the foundling home in person, actually left the baby in a basket at the orphanage doorstep, as though he had been abandoned there, so that they could appear at the orphanage the following day (S No. 130/3, Jul '59: "The Town That Hated Superman!")—or several days later (S No. 146/1, Jul '61: "The Story of Superman's Life!")—to adopt him for their own. Each year, Superman puts on a spectacular performance of super-feats for the orphanage's youngsters (Act No. 273, Feb '61: "The World of Mr. Mxyzptlk!").

SMARTYPANTS. A brilliant but spoiled little girl—a protégé of Prof. C. C. Skynhedd, who believes that children will never fulfill their potential unless their every whim is granted—who drives SUPERMAN crazy with her nagging demands until the Man of Steel finally cracks down on this runaway permissiveness in January-February 1949 (S No. 56/3: "Smartypants!").

SMATTEN, JON. A cunning "renegade scientist"—headquartered in a "hidden laboratory" located in a "hide-out cave concealed by lead-ore rock" to protect it from the penetrating gaze of SUPERMAN's X-ray vision—who, having come upon some space-drift wreckage from the exploded planet KRYPTON containing a supply of kryptium, Krypton's "strongest metal," fashions the virtually indestructible "super-metal" into an ingenious robot in the form of an armored knight and sends it forth to annihilate Superman. Superman demolishes the awesome kryptium robot and apprehends its creator in October 1965 (Act No. 329: "The Ultimate Enemy!").

SMIGGS, SAMUEL (Professor). The "wacky wizard of science" who is the inventor of the "if-machine," an ingenious device whose "radiation can change history by reaching through the past to make things happen differently!" When the "Bullet" Barris gang attempt to steal the machine, they are apprehended by SUPERMAN, but a ricocheting bullet strikes the device and damages it beyond any hope of repair (WF No. 38, Jan/Feb '49: "If There Were No Superman").

SMILTER, JOHN. A cunning criminal who, clad in a flame-resistant asbestos suit, ignites a parked fuel truck with incendiary bullets and then lunges through the resulting flames to steal the priceless Fabian diamonds from a dockside customs office. Smilter and his accomplice are apprehended by BATMAN and SUPERMAN in May-June 1952, however, while attempting to escape by helicopter from the deck of the cruise ship VARANIA (S No. 76/1: "The Mightiest Team in the World!").

SMIRT, JAMES. An unscrupulous businessman and generally "shady character," hired by some METROPOLIS racketeers to discredit SUPERMAN's testimony at their upcoming trial, who concocts an elaborate scheme designed to make Superman appear unreliable and irresponsible, first by tricking Superman into publishing his autobiography, principally accounts of his past cases, in the pages of the DAILY PLANET, and then by using kidnapping and terror tactics to force innocent persons to confess that it was they who committed the crimes recounted in the autobiography, and not the various criminals apprehended by Superman. The scheme is ultimately thwarted by Superman, who apprehends Smirt and his gangland cohorts in July-August 1953 (WF No. 65: "The Confessions of Superman!").

SMITH (Mr.). An alias employed by LEX LUTHOR in November-December 1952 when he has a massive fortresslike citadel constructed on a lonely mountaintop overlooking METROPOLIS as part of his elaborate scheme to bilk "some of the richest men in the country" of half their possessions and property (S No. 79/1: "Citadel of Doom!").

SMITH, JEFFERSON. The bogus private detective who is secretly the TOP (Act No. 48, May '42: "The Adventure of the Merchant of Murder").

SMITH, JONAS. A notorious confidence man, swindler, and extortionist—better known to the authorities as "Swindler" Smith—who, posing as a legitimate real estate developer, erects "an exact replica of a Kryptonian city" on an offshore island— renamed Krypton Island—not far from METROPOLIS, ostensibly for the purpose of establishing a futuristic model community as a tribute to SUPERMAN, but in reality as part of a cunning scheme to trick Superman into using his mighty super-powers to transform a dozen lumps of coal into flawless, priceless diamonds for the enrichment of Jonas Smith and his henchmen. The scheme is thwarted, however, by Superman, who apprehends Smith and his cohorts in November 1958 (Act No. 246: "Krypton on Earth!"). (See also KRYPTONOPOLIS.)

SMITH, "SAD SAM." An unhappy, wheelchair-bound billionaire who, having never in his life known the joy of laughter, promises to donate $1,000,000,000 to the Metropolis Orphan Fund if any man in METROPOLIS can make him laugh. Although many famous comics try and fail, Clark Kent ultimately succeeds, albeit by accident, when an unexpected emergency forces him to change to SUPERMAN in Smith's presence and Smith, far from realizing that he has suddenly become privy to Superman's secret identity, begins to laugh uproariously at the very suggestion that meek Clark Kent could possibly be Superman (S No. 136/3, Apr '60: "The Super-Clown of Metropolis!").

SMYTHE (Professor). An alias employed by the PRANKSTER in November-December 1949 when he poses as an inventor as part of his scheme to kidnap LOIS LANE (S No. 61/1: "The Prankster's Radio Program!").

SMYTHE, CASPER. The meek employee of Lacey's Department Store who is secretly SIR GAUNTLET (S No. 21/3, Mar/Apr '43: "The Robber Knight").

SNAGRIFF. A winged dinosaurlike creature of the planet KRYPTON which, many years ago, prior to Krypton's destruction, was injected by the scientist JOR-EL with an experimental life-prolonging serum and then catapulted into outer-space exile on Koron, a natural satellite of Krypton, after it had been discovered that an unwanted side effect of the as yet unperfected serum had been to transform the snagriff into a metallic monster with a voracious appetite for minerals and metals. Hurled violently from its orbit soon afterward by the cataclysmic explosion that destroyed Krypton, Koron careened wildly through space, passing ultimately within a short distance of the planet Earth—thus enabling the snagriff to leap onto the Earth—where, like any native of Krypton, it acquired awesome super-powers identical to SUPERMAN's. In September-October 1952 the super-powered snagriff runs amok on its newly adopted planet—voraciously consuming an ocean liner, gold bullion from the Federal Gold Reserve, and tons of scrap metal, and leaving havoc and destruction in its wake—until finally, after having swallowed six atomic bombs, it is carried high into the air by Superman, where the heat of the creature's body detonates the A-bombs, utterly destroying it (S No. 78/1: "The Beast from Krypton!").

"SNAKE, THE." A cunning murderer—clad in a scaly, yellow, orange-spotted costume resembling the skin of a giant snake—who kills his victims with double-pronged lances tipped with the venom of a deadly serpent. He is in reality Bill Chantey, the foreman of the Allerton Construction Company's Holloway Tunnel project—and a longtime collector of snakes—whose bitterness at being repeatedly passed over for promotion ("For years I slaved to make the *Allerton Construction Company* a success, and yet it was always others who got the big promotions. I vowed to ruin the company at any cost!") leads him to brutally murder several of his company's sandhogs before he is finally hospitalized after being accidentally bitten by one of his own poisonous snakes during a climactic confrontation with SUPERMAN (S No. 18/4, Sep/Oct '42: "The Snake").

SNAPINN, STEVEN. A METROPOLIS Little Leaguer who saves SUPERMAN's life when he finds him lying helpless beside a chunk of KRYPTONITE presented to him by BIZARRO in a moment of twisted mirth in November 1962 (S No. 157/3: "Superman's Day of Doom!").

SNELLING (Professor). A "noted historian" and newly installed resident of SMALLVILLE—the author of a forthcoming book called *The Life and Times of Superman*—who, having unwittingly purchased for his own the very home where SUPERMAN resided as a youngster, is prevented from uncovering a series of damaging clues to Superman's secret identity still remaining in the house, such as the cast-iron teddy bear Superman played with as an infant, only by the quick-witted and surreptitious intervention of Superman (S No. 90/2, Jul '54: "Superman's Secret Past!"). This text is contradicted by Action Comics No. 288, which asserts that the Smallville home of JONATHAN AND MARTHA KENT, Superman's foster parents, was bequeathed to Clark Kent and remains in his possession (May '62: The Man Who Exposed Superman!").

SNELLING, CASPAR (Professor). A world-renowned scientist and scholar who, rebuffed by his girl friend for being "such a mousy little fellow" and humiliated by his students when they abandon one of his lectures in droves in order to catch a glimpse of SUPERMAN, constructs a remote-controlled "atomic-powered steel robot" in his own likeness, endowed with super-strength and the power of flight, and sends it forth to perform a series of super-feats in an effort to persuade the public that he has become endowed with super-powers so that they will accord him the respect and admiration they have denied him in his intellectual pursuits. Forced to intervene, however, when the Snelling robot causes a series of accidental near-disasters through the inadvertent misuse of its awesome powers, Superman employs an elaborate ruse to persuade Professor Snelling to destroy his robot and to help him win the hand of his reluctant fiancée (S No. 85/3, Nov/Dec '53: "The Weakling Who Became a Superman!").

SNIDE, GUS. A vicious racketeer who concocts a scheme to seize control of the truck drivers' union and send all the city's truck drivers out on strike. "The city's food distribution will be paralyzed!" gloats Snide. "People have got to eat, and the employers will be forced to pay any blackmail we demand!" Snide and his henchmen are apprehended by SUPERMAN in Spring 1940 (S No. 4/4).

SNIGGLE (Mr.). The leader of a gang of criminals who are determined, by fair means or foul, to seize control of the Super-Moving Company—a METROPOLIS moving company specializing in the use of advanced engineering techniques for moving especially heavy objects from one place to another—as part of a larger scheme to steal $50,000,000 in cash from a load of heavy bank vaults that the Super-Moving Company has recently contracted to move. Sniggle and his henchmen are apprehended by SUPERMAN in May 1944 (Act No. 72: "Superman and the Super-Movers!").

SNIVELY, EPHRAIM ("Professor"). A renegade scientist who, during a period when the Earth is passing through a shower of KRYPTONITE dust in space—temporarily robbing SUPERMAN of his super-powers and forcing him to rely on hastily constructed "super-machines" to perform his customary super-tasks—sets in operation a mammoth air-pump designed to draw in all the kryptonite dust from miles around until enough of it has been accumulated to annihilate Superman. The scheme is thwarted in the nick of time by LOIS LANE, who apprehends Snively and his accomplice as Superman lies stricken with kryptonite-induced paralysis outside the villains' warehouse hideout (S No. 116/3, Sep '57: "The Mechanized Superman!").

SOCIETY OF ADVENTURERS, THE. A club in METROPOLIS which was founded by men who, in the words of one member, "formed our club so we could undertake dangerous tasks!" SUPERMAN is made an honorary member of the club in August 1953 (Act No. 183: "The Perfect Plot to Kill Superman!").

SPEARS (Captain). The unscrupulous captain of a gold-carrying freighter who masterminds an elaborate scheme to attack his own vessel with a mechanical sea serpent and sink it on a shallowly submerged rock in the mid-Atlantic so that the gold may be easily salvaged by himself and his waiting henchmen. Spears and his cohorts are apprehended by SUPERMAN in March-April 1946 (S No. 39/2: "The Monster of China Deep!").

SPHINX, THE. A mythological monster with the head of a human being and the body of a lion. The creature is famous in Greek legend and well known in the art of the ancient Near East, the largest and earliest known example being the Great Sphinx at Giza, in Egypt, dating from the reign of Khafre, the fourth Pharaoh of the 4th dynasty of Egypt, who reigned probably *ca.* 2540–*ca.* 2514 B.C. Known to be a portrait statue of Khafre himself, the Great Sphinx is one of the world's great monuments. It is this sphinx to which the remainder of this article refers.

Superman holds aloft a cement replica of the Sphinx, which he has constructed as part of his elaborate ruse to outwit renegade scientist Lex Luthor, 1954

In July-August 1953 "THE BRAIN" destroys the Sphinx and two other world-famous monuments as part of an elaborate scheme to steal $50,000,000 in precious gems lent to METROPOLIS by the Maharajah of Ipostan, but SUPERMAN restores the monuments and ultimately takes "The Brain" into custody (S No. 83/1: "Destination X!").

By July 1954 LEX LUTHOR and his henchmen have planted explosives on the Sphinx—and on many other world-famous monuments—as part of an elaborate scheme to extort millions of dollars from the governments of the world (S No. 90/3: "The Titanic Thefts!"). During this same period, the Sphinx is stolen—along with other world-famous monuments—by the Kryptonian villain MALA as part of the villain's elaborate scheme to wreak vengeance on Superman by destroying the planet Earth (Act No. 194, Jul '54: "The Outlaws from Krypton!").

In January 1960 a sudden "earth tremor" threatens to topple the Sphinx, but Superman and SUPERGIRL resteady the ancient monument on its foundations before any harm can come to it (Act No. 260: "Mighty Maid!"). During this same period, while impersonating Superman, the Kandorian scientist KULL-Ex seizes the Sphinx and the PYRAMIDS and piles them up like children's blocks in the Egyptian desert sand as part of his scheme to make Superman the most hated man on Earth (S No. 134, Jan '60: chs. I-III—"The Super-Menace of Metropolis!"; "The Revenge Against Jor-El!"; "The Duel of the Supermen!").

In December 1962 Superman destroys the Sphinx—and several other world-famous landmarks—after being driven temporarily berserk by a diabolical "telepathic-hypnotic weapon" fired at him by members of the SUPERMAN REVENGE SQUAD. After the villains have been defeated, however, Superman promises to repair the damage (Act No. 295: "Superman Goes Wild!").

SPHINX GANG, THE. A gang of criminals who conceal their identities beneath gray hoods resembling the heads of mythical sphinxes. The leader of the mob is gangster Al Regan. The entire Sphinx Gang is apprehended in February 1964 through the heroic efforts of BATMAN, ROBIN, and SUPERMAN (WF No. 139: "The Ghost of Batman!").

SPRUCE, LUCIUS. The dapper, monocled criminal who is the leader of the Hobby-Nappers, a gang of thieves who break into the homes of hobbyists of all kinds, steal their collections, and hold the collections for ransom. Spruce and his henchmen are apprehended by SUPERMAN in June 1944 (Act No. 73: "The Hobby Robbers!").

SPULBY, SAM. A dapper, middle-aged man who, in May 1955, becomes SUPERMAN's ally in an elaborate ruse designed to protect the Earth from an impending interplanetary invasion by preventing Earth's would-be conquerors, now poised for the attack, from learning the true effects of the "beam of counter energy" they have been aiming at Superman, i.e., its ability to prevent Superman from exercising any of his super-powers except while he is upside down. The ruse, in which Superman pretends that Spulby has acquired some secret hold over him which obliges him to obsequiously carry out every menial, humiliating task that Spulby assigns to him, is specifically designed to enable Superman to carry out his everyday tasks in an upside-down position until such time as the aliens have abandoned their plans to invade the Earth in the mistaken belief that their unearthly counter-energy weapon possesses insuffi-

cient power to incapacitate Superman (Act No. 20 "The Man Who Could Make Superman Do Any thing!").

SQUIFFLES, THE. Evil little green elflike creatures whose ruler, Ixnayalpay, makes a secret pac with ADOLF HITLER to lead his Squiffles in sabotaging America's aircraft industry in return for demon possession of Der Fuehrer's body. By pestering U.S pilots and distracting them from their controls, th Squiffles cause a series of disastrous military aircraf crashes in May-June 1943, but with the aid of the goo elves, known as Gremlins, SUPERMAN ultimately defeats the Squiffles and prevents them from demoishing an armada of American bombers en route t aid England. The text describes the story as "fantasy," rather than a recounting of actual event (S No. 22/1: "Meet the Squiffles!").

SQUIRE, THE. The young Englishman who is th crime-fighting companion of the KNIGHT. The Knigh is in reality the Earl of Wordenshire, and the Squire i his young son Cyril (BM No. 62/2, Dec/Jan '50-'51 "The Batman of England!").

STANDARD ELECTRONICS PRODUCTS. Th electronics firm that serves as a front for LEX LUTHOR's criminal activities in May 1951. It is whil snooping around the firm in an effort to unearth information about Luthor that LOIS LANE throws the switch on the renegade scientist's latest inventior and finds herself temporarily endowed with super powers similar to SUPERMAN's (Act No. 156: "The Gir of Steel!").

STARK, STANLEY. "A shady scientist with a [prison] record" who is the "wealthy brain" behind a series of "astounding robberies" that plague METROPOLIS in October 1954, robberies in which the only things stolen are shirts and jackets monogrammed with the letter "S," including a jacket belonging to a fireman on the ferryboat *Susquehanna*, a polo shirt belonging to a player on the Skylarks polo team, and finally the famous S-monogrammed shirt belonging to SUPERMAN. Even Stark's hired henchmen are not privy to the real motive behind the thefts—to enable Stark to "analyze and reproduce the indestructible fabric" of Superman's shirt so that he can make "a fortune selling garments of this fabric to criminals"— but Superman ultimately solves the riddle and apprehends Stark and his gangland cohorts (Act No. 197: "The Stolen 'S' Shirts").

STATUE OF LIBERTY, THE. A colossal statue in New York harbor which commemorates the birth of the United States and the continuing friendship between France and the United States. Sculpted by Frederic Auguste Bartholdi, the statue, dedicated on October 28, 1886, is one of the world's great monuments. According to at least two texts, the Statue of Liberty stands in Metropolis Harbor, one of numerous indications that fictional METROPOLIS is intended to represent New York City (Act No. 143, Apr '50: "The Bride of Superman!"; Act No. 146, Jul '50: "The Statues That Came to Life!"). Action Comics No. 146 refers to the statue as "...the woman who

Superman soars skyward with the Statue of Liberty, 1954

stands first in the hearts of all Americans, a symbol of freedom and tolerance," and SUPERMAN has described the statue as "the only girl in the world who means more to me than Lois Lane!" (Act No. 146, Jul '50: "The Statues That Came to Life!").

An attempt by EMIL LORING to destroy the Statue of Liberty is thwarted by Superman in January 1943 (Act No. 56: "Design for Doom!").

In July 1950 LEX LUTHOR brings the Statue of Liberty temporarily to life with his miraculous "life-ray gun." As the statue strolls through Metropolis Harbor, threatening, because of its titanic size, to swamp an excursion ship in its path, Superman averts the impending disaster by lifting the vessel high over his head and carrying it out of harm's way (Act No. 146: "The Statues That Came to Life!").

By July 1954 Lex Luthor and his henchmen have planted explosives in the Statue of Liberty—and in many other world-famous monuments—as part of an elaborate scheme to extort millions of dollars from the governments of the world (S No. 90/3: "The Titanic Thefts!").

STEFFENS (Professor). An unscrupulous scientist affiliated with the Metropolis Museum of Natural History who, having discovered a "prehistoric man" preserved intact inside an Alaskan glacier—and having successfully brought this so-called Dawn Man back to life—joins forces with a gang of criminals led by underworld figure Duke Brady in an elaborate scheme to impersonate the Dawn Man in a series of spectacular robberies. In Brady's words:

> It seemed like a swell opportunity.... All this publicity about the *Dawn Man*. I suggested we fix up one of our mobsters to look like the prehistoric man and have him pull jobs for us. The victims would be too scared at the sight of him to put up much opposition.

Even SUPERMAN is misled initially ("That prehistoric man is a definite menace. I can't permit his violences to continue," muses the Man of Steel), but the real Dawn Man eventually kills Professor Steffens and the gangland impersonator in a fit of anger, and Duke Brady and his remaining henchmen are apprehended by Superman (Act No. 44, Jan '42).

STEPHENS, "RAGS." The leader of a gang of protection racketeers who extort money from businessmen exhibiting their wares at the Metropolis Fair until they are finally apprehended by SUPERMAN in July 1955 (S No. 98/1: "Superman's Secret Life!").

STER, FRANK (Mr.). One of several aliases employed by the PRANKSTER in November-December 1949 as part of his scheme to buy up all the radio time on every radio station in METROPOLIS (S No. 61/1: "The Prankster's Radio Program!").

STONE, NICK. The leader of a gang of criminals whose plot to steal the priceless Rhanee Jewels from an exhibition at the New York World's Fair is thwarted by SUPERMAN in 1939 (NYWF No. 1).

STONY VOICE (Chief). The tribal name bestowed on PERRY WHITE when he is made an honorary Indian chief in January 1955 (Act No. 200: "Tests of a Warrior!").

STRADI (Colonel). A ruthless prison commandant on the "island republic" of Voroda whose plot to overthrow his nation's democracy and establish himself as dictator is thwarted by SUPERMAN in August 1960 (S No. 139/2: "The Jolly Jailhouse!").

STREAKY (the Super-Cat). LINDA LEE's pet cat, an ordinary orange feline—with a white, lightning-like streak on either side of its body—that becomes endowed with temporary super-powers as the result of its exposure to "X-kryptonite," a bizarre form of KRYPTONITE inadvertently created by SUPERGIRL while experimenting with green kryptonite. Streaky the Super-Cat wears a red cape and is a member of the LEGION OF SUPER-PETS.

In July 1962 Streaky becomes temporarily endowed with "the power to speak intelligently" when the mischievous MR. MXYZPTLK unleashes a magical "zoophonic force" upon the city of METROPOLIS (S No. 154/1: "The Underwater Pranks of Mr. Mxyzptlk!").

When Metropolis television station WMET-TV inaugurates its new "Our American Heroes" series with a program honoring Superman, "our greatest American hero," Streaky appears on the show along with three of the other super-pets—BEPPO THE SUPER-MONKEY, COMET THE SUPER-HORSE, and KRYPTO THE SUPERDOG—to help pay tribute to the Man of

*A flabbergasted airline pilot reacts to
Streaky the Super-Cat, 1960*

Steel (Act No. 309, Feb '64: "The Superman Super-Spectacular!").

In April 1965 Streaky journeys through the time barrier to the mid-nineteenth century to help Superman and the other super-pets teach a well-deserved lesson to "cruel junkman" CYRUS ATWILL (S No. 176/1: "The Revenge of the Super-Pets!").

STRIKER, JOE "THE ELEPHANT." A METROPOLIS "racketeer boss" who is apprehended along with his henchmen by SUPERMAN in June 1951 while attempting to stage a payroll robbery at the offices of the DAILY PLANET. Superman's efforts to capture the criminals are severely hampered by the fact that Vince Ellery, a reporter for a rival newspaper who is convinced that Clark Kent is Superman, has forced Kent to agree to wear, for a twenty-four-hour period, a pair of electronic ankle bracelets whose "mechanism...will register...if you leave the ground to fly in the air--or if you race at a speed faster than can a normal man," thus seriously inhibiting Superman in the use of his powers lest he risk betraying the secret of his dual identity (Act No. 157: "The Superman Who Couldn't Fly!").

STRONG, PAUL. A local blacksmith in the Western town of Powder Valley, and the secret leader of the gang of rustlers whose thefts have been plaguing the community. Strong and his henchmen are apprehended by SUPERMAN in July 1949 (Act No. 134: "Super-Cowboy!").

STRONGARM BANDIT, THE. A mysterious masked bandit of incredible strength who commits a series of crimes in METROPOLIS while clad in the costume of a circus strong man. The villain, who turns out to be an unnamed circus clown attempting to throw suspicion on a circus strong man named Herculo, is finally apprehended by Herculo himself as the result of a clever ruse devised by CLARK KENT (Act No. 28, Sep '40).

SUN BOY (or Sunboy). A member of the LEGION OF SUPER-HEROES. A native of the planet Earth, Sun Boy possesses the "power of creating solar heat," the ability to radiate intense heat from his body (S No.

156, Oct '62: "The Last Days of Superman!" pts. III—"Superman's Death Sentence!"; "The Super Comrades of All Time!"; "Superman's Last Day of Life!"). Sun Boy's real name is Dirk Morgna.

In April 1962 Sun Boy is among the six Legionnaires who play an elaborate hoax on SUPERMAN and SUPERGIRL as a prelude to celebrating the anniversary of Supergirl's arrival on Earth (S No. 152/1: "The Robot Master!"). (See LEGION OF SUPER-HEROES, THE.)

In October 1962, when Superman is believed to be dying of an incurable malady, Sun Boy is among the Legionnaires who are summoned to the twentieth century by Supergirl to help carry out the gigantic super-tasks that Superman hopes to fulfill as his final legacy to humanity, including the destruction of a "vast cloud of fungus in distant space, that will some day reach Earth and blight all plant life," and the melting of the Antarctic ice, "to make Antarctica a fit place for millions to live in the future," thus ensuring "a home for Earth's expanding population...!" (S No. 156: "The Last Days of Superman!" pts. I-III—"Superman's Death Sentence!"; "The Super-Comrades of All Time!"; "Superman's Last Day of Life!").

When METROPOLIS television station WMET-TV inaugurates its new "Our American Heroes" series with a program honoring Superman, "our greatest American hero," Sun Boy is among the Legion representatives who journey to the twentieth century to appear on the show and thus help pay tribute to the Man of Steel (Act No. 309, Feb '64: "The Superman Super-Spectacular!").

SUPER-APE. A mighty gorilla—an orphaned survivor of the exploded planet KRYPTON, endowed with the power of human speech as well as with all the super-powers of SUPERMAN—which Superman encounters during an expedition to the "untracked jungles" of Africa, where Super-Ape serves as the noble protector of the jungle's wildlife much as Superman protects the people of METROPOLIS.

Before the death of his native planet Krypton, Super-Ape was an experimental animal in the laboratory of the Kryptonian scientist Shir Kan, a colleague of JOR-EL who, concerned over Jor-El's warnings of the impending doom of the planet, launched a fleet of ape-carrying "experimental rockets" into outer space, each rocket toward a different planet, in an effort to determine whether Kryptonians could safely withstand the rigors of an interplanetary migration.

Shir Kan's effort, however, was too little, too late, and Shir Kan perished when Krypton exploded; but Super-Ape crash-landed in Earth's African jungle, where he was adopted by a pair of African apes and grew to maturity with physical and mental powers identical to Superman's.

In July 1956 Superman joins forces with Super-Ape to apprehend a pair of "illegal trappers and animal smugglers" named John Trask and Paul Spender, and then rockets into outer space, where he cates all the rest of Shir Kan's apes—now grown to naturity on various distant planets—and establishes new home for them on a lush, uninhabited planet in he farthest reaches of space. "Thanks, **Superman**," ays Super-Ape, "...I will never forget you for this! I m with my own folk again!" (Act No. 218: "The Super-Ape from Krypton").

SUPERBOY. The teen-aged SUPERMAN (*see* SUPER-MAN [section I, the man himself (as Superman)]).

SUPER-CAT. *See* STREAKY (THE SUPER-CAT).

SUPER-DOG. *See* KRYPTO (THE SUPERDOG).

SUPER-GIRL. A lovely blond super-heroine—endowed with super-powers identical to SUPERMAN's and clad in a red-and-blue costume featuring a red cape, miniskirt, and high-heeled boots, with a red etter "S" on a yellow field emblazoned on her chest—who materializes out of nowhere in August 1958 in response to JIMMY OLSEN's wish on a magic Indian totem for a "super-girl" to appear as a fitting companion for Superman. The newly arrived super-heroine proves more of a hindrance than a help to Superman, however, due to her inexperience in using super-powers and her inadvertent near-betrayal of Superman's secret identity. Ultimately, in a final act of heroism and redemption, she courageously overexposes herself to KRYPTONITE while saving the life of Superman, and, mortally weakened, prevails upon Jimmy Olsen to use his magic totem to dispatch her "back into the mysterious limbo from which she came..." (S No. 123: chs. 1-3—"The Girl of Steel"; "The Lost Super-Powers"; "Superman's Return to Krypton"). Super-Girl is not to be confused with SUPERGIRL.

Superman introduces Super-Girl to Lois Lane and Jimmy Olsen, 1958

SUPERGIRL. A lovely blond super-heroine who functions periodically, from May 1959 onward, as SUPERMAN's companion in super-heroic adventure. She is in reality Kara, Superman's first cousin, the daughter of the Kryptonian scientist ZOR-EL and

his wife ALURA. Born and raised on ARGO CITY, a city of the planet KRYPTON which survived the death of its native planet when it was hurled into outer space, people and buildings alive and intact, by the force of the cataclysm that destroyed Krypton, she was—at the age of fifteen—launched toward Earth in a small rocket ship by her father Zor-El when the city faced extinction due to KRYPTONITE poisoning.

On Earth, where, like any Kryptonian survivor, she acquired super-powers identical to Superman's, she assumed the secret alternate identity of Linda Lee, an orphan at the Midvale Orphanage, concealing her blond hair beneath a brunette wig and functioning as Supergirl only in secret, at Superman's insistence, until such time as she could learn to use her super-powers properly. Adopted by Fred and Edna Danvers, she attended Midvale High School as Linda Lee Danvers, graduated in 1964, and then went on to attend Stanhope College on a scholarship, graduating in 1971. Presented to the world by Superman in 1962, she has, since that time, performed super-heroic feats openly as Supergirl, while retaining the secrecy of her dual identity.

Supergirl's alternate identity is a closely held secret, but it is known to Superman, to her foster parents the Danverses (Act No. 285, Feb '62: "The World's Greatest Heroine!"; and others), and to the LEGION OF SUPER-HEROES, of which she served as a member until resigning her membership at the age of twenty-one (S No. 152/1, Apr '62: "The Robot Master!"; and others). Supergirl is fully aware that

Supergirl

Superman meets Supergirl, 1959

her cousin Superman is secretly Clark Kent. According to the Supergirl story in Action Comics No. 270, she has also been entrusted with the secret identities of BATMAN and ROBIN (Nov '60: "Supergirl's Busiest Day!"). Like all Kryptonian survivors, Supergirl is vulnerable to kryptonite. COMET THE SUPER-HORSE is Supergirl's pet and equine companion. STREAKY, the orange cat that acquires temporary super-powers as the result of its exposure to "X-kryptonite," is Linda Lee Danvers's pet cat.

In the texts, Supergirl is alternatively referred to as the Girl of Steel. Action Comics No. 285 describes Superman and Supergirl as "the two mightiest crusaders in the entire universe" (Feb '62: "The World's Greatest Heroine!"). Superman, who has dedicated a room to Supergirl in his FORTRESS OF SOLITUDE (S No. 142/3, Jan '61: "Flame-Dragon from Krypton"), has described his cousin this way:

> Physically, she's the mightiest female of all time! But at heart, she's as gentle and sweet and is [sic] quick to tears--as any ordinary girl! I guess that's why everyone who meets her loves her! [Act No. 285, Feb '62: "The World's Greatest Heroine!"].

Supergirl's red, yellow, and blue costume—which was originally fashioned by her mother Alura prior to her flight from doomed Argo City—is a female counterpart of Superman's own.

Most of what is known concerning Supergirl's origin is contained in the Supergirl story in Action Comics No. 252. In May 1959 a small rocket ship crash-lands on the outskirts of METROPOLIS and a teen-aged girl, clad in a costume clearly modeled after Superman's, emerges smiling and unhurt from the wreckage. As Superman listens in amazement to her story, the girl explains that she too is Kryptonian, although she was born on floating Argo City long after the planet Krypton exploded. When, years later, after his young daughter had become a teen-ager, the scientist Zor-El realized that Argo City's entire population would, within about one month's time, succumb to deadly kryptonite poisoning, he began desperately racing against time to construct a rocket ship to carry his daughter to another world. It was while scanning the universe through a "super-space telescope" in search of a suitable world to which young Kara could be sent that Kara and her mother discovered Earth, became aware of Superman and his exploits, and realized that Earth's greatest hero was a Kryptonian like them. Kara's mother decided to send her teen-aged daughter to Earth, clad in a costume that would make her easily recognizable to Superman as a fellow native of Krypton. And so, soon afterward, Zor-El placed his young daughter inside his small rocket ship and launched her toward Earth, while behind her, on Argo City, virtually the entire population lay dead or dying of kryptonite poisoning.

It is only as the newly arrived orphan from space concludes her narrative that Superman realizes that she is his cousin, the daughter of Zor-El, his father's brother (*see* JOR-EL). Overjoyed at having encountered a kinswoman from his native planet, Superman advises her that she can use her super-powers to aid humanity, as he does, but that first she must undergo a prolonged period of training so that she may learn to use her powers wisely.

After exchanging her colorful Supergirl costume for ordinary Earth girls' clothing and concealing her blond hair beneath a brown, pigtailed wig, Kara registers at the Midvale Orphanage in the Metropolis suburb of Midvale, employing the alias Linda Lee. Someday, promises Superman faithfully, the world will learn of her existence, but "for a long time to come," he adds, "you'll live here quietly as an 'ordinary' girl until you get used to earthly things!" (Act No. 252: "The Supergirl from Krypton!").

In January 1960 Supergirl assumes the alternate identity of MIGHTY MAID in order to help Superman thwart the schemes of a band of extraterrestrial aliens bent on destroying the Earth (Act No. 260: "Mighty Maid!"). During this same period, Supergirl helps Superman convince the Kandorian scientist KULL-EX that his bitter grudge against Superman's father is completely unfounded (S No. 134, Jan '60: chs. I-III—"The Super-Menace of Metropolis!"; "The Revenge Against Jor-El!"; "The Duel of the Supermen!").

Inside her room at the Midvale Orphanage, Linda Lee uses her super-strength to repair the bent leg of her cot, 1959

In August 1960, after exposure to red kryptonite has brought about the sudden, accelerated growth of Superman's hair, beard, and fingernails, Supergirl and KRYPTO THE SUPERDOG lend the Man of Steel a helping hand by using the combined power of their X-ray vision to disintegrate the virtually indestructible hair and fingernails, thus restoring Superman to his normal appearance (S No. 139/3: "The Untold Story of Red Kryptonite!").

In October 1960 Supergirl becomes embroiled in the bizarre adventure surrounding the infant son of BIZARRO and BIZARRO-LOIS (S No. 140: pts. I-III—"The Son of Bizarro!"; "The 'Orphan' Bizarro!"; "The Bizarro Supergirl!"). (*See* BIZARRO.)

In January 1961 Supergirl helps Batman, Superman, and Krypto the Superdog carry out an elaborate, and ultimately successful, ruse to protect the secret of Superman's identity (S No. 142/3: "Flame-Dragon from Krypton!").

In April 1961, at the Fortress of Solitude, Supergirl, Superman, and Krypto the Superdog all experience the same "red kryptonite hallucination" simultaneously as the result of their simultaneous exposure to red-kryptonite dust. In the hallucinatory fantasy, which is also referred to as a dream, the Earth is destroyed by a titanic explosion caused by Superman's careless tinkering with an extraterrestrial device; Supergirl, Superman, and Krypto, the sole survivors of the cataclysm, are taken into custody by the Cosmic Police, who charge Superman with "criminal negligence" in the destruction of Earth; stripped of their super-powers by an interplanetary tribunal, the now-powerless heroes are banished to a desolate "primordial planet," inhabited by ferocious prehistoric beasts, where they are forced to live as cave dwellers, in continual terror, until finally Supergirl and Krypto are annihilated by a terrifying "lightning-monster" and the shock of this grisly event brings the nightmarish dream to an end and snaps the three hallucinators back to reality (S No. 144/3: "The Orphans of Space!").

In May 1961 Supergirl joins forces with the SUPERMEN EMERGENCY SQUAD to carry out an elaborate, and ultimately successful, ruse designed to persuade JOHN KILEY and his cohorts that Kiley was only experiencing a drug-induced hallucination when he saw Clark Kent change into Superman (Act No. 276: "The War Between Supergirl and the Supermen Emergency Squad!").

In July 1961 Supergirl uses a chunk of white kryptonite to destroy the diabolical extraterrestrial "plant intelligence" that has seized control of the body of PERRY WHITE (Act No. 278: "The Super Powers of Perry White!").

In January 1962 Supergirl joins forces with Superman and Krypto the Superdog to prevent the PHANTOM ZONE prisoners from escaping the Phantom Zone (Act No. 284: "The Babe of Steel!"). During this same period, Supergirl, Superman, and Krypto the Superdog stand before the bottle city of KANDOR, in the Fortress of Solitude, and bow their heads solemnly for one full minute of silence to commemorate the anniversary of the destruction of Krypton. Afterward, the three Kryptonian survivors soar into outer space, where, in a "distant solar system," they use their mighty super-powers to transform an

Linda Lee changes to Supergirl, 1959

uninhabited planet into an exact duplicate of Krypton—and populate it with humanoid androids in the image of Jor-El, LARA, and other Kryptonians—as a planet-sized memorial to their exploded world (S No. 150/1, Jan '62: "The One Minute of Doom!").

In February 1962, after keeping Supergirl's presence on Earth a secret for almost three full years, Superman proudly proclaims her existence to the world, touring the world with her "to tumultuous applause," presenting her at the White House to President JOHN F. KENNEDY, introducing her at a special session of the United Nations, where she "receives a standing ovation from the distinguished representatives of member nations...."

"Everywhere," notes the text, "millions eagerly turn out for a glimpse of the two mightiest crusaders in the entire universe! Never before has there been such excitement, as the entire world thrills to the discovery that a girl with super-powers exists on Earth...."

"Supergirl," remarks President Kennedy, "I know you'll use your super-powers not only to fight crime, but to preserve peace in our troubled world!"

"Thank you, Mr. President!" replies Supergirl graciously. "...I will!"

At the United Nations, Supergirl is presented with a special "golden certificate" identical to one already possessed by Superman, empowering her to enter and leave member countries without a visa and to make arrests wherever she travels.

Inside the bottle city of Kandor, the Kandorians celebrate Supergirl's public debut by using their tiny rocket ships to skywrite a congratulatory message to her across the Kandorian sky, while in ATLANTIS, the Atlanteans commemorate the occasion with the unveiling of a gigantic undersea statue of a mermaid Supergirl (Act No. 285: "The World's Greatest Heroine!").

In March 1962 Supergirl soars into outer space with the bottle city of Kandor cradled in her arm after "telling the Kandorians that she would journey to scores of planets in space to find a scientist who could enlarge their miniature city!" (Act No. 286: "The Jury of Super-Enemies!"). Supergirl's quest, however, is apparently unsuccessful, for as of the late 1970s Kandor has still not been enlarged.

In April 1962 the LEGION OF SUPER-HEROES play an elaborate hoax on Superman and Supergirl as their playful way of commemorating the anniversary of Supergirl's arrival on Earth (S No. 152/1: "The Robot Master!").

In July 1962, during a period when Superman is periodically seized by an overpowering compulsion to commit evil acts as the result of the appearance over Earth of a mysterious blue comet, Supergirl, responding to an urgent telepathic summons from LORI LEMARIS, races to Atlantis to repair a vital chemical plant demolished by Superman and to prevent the Man of Steel from wreaking further destruction in the undersea realm. Later, after having been alerted to the true explanation behind Superman's senseless acts of destruction by the Kandorian scientist LON-Es, Supergirl brings about the blue comet's destruction, thereby curing Superman of his insane compulsion (S No. 154/2: "Krypton's First Superman!"). (See MAG-EN.)

In October 1962, after exposure to red kryptonite has temporarily transformed Superman into two separate individuals, a mature, responsible Clark

Supergirl in flight over Midvale, 1959

Kent and an unprincipled, irresponsible Superman, Supergirl is imprisoned in the Phantom Zone by the arrogant Superman in order to prevent her from interfering with his plan to keep the personalities of Clark Kent and Superman separate forever. Ultimately, however, Clark Kent frees Supergirl from the Phantom Zone, and soon afterward he succeeds in bringing about the reuniting of Clark Kent and

Superman into a single individual (Act No. 293: "The Feud Between Superman and Clark Kent!"). During this same period, when Superman is believed to be dying of exposure to VIRUS X, an incurable Kryptonian malady, Supergirl supervises, and joins forces with, the various "super-comrades"—including Krypto the Superdog, the Legion of Super-Heroes, the Supermen Emergency Squad, several of Superman's Superman-robots, and Lori Lemaris and the mer-people of Atlantis—in carrying out the gigantic super-tasks that Superman hopes to fulfill as his final legacy to humanity, viz., the construction of an elaborate "canal system for irrigating desert lands," to meet mankind's future needs for arable land; the destruction of a "faraway planet" that would otherwise collide with Earth "in far future times"; the destruction of a "vast cloud of fungus in distant space, that will some day reach Earth and blight all plant life"; the melting of the Antarctic ice, "to make Antarctica a fit place for millions to live in the future," thus ensuring "a home for Earth's expanding population"; and the injection of a colossal sea monster—which has been growing to ever more titanic size due to the stimulation of undersea radioactivity—with a special "shrinking formula" so that it will not one day become so terrifyingly gargantuan that it menaces the safety of Earth.

Sometime later, the super-tasks completed, Supergirl flashes through the time-space barrier, to the planet Krypton at a time prior to its destruction, in an unsuccessful effort to find a cure for Virus X. Ultimately, however, it becomes clear that Superman is not suffering from exposure to Virus X at all, but rather from the effects of a tiny nugget of kryptonite that has somehow become lodged in JIMMY OLSEN's camera. Once the kryptonite nugget has been removed and Superman is fast on the way to being restored to full health, Supergirl joins forces with Krypto the Superdog to preserve the secret of Superman's dual identity by using the awesome power of their combined heat vision to eradicate the name Clark Kent from the farewell message to mankind that Superman had earlier inscribed on the face of the MOON (S No. 156, Oct '62: "The Last Days of Superman!" pts. I-III—"Superman's Death Sentence!"; "The Super-Comrades of All Time!"; "Superman's Last Day of Life!").

In November 1962, when Superman Day is celebrated in Metropolis, Supergirl journeys to Metropolis to attend the festivities, bringing with her a life-sized statue of Superman—fashioned out of solid diamond—that she has carved in his honor. Plans are made to display the magnificent statue in Metropolis's SUPERMAN MUSEUM (S No.157/3: "Superman's Day of Doom!").

In May 1963 Supergirl helps Superman carry out an elaborate, and ultimately successful, ruse designed to enable him to preserve the secret of his dual identity (S No. 161/2: "Superman Goes to War!"). During this same period, Superman makes a time-journey to Metropolis one million years in the future,

where he encounters a lifelike Supergirl android created by the people of the far-distant future (Act No. 300, May '63: "Superman Under the Red Sun!").

In August 1963, after exposure to red kryptonite has temporarily transformed Superman into a fearsome Kryptonian "drang" (see KRYPTON), and the U.S. Armed Forces, unaware that the hideous monster is actually Superman, are on the verge of destroying it, it is Supergirl who provides Superman with the crucial assistance he needs to alert his attackers to his true identity and get them to hold their fire (Act No. 303: "The Monster from Krypton!").

© NPP 1975

Supergirl, 1975

When Metropolis television station WMET-TV inaugurates its new "Our American Heroes" series with a program honoring Superman, "our greatest American hero," Supergirl appears on the show along with Superman's other friends and admirers to help pay tribute to the Man of Steel (Act No. 309, Feb '64: "The Superman Super-Spectacular!").

In June 1964 Supergirl rescues Batman, LOIS LANE, Lori Lemaris, Jimmy Olsen, and Perry White from a cave beneath Metropolis, where they have been imprisoned in a state of suspended animation by the SUPERMAN REVENGE SQUAD (Act No. 313: "The End of Clark Kent's Secret Identity!"). (See SUPERMAN REVENGE SQUAD, THE.)

In March 1965, after members of the SUPERMAN REVENGE SQUAD have used a diabolical "cowardice ray" to transform Superman into a craven coward whenever he is dressed in the clothing of his Clark Kent identity, Supergirl successfully snaps Clark Kent out of his state of artificially induced cowardice by ingeniously creating an elaborate web of circumstances which forces Superman to perform a super-heroic feat while dressed as Clark Kent (Act No. 322: "The Coward of Steel!").

In April 1965 Supergirl accompanies Superman to the bottle city of Kandor to take part in the ceremonies marking the Day of Truth (S No. 176/3: "Superman's Day of Truth!"). (*See* KRYPTON.)

SUPER-HORSE. *See* COMET (THE SUPER-HORSE).

SUPERMAN. A world-famous crime-fighter and adventurer who has, for four full decades, battled the forces of crime and injustice with the aid of an awesome array of superhuman powers, including X-ray vision, the power of flight, and strength far beyond that of any ordinary mortal. Born on the planet KRYPTON, the son of the scientist JOR-EL and his wife LARA, he was launched into outer space in an experimental rocket ship to enable him to escape the cataclysm that destroyed his native planet, and, arriving on Earth, was taken into the home of JONATHAN AND MARTHA KENT, who named him Clark Kent and raised him to manhood as their adopted son. Endowed with mighty super-powers in the alien environment of Earth, this orphan from Krypton—named Kal-El by his parents—has, since mid-1938, battled the forces of evil as Superman,

Superman

© NPP 1976

while concealing his true, extraterrestrial identity beneath the alternate identity of Clark Kent, mild mannered reporter for the Metropolis DAILY PLANET more recently a full-time newscaster for METROPOLIS television station WGBS-TV.

Superman is "Earth's mightiest hero" (S No. 128/1, Apr '59: chs. 1-2—"Superman versus the Futuremen"; "The Secret of the Futuremen"), a "colorfully-costumed, mighty-sinewed man of might" engaged in "an unrelenting battle against the forces of evil" (S No. 21/4, Mar/Apr '43: "The Ghost of Superman!"). He is "the world's number one champion of justice and fair play" (S No. 130/3, Jul '59: "The Town That Hated Superman!") and "mankind's foremost crusader for good" (S No. 181/2, Nov '65: "The Superman of 2965!"), "a fighting champion of justice who is famous the world over" (Act No. 45, Feb '42). Described as "the world's most dynamic man" (WF No. 8, Win '42: "Talent, Unlimited!") and the "world's mightiest mortal" (WF No. 116, Mar '61: "The Creature from Beyond!"; and others), he is "mankind's greatest friend" (Act No. 310, Mar '64: "Secret of Kryptonite Six!"), a "mighty foe of all evil" (Act No. 91, Dec '45: "The Ghost Drum!"), a super-powered "savior of the helpless and oppressed" (Act No. 18, Nov '39).

Superman No. 1/1 calls Superman "the greatest exponent of justice the world has ever known" (Sum '39), and other texts describe him as "the law's most powerful defender" (Act No. 177, Feb '53: "The Anti-Superman Weapon"), as "the greatest of all heroes" (Act No. 210, Nov '55: "Superman in Superman Land"), and as a "defender of democracy" (S No. 13/1, Nov/Dec '41) who has chosen to "dedicate [his] powers to the good of all humanity!" (S No. 121/1, May '58: "The Bride of Futureman!"). "There is one man that people throughout the world honor and respect," notes Superman No. 128/1, "--and that man is Superman!" (Apr '59: chs. 1-2—"Superman versus the Futuremen"; "The Secret of the Futuremen").

Superman is "an incredibly muscular figure" (WF No. 6, Sum '42: "Man of Steel versus Man of Metal!"), "indestructible and cosmic in his gigantic strength" (Act No. 131, Apr '49: "The Scrambled Superman!"), a tireless "sentinel for the world" (Act No. 282, Nov '61: "Superman's Toughest Day!") whose "incredible super-powers...have made him a living legend...!" (S No. 160/1, Apr '63: pts. I-II—"The Mortal Superman!"; "The Cage of Doom!"). He is also the "most famous man in America" (Act No. 143, Apr '50: "The Bride of Superman!"), "patriot number one" (S No. 12/3, Sep/Oct '41), the indefatigable "foe of all interests and activities subversive to this country's best interests" (S No. 10/4, May/Jun '41). Everywhere, "in big cities...small towns...rural villages...the name of Superman is honored and loved!" (S No. 130/3, Jul '59: "The Town That Hated Superman!").

Indeed, "throughout the universe, Superman is hailed as a mighty champion of justice" (Act No. 319, Dec '64: "The Condemned Superman!"), as a "chamion of the weak and helpless" (Act No. 4, Sep '38) whose life is a "constant battle against evil..." (Act No. 280, Sep '61: "Brainiac's Super-Revenge!"). "Not only on Earth is **Superman** the greatest and most acclaimed of heroes," proclaims Superman No. 168, "but on many other worlds across the universe as well!" (Apr '64: pts. I-II—"Luthor--Super-Hero!"; 'Lex Luthor, Daily Planet Editor!").

"Everyone knows that **Superman** is the greatest hero of all time!" states Superman No. 165/1. "A man who can move mountains, even **planets**...a man who has defeated the worst villains in history!" (Nov '63: pts. I-II—"Beauty and the Super-Beast!"; "Circe's Super-Slave").

"Today," notes Superman No. 144/2, **"Superman** is the most famous crusader in the world, idolized everywhere for unselfishly using his incredible super-powers in behalf of justice" (Apr '61: "Superboy's First Public Appearance!").

In addition, the texts contain these descriptions: Action Comics No. 6, November 1938:

Dedicated to assisting the helpless and oppressed, is a mystery-man named SUPERMAN. Possessing super-strength, he can jump over a ten-story building, leap an eighth of a mile, run faster than an express train, lift tremendous weights, and crush steel in his bare hands!-- His amazing feats of strength become more apparent day after day!

Action Comics No. 7, December 1938; and others:

Friend of the helpless and oppressed is SUPERMAN, a man possessing the strength of a dozen Samsons! Lifting and rending gigantic weights, vaulting over skyscrapers, racing a bullet, possessing a skin impenetrable to even steel, are his physical assets used in his one-man battle against evil and injustice!

Action Comics No. 8, January 1939:

Leaping over towering buildings, rending steel in his bare hands, lifting incredible weights high overhead, impervious to bullets because of an unbelievably tough skin, racing at a speed hitherto unwitnessed by mortal eyes... these are the miraculous feats of strength which assist SUPERMAN in his one-man battle against the forces of evil and oppression!

Action Comics No. 27, August 1940:

Heartless criminals exploit the helpless and unfortunate! Clark Kent and his dual self, dynamic SUPERMAN, battle side by side with pretty Lois Lane, courageous girl reporter, to stamp out the evil geniuses of crime and corruption!

Superman No. 10/4, May-June 1941:

Foe of all interests and activities subversive to this country's best interests, SUPERMAN loses no time in going into action when he encounters a menace to American democracy. Super-strength clashes with evil super-cunning in another thrilling, dramatic adventure of today's foremost hero, the daring, dynamic *MAN OF TOMORROW*--SUPERMAN!!

Superman No. 16/4, May-June 1942: "Racket on Delivery":

No sterner or more courageous battler in behalf of justice is there than **Superman**, amazingly strong champion of the helpless and oppressed!

Superman No. 25/1, November-December 1943: "The Man Superman Refused to Help!":

Superman, amazing nemesis of evildoers, champion of the helpless and oppressed, comes to the aid of all worthy individuals in need of assistance.

Superman No. 64/1, May-June 1950: "Professor Lois Lane!":

Faster than a speeding bullet! Able to hurdle the highest mountain! More powerful than an atomic cyclotron! That's **Superman**, eternal foe of the underworld, champion of the underdog!

Action Comics No. 204, May 1955: "The Man Who Could Make Superman Do Anything!":

Faster than a speeding bullet! More powerful than a locomotive! Able to leap the highest mountain! That's **Superman**, the world's mightiest mortal.

Superman No. 96/1, March 1955: "The Girl Who Didn't Believe in Superman!":

From the jungle-wilds of Africa, to the skyscrapers of New York, the name of **Superman** has spread its fame! His Herculean strength, his super-battles against evil, are familiar to all....

Superman No. 120/3, March 1958: "The Human Missile":

Stronger than the very gravity that holds Earth in place...faster than the swiftest jet...more invulnerable than a mile-thick slab of steel, the incredible **Superman** can scoff at all weapons aimed at him!

Superman No. 152/2, April 1962: "Superbaby Captures the Pumpkin Gang!":

Today the whole world rings with **Superman**'s fame! In the far corners of the Earth men tell of how the **Man of Steel** uses his fantastic super-powers to help the forces of law and order against evildoers!

Friend and foe alike have paid tribute to Superman's heroism, and the texts have hailed him as "a giant among men" (S No. 70/2, May/Jun '51: "The Life of Superman!") and as the "mightiest of mortals" (S No. 84/2, Sep/Oct '53: "A Doghouse for Superman!"). An unidentified U.S. Navy admiral once described Superman as "the greatest hero of all time" (Act No. 284, Jan '62: "The Babe of Steel!"), and the master of ceremonies on a television special glowingly introduced him as "our greatest American hero"

(Act No. 309, Feb '64: "The Superman Super-Spectacular!").

"How fortunate we are here in America to have someone of **Superman's** calibre to aid us!" remarked Secretary of the Navy Hank Fox in March-April 1942., "In my opinion, he's worth *several* armies and navies!" (S No. 15/2).

JIMMY OLSEN has called Superman "the champion of justice and the enemy of evil all over the world" (S No. 176/2, Apr '65: "Tales of Green Kryptonite No. 2"), and LOIS LANE has described him as "the smartest, handsomest, strongest man in the universe" (S No. 176/3, Apr '65: "Superman's Day of Truth!") and as an "--American crusader, crime's greatest foe, enemy of all injustice, the most powerful force for good the world has ever seen...!" (S No. 17/1, Jul/Aug '42: "Man or Superman?").

In May 1962, an unidentified escapee from the PHANTOM ZONE refers to Superman as "Earth's greatest defender" (S No. 153/3: "The Town of Supermen!"), and in August 1964 the extraterrestrial gambler Rokk (*see* ROKK AND SORBAN) calls Superman the "guardian of Earth" (S No. 171/1: "Superman's Sacrifice!").

"Though he wasn't born on this world," notes scientist MEL EVANS at the annual Superman's Earthday celebration in SMALLVILLE in April 1960, "he has become Earth's greatest and most generous citizen!" (S No. 136/2: "The Secret of Kryptonite!").

Indeed, preliminary indications are that Superman's fame will be even greater in the future than it is today. A scientist of the thirtieth century A.D. has called Superman "the greatest hero in history" (WF No. 91, Nov/Dec '57: "The Three Super-Sleepers!"), and a man of the fiftieth century A.D. has echoed the sentiment, describing Superman as "the greatest hero in Earth's history" (S No. 122/1, Jul '58: "The Secret of the Space Souvenirs").

In the texts, Superman is frequently referred to as the Man of Steel and the Man of Tomorrow. He is also referred to as the Action Ace, the Champion of Democracy, and the King of Speed.

In addition, the texts describe Superman as a "champion of justice" (S No. 9/1, Mar/Apr '41), an "amazing champion of the helpless and oppressed" (S No. 13/4, Nov/Dec '41), "the world's foremost crime crusader" (S No. 18/3, Sep/Oct '42: "The Man with the Cane"), "the world's foremost justice-dispenser" (S No. 25/1, Nov/Dec '43: "The Man Superman Refused to Help!"), "Earth's mightiest warrior" (S No. 38/1, Jan/Feb '46: "The Battle of the Atoms!"), "the world's mightiest citizen" (S No. 40/2, May/Jun '46: "A Modern Marco Polo!"), the "world's mightiest being" (S No. 65/3, Jul/Aug '50: "Three Supermen from Krypton!"), "the world's most famous citizen" (Act No. 150, Nov '50: "The Secret of the 6 Superman Statues!"), "the most amazing human of our century" (Act No. 171, Aug '52: "The Secrets of Superman!"), "the world's mightiest defender of justice" (Act No. 178, Mar '53: "The Sandman of Crime!"), "the mightiest man alive" (Act No. 181, Jun

'53: "The New Superman"), "the world's mightiest man" (Act No. 182, Jul '53: "The Return of Planet Krypton!"; and others), "Earth's mightiest champion of justice" (Act No. 225, Feb '57: "The Death of Superman"), the "mightiest human being in all the world" (Act No. 235, Dec '57: "The Super-Prisoner of Amazon Island"), "Earth's mighty champion" (Act No. 242, Jul '58: "The Super-Duel in Space"), "the mightiest man on Earth" (Act No. 247, Dec '58: "Superman's Lost Parents!"; and others), "the Earth's most powerful man" (Act No. 269, Oct '60: "The Truth Mirror!"), a "famed battler against crime and injustice" (Act No. 287, Apr '62: "Perry White's Manhunt for Superman!"), "Earth's protector" and "the heroic champion of Earth" (Act No. 327, Aug '65: "The Three Generations of Superman!"), "the world's greatest hero" (Act No. 328, Sep '65: "Superman's Hands of Doom!"), "a defender of the weak and oppressed" and "the mightiest of all men" (S No. 164/1, Oct '63: pts. I-II—"The Showdown Between Luthor and Superman!"; "The Super-Duel!"), the "greatest lawman of them all" (S No. 178/2, Jul '65: "When Superman Lost His Memory!"), and as "a defender of the helpless, [and] a champion of the underdog" (S No. 146/1, Jul '61: "The Story of Superman's Life!").

A. ORIGIN
  1. The Original Account
  2. Addenda and Revisions
B. THE SECRET IDENTITY
C. THE COSTUME
D. THE FORTRESS OF SOLITUDE
E. THE SUPER-POWERS
  1. Derivation of the Super-Powers
  2. Super-Speed and the Power of Flight
  3. Super-Strength
  4. Invulnerability
  5. X-Ray Vision and the Other Optical Powers
  6. Super-Hearing
  7. Super-Breath and Related Powers
  8. Vocal and Ventriloquistic Powers
  9. Mental and Intellectual Powers
  10. Miscellaneous Powers
F. THE VULNERABILITIES
  1. Kryptonite
    a. *Green Kryptonite*
    b. *Red Kryptonite*
    c. *Gold Kryptonite*
    d. *Blue Kryptonite*
    e. *White Kryptonite*
  2. Magic
  3. Virus X
  4. Other Vulnerabilities
G. THE EQUIPMENT
  1. Lead Armor
  2. Dummies, Robots, and Androids
  3. Miscellaneous Equipment
H. THE MAN HIMSELF (as Clark Kent)
I. THE MAN HIMSELF (as Superman)

J. THE WOMEN OF THE CHRONICLES
   1. The Relationship with Lois Lane
   2. The Relationship with Lana Lang
   3. The Relationship with Lori Lemaris
   4. The Relationship with Lyla Lerrol
   5. The Relationship with Sally Selwyn
K. THE RELATIONSHIP WITH THE LAW-
   ENFORCEMENT ESTABLISHMENT
L. THE TEXTS
   1. Locales
   2. Developments
      a. *The Early Adventures*
      b. *The Wartime Adventures*
      c. *The Postwar Adventures*
      d. *The Later Adventures*

A. Origin. "Out of the infinite reaches of interstellar space came **Superman**, son of the doomed planet Krypton, to fight the forces of evil upon Earth…!" (Act No. 63, Aug '43: "When Stars Collide!").

1. The Original Account. "As a distant planet was destroyed by old age, a scientist placed his infant son within a hastily devised space-ship, launching it toward Earth!

"When the vehicle landed on Earth, a passing motorist, discovering the sleeping babe within, turned the child over to an orphanage.

"Attendants, unaware the child's structure was millions of years advanced of their own, were astounded at his feats of strength.

"When maturity was reached, he discovered he could easily: leap ⅛th of a mile; hurdle a twenty-story building…raise tremendous weights…run faster than an express train…and that nothing less than a bursting shell could penetrate his skin!

"Early, Clark decided he must turn his titanic strength into channels that would benefit mankind. And so was created…

"SUPERMAN! Champion of the oppressed, the physical marvel who had sworn to devote his existence to helping those in need!" (Act No. 1, Jun '38).

2. Addenda and Revisions. Since the appearance of this original account forty years ago, the story of Superman's origin has been greatly revised and expanded to accommodate a wealth of new detail. Later texts, for example, gave the name of Superman's native planet as KRYPTON and described its people and civilization in great detail. Superman's parents, JOR-EL and LARA, were introduced, and the events leading up to the cataclysm that destroyed Krypton were extensively chronicled. The "passing motorist" who found the infant Superman became a couple, JONATHAN AND MARTHA KENT, who adopted the orphan from space and named him Clark Kent. Conflicting accounts were offered of the infant's brief stay in the orphanage, including how long he remained there and whether his super-powers were actually revealed there. Later texts asserted that Superman embarked upon his super-heroic career while still a youngster in SMALLVILLE rather than

waiting until "maturity was reached." And, finally, the range and extent of his superhuman powers were continually expanded and the explanation of how he acquired them was periodically revised (*see* section E, the super-powers). For complete accounts and analyses of all the supplementary data concerning Superman's origin, consult the various entries cross-referenced above.

B. The Secret Identity. "The fact that Clark Kent, newspaper reporter, and **Superman**, the mighty Man of Steel, are one and the same person, is the most closely guarded secret in the world!" (Act No. 189, Feb '54: "Clark Kent's New Mother and Father!").

Within days of his arrival on the planet Earth, the infant Superman had two identities: on the one hand he was Kal-El, an orphaned native of the exploded planet KRYPTON, and on the other hand he was Clark Kent, the adopted son of JONATHAN AND MARTHA KENT. It was the Kents, in fact, who urged upon him the importance of keeping his super-powers secret and of using them to aid humanity.

"Now listen to me, Clark!" cautioned Jonathan Kent, while Clark was still a youngster. "This great strength of yours--you've got to hide it from people or they'll be scared of you!"

"But when the proper time comes," added Martha Kent, "you must use it to assist humanity" (S No. 1/1, Sum '39).

There were also other reasons for keeping Clark's super-powers secret: Jonathan Kent feared that unscrupulous individuals would try "to exploit his super-powers for evil purposes" (WF No. 57, Mar/Apr '52: "The Artificial Superman!"), and Clark himself soon realized that if he used his super-powers openly against the underworld, his foster parents would inevitably become the helpless targets of gangland retribution (S No. 146/1, Jul '61: "The Story of Superman's Life!"; and others).

In addition, the use of an alternate identity gives Superman the advantage of surprise over the criminal element and enables him to conduct investigations discreetly as journalist Clark Kent. "If, by accident, Lois [Lane] ever reveals my secret to the world," muses Superman during an anxious moment in October 1960, "my undercover role as Clark Kent will be ruined. I'll no longer be able to investigate criminals as 'meek' Clark Kent so that they can later be captured by **Superman**! And it may take me years to set up a new identity!" (Act No. 269: "The Truth Mirror!").

And Action Comics No. 61 observes that

The matter of **Superman's** secret identity is one of utmost importance. Disguised as Clark Kent, the **Man of Tomorrow** finds it possible, secretly, to ferret out crimes that need solving, and injustices that cry out to be righted [Jun '43: "The Man They Wouldn't Believe!"].

Perhaps the most important advantage of a secret identity, however, is that it affords Superman a

Just before the doomed planet, KRYPTON, exploded to fragments, a scientist placed his infant son within an experimental rocket-ship, launching it toward Earth!

When the vessel reached our planet, the child was found by an elderly couple, the Kents.

LOOK, MARY! -- IT'S A CHILD!

THE POOR THING! -- IT'S BEEN ABANDONED!

The infant was turned over to an orphan asylum, where it astounded the attendants with its feats of strength.

WE -- WE COULDN'T GET THAT SWEET CHILD OUT OF OUR MIND.

WE'VE COME TO ADOPT HIM IF YOU'LL PERMIT US.

I BELIEVE IT CAN BE ARRANGED. ('-- WHEW! THANK GOODNESS THEY'RE TAKING HIM AWAY BEFORE HE WRECKS THE ASYLUM!')

The love and guidance of his kindly foster-parents was to become an important factor in the shaping of the boy's future.

NOW LISTEN TO ME CLARK! THIS GREAT STRENGTH OF YOURS -- YOU'VE GOT TO HIDE IT FROM PEOPLE OR THEY'LL BE SCARED OF YOU!

BUT WHEN THE PROPER TIME COMES, YOU MUST USE IT TO ASSIST HUMANITY.

As the lad grew older, he learned to his delight that he could hurdle skyscrapers . . .

. . . leap an eighth of a mile . . .

. . . raise tremendous weights . . .

. . . run faster than a streamline train --

. . . and nothing less than a bursting shell could penetrate his skin!

WHAT TH' — ? THIS IS THE SIXTH HYPODERMIC NEEDLE I'VE BROKEN ON YOUR SKIN!

TRY AGAIN, DOC!

The passing away of his foster-parents greatly grieved Clark Kent. But it strengthened a determination that had been growing in his mind.

Clark decided he must turn his titanic strength into channels that would benefit mankind

And so was created--

SUPERMAN

CHAMPION OF THE OPPRESSED, THE PHYSICAL MARVEL WHO HAD SWORN TO DEVOTE HIS EXISTENCE TO HELPING THOSE IN NEED!

© NPP 1939

An early version of Superman's origin, published in 1939

Clark Kent changes to Superman in an empty storeroom at the Daily Planet, *1940*

haven of refuge from his life as a super-hero, enabling him to escape the adulators and curiosity seekers and to relate to ordinary Earth folk on everyday human terms.

Several texts, in fact, deal explicitly with the question of why it is important to Superman to maintain a secret identity. Superman No. 127/1 describes a series of events, purported to have taken place sometime in the past, when, after eyewitnesses had seen Clark Kent apparently "perish" in an accidental explosion, Superman had decided to allow his mild-mannered alter ego to remain "dead" and to live out his life openly as Superman, sharing an apartment with his friend JIMMY OLSEN. Before long, however, the disadvantages of the arrangement had become apparent to all concerned: the telephone in Jimmy's apartment rang constantly; the street outside became a mob scene as gawkers and favor seekers descended on Superman's new home; and criminals, now aware of the location of Superman's residence, concocted a plot to lure the Man of Steel into a deadly KRYPTONITE ambush. Indeed, the problems of living without a dual identity soon became so severe that Superman ultimately felt compelled to resolve the dilemma by resurrecting Clark Kent—i.e., by devising a plausible explanation to account for Kent's having survived the explosion that had apparently killed him—so that he could resume his accustomed dual life (Feb '59: "When There Was No Clark Kent!").

Action Comics No. 305 offers a series of hypothetical, "imaginary" vignettes calculated to drive home the importance of Superman's secret identity. In one vignette, the teen-aged Superman reveals his secret identity to the world, only to have his foster parents, Jonathan and Martha Kent, brutally gunned down by vengeful hoodlums while he is away from home on a super-heroic mission. In another vignette, after having rented an apartment in METROPOLIS in his Superman identity, the Man of Steel is besieged by curiosity seekers and, emerging one afternoon from his apartment, walks headlong into a kryptonite ambush devised by LEX LUTHOR, who leaves the

stricken Superman lying helpless on the pavement while he rushes off to perpetrate a million-dollar jewel heist. Superman attempts to resolve the dilemma of apartment living by taking up residence in his FORTRESS OF SOLITUDE, but the barrenness of the Arctic wastes is lonely and depressing, and Superman soon longs for the comfort of human companionship.

In another imaginary vignette, Jimmy Olsen stumbles onto the knowledge that someone on the staff of the DAILY PLANET is secretly Superman, although he does not learn exactly who. Jimmy's knowledge, however, falls into the hands of gangsters, who set up a round-the-clock surveillance of the Daily Planet Building and, when they learn finally that Clark Kent is Superman, lure Superman into a diabolical gold-kryptonite trap, thereby robbing Superman permanently of his mighty super-powers.

And, finally, in the last imaginary vignette, Clark Kent reveals his secret identity to the world when he openly uses his super-powers to thwart an attempted holdup. But when Superman attempts to establish a new civilian identity to replace the one that has now been exposed, he finds, to his dismay, that the complexities of modern life—the difficulties of obtaining a birth certificate and other valid identification to authenticate his new identity, and the need to establish a job history so that his new persona can obtain employment—make it virtually impossible for him to create a new identity as effective and substantial as the one he enjoyed as Clark Kent (Oct '63: "Why Superman Needs a Secret Identity!").

Clark Kent changes to Superman in an empty office at the Daily Planet, *1955*

Because the secret of Superman's dual identity is one the underworld would pay any price to obtain, to say nothing of the countless law-abiding individuals who would like to solve the mystery for purely egotistical reasons, the protection of his secret identity remains one of Superman's constant preoccupations. The texts repeatedly refer to Superman's secret identity as "the most closely guarded secret of the 20th century" (Act No. 171, Aug '52: "The Secrets of Superman!"), "the best-kept secret in the world" (S No. 102/2, Jan '56: "The Midget Menace"), "the world's best-kept secret" (S No. 126/1, Jan '59: "Superman's Hunt for Clark Kent!"), and "the greatest mystery of all time" (Act No. 297, Feb '63: "The Man Who Betrayed Superman's Identity!"; S No. 180/1, Oct '65: "Clark Kent's Great Superman Hunt!").

"One of the most closely guarded of secrets is the secret identity of **Superman!**" notes Action Comics No. 250. "...[N]o eye has ever seen the truth--that mild-mannered reporter Clark Kent masks the Herculean person of **Superman!**" (Mar '59: "The Eye of Metropolis!").

To conceal the fact that Clark Kent is secretly Superman, the Man of Steel has endowed his Clark Kent persona with an array of qualities and traits which are diametrically opposed to the ones he displays in his role as a super-hero. Indeed, the Clark Kent persona is meek, timid, ineffectual, submissive, mild-mannered, cowardly, even "spineless" (Act No. 1, Jun '38; and others). Clark Kent is weak, sickly, subject to fainting and dizzy spells, mildly hypochondriacal. When trouble comes, he runs away, or "dives for cover under a nearby table..." (Act No. 22, Mar '40).

The Man of Steel "has always hidden his **Superman** identity," notes Action Comics No. 324, "under the pose of a timid mouse, a trembling coward whom anyone could push around" (May '65: "The Secret Life of Clark Kent!"). Clark Kent tends to rationalize his timid persona as "the perfect camouflage for my real identity as **Superman!**" (Act No. 166, Mar '52: "The Three Scoops of Death!"). Granting, however, that Superman needs a dual identity, it seems nonetheless certain that his reasons for creating and maintaining this particular persona are largely unconscious and reveal a very great deal about the personality and inner life of Superman (see section I, the man himself [as Superman]).

"Everyone knows the world's most guarded secret is **Superman's** secret identity!" observes Action Comics No. 288. "Many men have tried to learn that secret, but failed!" (May '62: "The Man Who Exposed Superman!").

The most persistent seeker after Superman's secret, however, has not been a man, but a woman. "For years," notes Superman No. 135/1, "lovely **Lois Lane** has often wondered if her fellow reporter, meek, mild **Clark Kent**, is not in reality dynamic **Superman** in disguise!" (Feb '60: "When Lois First Suspected Clark Was Superman!").

LOIS LANE first encounters Superman in June 1938 (Act No. 1), yet it is not until June 1940 that she expresses even a mild interest in learning his secret identity (Act No. 25), and not until November-December 1940 that she expresses a real desire to ferret it out (S No. 7/2). In July-August 1941, for the

Lois Lane actively begins to suspect that Clark Kent is secretly Superman, 1942

© NPP 1942

first time in the chronicles, Lois Lane speculates that Clark Kent might possibly be Superman (S No. 11/1), but not until July-August 1942 does she actively begin to suspect "that Clark Kent and **Superman** are one and the same!" (S No. 17/1: "Man or Superman?").

Since that time, the discovery of Superman's secret identity has remained Lois Lane's constant preoccupation, although the texts are divided on the question of whether she would actually publish the secret if she were to learn it (S No. 75/3, Mar/Apr '52: "The Man Who Stole Memories!"; and others) or whether she would keep the secret to herself in order to avoid damaging the Man of Steel's super-heroic career (S No. 78/3, Sep/Oct '52: "The Girls in Superman's Life!"; and others). Superman No. 145/1 asserts that the psychological pressure of keeping the secret would be more than Lois Lane could bear (May '61: "The Secret Identity of Superman!"; see also Act No. 198, Nov '54: "The Six Lives of Lois Lane!"), and Clark Kent expresses this opinion on the question in March-April 1952: "If Lois exposes my secret identity," he muses, "it will give her the world's greatest scoop! She couldn't resist that!" (S No. 75/3: "The Man Who Stole Memories!").

However, despite Lois Lane's persistent efforts to verify her suspicion that Clark Kent is secretly Superman, the Man of Steel has always managed, often through the use of elaborate ruses, to persuade her that her suspicions were groundless, or at the very least not conclusively proven. "Sometimes," mused Clark Kent on one occasion, "Lois strains my ingenuity more than all the crooks in Metropolis!" (S No. 81/2, Mar/Apr '53: "20,000 Leagues Under the Sea with Superman").

In addition to employing elaborate ruses, many of them extremely intricate and convoluted, to prevent Lois Lane from penetrating his secret (Act No. 139, Dec '49: "Clark Kent...Daredevil!"; and many others), Superman contrives to protect his secret from Lois in other, subtler ways: by speaking of Clark

Kent, in the early years of the chronicles, in a disparaging way (Act No. 26, Jul '40; and others); by making it appear, as Clark Kent, that he is jealous of Lois Lane's interest in Superman and even secretly envious of Superman's powers (S No. 104/3, Mar '56: "The Super-Family from Outer Space"; and others); and by designing lifelike robots of Clark Kent and Superman that are so unbelievably sophisticated that one of them can actually spend an entire afternoon with Lois Lane without her even suspecting that she is not in the company of a real human being (Act No. 282, Nov '61: "Superman's Toughest Day!"; and others).

And Superman's painstaking efforts have clearly paid off, because "For years, despite her great efforts, inquisitive reporter Lois Lane has been unable to discover the secret of Superman's real identity" (Act No. 269, Oct '60: "The Truth Mirror!").

Nevertheless, the pressure of maintaining the secrecy of his dual identity exerts a great psychic toll on Superman and there are numerous indications that, in his heart of hearts, he would like Lois Lane to find him out. He has been sorely tempted to share his secret with her on several occasions (S No. 6/4, Sep/Oct '40; and others), and he has had dreams (S No. 19/2, Nov/Dec '42) and fantasies (S No. 34/2, May/Jun '45: "The Canyon That Went Berserk!") in which she discovers that Clark Kent is secretly Superman. "She's a great girl," muses Clark Kent silently in September-October 1941. "What a temptation it is to inform her who I really am!" (S No. 12/3). Clark Kent certainly wants Lois Lane at least to suspect that he is Superman, if only because he regards being dismissed as a possible suspect as something of a put-down (S No. 135/1, Feb '60: "When Lois First Suspected Clark Was Superman!").

In one early adventure, in 1943, Superman actually reveals his secret identity to Lois Lane—and asks her to marry him—in an effort to get her to abandon her announced plans to marry irresponsible playboy CRAIG SHAW. "I've known Lois for years," thinks Superman desperately, "--never declared my feelings—took her for granted... it never occurred to me that some day she might marry someone else....

"I can't let her go like this! She means too much to me! And yet--WHAT CAN I DO???

"Blowing off steam won't do any good. Somehow, I must win Lois for myself. But how? By proposing as Clark Kent?

"No. That wouldn't do--she despises Clark's meek character, and would turn him down. —There's only one thing I can do! Reveal my secret to Lois! Once she learns Clark Kent and Superman are one and the same, perhaps she'll forget Craig Shaw and marry me!"

Late that night, when Lois returns home from a lavish night on the town with Craig Shaw, she finds Clark Kent waiting in front of her apartment building. "I've been waiting for hours, Lois," he remarks. "There's something I must tell you!"

Together the two enter the elevator and ride it to the roof of Lois's building. "Better prepare yourself,

Lois," warns Kent. "What I have to say will shock and amaze you."

"What did you want to tell me, Clark?" asks Lois when they arrive on the roof.

"Just this!" replies Kent. "I'm not the quiet frightened little chap you believe I am. Far from it! The truth is--I AM SUPERMAN!"

But Lois only laughs in Kent's face, unable to believe that meek Clark Kent is actually the Man of Steel.

"But you don't understand, Lois," stammers Kent. "This is no hoax. I'm SUPERMAN! I've learned of your engagement to Craig, and I want you to marry me instead of him!"

Kent tries everything he can think of to convince Lois that he is actually Superman, but circumstances conspire to prevent him from doing so. He leaps off the roof to demonstrate his invulnerability, only to land atop a cushiony truckload of mattresses passing down the street below. He shoots himself with a pistol to prove that he cannot be harmed, only to discover that the pistol he selected was loaded only with blanks. To make matters worse, it is April Fool's Day, leading Lois to the erroneous conclusion that Kent is trying to make her the butt of an April Fool's gag.

Ultimately, Superman learns that Lois never intended to marry Craig Shaw after all, but had only encouraged Shaw's attentions as a means of enabling her to verify her suspicion that his ostentatious wealth derived from criminal activity. Superman ultimately apprehends Shaw and his henchman and, by means of an elaborate ruse, successfully persuades Lois Lane, at least for the time being, that Clark Kent and Superman are two different persons (Act No. 61, Jun '43: "The Man They Wouldn't Believe!").

Lois Lane learns Superman's secret identity in March 1951 when, while she and Clark Kent are spending a week alone on an uninhabited South Sea island as part of a contest sponsored by the Daily Planet to determine "who's more able to live alone under primitive conditions--the man or the woman," she actually sees Clark Kent changing to Superman. Superman ultimately salvages his secret, however, by tricking Lois Lane into believing that what she thought was Clark Kent changing to Superman was actually only a "delirious hallucination" brought on by a tropical fever (Act No. 154: "Miss Robinson Crusoe!").

Superman deliberately reveals his secret identity to Lois Lane in August 1954 in a desperate effort to shock her out of an amnesic state brought on by the trauma of having witnessed what she believed was the death of Clark Kent during a scuffle with criminals. As luck would have it, Superman's ploy successfully restores Lois's memory without betraying his dual identity, because Lois incorrectly interprets Superman's secret-identity revelation as meaning that the reason Clark Kent did not die in the scuffle is that Superman was impersonating Kent at the time (Act No. 195: "Lois Lane--Wanted!").

By November 1954 Lois Lane's mind has become seriously unbalanced as the result of her having

Lois Lane is convinced that she has learned Superman's secret at last,
but Jimmy Olsen and Clark Kent have the last laugh, 1962

inadvertently stumbled upon Superman in the act of changing into his Clark Kent identity. Because Lois experienced this trauma of discovery during a period when she was writing a series of newspaper articles on the "Great Women of History," Lois begins acting out a series of bizarre delusions, punctuated by brief interludes of sanity, in which she believes she is, and behaves as though she were, various famous women of history, including Florence Nightingale, Betsy Ross, Barbara Frietchie, Annie Oakley, Madame Curie, and Queen Isabella of Spain. Finally, however, Lois's delusions end of their own accord, and Superman, through an elaborate ruse, succeeds in persuading her that she never really did learn his secret at all (Act No. 198: "The Six Lives of Lois Lane!").

Lois Lane learns that Clark Kent is Superman in March 1955, when, having acquired a pair of experimental eyeglasses that endow her with the power of X-ray vision, she peers through Clark Kent's street clothes and sees his Superman costume underneath. Kent successfully safeguards his secret, however, by duping Lois into believing that Superman only loaned him his invulnerable costume to protect him from an anticipated attempt on his life by a gangland assassin (Act No. 202: "Lois Lane's X-Ray Vision!").

Lois Lane stumbles upon virtually irrefutable evidence linking Clark Kent with Superman when she discovers a highly sophisticated Clark Kent robot hidden behind a secret panel in a supply room at the *Daily Planet* in May 1958. Correctly deducing that this must be the robot Clark Kent uses to stand in for him at the *Daily Planet* whenever it is necessary for him to be elsewhere as Superman, Lois devises a scheme to trap Superman into openly admitting his secret. The Man of Steel succeeds, however, by means of an intricately convoluted ruse, in convincing Lois that she has not really learned his secret after all (Act No. 240: "Secret of the Superman Sphinx").

Clark Kent deliberately reveals his secret identity to Lois Lane in September 1958 when the two find themselves marooned on an island from which even Superman cannot escape, due to the fact that the island's volcano, which has a fallen kryptonite meteor lodged in its crater, is spewing fine particles of kryptonite dust into the surrounding air. Believing himself trapped on the island for life, Superman decides to make Lois's life a happy one by divulging the secret of his dual identity and arranging for them to be married by the island's local native chief. On the day of the scheduled wedding, however, Superman discovers that the volcano is no longer filling the air with kryptonite dust and that escape from the island is therefore possible. Ultimately, through an elaborate ruse, he succeeds in persuading Lois to withdraw from the marriage voluntarily as well as in tricking her into believing that Clark Kent had only been deceiving her when he confided to her that he was secretly Superman (S No. 124/2: "Mrs. Superman").

Lois Lane successfully tricks Superman into divulging his secret identity to her in April 1959 by

concealing her true identity beneath a blond wig and Kryptonian-style clothing and, employing the alias Rama, posing as a survivor of the exploded planet Krypton. Realizing soon afterward, however, that Lois Lane has duped him, Superman enlists the aid of his friend Bruce Wayne, the man who is secretly BATMAN, in an elaborate and ultimately successful ruse designed to persuade Lois that Clark Kent and Superman are two different men and that Superman was only playing a prank on Lois when he "pretended" to tell her his secret identity (S No. 128/2: "The Sleeping Beauty from Krypton!").

Throughout the years, numerous individuals besides Lois Lane have attempted to learn the secret of Superman's identity, or to confirm their suspicions that Clark Kent is Superman, only to be outwitted by the Man of Steel, often through the use of elaborate ruses.

LANA LANG has strongly suspected that Clark Kent is Superman ever since their childhood days in SMALLVILLE, but Superman has always managed to convince her that her suspicions were groundless, or at the very least not conclusively proven (S No. 78/3, Sep/Oct '52: "The Girls in Superman's Life!"; and others).

INSPECTOR ERSKINE HAWKINS of Scotland Yard has made a series of ingenious attempts to prove that Clark Kent is Superman, but Superman has always managed to outwit the great sleuth, often through the use of elaborate ruses (Act No. 100, Sep '46: "The Sleuth Who Never Failed!"; and others).

LEX LUTHOR learns Superman's secret identity in October 1948 when one of his henchmen sees Clark Kent change to Superman in a darkened alley. Captured sometime later by Superman, the criminals attempt to use their secret knowledge to blackmail the Man of Steel into giving them their freedom, but, through a ruse, Superman succeeds in convincing them that Clark Kent and Superman are two different persons (Act No. 125: "The Modern Nostradamus!").

Newsman Vince Ellery, a reporter for a Metropolis newspaper that is a rival of the *Daily Planet*, attempts to prove his conviction that Clark Kent is Superman by forcing Kent to wear, for a twenty-four-hour period, a pair of electronic ankle bracelets whose "mechanism...will register...if you **leave the ground** to fly in the air--or if you race at a speed faster than can a normal man!" Wearing the special ankle bracelets greatly limits Superman in the use of his super-powers, but he manages to perform his customary super-chores during the twenty-four hours without betraying his dual identity (Act No. 157, Jun '51: "The Superman Who Couldn't Fly!").

Metropolis gangster "HATCHET" KAIMS is offered $50,000 by the city's underworld chieftains to unravel the secret of Superman's identity, but the Man of Steel apprehends Kaims and his cohorts when they start a fire in Clark Kent's apartment building in an unsuccessful effort to discover which of its tenants is secretly Superman (S No. 74/3, Jan/Feb '52: "The Secret of Superman's Home!").

JOE HARRIS becomes convinced that he has

learned Superman's secret identity when a complex series of circumstances combine to persuade him that the Man of Steel is secretly an F.B.I. agent named Henry Smithers. Harris confides his conclusions to Superman and promises faithfully to keep his secret, and Superman, for his part, allows Harris to go on thinking that he has unraveled the secret of his dual identity (S No. 76/2, May/Jun '52: "The Misfit Manhunter!").

In September-October 1952 a gang of criminals, convinced that one of the members of the ATLAS CLUB must secretly be Superman, begins trying systematically to murder them all in an effort to determine which of them is invulnerable. However, Superman— who is not a member of the club in either of his identities—thwarts the various murder attempts and ultimately apprehends the criminals (S No. 78/2: "The Strong Man Club!").

An unidentified former gangster residing in MAPLEVILLE attempts to unravel the secret of Superman's identity by making him a gift of a bloodhound named Sniffer in hopes of later using the dog's acute sense of smell to root out Superman in his civilian identity. The dog succeeds in pursuing Superman's scent as far as the Daily Planet Building—where Superman works in his Clark Kent identity—but Kent throws the canine off his trail by means of a ruse and thereby thwarts the gangster's attempt to learn his secret identity (Act No. 179, Apr '53: "Super Manor!").

MR. MXYZPTLK attempts to sabotage Superman's super-heroic career in May-June 1953 by forcing him to publicly divulge his secret identity, but Superman successfully outwits the imp and banishes him back into his home dimension (S No. 82/2: "The Unemployed Superman").

The members of the ROUND TABLE CLUB, of which Clark Kent has recently become a member, learn that Kent is secretly Superman when Kent's suit of knightly armor is burned away by the breath of a fire-breathing prehistoric monster, revealing his Superman costume underneath. By means of an elaborate ruse, however, Superman successfully dupes the club members into believing that he was impersonating Clark Kent at the time Kent was seemingly exposed as Superman (S No. 86/1, Jan '54: "The Dragon from King Arthur's Court!").

The PROFESSOR attempts to track down Superman in his alternate identity in March 1954 with the aid of a dog that has developed an unbounded affection for Superman, but the Man of Steel apprehends the Professor and his henchmen and finds the dog a new home in France, where his unflagging devotion will pose less of a hazard to Superman's secret (S No. 88/2: "The Dog Who Loved Superman!").

While impersonating Clark Kent in July 1954, the super-powered villain MALA—who does not suspect that Clark Kent is secretly Superman—proclaims to the world that he, "Kent," is Superman as a means of throwing the public off the track concerning his own villainous identity while at the same time creating what he imagines will be a minor nuisance for

Superman. The widespread conviction that Kent is Superman presumably vanishes, however, when the public learns that, at the time the "revelation" was made, Kent was being impersonated by a villain with super-powers (Act No. 194: "The Outlaws from Krypton!").

PROFESSOR SNELLING, the author of a forthcoming book entitled The Life and Times of Superman, nearly uncovers Superman's secret while residing in Smallville, but Superman intervenes successfully to prevent the professor from learning his secret (S No. 90/2, Jul '54: "Superman's Secret Past!").

"THE THINKER" learns Superman's secret identity when one of his henchmen, in the act of impersonating Jimmy Olsen, stumbles upon evidence indicating Clark Kent is Superman. Through an elaborate ruse, however, Superman convinces the criminals that the evidence they have obtained is inauthentic (S No. 93/2, Nov '54: "Jimmy Olsen's Double!").

Journalist MONA MILES becomes suspicious that Clark Kent is Superman and launches a one-woman investigation to prove her suspicion correct. Through an elaborate ruse, however, Superman manages to persuade the resourceful newswoman that he has no single secret identity, but rather that he assumes new identities at random, changing to a different one every few days (S No. 99/2, Aug '55: "The 1,000 Lives of Superman!").

Mr. Mxyzptlk becomes suspicious that Clark Kent is Superman and attempts to trick Kent into betraying his secret in September 1955, but Kent successfully outwits the imp and, as Superman, succeeds in banishing Mr. Mxyzptlk back into his home dimension (Act No. 208: "The Magic of Mr. Mxyztplk").

FLOYD FOWLER correctly establishes that Clark Kent is Superman by comparing Kent's fingerprints with those of the infant Superman found embedded in a fragment of the rocket ship that first brought Superman to Earth from Krypton. Superman ultimately outwits Fowler and safeguards his secret, however, by altering the fingerprint evidence with his X-ray vision so as to make it appear that Fowler has erred in identifying Kent with Superman (S No. 100/3, Sep '55: "The Clue from Krypton").

In May 1956, while working as a reporter at the Daily Planet under a secret identity, Mr. Mxyzptlk becomes suspicious that Clark Kent is secretly Superman and attempts to trick Kent into betraying his secret. Kent successfully outwits the imp, however, and, as Superman, succeeds in banishing Mr. Mxyzptlk back into his home dimension (S No. 105/2: "Mr. Mxyztplk's Secret Identity").

DANDY JIM learns Superman's secret identity in August 1956 when two of his henchmen see the watery reflection of Superman changing to Clark Kent beneath a deserted wharf. By means of an elaborate ruse, however, Superman manages to dupe the criminals into believing they have made a mistake (S No. 107/2: "The Impossible Haircut").

PROFESSOR MARTIN, a "notorious criminal scientist," perpetrates an elaborate hoax on Superman in September 1956 in an attempt to unravel his secret identity, but Superman thwarts Martin's efforts and takes him into custody (S No. 108/1: "The Brain from the Future"). During this same period, a group of Metropolis policewomen make a series of resourceful attempts to verify their suspicion that Clark Kent is Superman, but Superman adoitly outwits them at every turn, thereby preserving the secret of his dual identity (S No. 108/3, Sep '56: "The Girl Cops of Metropolis!").

THAD LINNIS tricks Superman into believing that he has learned his secret identity as part of a scheme to blackmail the Man of Steel into leaving Metropolis while he and his henchmen loot the city with a powerful "super-tank." Superman ultimately learns that Linnis is only bluffing, however, and joins forces with Batman and ROBIN to take the gangster and his henchmen into custody (WF No. 84, Sep/Oct '56: "The Super-Mystery of Metropolis!").

In February 1957, during a period when Superman's personality is imprisoned in the mind of Jimmy Olsen, and vice versa, as the result of both men's having unwittingly exposed themselves to the effects of a Saturnian "mentality exchanger," Jimmy Olsen uncovers evidence that convinces him that Clark Kent is secretly Superman. By means of an elaborate ruse, however, Superman succeeds in tricking his young pal into believing that he has made a mistake (S No. 111/1: "The Non-Super Superman").

JUDD KENT, who actually stumbled upon the secret of Superman's identity while masquerading as Clark Kent's cousin many years ago, attempts to blackmail Superman into breaking him out of prison by threatening to reveal his secret to the world. Superman defies Kent's blackmail attempt, however, and successfully neutralizes the effects of Kent's claim by ingeniously amassing a body of bogus evidence calculated to refute the suggestion that Clark Kent and Superman are one and the same man (S No. 111/2, Feb '57: "Clark Kent's Crooked Cousin").

"MANY-FACES" FULTON concocts an elaborate scheme to learn Superman's secret identity in hopes of collecting the $1,000,000 being offered for the secret by an underworld syndicate. Superman thwarts the scheme, however, and apprehends Fulton in August 1957 (S No. 115/2: "Jimmy Olsen's Lost Pal").

After acquiring temporary super-powers in September-October 1957, BATWOMAN makes a determined effort to uncover the secret identities of Batman, Robin, and Superman. The three crimefighters outwit her at every turn, however, and before long Batwoman's super-powers have faded and vanished, without her having learned the secrets she sought (WF No. 90: "The Super-Batwoman!").

TORM learns Superman's secret identity in October 1957 by comparing Superman's fingerprints with those of Clark Kent, but Superman succeeds ultimately in destroying the fingerprint evidence, leaving Torm with no proof whatever that Clark Kent is Superman (Act No. 233: "The Land of a Million Supermen").

PROFESSOR THADDEUS V. MAXWELL, "one of the most brilliant men in the world," made a series of ingenious attempts to unravel Superman's secret identity while Clark Kent was a student at METROPOLIS UNIVERSITY. The Man of Steel successfully thwarted those attempts, however, and prevented Professor Maxwell from learning his secret (S No. 125/2, Nov '58: "Clark Kent's College Days").

CEDRIC AND MILLICENT CARSON, a pair of "scheming actors," successfully dupe Superman into revealing his secret identity by impersonating his foster parents, Jonathan and Martha Kent. The Carsons attempt to extort $5,000,000 from the Man of Steel as their price for keeping their knowledge secret, but Superman thwarts the extortion scheme by using his command of "super-hypnotic forces" to erase all memory of his secret identity from the villainous actors' minds (Act No. 247, Dec '58: "Superman's Lost Parents!").

Television interviewer JOHN BATES invites Clark Kent to appear on his talk show, "The Eye of Metropolis," with the clear intention of using the occasion as an opportunity to confirm his suspicion that Clark Kent is Superman. Bates's penetrating interview provides Clark Kent with some uncomfortable moments, but Kent nevertheless succeeds in convincing his interrogator, and millions of television viewers as well, that mild-mannered Clark Kent could not possibly be Superman (Act No. 250, Mar '59: "The Eye of Metropolis!").

The entire world learns Superman's secret identity in January 1961 when a blast of "fire-breath" belched forth by a Kryptonian "flame dragon" (see FLAME DRAGON) scorches away Clark Kent's street clothes in full view of Lois Lane and other onlookers, revealing his Superman costume underneath. Superman manages to preserve his secret, however, by means of an elaborate ruse involving Batman, SUPERGIRL, and KRYPTO THE SUPERDOG (S No. 142/3: "Flame-Dragon from Krypton").

JOHN KILEY successfully tricks Clark Kent into revealing his secret identity as the first step in a diabolical scheme to lure Superman to his doom in a kryptonite deathtrap, but Superman thwarts the scheme—and protects the secret of his dual identity—by enlisting the aid of Supergirl and the SUPERMEN EMERGENCY SQUAD in an elaborate ruse designed to persuade the villain that when he thought he saw Clark Kent changing to Superman he was actually only experiencing a drug-induced hallucination (Act No. 276, May '61: "The War Between Supergirl and the Supermen Emergency Squad!").

Two members of the ANTI-SUPERMAN GANG learn Superman's secret identity in April 1962 with the aid of a tiny television transmitter that they have concealed inside a "special medallion" that Superman has agreed to wear around his neck to help promote a Greater Metropolis Fund charity drive. The villains attempt to cap their scheme by killing Clark Kent with kryptonite, but the Man of Steel thwarts the attempt on his life and, through an elaborate ruse, tricks the criminals into believing they have erred in identifying Clark Kent with Superman (S No. 152/3: "The TV Trap for Superman!").

Ex-convict HAL COLBY attempts to unravel the secret of Superman's identity, both to wreak vengeance on Superman for a past defeat and to collect the $1,000,000 reward being offered him for the secret by "the leaders of the nation's crime syndicate," but the Man of Steel thwarts the scheme in May 1962 (Act No. 288: "The Man Who Exposed Superman!").

GENERAL PEDRO VALDEZ and his cohorts stumble upon the secret of Superman's identity and attempt to lure him into a kryptonite deathtrap, but the Man of Steel thwarts the attempt on his life and, with the aid of Superman look-alike MANUEL BAEZA, succeeds in convincing the villains that Clark Kent and Superman are two different persons (Act No. 306, Nov '63: "The Great Superman Impersonation!").

"Mysterious gangland czar" HERB FARR threatens to murder Lois Lane unless Clark Kent—who is widely known as a close friend of Superman—agrees to divulge Superman's secret identity. By means of an elaborate ruse, however, Superman succeeds in apprehending Farr and his henchmen and in rescuing Lois Lane from their clutches (S No. 180/1, Oct '65: "Clark Kent's Great Superman Hunt!").

A number of trusted individuals are actually privy to Superman's secret, including Batman and Robin (S No. 76/1, May/Jun '52: "The Mightiest Team in the World!"; and others), Supergirl (Act No. 285, Feb '62: "The World's Greatest Heroine!"; and others), Krypto the Superdog (S No. 142/1, Jan '61: "Lois Lane's Secret Helper!"; and others), and Superman's various Superman robots (S No. 163/1, Aug '63: "Wonder-Man, the New Hero of Metropolis!"; and others). PETE ROSS knows Superman's secret, but Superman does not know he knows it (Act No. 309, Feb '64: "The Superman Super-Spectacular!").

Other individuals or groups of individuals have learned Superman's secret or been entrusted with it, but they have invariably been inhabitants of distant planets, alien dimensions, other eras, or remote civilizations not likely to communicate their knowledge to Superman's contemporaries.

WILLIAM SHAKESPEARE deduces that Clark Kent is Superman—and even contemplates writing a play about it—during a time-journey by Superman to the city of London in the year 1601. Superman manages to convince the renowned dramatist, however, of the importance of keeping his dual identity secret (S No. 44/3, Jan/Feb '47: "Shakespeare's Ghost Writer!").

The inhabitants of the planet Skar, including VITOR VALL and his family, know that Clark Kent is Superman as the result of having observed his exploits by means of sophisticated space "scanners" (S No. 104/3, Mar '56: "The Super-Family from Outer Space").

The people of the sixtieth century A.D., including the historian KA THAR, know that Clark Kent is Superman (WF No. 81, Mar/Apr '56: "The True History of Superman and Batman!").

The SUPERMAN OF 2956 is fully aware that Clark Kent is secretly Superman (Act No. 215, Apr '56: "The Superman of Tomorrow").

Superman reveals his secret identity to ZOLL ORR and his son Kell Orr during a visit to the planet XENON in February 1958 (S No. 119: "The Second Superman!" chs. 1-3—"The World That Was Krypton's Twin"; "A Double for Superman"; "Superman's Mightiest Quest").

LORI LEMARIS knows that Clark Kent is Superman as the result of having read his mind by means of her telepathic powers (S No. 129/3, May '59: "The Girl in Superman's Past!"; and others). Since all ATLANTIS's mer-people possess powers identical to Lori's, it is entirely possible that every Atlantean is privy to the secret of Superman's dual identity (S No. 135/2, Feb '60: "Superman's Mermaid Sweetheart!"; and others).

Because BIZARRO possesses "a dim copy of Superman's memory," he knows that Clark Kent is secretly Superman (Act No. 255, Aug '59: "The Bride of Bizarro!"). Moreover, since all the male inhabitants of the planet HTRAE are duplicates of the original Bizarro, it is virtually certain that every one of them is privy to Superman's secret (Act No. 263, Apr '60: "The World of Bizarros!"; and others).

PRINCESS JENA, of the planet ADORIA, is fully aware that Clark Kent is secretly Superman (Act No. 266, Jul '60: "The Captive of the Amazons").

JAN-DEX and Zo-Gar, a pair of evil extraterrestrial "chameleon men" from the thirtieth century A.D., know that Clark Kent is Superman as the result of having been told the secret by COSMIC KING and LIGHTNING LORD (Act No. 283, Dec '61: "The Red Kryptonite Menace!"), two members of the LEGION OF SUPER-VILLAINS, an organization of twenty-first century A.D. super-criminals who also know the secret (S No. 147/3, Aug '61: "The Legion of Super-Villains!").

All of the members of the SUPERMAN REVENGE SQUAD know that Clark Kent is Superman (Act No. 286, Mar '62: "The Jury of Super-Enemies!"; and others), as do all the members of the LEGION OF SUPER-HEROES (S No. 152/1, Apr '62: "The Robot Master!"; and others).

The inhabitants of the PHANTOM ZONE know that Clark Kent is Superman as the result of their unique ability to observe everything that takes place in the physical universe (S No. 157/1, Nov '62: "The Super-Revenge of the Phantom Zone Prisoner!").

ROKK AND SORBAN, a pair of "interplanetary gamblers" from the planet Ventura, are fully aware that Clark Kent is Superman (S No. 171/1, Aug '64: "Superman's Sacrifice!").

Superman reveals his secret identity to Peter Fry, one of the inhabitants of secluded CRATER VALLEY, during a visit there in May 1965 (Act No. 324: "The Secret Life of Clark Kent!").

In addition, Superman's secret identity is known to all the inhabitants of the bottle city of KANDOR (S No. 179/2, Aug '65: "The Menace of Gold Kryptonite!").

More than a dozen individuals have deduced or otherwise come into possession of Superman's secret, but they have all taken their knowledge to the grave with them or developed amnesia before they could betray the secret.

Superman's foster parents, JONATHAN AND MARTHA KENT, encouraged him to maintain the secrecy of his dual identity and guarded the secret faithfully until their deaths (S No. 105/1, May '56: "Superman's 3 Mistakes!"; and others).

An unidentified burglar stumbles upon Superman's secret identity in September-October 1940 when, while hiding in a closet in Clark Kent's apartment, he sees Clark Kent change into Superman. The burglar dies moments later, however, when, while racing frantically out of the apartment building in a desperate effort to escape from Superman, he trips down a flight of stairs and breaks his neck (S No. 6/3; see also S No. 48/3, Sep/Oct '47: "The Rarest Secret in the World!").

When young Latin American intern Pedro Carlos, who is dying of the ghastly "yellow plague" (see QUASMANIA) that has broken out in Metropolis, refuses to tell Clark Kent what he knows of the plague and its origins, Kent wins the dying man's confidence by opening his shirtfront to reveal his Superman costume underneath. Carlos readily provides Superman with the information he seeks, then dies moments later, within seconds of having learned Superman's secret (S No. 11/3, Jul/Aug '41).

Window washer John Forrest stumbles upon the secret of Superman's identity when he peers through a window at the Daily Planet and sees Superman changing to Clark Kent. The shock of this discovery sends Forrest reeling backward off his window ledge and plummeting toward the pavement, but Superman rescues him before he hits the sidewalk. The unconscious Forrest is rushed to the hospital, with Superman fearful that he will reveal his identity the moment he regains consciousness. Awakening in his hospital bed, however, Forrest identifies himself as Eric Joyce, a Metropolis banker who vanished years ago after a blow on the head afflicted him with temporary amnesia. Now cured by the trauma of his recent fall, Joyce recalls nothing of his life as window washer "Forrest," including his briefly held knowledge of Superman's identity (S No. 48/3, Sep/Oct '47: "The Rarest Secret in the World!").

SUSAN SEMPLE, a switchboard operator at the Daily Planet, learns Superman's secret identity when "a strange experiment" endows her with extraordinary extrasensory powers. Twenty-four hours later, however, Susan Semple's powers vanish, leaving her with no recollection whatever of Superman's secret (Act No. 163, Dec '51: "The Girl of Tomorrow").

The infant son of MR. AND MRS. ROGER BLISS learns Superman's secret identity when, after having acquired temporary super-powers as the result of ingesting the contents of some Kryptonian "condensed food" cylinders, he peers through Clark Kent's street clothes with his X-ray vision and sees Kent's Superman costume underneath. Before long, however, the infant's temporary super-powers have faded and vanished, and Clark Kent expresses confidence that the child will have forgotten everything he learned during the period he was endowed with super-powers (Act No. 217, Jun '56: "The Amazing Super-Baby").

Newspaper tycoon HENRY FURST dupes Clark Kent into revealing his secret identity by means of an elaborate ruse in February 1958. Fortunately for Superman, however, a special drug Furst ingested to enable him to carry out his ruse turns out to have "hallucinatory side-effects," and Furst recovers from its influence with only a mistaken recollection of what Clark Kent revealed to him (Act No. 237: "Superman's Exposed Identity").

SUPER-GIRL, a lovely blond super-heroine who materializes out of nowhere in August 1958 in response to Jimmy Olsen's wish on a magic totem, learns Superman's secret identity when she peers through Clark Kent's street clothes with her X-ray vision and sees his Superman costume underneath. Soon afterward, however, in an ultimate act of heroism, Super-Girl sacrifices her existence in order to save the life of Superman (S No. 123: chs. 1-3—"The Girl of Steel"; "The Lost Super-Powers"; "Superman's Return to Krypton").

SUPER-MENACE has learned, by means of his own super-powers, that Clark Kent is secretly Superman, but his knowledge vanishes with him when he abandons his human form and transforms himself into "pure energy" (S No. 137, May '60: chs. I-III—"The Super-Brat from Krypton"; "The Young Super-Bully"; "Superman vs. Super-Menace!").

While inhabiting the body of PERRY WHITE, the diabolical "plant intelligence" XASNU learns the secret of Superman's identity when it peers through Clark Kent's street clothes with its X-ray vision and sees Kent's Superman costume underneath. Supergirl ultimately destroys Xasnu, however, with a chunk of white kryptonite, and Perry White, recovering from his ordeal, retains no recollection whatever of the events that occurred during the period when the sinister "plant alien" was inhabiting his body (Act No. 278, Jul '61: "The Super Powers of Perry White!").

QUEX-UL has learned the secret identities of both Superman and Supergirl as the result of having observed them while serving out his term in the Phantom Zone, but Quex-Ul is afflicted with "permanent amnesia" in November 1962 as the result of his exposure to gold kryptonite and retains no recollection whatever of his origins or of Superman's and Supergirl's dual identities (S No. 157/1: "The Super-Revenge of the Phantom Zone Prisoner!").

Perry White discovers Superman's secret identity during a period when he is suffering from temporary amnesia. With some help from Clark Kent, White soon regains his memory, but he retains no recollection whatever of Superman's secret or of the events that occurred while he was afflicted with amnesia (Act No. 297, Feb '63: "The Man Who Betrayed Superman's Identity!").

WONDER-MAN knows that Clark Kent is secretly

Superman as the result of having once been one of Superman's Superman-robots, but Wonder-Man perishes, taking Superman's secret with him, as the result of the Superman Revenge Squad's having deliberately endowed him with a defective "android body" (S No. 163/1, Aug '63: "Wonder-Man, the New Hero of Metropolis!").

Superman entrusts President JOHN F. KENNEDY with the secret of his dual identity so that the President can impersonate him briefly by appearing on a television show disguised as Clark Kent (Act No. 309, Feb '64: "The Superman Super-Spectacular!"; see also S No. 170/1, Jul '64: "Superman's Mission for President Kennedy!"). President Kennedy was assassinated in Dallas, Texas, in November 1963, and presumably guarded Superman's secret faithfully until his death.

Joe Meach learns Superman's secret identity when a freak accident transforms him into the COMPOSITE SUPERMAN, but Meach's powers ultimately vanish, leaving him with no recollection whatever of the secret he learned (WF No. 142, Jun '64: "The Origin of the Composite Superman!" pts. I-II—"The Composite Superman!"; "The Battle Between Titans!").

ADAM NEWMAN knows that Clark Kent is secretly Superman as the result of having been originally created by Superman as a Superman android, but Adam Newman perishes, taking Superman's secret with him, after being mortally wounded while battling a runaway nuclear pile (S No. 174/1, Jan '65: pts. 1-2—"Clark Kent's Incredible Delusion!"; "The End of a Hero!").

Metropolis billionaire "SAD SAM" SMITH should know that Clark Kent is Superman, because an unexpected emergency forces Kent to change to Superman directly in front of Smith in April 1960. Smith, however, cannot even imagine Clark Kent being Superman, and he assumes that Kent's change of costume was only an ingenious attempt to make him laugh (S No. 136/3: "The Super-Clown of Metropolis!").

Interestingly, several dogs have learned Superman's secret identity in the sense that they have recognized, by means of their canine sense of smell, that Clark Kent and Superman are one and the same man.

Lois Lane's dog Flip, a black-and-white spaniel, knows that Clark Kent is Superman and once put his knowledge to good use by summoning Clark Kent to the rescue after Lois Lane had been taken captive by a gang of dognappers (S No. 31/2, Nov/Dec '44: "A Dog's Tale!").

A bloodhound named Sniffer learns that Clark Kent is Superman when an unidentified gangster gives him to Superman as a pet during the period when Superman is residing in the town of MAPLEVILLE. The gangster attempts to use the dog to sniff out Superman in his other identity, but Kent throws Sniffer off his trail by means of a clever ruse and the gangster fails in his attempt to learn Superman's secret (Act No. 179, Apr '53: "Super Manor!").

Reginald Chauncey Applethwaite III, a golden-haired cocker spaniel belonging to a criminal known as the PROFESSOR, becomes so grateful to Superman for rescuing it from a caved-in rabbit burrow that it wags its tail exuberantly whenever it senses Superman in the vicinity. The Professor attempts to capitalize on the spaniel's affection for Superman by using it to sniff out Superman in his other identity, but Superman apprehends the Professor and his henchmen and finds Reginald a new home in France, where his unflagging devotion will pose less of a hazard to the secret of his dual identity (S No. 88/2, Mar '54: "The Dog Who Loved Superman!").

C. The Costume. "But once he is out of view...the timid reporter switches to a colorful costume known with fear, admiration, and respect in every corner of the globe!" (S No. 16/4, May/Jun '42: "Racket on Delivery").

In the course of four full decades, Superman's chroniclers have portrayed him in a variety of artistic styles, yet the basic details of his costume have remained substantially unchanged. Superman wears a blue costume complemented by red trunks, red boots, and a long, flowing red cape. A yellow belt encircles his waist, and there is a highly stylized Superman insignia—consisting of a large red letter "S" inscribed within a yellow shield, which is bordered in red—emblazoned on his chest. The back of Superman's cape bears a similar insignia, except that this one consists of a yellow letter "S" inscribed within a yellow shield bordered in yellow.

Superman as he was portrayed in 1938. Note the crudely drawn "S" insignia emblazoned on his chest

What minor changes there have been in Superman's costume over the years have generally been in terms of coloring. His boots, for example, which are blue in a number of very early adventures (Act No. 4, Sep '38; Act No. 5, Oct '38) and yellow in at least one other (Act No. 7, Dec '38), have been consistently colored red since the end of the 1930s.

The stylized "S" insignia on Superman's chest,

small and somewhat crudely portrayed in Superman's earliest adventures, soon becomes larger, more highly stylized, and more distinct. In a number of early adventures (e.g., Act No. 18, Nov '39), the yellow shield lacks the distinctive red border, but the red border has become standard by the beginning of the 1940s.

Inconsistencies persist for nearly twenty years, however, regarding the coloring of the insignia on Superman's cape. Missing from Superman's costume entirely in a number of texts (S No. 35/2, Jul/Aug '45: "Like Father, Like Son!"; and others), it is sometimes portrayed as a blue "S" on a yellow shield (S No. 11/2, Jul/Aug '41; and others), sometimes as a yellow "S" on a blue shield (Act No. 74, Jul '44: "Courtship of Adelbert Dribble!"; and others), sometimes as a red "S" on a yellow shield (S No. 12/3, Sep/Oct '41; and others), sometimes as a yellow "S" on a red shield (S No. 52/3, May/Jun '48: "Superman in Valhalla!"; and others), and sometimes as a yellow "S" on a yellow shield (S No. 22/2, May/Jun '43: "The Luck of O'Grady"; and others).

Often, the cape insignia is portrayed inconsistently within the confines of a single story (S No. 20/4, Jan/Feb '43: "Not in the Cards"; and others). Not until the late 1950s does a yellow letter "S" inscribed within a yellow shield become the standardized form of the insignia emblazoned on the back of Superman's cape (Act No. 233, Oct '57: "The Land of a Million Supermen"; and others).

© NPP 1978

Superman as he is being portrayed in the 1970s. The "S" insignia on his chest is now distinctive and highly stylized

In the texts, Superman's costume is referred to as his "invulnerable uniform" (Act No. 236, Jan '58: "Superman's New Uniform!"), his "action costume" (S No. 142/2, Jan '61: "Superman Meets Al Capone!"), his "action suit" (S No. 129/2, May '59: "Clark Kent, Fireman of Steel!"), his "super-costume" (S No. 129/3, May '59: "The Girl in Superman's Past!"), his "super-uniform" (S No. 134, Jan '60: chs. I-III—"The Super-Menace of Metropolis!"; "The Revenge Against Jor-El!"; "The Duel of the Supermen!"), and as his "super-suit" (Act No. 247, Dec '58: "Superman's Lost Parents!"; and others).

The origin of Superman's costume has been treated inconsistently in the chronicles, although there is virtually unanimous agreement among the texts that the costume is as "indestructible" (WF No. 29, Jul/Aug '47: "The Books That Couldn't Be Bound!"; and many others) as the Man of Steel himself. In Summer 1940 Superman describes his costume as "constructed of a cloth I invented myself which is immune to the most powerful forces!" (S No. 5/3). Indeed, seven years later, after LOIS LANE has borrowed his cape and used it as binding material for her scrapbook of Superman photos, Superman accepts the loss with equanimity. "Hm," he muses thoughtfully, "—well I guess I can weave a new cloak..." (WF No. 29, Jul/Aug '47: "The Books That Couldn't Be Bound!").

By the early 1950s, however, the texts have begun to describe Superman's costume as having been fashioned by Martha Kent (see KENT, JONATHAN AND MARTHA [MR. AND MRS.]) out of the colored blankets she and her husband found wrapped around the infant Superman when he arrived on Earth in a rocket from the doomed planet KRYPTON (S No. 73/2, Nov/Dec '51: "The Mighty Mite!"; and others).

Subsequent texts describe Superman's costume as having been fashioned from "a rare material from Krypton" (S No. 81/2, Mar/Apr '53: "20,000 Leagues Under the Sea with Superman"), "impenetrable material from **Krypton**" (WF No. 127, Aug '62: "The Sorcerer from the Stars!"), "indestructible material" (Act No. 199, Dec '54: "The Phantom Superman!"; and others), and "indestructible cloth woven on the planet **Krypton**" (Act No. 236, Jan '58: "Superman's New Uniform!"). Superman No. 112/2 offers this observation:

> Indestructible as time itself, **Superman's** costume, woven of strange cloth from his native planet, Krypton, has aided him in unqiue ways, many times in the past [Mar '57: "Superman's Fatal Costume"].

The implication of these texts is clearly that the indestructible quality of Superman's costume owes itself to the special properties of the Kryptonian material from which it was fashioned. "...[Y]ou see," explains Superman in October 1954, "my costume is of fabric that came with me from the planet Krypton when I was an infant! It's an indestructible **super-fabric!**" (Act No. 197: "The Stolen 'S' Shirts"). And in January 1958 he adds: "My uniform was made of indestructible cloth woven on the planet **Krypton** where I was born--cloth which was found in the rocket that brought me to Earth!" (Act No. 236: "Superman's New Uniform!").

More recent texts, however, have greatly modified

this position. Although Superman's costume is still described as having been fashioned from a "synthetic fiber of Krypton" (S No. 143/3, Feb '61: "Bizarro Meets Frankenstein!") whose unique properties "can't be duplicated" (S No. 112/2, Mar '57: "Superman's Fatal Costume"), this cloth is now said to have acquired its indestructibility just as Superman acquired his super-powers (see section E, the super-powers)—as the result of having been transported from the planet Krypton to the vastly different environment of Earth (Act No. 326, Jul '65: "The Legion of Super-Creatures!"; and others).

According to Superman No. 146/1, Martha Kent was moved to fashion a super-playsuit for the infant Superman because the child was constantly destroying his store-bought clothes by engaging in various forms of super-powered play. Fortunately, the Kents had had the foresight to save the three blankets—one red, one blue, and one yellow—in which the infant Superman had been swathed when he arrived on Earth in his rocket. Because the blanket material was indestructible and therefore could not be cut by any scissors, the Kents unraveled some loose ends and then coaxed their super-powered infant into using the heat of his X-ray vision to cut the unraveled thread so that Martha Kent could use it to sew the Kryptonian blankets into a super-playsuit. Years later, Martha Kent unraveled the playsuit and rewove the thread into Superman's now-famous costume (Jul '61: "The Story of Superman's Life!"; and others). According to one of the stories in Superman Annual No. 8, the young Superman used "strips of rubber padding" salvaged from the wreckage of his rocket to fashion a pair of bright red boots, while a yellow strap, also salvaged from the rocket, became his belt (Win '63-'64: "The Origin of Superman's Super-Costume!").

Superman's costume is, by all accounts, absolutely indestructible. Fire cannot burn it (WF No. 11, Fall '43: "The City of Hate!"; and others); the strongest shears cannot cut it (WF No. 29, Jul/Aug '47: "The Books That Couldn't Be Bound!"); neither bullets (Act No. 202, Mar '55: "Lois Lane's X-Ray Vision!"; and others) nor lightning (Act No. 197, Oct '54: "The Stolen 'S' Shirts"; and others) can make a mark on it. "...[N]othing can destroy it" (S No. 120/3, Mar '58: "The Human Missile"), not even the force of six atomic bombs exploding inside it (S No. 78/1, Sep/Oct '52: "The Beast from Krypton!"; see also S No. 146/2, Jul '61: "Superman's Greatest Feats!").

So long as it remains on Earth, or in some other environment where Superman would ordinarily have super-powers, Superman's costume retains its indestructibility. This remains true even if, for some reason or other, Superman has temporarily lost his powers. On such an occasion, Superman remains invulnerable to bullets and other weapons that strike his costume, but vulnerable to any weapons that may strike his head or other exposed parts of his body (WF No. 77, Jul/Aug '55: "The Super Bat-Man!"; and others). Similarly, the costume retains its indestructibility even if someone other than Superman wears it,

rendering the wearer invulnerable to bullets and other weapons so long as the weapons strike the costume and not the wearer. The costume protects BATMAN from being killed by bullets, for example, when he poses as Superman in July-August 1954 (WF No. 71: "Batman—Double for Superman!"); it protects LEX LUTHOR from being killed by bullets when he impersonates Superman in January 1958 (Act No. 236: "Superman's New Uniform!").

In addition to being indestructible, Superman's costume possesses remarkable resiliency. It "can stretch indefinitely without losing its strength" (S No. 81/2, Mar/Apr '53: "20,000 Leagues Under the Sea with Superman"; and others) and, according to Superman No. 78/1, "loses none of its strength when stretched!" (Sep/Oct '52: "The Beast from Krypton!"). Stretching the cape or costume, however, requires super-strength (Act No. 246, Nov '58: "Krypton on Earth!"; and others), and only Superman is "strong enough to stretch it!" (WF No. 127, Aug '62: "The Sorcerer from the Stars!").

KRYPTONITE radiations, however, can penetrate the costume, and objects from the planet Krypton—all of which, like the costume itself, immediately become indestructible in the alien environment of Earth—can rip or tear the costume just as they would have been able to do on Krypton, where neither costume nor object was "super." In October 1965, for example, on Earth, a sword made of kryptium, Krypton's "strongest metal," easily slashes a gaping hole in Superman's costume. This is because the materials used to make both sword and costume retain, on Earth, durability proportional to that which they originally possessed on Krypton (Act No. 329: "The Ultimate Enemy!").

It is this phenomenon to which Superman refers in February 1962, when, after having been bitten severely on the hand by a Kryptonian "flame dragon" (see FLAME DRAGON), he remarks that "The beast's bite penetrated my skin...which is invulnerable to everything except the bite of a Kryptonian creature who would have normally been stronger than me if both of us were on Krypton, minus our super-strength!" (S No. 151/3: "Superman's Greatest Secret!"). Just as the flame dragon's bite penetrated Superman's invulnerable skin, so could it also have penetrated his indestructible costume.

In July 1957 Superman observes that "...it's impossible for threads to unravel from my costume" (S No. 114/2: "The Man Who Discovered Superman's Identity"), but in January 1959 he modifies this observation somewhat when he muses to himself that "My super-garb can't tear, because it's made of indestructible material! But by using my super-strength, I can unravel some thread...!" (Act No. 248: "The Man No Prison Could Hold!").

According to the most recent explanation of Superman's powers, Superman derives his super-powers, in part, from the peculiar radiations of Earth's yellow sun. On planets revolving about a red sun, however, such as the planet LEXOR, or the planet

Krypton before it exploded, Superman has no super-powers. Similarly, on red-sun planets, Superman's costume loses its indestructibility and can be torn and damaged like any ordinary garment on Earth. If Superman's costume is ripped or damaged during a visit to a red-sun world—or during a visit to the bottle city of KANDOR, where red-sun conditions prevail—Superman must take care to repair the damage before returning to Earth, where the costume will once again become indestructible and therefore impossible to cut and sew (Act No. 236, Jul '65: "The Legion of Super-Creatures!"; and others).

While assuming the role of newsman Clark Kent, Superman wears his costume beneath his street clothes (Act No. 171, Aug '52: "The Secrets of Superman!"; and many others). Although he can easily change identities at super-speed, "so swiftly that no eye notices the motion" (Act No. 64, Sep '43: "The Terrible Toyman!"), Kent usually changes to Superman in some easily accessible, secluded place, such as a "deserted alley" (S No. 9/1, Mar/Apr '41; and many others), an "empty hallway" (S No. 19/1, Nov/Dec '42: "Case of the Funny Paper Crimes"), a "convenient doorway" (Act No. 155, Apr '51: "The Cover Girl Mystery!"; and others), a quiet "corner alcove" (S No. 181/1, Nov '65: pts. I-II—"The Super-Scoops of Morna Vine!"; "The Secret of the New Supergirl!"), and, most frequently of all, an unused "storage closet" at the DAILY PLANET (Act No. 181, Jun '53: "The New Superman"; and many others). Only very rarely, despite the stereotype, has Clark Kent ever changed into his Superman costume inside a phone booth (S No. 60/3, Sep/Oct '49: "Superman Fights the Super-Brain!"; and others).

In a deserted alleyway, Clark Kent changes into the world's most famous action costume, 1948

The moment when Clark Kent changes to Superman is a moment of high drama. Here is how a number of texts have described it:

That evening... within the privacy of Clark Kent's apartment, a miraculous transformation occurs!--Off come glasses and street-clothes...Clark's meek figure

straightens erect... and a few instants later the retiring reporter is replaced by the dynamic **SUPERMAN!** One lithe step brings the Man of Steel to his open window... and in another moment his tremendously powerful muscles fling him out into the night like a living projectile! [Act No. 7, Dec '38].

...[I]n a nearby deserted alley, Clark Kent removes his outer civilian garments, transforming himself into the champion of justice....**SUPERMAN!** [S No. 9/1, Mar/Apr '41].

In a secluded alleyway, Clark swiftly doffs his outer garments, revealing the colorful costume of--**Superman,** the Man of Steel...[Act No. 232, Sep '57: "The Story of Superman, Junior"].

Clark Kent's street clothes are "made of super-compressible material" to enable Superman to conceal them in the "secret pouch of his cape" (Act No. 313, Jun '64: "The End of Clark Kent's Secret Identity!"). In addition, they have been specially treated to make them "friction-proof" (Act No. 322, Mar '65: "The Coward of Steel!") and fireproof (S No. 178/2, Jul '65: "When Superman Lost His Memory!") so that, if the occasion demands it, Superman can fly through the air or perform super-feats in his Clark Kent identity without fear of his clothing burning up from air friction or being otherwise destroyed.

Clark Kent's eyeglasses—which one text refers to as his "indestructible super-glasses" (S No. 133/1, Nov '59: "The Super-Luck of Badge 77")—are "made of a super-plastic from the planet Krypton," thus enabling Kent to stand in the midst of a raging fire, or focus his X-ray vision through the lenses at full power, without fear of their melting from the intense heat (S No. 129/2, May '59: "Clark Kent, Fireman of Steel!"; and others).

According to Superman No. 130/1, Superman, while he was still a youngster in SMALLVILLE, used the "plexiglass shield" from the wreckage of the rocket ship that had brought him to Earth to fashion the eyeglass lenses he now wears in his role as Clark Kent. "These super-plastic lenses don't melt when I project my X-ray vision through them!" thought young Clark Kent at the time. "Ordinary Earth glasses would! As for the rims, my X-rays never touch them!" (Jul '59: "The Curse of Kryptonite!").

Superman No. 146/1 confirms this account, adding that the smashing of the rocket's "super-plexiglass" shield when the rocket crash-landed produced four "fairly round pieces" ideal for use as eyeglass lenses. "What luck!" thought the young Clark Kent as he examined what remained of the wreckage. "When the super-plexiglass smashed, four fairly round pieces were formed! I can make plastic frames to conceal the uneven ridges! I'll have glasses...both for my boyhood and manhood...that are impervious to my X-ray vision!" (Jul '61: "The Story of Superman's Life!"; *see also* Act No. 288, May '62: "The Man Who Exposed Superman!").

In the early texts of the Superman chronicles, Superman is described as concealing his Clark Kent clothing "beneath his cloak" (WF No. 2, Sum '41) or underneath his cape (S No. 30/1, Sep/Oct '44: "Superman Alias Superman!") whenever he goes into action in his Superman identity. By the mid-1950s, however, the hiding place for Clark Kent's street clothes has begun to be described as a hidden pocket inside Superman's cape (WF No. 68, Jan/Feb '54: "The Menace from the Stars!"; and others), or, more specifically, as "a secret pouch in the lining of his cape..." (Act No. 252, May '59: "The Menace of Metallo!"; and others).

The most thorough description of exactly how Clark Kent disposes of his street clothes when he changes to Superman appears in Action Comics No. 252:

> Moments later, the shy reporter becomes **Superman, Man of Steel!** With one squeeze of his mighty fingers, he compresses Clark Kent's resilient clothing and special fibre shoes into a compact ball!
> The next moment, **Superman** thrusts his compressed Clark Kent clothes into a secret pouch in the lining of his cape... [May '59: "The Menace of Metallo!"].

In the early days of Superman's career, before his ability to fly was definitely established, Superman occasionally glided through the air, using his cape to catch the wind as though it were a sail. "Seizing the sides of his cape," notes Superman No. 6/3, "**SU-PERMAN** navigates it like a sail so that he swoops out of sight in a giant curve...!" (Sep/Oct '40). Action Comics No. 48 contains this description: "Moments later, as **Superman** drifts leisurely over the **Speed Motors** building, using his wide-spread cape like a sail..." (May '42: "The Adventure of the Merchant of Murder").

When Superman flies visitors to his FORTRESS OF SOLITUDE, he wraps them in his "weather-proof, indestructible cape" to protect them against freezing to death in the sub-zero Arctic cold (Act No. 253, Jun '59: "The War Between Superman and Jimmy Olsen!"; and others) as well as against the potentially fatal "friction caused by **Superman's** flight" (Act No. 302, Jul '63: "The Amazing Confession of Super-Perry White!"). Visitors who have been flown to the Fortress of Solitude wrapped in Superman's cape have included Lois Lane (Act No. 274, Mar '61: "The Reversed Super-Powers!"), PERRY WHITE (Act No. 302, Jul '63: "The Amazing Confession of Super-Perry White!"), and JIMMY OLSEN (Act No. 253, Jun '59: "The War Between Superman and Jimmy Olsen!"; S No. 158, Jan '63: "Superman in Kandor" pts. I-III— "Invasion of the Mystery Super-Men!"; "The Dynamic Duo of Kandor!"; "The City of Super-People!").

The texts describe several methods by which Superman has cleaned his costume. To burn away some "kryptonite solution" sprayed onto his costume by STANLEY STARK's henchmen, Superman allows the costume to be struck by a bolt of lightning (Act No. 197, Oct '54: "The Stolen 'S' Shirts"). According to Action Comics No. 247, the Fortress of Solitude contains, among its many wonders, a swimming pool filled with molten lava which, as Superman swims in it, "burns off any stains and cleans [his] super-suit"

(Dec '58: "Superman's Lost Parents!"). Superman No. 134 shows Superman cleaning his costume in the Fortress of Solitude by standing in the white-hot flame of a "super-blowtorch" (Jan '60: chs. I-III— "The Super-Menace of Metropolis!"; "The Revenge Against Jor-El!"; "The Duel of the Supermen!"). In March 1962, at Superman's request, Jimmy Olsen uses an acetylene torch at the Fortress of Solitude to burn away the dirt stains on Superman's costume (Act No. 286: "The Jury of Super-Enemies!").

Superman possesses a number of duplicate costumes (S No. 74/3, Jan/Feb '52: "The Secret of Superman's Home!"; and others), one of which he carries around with him in the secret pouch in the lining of his cape (WF No. 138, Dec '63: "The Secret of the Captive Cavemen!"). These duplicates, however, are made only of ordinary cloth and are, therefore, not indestructible (S No. 172, Oct '64: pts. I-III—"The New Superman!"; "Clark Kent—Former Superman!"; "The Struggle of the Two Supermen!"; and others).

An elaborate scheme by Stanley Stark to steal the shirt from Superman's costume—so that he can "analyze and reproduce [its] indestructible fabric"— is thwarted by Superman in October 1954 (Act No. 197: "The Stolen 'S' Shirts").

LEX LUTHOR makes a detailed spectroscopic analysis of Superman's costume in March 1957 as the first step in an elaborate scheme to demoralize Superman while he and his henchmen commit a series of crimes, but Superman ultimately thwarts the scheme and apprehends Luthor and his henchmen (S No. 112/2: "Superman's Fatal Costume").

By impersonating Professor Xavier Carlton, a "renowned nuclear scientist," Lex Luthor tricks Superman into briefly lending him his costume for use in an atomic experiment in January 1958, and then, when the time comes to return the super-costume, surreptitiously replaces it with a duplicate made of ordinary material. This theft of Superman's costume is merely the first phase of Luthor's intricately convoluted scheme to destroy the Man of Steel, but Superman ultimately recovers his costume and apprehends the villain (Act No. 236: "Superman's New Uniform!").

"GADGET" GRIM, the inventor of a special magnet designed to attract the cloth of Superman's costume, attempts to use the magnet to help him commit a series of crimes, but Superman apprehends Grim and his henchmen in March 1958 (S No. 120/3: "The Human Missile").

By January 1965 ADAM NEWMAN has rendered Superman's costume temporarily invisible by means of a special "ray" as part of his elaborate scheme to trick Clark Kent into believing that Adam Newman is the only real Superman and that all Kent's own recollections of an action-filled life as Superman have only been symptoms of a pathetic delusion (S No. 174/1: pts. 1-2—"Clark Kent's Incredible Delusion!"; "The End of a Hero!").

D. The Fortress of Solitude. "Deep in the core of a mountainside in the desolate Arctic wastes lies **Superman's Fortress of Solitude**, where the **Man of**

Steel conducts incredible experiments, keeps strange trophies, and pursues astounding hobbies!" (Act No. 241, Jun '58: "The Super-Key to Fort Superman").

Carved into the rock face of an "ice-covered mountain" (Act No. 282, Nov '61: "Superman's Toughest Day!") not far from the North Pole (Act No. 243, Aug '58: "The Lady and the Lion"; and others) lies Superman's Fortress of Solitude, a "secret and solitary home" (Act No. 251, Apr '59: "The Oldest Man in Metropolis!") where Superman can relax, perform scientific experiments, and escape, if only temporarily, the demands and distractions of the everyday world.

Here in this "secret sanctum" (Act No. 326, Jul '65: "The Legion of Super-Creatures!"), far from civilization, are the fabulous trophy room, housing the hard-won memorabilia of more than a thousand adventures; the workshop and super-laboratory, where Superman labors in search of an antidote to KRYPTONITE and performs other experiments; the gymnasium and recreation facilities, where Superman exercises, relaxes, and indulges in a variety of super-hobbies; the interplanetary zoo, containing live species of wildlife from distant planets; special rooms and memorials in honor of Superman's parents, foster parents, and closest friends; the bottle city of KANDOR, a city of the planet KRYPTON that was reduced to microscopic size and stolen by the space villain BRAINIAC sometime prior to the death of Krypton; special monitors for communicating with Kandor, the undersea realm of ATLANTIS, the PHANTOM ZONE, distant planets, and alien dimensions; Superman's Superman-robots and other special equipment; and numerous other rooms, exhibits, weapons, machines, and scientific devices. Indeed, since the invasion of the Fortress by an outsider could result in the placing of these devices in the hands of evildoers—as well as endanger Superman's secret identity—the exact location of the Fortress remains one of the world's most closely guarded secrets.

In the texts, the Fortress of Solitude is referred to as Superman's "mountain fortress of silence and solitude" (Act No. 241, Jun '58: "The Super-Key to Fort Superman"), his "super-hideaway" (Act No. 243, Aug '58: "The Lady and the Lion"), and his "secret Arctic headquarters" (Act No. 311, Apr '64: "Superman, King of Earth!").

"Whenever Superman wants to get away from it all," notes Action Comics No. 261, "he retires to his secret sanctuary, the Fortress of Solitude, the most glamorous hideaway in the entire universe!" (Feb '60: "Superman's Fortresses of Solitude!").

In Superman's words:

This is the one place where I can relax and work undisturbed! No one suspects its existence, and no one can penetrate the solid rock out of which it is hewn! Here I can keep the trophies and dangerous souvenirs I've collected from other worlds. Here I can conduct secret experiments with my super-powers...and keep souvenirs of my best friends! [Act No. 241, Jun '58: "The Super-Key to Fort Superman"].

Superman approaches his Fortress of Solitude, 1964

Superman's Fortress of Solitude is not mentioned in the chronicles, at least by that name, until May-June 1949 (S No. 58/3: "The Case of the Second Superman"), but its existence is foreshadowed in a number of earlier texts.

In January 1941 a reference is made to Clark Kent's "laboratory," but the text contains no indication of where it is located (Act No. 32).

In July-August 1942 Superman completes construction of a huge "mountain retreat," a gigantic "mansion"—situated atop a "remote mountain-peak"—whose ornate facade features a huge Superman emblem patterned after the one emblazoned on his chest. "An excellent location for the secret citadel I recently built for myself," thinks Superman as he flies toward his retreat, "--but there's still some work to be done before I can consider it completed!"

"Streaking into action," notes the text, "Superman swarms over the structure, hands flying like piston rods, until the mansion is completed...." The newly completed citadel features a collection of trophies of Superman's past adventures; a fully equipped gymnasium, where Superman "indulges in acrobatics that would cause any gym enthusiast to doubt his eyesight"; and a circular running track, around which Superman "races at so great a speed there appears to be one continuous body girdling the track!" (S No. 17/3: "Muscles for Sale!").

In Fall 1942 Superman visits his mountain retreat once again, this time to exercise, "relax and catch up on [his] reading schedule!" The sanctuary, built into the side of a huge mountain, can be entered by means of an ordinary doorway, but the Superman emblem above the door, which is on hinges, functions as an emergency doorway, enabling Superman to exit from his mountain hideaway at super-speed (WF No. 7: "The Eight Doomed Men"). This mountain sanctuary also appears in several later texts, where it is referred to as Superman's "secret mountain-retreat" (Act No.

53, Oct '42: "The Man Who Put Out the Sun!"), his "mountain retreat" (S No. 21/3, Mar/Apr '43: "The Robber Knight"), and his "mountain hideaway" (S No. 21/4, Mar/Apr '43: "The Ghost of Superman!").

In Fall 1943 a reference is made to Superman's "hidden laboratory," containing an array of scientific apparatus as well as the Man of Steel's "private files, one of the most extensive newspaper clipping morgues in the world" (WF No. 11: "The City of Hate!"). This laboratory is presumably located in Superman's mountain retreat, but this is never explicitly stated.

In November-December 1943 the mountain retreat reappears, this time stocked with the necessary materials for fashioning disguises (S No. 25/3: "King of the Comic Books").

In May-June 1949 the name Fortress of Solitude is employed for the first time in the chronicles, and, also for the first time, Superman's sanctuary is depicted as being located in a region of ice and snow, described only as "the polar wastes." "I built it here in the polar wastes," explains Superman, "because the intense cold keeps away snoopers." During this period, the Fortress has its first outside visitor: REGOR, the "super-champion" of the planet UUZ (S No. 58/3: "The Case of the Second Superman").

Following this first appearance, however, the name Fortress of Solitude does not reappear in the chronicles for another nine years. In the interim, texts refer to it as Superman's "private retreat," "secret hideaway" (Act No. 149, Oct '50: "The Courtship on Krypton!"), "secret workshop" (S No. 81/1, Mar/Apr '53: "Superman's Secret Workshop"), "secret mountain hideaway" (WF No. 69, Mar/Apr '54: "Jor-El's Last Will!"), and "secret eyrie" (S No. 108/2, Sep '56: "Perry White, Jr., Demon Reporter!").

By October 1950 the facilities of Superman's private retreat have come to include a fully equipped laboratory and a "special police radio" for intercepting emergency calls. When Superman takes LOIS LANE there for a visit during this period, he keeps her eyes covered during the journey, because, in his words, "The location of my hideaway must remain a secret...!" (Act No. 149: "The Courtship on Krypton!").

The location of the mountain sanctuary does not remain secret for long, however. LEX LUTHOR locates and invades it in March-April 1953 (S No. 81/1: "Superman's Secret Workshop"), and the entire world learns its location—here described as in or near Mount Kadens—when the pilots of a search plane discover it in March-April 1954. "Once Superman's location is known," notes the text, "he is bombarded with pamphlets, and broadcast appeals for aid!" (WF No. 69: "Jor-El's Last Will!").

It is not until June 1958, nine years after the name Fortress of Solitude first appears in the chronicles, that the texts introduce the sprawling Arctic sanctuary—situated "deep in the core of a mountainside in the desolate Arctic wastes"—on which all subsequent renditions of the Fortress have been based (Act No. 241: "The Super-Key to Fort Superman").

Located inside "a desolate mountain top in the Arctic" (Act No. 241, Jun '58: "The Super-Key to Fort Superman"; and others), either "at the North Pole" (Act No. 242, Jul '58: "The Super-Duel in Space") or near it (Act No. 243, Aug '58: "The Lady and the Lion"; and others), the Fortress of Solitude was hollowed out of solid "rock cliff" by Superman (Act No. 300, May '63: "Superman Under the Red Sun!"; and others) with his bare hands. "Here I can get away from the world at times," thought Superman as he gouged away the solid rock, "...keep a super-trophy collection...stock an interplanetary zoo of strange animals...perform dangerous experiments...all kinds of things!" (S No. 176/2, Apr '65: "Tales of Green Kryptonite No. 2").

The Fortress is three stories high and features gigantic, museumlike, high-ceilinged rooms (LC No. C-48, Oct/Nov '76). The roof—which contains a huge, electronically operated observation dome (S No. 134, Jan '60: chs. I-III—"The Super-Menace of Metropolis!"; "The Revenge Against Jor-El!"; "The Duel of the Supermen!")—and the walls have been insulated, since April 1961, with a "thick coating of lead" to prevent kryptonite radiation from penetrating the Fortress (S No. 144/3: "The Orphans of Space!"). Superman added a special annex to the Fortress for SUPERGIRL in February 1962 (Supergirl story in Act No. 285: "The Infinite Monster!"; see also LC No. C-48, Oct/Nov '76) and has shared the Fortress with her since that time (S No. 152/1, Apr '62: "The Robot Master!"; and others).

Entrance to the Fortress is achieved by means of a massive metal door set into the face of the ice-encrusted rock cliff. "Sheltered from view by jutting rocks," the door is "so heavy that no human on Earth could move it an inch!"

Pointing toward the door, from atop a nearby peak, is a gigantic, golden, arrow-shaped key that fits neatly into a matching keyhole at the center of the massive door. "From above," muses Superman in June 1958, "this looks like a luminous arrow marker to guide planes over this lonely region! No one would suspect it's really a key--a super-key that weighs tons--and that no one else can lift!" (Act No. 241: "The Super-Key to Fort Superman"; and many others).

"Only this giant key," notes Action Comics No. 243, "can unlock the super-hideaway which is barred to the rest of the world!" (Aug '58: "The Lady and the Lion").

Indeed, even if evildoers were to discern the true function of the gigantic "airplane marker," its gigantic weight alone would prevent them from using it to invade the Fortress (Act No. 245, Oct '58: "The Shrinking Superman!"; and others).

Although its primary function is to lock and unlock the massive Fortress door, the giant key apparently does serve a useful purpose as an "airline guidepost" as well (Act No. 243, Aug '58: "The Lady and the Lion"; and others), its luminosity enabling it to serve as a beacon for air traffic even at night (Act No. 282, Nov '61: "Superman's Toughest Day!"; and others).

"I purposely disguised it as an airplane marker!" observes Superman in a flashback sequence in April 1965. "Installed on this mountain peak, it will guide pilots safely through this desolate wilderness!" (S No. 176/2: "Tales of Green Kryptonite No. 2").

By the late 1970s, however, the giant key has ceased to serve as an airline guidepost, having been moved from its old position atop a mountain peak facing the Fortress to a new position, resting vertically on brackets, directly to the left of the Fortress door (LC No. C-48, Oct/Nov '76; and others). One text describes the giant key as literally made out of gold, but this assertion seems so improbable that it may well be erroneous (Act No. 291, Aug '62: "The New Superman!").

The massive front door can be opened only by means of this gigantic key

Inside the Fortress of Solitude are the myriad rooms, exhibits, and special facilities that combine to make the Fortress the world's most incredible sanctuary.

When Superman "needs exercise worthy of his super-muscles" (Act No. 247, Dec '58: "Superman's Lost Parents!"), there are the extraordinary facilities of his "super-gym" (Act No. 245, Oct '58: "The Shrinking Superman!"), where the Man of Steel can swim in a private swimming pool filled with molten lava, engage in a super-tug of war with a dozen "atomic-powered robots" (Act No. 247, Dec '58: "Superman's Lost Parents!"), or spar a few rounds with an atomic-powered robot that is easily twelve feet tall. "Goodness!" exclaims Lois Lane in October 1958. "The robot's punch would cave in the side of a battleship! **Superman** doesn't feel it!" (Act No. 245: "The Shrinking Superman!").

For recreation, Superman bowls in the Fortress's giant bowling alley, filled with gigantic, oversized pins (Act No. 245, Oct '58: "The Shrinking Super-

man!"), or matches wits in a game of "super-chess with a great robot he has built as a playmate for himself...." "This robot possesses a super-electronic brain!" muses Superman in June 1958. "He can think and play with the speed of lightning, and plans a million moves at once! It's tough beating him!" But Superman does beat him, in "a game that's played so fast the pieces move in a blur of speed...."

Superman also pursues his own private "super-hobbies" at the Fortress, such as painting. During a visit there in June 1958, for example, Superman—hovering in midair, brush in hand, before a giant canvas—paints a picture of a Martian landscape while simultaneously verifying every detail of the real Martian landscape by homing in on MARS with his telescopic vision (Act No. 241: "The Super-Key to Fort Superman").

Superman also records his latest adventures in his own secret diary, a gigantic book, made of metal, which Superman inscribes with his fingernail while hovering in midair high off the Fortress floor. "There's no chance my diary will ever be destroyed!" muses Superman in June 1958. "The pages are made of metal and I engrave all my entries with my fingernails! And there's no danger that anyone will ever read these pages. I write everything in Kryptonese, the language of the planet on which I was born!" (Act No. 241: "The Super-Key to Fort Superman").

Elsewhere in the Fortress is the fully equipped "super-laboratory" (S No. 126/1, Jan '59: "Superman's Hunt for Clark Kent!"; and others), where the Man of Steel performs ceaseless experiments in search of an antidote to kryptonite, eyeglasses that will enable his X-ray vision to penetrate lead (Act No. 241, Jun '58: "The Super-Key to Fort Superman"; and others), a safe means of enlarging the city of Kandor (S No. 158, Jan '63: "Superman in Kandor" pts. I-III— "Invasion of the Mystery Super-Men!"; "The Dynamic Duo of Kandor!"; "The City of Super-People!"; and others), and other discoveries. To aid him in research, Superman keeps samples of green kryptonite on hand at the Fortress (S No. 134, Jan '60: chs. I-III—"The Super-Menace of Metropolis!"; "The Revenge Against Jor-El!"; "The Duel of the Supermen!"). Inside a locked safe, he keeps samples of red kryptonite, each wrapped in a "protective lead covering" and labeled according to the ways in which they have, at one time or another, affected either him, Supergirl, or KRYPTO THE SUPERDOG (Act No. 284, Jan '62: "The Babe of Steel!"; see also Act No. 300, May '63: "Superman Under the Red Sun!").

The Fortress of Solitude also boasts an elaborately equipped workshop (Act No. 264, May '60: "The Superman Bizarro!"), where Superman keeps his "super tool-chest" (Act No. 245, Oct '58: "The Shrinking Superman!"), an oversized chest filled with gigantic versions of ordinary tools, which, in Superman's words, "come in handy for super-jobs...!" (S No. 176/2, Apr '65: "Tales of Green Kryptonite No. 2"). These tools were first used by

Superman in March-April 1953 (S No. 81/1: "Superman's Secret Workshop").

Another room in the Fortress serves as the repository for the many plaques, trophies, and other awards that have been bestowed on Superman in the course of his career (Act No. 243, Aug '58: "The Lady and the Lion"). This may be the room where Superman has hung the special "golden certificate"

AND PRESENTLY, INSIDE HIS OWN SUPER-LABORATORY, AS HE USES HIS AMAZING X-RAY VISION...

OH-OOH! ACCORDING TO THIS COSMO-SPECTRUM ANALYSIS, THERE'S A VERY STRANGE COMBINATION OF ELEMENTS IN THIS VITAMIN! IN FACT, IT CONTAINS ISOTOPES RESEMBLING *KRYPTONITE* WHICH MAY EVEN AFFECT *ME!*

© NPP 1959

Superman at work in the Fortress's "super-laboratory," 1959

awarded him by the United Nations, empowering him to apprehend criminals in U.N. member nations and to enter and leave those nations without a passport. A similar certificate, conferred upon Supergirl by the U.N. in February 1962, hangs on a wall of the Fortress alongside Superman's own (Act No. 285: "The World's Greatest Heroine!").

Among the most colorful areas of the Fortress are the "interplanetary zoo" (Act No. 241, Jun '58: "The Super-Key to Fort Superman"; and others), housing a Kryptonian "metal-eater" (S No. 179/2, Aug '65: "The Menace of Gold Kryptonite!") and other live extraterrestrial fauna (LC No. C-48, Oct/Nov '76; and others), and the Hall of Interplanetary Monsters, featuring either models or stuffed specimens of fearsome extraterrestrial creatures (Act No. 261, Feb '60: "Superman's Fortresses of Solitude!").

Many of the rooms in the Fortress have been set aside as tributes to Superman's friends and loved ones.

The Lois Lane Room is filled, in Superman's words, with "souvenirs and trophies of our past adventures together," including a lifelike wax statue of Lois (S No. 129/1, May '59: "The Ghost of Lois Lane"; and others), several life-size photographs of Lois and Superman (Act No. 241, Jun '58: "The Super-Key to Fort Superman"; Act No. 245, Oct '58: "The Shrinking Superman!"), and a lock of Lois Lane's hair, encased in glass. The room is decorated with rare flowers (S No. 152/1, Apr '62: "The Robot

Master!"), and around the neck of the statue is an as-yet-incomplete necklace of perfectly matched pearls which Superman intends as a final gift for Lois in the event of his untimely death (Act No. 241, Jun '58: "The Super-Key to Fort Superman").

"A...A Lois Lane Room?" exclaims Lois happily when she first visits the room in October 1958. "You've collected trophies of me!"

"Why not, Lois?" replies Superman. "After all, you're one of my closest friends!"

"I...I wish I were more than a close friend...his wife!" sighs Lois silently (Act No. 245: "The Shrinking Superman!").

The Jimmy Olsen Room contains, among other trophies and souvenirs, a lifelike wax statue of JIMMY OLSEN and a luxurious handmade sports car which Superman is building as a final gift for Jimmy (Act No. 241, Jun '58: "The Super-Key to Fort Superman"; and others).

The Perry White Room contains a detailed scale model of PERRY WHITE's one-story suburban home and other mementoes (Act No. 278, Jul '61: "The Super Powers of Perry White!"; *see also* S No. 152/1, Apr '62: "The Robot Master!").

The Batman Room (Act No. 241, Jun '58: "The Super-Key to Fort Superman"), also referred to as the Batman and Robin Room, contains lifelike wax statues of BATMAN and ROBIN, as well as statues of their alter egos, Bruce Wayne and Dick Grayson (S No. 142/3, Jan '61: "Flame-Dragon from Krypton"); trophies of past cases Superman and Batman worked on together; an array of superscientific criminological apparatus, including a "lightning fingerprint classifier," an "electronic clue analysis" machine, and a "crime probability predictor"; and an ultra-sophisticated "robot detective" which Superman is constructing as a final gift for Batman. "This 'robot detective' should help Batman," muses Superman in June 1958, "...if ever I can't help him any more!" (Act No. 241: "The Super-Key to Fort Superman"; *see also* WF No. 100, Mar '59: "The Dictator of Krypton City!"). Because an outsider who entered this room would learn Batman's and Robin's secret identities, Superman has installed a special "protective device" designed to destroy his friends' statues instantly—thereby safeguarding their secret identities—in the event an intruder attempts to force his way into the locked room (S No. 142/3, Jan '61: "Flame-Dragon from Krypton").

The Supergirl Room, which contains a lifelike wax statue of Supergirl and other mementoes, is similarly equipped with a protective device to prevent an unauthorized intruder from learning the secret of her dual identity (S No. 142/3, Jan '61: "Flame-Dragon from Krypton").

The Jor-El and Lara Room, set aside as a memorial to Superman's parents (Act No. 247, Dec '58: "Superman's Lost Parents!"), contains lifelike wax statues of JOR-EL clutching a scientific blueprint and of LARA holding the infant Superman, and a model of the rocket that carried the infant Superman to Earth after Krypton exploded (Act No. 273, Feb '61: "The World of Mr. Mxyzptlk!").

Another room in the Fortress, set aside as a memorial to Superman's foster parents, JONATHAN AND MARTHA KENT, features a lifelike wax tableau of SUPERBOY and the Kents sharing a meal together in their family home in SMALLVILLE (Act No. 247, Dec '58: "Superman's Lost Parents!").

To help safeguard the secret of his dual identity, Superman has also created a Clark Kent Room, complete with a lifelike wax statue of Clark Kent and other mementoes, modeled after the rooms in the Fortress set aside to honor his closest friends. "Clark is known to be a friend of Superman," observes Superman in June 1958, "and if some unexpected earthquake ever opened my secret cave to a stranger that wax Clark would help preserve the secret of my identity!" (Act No. 241: "The Super-Key to Fort Superman"). Superman No. 152/1 adds this observation on the usefulness of the Clark Kent Room: "If intruders found rooms honoring all of [Superman's] friends but Kent," notes the text, "they'd suspect Kent was secretly Superman!" (Apr '62: "The Robot Master!").

Among the Fortress's "secret rooms," however, is a special Superman Room, containing lifelike wax statues of Clark Kent and Superman together with inscriptions revealing Superman's secret identity. Like the rooms set aside in honor of Supergirl and Batman and Robin, the Superman Room is equipped with a special explosive protective device designed to destroy the statues and their identity-revealing inscriptions in the event an intruder forces his way into the room (S No. 142/3, Jan '61: "Flame-Dragon from Krypton").

The Krypton Room, set aside in memory of Superman's exploded native planet, contains a scale model of Krypton (Act No. 278, Jul '61: "The Super Powers of Perry White!") along with a "3-dimensional tableau of the exact moment that the planet Krypton exploded!" The tableau depicts the destruction of the planet and the escape of the infant Superman in a tiny rocket (Act No. 261, Feb '60: "Superman's Fortresses of Solitude!").

Rooms are not generally set aside to memorialize the exploits of villains, but the Fortress does contain a Brainiac Room. In it are a lifelike wax statue of Brainiac, a model of his "space-time craft," and an array of complex machinery identified as "experiments aimed at penetrating Brainiac's force-field" (Act No. 275, Apr '61: "The Menace of Red-Green Kryptonite!").

In November 1962 Superman completes construction of a new Hall of Enemies, filled with colorful wax busts of such infamous villains and villainesses as MR. MXYZPTLK, SATURN QUEEN, JAX-UR, Brainiac, and Lex Luthor (Act No. 294: "The Kryptonite Killer!").

"Forbidden weapons of crimedom" (Act No. 241, Jun '58: "The Super-Key to Fort Superman") and other "unknown, dangerous machines" (WF No. 100,

Mar '59: "The Dictator of Krypton City!"), many of them confiscated by Superman from his most dangerous foes, are also on display in the Fortress. Among them are a "strange apparatus" created by Lex Luthor, designed "to summon beings from the fourth dimension" (Act No. 241, Jun '58: "The Super-Key to Fort Superman"), an apparent reference to the "fourth dimensional ray machine" employed by Lex Luthor in November 1957 (S No. 117/2: "The Secret of Fort Superman"); the ingenious "duplicator ray" (S No. 140, Oct '60: pts. I-III—"The Son of Bizarro!"; "The 'Orphan' Bizarro!"; "The Bizarro Supergirl!") with which Lex Luthor brought BIZARRO into being in July 1959 (Act No. 254: "The Battle with Bizarro!"); the "matter-radio" apparatus built by criminals from blueprints stolen from PROFESSOR AMOS DUNN (Act No. 281, Oct '61: "The Man Who Saved Kal-El's Life!"); the "enlarging ray" (S No. 158, Jan '63: "Superman in Kandor" pts. I-III—"Invasion of the Mystery Super-Men!"; "The Dynamic Duo of Kandor!"; "The City of Super-People!") employed by the Kandorian "renegade scientist" ZAK-KUL in October 1958 (Act No. 245: "The Shrinking Superman!"); and the portable raygunlike "shrinking ray" that Superman once confiscated from Brainiac (S No. 158, Jan '63: "Superman in Kandor" pts. I-III—"Invasion of the Mystery Super-Men!"; "The Dynamic Duo of Kandor!"; "The City of Super-People!"; and others).

One text refers to a room in the Fortress housing an array of "super inventions," among them a device created by Superman "whose vibrations can shatter any known substance to dust," but it is unclear whether this display consists solely of Superman's own inventions or whether it also includes inventions created by others (Act No. 278, Jul '61: "The Super Powers of Perry White!").

The largest room of the Fortress is probably the gigantic trophy room, where the trophies of Superman's innumerable exciting adventures are on display (WF No. 99, Feb '59: "Batman's Super-Spending Spree!"; LC No. C-48, Oct/Nov '76). Among them are a giant jack-in-the-box confiscated from Lex Luthor (Act No. 241, Jun '58: "The Super-Key to Fort Superman"), perhaps the one he used during his short-lived alliance with the PRANKSTER and the TOYMAN in March 1954 (S No. 88/3: "The Terrible Trio!"); an ingenious "face-molding instrument"—described as a sort of "electronic plastic surgery" machine—which was confiscated from an unidentified villain by Superman sometime in the past and which Zak-Kul uses to transform himself into a Superman look-alike in October 1958 (Act No. 245: "The Shrinking Superman!"); a "chameleon jewel" from the planet VENUS (Act No. 253, Jun '59: "The War Between Superman and Jimmy Olsen!"); an exotic "rainbow space jewel," whose baleful radiations can transform an ordinary human being into a "ghastly monster" (S No. 151/1, Feb '62: "The Three Tough Teen-Agers!"); a "projector for dematerializing any matter for one minute," and an anti-gravity "flying belt" presented to Superman as a gift by

unidentified extraterrestrial aliens (Act No. 302, Jul
'63: "The Amazing Confession of Super-Perry
White!"); a "telepathic-sending trophy," for commu-
nicating telepathically (Act No. 303, Aug '63: "The
Monster from Krypton!"); and a "force-radiating
instrument," in the form of a wristlet, capable of
transforming a human being into a "metalloid" (see
THAN-AR) (WF No. 143, Aug '64: "The Feud Between
Batman and Superman!" pts. I-II—no title; "The
Manhunters from Earth!").

Superman's grisliest "trophy" is the body of his
friend AR-VAL, now turned to solid stone, which
reposes in a glass case in the Fortress of Solitude
awaiting the day when Superman will succeed in
bringing him back to life (see also LUTHOR, LEX) (S
No. 172, Oct '64: pts. I-III—"The New Superman!";
"Clark Kent—Former Superman!"; "The Struggle of
the Two Supermen!").

"The most amazing exhibit in [the] Fortress" (Act
No. 243, Aug '58: "The Lady and the Lion") and "the
prize of [Superman's] collection" (Act No. 253, Jun
'59: "The War Between Superman and Jimmy
Olsen!") is the bottle city of Kandor, a city of the
planet Krypton which survived the destruction of its
native planet as the result of having been stolen
sometime prior to the cataclysm by the space villain
Brainiac, who reduced the city to microscopic size and
preserved it, people and buildings alive and intact,
inside a glass bottle aboard his spacecraft, where it
remained for many years until it was finally
recovered by Superman in July 1958 (Act No. 242:
"The Super-Duel in Space").

Safeguarding the city of Kandor and its lilliputian
population is one of Superman's gravest responsibilities. "I have to check that city-in-the-bottle regularly," muses the Man of Steel in January 1960, "to see
that the tiny people inside it are safe!" (S No. 134: chs.
I-III—"The Super-Menace of Metropolis!"; "The
Revenge Against Jor-El!"; "The Duel of the Supermen!").

To aid him in his task of defending Earth and
combatting injustice throughout the universe, Superman has equipped his Fortress with a unique array of
superscientific apparatus.

Superman's "super-univac," described as a gigantic "super-analyzing machine," is, beyond any doubt,
the most advanced computer on Earth. In October
1959, on the basis of photographic data fed into it by
Superman, it provides a detailed account of how
Superman's life would have unfolded if Krypton had
not exploded and Superman had never been sent to
Earth (S No. 132: "Superman's Other Life!" pts. 1-3—
"Krypton Lives On!"; "Futuro, Super-Hero of Krypton!"; "The Superman of Two Worlds!"). In June 1960,
after meeting HYPER-MAN, Superman uses his super-
univac to "work out a complete history of [Hyper-
Man's] future life for [Superman's] files," proof that
the giant computer can accurately foretell future
events (Act No. 265: "The 'Superman' from Outer
Space!").

Elsewhere in the Fortress, a bank of sophisticated

"world-monitor instruments" (S No. 153/2, May '62:
"The Secret of the Superman Stamp!") alerts Superman to emergencies and impending emergencies
around the world. Superman No. 138/1 depicts a
"world-wide alarm system" consisting of two gigantic hemispheric maps, dotted with red "pins," wired
into a loud clanging alarm. In the event of an
emergency anywhere on Earth, the pin at the
appropriate trouble spot lights up on the map, and the
alarm bell rings loudly, alerting Superman to the
danger (Jul '60: "Titano the Super-Ape!").

At least two texts depict a "monitoring machine"
equipped with five red lights which light up to
indicate the following types of emergencies: Kandor
Emergency, Outside Fortress Emergency, White
House Emergency, Interplanetary Emergency, and
Daily Planet Emergency (S No. 144/3, Apr '61: "The
Orphans of Space!"; S No. 152/1, Apr '62: "The Robot
Master!"). A "special alarm" sounds at the Fortress to
warn of an assault on FORT KNOX in June 1961 (Act
No. 277: "The Conquest of Superman!"), and one of
Superman's special devices, referred to only as an
"emergency monitor," alerts him to an "impending
danger" to the U.S. town of Littledale in May 1962 (S
No. 153/1: "The Day Superman Broke the Law!"). A
complex electronic graph-inscribing device, described only as one of Superman's "world-monitor
instruments," alerts the Man of Steel to the presence
of "dangerous subterranean activity"—in this case, a
geyser of boiling water unleashed by an earth
tremor—in Rangoon, Burma, in May 1962 (S No.
153/2: "The Secret of the Superman Stamp!"). By
July 1965 Superman has installed a "world monitor
screen" in his Fortress consisting of four wall-
mounted telescreens augmented by a bank of complex
electronic machinery (Act No. 326: "The Legion of
Super-Creatures!").

To enable him to cope with interplanetary emergencies, Superman has equipped his Fortress with an
"interplanetary alarm" which "automatically registers the entrance of any alien invader or space ship
into Earth's atmosphere" (Act No. 276, May '61: "The
War Between Supergirl and the Supermen Emergency Squad!"), as well as with a wall-mounted "space
monitor," with which he can communicate with the
inhabitants of distant worlds (Act No. 294, Nov '62:
"The Kryptonite Killer!") or observe events on distant
planets (Act No. 304, Sep '63: "The Interplanetary
Olympics!"). A so-called "inter-galactic danger detector," consisting of a gigantic wall-mounted telescreen
augmented by a bank of electronic machinery, has
been installed in the Fortress by April 1964 (Act No.
311: "Superman, King of Earth!").

Clocks mounted on the wall of the Fortress alert
Superman to the time of day on Venus, Jupiter, and
other distant planets (S No. 150/1, Jan '62: "The One
Minute of Doom!"), and a special "seismic map"
pinpoints the exact location of any atomic explosion
or other major disturbance (Act No. 328, Sep '65:
"Superman's Hands of Doom!").

The Fortress's "Atlantis monitor" enables Super-

man to observe events in the undersea realm of
Atlantis (Act No. 310, Mar '64: "Secret of Kryptonite
Six!"), and a sophisticated "interdimensional monitor" enables him to communicate, both visually and
orally, with the inhabitants of the fifth dimension
and presumably other extradimensional worlds
as well (S No. 174/2, Jan '65: "Super-
Mxyzptlk ... Hero!").

The Fortress also houses the "Kandor-scope" and
other devices necessary for communicating with the
inhabitants of Kandor (S No. 151/3, Feb '62: "Superman's Greatest Secret!"; and others); the various
shrinking rays, exchange rays, and other apparatus
which Superman has employed to enable him to enter
and leave the tiny city (S No. 158, Jan '63: "Superman
in Kandor" pts. I-III—"Invasion of the Mystery
Super-Men!"; "The Dynamic Duo of Kandor!"; "The
City of Super-People!"; and many others); and the
special "anti-gravity shoes" which any ordinary
earthling must wear if he is to walk comfortably in
Kandor's alien environment (S No. 158, Jan '63:
"Superman in Kandor" pts. I-III—"Invasion of the
Mystery Super-Men!"; "The Dynamic Duo of Kandor!"; "The City of Super-People!"; see also WF No.
143, Aug '64: "The Feud Between Batman and
Superman!" pts. I-II—no title; "The Manhunters from
Earth!"). (See KANDOR.)

In addition, the Fortress houses the "zone-ophone"
and other devices needed for observing events taking
place in the Phantom Zone and communicating with
its inhabitants (S No. 157/1, Nov '62: "The Super-
Revenge of the Phantom Zone Prisoner!"; and
others); the "Phantom Zone projector" and other
devices needed to project individuals into the Phantom Zone or release them from it (Act No. 284, Jan '62:
"The Babe of Steel!"; and many others); and the
complete "microfilm gallery of Phantom Zone
criminals" presented to Superman by Kandorian
law-enforcement officials (S No. 164/2, Oct '63: "The
Fugitive from the Phantom Zone!"). (See PHANTOM
ZONE, THE.)

To enable Superman to broadcast important
messages to the world at a moment's notice, the
Fortress is equipped with a sophisticated "super-
telecaster" with which the Man of Steel can black out
every television program in the world and broadcast
his own announcements over every network simultaneously. Superman uses this apparatus to broadcast KULL-EX's confession to the world in January
1960, so that people everywhere will know that the
destructive acts attributed to Superman were actually
performed by Kull-Ex (S No. 134: chs. I-III—"The
Super-Menace of Metropolis!"; "The Revenge Against
Jor-El!"; "The Duel of the Supermen!"). He uses it
again in February 1962, this time to make Supergirl's
existence known to the world (Act No. 285: "The
World's Greatest Heroine!").

A powerful "super-telescope," located elsewhere in
the Fortress, is capable of such incredible magnification that Superman can actually use it to seek out
individual persons on far-distant planets (Act No.

243, Aug '58: "The Lady and the Lion"). It is through
this telescope that Superman photographs the newly
erected statue of Lex Luthor on the planet LEXOR in
October 1963 (S No. 164: pts. I-II—"The Showdown
Between Luthor and Superman!"; "The Super-
Duel!").

Other important apparatus housed in the Fortress
includes a "time-space viewer," which "picks up light
and sound waves from the past" and thus enables one
to view selected historical events (WF No. 146, Dec
'64: "Batman, Son of Krypton!" pts. I-II—no title;
"The Destroyer of Krypton!"); a "psycho-locator,"
built by the scientists of Kandor, which, through the
electronic analysis and long-distance sensing of
brain-wave patterns, can locate a selected individual
"anywhere in space and time" (S No. 168, Apr '64: pts.
I-II—"Luthor--Super-Hero!"; "Lex Luthor, Daily
Planet Editor!"); a spherical, transparent "time
capsule," for traveling through space and time (Act
No. 310, Mar '64: "Secret of Kryptonite Six!"); and a
special ray-device capable of endowing an ordinary
individual with super-powers for a period of twenty-
four hours (WF No. 109, May '60: "The Bewitched
Batman!").

Many of Superman's "super-robots" (S No. 134,
Jan '60: chs. I-III—"The Super-Menace of Metropolis!"; "The Revenge Against Jor-El!"; "The Duel of the
Supermen!"; and many others)—and the special lead
armor which Superman often wears when dealing
with kryptonite (Act No. 241, Jun '58: "The Super-Key
to Fort Superman"; and others)—are also kept at the
Fortress of Solitude. (See section G, the equipment.)

The Fortress is also equipped with various facilities with which Superman can clean the stains off his
indestructible costume (see section C, the costume).
He can take a dip, fully clothed, in his lava-filled

Inside the Fortress, Superman uses a "super-
blowtorch" to burn the dirt and stains off his
indestructible costume, 1960

swimming pool (Act No. 247, Dec '58: "Superman's Lost Parents!"); take a "shower" beneath the white-hot flame of a special "super-blowtorch" (S No. 134, Jan '60: chs. I-III—"The Super-Menace of Metropolis!"; "The Revenge Against Jor-El!"; "The Duel of the Supermen!"); or burn away the dirt and grime with an ordinary acetylene torch (Act No. 286, Mar '62: "The Jury of Super-Enemies!").

The precise location of the Fortress of Solitude is one of the world's most closely guarded secrets. In June 1958 Superman observes to himself that "No one suspects its existence," although the text also notes that Superman has already entrusted his "crime-fighting friend, the **Batman**," with its precise location and given him free access to "all [its] secrets" (Act No. 241: "The Super-Key to Fort Superman").

By late 1958 both Jimmy Olsen (Act No. 244, Sep '58: "The Super-Merman of the Sea") and Lois Lane have clearly learned that the Fortress exists and that it has an Arctic location, although its exact location remains a mystery to them. Lois Lane tours the Fortress as Superman's guest in October 1958 so that she can "write it up as a newspaper feature" for the DAILY PLANET, suggesting that the entire world will soon know of the Fortress's existence (Act No. 245: "The Shrinking Superman!").

Indeed, by February 1960 Superman has temporarily transported the entire Fortress to a site "on the outskirts of Metropolis" and has begun conducting guided tours through it with the proceeds earmarked for charity. However, Superman warns the throngs of visitors that "some of the rooms contain super-secrets, which no other person must ever learn!" These rooms, explains the Man of Steel, "are forbidden to all visitors!" (Act No. 261: "Superman's Fortresses of Solitude!"). By August 1960 it appears to be public knowledge that Superman's Fortress of Solitude is situated somewhere in the Arctic (S No. 139/3: "The Untold Story of Red Kryptonite!").

Although the entire world now knows of the Fortress's existence, however, its exact location is known only to a trusted few. These include Batman and Robin (WF No. 100, Mar '59: "The Dictator of Krypton City!"; and others), Supergirl and Krypto the Superdog (S No. 134, Jan '60: chs. I-III—"The Super-Menace of Metropolis!"; "The Revenge Against Jor-El!"; "The Duel of the Supermen!"; and many others), and the LEGION OF SUPER-HEROES (S No. 152/1, Apr '62: "The Robot Master!").

Other individuals besides these have visited the Fortress as Superman's guests, but they have been kept ignorant of its precise location. These include Lois Lane (Act No. 245, Oct '58: "The Shrinking Superman!"), Jimmy Olsen (Act No. 253, Jun '59: "The War Between Superman and Jimmy Olsen!"; Act No. 286, Mar '62: "The Jury of Super-Enemies!"), Hyper-Man (Act No. 265, Jun '60: "The 'Superman' from Outer Space!"), the infant son of Bizarro and BIZARRO-LOIS (S No. 140, Oct '60: pts. I-III—"The Son of Bizarro!"; "The 'Orphan' Bizarro!"; "The Bizarro Supergirl!"), a teen-ager named Artie (S No. 151/1,

Feb '62: "The Three Tough Teen-Agers!"), Perry White (Act No. 302, Jul '63: "The Amazing Confession of Super-Perry White!"), and LANA LANG (Act No. 304, Sep '63: "The Interplanetary Olympics!"). CEDRIC AND MILLICENT CARSON tour the Fortress in December 1958 while posing as Jonathan and Martha Kent, but Superman ultimately uses his command of "super-hypnotic forces" to erase from their minds all recollection of the secrets they learned there (Act No. 247: "Superman's Lost Parents!").

Visitors to the Fortress, unless they possess super-powers of their own, are taken there wrapped in Superman's "weather-proof, indestructible cape" to protect them against freezing to death in the sub-zero Arctic cold (Act No. 253, Jun '59: "The War Between Superman and Jimmy Olsen!"; and others) as well as against the potentially fatal "friction caused by Superman's flight" (Act No. 302, Jul '63: "The Amazing Confession of Super-Perry White!").

Because it could be calamitous if villains were to succeed in penetrating the Fortress, a network of alarms and security devices has been installed to safeguard Superman's sanctuary against intruders. "Booby traps" of an unspecified nature have been installed inside the lock of the massive front door (Act No. 300, May '63: "Superman Under the Red Sun!"), and an electric-eye beam, crossing the door in front of the door's gigantic keyhole inside the Fortress, sets off a "super-sonic alarm" audible to Superman at any distance (WF No. 153, Nov '65: "The Saga of Superman vs. Batman!" pts. I-II—"The Clash of Cape and Cowl!"; "The Death of a Hero!"). In the 1970s a hidden "mirage projector" was installed to disguise the Fortress's entranceway completely, creating the illusion of an ice-covered rock cliff where, in actuality, the massive front door and gigantic key are located (LC No. C-48, Oct/Nov '76).

In addition, the Fortress is guarded in Superman's absence by the SUPERMEN EMERGENCY SQUAD (Act No. 303, Aug '63: "The Monster from Krypton!"), and explosive "protective devices," installed in the Fortress's "secret rooms," will destroy any evidence of Superman's secret identity, or those of his various super-friends, in the event an intruder attempts to force open their doors without knowing the "secret combinations of the doors' locks" (S No. 142/3, Jan '61: "Flame-Dragon from Krypton").

Although the walls of the Fortress have been insulated with a "thick coating of lead" since April 1961 to prevent kryptonite radiation from penetrating the Fortress (S No. 144/3: "The Orphans of Space!"), Superman has installed both a "kryptonite detector" (Act No. 243, Aug '58: "The Lady and the Lion") and a "red kryptonite detector" to detect the presence of unwanted kryptonite inside the Fortress (S No. 154/2, Jul '62: "Krypton's First Superman!").

A special "super-fumigation system," mounted in the Fortress walls, releases "jets of antibiotic gases" into the air to ensure that no extraterrestrial microbes—carried unwittingly into the Fortress by Superman or by new additions to his interplanetary

FAR TO THE NORTH, IN THE UNINHABITED ARCTIC WASTES, STANDS A LOFTY CLIFF. IT LOOKS LIKE ANY OTHER ICE-ENCRUSTED ROCK MASS — BUT HOW DIFFERENT IT *IS!* FOR A HIDDEN MIRAGE PROJECTOR CAUSES THE ILLUSION OF A SOLID ICE FACE, DISGUISING A LEDGE, WHERE A MASSIVE DOOR IS SET INTO THE SOLID ROCK. AND BEHIND THAT DOOR-- WHICH CAN ONLY BE OPENED BY A KEY SO HUGE ONLY *SUPERMAN* OR *SUPERGIRL* COULD LIFT IT FROM WHERE IT STANDS ON THE LEDGE-- IS THE SECRET SANCTUARY OF THE *MAN OF STEEL!*

1st LEVEL

the FORTRESS OF SOLITUDE

THE *FORTRESS* IS THREE STORIES HIGH -- BUT THERE ARE NO STAIRS! ONLY SOMEONE WHO CAN *FLY,* LIKE *SUPERMAN,* CAN REACH THE UPPER FLOORS...

NOTES:

Ⓐ THE TOP STORY CONTAINS *SUPERMAN'S* PRIVATE QUARTERS, WHERE HE CAN RETIRE TO SHUT OUT THE WORLD FOR A SHORT TIME.

Ⓑ AT ONE SIDE APART FROM THE REST, IS A PRIVATE MODULAR APARTMENT FOR *SUPERGIRL,* WHICH SHE HERSELF DESIGNED AND FURNISHED.

Ⓒ DEEP IN THE EARTH, FAR BELOW THE FORTRESS, IS THE *DISINTEGRATION PIT.*

① THE TROPHY ROOM IS FILLED WITH MEMORABILA OF THE NUMEROUS ADVENTURES THAT THE *MAN OF STEEL* HAS HAD.

GIANT ARROW KEY ONE TIME USED AS AIR ROUTINE SIGNALING.

Ⓐ SIDE Ⓑ

FRONT

TOP

REAR

Ⓐ & Ⓑ SECRET COMPARTMENTS

N-1621

② COMMUNICATIONS ROOM

③ STATUES OF JOR-EL AND LARA

④ KRYPTONIAN MEMORIAL

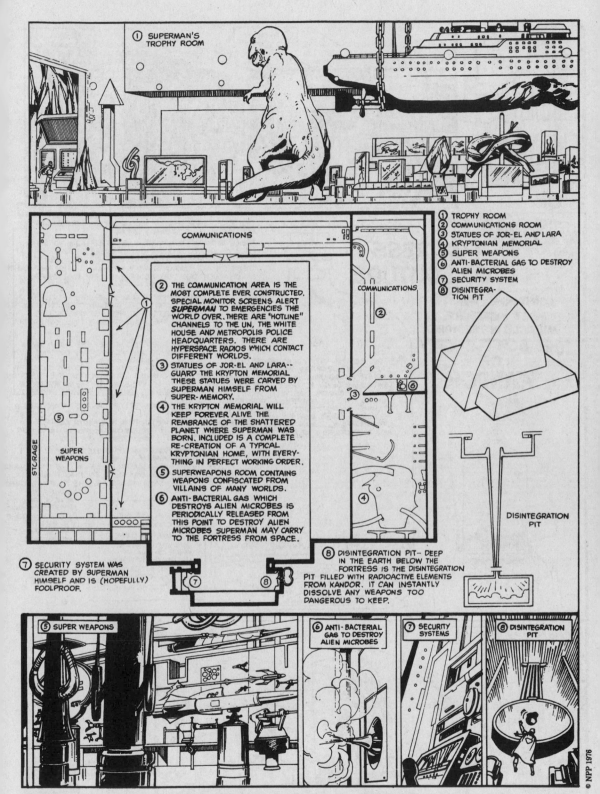

① SUPERMAN'S TROPHY ROOM

COMMUNICATIONS

① TROPHY ROOM
② COMMUNICATIONS ROOM
③ STATUES OF JOR-EL AND LARA
④ KRYPTONIAN MEMORIAL
⑤ SUPER WEAPONS
⑥ ANTI-BACTERIAL GAS TO DESTROY ALIEN MICROBES
⑦ SECURITY SYSTEM
⑧ DISINTEGRATION PIT

COMMUNICATIONS

② THE COMMUNICATION AREA IS THE MOST COMPLETE EVER CONSTRUCTED. SPECIAL MONITOR SCREENS ALERT *SUPERMAN* TO EMERGENCIES THE WORLD OVER. THERE ARE "HOTLINE" CHANNELS TO THE UN, THE WHITE HOUSE AND METROPOLIS POLICE HEADQUARTERS. THERE ARE HYPERSPACE RADIOS WHICH CONTACT DIFFERENT WORLDS.

③ STATUES OF JOR-EL AND LARA-- GUARD THE KRYPTON MEMORIAL THESE STATUES WERE CARVED BY SUPERMAN HIMSELF FROM SUPER-MEMORY.

④ THE KRYPTON MEMORIAL WILL KEEP FOREVER ALIVE THE REMBRANCE OF THE SHATTERED PLANET WHERE SUPERMAN WAS BORN. INCLUDED IS A COMPLETE RE-CREATION OF A TYPICAL KRYPTONIAN HOME, WITH EVERY-THING IN PERFECT WORKING ORDER.

⑤ SUPERWEAPONS ROOM CONTAINS WEAPONS CONFISCATED FROM VILLAINS OF MANY WORLDS.

⑥ ANTI-BACTERIAL GAS WHICH DESTROYS ALIEN MICROBES IS PERIODICALLY RELEASED FROM THIS POINT TO DESTROY ALIEN MICROBES SUPERMAN MAY CARRY TO THE FORTRESS FROM SPACE.

STORAGE

SUPER WEAPONS

⑤

DISINTEGRATION PIT

⑦ SECURITY SYSTEM WAS CREATED BY SUPERMAN HIMSELF AND IS (HOPEFULLY) FOOLPROOF.

⑧ DISINTEGRATION PIT-- DEEP IN THE EARTH BELOW THE FORTRESS IS THE DISINTEGRATION PIT FILLED WITH RADIOACTIVE ELEMENTS FROM KANDOR. IT CAN INSTANTLY DISSOLVE ANY WEAPONS TOO DANGEROUS TO KEEP.

⑤ SUPER WEAPONS

⑥ ANTI-BACTERIAL GAS TO DESTROY ALIEN MICROBES

⑦ SECURITY SYSTEMS

⑧ DISINTEGRATION PIT

Floor plan of the Fortress of Solitude's first level

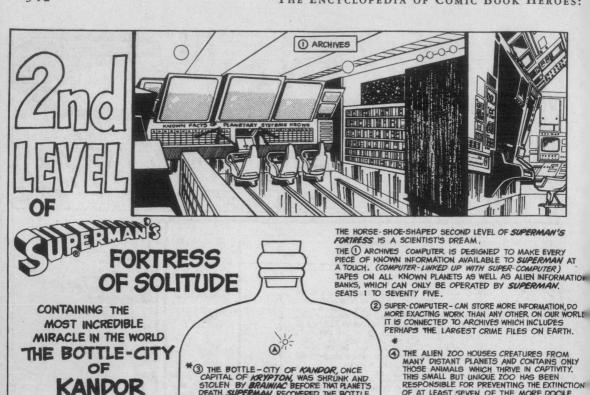

2nd LEVEL OF SUPERMAN'S FORTRESS OF SOLITUDE

CONTAINING THE MOST INCREDIBLE MIRACLE IN THE WORLD

THE BOTTLE-CITY OF KANDOR

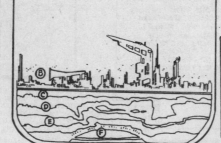

* ③ THE BOTTLE-CITY OF *KANDOR*, ONCE CAPITAL OF *KRYPTON*, WAS SHRUNK AND STOLEN BY *BRAINIAC* BEFORE THAT PLANET'S DEATH. *SUPERMAN* RECOVERED THE BOTTLE IN WHICH *KANDOR* WAS KEPT, AND PLACED IT IN HIS *FORTRESS* FOR SAFE-KEEPING. TANKS KEEP IT SUPPLIED WITH AN ATMOSPHERE EXACTLY LIKE THAT OF *KRYPTON*. IT HAS ARTIFICIAL GRAVITY AND A MINIATURE RED SUN, TOO.

THE HORSE-SHOE-SHAPED SECOND LEVEL OF *SUPERMAN'S FORTRESS* IS A SCIENTIST'S DREAM.

THE ① ARCHIVES COMPUTER IS DESIGNED TO MAKE EVERY PIECE OF KNOWN INFORMATION AVAILABLE TO *SUPERMAN* AT A TOUCH. (COMPUTER-LINKED UP WITH SUPER-COMPUTER) TAPES ON ALL KNOWN PLANETS AS WELL AS ALIEN INFORMATION BANKS, WHICH CAN ONLY BE OPERATED BY *SUPERMAN*. SEATS 1 TO SEVENTY FIVE.

② SUPER-COMPUTER — CAN STORE MORE INFORMATION, DO MORE EXACTING WORK THAN ANY OTHER ON OUR WORLD. IT IS CONNECTED TO ARCHIVES WHICH INCLUDES PERHAPS THE LARGEST CRIME FILES ON EARTH.

④ THE ALIEN ZOO HOUSES CREATURES FROM MANY DISTANT PLANETS AND CONTAINS ONLY THOSE ANIMALS WHICH THRIVE IN CAPTIVITY. THIS SMALL BUT UNIQUE ZOO HAS BEEN RESPONSIBLE FOR PREVENTING THE EXTINCTION OF AT LEAST SEVEN OF THE MORE DOCILE SPECIES OF ANIMALS ON OTHER PLANETS.

⑤ *SUPERMAN'S* LAB HAS SPECIAL EQUIPMENT MORE ADVANCED THAN ANYTHING ELSEWHERE ON EARTH. FEW SCIENTISTS COULD EVEN GUESS THE *USES* OF MANY ITEMS KEPT HERE.

⑥ THE *PHANTOM ZONE VIEWER* PERMITS *SUPERMAN* TO KEEP TABS ON THE *KRYPTONIAN* VILLAINS WHO WERE PUNISHED BY BEING BANISHED TO THAT TWILIGHT DIMENSION. NEARBY IS THE (OLD-FASHIONED LOOKING BUT THE LESS EFFECTIVE) *PROJECTOR* WHICH CAN SEND ANYONE INTO INTO THE ZONE OR *FREE* THAT PERSON.

A. ARTIFICIAL RED SUN.
B. CITY OF KANDOR.
C. SOIL AND RAW ELEMENTS.
D. UNSTABLE COMPOUND WHICH ORIGINALLY DESTROYED KRYPTON.
E. UNKNOWN BUT UNIQUELY KRYPTONIAN COMPOUNDS.
F. PLANET'S CORE ELEMENTS.

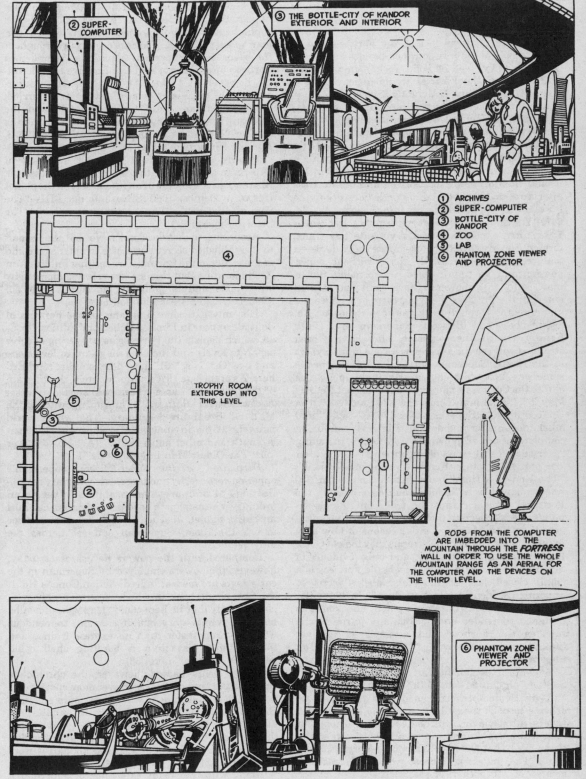

Floor plan of the Fortress of Solitude's second level

zoo—will escape the Fortress to unleash a deadly epidemic on Earth (S No. 176/2, Apr '65: "Tales of Green Kryptonite No. 2"; *see also* LC No. C-48, Oct/Nov '76).

Since the massive door of the Fortress weighs many tons, and the only entrance, besides the door, is "through fifty feet of solid rock," unauthorized infiltration of the Fortress would appear to be a virtual impossibility. In June 1958, however, as part of a friendly joke he plays on Superman in commemoration of "the anniversary of [Superman's] arrival on Earth from the planet Krypton," Batman successfully infiltrates the Fortress by hollowing out the tip of the giant key with an acetylene torch, hinging a secret panel in the key and concealing himself inside it, and then dropping unobserved into the Fortress after Superman, on one of his periodic visits to the Fortress, has inserted the key into the lock (Act No. 241: "The Super-Key to Fort Superman"). In October 1962, after exposure to red kryptonite has transformed Superman into two separate individuals—a mature, responsible Clark Kent, without super-powers, and an unprincipled, irresponsible Superman, with super-powers—Clark Kent succeeds in entering the Fortress by flying there in a helicopter and crawling through the gigantic keyhole (Act No. 293: "The Feud Between Superman and Clark Kent!"). On another occasion, after having been stranded without his super-powers one million years in the future, Superman enters the Fortress in the same way, after climbing painstakingly up the rock cliff to the Fortress's massive front door (Act No. 300, May '63: "Superman Under the Red Sun!").

According to Superman No. 174/1, "tapes" and other documents inside the Fortress contain a complete record of Superman's entire life, including "every detail and secret of Superman's past..." (Jan '65: pts. 1-2—"Clark Kent's Incredible Delusion!"; "The End of a Hero!"), but Action Comics No. 330 refers instead to a "hidden vault deep beneath the Fortress" which, claims the text, contains Superman's "super-secret file" on himself, including Jonathan and Martha Kent's account of how they found him as a baby, photographs they took of Clark Kent changing to Superboy, and other evidence of Superman's secret identity. Inside the Fortress is a small closed box bearing this label: "Secret of Superman's Identity/Do Not Open!" In actuality, however, this box contains a potent knockout gas designed to render unconscious any intruder who invades the Fortress and attempts to uncover Superman's secret (Nov '65: "The Strange 'S' Spell on Superman!").

Superman establishes an undersea Fortress of Solitude—hollowed out of the side of an undersea cliff—in September 1958 as part of his elaborate scheme to trick the evil VUL-KOR and his daughter Lya-La into believing that he has decided to abandon the surface world forever in favor of a new life on the ocean floor (Act No. 244: "The Super-Merman of the Sea"). The undersea Fortress, which is reportedly located at the bottom of the Sargasso Sea, at 28°

North latitude, 50° West longitude (S No. 176/3, Apr '65: "Superman's Day of Truth!"), is stocked with numerous exotic "ocean relics" and equipped with sophisticated monitoring apparatus to enable Superman to keep abreast of events occurring throughout the seven seas. Superman abandons the undersea Fortress after Vul-Kor and Lya-La have been defeated, however (Act No. 244, Sep '58: "The Super-Merman of the Sea"; *see also* Act No. 265, Jun '60: "The 'Superman' from Outer Space!"), and the structure is now used by the mer-people of Atlantis as "a showplace and a tourist attraction!" (S No. 176/3, Apr '65: "Superman's Day of Truth!").

Bizarro builds himself a crude imitation of Superman's Fortress, the so-called FORTRESS OF BIZARRO, in the middle of an arid desert on the planet HTRAE in October 1960 (S No. 140: pts. I-III—"The Son of Bizarro!"; "The 'Orphan' Bizarro!"; "The Bizarro Supergirl!").

According to Action Comics No. 261, Superman first established secret Fortresses in outer space and at the center of the Earth before settling finally on an Arctic location, but this assertion is unsupported by other texts and is probably inaccurate (Feb '60: "Superman's Fortresses of Solitude!").

The only extensive diagrams of the Fortress of Solitude appear in Limited Collectors' Edition No. C-48, which depicts the Fortress as consisting of three separate levels and includes diagrams of levels one and two (Oct/Nov '76). These diagrams are reprinted here. As of the late 1970s, unfortunately, the diagram of the third level has not been published.

E. The Super-Powers. "The super-powers of the Man of Steel are legendary! The whole world marvels at his invulnerability, super-speed, super-strength and other super-skills!" (Act No. 251, Apr '59: "The Oldest Man in Metropolis!").

1. Derivation of the Super-Powers. Superman's super-powers are, by and large, extraordinary magnifications of ordinary human abilities. Just as an ordinary man can hurl a baseball, Superman can hurl an entire planet. Just as an ordinary man can see across the room, Superman can see across the universe.

Compared with the powers he possesses today, however, the powers employed by Superman in the early texts are modest indeed. Action Comics No. 1, the first comic book in which Superman appeared, claimed only that its hero could "leap ⅛th of a mile; hurdle a twenty-story building...raise tremendous weights...run faster than an express train...and that nothing less than a bursting shell could penetrate his skin!" (Jun '38).

As the years passed, however, the chroniclers endowed the Man of Steel with ever more spectacular powers to enable him to meet ever more exacting challenges. Today Superman can withstand the heat at the core of the sun, soar through the air at a speed thousands of times the speed of light, and extinguish a star with a puff of his breath as though it were merely a candle on a birthday cake.

Along with the steady expansion of Superman's

powers has come a series of changing explanations of how he came to acquire those powers. Action Comics No. 1, for example, contains this "scientific explanation of Clark Kent's amazing strength":

Kent had come from a planet whose inhabitants' physical structure was millions of years advanced of our own. Upon reaching maturity, the people of his race became gifted with titanic strength!
--Incredible? No! For even today on our world exist creatures with **super-strength!**
The lowly ant can support weights hundreds of times its own. The grasshopper leaps what to man would be the space of several city blocks [Jun '38].

For approximately the first decade of Superman's career, the texts advanced the thesis that Superman's powers were merely those possessed by all the inhabitants of his native planet. These texts described the men and women of KRYPTON as a "super-race" (S No. 73/2, Nov/Dec '51: "The Mighty Mite!") who were gifted with X-ray vision and other powers and who were "thousands of eons" ahead of earthlings, both mentally and physically (S No. 53/1, Jul/Aug '48: "The Origin of Superman!").

According to Superman No. 33/1, "... **Superman**--a native of the ill-fated planet of Krypton---is of a different structure than the natives of Earth! Neither his mind nor his body are susceptible to the influences that can overcome other human beings!" (Mar/Apr '45: "Dimensions of Danger!").

"Where we come from," gloats the Kryptonian villain U-BAN in July-August 1950, "**everyone** has see-through vision, extra-strength and extra-speed!" (S No. 65/3: "Three Supermen from Krypton!").

By the late 1940s, however, the texts had begun to describe the people of Krypton as more or less ordinary human beings and to attribute Superman's powers to the vast differences between the gravitational pull and atmospheric conditions of Krypton and those of the planet Earth. In the words of Superman No. 58/3:

Everyone knows that **Superman** is a being from another planet, unburdened by the vastly weaker gravity of Earth. But not everyone understands how gravity effects [sic] strength! If you were on a world smaller than ours, you could jump over high buildings, lift enormous weights ... and thus duplicate some of the feats of the **Man of Steel!** [May/Jun '49: "The Case of the Second Superman"].

Subsequent texts continued to cite the importance of the gravitational difference between Earth and Krypton while laying increasingly greater stress on the significance of Krypton's "unique atmosphere" in accounting for the awesome powers a Kryptonian acquired once he was free of his native planet. "Obviously, Krypton is such an unusual planet," Superman's father, JOR-EL, once noted, "that when a native Kryptonian is elsewhere, free of Krypton's unique atmosphere and tremendous gravitational pull, he becomes a **superman!**" (S No. 113, May '57:

chs. 1-3—"The Superman of the Past"; "The Secret of the Towers"; "The Superman of the Present").

·Since, according to this theory, Superman owes the existence of his super-powers to the fact that he is no longer on the planet Krypton, it follows that Superman has no super-powers wherever atmospheric and gravitational conditions prevail that are identical to those of his native planet.

Indeed, during a visit to a man-made duplicate of the planet Krypton in July 1953, Superman finds that he can no longer fly, "since [the planet's] tremendous gravitational power neutralizes [his] strength!"

"And, because of the greater atmospheric density on this world," notes Superman, "I can't (ugh) use my X-ray vision here either!" And moments later he adds, "I--I could stay under water almost indefinitely on Earth---but not on [the duplicate] Krypton! Because of the greater exertion, I need more oxygen!" (Act No. 182: "The Return of Planet Krypton!").

An identical loss of his super-powers befalls Superman whenever he journeys through the time barrier to Krypton at a time prior to its destruction or pays a visit to the bottle city of KANDOR. "... [W]here Krypton's non-earthly gravity conditions are in force," muses Superman during a visit to Kandor in October 1958, "I have no super-powers! I-I'm just an **ordinary man!**" (Act No. 245: "The Shrinking Superman!").

According to a revised theory of Superman's powers, first advanced in 1960, the Man of Steel derives his super-powers "partly from [the] lesser gravity" of Earth, and partly from unique "**ultra solar rays** that penetrate Earth day and night!"

"These rays," explains Superman to SUPERGIRL in March 1960, "can only affect people who were born in other solar systems than Earth's! And only **yellow** stars like Earth's sun emit those super-energy rays! On planets of non-yellow suns, we would **not** be super-powered, even under low gravity!" (Supergirl story in Act No. 262: "Supergirl's Greatest Victory!").

This theory is restated in Superman No. 141. "What gave me super-powers on Earth," explains Superman, "was Earth's lesser gravity and the fact that, unlike **Krypton's** red sun, Earth's solar system has a **yellow** sun.... Only yellow stars radiate super-energy rays which give super-powers to people born in other solar systems!" (Nov '60: pts. I-III—"Superman Meets Jor-El and Lara Again!"; "Superman's Kryptonian Romance!"; "The Surprise of Fate!").

Superman No. 146/1 refines this theory still further, attributing Superman's "muscular powers"—super-strength, super-breath, super-speed, and the power of flight—to Earth's light gravity, and his "super-senses and mental powers"—X-ray vision and other optical powers, super-hearing, and various intellectual powers—to the ultra solar rays of Earth's yellow sun. In a flashback sequence, Superman explains that, as the result of his having been born

on a giant world with heavy gravity, my muscles automatically became super-strong in Earth's light gravity! I'm like the ant, which, if it were man-sized, could carry a locomotive! Grasshoppers could leap over buildings!

Now notice that **Krypton** had a **red sun**...! But only the **ultra solar rays** of Earth's **yellow** sun can super-energize my brain and five senses to give me the other non-muscular super-powers!

Also, those yellow-sun rays, which only **tan** Earth people's skin, **hardened** mine like steel! Radium rays...lightning...fire...**nothing** can harm me! [Jul '61: "The Story of Superman's Life!"].

In the logic of this latest refinement, all Kryptonian objects acquire indestructibility in the yellow-sun environment of Earth, and all native Kryptonians—such as Supergirl or KRYPTO THE SUPERDOG—acquire super-powers identical to Superman's. However, the indestructibility of these objects and the super-powers of the various Kryptonian survivors remain proportional to what they would have been had they remained in their native Kryptonian environment. Superman is stronger than Supergirl, for example, just as an ordinary human male is normally stronger than his female counterpart. Similarly, a Kryptonian gorilla on Earth would be stronger than Superman, just as an ordinary gorilla is more powerful than an ordinary man.

It is this phenomenon to which Superman refers in February 1962, when, after having been bitten severely on the hand by a Kryptonian "flame dragon" (*see* FLAME DRAGON), he remarks that "The beast's bite penetrated my skin...which is invulnerable to everything except the bite of a Kryptonian creature who would have normally been stronger than me if both of us were on **Krypton**, minus our super-strength!" (S No. 151/3: "Superman's Greatest Secret!").

Because Superman is now said to derive his powers, in part, from the "ultra solar rays" of Earth's yellow sun, he has no powers on any planet revolving about a red sun, such as the planet LEXOR (Act No. 318, Nov '64: "The Death of Luthor!"; and others) or the world of the THORONES (Act No. 321, Feb '65: "Superman--Weakest Man in the World!").

The mighty super-powers that Superman employs today are the products of a gradual evolution spanning four decades of texts. Following is an inventory of Superman's super-powers, along with the history and evolution of each super-power.

2. Super-Speed and the Power of Flight. In the early years of his super-heroic career, Superman was not endowed with the power of flight. Although he possessed superhuman speed, he moved from place to place by running or by executing gigantic leaps. Month by month, however, Superman's running speed increased, along with the length of his leaps and the complexity of the aerial maneuvers he was able to perform once he had left the ground. The transition from leaping to actual flying was extraordinarily gradual and was punctuated with a great deal of inconsistency. In March-April 1941, for example, Superman "streaks thru [sic] the clouds like a skyrocket gone wild..." (S No. 9/3), clearly suggesting flying rather than leaping, but in November 1942 he seats LOIS LANE in a rowboat and swims through the water, propelling the rowboat ahead of him, as his only means of ferrying her out to a besieged cargo vessel without getting her wet (Act No. 54: "The Pirate of Pleasure Island"). Not until May 1943, in fact, is Superman explicitly referred to as a "being who can fly like a bird" (Act No. 60: "Lois Lane--Superwoman!"), and not until later that same year can it be said, without qualification, that Superman actually possesses the power of flight (Act No. 65, Oct '43: "The Million-Dollar Marathon!"; and others).

Following is a chronological survey of the textual

With Lois Lane cradled in his arms, Superman outraces a raging flood, 1938

data relating to Superman's speed and power of flight, with specific attention to whatever data exist concerning the precise limitations and extents of those powers. By following the growth and development of these abilities, one can trace their gradual expansion as it unfolded in the chronicles.

In June 1938 Superman is described as being able to "leap ⅛th of a mile; hurdle a twenty-story building...[and] run faster than an express train...!" (Act No. 1). Action Comics No. 11 notes that he "...races toward a distant oil town at a speed that would outdistance the fastest streamline limited--" (Apr '39).

In July 1938 Superman leaps from the ground to the top of the WASHINGTON MONUMENT (Act No. 2).

In August 1938 Superman is described as running "at a terrific pace that not even the fastest auto or airplane could duplicate!" (Act No. 3).

In October 1938 Superman is described as covering "huge distances...with giant leaps." "From atop the great *Daily Star* building," notes Action Comics No. 5, "a weird figure leaps out into the night! Huge distances are swiftly covered by it with giant leaps...."

Not yet endowed with the power of flight, Superman moves from place to place in gigantic running leaps, 1938

In December 1938 Superman is described as being capable of "racing a bullet" and of running so swiftly that "he appears to be a blurred streak of motion!" (Act No. 7).

In June 1939 Superman leaps off a rooftop while grasping a racketeer under one arm, "but his great flying leap [is] deflected" when the racketeer attempts, in midair, to stab him with a knife. As "the two figures catapult toward the far distant streets below--- SUPERMAN succeeds in grasping a window-sill with one outflung hand--but the racketeer continues downward toward his doom--!" (Act No. 13).

In November 1939, "...high overhead in the sky, SUPERMAN trails [a blackmailer's] auto," but he does so by means of gigantic leaps and not by flying (Act No. 18).

In Winter 1940 Superman swims underwater faster than a motorboat (S No. 3/4).

In January 1940 "SUPERMAN, a vertible [sic] human fly, swiftly scales the side of [a tall] building" and later swims underwater as fast as a submarine (Act No. 20).

In Spring 1940 Superman leaps "into the stratosphere-- and beyond" in a contest with LEX LUTHOR to determine "who can rise the highest above the Earth, and still return safely," and runs across the surface of the ocean while racing Luthor around the world (S No. 4/1). During this same period, Superman runs the entire distance from METROPOLIS to Oklahoma, "fleetly covering miles in seconds..." (S No. 4/2, Spr '40).

In August 1940 Superman catches a bullet in midair and then flips it like a marble to deflect a second oncoming bullet (Act No. 27).

In September 1940 Superman runs, a mile in one second flat (Act No. 28).

In September-October 1940 "SUPERMAN speeds thru [sic] the sky at such a terrific speed, his figure appears to blur." "Just look at [him] soaring through the sky---it's **incredible**!" exclaims an airline pilot from the cockpit of his plane. Indeed, "...tho [sic] the plane hits as high a speed as 250 miles per hour, **Superman** easily outdistances it..." (S No. 6/1). During this same period, Superman is described as "zooming thru [sic] the sky like a rocket..." (S No. 6/2, Sep/Oct '40), but he still lacks the power of self-sustained flight, for, at one point, "Seizing the sides of his cape," he "navigates it like a sail" to enable him to soar through the air (S No. 6/3, Sep/Oct '40).

In March-April 1941 Superman "streaks thru [sic] the clouds like a skyrocket gone wild," covering "hundreds of miles in minutes" (S No. 9/3). The references to Superman's flying, however, are never truly explicit. "A great leap," notes one text for this period, "carries Superman...out thru [sic] the window and over the city..." (S No. 9/4, Mar/Apr '41).

In May-June 1941 Superman appears to hover in midair (S No. 10/1), and in July-August 1941 he changes course in midair and executes elaborate aerial maneuvers (S No. 11/2; *see also* S No. 12/3, Sep/Oct '41).

In July-August 1941 Superman burrows through the Earth to reach an underground spring, moving "faster and more silently than any excavating machine ever invented by man!" (S No. 11/3). "Down into the Earth goes **Superman**," notes another text, describing a similar feat several years later, "boring through concrete, rock and earth with express-train speed!" (Act No. 69, Feb '44: "The Lost-and-Found Mystery!").

In November-December 1941 Superman is described as moving at "super-speed" (S No. 13/1).

In December 1941 Superman gives every indication of actual flight when he hoists a crippled airliner over his head and hurtles through the sky with it. "Thru [sic] the fleecy clouds he speeds at a speed so great," notes the text, "the plane's wings strain at their supports..." (Act No. 43).

Superman overtakes a streamline train...

In the ensuing year, however, events occur which make it appear that Superman cannot fly, as when he scales the outer wall of a skyscraper to reach an upper story (Act No. 44, Jan '42; Act No. 56, Jan '43: "Design for Doom!"); "springs" out over the ocean with a seagoing ark and then, setting it down in the water, "swims at great speed, shoving the ancient vessel before him..." rather than flying through the air with it (Act No. 45, Feb '42); glides through the air, "using his wide-spread cape like a sail..." (Act No. 48, May '42: "The Adventure of the Merchant of Mur-

der"); places Lois Lane inside a rowboat as his only means of carrying her out over the ocean without getting her wet (Act No. 54, Nov '42: "The Pirate of Pleasure Island"); and races from the U.S.A. to Africa in "minutes" in a posture that suggests he is leaping through the air as opposed to actually flying (Act No. 56, Jan '43: "Design for Doom!").

In January-February 1942, in order to extinguish a fire at a lavish mansion, Superman "races about the mansion with such terrific speed that a vacuum is created--and the fire goes out..." (S No. 14/2).

In May-June 1942, while attempting to elude a policeman in his role as Clark Kent, Superman races around a corner and "increases speed so that he equals the pace of light itself...!" (S No. 16/1: "The World's Meanest Man"; *see also* S No. 19/3, Nov/Dec '42).

In September-October 1942 Superman outraces electric current to its destination in order to prevent the explosion of a charge of dynamite. It is, notes the text, "one of the most unusual races since the world began--man versus electricity--for **Superman** is racing the current in the wire to its destination...!" (S No. 18/1: "The Conquest of a City").

In May 1943 a villain appearing in one of Lois Lane's dreams refers to Superman as a "being who can fly like a bird!" (Act No. 60: "Lois Lane--Superwoman!").

In July 1943, while carrying another man, Superman dives through a plate-glass window with such lightning celerity that the pane of glass does not even shatter. "Increasing his speed beyond all known limits," notes the text, "**Superman** performs a scientific miracle! So swiftly is the glass penetrated that its molecular structure is undisturbed, and even after two men have passed through, it remains intact!" (Act No. 62: "There'll Always Be a Superman!").

By October 1943 Superman has clearly acquired,

...and passes it as though it were standing still, 1938

without qualification, the power of flight (Act No. 65: "The Million-Dollar Marathon!"; and others).

In Winter 1943, by "spiraling upward with terrific speed, Superman creates a miniature cyclone to clear the street of [poison] gas..." (WF No. 12: "The Man Who Stole a Reputation!").

A text for May-June 1944 contains this description of Superman's successful effort to combat a cyclone:

> Abruptly, a crimson-and-blue figure darts into the spinning vortex of dust and debris!
> Hurtling at dizzy speed, Superman breasts the terrific air currents, spiraling in the opposite direction to the whirlwind's motion....
> And as air flows into the vacuum left in his wake, the rushing wind is stopped dead, cutting the "twister" in half!

"That does it," notes Superman with satisfaction. "The force of the top and bottom parts [of the cyclone] will be spent in a few minutes, and the storm will be over!" (S No. 28/1: "Lambs versus Wolfingham!").

In October 1944 Superman swims through the Atlantic towing a long line of lifeboats at a speed sixty times that of an ocean liner (Act No. 77: "The Headline Hoax!").

In November-December 1944 Superman reconstructs a brontosaurus skeleton at super-speed, completing in three minutes a task that would have taken a team of scientists months. "Geared to the speed of light," notes the text, "Superman's arms spin like windmill blades in a cyclone..." (S No. 31/3: "The Treasure House of History!").

In July-August 1945 Superman flies from Metropolis to Burma "in the wink of an eye!" "Light travels 186,000 miles a second, but has nothing on Superman," notes the text, "who finds himself hovering over the jungles of distant Burma in the wink of an eye!" (S No. 35/3: "The Genie of the Lamp!").

In November-December 1946 Superman demonstrates the ability to stand invisibly in one spot by "oscillating his body so fast that the human eye cannot see him!" (S No. 43/1: "The Invention of Hector Thwistle!"). During this same period, Superman protects bystanders at a navy yard from the effects of a devastating explosion by spinning around the blast area at super-speed. "...[W]ith the speed of light," notes the text, "Superman makes a wall of his revolving body, through which the expanding gases of the explosive cannot penetrate! Then, funneling upward, Superman directs the blast toward the sky!" (S No. 43/3, Nov/Dec '46: "The Molten World!").

In August 1947 Superman successfully photographs a series of past events by flying into outer space faster than the speed of light and overtaking the light waves leaving Earth which contain the images of the events he wants to record on film (Act No. 111, Aug '47: "Cameras in the Clouds!"; and others).

In a text dated September-October 1947 Superman single-handedly constructs an entire underground city in a matter of seconds (S No. 48/1: "The Man Who Stole the Sun!"). During this same period, Superman

uses his command of super-speed to travel through the time barrier into the past. "Through a deserted sky rockets the Man of Steel at super-speed," notes the text, "following a weird mathematical design ...An abrupt angular turn...and he vanishes into the time-dimension!" (S No. 48/2, Sep/Oct '47: "Autograph, Please!").

Other texts contain these descriptions of how Superman's speed enables him to travel in time:

> Time seems to stand still, becomes an endless highway, as Superman streaks backward at cosmic speed...faster...faster...ever faster...[Act No. 132, May '49: "The Secret of the Kents!"].
> ...[T]ime seems to stand still as Superman races at cosmic velocity, passing the speed of light years in instants. Faster...faster...until Superman breaks through the time barrier...[S No. 61/3, Nov/Dec '49: "Superman Returns to Krypton!"].

> Round and round whirls the Man of Steel--faster than the speed of light, faster than time itself! [S No. 89/1, May '54: "Captain Kent the Terrible!"].

> Out into space streaks Superman, faster than the speed of light--faster than time itself--breaking the barrier between our era and the world of the past...[S No. 92/2, Sep '54: "Superman's Sweetheart!"].

Virtually all texts agree that to penetrate the time barrier, Superman must move at a speed exceeding that of light (S No. 95/1, Feb '55: "Susie's Enchanted Isle"; and others). "When I fly at super-speed and

Flashing through space faster than the speed of light, Superman penetrates the time barrier en route to the planet Krypton at a time prior to its destruction. Since Superman will have no super-powers on Krypton, he wears a special anti-gravity belt designed to enable him to escape from Krypton's red-sun solar system, 1962

exceed the velocity of light," observes Superman in July 1959, "I can cross over the time-barrier to any past or future time I choose!" (S No. 130/3: "The Town That Hated Superman!").

In May 1948 Superman swims up NIAGARA FALLS at such phenomenal speed that the water about him vaporizes into clouds of steam (Act No. 120: "Superman, Stunt Man!").

In July-August 1950, without even flying at top speed, Superman makes a round-trip journey to a planetoid 5,000,000,000 miles away from Earth in five seconds flat, a speed more than 10,000 times the speed of light (S No. 65/1: "The Testing of Superman!").

In May 1957 Superman travels through outer space at an even more spectacular speed, traversing "in split seconds" vast distances that light travels only in years. "Light-years of distance dissolve in split seconds," notes the text, "as the **Man of Steel** flashes onward--out of our solar system...out of our island-universe!" (S No. 113: chs. 1-3—"The Superman of the Past"; "The Secret of the Towers"; "The Superman of the Present").

3. *Super-Strength.* "There have been many strong men in the world--but none with the amazing power of **Superman**, whose rippling steel muscles can blast boulders to dust and move mountains!" (S No. 112/3, Mar '57: "The Three Men of Steel!").

Like Superman's other powers, his strength has, in the course of four decades, been continually magnified. The chronology that follows traces the growth of

kicks a circus wagon high into the sky (Act No. 7).

In May 1939 Superman smashes his way through a brick wall (Act No. 12).

In a text dated Summer 1939, Superman crushes a gun barrel out of shape by squeezing it with one hand (S No. 1/1). Superman No. 2/3 records a similar feat, noting that Superman "crushes [the] pistol into a shapeless pulp!" (Fall '39: "Superman and the Skyscrapers").

In July 1939 the ULTRA-HUMANITE imprisons Superman in a block of crystal, but the Man of Steel "flexes his great muscles and the crystal block explodes!" (Act No. 14).

In Spring 1940, when METROPOLIS is ravaged by a man-made earthquake, "...**Superman** supports tottering buildings while terrified occupants dash to safety!" (S No. 4/1).

In July 1940 Superman demolishes a house with a single blow of his fist (Act No. 26).

In August 1940 Superman sticks a "red hot poker" into his mouth and bites off the end with his powerful teeth (Act No. 27).

In January-February 1941 Superman hurls a boulder "as large as a house" (S No. 8/1).

In an early display of his titanic strength, Superman demolishes a door made of solid steel, 1938

Superman's strength as it unfolded in the chronicles.

In June 1938 Superman, described as a man of "titanic strength" with the ability to "raise tremendous weights," lifts an automobile over his head with one hand, shakes its hoodlum occupants out onto the ground, and then smashes the car to bits against the base of a cliff (Act No. 1).

In October 1938 Superman diverts the raging floodwaters of the VALLEYHO DAM away from the town of Valleyho by shoving an entire mountain peak into the path of the "great, irresistible flood of onrushing water" (Act No. 5).

In December 1938 Superman, here described as "a man possessing the strength of a dozen Samsons,"

In April 1941, when an airliner is unable to make a proper takeoff due to rough terrain, Superman seizes the airplane in his hands and hurls it skyward (Act No. 35).

In May 1941, in the skies over Metropolis, Superman plows into an armada of enemy aircraft and "sends the enemy planes whirling off like bowling-pins!" (Act No. 36).

In September 1941 Superman swims through a raging flood using only one hand, while holding a mansion aloft with the other hand. To divert the floodwaters, Superman "digs a huge, mile-long ditch with his bare hands in a matter of moments..." (Act No. 40).

Overtaking a speeding car filled with hoodlums, Superman shakes out the passengers and smashes the vehicle to bits against a cliff, 1938

In September-October 1941 Superman single-handedly captures a seagoing submarine and drags it back onto dry land (S No. 12/1).

In November-December 1941 Superman soars through the air carrying a car (S No. 13/1).

In March-April 1942 Superman seizes a set of brass knuckles and "crushes the cowardly instrument in his palm as easily as tho [sic] the metal were putty..." (S No. 15/1).

In April 1942 Superman smashes his way through the side of a mountain (Act No. 47: "Powerstone").

In July 1942, while clinging to the side of a moving train, "**Superman** performs an amazing stunt--he *opens a Pullman window*...!" (Act No. 50).

In July-August 1942 Superman leaps from the roof of a skyscraper and "crashes to the ground, uninjured by the great fall because of his tremendously powerful muscles..." (S No. 17/2: "The Human Bomb").

In September 1942 Superman wrenches apart a

pair of twin mountain peaks with his bare hands (Act No. 52: "The Emperor of America").

In November-December 1942 "**Superman** tears open [a] metal armored car as casually as a housewife would open a can of sardines..." (S No. 19/3).

In July 1943, when Superman acts to avert the collapse of a massive undersea cavern, his "mighty shoulders bear the weight of thousands of tons of rock, and the terrific pressure of the ocean above it..." (Act No. 62: "There'll Always Be a Superman!").

In July-August 1943 Superman hits a baseball so hard it circles the world (S No. 23/4: "Danger on the Diamond!"; *see also* S No. 61/2, Nov/Dec '49: "The Courtship of the Three Lois Lanes!").

In August 1943, in a head-on collision, Superman demolishes "a tremendous meteor" hurtling toward Metropolis. As the "fiery projectile of doom hurtles through the black void of the night" toward the helpless city below, Superman launches himself into

Superman gives a gang of toughs "the severest thrashing of their lives," 1938

the sky to intercept it. "Of all the famous contests the Earth has seen," notes the text, "none could have surpassed this amazing charge of a puny figure against a vast mass of sizzling rock!" As Superman collides with the oncoming meteor, "a terrible blast rocks the Earth and sky," shattering the meteor but leaving Superman unharmed (Act No. 63: "When Stars Collide!").

In October 1944 Superman flies an entire steel mill—including the acre of land on which it is situated—through the air from one place to another. "An acre of land and buildings containing thousands of tons of machinery," notes the text, "are transported across mountains by the mighty **Man of Steel!**" (Act No. 77: "The Headline Hoax!").

In March-April 1946 Superman uses his super-strength to mend a gaping hole in the hull of a sunken freighter, welding the torn steel plates into place "by rubbing them with [his] hands till they're white-hot!" (S No. 39/2: "The Monster of China Deep!"). Later

Superman smashes aside an avalanche of raining boulders, 1940

texts refer to this process as the application of "super-friction" (S No. 84/3, Sep/Oct '53: "Lois Lane, Policewoman!"; and others).

In May-June 1946 Superman uses his "mighty fists" to pulverize large boulders into a "blizzard of dust" (WF No. 22: "The Siege of Aurora Roost!").

In December 1947 Superman transforms a lump of coal into a glittering diamond by squeezing it in his mighty fist. In the words of the text: "Incalculable tons of pressure exerted by the **Man of Steel's** mighty fist duplicates the work of eons to fuse the opaque coal carbons into... the translucent perfection of a glittering diamond!" (Act No. 115: "The Wish That Came True!"; and others).

In January-February 1948 Superman uses the super-pressure of his thumbnail to cut sheet metal (S No. 50/2: "The Slogans That Came Too True!").

In a text dated February 1948, Superman fells trees with his bare hands and then uses the edge of his hand like a metal tool to transform the fallen timber into neatly hewn planks (Act No. 117: "Christmas-town, U.S.A.!").

In June 1948 Superman hurls a giant ocean liner the entire length of Metropolis (Act No. 121: "Superman versus Atlas!").

In May-June 1949 Superman single-handedly creates a sun for the planet Uuz by crashing its two uninhabited moons together—"With cosmic speed," notes the text, "the **Man of Tomorrow** crashes the lifeless worlds together...creating a blaze of atomic power"—and then fueling the resultant blaze with drifting meteors (S No. 58/3: "The Case of the Second Superman").

In January 1950, working only with his bare hands, Superman "cold-welds [metal] ore into a molten mass of pliable metal...then forces it into thin wire strands" for the construction of a wire fence (Act No. 140: "Superman Becomes a Hermit!").

In March-April 1950 Superman blasts apart a log jam by diving underwater and clapping his hands. "Diving below the jam," notes the text, "**Superman applauds** — and the titanic pressure blasts the logs apart!" (S No. 63/3: "Miss Metropolis of 1950").

In September-October 1950 Superman mines more than 1,000,000,000 tons of coal in a single day (S No. 66/2: "The Last Days of Superman!").

In November 1950 Superman flies through the air carrying a 1,000-ton vault (Act No. 150: "The Secret of the 6 Superman Statues!").

In May-June 1951 Superman hurls a Metropolis skyscraper into orbit around the Earth long enough to enable him to repair its foundation (S No. 70/2: "The Life of Superman!").

In November-December 1951 Superman transforms an abandoned coal mine into a diamond mine by pummeling the mine's walls with mighty blows of his fists. "Diamonds are simply bits of coal subjected to **tremendous pressure** over thousands of years!" observes Superman. "My fists speed things up a bit!" (S No. 73/1: "Hank Garvin, Man of Steel!").

In January 1952 Superman uses his super-

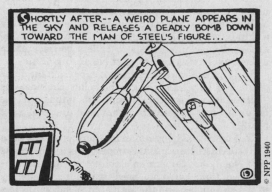

When "a weird plane appears in the sky and releases a
deadly bomb down toward the Man of Steel's figure…"

In an awesome display of super-strength, Superman
wrenches apart a pair of mountain peaks, 1942

…the Man of Steel catches the missile…

…and hurls it "back to its source"
with deadly accuracy, 1940

strength to squeeze sand into molten silicon (Act No.
164: "Superman's Hall of Trophies!"; see also Act No.
248, Jan '59: "The Man No Prison Could Hold!").

In March-April 1952, when an overloaded dynamo
at a Metropolis power plant plunges the city into a
paralyzing blackout, "Superman hurls [large] boulders through the atmosphere with such terrific speed
that they heat up and burn, disintegrating like fiery
comets" and producing enough light to illuminate the
entire city (S No. 75/3: "The Man Who Stole Memories!").

In May-June 1952, while putting on an exhibition
of his super-strength for passengers aboard the cruise
ship VARANIA, Superman juggles three massive
icebergs (S No. 76/1: "The Mightiest Team in the
World!").

In November 1953, when "a great dark star that's
rushing through the solar system" begins "causing
Earth to spin faster" on its axis, Superman finds
himself confronted by "the greatest challenge of his
career," that of devising a means of "slowing down
the Earth!" After fashioning a gigantic metal drill
from ore-bearing rock, Superman drills through the
Earth to "the red-hot rocks inside Earth's crust," and
then, "using his own body as a high-speed chisel,"
gouges a canal from the sea to the hole he has drilled
in the Earth. When the seawater rushing through
Superman's man-made canal washes over the red-hot
rocks at the Earth's core, the result is a "continuous
blast of steam [that] makes a great jet-blast,
pushing against the rotating Earth to slow it down!"
"When it's back to normal," notes Superman, "I can
close off the canal!" (Act No. 186: "Haunted Superman!").

In November-December 1953, while carrying out
the restoration of John Paul Jones's famous vessel,
the Bonhomme Richard, Superman saws the lumber
he needs by using the edge of his hand like a high-
speed buzz saw. "My hand makes a good buzzsaw
when I vibrate it at super-speed!" observes Superman. "Once I've cut enough planks, I can restore the
ship to its original appearance!" (S No. 85/2: "Clark
Kent, Gentleman Journalist!").

In July 1954 Superman transforms an entire
asteroid into a single gigantic diamond by subjecting
it to awesome "super-force" (S No. 90/1: "Superman's
Last Job!").

In September 1954 Superman hurls a chunk of
KRYPTONITE millions of miles into outer space (S No.
92/3: "Superman's Last Hour!").

In January 1955 Superman flies through the air
carrying a gigantic "hunk of ice mountain" from the

Arctic Circle weighing "a few million tons" (Act No. 200: "Tests of a Warrior!").

In January 1957 Superman hurls an uninhabited planet through space (S No. 110/2: "The Mystery Superman!").

In June 1957 Superman polishes a mammoth chunk of MOON rock into a gigantic mirror with the super-friction of his hands (Act No. 229: "The Superman Satellite").

In June 1958 Superman produces a small earthquake with "a super-clap of [his] hands" (Act No. 241: "The Super-Key to Fort Superman").

Superman battles a swarm of flaming meteors, 1956

In February 1959 Superman hurls a giant ape (*see* TITANO) "across the time barrier into the prehistoric past," a feat that requires him to throw the beast at faster-than-light speed while imparting to the animal that "certain spin" necessary to propel the ape across the time barrier (S No. 127/3: "Titano the Super-Ape!").

By July 1962 Superman's strength has become so awesomely colossal that he could, if he chose, destroy the Earth by ramming it in a head-on collision (S No. 154/2: "Krypton's First Superman!").

In March 1965 Superman seizes a spacecraft manned by members of the SUPERMAN REVENGE SQUAD and hurls it into "a far-distant galaxy" light-years away from Earth (Act No. 322: "The Coward of Steel!").

4. *Invulnerability.* "Fire can't burn him, knives can't cut him, bullets can't hurt him.... In fact, there's nothing known to man that can harm even a hair of Superman's head!" (S No. 107/2, Aug '56: "The Impossible Haircut").

"Of all the awesome capabilities of Superman," notes Action Comics No. 290, "one of the most important is his invulnerability!" (Jul '62: "Half a Superman!"). The chronology that follows traces the development of Superman's invulnerability as it unfolded in the chronicles. (*See also* section F, the vulnerabilities.)

In June 1938 a "bullet ricochets off Superman's tough skin" and a knife blade shatters when it strikes

his body. "...[N]othing less than a bursting shell," notes the text, "could penetrate his skin!" (Act No. 1). Subsequent texts describe Superman as "possessing a skin impenetrable to even steel" (Act No. 7, Dec '38) and as being "impervious to bullets because of an unbelievably tough skin" (Act No. 8, Jan '39).

In July 1938, when Superman leaps from the dome of the U.S. Capitol to the ground below, the sidewalk "bursts into fragments" from the impact of his landing, but Superman remains unharmed (Act No. 2).

In August 1938 Superman is described as having a "physical structure" that is impervious to poison gas (Act No. 3), but Superman's ability to withstand the effects of toxic gases has been treated inconsistently in the chronicles, and the Man of Steel succumbs to a debilitating "serum-gas" as late as the mid-1960s (S No. 167, Feb '64: "The Team of Luthor and Brainiac!" pts. I-III—"The Deadly Duo!"; "The Downfall of Superman!"; "The Hour of Kandor's Vengeance!").

In September 1938 Superman makes a remark indicating that he would be killed if run over by an express train (Act No. 4).

In January 1939 Superman withstands a barrage of machine-gun fire, and a monkey wrench is bent out of shape when it strikes his head (Act No. 8).

In June 1939 a buzz saw shatters against Superman's skin: "Against the mighty saw moves the Man of Steel--a great rasping--the sound of cracking metal--and the saw explodes into a thousand fragments—!" The text makes it clear, however, that Superman could be killed in a fire, and he is knocked unconscious by an elecrical charge sufficient "to kill five-hundred men!" (Act No. 13).

In Fall 1939, when a professional prizefighter punches Superman in the course of a bout, "it feels to him as tho [sic] he were battering a stone wall!" (S No. 2/1). During this same period, steel bayonets crumple against Superman's "super-tough skin" and he exhibits invulnerability to poison gas, but he is knocked momentarily unconscious by a small bomb dropped from an airplane (S No. 2/2, Fall '39: "Superman Champions Universal Peace!"), and when NAT GRAYSON tries to destroy him in a bomb-laden booby trap, "Only a swift sideward leap saves *SUPERMAN* from annihilation..." (S No. 2/3, Fall '39: "Superman and the Skyscrapers").

In October 1939 Superman extinguishes a raging fire "...aided by his amazing resistance to flame and pain...!" (Act No. 17).

In December 1939 Superman survives a deadly plague epidemic thanks to his "super-resistance to disease," but is stunned into unconsciousness by the ULTRA-HUMANITE's cannonlike "electric-gun." Superman successfully resists an attempt by the Ultra-Humanite to hypnotize him during this period (Act No. 19), but Superman's ability to resist hypnosis is treated inconsistently in the early texts, and there are a number of occasions when villains successfully hypnotize him (Act No. 25, Jun '40; and others).

In Spring 1940 Superman survives the explosion of a hand grenade hurled at him by LEX LUTHOR (S No.

4/1), withstands "a terrific barrage of electricity bolts," and remains unharmed despite his having "swallowed enough poison to kill a hundred men!" (S No. 4/3). He is, however, knocked unconscious by "a powerful new gas [which] is released in his face" by Lex Luthor (S No. 4/1).

In June 1940 Superman is temporarily paralyzed

knocked unconscious by the "blinding rays" of ZOLAR's "globe gun," a hideous implement of destruction capable of disintegrating an ordinary human being (Act No. 30).

In November-December 1940 Superman is knocked unconscious by the diabolical gas developed by the evil scientist KOTZOFF (S No. 7/2).

"Possessing a skin impenetrable to even steel," Superman leaps skyward to challenge an enemy aircraft...

...and emerges victorious as the airplane falls to its doom, "its propeller shattered upon Superman's skin," 1938

by the evil MEDINI's awesome "hypnotic power" (Act No. 25).

In Summer 1940 Superman extinguishes flaming torches with his bare hands (S No. 5/1) and demolishes an airplane in a head-on aerial collision (S No. 5/3).

In August 1940 Superman bites off the end of a "red hot poker" and remains unharmed (Act No. 27).

In a text dated November 1940, Superman is

In January-February 1941 Superman chews up a pocket knife and swallows it (S No. 8/3).

In Spring 1941 Superman succumbs to "overpowering weakness" after being exposed to a dose of the RAINMAKER's "radical new paralysis gas" sufficient to kill 1,000 ordinary men (WB No. 1).

In April 1941 Superman survives a powerful explosion of nitroglycerine (Act No. 35).

In May-June 1941 Superman is knocked unconscious by explosions that bury him under tons of rock (S No. 10/1), but deadly gas has no effect on him whatever (S No. 10/4).

In September-October 1941 a torpedo fired from a submarine explodes harmlessly against Superman's chest (S No. 12/1), but the Man of Steel is knocked unconscious by Lex Luthor's diabolical "paralysis gun" (S No. 12/4).

In November 1941, after being "bombarded by a terrific wave of electricity" unleashed by Lex Luthor, Superman finds himself simultaneously paralyzed and hypnotized, the victim of a diabolical form of "electrical hypnosis." "You'll find you can't move unless I will it!" gloats the villain. "You see, I've discovered many things about the mysterious force called electricity!" (Act No. 42).

In November-December 1941 Superman is both paralyzed and hypnotized by the "vari-colored beams of light" unleashed against him by "The Light" (see

In March-April 1942 Superman withstands the effects of a "tremendously powerful [artillery] shell" fired at him by the military forces of OXNALIA. "The bomb hasn't been invented yet that can make the slightest impression on me!" observes Superman (S No. 15/3). During this same period, Superman is momentarily stopped in his tracks by "THE EVOLU-TION KING's" diabolical "paralyzing ray" (S No. 15/4, Mar/Apr '42).

In April 1942 Superman plows through molten metal and emerges unharmed (Act No. 47: "Power-stone").

In May 1942 Superman is unhurt when a building collapses on top of him (Act No. 48: "The Adventure of the Merchant of Murder").

In May-June 1942 Superman is temporarily paralyzed by MISTER SINISTER's diabolical "force ray" (S No. 16/3: "Case of the Runaway Skyscrap-ers").

Superman easily withstands gunfire, 1939

LUTHOR, LEX) (S No. 13/1). During this same period, however, Superman plummets into a volcanic crater filled with boiling lava and emerges unharmed (S No. 13/4, Nov/Dec '41; see also Act No. 133, Jun '49: "The World's Most Perfect Girl!").

In January-February 1942 Superman withstands "a great blast of electricity" estimated at "a couple [of] million volts," but he is momentarily paralyzed by "a weird, enchanting melody" played on the piano by RUDOLPH KRAZINSKI (S No. 14/1).

In February 1942 Superman lapses into uncon-sciousness after being tricked into drinking a native African "witch-potion" (Act No. 45).

In June 1942 Superman is momentarily dazed by poison gas (Act No. 49: "The Puzzler!!").

In September 1942 Superman withstands the impact of a bolt of lightning (Act No. 52: "The Emperor of America"). One year later, Superman becomes dazed and groggy after being struck by a bolt of man-made lightning (S No. 25/4, Nov/Dec '43: "Hi-Jack--Jackal of Crime!"), but a subsequent text explains away this apparent discrepancy by noting that that particular bolt of artificial lightning had an adverse effect on Superman only because it "was lucky enough to strike the base of [his] brain!" (S No. 29/2, Jul/Aug '44: "The Tycoon of Crime!").

BUT KENDRICKS FIRES IN UNREASONING TERROR...!

THE BULLETS-- THEY GLANCED OFF YOU LIKE PEAS...!

YOU'D BE BETTER OFF WITH A PEA-SHOOTER, AT THAT!

Mistaking Superman for a vicious killer, a wealthy jewel merchant blazes away at him "in unreasoning terror," but the bullets merely bounce off Superman's impenetrable skin, 1941

In September-October 1942 Superman is momentarily frozen in his tracks by Lex Luthor's diabolical "freezing-ray," but the Man of Steel successfully throws off the effects of "the cold ray" by "straining with all his might" (S No. 18/2).

In January 1943 Superman is momentarily dazed by the explosions of EMIL LORING's "radio-controlled bombs" (Act No. 56: "Design for Doom!").

In February 1943 Superman accidentally knocks himself unconscious with a blow to his own chin (Act No. 57: "Crime's Comedy King!"; *see also* Act No. 145, Jun '50: "Merton Gloop and His Magic Horseshoe!").

In August 1943 Superman is knocked unconscious and afflicted with temporary amnesia by the "weird rays" emanating from a cosmic collision in outer space. In the words of the text:

Flaming havoc fills a vast area of the universe as monstrous suns crash head-on! Vibrating at frequencies infinitely greater than those of electricity, showers of invisible rays are loosed in all directions!

The cruder senses of ordinary mortals are undisturbed by the phenomenon, but the super-sensitive nerve structure of the **Man of Tomorrow** is shaken like the rigging of a gale-tossed ship...and mighty forces from infinity bring about what all the evil genius of the underworld has failed to accomplish...THE COLLAPSE OF A GIANT....

It soon becomes apparent, however, that "the shock of that [interstellar] collision has hurled a tremendous meteor into Earth's gravity field," a meteor which will demolish half of METROPOLIS unless Superman destroys it in time. And so, as the "fiery projectile of doom hurtles through the black void of the night" toward the helpless city far below, Superman launches himself into the sky to intercept it. "Of all the famous contests the Earth has seen,"

notes the text, "none could have surpassed this amazing charge of a puny figure against a vast mass of sizzling rock!"

As Superman collides with the oncoming meteor, "a terrible blast rocks the Earth and sky," and "as the force of bursting suns paralyzed **SUPERMAN'S** memory, so the shattering of a meteor restores it...!" (Act No. 63: "When Stars Collide!").

In September 1943 a U.S. soldier remarks that "not even our biggest shells can hurt **Superman!**" (Act No. 64: "The Terrible Toyman!").

In March-April 1944 Superman swims unharmed through a tank of deadly acid and withstands "white-hot blasts of oxyacetylene flame" (S No. 27/1: "The Palace of Perilous Play!").

In July-August 1944 Superman withstands the heat of "thermite flame, the hottest substance known," but he is temporarily hypnotized by the TYCOON OF CRIME's diabolical color wheel (S No. 29/2: "The Tycoon of Crime!").

In November-December 1944 Superman withstands the "terrible vibrations" of Lex Luthor's gigantic tuning fork (S No. 31/1: "Tune Up for Crime!"). In a text for this same period, however, "**Superman**'s iron frame staggers under the stunning impact of sunlight...concentrated sunlight," unleashed by an ancient "sun-cannon" wielded by the inhabitants of a lost Mayan civilization. This "ancient weapon of the sun-worshipping Mayans paralyzes the energies of even a **Superman**," notes the text, "...so powerful is [sic] the concentrated rays of the heat-giving, life-giving core of the solar system!" (S No. 31/3, Nov/Dec '44: "The Treasure House of History!").

A text dated January-February 1945 notes that "Unlike ordinary people, the **Man of Steel** can do without food if necessary..." (S No. 32/1: "Superman's Search for Clark Kent!"), but a later text contradicts this, noting that Superman could indeed "starve to death" (Act No. 161, Oct '51: "Exit—Superman!"). Two texts in the 1960s, however, support the contention of the first text: In August 1964 Superman notes that he can "live interminably without any food!" (S No. 171/2: "The Curse of Magic!"). And in April 1965 he makes this observation: "Since I'm invulnerable, I could go indefinitely without eating--but I'd rather not!" (Act No. 323: "Clark Kent in the Big House!").

In September-October 1945 Superman holds open an earthquake fissure with his bare hands until LOIS LANE has had a chance to climb to safety. "The most powerful muscles on Earth," notes the text, "withstand the tremendous pressure of thousands of tons of rock!" "If the fissure had closed on me," remarks Superman, "the only damage would have been to the rock!" (S No. 36/1: "Mr. Mxyztplk's Mistake!"). During this same period, Superman is unaffected by knockout gas (S No. 36/3, Sep/Oct '45: "Clark Kent, Star Reporter!").

In January-February 1946 Superman easily withstands the explosive impact of Lex Luthor's grenade-sized "atomic bomb," but he is stunned into unconsciousness by the villain's diabolical "molecular impulsion beam" (S No. 38/1: "The Battle of the Atoms!").

In May 1946 Superman notes that he is "invulnerable to [poison] gas" (Act No. 96: "Haircut--And a Close Shave!").

In October 1946 Superman flies onto an atomic-bomb test site and withstands the successive impact of two atomic bombs. He proves vulnerable, however, to the insanity-inducing drug employed by gang chief SPECS DOUR (Act No. 101: "Crime Paradise!").

In November-December 1946 Superman withstands the intense heat at the Earth's molten core (S No. 43/3: "The Molten World!").

In March-April 1947 Superman succumbs to the effects of a suspended-animation gas employed by an extradimensional alien (S No. 45/3: "The Case of the Living Trophies!").

In November-December 1947 Superman is temporarily weakened by a dose of the diabolical "radiation gas" unleashed by the GARGOYLE (S No. 49/2: "Clark Kent's Most Dangerous Assignment!").

In September 1948 Superman survives the cataclysmic explosion of an atomic pile: "Abruptly the atom pile explodes in an incredible cataclysm of power that almost rocks the solar system!....But though the blast sends him hurtling through space, Superman proves mightier even than atomic power!" (Act No. 124: "A Superman of Doom!").

In July 1950 Superman swims underwater "thousands of fathoms deep, down to the ocean bed itself," and suffers no ill effects from the crushing water pressure (Act No. 146: "The Statues That Came to Life!").

In July-August 1950 Superman withstands the heat at the rim of the sun (S No. 65/1: "The Testing of

Superman!"), estimated in a subsequent text at "a few billion degrees" (S No. 72/3: "The Flight of the Failures!").

In January 1951 Superman describes himself as being "invulnerable to *any* gas...!" (Act No. 152: "The Sleep That Lasted 1000 Years").

Although severely stunned by the blast, Superman nevertheless survives the awesome explosive impact of Lex Luthor's diabolical "molecular impulsion beam," 1946

In August-September 1951 Superman's coordination is adversely affected by unknown radiations unleashed by the explosion of a planet in outer space (WF No. 53: "The City That Was for Sale!").

In October 1951 Superman withstands the heat at the core of the sun (Act No. 161: "Exit—Superman!"). "Out in space, a blue-red costumed figure flashes into the very core of the sun," notes Superman No. 117/3, describing a similar event six years later, "...and is

Superman saves the life of Tom Trent by absorbing the full impact of a lightning bolt on his invulnerable chest, 1947

swallowed by licking tongues of blinding, blazing flame that can sear a planet to ash in a moment..." (Nov '57: "The Man with the Zero Eyes!").

In October-November 1951 Superman suffers no ill effects whatever after drinking a liquid "concocted of every deadly microbe known to man" (WF No. 54: "The Superman Who Avoided Danger!"). Indeed, by this date, Superman's "Herculean body" has become "immune to all ills" and "it's impossible for [him] to get sick" (S No. 81/2, Mar/Apr '53: "20,000 Leagues Under the Sea with Superman"). According to Superman No. 160/1, "...Superman's super-body is immune to infection and illness!" (Apr '63: pts. I-II— "The Mortal Superman!"; "The Cage of Doom!"). Superman is not immune, however, to certain extraterrestrial illnesses, such as the mysterious space virus that temporarily transforms his X-ray vision into "deep-freeze" vision in November 1957 (S No. 117/3: "The Man with the Zero Eyes!"), and VIRUS X, native to the planet KRYPTON (S No. 156, Oct '62: "The Last Days of Superman!" pts. I-III— "Superman's Death Sentence!"; "The Super-Comrades of All Time!"; "Superman's Last Day of Life!").

In May 1953 Superman withstands a barrage of 450,000,000 volts of electricity (Act No. 180: "The Super-Telethon").

In June 1953 Superman is adversely affected by the weird "super-cosmic rays" emanating from a "huge whirlpool of flaming gases" in the "vast loneliness of interstellar space." Realizing that "the super-cosmic rays that bother me now could destroy the world in time," Superman obliterates the "swirling inferno" of gases by devising a colossal "super-bomb" whose explosion scatters the gases throughout the universe. "WOW! Not even I could have survived a blast like that!" muses Superman aloud, as he hurls himself free of the blast area at the last possible instant. "Now there'll be tatters of flame all over the universe...but no single concentration of rays strong enough to matter!" (Act No. 181: "The New Superman").

In February 1954 Superman withstands the explosion of a hydrogen bomb, although it does leave him with "a slight headache" (S No. 87/1: "The Thing from 40,000 A.D.!").

In August 1954 Superman withstands a barrage of "man-made electrical force" sufficient to "fry Mount Everest to ash!" (S No. 91/1: "The Superman Stamp!").

In May 1955 Superman is adversely affected by a "beam of counter energy" unleashed by extraterrestrial aliens bent on conquering the Earth (Act No. 204: "The Man Who Could Make Superman Do Anything!").

In September 1957 Superman is adversely affected by poisonous meteoric dust from outer space (Act No. 232: "The Story of Superman, Junior").

In November 1957 Superman proves vulnerable to the effects of a bizarre somnabulism-inducing radiation emitted by a relic recovered from sunken

Quex-Ul batters Superman with a locomotive, but only the locomotive suffers damage, 1962

ATLANTIS (S No. 117/1: "Clark Kent, Man of Mystery").

In April 1958 Superman withstands "the mightiest atomic explosion of all time," created by detonating an entire planetoid composed of "almost pure uranium" (Act No. 239: "Superman's New Face").

In July 1958 Superman makes a remark indicating that he is potentially vulnerable to the intense heat of his own X-ray vision (Act No. 242: "The Super-Duel in Space").

In August 1958 Superman describes himself as being "invulnerable to any poisons or serums!" (Act No. 243: "The Lady and the Lion").

In January 1959 Superman withstands a barrage of 10,000,000,000 volts of electricity (S No. 126/1: "Superman's Hunt for Clark Kent!").

In April 1959 Superman is adversely affected by PROF. VANCE's "new vitamin serum," but only because "it contains isotopes resembling kryptonite" (Act No. 251: "The Oldest Man in Metropolis!").

A text dated April 1960 observes that the rifle-like "non-super-ray" weapon employed by the Bizarros of the planet HTRAE could permanently rob Superman of his super-powers (Act No. 263: "The World of Bizarros!"; see also Act No. 264, May '60: "The Superman Bizarro!"). Another text for this period strongly implies that Superman is invulnerable to the aging process and therefore immortal (S No. 136/1, Apr '60: "The Man Who Married Lois Lane!"), but Superman No. 181/2 contradicts this, noting that "Though Superman is the mightiest man on Earth, even he cannot live forever!" (Nov '65: "The Superman of 2965!").

In August 1960 Superman is afflicted with temporary amnesia as the result of having absorbed the full impact of a volcanic eruption (WF No. 111: "Superman's Secret Kingdom!").

In December 1960, during a visit to the planet ZORON, Superman discovers that a strange green mist surrounding the planet, composed of a substance similar in atomic structure to kryptonite, completely robs him of his super-powers so long as he remains there (WF No. 114: "Captives of the Space Globes!").

In April 1961 Superman is adversely affected by BERT TALBOT's diabolical Weapon X (S No. 144/1: "The Super-Weapon!").

In June 1961, during a visit to the extradimensional world of XERON, Superman discovers that the alien environment somehow alters and distorts his super-powers, so that his X-ray vision freezes things instead of heating them, and his super-breath sets things aflame (WF No. 118: "The Creature That Was Exchanged for Superman!").

In December 1962 Superman proves vulnerable to the diabolical "telepathic-hypnotic weapon" employed by members of the SUPERMAN REVENGE SQUAD (Act No. 295: "Superman Goes Wild!").

In February 1964 Superman is temporarily robbed of his super-powers by means of a diabolical "serum-gas" devised by Lex Luthor and BRAINIAC (S No. 167: "The Team of Luthor and Brainiac!" pts. I-III—"The Deadly Duo!"; "The Downfall of Superman!"; "The Hour of Kandor's Vengeance!").

In October 1964 Superman is robbed of his super-powers by the baleful radiations of a mysterious green comet, but his powers are ultimately restored to him through the heroic sacrifice of AR-VAL (S No. 172: pts. I-III—"The New Superman!"; "Clark Kent—Former Superman!"; "The Struggle of the Two Supermen!").

In March 1965 Superman proves vulnerable to the diabolical "cowardice projector" employed by members of the Superman Revenge Squad. The weapon "works on people from Krypton," notes the text, because it was "built from machinery stolen from Krypton before that planet exploded...!" (Act No. 322: "The Coward of Steel!").

A text dated April 1965 notes that Superman is "invulnerable to drowning, [and] can remain underwater as long as he wishes!" (Act No. 323: "Clark Kent in the Big House!"). (See also section E 7, super-breath and related powers.)

In July 1965 Superman finds that monsters from the planet GIANTIA become even more powerful than he is upon reaching Earth because their native planet is even larger than Krypton was and revolves about a larger red sun (Act No. 326: "The Legion of Super-Creatures!").

Because Superman is invulnerable, he cannot blush (Act No. 298, Mar '63: "Clark Kent, Coward!"; Act No. 317, Oct '64: "Superman's Rainbow Face!") or perspire (S No. 170/1, Jul '64: "Superman's Mission for President Kennedy!"; Act No. 322, Mar '65: "The Coward of Steel!"). Because his "skin is never affected by sun," he is impervious to sunburn (Act No. 262, Mar '60: "When Superman Lost His Powers!"; see also Act No. 308, Jan '64: "Superman Meets the Goliath-Hercules!").

Superman's hair is indestructible (Act No. 222, Nov '56: "The Duplicate Superman"; and many others) and can neither "be cut or grow...in Earth's atmosphere!" (S No. 132, Oct '59: "Superman's Other Life!" pts. 1-3—"Krypton Lives On!"; "Futuro, Super-Hero of Krypton!"; "The Superman of Two Worlds!"; and many others).

Any attempt to cut Superman's hair by ordinary means results only in the shattering of whatever scissors are being used (S No. 180/1, Oct '65: "Clark Kent's Great Superman Hunt!"; and others), but Superman can cut his own hair when absolutely necessary by subjecting it to the concentrated power of his own X-ray vision (S No. 107/2, Aug '56: "The Impossible Haircut"). In a red-sun environment, however, where Superman has no super-powers, his

Clark Kent reflects on his "super-resistance to disease," 1939

hair loses its indestructibility and begins to grow (Act No. 300, May '63: "Superman Under the Red Sun!"; and others). If Superman undertakes a mission to a red-sun planet, it is best for him to shave and trim his hair before returning to the yellow-sun environment of Earth, where his hair will once again become indestructible (S No. 171/3, Aug '64: "The Nightmare Ordeal of Superman").

Similarly, Superman's fingernails and toenails, which are indestructible and do not grow in the earthly environment, do grow and are destructible on planets revolving about a red sun (Act No. 300, May '63: "Superman Under the Red Sun!"; S No. 171/3, Aug '64: "The Nightmare Ordeal of Superman").

5. X-Ray Vision and the Other Optical Powers. "With telescopic vision, he has spanned the solar system--his microscopic vision has seen the tiniest dust particle--while his X-ray vision has pierced every substance except lead!" (Act No. 227: "The Man with the Triple X-Ray Eyes").

Today's Superman possesses a wide range of optical super-powers, including X-ray vision, which enables him to see through all substances except lead; telescopic vision, which enables him to focus on objects millions of miles away; super-vision, a combination of X-ray vision and telescopic vision, which enables him to perform such optical feats as peering through the wall of a house thousands of miles away; microscopic vision, which enables him to examine the tiniest atomic particles; heat vision, which enables him to apply intense heat to any substance except lead; infrared vision, which enables him to see objects lying outside the visible spectrum at its red end; radar vision, a term denoting infrared vision used at low power, which enables him to see in pitch darkness; and photographic vision, which enables him to perform such feats as memorizing whole books at a single glance (*see also* section E 9, mental and intellectual powers).

In Superman's earliest adventures, however, he exhibited no special optical powers, and the vision abilities he employs today are the products of a gradual evolution spanning many years of texts. Tracing the evolution of these abilities is difficult, for the terminology used to describe them is often haphazard and confusing. "Telescopic X-ray vision," for example, used as a general term in many early texts to denote Superman's ability both to see through objects and to see objects from far away (S No. 11/2, Jul/Aug '41; and others), later comes to refer to the use of both these visions simultaneously (Act No. 260, Jan '60: "Mighty Maid!"; and many others), a usage which is in turn supplanted by the term "supervision" (Act No. 281, Oct '61: "The Man Who Saved Kal-El's Life!"; and many others).

"Super-vision," however, both with and without the hyphen, has been employed at various times in the chronicles as a synonym for telescopic vision (S No. 4/2, Spr '40; Act No. 186, Nov '53: "Haunted Superman!"); as a means of describing Superman's ability to perform some complex optical feat, such as tracing television broadcast signals to their source (Act No. 273, Feb '61: "The World of Mr. Mxyzptlk!"; and others); and as a term denoting a combination of X-ray vision and telescopic vision, the meaning it has today.

Similarly, Superman used his X-ray vision to analyze the chemical composition of substances (Act No. 29, Oct '40), to melt solid objects (Act No. 145, Jun '50: "Merton Gloop and His Magic Horseshoe!"; and many others), and to see in pitch darkness (Act No. 167, Apr '52: "The Machines of Crime!") long before the more specialized terms microscopic vision, heat vision, and radar vision ever appeared in the chronicles.

Some terms, such as "super-sensory sight" (Act No. 43, Dec '41), "super-sensory vision" (Act No. 53, Oct '42: "The Man Who Put Out the Sun!"), and "supernormal vision" (S No. 26/4, Jan/Feb '44: "The Quicksilver Kid!") are used in the texts without ever being defined precisely. Given that these difficulties exist, however, the chronology that follows traces the development of Superman's optical powers as it unfolded in the chronicles.

In April 1939 Superman exhibits a superhuman optical ability—here referred to as "X-ray eyesight"—for the first time in the chronicles, but it is unclear whether this super-power actually enables Superman to peer through a solid object or whether it merely enables him to see a longer distance than an ordinary man (Act No. 11).

In November 1939 Clark Kent peers through the brick wall of a house with his "X-ray eyes" in order to determine what is going on inside (Act No. 18). A subsequent text notes that Kent's "eyes glow weirdly as he makes use of their X-ray ability" (Act No. 24, May '40).

In January 1940 reference is made both to Superman's "X-ray vision" and "telescopic-vision," but, as in many texts of this early period, the terms are used haphazardly, with little real distinction being drawn between them (Act No. 20).

In Spring 1940 reference is made to Clark Kent's "supervision," which enables him to view events occurring far out at sea (S No. 4/2).

In May 1940 reference is made to Superman's "microscopic vision," which enables him to spot a spent bullet embedded in the floor in the far corner of a room (Act No. 24).

In Summer 1940 reference is made to Superman's "telescopic X-ray vision" (S No. 5/3), but here, as in many early texts (S No. 8/1, Jan/Feb '41; and others), the term is never clearly defined, and no real effort is made to distinguish between X-ray vision and telescopic vision. In one such text, for example, Superman spies a gangster hiding inside a trash can by means of his "telescopic X-ray vision" (S No. 8/4, Jan/Feb '41).

In September-October 1940 Clark Kent's microscopic vision enables him to make out a strangler's fingerprints on a murder victim's throat (S No. 6/4).

In October 1940, by examining some "aspirin tablets" with his X-ray vision, Clark Kent is able to discern that they are not aspirins at all, but a slow-acting poison (Act No. 29). A similar situation occurs five months later: "Hanging outside the office window," notes the text, "SUPERMAN'S X-ray vision enables him to see that Laurey [*see* LAUREY, JIM]) is offering his niece a POISONED DRINK!" (Act No. 34, Mar '41).

In January-February 1942, while pretending to be asleep, Clark Kent observes the goings-on around him by peering through his own eyelids with his X-ray vision (S No. 14/1; *see also* S No. 21/1, Mar/Apr '43).

In September-October 1942 Clark Kent visits the observatory of an eminent astronomer and peers at a meteor through his powerful telescope. "But, unknown to the astronomer," notes the text, "Clark's vision is even more powerful than the telescope's. The reporter is able to scan the space-wanderer's surface with almost microscopic thoroughness..." (S No. 18/2).

In October 1942 Superman's "super-sensory vision" enables him to see in total darkness (Act No. 53: "The Man Who Put Out the Sun!").

In May-June 1943 Clark Kent's "marvelous microscopic eyesight" enables him to read the faint traces of a message remaining on a burnt piece of paper (S No. 22/4: "A Modern Robin Hood!").

In July-August 1943, during a period when the texts are still employing the term "telescopic X-ray vision" to designate Superman's X-ray and telescopic optical powers generally, "Superman's telescopic X-

Spying a weakened girder with his X-ray vision...

ray vision stabs through mountains as if they were crystal lenses..." (S No. 23/1: "America's Secret Weapon!").

In January-February 1944, when MERCURY, the mythological messenger of the gods, performs acts of mischief in METROPOLIS while moving about at invisible super-speed, "Only Clark's [Clark Kent's] eyes, capable of supernormal vision, can see the mischief-maker..." (S No. 26/4: "The Quicksilver Kid!").

.. Superman rescues Lois Lane from being crushed to death by a collapsing building, 1952

In February 1944 reference is made to the fact that Superman's X-ray vision cannot penetrate lead (Act No. 69: "The Lost-and-Found Mystery!").

In March-April 1945 Clark Kent learns the contents of a letter that a murder victim was writing just before his death by using his microscopic vision to read "the almost imperceptible indentations formed in the desk blotter by the pressure of the dead man's pen!" (S No. 33/3: "The Compass Points to Murder!").

In May-June 1946 Superman uses his X-ray vision like an X-ray machine to guide a surgeon in the performance of a delicate surgical operation (S No. 40/2: "A Modern Marco Polo!").

In November 1948 Superman analyzes chemical crystals with his microscopic vision (Act No. 126: "Superman on Television!").

In July 1949 Superman's X-ray vision enables him to read, at super-speed, a pile of unopened letters on PERRY WHITE's desk (Act No. 134: "Super-Cowboy!").

In July-August 1949 Superman melts an Arctic glacier by bombarding it with "the full strength of [his] X-ray powers." "Under the terrific heat of the X-ray beams," notes the text, "the huge glacier is soon dissolved..." (S No. 59/2: "The Man of Steel's Super Manhunt!"; *see also* Act No. 180, May '53: "The Super-Telethon").

In December 1949 Superman uses the heat of his X-ray vision to set a wooden bridge afire (Act No. 139: "Clark Kent...Daredevil!").

In March-April 1950 Superman renders some gems radioactive by bombarding them "with a charge of radioactivity from [his] X-ray eyes!" (S No. 63/2: "The Wind-Up Toys of Peril!").

In October-November 1950 Superman examines the molecules of newly processed steel with his microscopic vision, observing that this super-power enables him to "see what even the best microscope can't detect, because my vision is at least a thousand times more powerful!" (WF No. 48: "The Great Steel Mystery!").

In February 1951 reference is made to Superman's "telescopic X-ray vision," here, as in other texts of this period, denoting telescopic vision and X-ray vision used simultaneously (Act No. 153: "The 100 Deaths of Clark Kent!").

In March 1951 Superman's "super-microscopic vision" enables him to discern that a brook "contains harmful bacteria" and is therefore unfit for drinking (Act No. 154: "Miss Robinson Crusoe!").

In November-December 1951 Superman reads through Metropolis's entire archive of municipal records by spreading them out in stacks and then flying over them. "With my telescopic vision," notes Superman, "I can study thousands of records at once, from up here, just like an aerial camera takes in several square miles of land on one picture!" (S No. 73/1: "Hank Garvin, Man of Steel!").

In April 1952, while conducting an underwater search, Superman uses his X-ray vision to illuminate the ocean floor. "By concentrating," notes Superman,

"I can lengthen the waves of my *X-ray vision* enough for them to become *light rays* and illuminate the ocean floor!" (Act No. 167: "The Machines of Crime!").

In September-October 1952 Superman uses the heat of his X-ray vision to disintegrate a pile of falling lumber (S No. 78/2: "The Strong Man Club!").

In February 1953 Superman uses the heat of his X-ray vision to detonate an arsenal of explosives (Act No. 177: "The Anti-Superman Weapon").

In March-April 1953 Superman melts a bullet in midair with the heat of his X-ray vision (S No. 81/3: "The Superwoman from Space").

In April 1953, within the space of "a few minutes," Superman reads approximately half a million unopened letters with the aid of his X-ray vision (Act No. 179: "Super Manor!").

In October 1953 Clark Kent's telescopic vision enables him to observe a meteor "almost a million miles away" in space (Act No. 185: "Superman's Million Dollar Photos!").

In November 1953 Superman is described as possessing "a super vision that outmatches the greatest telescopes in the world." The reference is presumably to Superman's telescopic vision, but this is never actually stated (Act No. 186: "Haunted Superman!").

In July 1954, while sitting in a home on the outskirts of Metropolis, Superman uses his telescopic X-ray vision to read several books in a Parisian library (S No. 90/1: "Superman's Last Job!").

In September-October 1954, while being held captive by criminals in a moving auto, Clark Kent activates a teletype machine at the DAILY PLANET "by controlling the impulses of the [electric] current with [his] X-ray vision!" (WF No. 72: "Fort Crime!").

A text dated November 1954 provides evidence of Superman's ability to control the heat-intensity of his X-ray vision. "Turning on the full strength of his X-ray vision," notes the text, "Clark [Kent] focuses its burning intensity on a minor cog of the machine..." (Act No. 198: "The Six Lives of Lois Lane!").

In March 1955 Superman observes that he can "see things with [his] X-ray vision that no standard X-ray machine can!" (S No. 96/1: "The Girl Who Didn't Believe in Superman!").

In October 1955, while standing on a planetoid in outer space, Superman uses the heat of his X-ray vision to melt a meteor hundreds of thousands of miles away (Act No. 209: "The Man Who Was Mightier Than Superman").

In August 1956 Superman cuts his own indestructible hair with the concentrated heat of his X-ray vision (S No. 107/2: "The Impossible Haircut!").

In March 1957, while seated at his desk at the *Daily Planet*, Clark Kent demonstrates the ability to "send his telescopic vision far across space" and actually locate a selected individual on a far-distant planet (Act No. 226: "The Invulnerable Enemy").

In November 1957 "the full force of **Superman**'s amazing X-ray vision...emits the scorching heat of a

Scanning a desert region with his X-ray vision, Superman spots a green-kryptonite meteor buried beneath the ground, 1953

million blast furnaces!" (S No. 117/3: "The Man with the Zero Eyes!").

In December 1957 Superman creates a man-made comet by fusing together several meteors, subjecting them to the awesome heat of his X-ray vision, and then hurling them through space. "The heat of my X-rays turned it [the comet] red-hot," muses Superman, "causing hot sparks to stream out behind for millions of miles!" (Act No. 235: "The Super-Prisoner of Amazon Island").

In July 1958 Superman suggests that the reflected "super-heat" of his X-ray vision could harm even him (Act No. 242: "The Super-Duel in Space").

In February 1959 Superman actually "projects his telescopic vision across the time barrier" in order to locate TITANO in the prehistoric past (S No. 127/3: "Titano the Super-Ape!").

In April 1960 Superman demonstrates the ability to analyze the age of a document with his microscopic vision (S No. 136/1: "The Man Who Married Lois Lane!") and burns an inscription into a stone tablet with the heat of his X-ray vision (S No. 136/2: "The Secret of Kryptonite!").

A text dated July 1960 describes Superman as having "photographic eyes," a reference to his capacity for instantaneous memorization (S No. 138/1: "Titano the Super-Ape!").

In February 1961 Superman demonstrates the ability to turn the waters of an entire bay to steam with the heat of his X-ray vision (WF No. 115: "The Curse That Doomed Superman!").

In April 1961 reference is made to Superman's "amazing heat vision," a new term denoting X-ray vision used to produce heat. Superman uses his heat vision during this period to disintegrate a falling chandelier before it can hit the floor (Act No. 275: "The Menace of Red-Green Kryptonite!"). One month later, he uses it to generate "millions of degrees" of heat (S No. 145/2, May '61: "The Interplanetary Circus!").

In October 1961 Superman scans the entire city of Metropolis with his "super-vision"—here used to designate a combination of telescopic vision and X-ray vision—until he locates the one individual for whom he is searching (Act No. 281: "The Man Who Saved Kal-El's Life!").

In February 1962 Superman uses his microscopic vision to analyze the chemical composition of a fraudulent "magic elixir" (S No. 151/2: "The Man Who Trained Supermen!").

In October 1962, while hovering in outer space, Superman uses his heat vision to char a message to mankind into the side of the MOON (S No. 156: "The Last Days of Superman!" pts. I-III—"Superman's Death Sentence!"; "The Super-Comrades of All Time!"; "Superman's Last Day of Life!").

In March 1963 Clark Kent stares at the ground and focuses "the awesome power" of his heat vision all the way through to the opposite side of the Earth in order to melt a gigantic glacier in the Arctic, thousands of miles away (Act No. 298: "Clark Kent, Coward!").

In April 1964 Superman uses his telescopic vision to read the lips of individuals on a far-distant planet as well as to scan the entire Earth in order to satisfy himself that the one individual for whom he is searching is nowhere on the planet (S No. 168: pts. I-II—"Luthor--Super-Hero!"; "Lex Luthor, Daily Planet Editor!").

6. Super-Hearing. Today Superman's super-hearing—ordinary human hearing multiplied countless thousands of times—enables Superman to "detect the footfall of an ant 1,000 miles away" (S No. 117/3, Nov '57: "The Man with the Zero Eyes!") or trace the source of sound waves across millions of miles of interstellar space (Act No. 260, Jan '60: "Mighty Maid!").

In his very earliest adventures, however, Superman exhibited no special aural powers, and the super-hearing he employs today is the product of a gradual evolution spanning many years of texts. The term "super-hearing" first appears in the chronicles in Fall 1939 (S No. 2/3: "Superman and the Skyscrapers"). Nevertheless, during the first two decades of Superman's career, the texts also employ such other descriptive terms as "super-acute hearing" (Act No. 11, Apr '39; S No. 2/1, Fall '39), "super-sensitive hearing" (S No. 5/4, Sum '40; and others), "hyper-keen hearing" (Act No. 97, Jun '46: "The Magician's Convention!"), and "super-keen hearing" (Act No. 221, Oct '56: "Superman's New Super-Power"). Given that this mélange of terminology exists, however, the chronology that follows traces the development of Superman's aural powers as it unfolded in the chronicles.

In January 1939 Superman is described as having "sensitive ears," which enable him to hear things ordinary human beings cannot (Act No. 8).

In April 1939 reference is made to Superman's "super-acute hearing" (Act No. 11), which, in a subsequent text, enables him to overhear a conversation taking place in a nearby building (S No. 2/1, Fall '39).

In Fall 1939 reference is made to Superman's "super-hearing" (S No. 2/3: "Superman and the Skyscrapers").

Not yet endowed with super-hearing, Superman clings to the outer wall of a Washington, D.C., apartment building in order to eavesdrop on villains plotting to embroil the United States in World War II, 1938

In Summer 1940 reference is made to Superman's "super-sensitive hearing" (S No. 5/4; see also S No. 14/1, Jan/Feb '42).

In November-December 1940 Superman's "super-sensitive ears" enable him to "pick up radio waves" so that he can listen in on a radio news broadcast without a radio (S No. 7/1).

In January-February 1942 Superman's super-sensitive hearing enables him to trace radio waves to their source (S No. 14/1).

In May-June 1942 Clark Kent's super-sensitive hearing enables him to listen in on police radio calls without a radio (S No. 16/2). "Using his super-hearing," notes Action Comics No. 195, describing an identical feat twelve years later, "the Man of Steel tunes in on police short-wave broadcasts without using a receiving set" (Aug '54: "Lois Lane--Wanted!").

In July-August 1942, while Superman is relaxing at his secret mountain retreat (see section D, the Fortress of Solitude), his super-sensitive hearing enables him to overhear a police short-wave broadcast miles away in METROPOLIS (S No. 17/3: "Muscles for Sale!").

In June 1946 Superman's "hyper-keen hearing" enables him to trace a telephone call across the phone wires to its source (Act No. 97: "The Magician's Convention!").

In July-August 1950 Superman's super-hearing

enables him to hear the low humming sound of a machine 1,500 miles away (S No. 65/3: "Three Supermen from Krypton!").

In May 1953 Superman exhibits the ability to focus his super-hearing so precisely that, while flying high over Metropolis, he can eavesdrop on a conversation taking place in one specific apartment (Act No. 180: "The Super-Telethon").

In March-April 1955 Superman notes that his super-hearing "can pick up explosions anywhere in the world!" (WF No. 75: "The New Team of Superman and Robin!").

In May 1955, while Clark Kent is interviewing the warden at Metropolis Jail, his super-hearing enables him to eavesdrop on every single conversation taking place in the building simultaneously (S No. 97/3: "Superboy's Last Day in Smallville!").

In November 1957 Superman observes that his super-hearing "can detect the footfall of an ant 1,000 miles away ..." (S No. 117/3: "The Man with the Zero Eyes!").

In January 1960 Superman's super-hearing enables him to trace sound waves to their ultimate source: "a space ship millions of miles from Earth ..." (Act No. 260: "Mighty Maid!").

In December 1960, while stranded in the Sahara Desert, Superman can hear Big Ben chiming the hour in London (Act No. 271: "Voyage to Dimension X!").

7. *Super-Breath and Related Powers.* Like Superman's other super-powers, his super-breath and related powers have undergone continual expansion and magnification. The chronology that follows traces the development of these powers as it unfolded in the chronicles.

A text dated August 1939 notes that Superman "can hold his breath for hours underwater ..." (Act No. 15).

In January 1940 Superman blows out a flaming torch with a powerful puff of his breath (Act No. 20).

A text dated March 1941 notes that Superman's lungs can withstand any air pressure, no matter how great (Act No. 34), and a later text observes that Superman can swim "thousands of fathoms deep, down to the ocean bed itself," without suffering any ill effects (Act No. 146, Jul '50: "The Statues That Came to Life!").

In June 1941 Superman extinguishes a raging fire with "a terrific gust of breath" (Act No. 37).

In September-October 1947 Superman extinguishes a small bonfire by inhaling the flames (S No. 48/2: "Autograph, Please!").

In November-December 1947, when the TOYMAN attempts to make good his escape astride a rocket-powered hobbyhorse, Superman draws him back to earth with a deep inhalation of breath (S No. 49/1: "Toyman and the Gadgets of Greed!").

In March-April 1948 Superman notes that he "can hold [his] breath indefinitely" (S No. 51/3: "The Man Who Bossed Superman!"), but a text five years later contradicts this, strongly suggesting that Superman cannot even stay underwater a full twenty-four hours

without the aid of an external air supply (S No. 81/2, Mar/Apr '53: "20,000 Leagues Under the Sea with Superman").

In March-April 1949, after having been locked inside a skyrocket by LEX LUTHOR, Superman uses his super-breath "in place of rocket fuel" to launch the skyrocket into the stratosphere. "And with super-breath," notes the text, "the Man of Steel lifts the projectile into the sky!" (S No. 57/1: "The Menace of the Machine Men!"). Superman performs a similar feat in July 1960, climbing into the exhaust apparatus of a jet aircraft disabled in midair and using his "superbreath as jet propulsion" to guide it to a safe landing (Act No. 266: "The Captive of the Amazons").

In July-August 1949 Superman uses his super-breath to inflate Navy surplus observation blimps as though they were toy balloons (S No. 59/2: "The Man of Steel's Super Manhunt!").

In September-October 1949 Superman extinguishes a chemical fire by inhaling all the air around it. "... [T]he deadly flames are no menace to **Superman**," notes the text, "who smothers them by momentarily drawing all the air in the room into his own mighty lungs!" (S No. 60/2: "The Men Who Had to Guard Superman!").

In March 1950 Superman propels a Naval training vessel through the water with a blast of his super-breath (Act No. 142: "The Conquest of Superman!").

In March-April 1950 Superman rescues the workers in a rubber factory from deadly sulfur dioxide by inhaling all the gas in the factory and exhaling it out an open window (S No. 63/1: "Achilles *versus* Superman!").

In November-December 1950 Superman makes an ordinary man appear to fly by propelling him through the air with puffs of his super-breath (S No. 67/3: "Clark Kent's Twin!"; *see also* S No. 81/3, Mar/Apr '53: "The Superwoman from Space").

In December 1951-January 1952, while standing on the ground, Clark Kent uses puffs of his super-breath to enable a disabled airplane to glide to a safe landing (WF No. 55: "The City That Exiled Superman!").

In May-June 1953 Superman freezes streams of water from high-pressure hoses by inhaling sub-zero air high in the stratosphere and then exhaling it at the gushing water (WF No. 64: "The Death of Lois Lane").

In July 1953 Superman notes that he can "stay under water almost indefinitely" (Act No. 182: "The Return of Planet Krypton!").

In July 1954 Superman paints a house by using his super-breath to blow paint out of a paint bucket onto the house. "**Super-breath** comes in handy in many ways," muses Superman, "... but this is the first time I've used it as a **paint sprayer!**" (S No. 90/1: "Superman's Last Job!").

In August 1954, far out in space, Superman extinguishes a star with a blast of his super-breath (S No. 91/1: "The Superman Stamp!").

In May 1958 Superman hypnotizes ELDREDGE

CORAM by using his super-breath to oscillate a wall mirror in such a way that it flashes in Coram's eyes and places him in a hypnotic trance (S No. 121/2: "The Great Superman Swindle").

In May 1959 Clark Kent extinguishes a fire at the SUPERMAN MUSEUM by using the "super-cooling" power of his super-breath to lower the temperature in the museum to below freezing, thereby snuffing out the flames (S No. 129/2: "Clark Kent, Fireman of Steel!").

In July 1959 Superman halts a massive tidal wave by freezing it into "a solid iceberg" with a blast of his super-breath (Act No. 254: "The Battle with Bizarro!"). In January 1961 Superman defeats a fearsome Kryptonian "flame dragon" (see FLAME DRAGON) by splashing the creature with an ocean wave and then quick-freezing the water around the beast into "a great mass of ice" with a mighty blast of his "super-cold breath" (S No. 142/3: "Flame-Dragon from Krypton").

In November 1959 Superman creates a cooling shower of rain for U.S. soldiers on a thirty-mile hike by using his "powerful vacuum breath" to draw a stream of water from a nearby lake. On another occasion during this period, Superman helps some soldiers at an Army firing range improve their scores in marksmanship by using his super-breath to deflect their bullets into the bull's-eyes of their targets (S No. 133/3: "Superman Joins the Army!").

In March 1960 JIMMY OLSEN remarks that "Superman can live for years underwater!" (Act No. 262: "When Superman Lost His Powers!").

In October 1960, after engraving an inscription with his fingernail into the frame of a mirror, Superman blows on the inscription with his super-breath in order to imbue it with an antique appearance. "The force of my super-breath will create an artificial aging effect," observes Superman, "so the writing will appear centuries-old!" (Act No. 269: "The Truth Mirror!").

In February 1961, after MR. MXYZPTLK has loosed a cloud of "magic sneezing powder" on METROPOLIS, Superman finds himself forced to give vent to a "super-sneeze" that literally destroys an entire "distant solar system" (Act No. 273: "The World of Mr. Mxyzptlk!").

In April 1963 Superman disarms a gang of bank robbers by using his "super-cold breath" to freeze the air around their guns into blocks of ice. "Puffing my super-cold breath at them," muses Superman, "I've condensed the moisture in the air around their guns into ice! Now that their numb fingers can't pull triggers, innocent bystanders won't get hurt!" (S No. 160/2: "The Super-Cop of Metropolis!").

A text dated April 1965 notes that Superman is "invulnerable to drowning, [and] can remain underwater as long as he wishes!" (Act No. 323: "Clark Kent in the Big House!").

8. Vocal and Ventriloquistic Powers. Like Superman's other super-powers, his vocal and ventriloquistic powers have been continually magnified and expanded in the course of his career. The chronology that follows traces their development as it unfolded in the chronicles.

In November-December 1941 Superman employs ordinary ventriloquism to distract the attention of criminals holding LOIS LANE captive (S No. 13/1).

In March-April 1942 Superman exhibits the ability to mimic voices when he "expertly disguises his voice so that it sounds exactly like [a] gang-leader's..." (S No. 15/4).

In September-October 1942, in order to warn the people of METROPOLIS of a Nazi invasion, "...Superman shouts a warning in such dynamic tones his voice carries for miles..." (S No. 18/1: "The Conquest of a City"; see also Act No. 125, Oct '48: "The Modern Nostradamus!").

In May-June 1943 Superman summons police to an underworld hideout by "broadcasting his voice with the aid of his super-powers so that it materializes in police radio sets..." (S No. 22/4: "A Modern Robin Hood!").

In March 1944 Clark Kent employs ventriloquism in order to make a Superman dummy appear to talk (Act No. 70: "Superman Takes a Holiday!").

In November-December 1947 Superman shatters a thousand-ton block of ice into tiny fragments with a mighty shout (S No. 49/2: "Clark Kent's Most Dangerous Assignment!").

In September 1948 Superman deliberately topples several Metropolis buildings by using his voice to produce musical notes of extraordinarily high intensity and pitch (Act No. 124: "A Superman of Doom!").

In January 1950 reference is made to Superman's "super-voice" (Act No. 140: "Superman Becomes a Hermit!").

In January-February 1950 Superman ventriloquizes over a considerable distance in order to make a painted image of himself appear to talk and in order to make his voice materialize from a police-car radio (S No. 62/2: "The People vs. Superman!"). This technique, which later becomes known as "super-ventriloquism," enables Superman to project his voice over immense distances and yet have his voice heard only by those whom he is directly addressing (Act No. 278, Jul '61: "The Super Powers of Perry White!"; and many others).

In July-August 1950 one of Superman's super-yells is monitored at over 1,000,000 decibels (S No. 65/1: "The Testing of Superman!"). One later text notes that "Superman's tremendous shout echoes like a thousand thunderstorms in the sky" (Act No. 183, Aug '53: "The Perfect Plot to Kill Superman!"), while another observes that his "super-voice...resounds like 1,000 loudspeakers," enabling everyone within a five-mile radius to hear it (S No. 113, May '57: chs. 1-3—"The Superman of the Past"; "The Secret of the Towers"; "The Superman of the Present").

In August 1950, while standing with Lois Lane in an office at the DAILY PLANET, Superman uses ventriloquism to make Clark Kent's voice come over the telephone so that Lois will believe Kent and Superman are two different men (Act No. 147: "Superman Becomes Miss Lovelorn!").

In September 1955 Superman shatters a diamond into powder by using his super-voice to produce extraordinarily high-pitched musical notes (S No. 100/3: "The Clue from Krypton").

In July 1961 Superman converses with SUPERGIRL over an immense distance by means of super-ventriloquism, a voice-throwing technique that enables them to converse over long distances without being overheard by anyone in between (Act No. 278: "The Super Powers of Perry White!").

In July 1962 Superman summons KRYPTO THE SUPERDOG by means of super-ventriloquism (Act No. 290: "Half a Superman!"), but in November 1963 he speaks of summoning Krypto "via supersonic ventriloquism," a technique that enables him to throw his voice at such a high pitch that only Krypto's super-canine hearing could possibly hear it (S No. 165/1: pts. I-II—"Beauty and the Super-Beast!"; "Circe's Super-Slave").

9. *Mental and Intellectual Powers.* Along with his other super-powers, Superman also possesses a "super-intellect" (Act No. 140, Jan '50: "Superman Becomes a Hermit!"; and others) and other superhuman mental powers. The following chronology traces the development of those powers as it unfolded in the chronicles.

In Spring 1940 Clark Kent exhibits the ability "to temporarily halt the beating of his heart" (S No. 4/1). On several occasions in subsequent years, Superman employs this unique ability in order to enable him to feign death. Superman No. 21/4 alludes to Superman's having temporarily "halted the beating of his heart-[and] put himself into a state of suspended animation" (Mar/Apr '43: "The Ghost of Superman!"), and World's Finest Comics No. 54 cites Superman's ability "to control [his] heart action" in order to simulate the signs of death (Oct/Nov '51: "The Superman Who Avoided Danger!"). Control of one's heartbeat would seem to involve mental control of one's physical functions, but in his only clear description of this feat, Superman describes it as one of "super-muscular control." "To make you think I had 'died,'" he remarks to a group of captured criminals in January 1958, "I used super-muscular control to stop my heart from beating--just as I'm doing now to make it beat faster and louder, listen!" (S No. 118/3: "The Death of Superman!").

In Summer 1940 Superman is described as possessing a "photographic memory" (S No. 5/1; and others).

In January 1941 Superman cures LOIS LANE of her amnesia by means of hypnosis (Act No. 32), and a month later, as Clark Kent, he hypnotizes Lois into forgetting the super-feats he is about to perform so that he can rescue her from a burning cabin in his role as Clark Kent without betraying his dual identity (Act No. 33, Feb '41). "Swiftly Clark focuses his eyes hypnotically upon Lois Lane," observes Superman No. 13/2, describing a similar event some nine months later, "so that she is swiftly and painlessly rendered unconscious..." (Nov/Dec '41).

In July-August 1941 Clark Kent uses his potent hypnotic powers to hypnotize an entire group of South American Indians holding him captive (S No. 11/3).

In September-October 1941 Clark Kent's "super-sensory powers" inform him that a native ornamental doll is "coated with a deadly poison" fatal to the touch, but the precise nature of Kent's super-sensory powers is never delineated (S No. 12/1). Superman performs an almost identical feat earlier in 1941, however, by means of his X-ray vision (Act No. 34, Mar '41). (*See also* section E 5, X-ray vision and the other optical powers.)

In January-February 1942 Superman is able to converse fluently with a mermaid despite the fact that her tongue is completely foreign to him because his "advanced intellect instantly comprehends [her] strange language..." (S No. 14/3; *see also* Act No. 214, Mar '56: "Superman, Super-Destroyer").

In June 1942 Superman defeats a "checkers expert" at a game of checkers despite having "only played the game once before" (Act No. 49: "The Puzzler!!").

In July 1943 Superman is described as having a "super-brain" (Act No. 62: "There'll Always Be a Superman!"; and others). Subsequent texts refer to Superman as having a "super-intellect" (Act No. 140, Jan '50: "Superman Becomes a Hermit!"; and others) and a "super-mind" (Act No. 186, Nov '53: "Haunted Superman!"; WF No. 93, Mar/Apr '58: "The Boss of Batman and Superman").

In January-February 1945 Superman visits the public library and reads through a mountain of books and articles about himself in only five minutes (S No. 32/1: "Superman's Search for Clark Kent!"), and in November-December 1945 he is described as reading a 500-page book in ten seconds flat (S No. 37/1: "The Dangerous Dream!").

In March-April 1947 Superman uses his power of "telepathic will-control" to force an extradimensional alien to do his bidding. Under the compelling influence of Superman's "mental assault," the alien obeys the Man of Steel's mental command without even being aware that his actions are being determined by an outside influence (S No. 45/3: "The Case of the Living Trophies!"). This super-power, however, never reappears in the chronicles and is no longer part of Superman's arsenal of powers.

In September-October 1947 Superman is described as having a "super-instinct" that alerts him to the fact that someone is watching him (S No. 48/3: "The Rarest Secret in the World!"; *see also* S No. 138/3, Jul '60: "The Mermaid from Atlantis!").

In July-August 1948 Superman demonstrates the ability to solve complex mathematical equations with the speed and accuracy of a "giant computing machine" (S No. 53/2: "The Oracle from Metropolis!").

In August 1949 Superman pores over "thousands of detailed geological maps" in the space of one minute (Act No. 135: "The Case of the Human Statues!").

In July-August 1950 Superman's super-intellect enables him to solve, in seconds, "a complicated mathematical problem" that the Metropolis Science Foundation's "mighty electronic brain" takes ten minutes to solve (S No. 65/1: "The Testing of Superman!").

In September 1950 Superman's "super reading-speed" enables him to read through the contents of an entire historical archive in the space of five minutes (Act No. 148: "Superman, Indian Chief!").

In July-August 1951 Clark Kent memorizes a 400-page book in a matter of seconds (S No. 71/1: "Clark Kent's Super-Masquerade!").

In September-October 1951 Superman comments that, for the sake of "convenience," he has "memorized the entire [METROPOLIS] phone book" (S No. 72/2: "The Private Life of Perry White!").

In November 1953 Superman is described as having a "super-memory" (Act No. 186: "Haunted Superman!"; and others).

In March-April 1954 Superman's "super-intelligence" enables him to solve a complex equation that involves "dealing with mathematical ideas unknown to ordinary men" (WF No. 69: "Jor-El's Last Will!").

In March 1955 Superman memorizes all the existing books on eye surgery preparatory to performing "a complicated eye operation" (S No. 96/1: "The Girl Who Didn't Believe in Superman!").

In April 1955 Superman is described as having used his photographic memory to memorize all the files of the DAILY PLANET (Act No. 203: "The International Daily Planet!").

In May 1955 Superman is described as having a "super-photographic memory" (S No. 97/1: "The Amazing Professor Memory!").

In May 1956 Superman is described as being able to "recall every action of his life . . . with his super-human memory!" (S No. 105/1: "Superman's 3 Mistakes!"; and others). Subsequent texts refer to Superman's "power of total memory" (S No. 156, Oct '62: "The Last Days of Superman!" pts. I-III—"Superman's Death Sentence!"; "The Super-Comrades of All Time!"; "Superman's Last Day of Life!") or "total-recall memory" (S No. 172, Oct '64: pts. I-III—"The New Superman!"; "Clark Kent—Former Superman!"; "The Struggle of the Two Supermen!"; and others), noting that it enables the Man of Steel to remember everything he ever said or did (WF No. 146, Dec '64: "Batman, Son of Krypton!" pts. I-II—no title: "The Destroyer of Krypton!"; and others).

In February 1957 Superman's photographic memory enables him to draw a photographic likeness of a man whom he has not seen since childhood (S No. 111/2: "Clark Kent's Crooked Cousin").

In January 1958 Superman is able to match up a suspect's fingerprints with those on file in Washington, D.C., as the result of having used his super-memory to memorize the entire fingerprint file of the F.B.I. (S No. 118/3: "The Death of Superman!"; see also Act No. 246, Nov '58: "Krypton on Earth!").

In June 1958, while relaxing at his Fortress of Solitude (see section D, the Fortress of Solitude), Superman defeats "a great robot he has built" in a game of "super-chess" despite the fact that the robot—which "possesses a super-electronic brain"—can "think and play with the speed of lightning, and plans a million moves at once!" (Act No. 241: "The Super-Key to Fort Superman").

In December 1958 Superman demonstrates his command of powerful "super-hypnotic forces" (Act No. 247: "Superman's Lost Parents!").

In November 1960 Superman is described as having mastered Kryptonese, the language of KRYPTON, "through his memory's power of total recall" (S No. 141: "Superman's Return to Krypton!" pts. I-III—"Superman Meets Jor-El and Lara Again!"; "Superman's Kryptonian Romance!"; "The Surprise of Fate!").

In August 1961 Superman is described, albeit in an "imaginary tale," as being able to speak "all languages, living or dead" (Act No. 279: "The Super-Rivals!").

A text dated August 1963 notes that Superman "possesses the super-intellect of a score of the world's most brilliant minds put together . . ." (S No. 163/2: "The Goofy Superman!").

In May 1965 Superman is described as being able to alter his own brain-wave patterns by "super-mental control" (WF No. 149: "The Game of Secret Identities!" pts. I-II—no title; "The Super-Detective!").

10. *Miscellaneous Powers.* In addition to the super-powers enumerated in the foregoing subsections, Superman has displayed other unique abilities that are not readily classifiable.

Several texts describe Superman as possessing "super-senses," which, among other things, enable him to sense the presence of an "electrical discharge" (Act No. 38, Jul '41) or the close proximity of LORI LEMARIS (S No. 135/2, Feb '60: "Superman's Mermaid Sweetheart!").

Superman's "supersensitive nostrils" (WF No. 26, Jan/Feb '47: "The Confessions of Superman!") enable him to detect the faint odor of nitroglycerine in a cache of dynamite (Act No. 288, May '62: "The Man Who Exposed Superman!") or to stand atop a METROPOLIS skyscraper and pinpoint LOIS LANE's exact location by the scent of her perfume (Act No. 195, Aug '54: "Lois Lane--Wanted!").

According to one text, Superman possesses a "super-sensitive nerve structure," rendering him extraordinarily sensitive to the effects of cosmic disturbances (Act No. 63, Aug '43: "When Stars Collide!"). Another text notes that Superman's "fingers are super-sensitive," enabling him to distinguish between types of metal ores by their touch even when he cannot see them (Act No. 227, Apr '57: "The Man with the Triple X-Ray Eyes").

Superman's "super-coordination" enables him to sign two autographs simultaneously, one with each hand (S No. 180/1, Oct '65: "Clark Kent's Great Superman Hunt!"), and a transfusion of his alien blood has the power to make a critically ill person well again within a matter of moments (S No. 6/4, Sep/Oct '40).

Superman No. 133/2 asserts that Superman could consume virtually endless quantities of food (Nov '59: "How Perry White Hired Clark Kent!"), and Action Comics No. 306 suggests that Superman can perform feats of lovemaking of which an ordinary man would be quite incapable: forced into the position of having to kiss Lois Lane beneath the mistletoe at a DAILY PLANET Christmas party in 1963, Clark Kent mischievously decides to "shock the daylights out of Lois by giving her a **super-kiss**," in the manner of Superman, instead of the mild-mannered kiss she would be likely to expect from Clark Kent. Indeed, when Kent finally releases Lois from his embrace after giving her a super-soulful kiss, Lois is glassy-eyed and on the verge of swooning.

"Holy Toledo, Clark," exclaims someone at the party,"--where'd you learn to kiss like **that?**"

"Yes," stammers Lois, plainly impressed, "for a while I thought you were--er--someone else! Where'd you pick up this technique?"

"Maybe it's a sort of hidden talent!" replies Kent. "After all, you don't know everything about me!" And then Kent thinks: "True indeed! Lois would pass out if she knew it was **Superman**, my other identity, who kissed her!" (Nov '63: "The Great Superman Impersonation!").

One super-power that has long since been discarded by the chroniclers is Superman's ability, displayed on a number of occasions in the 1940s, to radically alter his facial characteristics and even his size through what was described as "superb muscular control" (S No. 26/1, Jan/Feb '44: "The Super Stunt Man!") of his "plastic features" (Act No. 55, Dec '42: "A Goof Named Tiny Rufe"; and others).

In the very earliest texts, Superman could alter his appearance only with the aid of makeup (S No. 2/1, Fall '39; and others). In September-October 1942, however, Superman No. 18/4 notes that "Assuming another identity is a simple matter for Clark Kent.--Working clothes--features twisted into another facial appearance--and the trick is done!" ("The Snake").

Several months later, in December 1942, Superman is described as disguising his facial appearance by "twisting his own plastic features" (Act No. 55: "A Goof Named Tiny Rufe"). In July-August 1943, in order to impersonate pitcher Tom Marin, "the **Man of Tomorrow** twists his plastic features into a perfect resemblance of Tom Marin's face..." (S No. 23/4: "Danger on the Diamond!").

In March-April 1947 Superman carries his power of disguise a step further when, by what the text describes only as "twisting" and "turning," he "alters [both] his size and appearance" in order to impersonate a white-skinned extradimensional alien who bears no resemblance whatever to a human being (S No. 45/3: "The Case of the Living Trophies!").

This bizarre super-power appears in the chronicles

for the last time in December 1947, however, when Superman uses it to disguise himself as a criminal (Act No. 115: "The Wish That Came True!"). Since that time, Superman has employed disguises on numerous occasions, but these disguises have always been achieved through costumes, makeup, and other conventional means.

F. The Vulnerabilities. Despite his awesome super-powers (*see* section E, the super-powers), Superman continues to be afflicted with certain important vulnerabilities. The pages that follow are devoted to an examination of these vulnerabilities. (*See also* section E 4, invulnerability.)

1. Kryptonite. The term *kryptonite* is used in the chronicles to designate any surviving fragment of the exploded planet KRYPTON. There are five distinct varieties of kryptonite (green, red, gold, blue, and white), the first three of which are toxic to Superman as well as to all other surviving natives of Krypton. By far the most common variety is green kryptonite. Indeed, whenever the word *kryptonite* appears in this encyclopedia without a specific color designation, it is green kryptonite that is being referred to.

a. GREEN KRYPTONITE. "What poison is to the average human being, **green kryptonite** is to **Superman!** Indeed, the only thing the **Man of Steel** has to fear in the entire universe is the ghastly green substance which was flung into space when the planet **Krypton** exploded!" (Act No. 291, Aug '62: "The New Superman!").

When the planet Krypton exploded into fragments as the result of a cataclysmic chain reaction originating at the planet's core, all of Krypton's atomic elements "fused to become one deadly compound," a compound later to become known as kryptonite (S No. 61/3, Nov/Dec '49: "Superman Returns to Krypton!"). Sent hurtling into outer space by the force of the cataclysm, these "dazzling particles" of the demolished planet, all "laden with cosmic energy," were scattered throughout the far reaches of the universe in the form of meteors and meteoric fragments, emitting a deadly radiation to which only Kryptonian survivors are vulnerable (Act No. 141, Feb '50: "Luthor's Secret Weapon").

"When a radioactive chain reaction exploded my native planet **Krypton**, long ago," notes Superman in August 1960, "chunks of **green kryptonite** were formed! They scattered throughout space as meteors!

"Their peculiar radioactive rays can bring **kryptonite-fever** and death to any person from **Krypton**...but are **harmless** to Earth people!" (S No. 139/3: "The Untold Story of Red Kryptonite!").

In the texts, green kryptonite is referred to as "the strange element given off by the explosion of the planet Krypton" (Act No. 141, Feb '50: "Luthor's Secret Weapon"); "the deadly rock-like element from the exploded planet Krypton whose radiations can paralyze **Superman**" (Act No. 142, Mar '50: "The Conquest of Superman!"); "the one substance...that can overpower the **Man of Steel**" (Act No. 152, Jan '51: "The Sleep That Lasted 1000 Years"); "the rare

In an unsuccessful effort to build up an immunity to green kryptonite, Superman deliberately exposes himself to the baleful radiations of a kryptonite meteor, 1953

element, whose mysterious radiation is the only known force capable of overcoming Superman" (WF No. 50, Feb/Mar '51: "Superman Super-Wrecker"); "a baleful new element whose rays affect only natives of Krypton" (Act No. 158, Jul '51: "The Kid from Krypton!"); "the meteor metal caused by the explosion of *Superman*'s native planet" (WF No. 56, Jan/Feb '52: "The Superman Pageant!"); "the rare element from the shattered planet Krypton whose radiations have a deadly effect on **Superman**" (Act No. 174, Nov '52: "The Man Who Shackled Superman!"); the "one element in all the universe [that] can overcome" Superman (Act No. 181, Jun '53: "The New Superman"); "the one substance that can destroy" Superman (Act No. 235, Dec '57: "The Super-Prisoner of Amazon Island"); "the one substance in the universe feared by Superman" (Act No. 236, Jan '58: "Superman's New Uniform!"); and "Superman's one fatal flaw" (S No. 136/2, Apr '60: "The Secret of Kryptonite!").

In the words of Superman No. 84/2:

Kryptonite, the radioactive particles of the former planet Krypton on which **Superman** was born, and which later exploded, is the one substance in the universe that can affect the mighty **Man of Steel!** Since kryptonite fragments still float in space after the explosion of the planet, some particles often find their way to Earth embedded in meteors! [Sep/Oct '53: "A Doghouse for Superman!"].

"Bullets!... Fire!... Bombs!... Acid! I'm immune to them all!" muses Superman ruefully in July 1959. "But **kryptonite** is my Achilles heel... the only substance in the universe that can harm me! It was originally formed years ago... when the planet Krypton, the world on which I was born, blew up! A nuclear chain-reaction converted every chunk of the

exploding world into glowing green **kryptonite**!" (S No. 130/1: "The Curse of Kryptonite!").

Recent texts assert that the entire planet Krypton and every single thing on it was transformed into kryptonite by the force of the cataclysm (Act No. 314, Jul '64: "The Day Superman Became the Flash!"; and many others). Numerous earlier texts, however, maintain that whereas the planet itself was transformed into kryptonite, its buildings and other artifacts of civilization were not (S No. 74/1, Jan/Feb '52: "The Lost Secrets of Krypton!"; and many others).

Green kryptonite is a radioactive (S No. 89/3, May '54: "One Hour to Doom!") metal (WF No. 56, Jan/Feb '52: "The Superman Pageant!") which is characterized by a distinctive "greenish glow" (Act No. 235, Dec '57: "The Super-Prisoner of Amazon Island"; and others) and "has certain properties similar to radium...!" (Act No. 167, Apr '52: "The Machines of Crime!"). Colored red in its initial textual appearance (S No. 61/3, Nov/Dec '49: "Superman Returns to Krypton!"), green kryptonite has been colored green in every text since then. Although Action Comics No. 158 states flatly that "No substance will screen kryptonite's rays--not even supermanium" (*see* SUPERMANIUM) (Jul '51: "The Kid from Krypton!"), innumerable texts have maintained since then that green-kryptonite radiations are unable to penetrate lead (S No. 92/3, Sep '54: "Superman's Last Hour!"; and many others).

In March-April 1954 Superman neutralizes the radioactivity of a green-kryptonite meteor merely by plunging it into the ocean (WF No. 69: "Jor-El's Last Will!"), but the notion that the baleful effects of kryptonite can be neutralized by seawater is contradicted by numerous other texts: "Ah! My X-ray vision shows a **kryptonite** meteor that fell to the sea bottom!" muses Superman in December 1958. "But to pick it up, I'll need the protection of lead, which alone can stop the deadly radiations!" (Act No. 247: "Superman's Lost Parents!"; and many others).

According to Action Comics No. 158, powerful acids and even man-made lightning cannot destroy green kryptonite (Jul '51: "The Kid from Krypton!"), but Superman has successfully melted the substance with his X-ray vision (Act No. 252, May '59: "The Menace of Metallo!"; and others) and green-kryptonite meteors dissolve completely when subjected to the searing heat at the core of the sun (WF No. 61, Nov/Dec '52: "Superman's Blackout!"; *see also* Act No. 161, Oct '51: "Exit—Superman!"). The reason green-kryptonite meteors do not burn up from air friction when they enter Earth's atmosphere is that "kryptonite can't combine chemically with oxygen, which causes combustion!" (S No. 130/1, Jul '59: "The Curse of Kryptonite!"; *see also* Act No. 267, Aug '60: "Hercules in the 20th Century!").

Assuming that the necessary advanced technology were available to utilize it, green kryptonite could become an invaluable source of atomic power. It retains its radioactivity "for centuries" (Act No. 161,

Oct '51: "Exit—Superman!") and is described as a more potent power source than uranium (Act No. 252, May '59: "The Menace of Metallo!"). Its principal drawback appears to be that it "crumbles and destroys any generator" in which it is utilized (Act No. 224, Jan '57: "The Secret of Superman Island!"), but this has not prevented at least one group of extraterrestrial aliens from developing a powerful "rocket fuel composed of liquid green kryptonite" (Act No. 296, Jan '63: "The Invasion of the Super-Ants!"). Green kryptonite also has properties that nourish the development of certain forms of plant life (Act No. 169, Jun '52: "Caveman Clark Kent!").

Although numerous texts describe green kryptonite as an exceedingly rare substance (Act No. 181, Jun '53: "The New Superman"; and many others), noting that "**Kryptonite** meteors that [fall] on Earth are rare" (Act No. 238, Mar '58: "The Super-Gorilla from Krypton"), other texts, admittedly fewer in number, maintain that "Kryptonite meteors often fall from space" (S No. 134, Jan '60: chs. I-III—"The Super-Menace of Metropolis!"; "The Revenge Against Jor-El!"; "The Duel of the Supermen!") and that "particles [of kryptonite] often find their way to Earth embedded in meteors!" (S No. 84/2, Sep/Oct '53: "A Doghouse for Superman!"). On balance, however, the evidence of the texts is that green kryptonite is "very rare" and not easily acquired (S No. 128/1, Apr '59: chs. 1-2—"Superman versus the Futuremen"; "The Secret of the Futuremen"; and others).

It is presumably the scarcity of green kryptonite—combined with its crushingly debilitating effect on Superman—that has motivated a number of villains to find ways to synthesize it. LEX LUTHOR creates the first synthetic kryptonite in February 1950 by ingeniously fusing together "a mammoth pearl from one of the giant oysters miles down under the sea"; "a couple of handfuls of dust from the dark side of the moon"; "pollen from the man-eating homocessandi plant deep in the Asiatic jungles"; and "a bit of the rare chemical binarium, preserved in the soil by a thousand years of glacial frost" (Act No. 141: "Luthor's Secret Weapon").

DR. VALLIN devises a formula for synthesizing green kryptonite in January-February 1952 that calls for stockpiling gold, silver, lead, and bismuth and then "fusing the...ore with acid and crackling electricity" (WF No. 56: "The Superman Pageant!").

A third method of synthesizing kryptonite, successfully employed by Lex Luthor in August 1953, is based on Luthor's observation that

> Each piece of metal that strikes **Superman**'s invulnerable body undergoes a slight chemical change! To a minute degree, it acquires the properties of kryptonite, but its presence is so faint that it can only be detected by means of a spectroscope!
> Kryptonite is the one material that can harm **Superman**! By refining tons of this metal, I'll be able to extract kryptonite---just as radium is obtained by refining tons of uranium ore! [Act No. 183: "The Perfect Plot to Kill Superman!"].

Whether the kryptonite is natural or synthetic, however, its effects on Superman are devastating, although they do vary according to the amount of kryptonite involved and Superman's distance from it. Large meteors produce the worst effects, but close proximity to even a small quantity of green kryptonite—such as a piece the size of a large decorative gem—is sufficient to make Superman feel "like a feeble old man," incapable of even touching the kryptonite without losing consciousness (S No. 61/3, Nov/Dec '49: "Superman Returns to Krypton!").

"As soon as I approach kryptonite," observes Superman in April 1952, "I become weak!" (Act No. 167: "The Machines of Crime!"). Other texts refer to such symptoms as "dizzy spells," exhaustion, and grogginess (Act No. 169, Jun '52: "Caveman Clark Kent!"; and many others); nausea (S No. 81/2, Mar/Apr '53: "20,000 Leagues Under the Sea with Superman"); loss of consciousness (S No. 66/2, Sep/Oct '50: "The Last Days of Superman!"; and many others); and temporary impairment—or even complete loss—of memory (S No. 71/1, Jul/Aug '51: "Clark Kent's Super-Masquerade!"; and others). Typically, Superman's pupils become dilated, his pulse rate falls below normal, and his respiratory rate is reduced by half (S No. 66/2, Sep/Oct '50: "The Last Days of Superman!").

If lured to within close proximity of a fairly large chunk of green kryptonite, such as a meteoric fragment about the size of a basketball, Superman suffers a nearly total loss of his super-strength accompanied by an agonizing semi-paralysis—referred to in the texts as a "kryptonite paralysis" (Act No. 218, Jul '56: "The Super-Ape from Krypton"; and others)—and the drastic diminution of all his super-powers.

For the effects of the kryptonite to prove fatal may take hours (S No. 92/3, Sep '54: "Superman's Last Hour!"; and others) or even days, but gradually, under "constant exposure" to the kryptonite radiations, Superman's "mighty body becomes emaciated and his keen mind grows dim..." (S No. 77/2, Jul/Aug '52: "The Greatest Pitcher in the World!"; and others).

As the last vestiges of his mighty powers begin slowly waning, Superman "begins to feel pain from the steady exposure to the kryptonite," and he lapses into a potentially fatal "kryptonite fever," similar in many respects to that which afflicts ordinary people who have been "over-exposed to **radium** rays!" Even if drugs were available to treat the illness, they could not be injected, for "the hypodermic needles [would] only bend" against Superman's invulnerable skin.

"The kryptonite radiations will soon penetrate my otherwise invulnerable skin and change the red corpuscles of my bloodstream to green!" thinks Superman desperately in July 1959 as he suffers the agonizing effects of exposure to a green-kryptonite meteor. "I'll become a victim of blood-poisoning!" (S No. 130/1: "The Curse of Kryptonite!").

Indeed, if Superman were not rescued from the baleful radiations in time, his body would begin to exude a greenish glow, like that of the deadly kryptonite itself, and he would lapse into a coma and die. Superman has never succumbed to this terrible fate, but other Kryptonian survivors have, including KING KRYPTON (Act No. 238, Mar '58: "The Super-Gorilla from Krypton") and virtually all the inhabitants of ARGO CITY (Supergirl story in Act No. 252, May '59: "The Supergirl from Krypton!").

Superman has, however, amazing recuperative powers. Although, on a number of occasions, he has remained physically weak for a short time after having suffered the effects of kryptonite exposure (S No. 66/2, Sep/Oct '50: "The Last Days of Superman!"; and others), in the vast majority of cases he recovers his full powers within moments after the debilitating kryptonite has been removed from his presence (Act No. 141, Feb '50: "Luthor's Secret Weapon"; and many others).

The texts are divided, however, on the question of whether green-kryptonite radiations are capable of weakening Superman to the point of robbing of him of his invulnerability—thereby rendering him vulnerable to guns, bombs, and other ordinary weapons (WF No. 87, Mar/Apr '57: "The Reversed Heroes!"; and others)—or whether, as most texts dealing with this question contend, Superman retains his invulnerability despite prolonged exposure to kryptonite and can only be killed by the kryptonite itself (Act No. 299, Apr '63: "The Story of Superman's Experimental Robots!"; and many others).

In situations in which Superman has no super-powers, such as that which exists in October 1964, after the Man of Steel has been stripped of his powers by the baleful radiations of a mysterious green comet, he becomes immune to green-kryptonite radiations until such time as his super-powers have been restored to him (S No. 172: pts. I-III—"The New Superman!"; "Clark Kent—Former Superman!"; "The Struggle of the Two Supermen!"; and others).

Once having been lured into a kryptonite death-trap, Superman has coped with the deadly substance in a variety of ways, such as by using his waning X-ray vision to melt an object containing lead around the kryptonite, thereby shielding himself from its radiations (S No. 145/1, May '61: "The Secret Identity of Superman!"), or by burning a hole in the floor with his weakened X-ray vision in order to make the kryptonite fall safely out of life-threatening range (S No. 77/2, Jul/Aug '52: "The Greatest Pitcher in the World!"). On one occasion, Superman successfully wards off the agonizing pain induced by green-kryptonite exposure—albeit only for a few crucial moments—by literally hypnotizing himself into not feeling the pain (Act No. 278, Jul '61: "The Super Powers of Perry White!").

Superman has had some success with melting small chunks of kryptonite with his X-ray vision (Act No. 252, May '59: "The Menace of Metallo!"), but this technique is inadequate for dealing with larger

masses of the substance, such as, for example, an entire kryptonite meteor or meteorite (Act No. 254, Jul '59: "The Battle with Bizarro!"; S No. 130/1, Jul '59: "The Curse of Kryptonite!").

Because green kryptonite is the bane of his existence, Superman has conducted numerous experiments in search of an antidote, but all his efforts have ended in failure (Act No. 158, Jul '51: "The Kid from Krypton!"; and others). He has also experimented with building up an immunity to the substance through controlled exposure to it, but these attempts, too, have been unsuccessful (S No. 84/2, Sep/Oct '53: "A Doghouse for Superman!"). Superman has, however, successfully devised a suit of special lead armor (see section G1, lead armor) to enable him to experiment with the substance (Act No. 241, Jun '58: "The Super-Key to Fort Superman"; Act No. 249, Feb '59: "The Kryptonite Man!") as well as a special "kryptonite detector" (Act No. 243, Aug '58: "The Lady and the Lion")—also referred to as a "K-detector"—which "detects kryptonite as a Geiger counter does uranium" (Act No. 158, Jul '51: "The Kid from Krypton!").

For handling green kryptonite without his special lead armor, Superman has employed remote-controlled robots (Act No. 158, Jul '51: "The Kid from Krypton!"), gigantic shovels (S No. 71/1, Jul/Aug '51: "Clark Kent's Super-Masquerade!") and tongs (S No. 113, May '57: chs. 1-3—"The Superman of the Past"; "The Secret of the Towers"; "The Superman of the Present"; and others), and other special tools (S No. 115/2, Aug '57: "Jimmy Olsen's Lost Pal"; and others) designed to enable him to handle, or dispose of, the kryptonite without venturing too close to it. According to Superman No. 130/1, Superman remains safe from harm as long as he remains "at least 100 feet from the radiations..." (Jul '59: "The Curse of Kryptonite!").

b. RED KRYPTONITE. "When an atomic explosion destroyed **Krypton** long ago, chunks of **green kryptonite** were formed and scattered throughout space as meteors! But one flock of these meteors went through a strange cosmic cloud and turned to **red kryptonite**! Ever since then, **red kryptonite** has always had peculiar, unpredictable effects on **Superman!**" (Act No. 283, Dec '61: "The Red Kryptonite Menace!").

When the mighty world of KRYPTON exploded into stardust as the result of a cataclysmic chain reaction originating at the planet's core, the entire planet was transformed into "green, radioactive fragments, later to be known as kryptonite" (see section F 1 a, green kryptonite). In the course of their endless journey through space, however, "one flock of green kryptonite meteorites later passed through a radioactive cosmic cloud to become red kryptonite," a baleful new substance to which Superman and all other surviving natives of Krypton are vulnerable (S No. 146/1, Jul '61: "The Story of Superman's Life!"; and others).

Unlike green kryptonite, which severely impairs

Kryptonite!"), "the eerie substance that always affects survivors of the planet **Krypton** in an unpredictable way" (Act No. 290, Jul '62: "Half a Superman!"), "the uncanniest element in the universe" (Act No. 293, Oct '62: "The Feud Between

IF MY GUESS IS RIGHT, THIS SUPER-POWERFUL ACID WILL REACT WITH THE **RED KRYPTONITE**, CREATING FUMES THAT WILL IMMUNIZE ME FOREVER AGAINST THE EFFECTS OF **ALL** VARIETIES OF **RED K!**

SNIFF!

© NPP 1964

In an unsuccessful attempt to immunize himself against the effects of red kryptonite, Superman performs an experiment in the "super-laboratory" at his Fortress of Solitude, 1964

Superman and Clark Kent!"), and "the sinister scarlet mineral" (Act No. 330, Nov '65: "The Strange 'S' Spell on Superman!").

Action Comics No. 259 describes red kryptonite as

the dread substance that was formed many years ago when fragments of the destroyed planet **Krypton**, converted to **green kryptonite** by nuclear fission, passed through a strange cosmic cloud.... **Green kryptonite** can kill **Superman**! **Red kryptonite** does weird, unpredictable things to the **Man of Steel**...[Dec '59: "The Revenge of Luthor!"].

Red kryptonite is a great deal rarer than green kryptonite (S No. 128/1, Apr '59: chs. 1-2—"Superman versus the Futuremen"; "The Secret of the Futuremen"). Action Comics No. 283 notes that although "everything that existed on **Krypton** before it exploded is [now] indestructible," red kryptonite "lost its indestructibility while traveling through that cosmic cloud" and can therefore be broken up into smaller pieces. In addition, "red kryptonite can easily be burned or melted by friction or intense heat!" (Dec '61: "The Red Kryptonite Menace!").

It is unclear, however, whether lead shields red-kryptonite radiations as it does those of green kryptonite. Superman No. 139/3 states flatly that "lead can't stop red kryptonite rays" (Aug '60: "The Untold Story of Red Kryptonite!"), but other texts assert just as flatly that red-kryptonite radiations

Superman's strength and other super-powers and is potentially fatal, red kryptonite afflicts Superman with bizarre and unpredictable—albeit temporary and nonfatal—symptoms, as when it makes his hair and fingernails grow uncontrollably (S No. 139/3, Aug '60: "The Untold Story of Red Kryptonite!"), endows him with the power of "mental telepathy" (WF No. 115, Feb '61: "The Curse That Doomed Superman!"), and transforms him into a terrifying Kryptonian monster known as a "drang" (*see* KRYPTON) (Act No. 303, Aug '63: "The Monster from Krypton!").

On other occasions, exposure to red kryptonite has caused Superman to experience terrifying nightmares (Act No. 286, Mar '62: "The Jury of Super-Enemies!"; and others); made flame shoot out of his mouth and endowed him with the power to make his wishes come true (Act No. 283, Dec '61: "The Red Kryptonite Menace!"); transformed him into an infant with the mind of an adult (Act No. 284, Jan '62: "The Babe of Steel!"); robbed him of his invulnerability along the entire left side of his body (Act No. 290, Jul '62: "Half a Superman!"); made him immune to green kryptonite but vulnerable, in turn, to silver, gold, aluminum, and diamond (Act No. 291, Aug '62: "The New Superman!"); transformed him into two separate individuals, a mature, responsible Clark Kent and an unprincipled, irresponsible Superman (Act No. 293, Oct '62: "The Feud Between Superman and Clark Kent!"); endowed him with the head and antennae of a giant ant (Act No. 296, Jan '63: "The Invasion of the Super-Ants!"); robbed him of his invulnerability and super-powers (S No. 160/1, Apr '63: pts. I-II—"The Mortal Superman!"; "The Cage of Doom!"); driven him insane for a period of forty-eight hours (S No. 163/2, Aug '63: "The Goofy Superman!"); robbed him of his super-powers and afflicted him with total amnesia (S No. 165/2, Nov '63: "The Sweetheart Superman Forgot!"); transformed him into two separate individuals, a mature, responsible Clark Kent and a heroic Superman (Act No. 311, Apr '64: "Superman, King of Earth!"; Act No. 312, May '64: "King Superman versus Clark Kent, Metallo"); robbed him of all his super-powers with the exception of his "various vision abilities" (S No. 168, Apr '64: pts. I-II—"Luthor--Super-Hero!"; "Lex Luthor, Daily Planet Editor!"); made his face literally change color to reflect his emotions, as when it turns green with envy and blue with grief (Act No. 317, Oct '64: "Superman's Rainbow Face!"); made it impossible for him to speak or write except in Kryptonese, the language of Krypton (S No. 177/1, May '65: "Superman's Kryptonese Curse!"); and transformed him into a towering giant, bereft of his super-powers (Act No. 325, Jun '65: "The Skyscraper Superman!").

In the texts, red kryptonite is referred to as "the substance which has terrible and unpredictable effects on *Superman*" (WF No. 115, Feb '61: "The Curse That Doomed Superman!"), "the mysterious substance which always has an unexpected effect on him" (Act No. 275, Apr '61: "The Menace of Red-Green

cannot penetrate lead (Act No. 284, Jan '62: "The Babe of Steel!"; and others).

"There's no red kryptonite here in the Fortress [of Solitude] and we couldn't have been affected by any outside [red] kryptonite," remarks Superman to SUPERGIRL and KRYPTO THE SUPERDOG in April 1961, "because the Fortress walls are coated with lead! Kryptonite radiations can't pass through lead!" (S No. 144/3: "The Orphans of Space!").

For Superman, the first noticeable symptom of red-kryptonite exposure is a "peculiar tingling sensation" (Act No. 317, Oct '64: "Superman's Rainbow Face!"; and others) "throughout [his] body" which informs him that he has come in contact with the dreaded substance and that it will affect him in some bizarre way almost "any second" (Act No. 283, Dec '61: "The Red Kryptonite Menace!"; and others).

"Oh-oh!" thinks Superman to himself in April 1962. "I'm getting the tingling sensation that always signals the onset of another red kryptonite effect!" (Act No. 287: "Perry White's Manhunt for Superman!").

Usually, the effects of red-kryptonite exposure become immediately apparent. Often, however, the red kryptonite produces "a delayed reaction" (S No. 142/3, Jan '61: "Flame-Dragon from Krypton"; and others), so that whatever bizarre symptoms ultimately afflict Superman do not make themselves felt until some time later (S No. 139/3, Aug '60: "The Untold Story of Red Kryptonite!"; and others).

Whatever the effects of red-kryptonite exposure, they "almost always last 24 hours, at least" (S No. 177/1, May '65: "Superman's Kryptonese Curse!"), and usually wear off within forty-eight hours (S No. 165/2, Nov '63: "The Sweetheart Superman Forgot!"; S No. 168, Apr '64: pts. I-II—"Luthor--Super-Hero!"; "Lex Luthor, Daily Planet Editor!").

On at least one occasion, however, the effects of exposure to red kryptonite persisted for seventy-two hours (Act No. 293, Oct '62: "The Feud Between Superman and Clark Kent!"), and Superman No. 165/2 reports the existence of "a freak type which...does not wear off for weeks!" (Nov '63: "The Sweetheart Superman Forgot!").

As a general rule, "each strange effect caused by red kryptonite can only work once on Superman, after which he gains immunity from it!" Once having been transformed into an infant by red kryptonite, for example, Superman is unlikely ever to be transformed into an infant again. In Clark Kent's words, "...red k has affected me in many ways! Luckily, the same kind of change can't work on me twice!" (Act No. 325, Jun '65: "The Skyscraper Superman!"; and others).

Near duplications of past effects do occur, however. In October 1962, for example, exposure to red kryptonite transforms Superman into two separate individuals, a mature, responsible Clark Kent and an unprincipled, irresponsible Superman (Act No. 293: "The Feud Between Superman and Clark Kent!"). Eighteen months later, in April 1964, red-kryptonite exposure once again transforms Superman into two

separate persons, a Clark Kent and a Superman, but this time both Kent and Superman are heroic and responsible (Act No. 311: "Superman, King of Earth!"; see also Act No. 312, May '64: "King Superman versus Clark Kent, Metallo"). And there are other exceptions: in November 1963, for example, Superman is exposed to "a freak type" of red kryptonite which does afflict him with previously experienced effects (S No. 165/2: "The Sweetheart Superman Forgot!").

Another important principle of red-kryptonite exposure is that any given red-kryptonite meteor can afflict Superman with only one effect, after which it can never affect him again (Act No. 283, Dec '61: "The Red Kryptonite Menace!"; and others). As BATMAN explains it in March 1964, "...each piece of red kryptonite can only affect Superman once...then he has no reaction to it!" (WF No. 140: "The Clayface Superman!").

Even after a given sample of red kryptonite has affected Superman once, however, and thereby lost its power ever to affect him again, it is still capable of affecting all other Kryptonian survivors—such as Supergirl or Krypto the Superdog—one time each, although it will always affect them exactly as it did Superman. If Superman knows, for example, that a given red-kryptonite sample—one to which he himself has never been exposed—once transformed Supergirl into an infant, then he also knows that exposure to this identical sample will also transform him into an infant and that it will transform Krypto the Superdog into a pup (Act No. 284, Jan '62: "The Babe of Steel!"; and others).

A good illustration of this principle in action occurs in March 1962, when, after having lured Krypto into a trap and taken him captive, members of the SUPERMAN REVENGE SQUAD use him as a sort of super-canine guinea pig to enable them to ascertain, in advance, exactly what kinds of bizarre effects red-kryptonite samples in their possession will have on Superman (Act No. 286: "The Jury of Super-Enemies!").

Because his vulnerability to red kryptonite is a constant hazard, Superman has conducted numerous experiments in hopes of immunizing himself against its effects. All these efforts have been unsuccessful (Act No. 311, Apr '64: "Superman, King of Earth!"), but Superman has succeeded in devising a special "red kryptonite detector" to enable him to detect its presence (S No. 154/2, Jul '62: "Krypton's First Superman!").

Red kryptonite has been successfully synthesized on several occasions, notably by Professor Benet, a Nobel Prize-winning chemist, in August 1962 (Act No. 291: "The New Superman!"), and by LEX LUTHOR in April 1964 (S No. 168: pts. I-II—"Luthor--Super-Hero!"; "Lex Luthor, Daily Planet Editor!").

c. GOLD KRYPTONITE. This rare variety of kryptonite, to which all surviving natives of KRYPTON are vulnerable, would permanently rob Superman of his super-powers were he ever to be exposed to its baleful radiations.

Because gold kryptonite has appeared in the chronicles only infrequently, data concerning it is sparse beyond the fact that its radiations can be shielded by lead (S No. 157/1, Nov '62: "The Super-Revenge of the Phantom Zone Prisoner!"; S No. 179/2, Aug '65: "The Menace of Gold Kryptonite!") and that a Kryptonian's loss of super-powers due to gold-kryptonite exposure would invariably be inherited by his or her offspring, thereby rendering the offspring incapable of acquiring super-powers in those environments—like that of Earth—where Kryptonian survivors normally acquire them (S No. 179/2, Aug '65: "The Menace of Gold Kryptonite!").

Several Kryptonian survivors have lost their super-powers through exposure to gold kryptonite, including the Kryptonian scientist Quex-Ul, released from the Phantom Zone in November 1962 (S No. 157/1: "The Super-Revenge of the Phantom Zone Prisoner!"), and a Kandorian couple (see Kandor) named Jay-Ree and Joenne. Other than loss of their super-powers, the Kandorian couple appear to have experienced no ill effects from their gold-kryptonite exposure (S No. 179/2, Aug '65: "The Menace of Gold Kryptonite!"), but Quex-Ul's loss of super-powers was accompanied by "permanent amnesia" resulting from damage inflicted by the gold kryptonite to "some of his brain's memory cells" (S No. 157/1, Nov '62: "The Super-Revenge of the Phantom Zone Prisoner!").

d. BLUE KRYPTONITE. This form of kryptonite, also known as "Bizarro kryptonite" because it emits radiations to which only Bizarro creatures are vulnerable, was first brought into being by Superman in October 1960 as a means of thwarting an invasion of Earth by Bizarros from the planet Htrae. By focusing Lex Luthor's "duplicator ray"—an ingenious device designed to create imperfect molecular duplicates of either animate or inanimate objects—on a mound of green kryptonite (see section F 1 a, green kryptonite), Superman produces a new, imperfect form of kryptonite that is harmless to Kryptonian survivors but deadly to Bizarros. One unfortunate Bizarro creature, a Bizarro-Supergirl, succumbs to the fatal effects of blue-kryptonite poisoning in October 1960 (S No. 140: pts. I-III—"The Son of Bizarro!"; "The 'Orphan' Bizarro!"; "The Bizarro Supergirl!"; see also Act No. 278, Jul '61: "The Super Powers of Perry White!").

e. WHITE KRYPTONITE. This scarce form of kryptonite, which is harmless to Superman and all other Kryptonian survivors but emits a radiation that "destroys all plant life," was brought into being when a flock of green-kryptonite meteors (see section F 1 a, green kryptonite) passed through a weird "space cloud" somewhere in the vast reaches of interstellar space. Supergirl uses a chunk of white kryptonite to destroy the diabolical extraterrestrial "plant intelligence" Xasnu in July 1961 (Act No. 278: "The Super Powers of Perry White!").

2. Magic. Although this subject is not treated in the chronicles with absolute consistency, it is generally agreed that Superman's power of invulnerability does not protect him from magic. As Superman notes ruefully in August 1964, "... my invulnerability can't protect me from magic or a sorcerer's spell!" (S No. 171/2: "The Curse of Magic!"). Following is a brief chronological survey of the effects of magic on Superman as they are recorded in the chronicles.

In January-February 1942 Akthar "places Superman under a strange spell" that paralyzes him completely, but the Man of Steel shakes off the effects of his paralysis by "concentrating mightily" (S No. 14/3).

In May-June 1943 the Squiffles put a spell on Superman which makes him dizzy and fogs his mind, but the sight of Lois Lane hurtling toward seemingly certain doom "supplies the urge that is powerful enough to break the Man of Steel's mental thralldom!" The text describes this story as a "fantasy," however, rather than a recounting of actual events (S No. 22/1: "Meet the Squiffles!").

In January-February 1944 Superman is unaffected by the magic power of Mercury's magic staff (S No. 26/4: "The Quicksilver Kid!").

In March-April 1945 Superman proves impervious to Mr. Mxyzptlk's attempts to hypnotize him, but he is stymied by the magical conditions that prevail in the "multi-dimensional" Land of Zrfff (S No. 33/1: "Dimensions of Danger!").

In September-October 1950 Superman is transformed into an infant with the mind of an adult by magic elixir from the legendary Fountain of Youth (S No. 66/1: "The Babe of Steel!").

In August 1958 Superman proves vulnerable to the magic power of Jimmy Olsen's ancient Indian totem (S No. 123: chs. 1-3—"The Girl of Steel"; "The Lost Super-Powers"; "Superman's Return to Krypton").

In February 1960 Mr. Mxyzptlk temporarily places Superman under his hypnotic control by means of "5th dimensional hypnotism" (S No. 135/3: "The Trio of Steel!").

In September 1960 Superman proves vulnerable to the magical "Olympus powers" conferred upon Hercules by the ancient gods and heroes dwelling on Mt. Olympus (Act No. 268: "Superman's Battle with Hercules!").

In February 1961, after inhaling a cloud of Mr. Mxyzptlk's "magical sneezing powder," Superman unleashes a gargantuan "super-sneeze" that literally destroys "a distant solar system." "You're invulnerable to everything," remarks the mischievous imp, "except my magical powers!" (Act No. 273: "The World of Mr. Mxyzptlk!").

In July 1962, however, when Mr. Mxyzptlk unleashes a "second childhood gas" which infantalizes everyone in Metropolis, Superman remains unaffected because of his "invulnerable body" (S No. 154/1: "The Underwater Pranks of Mr. Mxyzptlk!").

In August 1964 Superman proves vulnerable to Mr. Mxyzptlk's "curse of magic" (S No. 171/2: "The Curse of Magic!").

In January 1965 Superman outwits a trio of extradimensional villains who possess, in his own words, "magical powers that even my invulnerable body cannot withstand!" (Act No. 320: "The Three Super-Enemies!").

3. *Virus X.* This deadly Kryptonian virus, for which no cure has ever been discovered, is described in Superman No. 156 as "a contagion fatal in 30 days to any native of Krypton...." Because living X viruses—if, indeed, any survived the destruction of Superman's native planet—would acquire super-virulence in the alien environment of Earth in the same manner whereby Superman acquired his super-powers, Superman and all other surviving natives of KRYPTON are vulnerable to this killer virus just as they would have been had Krypton never exploded and they, and the virus, remained on Krypton.

In his experiments with Virus X prior to the death of Krypton, the Kryptonian scientist Tharb-El discovered that he could destroy the virus with "element 202." Because element 202 is fatal to human beings, however, Tharb-El was unsuccessful in his efforts to produce a viable cure (Oct '62: "The Last Days of Superman!" pts. I-III—"Superman's Death Sentence!"; "The Super-Comrades of All Time!"; "Superman's Last Day of Life!").

4. *Other Vulnerabilities.* In addition to the vulnerabilities enumerated in the preceding subsections, there remain other situations in which Superman is vulnerable. He is susceptible to being overpowered and even destroyed by other Kryptonian survivors (S No. 151/3, Feb '62: "Superman's Greatest Secret!"; and others) or by Kryptonian machinery and weapons to which he would have been vulnerable on Krypton (Act No. 329, Oct '65: "The Ultimate Enemy!"; and others). He could be destroyed by alien monsters which, because of the peculiarities of their own native planets, acquire super-powers even greater than Superman's in the alien environment of Earth (Act No. 326, Jul '65: "The Legion of Super-Creatures!").

Superman loses his super-powers completely upon entering a solar system whose planets revolve about a red sun (S No. 164/1, Oct '63: pts. I-II—"The Showdown Between Luthor and Superman!"; "The Super-Duel!"; and others). And he is susceptible to losing his super-powers completely, or having them drastically curtailed, if he visits a planet revolving about any non-yellow sun, even if that sun's color has been changed from yellow to another color by artificial means, such as by using a "colossal blue filter" mounted atop a "robot-controlled space-station" to transform a yellow sun into a green one (S No. 155/1, Aug '62: pts. I-II—"Superman Under the Green Sun!"; "The Blind Superman!"; and others).

Perhaps Superman's greatest vulnerability is that his friends and loved ones do not possess super-powers, a fact which evildoers continually attempt to capitalize on—although invariably without success—in an effort to prevent Superman from apprehending them or to force him to do their bidding.

And "...despite all his tremendous super-powers, the Man of Steel has never been able to prevent a

tragedy of the past, no matter how much he has tried! Always, fate has successfully resisted his attempts to change history!" (S No. 146/2, Jul '61: "Superman's Greatest Feats!"; and others).

G. *The Equipment.* Most of the special apparatus employed by Superman has already been enumerated and described in the section of this article devoted to the Fortress of Solitude (*see* section D, the Fortress of Solitude). Other equipment used by Superman in the course of his career falls into the following general categories: 1) lead armor; 2) dummies, robots, and androids; and 3) miscellaneous equipment.

1) *Lead Armor.* In September 1948, after the cataclysmic explosion of an atomic reactor has temporarily rendered Superman so dangerously radioactive that he cannot come close to people without destroying them, the Man of Steel fashions himself a thick lead armor suit out of molten metal to enable him to shield those with whom he comes in contact from the deadly "radioactive rays" emanating from his body. "I couldn't permit eye-holes in this suit," notes Superman as he flies through the air in his armor suit, "...fatal radioactive rays could seep through them. I'll see with my X-ray vision!" (Act No. 124: "A Superman of Doom!"). This text clearly ignores the fact that Superman's X-ray vision cannot penetrate lead.

In June 1958 Superman dons a suit of lead armor while experimenting with KRYPTONITE at his Fortress of Solitude. "In this lead armor," observes Superman, "I'm immune to kryptonite rays...and can study it

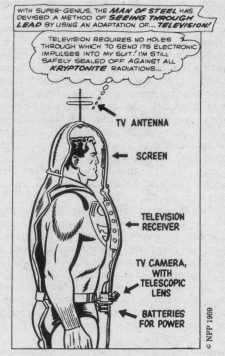

WITH SUPER-GENIUS, THE *MAN OF STEEL* HAS DEVISED A METHOD OF *SEEING THROUGH LEAD* BY USING AN ADAPTATION OF... *TELEVISION!*

TELEVISION REQUIRES NO HOLES THROUGH WHICH TO SEND ITS ELECTRONIC IMPULSES INTO MY SUIT! I'M STILL SAFELY SEALED OFF AGAINST ALL *KRYPTONITE* RADIATIONS...

TV ANTENNA

SCREEN

TELEVISION RECEIVER

TV CAMERA, WITH TELESCOPIC LENS

BATTERIES FOR POWER

© NPP 1959

Cutaway diagram of Superman's lead armor, 1959

to see if I can overcome its dangerous effect on me" (Act No. 241: "The Super-Key to Fort Superman").

In February 1959, after LEX LUTHOR has transformed himself into a kryptonite menace by ingesting a diabolical "liquid kryptonite" serum, Superman flees to his Fortress of Solitude and hastily dons his suit of lead armor, here referred to as a "leaden suit." This lead suit, a diagram of which appears below, utilizes a television camera and receiver to enable Superman to "see" outside the suit despite its being composed entirely of lead. Luthor destroys the effectiveness of this lead armor by using sophisticated "super-electronic apparatus" aboard his "Luthor satellite" to transform the armor into common glass, but the Man of Steel fashions himself another lead suit out of lead ore he finds on the MOON (Act No. 249: "The Kryptonite Man!").

By July 1960 Superman has taken to hiding his leaden suit among a pile of old crates in "an unused storage room" at the DAILY PLANET. The Man of Steel dons the lead armor during this period in the hope that it will protect him against TITANO's deadly "kryptonite-vision," but the lead suit is destroyed by air friction when Superman swerves aside in midair at super-speed to avoid being swatted by one of Titano's gargantuan paws (S No. 138/1: "Titano the Super-Ape!").

By October 1960 Superman has apparently constructed a new suit of lead armor, for he uses a television-equipped lead suit stored at his Fortress of Solitude to enable him to gather a supply of green-kryptonite meteors—from which he in turn creates a supply of "Bizarro kryptonite," or "blue kryptonite"—to turn back an army of Bizarros (see BIZARRO) advancing toward Earth (S No. 140: pts. I-III—"The Son of Bizarro!"; "The 'Orphan' Bizarro!"; "The Bizarro Supergirl!").

In July 1961 Superman dons his suit of television-equipped lead armor as protection against the kryptonite weapons wielded by PERRY WHITE, whose body has been taken over by a diabolical "plant intelligence" from another planet (Act No. 278: "The Super Powers of Perry White!").

According to Superman No. 130/1, Superman, clad in his lead armor and armed with a gigantic net, once attempted, in his own words, "a super-task that proved even too much for me…hunting down all kryptonite meteors in space" in an effort to rid himself, once and for all, of the deadly threat posed by the existence of kryptonite. Superman accumulated literally thousands of kryptonite meteors, but he soon discovered, to his chagrin, that "there are countless other [meteor] swarms, scattered in every galaxy! It's an impossible job to gather all the kryptonite in the universe!" (Jul '59: "The Curse of Kryptonite!").

2) *Dummies, Robots, and Androids.* Almost from the beginning of his long career, Superman has employed dummies and robots of Clark Kent and Superman—as well as of his loved ones and closest friends—to help him carry out his customary super-tasks and protect the secret of his dual identity. Today these so-called "super-robots"—which are housed both at the Fortress of Solitude and behind a secret panel in Clark Kent's METROPOLIS apartment—are immensely sophisticated and complex, possessing mighty super-powers and capable of human emotion, independent thought, and autonomous action. In the early years of the chronicles, however, this was not the case, and the complex robots that exist today are the products of a gradual evolution spanning many years of texts.

In March 1944 Clark Kent uses a Superman dummy to help him outwit the THINKER, employing ventriloquism to make the dummy appear to talk (Act No. 70: "Superman Takes a Holiday!").

In September-October 1949 Superman employs a Superman robot in an elaborate scheme to dupe a band of aliens from the planet URANUS into believing that all earthlings are actually robots. Superman makes his robot appear lifelike by manipulating it like a puppet at invisible super-speed while employing ventriloquism to make it talk (WF No. 42: "The Alphabetical Animal Adventure!").

In February 1951 Clark Kent employs a Superman balloon to make it appear that Superman is flying overhead, keeping on eye on Kent as he walks down the street (Act No. 153: "The 100 Deaths of Clark Kent!"). He uses a similar balloon, employing ventriloquism to make it talk, in September-October 1952 in order to dupe LOIS LANE and LANA LANG into believing that Clark Kent and Superman are two different persons (S No. 78/3: "The Girls in Superman's Life!").

In July 1951 Superman constructs a pair of gigantic "remote-controlled robots" to enable him to experiment with KRYPTONITE without coming close to it (Act No. 158: "The Kid from Krypton!").

In February 1952 Superman employs a lifelike robot—which assumes the role of an outlaw from the planet MERCURY—as part of his elaborate ruse to apprehend the CRIME CZAR. Superman operates the robot, which is made of a "super-hard" Mercurian metal, by means of a "tiny control panel" strapped beneath his sleeve and makes it talk by means of ventriloquism (Act No. 165: "The Man Who Conquered Superman!"). During this same period, Superman accompanies Lois Lane and her friend Lorraine Jennings on a double date, both as Clark Kent and as Superman, by using a lifelike remote-controlled robot to stand in for Clark Kent, endowing it with speech by means of ventriloquism. The text in which these events occur is dated May-June 1952, but the story itself is set in February, in the period surrounding Valentine's Day (S No. 76/3: "Mrs. Superman!").

In May 1956 Clark Kent employs a Superman robot in a ruse to protect his secret identity. Kent refers to it as "that **Superman**-robot I always keep around for emergencies," but no additional information about the robot is provided in the text (S No. 105/1: "Superman's 3 Mistakes!").

In January 1957 Superman uses a remote-controlled Superman robot to battle LEX LUTHOR so that he will not have to risk becoming exposed to the kryptonite in Luthor's possession. The robot exhibits some of Superman's super-powers—it can fly, for example, and has superhuman strength—but it is not nearly as powerful as Superman (S No. 110/3: "The Defeat of Superman").

By February 1957 Superman has secretly gone into hiding—and constructed a lifelike Superman robot to take his place—as part of an elaborate, and ultimately successful, ruse to recover several million dollars in stolen loot. The robot is extremely lifelike and exhibits a number of Superman's powers. It is ultimately destroyed, however, after being lured into an explosives-laden trap by a gang of criminals. No information on the operation of the robot is provided in the text (Act No. 225: "The Death of Superman").

In March 1958 Superman employs a Superman robot in a ruse designed to enable him to apprehend "GADGET" GRIM (S No. 120/3: "The Human Missile").

By May 1958 Superman has succeeded in devising robots so unbelievably sophisticated that his Clark Kent robot—kept concealed behind a secret panel in a supply room at the DAILY PLANET—is actually capable of carrying on his duties at the Daily Planet whenever his presence is required elsewhere as Superman. "The robot Clark will replace me here in the office, as usual!" thinks Superman. "Remote-control impulses from my X-ray eyes will guide him and operate his voice-box!" Superman also utilizes a sophisticated Superman robot during this period to carry out a mission in outer space (Act No. 240: "Secret of the Superman Sphinx").

In June 1958, during a visit to his Fortress of Solitude, Superman matches wits in a game of "super-chess with a great robot he has built as a playmate for himself...." "This robot possesses a super-electronic brain!" notes Superman. "He can think and play with the speed of lightning, and plans a million moves at once! It's tough beating him!" But Superman does beat him, in "a game that's played so fast the pieces move in a blur of speed..." (Act No. 241: "The Super-Key to Fort Superman").

In October 1958, while touring the Fortress of Solitude with Lois Lane, Superman spars with an "atomic-powered robot" that is easily twelve feet tall. "Goodness!" exclaims Lois Lane. "The robot's punch would cave in the side of a battleship! Superman doesn't feel it!" (Act No. 245: "The Shrinking Superman!"). On a subsequent visit to his Fortress, Superman exercises his "super-muscles" by engaging in a super-tug of war with a dozen atomic-powered robots (Act No. 247, Dec '58: "Superman's Lost Parents!").

By December 1958 Superman has begun housing several Superman robots in a secret closet in Clark Kent's apartment, each equipped to duplicate one of Superman's super-powers, such as super-strength, the power of flight, X-ray vision, or super-breath. "Each is designed to use one of my super-powers when needed!" notes Superman. "I send out the robots when Clark's absence would be suspicious! Or when I suspect that criminals are waiting to use kryptonite against me!" (Act No. 247: "Superman's Lost Parents!").

By January 1960 Superman has clearly increased the complexity of his robots even further, for he is now quoted in the Daily Planet as saying that "my robots...possess all my super-powers..." (Act No. 260: "Mighty Maid!").

In February 1960, when Superman conducts guided tours through his Fortress of Solitude for the benefit of charity, two of his Superman robots stand outside, scanning the incoming crowds with their X-ray vision to ensure that no bombs or other dangerous devices are carried into the Fortress. Indications are that the robots are carrying out their duties autonomously, without any outside help from Superman (Act No. 261: "Superman's Fortresses of Solitude!").

In April 1960, while Superman is away on the planet HTRAE, his Clark Kent robot stands in for him at the Daily Planet, performing his reportorial chores on his own without any guidance whatever from the Man of Steel (Act No. 263: "The World of Bizarros!"). Indeed, a text for May 1960 asserts that the Clark Kent robot is actually capable of writing up original news stories and performing other complex tasks (Act No. 264: "The Superman Bizarro!").

In June 1960 Superman, busily occupied with putting on a demonstration of his super-powers for children at a local hospital, dispatches a Clark Kent robot to keep a lunch date with Lois Lane, confident that the robot is so thoroughly lifelike that Lois will not be able to tell it from a real human being (Act No. 265: "The 'Superman' from Outer Space!").

In March 1961 one of Superman's Superman-robots, acting entirely on its own volition, carries out an intricately convoluted ruse involving human emotion, sophisticated independent thinking, and the ability to invent and construct complex scientific devices (Act No. 274: "The Reversed Super-Powers!"). (See SUPERMAN ROBOT Z.)

In November 1961, a Clark Kent robot, doubling for the real Clark Kent on a date with Lois Lane while Superman is occupied elsewhere, engages in original conversation, reacts emotionally, and copes with several unanticipated emergencies without any outside assistance from Superman (Act No. 282: "Superman's Toughest Day!").

By January 1965 Superman has succeeded in devising an "android" that is so unbelievably lifelike as to be virtually human. "A few weeks ago," notes the text, Superman decided that "My secret identity would be safer if I had perfect, flesh-like doubles of myself to substitute for me in emergencies, instead of Superman robots. I'll manufacture a synthetic android and try it out."

Working alone at his Fortress of Solitude, Superman had created a lifelike android and subjected it to a series of grueling tests. The android was totally lifelike and possessed all of Superman's super-powers, but Superman's tests revealed that its coordination was poor, making it unreliable in emergencies, and that its "artificial nerves would be harmed by a very great electric force!"

Superman discarded the android and resolved not to manufacture any more like it, but the android was so sophisticated, and so nearly human in its makeup, that it reacted bitterly to having been rejected and, acting entirely on its own volition, concocted an intricately convoluted scheme for wreaking vengeance on Superman (S No. 174/1: pts. 1-2—"Clark Kent's Incredible Delusion!"; "The End of a Hero!"). (See NEWMAN, ADAM.)

For the last two decades, Superman's sophisticated "super-robots" (Act No. 258, Nov '59: "The Menace of Cosmic Man!"; and others) have been housed in two principal locations: the Fortress of Solitude (S No. 134, Jan '60: chs. I-III—"The Super-Menace of Metropolis!"; "The Revenge Against Jor-El!"; "The Duel of the Supermen!"; and many others) and the secret closet in Clark Kent's Metropolis apartment (Act No. 247, Dec '58: "Superman's Lost Parents!"; and many others).

Standing before the hidden closet in Clark Kent's Metropolis apartment, Superman uses his X-ray vision to activate one of his "super-robots"

The closet, which is referred to as a "secret closet" (Act No. 282, Nov '61: "Superman's Toughest Day!"; and others) and as a "secret trophy closet" (S No. 126/1, Jan '59: "Superman's Hunt for Clark Kent!"), is concealed behind "a fake wall" which slides open at the touch of a secret button (S No. 174/1, Jan '65: pts. 1-2—"Clark Kent's Incredible Delusion!"; "The End of a Hero!") mounted on the apartment wall (S No. 126/1, Jan '59: "Superman's Hunt for Clark Kent!").

The fake wall also slides open when a special box on Clark Kent's table is opened. In the event an intruder inadvertently activates this sliding-wall mechanism and discovers the secret closet, however, a special security device on the closet door makes the phone in the apartment ring. When the intruder answers, he hears the voice of Superman, on a prerecorded tape, asking Clark Kent to return the

robots he has recently "borrowed." When PERRY WHITE stumbles upon the secret closet in February 1963, this elaborate ploy makes him doubt whether he has actually unearthed the secret of Superman's dual identity (Act No. 297: "The Man Who Betrayed Superman's Identity!").

The robots used most often by Superman have been robots of Superman and Clark Kent, but the Man of Steel has also used robots of JONATHAN AND MARTHA KENT (Act No. 247, Dec '58: "Superman's Lost Parents!"), Lois Lane and Lana Lang (S No. 150/2, Jan '62: "The Duel Over Superman!"), SUPERGIRL and KRYPTO THE SUPERDOG (S No. 177/1, May '65: "Superman's Kryptonese Curse!"), and robots of himself both as a teen-ager and as a super-baby (S No. 135/3, Feb '60: "The Trio of Steel!").

The robots address Superman as "master" (Act No. 261, Feb '60: "Superman's Fortresses of Solitude!"; and many others), and Superman addresses them, when he addresses them verbally, either by a number, such as Robot One (S No. 126/1, Jan '59: "Superman's Hunt for Clark Kent!"), or by a letter of the alphabet, such as Robot Y (Act No. 261, Feb '60: "Superman's Fortresses of Solitude!"; see also Act No. 274, Mar '61: "The Reversed Super-Powers!").

The chronicles contain little real information concerning the workings of Superman's robots beyond that they run on sophisticated batteries (Act No. 274, Mar '61: "The Reversed Super-Powers!"; Act No. 292, Sep '62: "When Superman Defended His Arch-Enemy!"), that they contain complex "circuits and energy cells" (S No. 181/1, Nov '65: pts. I-II—"The Super-Scoops of Morna Vine!"; "The Secret of the New Supergirl!"), and that each is controlled by an "electronic control center" located somewhere in its body (S No. 177/1, May '65: "Superman's Kryptonese Curse!").

Superman can activate and control his robots either with verbal commands (Act No. 251, Apr '59: "The Oldest Man in Metropolis!"; and others) or by means of his X-ray vision (Act No. 265, Jun '60: "The 'Superman' from Outer Space!" and others). Even from a long distance away, Superman can summon his robots into action either with his X-ray vision (Act No. 265, Jun '60: "The 'Superman' from Outer Space!"; and others) or with a "ventriloquistic signal" (S No. 156, Oct '62: "The Last Days of Superman!" pts. I-III—"Superman's Death Sentence!"; "The Super-Comrades of All Time!"; "Superman's Last Day of Life!"). In the event of an emergency, Superman's robots can also be activated by the SUPERMEN EMERGENCY SQUAD (Act No. 292, Sep '62: "When Superman Defended His Arch-Enemy!"), but they will not respond to anyone's voice but Superman's (Act No. 302, Jul '63: "The Amazing Confession of Super-Perry White!").

This latter form of security, however, is not without its drawbacks. On one occasion, for example, after a "new vitamin serum" developed by PROF. VANCE has temporarily transformed him into a white-haired old man, Superman finds that his robots will not obey him because "the vibrations of [his] aged voice are too cracked and weak to transmit the proper signals" (Act No. 251, Apr '59: "The Oldest Man in Metropolis!"). And several years later, when exposure to red kryptonite temporarily robs him of his super-powers and he is freezing to death outside the Fortress of Solitude, Clark Kent finds that his robots will not leave the Fortress to help him because they believe the quavering voice they hear calling for help could not possibly be Superman's (S No. 160/1, Apr '63: pts. I-II—"The Mortal Superman!"; "The Cage of Doom!").

Even if a villain could succeed in commandeering one of Superman's robots, there are indications that the robots, having been "created only to do good deeds," would refuse to perform evil ones (Act No. 312, May '64: "King Superman versus Clark Kent, Metallo"). In addition, Superman has installed a special self-destruct mechanism in each of his robots—designed to destroy completely any robot that becomes disabled while performing a mission—to prevent unscrupulous individuals from cannibalizing the parts of disabled robots and using the sophisticated circuitry for evil ends (S No. 181/1, Nov '65: pts. I-II—"The Super-Scoops of Morna Vine!"; "The Secret of the New Supergirl!").

Even though Superman's robots have, for nearly two decades, possessed all of Superman's super-powers (Act No. 260, Jan '60: "Mighty Maid!"), they are not, by any means, as powerful or as indestructible as Superman himself. Even Superman's best robots have been crushed by undersea water pressure (S No. 139/3, Aug '60: "The Untold Story of Red Kryptonite!"), demolished by the "flame-breath" of a Kryptonian "flame dragon" (see FLAME DRAGON) (S No. 142/3, Jan '61: "Flame-Dragon from Krypton"), destroyed by a powerful electromagnet (S No. 147/1, Aug '61: "The Great Mento!") or repelled by "a powerful anti-magnetic device" (S No. 148/1, Oct '61: "The 20th Century Achilles!"), blacked out by sophisticated "electronic machinery" (Act No. 276, May '61: "The War Between Supergirl and the Supermen Emergency Squad!"), shattered by Lex Luthor's "vibro-gun" (Act No. 292, Sep '62: "When Superman Defended His Arch-Enemy!"), short-circuited by "electromagnetic disturbances" arising from "sudden sunspot activity" (S No. 156, Oct '62: "The Last Days of Superman!" pts. I-III—"Superman's Death Sentence!"; "The Super-Comrades of All Time!"; "Superman's Last Day of Life!"), rendered inoperable by a sophisticated "inhibitor invention" (Act No. 320, Jan '65: "The Three Super-Enemies!"), destroyed by "undersea monsters" (S No. 181/1, Nov '65: pts. I-II—"The Super-Scoops of Morna Vine!"; "The Secret of the New Supergirl!"), or had their motors destroyed by a super-powered villain's X-ray vision (S No. 134, Jan '60: chs. I-III—"The Super-Menace of Metropolis!"; "The Revenge Against Jor-El"; "The Duel of the Supermen!"). And, although Superman's own costume is indestructible, the ones worn by his Super-

man robots are not (Act No. 312, May '64: "King Superman versus Clark Kent, Metallo").

Because Superman's robots are not vulnerable to kryptonite (S No. 130/1, Jul '59: "The Curse of Kryptonite!"; and others), they are extremely useful in certain emergencies in which Superman's life would otherwise be in jeopardy (S No. 139/3, Aug '60: "The Untold Story of Red Kryptonite!"; and others). Superman has programmed his Superman robots to feign vulnerability to kryptonite in public, however, to prevent outsiders from distinguishing the real Superman from his robot surrogates. This programming strategy enables Superman to use his robots to help protect his secret identity by standing in for him as Superman, while preventing those whom he is trying to dupe from realizing that they are dealing only with a Superman robot (S No. 130/1, Jul '59: "The Curse of Kryptonite!"; Act No. 277, Jun '61: "The Conquest of Superman!"). It is common knowledge, however, that Superman has and uses Superman robots (Act No. 260, Jan '60: "Mighty Maid!"; and others). All newly constructed Superman robots are forced to undergo a period of arduous training before they are permitted to work alongside Superman's other robots on an equal footing (Act No. 277, Jun '61: "The Conquest of Superman!").

Over the years, a number of present and former Superman robots have played important roles in the chronicles, including Superman Robot Z (Act No. 274, Mar '61: "The Reversed Super-Powers!"), WONDER-MAN (S No. 163/1, Aug '63: "Wonder-Man, the New Hero of Metropolis!"), and Adam Newman (S No. 174/1, Jan '65: pts. 1-2—"Clark Kent's Incredible Delusion!"; "The End of a Hero!").

3. *Miscellaneous Equipment.* In his unceasing war against evil and injustice, Superman has also employed a variety of miscellaneous apparatus.

By January 1941 Superman has devised the "krypto-raygun," a "startling invention with which [he] can snap pictures--they are developed right in the gun--and can be flashed upon a wall!" Superman uses the krypto-raygun—a combination still camera, developing mechanism, and projector in the shape of a raygun—to accumulate incriminating photographic evidence of the illegal gambling taking place at the Preston Club (see PRESTON [MR.]) in January 1941 (Act No. 32).

In August 1948 Superman uses a miniature camera concealed inside a special ring to keep an incriminating photographic record of the attempts on his life made by SKID RUSSELL and his fellow METROPOLIS "crime kings" (Act No. 123: "50 Ways to Kill Superman!").

In July 1951, in the course of conducting a series of unsuccessful experiments "to find some way to fight against the power of kryptonite," Superman devises a so-called "K-detector," which "detects kryptonite as a Geiger counter does uranium!" (Act No. 158: "The Kid from Krypton!"). This device, which is also referred to as a "kryptonite detector," is now housed in the Fortress of Solitude (Act No. 243, Aug '58: "The Lady and the Lion") along with Superman's "red kryptonite detector" (S No. 154/2, Jul '62: "Krypton's First Superman!").

In September 1957, during a period when Superman is temporarily bereft of his super-powers as the result of Earth's passing through a shower of kryptonite dust in space, the Man of Steel successfully carries out his customary super-tasks with the aid of an armada of ingenious "super-machines" that he had hastily constructed in anticipation of the crisis. Among them are an armored tanklike vehicle equipped with a power scoop, a battering ram, and maneuverable mechanical arms; a colossal earth-boring machine; a tanklike vehicle equipped with a gigantic electromagnet; a "massive super-insulated suit," designed to render Superman invulnerable to fire and other dangers; a jet-motor harness to endow him with the power of flight; and various telescopes, fluoroscopes, and microphones designed to duplicate, as nearly as possible, Superman's super-vision and super-hearing (S No. 116/3: "The Mechanized Superman!").

In December 1959 Superman and BATMAN wear special "wrist-radios" designed to enable them to communicate with one another while Superman is in Metropolis and Batman is in GOTHAM CITY (WF No. 106: "The Duplicate Man!").

In November 1962, during a time-journey he makes to the planet KRYPTON prior to its destruction, Superman—knowing that he will have no super-powers in Krypton's red-sun environment—wears a special "anti-gravity belt" designed to enable him to escape from the planet so that, once having departed Krypton's solar system and regained his powers, he can return through the time barrier at super-speed to the year 1962 (S No. 157/1: "The Super-Revenge of the Phantom Zone Prisoner!"). Similarly, when Superman and JAX-UR undertake a time-journey to Krypton in March 1964, they make the trip in a spherical, transparent "time capsule" so that they will not become marooned on Krypton after losing their super-powers there (Act No. 310: "Secret of Kryptonite Six!").

In May 1965, as a means of testing the security of his secret identity, Superman uses a "selective amnesia-inducer" to erase from the minds of Batman and ROBIN the knowledge that Clark Kent is secretly Superman. Despite this selective loss of memory, the Dynamic Duo are able to deduce Superman's secret on their own, but when the roles are reversed, and the selective amnesia-inducer is used to erase Superman's knowledge of the Dynamic Duo's identities, Superman is unable to discover, try though he might, that Batman and Robin are secretly Bruce Wayne and Dick Grayson (WF No. 149: "The Game of Secret Identities!" pts. I-II—no title; "The Super-Detective!").

Two 1955 texts feature the so-called "super-signal," a giant searchlight that casts a circle of light against the sky containing a stylized "S" insignia patterned after the one emblazoned on Superman's chest. In January-February 1955 Superman refers to it as "the emergency signal Batman and I agreed on in case of a crisis," clearly implying that the super-signal is a device with which Batman summons Superman (WF No. 74: "The Contest of Heroes!"). In May-June 1955, however, LOIS LANE displays the special searchlight to Batman and Robin, describing it as "the S-signal which we use to call Superman," clearly suggesting that the super-signal is a device used by the officials of Metropolis to summon Superman (WF No. 76: "When Gotham City Challenged Metropolis!"). The super-signal, in any event, never takes hold as a permanent feature and soon disappears from the chronicles entirely.

H. The Man Himself (as Clark Kent). The chief protagonist of the Superman chronicles is in one sense really two men. He is, of course, Superman, the world's mightiest hero, but he is also Clark Kent, mild-mannered journalist, for more than thirty years the star reporter of the DAILY PLANET, more recently a full-time newscaster for METROPOLIS television station WGBS-TV (S No. 233, Jan '71: "Superman Breaks Loose"; and many others).

Clark Kent has black hair and blue eyes. He is 6'2" tall, with a chest measurement of 44" and a waist measurement of 34" (Act No. 297, Feb '63: "The Man Who Betrayed Superman's Identity!"; S No. 178/1, Jul '65: "Project Earth-Doom!"). According to one text, his "blood conforms to ALL FOUR types!" (S No. 6/4, Sep/Oct '40).

Clark Kent scans an edition of the Daily Star, *1938*

Since Clark Kent and Superman are one and the same man, it is not surprising that some have noticed a strong resemblance between them. In February 1963 PERRY WHITE observes that Clark Kent "strongly resembles Superman" (Act No. 297: "The Man Who Betrayed Superman's Identity!"), and in November 1963 GENERAL PEDRO VALDEZ informs Kent that

Clark Kent, 1941

Clark Kent phones in a news story about Superman, 1942

"Without glasses and dressed like **Superman**, you could pass anywhere as his double!" (Act No. 306: "The Great Superman Impersonation!").

"Hmm...there is a resemblance!" notes LOIS LANE in December 1965. "That's why I've often suspected Clark might be **Superman**!" (Act No. 331: "Clark Kent's Masquerade as Superman!"). Despite this perceived resemblance, however, Clark Kent has succeeded in keeping his dual identity one of the world's most closely guarded secrets (*see* section B, the secret identity).

The identity of Clark Kent was conferred upon the infant Superman by JONATHAN AND MARTHA KENT, who adopted the orphan from the doomed planet KRYPTON soon after the rocket that had brought him safely to Earth had landed in an open field (Act No.

141, Feb '50: "Luthor's Secret Weapon") on the outskirts of SMALLVILLE (WF No. 57, Mar/Apr '52: "The Artificial Superman!"; and others). The proud foster parents named their new son Clark, which was Martha Kent's maiden name (S No. 146/1, Jul '61: "The Story of Superman's Life!"; and others).

Clark Kent's early childhood years were spent on his foster parents' farm outside of Smallville (S No. 152/2, Apr '62: "Superbaby Captures the Pumpkin Gang!"; and others). By the time Clark was old enough to attend elementary school, the Kents had sold their farm and moved to Smallville, where Jonathan Kent opened up a general store (S No. 146/1, Jul '61: "The Story of Superman's Life!"; and others).

According to Superman No. 46/3, Clark Kent

Lois Lane and Clark Kent peruse the comics page of the Daily Planet, *1942*

attended high school at Metropolis High, where he was nicknamed "Specs" and became known as his class's "quietest boy" (May/Jun '47: "That Old Class of Superboy's!"). However, numerous other texts assert, far more plausibly, that Clark Kent grew up in Smallville, attending Smallville High School (WF No. 69, Mar/Apr '54: "Jor-El's Last Will!"; and others) and working afternoons after school in his foster father's general store (S No. 116/2, Sep '57: "Disaster Strikes Twice"). His high-school principal thought of him as "the shyest boy in our graduating class" (S No. 125/2, Nov '58: "Clark Kent's College Days"), but his senior class yearbook described him this way: "highest grades--boy most likely to become famous--" (S No. 144/2, Apr '61: "Superboy's First Public Appearance!").

Following his graduation from Smallville High School, Clark Kent attended college at METROPOLIS UNIVERSITY (S No. 125/2, Nov '58: "Clark Kent's College Days"; and others). He lived in a dormitory, joined a fraternity (S No. 129/3, May '59: "The Girl in Superman's Past!"), and yelled his heart out as a cheerleader for the college football team (S No. 125/2, Nov '58: "Clark Kent's College Days").

He had already decided upon a career in journalism (Act No. 144, May '50: "Clark Kent's Career!"). Nevertheless, he studied advanced science under PROFESSOR THADDEUS V. MAXWELL (S No. 125/2, Nov '58: "Clark Kent's College Days") and took courses in biology, astronomy, art, music, and other subjects. In his senior year he had a bittersweet romance with LORI LEMARIS (S No. 129/3, May '59: "The Girl in Superman's Past!").

Following his college graduation, Clark Kent returned to Smallville, but not long afterward, both his foster parents passed away. It was a bereaved Clark Kent who departed Smallville to embark on his chosen career as a newspaper reporter in Metropolis

Lois Lane and Clark Kent, 1946

(S No. 146/1, Jul '61: "The Story of Superman's Life!").

Kent actually began his journalistic career as a reporter for the DAILY STAR, the forerunner in the chronicles of the *Daily Planet*. By thwarting a lynching at the county jail as Superman, and then phoning in an exclusive account of the events as would-be reporter Clark Kent, Kent persuaded the paper's editor to hire him despite his lack of experience (S No. 1/1, Sum '39). These events are chronicled in two pages of illustrations accompanying this section. Since the appearance of this early account, however, two other, widely disparate, texts have appeared purporting to tell the true story of how

Clark Kent examines the "powerstone," 1942

Clark Kent, 1952

Clark Kent came to acquire his job as a newspaper reporter (Act No. 144, May '50: "Clark Kent's Career!"; S No. 133/2, Nov '59: "How Perry White Hired Clark Kent!"). Both these accounts may safely be regarded as spurious. (*See* DAILY PLANET.)

Working as a reporter for a major newspaper enables Clark Kent to "investigate criminals without their suspecting [he's] really **Superman**" (S No. 133/2, Nov '59: "How Perry White Hired Clark Kent!") and provides him with "the best opportunity for being free to help people as **Superman**" without having to explain his frequent absences from his place of employment (Act No. 144, May '50: "Clark Kent's Career!"; and others). "As a reporter," notes Kent in December 1949, "I have a hundred underworld and police contacts that make it easier for Superman to fight crime!" (Act No. 139: "Clark Kent...Daredevil!").

Over and above its usefulness to him in his career as Superman, it is clear that Clark Kent values his career in journalism purely for its own sake. "Just remember," exclaims Kent to newsboy TOMMY BLAKE in Summer 1945, "a good reporter gets the news...and gets it first! But there's more to being a reporter than that!

"He lives by the deadline! The thunder of the presses is the pounding of his heart! And most important--all his personal feelings remain in the background! It's his story that counts! Always remember that!" (WF No. 18: "The Junior Reporters!").

According to Superman No. 25/2, Clark Kent tried to enlist in the U.S. Army during World War II, only to be rejected on the ground of faulty eyesight when, in the midst of his preinduction eye exam, he absentmindedly peered through the wall of the examining room with his X-ray vision and, instead of reading aloud the letters of his own eye chart, recited those on a different eye chart posted on a wall in the adjoining room. Kent might have renewed his efforts to join the Armed Forces had he not soon realized that, as Superman, he "could be of more value on the home front operating as a free agent" (Nov/Dec '43: "I Sustain the Wings!").

And so, for more than three continuous decades, Clark Kent has been the *Daily Planet*'s "star reporter" (Act No. 25, Jun '40; and others). Renowned for his ability to root out local news (S No. 44/3, Jan/Feb '47: "Shakespeare's Ghost Writer!"; and others), particularly stories dealing with crime and corruption (S No. 83/3, Jul/Aug '53: "Clark Kent---Convict!"; and others), he has performed in numerous other capacities for the *Daily Planet*, including that of war correspondent (Act No. 23, Apr '40), lovelorn editor (S No. 18/3, Sep/Oct '42: "The Man with the Cane"; and others), editor of the *Daily Planet*'s Bombay edition (Act No. 203, Apr '55: "The International Daily Planet!"), and editor of the entire newspaper in the absence of editor Perry White (Act No. 297, Feb '63: "The Man Who Betrayed Superman's Identity!").

In pursuit of a news story, Clark Kent has enlisted in the Army Air Force cadet training program (S No. 25/2, Nov/Dec '43: "I Sustain the Wings!"); worked as a private detective (WF No. 45, Apr/May '50: "Lois Lane and Clark Kent, Detectives!"), a fireman (S No. 129/2, May '59: "Clark Kent, Fireman of Steel!"), and a policeman (S No. 84/3, Sep/Oct '53: "Lois Lane, Policewoman!"; S No. 133/1, Nov '59: "The Super-Luck of Badge 77"); joined the Marines (S No. 179/3, Aug '65: "Private Kent, the Fighting Marine!"); and even become a skid row bum (S No. 89/2, May '54: "Superman of Skid Row!"). He has been a police commissioner (Act No. 37, Jun '41), a department store clerk (Act No. 21/3, Mar/Apr '43: "The Robber Knight"), a sheriff (WF No. 30, Sep/Oct '47: "Sheriff Clark Kent"), a vacuum cleaner salesman (S No. 79/2, Nov/Dec '52: "The End of the Planet!"), and a disc jockey (S No. 84/1, Sep/Oct '53: "Superman's Other Life!"). Clark Kent has even gone to prison

At bedtime, Clark Kent relaxes with a book in his Metropolis apartment, 1959

voluntarily to investigate a series of prison riots (S No. 83/3, Jul/Aug '53: "Clark Kent---Convict!") and to learn where a hardened convict hid $1,000,000 in stolen loot (Act No. 323, Apr '65: "Clark Kent in the Big House!").

Clark Kent is described as the *Daily Planet*'s "foremost reporter" in Superman No. 12/2 (Sep/Oct '41), and as its "ace reporter" in Action Comics No. 105 (Feb '47: "The Man Who Hated Christmas!") and in numerous other texts.

"Well known to millions of **Daily Planet** readers," notes Superman No. 83/3, "is famed feature reporter Clark Kent! Many times, in his fearless newspaper articles, Clark Kent has helped to expose crime and corruption!" (Jul/Aug '53: "Clark Kent---Convict!").

Indeed, just as the underworld has made countless attempts to assassinate Superman, so have they made innumerable attempts to wreak vengeance on

Clark Kent does some super-baby-sitting, 1941

By thwarting a lynching as Superman, and then phoning in the story
as would-be reporter Clark Kent, Kent earns a reporter's job on the
Daily Star, the forerunner of the Daily Planet in the chronicles

Clark Kent for the courageous exposés appearing under his byline (S No. 15/4, Mar/Apr '42; and many others).

"To Daily Planet readers," observes Superman No. 98/2, "the name of Clark Kent signed over a story has always meant integrity and honesty! His newspaper reporting on crime has won him countless awards!" (Jul '55: "Clark Kent Outlaw!").

These awards have included "the annual trophy for prize reporting," presented to him at a "newspapermen's banquet" in Metropolis Hall in May-June 1950, and the honorary professorship in journalism at QUINN COLLEGE that he receives soon afterward (S No. 64/1: "Professor Lois Lane!"); the annual Reporter's Award, in the form of a gold typewriter, presented to him in June 1954 for having written "the best story of the year" (Act No. 193: "The Golden Superman!"; see also S No. 98/2, Jul '55: "Clark Kent Outlaw!"); the coveted Superman Medal, awarded annually by the Metropolis Police Department "to the person whose heroism...helped Superman the most" during the preceding year, presented to Clark Kent in August 1955 "for risking his life so he could act as [an] undercover agent and help Superman break a big crime combine..." (Act No. 207: "The Four Superman Medals!"); the Reporter of the Year award, presented to him just prior to March 1959 (Act No. 250: "The Eye of Metropolis!"); and the National Publishers' Prize, awarded to him in August 1964 for his "big expose of the hot car racket" (S No. 171/2: "The Curse of Magic!"). Ironically and somewhat ludicrously, Clark Kent is selected as "the ideal average American" in a contest sponsored by the Daily Planet in January 1946 (Act No. 92: "The Average American!").

In addition to wearing ordinary street clothes and slightly altering his facial appearance with eyeglasses to conceal the fact that he is secretly Superman, Clark Kent exhibits qualities of personality far removed from the ones he displays as a superhero. The chronicles repeatedly describe Clark Kent as "meek" (S No. 7/1, Nov/Dec '40; and many others), "timid" (WB No. 1, Spr '41; and many others), "mild-mannered" (Act No. 169, Jun '52: "Caveman Clark Kent!"; and many others), "sickly" (S No. 106/2, Jul '56: "The Thefts of Clark Kent"), "weak" (S No. 155/1, Aug '62: pts. I-II—"Superman Under the Green Sun!"; "The Blind Superman!"; and others), "cowardly" (Act No. 322, Mar '65: "The Coward of Steel!"; and others), "submissive" (S No. 155/1, Aug '62: pts. I-II—"Superman Under the Green Sun!"; "The Blind Superman!"), and even "spineless" (Act No. 1, Jun '38; and others).

Clark Kent is afraid of dogs (S No. 31/2, Nov/Dec '44: "A Dog's Tale!"), afraid of heights (S No. 136/3, Apr '60: "The Super-Clown of Metropolis!"; and others), willing to let almost anyone push him around (Act No. 1, Jun '38; and many others).

Kent tends to rationalize his meek behavior—which is a caricature of a timid person's behavior rather than a skillful imitation of it—as "the perfect camouflage for my real identity as Superman" (Act No. 166, Mar '52: "The Three Scoops of Death!" but there is a deeper significance behind the choice c traits with which Superman has equipped his alte ego, for this selection reveals a great deal about th personality and inner life of Superman (see section i the man himself [as Superman]).

Clark Kent lives in apartment 3-B at 344 Clinto Street (S No. 112/1, Mar '57: "Superman's Neigh bors"), a high-rise apartment building (WF No. 92 Jan/Feb '48: "The Boy from Outer Space!"; ane others) in the midtown area (S No. 8/2, Jan/Feb '41 of Metropolis (S No. 15/2, Mar/Apr '42; and many others), "across town" from the Daily Planet Build ing (S No. 181/1, Nov '65: pts. I-II—"The Super Scoops of Morna Vine!"; "The Secret of the New Supergirl!") and not far from the apartment building where Lois Lane lives (S No. 40/1, May/Jun '46: "The Mxyztplk-Susie Alliance!"). World's Finest Comics No. 35 portrays Clark Kent as residing in a house at 906 Warmon as opposed to an apartment, but this information is almost certainly erroneous (Jul/Aug '48: "Daddy Superman!").

One room of Kent's apartment houses his extensive collection of antique clocks (Act No. 73, Jun '44: "The Hobby Robbers!"). A "fake wall" in the apartment, which slides open at the touch of a secret button (S No. 174/1, Jan '65: pts. I-II—"Clark Kent's Incredible Delusion!"; "The End of a Hero!") mounted on the apartment wall (S No. 126/1, Jan '59: "Superman's Hunt for Clark Kent!"), conceals a "secret closet" (Act No. 282, Nov '61: "Superman's Toughest Day!"; and others)—or "secret trophy closet" (S No. 126/1, Jan '59: "Superman's Hunt for Clark Kent!")—housing a number of Superman's sophisticated robots (Act No. 247, Dec '58: "Superman's Lost Parents!"; and many others), several numbered boxes of Superman trophies and samples of KRYPTONITE (S No. 126/1, Jan '59: "Superman's Hunt for Clark Kent!"), and various other "Superman mementoes" (Act No. 325, Jun '65: "The Skyscraper Superman!"). When he is not wearing his Superman costume, Clark Kent sometimes hangs it in this secret closet (S No. 71/1, Jul/Aug '51: "Clark Kent's Super-Masquerade!").

Clark Kent has been a member of the ANTI-SUPERMAN CLUB (S No. 71/2, Jul/Aug '51: "The Anti-Superman Club!"), the ATLAS CLUB (S No. 78/2, Sep/Oct '52: "The Strong Man Club!"), and the ROUND TABLE CLUB (S No. 86/1, Jan '54: "The Dragon from King Arthur's Court!"). He was honored as the Meek Man's Hero of the Week by the METROPOLIS MEEK MAN'S CLUB in November 1955 (S No. 101/2: "The Meek Man's Club").

Clark Kent's closest friends are Lois Lane (see also section J 1, the relationship with Lois Lane), JIMMY OLSEN, and Perry White. His living Kent-family relatives include his cousin "Digger" Kent, a gold prospector; his cousin Louis Pasteur Kent, a country doctor; his cousin Titus Kent, a wheelchair-bound recluse who lost his entire fortune during the great

Depression; his first cousin Carol Kent, an actress (Act No. 132, May '49: "The Secret of the Kents!"); and his aunt MINERVA KENT, his foster father's younger sister (Act No. 160, Sep '51: "Superman's Aunt Minerva!"). (*See also* KENT, JONATHAN AND MARTHA [MR. AND MRS.].)

Because Clark Kent is widely known as Super-

Superman

man's "best friend" (S No. 178/2, Jul '65: "When Superman Lost His Memory!"; and others), people often contact Kent, usually at the *Daily Planet*, as the most reliable means of getting in touch with Superman (S No. 57/3, Mar/Apr '49: "The Son of Superman!"; and many others).

In January 1971 the president of the Galaxy Broadcasting System, which owns the *Daily Planet*, removes Clark Kent from the *Planet* staff and installs him as a full-time newscaster on another Galaxy property, Metropolis television station WGBS-TV, a post Kent continues to occupy as of the late 1970s (S No. 233: "Superman Breaks Loose"; and others).

I. The Man Himself (as Superman). Superman, the world-famous crime-fighter and adventurer who masks his true identity beneath the mild-mannered guise of his alter ego, journalist Clark Kent, is the hero of the Superman chronicles and the veteran of well over a thousand adventures. He is the close friend and frequent crime-fighting ally of BATMAN, the cousin and crime-fighting ally of SUPERGIRL, the owner of KRYPTO THE SUPERDOG, and the close personal friend of JIMMY OLSEN and PERRY WHITE.

Operating from the Fortress of Solitude, his impenetrable secret sanctuary located in the barren Arctic wastes (*see* section D, the Fortress of Solitude), Superman wages unrelenting warfare against the forces of evil and injustice, aided by his mighty super-powers (*see* section E, the super-powers) and by a sophisticated arsenal of special equipment (*see* section G, the equipment).

Superman's most important relationship is the one he shares with LOIS LANE, but Superman has also enjoyed romantic involvements with such beautiful, talented, and fascinating women as LANA LANG, LORI LEMARIS, LYLA LERROL, and SALLY SELWYN (*see* section J, the women of the chronicles).

Amid the crumbling ruins of a dying Krypton, Jor-El and Lara launch their son Kal-El, the infant Superman, toward a safe haven on Earth

Superman easily withstands a barrage of machine-gun fire, 1938

It is common knowledge in the world of the chronicles that Superman has another identity, but exactly who he is when he is not being Superman is one of the world's most closely guarded secrets (*see* section B, the secret identity).

Superman is "over 30 years of age" (S No. 180/1, Oct '65: "Clark Kent's Great Superman Hunt!"), with black hair and blue eyes (Act No. 297, Feb '63: "The Man Who Betrayed Superman's Identity!"; S No. 178/1, Jul '65: "Project Earth-Doom!"). Described as "an incredibly muscular figure" (WF No. 6, Sum '42: "Man of Steel versus Man of Metal!") with "a physique of magnificent symmetry" (S No. 54/1, Sep/Oct '48: "The Wrecker"), he is 6'2" tall, with a chest measurement of 44" and a waist measurement of 34" (Act No. 297, Feb '63: "The Man Who Betrayed Superman's Identity!"; S No. 178/1, Jul '65: "Project Earth-Doom!"). Because he was born on the distant planet KRYPTON, "his atomic structure is different from that of ordinary people" (S No. 38/1, Jan/Feb '46: "The Battle of the Atoms!"; and others), and his blood, according to one text, "conforms to all ALL FOUR types" (S No. 6/4, Sep/Oct '40).

A U.S. Army doctor once described Superman as "the finest physical specimen on Earth" (S No. 133/3, Nov '59: "Superman Joins the Army!"), and Lois Lane has referred to him as "the smartest, handsomest, strongest man in the universe" (S No. 176/3, Apr '65: "Superman's Day of Truth!").

The son of the Kryptonian scientist JOR-EL and his wife, LARA, Superman was born in the Kryptonian city of KRYPTONOPOLIS (SA No. 5, Sum '62; and others) during the month of October (Act No. 149, Oct '50: "The Courtship on Krypton!"), in the year 1920 (S No. 181/2, Nov '65: "The Superman of 2965!").

According to Superman No. 75/1, the proud parents named their son Jor-El, 2nd (Mar/Apr '52: "The Prankster's Star Pupil!"), but an overwhelming preponderance of texts assert that they named him

Kal-El (S No. 113, May '57: chs. 1-3—"The Superman of the Past"; "The Secret of the Towers"; "The Superman of the Present"; and others). By all accounts, the dark-haired youngster bore an "unmistakable" resemblance to his father (S No. 77/1, Jul/Aug '52: "The Man Who Went to Krypton!"; and others).

As the newest member of the so-called House of El, Superman was born into a family with a centuries-long heritage of achievement in the fields of science, statesmanship, and exploration. His ancestry teemed with such men of lasting distinction as Val-El, an explorer and discoverer who was the moving force behind Krypton's great Age of Exploration; Sul-El, the inventor of Krypton's first telescope, who charted many far-off stars, including Earth's sun; Tala-El, the author of Krypton's planet-wide constitution; Hatu-El, a scientist and inventor who discovered the nature of electricity and devised Krypton's first electromagnet and electric motor; and Gam-El, the father of modern Kryptonian architecture (SF No. 172, Aug/Sep '75; and others). Superman's paternal grandfather had pioneered the science of space travel on Krypton by journeying to Earth and back in an experimental spacecraft of his own design (S No. 103/1, Feb '56: "The Superman of Yesterday"), although knowledge of the craft's construction had apparently been lost to Kryptonians by the time Superman was born (Act No. 158, Jul '51: "The Kid from Krypton!"; and others).

Superman's uncle Nim-El, his father's identical twin brother, was a distinguished weapons scientist. Superman's uncle ZOR-EL, another of Jor-El's brothers, had embarked upon a distinguished career in climatography. Zor-El and the woman he would later marry, ALURA, survived the death of Krypton and now reside in KANDOR. Their daughter Kara, known to the world as Supergirl, is Superman's first cousin (Act No. 285, Feb '62: "The World's Greatest Her-

Coming upon a "torturer's inquisition"
in the midst of the San Montè war...

oine!"; and others). VAN-ZEE, "a distant kinsman" of Superman's, resides in Kandor with his wife, SYLVIA (S No. 158, Jan '63: "Superman in Kandor" pts I-III—"Invasion of the Mystery Super-Men!"; "The Dynamic Duo of Kandor!"; "The City of Super-People!").

While Superman was still an infant, his native planet exploded into fragments as the result of a cataclysmic chain reaction originating at the planet's core, but not before his parents had placed him in an experimental rocket ship and launched him toward the safety of the planet Earth. There the Kryptonian infant Kal-El, who would one day be known throughout the universe as Superman, was found and adopted—and renamed Clark Kent—by a kindly couple, JONATHAN AND MARTHA KENT (S No. 53/1, Jul/Aug '48: "The Origin of Superman!"; and others).

It was the Kents, in fact, who urged upon their adopted son the importance of keeping his superpowers secret and of using them to aid humanity. "Now listen to me, Clark!" cautioned Jonathan Kent, while Clark was still a youngster. "This great strength of yours--you've got to hide it from people or they'll be scared of you!"

"But when the proper time comes," added Martha Kent, "you must use it to assist humanity" (S No. 1/1, Sum '39).

According to the earliest accounts, Clark Kent embarked on his super-heroic career as Superman only after reaching adulthood (S No. 1/1, Sum '39; and others), and first learned of his extraterrestrial origins as late as November-December 1949, when, after having already functioned as a super-hero for more than a decade, he journeyed through the barriers of time and space—to the planet Krypton prior to its destruction—and actually witnessed the cataclysm that destroyed his native planet. He also witnessed the aftermath of that cataclysm, including his arrival on Earth in a rocket and his adoption by the Kents.

"That old couple...they're my *foster parents!*" thinks Superman excitedly as he watches Jonathan and Martha Kent lift his infant self gently from the rocket that has just brought him to Earth. "I'm Clark Kent! Then that's me... *that infant is me back in the past!*

"Now I understand why I'm different from earthmen! I'm not really from Earth at all — I'm from another planet — the planet Jor-El called **Krypton!!**"

"So at last," notes the textual narrative, "after all these years, **Superman** is at last aware of his birthplace, and why he is the strongest man on Earth!" (S No. 61/3: "Superman Returns to Krypton!").

In the years that followed, however, these early accounts underwent substantial revision. In the newer version, Superman was portrayed as having battled crime and injustice as a youngster—as Superboy—prior to embarking on his adult crime-fighting career as Superman (S No. 72/2, Sep/Oct '51: "The Private Life of Perry White!"; and many others), and he was described as having learned of his extraterrestrial origins while still a boy "by overtaking and photographing light rays that had left **Krypton** before it exploded" (S No. 132, Oct '59: "Superman's Other Life!" pts. 1-3—"Krypton Lives On!"; "Futuro, Super-Hero of Krypton!"; "The Superman of Two Worlds!"; and others). In addition, it was stated that "Because of his super-memory, **Superman** can recall all the incidents of his childhood!"

(Act No. 288, May '62: "The Man Who Exposed Superman!"; and others).

Despite this revision, however, all the texts of the Superman chronicles agree that Superman has lived a double life since the onset of his super-heroic career, using his super-powers openly only as Superboy or Superman while concealing his true, extraterrestrial identity beneath the deceptive guise of mild-mannered Clark Kent.

There are advantages to maintaining two separate identities: the Clark Kent persona enables Superman to catch the criminal element unawares and to safeguard his friends and intimates against gangland reprisals; it affords him a refuge from his life as a super-hero, making it possible for him to escape the ever-present adulators and curiosity seekers and to relate to ordinary Earth folk on everyday human terms.

None of this, however, serves to explain the constellation of personality characteristics with which Superman has chosen to equip his Clark Kent persona, even though he tends to rationalize his meek, cowardly behavior as "the perfect camouflage for my real identity as Superman" (Act No. 166, Mar '52: "The Three Scoops of Death!").

There are, however, deeper reasons behind Superman's creation of the meek Clark Kent persona, reasons which go to the very heart of Superman's unconscious life. It is incorrect, first of all, to think of Superman as the real person and of Clark Kent as only a shallow persona, for the psychological truth is very nearly the opposite: in Superman's mind, Clark Kent is the real person and Superman is the masquerade.

Clark Kent is the outward expression of Superman's inner self. He is Superman's internal experience of who he really is. For despite his vast powers, Superman sees himself as weak and inadequate. If it is difficult to comprehend how a being so nearly

omnipotent as Superman can possibly feel so impotent and powerless, it must be remembered that Superman is not an earthman, but a Kryptonian. On the planet Krypton, where he was born, Superman had no special powers. He acquired his super-powers, the powers that transformed him into a "superman," only by virtue of having been transplanted to the alien environment of Earth.

An ordinary man in Lilliput may be a giant to the Lilliputians, but he will continue to see himself as ordinary, for the standards by which he measures himself will not be Lilliputian standards, but rather the standards of the country from which he came. On Krypton, Superman was a helpless infant—helpless to prevent the cataclysm that destroyed his native planet; helpless to rescue the Kryptonian people; helpless to save his own parents from doom. The one time in his life when power really mattered, Superman was an impotent witness to planet-shattering events.

Superman is among the last remaining survivors of a perished civilization. Like most survivors, he feels immense guilt at having been powerless to save those who did not survive, and immense anger at having been "abandoned" by them. As the planet Krypton shuddered and rumbled toward the doomsday cataclysm, Superman was not really "super" at all; he was cringing Clark Kent, spinelessly fleeing the scene of terrifying events he could not even hope to control. And while he fled to safety, others died.

Like most youngsters orphaned in childhood, Superman appears to have experienced the death of his parents as a personal desertion. In the unconscious mind of the infant Superman, he was unworthy of his parents' lasting love and so they deserted him. The deep inner feelings of worthlessness and self-loathing engendered by this unconsciously perceived rejection find their outward expression in the personality of Clark Kent, who continually

...*Superman hurls the offending torturer to his doom "as tho* [sic] *he were hurling a javelin," 1938*

Superman uses vigilante techniques, typical of his early period, to extort information from Washington lobbyist Alex Greer, 1938

Bending an iron bar in his bare hands, Superman terrifies munitions magnate Emil Norvell into doing his bidding, 1938

reinforces and confirms his own lowly estimation of himself by arousing the loathing and contempt of others through his cringing, unmanly behavior. On the other hand, Superman's mortal anger at his parents for having "rejected" him finds socially acceptable expression in the personality of Superman, who has sublimated his enormous aggressive impulses to the task of battling evildoers and apprehending criminals.

The horrendous cataclysm that destroyed Krypton occurred at a time when the infant Superman was grappling with the agonizing complexity of his affectional and erotic feelings toward Lara, his mother. In Oedipal terms, the infant Superman wished his father dead so that he could possess his mother. And then, all at once, the first part of the forbidden fantasy came true: the entire planet exploded and his father perished. Even adults often fear the consequences of a forbidden fantasy, but for a babe in arms to wish his father dead and then have the wish come true produces an unendurable agony of guilt, engendering, deep within the unconscious, the conviction that one's innermost needs and feelings are cataclysmically destructive, that one's most deeply felt wishes are irredeemably evil. The personality of Clark Kent is Superman's way of denying his awesome power, of protecting the universe from his awesomely destructive fantasies of death and cataclysm.

The rocket that carried Superman safely to Earth had room for two passengers. When the doomsday came and the planet Krypton rumbled toward destruction, Superman's father, Jor-El, urged his wife Lara to climb aboard the rocket and escape to Earth with their infant son. It must have been an agonizing

moment for Superman. Wrapped in a blanket in his mother's arms, he could feel her literally within his grasp. And yet, given the chance to escape to Earth with her son, Lara chose instead to die with Jor-El. It would be impossible to overestimate the importance of this event in shaping Superman's emotional life, particularly his relationships with Lois Lane and the various other women with whom he has shared romantic involvements (*see* section J, the women of the chronicles).

Throughout the chronicles, Superman expresses the desire to be loved as Clark Kent. If Clark Kent were merely a masquerade—a convenient disguise behind which Superman could conceal his true identity—Superman would feel no need to have his alter ego loved and appreciated. When Clark Kent is viewed as Superman's inner self, however, it becomes immediately apparent why Superman is so anxious to win acceptance in this identity.

Nevertheless, the Superman/Clark Kent split produces serious conflicts for Superman, for Superman personifies strength, control, omnipotence, and perfection, while Clark Kent personifies weakness, cowardice, helplessness, and inadequacy. Although Superman wants desperately to be accepted as Clark Kent, he also loathes Clark Kent and the qualities he represents. Superman's desire for control and omnipotence forces him to deny his human vulnerability. Superman expresses his humanity only in the guise of Clark Kent. Only as Clark Kent is Superman truly human and truly vulnerable. Yet Clark Kent's brand of humanity is a flawed one, for Clark Kent is a sad caricature that identifies vulnerability with weakness, humanity with cowardice.

Finally, Superman's dual personality must also be viewed in light of his upbringing by Jonathan and Martha Kent. Superman's real parents were larger than life. Jor-El was his planet's foremost scientist; Lara was a great beauty and an intellectual as well. The Kents, on the other hand, were ordinary, undistinguished people, the owners of a family farm and later the proprietors of a small-town general store. If Superman is the son of Jor-El and Lara, then Clark Kent is the son of Jonathan and Martha Kent. Although, in actuality, the Kents appear to have loved their adopted son as though he were their own flesh and blood, it seems probable that the infant Superman unconsciously despised the Kents for being ordinary and elderly, for compromising his exalted Kryptonian heritage, and for not loving him as much as, in his child's imagination, his real parents would have loved him had they only lived. Superman's unconscious hatred of the Kents finds expression in the personality of Clark Kent, which is in many ways a distorted caricature of Jonathan Kent. Superman, after all, is the great man that he might have been had he grown to maturity on Krypton. Clark Kent is the bumbling son of a small-time farmer whose greatest achievement in life was operating a general store.

"Today," notes Superman No. 144/2, "**Superman**

Superman brings an end to the San Monte war by threatening to beat up the opposing commanders unless they agree to settle the conflict, 1938

is the most famous crusader in the world, idolized everywhere for unselfishly using his incredible super-powers in behalf of justice" (Apr '61: "Superboy's First Public Appearance!").

But Superman was not always famous. In the early days of his career, he actively sought anonymity (Act No. 1, Jun '38; and others) and was relieved when newspaper accounts of important events omitted mention of his participation in them (S No. 1/1, Sum '39). Early texts describe him as a "mystery-man" (Act No. 6, Nov '38; and others) and, even as late as September-October 1941, many of the people he encountered expressed surprise that he was more than a "legendary character" (S No. 12/1; and others).

In February 1942, Action Comics No. 45 describes Superman as "a fighting champion of justice who is famous the world over," but even as late as October 1945 there were people who doubted Superman's existence (Act No. 89: "The King of Color!").

In general, however, since the early 1940s, Super-man has been known "in every corner of the globe" (S No. 16/4, May/Jun '42: "Racket on Delivery"), receiving literally tons of fan mail (Act No. 179, Apr '53: "Super Manor!") and being continually besieged by youngsters seeking his autograph (S No. 20/1, Jan/Feb '43: "Superman's Secret Revealed!").

In the words of Superman No. 96/1:

From the jungle-wilds of Africa, to the skyscrapers of New York, the name of Superman has spread its fame! His Herculean strength, his super-battles against evil, are familiar to all...[Mar '55: "The Girl Who Didn't Believe in Superman!"].

Other texts contain these comments:

Beyond any doubt, the most famous man on Earth is Superman, super-powerful foe of evil and champion of justice! For years, he has been hailed as the world's mightiest hero! [S No. 150/3, Jan '62: "When the World Forgot Superman!"].

Today the whole world rings with Superman's fame! In the far corners of the Earth men tell of how the Man of Steel uses his fantastic super-powers to help the forces of law and order against evildoers! [S No. 152/2, Apr '62: "Superbaby Captures the Pumpkin Gang!"].

Just as Superman's fame has increased over the years, so too have his methods of dealing with evildoers changed. Sought by the police in the early days of his career for working beyond the pale of legitimate authority (see section K, the relationship with the law-enforcement establishment), Superman was not averse to killing his adversaries whenever he felt the situation demanded it.

In July 1938, while attempting to bring an end to the SAN MONTÉ war, Superman—in a sequence reprinted in these pages—deliberately takes the life of a military torturer, seizing him in one hand and hurling him bodily through the air, as though, in the words of the text, "he were hurling a javelin" (Act No. 2).

In June 1939 Superman leaps high into the air to intercept a bizarre aircraft carrying the ULTRA-HUMANITE and his henchmen. "Deliberately," notes the text, "Superman crashes into the plane's propellor--- down toward the distant Earth hurtle both doomed plane and Man of Steel---'The Ultra-Humanite's' vessel crumples sickeningly as it strikes the ground with a thunderous crash---!" The Ultra-Humanite somehow manages to escape, but his hirelings are dead in the wreckage (Act No. 13).

In Spring 1940 Superman deliberately electrocutes J. F. CURTIS (S No. 4/3).

In January-February 1941 Superman drowns the horde of zombielike human giants created by PRO-FESSOR ZEE and Dr. Cardos (S No. 8/1).

In March-April 1941, when racketeer JOE GATSON fires a bullet at a young woman, Superman kills Gatson by hurling him into the bullet's path (S No. 9/2).

In November 1941 Superman kills one of LEX LUTHOR's henchmen by hurling him bodily out of an upper-story window (Act No. 42).

In January-February 1942 Superman deliberately electrocutes "THE LIGHTNING MASTER" (S No. 14/4).

By January-February 1943, however, Superman's attitude toward the taking of human life has changed drastically. "I'd like to attend to the Puzzler," he muses grimly, after the villain has deliberately sent a carload of his own henchmen hurtling off a bridge in order to divert the Man of Steel from pursuing him while he makes his escape, "--but above all I must save human life...no matter how little those thugs deserve it..." (S No. 20/4: "Not in the Cards").

By November 1943 the taking of a human life, no matter how villainous, has become deeply repugnant to Superman's moral code. Indeed, a text for this period refers erroneously to Superman as a hero "who in all his epic adventures has never taken a human life..." (Act No. 66: "The Boy Who Came Back!").

Throughout his career, Superman has frequently resorted to violence and the threat of violence to extort information and confessions from criminal suspects. Following are some examples of particularly flagrant violations of civil liberties perpetrated by Superman in the course of his career.

In June 1938, in a two-page sequence reprinted here, Superman uses violent means to extort information from lobbyist ALEX GREER (Act No. 1).

In July 1938, in a one-page sequence reprinted here, Superman brings an end to the San Monté war by threatening to beat up the opposing commanders unless they agree to settle the conflict (Act No. 2).

In September 1938, after disguising himself as Cordell University football player Tommy Burke so that he can impersonate Burke in an upcoming championship game, Superman puts the real Burke out of action—without his consent—by jabbing him with a hypodermic needle containing a knockout drug and then locking him in his apartment (Act No. 4).

In December 1938 Superman extorts information from DEREK NILES's henchman Trigger by tossing

Superman extorts a murder confession from nightclub singer Bea Carroll

him high into the air and threatening to let him hit the ground unless he agrees to tell what he knows (Act No. 7).

In May 1939 Superman demolishes an automobile factory and commits numerous other illegal acts

Assigned to cover a wife beating for the Daily Star...

when he declares war on defective cars and "homicidal drivers" (Act No. 12). (*See* section L 2 a, the early adventures.)

In a one-page sequence reprinted here, Superman terrifies nightclub singer BEA CARROLL into signing a murder confession by crushing the barrel of her automatic pistol in the palm of his hand and then threatening to do the same to her arm (S No. 1/1, Sum '39).

In July 1939 Superman extorts a confession from a

villain by dangling him out of an upper-story window (Act No. 14).

In September 1939 Superman intimidates ME-TROPOLIS's illegal gambling czars into leaving town en masse by threatening to track down any man who remains behind "and end his life with my own hands!" (Act No. 16).

In Fall 1939 Superman brings an end to the senseless civil war ravaging far-off Boravia by threatening to kill the opposing negotiators unless they agree to resolve the conflict immediately (S No. 2/2: "Superman Champions Universal Peace!"). During this same period, Superman uses violent means to extort information from several hoodlums, then forces NAT GRAYSON to sign a confession by strangling him by the throat until he agrees to confess (S No. 2/3, Fall '39: "Superman and the Skyscrapers").

In November 1939 Superman demolishes the plant and equipment of MR. HAMILTON's *Morning Herald* and frightens Hamilton and his cohorts into leaving town. "If you're smart," warns Superman, "you won't be in this city tomorrow!" (Act No. 18).

In April 1940, while attempting to bring a halt to the bloody war raging between the nations of GALONIA and TORAN, Superman extorts information from one of the opposing generals by threatening to kill him unless he agrees to tell what he knows. "Either answer my question," demands Superman, **"or have your brains dashed out against that wall!"** (Act No. 23).

In January-February 1941 Superman extorts a confession from JEFF CARLTON at gunpoint (S No. 8/2).

In May-June 1941 Superman extorts a confession from GRADY by dangling him out of a window and threatening to drop him and then flying through the air with him while performing aerial acrobatics. "Out

...Clark Kent arrives on the scene as Superman and administers a well-deserved thrashing to the brutal wife beater...

...before the terrified man faints dead away in his arms, 1938

into the empty air leaps the mighty *Man of Steel*," notes the textual narrative, "with his craven, screeching burden..." (S No. 10/2). During this same period, Superman uses similar techniques to extort a confession from RIGHAB BEY (S No. 10/3, May/Jun '41).

In Summer 1941 Superman extorts information from one of "THE UNKNOWN X's" henchmen by flying into the air with him and threatening to drop him into the whirling propeller of an airplane unless the terrified criminal agrees to tell what he knows (WF No. 2).

In July 1941 Superman hypnotizes HAROLD MORTON into making a full confession of his crimes (Act No. 38).

In July-August 1941 Superman uses a chilly ride through the upper atmosphere to frighten a confession out of COUNT TONY BERGAC (S No. 11/4).

In September 1941 Superman threatens a crooked gambler with death unless he agrees to allow one of his victims to win back the money she has lost (Act No. 40).

In November-December 1941 Superman extorts information from one of Lex Luthor's henchmen by dropping him from a great height and threatening to let him fall to his doom unless he agrees to talk (S No. 13/1).

In December 1941 Superman extorts information from a group of hoodlums by threatening to hurl them into the path of an oncoming locomotive (Act No. 43).

In July 1942 Superman uses the threat of violence to extort information from "big-time gambler" Mike Caputo. "Up into the sky hurtles **Superman** with his shrieking captive..." notes the text. "You know what I'm capable of doing, Mike," threatens Superman. "Do I have to put you thru [sic] the works or--" "Oh-hhh--my head," groans Caputo dazedly, "--the dizziness...I'll tell you anything!" (Act No. 50).

In November-December 1942 Superman extorts a confession from MR. Z by leaping with him out of an

upper-story window, holding his head under an open fire hydrant, and threatening to allow him to be run over by an oncoming car (S No. 19/3).

In January 1943 Superman extorts information from a criminal by dropping him out of an upper-story window and promising to catch him before he hits the ground only if he agrees to talk (Act No. 56: "Design for Doom!").

In November-December 1944 Superman extorts a written confession from ROCKY GRIMES by threatening to attack him with a rabid dog (S No. 31/2: "A Dog's Tale!").

In September-October 1946 Superman extorts a confession from POSY EDWARDS by locking him in the gorilla cage at the Metropolis Zoo (WF No. 24: "Impossible but True!").

In November 1950 Superman deliberately tricks MORKO and his henchmen into attacking him in the belief that they are only destroying a lifeless Superman statue so that he can haul them off to jail

Superman orders Metropolis's gambling czars to clear out of town, 1939

Superman, 1941

Superman in action, 1941

on a trumped-up charge of assault and battery (Act No. 150: "The Secret of the 6 Superman Statues!").

In November-December 1952 Superman threatens to drop a huge meteor on Lex Luthor and his henchmen unless they agree to surrender and confess their crimes (S No. 79/1: "Citadel of Doom!").

In May-June 1953 Superman offers to rescue JOHN MADDERS and his henchman from being buried alive by a collapsing building only if they agree to confess their crimes (WF No. 64: "The Death of Lois Lane").

In July 1960 Superman, posing as the Devil, extorts a confession from "DUKE" HASKELL and "Lefty" Montez by transporting them to the depths of a dying volcano and threatening to keep them in "Hell" forever unless they agree to confess their crimes (S No. 138/2: "Superman's Black Magic!").

In January 1961 Superman employs an elaborate ruse involving entrapment to enable the Metropolis police force to apprehend the "ACE" RUGGLES gang (Act No. 272: "Superman's Rival, Mental Man!").

In September 1965 Superman extorts a confession from MR. GIMMICK and his cohorts by threatening to destroy them in a "super-atomic" explosion (Act No. 328: "Superman's Hands of Doom!").

Superman is a man of high ideals, and much of his behavior is motivated by an abiding sense of honor and principle. Among his deeply held convictions is the sacredness of human life, which, except for the first four years of his crime-fighting career, forbids him from taking a human life, even that of the vilest villain (S No. 172, Oct '64: pts. I-III—"The New Superman!"; "Clark Kent—Former Superman!"; "The Struggle of the Two Supermen!"; and many others).

Superman always keeps his word (S No. 147/3, Aug '61: "The Legion of Super-Villains!"; and others), and "it's against [his] code to resist the law," even

when the law seems unreasonable or unjust (Act No. 264, May '60: "The Superman Bizarro!").

Superman is vigorously opposed to slot machines (S No. 5/1, Sum '40) and all other forms of gambling (Act No. 32, Jan '41), for he regards gambling as "a parasitic vice that has no place in a decent town" (Act No. 16, Sep '39).

One of Superman's most deeply held convictions is that he must never use his super-powers for profit or personal aggrandizement (Act No. 120, May '48: "Superman, Stunt Man!"; and many others). He has always rejected remuneration for his super-heroic deeds (Act No. 24, May '40; and many others), although he has, on occasion, performed services for others in return for the promise of contributions to charity (Act No. 40, Sep '41; and others).

Although Superman No. 114/3 asserts that Superman accepts rewards for the criminals he captures and then, in turn, donates them to charity (Jul '57: "Superman's Billion-Dollar Debt!"), numerous other

Superman, 1941

texts contradict this, insisting that Superman "has always arrested wanted criminals without ever claiming the rewards offered for their capture!" (S No. 102/1, Jan '56: "Superman for Sale"; and many others). On occasion, projects in which Superman becomes involved—such as the writing of his autobiography in January-February 1947—do produce income, but such income is, without exception, donated to charity (WF No. 26: "The Confessions of Superman!"; and others).

Indeed, virtually from the onset of his career, but particularly since the early 1950s, Superman has displayed unstinting devotion to worthy causes, staging spectacular exhibitions of his super-powers

Superman hurdles a gangster's auto, 1938

at orphanages and other institutions (S No. 73/2, Nov/Dec '51: "The Mighty Mite!"; and others); appearing on telethons (Act No. 180, May '53: "The Super-Telethon"; S No. 127/3, Feb '59: "Titano the Super-Ape!"); making public-service films (S No. 143/3, Feb '61: "Bizarro Meets Frankenstein!"); building orphan asylums (S No. 147/3, Aug '61: "The Legion of Super-Villains!"); conducting guided tours for charity through his Fortress of Solitude (Act No. 261, Feb '60: "Superman's Fortresses of Solitude!") and otherwise donating his super-services (WF No. 49, Dec/Jan '50-'51: "The Men Who Shot Superman!"; and many others); and helping to promote innumerable charity drives (S No. 152/3, Apr '62: "The TV Trap for Superman!"; and others), particularly those sponsored by the DAILY PLANET (S No. 160/1, Apr '63: pts. I-II—"The Mortal Superman!"; "The Cage of Doom!"; and others).

During the first three years of his career, more than any other period since, Superman exhibited an abiding concern for such pressing social issues as wife beating (Act No. 1, Jun '38), mine safety (Act No. 3, Aug '38, juvenile delinquency and urban renewal

(Act No. 8, Jan '39), prison reform (Act No. 10, Mar '39), traffic safety (Act No. 12, May '39), crooked unions (Act No. 13, Jun '39), illegal gambling (Act No. 16, Sep '39), corrupt municipal government (S No. 7/3, Nov/Dec '40), and the rights of accused persons to fair and impartial justice (S No. 1/1, Sum '39). Frequently, Superman fought for radical social change in ways that put him at odds with legitimate authority (Act No. 8, Jan '39; and others). Since the end of 1940, however, Superman has been the ally of the establishment and has seldom concerned himself with social issues other than combatting crime.

Similarly, Superman's early adventures often revolved around his efforts to help individuals in trouble: a circus owner threatened with the loss of his circus (Act No. 7, Dec '38), an escapee from a brutal chain gang (Act No. 10, Mar '39), a washed-up prizefighter (S No. 2/1, Fall '39), a gambler despondent over his losses (Act No. 16, Sep '39), a zoo keeper who has lost his job because "the war in Europe is making it almost impossible" to obtain new animals for the zoo (Act No. 45, Feb '42). On more than half a dozen occasions during the first decade of his career, Superman first became embroiled in an adventure as the result of having saved the life of a would-be suicide (Act No. 16, Sep '39; and others). In the last three decades, would-be suicides have rarely appeared in the chronicles, and Superman's adventures have only infrequently centered around his efforts to help individuals with their personal problems.

Superman regularly patrols Metropolis—sometimes at night (S No. 114/1, Jul '57: "Superman's Billion-Dollar Debt!"; and others), and sometimes during the daylight hours (WF No. 96, Sep '58: "The Super-Foes from Planet X"; and others)—in search of crimes in progress and other emergencies requiring his attention. Because Superman is widely known as

Superman, 1938

Clark Kent's "best friend" (S No. 178/2, Jul '65: "When Superman Lost His Memory!"; and others), individuals seeking Superman's help often contact him through Clark Kent at the *Daily Planet* (S No. 57/3, Mar/Apr '49: "The Son of Superman!"; and many others).

For recreation and relaxation, Superman avails himself of the various hobbies and recreational facilities in his Fortress of Solitude (Act No. 241, Jun '58: "The Super-Key to Fort Superman"; and others), relaxes with an issue of Action Comics (Act No. 45, Feb '42), or knits, a pastime he has described as "a wonderful tonic for the nerves...." "Yes!" notes the textual narrative of Superman No. 32/1. "**Superman**, the greatest man's man of all, knits with a skill far surpassing the most expert woman!" (Jan/Feb '45: "Superman's Search for Clark Kent!"). Superman is also the inventor of SUPERMANIUM, "the hardest substance in existence" (WF No. 41, Jul/Aug '49: "The Discovery of Supermanium!"; and others).

On approximately half a dozen occasions between 1942 and 1948, Superman has launched himself into the sky with the cry "Up-up-and **away!**" (Act No. 65, Oct '43: "The Million-Dollar Marathon!"; and others), but the phrase has appeared in the chronicles only rarely over the last three decades.

Although Superman "hates being glorified" (S No. 70/2, May/Jun '51: "The Life of Superman!") and has always modestly shunned the spotlight of public acclaim, few individuals in history have been accorded such widespread honor and distinction. His exploits have been celebrated and immortalized in virtually every known medium: on radio, on "The Adventures of Superman" series (S No. 39/1, Mar/Apr '46: "The Big Superman Broadcast!") and on the "Thrill-a-Minute Program" (S No. 61/1, Nov/Dec '49: "The Prankster's Radio Program!"); on television, on station WMET-TV's "Our American Heroes" series (Act No. 309, Feb '64: "The Superman Super-Spectacular!"); and on film, in Superman animated cartoons (S No. 19/4, Nov/Dec '42: "Superman, Matinee Idol"), a Superman newsreel (S No. 98/3, Jul '55: "The Amazing Superman Newsreel!"), and in such live-action movies as JACK ALLEN's *Superman in Valhalla* (S No. 52/3, May/Jun '48: "Superman in Valhalla!") and CHARLES LAMONT's *The Life of Superman* (S No. 70/2, May/Jun '51: "The Life of Superman!").

Superman has been the recipient of numerous awards, trophies, citations, and other honors, including Metropolis's Outstanding Citizen Award for 1954, presented to Superman "in honor of [his] conspicuous efforts to improve Metropolis" (S No. 93/2, Nov '54: "Jimmy Olsen's Double!"); the plaque awarded him in August 1958 in recognition of his efforts on behalf of Metropolis's orphans (Act No. 243: "The Lady and the Lion"); the golden Superman statuette presented to Superman by the president of BORKIA in November 1959 in appreciation of his having thwarted the dictatorial ambitions of GENERAL MALVIO (Act No. 258: "The Menace of Cosmic Man!"); the certificate of

© NPP 1972

Superman, 1972

honorary citizenship "in all the countries of the United Nations" awarded Superman by the U.N. (S No. 146/1, Jul '61: "The Story of Superman's Life!"); and "the key to the city" presented to Superman by the mayor of Metropolis in September 1965 (Act No. 328: "Superman's Hands of Doom!"). Each year, in Superman's honor, the Metropolis Police Department awards a Superman Medal "to the person whose heroism...helped **Superman** the most" during the preceding year (Act No. 207, Aug '55: "The Four Superman Medals!"). All of Superman's plaques and awards are housed in a room set aside for them in his Fortress of Solitude (Act No. 243, Aug '58: "The Lady and the Lion").

Statues and other artistic tributes to Superman abound, particularly in Metropolis, including the statue of Superman in the Metropolis Hall of Fame (Act No. 297, Feb '63: "The Man Who Betrayed Superman's Identity!"), the "colossal steel statue of **Superman**" in Metropolis Park (WF No. 28, May/Jun '47: "Superman's Super-Self!"; and others), the monumental statue of Superman towering over Metropolis Harbor like the legendary Colossus of Rhodes (WF No. 23, Jul/Aug '46: "The Colossus of Metropolis!"; *see also* Act No. 146, Jul '50: "The Statues That Came to Life!"), and the marble statue of Superman unveiled in Planet Square in January-February 1946 (S No. 38/3: "The Man of Stone!"; S No. 69/1, Mar/Apr '51: "The Prankster's Apprentice!").

Other artistic tributes to Superman include the monumental Superman statue blasted out of an entire mountaintop somewhere in the United States by members of the SUPER-SAVED CLUB in July-August 1949 (WF No. 41: "The Discovery of Supermanium!"); the colossal head of Superman, carved into the side of a mountain, which appears briefly in Action Comics No. 282 (Nov '61: "Superman's Toughest Day!"); the huge bronze statue of Superman constructed atop a penitentiary roof by the TOYMAN as part of a prison-escape scheme in March-April 1950 (S No. 63/2: "The Wind-Up Toys of Peril!"); the various Superman statues in the bottle city of Kandor (S No. 158, Jan '63: "Superman in Kandor" pts. I-III—"Invasion of the Mystery Super-Men!"; "The Dynamic Duo of Kandor!"; "The City of Super-People!"); and the standing statue of SUPERBOY in the town of SMALLVILLE (S No. 97/3, May '55: "Superboy's Last Day in Smallville!").

A heroic portrait of Superman, commissioned by Metropolis's mayor and city council in April 1946, is defaced by the PRANKSTER prior to its unveiling as part of his scheme to humiliate Superman (Act No. 95: "The Laughing Stock of Metropolis!").

Two commemorative stamps have been issued in honor of Superman, one by the U.S. Government (S No. 91/1, Aug '54: "The Superman Stamp!"), the other by the city of Rangoon, Burma (S No. 153/2, May '62: "The Secret of the Superman Stamp!").

Buildings and public places dedicated to Superman or devoted to his exploits include the Superman School for Officers' Training, "the nation's largest army officers' training center," constructed single-handedly by Superman, at super-speed, as a favor to the U.S. Army in December 1943 (Act No. 67: "Make Way for Fate!"); the SUPERMAN LAND amusement park, "the most colossal, super-stupendous amusement park in the world" (Act No. 210, Nov '55: "Superman in Superman Land"); JONAS SMITH's Krypton Island, now renamed Kryptonopolis (Act No. 246, Nov '58: "Krypton on Earth!"); Superman Skytower, an unfinished Metropolis skyscraper which is completed single-handedly by Superman in September 1958 (S No. 124/3: "The Steeplejack of Steel"); and Metropolis's famed SUPERMAN MUSEUM, which houses an extensive collection of Superman memorabilia (S No. 150/3, Jan '62: "When the World Forgot Superman!"; and many others).

The inhabitants of a far-distant planet once reshaped their entire world into a colossal three-dimensional portrait of Superman in gratitude for his having liberated them from the oppressive yoke of a "power-mad" dictator (see DRAGO [alien dictator]) (S No. 155/1, Aug '62: pts. I-II—"Superman Under the Green Sun!"; "The Blind Superman!"); and a distinctive man-made island (see SUPERMAN ISLAND), fashioned in the Man of Steel's own image off the coast of Metropolis and then hurled into outer space by Superman in January 1957, now wanders the universe as "a Superman star" (Act No. 224: "The Secret of Superman Island!").

Both in Metropolis and in Smallville, special holidays have been set aside in honor of Superman. Metropolis has celebrated Superman Day on at least two separate occasions (S No. 157/3, Nov '62: "Superman's Day of Doom!"; Act No. 328, Sep '65:

Superman, 1948

© NPP 1948

"Superman's Hands of Doom!"), and in Smallville, Superboy Day is celebrated annually (S No. 116/2, Sep '57: "Disaster Strikes Twice"), as is Superman's Earthday, "the anniversary of the day [Superman] landed on Earth from the doomed planet, **Krypton!**" (S No. 136/2, Apr '60: "The Secret of Kryptonite!").

Superman has been made an Indian chief (Act No. 148, Sep '50: "Superman, Indian Chief!"), held the rank of general in the U.S. Army (S No. 133/3, Nov '59: "Superman Joins the Army!"), and served as chairman of the Phantom Zone Parole Board in the bottle city of Kandor (Act No. 310, Mar '64: "Secret of Kryptonite Six!").

He is an honorary member of the SOCIETY OF ADVENTURERS (Act No. 183, Aug '53: "The Perfect Plot to Kill Superman!"), the chairman (see LIGHTNING-MAN) of the Club of Heroes (WF No. 89, Jul/Aug '57: "The Club of Heroes!"), and a member of an organization of heroes known as the Justice

Superman, 1947

© NPP 1947

League of America (Act No. 314, Jul '64: "The Day Superman Became the Flash!"; and others). From Winter 1940, the date of its founding (AS No. 3), through February-March 1951, Superman served as an honorary member of the Justice Society of America (AS No. 57), an organization of heroes described as "the mightiest champions of right and justice in the world!" (AS No. 3). As a teen-ager, Superman was a member of the LEGION OF SUPER-HEROES (S No. 147/3, Aug '61: "The Legion of Super-Villains!"). Clubs formed in honor of Superman include the SUPER-SAVED CLUB (WF No. 41, Jul/Aug '49: "The Discovery of Supermanium!") and the SUPER SORORITY (Act No. 235, Dec '57: "The Super-Prisoner of Amazon Island").

Future generations will have little difficulty familiarizing themselves with Superman's exploits. The public library contains a veritable mountain of information about Superman: "volume upon volume--books, magazines, newspapers, articles--all telling of the countless and incredible exploits of Super-man!" (S No. 32/1, Jan/Feb '45: "Superman's Search for Clark Kent!").

Superman has written three autobiographies. The first, entitled The Confessions of Superman, was published by BENNY CALL in January-February 1947 (WF No. 26: "The Confessions of Superman!"); the second, written for the Daily Planet in return for a $50,000 charitable contribution, appeared in July-August 1953 (WF No. 65: "The Confessions of Superman!"); and the third, entitled I Superman, was published "a few years" prior to September 1955 (S No. 100/3: "The Clue from Krypton").

In addition, a time capsule containing a newsreel account of Superman's exploits was buried on the site of the 1939 New York World's Fair (S No. 59/3, Jul/Aug '49: "The City That Forgot Superman"), and in August 1952 Superman buries a second time capsule, containing a "complete picture record" of his life, abilities, and exploits (Act No. 171: "The Secrets of Superman!"). A time capsule buried by the Metropolis Museum in July 1958 contains a series of exotic "space trophies" designed to serve as "a living memorial" to Superman's achievements (S No. 122/1: "The Secret of the Space Souvenirs").

In September 1965, in conjunction with the festivities marking the celebration of Metropolis's Superman Day, Superman "uses his awesome strength like a pile-driver" to ram a Superman time capsule—marked Superman Time Capsule 1965—deep into the Earth, "down beside the many other capsules that mark his career...." Visible in a hollow deep underground are four other time capsules—labeled 1961, 1962, 1963, and 1964, respectively—suggesting that a new time-capsule record of Super-man's exploits is buried each year (Act No. 328: "Superman's Hands of Doom!").

Indeed, indications are that the memory of Superman's mighty deeds will live forever. During a brief sojourn in the world of 2957 A.D., Superman, Batman, and ROBIN are feted as great heroes by

worlds throughout the solar system (WF No. 91, Nov/Dec '57: "The Three Super-Sleepers!"). In the fiftieth century A.D., Superman will be acclaimed as "the greatest hero in Earth's history" (S No. 122/1, Jul '58: "The Secret of the Space Souvenirs"). Even in the world of 824,057 A.D.—more than 800,000 years in the future—lifelike androids of Superman's friends and adversaries, created by the people of the far-distant future, will still march in Metropolis's annual Superman Commemoration Parade "as immortal memorials of the greatest hero of this world" (Act No. 300, May '63: "Superman Under the Red Sun!").

Superman's most famous alternate identity is that of Clark Kent, but Superman has employed numerous aliases and alternate identities in the course of his career, including those of TOM DALY (Act No. 10, Mar '39), KENNETH CLARKSON (S No. 42/3, Sep/Oct '46: "The Death of Clark Kent!"), BUD MACK (S No. 77/2, Jul/Aug '52: "The Greatest Pitcher in the World!"), CHARLIE KENDALL (S No. 89/2, May '54: "Superman of Skid Row!"), MENTAL-MAN (Act No. 196, Sep '54: "The Adventures of Mental-Man!"), LIGHTNING-MAN (WF No. 89, Jul/Aug '57: "The Club of Heroes!"), KIRK BRENT (S No. 124/3, Sep '58: "The Steeplejack of Steel"), KENT CLARK (S No. 130/3, Jul '59: "The Town That Hated Superman!"), the ALCHEMIST (BM No.

Superman in flight over Metropolis, 1952

140/2, Jun '61: "The Charmed Life of Batman!"), TIGERMAN (WF No. 119, Aug '61: "The Secret of Tigerman!"), NIGHTWING (S No. 158, Jan '63: "Super-man in Kandor" pts. I-III—"Invasion of the Mystery Super-Men!"; "The Dynamic Duo of Kandor!"; "The City of Super-People!"; WF No. 143, Aug '64: "The Feud Between Batman and Superman!" pts. I-II—no title; "The Manhunters from Earth!"), JIM WHITE (S No. 165/2, Nov '63: "The Sweetheart Superman Forgot!"; S No. 169/2, May '64: "The Man Who Stole Superman's Secret Life!"), and BRAD DEXTER (Act No. 322, Mar '65: "The Coward of Steel!").

The cover of Action Comics No. 1, the first comic book in which Superman appeared

Interestingly, nearly a score of men have been perfect or near-perfect Superman look-alikes, including Miggs, a hoodlum in the employ of MR. KEELE (S No. 36/3, Sep/Oct '45: "Clark Kent, Star Reporter!"); an unidentified member of the Rockdust Bandits, a gang of criminals led by CATAWAMPUS JONES (WF No. 30, Sep/Oct '47: "Sheriff Clark Kent"); ironworker JOE POLESKI (S No. 67/3, Nov/Dec '50: "Clark Kent's Twin!"); reporter JACK WILDE (Act No. 171, Aug '52: "The Secrets of Superman!"); underworld assassin DASHER DRAPE (WF No. 63, Mar/Apr '53: "Clark Kent, Gangster"); naval pilot Guy Vandevier, the son of MR. AND MRS. JOHN VANDEVIER (Act No. 189, Feb '54: "Clark Kent's New Mother and Father!"); the Kryptonian villain MALA (Act No. 194, Jul '54: "The Outlaws from Krypton!"); the unidentified citizen of Metropolis, suffering from amnesia, whom Superman uses as a Clark Kent stand-in when, in August 1955, he is forced to attend an awards dinner simultaneously both as Clark Kent and as Superman (Act No. 207: "The Four Superman Medals!"); Mr. Cranston, a substitute teacher in the Metropolis school system (S No. 100/2, Sep '55: "Superman--Substitute Teacher"); Kell Orr, the son of ZOLL ORR (S No. 119, Feb '58: "The Second Superman!" chs. 1-3—"The World That Was Krypton's Twin"; "A Double for Superman"; "Superman's Mightiest Quest"); "average American" HARRY WINTERS (S No. 127/2, Feb '59: "The Make-Believe Superman!"); John Corben, alias METALLO (Act No. 252, May '59: "The Menace of Metallo!"); HYPER-MAN, a super-hero on the planet Oceania (Act No. 265, Jun '60: "The 'Superman' from Outer Space!"); VAN-ZEE, a "distant kinsman" of Superman's residing in Kandor (S No. 158, Jan '63: "Superman in Kandor" pts. I-III—"Invasion of the Mystery Super-Men!"; "The Dynamic Duo of Kandor!"; "The City of Super-People!"); the Superman look-alike, also named Superman, whom Batman encounters during a visit to an extradimensional parallel world in September 1963 (WF No. 136: "The Batman Nobody Remembered!"); MANUEL BAEZA, a citizen of the "tiny South American republic" of El Salmado (Act No. 306, Nov '63: "The Great Superman Impersonation!"); and VOL-DON, Clark Kent's double in the Kandorian LOOK-ALIKE SQUAD (S No. 177/1, May '65: "Superman's Kryptonese Curse!").

A number of individuals have transformed themselves into Superman look-alikes by means of plastic surgery, including gangster BLACKY BARTON (S No. 118/3, Jan '58: "The Death of Superman!"); the renegade Kandorian scientist ZAK-KUL (Act No. 245, Oct '58: "The Shrinking Superman!"); GYPO, a henchman of LEX LUTHOR (Act No. 271, Dec '60: "Voyage to Dimension X!"); and onetime Superman admirer NED BARNES (S No. 169/2, May '64: "The Man Who Stole Superman's Secret Life!").

SUPER-MENACE, "an unearthly force manifested into human form," is an exact double of Superman (S No. 137, May '60: chs. I-III—"The Super-Brat from Krypton"; "The Young Super-Bully"; "Superman vs. Super-Menace!"), and ADAM NEWMAN is an exact

double of Superman because he is actually a lifelike android created by Superman in his own image (S No. 174/1, Jan '65: pts. 1-2—"Clark Kent's Incredible Delusion!"; "The End of a Hero!").

BIZARRO is a "grotesque, imperfect double" of Superman (Act No. 263, Apr '60: "The World of Bizarros!"; and others), as are all the male inhabitants of the planet HTRAE (S No. 140, Oct '60: pts. I-III—"The Son of Bizarro!"; "The 'Orphan' Bizarro!"; "The Bizarro Supergirl!"; and others).

J. The Women of the Chronicles. The sudden, violent loss of his mother while he was still an infant, during a period of his life when his psyche was grappling with the complexity of his affectional and erotic feelings for her, has left Superman with a deep reservoir of unconscious hostility toward women. Like many orphaned children, he saw the death of his mother as a personal desertion. He loved and needed his mother, and yet she left him. The death of a loved one, particularly a parent, is always painful, but for the infant Superman the unconsciously perceived desertion was an unendurable agony.

The precise circumstances of this "desertion" were particularly traumatic: the rocket that carried the infant Superman safely away from the cataclysm that destroyed KRYPTON had room for two passengers. His father, JOR-EL, urged his wife LARA to climb aboard the rocket and escape to Earth with their infant son. But Lara, presented with the clear, conscious choice of either fleeing Krypton with Superman or remaining behind with Jor-El, literally chose to die with Jor-El rather than to live with Superman.

For Superman, it was a shattering rejection, one that continues to exert its influence over his entire emotional life. Unconsciously, Superman hates his mother for having abandoned him, and hates himself for having been unworthy of her lasting love.

The mortal anger engendered by this unconsciously perceived rejection finds socially acceptable expression in Superman's unrelenting war against villainy and injustice. Superman is a man of enormous aggressive instincts. He could have chosen to use this aggression destructively—in the pursuit of personal power and self-aggrandizement—or he could have turned his awesome power against himself. Instead, Superman chose to use his aggression heroically, to battle the forces of evil and oppression. In choosing to live his life as a hero, rather than as a murderer or power-made dictator, Superman has resolved his inner conflict constructively, but only at the cost of being unable to deal openly with his vulnerability, of being unable to share intimacy with another human being.

The persona of Clark Kent is Superman's unsuccessful attempt to resolve his need for intimacy and closeness. Only as Clark Kent is Superman truly human, even if Clark Kent's brand of humanity is really little more than a caricature consisting mainly of foibles.

It is simplistic to view Superman as a masochist unconsciously seeking out punishment in his role as

Clark Kent. Rather, Clark Kent represents Superman's inner view of himself as inadequate and undesirable (see section I, the man himself [as Superman]).

Because the inner Superman sees himself as Clark Kent rather than as the omnipotent hero idolized by the public, it is as Clark Kent that Superman yearns to be loved. That is why Superman pursues LOIS LANE as Clark Kent and remains cool toward her as Superman. Superman desperately wants Lois Lane to fall in love with Clark Kent, because, unconsciously, he feels that Clark Kent is the real Superman.

Of course, the catch is that, despite his achievements as a journalist, Clark Kent is cowardly and undesirable. Inevitably, Lois Lane rejects him in favor of the far more glamorous Superman. Since Superman created the Clark Kent persona, he must bear the responsibility, albeit on an unconscious level, for the qualities of personality that Clark Kent exhibits. Since Superman created the personality that Lois Lane continually rejects, Superman also bears the responsibility for these rejections. Indeed, Superman courts the rejections, for this neurotic drama of courtship and inevitable rejection is, for Superman, a reenactment of his childhood rejection by his mother. At the same time, Superman has the "last laugh" on Lois, for he knows that Clark Kent is secretly Superman. By having the last laugh on Lois, Superman expresses his contempt for her, and, by extension, his contempt toward his mother for having rejected him.

As an infant in the throes of the Oedipal conflict, Superman wished his father dead so that he could possess his mother. And then the first part of the forbidden fantasy came true: the planet Krypton exploded into stardust, and his father perished along with virtually the entire population.

The actual fulfillment of his murderous infantile wish has left Superman with an abiding legacy of deep-seated guilt, with the unconscious conviction that his deepest yearnings are evil and awesomely destructive. The persona of Clark Kent is Superman's way of denying his power, of protecting the universe against himself.

If, deep within his psyche, a man believes that his wishes are capable of destroying those he loves, he will, unconsciously, take steps to see to it that no one falls in love with him. By pursuing Lois Lane as Clark Kent—and not as Superman—Superman assures himself of being rejected while at the same time protecting Lois from the evil, destructive creature he knows he really is. Superman's most persistent rationalization for his unwillingness to become emotionally involved with women is his fear that they will become the targets of gangland retribution. Because this fear is not entirely without its rational basis, it serves to validate Superman's internal conviction that his love is destructive and thus to reinforce his neurotic determination not to allow himself to become vulnerable to a woman.

Superman's world is a world from which women have been all but excluded, one in which meaningful relationships with them are all but impossible. To protect himself from the joys and pains of adult romantic involvement, Superman has erected a wall of rationalizations designed to make it impossible for him to experience emotional involvement.

Superman frequently bemoans the fact that he cannot marry because his wife would become the target of underworld reprisals (S No. 129/3, May '59: "The Girl in Superman's Past!"; and many others), yet his long-lived—and extraordinarily complex—relationship with Lois Lane has as one of its central elements the fact that he must continually rescue her from the jaws of death.

Sometimes, Superman pleads duty to mankind as his excuse for avoiding involvement, arguing that "...I can't consider marriage while I have my duties to perform on Earth!" (S No. 136/1, Apr '60: "The Man Who Married Lois Lane!"; and others). Yet on those occasions when Superman could feel subconsciously secure that his relationship of the moment—e.g., his relationship with LORI LEMARIS—would not survive, he has expressed the willingness to abandon his super-heroic career in favor of matrimony (S No. 129/3, May '59: "The Girl in Superman's Past!"; and others).

For both Clark Kent and Superman, women are a source of anxiety, confusion, hostility, and bewilderment. "Females are a puzzle," muses Clark Kent in January 1940 (Act No. 20). In July-August 1943, when Kent is forced to attend a fashion show featuring lovely models in revealing evening gowns, he becomes noticeably embarrassed and ill at ease (S No. 23/3: "Fashions in Crime!").

"Women!" exclaims Clark Kent bewilderedly in September-October 1945. "No man can figure them out...not even a Superman!" (S No. 36/3: "Clark Kent, Star Reporter!"). Clark Kent repeats this sentiment in March-April 1947. "Whew!" he muses. "Whoever understands a woman is a better man than Superman!" (S No. 45/1: "Lois Lane, Superwoman!").

Occasionally, however, despite his bewilderment and discomfort, Superman allows himself a flash of poignant near-insight. "How ironic!" muses the Man of Steel sadly in May 1964, after he has fled his romantic involvement with lovely SALLY SELWYN. "Mighty Superman can help everyone...but when it comes to my own happiness--I can't help--myself!" (S No. 169/2: "The Man Who Stole Superman's Secret Life!").

Five women play important roles in the Superman chronicles during the first three decades of Superman's career. The following pages are devoted to an examination of Superman's relationships with these women, both in his role as Clark Kent and in his role as Superman.

1. The Relationship with Lois Lane. Superman and LOIS LANE first make one another's acquaintance in June 1938 (Act No. 1) and embark on a neurotic, unfulfilling relationship that has already endured for four full decades.

Almost from the moment of their first encounter,

Lois Lane's first encounter with Superman, 1938

Lois Lane is in love with Superman. She refers to him as her "dream-lover" (Act No. 7, Dec '38), "the only man I'll ever love" (S No. 14/4, Jan/Feb '42), "my dream man" (Act No. 72, May '44: "Superman and the Super-Movers!"), "the world's *only* ideal man" (S No. 55/1, Nov/Dec '48: "Prankster's Second Childhood"), "the handsomest man on Earth" (S No. 67/2, Nov/Dec '50: "The City Under the Sea!"), "the **only** man I could ever love" (Act No. 254, Jul '59: "The Battle with Bizarro!"), "the good, gentle, gallant man I love" (S No. 134, Jan '60: chs. I-III—"The Super-Menace of Metropolis!"; "The Revenge Against Jor-El!"; "The Duel of the Supermen!"), "the man I love" (S No. 153/3, May '62: "The Town of Supermen!"), "the smartest, handsomest, strongest man in the

universe" (S No. 176/3, Apr '65: "Superman's Day of Truth!"), and "the only man I ever loved" (S No. 177/2, May '65: "The Menace Called 'It'!"). In the words of Superman No. 61/2, "Everyone knows that the one love of Lois Lane's life is...**Superman!**" (Nov/Dec '49: "The Courtship of the Three Lois Lanes!").

For decades, Lois Lane's foremost ambition has been to become the wife of Superman (S No. 46/2, May/Jun '47: "High Man on a Flagpole!"; and many others).

"Each morning as reporter Lois Lane of the Metropolis Daily Planet awakens," notes Action Comics No. 149, "she recites the same greeting and the same wish to a *picture* [of Superman] *on the wall!*" "Good morning, **Superman**..." sighs Lois hopefully, "...perhaps, someday, instead of just greeting your photograph, my dream will come true and I'll really be **married** to you..." (Oct '50: "The Courtship on Krypton!").

"Lois has always dreamed that **Superman** would one day marry her...!" notes Superman No. 121/1 (May '58: "The Bride of Futureman!").

"For years," adds Action Comics No. 260, "the girl reporter has had her heart set upon becoming **Mrs. Superman!**" (Jan '60: "Mighty Maid!").

"What would [Lois Lane] want to see **most** in her future?" asks Superman No. 131/2. "Becoming the wife of **Superman**, of course!" (Aug '59: "Superman's Future Wife!").

And in the words of Superman No. 136/1, "For years, Lois has hoped to become **Superman's** bride...!" (Apr '60: "The Man Who Married Lois Lane!").

"Oh, how I wish he'd fall in love with me--and ask me to marry him!" sighs Lois Lane forlornly in July

Covering miles in mighty leaps—because at this early stage of his career he cannot fly—Superman returns Lois Lane to the city's outskirts following their initial encounter. But Lois's editor refuses even to believe that the Man of Steel exists, 1938

*After rescuing Lois Lane from a firing squad in 1938,
Superman refuses to satisfy her curiosity concerning his
origins...*

...or even to tell her when she will see him again

1955. "I know it's too much to wish for, but it would be
wonderful to be the wife of **Superman**..." (Act No.
206: "Superman Marries Lois Lane!").

Never has a woman pursued a man as relentlessly
as Lois Lane has pursued Superman. In the words of
Superman No. 76/3:

> No female in the history of the world--from Helen of
> Troy or Cleopatra right up to the No. 1 glamor girl of the
> 20th century--ever pursued any man as determinedly as
> Lois Lane chases Superman! **Every year is Leap Year**
> as far as Lois' pursuit of Superman is concerned!
> [May/Jun '52: "Mrs. Superman!"].

In an effort to lure Superman into matrimony, Lois
Lane has tried virtually every ploy imaginable, from
dyeing her hair to alter her appearance (S No. 61/2,
Nov/Dec '49: "The Courtship of the Three Lois
Lanes!"), to feigning interest in other men (S No.
55/2, Nov/Dec '48: "The Richest Man in the World!";
and others), to contriving elaborate scenarios calculated to enable her to impress Superman with her
skills as a wife and homemaker (Act No. 149, Oct '50:
"The Courtship on Krypton!"; and others).

All Lois's stratagems, however, have ended in
failure. Although Superman does display a certain
amount of sexual interest in Lois Lane in the very
early texts (Act No. 5, Oct '38; and others), he
invariably frustrates her either by fleeing the scene
as she attempts to express her love for him or by
dampening her ardor with a show of apparent
indifference (S No. 5/2, Sum '40; and others).
Moreover, Superman's early alternating displays of
sexual interest and disinterest are soon replaced by
an attitude of friendly concern of the type a man
might express for a girl much younger than himself or
for the wife of a close friend (Act No. 129, Feb '49:
"Lois Lane, Cavegirl!"; and many others).

Whatever his behavior toward Lois Lane, however, the texts make it abundantly clear that
Superman does love her. He is jealous of her
occasional involvements with other men (Act No. 61,
Jun '43: "The Man They Wouldn't Believe!"; and
others) and heartbroken when she actually marries
one of them (S No. 136/1, Apr '60: "The Man Who
Married Lois Lane!"). He has gone to great lengths to
protect her from being maneuvered into marriages
she does not want (S No. 51/1, Mar/Apr '48: "Mr.
Mxyztplk Seeks a Wife!"; and others). World's Finest
Comics No. 36 describes Lois Lane as "the one person
for whom [Superman] cares most" (Sep/Oct '48: "Lois
Lane, Sleeping Beauty").

As Jimmy Olsen looks on from the cockpit of the Daily
Planet's *Flying Newsroom helicopter, Lois Lane expresses
her long-held desire to become Superman's wife. But a cool
rebuff is the Man of Steel's only response, 1958*

"Why couldn't I have led a normal life and--(choke) married her!" pines Superman in May 1959, after Lois Lane has apparently perished in an accidental explosion. "Yes--if things had been different, she'd have been my--wife!" (S No. 129/1: "The Ghost of Lois Lane").

Yet because Superman refuses to respond to her in a normal, healthy fashion, Lois Lane finds her love for Superman constantly frustrated. And so, like a girl at the beach who finds that the only way she can arouse the attention of the handsome lifeguard is by swimming out into deep water and pretending to be drowning, Lois Lane recklessly plunges into danger as her only means of getting Superman to display an interest in her. "The greatest joy in my life occurs

Lois Lane is well aware that Superman welcomes the opportunity to rescue her. "**Superman**--stop pretending!" she scolds in May-June 1951. "You know you like protecting me...!" (S No. 70/1: "Lois Lane Meets Annie Oakley!"). What is more, Lois has correctly perceived, despite Superman's feigned indifference, that the Man of Steel harbors a strong affection for her.

"You're a strange fellow--outside of your super-strength, I mean," she remarks in September-October 1940. "You continually act as tho [sic] I don't mean a thing to you, and yet you always manage to show up and help me when I get into difficulties!"

"I'd do the same for anyone in trouble!" replies Superman.

Lois Lane thinks she has exacted a pledge of matrimony from Superman, but Superman, ever wary of emotional involvement, wriggles free, 1959

whenever you enter into it!" exclaims Lois to Superman in March-April 1943. "Why don't you do so more often?"

"I'll take the matter under consideration!" replies Superman. "Now try and stay out of mischief--and don't go around picking arguments with desperate characters...."

"Why not," replies Lois Lane, "--if it gives me a chance to encounter you!?" (S No. 21/2: "The Four Gangleaders").

Indeed, although Superman frequently complains at being forced to keep a constant eye on Lois (WF No. 42, Sep/Oct '49: "The Alphabetical Animal Adventure!"; and many others), the evidence is overwhelming that he loves every minute of it, for rescuing Lois Lane from danger enables Superman to be near Lois—and to express concern for her—without becoming involved with her in a committed relationship. "Twenty to one Lois is in a tough jam right now!" thinks Superman to himself in August 1940. "That gal's a natural for getting involved in mischief--but that's just what I like about her!" (Act No. 27).

"But sometimes," continues Lois, "I seem to sense that you care for me more than you want me to believe!"

"There is no time for talk of that sort!" retorts Superman, cutting short the conversation (S No. 6/1).

In Summer 1943 Lois Lane makes a similar remark. "Sometimes, **Superman**," she observes, "I come to the conclusion that you care for me very much."

"Isn't there an old saying--'Don't leap to conclusions,'" replies Superman (WF No. 10: "The Insect Terror!").

Because Superman harbors a great deal of unconscious hostility toward women, he often expresses hostility toward Lois Lane through other means than outright rejection. Lois Lane is in love with Superman, and therefore extremely jealous of his attentions to other women (Act No. 130, Mar '49: "Superman and the Mermaid!"; and many others), yet despite Lois's jealousy Superman often devises elaborate ruses—for the ostensible purpose of apprehending criminals—in which he causes Lois anguish

Under the baleful sway of Mr. Mxyzptlk's "5th dimensional hypnotism,"
Superman becomes temporarily transformed into a "super-heel," proposing to
Lois Lane and then, seconds later, laughing cruelly in her face, 1960

and heartache by pretending to have fallen in love with another woman (S No. 120/1, Mar '58: "The Day That Superman Married"; and many others). Since Superman, with all his mighty super-powers, could presumably devise other means for achieving his stated objectives, these ruses which so upset Lois can only be viewed as unconscious attempts to hurt her.

On other occasions, usually in the name of teaching Lois Lane some sort of lesson in character, Superman works behind the scenes to maneuver Lois toward marriage to some horribly unattractive individual. Only at the last minute, after Lois has been forced to suffer the anguish of an impending marriage to a man she does not want, does Superman intervene to undo the complex situation and extricate Lois from her agonizing predicament (S No. 54/3, Sep/Oct '48: "Her Majesty Lois Lane!"; and others).

Lois, for her part, seethes with unconscious resentment toward Superman for titillating and then rejecting her and for trifling with her feelings. She expresses this resentment in many ways. On one occasion, Lois fakes her own death in an explosion, telling herself that she is doing Superman a favor by ensuring that the underworld will no longer be able to use her as a hostage against him. Lois's underlying motive, however, is clearly to lash out at Superman by making him feel anguished and guilt-ridden by her "death" (WF No. 64, May/Jun '53: "The Death of Lois Lane"). On another occasion, after Superman has been temporarily transformed into an infant with the mind of an adult, Lois deliberately tries to humiliate him in public in an effort to wreak what she herself candidly refers to as her "revenge on **Superman**" for his past treatment of her (S No. 66/1, Sep/Oct '50: "The Babe of Steel!").

On more than one occasion, Lois has gone so far as

to accept marriage proposals from men she did not love purely for the purpose of spiting Superman (S No. 121/1, May '58: "The Bride of Futureman!"; S No. 136/1, Apr '60: "The Man Who Married Lois Lane!").

"Why shouldn't I accept this gorgeous hunk of man as a husband?" muses Lois Lane bitterly as she contemplates a proposal of marriage from X-PLAM— a proposal she ultimately accepts—in April 1960.

As a stunned Lana Lang eavesdrops on their hospital-room conversation, Superman proposes to Lois Lane in an "imaginary tale," 1965

"I've passed up too many chances to marry because of my love for **Superman**! I've turned down every proposal of marriage, hoping **Superman** would marry me some day! Once and for all, I'll show **Superman** I won't die of a bleeding heart because he never returned my love!" (S No. 136/1: "The Man Who Married Lois Lane!").

Lois Lane's relationship with Clark Kent is also fraught with hostility. Both Clark Kent and Lois are reporters for the same METROPOLIS newspaper, and their reportorial rivalry is a keen one. Lois, in particular, is fiercely, even unscrupulously competitive, resorting to such tactics as intercepting Kent's telephone messages (S No. 14/4, Jan/Feb '42; and others), sending him off on wild-goose chases (Act No. 5, Oct '38; and others), and even seducing him into letting her accompany him on an interview and then slipping knockout drops in his drink so that she can cover the story alone (Act No. 6, Nov '38).

In the largest sense, however, the Lane-Kent reportorial rivalry is a sham, for the headline stories for which they compete so assiduously are invariably stories about Superman, and the outcome of the contest to determine which of them can publish a particular story first is just as invariably determined by whether Superman decides to give Lois Lane an exclusive account or to write it up himself as reporter Clark Kent.

Indeed, even in the journalistic arena, Superman makes a fool of Lois and thereby expresses his contempt for her. Typically, the pattern of reportorial

Superman and Lois Lane remain as far removed from true emotional involvement today as they have ever been...

...but in the 1970s, surface intimacy is portrayed more frequently than in the texts of previous decades

rivalry is as follows: (a) when the action begins, Clark Kent feigns cowardice, thereby arousing Lois Lane's scorn and disgust, so that he can slip away and change to Superman; (b) with Kent having fled the scene, Lois remains in the thick of the action, risking her life to get the big story, invariably committing some recklessly daring act which makes it necessary for Superman to come to her rescue; and (c) returning to the DAILY PLANET with her exclusive, first-hand view of the headline-making events, she finds, to her astonishment and chagrin, that Kent has somehow managed to beat her into print with the story. Lois usually tries to minimize Kent's victory by attributing it to dumb luck or outside help from Superman. Kent, however, does not hesitate to rub salt in Lois's wound. "When you get to be as good a reporter as I am, Lois," he remarks in Winter 1943, "maybe you'll develop a nose for news, too!" (WF No. 12: "The Man Who Stole a Reputation!"; and others).

In addition to their professional relationship, Clark Kent and Lois Lane share a personal relationship, for although Superman rejects Lois Lane as Superman, he pursues her slavishly in his role as Clark Kent.

Clark Kent has dated Lois Lane for four full decades (Act No. 1, Jun '38; and many others). He is gleeful when she consents to go out with him (Act No. 27, Aug '40; and others), forlorn and dejected when she turns him down (S No. 3/4, Win '40; and others). On half a dozen occasions, he has hinted at his desire to marry her (S No. 27/4, Mar/Apr '44: "Dear Diary!"; and others) or proposed outright (S No. 123, Aug '58: chs. 1-3—"The Girl of Steel"; "The Lost Super-Powers"; "Superman's Return to Krypton"; and others), but Lois has always rejected his proposals.

Consciously, Superman tells himself that he would like to win Lois in his Clark Kent identity so that he could feel confident she truly loved him for himself, and not for his fame and super-powers. But Lois Lane is plainly bedazzled by Superman's fame and powers. In March 1961, for example, when one of Superman's Superman-robots (see SUPERMAN ROBOT Z), acting entirely on its own volition, impersonates Superman and, after feigning the loss of its super-powers, asks Lois to marry him, Lois becomes exultant at first, then hesitant. "At last!" she thinks to herself. "**Superman** is proposing marriage! This is what I've wanted to hear for years, and years.... Wait! I...I mustn't accept so quickly! Will I **remain** in love with a **Superman** who has **no** mighty powers? I...I don't know...!" Indeed, Lois asks for time to consider the proposal and ultimately turns "Superman" down (Act No. 274: "The Reversed Super-Powers!").

In his contemplative moments, Clark Kent realizes that Lois Lane loves Superman not for his personal qualities, but for the aura of glamor that surrounds his super-heroic feats.

"...I'm always afraid girls don't love me for myself--are merely dazzled by my fame and super-powers," he muses silently in November 1963. "I wonder how it would feel to be really loved for--myself??! I guess...I'll never know....'It would be nice if there were such a girl! No such luck!" (S No. 165/2: "The Sweetheart Superman Forgot!").

Indeed, by selecting, as the foremost object of his affections, a woman dazzled by his fame and blind to his personal qualities, Superman serves to confirm his worst suspicions about women and to fuel his unconscious hatred of them. In point of fact, however, Superman's real reasons for pursuing Lois Lane as

Clark Kent have nothing to do with his conscious desire to find a mate who will love him for himself. This is amply demonstrated by at least two texts in which Lois, in a rare change of mood, pursues Clark Kent with matrimony in mind, only to have Kent devise new excuses for rejecting her (S No. 58/2, May/Jun '49: "Lois Lane Loves Clark Kent!"; Act No. 176, Jan '53: "Muscles for Money").

The real reasons why Superman pursues Lois Lane so assiduously as Clark Kent are inextricably bound up with Superman's unconscious desire for rejection, for Lois Lane's repeated rejections of Kent serve to confirm his inner feelings of worthlessness and self-loathing; to "protect" Lois from what Superman unconsciously perceives as his evil, destructive desire for her; to insulate him against the

Clark Kent asks Lois Lane for a date, 1938

agonies of mature emotional involvement; and to re-create the traumatic feelings of desertion and abandonment caused by his mother's "rejection" of him at the time of Krypton's destruction.

By making Clark Kent as unattractive as possible, Superman ensures that Lois Lane will always reject him. Over and above the need to appear timid in order to protect the secret of his dual identity, Kent literally searches for opportunities to "convince Lois [he's] yellow clear thru [sic]" (S No. 12/3, Sep/Oct '41) and to "sabotage Clark Kent in Lois' estimation" (S No. 17/3, Jul/Aug '42: "Muscles for Sale!"). Invariably, this behavior arouses the disdain and contempt of the very woman Kent claims he is trying to attract.

To make matters worse, Superman openly disparages Clark Kent in the early texts, contemptuously referring to him as Lois Lane's "weak-kneed boyfriend" (S No. 12/4, Sep/Oct '41) and otherwise heaping abuse upon him.

"Good heavens," exclaims Lois to Superman in

On his first date with Lois Lane, Clark Kent takes her dancing. But Kent's cowardly demeanor sickens Lois, and she stalks angrily off the dance floor, scornfully denouncing him as "a spineless, unbearable coward," 1938

July 1940, "--I just remembered--Clark [is] back there, at the mercy of those dangerous men--you've got to save him, too!"

"I don't think that cowardly weakling is worth saving," replies Superman, "but I'll do it for you!" (Act No. 26).

Is it any wonder, then, that Lois is forever making unfavorable comparisons between Clark Kent and Superman?

"I like you, Clark," admits Lois in May 1943, "but how could I really care for a man like you when I've associated with someone as confident, outspoken, and assertive as SUPERMAN! I'll care for you when you're like SUPERMAN...which will be NEVER!" (Act No. 60: "Lois Lane--Superwoman!").

In August 1946 Lois kisses Clark Kent gently on the cheek in gratitude for his having agreed to let her take full credit for an important news story they worked on together. "I'm the happiest man in the world!" beams Kent. "...You must like me a lot to—"

"The least little bit, maybe," interrupts Lois, "...but how could I ever admire you, with Superman to compare you with?" (Act No. 99: "The Talisman of Trouble!").

A similar exchange follows Clark Kent's capture of CATAWAMPUS JONES in September-October 1947. "I must admit that—that I'm proud of you!" remarks Lois.

"Do you really mean it, Lois?" asks Clark Kent happily.

"Of course, there's no comparison with Superman!" adds Lois (WF No. 30: "Sheriff Clark Kent").

"Clark Kent, you're the original timid soul!" remarks Lois in September-October 1949. "No wonder I prefer Superman!" (S No. 60/2: "The Men Who Had to Guard Superman!").

In August 1958, after Clark Kent has asked her to marry him, Lois Lane makes this reply: "It's sweet of you, Clark...but I could only marry you if you were really Superman!" (S No. 123: chs. 1-3—"The Girl of Steel"; "The Lost Super-Powers"; "Superman's Return to Krypton").

Although he persists, nevertheless, in his hopeless efforts to win Lois Lane away from his super-heroic alter ego, Clark Kent is fully aware that he cannot possibly succeed. Indeed, Clark Kent persists in his efforts only because he knows he is doomed to fail. "...I guess until you can forget Superman," he remarks to Lois in July-August 1944, "I don't stand a chance!" (S No. 29/3: "The Pride of the Kents!").

"Isn't he magnificent?" exclaims Lois Lane, referring to Superman, in January-February 1948.

"What chance is there for a plain fellow like me?" asks Clark Kent dejectedly (S No. 50/2: "The Slogans That Came Too True!").

In July-August 1951 Lois Lane meets Clark Kent for a date and asks, "Did you see Superman today, Clark? Did you talk to him?"

"There you go, raving about Superman again!" complains Kent. "How about devoting a little attention to me?"

"Clark, you're a nice fellow," replies Lois, "but there's nothing super about you!"

"The same old trouble!" muses Kent sadly. "She's so smitten by my Superman identity that she can't see me as Clark Kent!" (S No. 71/2: "The Anti-Superman Club!").

Particularly in the early texts, Lois despises Clark Kent and is openly contemptuous of him, referring to him as a "spineless, unbearable coward" (Act No. 1, Jun '38), a "worm" (S No. 3/4, Win '40), and a "weak-kneed pantywaist" (S No. 8/3, Jan/Feb '41). Over the years, Lois's open contempt for Kent has mellowed into a genuine fondness for him, but Lois continues to despise Clark Kent for his cowardice (S No. 16/1, May/Jun '42: "The World's Meanest Man"; and many others), openly referring to him as a "spineless jellyfish" as late as March 1965 (Act No. 322: "The Coward of Steel!").

Through all the indignities, however, Clark Kent continues to pursue Lois slavishly. "How about having lunch with me today, Lois?" he asks hopefully in Winter 1940.

"Sorry," replies Lois, "—not interested!"

"Aw, come on!" pleads Kent. "--I'm not poison ivy!"

Following the incident at the nightclub, Clark Kent begs Lois Lane to forgive him, but "Lois treats Clark colder than ever," 1938

"For once and all," says Lois scornfully, "will you please let it register in that thick dome of yours that I dislike you heartily! Understand?" (S No. 3/1).

Although Clark Kent rationalizes his need to play the coward on the ground that it helps him protect his secret identity, there is no way of easily rationalizing his openly stated desire to fool Lois into believing that she has him wrapped around her little finger. In November 1938, for example, after learning that Kent is scheduled to interview Superman, Lois seduces

Kent into making a date with her as the first step in her scheme to pirate Kent's interview.

"I'll be waiting for you tonight!" she calls out brightly after the arrangements have been made.

"I'll be there!" replies Kent happily.

"—How easily I can twist you around my finger!—" thinks Lois to herself.

"—How easy you are to convince that I'm putty in your hands!—" thinks Kent almost simultaneously (Act No. 6).

Kent's desire to make Lois Lane believe that he is "putty in [her] hands" can only be explained in terms of his anger toward her. Kent hates Lois for continually rejecting him, for being infatuated with the fame and glamor of his super-heroic alter ego, for being indifferent to the needs of the flesh-and-blood human being whose heart beats beneath the flashy red-and-blue costume. Both as Clark Kent and as Superman, he expresses this hatred in many ways: by rejecting Lois as Superman, by scooping her as Clark Kent, by deceiving her as to his true identity, by making her believe that he slavishly adores her while, in actuality, he laughs behind her back.

The mutual contempt at play in the Kent-Lane relationship is well illustrated by an exchange that takes place in February 1939, shortly after Kent has put on a display of cowardice when confronted by an angry police detective at a press conference.

"Don't forget, Lois," remarks Kent, following the press conference, "—you--er--promised me I could take you to a movie tonight."

"Clark Kent," fumes Lois, "--I DESPISE YOU!"

"WHAT!" exclaims Kent, taken aback. "—But—but you've been so friendly lately, I—uh—was beginning to hope--"

"I absolutely loathe you!" cries Lois. "You contemptible weakling! —Don't you dare even to talk to me any more!"

"You don't fool me!" accuses Kent. "It's someone else!—Tell me, Lois! Who is this person whom you love!"

"Don't be silly!" denies Lois. "Why--!"

"Don't lie!" interrupts Kent. "I've watched you when you've thought you were alone. A tender faraway look creeps into your eyes. You're thinking of HIM!"

"Peeping and snooping, eh?" accuses Lois scornfully. "I might have expected it of you! Yes! There is someone!"

"WHO?" demands Kent.

"He's grand! He's glorious! He's terrific!" replies Lois triumphantly. "—He's everything you're not! Brave, bold, handsome--superb!"

"Who is he?" demands Kent again.

"SUPERMAN!" shrieks Lois at the top of her lungs.

"S-SUPERMAN?" echoes Kent, seemingly stunned by this crushing news.

"Yes," replies Lois tartly. "—Now go away and don't bother me!"

"Dazed—bewildered—crushed," notes the textual narrative, "—Kent walks slowly off."

"Maybe I was too harsh with him," thinks Lois to herself. "But I can't help it. He sickens me!"

Kent, meanwhile, shuffles sadly toward an empty office, walks inside, and shuts the door behind him. "But once the door is shut behind him," notes the narrative text, "an amazing thing occurs—his woeful expression disappears! He clutches his sides and doubles! Then shrieks with--LAUGHTER!" For Clark Kent knows that he has made a fool of Lois. Clark Kent knows that he is secretly Superman (Act No. 9).

Although the basic dynamic of the Kent-Lane relationship has remained unchanged since 1939, Lois Lane's feelings for Clark Kent have, in the intervening years, mellowed considerably. By the early 1940s she has grown genuinely fond of him, and

Clark Kent asks Lois Lane for a lunch date, but Lois turns him down cold, 1939

on a number of occasions, when it appears he has perished, she is genuinely grief-stricken. On one such occasion, she recalls him as having been a fine person, kind and generous (S No. 20/1, Jan/Feb '43: "Superman's Secret Revealed!"), and on another she describes him as "the grandest person I've ever known," next to Superman (S No. 24/4, Sep/Oct '43: "Suicide Voyage!").

When Clark Kent is fired from the *Daily Planet* in November-December 1947, it is Lois Lane who helps him regain his job (S No. 49/2: "Clark Kent's Most Dangerous Assignment!"). In a dream she has in July 1955, Lois thinks of Superman and Clark Kent as her "two favorite men" (Act No. 206: "Superman Marries Lois Lane!").

Lois Lane is well aware that she often treats Clark Kent shabbily, and every now and then she shows pangs of remorse. "G-Goodbye, Clark," she sobs in March-April 1948, when she thinks she and Kent are about to die at the hands of the villainous MR. OHM. "I-I'm s-sorry I've ever been mean to you!" (S No. 51/2: "The Magnetic Mobster!").

Typically, however, Lois's attitude toward Clark Kent's feelings is somewhat more cavalier. "Clark's nice...! I should treat him better!" she confides to PEGGY WILKINS in July-August 1950. "But how can I--when I'm in love with **Superman?** (sigh!!) **Superman's really super!**" (S No. 65/2: "Superman's Sweetheart!").

Despite her romantic interest in Superman and her lack of interest in Clark Kent, however, Lois Lane is extremely possessive of Clark Kent and spitefully jealous of any other woman who shows an interest in him (Act No. 94, Mar '46: "Battle of the Redwoods!"; and many others).

In November-December 1950, for example, during a visit to the subsea realm of ATLANTIS, Lois becomes visibly jealous over Clark Kent's involvement with lovely QUEEN PARALEA, and visibly relieved when the queen's plans to marry Kent are abruptly cancelled (S No. 67/2: "The City Under the Sea!").

Lois Lane's jealousy is even more nakedly expressed in May-June 1953, when Clark Kent falls under the admiring eye of lovely WAC sergeant Gloria Mulvaney. In an effort to keep Kent away from the sergeant, whom Kent has met while researching a newspaper article on the WACs, Lois persuades *Daily Planet* editor Perry White to remove Kent from the story so that she can cover it herself. "Even if Clark isn't the man of my dreams," huffs Lois, "I don't want to see him fall into the clutches of that blonde vampire!"

A short while later, however, from the vantage point of an airborne weather balloon, Lois spies the WAC sergeant once again flirting with Kent. "Ohhh!" fumes Lois angrily. "Sergeant Mulvaney...[is] trying to steal Clark Kent away from me! If I had that blonde vampire here now, I'd-I'd tear her eyes out!" (S No. 82/1: "Lois Lane Joins the WACS!").

The question arises: if Lois Lane is infatuated with Superman and indifferent to Clark Kent, why does it

Alone in her automobile, Lois Lane reflects on her feelings for Clark Kent and Superman, 1952

upset her to see Kent involved with another woman? The answer is that, subconsciously, Lois Lane knows that Kent is Superman and that to lose the mild-mannered reporter to another woman is also to lose the Man of Steel.

Ever since the early 1940s, Lois has struggled to learn the secret of Superman's identity (*see* section B, the secret identity). Indeed, Lois Lane's efforts to learn Superman's secret, and Superman's constant efforts to protect it, are yet another way in which hostility is expressed in the Superman-Lois Lane relationship.

Superman's secret identity is vital to the continuation of his super-heroic career, yet Lois Lane seeks not only to unravel that secret, but to proclaim it to the world (S No. 75/3, Mar/Apr '52: "The Man Who Stole Memories!"; and others). Even if she were to agree to withhold the secret from publication to avoid damaging Superman's career (S No. 78/3, Sep/Oct '52: "The Girls in Superman's Life!"; and others), the indications are that her unconscious desire to reveal the secret is so overpowering that she would be psychologically incapable of remaining silent (Act No. 198, Nov '54: "The Six Lives of Lois Lane!"; S No. 145/1, May '61: "The Secret Identity of Superman!").

By revealing Superman's secret and thereby bringing an end to his career as a super-hero, Lois Lane would be removing the sole obstacle to a permanent relationship between them, i.e., Superman's need to remain unencumbered so that he can continue to battle injustice as Superman. But the removal of this obstacle would be at the cost of bringing an end to the heroic Superman side of Superman's dual life. Ironically, Lois would be winning Superman only by "destroying" him. Her prize would not be the omnipotent Superman of her fantasies, but the inadequate Clark Kent whom she continually scorns. Seen in this light, Lois Lane's attempts to ferret out Superman's secret represent a destructive attempt by Lois to lash out at Superman for rebuffing her by bringing an end to his super-heroic career.

Despite Lois Lane's persistent efforts to learn his secret, however, Superman continually outwits her, often through the use of elaborate ruses. By thwarting her attempts to unravel his secret while associating with her on a daily basis as reporter Clark Kent, Superman expresses his contempt for her. And, surely, in his heart of hearts, Superman must harbor the very thought that millions of his readers have had for decades: what an idiot Lois Lane must be if she cannot even recognize the man of her dreams when he merely exchanges his costume for a business suit and a pair of eyeglasses!

In fact, however, although Superman has always managed to persuade Lois Lane that her suspicions concerning his secret identity were groundless, or at the very least not conclusively proven, there is ample support for the view that, despite all of Superman's ingenious ruses, Lois Lane is aware, at least subconsciously, that Clark Kent and Superman are one and the same man. In February-March 1950, for example, Lois Lane has a dream in which Clark Kent is revealed as Superman (WF No. 44: "The Revolt of the Thought Machine!"), suggesting an inner awareness of Superman's secret.

On a number of occasions, Lois has stumbled on virtually irrefutable proof that Clark Kent is Superman, only to allow herself to be led astray—even to the point of denying the evidence of her own senses—by a transparent ruse or flimsy explanation. On several occasions, Superman has deliberately revealed his identity to Lois for one reason or another, only to attempt to back away from his revelation later with the aid of some wholly unconvincing excuse. In October 1962, during a period when Superman is believed to be dying of an incurable malady, Lois becomes convinced that Clark Kent is secretly Superman, but she later gallantly offers to "forget" her suspicions—as if that would be possible for *any* human being—as her way of expressing her happiness at learning that Superman is not going to die after all (S No. 156: "The Last Days of Superman!" pts. I-III—"Superman's Death Sentence!"; "The Super-Comrades of All Time!"; "Superman's Last Day of Life!"). (*See also* section B, the secret identity.)

It is her subconscious awareness that Clark Kent is secretly Superman that accounts for the jealousy Lois Lane feels toward the various other women who, from time to time, enter Clark Kent's life.

All in all, Superman's relationship with Lois Lane is an exercise in frustration for both parties. Its gratifications are neurotic and almost wholly unconscious. The relationship denies Lois Lane the married life she claims to seek, while denying Superman the joys of ordinary life that he claims to envy. "If only I could be married some day," muses Clark Kent poignantly in October 1964. "What a thrill it would be to fly my bride across the threshold into my Fortress of Solitude! Our own home... quiet evenings togeth-er... maybe a super-baby to increase our joy... but it's all impossible!" (Act No. 317: "Superman's Rainbow Face!").

2. *The Relationship with Lana Lang.* Lovely red-haired LANA LANG, a newscaster for METROPOLIS television station WMET-TV (LL No. 68, Sep/Oct '66; and others), is really little more than a psychological carbon copy of LOIS LANE. Although, as an adult, she appears sporadically in the chronicles as one of Superman's "best friends" (S No. 156, Oct '62: "The Last Days of Superman!"; pts. I-III—"Superman's Death Sentence!"; "The Super-Comrades of All Time!"; "Superman's Last Day of Life!") and as Lois Lane's "arch-rival" for his affections (Act No. 279, Aug '61: "The Super-Rivals!"; and others), Lana Lang's principal relationship with Superman occurred during their teen-age years, when, as a member of Clark Kent's class (S No. 144/2, Apr '61: "Superboy's First Public Appearance!") at Smallville High School (Act No. 305, Oct '63: "Why Superman Needs a Secret Identity!"), she had a "crush" on Superboy, i.e., the teen-aged Superman (S No. 97/3, May '55: "Superboy's Last Day in Smallville!"), was alternately friendly to, and contemptuous of, mild-mannered Clark Kent, and generally "tormented and pestered" them both in her never-ending quest for the secret of Superboy's dual identity (S No. 78/3, Sep/Oct '52: "The Girls in Superman's Life!").

Indeed, the obvious parallel between Lana Lang's relationship with the teen-aged Superboy and Lois Lane's relationship with the adult Superman has not been lost on the chroniclers. "Superman has had his troubles from the reckless rashness of Lois Lane," notes the textual narrative of Superman No. 78/3, "... but that's nothing new to him! For years ago in Smallville, when he was Superboy, pretty, prying, pestiferous Lana Lang also used to give him head-aches!" (Sep/Oct '52: "The Girls In Superman's Life!").

Lana Lang's appearance in the chronicles as one of Superman's most enduring relationships—second only to the one he shares with Lois Lane—dramatically attests to the irresistible psychological appeal this type of relationship has for Superman.

3. *The Relationship with Lori Lemaris.* Lovely brown-haired LORI LEMARIS, a mermaid from the subsea realm of ATLANTIS, first became involved with Clark Kent, the man who is secretly Superman, while both were students at METROPOLIS UNIVERSITY. Kent "dated her steadily" during this period, falling, day by day, ever more hopelessly in love with her. Finally, Kent decided to ask Lori to marry him. Convinced that it would be impossible for him to assume the responsibilities of marriage while at the same time carrying on his work as Superman, Kent was prepared to abandon his super-heroic role forever and to live out his life with Lori as plain Clark Kent.

In this case, there was no question of Lori's being dazzled by Superman and repelled by Clark Kent, for Lori's telepathic powers, common to all Atlanteans, had made her immediately privy to Superman's

Superman and Lori Lemaris, 1960

secret. But because, unconsciously, Superman fears emotional involvement and desires rejection, he had unconsciously selected, as the object of his affections, a woman whose own needs would cause her to reject him.

Indeed, this is exactly what happened. Although, superficially, the love between Clark Kent and Lori Lemaris was mutual, she ultimately rejected his proposal of marriage—and, in fact, deserted the relationship entirely—on the rather vague, flimsy ground that her duty required her to return to Atlantis (S No. 129/3, May '59: "The Girl in Superman's Past!").

The neurotic pattern of this relationship reasserts itself in February 1960, when, after having not seen Lori Lemaris since his senior year at college, Superman initiates the relationship again. Once again Superman proposes marriage; once again, Lori rejects him. But finally Lori succumbs to Superman's ardor and the lovely mermaid agrees to become his wife. Lori's assent, however, is only the prelude to an even more crushing rejection, for soon afterward, Lori becomes hopelessly paralyzed as the result of a vengeful attack by an evil fisherman, and after Superman has scoured the universe in order to locate a surgeon capable of curing his beloved's paralysis, Lori renounces her engagement to Superman and marries the surgeon (S No. 135/2: "Superman's Mermaid Sweetheart!").

Superficially, the pattern is different from the one Superman enacts and reenacts with LOIS LANE, but the end result is exactly the same. Dreading involvement and gratified by rejection, Superman unconsciously creates situations in which his conscious desire for love is bound to be thwarted.

4. *The Relationship with Lyla Lerrol.* Superman embarks on a passionate, poignant romance with "hauntingly beautiful" Kryptonian actress LYLA LERROL during a time-journey he makes to the planet KRYPTON at a time preceding its destruction. The love Superman shares with the glamorous actress is intoxicatingly intense. It is a relationship of mutual commitment and neither party may fairly be said to reject the other (S No. 141, Nov '60: "Superman's Return to Krypton!" pts. I-III—"Superman Meets Jor-El and Lara Again!"; "Superman's Kryptonian Romance!"; "The Surprise of Fate!").

Once again, however, Superman has initiated a relationship certain to be unenduring. Krypton, as he well knows, is doomed to destruction, along with Lyla Lerrol and virtually all its inhabitants. And, as bitter experience has taught Superman many times before, even his mighty super-powers do not enable him to change the course of history (S No. 146/2, Jul '61: "Superman's Greatest Feats!"; and others). It is as though Superman had chosen the love of his life from a terminal cancer ward: no matter which mate he selected, their relationship could not possibly endure.

5. *The Relationship with Sally Selwyn.* Superman falls in love with SALLY SELWYN, the lovely blond-haired daughter of an immensely wealthy landowner and industrialist, in November 1963, when, after having been temporarily robbed of his super-powers and afflicted with total amnesia as the result of exposure to red KRYPTONITE, he wanders onto the Selwyn estate, clad in the clothing and eyeglasses he customarily wears in his role as Clark Kent.

The relationship that develops between the amnesic Superman and the millionaire's daughter is intense yet affectionate, powerful yet at the same time touchingly romantic. Of all the relationships Superman shares with women during the first three decades of his career, this one seems the most mature and genuinely loving (S No. 165/2: "The Sweetheart Superman Forgot!").

Superman No. 169/2 describes Sally Selwyn as "the one girl who ever loved Clark Kent for himself, not because he was secretly **the Man of Steel**" (May '64: "The Man Who Stole Superman's Secret Life!"), but this statement is not, strictly speaking, correct. In the course of his romance with Sally Selwyn, Superman does indeed wear the clothing and eyeglasses characteristic of his role as reporter Clark Kent, but he does not exhibit the spineless timidity which LOIS LANE finds so repellingly offensive.

The Clark Kent who romances Sally Selwyn is the perfect blend of both Clark Kent and Superman—"kind, as well as manly," gentle yet forthright, individualistic and courageous.

The fatal flaw in the relationship is that Superman is psychologically free to abandon his oppressive Clark Kent-Superman duality only so long as he is afflicted with total amnesia. Having forgotten completely who he really is—that he is an alien from outer space with superhuman powers—Superman becomes somehow free to merge the extremes of his tortured personality into a single wholesome individual. As the relationship proceeds, the amnesic Superman presents his beloved with an engagement

A tearful Sally Selwyn recalls her lost romance with the man she knew only as "Jim White," unaware that her beloved "Jim" was actually Superman suffering from red-kryptonite-induced amnesia, 1963

ring and the couple tentatively plan their marriage. When the baleful effects of the red kryptonite wear off, however, Superman is far from the Selwyn estate. With his super-powers now returned to him and his memory restored, he returns to his accustomed double life as a world-renowned super-hero and mild-mannered reporter. Tragically, the entire period of his romance with Sally Selwyn remains a complete blank in his memory (S No. 165/2, Nov '63: "The Sweetheart Superman Forgot!").

The crucial role played by Superman's amnesia in enabling him to share a true emotional commitment with Sally Selwyn becomes poignantly evident six months later, in May 1964, when Clark Kent, no longer suffering from loss of memory, encounters Sally Selwyn by accident not far from her home. Up until now, the Man of Steel has had no recollection whatever of his romance with Sally, but as she takes him in her arms and kisses him passionately, "Suddenly, by an inexplicable trick of the mind, Sally's ardent kiss causes forgotten memories deep within Clark's subconscious to flow back into consciousness...."

"Great Scott!" thinks Clark Kent with a start. "I remember everything now--everything!"

Kent's initial decision is to marry Sally, to tell her that he loves her and wants her for his bride. But it was only Superman's amnesic state that had allowed him to overcome his unconscious fear of intimacy. Ultimately, as he has done so often with Lois Lane, Superman flees this relationship and the emotional involvement it represents, rationalizing that he can never marry due to the fact that his wife would inevitably become the target of underworld retribution (S No. 169/2: "The Man Who Stole Superman's Secret Life!").

K. The Relationship with the Law-Enforcement Establishment. "As a champion of justice, **Superman** has constantly fought the forces of crime! To people everywhere, he is the living symbol of law and order!" (S No. 153/1, May '62: "The Day Superman Broke the Law!").

Four full decades of super-heroic adventure have made Superman "the most famous crusader in the world, idolized everywhere for unselfishly using his incredible super-powers in behalf of justice" (S No. 144/2, Apr '61: "Superboy's First Public Appearance!").

For years, the Man of Steel has worked hand in hand with the police (S No. 116/1, Sep '57: "The Ray That Changed Superman"; and many others), as well as the U.S. Army (S No. 23/1, Jul/Aug '43: "America's Secret Weapon!"; and many others), the U.S. Navy (S No. 15/2, Mar/Apr '42; *see also* Act No. 149, Oct '50: "The Courtship on Krypton!"), the F.B.I. (S No. 25/1, Nov/Dec '43: "The Man Superman Refused to Help!"; and others), the Treasury Department (S No. 102/1, Jan '56: "Superman for Sale"), the Secret Service (Act No. 256, Sep '59: "The Superman of the Future!"), and several U.S. Presidents (S No. 170/1, Jul '64: "Superman's Mission for President Kennedy!"; and others).

Although Superman apparently lacks jurisdiction to apprehend criminals outside Earth's solar system (Act No. 292, Sep '62: "When Superman Defended His Arch-Enemy!"), he has been awarded honorary citizenship "in all the countries of the United Nations" (S No. 146/1, Jul '61: "The Story of Superman's Life!"), along with a special "golden certificate" empowering him to apprehend criminals in U.N. member nations and to travel in and out of those nations without a passport (Act No. 285, Feb '62: "The World's Greatest Heroine!").

METROPOLIS law-enforcement officials can summon Superman into action either with the aid of the "super-signal" (*see* section G, the equipment) or by means of a large loudspeaker mounted atop the roof of police headquarters (S No. 114/1, Jul '57: "The Soundproof Superman"; *see also* S No. 101/1, Nov '55: "Luthor's Amazing Rebus"), and "every [foreign] nation knows exactly how to get in touch with **Superman** through the White House!" (Act No. 306, Nov '63: "The Great Superman Impersonation!").

Superman has been the recipient of numerous awards, trophies, citations, and other honors, including the commemorative stamp issued in his honor by the U.S. government (S No. 91/1, Aug '54: "The Superman Stamp!"), Metropolis's Outstanding Citizen Award for 1954 (S No. 93/2, Nov '54: "Jimmy Olsen's Double!"), and "the key to the city" presented to him by the mayor of Metropolis in September 1965 (Act No. 328: "Superman's Hands of Doom!").

Metropolis has celebrated Superman Day on at least two separate occasions (S No. 157/3, Nov '62: "Superman's Day of Doom!"; Act No. 328, Sep '65: "Superman's Hands of Doom!"), and each year, in Superman's honor, the Metropolis Police Department awards a Superman Medal "to the person whose heroism...helped **Superman** the most" during the preceding year (Act No. 207, Aug '55: "The Four Superman Medals!").

Artistic tributes to Superman include the statue of Superman in the Metropolis Hall of Fame (Act No. 297, Feb '63: "The Man Who Betrayed Superman's Identity!"), the "colossal steel statue of **Superman**" in Metropolis Park (WF No. 28, May/Jun '47: "Superman's Super-Self!"; and others), the monumental statue of Superman towering over Metropolis Harbor like the legendary Colossus of Rhodes (WF No. 23, Jul/Aug '46: "The Colossus of Metropolis!"; see also Act No. 146, Jul '50: "The Statues That Came to Life!"), and the marble statue of Superman unveiled in Planet Square in January-February 1946 (S No. 38/3: "The Man of Stone!"; S No. 69/1, Mar/Apr '51: "The Prankster's Apprentice!"). (See also section I, the man himself [as Superman].)

Superman has not always enjoyed the approval of established authority, however, although he has generally enjoyed the admiration of the press (Act No. 9, Feb '39) and of the average policeman (S No. 13/3, Nov/Dec '41; and others).

In the early days of his career, Superman was a vigilante "mystery-man" (Act No. 6, Nov '38; and others) who freely resorted to violence and the threat of violence in order to extort information and confessions from criminal suspects (S No. 1/1, Sum '39; and many others), demolished private property and committed other gross violations of individual rights (Act No. 12, May '39; and others), and meted out death to his adversaries whenever he felt the situation demanded it (Act No. 2, Jul '38; and others).

Pursued by the police during this early period for flouting the law and working beyond the pale of legitimate authority (Act No. 9, Feb '39; and others), Superman was sought as a fugitive until mid-1942, by which time, although no explanation for the change-over is actually given, he has clearly won the approval of the law-enforcement establishment (S No. 17/4, Jul/Aug '42: "When Titans Clash!"; and others).

Following is a chronological listing of the textual data relating to Superman's relationship with the law-enforcement establishment.

In June 1938, having obtained the evidence necessary to exonerate EVELYN CURRY of the charge of murder and rescue her from death in the electric chair, Superman barges into the governor's home just before midnight, manhandles the governor's personal servant and smashes down the door to his bedroom, and, with only moments to go before Evelyn Curry's scheduled execution, persuades the governor to put through a life-saving call to the death house. "Gentlemen," exclaims the governor to the members of his staff the following morning, "I still can't believe my senses! **He's not human!**—Thank heaven he's apparently on the side of law and order!" (Act No. 1).

In January 1939 Superman, convinced that

juvenile delinquency is caused not so much by bad youngsters as by the stifling slum environment in which many city youths must dwell, overtakes a paddy wagon taking an arrested delinquent to jail and forcibly rescues him from the clutches of the enraged police in a bid to save the boy from a life of imprisonment.

"It's not entirely your fault that you're delinquent," remarks Superman, "--it's these slums—your poor living conditions—if there was only some way I could remedy it--!"

Then, as luck would have it, the headline on a local newspaper catches Superman's eye. "Cyclone Hits Florida," it screams. "Cities Laid Waste!" The story beneath the headline details plans by the U.S. government to erect modern housing projects on the sites of buildings destroyed by the cyclone.

Inspired by the newspaper article, Superman passes the word to the residents of the city's slums to gather up their possessions and evacuate their homes immediately. Then, with the dilapidated slum dwellings safely emptied of their occupants, he whirls through the area like "a one-man cyclone," single-handedly demolishing every structure in sight with hammerlike blows of his mighty fists. "So the government rebuilds destroyed areas with modern cheap-rental apartments, eh?" says Superman to himself. "Then here's a job for it!—When I finish, this town will be rid of its filthy crime-festering slums!"

Superman's unorthodox approach to slum clearance, however, does not endear him to the authorities, and as word of his devastation spreads, scores of policemen and firemen, a contingent of National Guardsmen, and finally "a squadron of aerial-bombers" are ordered into the disaster area with orders to annihilate Superman and put an end to the destruction. But the machine-gun bullets of the National Guardsmen merely bounce off Superman's chest like pebbles, and the bombs unleashed by the bombers serve only to hasten the completion of his remarkable task.

Nimbly, he races thru [sic] the streets, explosions dodging his footsteps as the frantic aviators seek desperately to eliminate him....

And then finally, his task completed, "SUPERMAN vanishes from sight. Behind him he leaves what formerly were the slums, but now, a desolate shambles...."

Soon afterward, as Superman had anticipated, the federal government initiates a campaign of massive aid in the disaster-stricken area. "Emergency squads commence erecting huge apartment-projects... and in time the slums are replaced by splendid housing conditions."

Officially, of course, this unauthorized act of slum demolition has made an outlaw out of Superman, but even the authorities are privately elated. "...We'll spare no effort to apprehend SUPERMAN," vows the police chief, "--but off the record...I think he did a splendid thing and I'd like to shake his hand!" (Act No. 8).

In February 1939 the police chief summons newsmen to his office "to witness an announcement of unusual importance."

"I'll come to the point at once!" he remarks. "As you know, a man possessed of super-strength named SUPERMAN has torn down our slum area, causing modern apartments to replace crowded tenements."

"Good for him!" cries one reporter.

"What the world needs is a couple more guys like him!" exclaims another.

"Regardless of his motives and our personal approval of them," scolds the police chief, "the fact remains that he has wantonly destroyed public property and must pay the full penalty to the law just like any other transgressor!"

In hopes of apprehending Superman, the police chief has imported, from Chicago, Detective Captain Reilly, a "conceited windbag" who is, nevertheless, famous for having successfully captured every one of the 800 fugitives he has been assigned to track down. Repeatedly outwitted by Superman, however, Reilly suffers his worst humiliation when he lunges headlong at Superman and knocks himself unconscious against Superman's "super-tough" skin (Act No. 9).

In March 1939 Superman drags a pusillanimous governor out of bed in the middle of the night so that he can force him to witness, firsthand, the brutal treatment of inmates of the Coreytown prison (Act No. 10). (See WYMAN [SUPERINTENDENT].)

In May 1939 Superman forcibly smashes his way into a broadcasting studio, shoving aside the startled announcer and seizing control of the microphone. "Attention, citizens of this city!" he proclaims to the city's stunned radio audience. "A warning from Superman--pay close heed!" And then, Superman issues the following announcement:

The auto-accident death rate of this community is one that should shame us all! It's constantly rising and due entirely to reckless driving and inefficiency! More people have been killed needlessly by autos than died during the World War!

From this moment on, I declare war on reckless drivers--henceforth, homicidal drivers answer to me!

Racing at top speed to the county jail, Superman swoops down on "the great lot where the autos of traffic violators are temporarily stored. Leaping at the massed cars, Superman commences to systematically smash and tear them to a pulp!"

"Yes-sir-ee!" exclaims Superman, as he gleefully demolishes the automobiles. "I think I'm going to enjoy this private little war!"

Next, Superman visits "a used-car lot which sells completely dilapidated autos." "You call these 'cars'?" he cries to the horrified lot owner. "They're nothing but accidents looking for a place to happen!-- If they weren't so dangerous they'd actually be funny!" And then, as he wades into the used cars, smashing them into useless scrap with mighty blows

of his fists, Superman exclaims, "Sorry if this is tough on your pocketbook, but I'm thinking of the lives to be saved!"

Soon afterward, "...the Man of Steel swoops down from the skies toward the Bates Motor Company's great factory" and brazenly barges into the office of Mr. Bates himself. "...You use inferior metals and parts so as to make higher profits at the cost of human lives!" accuses Superman. And then, as the flabbergasted automobile magnate looks on in horror, "Gleefully, Superman runs amuck, destroying the factory's manufacturing equipment" with his bare hands, reducing the entire factory to a mass of rubble.

A short while later, Superman abducts the city's mayor and drags him to the city morgue. "By not seeing to it that the speed laws were strictly enforced," intones Superman, "you doomed many to death!"

Indeed, peering through a glass partition inside the morgue, the mayor can see "the bodies of auto victims--maimed---horrible!" "They," remarks Superman grimly, "are men you killed!"

Jolted out of his complacency by this grisly spectacle, the mayor promises to see to it that the city's traffic regulations are henceforth strictly enforced, and soon afterward initiates "a great traffic improvement drive...!" (Act No. 12).

In September 1939, convinced that "gambling is a parasitic vice that has no place in a decent town," Superman launches a one-man crusade against illegal gambling, single-handedly demolishing virtually every crooked casino in Metropolis. Tearing open the safe in one gambling czar's office, Superman seizes the hoard of cash inside and, soaring high into the air with it, sends an armful of "fluttering bills" raining down on the grateful inhabitants of "a poor section of the city."

When he learns that the city's big-time gamblers are receiving protection from a corrupt police commissioner, Superman confronts the official ("Commissioner, you're a clever man," threatens Superman, "and so I won't bandy words. --Either do as I tell you, or prepare to meet your end!"), forces him to call a mass meeting of Metropolis's gambling czars, and then terrorizes the commissioner into resigning his office—and the gamblers into leaving town—by threatening to track down any man who remains behind "...and end his life with my own hands!" (Act No. 16).

In Fall 1939 Superman strangles NAT GRAYSON by the throat until he agrees to make a full confession of his crimes and then departs through an open window to avoid a run-in with arriving police. "Remember!" warns Superman as he makes his exit. "If you don't confess, I'll come back and dish out the justice you deserve with my bare hands!" (S No. 2/3: "Superman and the Skyscrapers").

In December 1939, when a chemical company refuses to sell PROFESSOR HENRY TRAVERS the chemicals he needs to carry on his experiments in search of a cure for the ghastly "purple plague" unleashed against Metropolis by the ULTRA-HUMANITE, Superman breaks into the chemical plant at night and steals the materials Travers needs. "Here are the chemicals..." exclaims Superman to the astonished young scientist. "Never mind how I got them! Get to work!" (Act No. 19).

In February 1940 Superman becomes embroiled, against his will, in a pitched battle with Metropolis police and National Guardsmen when circumstances force him to steal a display of priceless crown jewels in an attempt to ransom captive scientist TERRY CURTIS from the clutches of the Ultra-Humanite (Act No. 21).

In September-October 1940, after LOIS LANE has been wrongfully charged with murder and placed under arrest, Superman swoops down on the police car carrying her to jail and races away with her amid a fusillade of police bullets (S No. 6/1).

In October 1940 an unidentified policeman attempts to place Superman under arrest, but Superman easily makes good his escape (Act No. 29).

In January-February 1941, after Superman has helped thwart a robbery, a policeman on the scene attempts to arrest him, but Superman easily escapes (S No. 8/4).

In June 1941 Superman is apparently still being sought for working outside the law, for SERGEANT CASEY makes an unsuccessful attempt to take him into custody (Act No. 37).

In July 1941 Sergeant Casey, suspicious that Superman may somehow be implicated in a recent wave of mysterious robberies (see MORTON, HAROLD), attempts to place him under arrest, but the Man of Steel easily shatters his handcuffs and escapes, and by the conclusion of the adventure his innocence has been clearly established (Act No. 38).

In August 1941, after a dying watchman, mortally wounded by a mysterious bandit, has muttered something about his assailant's having been invulnerable to bullets, Sergeant Casey attempts to arrest Superman for the crime. The Man of Steel escapes, however, and ultimately succeeds in proving his innocence (Act No. 39). (See BRYSON, BRETT.)

In November-December 1941, while searching for clues at the home of a recently murdered millionaire, Superman is surprised by the police, who attempt to arrest him in the apparent belief that he may have been responsible for the millionaire's murder. Superman eludes his would-be captors, however, by burrowing beneath the ground like a human drill and then returning to the surface at a different spot and flying away. "It would be useless to attempt to reason with them!" thinks Superman to himself (S No. 13/2). During this same period, however, when Superman turns a captured foreign spy chief over to the police, one of them remarks admiringly, "If we could only draft you into the force!" (S No. 13/3, Nov/Dec '41).

In January-February 1942 Superman traces the license number of RUDOLPH KRAZINSKI's automobile by surreptitiously breaking into the city's Auto License Bureau and rifling the files, a certain

indication that Superman does not yet enjoy the cooperation of the law-enforcement establishment (S No. 14/1). Moreover, during this same period, Superman abruptly breaks off his interrogation of JIM BALDWIN's hired henchmen and flees through an open window in order to avoid a run-in with arriving police (S No. 14/2, Jan/Feb '42).

In March-April 1942, after Superman has thwarted an attempt by NAPKAN saboteurs to sink a newly christened American battleship, Secretary of the Navy Hank Fox pays the Man of Steel this tribute: "How fortunate we are here in America," he remarks, "to have someone of Superman's calibre to aid us! In my opinion, he's worth several armies and navies!" (S No. 15/2).

In April 1942, when Superman attempts to thwart LEX LUTHOR's robbery of a Metropolis bank, policemen arriving on the scene begin shooting at Superman in the belief that he must have been responsible for setting off the bank's alarm. Superman easily eludes the police, but Luthor capitalizes on the confusion in order to make good his escape (Act No. 47: "Powerstone").

In May-June 1942, after Superman has apprehended CHARLIE GRAYSON, Sergeant Casey asks admiringly, "What would the police force do without you?" "No doubt get along very nicely!" replies Superman (S No. 16/1: "The World's Meanest Man").

In Summer 1942, after METALO has used his awesome super-strength to steal an entire mail car from the Metropolis train terminal, Superman is accused of having committed the crime. Superman ultimately defeats Metalo, however, and establishes his innocence (WF No. 6: "Man of Steel versus Man of Metal!").

In July-August 1942 Superman apprehends a group of Lex Luthor's henchmen and turns them over to the police. "If you keep up this super crook-catching," remarks one officer, "the force will have to retire!" "Always glad to help the police!" replies Superman (S No. 17/4: "When Titans Clash!").

By January-February 1943 Superman's era as a fugitive has apparently ended, for as he helps the police apprehend the LEOPARD's henchmen, one officer remarks, "To think we once considered him outside the law!" (S No. 20/3: "Lair of the Leopard!").

In May-June 1943 the nation is plunged into chaos as the result of the PRANKSTER's having copyrighted the English alphabet. "—What can I do?" thinks Clark Kent helplessly. "The Prankster has the law on his side, and I won't flout justice at any cost!—" (S No. 22/3: "The Great ABC Panic!").

In July-August 1943 Superman, by now clearly an American hero, is cheered enthusiastically by American troops when he makes an appearance at a U.S. army base. "—American soldiers cheering me, when all the civilized peoples in the world are cheering them!" thinks Superman proudly. "It's the grandest tribute I've ever had!—" (S No. 23/1: "America's Secret Weapon!").

In August 1943, while suffering from temporary

amnesia induced by a shower of "weird rays" from outer space, Superman commits a series of criminal acts under the evil influence of "PROFESSOR" PRALINE. For a time, the authorities are convinced that Superman has joined forces with the underworld, but Superman ultimately regains his memory and apprehends Praline and his henchmen (Act No. 63: "When Stars Collide!").

In January-February 1950 Superman is convicted and sentenced to life imprisonment for the murder of Clark Kent, but the Man of Steel is exonerated when it becomes clear that he only faked Kent's death as part of an elaborate ruse to enable the Metropolis police to apprehend the ACE (S No. 62/2: "The People vs. Superman!").

In December 1951-January 1952 Superman is exiled from Metropolis by the Metropolis city council after the "DUDE" VORMAN gang has framed him for a series of irresponsible acts. Superman ultimately apprehends the Vorman gang, however, and establishes his innocence (WF No. 55: "The City That Exiled Superman!").

In January 1953 Superman astounds the authorities by greedily demanding fees and rewards for what have hitherto been his gratuitous services. Superman is only feigning avarice, however, as part of his plan for apprehending the MILLION-DOLLAR MARVIN gang (Act No. 176: "Muscles for Money").

In September-October 1953 Superman is widely suspected of being a Metropolis gang czar as the result of an elaborate scheme devised by gangster HARRY "KING" SAPHIRE. Superman ultimately exonerates himself of the charge, however, and apprehends Saphire (WF No. 66: "Superman, Ex-Crimebuster!").

In May-June 1954, during a period when Superman is blacking out for an hour every afternoon as the result of the presence in Earth's solar system of a KRYPTONITE-laden asteroid, a pair of criminals named Benny and Red begin capitalizing on the Man of Steel's daily blackouts in order to implicate him in a series of crimes. For a time, Superman is widely believed to have developed a "Jekyll-Hyde personality" that causes him to turn evil for an hour each day, but Superman ultimately establishes his innocence, destroys the kryptonite-laden asteroid, and apprehends the criminals (WF No. 70: "The Two Faces of Superman!").

In July-August 1956 Superman is an "honored guest"—along with BATMAN and ROBIN—at GOTHAM CITY's annual police ball (WF No. 83: "The Case of the Mother Goose Mystery!").

In April 1959 VARD and Boka, a pair of diabolical "futuremen" from the year 2000 A.D., successfully trick the F.B.I. and other law-enforcement authorities into believing that Superman is actually a fugitive "renegade scientist" from their own future era. The villains plan to make Superman their unwilling ally in a heinously vicious scheme to blackmail the Earth, but the Man of Steel ultimately defeats the futuremen and exonerates himself of the bogus charges against

him (S No. 128/1: chs. 1-2—"Superman versus the Futuremen"; "The Secret of the Futuremen").

When the Metropolis Police Department stages its gala Policemen's Benefit Show at Metropolis Stadium, Superman contributes a dazzling performance of super-powered feats (S No. 133/1, Nov '59: "The Super-Luck of Badge 77").

In January 1960 the name of Superman becomes anathema to the people of Earth when the Kandorian scientist KULL-EX impersonates him while committing a series of insanely destructive acts. Superman ultimately prevails upon Kull-Ex to confess his misdeeds, however, and the Man of Steel is exonerated of any wrongdoing (S No. 134: chs. I-III—"The Super-Menace of Metropolis!"; "The Revenge Against Jor-El!"; "The Duel of the Supermen!").

In December 1962 Superman becomes transformed from a beloved hero into "the most feared and hated person on Earth" when he commits a series of insanely destructive acts while under the baleful influence of a diabolical "telepathic-hypnotic weapon" beamed at him by members of the SUPERMAN REVENGE SQUAD. Superman ultimately defeats the villains, however, and exonerates himself of any wrongdoing (Act No. 295: "Superman Goes Wild!").

In April 1963, at the ceremonies marking Police Day at Metropolis Stadium, Superman is on hand to present a gigantic police badge to the heroic policemen who make up Metropolis's police force (S No. 160/2: "The Super-Cop of Metropolis!").

In June 1963 Superman is convicted and sentenced to life imprisonment for the murder of Clark Kent, but the Man of Steel is exonerated when it becomes clear that he only faked Kent's death as part of an elaborate ruse to enable the Metropolis police to apprehend COUNT X and his underworld cohorts (Act No. 301: "The Trial of Superman!").

In the spring of 1964 Superman astounds the world by demanding that the United Nations agree to crown him King of Earth (Act No. 311, Apr '64: "Superman, King of Earth!"), but the Man of Steel has only assumed the pose of a "power-hungry madman" as part of his plan to thwart an impending alien invasion from the planet BXPA (Act No. 312, May '64: "King Superman versus Clark Kent, Metallo").

L. The Texts. 1. Locales. In the course of a career spanning four full decades of adventure, Superman has traveled to the four corners of the Earth, to distant planets and alien dimensions, back into the past and forward into the future, and throughout his adopted country, the United States of America. By and large, however, the adventures of Superman take place in and around METROPOLIS, the resident city of Superman and the place where he makes his home as journalist Clark Kent. The textual evidence is overwhelming that Metropolis is modeled after, and fully intended to represent, the city of New York. (See METROPOLIS.)

2. Developments. a. THE EARLY ADVENTURES. In June 1938, in a text which offers the first account of

Superman's origin (see section A, origin), Superman rescues EVELYN CURRY from the electric chair, administers a well-deserved thrashing to an unidentified wife beater, rescues Lois Lane from a gang of hoodlums, and travels to Washington, D.C., for a confrontation with lobbyist ALEX GREER (Act No. 1).

In July 1938 Superman matches wits with EMIL NORVELL and brings an end to the SAN MONTÉ war (Act No. 2).

In August 1938 Superman teaches a richly deserved lesson to THORNTON BLAKELY (Act No. 3).

In September 1938 Superman thwarts the unscrupulous schemes of COACH RANDALL (Act No. 4).

In October 1938 Superman copes with the emergency of the VALLEYHO DAM (Act No. 5).

In November 1938 Superman matches wits with NICK WILLIAMS (Act No. 6).

In December 1938 Superman battles DEREK NILES (Act No. 7).

In January 1939 Superman thwarts the sinister schemes of GIMPY, "loathsome corrupter of youth..." (Act No. 8).

In February 1939 Superman matches wits with DETECTIVE CAPTAIN REILLY (Act No. 9).

In March 1939 Superman fights for prison reform (see WYMAN [SUPERINTENDENT]) (Act No. 10).

In April 1939 Superman thwarts the sinister machinations of two crooked stockbrokers (see RAMSEY, HOMER) (Act No. 11).

In May 1939, after a personal friend has been run down by a speeding auto, Superman launches a one-man war against reckless drivers. In Superman's words:

> The auto-accident death rate of this community is one that should shame us all! It's constantly rising and due entirely to reckless driving and inefficiency! More people have been killed needlessly by autos than died during the World War!
>
> From this moment on, I declare war on reckless drivers--henceforth, homicidal drivers answer to me!

Racing at top speed to the county jail, Superman swoops down on "the great lot where the autos of traffic violators are temporarily stored. Leaping at the massed cars, Superman commences to systematically smash and tear them to a pulp!"

"Yes-sir-ee!" exclaims Superman as he gleefully demolishes the automobiles. "I think I'm going to enjoy this private little war!"

Next, Superman visits "a used-car lot which sells completely dilapidated autos." "You call these 'cars'?" he cries to the horrified lot owner. "They're nothing but accidents looking for a place to happen!-- If they weren't so dangerous they'd actually be funny!" And then, as he wades into the used cars, smashing them into useless scrap with mighty blows of his fists, Superman exclaims, "Sorry if this is tough on your pocketbook, but I'm thinking of the lives to be saved!"

Soon afterward, "...the Man of Steel swoops down from the skies toward the Bates Motor Company's

great factory" and brazenly barges into the office of Mr. Bates himself. "...You use inferior metals and parts so as to make higher profits at the cost of human lives!" accuses Superman. And then, as the flabbergasted automobile magnate looks on in horror, "Gleefully, Superman runs amuck, destroying the factory's manufacturing equipment" with his bare hands, reducing the entire factory to a mass of rubble.

A short while later, Superman abducts the city's mayor and drags him to the city morgue. "By not seeing to it that the speed laws were strictly enforced," intones Superman, "you doomed many to death!"

Indeed, peering through a glass partition inside the morgue, the mayor can see "the bodies of auto victims--maimed---horrible!" "They," remarks Superman grimly, "are men you killed!"

Jolted out of his complacency by this grisly spectacle, the mayor promises to see to it that the city's traffic regulations are henceforth strictly enforced, and soon afterward initiates "a great traffic improvement drive...!" (Act No. 12).

In June 1939 Superman battles the ULTRA-HUMANITE (Act No. 13).

In Summer 1939, in a text which offers a slightly expanded version of Superman's origin, the story of Superman's efforts to rescue EVELYN CURRY from the electric chair is reprinted, in expanded form, from Action Comics No. 1 (Jun '38) (S No. 1/1); the story of Superman's encounter with EMIL NORVELL and adventure in SAN MONTÉ is reprinted verbatim from Action Comics No. 2 (Jul '38) (S No. 1/2); the story of Superman's meeting with THORNTON BLAKELY is reprinted verbatim from Action Comics No. 3 (Aug '38) (S No. 1/3); and the story of Superman's efforts to thwart the schemes of COACH RANDALL is reprinted verbatim from Action Comics No. 4 (Sep '38) (S No. 1/4).

In July 1939 Superman matches wits with the ULTRA-HUMANITE (Act No. 14).

In August 1939 Superman lends KIDTOWN a helping hand (Act No. 15).

In September 1939, convinced that "gambling is a parasitic vice that has no place in a decent town," Superman launches a one-man crusade against illegal gambling, single-handedly demolishing virtually every crooked casino in Metropolis, forcing the city's corrupt police commissioner to resign, and persuading Metropolis's gambling czars to leave town en masse by threatening to murder those who remain behind (Act No. 16).

In Fall 1939 Superman lends a helping hand to LARRY TRENT (S No. 2/1), matches wits with LUBANE (S No. 2/2: "Superman Champions Universal Peace!"), and thwarts the unscrupulous machinations of NAT GRAYSON (S No. 2/3: "Superman and the Skyscrapers").

In October 1939 Superman battles the ULTRA-HUMANITE (Act No. 17).

In November 1939 Superman matches wits with MR. HAMILTON (Act No. 18).

In December 1939 Superman thwarts the sinister schemes of the ULTRA-HUMANITE (Act No. 19).

Sometime during 1939, Superman attends the New York World's Fair and matches wits with NICK STONE (NYWF).

In Winter 1940 Superman thwarts the unscrupulous machinations of SUPERINTENDENT LYMAN (S No. 3/1); the story of Superman's adventure at the VALLEYHO DAM is reprinted verbatim from Action Comics No. 5 (Oct '38) (S No. 3/2); the story of Superman's encounter with NICK WILLIAMS is reprinted verbatim from Action Comics No. 6 (Nov '38) (S No. 3/3); and Superman matches wits with LEW FRAWLEY (S No. 3/4).

In January 1940 Superman battles the ULTRA-HUMANITE (Act No. 20).

In February 1940 Superman renews his battle with the ULTRA-HUMANITE (Act No. 21).

In March 1940 Superman struggles to bring an end to the war raging between TORAN and GALONIA (Act No. 22).

In April 1940 Superman battles LEX LUTHOR (Act No. 23).

In Spring 1940 Superman matches wits with LEX LUTHOR (S No. 4/1; S No. 4/2), thwarts the sinister machinations of J. F. CURTIS (S No. 4/3), and battles GUS SNIDE (S No. 4/4).

In May 1940 Superman meets PETER CARNAHAN (Act No. 24).

In June 1940 Superman matches wits with MEDINI (Act No. 25).

In Summer 1940 Superman battles "SLUG" KELLY (S No. 5/1), thwarts the unscrupulous machinations of ALEX EVELL (S No. 5/2), matches wits with LEX LUTHOR (S No. 5/3), and meets PROFESSOR CARL GRINSTEAD (S No. 5/4).

In July 1940 Superman matches wits with "PROFESSOR" CLARENCE COBALT (Act No. 26).

In August 1940 Superman meets MR. AND MRS. TWEED (Act No. 27).

In September 1940 Superman copes with the crimes of the STRONGARM BANDIT (Act No. 28).

In September-October 1940 Superman investigates the murder of NORVAL (S No. 6/1), matches wits with "BRUTE" BASHBY (S No. 6/2), provides some much-needed aid to the small South American country of SAN CALUMA (S No. 6/3), and thwarts the sinister machinations of a construction tycoon named JACKSON (S No. 6/4).

In October 1940 Superman matches wits with MARTIN (Act No. 29).

A text for November 1940 recounts the story of Superman's battle with the diabolical ZOLAR (Act No. 30).

In November-December 1940 Superman matches wits with NICK NORTON (S No. 7/1), thwarts the sinister machinations of the evil KOTZOFF (S No. 7/2), meets BERT RUNYAN (S No. 7/3), and battles the BLACK GANG (S No. 7/4).

In December 1940 Superman matches wits with BARON MUNSDORF (Act No. 31).

Sometime during 1940, Superman attends the New York World's Fair and apprehends the BLACKIE SARTO gang (NYWF).

In January 1941 Superman matches wits with MR. PRESTON (Act No. 32).

In January-February 1941 Superman thwarts the fiendish schemes of PROFESSOR ZEE (S No. 8/1), matches wits with JEFF CARLTON and the evil SAGDORF (S No. 8/2), battles the wily JACKAL (S No. 8/3), and apprehends JOHN PERRONE (S No. 8/4).

In February 1941 Superman matches wits with BRETT HALL (Act No. 33).

In March 1941 Superman thwarts the unscrupulous schemes of JIM LAUREY (Act No. 34).

In March-April 1941 Superman battles DERWING (S No. 9/1), matches wits with JOE GATSON (S No. 9/2), and thwarts the machinations of the evil JACKSON (S No. 9/4).

In Spring 1941 Superman meets the RAINMAKER (WB No. 1).

In April 1941 Superman matches wits with BROCK WALTERS (Act No. 35).

In May 1941 Superman thwarts the sinister machinations of STUART PEMBERTON (Act No. 36).

In May-June 1941 Superman battles LEX LUTHOR (S No. 10/1), matches wits with GRADY (S No. 10/2), smashes the spy ring headed by RIGHAB BEY (S No. 10/3), and matches wits with KARL WOLFF (S No. 10/4).

In June 1941 Superman thwarts the unscrupulous schemes of POLICE COMMISSIONER KENNEDY (Act No. 37).

In Summer 1941 Superman battles "THE UNKNOWN X" (WF No. 2).

In July 1941 Superman matches wits with HAROLD MORTON (Act No. 38).

In July-August 1941 Superman thwarts the fiendish schemes of ROLF ZIMBA (S No. 11/1), meets GRANT FELLOWS (S No. 11/2), visits QUASMANIA (S No. 11/3), and matches wits with COUNT TONY BERGAC (S No. 11/4).

In August 1941 Superman meets BRETT BRYSON (Act No. 39).

In September 1941 Superman teaches a much-needed lesson to NANCY THORGENSON (Act No. 40).

In September-October 1941 Superman matches wits with CARL BOGART (S No. 12/1), apprehends an unidentified gangster who commits murders-for-hire and contrives to make the crimes look like suicides or accidents (S No. 12/2), apprehends CALVIN DENBY (S No. 12/3), and matches wits with LEX LUTHOR (S No. 12/4).

In Fall 1941 Superman thwarts the unscrupulous machinations of THORNTON BIGSBY (WF No. 3: "The Case of the Death Express").

In October 1941 Superman matches wits with RALPH COWAN (Act No. 41).

In November 1941 Superman battles LEX LUTHOR (Act No. 42).

In November-December 1941 Superman thwarts the sinister machinations of LEX LUTHOR (S No.

13/1), battles "THE ARCHER" (S No. 13/2), meets MRS. CLARA PIERSON (S No. 13/3), and matches wits with the villainous KYACK (S No. 13/4).

b. THE WARTIME ADVENTURES. In December 1941 Superman matches wits with DUTCH O'LEARY (Act No. 43).

In Winter 1941 Superman meets DAN BRANSOM (WF No. 4: "The Case of the Crime Crusader").

In January 1942 Superman matches wits with PROFESSOR STEFFENS (Act No. 44).

In January-February 1942 Superman thwarts the sinister machinations of RUDOLPH KRAZINSKI (S No. 14/1), matches wits with JIM BALDWIN (S No. 14/2), meets AKTHAR (S No. 14/3), and battles "THE LIGHTNING MASTER" (S No. 14/4).

In February 1942 Superman meets COUNT VON HENZEL (Act No. 45).

In March 1942 Superman battles the DOMINO (Act No. 46: "The Devil's Playground").

In March-April 1942 Superman matches wits with BILL TALLEY (S No. 15/1), battles the forces of NAPKAN (S No. 15/2), journeys to OXNALIA (S No. 15/3), and thwarts the fiendish schemes of "THE EVOLUTION KING" (S No. 15/4).

In Spring 1942 Superman matches wits with LEMUEL P. POTTS (WF No. 5: "The Case of the Flying Castle").

In April 1942 Superman battles LEX LUTHOR (Act No. 47: "Powerstone").

In May 1942 Superman thwarts the schemes of the TOP (Act No. 48: "The Adventure of the Merchant of Murder").

In May-June 1942 Superman matches wits with CHARLIE GRAYSON (S No. 16/1: "The World's Meanest Man"), meets TOM NELSON and STAN EMERSON (S No. 16/2), battles MISTER SINISTER (S No. 16/3: "Case of the Runaway Skyscrapers"), and thwarts the sinister machinations of VERNON HALE (S No. 16/4: "Racket on Delivery").

In June 1942 Superman battles the PUZZLER (Act No. 49: "The Puzzler!!").

In Summer 1942 Superman meets METALO (WF No. 6: "Man of Steel versus Man of Metal!").

In July 1942 Superman lends a helping hand to STAN DOBORAK (Act No. 50).

In July-August 1942 Superman battles the TALON (S No. 17/1: "Man or Superman?"), apprehends WATKINS (S No. 17/2: "The Human Bomb"), matches wits with JAKE MASSEY (S No. 17/3: "Muscles for Sale!"), and thwarts the fiendish schemes of LEX LUTHOR (S No. 17/4: "When Titans Clash!").

In August 1942 Superman meets the PRANKSTER (Act No. 51: "The Case of the Crimeless Crimes").

A text for September 1942 recounts the story of Superman's battle with the EMPEROR OF AMERICA (Act No. 52: "The Emperor of America").

In September-October 1942 Superman matches wits with CARL BLAND (S No. 18/1: "The Conquest of a City"), battles LEX LUTHOR (S No. 18/2: "The Heat Horror"), meets the MAN WITH THE CANE (S No. 18/3: "The Man with the Cane"), and thwarts the schemes

of "THE SNAKE" (S No. 18/4: "The Snake").

In Fall 1942 Superman apprehends JENKINS (WF No. 7: "The Eight Doomed Men").

In October 1942 Superman battles the NIGHT-OWL (Act No. 53: "The Man Who Put Out the Sun!").

In November 1942 Superman meets STANLEY FINCHCOMB (Act No. 54: "The Pirate of Pleasure Island").

In November-December 1942 Superman battles FUNNYFACE (S No. 19/1: "The Case of the Funny Paper Crimes"), matches wits with SKEET MONAHAN (S No. 19/2), thwarts the sinister machinations of MR. Z (S No. 19/3), and, as Clark Kent, takes in a Superman animated cartoon at the Empire Theater with Lois Lane (S No. 19/4: "Superman, Matinee Idol").

In December 1942 Superman thwarts the unscrupulous machinations of cartoonist AL HATT (Act No. 55: "A Goof Named Tiny Rufe").

In Winter 1942 Superman lends a helping hand to five deserving youngsters aspiring to careers in the arts (WF No. 8: "Talent, Unlimited!").

In January 1943 Superman matches wits with EMIL LORING (Act No. 56: "Design for Doom!").

In January-February 1943 Superman battles "IRONJAW" GROGAN (S No. 20/1: "Superman's Secret Revealed!"), thwarts the fiendish machinations of HERR FANGE (S No. 20/2: "Destroyers from the Depths"), meets the LEOPARD (S No. 20/3: "Lair of the Leopard!"), and battles the PUZZLER (S No. 20/4: "Not in the Cards").

In February 1943 Superman matches wits with the PRANKSTER (Act No. 57: "Crime's Comedy King!").

In March 1943 Superman meets ADONIS (Act No. 58: "The Face of Adonis!").

In March-April 1943 Superman thwarts the sinister schemes of CARLTON GRAUL (S No. 21/1), matches wits with CHARLES CLAYTON (S No. 21/2: "The Four Gangleaders"), battles SIR GAUNTLET (S No. 21/3: "The Robber Knight"), and outwits "BLINKY" MOXBY (S No. 21/4: "The Ghost of Superman!").

In Spring 1943 Superman meets JANE CARTRIGHT (WF No. 9: "One Second to Live!").

In April 1943, in his Clark Kent identity, Superman baby-sits with SUSIE TOMPKINS (Act No. 59: "Cinderella--a la Superman!").

In May 1943 LOIS LANE dreams that a transfusion of Superman's blood has endowed her with superpowers (Act No. 60: "Lois Lane--Superwoman!").

In May-June 1943 Superman meets the SQUIFFLES (S No. 22/1: "Meet the Squiffles!"), lends a helping hand to "LUCKY" O'GRADY (S No. 22/2: "The Luck of O'Grady"), matches wits with the PRANKSTER (S No. 22/3: "The Great ABC Panic!"), and battles ROBIN HOOD (S No. 22/4: "A Modern Robin Hood!").

A text for June 1943 recounts the story of Superman's encounter with CRAIG SHAW (Act No. 61: "The Man They Wouldn't Believe!").

In Summer 1943 Superman thwarts the schemes of

"THE INSECT MASTER" (WF No. 10: "The Insect Terror!").

A text for July 1943 recounts the story of Superman's battle with ADMIRAL VON STORFF (Act No. 62: "There'll Always Be a Superman!").

In July-August 1943 Superman helps train American troops for the war against Fascism by participating in mock-warfare exercises at a United States army base (S No. 23/1: "America's Secret Weapon!"), matches wits with RAYMOND LOCK (S No. 23/2: "Habitual Homicide"), battles the DUDE (S No. 23/3: "Fashions in Crime!"), and lends a helping hand to TOM MARIN (S No. 23/4: "Danger on the Diamond!").

In August 1943 Superman thwarts the sinister machinations of "PROFESSOR" PRALINE (Act No. 63: "When Stars Collide!").

In September 1943 Superman battles the TOYMAN (Act No. 64: "The Terrible Toyman!").

In September-October 1943 Superman meets LOUIE DOLAN (S No. 24/2: "The King of Crackpot Lane"), battles the COBRA KING (S No. 24/3: "Surprise for Superman!"), and comes to the aid of COLONEL RANDALL (S No. 24/4: "Suicide Voyage!").

In Fall 1943 Superman thwarts the sinister machinations of CHARLIE FROST (WF No. 11: "The City of Hate!").

In October 1943 Superman meets TRUMAN TREADWELL (Act No. 65: "The Million-Dollar Marathon!").

In November 1943 Superman thwarts the schemes of MR. ANNISTER (Act No. 66: "The Boy Who Came Back!").

In November-December 1943 Superman comes to the aid of MAJOR JONATHAN RAMSEY (S No. 25/1: "The Man Superman Refused to Help!"), makes the acquaintance of HENRY JONES (S No. 25/3: "King of the Comic Books"), matches wits with HI-JACK (S No. 25/4: "Hi-Jack--Jackal of Crime!"), and, as Clark Kent, enlists in the Army Air Force cadet training program at Yale University so that he can accurately assess the thoroughness and effectiveness of the program in an article for the *Daily Planet* (S No. 25/2: "I Sustain the Wings!").

In December 1943 Superman apprehends underworld fence Reginald Sykes and four of his cohorts; single-handedly constructs, at super-speed, "the nation's largest army officers' training center"— christened the Superman School for Officers' Training by the government—as a favor to the U.S. Army; and helps settle a foolish quarrel between Martha Hoskins and Samuel Rayburn that has caused the stubborn couple to keep postponing their wedding for thirty years despite the fact that they are deeply in love (Act No. 67: "Make Way for Fate!").

In Winter 1943 Superman meets the LYNX (WF No. 12: "The Man Who Stole a Reputation!").

In January 1944 Superman apprehends the Beaker Beales gang (Act No. 68: "Superman Meets Susie!").

In January-February 1944 Superman lends a helping hand to "DAREDEVIL" DOLAN (S No. 26/1: "The Super Stunt Man!"), matches wits with J.

WILBUR WOLFINGHAM (S No. 26/2: "Comedians' Holiday!"), makes the acquaintance of ANDY HOOPS (S No. 26/3: "Superman's Master!"), and becomes embroiled in conflict with the Roman god MERCURY (S No. 26/4: "The Quicksilver Kid!").

In February 1944 Superman battles the PRANKSTER (Act No. 69: "The Lost-and-Found Mystery!").

In March 1944 Superman matches wits with the THINKER (Act No. 70: "Superman Takes a Holiday!").

In March-April 1944 Superman thwarts the schemes of the TOYMAN (S No. 27/1: "The Palace of Perilous Play!"); rescues Lois Lane, two lumbermen, and a paper mill engineer from a burning North Woods cabin (S No. 27/2: "When Giants Meet!"); and meets HIRAM PARDEE (S No. 27/3: "Robbers' Roost!"). A text for this same period recounts the story of Superman's encounter with GOLDIE GATES (S No. 27/4, Mar/Apr '44: "Dear Diary!").

In Spring 1944 Superman matches wits with DELMAR "DICE" DIMANT and his cohorts (WF No. 13: "The Freedom of the Press!").

A text for April 1944 recounts the story of Superman's encounter with the evil COUNT D'ORT (Act No. 71: "Valentine Villainy!").

In May 1944 Superman thwarts the unscrupulous schemes of MR. SNIGGLE (Act No. 72: "Superman and the Super-Movers!").

In May-June 1944 Superman matches wits with J. WILBUR WOLFINGHAM (S No. 28/1: "Lambs versus Wolfingham!"), battles BIG JOE REEFER (S No. 28/2: "The Golden Galleons!"), and meets HERCULES (S No. 28/3: "Stand-In for Hercules!").

In June 1944 Superman matches wits with LUCIUS SPRUCE (Act No. 73: "The Hobby Robbers!").

In Summer 1944 Superman battles the AL BANDAR gang (WF No. 14: "Desert Town!").

In July 1944 Superman makes the acquaintance of ADELBERT DRIBBLE (Act No. 74: "Courtship of Adelbert Dribble!").

In July-August 1944 Superman matches wits with the PRANKSTER (S No. 29/1: "The Wizard of Wishes!"), thwarts the nefarious schemes of the TYCOON OF CRIME (S No. 29/2: "The Tycoon of Crime!"), and meets DUDLEY KENT (S No. 29/3: "The Pride of the Kents!").

In August 1944 Superman matches wits with JOHNNY AESOP (Act No. 75: "Aesop's Modern Fables").

A text for September 1944 recounts the story of Superman's encounter with ROGER CARSON (Act No. 76: "A Voyage to Destiny!").

In September-October 1944 Superman battles SILVER FOXX (S No. 30/1: "Superman Alias Superman!"), comes to the aid of an enterprising young trucker whose girl friend's wealthy father is opposed to the trucker's plans to marry his daughter (S No. 30/2: "The King's Substitute!"), and copes with the magical mischief of MR. MXYZPTLK (S No. 30/3: "The Mysterious Mr. Mxyztplk!").

In Fall 1944 Superman matches wits with DERBY BOWSER (WF No. 15: "The Rubber Band").

In October 1944 Superman battles the PRANKSTER (Act No. 77: "The Headline Hoax!").

In November 1944 Superman lends a helping hand to the owner and patrons of SERGEI'S BORSHT BOWL (Act No. 78: "The Chef of Bohemia!").

In November-December 1944 Superman thwarts the sinister schemes of LEX LUTHOR (S No. 31/1: "Tune Up for Crime!"). Other texts for this period recount the stories of Superman's encounters with ROCKY GRIMES (S No. 31/2, Nov/Dec '44: "A Dog's Tale!") and MR. VAN CROFT (S No. 31/3, Nov/Dec '44: "The Treasure House of History!").

In December 1944 Superman matches wits with J. WILBUR WOLFINGHAM (Act No. 79: "The Golden Fleece!").

A text for Winter 1944 recounts the story of Superman's efforts to help an aspiring young songwriter publish his songs and win the heart of the pretty secretary at the song publishing company (WF No. 16: "Music for the Masses").

In January 1945 Superman copes with the magical mischief of MR. MXYZPTLK (Act No. 80: "Mr. Mxyztplk Returns!").

In January-February 1945 Superman apprehends MART MINK (S No. 32/1: "Superman's Search for Clark Kent!"), matches wits with TED SWAN (S No. 32/2: "Crime on Skis!"), and battles the TOYMAN (S No. 32/3: "Toys of Treachery!").

In February 1945 Superman meets JOHN NICHO-LAS (Act No. 81: "Fairyland Isle!").

In March 1945 Superman battles the WATER SPRITE (Act No. 82: "The Water Sprite!").

In March-April 1945 Superman visits the bizarre home dimension of MR. MXYZPTLK (S No. 33/1: "Dimensions of Danger!"), flies through a raging hurricane to deliver a supply of serum needed to combat an epidemic in the town of Middletown (S No. 33/2: "The Country Doctor!"), and solves the murder of Elias Carp (see CHATE [CAPTAIN]) (S No. 33/3: "The Compass Points to Murder!").

In Spring 1945 Superman meets "EASY" PICKINS (WF No. 17: "The Great Godini!").

In April 1945 Superman meets HOCUS AND POCUS (Act No. 83: "Hocus & Pocus... Magicians by Accident!").

In May 1945 Superman apprehends the DAPPER gang (Act No. 84: "Tommy Gets a Zero!").

In May-June 1945 Superman battles LEX LUTHOR (S No. 34/3: "When the World Got Tired!") and, as Clark Kent, serves as a war correspondent for the *Daily Planet* aboard the Navy destroyer U.S.S. *Davey Jones* somewhere in the Pacific (S No. 34/1: "The United States Navy!"). During this same period, while visiting a fortune teller with Lois Lane, Clark Kent peers into the fortune teller's crystal ball and sees, enacted in the crystal ball, an action-packed adventure in which, as Superman, he thwarts a scheme by senile prospector Pick Perkins and his underworld allies to frighten tourists away from Crazy Canyon—a "rugged canyon" in the western United States "in which are steaming geysers,

colorful cliffs, [and] volcanic mountains"—so that they can buy up the canyon for a fraction of its worth and freely mine the vein of gold that Perkins has discovered in one of the canyon's volcanoes. In the course of this imaginary adventure, Lois Lane discovers, beyond any doubt, that Clark Kent is secretly Superman. "--Wonder if my subconscious mind made up that yarn, or if Lois will really learn the truth about me some day?" muses Kent soon afterward, as he and Lois depart the fortune teller's. "...Only time can tell!--" (S No. 34/2, May/Jun '45: "The Canyon That Went Berserk!").

In June 1945 Superman matches wits with the TOYMAN (Act No. 85: "The Puzzle in Jade!").

In Summer 1945 Superman meets TOMMY BLAKE (WF No. 18: "The Junior Reporters!").

A text for July 1945 recounts the story of Superman's encounter with the WIZARD OF WOKIT (Act No. 86: "The Enchanted Mountain!").

In July-August 1945 Superman thwarts the schemes of J. WILBUR WOLFINGHAM (S No. 35/1: "Fame for Sale!"), matches wits with JED SCAPELY (S No. 35/2: "Like Father, Like Son!"), and teaches a much-needed lesson to BERNARD DEMAREST, JR. (S No. 35/3: "The Genie of the Lamp!").

In August 1945 Superman apprehends a gang of truck hijackers (Act No. 87: "Danger Highway!").

In September 1945 Superman becomes embroiled in an adventure with HOCUS AND POCUS (Act No. 88: "The Adventure of the Stingy Men!").

In September-October 1945 Superman copes with the magical mischief of MR. MXYZPTLK (S No. 36/1: "Mr. Mxyztplk's Mistake!"), meets GLORIA ALLURE (S No. 36/2: "Glory for Gloria!"), and thwarts the unscrupulous machinations of MR. KEELE (S No. 36/3: "Clark Kent, Star Reporter!").

In Fall 1945, while in a hypnotic trance, Lois Lane fantasizes that she and Superman are sharing an adventure together in the days of the Greek mythological heroes (WF No. 19: "The Battle of the Zodiac!").

In October 1945 Superman matches wits with SLIPPERY ANDY (Act No. 89: "The King of Color!").

In November 1945 Superman battles HORACE RIKKER and his Amphi-Bandits (Act No. 90: "Rookery for River Rats!").

In November-December 1945 Superman lends a helping hand to JOHNNY FRAY (S No. 37/1: "The Dangerous Dream!"), matches wits with the PRANK-STER (S No. 37/2: "Pranks for Profit!"), and comes to the aid of SINBAD (S No. 37/3: "The Rubbish Robbers!").

In December 1945 Superman battles "DAVEY JONES" (Act No. 91: "The Ghost Drum!").

In Winter 1945 Superman matches wits with the TOYMAN (WF No. 20: "The Toyman: Super-Scientist!").

c. THE POSTWAR ADVENTURES. In January 1946 Superman thwarts the schemes of NORMIE NORMAN (Act No. 92: "The Average American!").

In January-February 1946 Superman battles LEX LUTHOR (S No. 38/1: "The Battle of the Atoms!"), meets MR. BURTON (S No. 38/2: "The Bad Old Knights!"), and apprehends GOON MCGLOON and Literary Link (S No. 38/3: "The Man of Stone!").

A text for February 1946 recounts the story of how, during Christmas 1945, Superman traveled around the globe, playing Santa Claus to the world's children (Act No. 93: "Christmas 'Round the World!").

In March 1946 Superman thwarts the unscrupulous machinations of BULLWER "BULL" RYLIE (Act No. 94: "Battle of the Redwoods!").

In March-April 1946 Superman matches wits with CAPTAIN SPEARS (S No. 39/2: "The Monster of China Deep!"), thwarts the schemes of J. WILBUR WOLFINGHAM (S No. 39/3: "Swindle in Sweethearts!"), and lends a helping hand to BILL MINTON (WF No. 21: "The Plane of Tomorrow!"). A text for this same period recounts the story of Superman's encounter with BOSS BIGGINS (S No. 39/1, Mar/Apr '46: "The Big Superman Broadcast!").

In April 1946 Superman matches wits with the PRANKSTER (Act No. 95: "The Laughing Stock of Metropolis!").

A text for May 1946 recounts the story of Superman's encounter with MISTER TWISTER (Act No. 96: "Haircut--And a Close Shave!").

In May-June 1946 Superman copes with the exasperating alliance of Susie Tompkins and MR. MXYZPTLK (S No. 40/1: "The Mxyztplk-Susie Alliance!") and meets KUBLAI KHAN (S No. 40/2: "A Modern Marco Polo!"). A text for this same period recounts the story of Superman's encounter with PROFESSOR WALTER WHIFFENSNIFF (S No. 40/3, May/Jun '46: "There Is No Superman!").

In June 1946 Superman becomes embroiled in an adventure with HOCUS AND POCUS (Act No. 97: "The Magician's Convention!").

In July 1946 Superman becomes involved in the hijinks of SUSIE TOMPKINS (Act No. 98: "Starring Susie!").

In July-August 1946 Superman matches wits with the PRANKSTER (S No. 41/1: "Too Many Pranksters!"), meets PAT MALARKEY (S No. 41/2: "Clark Kent's Bodyguard!"), comes to the aid of ALICE NEAL (S No. 41/3: "A Modern Alice in Wonderland!"), and helps a trio of former stars of the silent screen make a comeback in a "talkie" that they themselves produce (WF No. 23: "The Colossus of Metropolis!").

In August 1946 Superman matches wits with KEITH LANGWELL (Act No. 99: "The Talisman of Trouble!").

In September 1946 Superman makes the acquaintance of INSPECTOR ERSKINE HAWKINS (Act No. 100: "The Sleuth Who Never Failed!").

In September-October 1946 Superman thwarts the nefarious schemes of J. WILBUR WOLFINGHAM (S No. 42/1: "The Men Who Wouldn't Quit!"), apprehends BURTON CROWTHER (S No. 42/2: "A Legend Comes True!"), temporarily adopts the alternate identity of KENNETH CLARKSON (S No. 42/3: "The Death of Clark Kent!"), and matches wits with POSY EDWARDS (WF No. 24: "Impossible but True!").

In October 1946 Superman apprehends SPECS DOUR (Act No. 101: "Crime Paradise!").

In November 1946 Superman copes with the magical mischief of MR. MXYZPTLK (Act No. 102: "Mr. Mxyztplk and His Wonderful Lamp!").

In November-December 1946 Superman meets HECTOR THWISTLE (S No. 43/1: "The Inventions of Hector Thwistle!"), apprehends JOE CORCORAN (S No. 43/2: "Lois Lane, Actress!"), battles LEX LUTHOR (S No. 43/3: "The Molten World!"), and matches wits with ED ROOK (WF No. 25: "Mad Weather in Metropolis!").

In December 1946 Superman encounters the sole remaining survivors of tenth-century QUETZATLAN (Act No. 103: "The Road to Happiness!").

In January 1947 Superman matches wits with the PRANKSTER (Act No. 104: "Candytown, U.S.A.").

In January-February 1947 Superman battles the TOYMAN (S No. 44/1: "Playthings of Peril!"), matches wits with SAMUEL C. OWENS (S No. 44/2: "The Men Who Didn't Die on Time!"), meets WILLIAM SHAKESPEARE during a time-journey to London in the year 1606 (S No. 44/3: "Shakespeare's Ghost Writer!"), and makes the acquaintance of BENNY CALL (WF No. 26: "The Confessions of Superman!").

A text for February 1947 recounts the story of Superman's encounter with JASPER RASPER (Act No. 105: "The Man Who Hated Christmas!").

In March 1947 Clark Kent temporarily assumes the title of BARON EDGESTREAM (Act No. 106: "His Lordship, Clark Kent!").

In March-April 1947 Superman becomes embroiled in an adventure with HOCUS AND POCUS (S No. 45/1: "Lois Lane, Superwoman!"), thwarts the unscrupulous machinations of HUGH ROWLAND (S No. 45/2: "Showdown on the Showboat!"), meets NELSON SWAYNE (WF No. 27: "The Man Who Out-Supered Superman!"), and defeats an unidentified extradimensional alien who has abducted Lois Lane and four other people and placed them on display in his home dimension in his own private museum (S No. 45/3: "The Case of the Living Trophies!").

In April 1947 Superman matches wits with J. WILBUR WOLFINGHAM (Act No. 107: "Journey into Ruin!").

In May 1947 Superman meets VINCE VINCENT (Act No. 108: "The Great Crasher!").

In May-June 1947 Superman copes with the magical mischief of MR. MXYZPTLK (S No. 46/1: "Mr. Mxyztplk Goes to College!"), meets TOM TRENT (S No. 46/2: "High Man on a Flagpole!"), battles LEX LUTHOR (WF No. 28: "Superman's Super-Self!"), and helps some of Clark Kent's former high school classmates achieve their unfulfilled ambitions (S No. 46/3: "That Old Class of Superboy's!").

In June 1947 Superman matches wits with the PRANKSTER (Act No. 109: "The Man Who Robbed the Mint!").

In July 1947 Superman receives some crook-catching assistance from SUSIE TOMPKINS (Act No. 110: "Mother Goose Crimes!").

In July-August 1947 Superman battles the TOY-MAN (S No. 47/1: "The Toyman's Castle!"), becomes embroiled in an adventure with SUSIE TOMPKINS (S No. 47/2: "Susie Reforms!"), lends a helping hand to BARNEY VELLUM (WF No. 29: "The Books That Couldn't Be Bound!"), and suffers through a day of bad luck, both as Clark Kent and as Superman, in which just about everything seems to go wrong (S No. 47/3: "Superman's Unlucky Day!").

In August 1947 Superman comes to the aid of GI NEWSREEL, INC. (Act No. 111: "Cameras in the Clouds!").

In September 1947 Superman copes with the magical mischief of MR. MXYZPTLK (Act No. 112: "The Cross-Country Chess Crimes!").

In September-October 1947 Superman lends a helping hand to JOHNNY TERRILL (S No. 48/2: "Autograph, Please!"), matches wits with "FAT-HEAD" GURNEY (S No. 48/3: "The Rarest Secret in the World!"), and battles CATAWAMPUS JONES and his Rockdust Bandits (WF No. 30: "Sheriff Clark Kent!"). A text for this same period recounts the story of a battle between Superman and LEX LUTHOR (S No. 48/1: "The Man Who Stole the Sun!").

In October 1947 Superman stands before a mirror and hypnotizes himself into believing, for a period of twenty-four hours, that he is just an ordinary human being, without super-powers, so that he can see how it feels to be just an "ordinary guy." Ultimately, however, Superman concludes that "there's no such thing as an ordinary man. Everyone has some special talents that he can develop and learn to use" (Act No. 113: "Just an Ordinary Guy!").

A text for November 1947 recounts the story of Superman's battle with MIKE CHESNEY and response to a lecture delivered by DR. CARL SAND (Act No. 114: "The Man Who Was Honest!").

In November-December 1947 Superman matches wits with the TOYMAN (S No. 49/1: "Toyman and the Gadgets of Greed!"), battles the GARGOYLE (S No. 49/2: "Clark Kent's Most Dangerous Assignment!"), and thwarts the unscrupulous machinations of the editor and publisher of the Metropolis EXAMINER (S No. 49/3: "Lois Lane, Globe-Trotter!"). A text for this same period recounts the details of a criminal's nightmare about Superman (WF No. 31, Nov/Dec '47: "Superman's Super-Rival!").

In December 1947 Superman restores the lost faith of ARTHUR PARRISH (Act No. 115: "The Wish That Came True!").

In January 1948 Superman thwarts the sinister schemes of J. WILBUR WOLFINGHAM (Act No. 116: "The Wizard of Winter!").

In January-February 1948 Superman matches wits with JASPER HAWK (S No. 50/1: "The Task That Stumped Superman!"), battles the PRANKSTER (S No. 50/2: "The Slogans That Came Too True!"), helps three hunters gain admission to the HUNTERS' CLUB (S No. 50/3: "The Hunters' Club!"), and thwarts the sinister machinations of the evil high priest NA-TSE during a time-journey to Egypt in the twenty-sixth

century B.C. (WF No. 32: "The Seventh Wonder of the World!").

A text for February 1948 recounts the story of how, on Christmas Eve 1947, Superman made it possible for the people of Christmastown, in Central Valley, to hold their gala annual Christmas festival as scheduled despite Central Valley's having been inundated by a flash flood (Act No. 117: "Christmastown, U.S.A.!").

In March 1948 Superman exonerates his alter ego, Clark Kent, of responsibility for the death of SLUGGER MAULL (Act No. 118: "The Execution of Clark Kent!").

In March-April 1948 Superman copes with the magical mischief of MR. MXYZPTLK (S No. 51/1: "Mr. Mxyztplk Seeks a Wife!"), battles MR. OHM (S No. 51/2: "The Magnetic Mobster!"), outwits "PUDGE" PURDY (S No. 51/3: "The Man Who Bossed Superman!"), and apprehends the WHITEY CRONIN gang (WF No. 33: "Superman Press, Inc.!").

In April 1948 Superman comes to the aid of JIM BANNING (Act No. 119: "Superman for a Day!").

In May 1948 Superman thwarts the unscrupulous machinations of MIKE FOSS (Act No. 120: "Superman, Stunt Man!").

In May-June 1948 Superman battles the PRANK-STER (S No. 52/1: "Preview of Plunder"), meets HIRAM BROWNLEE (S No. 52/2: "Superman Turns on the Heat!"), makes the acquaintance of JACK ALLEN (S No. 52/3: "Superman in Valhalla!"), and, with the aid of an unidentified actor hired to portray Superman in a charity benefit, apprehends a gang of Fascists responsible for hurling a bomb into the midst of a parade being held to promote international goodwill (WF No. 34: "The Un-Super Superman!").

In June 1948 Superman thwarts the nefarious schemes of WILLIAM SHARP (Act No. 121: "Superman versus Atlas!").

In July 1948 Superman matches wits with CHARLEY CARSON (Act No. 122: "The Super Sideshow!").

In July-August 1948 Superman's origin is extensively recounted (S No. 53/1: "The Origin of Superman!"), and Superman meets MIKE MOONEY (S No. 53/2: "The Oracle from Metropolis!"), battles the EYE (S No. 53/3: "A Job for Superhombre!"), and undergoes a series of minor trials and tribulations while baby-sitting with a pair of twin baby boys mistakenly deposited on Clark Kent's doorstep (WF No. 35: "Daddy Superman!").

In August 1948 Superman battles SKID RUSSELL and his cohorts (Act No. 123: "50 Ways to Kill Superman!").

In September 1948 crime goes on a rampage in the city of Metropolis after the cataclysmic explosion of an atomic reactor has rendered Superman temporarily radioactive, making it impossible for him to come close to people without destroying them. Ultimately, however, the Man of Steel succeeds in ridding himself of his deadly radioactivity, enabling him to halt the crime wave and apprehend the criminals responsible for it (Act No. 124: "A Superman of Doom!").

In September-October 1948 Superman battles the WRECKER (S No. 54/1: "The Wrecker"), teaches LOIS LANE a well-deserved lesson (S No. 54/3: "Her Majesty Lois Lane!"), comes to the aid of a playwright named BLANDING (WF No. 36: "Lois Lane, Sleeping Beauty"), and, as Clark Kent, lends a helping hand to RICHARD WONG (S No. 54/2: "The Secret of the Chinese Dragon!").

In October 1948 Superman matches wits with LEX LUTHOR (Act No. 125: "The Modern Nostradamus!").

In November 1948 Superman battles the CHAMELEON (Act No. 126: "Superman on Television!").

In November-December 1948 Superman thwarts the schemes of the PRANKSTER (S No. 55/1: "Prankster's Second Childhood"), meets STEPHEN VAN SCHUYLER III (S No. 55/2: "The Richest Man in the World!"), puts in a good word for JONATHAN TRUNDLE (S No. 55/3: "Too Many Heroes!"), and spends a hectic day with five reporters from the DAILY PLANET (WF No. 37: "The Superman Story!").

In December 1948 Superman meets RALPH EDWARDS (Act No. 127: "Superman Takes the Consequences!").

In January 1949 Superman thwarts the sinister machinations of "ACES" DUCEY (Act No. 128: "The Adventure of Little Red!").

In January-February 1949 Superman battles the PRANKSTER (S No. 56/1: "The Prankster Picks a Partner!"), lends a helping hand to F. P. CROTCHETT (S No. 56/2: "The Man Who Couldn't Laugh!"), meets SMARTYPANTS (S No. 56/3: "Smartypants!"), and apprehends the "Bullet" Barris gang when they attempt to steal PROFESSOR SAMUEL SMIGGS's "if-machine" (WF No. 38: "If There Were No Superman").

In February 1949 Superman meets GOB-GOB (Act No. 129: "Lois Lane, Cavegirl!").

In March 1949 Superman matches wits with CAPTAIN KIDDER (Act No. 130: "Superman and the Mermaid!").

In March-April 1949 Superman battles LEX LUTHOR (S No. 57/1: "The Menace of the Machine Men!"), meets LOIS 4XR during a time-journey to the year 2949 A.D. (S No. 57/2: "Every Man a Superman!"), becomes the foster father of TOMMY SUPERMAN (S No. 57/3: "The Son of Superman!"), and matches wits with BIG JIM MARTIN (WF No. 39: "The Fatal Forecasts!").

In April 1949 Superman battles LEX LUTHOR (Act No. 131: "The Scrambled Superman!").

In May 1949 Superman learns the story of ELY KENT (Act No. 132: "The Secret of the Kents!").

In May-June 1949 Superman matches wits with TINY TRIX (S No. 58/1: "Tiny Trix, the Bantam Bandit!"), becomes embroiled in a dilemma involving LOIS LANE (S No. 58/2: "Lois Lane Loves Clark Kent!"), meets REGOR (S No. 58/3: "The Case of the Second Superman"), and battles CHECK (WF No. 40: "The Two Lois Lanes!").

In June 1949 Superman thwarts the unscrupulous machinations of EMMA BLOTZ (Act No. 133: "The World's Most Perfect Girl!").

In July 1949 Superman matches wits with PAU[..] STRONG (Act No. 134: "Super-Cowboy!").

In July-August 1949 Superman becomes embroile[..] in an adventure with LOIS LANE (S No. 59/1: "Loi[..] Lane—Queen of the Amazons!"), meets ALAN SHO[..] WELL (S No. 59/3: "The Man of Steel's Supe[..] Manhunt!"), copes with the magical mischief of MR[..] MXYZPTLK (S No. 59/3: "The City That Forgo[..] Superman"), and thwarts the unscrupulous machina[..] tions of JAMES HARVEY THORBEN (WF No. 41: "Th[..] Discovery of Supermanium!").

In August 1949 Superman matches wits with JOH[..] MORTON (Act No. 135: "The Case of the Huma[..] Statues!").

In September 1949 Superman rescues Metropoli[..] from destruction by "a giant swarm of meteors[..] hurtling toward the Earth (Act No. 136: "Superman Show-Off!").

In September-October 1949 Superman matche[..] wits with HOLLIS SHORE (S No. 60/1: "The Tw[..] Identities of Superman!"), meets PROFESSOR JOHN[..] (S No. 60/2: "The Men Who Had to Guard Super[..] man!"), battles the TOYMAN (S No. 60/3: "Superma[..] Fights the Super-Brain!"), and outwits a band o[..] robot aliens from the planet URANUS (WF No. 42[..] "The Alphabetical Animal Adventure!").

In October 1949 Superman comes to the aid o[..] PERCIVAL WINTERS (Act No. 137: "The Man with the[..] Charmed Life!").

In November 1949 Superman lends a helping hand[..] to HERBERT BINKLE (Act No. 138: "Superman Scoop[..] Parade").

In November-December 1949 Superman battles[..] the PRANKSTER (S No. 61/1: "The Prankster's Radio[..] Program!"), becomes embroiled in an adventure[..] involving LOIS LANE (S No. 61/2: "The Courtship of[..] the Three Lois Lanes!"), and matches wits with[..] SWAMI RIVA (S No. 61/3: "Superman Returns to[..] Krypton!").

In December 1949 Clark Kent takes steps to[..] assuage the dissatisfaction of J. WIMMER (Act No.[..] 139: "Clark Kent...Daredevil!").

In December 1949-January 1950 Superman[..] matches wits with J. WILBUR WOLFINGHAM (WF No.[..] 43: "When Metropolis Went Mad!").

In January 1950 Superman rescues the world from[..] destruction by a terrifying form of extraterrestrial[..] plant life—Superman dubs it "the creeping death"—[..] which falls to Earth inside a meteor and, as it grows,[..] "wreaks complete destruction on everything it[..] passes!" (Act No. 140: "Superman Becomes a Hermit!").

In January-February 1950 Superman battles[..] MARTLER (S No. 62/1: "Black Magic on Mars!"),[..] matches wits with the ACE (S No. 62/2: "The People[..] vs. Superman!"), and copes with the magical mischief[..] of MR. MXYZPTLK (S No. 62/3: "Mr. Mxyztplk,[..] Hero!").

In February 1950 Superman battles LEX LUTHOR[..] (Act No. 141: "Luthor's Secret Weapon").

A text for February-March 1950 recounts a dream[..] of Lois Lane's in which Superman battles a gigantic electronic brain that has come miraculously to life (WF No. 44: "The Revolt of the Thought Machine!").

In March 1950 Superman matches wits with DAN THE DIP and his cohorts (Act No. 142: "The Conquest of Superman!").

In March-April 1950 Superman battles JOHN ACHILLES (S No. 63/1: "Achilles *versus* Superman!"), thwarts the schemes of the TOYMAN (S No. 63/2: "The Wind-Up Toys of Peril!"), and makes the acquaintance of ELLEN BOND (S No. 63/3: "Miss Metropolis of 1950").

In April 1950 Superman launches an apparent romance with NIKKI LARUE (Act No. 143: "The Bride of Superman!").

In April-May 1950 Clark Kent and Lois Lane open a private detective agency (*see* LOIS LANE AND CLARK KENT, PRIVATE DETECTIVES) (WF No. 45: "Lois Lane and Clark Kent, Detectives!").

A text for May 1950 purports to tell the true story of how Clark Kent came to acquire his reporter's job on the DAILY PLANET (Act No. 144: "Clark Kent's Career!").

In May-June 1950 Clark Kent and Lois Lane become honorary professors of journalism at QUINN COLLEGE (S No. 64/1: "Professor Lois Lane!"), the world is threatened with disaster because of an invention created by DR. JOHN DORSEY (S No. 64/2: "The Isle of Giant Insects!"), and Superman matches wits with the PRANKSTER (S No. 64/3: "The Free-for-All Crimes!").

In June 1950 Superman meets MERTON GLOOP (Act No. 145: "Merton Gloop and his Magic Horseshoe!").

In June-July 1950 Superman battles MISTER SEVEN (WF No. 46: "The Seven Crimes of Mister 7!").

In July 1950 Superman matches wits with LEX LUTHOR (Act No. 146: "The Statues That Came to Life!").

In July-August 1950 Superman meets DR. EPHRAIM POTTS (S No. 65/1: "The Testing of Superman!"), appears to develop a romantic interest in PEGGY WILKINS (S No. 65/2: "Superman's Sweetheart!"); and battles MALA and his villainous brothers (S No. 65/3: "Three Supermen from Krypton!").

In August 1950 Superman matches wits with "CHECKS" ROSS and his Blackout Bandits (Act No. 147: "Superman Becomes Miss Lovelorn!").

In August-September 1950 Clark Kent and Lois Lane recall Superman's dramatic capture of the Eddie Fisk gang during the period when, according to this text, Lois Lane was working as a waitress at HARRY'S DOG HOUSE (WF No. 47: "The Girl Who Hated Reporters!").

In September 1950 Superman thwarts the unscrupulous machinations of HENRY MEECHER (Act No. 148: "Superman, Indian Chief!").

In September-October 1950 Superman matches wits with the PRANKSTER (S No. 66/1: "The Babe of Steel!") and lends a helping hand to FINNEY FLOOR (S No. 66/3: "The Machine That Played Cupid!"). During this same period, after Clark Kent has

suffered a series of fainting spells and doctors have diagnosed his condition as Walker's disease, an incurable fatal illness, Superman decides to use what he believes are his last remaining days of life to carry out a series of gigantic super-tasks as his final legacy to mankind, including the stockpiling of vast amounts of coal and oil—and the construction of a gigantic solar-power plant—to meet mankind's energy needs in the year 2000 A.D., and the destruction of a barren planet in outer space that threatens to collide with Earth in the year 1987. Ultimately, however, having completed these tasks, Superman learns that he is not dying at all, but rather suffering from the debilitating effects of a tiny fragment of kryptonite that has become accidentally lodged in the camera of a *Daily Planet* cameraman, thereby weakening Clark Kent with its baleful radiations whenever he reports to work at the *Planet*. Indeed, once the offending kryptonite fragment has been disposed of, Kent is restored to perfect health (S No. 66/2, Sep/Oct '50: "The Last Days of Superman!").

In October 1950 Superman thwarts a series of attempts by LOIS LANE to maneuver him into matrimony (Act No. 149: "The Courtship on Krypton!").

In October-November 1950 Superman thwarts the unscrupulous machinations of MARVIN BLAIR (WF No. 48: "The Great Steel Mystery!").

In November 1950 Superman matches wits with MORKO (Act No. 150: "The Secret of the 6 Superman Statues!").

In November-December 1950 Superman meets PERRY COMO (S No. 67/1: "Perry Como, I Love You!"), visits the undersea realm of QUEEN PARALEA (S No. 67/2: "The City Under the Sea!"), and makes the acquaintance of JOE POLESKI (S No. 67/3: "Clark Kent's Twin!").

In December 1950 Superman battles the formidable alliance of MR. MXYZPTLK, Lex Luthor, and the Prankster (Act No. 151: "Superman's Super-Magic Show!").

In December 1950-January 1951 Superman meets the members of the METROPOLIS SHUTTERBUG SOCIETY (WF No. 49: "The Men Who Shot Superman!").

In January 1951 Superman matches wits with DR. DORROW (Act No. 152: "The Sleep That Lasted 1000 Years").

In January-February 1951 Superman battles LEX LUTHOR (S No. 68/1: "The Six Elements of Crime!"), makes the acquaintance of KING HARRUP II (S No. 68/2: "Lois Lane's Royal Romance!"), and matches wits with JUDD BIXBY (S No. 68/3: "Superman, Hotel Manager!").

In February 1951 Superman defeats the KINGPIN (Act No. 153: "The 100 Deaths of Clark Kent!").

In February-March 1951 Superman lends a helping hand to BEN DRILL (WF No. 50: "Superman Super-Wrecker").

In March 1951 Superman thwarts the unscrupulous machinations of HARRY REED (Act No. 154: "Miss Robinson Crusoe!").

In March-April 1951 Superman battles the PRANK-STER and his cunning apprentice (S No. 69/1: "The Prankster's Apprentice!"), meets SANDOR SANDOR (S No. 69/2: "Sandor Sandor, Genius!"), and matches wits with INSPECTOR ERSKINE HAWKINS (S No. 69/3: "The Man Who Didn't Know He Was Superman!").

In April 1951 Superman apprehends ANDREW ARVIN (Act No. 155: "The Cover Girl Mystery!").

In April-May 1951 Superman becomes embroiled in an adventure involving LOIS LANE (WF No. 51: "The Amazing Talents of Lois Lane!").

In May 1951 Superman battles LEX LUTHOR (Act No. 156: "The Girl of Steel!").

In May-June 1951 Superman meets ANNIE NICHOLS (S No. 70/1: "Lois Lane Meets Annie Oakley!"), lends a helping hand to CHARLES LAMONT (S No. 70/2: "The Life of Supermen!"), and matches wits with the PRANKSTER (S No. 70/3: "The Pied Piper Prankster!").

In June 1951 Superman apprehends JOE "THE ELEPHANT" STRIKER and his henchmen (Act No. 157: "The Superman Who Couldn't Fly!").

In June-July 1951 Superman thwarts the nefarious schemes of J. WILBUR WOLFINGHAM (WF No. 52: "The Man Who Swindled Superman!").

In July 1951 Superman matches wits with KANE KORREL (Act No. 158: "The Kid from Krypton!").

In July-August 1951 Superman matches wits with R24 (S No. 71/1: "Clark Kent's Super-Masquerade!"), comes to the aid of the ANTI-SUPERMAN CLUB (S No. 71/2: "The Anti-Superman Club!"), and battles LEX LUTHOR (S No. 71/3: "The Man Who Stole the Oceans!").

In August 1951 Superman makes the acquaintance of OSWALD WHIMPLE (Act No. 159: "The Man Who Owned Superman").

In August-September 1951 Superman thwarts the unscrupulous machinations of ELIAS TOOMEY (WF No. 53: "The City That Was for Sale!").

In September 1951 Superman meets MISS MINERVA KENT (Act No. 160: "Superman's Aunt Minerva!").

In September-October 1951 Superman battles the PRANKSTER (S No. 72/1: "The Unfunny Prankster!"), closes down the UNIVERSAL INSURANCE COMPANY (S No. 72/2: "The Private Life of Perry White!"), and meets HARVEY FOLLENSBY (S No. 72/3: "The Flight of the Failures!").

In October 1951 Superman meets ANTARA (Act No. 161: "Exit—Superman!").

In October-November 1951 Superman apprehends FINGERS FELTON and Lefty Louie (WF No. 54: "The Superman Who Avoided Danger!").

In November 1951 Superman encounters "IT" (Act No. 162: "IT!").

In November-December 1951 Superman closes down GLOBAL ENTERPRISES, INC. (S No. 73/1: "Hank Garvin, Man of Steel!"), matches wits with "THE INSIDER" (S No. 73/3: "Perry White vs. Clark Kent!"), and recalls some of his own experiences as an orphan while putting on a one-man circus for the youngsters at the Metropolis Orphan Asylum (S No. 73/2: "The Mighty Mite!").

In December 1951 Superman matches wits with SUSAN SEMPLE and, with her help, apprehends the VINCE MOON gang (Act No. 163: "The Girl of Tomorrow").

In December 1951-January 1952 Superman battles "DUDE" VORMAN (WF No. 55: "The City That Exiled Superman!").

In January 1952 Superman meets STEFAN ANDRIESSEN (Act No. 164: "Superman's Hall of Trophies!").

In January-February 1952 Superman matches wits with LEX LUTHOR (S No. 74/1: "The Lost Secrets of Krypton!"), meets ERNEST GADDEN (S No. 74/2: "Superman's Masters!"), apprehends "HATCHET" KAIMS (S No. 74/3: "The Secret of Superman's Home!"), and battles DR. VALLIN (WF No. 56: "The Superman Pageant!").

In February 1952 Superman matches wits with the CRIME CZAR (Act No. 165: "The Man Who Conquered Superman!").

In March 1952 Superman battles LEX LUTHOR (Act No. 166: "The Three Scoops of Death!").

In March-April 1952 Superman thwarts the nefarious schemes of the PRANKSTER (S No. 75/1: "The Prankster's Star Pupil!"), puts MR. JASSON out of business (S No. 75/2: "Superman--Thrill Salesman!"), apprehends the MOOSE COLLINS gang (S No. 75/3: "The Man Who Stole Memories!"), and meets VANCE CORLIN (WF No. 57: "The Artificial Superman!").

In April 1952 Superman investigates the mysterious PROFESSOR NERO and lends a helping hand to a group of "weird insect beings" from a distant planet who have been stranded on the ocean floor, without the necessary rocket fuel to launch themselves back into outer space, ever since their spaceship "was caught by the Earth's gravity and crashed in the sea!" (Act No. 167: "The Machines of Crime!").

In May 1952 Superman matches wits with OLAV (Act No. 168: "The Menace of Planet Z!").

In May-June 1952 Superman and Batman apprehend JOHN SMILTER, and learn each other's secret identity while vacationing aboard the coastal cruiseship VARANIA (S No. 76/1: "The Mightiest Team in the World!"), and Superman lends a helping hand to JOE HARRIS (S No. 76/2: "The Misfit Manhunter!") and thwarts the nefarious schemes of MR. FENTON (WF No. 58: "'Scoop' Smith, Boy Reporter!"). Another text for this period recounts the story of Superman's capture of "SHUT-EYE" COLLINS and of LOIS LANE's attempt to marry Clark Kent off to her friend Lorraine Jennings (S No. 76/3, May/Jun '52: "Mrs. Superman!").

In June 1952 Clark Kent and Lois Lane meet the caveman inventor LARS (Act No. 169: "Caveman Clark Kent!").

A text for July 1952 recounts the story of Superman's encounter with DR. HUGO RENALDO (Act No. 170: "The Mad Artist of Metropolis!").

In July-August 1952 Superman meets PROFESSOR WILLIAM ENDERS (S No. 77/1: "The Man Who Went to Krypton!"), matches wits with the FIXER (S No. 77/2:

"The Greatest Pitcher in the World!"), and battles LEX LUTHOR (WF No. 59: "Superman's Super Hold-Up!"). During this same period, Clark Kent and Lois Lane journey by time machine to Jamestown, Virginia, in the year 1609, where, as Superman, Kent helps forge a permanent peace between the white settlers and the Indians (S No. 77/3, Jul/Aug '52: "Superman Meets Pocahontas!").

In August 1952 Superman buries a time capsule containing a "complete picture record" of his life, abilities, and exploits for the edification of "future generations" (Act No. 171: "The Secrets of Superman!").

In September 1952 Superman becomes embroiled in an adventure involving LOIS LANE (Act No. 172: "Lois Lane...Witch!").

In September-October 1952 Superman battles a Kryptonian "snagriff" (see SNAGRIFF) (S No. 78/1: "The Beast from Krypton!"), comes to the aid of the ATLAS CLUB (S No. 78/2: "The Strong Man Club!"), becomes embroiled in an adventure involving "LENS" LEWIS and LANA LANG (S No. 78/3: "The Girls in Superman's Life!"), and matches wits with J. WILBUR WOLFINGHAM (WF No. 60: "The Swindler Who Was Honest!").

In October 1952 Superman thwarts the evil machinations of "DRAGON" LANG (Act No. 173: "Superman's Invulnerable Foe!").

In November 1952 Superman battles the so-called "miracle twine gang" (see MIRACLE TWINE GANG, THE) (Act No. 174: "The Man Who Shackled Superman!").

In November-December 1952 Superman matches wits with LEX LUTHOR (S No. 79/1: "Citadel of Doom!"); thwarts the unscrupulous schemes of JOHN WILTON (S No. 79/2: "The End of the Planet!"); visits England, the home of INSPECTOR ERSKINE HAWKINS (S No. 79/3: "The Revenge That Took 300 Years!"); and apprehends a pair of criminals named Mike and Corky—and destroys a meteor hurtling toward Earth—despite the severe limitations that have been imposed on his activities by the baleful effects of three kryptonite meteors, which, having plunged into the sun, have temporarily contaminated the sun's rays, causing Superman to become seriously weakened— even to the point of paralysis—whenever he is in direct sunlight (WF No. 61: "Superman's Blackout!").

In December 1952 Superman matches wits with JOHN VINDEN (Act No. 175: "5 Against Superman!").

In January 1953 Superman apprehends the MILLION-DOLLAR MARVIN gang (Act No. 176: "Muscles for Money").

In January-February 1953 Superman meets HALK KAR (S No. 80/1: "Superman's Big Brother!"), battles BIG-NOISE NELSON (S No. 80/2: "The Big Noise of Metropolis!"), matches wits with LEX LUTHOR (WF No. 62: "The Seven Secrets of Superman"), and lends a helping hand to three bizarre fire-creatures— described as "some weird kind of fire life"—which have been helplessly stranded on the Earth's surface ever since a powerful volcanic eruption hurled them from their own world inside the Earth's core (S No.

80/3: "The Men of Fire").

In February 1953 Superman matches wits with the "GENERAL" (Act No. 177: "The Anti-Superman Weapon").

In March 1953 Superman apprehends PROFESSOR SANDS (Act No. 178: "The Sandman of Crime!").

In March-April 1953 Superman battles LEX LUTHOR (S No. 81/1: "Superman's Secret Workshop"), matches wits with LITTLE DAN WHEELER (S No. 81/2: "20,000 Leagues Under the Sea with Superman"), meets THARKA (S No. 81/3: "The Superwoman from Space"), and, as Clark Kent, impersonates DASHER DRAPE (WF No. 63: "Clark Kent, Gangster").

In April 1953 Superman establishes a residence in the town of MAPLEVILLE (Act No. 179: "Super Manor!").

In May 1953 Superman matches wits with the SYNDICATE OF FIVE (Act No. 180: "The Super-Telethon").

In May-June 1953 Superman copes with the magical mischief of MR. MXYZPTLK (S No. 82/2: "The Unemployed Superman"); rescues Perry White, Lois Lane, and the rest of the Daily Planet's reportorial staff after the bus carrying them on their annual picnic has been buried by a landslide, and single-handedly gathers the news for the newspaper's forthcoming edition (S No. 82/3: "The Super-Reporter of Metropolis"); thwarts the nefarious schemes of JOHN MADDERS (WF No. 64: "The Death of Lois Lane"); and, after Lois Lane has joined the WACs in order to write a series of articles on the subject for the Daily Planet, uses his super-powers to protect her from the petty vindictiveness of a lovely WAC sergeant jealous of Lois's close friendship with Clark Kent (S No. 82/1: "Lois Lane Joins the WACS!").

In June 1953 Superman matches wits with DIAMOND DAVE DELANEY (Act No. 181: "The New Superman").

In July 1953 Superman defeats a band of evil "space raiders" from a distant galaxy who attempt to deceive the Man of Steel into believing that they are survivors of his own native planet, Krypton, as part of their diabolical scheme to conquer the Earth (Act No. 182: "The Return of Planet Krypton!").

In July-August 1953 Superman battles "THE BRAIN" (S No. 83/1: "Destination X!"), meets GRETA GAGE (S No. 83/2: "The Search for the Bravest Woman!"), thwarts the nefarious schemes of PHIL CASAN (S No. 83/3: "Clark Kent--Convict!"), and matches wits with JAMES SMIRT (WF No. 65: "The Confessions of Superman!").

In August 1953 Superman battles LEX LUTHOR (Act No. 183: "The Perfect Plot to Kill Superman!").

In September 1953 Superman comes to the aid of DONALD WHITMORE (Act No. 184: "The Covered Wagon of Doom!").

In September-October 1953 Superman meets the "yeast-men" (see YEAST-MEN) (S No. 84/2: "A Doghouse for Superman!"), matches wits with HARRY "KING" SAPHIRE (WF No. 66: "Superman, Ex-Crimebuster!"), and, during a period when Clark Kent and Lois Lane are working as temporary police officers so that they can write an article on their experience for the *Daily Planet*, apprehends fugitive bank robber "Cracker" Moreau and a gang of criminals led by "crafty crime-planner" "Silver" Skene (S No. 84/3: "Lois Lane, Policewoman!"). During this same period, Superman journeys through the time barrier to the day when, as Clark Kent, he first arrived in Metropolis to begin his career as a newspaper reporter, hoping, in this way, to be able to "start life anew" in a new occupation and thus escape Lois Lane's constant attempts to unravel the secret of his dual identity. Embarking upon a new career as a midnight-to-morning disc jockey, however, Kent finds himself saddled with a female assistant who is even more determinedly curious than Lois Lane, and when this assistant finally quits her job—after Kent has successfully deceived her into believing that he is not really Superman—Kent learns, to his dismay, that her replacement is none other than Lois Lane, who, in this alternate replay of Clark Kent's life, has just quit her job at the *Daily Planet* in order to come to work at the radio station which employs Clark Kent. "...I guess even **Superman** can't escape fate!" muses ᴷent ruefully, as he prepares to journey forward through the time barrier in order to resume the old life he left behind. "I might as well go back in time...at least, I'm familiar with the problems there!" (S No. 84/1, Sep/Oct '53: "Superman's Other Life!").

In October 1953 Superman thwarts the unscrupulous machinations of ISAAH PENDLETON (Act No. 185: "Superman's Million Dollar Photos!").

In November 1953, after the Earth's rate of rotation has been vastly speeded up as a consequence of forces unleashed by "a great **dark star** that's rushing through the solar system," Superman, facing what the text describes as "the greatest challenge of his career," rescues the Earth from imminent disaster by single-handedly slowing down the Earth and restoring its rotation rate to normal (Act No. 186: "Haunted Superman!").

In November-December 1953 Superman battles LEX LUTHOR (S No. 85/1: "Luthor—Hero!"), meets GRISELDA GRAY (S No. 85/2: "Clark Kent, Gentleman Journalist!"), lends a helping hand to PROFESSOR CASPAR SNELLING (S No. 85/3: "The Weakling Who Became a Superman!"), and makes the acquaintance of CURTIS GALLOWAY (WF No. 67: "Metropolis--Crime Center!").

In December 1953 Superman matches wits with SILVER (Act No. 187: "Superman's New Super Powers!").

In January 1954 Superman battles the CUSHIONS RAYMOND gang (Act No. 188: "The Spectral Superman!"), meets the members of the ROUND TABLE CLUB (S No. 86/1: "The Dragon from King Arthur's Court!"), copes with the magical mischief of MR. MXYZPTLK (S No. 86/3: "The Fourth Dimension Gazette!"), and, after capturing a gang of criminals known as the Gaspipe Gang, apprehends the unidentified perpetrators of an unsolved jewel robbery (*see* OLSEN, JIMMY) (S No. 86/2: "Jimmy Olsen...Editor!").

In January-February 1954 Superman demolishes a gigantic asteroid whose presence in Earth's solar system has been causing monumental catastrophes on Earth—including tidal waves, cyclones, and other disasters—and suffers through a period of near-total amnesia induced by the unearthly elements contained in the asteroid, including, apparently, "a variety of kryptonite" (WF No. 68: "The Menace from the Stars!").

In February 1954 Superman makes the acquaintance of MR. AND MRS. JOHN VANDEVIER (Act No. 189: "Clark Kent's New Mother and Father!"), encounters "the thing" (*see* "THING, THE") (S No. 87/1: "The Thing from 40,000 A.D.!"), protects CYRUS WALTERS's gem collection (S No. 87/2: "Superman's Super-Boners!"), and matches wits with the PRANKSTER (S No. 87/3: "The Prankster's Greatest Role!").

In March 1954 Superman copes with the magical mischief of MR. MXYZPTLK (Act No. 190: "The Boy Who Saved Superman!"), thwarts the nefarious schemes of the PROFESSOR (S No. 88/2: "The Dog Who Loved Superman!"), battles the formidable alliance of LEX LUTHOR, the Toyman, and the Prankster (S No. 88/3: "The Terrible Trio!"), and, during a period when, as Clark Kent, he is serving brief stints as a construction worker, steelworker, and truck driver in preparation for writing a series of articles for the *Daily Planet* on the world's "toughest jobs," frightens the unscrupulous chief engineer of a subway tunnel project—who has been defrauding his contractor by using substandard cement on the project and pocketing the difference—into making a full confession of his crimes (S No. 88/1: "The Toughest Job in the World!").

In March-April 1954 Superman unearths JOR-EL's last will and testament (WF No. 69: "Jor-El's Last Will!").

In April 1954 Superman matches wits with VIC VORDEN (Act No. 191: "Calling Doctor Superman!").

In May 1954 Superman teaches a much-needed lesson to JASPER COLDSTONE (Act No. 192: "The Man Who Sped Up Superman!"), meets QUEEN ELIZABETH I during a time-journey to England in the year 1588 (S No. 89/1: "Captain Kent the Terrible!"), matches wits with ED MAIN (S No. 89/2: "Superman of Skid Row!"), and battles LEX LUTHOR (S No. 89/3: "One Hour to Doom!").

In May-June 1954 Superman demolishes a kryptonite-laden asteroid which, as it orbits the moon, has been causing him to black out for an hour every afternoon, and apprehends a pair of criminals named Benny and Red who have been capitalizing on his daily blackouts in order to implicate him in a series of crimes (WF No. 70: "The Two Faces of Superman!").

In June 1954 Superman matches wits with BEETLES BROGAN (Act No. 193: "The Golden Superman!").

In July 1954 Superman battles MALA and his villainous brothers (Act No. 194: "The Outlaws from Krypton!"), apprehends RED and his cohorts (S No. 90/1: "Superman's Last Job!"), outwits PROFESSOR

SNELLING (S No. 90/2: "Superman's Secret Past!"), and thwarts the sinister machinations of LEX LUTHOR (S No. 90/3: "The Titanic Thefts!").

In July-August 1954 Superman joins forces with Batman and Robin to apprehend a gang of criminals and prevent Lois Lane from unraveling the secret of his dual identity (WF No. 71: "Batman—Double for Superman!").

In August 1954 Superman becomes embroiled in an adventure involving the TIGER WOMAN and LOIS LANE (Act No. 195: "Lois Lane--Wanted!"), meets WILLIS FOTHERINGAY (S No. 91/1: "The Superman Stamp!"), joins forces with a Federal agent employing the alias DOC MERLIN (S No. 91/2: "The Lazy Man's Best Friend!"), and lends a helping hand to PERRY WHITE (S No. 91/3: "Great Caesar's Ghost!").

In September 1954 Superman assumes the role of MENTAL-MAN (Act No. 196: "The Adventures of Mental-Man!"), matches wits with JIGGER BENSON (S No. 92/1: "The Impossible Headlines!"), meets DUKE GLENNON during a time-journey to Belford, England, in the twelfth century A.D. (S No. 92/2: "Superman's Sweetheart!"), and battles "NAILS" HARRIGAN (S No. 92/3: "Superman's Last Hour!").

In September-October 1954 Batman, Robin, and Superman apprehend the HEAVY WEAPONS GANG (WF No. 72: "Fort Crime!").

In October 1954 Superman matches wits with STANLEY STARK (Act No. 197: "The Stolen 'S' Shirts").

In November 1954 Superman humors LOIS LANE during a period when she is suffering from a series of delusions (Act No. 198: "The Six Lives of Lois Lane!"), meets WILMINGTON WAFFLE (S No. 93/1: "The Super-Joke on Superman!"), matches wits with "THE THINKER" (S No. 93/2: "Jimmy Olsen's Double!"), and lends a helping hand to ALFRED HUNTLEY (S No. 93/3: "The Man Superman Feared!").

In November-December 1954 Batman, Robin, and Superman battle the FANG (WF No. 73: "Batman and Superman, Swamis, Inc!").

In December 1954 Superman thwarts the nefarious schemes of LEX LUTHOR (Act No. 199: "The Phantom Superman!").

In January 1955 Superman matches wits with MORWATHA (Act No. 200: "Tests of a Warrior!"), encounters a band of aliens from the planet BLANTH (S No. 94/2: "The Men Without a World!"), meets the lovely MARYBELLE (S No. 94/3: "Clark Kent's Hillbilly Bride!"), and apprehends a gang of criminals who are attempting to frighten the people of Metropolis into evacuating the city so that they can loot it unimpeded (S No. 94/1: "Three Dooms for Metropolis!").

In January-February 1955 Batman, Robin, and Superman help an extraterrestrial youngster stranded on Earth find his way home again (WF No. 74: "The Contest of Heroes!").

In February 1955 Superman matches wits with BENNY THE BRUTE (Act No. 201: "The Challenge of Stoneman!"), copes with the antics of SUSIE TOMPKINS (S No. 95/1: "Susie's Enchanted Isle"), meets

POINTDEXTER WELLS (S No. 95/2: "The Practical Joker!"), and becomes embroiled in an adventure involving JIMMY OLSEN (S No. 95/3: "Jimmy Olsen, Super-Reporter!").

In March 1955 Superman struggles to safeguard the secret of his dual identity against LOIS LANE's newly acquired X-ray vision (Act No. 202: "Lois Lane's X-Ray Vision!"), meets ALICE NORTON (S No. 96/1: "The Girl Who Didn't Believe in Superman!"), copes with the magical mischief of MR. MXYZPTLK (S No. 96/2: "Mr. Mxyztplk--Mayor of Metropolis!"), and lends a helping hand to JOHN GRISWOLD (S No. 96/3: "The Collector of Celebrities!").

In March-April 1955 Batman, Robin, and Superman battle the PURPLE MASK MOB (WF No. 75: "The New Team of Superman and Robin!").

In April 1955 Superman meets PIETRO PARESCA (Act No. 203: "The International Daily Planet!").

In May 1955 Superman receives some assistance from SAM SPULBY (Act No. 204: "The Man Who Could Make Superman Do Anything!"), meets PROFESSOR MEMORY (S No. 97/1: "The Amazing Professor Memory!"), matches wits with DAN WHEELER (S No. 97/2: "The Big Game Hunt of Metropolis!"), and visits SMALLVILLE (S No. 97/3: "Superboy's Last Day in Smallville!").

In May-June 1955 Superman engages in a contest with Batman and Robin (see VOHR [PROFESSOR]) (WF No. 76: "When Gotham City Challenged Metropolis!").

In June 1955 Superman comes to the aid of FRED CARSON (Act No. 205: "Sergeant Superman").

In July 1955 Superman figures prominently in one of LOIS LANE's dreams (Act No. 206: "Superman Marries Lois Lane!"), matches wits with "RAGS" STEPHENS (S No. 98/1: "Superman's Secret Life!"), apprehends the "BIG GUY" (S No. 98/2: "Clark Kent Outlaw!"), and, while attending the showing of a Superman newsreel with Lois Lane in his Clark Kent identity, slips into the projection booth and alters the film slightly in order to eradicate a minute clue which, if noticed, could endanger the secret of his dual identity (S No. 98/3: "The Amazing Superman Newsreel!").

In July-August 1955 Batman, Robin, and Superman match wits with PROFESSOR PENDER (WF No. 77: "The Super Bat-Man!").

In August 1955 Superman battles the MIDNITE GANG (S No. 99/1: "The Camera Club Scoops!"), meets MONA MILES (S No. 99/2: "The 1,000 Lives of Superman!"), becomes embroiled in an adventure involving LOIS LANE (S No. 99/3: "The Incredible Feats of Lois Lane!"), and, as Clark Kent, is awarded the coveted Superman Medal, a medal awarded annually by the Metropolis Police Department "to the person whose heroism...helped **Superman** the most" during the preceding year (Act No. 207: "The Four Superman Medals!").

In September 1955 Superman copes with the magical mischief of MR. MXYZPTLK (Act No. 208: "The Magic of Mr. Mxyztplk"), apprehends RED ANSON (S No. 100/1: "The Toy Superman Contest"), thwarts the unscrupulous machinations of FLOYD FOWLER (S No. 100/3: "The Clue from Krypton"), and, while serving a one-day stint, in disguise, as a substitute schoolteacher, surreptitiously uses his super-powers to teach a well-deserved lesson in good manners to a group of mischievous schoolchildren (S No. 100/2: "Superman--Substitute Teacher").

In September-October 1955 Batman, Robin, and Superman apprehend the VARREL MOB (WF No. 78: "When Superman's Identity Is Exposed!").

In October 1955 Superman matches wits with "DOC" WINTERS (Act No. 209: "The Man Who Was Mightier Than Superman").

In November 1955 Superman encounters LEX LUTHOR at SUPERMAN LAND (Act No. 210: "Superman in Superman Land"), battles LEX LUTHOR (S No. 101/1: "Luthor's Amazing Rebus"), meets the members of the METROPOLIS MEEK MAN'S CLUB (S No. 101/2: "The Meek Man's Club"), and sets in motion an elaborate ruse involving the "rainbow doom" (see RAINBOW DOOM, THE) (S No. 101/3: "The Rainbow Doom").

In November-December 1955 Batman, Robin, and Superman journey into the distant past, where they encounter the legendary ALADDIN (WF No. 79: "The Three Magicians of Bagdad!").

In December 1955 Superman lends a helping hand to the DAILY PLANET (Act No. 211: "The Superman Spectaculars").

In January 1956 Superman matches wits with THORNE VARDEN (Act No. 212: "The Superman Calendar"), organizes the SUPERMAN STOCK COMPANY (S No. 102/1: "Superman for Sale"), outwits a band of aliens from the planet THURA (S No. 102/2: "The Midget Menace"), and thwarts a scheme concocted by SOAPY MARTIN (S No. 102/3: "The Million-Dollar Mistake").

In January-February 1956 Batman, Robin, and Superman apprehend the MOLE (WF No. 80: "The Super-Newspaper of Gotham City").

In February 1956 Superman matches wits with PAUL PAXTON (Act No. 213: "Paul Paxton Alias Superman!"), meets JEREMY BIRD (S No. 103/1: "The Superman of Yesterday"), copes with the magical mischief of MR. MXYZPTLK (S No. 103/2: "The Revenge of Mr. Mxyzptlk!"), and becomes embroiled in an adventure involving the GREAT COSMO (S No. 103/3: "The Man Who Could Read Superman's Mind!").

In March 1956 Superman embarks on a demolition project at the behest of EBENEEZER WALKER (Act No. 214: "Superman, Super-Destroyer"), copes with the newly acquired super-intellect of LOIS LANE (S No. 104/1: "Lois Lane, Super-Genius"), matches wits with ED ROWSE (S No. 104/2: "Clark Kent Jailbird!"), and makes the acquaintance of extraterrestrial alien VITOR VALL (S No. 104/3: "The Super-Family from Outer Space").

In March-April 1956 Batman, Robin, and Superman meet KA THAR (WF No. 81: "The True History of Superman and Batman!").

In April 1956 Superman meets the SUPERMAN OF 2956 during a time-journey to Metropolis in the thirtieth century A.D. (Act No. 215: "The Superman of Tomorrow").

In May 1956 Superman destroys an arsenal of Kryptonian "war weapons" launched into outer space by JOR-EL (Act No. 216: "The Super-Menace of Metropolis"), struggles to uncover the identity of the author of a mysterious anonymous letter (see KENT, JONATHAN AND MARTHA [MR. AND MRS.]) (S No. 105/1: "Superman's 3 Mistakes!"), copes with the magical mischief of MR. MXYZPTLK (S No. 105/2: "Mr. Mxyztplk's Secret Identity"), and matches wits with the tyrannical ELDRIC (S No. 105/3: "Superman, Slave!").

In May-June 1956 Batman, Robin, and Superman journey into the past, where they encounter the THREE MUSKETEERS (WF No. 82: "The Three Super-Musketeers!").

In June 1956 Superman meets MR. AND MRS. ROGER BLISS (Act No. 217: "The Amazing Super-Baby").

In July 1956 Superman encounters the incredible SUPER-APE (Act No. 218: "The Super-Ape from Krypton"), meets DR. REESE KEARNS (S No. 106/1: "Superman's First Exploit"), matches wits with "BULLETS" BARTON (S No. 106/2: "The Thefts of Clark Kent"), and battles LEX LUTHOR (S No. 106/3: "The Super-Outlaw of Metropolis").

In July-August 1956 Batman, Robin, and Superman are honored guests at Gotham City's annual policemen's ball (WF No. 83: "The Case of the Mother Goose Mystery!").

In August 1956 Superman apprehends ART SHALER (Act No. 219: "Superman's Treasure Hoard"), meets HAL HANNON (S No. 107/1: "The Make-Believe Superman"), and battles the renegade scientist DRAGO during a brief sojourn in the thirtieth century A.D. (S No. 107/3: "Rip Van Superman!"). A text for this same period recounts the story of Superman's encounter with DANDY JIM (S No. 107/2, Aug '56: "The Impossible Haircut"). When, in the midst of a hurricane, Batman loses a bat-cape with his real name—Bruce Wayne—sewn inside it, Clark Kent finds the lost cape and uses his X-ray vision to burn away the telltale writing to help safeguard the secret of Batman's identity (BM No. 101/3, Aug '56: "The Great Bat-Cape Hunt!").

In September 1956 Superman journeys to the planet THON (Act No. 220: "The Interplanetary Olympics"), thwarts the sinister machinations of PROFESSOR MARTIN (S No. 108/1: "The Brain from the Future"), matches wits with MR. WHEELS (S No. 108/2: "Perry White, Jr., Demon Reporter!"), and successfully thwarts a series of ingenious attempts by Metropolis's policewomen to unravel the secret of his dual identity (S No. 108/3: "The Girl Cops of Metropolis!").

In September-October 1956 Batman, Robin, and Superman apprehend the THAD LINNIS gang (WF No. 84: "The Super-Mystery of Metropolis!").

In October 1956 Superman matches wits with JAY VORRELL (Act No. 221: "Superman's New Super-Power").

In November 1956 Superman meets ABNER HOKUM (S No. 109/1: "The Man Who Stole Superman's Powers"), lends a helping hand to PAUL BERG (S No. 109/2: "The Puppet with X-Ray Eyes"), and battles a series of disasters—all of them eerie repetitions of such famous disasters of history as the San Francisco earthquake—which have been caused, more or less playfully, without any real malicious intent, by extraterrestrial creatures millions of light-years away from Earth, creatures, in Superman's words, "with undreamed of powers, who take a peculiar delight in using those powers to act like--like--cosmic apes-- imitating what they see on other worlds" (S No. 109/3: "The Duplicate Disasters"). During this same period, Superman is miraculously split into two virtually identical Supermen by the awesome explosive force of a powerful "Q-bomb," a "new government weapon" with the explosive power of 100 hydrogen bombs. The two Supermen work together as a super-heroic team until one of them finally sacrifices his life to save the other from the effects of a gigantic kryptonite meteor hurtling toward Earth (Act No. 222, Nov '56: "The Duplicate Superman").

In November-December 1956 Batman, Robin, and Superman meet PRINCESS VARINA (WF No. 85: "The Super-Rivals!").

In December 1956, "far out in space," Superman comes upon a journal and some films made by his father, JOR-EL (Act No. 223: "The First Superman of Krypton").

d. THE LATER ADVENTURES. In January 1957 Superman creates SUPERMAN ISLAND (Act No. 224: "The Secret of Superman Island!"), apprehends LES KEEGAN (S No. 110/1: "The Secret of the Superman Trophy"), visits HIGHVILLE (S No. 110/2: "The Mystery Superman!"), and battles LEX LUTHOR (S No. 110/3: "The Defeat of Superman").

In January-February 1957 Batman, Robin, and Superman thwart the unscrupulous machinations of HENRY BARTLE (WF No. 86: "The Super-Show of Gotham City").

In February 1957 Superman helps bring about the capture of BLACKY BAIRD (S No. 111/1: "The Non-Super Superman"), meets JUDD KENT (S No. 111/2: "Clark Kent's Crooked Cousin"), employs the alias MYSTO THE GREAT (S No. 111/3: "The Magical Superman"), and fakes his own death as part of an elaborate, and ultimately successful, ruse designed to enable him to discover the whereabouts of several million dollars in loot stolen years ago in an armored-car robbery but never recovered (Act No. 225: "The Death of Superman").

In March 1957 Superman battles LEX LUTHOR (S No. 112/2: "Superman's Fatal Costume") and apprehends PROFESSOR WILTON (S No. 112/3: "The Three Men of Steel!"). Other texts for this same period recount the story of an encounter between Superman and LEX LUTHOR (Act No. 226, Mar '57: "The

Invulnerable Enemy") and describe the sundry secret ways in which Superman lends a helping hand to his neighbors at 344 Clinton Street in Metropolis, where he rents an apartment in his role as Clark Kent. "Yes," notes the text, "unknown to themselves, the people of 344 Clinton Street lead strangely enriched lives," for Superman has appointed himself their guardian angel, and, as a result, "a special kind of magic weaves a kinder fate for them," protecting them from harm, helping to make their unfulfilled wishes come true. "Behind closed walls," continues the text, "the comedies and tragedies of life at 344 Clinton Street go on--but no matter how thick the walls, they cannot shut out Superman's sympathy with his fellow men..." (see also ROSS, ALEXANDER) (S No. 112/1, Mar '57: "Superman's Neighbors").

In March-April 1957 Superman narrates the story of a past encounter that he, Batman, and Robin had with the villainous ELTON CRAIG (WF No. 87: "The Reversed Heroes!").

In April 1957 Superman carries on his normal duties in Metropolis, apprehending criminals and performing super-heroic feats, despite the severe limitations that have been imposed on his activities by a freak accident involving a malfunctioning X-ray machine which has had the effect of so greatly intensifying the power of Superman's X-ray vision that, until the effects of the mishap wear off and his eyesight returns to normal, Superman must keep his eyes constantly closed, or covered by lead goggles, to avoid incinerating anything he looks at (Act No. 227: "The Man with the Triple X-Ray Eyes").

In May 1957 Superman recovers a Kryptonian "mind-tape" recorded by JOR-EL, meets QUEEN LATORA, apprehends an unidentified deranged scientist attempting to destroy Metropolis (S No. 113: chs. 1-3--"The Superman of the Past"; "The Secret of the Towers"; "The Superman of the Present"), and captures JAY AMERY and his henchman at the SUPERMAN MUSEUM (Act No. 228: "Superman's Super Skyscraper").

In May-June 1957 Batman, Robin, and Superman match wits with LEX LUTHOR and the Joker (WF No. 88: "Superman's and Batman's Greatest Foes!").

In June 1957 Superman comes to the aid of DR. JOHN HALEY (Act No. 229: "The Superman Satellite").

In July 1957 Superman battles BART WELLINS (Act No. 230: "Superman Loses His Powers"), matches wits with MENTO (S No. 114/2: "The Man Who Discovered Superman's Identity"), meets JASON HAWKER (S No. 114/3: "Superman's Billion-Dollar Debt!"), and carries on his normal crime-fighting duties in Metropolis despite the fact that exposure to the sound of a gigantic explosion in a tightly enclosed space has had the effect of so greatly intensifying his super-hearing that even the sound of an ant walking is unbearably painful, forcing him to cover his head with a special plastic helmet—rendering him stone deaf so long as he wears it—until the effects of the explosion have worn off and his hearing has returned to normal (S No. 114/1: "The Soundproof Superman").

In July-August 1957 Batman, Robin, and Superman become embroiled in an adventure involving the amazing LIGHTNING-MAN (WF No. 89: "The Club of Heroes!").

In August 1957 Superman apprehends the SEAL GANG (see also OLSEN, JIMMY) (Act No. 231: "Sir Jimmy Olsen, Knight of Metropolis"), meets TOM AND TINA THUMB (S No. 115/1: "The Midget Superman"), matches wits with "MANY-FACES" FULTON (S No. 115/2: "Jimmy Olsen's Lost Pal"), and battles the ORGANIZER (S No. 115/3: "The Three Substitute Supermen!").

In September 1957 Superman meets JOHNNY KIRK (Act No. 232: "The Story of Superman, Junior"), matches wits with REX MALCOLM (S No. 116/1: "The Ray That Changed Superman"), survives a heinous scheme concocted by "PROFESSOR" EPHRAIM SNIVELY (S No. 116/3: "The Mechanized Superman!"), and, during a visit to Smallville, where he spent his boyhood, persuades a group of the town's prominent citizens that it would be unwise of him to accede to their request that he leave Metropolis in favor of renewed residence in Smallville. "...[Y]ou can't turn the calendar back!" explains Superman. "We all have to face new responsibilities, and enjoy life through them!" (S No. 116/2: "Disaster Strikes Twice").

In September-October 1957 Batman, Robin, and Superman find themselves forced to cope with a super-powered BATWOMAN (WF No. 90: "The Super-Batwoman!").

In October 1957 Superman battles the tyrannical TORM (Act No. 233: "The Land of a Million Supermen").

In November 1957 Superman meets GOLLO (Act No. 234: "The Creature of 1,000 Disguises"), battles LEX LUTHOR (S No. 117/2: "The Secret of Fort Superman"), matches wits with REX CHALMERS (S No. 117/3: "The Man with the Zero Eyes!"), and carries out an elaborate, and ultimately successful, ruse designed to enable him to partially obliterate the signatures of Clark Kent and Superman on a testimonial plaque awarded to Perry White so as to prevent anyone from ever comparing the two signatures and thereby deducing that Clark Kent and Superman are actually the same man (S No. 117/1: "Clark Kent, Man of Mystery").

In November-December 1957 Batman, Robin, and Superman apprehend RICK HARBEN and match wits with ROHTUL (WF No. 91: "The Three Super-Sleepers!").

In December 1957 Superman matches wits with QUEEN ELSHA (Act No. 235: "The Super-Prisoner of Amazon Island").

In January 1958 Superman battles LEX LUTHOR (Act No. 236: "Superman's New Uniform!"), becomes embroiled in an adventure involving JIMMY OLSON (S No. 118/2: "The Boy Napoleon"), matches wits with BLACKY BARTON (S No. 118/3: "The Death of Superman!"), and copes with the destructive antics of

a gigantic dinosaurlike prehistoric beast, in hibernation for centuries in a subterranean cavern until its recent escape from the Earth's depths, which, although it is generally friendly and means no harm, threatens to wreak untold disaster because of its dragonlike flame-breath and its gargantuan size (S No. 118/1: "The Prehistoric Pet").

In January-February 1958 Batman, Robin, and Superman meet SKYBOY (WF No. 92: "The Boy from Outer Space!").

In February 1958 Superman thwarts the unscrupulous machinations of HENRY FURST (Act No. 237: "Superman's Exposed Identity") and meets ZOLL ORR (S No. 119: "The Second Superman!" chs. 1-3—"The World That Was Krypton's Twin"; "A Double for Superman"; "Superman's Mightiest Quest").

In March 1958 Superman encounters KING KRYPTON (Act No. 238: "The Super-Gorilla from Krypton"), matches wits with "COUP" COLBY (S No. 120/1: "The Day That Superman Married"), meets AL JONES (S 120/2: "The Super-Feats Superman Forgot"), and battles "GADGET" GRIM (S No. 120/3: "The Human Missile").

In March-April 1958 Batman, Robin, and Superman thwart the schemes of VICTOR DANNING (WF No. 93: "The Boss of Batman and Superman").

In April 1958 Superman finds the secret of his dual identity in jeopardy after a bizarre series of circumstances, culminating in the explosion of an experimental atomic generator, has caused tiny fragments of kryptonite to become embedded in his forehead, spelling out the name Clark Kent. For a time Superman is compelled to hide his face—first with cloth bandages and later with a metal mask—to avoid people's seeing it and learning his secret, but ultimately he succeeds in burning the kryptonite particles out of his skin by deliberately exposing himself to an awesome atomic explosion in space, described by the text as "the mightiest atomic explosion of all time" (Act No. 239: "Superman's New Face").

In May 1958 Superman meets XL-49 (S No. 121/1: "The Bride of Futureman!"), thwarts the unscrupulous machinations of ELDREDGE CORAM (S No. 121/2: "The Great Superman Swindle"), matches wits with "HONEST" JOHN (S No. 121/3: "Jimmy Hits the Jackpot"), and, after Lois Lane has inadvertently stumbled upon an all-but-certain clue to Superman's secret identity by discovering a highly sophisticated Clark Kent robot hidden behind a secret panel in the wall of a supply room at the Daily Planet, carries out an intricately convoluted, but nonetheless successful, ruse designed to convince Lois Lane that she has not really learned his secret at all, while at the same time carrying out a completely unrelated mission, the testing of some highly classified "heat ray weapons" for the U.S. government (Act No. 240: "Secret of the Superman Sphinx").

In May-June 1958 Batman, Robin, and Superman battle LEX LUTHOR (WF No. 94: "The Origin of the Superman-Batman Team!").

In June 1958 Superman begins receiving taunting messages from an anonymous adversary who can enter and leave his Fortress of Solitude at will and who has clearly penetrated the secret of his dual identity. The mysterious intruder, however, turns out to be none other than Batman, who had decided to present his friend Superman with the enigma of an anonymous adversary as his good-humored way of helping the Man of Steel celebrate "the anniversary of [his] arrival on Earth from the planet Krypton!" (Act No. 241: "The Super-Key to Fort Superman").

In July 1958 Superman battles BRAINIAC (Act No. 242: "The Super-Duel in Space"), figures prominently in one of JIMMY OLSEN's dreams (S No. 122/2: "Superman in the White House!"), meets PVT. JONES (S No. 122/3: "The Super-Sergeant"), and, acting under a strange compulsion that he cannot explain, journeys to eight different planets and satellites the first letter of whose names, taken together, spell out the name Superman—viz., Saturn, Uranus, Pluto, Earth, Rhea (one of Saturn's moons), Mars, Ariel (one of Uranus's moons), and Neptune—in order to accumulate a series of exotic "space trophies" for inclusion in a time capsule which the Metropolis Museum plans to bury in the ground as a gift for the people of the fiftieth century A.D. The nature of the compulsion to gather the trophies becomes plain soon afterward, when the "dream-like vision" of a fiftieth-century man appears to Clark Kent in his sleep. "We of the 50th century compelled you to gather the space trophies!" explains the vision. "You see, we wanted them as a living memorial to the greatest hero in Earth's history! But we knew you would be too modest to comply if we asked you directly! So we sent mental commands across the time barrier to your mind, powered by kryptonite, so that you were forced to obey! When we open the time capsule tomorrow, in our age, we will find your space trophies, which will spell out your own name in your honor!" (S No. 122/1: "The Secret of the Space Souvenirs").

In July-August 1958 Batman, Robin, and Superman fall under the baleful influence of a pair of aliens from the planet XLYM (WF No. 95: "The Battle of the Super-Heroes!").

In August 1958 Superman encounters a descendant of the enchantress CIRCE (Act No. 243: "The Lady and the Lion") and becomes embroiled in an adventure involving JIMMY OLSEN (S No. 123: chs. 1-3—. "The Girl of Steel"; "The Lost Super-Powers"; "Superman's Return to Krypton").

In September 1958 Superman matches wits with VUL-KOR and his daughter Lya-La (Act No. 244: "The Super-Merman of the Sea"), apprehends "BULL" MATHEWS (S No. 124/1: "The Super-Sword"), becomes embroiled in an adventure involving LOIS LANE (S No. 124/2: "Mrs. Superman"), thwarts the schemes of BART BENSON (S No. 124/3: "The Steeplejack of Steel"), and, together with Batman and Robin, lends a helping hand to a band of extraterrestrial aliens who have journeyed to the planet Earth (WF No. 96: "The Super-Foes from Planet X").

In October 1958 Superman matches wits with ZAK-KUL (Act No. 245: "The Shrinking Superman!") and joins forces with Batman and Robin to battle the CONDOR GANG (WF No. 97: "The Day Superman Betrayed Batman!").

In November 1958 Superman meets JONAS SMITH (Act No. 246: "Krypton on Earth!"), figures prominently in one of LOIS LANE's dreams (S No. 125/1: "Lois Lane's Super-Dream"), and, as Clark Kent, recalls his experiences with PROFESSOR THADDEUS V. MAXWELL (S No. 125/2: "Clark Kent's College Days"). During this same period, Superman loses all his accustomed super-powers—and acquires a mysterious new power: the ability to materialize and control, merely by willing it, a tiny duplicate of himself which is endowed with all his familiar super-powers—as the result of having come into physical contact with a weird extraterrestrial spacecraft. In Superman's words:

The people who made that space ship were very advanced in science! They must have developed a force that enabled them to project an image of themselves anywhere they wanted!

It's like telepathy! All my powers are embodied in that midget duplicate of myself which I can project anywhere!

The only trouble is that my powers have been transferred to that doll-sized replica of the real me, so that while I have the "new" power, it has absorbed all my old ones!

For a time, Superman apprehends criminals and performs his customary super-tasks using his doll-sized replica in place of his vanished super-powers. Ultimately, however, the replica sacrifices its existence to rescue Superman from the effects of a deadly kryptonite meteor, and, with the replica gone, Superman discovers, to his great relief, that his old super-powers have been completely restored to him (S No. 125/3, Nov '58: "Superman's New Power!").

In December 1958 Superman matches wits with CEDRIC AND MILLICENT CARSON (Act No. 247: "Superman's Lost Parents!") and joins forces with Batman and Robin to battle the MOONMAN (WF No. 98: "The Menace of the Moonman!").

In January 1959 Superman thwarts the nefarious schemes of VON KAMP (Act No. 248: "The Man No Prison Could Hold!"), assumes the alternate identity of CLARENCE KELVIN (S No. 126/1: "Superman's Hunt for Clark Kent!"), apprehends the FALLON gang (S No. 126/2: "The Spell of the Shandu Clock"), and teaches a well-deserved lesson to LOIS LANE (S No. 126/3: "The Two Faces of Superman!").

In February 1959 Superman matches wits with LEX LUTHOR (Act No. 249: "The Kryptonite Man!"), recalls a series of past events which clearly demonstrated the importance of his maintaining a secret identity (see section B, the secret identity) (S No. 127/1: "When There Was No Clark Kent!"), meets HARRY WINTERS (S No. 127/2: "The Make-Believe Superman!"), battles TITANO (S No. 127/3: "Titano the Super-Ape!"), and, together with Batman and Robin, becomes embroiled in an adventure involving the bizarre last will and testament of eccentric millionaire CARL VERRIL (WF No. 99: "Batman's Super-Spending Spree!").

In March 1959 Superman joins forces with Batman and Robin to battle LEX LUTHOR (WF No. 100: "The Dictator of Krypton City!"), and, as Clark Kent, outwits JOHN BATES (Act No. 250: "The Eye of Metropolis!").

In April 1959 Superman meets VARD and Boka (S No. 128/1: chs. 1-2—"Superman versus the Futuremen"; "The Secret of the Futuremen") and struggles to safeguard the secret of his dual identity (see LOIS LANE) (S No. 128/2: "The Sleeping Beauty from Krypton!"). A text for this same period recounts the story of Superman's encounter with PROF. VANCE (Act No. 251, Apr '59: "The Oldest Man in Metropolis!").

In May 1959 Superman battles METALLO (Act No. 252: "The Menace of Metallo!"), meets PROFESSOR GRAIL (S No. 129/1: "The Ghost of Lois Lane"), and, as Clark Kent, outwits FIRE CHIEF HOGAN (S No. 129/2: "Clark Kent, Fireman of Steel!") and recalls his romance with LORI LEMARIS (S No. 129/3: "The Girl in Superman's Past!"). During this same period, Superman joins forces with Batman and Robin to battle the ATOM-MASTER (WF No. 101, May '59: "The Menace of the Atom-Master!"), and the Supergirl story in Action Comics No. 252 recounts the story of Superman's first encounter with SUPERGIRL (May '59: "The Supergirl from Krypton!").

In June 1959 Superman matches wits with EL GAR KUR (Act No. 253: "The War Between Superman and Jimmy Olsen!") and joins forces with Batman and Robin to apprehend the JO-JO GROFF gang (WF No. 102: "The Caveman from Krypton!").

In July 1959 Superman battles BIZARRO (Act No. 254: "The Battle with Bizarro!"), is rescued by KRYPTO THE SUPERDOG (S No. 130/1: "The Curse of Kryptonite!"), matches wits with MARK MULLOY (S No. 130/2: "The Super-Servant of Crime"), and pays a visit to CYRUSVILLE (S No. 130/3: "The Town That Hated Superman!").

In August 1959 Superman battles BIZARRO (Act No. 255: "The Bride of Bizarro!"), copes with the magical mischief of MR. MXYZPTLK (S No. 131/1: "The Menace of Mr. Mxyzptlk!"), and joins forces with Batman and Robin to outwit ATKINS and Bork (WF No. 103: "The Secret of the Sorcerer's Treasure!"). Other texts for this period recall Lois Lane's visit to the New England town of WICKSVILLE (S No. 131/2, Aug '59: "Superman's Future Wife!") and recount a series of super-favors which Superman performed for three complete strangers while he was a youngster in Smallville, unaware that those strangers—Jimmy Olsen, Lois Lane, and Perry White—would one day figure prominently in his adult life (S No. 131/3, Aug '59: "The Unknown Super-Deeds!").

In September 1959 Superman matches wits with DIRK FOLGAR (Act No. 256: "The Superman of the Future!") and joins forces with Batman and Robin to thwart the schemes of LEX LUTHOR (WF No. 104: "The Plot to Destroy Superman!").

In October 1959 Superman battles LEX LUTHOR (Act No. 257: "The Reporter of Steel!") and, at the suggestion of Batman and Robin, feeds photographic data concerning life on the planet Krypton into the "super-univac" in his Fortress of Solitude together with the question, "What would Superman's other life have been, if Krypton had not exploded?" The answer, according to the super-univac, is that much about Superman's might-have-been life would have paralleled his real one, with Superman eventually acquiring super-powers on his native planet and assuming the role of Krypton's super-hero (S No. 132: "Superman's Other Life!" pts. 1-3—"Krypton Lives On!"; "Futuro, Super-Hero of Krypton!"; "The Superman of Two Worlds!").

In November 1959 Superman defeats GENERAL MALVIO (Act No. 258: "The Menace of Cosmic Man!"), meets CAPTAIN JONATHAN GRIMES (S No. 133/3: "Superman Joins the Army!"), and, together with Batman and Robin, matches wits with the evil KHALEX (WF No. 105: "The Alien Superman!"). Other texts for this period provide what purports to be the true account of how Clark Kent came to acquire his reporter's job on the DAILY PLANET (S No. 133/2, Nov '59: "How Perry White Hired Clark Kent!") and recount the story of a three-day period during which Clark Kent worked as a patrolman on the Metropolis police force so that he could write an article about his experience for the *Daily Planet* (S No. 133/1, Nov '59: "The Super-Luck of Badge 77").

In December 1959 Superman is plagued by a frightening "super-nightmare" involving LEX LUTHOR (Act No. 259: "The Revenge of Luthor!") and joins forces with Batman and Robin to defeat the DUPLICATE MAN (WF No. 106: "The Duplicate Man!").

In January 1960 Superman meets MIGHTY MAID (Act No. 260: "Mighty Maid!") and matches wits with KULL-EX (S No. 134: chs. I-III—"The Super-Menace of Metropolis!"; "The Revenge Against Jor-El!"; "The Duel of the Supermen!").

In February 1960 Superman thwarts the schemes of the ANTI-SUPERMAN GANG (Act No. 261: "Superman's Fortresses of Solitude!"), renews his relationship with LORI LEMARIS (S No. 135/2: "Superman's Mermaid Sweetheart!"), copes with the magical mischief of MR. MXYZPTLK (S No. 135/3: "The Trio of Steel!"), and, together with Batman and Robin, annihilates an awesomely destructive "creature of energy" spawned by the "alien gases" of a "strange fireball" from outer space (WF No. 107: "The Secret of the Time Creature!"). A text for this same period tells what purports to be the true story of how Lois Lane first came to suspect that Clark Kent might secretly be Superman (see section B, the secret identity) (S No. 135/1, Feb '60: "When Lois First Suspected Clark Was Superman!").

In March 1960, together with Batman and Robin, Superman meets an alien movie producer from the planet KZOTL (WF No. 108: "The Star Creatures!"), and, while covering the exploration of an Aztec tomb in his role as Clark Kent, is suddenly overcome—along with his companions Lois Lane, Jimmy Olsen, and Perry White—by noxious, "evil-smelling vapors" which catapult them all into a frightening two-day adventure in a bizarre fantasy world—a world where Superman has no super-powers—which may be a real adventure but which the text suggests may also be a strange nightmare somehow experienced simultaneously by all four tomb explorers (Act No. 262: "When Superman Lost His Powers!").

In April 1960 Superman visits the Bizarro world (see BIZARRO) (Act No. 263: "The World of Bizarros!"), meets X-PLAM (S No. 136/1: "The Man Who Married Lois Lane!"), encounters MEL EVANS during a visit to SMALLVILLE (S No. 136/2: "The Secret of Kryptonite!"), and lends a helping hand to "SAD SAM" SMITH (S No. 136/3: "The Super-Clown of Metropolis!").

In May 1960 Superman concludes his adventure on the Bizarro world (see BIZARRO) (Act No. 264: "The Superman Bizarro!"), battles SUPER-MENACE (S No. 137: chs. I-III—"The Super-Brat from Krypton"; "The Young Super-Bully"; "Superman vs. Super-Menace!"), and, together with Batman and Robin, becomes embroiled in a bizarre adventure involving a centuries-old trap set by the sorcerer FANGAN (WF No. 109: "The Bewitched Batman!").

In June 1960 Superman meets HYPER-MAN (Act No. 265: "The 'Superman' from Outer Space!") and, together with Batman, battles and defeats an extraterrestrial alien who has stolen part of Robin's life force (WF No. 110: "The Alien Who Doomed Robin!").

In July 1960 Superman matches wits with PRINCESS JENA (Act No. 266: "The Captive of the Amazons"), battles TITANO (S No. 138/1: "Titano the Super-Ape!"), outwits "DUKE" HASKELL and "Lefty" Montez (S No. 138/2: "Superman's Black Magic!"), and thwarts a well-intentioned scheme of LORI LEMARIS's (S No. 138/3: "The Mermaid from Atlantis!").

In August 1960 Superman encounters HERCULES in the twentieth century (Act No. 267: "Hercules in the 20th Century!"), meets BRETT RAND (S No. 139/1: "The New Life of Super-Merman!"), matches wits with COLONEL STRADI (S No. 139/2: "The Jolly Jailhouse!"), and joins forces with Batman and Robin to apprehend FLOYD FRISBY (WF No. 111: "Superman's Secret Kingdom!"). During this same period, Superman rescues the crew of a bathyscaphe trapped in an underwater crevasse ten miles down, and, after exposure to a submerged red-kryptonite meteor has brought about the sudden, accelerated growth of his hair, beard, and fingernails, summons the aid of Supergirl and Krypto the Superdog, who use the combined power of their X-ray vision to disintegrate the Man of Steel's virtually indestructible hair and fingernails, thus restoring Superman to his normal appearance (S No. 139/3, Aug '60: "The Untold Story of Red Kryptonite!").

In September 1960 Superman battles HERCULES (Act No. 268: "Superman's Battle with Hercules!").

In October 1960 Superman thwarts an attempt by LOIS LANE to learn his secret identity (Act No. 269: "The Truth Mirror!") and becomes embroiled in an adventure involving BIZARRO (S No. 140: pts. I-III—"The Son of Bizarro!"; "The 'Orphan' Bizarro!"; "The Bizarro Supergirl!").

In November 1960 Superman embarks on a passionate romance with LYLA LERROL during a time-journey to the planet Krypton at a time prior to its destruction (S No. 141: "Superman's Return to Krypton!" pts. I-III—"Superman Meets Jor-El and Lara Again!"; "Superman's Kryptonian Romance!"; "The Surprise of Fate!"), and, together with Batman and Robin, endures the magical mischief of MR. MXYZPTLK and Bat-Mite (WF No. 113: "Bat-Mite Meets Mr. Mxyzptlk!"). During this same period, Clark Kent falls asleep and has a disturbing dream in which, as Superman, he has crashed through the time barrier into the future to discover, to his chagrin, that the time-journey has somehow transformed him into a feeble old man and that he is now living in the time of his own old age, living out his twilight years as a pathetic, "old, broken-down has-been" of a super-hero, long since deprived of his mighty super-powers as the result of his numerous past exposures to kryptonite.

In the dream, Perry White, now deceased, has been replaced as editor-in-chief of the *Daily Planet* by a grown-up Jimmy Olsen; Superman's alter ego, Clark Kent, has retired from the *Daily Planet* on an old-age pension and his place on the staff has been taken by Linda Lee, once secretly Supergirl, now grown up into an adult Superwoman; Krypto the Superdog, now an aged canine, has, like Superman, lost all his super-powers and is now reduced to scrounging for garbage, and, as the aged Superman watches helplessly, is netted by the dogcatcher and dragged off to the pound; Lex Luthor is mayor of Metropolis, having received a full pardon for his crimes after discovering a cure for cancer; Jimmy Olsen and Lucy Lane are married and are raising two children, and Lana Lang is wedded to an unidentified millionaire; Superwoman has taken over Superman's Fortress of Solitude, filling it with trophies of her adventures while consigning Superman's trophies to a dusty storeroom, the city of Kandor is no longer tiny, having long since been enlarged to full size by Superman on a distant planet; an elderly Bizarro, having lost his super-powers during a visit to Earth, is serving a term for vagrancy in the Metropolis jail; and, finally, Lois Lane is a feeble old maid, living out her last years in loneliness and regret.

"I wasted my life waiting for you!" she explains to Superman pathetically. "But now we can still share our last years together, darling!" Indeed, just as the elderly Superman is on the verge of agreeing to marry Lois, Clark Kent begins to awaken from his nap and the images of his dream begin fading away. "Superman...you're fading away!" cries the dream-Lois desperately. "Please come back, my darling...please! I'll always love you...."

The following day, at the *Daily Planet*, the real Lois Lane beams happily over a bouquet of flowers just arrived by messenger. "Clark!" she exclaims. "This bouquet is from **Superman!** Goodness! Why is he suddenly treating me so nicely?"

"Who knows, Lois?" replies Clark Kent. "Maybe he...er...is thinking how lonely old age can be if he has no...uh...companion by his side!" (Act No. 270, Nov '60: "The Old Man of Metropolis!").

In December 1960 Superman matches wits with LEX LUTHOR (Act No. 271: "Voyage to Dimension X!") and, together with Batman and Robin, journeys to the planet Zoron for an encounter with the evil CHORN (WF No. 114: "Captives of the Space Globes!").

In January 1961 Superman carries out an elaborate ruse that culminates in the capture of the "ACE" RUGGLES gang (Act No. 272: "Superman's Rival, Mental Man!"), eludes a series of well-intentioned attempts by KRYPTO THE SUPERDOG to maneuver him into matrimony (S No. 142/1: "Lois Lane's Secret Helper!"), meets AL CAPONE during a time-journey to Chicago in the 1920s (S No. 142/2: "Superman Meets Al Capone!"), and battles an awesome Kryptonian "flame dragon" (*see* FLAME DRAGON) (S No. 142/3: "Flame-Dragon from Krypton").

In February 1961 Superman teaches a richly deserved lesson to MR. MXYZPTLK (Act No. 273: "The World of Mr. Mxyzptlk!"), thwarts a scheme by PROFESSOR OTTO JURIS (S No. 143/1: "The Great Superman Hoax!"), matches wits with CLIP CARSON (S No. 143/2: "Lois Lane's Lucky Day!"), encounters BIZARRO in Hollywood, California (S No. 143/3: "Bizarro Meets Frankenstein!"), and, together with Batman and Robin, thwarts an elaborate scheme by a gang of criminals to steal $500,000 in contributions earmarked for the Children's Charity Fund (WF No. 115: "The Curse That Doomed Superman!").

In March 1961 Superman is impersonated by SUPERMAN ROBOT Z (Act No. 274: "The Reversed Super-Powers!") and, together with Batman and Robin, encounters the weirdly transformed VANCE COLLINS (WF No. 116: "The Creature from Beyond!").

In April 1961 Superman battles BRAINIAC (Act No. 275: "The Menace of Red-Green Kryptonite!"); matches wits with BERT TALBOT (S No. 144/1: "The Super-Weapon!"); experiences, along with SUPERGIRL and KRYPTO THE SUPERDOG, a frightening "red kryptonite hallucination" induced by exposure to red-kryptonite dust (S No. 144/3: "The Orphans of Space!"); and, while traveling around the world taking photographs of DAILY PLANET branch offices and personnel in foreign countries to help commemorate the newspaper's centennial, recalls the days when, as a youth, he first made his super-powers known to the world (S No. 144/2: "Superboy's First Public Appearance!").

In May 1961 Superman matches wits with JOHN KILEY (Act No. 276: "The War Between Supergirl and the Supermen Emergency Squad!"), copes with the consequences of one of JIMMY OLSEN's inspirations (S No. 145/1: "The Secret Identity of Superman!"), thwarts an attempt by an unscrupulous alien ringmaster to force him to join his traveling "interplanetary circus" as the show's star attraction (S No. 145/2: "The Interplanetary Circus!"), and, together with Batman and Robin, battles LEX LUTHOR (WF No. 117: "The Super-Batwoman and the Super-Creature!"). A text for this same period, intended as a sort of April Fool's Day joke on the Superman readership, contains a host of ludicrous "errors"—such as a panel showing Clark Kent dressed in knickers and knee socks, and another showing the letter "S" emblazoned backwards on Superman's chest—and invites readers to compile a list of them, with a prize being offered to the reader who discovers the largest number (S No. 145/3, May '61: "The Night of March 31st!").

In June 1961 Superman battles LEX LUTHOR (Act No. 277: "The Conquest of Superman!"), employs the alias the ALCHEMIST (BM No. 140/2: "The Charmed Life of Batman!"), joins forces with Batman and Robin to thwart the dictatorial ambitions of VATHGAR (WF No. 118: "The Creature That Was Exchanged for Superman!"), and, after a weird mixture of "upper atmosphere" gas samples in a Gotham City laboratory has temporarily transformed Batman into a colossal giant, helps Batman protect the secret of his dual identity by disguising himself as Bruce Wayne, Batman's alter ego, and standing in for Wayne at a community fund dinner (Det No. 292: "The Colossus of Gotham City!").

In July 1961 Superman battles Xasnu, an extraterrestrial "plant intelligence" inhabiting the body of PERRY WHITE (Act No. 278: "The Super Powers of Perry White!"), responds to an urgent telepathic summons from LORI LEMARIS, and, in addition, journeys to an extradimensional parallel universe, where he finds, contrary to the natural laws that prevail in his own universe, that he can change history, and where he therefore avails himself of the opportunity to use his super-powers to undo some of the parallel universe's great historical disasters, including the sinking of Atlantis, the assassination of Abraham Lincoln, and the death of virtually the entire population of Krypton. These momentous changes in history have no effect whatever on Superman's own universe, however, where even Superman cannot alter the course of history (S No. 146/2: "Superman's Greatest Feats!"). During this same period, the story of Superman's origin and early life are recapitulated (S No. 146/1, Jul '61: "The Story of Superman's Life!").

In August 1961 Superman encounters HERCULES and Samson in an "imaginary tale" (Act No. 279: "The Super-Rivals!"), meets the GREAT MENTO (S No. 147/1: "The Great Mento!"), battles the LEGION OF SUPER-VILLAINS (S No. 147/3: "The Legion of Super-

Villains!"), and, together with Batman and Robin, thwarts the sinister schemes of GENERAL GRAMBLY (WF No. 119: "The Secret of Tigerman!"). During this same period, Krypto the Superdog encounters TITANO during a time-journey to the prehistoric past (S No. 147/2, Aug '61: "Krypto Battles Titano!").

In September 1961 Superman battles BRAINIAC (Act No. 280: "Brainiac's Super-Revenge!") and, together with Batman and Robin, defeats an unidentified criminal who has managed to bring to life three enchanted beings, all originally created by the ancient alchemist Albertus, who proceed to temporarily steal several of Superman's super-powers (WF No. 120: "The Challenge of the Faceless Creatures!").

In October 1961 Superman has an encounter with PROFESSOR AMOS DUNN (Act No. 281: "The Man Who Saved Kal-El's Life!"), matches wits with ACHILLES (S No. 148/1: "The 20th Century Achilles!"), copes with the magical mischief of MR. MXYZPTLK (S No. 148/2: "Mr. Mxyzptlk's Super-Mischief!"), and makes the acquaintance of RUPERT BRAND (S No. 148/3: "Superman Owes a Billion Dollars!").

In November 1961 Superman assigns one of his sophisticated Clark Kent robots to keep a date with Lois Lane so that he can remain free to spend the day performing his customary super-chores (Act No. 282: "Superman's Toughest Day!"), matches wits with LEX LUTHOR in an "imaginary tale" (S No. 149: pts. I-III—"Lex Luthor, Hero!"; "Luthor's Super-Bodyguard!"; "The Death of Superman!"), and, together with Batman and Robin, battles the villainous XANU (WF No. 121: "The Mirror Batman!").

In December 1961 Superman matches wits with JAN-DEX and ZO-GAR (Act No. 283: "The Red Kryptonite Menace!") and, together with Batman and Robin, thwarts the dictatorial ambitions of the villainous KLOR (WF No. 122: "The Capture of Superman!").

In January 1962 Superman struggles to thwart a possible mass escape from the PHANTOM ZONE (Act No. 284: "The Babe of Steel!"), thwarts a scheme by Lois Lane and LANA LANG to maneuver him into matrimony (S No. 150/2: "The Duel Over Superman!"), and, together with Supergirl and Krypto the Superdog, stands before the bottle city of Kandor, in the Fortress of Solitude, and bows his head solemnly for one full minute of silence to commemorate the anniversary of the destruction of Krypton. Afterward, the three Krypton survivors soar into outer space, where, in a "distant solar system," they use their mighty super-powers to transform an uninhabited planet into an exact duplicate of Krypton—and populate it with humanoid androids in the image of Jor-El, Lara, and other Kryptonians—as a planet-sized memorial to their exploded world (S No. 150/1: "The One Minute of Doom!"). A text for this same period recounts the story of an encounter between Superman and MR. MXYZPTLK (S No. 150/3, Jan '62: "When the World Forgot Superman!").

In February 1962 Superman proudly proclaims SUPERGIRL's existence to the world (Act No. 285: "The World's Greatest Heroine!"), matches wits with

CONRAD KRUGG (S No. 151/2: "The Man Who Trained Supermen!"), battles a Kryptonian flame dragon (see FLAME DRAGON) (S No. 151/3: "Superman's Greatest Secret!"), and, together with Batman and Robin, copes with the magical mischief of MR. MXYZPTLK and Bat-Mite (WF No. 123: "The Incredible Team of Bat-Mite and Mr. Mxyzptlk!"). During this same period, while Lois Lane is working as a schoolteacher in a problem school in order to gather information for a feature article on juvenile delinquency for the Daily Planet, Superman lends her a helping hand by using his mighty super-powers to teach a well-deserved lesson in good manners and respect for others to three rude troublemakers in her elementary-school class (S No. 151/1, Feb '62: "The Three Tough Teen-Agers!").

In March 1962 Superman becomes the target of a scheme by the SUPERMAN REVENGE SQUAD (Act No. 286: "The Jury of Super-Enemies!") and, together with Batman and Robin, thwarts the evil machinations of HROGUTH (WF No. 124: "The Mystery of the Alien Super-Boy!").

In April 1962 Superman thwarts a scheme by the SUPERMAN REVENGE SQUAD (Act No. 287: "Perry White's Manhunt for Superman!"), becomes the target of a well-intentioned hoax devised by the LEGION OF SUPER-HEROES (S No. 152/1: "The Robot Master!"), and matches wits with the ANTI-SUPERMAN GANG (S No. 152/3: "The TV Trap for Superman!"). A text for this same period recounts the story of how Superman, while still an infant, was inadvertently responsible for the capture of three fugitive criminals (S No. 152/2, Apr '62: "Superbaby Captures the Pumpkin Gang!").

In May 1962 Superman matches wits with HAL COLBY (Act No. 288: "The Man Who Exposed Superman!"), thwarts the schemes of COUNCILMAN FINCH (S No. 153/1: "The Day Superman Broke the Law!"), visits the town of DRYWOOD GULCH (S No. 153/3: "The Town of Supermen!"), and, together with Batman and Robin, thwarts the sinister machinations of JUNDY (WF No. 125: "The Hostages of the Island of Doom!"). During this same period, when the city of Rangoon, Burma, dispatches two officials to the United States to obtain "an inspiring picture of Superman" for use on Rangoon's forthcoming Superman commemorative stamp, Superman becomes anxious to dissuade the Burmese from selecting a frontal view of himself, for he fears that the Rangoon post-office cancellation, with its prominent double O, will in effect superimpose "eyeglasses" on his face and thereby jeopardize the secret of his dual identity. Superman is greatly relieved, therefore, when the Burmese finally select a photograph of him flying through the air, supporting a multiracial group of youngsters atop a gigantic slab of rock (S No. 153/2, May '62: "The Secret of the Superman Stamp!"). The story is in many respects similar to Superman No. 91/1 (Aug '54: "The Superman Stamp!"). (See FOTHERINGAY, WILLIS.)

In June 1962 Superman meets DEXTER WILLIS (Act No. 289: "The Super-Practical Joker!") and, together with Batman and Robin, battles LEX LUTHOR (WF No. 126: "The Negative Superman!").

In July 1962 Superman copes with the magical mischief of MR. MXYZPTLK (S No. 154/1: "The Underwater Pranks of Mr. Mxyzptlk!"), becomes the victim of a scheme devised by MAG-EN (S No. 154/2: "Krypton's First Superman!"), and successfully performs his customary round of super-chores despite the fact that exposure to red kryptonite has temporarily robbed him of his invulnerability along the entire left side of his body (Act No. 290: "Half a Superman!").

In August 1962 Superman matches wits with "DUDE" DUNN (Act No. 291: "The New Superman!"), battles DRAGO (S No. 155/1: pts. I-II—"Superman Under the Green Sun!"; "The Blind Superman!"), outwits DUKE MARPLE (S No. 155/2: "The Downfall of Superman!"), and, together with Batman and Robin, thwarts the schemes of the evil ZERNO (WF No. 127: "The Sorcerer from the Stars!").

In September 1962 Superman pursues LEX LUTHOR to the planet Roxar (Act No. 292: "When Superman Defended His Arch-Enemy!") and, together with Batman and Robin, thwarts the schemes of MOOSE MORANS (WF No. 128: "The Power That Transformed Batman!").

In October 1962 exposure to red kryptonite transforms Superman into two separate individuals, a mature, responsible Clark Kent and an unprincipled, irresponsible Superman. The arrogant Superman becomes ruthlessly determined to keep the personalities of Clark Kent and Superman separate forever, but Clark Kent ultimately succeeds, despite Superman's malevolent efforts, in bringing about the reuniting of Clark Kent and Superman into a single individual (Act No. 293: "The Feud Between Superman and Clark Kent!"). During this same period, after a series of complex circumstances have combined to mislead Superman into believing that he is dying of exposure to Virus X, an incurable Kryptonian malady, Superman calls on SUPERGIRL and his other "super-comrades" to help him carry out a series of gigantic super-tasks that he hopes to fulfill as his final legacy to humanity. Ultimately, however, after the tasks have been completed, it becomes clear that Superman is not suffering from exposure to Virus X at all, but rather from the effects of a tiny nugget of kryptonite that has somehow become lodged in Jimmy Olsen's camera. Indeed, once this kryptonite nugget has been removed from Superman's presence, Superman is, almost immediately, restored to full health (S No. 156, Oct '62: "The Last Days of Superman!" pts. I-III—"Superman's Death Sentence!"; "The Super-Comrades of All Time!"; "Superman's Last Day of Life!"). The story is in many respects similar to Superman No. 66/2 (Sep/Oct '50: "The Last Days of Superman!"), which has been summarized previously in this section.

In November 1962 Superman battles LEX LUTHOR (Act No. 294: "The Kryptonite Killer!"), releases QUEX-UL from the Phantom Zone (S No. 157/1: "The Super-Revenge of the Phantom Zone Prisoner!"), carries out an elaborate ruse with the aid of PROFESSOR VON SCHULTZ (S. No 157/2: "The Super-Genie of Metropolis!"), is nearly killed by BIZARRO (S No. 157/3: "Superman's Day of Doom!"), and, together with Batman and Robin, thwarts the sinister schemes of LEX LUTHOR and the Joke (WF No. 129: "Joker-Luthor, Incorporated!").

In December 1962 Superman matches wits with the SUPERMAN REVENGE SQUAD (Act No. 295: "Superman Goes Wild!").

In January 1963 Superman struggles to thwart the misguided schemes of THAN OL (S No. 158: "Superman in Kandor" pts. I-III—"Invasion of the Mystery Super-Men!"; "The Dynamic Duo of Kandor!"; "The City of Super-People!") and extends the hand of friendship to a band of gigantic red ants, emissaries of peace and brotherhood from a "distant world" where theirs is the "supreme race," who have been temporarily stranded on the planet Earth ever since their spacecraft crashed in a valley outside Metropolis while they were traveling from planet to planet preaching their message of peace (Act No. 296: "The Invasion of the Super-Ants!").

In February 1963 Superman becomes embroiled in an adventure involving PERRY WHITE (Act No. 297: "The Man Who Betrayed Superman's Identity!") and, together with Batman and Robin, battles the OCTOPUS (WF No. 131: "The Mystery of the Crimson Avenger!"). A text for this same period recounts, in an "imaginary tale," what might have happened if Earth had exploded instead of Krypton, and if the infant Lois Lane had been dispatched to Krypton in a rocket, endowed with super-powers, much as the infant Superman was sent in a rocket to Earth (S No. 159, Feb '63: "Lois Lane, the Super-Maid of Krypton!" chs. I-III—"Lois Lane's Flight from Earth!"; "The Female Luthor of Krypton!"; "The Doom of Super-Maid!").

In March 1963 Superman meets QUEEN LURA (Act No. 298: "Clark Kent, Coward!") and, together with Batman and Robin, captures DENNY KALE and Shorty Biggs (WF No. 132: "Batman and Robin, Medieval Bandits!").

In April 1963 Superman matches wits with "ROCKS" HANEY (S No. 160/1: pts. I-II—"The Mortal Superman!"; "The Cage of Doom!") and, with the aid of Perry White and the Metropolis police force, carries out an elaborate, and ultimately successful, ruse designed to enable him to apprehend a ring of foreign spies planning to steal the blueprints for a "new type of atomic war-head" developed by the U.S. government (S No. 160/2: "The Super-Cop of Metropolis!"). A text for this same period recounts the story of how, "many years ago," Superman triumphed over three of his own "experimental robots," which turned against him and tried to destroy him (Act No. 299, Apr '63: "The Story of Superman's Experimental Robots!").

In May 1963 Superman is lured into a trap by the SUPERMAN REVENGE SQUAD (Act No. 300: "Superman Under the Red Sun!"), returns to Smallville to commemorate the death of JONATHAN AND MARTHA KENT (S No. 161/1: "The Last Days of Ma and Pa Kent!"), and lends a helping hand to a band of aliens from the planet ZHOR (S No. 161/2: "Superman Goes to War!").

In June 1963 Superman matches wits with COUNT X (Act No. 301: "The Trial of Superman!") and, together with Batman and Robin, battles the BAND OF SUPER-VILLAINS (WF No. 134: "The Band of Super-Villains").

In July 1963 Superman impersonates Perry White as part of an elaborate, and ultimately successful, ruse to enable him to apprehend a ring of stock swindlers (Act No. 302: "The Amazing Confession of Super-Perry White!"). A text for this same period recounts, in an "imaginary tale," the events that ensue when the malfunctioning of a complex "brain-evolution machine" in the Fortress of Solitude accidentally transforms Superman into two identical Supermen—one clad in a blue costume, the other in a red one—each endowed with a super-intellect 100 times as powerful as that of the original. Armed with their vastly increased intellectual capacity as well as with their mighty super-powers, the two benevolent Supermen—referred to as Superman-Blue and Superman-Red—set out to fulfill a series of mighty super-tasks which Superman, working alone, has traditionally been unable to fulfill: together the two Supermen re-create the exploded planet Krypton to its last topographical detail; alter the atomic structure of kryptonite, rendering it harmless to Kryptonians; enlarge the bottle city of Kandor; provide a water-world home in outer space for Lori Lemaris and the other Atlantean mer-people; and bring about the total eradication of crime, warfare, and evil by flooding the Earth with a potent "anti-evil ray" of their own invention. These and other great tasks finally completed, Superman-Blue and Superman-Red marry Lana Lang and Lois Lane, respectively, and settle down to lives of wedded bliss (S No. 162, Jul '63: "The Amazing Story of Superman-Red and Superman-Blue!" pts. I-III—"The Titanic Twins!"; "The Anti-Evil Ray!"; "The End of Superman's Career!").

In August 1963 Superman is temporarily transformed into a Kryptonian "drang" (see KRYPTON) by exposure to red kryptonite (Act No. 303: "The Monster from Krypton!"), thwarts a scheme concocted by the SUPERMAN REVENGE SQUAD (S No. 163/1: "Wonder-Man, the New Hero of Metropolis!"), is incarcerated in the HAPPY ACRES STATE MENTAL REHABILITATION CENTER (S No. 163/2: "The Goofy Superman!"), and, together with Batman and Robin, meets JON DURR during a time-journey into the future (WF No. 135: "The Menace of the Future Man!").

In September 1963 Superman journeys to the "planetoid" VORN (Act No. 304: "The Interplanetary Olympics!"). During this same period, Batman encounters an extradimensional Superman during an unplanned visit to a parallel world (see RED RAVEN) (WF No. 136, Sep '63: "The Batman Nobody Remembered!").

In October 1963 Superman battles LEX LUTHOR (S No. 164/1: pts. I-II—"The Showdown Between Luthor and Superman!"; "The Super-Duel!") and matches wits with RAS-KROM (S No. 164/2: "The Fugitive from the Phantom Zone!"). A text for this same period describes Clark Kent's encounter with BENNY THE BLASTER and, in a series of "imaginary" vignettes, explains why it is essential for Superman to maintain a secret identity (Act No. 305, Oct '63: "Why Superman Needs a Secret Identity!").

In November 1963 Superman matches wits with the SUPERMAN REVENGE SQUAD (S No. 165/1: pts. I-II—"Beauty and the Super-Beast!"; "Circe's Super-Slave"), meets SALLY SELWYN (S No. 165/2: "The Sweetheart Superman Forgot!"), and, together with Batman and Robin, battles LEX LUTHOR (WF No. 137: "Superman's Secret Master!"). A text for this same period recounts the story of Superman's encounter with GENERAL PEDRO VALDEZ (Act No. 306, Nov '63: "The Great Superman Impersonation!").

In December 1963 Superman matches wits with "KING" KOBRA (Act No. 307: "Clark Kent—Target for Murder!") and, together with Batman and Robin, defeats GENERAL GROTE (WF No. 138: "The Secret of the Captive Cavemen!").

In January 1964 Superman encounters an extradimensional counterpart of the legendary HERCULES (Act No. 308: "Superman Meets the Goliath-Hercules!"), and an "imaginary tale," set in the near future, describes the heroic efforts of Superman's two sons—one of whom possesses super-powers, the other of whom does not—to defeat an escapee from the Phantom Zone bent on conquering the Earth (S No. 166: "The Fantastic Story of Superman's Sons!" pts. I-III—"Jor-El II and Kal-El II!"; "The New Nightwing and Flamebird!"; "Kal-El II's Mission to Krypton!").

In February 1964 Superman matches wits with LEX LUTHOR and Brainiac (S No. 167: "The Team of Luthor and Brainiac!" pts. I-III—"The Deadly Duo!"; "The Downfall of Superman!"; "The Hour of Kandor's Vengeance!") and, together with Batman and Robin, battles the SPHINX GANG (WF No. 139: "The Ghost of Batman!"). A text for this same period recounts the events surrounding Superman's appearance, as guest of honor, on the premiere program of Metropolis television station WMET-TV's "Our American Heroes" series (see LANG, LANA) (Act No. 309, Feb '64: "The Superman Super-Spectacular!").

In March 1964 Superman matches wits with JAX-UR (Act No. 310: "Secret of Kryptonite Six!") and, together with Batman and Robin, thwarts the sinister machinations of CLAYFACE (WF No. 140: "The Clayface Superman!").

In April 1964 Superman battles LEX LUTHOR (S No. 168: pts. I-II—"Luthor--Super-Hero!"; "Lex Luthor, Daily Planet Editor!") and sets in motion an elaborate ruse designed to thwart an invasion of Earth by the planet BXPA (Act No. 311: "Superman, King of Earth!").

In May 1964 Superman concludes his efforts to

thwart the invasion from BXPA (Act No. 312: "King Superman versus Clark Kent, Metallo"), copes with the magical mischief of MR. MXYZPTLK (S No. 169/1: "The Infernal Imp!"), pursues NED BARNES and renews his relationship with SALLY SELWYN (S No. 169/2: "The Man Who Stole Superman's Secret Life!"), and endures a BIZARRO invasion of Earth (S No. 169/3: "The Bizarro Invasion of Earth!"). During this same period, with the aid of Robin and Jimmy Olsen, Batman and Superman apprehend a pair of criminals who have kidnapped a prominent physicist and stolen his newly invented "invisibility de-visors" so that they can use the devices to render themselves invisible while they commit crimes (WF No. 141, May '64: "The Olsen-Robin Team versus 'The Superman-Batman Team!'").

In June 1964 Superman matches wits with the SUPERMAN REVENGE SQUAD (Act No. 313: "The End of Clark Kent's Secret Identity!") and, together with Batman and Robin, battles the COMPOSITE SUPERMAN (WF No. 142: "The Origin of the Composite Superman!" pts. I-II—"The Composite Superman!"; "The Battle Between Titans!").

In July 1964 Superman views a Kryptonian "video-recording" narrated by his father, JOR-EL (Act No. 314: "The Day Superman Became the Flash!"). Other texts for this same period recount the story of a mission Superman performed for President JOHN F. KENNEDY (S No. 170/1, Jul '64: "Superman's Mission for President Kennedy!") and describe a bizarre scheme by LEX LUTHOR to become the father of Superman (S No. 170/2, Jul '64: pts. I-II—"If Lex Luthor Were Superman's Father!"; "The Wedding of Lara and Luthor!").

In August 1964 Superman meets ZIGI AND ZAGI (Act No. 315: "The Juvenile Delinquents from Space!"), matches wits with ROKK AND SORBAN (S No. 171/1: "Superman's Sacrifice!"), copes with the magical mischief of MR. MXYZPTLK (S No. 171/2: "The Curse of Magic!"), journeys to a distant planet at the behest of DR. LURING (S No. 171/3: "The Nightmare Ordeal of Superman"), and, together with Batman and Robin, becomes embroiled in an adventure involving the Kandorian official THAN-AR (WF No. 143: "The Feud Between Batman and Superman!" pts. I-II—no title; "The Manhunters from Earth!").

In September 1964 Superman renews his acquaintance with ZIGI AND ZAGI (Act No. 316: "Zigi and Zagi's Trap for Superman!") and, together with Batman and Robin, battles the formidable alliance of CLAYFACE and Brainiac (WF No. 144: "The 1,001 Tricks of Clayface and Brainiac!" pts. I-II—no title; "The Helpless Partners!").

In October 1964 Superman struggles to thwart the sinister machinations of LEX LUTHOR and Brainiac (S No. 172: pts. I-III—"The New Superman!"; "Clark Kent—Former Superman!"; "The Struggle of the Two Supermen!"), and struggles through a period during which, as the result of his exposure to red kryptonite, his face literally changes color to reflect his emotions—so that when he is angry it turns purple, embarrassed it turns red, envious it turns green, and grief-stricken it turns blue—thus threatening to betray his dual identity to anyone, particularly Lois Lane, who might chance to perceive the same kinds of bizarre facial transformations taking place in both Clark Kent and Superman (Act No. 317: "Superman's Rainbow Face!").

In November 1964 Superman matches wits with LEX LUTHOR (Act No. 318: "The Death of Luthor!"), meets ED BABSON (S No. 173/1: "The 'Untouchable' Clark Kent!"), enlists the aid of his friend Batman in teaching a much-needed lesson to JIMMY OLSEN (S No. 173/3: "The Triumph of Luthor and Brainiac!"), and, together with Batman and Robin, thwarts the schemes of conquest devised by the masters of the planet VOR (WF No. 145: "Prison for Heroes!" pts. I-II—no title; "The Revenge of Superman!"). A text for this same period initiates a series of so-called "tales of kryptonite," short tales of Superman's life as "seen" through the "eyes" of a chunk of kryptonite (S No. 173/2, Nov '64: "Tales of Green Kryptonite No. 1").

In December 1964 Superman matches wits with LEX LUTHOR (Act No. 319: "The Condemned Superman!") and, together with Batman and Robin, learns the incredible story of DR. THOMAS ELLISON (WF No. 146: "Batman, Son of Krypton!" pts. I-II—no title; "The Destroyer of Krypton!").

In January 1965 Superman encounters ADAM NEWMAN (S No. 174/1: pts. 1-2—"Clark Kent's Incredible Delusion!"; "The End of a Hero!"), copes with some infuriating competition from MR. MXYZPTLK (S No. 174/2: "Super-Mxyzptlk...Hero!"), and defeats a trio of extradimensional villains—endowed with superhuman strength as well as magical powers—who are perfect look-alikes for the Hercules, Samson, and Atlas who inhabit various past eras in Superman's own dimension (Act No. 320: "The Three Super-Enemies!").

In February 1965 Superman encounters the THORONES after being lured into a trap by the FOUR GALACTIC THIEFMASTERS (Act No. 321: "Superman--Weakest Man in the World!"), figures prominently in an "imaginary tale" involving LEX LUTHOR (S No. 175: pts. I-III—"Clark Kent's Brother!"; "The Defeat of Superman!"; "The Luthor-Superman"), and, together with Batman, struggles to aid Robin and JIMMY OLSEN, whose minds have been "taken over and possessed" by some weirdly glowing jewels from a distant planet (WF No. 147: "The Doomed Boy Heroes!" pts. I-II—"The New Terrific Team!"; "The Doom of Jimmy Olsen and Robin!").

In March 1965 Superman becomes the target of a cunning scheme devised by the SUPERMAN REVENGE SQUAD (Act No. 322: "The Coward of Steel!"). During this same period, Batman and Superman are temporarily catapulted into a bizarre "parallel world...a world that's almost like Earth in every way, but in which history had a different course than on Earth!" On this parallel world, the counterparts of Batman and Superman are master criminals; Robin is

Batman's partner in crime; Jonathan and Martha Kent, Superman's foster parents, were notorious criminals in their day, as was Thomas Wayne, the father of Batman; Lex Luthor and Clayface, notorious villains on the world inhabited by the real Batman and Superman, are renowned champions of law and justice; Jimmy Olsen is Lex Luthor's pal; and Perry White is a prosecuting attorney. During their stay on the parallel world, Batman and Superman help their fellow lawmen—Lex Luthor and Clayface—apprehend the evil Batman and Superman before departing for home (WF No. 148, Mar '65: "Superman and Batman--Outlaw!" pts. I-II—"The Evil Superman and Batman"; "The Incredible New Super-Team!").

In April 1965 Superman matches wits with "BLACKY" BLAKE (Act No. 323: "Clark Kent in the Big House!"), teaches a well-deserved lesson to CYRUS ATWILL during a time-journey to the year 1866 (S No. 176/1: "The Revenge of the Super-Pets!"), and takes part in the ceremonies marking the Day of Truth in the bottle city of Kandor (see KRYPTON) (S No. 176/3: "Superman's Day of Truth!"). A text for this same period contains the second in the "tales of kryptonite" series (S No. 176/2, Apr '65: "Tales of Green Kryptonite No. 2").

In May 1965 Superman encounters "IT" (S No. 177/2: "The Menace Called 'It'!"), spends a night at the Fortress of Solitude with Jimmy Olsen and KRYPTO THE SUPERDOG (S No. 177/3: "When Jimmy Olsen Stole Krypto from Superman"), and, as Clark Kent, makes an unplanned visit to CRATER VALLEY (Act No. 324: "The Secret Life of Clark Kent!"). During this same period, when, as a means of testing the security of his secret identity, Superman uses a "selective amnesia-inducer" to erase from the minds of Batman and Robin the knowledge that Clark Kent is secretly Superman, the Dynamic Duo are nevertheless able to deduce Superman's secret on their own. When the roles are reversed, however, and the selective amnesia-inducer is used to erase Superman's knowledge of the Dynamic Duo's identities, Superman is unable to discover, try though he might, that Batman and Robin are secretly Bruce Wayne and Dick Grayson. "...Though he's the mightiest man in the world," remarks Robin privately to Batman, "he's not the greatest detective!" (WF No. 149, May '65: "The Game of Secret Identities!" pts. I-II—no title; "The Super-Detective!"). A text for this same period contains the third in the "tales of kryptonite" series (S No. 177/1, May '65: "Superman's Kryptonese Curse!").

In June 1965 Superman recalls a dip he once took in Krypton's SHRINKWATER LAKE and, through a ruse, succeeds in frightening away a band of extraterrestrial "space bandits" bent on looting Earth of its iron and steel objects by means of an awesomely powerful "super-magnet," despite the fact that exposure to red kryptonite has temporarily robbed him of his super-powers and transformed him into a towering giant (Act No. 325: "The Skyscraper

Superman!"). During this same period, Batman and Superman match wits with ROKK AND SORBAN (WF No. 150, Jun '65: pts. I-II—"The Super-Gamble with Doom!"; "The Duel of the Super-Gamblers!"),

In July 1965 Superman journeys to the planet GIANTIA (Act No. 326: "The Legion of Super-Creatures!"), thwarts the sinister machinations of TORR THE TERRIBLE (S No. 178/1: "Project Earth-Doom!"), and suffers through a period of near-total amnesia induced by exposure to a weird substance formed by the fusion of red kryptonite and gold kryptonite (S No. 178/2: "When Superman Lost His Memory!"). This latter story is in many respects similar to World's Finest Comics No. 68 (Jan/Feb '54: "The Menace from the Stars!"), which has been summarized previously in this section.

In August 1965 Superman matches wits with PETE COREY (S No. 179/1: "The Outlaw Fort Knox!"), meets SGT. BUCK BREWSTER (S No. 179/3: "Private Kent, the Fighting Marine!"), and, in an "imaginary tale" set in the future, after Superman has retired from crime-fighting and become a grandfather, joins forces with his infant grandson, Kal-El II, to defeat a band of extraterrestrial robots that have been dispatched to Earth by aliens from a distant planet as the advance guard of an impending interplanetary invasion (Act No. 327: "The Three Generations of Superman!"). A text for this same period contains the fourth in the "tales of kryptonite" series (S No. 179/2, Aug '65: "The Menace of Gold Kryptonite!").

In September 1965 Superman matches wits with MR. GIMMICK (Act No. 328: "Superman's Hands of Doom!") and, together with Batman and Robin, copes with the magical mischief of MR. MXYZPTLK and Bat-Mite (WF No. 152: "The Colossal Kids!" pts. I-II—no title; "The Magic of Bat-Mite and Mr. Mxyzptlk!").

In October 1965 Superman apprehends JON SMATTEN (Act No. 329: "The Ultimate Enemy!"), matches wits with HERB FARR (S No. 180/1: "Clark Kent's Great Superman Hunt!"), and visits FLORENA, the so-called "island of women" (S No. 180/2: "The Girl Who Was Mightier Than Superman!").

In November 1965 Superman receives some assistance from KRYPTO THE SUPERDOG (Act No. 330: "The Strange 'S' Spell on Superman!") and meets MORNA VINE (S No. 181/1: pts. I-II—"The Super-Scoops of Morna Vine!"; "The Secret of the New Supergirl!").

In December 1965 Superman matches wits with IRON IKE (Act No. 331: "Clark Kent's Masquerade as Superman!"). A text for this same period contains an "imaginary tale" in which Lois Lane appears as the wife of Clark Kent, and Kathy Kane appears as the wife of Bruce Wayne (see BATWOMAN, THE) (WF No. 154, Dec '65: "The Sons of Superman and Batman!" pts. I-II—no title; "The Junior Super-Team").

SUPERMAN, JUNIOR. The name given by SUPERMAN to his young foster son, JOHNNY KIRK (Act No. 232, Sep '57: "The Story of Superman, Junior").

SUPERMAN EMERGENCY SQUAD, THE. *See* SUPERMEN EMERGENCY SQUAD, THE.

SUPERMAN HALL OF TROPHIES. *See* SUPERMAN MUSEUM, THE.

SUPERMANIUM. A rare metallic element (S No. 68/1, Jan/Feb '51: "The Six Elements of Crime!"; and others) that is discovered by SUPERMAN in July-August 1949 and named in his honor by the members of the SUPER-SAVED CLUB. Superman refers to it as "the hardest substance in existence" (WF No. 41, Jul/Aug '49: "The Discovery of Supermanium!") and as "my invulnerable new element" (S No. 68/1, Jan/Feb '51: "The Six Elements of Crime!"), and the texts describe it as "the strongest metal known" (Act No. 289, Jun '62: "The Super-Practical Joker!") and as "the strongest metal known to science" (S No. 167, Feb '64: "The Team of Luthor and Brainiac!" pts. I-III—"The Deadly Duo!"; "The Downfall of Superman!"; "The Hour of Kandor's Vengeance!").

In July-August 1949, after an "eminent chemist" has reported the probable existence of a "super-hard" element, as yet undiscovered, whose unique properties would make it "extremely valuable for all sorts of industrial purposes," the members of the Super-Saved Club—acting at the urging of JAMES HARVEY THORBEN—decide to pool their financial resources and scientific and engineering expertise in order to locate and refine the new element. If successful, they plan to name it "supermanium" as a surprise tribute to Superman.

Officially, it is the members of the Super-Saved Club who locate the new element in a remote mountain region and refine the world's first sample of supermanium ore. In actuality, however, it is Superman, working behind the scenes with his super-powers so as not to spoil the club members' surprise for him, who locates the vein of supermanium ore and refines it, for the new substance is so unbelievably super-hard that it literally shatters the machinery with which the club members attempt to grind it, forcing Superman "to apply his full colossal strength" in order to refine the ore by hand. "Heat and pressure," thinks Superman as he bends to the task, "--I can supply more of them with my hands than any machine can!"

Having secretly refined the rare ore himself while contriving to make it appear that the Super-Saved Club's machinery has somehow done the job for them, Superman graciously allows the club's members to present him with the element they have named in his honor, promising that he will see to it that it is put to work in a multitude of ways "to save human drudgery!" (WF No. 41: "The Discovery of Supermanium!").

In January-February 1951 Superman fashions a vault out of supermanium for METROPOLIS's "famous radium institute" in order to prevent its priceless radium stockpile from being stolen by LEX LUTHOR (S No. 68/1: "The Six Elements of Crime!").

In June 1962 Superman employs invisibly fine wires fashioned out of supermanium to enable him to manipulate gigantic replicas of mythical monsters as though they were colossal marionettes (Act No. 289: "The Super-Practical Joker!").

In February 1964, when Lex Luthor arrives on the "prison planet" KRONIS to liberate BRAINIAC, he finds the notorious space villain locked in a "mighty cage"—fashioned by Superman from "an isotope of supermanium"—which his powerful "atomic torch" cannot even scratch. It is while Lex Luthor is attempting to free him from his supermanium prison that Brainiac remarks, incorrectly, that supermanium "is named after Superman because it was forged by him from the heart of a mighty star!" (S No. 167: "The Team of Luthor and Brainiac!" pts. I-III—"The Deadly Duo!"; "The Downfall of Superman!"; "The Hour of Kandor's Vengeance!").

SUPERMAN ISLAND. A distinctive man-made island, fashioned by SUPERMAN in his own image off the coast of METROPOLIS, where, despite the great personal danger to himself, the Man of Steel assembles a vast hoard of KRYPTONITE as his humanitarian response to a pronouncement by Professor Vanley of METROPOLIS UNIVERSITY to the effect that "kryptonite would yield perpetual atomic power" and therefore offer a permanent solution to mankind's growing energy needs. However, when Professor Vanley discovers that kryptonite "crumbles and destroys any generator" in which it is used and is therefore of no practical value as fuel, Superman tears Superman Island from its moorings and hurls it into outer space, where "It'll be a new star, wandering forever in the vast universe...a Superman star!" (Act No. 224, Jan '57: "The Secret of Superman Island!").

SUPERMAN LAND. "The most colossal, super-stupendous amusement park in the world," a "unique amusement park devoted to the exploits of a fabulous hero"—SUPERMAN. The park, which opens to an enthusiastic public in November 1955, includes such varied attractions as a gigantic statue of Superman standing guard over the main entrance; a fabulous "rocket room," where 3-D movie films and other special effects enable youngsters to experience the thrill of a make-believe journey through outer space to the planet KRYPTON; a DAILY PLANET building, containing lifelike wax dummies of Superman's "close friends" LOIS LANE, JIMMY OLSEN, PERRY WHITE, and CLARK KENT; a Superman Super-Powers Building, where papier-mâché barbells and X-ray special effects enable visitors to experience the thrill of simulated super-strength and X-ray vision; a Super-Shooting Gallery, where youngsters can fire guns and bows and arrows at a steel Superman dummy; a Superman Cartoon Festival Movie Theater, featuring Superman cartoons; a Superman Hall of Trophies, where youngsters can purchase Superman costumes and other super-souvenirs, and where a chunk of imitation KRYPTONITE is handed out free with every purchase; a Superman Land Post Office, where visitors can post letters stamped with a distinctive Superman stamp and cancelled with a special Superman cancellation; and a Superman

Merry-Go-Round, equipped with models of Superman in place of horses, so that youngsters can pretend to soar through the air atop a flying Superman. Disguised in a fake beard, moustache, and toupee, LEX LUTHOR invades Superman Land on its opening day as part of his latest scheme to destroy Superman (Act No. 210: "Superman in Superman Land").

SUPERMAN MUSEUM, THE. A museum in METROPOLIS, open to the public, which houses an extensive collection of SUPERMAN trophies and memorabilia. Founded in January 1952 by famed explorer STEFAN ANDRIESSEN (Act No. 164: "Superman's Hall of Trophies!"), it is located in the middle of Metropolis Park (S No. 150/3, Jan '62: "When the World Forgot Superman!") and attracts "hundreds of visitors" daily, all of whom pay an admission charge which is donated to charity (Act No. 185, Oct '53: "Superman's Million Dollar Photos!"). Superman No. 110/1 notes that

> There are many museums in the city of Metropolis, but the most famous is the one which is dedicated to **Superman** and contains sensational trophies of his amazing deeds! All of these exhibits are symbols of the **Man of Steel**'s victories over crime...[Jan '57: "The Secret of the Superman Trophy"].

Among the museum's numerous attractions are an extensive Superman Photo Gallery (Act No. 185, Oct '53: "Superman's Million Dollar Photos!"), weapons and other devices confiscated by Superman from LEX LUTHOR and other villains (S No. 101/1, Nov '55: "Luthor's Amazing Rebus"; and others), murals depicting Superman employing his various super-powers and an extensive file of Superman news stories (S No. 126/1, Jan '59: "Superman's Hunt for Clark Kent!"), a gallery of "souvenirs of other worlds" (S No. 129/2, May '59: "Clark Kent, Fireman of Steel!"), statuettes of the LEGION OF SUPER-HEROES

presented to Superman by the Legionnaires when he was a boy (WF No. 142, Jun '64: "The Origin of the Composite Superman!" pts. I-II—"The Composite Superman!"; "The Battle Between Titans!"), and statues of JOR-EL, LARA, and Superman himself at various stages of his life (S No. 150/3, Jan '62: "When the World Forgot Superman!"; and others), including the life-sized Superman statue carved out of solid diamond by SUPERGIRL in commemoration of Superman Day in November 1962 (S No. 157/3: "Superman's Day of Doom!"). Many of the trophies are extraordinarily valuable: in April 1959, one trophy alone is appraised at $35,000 (S No. 128/2: "The Sleeping Beauty from Krypton!").

The texts contain several references to a Superman Hall of Trophies (Act No. 185, Oct '53: "Superman's Million Dollar Photos!"; S No. 108/1, Sep '56: "The Brain from the Future!") and a Superman Trophy Hall (S No. 86/3, Jan '54: "The Fourth Dimension Gazette!"; S No. 110/1, Jan '57: "The Secret of the Superman Trophy"), but these would seem to be merely alternate names for the Superman Museum. The caretaker of the Superman Museum is Joe Meach, the man who achieves infamy as the COMPOSITE SUPERMAN (WF No. 142, Jun '64: "The Origin of the Composite Superman!" pts. I-II—"The Composite Superman!"; "The Battle Between Titans!").

In January 1952 STEFAN ANDRIESSEN, "the greatest explorer and adventurer of our times," assembles a large collection of Superman trophies and announces the dedication of a Superman Museum in the city of Metropolis (Act No. 164: "Superman's Hall of Trophies!").

In October 1953 a flaming meteor fragment from outer space hurtles through a window of the Superman Museum and starts a fire that destroys every single photograph in the Superman Photo Gallery

The Superman Museum

before firemen can bring the blaze under control. A new collection of Superman photos is soon under way, however, through the combined efforts of Superman and the museum's staff photographer (Act No. 185: "Superman's Million Dollar Photos!").

In November 1955 LEX LUTHOR commits a series of crimes designed to transform the Superman Museum into a memorial to his conquests instead of Superman's (S No. 101/1: "Luthor's Amazing Rebus").

In January 1957 escaped convict Les Keegan and two accomplices attempt to rob the Superman Museum as part of an elaborate scheme to blackmail the mayor of Metropolis, but all three criminals are apprehended by Superman (S No. 110/1: "The Secret of the Superman Trophy").

In May 1957, just outside Metropolis, Superman constructs a brand new Superman Museum in the form of a "miles-high structure" that towers above the surrounding countryside "far higher than any skyscraper." To the people of Metropolis, it appears that Superman's decision to build this ostentatious memorial to himself arises from unwholesome super-conceit, but the real function of the museum building is to serve as camouflage for a gigantic air shaft with which Superman intends to dispose of a deadly "poisonous chemical gas," which is seeping upward from the center of the Earth, without panicking the people of Metropolis. Once the toxic gas has been dissipated in the upper atmosphere, the Man of Steel dismantles the structure and converts it into "a much-needed housing project!" It is while this special Superman Museum is in operation that Superman apprehends "racket-leader" JAY AMERY and his henchman when they smuggle themselves into the building in an attempt to rob it (Act No. 228: "Superman's Super Skyscraper").

In January 1959, after Superman has become afflicted with temporary amnesia as the result of a mishap that occurs while he is experimenting with KRYPTONITE, the Man of Steel visits the Superman Museum in hopes of finding a clue to his own secret identity (S No. 126/1: "Superman's Hunt for Clark Kent!").

Superman spends some time in a Superman Museum during a time-journey to the year 2000 A.D., but it is uncertain whether this museum is the same as the Superman Museum now standing in Metropolis (S No. 128/1, Apr '59: chs. 1-2—"Superman versus the Futuremen"; "The Secret of the Futuremen").

In May 1959, while serving a stint as a "temporary fireman" so that he can write "a feature on the perils of fire-fighting" for the DAILY PLANET, Clark Kent extinguishes a fire at the Superman Museum with a blast of his super-breath (S No. 129/2: "Clark Kent, Fireman of Steel!").

In October 1959 a gang of criminals knock out the guards at the Superman Museum with "sleep-gas" and attempt to loot the building, but Clark Kent arrives on the scene and apprehends the criminals (Act No. 257: "The Reporter of Steel!").

In January 1960, during a period when the Kandorian scientist KULL-EX is committing insanely destructive acts while posing as Superman as part of his scheme to make "the name of Superman hated everywhere," the Superman Museum is forced to close after being all but demolished by angry mobs. Presumably the museum is rebuilt and reopened after Superman's name has been cleared, but this is never actually stated (S No. 134: chs. I-III—"The Super Menace of Metropolis!"; "The Revenge Against Jor-El!"; "The Duel of the Supermen!").

In May 1960, in a senseless act of destruction, SUPER-MENACE invades the Superman Museum and runs amok, smashing the museum's exhibits and shattering its statues of Superman with mighty blows of his fists (S No. 137: chs. I-III—"The Super-Brat from Krypton"; "The Young Super-Bully"; "Superman vs. Super-Menace!").

In a text dated January 1962, after MR. MXYZPTLK has used his "5th dimensional magic" to erase all memory of Superman's existence and all evidence of his heroic exploits, Superman returns to Earth from a mission in outer space to discover that the spot where the Superman Museum once stood is now occupied by an outer-space museum and that the statues of himself and his parents which once stood outside the museum have somehow been replaced by a statue of BATMAN. Once Superman has tricked Mr. Mxyzptlk into returning to his home dimension, however, the effects of the imp's magic vanish and the Superman Museum and the statues outside it are automatically restored to their proper place (S No. 150/3: "When the World Forgot Superman!").

In March 1962 Clark Kent muses to himself that the Superman Museum was dedicated only "yesterday," but this thought may safely be dismissed as erroneous (Act No. 286: "The Jury of Super-Enemies!").

In May 1964, during one of his mischievous forays through Metropolis, MR. MXYZPTLK transforms a globe of the planet KRYPTON—held aloft by a statue of Superman outside the Superman Museum—into a gigantic pumpkin, but the globe is automatically restored to its proper form once the imp has returned to his home dimension (S No. 169/1: "The Infernal Imp!").

In June 1964 a freak accident at the Superman Museum transforms caretaker Joe Meach into the COMPOSITE SUPERMAN (WF No. 142: "The Origin of the Composite Superman!" pts. I-II—"The Composite Superman!"; "The Battle Between Titans!").

SUPERMAN OF 2956. A costumed hero, clad in a costume identical to SUPERMAN'S, who enjoys a brief but colorful career as a crime-fighter in the thirtieth century A.D. with the aid of scientific gadgetry—including "concealed jet units for flight" and "a concealed degravitator to make heavy things light"—that enables him to simulate, albeit somewhat imperfectly, some of Superman's mighty super-powers. The Superman of 2956, also known as the "new Superman," is in reality Craig King, a mild-mannered "telenews reporter" for the Daily Solar System who assumed the role of thirtieth-century Superman at the behest of a delegation of "leading scientists" who provided him with his special super-power apparatus in the hope that he might be able to bring a halt to the mysterious "scientific thefts" that have been plaguing METROPOLIS.

Failing in his initial attempts to apprehend the criminals, however, the Superman of 2956 summons the real Superman to thirtieth-century Metropolis to help him, and, once the criminals have been apprehended, retires from crime-fighting, relieved that he will "never again have to imitate the man who can't be imitated--Superman!" (Act No. 215, Apr '56: "The Superman of Tomorrow"). (*See also* VAIL, VINSON.)

SUPERMANOR. The lavish mansion, donated by the people of MAPLEVILLE, where SUPERMAN sets up residence in April 1953 until an angry citizenry orders him out of town (Act No. 179: "Super Manor!"). (*See* MAPLEVILLE.)

SUPERMAN REVENGE SQUAD, THE. A loosely knit organization of extraterrestrial villains, founded originally by the warlike inhabitants of the planet Wexr II but now comprised of aliens from many planets, who have for years, ever since SUPERMAN was a teen-ager, sought to wreak vengeance on the Man of Steel in retaliation for his having repeatedly thwarted their attempts to subjugate peaceful planets and "dominate the universe" (Act No. 287, Apr '62: "Perry White's Manhunt for Superman!"; and others). In the words of one Squad member:

> We of the **Superman Revenge Squad** have tried for decades to get even with **Superman!** We have hated him ever since, as **Superboy**, he stopped [us] from conquering peaceful planets in outer space! Our squad has tried to destroy him many times--but we've always failed! [Act No. 295, Dec '62: "Superman Goes Wild!"].

The members of the Superman Revenge Squad are fully aware that Clark Kent is secretly Superman (Act No. 286, Mar '62: "The Jury of Super-Enemies!"; and others).

In March 1962 members of the Superman Revenge Squad set in motion an elaborate scheme to wreak vengeance on Superman by destroying the Earth (Act No. 286: "The Jury of Super-Enemies!"). "Only when his beloved Earth lies in smoking ruins," snarls their leader, a blue-skinned alien named Rava, "will he realize that we have finally repaid him for wrecking all our plans to dominate the universe!" (Act No. 287, Apr '62: "Perry White's Manhunt for Superman!").

The first phase of the villains' scheme involves surreptitiously exposing Superman to a variety of red KRYPTONITE whose effect they know, from having previously tested the substance on KRYPTO THE SUPERDOG, will be to make Superman experience terrifying nightmares set in the future. In one such nightmare, for example, Superman dreams that, in the distant future, the great-great-great-great-grandson of PETE ROSS and the great-great-great-granddaughter of LANA LANG are husband and wife, and that they attempt to destroy him by overexposure

to green kryptonite. The nightmares are frightening and deeply disturbing, but after having deduced that they are being caused by exposure to red kryptonite, Superman reasons that the nightmares are, after all, only harmless fantasies and that the effects of the red kryptonite will soon wear off (Act No. 286, Mar '62: "The Jury of Super-Enemies!").

It is then, however, that the Superman Revenge Squad initiates phase two of its scheme: the invasion of Metropolis by an army of extraterrestrial robots which shoot "jets of deadly anti-chlorophyl acid at the ground, converting the earth into a crawling blight that will spread like wildfire till not a blade of grass is left!" "Then," gloat the villains, "all humanity will starve to death!"

At first, as the ruthless extraterrestrial aliens had correctly anticipated, Superman assumes that the deadly robot invasion is merely another of his recurring red-kryptonite-induced nightmares. Ultimately, however, he realizes that the robot invasion is real and destroys the alien robots before they can overrun the Earth.

"Curse **Superman!**" mutters Rava angrily to his comrades, hovering high above the Earth in their flying-saucerlike spacecraft. "He's foiled us again! We'd better escape before he spots us and punishes us! But we of the **Superman Revenge Squad** will never give up hope! Some day we will execute the perfect revenge against **Superman!**" (Act No. 287, Apr '62: "Perry White's Manhunt for Superman!").

In December 1962 two members of the Superman Revenge Squad set out to "wreak a vengeance on Superman that is worse than death" by transforming him "from a hero beloved by all ... into the most feared and hated person on Earth!" Hovering just outside Earth's atmosphere in their flying-saucerlike spacecraft, the aliens employ a "telepathic signal gun"—a diabolical "telepathic-hypnotic weapon" which is specially "tuned to Superman's brain"—to bombard Superman's mind with a series of powerful "hypnotic commands" which the Man of Steel is powerless to disobey.

Under the baleful influence of the aliens' fiendish weapon, Superman embarks on a rampage of insanely destructive acts, demolishing the LEANING TOWER OF PISA, the SPHINX, and the EIFFEL TOWER; denouncing the United Nations on a television program devoted to the cause of international goodwill; maliciously shoving the MOON out of its proper orbit, causing massive tidal waves on the Earth's surface and an undersea disaster in ATLANTIS. Confident that they will succeed in their scheme to "humiliate Superman beyond his endurance" by forcing him to commit acts of destruction "that will disgrace him forever," the villains even go so far as to communicate with Superman by means of "a hypnotic-telepathic beam that penetrates [his] mind," informing him exactly what they have been doing to him and gloating over their ability to "compel him to do anything we want!" Indeed, before long, the villains have made Superman the most despised man on Earth.

Fortunately for Superman, however, the aliens periodically "turn off the telepathic beam and let Superman regain his sanity for a brief time" so that they can force him to endure the painful humiliation of being hated by almost everyone on Earth. It is during one of these periods of mental lucidity, while he is no longer under the baleful control of the villains' telepathic signal gun, that Superman enlists the aid of PERRY WHITE in a ruse designed to throw the Superman Revenge Squad members off their guard long enough for the SUPERMEN EMERGENCY SQUAD to apprehend them. By and large, the ruse succeeds, but as the Supermen Emergency Squad closes in on the aliens' spacecraft, the villains blow themselves and their craft to smithereens rather than submit to capture (Act No. 295: "Superman Goes Wild!").

In May 1963 two members of the Superman Revenge Squad, piloting their flying-saucerlike spacecraft at such "incredible velocity" that it hurtles across the time barrier, cunningly lure Superman into pursuing them into the distant future, to the vicinity of METROPOLIS one million years from now. In this far-future era, when Earth's sun is no longer yellow, but red, Superman realizes, to his horror, that he has completely lost his super-powers. "The sun ... it's red now, not yellow!" muses Superman ruefully as the villains soar away gloating in their spacecraft, confident that they have lured Superman into a deathtrap from which he cannot possibly escape. "In this far future [era], Earth's sun has become red as suns usually do as they get old! But ... but ... but under a red sun, like that of perished Krypton, I have no super-powers! Only the rays of a yellow sun give me powers!"

Stranded without his super-powers in this world of the far, far future, at a time when the Earth is a barren wasteland devoid of water and all that is left of the human race has long since migrated to more hospitable planets, Superman is literally "the last man on Earth," alone except for the weird creatures that have managed to adapt to a life without water. The only remaining vestiges of humanity are a half dozen lifelike androids of Superman's old friends and adversaries that were created by the people of the distant future to "march like real people in each year's Superman Commemoration Parade."

"What a mockery," sighs Superman dejectedly, "--I'm the last man on Earth with only androids of my past comrades for company! And I'll never escape from this dead world!"

Ultimately, however, after a perilous and arduous journey, Superman finally reaches the ruins of his FORTRESS OF SOLITUDE, clambering up the face of the jagged rock cliff and entering the Fortress through the massive keyhole. Inside the Fortress, after reducing himself to lilliputian size with the aid of a sample of red kryptonite that he knows will render him temporarily tiny, Superman climbs aboard a Kandorian (see KANDOR) rocket ship and skillfully pilots it back across the time barrier to the city of Metropolis in the year 1963. Once returned to the yellow-sun environment of twentieth-century Earth, Superman finds his super-powers restored to him, and once the effects of the red kryptonite have worn off, the Man of Steel returns to his normal size. "Will Earth really be like that a million years from now?" wonders Superman. "Or was that only one of many possible futures? I may never know--but I hope I'm never again the last man on Earth!" (Act No. 300: "Superman Under the Red Sun!").

By August 1963 several members of the Superman Revenge Squad have set in motion an intricately convoluted scheme to destroy Superman. To lay the groundwork for their complex scheme, the villains deliberately caused an "accident" in outer space in which Ajax, one of Superman's own Superman robots, was seriously damaged by a hurtling meteor. Taking the mortally injured robot aboard their spacecraft, the villains, feigning friendship, performed a delicate operation that transferred Ajax's super-sophisticated robot mind out of its robot body and into a "chemically-made android body" that is utterly lifelike.

"Our science," explained one of the aliens to Ajax, "enabled us to take only the contents of your mind and transfer them to the brain of this chemically-made android body ... which has super-powers! You talked during your coma and we learned that you were a robot-servant of Superman on Earth! But now that you are a person, you need not be his servant!"

"Why, that's right," exclaimed Ajax happily as he surveyed his unbelievably lifelike synthetic body, a body capable of human thought and human emotion, "...Superman was my master, but now I have no master!"

Overjoyed at the prospect of living out the remainder of his life as a true human being, Ajax could hardly wait to return to Earth to embark on a super-heroic career independent of Superman. The aliens renamed him WONDER-MAN and provided him with a colorful new costume "made of super-durable fabric." Warning him that Superman would be resentful of his new independence, they gave him a chunk of green kryptonite—harmless to Wonder-Man but potentially fatal to Superman—which he could use as a weapon against the Man of Steel in the event he attempted to interfere with Wonder-Man's super-heroic career.

Hovering outside the aliens' spacecraft preparatory to returning to Earth, however, Wonder-Man overheard the villains gloating over their plan. Their real motive in "helping" him, he learned, was to create a rival for Superman in the hope that this rivalry would result in a violent conflict between the two heroes in which Superman would be destroyed. Wonder-Man also learned that the villains had deliberately endowed him with a defective android body, thereby assuring his demise within the space of several days.

And so, having overheard the scheme, Wonder-Man returns to Metropolis, where he performs a series of stunning super-feats that soon have him eclipsing Superman as the city's foremost hero. Indeed, "...in the days that follow, **Superman** becomes half-forgotten and **Metropolis** honors **Wonder-Man** as its new hero!" Wonder-Man even goes so far as to make romantic overtures to LOIS LANE and to dispossess Superman from his Fortress of Solitude. In the inevitable confrontation that follows, Superman falls helpless to the ground, half-paralyzed by the baleful radiations emanating from Wonder-Man's chunk of green kryptonite. "Well, **Superman**, I've won our duel," sneers Wonder-Man, "...and I'm leaving you here with the kryptonite to keep you immobile...until you die from its deadly rays!"

No sooner has Wonder-Man departed than the Superman Revenge Squad members arrive on the scene in their spacecraft and begin to gloat over the fallen Superman. Wonder-Man's rivalry with Superman and the violent confrontation it provoked, however, were only part of Wonder-Man's own plan for luring the villains into the open where they could be easily apprehended. Streaking back to the scene, he hurls the debilitating green kryptonite far into outer space, and, when the villains attempt to flee in their spacecraft, he and Superman seize the craft and hurl it light-years away into the interstellar void. "It'll be years...years of prison in the ship," observes Superman, "...before they can brake the impetus of our mighty throw!"

Superman had already deduced that Wonder-Man was once a Superman robot and that his pretended ruthlessness was only a ploy to trap the villains. Now he proposes to reveal the true story of Wonder-Man's heroism to the world and to form an enduring super-heroic partnership with his former robot. But already Wonder-Man's time has run out, and he collapses, mortally stricken, in Superman's arms. "It has been wonderful to be human, even for a little while," whispers Wonder-Man, "...to have felt, thought and loved! Goodbye...**Superman**, my master...."

"Not your master now, **Wonder-Man**!" replies Superman gently. "You die as you lived, as a human being and as my friend!" (S No. 163/1: "Wonder-Man, the New Hero of Metropolis!").

In November 1963 Saturn Woman (see SATURN GIRL) becomes Superman's ally in an elaborate, and ultimately successful, ruse designed to prevent three members of the Superman Revenge Squad, hovering over Earth in their flying-saucerlike spacecraft, from learning the true effects of the diabolical "counter-energy ray" they recently fired at Superman, i.e., its ability to prevent Superman from exercising any of his super-powers except while he is upside down. The ruse, in which Saturn Woman, posing as the enchantress CIRCE, pretends to force Superman to carry out a series of menial, humiliating tasks—ostensibly in retaliation for his having once spurned her love—by threatening to use her magical powers to turn the Man of Steel into an animal if he fails to comply, is specifically designed to enable Superman to carry out his everyday tasks in an upside-down position until

such time as the effects of the villains' counter-energy ray have worn off and the Superman Revenge Squad members have fled into outer space, convinced that their weapon has had no effect whatever on Superman (S No. 165/1: pts. I-II—"Beauty and the Super-Beast!"; "Circe's Super-Slave"). The story is in many respects similar to Action Comics No. 204 (May '55: "The Man Who Could Make Superman Do Anything!"). (See SPULBY, SAM.)

By June 1964 two members of the Superman Revenge Squad—one of them known as the Android Master—have kidnapped BATMAN, Lois Lane, LORI LEMARIS, JIMMY OLSEN, and Perry White and replaced them with lifelike android impostors as part of an elaborate scheme to torment Superman and destroy his morale by making him believe that his closest friends have inexplicably turned against him, learning the secret of his dual identity, for example, and then demanding blackmail in exchange for their silence. Demoralized, for a time, at having been betrayed by his best friends, Superman eventually comes to realize that his friends are being impersonated by lifelike androids. Before long, SUPERGIRL has rescued his real friends from the cave beneath Metropolis where they have been imprisoned in a state of suspended animation, and the members of the Superman Revenge Squad, their scheme to break Superman's spirit thwarted, flee defeated into outer space (Act No. 313: "The End of Clark Kent's Secret Identity!").

In March 1965 two members of the Superman Revenge Squad, hovering above the Earth in their flying-saucerlike spacecraft, bombard Clark Kent—whom they know to be Superman—with a "cowardice ray" with the intention of transforming Superman into a cringing coward, only to discover, to their dismay, that their ray has malfunctioned, affecting "only the 'Clark Kent identity' part of his brain" and leaving the Superman portion unaffected. The effect of the ray barrage has therefore been to transform Superman into a craven coward, but only when he is dressed in the clothing of his Clark Kent identity. In the words of one of the villains, "He's still brave as **Superman**!"

Although Superman retains his super-powers in both identities and remains invulnerable to harm, the irrational fear and terror he experiences whenever he becomes Clark Kent represent a serious threat to his super-heroic career. Ultimately, however, Supergirl succeeds in curing him of the cowardice ray's effects, and when the villains return to Earth to bombard him with their ray again, Superman seizes their spacecraft and hurls it into "a far-distant galaxy" many light-years away, where the "outlaw vessel" is sure to be spotted and taken into custody by the "space police" (Act No. 322: "The Coward of Steel!").

SUPERMAN ROBOT Z. A SUPERMAN robot belonging to Superman that impersonates its master in March 1961 and uses a special invention to endow LOIS LANE with temporary super-powers identical to Superman's as part of an elaborate scheme to test the veracity of its long-held suspicion that Lois is nothing but a "scheming female" who has "for many years...sought to lure [Superman] into marriage ....not because of human love...but because she was dazzled by [his] super-powers and fame!" Judged by any reasonable standard, the errant robot proves its point, but Superman's reaction is to side with Lois and to promise to repair the robot so that it "follows orders better and doesn't interfere again with my private life!" (Act No. 274: "The Reversed Super-Powers!").

SUPERMAN STOCK COMPANY. A company organized by SUPERMAN in January 1956, ostensibly as a means of rewarding METROPOLIS's "model citizens" by allowing them to share in the proceeds (i.e., reward money and other income) of Superman's crime-fighting activities, but in reality as part of an elaborate scheme, devised in cooperation with agent Barclay of the U.S. Treasury Department, for tricking three prominent retired businessmen—all of them secret partners in a notorious Metropolis crime syndicate—into revealing the whereabouts of a hidden cache of ill-gotten loot. When the ruse finally succeeds, the Superman Stock Company is dissolved, and the three rackets czars—Henry Drebbin, Edward Jorgens, and Paul Quillan—are placed under arrest by T-man Barclay (S No. 102/1: "Superman for Sale").

SUPERMAN, TOMMY. The name given to a twelve-year-old orphan named Tommy after he has been legally adopted by SUPERMAN in March-April 1949. The bond between Superman and his adopted son becomes singularly strong, but when Tommy's safety is severely threatened by Superman's crime-fighting career, Superman reluctantly arranges for him to be newly adopted by a linotype operator at the DAILY PLANET (S No. 57/3: "The Son of Superman!").

SUPERMAN TOY-O-MAT, THE. A unique toy emporium—where skillfully crafted wind-up SUPERMAN toys are dispensed from coin-operated vending machines—which is founded by the TOYMAN in March-April 1950 as part of his elaborate scheme to loot the cashier's cage at the DAILY PLANET and steal a priceless diamond collection from the vault of the Strongbilt Construction Company (S No. 63/2: "The Wind-Up Toys of Peril!").

SUPERMAN TROPHY HALL. See SUPERMAN MUSEUM, THE.

SUPER-MENACE. An unearthly manifestation of "force" in the exact image of SUPERMAN that came into being completely by chance, many years ago, when the rocket ship carrying the infant Superman away from the exploding planet KRYPTON glanced against "the nose-cone of a giant space ship from another universe," accidentally jarring into operation one of its many "weird scientific devices" and, by so doing, bringing about the creation of "a duplicate of the rocket and everything inside it, including the tiny infant," except that the duplicate infant, destined to become known as Super-Menace, was merely "an unearthly force manifested into human form," devoid of either bones, arteries, or blood, but possessing physical features and super-powers identical to Superman's.

Arriving on Earth near the United States town of Brentstock, the infant Super-Menace was found and taken in by onetime "public enemy" "Wolf" Derek and his wife Bonnie, much as the infant Superman was found and adopted by JONATHAN AND MARTHA KENT, except that whereas the Kents raised Superman to be an implacable foe of evil and enemy of injustice, the Dereks raised Super-Menace "to admire crime, and to hate all that is decent in life," in the hope that one day, when he reached manhood, he would use his mighty super-powers to annihilate Superman and help his evil foster father become "the crime king of Earth."

Grown finally to manhood under the baleful influence of the Dereks, Super-Menace—an exact double of Superman except for his narrow black eye-mask—is easily "the world's mightiest criminal," a ruthless "super-outlaw" who represents "the most dangerous menace to law-and-order the world has ever known!"

Sent forth finally by Derek to seek out and annihilate Superman—after Derek has won the agreement of the "crime syndicate" to install him as its president as soon as his foster son has eliminated Superman—Super-Menace happens to overhear his evil foster father referring to him as a "freak" and gloating that he and Bonnie have only "pretended to love" him so that they could manipulate him into becoming their instrument for attaining power in the underworld.

Nevertheless, in the titanic battle with Superman that follows, Super-Menace finally emerges triumphant by trapping Superman amidst a swarm of deadly KRYPTONITE meteors. It is then, however, with Superman completely helpless and his life ebbing away beneath the baleful rays of the kryptonite, that Super-Menace, recalling what he has recently learned about "Wolf" Derek's secret contempt for him, makes a sudden, fateful decision. After first rescuing Superman from the death-dealing kryptonite by driving it far beneath the ground with mighty puffs of super-breath, Super-Menace races to the Dereks' hideout for a final, dramatic confrontation.

"I know everything, Wolf!" he cries. "I know how you twisted my mind into ways of crime...I know you secretly loathed me, while pretending fatherly love...."

"My life could've been a blessing," he continues moments later, "but you, with your rotten cunning, twisted it into...something terrible...."

And then, "suddenly, Super-Menace's form begins to glow and expand, as it turns into pure energy...."

"I'll abandon this 'human' form," cries Super-Menace, "and return to...pure force! And take you two with me!"

Instants later, as Superman arrives on the scene, all he sees is Super-Menace vanishing into nothingness in a blaze of incandescent light, and the

Dereks perishing with him in an unearthly explosion of energy, shrieking vainly for mercy.

"He's vanishing!" thinks Superman aloud. "There's...a pathetic quality about...'it'..." (S No. 137, May '60: chs. I-III—"The Super-Brat from Krypton"; "The Young Super-Bully"; "Superman vs. Super-Menace!").

SUPERMEN EMERGENCY SQUAD, THE. An elite corps of "tiny Supermen" (Act No. 291, Aug '62: "The New Superman!")—Kandorian men clad in red-and-blue costumes identical to SUPERMAN's—who monitor Superman's activities constantly by means of sophisticated "Earth monitor screens" in the bottle city of KANDOR (Act No. 276, May '61: "The War Between Supergirl and the Supermen Emergency Squad!"; and others) and periodically leave their bottle city to come to the aid of Superman in special emergencies. Because, like all Kandorians, they acquire super-powers identical to Superman's immediately upon departing the confines of their bottle city, where atmospheric conditions identical to those of their native planet Krypton prevail, they are a formidable fighting force, described in one text as "an intrepid army of super-powered, lilliputian Men of Steel" (Act No. 276, May '61: "The War Between Supergirl and the Supermen Emergency Squad!") and in another as "the tiny Supermen of Kandor" (S No. 167, Feb '64: "The Team of Luthor and Brainiac!" pts. I-III—"The Deadly Duo!"; "The Downfall of Superman!"; "The Hour of Kandor's Vengeance!").

Members of the Supermen Emergency Squad fly through the Fortress of Solitude's gigantic keyhole into the outside world, 1962

The Supermen Emergency Squad is also referred to as the Super*man* Emergency Squad (Act No. 291, Aug '62: "The New Superman!"; and others) or, simply, as the Emergency Squad (Act No. 303, Aug '63: "The Monster from Krypton!"; S No. 167, Feb '64: "The Team of Luthor and Brainiac!" pts. I-III—"The

Deadly Duo!"; "The Downfall of Superman!"; "The Hour of Kandor's Vengeance!"). The "captain" of the Supermen Emergency Squad is named Don-El (SA No. 5, Sum '62). VAN-ZEE is one of the Squad's members (S No. 148/2, Oct '61: "Mr. Mxyzptlk's Super-Mischief!"). Like all Kandorians (S No. 179/2, Aug '65: "The Menace of Gold Kryptonite!"), the members of the Supermen Emergency Squad are fully aware that Clark Kent is secretly Superman (Act No. 276, May '61: "The War Between Supergirl and the Supermen Emergency Squad!").

In their earliest textual appearances, the members of the Supermen Emergency Squad are described as having been specially selected for Squad membership on the basis of their close physical resemblance to Superman (Act No. 276, May '61: "The War Between Supergirl and the Supermen Emergency Squad!"; S No. 148/2, Oct '61: "Mr. Mxyzptlk's Super-Mischief!"), but this particular concept is soon discarded in favor of a Squad characterized by a more varied appearance (S No. 167, Feb '64: "The Team of Luthor and Brainiac!" pts. I-III—"The Deadly Duo!"; "The Downfall of Superman!"; "The Hour of Kandor's Vengeance!"; and many others). The Supermen Emergency Squad is not to be confused with the Kandorian LOOK-ALIKE SQUAD.

Seated at their monitor screens in the bottle city of Kandor, the Squad's "watchers" maintain a constant vigil over Superman's activities (S No. 167, Feb '64: "The Team of Luthor and Brainiac!" pts. I-III—"The Deadly Duo!"; "The Downfall of Superman!"; "The Hour of Kandor's Vengeance!"; and others). In emergencies, they are empowered to activate the Superman robots in the FORTRESS OF SOLITUDE (Act No. 292, Sep '62: "When Superman Defended His Arch-Enemy!"). Among their ongoing assignments is that of safeguarding the Fortress against intruders (S No. 160/1, Apr '63: pts. I-II—"The Mortal Superman!"; "The Cage of Doom!").

Their primary mission, however, is to fly into action the moment Superman summons them or to rush to his aid when they see him in jeopardy. When the watchers observe that Superman needs the Squad's assistance, they sound the emergency "siren-alert" that summons the Squad members into action. Hastily boarding a Kandorian rocket ship, the Squad members soar to the top of the bottle, to the place where the giant cork seals shut the entrance to the city. Exiting from the rocket ship, they cling to the smooth glass wall of the bottle by means of special suction cups affixed to their hands and feet while the rocket's pilot sprays them with a rare "enlarging gas," developed by a Kandorian scientist, which temporarily enlarges them from their customary microscopic size to "a few inches" in height.

Then, aided by their increased size and strength, the Squad members strain their backs against one side of the giant cork, prying it up just enough to enable them to crawl through the tiny gap into the Fortress of Solitude, where, freed from Kandor's Kryptonian atmosphere, they instantaneously acquire super-powers identical to Superman's and soar into the outside world through the gigantic keyhole in the Fortress of Solitude's massive front door (Act No. 276, May '61: "The War Between Supergirl and the Supermen Emergency Squad!"; and others). By August 1965 a special doorway has been installed in the giant cork to facilitate "easier exit from the... bottle" (S No. 179/2: "The Menace of Gold Kryptonite!").

In the vast majority of the texts in which they appear, the members of the Supermen Emergency wear red-and-blue costumes identical to Superman's (Act No. 276, May '61: "The War Between Supergirl and the Supermen Emergency Squad!"; and many others). On occasion, however, they have worn either costumes similar to Superman's, but lacking capes (S No. 158, Jan '63: "Superman in Kandor" pts. I-III—"Invasion of the Mystery Super-Men!"; "The Dynam-

Summoned into action by the men who man the Earth monitor screens in the bottle city of Kandor...

...the men of the Supermen Emergency Squad climb aboard their rocket ship for the flight to the bottle's rim...

ic Duo of Kandor!"; "The City of Super-People!"), or distinctive purple-and-red Kandorian costumes (S No. 156, Oct '62: "The Last Days of Superman!" pts. I-III—"Superman's Death Sentence!"; "The Super-Comrades of All Time!"; "Superman's Last Day of Life!"; and others).

In May 1961 the Supermen Emergency Squad joins forces with SUPERGIRL to carry out an elaborate, and ultimately successful, ruse designed to persuade JOHN KILEY and his cohorts that Kiley was only experiencing a drug-induced hallucination when he saw Clark Kent change into Superman (Act No. 276: "The War Between Supergirl and the Supermen Emergency Squad!").

In October 1961 the Supermen Emergency Squad helps Superman thwart the mischievous machinations of MR. MXYZPTLK (S No. 148/2: "Mr. Mxyzptlk's Super-Mischief!").

In August 1962, during a period when Superman's vulnerability to KRYPTONITE has been temporarily replaced by a vulnerability to gold, Superman is rescued from a potentially fatal overexposure to gold by members of the Supermen Emergency Squad (Act No. 291: "The New Superman!").

In October 1962, after exposure to red kryptonite has temporarily transformed Superman into two separate individuals, a mature, responsible Clark Kent and an unprincipled, irresponsible Superman, the entire city of Kandor is imprisoned in the PHANTOM ZONE by the arrogant Superman in order to prevent the Supermen Emergency Squad from interfering with his plan to keep the personalities of Clark Kent and Superman separate forever. Ultimately, however, Clark Kent frees Kandor from the Phantom Zone, and soon afterward he succeeds in bringing about the reuniting of Clark Kent and Superman into a single individual (Act No. 293: "The Feud Between Superman and Clark Kent!"). During this same period, when Superman is believed to be dying of an incurable malady, the Supermen Emergency Squad joins forces with KRYPTO THE SUPER-DOG, Supergirl, the LEGION OF SUPER-HEROES, several of Superman's Super-robots, and LORI LEMARIS and the mer-people of ATLANTIS to carry out two of the gigantic super-tasks that Superman hopes to fulfill as his final legacy to humanity, viz., the melting of the Antarctic ice, "to make Antarctica a fit place for millions to live in the future," thus ensuring "a home for Earth's expanding population," and the injection of a colossal sea monster—which has been browing to ever more titanic size due to the stimulation of undersea radioactivity—with a special "shrinking formula" so that it will not one day become so terrifyingly gargantuan that it menaces the safety of Earth (S No. 156, Oct '62: "The Last Days of Superman!" pts. I-III—"Superman's Death Sentence!"; "The Super-Comrades of All Time!"; "Superman's Last Day of Life!").

In December 1962 Superman enlists the aid of the Supermen Emergency Squad in apprehending two members of the SUPERMAN REVENGE SQUAD, but just

...where, clinging to the bottle's slippery glass walls with the aid of special suction cups affixed to their hands and feet, they push upward on the bottle's cork...

...and, after exiting from the bottle, are soon soaring through the Fortress of Solitude's gigantic keyhole into the freedom of the outside world, 1964

as the tiny Supermen are closing in on the villains' spacecraft, the villains blow themselves and their craft to smithereens rather than submit to capture (Act No. 295: "Superman Goes Wild!").

In January 1963, after Superman has been taken captive in Kandor by the "fanatic scientist" THAN OL, the Supermen Emergency Squad joins forces with JIMMY OLSEN and Van-Zee to engineer his successful escape (S No. 158: "Superman in Kandor" pts. I-III—"Invasion of the Mystery Super-Men!"; "The Dynamic Duo of Kandor!"; "The City of Super-People!").

In August 1963, after exposure to red kryptonite has temporarily transformed Superman into a horrifying Kryptonian monster known as a "drang," the Supermen Emergency Squad turns out in force to prevent the drang from entering the Fortress of Solitude, unaware that the monster is actually Superman. Ultimately, however, the effects of the red kryptonite wear off, restoring Superman to his normal human form (Act No. 303: "The Monster from Krypton!").

In February 1964 the Supermen Emergency Squad apprehend LEX LUTHOR and BRAINIAC and bring them to Kandor to stand trial for their crimes. The Kandorians are ultimately compelled to let the villains go free, however, in order to save the life of Superman (S No. 167: "The Team of Luthor and Brainiac!" pts. I-III—"The Deadly Duo!"; "The Downfall of Superman!"; "The Hour of Kandor's Vengeance!"). (*See* LUTHOR, LEX.)

SUPER-MONKEY. *See* BEPPO (THE SUPER-MONKEY).

SUPER-SAVED CLUB, THE. A club made up of people whose lives have been saved by Superman. Its chairman is LOIS LANE, whose "life has been saved [by Superman] more times than anyone!" An effort by unscrupulous tycoon JAMES HARVEY THORBEN to exploit the club members is thwarted by SUPERMAN in July-August 1949 (WF No. 41: "The Discovery of Supermanium!").

SUPER SORORITY, THE. "A club formed by girls in honor of Superman," all of whose members share the common experience of having at one time or another been rescued by SUPERMAN.

Its members include: scientist Dr. Edna Blaine, who was once rescued by Superman from her burning laboratory; animal trainer Julia Johns, rescued by Superman "from the fangs of a tiger"; opera singer Sonya Sophia, rescued by Superman when a stage collapsed beneath her; swimming champ Betty Dunn, rescued by Superman from a shark while swimming; and reporter Lois Lane, Super Sorority chairman, who has been rescued by Superman on innumerable occasions.

Stranded on lonely AMAZON ISLAND, thousands of miles from METROPOLIS, after their cabin cruiser has been blown off course by a violent ocean squall, the entire sorority is rescued by Superman in December 1957 (Act No. 235: "The Super-Prisoner of Amazon Island"). (*See also* ELSHA [QUEEN].)

SUSIE. *See* TOMPKINS, SUSIE.

SWAN, TED. The skiing and ice-skating instructor at the Sky Valley resort hotel, and the secret leader of a gang of smugglers who smuggle furs from Canada into the United States by having skiers carry them across the border at night. Swan is apprehended by SUPERMAN in January-February 1945 (S No. 32/2: "Crime on Skis!").

SWAYNE, NELSON. A scrawny, bespectacled milquetoast who, fed up with his girl friend's hero-worshipping idolization of SUPERMAN, publicly challenges Superman to a contest of super-feats and then, albeit with some occasional super-help from the sympathetic Man of Steel, proceeds to win the contest—and the overdue admiration of his girl friend—by using ingenuity and quick-wittedness to triumph over Superman in almost every event, as when he beats Superman at weight lifting by simply raising his hands above his head and announcing that he is supporting untold tons of empty air (WF No. 27, Mar/Apr '47: "The Man Who Out-Supered Superman!").

SYLVIA. The wife of VAN-ZEE and the mother of their young twins: a son, Lyle, and a daughter, Lili. Sylvia is "an exact double" of LOIS LANE. Born Sylvia DeWitt, a "rich young heiress" from "a bustling Midwestern city," Sylvia first meets Van-Zee—a citizen of KANDOR—during a period when Van-Zee is living in the world outside Kandor after having been accidentally enlarged to full human size by SUPERMAN by means of the ingenious enlarging ray developed by the renegade Kandorian scientist ZAK-KUL. After the couple have courted, married, and settled for a time on the planet VENUS—and Sylvia has given birth to their two children—Superman reduces the entire family to microscopic size with BRAINIAC's shrinking ray so that they can all live happily together in Van-Zee's native Kandor (LL No. 15, Feb '60: "The Super-Family of Steel!" pts. I-III—"Super-Husband and Wife!"; "The Bride Gets Super-Powers!"; "Secret of the Super-Family!").

It is in Kandor that the family now resides. Superman visits briefly with Van-Zee and Sylvia during an adventure in Kandor in January 1963 (S No. 158: "Superman in Kandor" pts. I-III—"Invasion of the Mystery Super-Men!"; "The Dynamic Duo of Kandor!"; "The City of Super-People!").

SYNDICATE OF FIVE, THE. The five gangland lieutenants of METROPOLIS "crime boss" Turk Kane who, having brutally murdered their leader in order to seize control of his underworld empire, attempt to capitalize on SUPERMAN's appearance on a charity telethon—a so-called "super-telethon," in which Superman performs requested super-feats in return for contributions to Worldwide Charities—by submitting a series of super-feat requests designed to help them locate the hiding place of their slain leader's reputed $10,000,000 treasure trove. Superman apprehends the Syndicate of Five in May 1953, and successfully raises his goal of $100,000,000 for Worldwide Charities (Act No. 180: "The Super-Telethon").

T

TAJ MAHAL, THE. A breathtakingly beautiful mausoleum which stands outside Agra, in India, on the south bank of the Jumna River. Begun in 1632 on the orders of the Mogul emperor Shah Jahan in memory of his beloved wife Arjumand Banu Begum (called Mumtaz Mahal, "chosen one of the palace"), who had died in childbirth one year earlier, the Taj Mahal complex took thousands of workmen 22 years to complete and stands as one of the world's greatest architectural masterpieces. By July 1954 LEX LUTHOR and his henchmen have planted explosives in the Taj Mahal—and in many other world-famous monuments—as part of an elaborate scheme to extort millions of dollars from the governments of the world (S No. 90/3: "The Titanic Thefts!").

TALBOT, BERT. A METROPOLIS gangster—until recently a cellmate of LEX LUTHOR at Metropolis Prison—who, having obtained from Luthor a blueprint for the construction of the diabolical Weapon X—a bazookalike weapon capable of accumulating and then unleashing the incredible "super-force" generated by Superman whenever he performs super-feats—with the understanding that Talbot will, upon his release from prison, build Weapon X and use it to break Luthor out of Metropolis Prison, instead double-crosses Luthor by constructing the weapon, tricking Superman into performing the super-feats necessary to charge the weapon's "power battery," and then leaving Luthor to rot in prison while he and his henchmen use Weapon X to commit a series of spectacular crimes. Ultimately, however, with the aid of JIMMY OLSEN, Superman succeeds in draining Weapon X of its awesome power and in apprehending Talbot and his henchmen in April 1961 (S No. 144/1: "The Super-Weapon!").

TALLEY, BILL. A ruthless protection racketeer who murders his own ex-wife to avoid alimony payments and then pins the crime on Sgt. Bob Branigan, "famous two-fisted fighter of the Metropolis police force." Talley and his henchmen are apprehended by Sgt. Branigan and SUPERMAN in March-April 1942 (S No. 15/1).

TALON, THE. The sinister mastermind behind a series of hideous attempts to sabotage and destroy the METROPOLIS subway system, including one attempt, thwarted by SUPERMAN, to electrocute entire trainloads of helpless subway passengers. Captured by Superman in July-August 1942, he is exposed as Albert Caldwell, the president of Metropolis Subway, Inc., a secret "Fascist sympathizer" and "fifth columnist" who, in Superman's words, "tried to sabotage the city's transportation system, so that the conquest of our nation by the Axis would be that much simpler" (S No. 17/1: "Man or Superman?").

TATE, ROGER. The alias employed by HERCULES in August 1960 when he obtains employment as a reporter on the DAILY PLANET during a visit to the twentieth century (Act No. 267: "Hercules in the 20th Century!").

TAYLOR, GEORGE. The editor of the DAILY STAR (S No. 2/2, Fall '39: "Superman Champions Universal Peace!"), the forerunner in the chronicles of the DAILY PLANET. When, beginning in Spring 1940, without any explanation having been given for the changeover, the name *Daily Star* disappears from the texts and the newspaper is referred to as the *Daily Planet* (S No. 4/1-4; *see also* Act No. 23, Apr '40), George Taylor remains its editor (Act No. 25, Jun '40; and others), a post he continues to occupy through November 1940 (Act No. 30). Then, in November-December 1940, a new *Daily Planet* editor appears in the person of PERRY WHITE (S No. 7/1; and others).

George Taylor, 1938

TERRILL, JOHNNY. A poor, crippled youngster, cured of his paralysis but lacking the self-confidence to get up and walk again, who finally surmounts his psychological disability with the help of SUPERMAN in September-October 1947 (S No. 48/2: "Autograph, Please!").

THAN-AR. An official of KANDOR and longtime friend of SUPERMAN, sometimes rendered Than-Kar, who agrees to transform himself temporarily into a "metalloid," or metal man—by means of a special "force-radiating instrument" capable of transforming human flesh into "invulnerable metal"—and to embark on a bogus crime rampage in Kandor as part

463

of an elaborate scheme devised by Superman for undoing the serious loss of morale and self-confidence recently suffered by BATMAN as the result of having been wounded by a ricocheting bullet during a battle with criminals. The plot becomes unexpectedly complicated, however, when Jhan-Ar, the evil brother of Than-Ar, steals the force-radiating instrument, manufactures a series of duplicate instruments with which he transforms himself and two accomplices into metalloids, and then unleashes a genuine metalloid menace in Kandor. The villains are ultimately defeated and apprehended by Batman and ROBIN, however, with the aid of Superman and JIMMY OLSEN, who function throughout most of the adventure in their Kandorian identities of NIGHTWING and FLAMEBIRD (WF No. 143, Aug '64: "The Feud Between Batman and Superman!" pts. I-II—no title; "The Manhunters from Earth!").

THAN OL. A "fanatic scientist" of KANDOR—"the only surviving city of lost Krypton"—who constructs a gigantic "enlarging-ray projector" to accomplish the long-hoped-for enlargement of the city, unaware that his enlarging apparatus contains a "fatal drawback" that will "bring doomsday" to the entire city and its populace by weakening the bonds between the city's atoms and causing it to disintegrate completely after only three hours' time.

Aware of the fatal danger inherent in Than Ol's enlarging process but helpless to prevent the headstrong Kandorians—who have become convinced that Superman's opposition to their plan stems only from petty personal jealousy—from using the flawed ray projector to enlarge their tiny city, Superman barely succeeds—with the aid of JIMMY OLSEN, NOR-KAN, VAN-ZEE, and the SUPERMEN EMERGENCY SQUAD—in reducing the city back to its former lilliputian size with the aid of a "shrinking ray" confiscated from BRAINIAC just as the three-hour time limit elapses and the city's buildings begin to disintegrate and collapse, just as Superman had warned.

"...I vow that I'll never cease trying to find a safe way to make you normal!" announces Superman to the now-remorseful Than Ol and his fellow Kandorians. "....I promise that some day Kandor will become big again, and will stay so forever!" (S No. 158, Jan '63: "Superman in Kandor" pts. I-III—"Invasion of the Mystery Super-Men!"; "The Dynamic Duo of Kandor!"; "The City of Super-People!"). Superman and Jimmy Olsen adopt their alternate Kandorian identities of NIGHTWING and FLAMEBIRD for the very first time during the course of this adventure.

THARKA. A lovely blond super-heroine from the far-distant planet Zor—clad in an orange minidress, green cape, and green gloves, with a white letter "T" on a black background emblazoned on her chest—who journeys to Earth in March-April 1953, as a gesture of interplanetary goodwill, with the intention of apprehending the "Bowtie" Barris gang, a gang of vicious criminals who, with the aid of a hijacked experimen-

tal tank, have been terrorizing METROPOLIS with a series of spectacular crimes. Complications arise for SUPERMAN, however, owing to the fact that although Tharka possesses super-powers on her home planet, she is only an ordinary human in Earth's greater gravity, and Superman feels compelled to aid the visiting heroine surreptitiously so that she will not appear to fail in her mission. Ultimately, he and Tharka apprehend the Barris gang, leaving Tharka free to return to Zor in triumph (S No. 81/3: "The Superwoman from Space").

THARLA. See ARDORA.

THARN. The boy from the planet Kormo who becomes known as SKYBOY (WF No. 92, Jan/Feb '58: "The Boy from Outer Space!").

THIEFMASTERS, THE. See FOUR GALACTIC THIEFMASTERS, THE.

"THING, THE." The name bestowed, for want of a better one, on "a shapeless blob of primeval matter"— a mass of "shapeless protoplasm" capable of assuming any form it pleases and of duplicating, down to the most minute detail, the characteristics of whatever being it has chosen to impersonate—which arrives in the twentieth century in February 1954, after having been banished from its own era—the year 40,000 A.D.—by a populace that had grown afraid of it. Temporarily stranded in the twentieth century, "The Thing" takes on the form of various individuals—including SUPERMAN—as part of its elaborate scheme to steal the advanced technological components necessary for the construction of a "time machine," with which it intends to return to its own era and set up a dictatorship. Superman ultimately destroys the creature, however, by luring it into the midst of a hydrogen-bomb explosion. "Whew! That H-bomb gave me a slight headache!" muses Superman. "But it finished my rival--completely! He couldn't adapt himself to an explosion of such magnitude!" (S No. 87/1: "The Thing from 40,000 A.D.!").

THINKER, THE. The "master strategist of the underworld," a brilliant "gang chieftain whose name has become legendary in underworld circles" for the "cunning generalship" with which he leads his men and the "clockwork precision" that characterizes his crimes. In March 1944 the Thinker and his henchmen stun METROPOLIS with a series of spectacular criminal escapades—including "one of the most carefully planned bank robberies in the archives of criminal history"—but it is SUPERMAN who inflicts the final humiliation by apprehending them all in his Clark Kent identity (Act No. 70: "Superman Takes a Holiday!").

"THINKER, THE." The "big brain of gangdom," and the leader of a gang of criminals who kidnap JIMMY OLSEN in November 1954 and replace him with a hoodlum look-alike named Baby-Face in the hope that the impersonation will enable them to obtain valuable information they can turn to their advantage. While impersonating Olsen, Baby-Face stumbles upon evidence indicating Clark Kent is

SUPERMAN, but Superman apprehends "The Thinker" and his henchmen and, through a ruse, convinces them that their evidence is inauthentic (S No. 93/2: "Jimmy Olsen's Double!").

THON. The tiny, far-distant planet which is the site of the Interplanetary Olympic Games in September 1956. Summoned to Thon to compete against other "super-Olympic contestants," SUPERMAN thwarts a scheme by two evil aliens to win the Olympics—along with the "giant power crystal," a glowing, "limitless source of energy" to be awarded to the victor's home planet—by entering a "powerful, remote-controlled robot" named Bronno, in place of a legitimate contestant (Act No. 220: "The Interplanetary Olympics").

THORBEN, JAMES HARVEY. An unscrupulous industrial tycoon who uses a ruse to gain admission to the ranks of the SUPER-SAVED CLUB in July-August 1949 as part of an elaborate scheme to trick the club's members into using their combined financial resources and scientific and engineering expertise to locate and refine a powerful new element, as yet undiscovered, whose probable existence has been recently reported by an "eminent chemist" and which Thorben suggests the club members name "supermanium" in honor of their hero, SUPERMAN. Somewhere in a remote mountain area, the club members' do indeed succeed in isolating SUPERMANIUM, "the hardest substance in existence," but when Thorben attempts to steal the "super-hard" element—described as "extremely valuable for all sorts of industrial purposes"—in order to turn its discovery to personal profit, he is apprehended by Superman, who promises that supermanium will be used in a multitude of ways to perform difficult tasks designed "to save human drudgery!" (WF No. 41: "The Discovery of Supermanium!").

THORGENSON, NANCY. The beautiful brown-haired daughter of Morgan Thorgenson, a METROPOLIS billionaire who promises to contribute $100,000 to SUPERMAN's favorite charity if Superman can succeed in curing his daughter of her headstrong, profligate ways. "The girl's stubborn, foolhardy," explains Thorgenson, "--spends money like it was water, gets into countless scrapes--I'm afraid she's headed for serious trouble--unless, that is--someone straightens her out."

"I see," replies Superman. "And you'd like to wish that job on me?"

"I've hired detectives by the dozens," continues Thorgenson. "It's done no good. I've pleaded--cajoled --threatened ... but she turns her charms on the men I hire and they begin to act like bashful schoolboys."

Unlike Thorgenson's detectives, however, Superman is immune to Nancy's womanly wiles, and ultimately he persuades her to abandon her decadent lifestyle, so that now she "devotes herself to important social work, aiding unfortunates."

"I've learned that there are more important things in life than night clubs and selfish living," explains Nancy (Act No. 40, Sep '41).

THORON. A far-distant planet, orbiting in the same solar system as that once occupied by the planet KRYPTON, which is described as "a smaller world than mighty Krypton--but still much larger than Earth!" Thoron is the home planet of the alien HALK KAR (S No. 80/1, Jan/Feb '53: "Superman's Big Brother!").

THORONES. The "ruthless, pitiless" inhabitants of a far-distant planet, revolving about a red sun, where Superman is left stranded by the FOUR GALACTIC THIEFMASTERS in February 1965. Bereft of his super-powers under the baleful rays of the red sun—and hurled into prison by the Thorones, all of whom possess super-powers similar to the ones he himself possesses on Earth—SUPERMAN seems helpless to combat the Thorones' impending invasion of Earth until finally, with the aid of a lovely Thorone named LAHLA, he succeeds in fleeing the Thorones' planet, recovering his powers, and permanently thwarting the Thorones' plans to conquer the Earth (Act No. 321: "Superman--Weakest Man in the World!").

THREE MUSKETEERS, THE. A trio of swash-buckling swordsmen—melancholy Athos, gigantic Porthos, and quick-witted Aramis—who, with their comrade D'Artagnan, play central roles in a series of famous historical romances by the French novelist Alexandre Dumas (1802-1870).

In May-June 1956 BATMAN, ROBIN, and SUPERMAN journey through the time barrier to France in the year 1696, during the reign of Louis XIV (1638-1715), where they encounter D'Artagnan and the Three Musketeers and help bring about the downfall of the king's "evil chancellor" BOURDET (WF No. 82: "The Three Super-Musketeers!").

THUMB, TOM AND TINA. A husband-and-wife team of midget actors who are the stars of *The Super-Rescue of Lois Lane, Girl Reporter*, an old-fashioned theatrical melodrama in which Tom, clad in a SUPERMAN costume and calling himself Super-Midget, dramatically rescues Tina, playing the part of LOIS LANE, from the clutches of the evil Goliath the Giant. When Tom temporarily grows to full adult size because of an accident inadvertently caused by Superman—thus preventing Tom from performing opposite his tiny wife in their upcoming performance—Superman summons his infant self from the past to play Super-Midget in Tom's stead, and later apprehends Goliath's unscrupulous press agent, Joe Trent, when he tries to murder Tom in a twisted effort to win fame and fortune for his client (S No. 115/1, Aug '57: "The Midget Superman").

THURA. A far-off planet in a distant solar system, inhabited by a green-skinned race of lilliputian super-scientists, which dispatches a delegation to Earth in January 1956 with instructions to study and ascertain the source of SUPERMAN's super-powers so that their own people will be able to duplicate these powers within themselves and thus more easily carry out the conquest of one of their neighboring planets. On Earth, having studied Superman at close range, the aliens succeed in temporarily endowing themselves

with super-powers identical to his, but Superman
tricks the aliens into believing that their efforts to
acquire super-powers have been unavailing, and the
would-be conquerors—whose super-powers will soon
wane—swiftly disembark for Thura, convinced that
their mission has ended in failure (S No. 102/2: "The
Midget Menace").

THWISTLE, HECTOR. A scatterbrained inventor—creator of such wacky devices as skis on
rollers for skiers who like to roller skate, and an alarm
clock that wakes you up by tickling the soles of your
feet—who helps SUPERMAN apprehend the entire Joe
Jipper gang, operators of the shady Joe Jipper
Promotion Company, after they have misrepresented
themselves as Thwistle's agents in order to be able to
use his inventions to commit spectacular crimes (S
No. 43/1, Nov/Dec '46: "The Inventions of Hector
Thwistle!").

TIGERMAN. An alias employed by SUPERMAN in
August 1961 when he dons a tiger-striped costume
and assumes the role of a hopelessly inept crime-
fighter as part of an elaborate scheme—devised with
the aid of BATMAN and ROBIN—to apprehend
GENERAL GRAMBLY and smash his Purple Legion
(WF No. 119: "The Secret of Tigerman!").

TIGER WOMAN, THE. "The most daring female
bandit in years," a "clever--and ruthless"
villainess—with a holstered gun at her waist, hoop
earrings, and a patch over one eye—who is a perfect
look-alike for LOIS LANE. The Tiger Woman and her
henchmen are apprehended by SUPERMAN following
an unsuccessful payroll robbery at the Crescent Steel
Works in August 1954 (Act No. 195: "Lois Lane--
Wanted!").

TITANO. The new name bestowed upon Toto, a
gentle performing chimpanzee, after a "strange
biological change"—triggered by his simultaneous
exposure to the radiations of two colliding meteors,
one of uranium, the other of KRYPTONITE—has transformed him into a gargantuan "super-ape" (S No.
127/3, Feb '59: "Titano the Super-Ape!"), a "menacing giant" (S No. 147/2, Aug '61: "Krypto Battles
Titano!") that towers over all but the tallest buildings
(S No. 138/1, Jul '60: "Titano the Super-Ape!"), that
can dangle railroad cars from his fingers as though
they were toys, and that is endowed with awesome
"kryptonite vision," i.e., "the strange power of
transmitting kryptonite radiations from his eyes!" (S
No. 127/3, Feb '59: "Titano the Super-Ape!").

In the words of Superman No. 147/2: "Taller than
a building, mightier than a thousand gorillas, is the
greatest, strongest ape on Earth...Titano!" (Aug
'61: "Krypto Battles Titano!").

In February 1959 Toto, a gentle performing
chimpanzee, renowned as "the smartest animal on
Earth" because of his ability to solve simple mathematical problems, is launched into Earth orbit for one
week in an experimental satellite as a combination
publicity stunt and scientific experiment. During his
week-long sojourn in space, however, Toto is bathed
in the radiations of two glowing meteors—one of

Clutching Lois Lane tightly in one of his massive paws,
Titano turns his deadly kryptonite vision on Superman,
1959

uranium, the other of kryptonite—that collide near
his satellite, and when he finally returns to Earth and
is released from the satellite a "strange biological
change" suddenly and instantaneously takes place,
catapulting him to titanic size and endowing him
with gargantuan strength and glowing "kryptonite
vision." It is in the immediate aftermath of this
astounding event that LOIS LANE christens the
mammoth creature Titano.

Although Titano's personality remains that of the
playful, gentle chimpanzee he was before his transformation, his colossal size and titanic strength have
made him a serious threat to human life, and
Superman, hampered in his efforts to capture or
subdue the beast because of its deadly kryptonite
vision, soon decides, albeit reluctantly, that the great
ape will have to be destroyed. Ultimately, however,
with the aid of Lois Lane, whom Titano trusts and
has come to befriend, Superman gets the super-ape to
don a pair of gigantic leaden eyeglasses so that, with
his kryptonite vision temporarily shielded, the Man
of Steel can pick the creature up and literally hurl him
"across the time barrier into the prehistoric past,"
where the gargantuan ape will be able to cavort
harmlessly with dinosaurs and other huge creatures
more nearly his own size (S No. 127/3: "Titano the
Super-Ape!").

In July 1960, while idly experimenting with an
extraterrestrial "time-transporter" at his FORTRESS
OF SOLITUDE, Superman accidentally uses the
strange device to transport Titano across the time

barrier from "the age of dinosaurs" to the twentieth century. For a time Titano runs amok in METROPOLIS, endangering life and property with his titanic strength and keeping Superman at bay with his kryptonite vision. Finally, however, Superman succeeds in knocking the great ape unconscious so that he can fly him safely back across the time barrier to the prehistoric past (S No. 138/1: "Titano the Super-Ape!").

A text dated January 1961 describes a brief encounter between Superman and Titano that takes place when Superman makes a time-journey to the prehistoric past to undertake a scientific measurement of one of Titano's gigantic footprints. Superman has finished measuring the footprint and is about to depart for the twentieth century when suddenly Titano appears on the scene and grazes Superman with the rays of his kryptonite vision.

"As a result of being exposed to Titano's kryptonite radiations," notes the textual narrative, "Superman's flight into the year 1960 is detoured" and he finds himself forced to make a temporary stopover in 1920s Chicago "until the effects of the kryptonite rays wear off!" It is during this stopover in Prohibition-era Chicago that Superman encounters gangster AL CAPONE (S No. 142/2: "Superman Meets Al Capone!"). Although this text is dated January 1961, the text repeatedly refers to the present as being the year 1960.

In August 1961 KRYPTO THE SUPERDOG, furious with Titano for having inadvertently trampled one of his favorite bones during one of his rampages through Metropolis, hurtles across the time barrier into the prehistoric past, determined to wreak a

"prankful vengeance" on the gigantic ape for destroying his beloved bone.

Arriving at last in the age of the dinosaurs, Krypto carries out a series of super-powered pranks calculated to infuriate Titano, only to have the colossal ape retaliate by bathing Krypto in the deadly glow of his kryptonite vision. Nevertheless, Krypto and the super-ape soon become fast friends, and both join forces to thwart the efforts of a band of extraterrestrial aliens to capture them as exhibits for their "spaceship zoo." Unfortunately, the friendship is not long-

... only to have the super-ape "burst the chains like so much string," 1959

lived, because Krypto finds himself forced to anger the gigantic ape deliberately as his only means of getting Titano to activate his kryptonite vision so that it can be employed as part of Krypto's clever ruse for driving the aliens away. "...The big ape!" thinks Krypto fondly as he returns across the time barrier to the twentieth century. "I kind of like him! He's stupid --but lovable!!" (S No. 147/2: "Krypto Battles Titano!").

TITUS, JOHN. The GOTHAM CITY millionaire who is secretly the Condor (WF No. 97, Oct '58: "The Day Superman Betrayed Batman!"). (*See* CONDOR GANG, THE.)

TOMPKINS, SUSIE. LOIS LANE's eight-year-old niece (Act No. 68, Jan '44: "Superman Meets Susie!"), a freckle-faced youngster with an overactive imagination who is forever making mischief by concocting tall tales. Her hair, which is sometimes red (Act No. 59, Apr '43: "Cinderella--a la Superman!"; and others) and sometimes brown (Act No. 68, Jan '44: "Superman Meets Susie!"; S No. 40/1, May/Jun '46: "The Mxyztplk-Susie Alliance!"), is usually worn in pigtails (Act No. 68, Jan '44: "Superman Meets Susie!"; and others), although not always (Act No. 59, Apr '43: "Cinderella--a la Superman!").

Susie, whom Lois Lane once describes as "my sister's little girl," lives somewhere out in "the

Shielding himself from Titano's kryptonite vision with a block of lead, Superman attempts to shackle the colossal ape with giant chains...

Susie Tompkins, 1947

country" and occasionally comes to METROPOLIS to visit her Aunt Lois (Act No. 68, Jan '44: "Superman Meets Susie!"; and others). The name of Susie's mother is never stated in the chronicles, but she is evidently married (Act No. 59, Apr '43: "Cinderella--a la Superman!") to a man named Tompkins (Act No. 98, Jul '46: "Starring Susie!") and is therefore not to be identified with Lois Lane's unmarried sister, LUCY LANE (S No. 147/1, Aug '61: "The Great Mento!"; and others).

The texts describe Susie as "Lois Lane's problem-niece" (Act No. 98, Jul '46: "Starring Susie!"), "Lois Lane's ultra-imaginative niece" (S No. 47/2, Jul/Aug '47: "Susie Reforms!"), "Lois Lane's ever-fibbing niece" (S No. 95/1, Feb '55: "Susie's Enchanted Isle"), and as "the girl who loves to tell whoppers" (S No. 40/1, May/Jun '46: "The Mxyztplk-Susie Alliance!"). Susie has an incurable penchant for "causing trouble by telling wild stories" (S No. 47/2, Jul/Aug '47: "Susie Reforms!"), concocted with the aid of what MR. MXYZPTLK has admiringly referred to as her "marvelous imagination."

"Some people can take a dash of imagination or leave it alone," notes Superman No. 40/1, "—but with Susie, one little touch goes right to her head, and grows and grows and grows!" (May /Jun '46: "The Mxyztplk-Susie Alliance!").

In April 1943, after reluctantly agreeing to baby-sit with Susie as a favor to Lois Lane, CLARK KENT dozes off on a couch while reading the youngster the story of Cinderella. "As Clark Kent drifts into dreamland," notes the text, "his mind is assaulted by a weird phantasmagoria.... And so begins one of the strangest dreams in all history!"

The dream is a retelling of "Cinderella," with SUPERMAN playing the role of the fairy godmother, using his super-powers instead of magic to perform the traditional magic feats.

"I had the funniest dream," remarks Kent to Lois Lane after he has finally been jolted awake. "I dreamt I was back in the days of CINDERELLA...that I was SUPERMAN...and that I aided her instead of the fairy godmother coming to her help...."

"The only thing funny about your dream," replies Lois sarcastically, "was the possibility of your being SUPERMAN!" (Act No. 59: "Cinderella--a la Superman!").

In January 1944 Susie reappears in the chronicles, causing mayhem and making mischief with her penchant for tall tales. Dialogue in this text creates the impression that Clark Kent and Susie have never met prior to this date, but there is no doubt whatever that the Susie of this text (Act No. 68: "Superman Meets Susie!") is identical to the Susie who appeared nine months earlier in Action Comics No. 59 (Apr '43: "Cinderella--a la Superman!").

In May-June 1946 Susie forms an outrageous alliance with the mischievous MR. MXYZPTLK (S No. 40/1: "The Mxyztplk-Susie Alliance!").

In July 1946, after having been ordered to bed without dinner as punishment for telling tall tales, Susie climbs out her bedroom window and runs away from home, determined to get back at her parents by running away to Hollywood to become a movie star. After a tired night of walking alone down a dark, lonely road, however, Susie falls asleep in the back seat of a parked car belonging to two criminals, who, upon hearing her story, decide to make her their dupe in a scheme to steal a priceless ruby from a millionaire living nearby.

By claiming to be Hollywood talent scouts and promising to make Susie a star, the thieves trick the youngster into agreeing to an "acting test" in which she is to gain entree to the millionaire's home by posing as an orphan and then rejoin them at the back door once the household is fast asleep. Susie plays her role to perfection, but no sooner has she opened the back door of the mansion to rejoin her "friends" than the two crooks take her captive, sneak into the mansion through the now-open back door, and pilfer the ruby from the millionaire's wall safe.

Now realizing, albeit belatedly, that her new-found companions are criminals, Susie snatches away the stolen ruby, kicks the crooks in the shins, and races away into the darkness. When, at dawn the next morning, Susie is befriended by the engineer of a passing train and given refuge aboard his locomotive, the criminals attempt to wreck the train in hopes of recovering the ruby, but Superman arrives on the scene in time to avert the train wreck and apprehend the evildoers. Susie, for her part, is soon safely back home again, where she is feted as a heroine for her courageous rôle in recovering the stolen ruby and helping to bring the two thieves to justice (Act No. 98: "Starring Susie!").

In July 1947 Lois Lane and Clark Kent take Susie to the Children's Theater at Thimble's Department Store for a scheduled theatrical rendition of the Mother Goose rhymes, only to have the colorfully costumed actors in the production turn out to be criminals bent on robbing the audience of their money and valuables. With some helpful assistance from Susie, however, Superman apprehends the troupe of stickup men and ties them up in a neat package for delivery to the police (Act No. 110: "Mother Goose Crimes!").

In July-August 1947 Susie finds herself in Dutch with Lois Lane when, after having promised faithfully not to tell any more fibs, she claims to have seen a pair of elephants flying through the air. Susie is vindicated soon afterward, however, when it is discovered that CRAWLEY and his cohorts recently stole the elephants by using winches and steel cable to haul them upward into a giant dirigible hidden out of sight among the clouds. Sometime later, while attending a lavish fashion show with Lois Lane, Susie is on the verge of being crushed to death by the charging elephants when Superman appears on the scene and rescues her from harm (S No. 47/2: "Susie Reforms!").

In February 1955, after idly pressing a button on a newly invented time machine, Susie suddenly finds herself whisked across the time barrier into the ancient past, to a sultan's palace in the fabled era of the *Arabian Nights*, where, in inimitable Susie fashion, she regales the sultan with extravagant fibs about a golden dragon that breathes golden flames, an enchanted river that comes wherever you call it, an exotic plant whose fibers can be woven into a magic carpet, and a fabulous genie that is hers to command.

So impressed is the sultan by these fantastic tales that he confiscates Susie's time machine in order to force her to use her "magic powers" to make them come true, thus forcing Superman, who has hurtled across the time barrier to rescue Susie at the request of a frantic Lois Lane, to assume the role of Susie's magic genie—and to exercise every last ounce of his super-ingenuity—in order to transform Susie's extravagant fantasies into realities so that the sultan will agree to relinquish the time machine and allow Susie to peacefully depart his kingdom (S No. 95/1: "Susie's Enchanted Isle").

TOOMEY, ELIAS. The unscrupulous president of the Readville Bank, who, having received advance notification of SUPERMAN's plan to renovate Readville in an effort to restore the vitality of the dying community and stem the tide of youthful migration to the "already overcrowded cities," buys up options on half the homes in Readville so that he can reap windfall profits when the rejuvenation wrought by Superman sends Readville's land values soaring. The scheme is thwarted by Superman, who uses an elaborate ruse to trick Toomey into tearing up his land options before rebuilding Readville and apprehending Toomey on an embezzlement charge (WF No. 53, Aug/Sep '51: "The City That Was for Sale!").

TOP, THE. The "avaricious owner of a second-hand auto business who deliberately and knowingly sells cars in seriously bad condition--a menace to life and limb!" The text describes him as a "breeder of mass murder," a "ruthless dealer in death who amasses his pernicious profits to the terrible tune of crashing cars, highway homicide, and hit-and-run horror...!" Through terror, treachery, and deceit, he has established himself as the undisputed overlord of a nationwide network of used car dealers who, under his direction, cosmetize the exteriors of demolished automobiles and then pass them along to the public at exorbitant profits, viciously indifferent to the fact that they are little more than deathtraps on wheels waiting to claim new victims.

The Top is in reality Jefferson Smith, a disarming, seemingly kindly man who passes himself off to CLARK KENT and LOIS LANE as a private detective engaged in investigating the city's used car racket.

In May 1942, after witnessing a fatal auto accident involving an inexcusable brake failure on a recently purchased used car, Clark Kent and Lois Lane become determined "to bust this vicious used car racket wide open" by using the power of the press to agitate for effective "city supervision of used car sales." In so doing, they run afoul of the Top and his cohorts, who are bent on using any means, from bribery to murder, to prevent them from publishing a series of damaging exposés in the pages of the DAILY PLANET.

After a final, climactic encounter at a used car lot, SUPERMAN cuts off the escape of the Top's hirelings by demolishing their getaway car with a mighty blow, but the Top makes a frantic dash for freedom by "leaping into one of the used car 'bargains' on the lot" and racing madly away. He has not gotten far, however, when "something goes wrong in the defective mechanism" of the car he has chosen for his getaway, and with "a sudden explosion--the car bursts into flames," dooming the Top to the very fate he has no viciously handed out to others.

"And so dies **the Top**," murmurs Superman grimly, "--a victim of one of his own imperfect cars!"

With the Top dead and his henchmen in custody, the Top's entire syndicate of used car dealerships collapses, and Clark Kent observes proudly that "All the used car dealers freed from **the Top's** evil influence have donated their imperfect cars to the government--the metal salvaged from them to be used for national defense!" (Act No. 48: "The Adventure of the Merchant of Murder").

TOPLIK, MAXY Z. The name which MR. MXYZPTLK legally adopts in his fifth-dimensional homeland before running for mayor of METROPOLIS in March 1955 (S No. 96/2: "Mr. Mxyztplk--Mayor of Metropolis!").

TOPSY-TURVY LAND. *See* ZRFFF, LAND OF.

TORAN. A brutal European aggressor nation which is at war with the peace-loving country of Galonia. Indeed, when "the armed battalions of Toran unexpectedly swoop down upon a lesser nation, Galonia," fears mount that "...once again the world is being flung into a terrible conflagration!" LOIS LANE and CLARK KENT are sent to Europe as war correspondents to cover the conflict for their newspaper, but it is SUPERMAN who thwarts an elaborate scheme to win "the sympathy of the democracies" for the Toranian cause (see LAVERNE, LITA) (Act No. 22, Mar '40). Only later does Superman learn that "a fiend named Luthor deliberately fomented this war for evil purposes" as part of his heinous scheme "to engulf the entire [European] continent in bloody warfare" (see LUTHOR, LEX) (Act No. 23, Apr '40).

TORM. The dictator of Borgonia, a tyrannical despot who, by means of an elaborate ruse, tricks SUPERMAN into using his awesome super-strength to transform a pile of worthless coal into a "glittering cascade" of priceless diamonds, "enough diamonds to make Torm the richest man in the world!" Ultimately, however, Superman turns the tables on the evil dictator, depriving him of his ill-gotten diamonds and toppling him from power by bringing about Borgonia's first truly free, democratic elections (Act No. 233, Oct '57: "The Land of a Million Supermen").

TORR (the Terrible). The power-hungry "space emperor"—so named "because of the many worlds he [has] vanquished and looted"—who is the ruler of Duplor, a far-distant planet, situated in the Duplor Galaxy, which is the home of the Duplorians, a humanoid "race of space conquerors," all of whom "look exactly alike" due to "an accident of evolution," who have "plundered countless planets" with the awesome "weapons of [their] super-science."

By July 1965, however, having gambled away virtually his entire "space empire" by wagering recklessly "with other space rulers, using whole worlds as stakes," Torr the Terrible has concocted an evil scheme of conquest known as Project Earth-Doom, a mad plot to "kidnap the Earth" and a dozen other planets by using the "volcanic forces" of these various worlds to power gigantic atomic engines designed to propel the captive planets out of their respective solar systems into a new galaxy being prepared by Torr's minions in the outer reaches of space, an artificially created galaxy which will enable the power-mad Torr to rule unchallenged over "the greatest space-domain in the universe."

After successfully thwarting the Duplorian scheme to kidnap Earth and other planets, SUPERMAN races to Duplor for a showdown with Torr the Terrible, only to find the villain—his sanity shattered by the strain of defeat—standing alone on a balcony, deprived of his empire and deserted by his followers, pathetically shouting orders to an army of inanimate robots, his only remaining subjects.

"Now **Duplor** is a huge asylum for a single madman!" muses Superman grimly. "Let it be a warning to all other would-be emperors . . . dreams of conquest are only madness!" (S No. 178/1: "Project Earth-Doom!").

TOTO. The gentle performing chimpanzee that is renamed TITANO after a "strange biological change" transforms him into a gargantuan "super-ape" (S No. 127/3, Feb '59: "Titano the Super-Ape!").

TOWER OF LONDON, THE. An ancient fortress

Superman soars skyward with the Tower of London, 1954

which stands on the southeast side of the city of London, on the north bank of the River Thames. Dating from the eleventh century A.D., it remains the most important secular monument in Britain and one of the world's great landmarks. By July 1954 LEX LUTHOR and his henchmen have planted explosives in the Tower of London—and in many other world-famous monuments—as part of an elaborate scheme to extort millions of dollars from the governments of the world (S No. 90/3: "The Titanic Thefts!").

TOYMAN, THE. A bespectacled, bulbous-nosed villain who "invents weird automatic toys . . . to help him execute bizarre crimes" (S No. 60/3, Sep/Oct '49: "Superman Fights the Super-Brain!"). He is "a crafty criminal with the face of a saint and an adding machine for a heart" (S No. 44/1, Jan/Feb '47: "Playthings of Peril!"), a "cunning creator of crime-toys" (S No. 63/2, Mar/Apr '50: "The Wind-Up Toys of Peril!") who is "publicity-mad as well as money-mad" (Act No. 64, Sep '43: "The Terrible Toyman!") and whose "tenderest spot-[is] his vanity" (S No. 63/2, Mar/Apr '50: "The Wind-Up Toys of Peril!"). Action Comics No. 64 describes him as

a wily old man who has devoted his life to the most intricate and amazing toys you've ever seen--and has learned so well to make them do his bidding that he [has become] a national menace! [Sep '43: "The Terrible Toyman!"].

The Toyman is "a kindly-seeming old man with bright, twinkling eyes" (Act No. 64, Sep '43: "The Terrible Toyman!"), a "nimble brain" (S No. 63/2, Mar/Apr '50: "The Wind-Up Toys of Peril!"), and shoulder-length hair which is sometimes blond (Act No. 64, Sep '43: "The Terrible Toyman!"; S No. 32/3, Jan/Feb '45: "Toys of Treachery!") or red (S No. 27/1, Mar/Apr '44: "The Palace of Perilous Play!"), but is most often colored brown (S No. 44/1, Jan/Feb '47: "Playthings of Peril!"; and others).

"In a cellar deep beneath the city streets, the **Toyman** has a secret workshop, tooled with the latest precision machinery...." (Act No. 64, Sep '43: "The Terrible Toyman!"). It is here that this "whimsical villain" (S No. 32/3, Jan/Feb '45: "Toys of Treachery!"), this bizarre "genius who never graduated from kindergarten" (S No. 47/1, Jul/Aug '47: "The Toyman's Castle!"), applies his "crafty genius" to transforming "objects of innocent amusement into fantastic tools of villainy" (S No. 27/1, Mar/Apr '44: "The Palace of Perilous Play!"), "not for the amusement of children, but for the consternation of their fathers!" (Act No. 64, Sep '43: "The Terrible Toyman!").

"As everyone knows," notes Superman No. 63/2, "the incredible **Toyman**'s business is creating treacherous toys for cunning crimes -- grim playthings for plunder!" (Mar/Apr '50: "The Wind-Up Toys of Peril!").

The texts describe the Toyman as a "whimsically sinister rugged individualist of crime" (Act No. 85, Jun '45: "The Puzzle in Jade!"), as a "gleeful gadgeteer," and as a "malevolent master of mechanical menace" (S No. 60/3, Sep/Oct '49: "Superman Fights the Super-Brain!").

The Toyman, 1943

In September 1943 a "queer old maker of toys" prepares to embark on a truly astonishing career in crime. "People have laughed," muses the villain aloud, "thinking me a harmless old eccentric! Little do they suspect that I have become the world's cleverest toymaker for reasons of my own! Riches and power shall be mine because of my ingenius [sic] toys! Then it will be my turn to laugh at the world! Ha-ha-ha-ha-ha-ha!"

In the days that follow, the Toyman and his henchmen commit two spectacular crimes, first robbing a bank by employing an army of ingenious toy soldiers to fire a barrage of sleeping gas into the bank building, then looting an armored truck of its cargo of currency by using a toy armored truck, filled with high explosives, to blast the money-laden vehicle over the side of a bridge. SUPERMAN thwarts the Toyman's third robbery and apprehends his henchmen, but the villain escapes to his secret subterranean workshop and takes LOIS LANE captive when she stumbles upon its location. He is about to annihilate her with his collection of radio-controlled dolls ("The only unpleasant thing about them," notes the Toyman dryly, "is that their fingers are sharpened to needle points and dipped in poison! The effect is swift, once your skin is pierced!"), when Superman arrives on the scene in the nick of time to apprehend the Toyman and rescue Lois from his clutches.

"I'm sure the warden at State Prison will appreciate your peculiar talents, **Toyman!**" remarks Superman as he carries the villain away to prison.

"I'll stay there just long enough to think of a plan to destroy you," retorts the villain, "and then I'll be back! How the world will laugh when **Superman** is defeated by a toy! Ha-ha-ha-ha-ha-ha-ha!" (Act No. 64: "The Terrible Toyman!").

Indeed, "even in prison, the **Toyman**'s uncanny skill wins him applause--and the freedom of the workshop," and in March-April 1944 he executes a dramatic escape by manufacturing a rocket-powered mechanical Superman and riding it to safety over the prison wall.

Sometime later, after disguising his true identity beneath a black wig, moustache, and Vandyke beard, the Toyman announces the opening of his $1 Palace of Play, an amusement parlor for the upper classes whose extravagant versions of traditional penny-arcade games cost $1 apiece to play. In addition to the profits he earns from his games, however, the Toyman also robs and swindles his patrons, such as by stealing their wallets and jewelry when they enter his parlor's photographic booth to have their pictures taken.

When Lois Lane pays a visit to the Toyman's lavish dollar arcade, the villain lures her to his private workshop and imprisons her in an airtight glass cylinder ringed with deathtraps in hopes of luring Superman to his doom, but Superman survives the barrage of "high-tension electric current" and other deadly booby traps, rescues Lois Lane from the cylinder, and takes the Toyman into custody (S No. 27/1: "The Palace of Perilous Play!").

In January-February 1945, after flying out of State Prison in a sophisticated model airplane he had ostensibly been building for the warden's son, the Toyman sets to work on an elaborate scheme designed to enable him to recover a fortune in jewels hidden during the French Revolution by the wealthy Count du Rochette but long since believed lost. To gain entree to the homes of the three wealthy METROPOLIS families who now own the three objects—a vase, a coach door, and a fountain statue—in which the eighteenth-century French nobleman hid his fabulous gems, but who have no inkling whatever of the riches the objects contain, the Toyman, adopting the alias Monsieur Printemps, obtains employment as a toy designer at Metropolis's largest toy store and soon persuades the wealthy families who own the objects he seeks to commission him to design a series of lavish, one-of-a-kind toys for their children. Gaining entree to his victims' homes by delivering these commissioned toys in person, the Toyman uses his intricate creations to help him steal the objects he seeks, as when he uses ingeniously constructed mechanical figures of Goldilocks and the Three Bears to knock the vase containing a portion of the Count du Rochette's treasure out an open window. Superman ultimately apprehends the Toyman, however, and returns him to prison (S No. 32/3: "Toys of Treachery!").

By June 1945 the Toyman has escaped from prison and embarked on a series of spectacular robberies involving the theft of relatively inexpensive jade objects, including a ring, a watch charm, and a pair of cuff links. Superman is puzzled by the Toyman's interest in these objects until he learns that the fragments of jade from which they were made once belonged to a notorious criminal, now deceased, who had inscribed on each fragment a small segment of a map to his vast hoard of stolen loot. The Toyman had learned of the map while an inmate in prison, but by the time he had escaped and set about finding the jade pieces, they had been sold to a jeweler and fashioned into inexpensive items of jewelry. The villain manages to recover several of the jade pieces and to take Lois Lane captive in hopes of forestalling interference from Superman, but the Man of Steel locates the Toyman's hideout, rescues Lois, and takes the villain into custody (Act No. 85: "The Puzzle in Jade!").

By Winter 1945 the Toyman has escaped from prison and set about continuing his villainous "march toward riches and power" by stealing "the finest ultra-modern scientific equipment the world has ever produced," including "valuable experimental equipment" en route by freighter to "the International Radiological Institute."

"Not all [Superman's] powers can stop me," gloats the villain, "when I have stolen the most advanced inventions of this new age and turned them to my own use!"

To facilitate his fiendish crimes, the Toyman employs radio-controlled torpedoes in the form of small-scale replicas of the conveyances he intends to rob, as when he disables a cargo plane by means of a radio-controlled torpedo shaped like an airplane. To make his escapes, the Toyman has devised a small but powerful "atomic-powered rocket ship."

Superman's efforts to apprehend the villain are complicated by the fact that the Toyman has stolen

an ingenious scientific device which "can be tuned to the personal wave-length of any individual—and detect the presence of that individual a mile away!" Once having been "set...to correspond with the electrical vibrations of your body," explains the device's inventor to Superman shortly following its theft, "it will warn him whenever you're within a mile of him—on land, sea or in the air!" Nevertheless, despite this handicap, Superman ultimately overtakes the Toyman's getaway rocket and takes the villain into custody (WF No. 20: "The Toyman: Super-Scientist!").

Seated astride his flying pogo stick, the Toyman makes a spectacular getaway, 1943

In January-February 1947 the Toyman, having already escaped from prison, concocts an intricately convoluted scheme for bilking six of Metropolis's wealthiest businessmen. After building a number of lavish, magnificent toys—such as an exact scale model of the Silver Streak, a new train recently put into operation by the Metropolis Railroad—the Toyman pays a series of calls on his unsuspecting victims and, posing as a shy philanthropist, asks the six businessmen to do him the favor of donating his lavish toys to Metropolis's poor children for him so that he himself can remain anonymous. The businessmen, overjoyed at the prospect of the free publicity the donations will bring them, eagerly agree, even going so far as to grant the Toyman's request that the businessmen allow the toys to be brought back to their respective business establishments in the event they require repairs so that the Toyman can make the repairs anonymously.

In due course, the toys are donated to some of Metropolis's neediest youngsters, and, also in due course, as the Toyman had cunningly planned from the very beginning, the toys break down and are returned to the businesses that donated them so that they may undergo repairs. Unbeknownst to the six businessmen, however, each toy has been specially designed to facilitate the robbery of the business to which it has been returned: the model of the Silver Streak, for example, is filled with explosives to enable the Toyman to blast open the railroad company's safe.

Although, for a time, the Toyman's spectacular crime spree continues unabated, Superman ultimately apprehends the villain and, with the aid of building materials donated by the Toyman's six intended victims, constructs new housing for the people of one of Metropolis's most impoverished slums (S No. 44/1: "Playthings of Peril!").

In July-August 1947, while serving a term in prison, the Toyman talks the warden into letting him organize a prison toy shop, where he soon begins manufacturing elaborate cops-and-robbers games—utilizing complex mechanical dolls—for sale in a Metropolis store featuring prison-made goods. Ostensibly, the games, in which tiny mechanical criminals are apprehended by tiny mechanical police, are designed to demonstrate the futility of crime, but in reality they are elaborate crime blueprints designed to instruct the Toyman's confederates outside the prison in the foolproof commission of spectacular crimes.

When Superman finally captures the villain's cohorts, the Toyman breaks out of prison by blasting a hole in the wall with an explosives-filled mechanical doll. At large once again, the Toyman embarks on an elaborate fortune-telling swindle which involves accumulating the signatures of prominent persons, ostensibly so that the Toyman's electronic swami can tell their fortunes, but in reality so that the villain can duplicate the collected signatures and use them for forgery.

Although the Toyman takes the precaution of kidnapping Lois Lane to prevent interference from Superman, the Man of Steel nevertheless apprehends the villain and frees Lois from her place of captivity, a fantastic castle hideaway filled with ingenious toys and marvelous mechanical devices (S No. 47/1: "The Toyman's Castle!").

In November-December 1947, while en route to State Prison in a prison van, the Toyman is rescued from police custody by Arnold Langs, an unscrupulous jeweler who plans to frame the Toyman for the grisly murders of four men, all of them potential witnesses to the fact that, sometime in the recent past, Langs swindled an insurance company out of thousands of dollars by pocketing a string of his own priceless pearls and then collecting the insurance.

Since Langs and his four intended victims, all of whom had seen the jeweler with the pilfered pearls in his possession after Langs had reported them stolen, were also witnesses against the Toyman at one of his recent trials, Langs plans to murder them all while making it appear that the Toyman killed them in retaliation for their testimony. After faking his own death in a manner calculated to implicate the Toyman, Langs brings about the death of two of his intended victims—one by means of a hand buzzer containing a poisoned needle, the other with a water

Lex Luthor, the Toyman, and the Prankster, 1954

pistol that shoots poison gas—and is prevented from killing the remaining two in similarly ghastly fashion only by the timely intervention of Superman.

For a time it appears to everyone concerned that the Toyman has embarked on a vengeful rampage, but Superman ultimately solves the complex riddle, apprehends Arnold Langs, and recaptures the Toyman and returns him to prison (S No. 49/1: "Toyman and the Gadgets of Greed!").

In September-October 1949 the Toyman and his underworld cohorts commit a pair of spectacular crimes—the looting of a jewelry store followed by the theft of an entire bank building—with the aid of an amazing "super-brain," an incredible machine invented by the Toyman, which, in the villain's words, "'thinks' automatically and answers in moments a problem that might puzzle us for days!"

"Even as the **Toyman** speaks into the [machine's] microphone," notes the text, "the electrical impulses [of his voice] operate machinery" beneath the machine's glass dome "which molds plastic miniatures" of all the people, places, and objects involved in the commission of a projected crime. "Miraculously, the amazing toy creates a model replica of all the factors in the crime drama being planned," acting out the crime-to-be in miniature, in advance, before the very eyes of the criminals, showing them how to execute every detail of the crime to perfection.

Even the remarkable super-brain, however, cannot hope to cope indefinitely with the super-ingenuity of Superman, and when the criminals attempt to carry out their third major robbery, the Man of Steel is on the scene to apprehend the Toyman's entire army of underworld cohorts. The Toyman does not participate in this last crime himself, but Superman apprehends him soon afterward at his secret hideout (S No. 60/3: "Superman Fights the Super-Brain!").

In March-April 1950, after obtaining permission from the warden to build a bronze statue of Superman atop the prison roof as an inspiration to his fellow convicts to mend their evil ways, the Toyman constructs an ingenious Superman statue whose arm is actually a steam-powered catapult and then catapults himself to freedom beyond the prison wall. At large once again, and determined to "stage crimes with toys that will make **Superman** look ridiculous before the whole world," the Toyman launches the Superman Toy-O-Mat, a unique toy emporium where skillfully crafted wind-up Superman toys are dispensed from coin-operated vending machines.

Among the toys on sale at the Superman Toy-O-Mat are a Superman doll that leaps over a model of the Daily Planet Building, and a second Superman doll that crashes through a model of the outer wall of the Strongbilt Construction Company. When, as the villain has anticipated, the business manager of the DAILY PLANET and the president of the Strongbilt Construction Company visit the Superman Toy-O-Mat and buy these toys to display in the offices of their respective companies, the Toyman sees to it that they receive special versions of the toys which have been filled with explosives and otherwise equipped to enable the Toyman to rob the two firms.

At a prearranged time, the Superman doll in the *Daily Planet*'s toy hurls itself through the glass window of the newspaper's cashier's cage, snatches the company payroll, and flies out the window with it to the waiting Toyman. And, that night, the Superman doll in the Strongbilt Construction Company toy blows open the firm's vault with a charge of high explosive, enabling the Toyman to steal the priceless diamond collection stored inside. Nevertheless, not long afterward, Superman trails the Toyman to his secret hideout, rescues Lois Lane from his clutches, and takes the villain into custody (S No. 63/2: "The Wind-Up Toys of Peril!").

In March 1954 the Toyman forms a temporary alliance with LEX LUTHOR and the PRANKSTER in an attempt to commit a series of spectacular crimes (S No. 88/3: "The Terrible Trio!"). (*See* LUTHOR, LEX.)

TRACY (Miss). An alias employed by LOIS LANE in February 1962 when she joins the teaching staff of Public School No. 84 in METROPOLIS in order to gather information for a newspaper article on juvenile delinquency in the classroom (S No. 151/1: "The Three Tough Teen-Agers!").

TRAVERS, HENRY (Professor). The brilliant young scientist who, with SUPERMAN's help, finally discovers a cure for the ghastly "purple plague" unleashed against METROPOLIS by the ULTRA-HUMANITE in December 1939 (Act No. 19).

TREADWELL, TRUMAN. A multimillionaire with a sardonic sense of humor who passes away in October 1943 leaving behind an estate of $3,000,000 and a bizarre will bequeathing it all to the children's hospital which employs his humanitarian nephew, Roger Treadwell, but only on the condition that Roger first fulfill the task of spending $1,000,000 in a single day, giving none of it away and spending no more than $1,000 on any single purchase. Roger Treadwell's ne'er-do-well cousin, Brandon Treadwell, "the

greatest rogue the Treadwells ever produced" and also the man designated to inherit the Treadwell fortune if Roger fails to meet the requirements of the will, hires gangster Tug Moxton and his henchmen to sabotage Roger's spending spree, but SUPERMAN—who has volunteered to help Roger for the good of charity by whisking him from place to place and helping him devise imaginative ways to spend the $1,000,000—thwarts the criminals' efforts and ultimately apprehends them. Now Truman Treadwell's fortune will be used to finance research into new cures for children's diseases, and Brandon Treadwell, left penniless, will be compelled to seek gainful employment (Act No. 65: "The Million-Dollar Marathon!").

TRENT, LARRY. A "stumble-bum" prizefighter bent on suicide—a man who was heavyweight champion of the world until the night his "crooked manager," Tom Croy, working "hand-in-glove with ruthless gangsters," slipped him a Mickey Finn on the night of an important bout—who stages a stunning comeback and recovers both his title and his dignity through the heroic efforts of SUPERMAN (S No. 2/1, Fall '39).

TRENT, TOM. The partner of a man named Quent in a local window-cleaning concern, and the rival of Arnold Carlyle for the hand of lovely Jean Dixon. When Jean agrees to marry Trent if he succeeds in beating Carlyle's world flagpole-sitting record, Trent willingly accepts the challenge, only to have his life threatened by a series of assassination attempts as he sits atop the flagpole. The principal suspect is rival suitor Carlyle, but SUPERMAN discovers that the real villain is Quent—who had been gambling away the profits of his and Trent's business—and takes him into custody (S No. 46/2, May/Jun '47: "High Man on a Flagpole!").

TREVOR, JAMES. The onetime movieland matinee idol who is secretly ADONIS (Act No. 58, Mar '43: "The Face of Adonis!").

TRIPLICATE GIRL. A member of the LEGION OF SUPER-HEROES. A native of the planet Cargg, Triplicate Girl possesses, like all the inhabitants of her native planet, the ability to split into three separate, identical individuals and then merge again at will. Triplicate Girl's real name is Luornu Durgo.

In October 1962, when SUPERMAN is believed to be dying of an incurable malady, Triplicate Girl is among the Legionnaires who are summoned to the twentieth century by SUPERGIRL to help carry out the gigantic super-tasks that Superman hopes to fulfill as his final legacy to humanity, including the destruction of a "vast cloud of fungus in distant space, that will some day reach Earth and blight all plant life," and the melting of the Antarctic ice, "to make Antarctica a fit place for millions to live in the future," thus ensuring "a home for Earth's expanding population...!" (S No. 156: "The Last Days of Superman!" pts. I-III—"Superman's Death Sentence!"; "The Super-Comrades of All Time!"; "Superman's Last Day of Life!"). In recent years, following the death of one of her three bodies at the hands of a villain, Triplicate Girl was renamed Duo Damsel.

TRIX, JOHN. The name which Mr. Mxyzptlk legally adopts in his fifth-dimensional homeland before journeying to Metropolis to pester and bedevil Superman in October 1961 (S No. 148/2: "Mr. Mxyzptlk's Super-Mischief!").

TRIX, TINY. A wily midget criminal—described in the text as a "puny pirate" and "dwarfed desperado"—who stages a series of spectacular if somewhat amusing thefts before he is finally apprehended by Superman in May-June 1949 (S No. 58/1: "Tiny Trix, the Bantam Bandit!").

TRUNDLE, JONATHAN. The executor of the estate of famous movie-villain Peter Lorloff, recently deceased, whose will bequeaths $1,000,000 to whoever performs the most heroic act during the week directly following Lorloff's death. Superman thwarts the efforts of some unscrupulous relatives to murder Lorloff's niece in order to seize the money for themselves, and persuades a judge to award the $1,000,000 to Trundle for risking his life to save the niece in a moment of great personal danger (S No. 55/3, Nov/Dec '48: "Too Many Heroes!").

TWEED (Mr. and Mrs.). The unscrupulous operators of the Brentwood Rehabilitation Home for "wayward youth," a "hypocritical couple whose sole interest is not in their young charges, but in inflating their bank account!" Under the evil stewardship of the Tweeds, the children at Brentwood are poorly fed and frequently beaten, must sleep huddled in groups "crammed together like cattle," and are forced to "labor from dawn to near midnight" making products that the Tweeds ultimately sell out of state. The Tweeds are apprehended by Superman in August 1940 (Act No. 27).

TYCOON OF CRIME, THE. A villain of cunning intellect and cultivated tastes who rules his gangland fiefdom from a lavishly appointed office—automated to fulfill his every need at the merest touch of a button—surrounded by a fabulous collection of the world's greatest artistic masterpieces, all surreptitiously stolen from museums and galleries and replaced by ingenious duplicates created by talented artisans in the Tycoon of Crime's own art-forgery factory. He is in reality Mr. Blob, an obese "tycoon of business" who retired from the Byzantine world of corporations "to enjoy my money in a life of crime." The Tycoon of Crime and his henchmen are put out of business by Superman in July-August 1944 (S No. 29/2: "The Tycoon of Crime!").

U

U-BAN. An evil survivor of the exploded planet KRYPTON who, along with his two villainous brothers, Kizo and MALA, battles SUPERMAN in July-August 1950 (S No. 65/3: "Three Supermen from Krypton!") and again in July 1954 (Act No. 194: "The Outlaws from Krypton!"). (*See* MALA.)

ULONDA. A fabulous "lost city," situated in "an unexplored portion of the Sahara Desert" and reputedly rich in stockpiled radium, which is the scene of a climactic battle between SUPERMAN and the villain ZOLAR (Act No. 30, Nov '40).

ULTRA. *See* ULTRA-HUMANITE, THE.

ULTRA-HUMANITE, THE. A fiendish "mad scientist" (Act No. 17, Oct '39), hopelessly paralyzed from the waist down and confined to a wheelchair, whose "great goal" is the "domination of the Earth" (Act No. 14, Jul '39; and others). Portrayed as nearly bald in two texts (Act No. 13, Jun '39; Act No. 19, Dec '39) and as completely bald in two others (Act No. 14, Jul '39; Act No. 17, Oct '39), he is "a mental giant"—the "head of a vast ring of evil enterprises"—whose "fiery eyes...burn with terrible hatred and sinister intelligence."

His real name is never stated in the chronicles, but he has been known as the Ultra-Humanite—Ultra, for short—ever since "a scientific experiment resulted in [his] possessing the most agile and learned brain on Earth!"

"—Unfortunately for mankind," proclaims the villain in June 1939, "I prefer to use this great intellect for crime. My goal? DOMINATION OF THE WORLD!!" (Act No. 13).

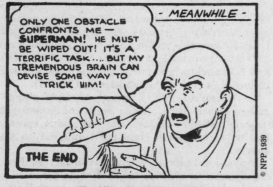

The Ultra-Humanite, 1939

In June 1939 SUPERMAN sets out to smash the so-called Cab Protective League, an underworld organization, headed by a racketeer named Reynolds, which is attempting to seize control of the city's lucrative taxi trade by launching a reign of terror against the independent cab companies, murdering their drivers and demolishing their taxicabs in an effort to coerce the independents into joining the League.

Finally defeated and apprehended by Superman, Reynolds is convicted of his crimes and sentenced to a term in the Sing Sing penitentiary. However, while en route to the prison by automobile, under police guard, Reynolds asks for, and receives, permission to smoke a cigarette, and within moments he has knocked his police escort unconscious by exhaling smoke from a specially prepared cigarette containing "a mysterious gas," hurled the unconscious policemen from the speeding car, and made good his escape.

Superman finally corners Reynolds at his secluded cabin hideout and is about to take him into custody when his attention is called to a second figure in the cabin, a "paralysed cripple" whose "fiery eyes ...burn with terrible hatred and sinister intelligence."

"So we meet at last, eh?" smiles the sinister paralytic. "It was inevitable that we should clash!"

"Who are you?" asks Superman.

"The head of a vast ring of evil enterprises," replies the paralytic, "--men like Reynolds are but my henchmen. You have interfered frequently with my plans, and it is time for you to be removed!"

"If what you say is true," retorts Superman, "then thanks for giving me the opportunity to capture you!"

"You may not find that task as simple as it appears on the surface," remarks the paralytic confidently. "You may possess unbelievable strength--but you are pitting yourself against a mental giant! I am known as 'the Ultra-Humanite.'"

As Superman lunges forward to grab him, the villain unleashes a barrage of electricity sufficient "to kill five-hundred men," and Superman, trapped "amidst a sheet of flame" produced by the high-voltage current coursing through the electrified floor, lapses into unconsciousness. With Superman now helpless, Reynolds and the Ultra-Humanite attempt to annihilate him with a buzz saw, but as "the mighty saw" makes contact with Superman's invulnerable skin, there is "a great rasping--the sound of cracking metal--and the saw explodes into a thousand fragments—!"

"Reynolds dies a horrible death," notes the text, "as one of the steely fragments pierces his throat---!"

Leaving Superman behind to perish in the blazing cabin, the villain's henchmen carry their crippled leader outside to a waiting aircraft, but Superman regains consciousness in the nick of time and leaps upward into the sky "out of reach of the hungry blaze."

"I'll bet that strange ship belongs to 'the Ultra-Humanite'!" cries Superman as he spies the weird aircraft carrying the villain and his henchmen. "--His fiendish deviltry is going to end RIGHT NOW!"

"Deliberately," observes the textual narrative, "Superman crashes into the plane's propellor---down toward the distant Earth hurtle both doomed plane and Man of Steel---'the Ultra-Humanite's' vessel crumples sickeningly as it strikes the ground with a thunderous crash---" but Superman remains unharmed.

"Strange," muses Superman grimly, as he searches painstakingly through the wreckage of the aircraft, "I can't find any trace of 'the Ultra-Humanite'! Well, that finishes his plan to control the Earth--- or does it?" (Act No. 13).

In July 1939, after scores of subway riders have been injured in the collapse of a subway tunnel, Superman discovers that Star, Inc., the firm that built the tunnel, defrauded the city by charging the city for expensive materials and then using substandard materials on the actual project. Before long, Superman has cornered Mr. Lyons, the head of Star, Inc., and forced him to sign a full confession of his crimes, but as he races after the speeding automobile in which Lyons's two henchmen are attempting to escape, one of the henchmen presses a button inside the car and the vehicle instantly becomes invisible.

"Those men wouldn't have the ingenuity to make that car invisible," muses Superman, "—there's something sinister behind this!"

Although the automobile has become invisible, however, it still leaves tire tracks, and Superman's pursuit of the vehicle soon leads him to a boarded-up shed in the countryside where the Ultra-Humanite is lying in wait for him.

As Superman barges headlong into the shed, the villain freezes him inside a block of crystal. "BEHOLD!" gloats the Ultra-Humanite. "My mortal foe imprisoned in crystal.... so that I can look upon him and laugh until eternity!

"When he destroyed my plane, he thought that I, too, had been eliminated! But unknown to SUPERMAN, I escaped with a parachute!

"He alone stood between me and my great goal!... DOMINATION OF THE EARTH! Now I can hasten my plans, unhampered!"

However, the villain has not reckoned on the Man of Steel's amazing recuperative powers. "As SUPERMAN revives, he flexes his great muscles and the crystal block explodes!"

Now realizing that capture is imminent unless he somehow escapes, the Ultra-Humanite presses a hidden button and vanishes mysteriously through the center of the floor. A search beneath the floorboards reveals nothing, and when Superman finally races outside, he finds that "the invisible car's gone! He's made good his escape!" Lyons's two

henchmen, however, are still inside the shed, and Superman swiftly apprehends them and turns them over to the authorities.

"The 'Ultra-Humanite' has got to be stopped before he succeeds in his mad plan to dominate the Earth," muses CLARK KENT afterward. "If not, the world will succumb to evil forces!"

"Only one obstacle confronts me—Superman!" thinks the villain aloud to himself in the safety and seclusion of some hidden laboratory. "He must be wiped out! It's a terrific task.... but my tremendous brain can devise some way to trick him!" (Act No. 14).

In October 1939, after quelling a raging fire aboard the steamship Clarion, Superman learns that the Clarion is the fourth Deering Lines ship to have recently been "deliberately destroyed" and that a mysterious extortionist has been demanding a payment of $5,000,000 in return for bringing the sabotage to a halt.

To compound the mystery, the Deering Lines' general manager has been receiving telephone calls from the extortionist that do not travel over the telephone company's wires, even though he does receive them on his regular office telephone. "Only one person could have accomplished the miraculous scientific feat of telephoning without using the telephone company's lines," thinks Clark Kent to himself, "...'Ultra,' the mad scientist who seeks domination of the Earth."

After trailing the Ultra-Humanite's henchmen to his secret laboratory hideout, Superman finally confronts the villain, who has been attempting to extort money from the Deering Lines in order to acquire the funds he needs "to continue my costly subversive activities."

Superman hurls himself at the Ultra-Humanite, but his hands only "pass thru [sic] 'Ultra's' figure" as "the scientist's body wavers" and then abruptly vanishes into thin air.

"Wh-What?" exclaims Superman, completely bewildered. "--Then it wasn't 'Ultra' who was here, after all--just a projected image of him!" Indeed, the Ultra-Humanite is still at large, but his plot to extort $5,000,000 from the Deering Lines has been thwarted, and his henchmen, apprehended by Superman, will be turned over to the authorities (Act No. 17).

In December 1939 a ghastly "purple plague" sweeps METROPOLIS, leaving death and suffering in its wake. "The new disease, without warning, spreads like wildfire...people drop right and left on the streets...."

Anyone unfortunate enough to contract the dread contagion dies swiftly, "a mass of purple, rotting blotches!" "Daily, the streets are clogged with death--wagons carting away load upon load of putrifying corpses...HORROR GRIPS THE CITY!!"

When Professor Henry Travers, a brilliant young scientist who "has a theory regarding this gruesome plague" and is on the verge of discovering a cure for it, is abducted by the Ultra-Humanite's henchmen and driven away in an automobile, Superman gives chase, only to be compelled to abandon the pursuit when the villains hurl Travers over the side of a cliff, forcing Superman to rescue Travers while his abductors escape.

"SUPERMAN, eh?" exclaims the Ultra-Humanite angrily, after his henchmen have told him of their run-in with Superman. "So he dares to interfere again! No freak of nature will stop me from achieving my goal! The human race shall be blotted out so that I can launch a race of my own---and no one--nothing--shall prevent it!"

And so, a short while later, as Superman departs Professor Travers's laboratory after having supplied the young scientist with the chemicals he needs to continue his experiments in search of a plague cure, the Ultra-Humanite's henchmen stun him into unconsciousness with their leader's cannonlike "electric-gun" and carry his limp body to the Ultra-Humanite's secret laboratory. There, the villain attempts to place the Man of Steel under his hypnotic control in order to force him to help his henchmen continue spreading the deadly plague germs throughout Metropolis.

Although unaffected by the hypnosis, Superman cleverly pretends to be hypnotized, biding his time until the villain's henchmen have flown him high into the air aboard a "fantastic airship of Ultra's creation" to help them ravage Metropolis with the purple plague. Then suddenly Superman leaps at the controls, smashing them to bits with mighty blows of his fist, sending the weird airship plummeting earthward, out of control. "NEXT STOP FOR THIS PLANE--ETERNITY!" cries Superman.

When Superman returns to the Ultra-Humanite's laboratory stronghold, the villain attempts to annihilate him with another blast of his electric-gun, but the gun misfires, exploding in the Ultra-Humanite's face, and the madman collapses lifeless to the laboratory floor. "Dead!" murmurs Superman, as he gazes down at the villain's corpse.

Professor Travers, meanwhile, aided by the materials supplied to him by Superman, has successfully developed a cure for the purple plague, thus ensuring that the dread disease will no longer continue to snuff out human lives (Act No. 19).

In January 1940 the Hollywood filmmaking community is stunned by the announcement that lovely brown-haired movie star Dolores Winters has abruptly decided to retire from the movie business. At the same time, the famed actress also announces her intention to hold a lavish farewell party aboard her yacht, the Sea-Serpent. And so, "that night..laughing and joking, a gay crowd composed of leading movie actors, writers, directors, and producers, loudly climb aboard the Sea-Serpent for a huge send-off party...."

While the party is in full swing, however, Dolores Winters slips away from the merrymakers and instructs her crewmen to lift anchor and head the yacht out toward the open sea. Before the astonished partygoers fully realize what is happening, hoodlums armed with machine guns interrupt the festivities to inform the horrified guests that they are all now prisoners.

"On board my vessel I hold captive some of the wealthiest people alive," proclaims Dolores Winters in a terse ship-to-shore message. "And if their relatives wish to see them again, they'll have to pay plenty!" The actress's price for releasing the kidnapped celebrities is $5,000,000 in cash, to be left inside a buoy at a designated spot.

After the friends and families of the kidnap victims have hastily raised the ransom money and deposited it inside the buoy, Superman hides underwater until a weird submarine arrives on the scene to collect it and then clings to the side of the vessel until it surfaces in an air-filled subsea cavern, where Dolores Winters and her henchmen are holding their victims captive. From his hiding place behind an outcropping of rock, Superman can see that each hostage has been forced to don a strange metal helmet wired to an electrical control panel.

Realizing, to his horror, that Dolores Winters intends to electrocute her captives now that the $5,000,000 ransom has been paid, Superman leaps from his place of concealment and hurls a huge stalagmite at the control board, smashing its wiring and rendering it inoperable. And then suddenly, as he stands face to face with the brown-haired actress, "SUPERMAN has a sudden burst of intuition...."

"Those evil blazing eyes," he exclaims, "...there's only one person on this Earth who could possess them...! ULTRA!"

"You are indeed perceptive, Superman!" replies Dolores Winters. "You thought you had killed me in our last encounter, didn't you? But look--as you can see, I'm very much alive!"

"But--I saw you die myself!" stammers Superman.

"My assistants, finding my body, revived me via adrenalin," explains the villain. "However, it was clear that my recovery could be only temporary. And so, following my instructions, they kidnapped Dolores Winters yesterday, and placed my mighty brain in her young vital body!"

Superman hurls himself at his evil foe, but the villain dives into the watery channel leading into the air-filled cavern and eludes Superman in the murky depths. Returning to the cavern, Superman finds that the kidnap victims have succeeded, on their own, in overpowering the Ultra-Humanite's henchmen and securing their freedom.

"...Is it the end?" wonders Clark Kent afterward. "Did Ultra escape? If so, will he continue his evil career? Only the future will tell!--" (Act No. 20).

In February 1940 Clark Kent is on the scene when a devastating accidental explosion virtually demolishes the laboratory of Terry Curtis, a brilliant young scientist. "For some time," explains Curtis, "I've been on the track of harnessing atomic energy. Today, in the midst of my experimentation, there came that terrific explosion! It looks like I'm upon the point of discovering a weapon that could destroy any matter it was leveled at!"

Not long afterward, "in a distant spot," the Ultra-

His "mighty brain" now transplanted into the "young vital body" of movie actress Dolores Winters, the Ultra-Humanite plots to gain control of a miraculous invention capable of "harnessing atomic energy," 1940

Inhabiting the body of Dolores Winters, the Ultra-Humanite dispatches powerful robots to destroy Superman, but in the ensuing battle, the Man of Steel "tears and smashes them together, wrecking them completely," 1940

Humanite—still inhabiting the body of actress Dolores Winters—peruses Clark Kent's account of the laboratory explosion in the pages of the DAILY STAR. "An atomic-disintegrator---hm-m..." muses the villain. "If I had it in my possession, nothing could stop me...nothing!"

And so, the following evening, the Ultra-Humanite and his henchmen abduct Curtis at gunpoint and force him "into a fantastic autogyro, [which] wings off into the night...." Held captive at the villain's laboratory stronghold, Curtis bravely refuses to carry on his atomic experiments for the Ultra-Humanite's benefit, but after being strapped into a chair and subjected to "several hours [of] 'persuasion'" beneath the villain's diabolical "torture-ray," the pain-wracked young scientist breaks down and agrees to do whatever the villain demands of him.

It is a week later when the Ultra-Humanite breaks in on all regularly scheduled radio programs to broadcast "a strange message to the city of Metropolis...."

"...$2,000,000 is to be delivered to me," intones the villain grimly, "or else I will destroy your city and every living soul in it! As a sample of my power I will destroy the Wentworth Tower at 2:00 p.m. this afternoon!"

Indeed, "at exactly two o'clock a strange airship appears over the Wentworth Tower...As a ray from it engulfs the massive edifice, the tower commences to crumble down toward the horrified spectators below...!"

After keeping the massive structure from toppling into the street long enough for endangered passersby to scramble to safety, Superman soars skyward in pursuit of the Ultra-Humanite's weird airship. Eluding the efforts of the Ultra-Humanite's henchmen inside the airship to annihilate him with the awesome atomic-disintegrator constructed for them under duress by scientist Terry Curtis, Superman silently clings to the aircraft until it "descends within an extinct volcano's crater, and enters a glass-sheathed city...."

Superman's arrival, however, has not gone unnoticed. Watching him enter the volcano crater by means of a special video-screen in his laboratory, the Ultra-Humanite dispatches fearsome metal robots to destroy the Man of Steel, but Superman "tears and smashes them together, wrecking them completely...."

Racing to the villain's secret laboratory, where the Ultra-Humanite is holding Curtis prisoner, Superman finds that the villain has "rigged up a photo-electric beam across the room." "If you break it," warns Curtis, "the city of Metropolis will automatically be destroyed!"

Momentarily stymied, Superman is compelled to accept the Ultra-Humanite's offer to set Curtis free in return for the Man of Steel's promise to steal him a set of priceless crown jewels on display in Metropolis. No sooner has Superman departed the stronghold, however, than the villain broadcasts a message to the Metropolis authorities, warning them of the theft of crown jewels that is about to take place.

"I don't understand," exclaims Curtis. "First you dispatch **SUPERMAN** to get the jewels for you, then you warn their owners that he's coming for them!"

"It will be interesting to observe what occurs," replies the villain slyly, "when the Man of Steel meets their resistance!"

Indeed, by the time Superman arrives at the building housing the crown jewels, a cordon of police and National Guardsmen has arrived on the scene to apprehend him, and Superman only escapes with the gems after a rousing battle against tear gas, small-arms and machine-gun fire, and cannon fire from an armada of military aircraft.

Soon afterward, when "the Man of Steel's figure descends down into the volcano's crater and into the glass-sheathed city" which serves as the Ultra-Humanite's stronghold, the villain attempts to destroy him in a deathtrap that sends powerful diamond drills boring into his body, and a henchman tries to annihilate him with the atomic-disintegrator. But Superman escapes the diamond-drill deathtrap and, seizing the atomic-disintegrator, "disintegrates the photo-electric connections" with which the Ultra-Humanite had threatened to obliterate Metropolis. Seeing that all is now lost, the villain "tears open a glass-sheeted window, and leaps down into the volcano's crater" to his apparent doom in the fiery depths of the volcano.

Seizing Curtis in one arm and leaping to the rim of the volcano, Superman hurls huge boulders down into the crater, reawakening the once-extinct volcano and causing the Ultra-Humanite's glass-sheathed city to be destroyed "in a devastating eruption."

"It all seems to have been a terrible nightmare!" exclaims Curtis once he and Superman have leaped clear of the volcano.

"Well," replies Superman thoughtfully, "leave it go at that. Forget you ever succeeded in disrupting the atom! Farewell!" (Act No. 21).

ULTRA-SUPERMAN, THE. An alias employed by SUPERMAN in September 1959 when he poses as the Superman of the year 100,000 A.D. as part of an elaborate plan to thwart an anticipated assassination attempt on the life of President DWIGHT D. EISENHOWER (Act No. 256: "The Superman of the Future!"). (*See* FOLGAR, DIRK.)

UNIVERSAL INSURANCE COMPANY. The front for a gang of protection racketeers who offer vandalism "insurance" to business firms and then vandalize those refusing to buy it. They are apprehended by SUPERMAN in September-October 1951 on a tip provided by WILL WHITE, the son of PERRY WHITE (S No. 72/2: "The Private Life of Perry White!").

"UNKNOWN X, THE." A mysterious criminal mastermind who commands "the most thorough organization of criminals the city has yet seen!" Under his canny leadership, "crimes are pulled at great rapidity by thugs wearing a distinctive armband" featuring a letter "X" inscribed in a large circle. "The Unknown X"—who is secretly Arthur Jameson, the chairman of the citizens' committee formed to combat the menace posed by "The Unknown X"—is apprehended by SUPERMAN in Summer 1941 (WF No. 2).

URANUS. The seventh planet from the sun. According to World's Finest Comics No. 42, Uranus is a planet populated entirely by robots (Sep/Oct '49: "The Alphabetical Animal Adventure!").

In September-October 1949 a band of robot aliens from the planet Uranus—who are "touring the solar system to secure specimens [of] animal life from each planet for Uranus' new *Interplanetary Zoo*"—orbit the Earth in their saucerlike spacecraft while using an ingenious "transport-ray" to capture various specimens of earthian wildlife and transport them into the hold of their spacecraft. SUPERMAN assists the aliens in their animal roundup but tricks them into agreeing to depart without a specimen of either a man or a woman by duping them into believing that earthlings, like Uranians, are merely robots and hence valueless as exhibits in a Uranian zoo (WF No. 42: "The Alphabetical Animal Adventure!").

In July 1958 Superman journeys to Uranus to obtain the fossil of an extinct six-legged Uranian horse, and later to Ariel, one of Uranus's moons, to obtain an exotic rainbow-hued flower. These are but two of a series of eight so-called "space trophies" which the Man of Steel gathers during this period for inclusion in a time capsule which the Metropolis Museum plans to bury in the ground as a gift for the people of the fiftieth century A.D. (S No. 122/1: "The Secret of the Space Souvenirs").

UUZ. An intensely cold, "undiscovered world far beyond Pluto's distant orbit," where the gravity is "far weaker than that of Earth" and where buildings and automobiles are made out of glass, which is opaque to the eyes of ordinary Uuzians. This far-distant planet, home of the "super-champion" REGOR, is the scene of SUPERMAN's battle with Bantor, "master of crime," in May-June 1949 (S No. 58/3: "The Case of the Second Superman"). (*See* REGOR.)

V

VAIL, VINSON. One of METROPOLIS's "leading scientists" in the thirtieth century A.D., and the secret leader of a gang of "mystery-thieves" who have perpetrated a rash of spectacular "scientific thefts" as a prelude to "the most titanic theft of all time": the theft of "the world's power-supply" in the form of the "great atomic plant" outside Metropolis, which "supplies power, by wireless, to every machine, car and plane on Earth," and without which the world would be helpless and ripe for a tyrannical takeover. Summoned to thirtieth-century Metropolis by the SUPERMAN OF 2956, SUPERMAN exposes Vail as the mastermind behind the mysterious thefts and swiftly apprehends him (Act No. 215, Apr '56: "The Superman of Tomorrow").

VAKOX (Professor). A renegade Kryptonian scientist who was banished into the PHANTOM ZONE prior to the death of KRYPTON as punishment for having contaminated Great Krypton Lake with a vial of his "life force" formula, thereby spawning the creation in the lake of a hideous multiheaded lizardlike monster. "If I ever get out of the Phantom Zone," vows Professor Vakox in January 1962, "I'd create terrible monsters who would destroy whole cities!"

Indeed, Professor Vakox and his fellow prisoners seem on the verge of escaping from the Phantom Zone during this period after "the electrical ions of the Aurora Borealis have opened a small hole in the Phantom Zone which is steadily widening," threatening to release the exiled "super-villains" into the earthly dimension as soon as it becomes "big enough for the Phantom Zone criminals to squeeze through!" Alerted to the threat, however, by their friend MON-EL, SUPERMAN, SUPERGIRL, and KRYPTO THE SUPER-DOG use the combined power of their X-ray vision to burn up the Aurora Borealis, thereby sealing up the opening through which Professor Vakox and his cohorts had hoped to make their escape (Act No. 284: "The Babe of Steel!").

VALDEZ, PEDRO (General). The secret police chief of the "tiny South American republic" of El Salmado, and the secret leader of a gang of "terrorists" bent on assassinating the nation's president and seizing control of the country.

At Christmastime 1963 General Valdez invites CLARK KENT to come to El Salmado to impersonate SUPERMAN and serve as bodyguard to the country's president, ostensibly because he feels that Kent's "amazing resemblance to Superman" will serve to discourage attempts on the president's life by terrorist assassins, but in reality because, by tricking the chief executive into believing that he now has Superman for a bodyguard, Valdez hopes to lull the president into relaxing all his other security measures so that he and his henchmen can kill him and set up a dictatorship.

Eventually, Valdez and his cohorts come to the startling realization that their Superman "impersonator" is actually Superman—and concoct a cunning scheme to lure him into a KRYPTONITE deathtrap—but Superman successfully thwarts the scheme and takes Valdez and his fellow plotters into custody (Act No. 306, Nov '63: "The Great Superman Impersonation!").

VALE (Professor). The elderly scientist who performs the brilliant life-saving operation that transforms John Corben into METALLO (Act No. 252, May '59: "The Menace of Metallo!").

VALE, VICKI. The lovely photographer who, during the course of her glamorous and exciting career, has been linked romantically with both BRUCE WAYNE and BATMAN. From October-November 1948 onward, she labors unceasingly to verify her suspicion that Bruce Wayne and Batman are one and the same man. In the words of Batman

Vicki Vale, 1957

No. 49/2, "Vicki will climb the highest mountain...[and] swim the deepest seas...just to get a picture!" ("The Scoop of the Century!"). She is continually risking her life to obtain sensational photographs for her magazine, and a fellow journalist has observed that "she handles the toughest assignments on the staff!" (BM No. 50/1, Dec/Jan '48-'49: "Lights—Camera—Crime!").

In November-December 1956 Vicki Vale and LOIS LANE become jealous and upset when it appears that both Batman and SUPERMAN have fallen in love with PRINCESS VARINA, the lovely brown-haired ruler of the "faraway kingdom of Balkania." In a meddlesome effort to place Princess Varina out of reach of the men they love, Vicki and Lois offer to help the princess elope with the man she really loves, an "officer of [the royal] guards" named Captain Stefan. Batman and Superman are compelled to thwart the elopement for the same reason that they have been so zealously courting the princess—because her marriage to the commoner Stefan would precipitate a civil war in her country—but they manage ultimately to make Stefan a hero in the eyes of his countrymen so that the Balkanian parliament will grant him permission to marry the princess (WF No. 85: "The Super-Rivals!").

In September 1963 Batman encounters a second Vicki Vale—this one a perfect look-alike for Lois Lane—during a visit to an extradimensional parallel world (WF No. 136: "The Batman Nobody Remembered!"). (For a complete account of the life and career of Vicki Vale, consult *The Encyclopedia of Comic Book Heroes: Volume I—Batman.*)

VALLEYHO DAM. A great dam situated above the town of Valleyho, which "cracking under the strain of a huge down pour [sic]," threatens to inundate the valley below it with a "great, irresistible flood of onrushing water"—"killing thousands and destroying the fertile land"—until the "weird figure" of SUPERMAN arrives on the scene to avert the "terrible disaster" and divert the raging "mountain of water" away from Valleyho (Act No. 5, Oct '38). The story is reprinted in Superman No. 3/2 (Win '40).

VALLIN (Dr.). A "brilliant scientist" turned criminal who concocts an elaborate scheme to annihilate SUPERMAN by "fusing" gold, silver, lead, and bismuth "with acid and crackling electricity" to produce a deadly sample of artificial KRYPTONITE. Vallin and his henchmen are apprehended by Superman in January-February 1952 (WF No. 56: "The Superman Pageant!").

VANCE (Prof.). A "famous scientist" whose hitherto untested "new vitamin serum," voluntarily ingested by Clark Kent, unexpectedly accelerates Kent's life cycle overnight, temporarily transforming him into a bent, gnarled, white-haired old man who looks and feels like a man of seventy and who, even as SUPERMAN, finds his awesome strength "terrifically weakened," his power of flight unsteady and erratic, and his capacity for exertion seriously impaired. Despite these debilitating geriatric handicaps, however, Superman still manages to apprehend an impressive assortment of criminals—including a modern-day pirate named Captain Cutlass, two department-store holdup men, and the Clock, a crook who "uses clocks in all his crimes"—before returning to his normal age and physical condition seventy-two hours later (Act No. 251, Apr '59: "The Oldest Man in Metropolis!").

VAN CROFT (Mr.). An unscrupulous trustee of the Metropolis Museum of Natural Science who, sometime in the past, "in the years before the war," masterminded a diabolical scheme to sabotage the museum's expeditions and murder its explorers in the hope that, by blaming these mishaps on the museum's director, he could persuade the board of trustees to oust the director and install him in his place, thus making it easy for him to enrich himself by embezzling funds from the museum's million-dollar annual budget. Van Croft's henchmen were apprehended by SUPERMAN, however, and Van Croft died when, while fleeing through the museum, he collided with the skeleton of a *Tyrannosaurus rex* and was crushed beneath the weight of the gigantic falling bones (S No. 31/3, Nov/Dec '44: "The Treasure House of History!").

VANDEVIER, JOHN (Mr. and Mrs.). A wealthy METROPOLIS couple who legally adopt CLARK KENT as their son in February 1954 in an effort to replace their real son, Guy Vandevier, a courageous naval pilot and Clark Kent look-alike who has been missing and presumed dead since being caught in a mid-ocean cyclone while flying home from Korea. Kent consents to the adoption in order to avoid damaging the health of the distraught Mrs. Vandevier, then has it legally nullified after SUPERMAN has located Guy Vandevier alive on a remote Pacific island and successfully reunited him with his grateful, happy parents (Act No. 189: "Clark Kent's New Mother and Father!").

VAN PRANK (Mr.). One of several aliases employed by the PRANKSTER in November-December 1949 as part of his scheme to buy up all the radio time on every radio station in METROPOLIS (S No. 61/1: "The Prankster's Radio Program!").

VAN SCHUYLER, STEPHEN, III. The world's richest man and "most eligible bachelor"—a world-famous explorer, renowned sportsman, and daring airplane stunt-flier—who has long loved LOIS LANE from afar and is determined to marry her until SUPERMAN proves to him that his real love is for his attractive secretary, Mary Jones, who, without her eyeglasses and with her hair restyled, is an almost perfect look-alike for Lois Lane (S No. 55/2, Nov/Dec '48: "The Richest Man in the World!").

VAN-ZEE (or Van Zee). A Kandorian scientist who is both a "distant kinsman" and an "exact double" of SUPERMAN (S No. 158, Jan '63: "Superman in Kandor" pts. I-III—"Invasion of the Mystery Super-Men!"; "The Dynamic Duo of Kandor!"; "The City of Super-People!"). Residing in the bottle city of KANDOR with his wife SYLVIA and their young twins—a son, Lyle, and a daughter, Lili (LL No. 15, Feb '60: "The Super-Family of Steel!" pts. I-III—"Super-Husband and Wife!"; "The Bride Gets Super-Powers!"; "Secret of the Super-Family!")—Van-Zee is also a member of the SUPERMEN EMERGENCY SQUAD (S No. 148/2, Oct '61: "Mr. Mxyzptlk's Super-Mischief!"). Van-Zee's father, NIM-ZEE, is "a distinguished member of the Kandorian Council," Kandor's governing body (S No. 151/3, Feb '62: "Superman's Greatest Secret!").

Van-Zee first meets Sylvia, his wife-to-be, during a period when he is living in the world outside Kandor after having been accidentally enlarged to full human size by Superman by means of the ingenious enlarging ray developed by the renegade Kandorian scientist ZAK-KUL. After the couple have courted, married, and settled for a time on the planet VENUS—

AND INSIDE THE MINIATURE BOTTLE-CITY OF *KANDOR*, IN THE FORTRESS, *VAN-ZEE* AND *SYLVIA* JOIN MILLIONS OF OTHER KANDORIANS IN AN IMPRESSIVE TRIBUTE...

WHY ARE THEY LOWERING THE KRYPTONIAN FLAG, MOMMY?

A GREAT MAN HAS DIED-- CHOKE! -- *SUPERMAN* WILL NEVER VISIT US... AGAIN... SOB!

© NPP 1961

In a public square in the bottle city of Kandor, Van-Zee and his wife Sylvia—and their twins, Lyle and Lili—mourn the death of Superman in an "imaginary tale," 1961

and Sylvia has given birth to their two children— Superman reduces the entire family to microscopic size with BRAINIAC's shrinking ray so that they can all live happily together in Van-Zee's native Kandor (LL No. 15, Feb '60: "The Super-Family of Steel!" pts. I-III—"Super-Husband and Wife!"; "The Bride Gets Super-Powers!"; "Secret of the Super-Family!").

In October 1961, when Superman carries out an elaborate ruse with the aid of a lifelike dummy of MR. MXYZPTLK animated by members of the Supermen Emergency Squad, it is Van-Zee who provides the dummy's voice (S No. 148/2: "Mr. Mxyzptlk's Super-Mischief!").

In January 1963 Van-Zee allies himself with Superman in his struggle to prevent the "fanatic scientist" THAN OL from bringing doom to the city of Kandor (S No. 158: "Superman in Kandor" pts. I-III— "Invasion of the Mystery Super-Men!"; "The Dynamic Duo of Kandor!"; "The City of Super-People!").

VARANIA. The name of a coastal cruise-ship on which, while vacationing separately as Bruce Wayne and Clark Kent in May-June 1952, BATMAN and SUPERMAN find themselves forced to share a cabin due to lack of space. In the course of the cruise, the two heroes learn each other's secret identity completely by accident when the light of a fire coming through a porthole suddenly and unexpectedly illuminates their cabin while they are surreptitiously changing into their costumes in the dark (S No. 76/1: "The Mightiest Team in the World!").

VARD. One of a pair of diabolical "futuremen"—his accomplice is named Boka—both inhabitants of Earth in the year 2000 A.D., who journey to the

twentieth century via time machine, temporarily rob SUPERMAN of his super-powers with blasts of red KRYPTONITE, and then carry him captive to the twenty-first century—a time when "the oceans are gone--accidentally dissolved by an atomic experiment," and mankind is threatened with imminent extinction due to the catastrophic scarcity of water. The villains have concocted an elaborate scheme to enrich themselves at the expense of the dying Earth by offering to force Superman to use his titanic super-strength to replenish Earth's bone-dry ocean beds with water from the "snowball" moons of the distant planet SATURN, but only if Earth authorities will first agree to pay them billions of dollars in blackmail. Escaping finally from his evil captors, however, Superman thwarts "this gigantic holdup of Earth" by apprehending the villains, then tows several of Saturn's frozen moons to Earth to enrich the planet's supply of life-giving water before returning to METROPOLIS in the twentieth century (S No. 128/1, Apr '59: chs. 1-2—"Superman versus the Futuremen"; "The Secret of the Futuremen").

VARDEN, THORNE. An unscrupulous calendar publisher who approaches SUPERMAN with an offer to manufacture and market a Superman calendar with all the profits earmarked for charity as part of a scheme to swindle Superman into performing a series of spectacular super-feats to illustrate the calendar and then keep the profits for himself. The scheme is thwarted by Superman (Act No. 212, Jan '56: "The Superman Calendar").

VARINA (Princess). The lovely brown-haired ruler of the "faraway kingdom" of Balkania, who visits the United States in November-December 1956, accompanied by Count Zitu, Balkania's prime minister, and Captain Stefan, an "officer of [the royal] guards" with whom she is deeply in love.

When BATMAN and SUPERMAN learn that Princess Varina is contemplating abdicating her throne in order to marry the commoner Stefan, and that such a move by the princess would inevitably plunge Balkania into a bloody civil war, they set in motion a complex scheme designed to prevent the princess from marrying Stefan—by pretending to be rivals for her affection themselves—while they search desperately for some means of sufficiently elevating Stefan's status in the eyes of Balkania's parliament to make it possible for the princess to marry him without abdicating her throne.

When the Pete Kaney gang attacks the princess's car in a brazen attempt to steal Balkania's royal jewels, Batman and Robin help Stefan apprehend the criminals while carefully contriving to remain unseen so that Stefan will receive all the credit for the capture. As Batman and Superman had hoped, Stefan's courageous efforts on behalf of the princess make him a hero to his native Balkanians, thus persuading the country's parliament to approve his marriage to the princess (WF No. 85: "The Super-Rivals!").

VARREL MOB, THE. A gang of GOTHAM CITY

criminals who are rumored to be setting a deadly trap for BATMAN. In order to distract Batman's attention from the Varrel Mob and keep him safely out of Gotham City while he hunts for the criminals alone, SUPERMAN devises an elaborate ruse to make Batman believe that some unknown person in METROPOLIS has correctly deduced that Clark Kent is Superman, and that Batman must therefore come to Metropolis immediately to help uncover the culprit's identity. Ultimately, however, Batman realizes what his friend Superman has done, and he and ROBIN return to Gotham City in time to help Superman apprehend the Varrel Mob (WF No. 78, Sep/Oct '55: "When Superman's Identity Is Exposed!").

VATHGAR. A ruthless villain on the extradimensional world of Xeron who masterminds a scheme to establish himself as the dictator of Xeron by transforming ordinarily harmless creatures called "skrans" into creatures of awesome destructiveness by feeding them iron ore—a substance which is exceedingly rare on Xeron, but which Vathgar hopes to obtain in quantity from the planet Earth—and then using the skrans to help him establish absolute dominion over Xeron and its people.

In June 1961, with the aid of a special machine designed to facilitate the passage of people or objects through the "space-time barrier," Vathgar transmits a single skran to Earth to ascertain whether Earth contains sufficient iron ore to fulfill the needs of his scheme. Vathgar's dictatorial ambitions are ultimately shattered, however, and his dangerous iron-fed skrans rendered completely harmless, through the heroic efforts of BATMAN, ROBIN, and SUPERMAN (WF No. 118: "The Creature That Was Exchanged for Superman!").

VELLUM, BARNEY. A METROPOLIS bookbinder whose hobby is binding books with odd materials appropriate to their contents, such as a horsehide binding for a book titled *The Jockey* and a binding of skunk skin for Hitler's *Mein Kampf*. When some acquaintances attempt to humiliate Vellum by ordering books bound in unobtainable materials, such as material from ATLANTIS for a book on *The Lost Continent*, SUPERMAN helps him obtain them, and Vellum gratefully returns the favor by binding LOIS LANE's scrapbook of Superman photos, intended as a surprise gift for Superman, in the colorful material of Superman's cape (WF No. 29, Jul/Aug '47: "The Books That Couldn't Be Bound!").

VEL QUENNAR. The highly esteemed Lexorian attorney who is appointed to defend SUPERMAN when the Man of Steel is brought to trial on the planet LEXOR on the charge of having deliberately murdered LEX LUTHOR, Lexor's greatest hero. Vel Quennar does not volunteer to defend Superman, whose cause seems hopeless, but once the court has appointed him to manage Superman's defense, he and his "young partner," Garn Abu, work on Superman's behalf with all the skill and resources at their command. It is Vel Quennar who suggests that they attempt to show the existence of extenuating circumstances by establish-ing that the Man of Steel was suffering from temporary insanity at the time he murdered Luthor (Act No. 318, Nov '64: "The Death of Luthor!"). Although Superman himself demolishes this defense by insisting on the witness stand that Luthor's death was an accident, he is ultimately pronounced not guilty and released from custody when it is discovered that Luthor has not died at all but merely been in a "deathlike trance" induced by a "coma drug" (Act No. 319, Dec '64: "The Condemned Superman!"). (*See* LUTHOR, LEX.)

VENTURA. The "gamblers' planet," a far-distant world whose entire civilization is preoccupied with games of chance and where "everyone is trained from childhood in the art of gambling." On the planet Ventura, "machines driven by a fusion-power center do all [the] work," leaving Venturans plenty of time "to do nothing but gamble!" Instead of being governed from a national capitol, Ventura is ruled from a "national casino!"

Ventura is the home of ROKK AND SORBAN, a pair of ruthlessly amoral interplanetary gamblers who are described as "the last surviving members of [Ventura's] hereditary ruling class!" (WF No. 150, Jun '65: pts. I-II—"The Super-Gamble with Doom!"; "The Duel of the Super-Gamblers!").

"We're the last of a dying race," explains Rokk in August 1964. "With our super-science, we have nothing to do but enjoy ourselves. But now all pastimes bore us! Only gambling is exciting!" (S No. 171/1: "Superman's Sacrifice!"). Sorban echoes this sentiment in June 1965. "With our super-science to support us," he declares, "we've no need to work, so we live for gambling!" (WF No. 150: pts. I-II—"The Super-Gamble with Doom!"; "The Duel of the Super-Gamblers!").

Because Ventura's "ancient race has developed astounding brain power," its members are possessed of awesome "super-mental powers," including the ability to obliterate entire planets, hypnotize entire world populations, and miraculously "alter the atomic structure" of substances with beams of "mental energy" that blaze forth from their eyes. SUPERMAN first matches wits with Rokk and Sorban in August 1964 (S No. 171/1: "Superman's Sacrifice!"). Superman journeys to Ventura in June 1965 in hopes of rescuing BATMAN from Rokk and Sorban's clutches (WF No. 150: pts. I-II—"The Super-Gamble with Doom!"; "The Duel of the Super-Gamblers!").

VENUS. The second planet from the sun. Action Comics No. 152 portrays Venusian civilization as a futuristic version of Earth's, and Venusians as humanoids who have adopted English as their planetary language (Jan '51: "The Sleep That Lasted 1000 Years"). Superman No. 151/1, on the other hand, portrays Venusian life humorously, depicting Venus as a world inhabited by cute "tomato girls," "pumpkin men," "cucumber men," and other comical "plant-beings" (Feb '62: "The Three Tough Teen-Agers!"). Venus is COSMIC KING's native planet (S

No. 147/3, Aug '61: "The Legion of Super-Villains!"), and the place where VAN-ZEE and SYLVIA lived prior to taking up residence in KANDOR (LL No. 15, Feb '60: "The Super-Family of Steel!" pts. I-III—"Super-Husband and Wife!"; "The Bride Gets Super-Powers!"; "Secret of the Super-Family!").

In November-December 1948 SUPERMAN journeys to Venus to obtain an exotic Venusian flower as a gift for LOIS LANE (S No. 55/2: "The Richest Man in the World!").

In January 1951 DR. DORROW attempts to exile Superman and Lois Lane to Venus by shutting them inside transparent cylinders filled with "suspended animation gas" and launching them into outer space, but Superman and Lois are released from their cylinders by friendly Venusians and soon succeed in returning to Earth (Act No. 152: "The Sleep That Lasted 1000 Years").

In February 1962 Superman flies a juvenile delinquent to Venus and threatens to abandon him there as part of his plan for teaching the young troublemaker a richly deserved lesson in good manners and respect for others (S No. 151/1: "The Three Tough Teen-Agers!").

VERGO. A far-distant planet, revolving about a dying sun, which is rescued from imminent extinction by SUPERMAN in May 1957 (S No. 113: chs. 1-3—"The Superman of the Past"; "The Secret of the Towers"; "The Superman of the Present"). (See LATORA [QUEEN].)

VERRIL, CARL. An eccentric millionaire who has recently died, leaving behind a bizarre will stipulating that his son Vincent must successfully squander $1,000,000 within four days' time in order to be entitled to inherit his remaining estate of $10,000,000. Verril's motive was to force his heir to experience one whirlwind spending spree to enable him to get any foolish spending notions he might have out of his system, but events become almost hopelessly complicated when Vincent Verril is hospitalized and therefore unable to embark on the spending spree; BATMAN is officially authorized to spend the $1,000,000 in Verril's stead; Vincent's cousin, who stands to inherit the remaining $10,000,000 if Batman fails, hires thugs to see to it that Batman's spending spree is unsuccessful; and SUPERMAN, unaware of the real motive behind Batman's reckless spending, secretly uses his super-powers to make Batman's deliberate wastefulness turn unwantedly profitable. Ultimately, however, Vincent's unscrupulous cousin is thwarted, Superman helps Batman spend the $1,000,000 by selling him some of his personal souvenirs of his own adventures and then contributing the proceeds to charity, and Vincent emerges from the hospital to inherit his father's $10,000,000 (WF No. 99, Feb '59: "Batman's Super-Spending Spree!").

VINCENT, VINCE. A "whacky character whose hobby is gaining entrance without invitation or paying admission," a likable and basically honest fellow whose clever gate-crashing antics—at wed-

dings, parties, and sporting events—have won him the appellation of the Great Crasher. In May 1947 Vincent is kidnapped by the Mugsy Magoon gang and forced to use his gate-crashing talents to help them commit a series of crimes, but SUPERMAN ultimately apprehends the gang with the aid of a subtle tip-off provided by the captive Vincent (Act No. 108: "The Great Crasher!").

VINDEN, JOHN. A "brilliant criminal scientist," just released from prison after serving a five-year term, who uses his "warped scientific genius" to endow four ordinary criminals with "artificial super-powers" similar to SUPERMAN's as part of his cunning scheme to defeat Superman and "loot the scientific world of Metropolis" in order to avenge himself on the city's scientific community, whom Vinden holds responsible for having sent him to prison. Vinden and his henchmen are apprehended by Superman in December 1952 (Act No. 175: "5 Against Superman!").

VINE, MORNA. The lovely brown-haired young woman who is the DAILY PLANET's "newest cub reporter" as well as the niece of wealthy Mark Vine, the Daily Planet's "biggest stockholder."

By November 1965, after having recovered the severed head of one of SUPERMAN's "super-robots" from the ocean bottom, where it lay in fragments after having been demolished in a battle with "undersea monsters"—and after having persuaded her scientist father to use the still-intact "circuits and energy cells" from the robot's head to create a pair of special earrings and "super-spectacles" designed to duplicate some of Superman's super-powers (X-ray vision, super-hearing, heat vision, and telescopic vision)—Morna has used her uncle's influence to obtain a cub reporter's post on the Daily Planet as part of her scheme to use her electronic super-powers to establish a reputation for herself as a "famous reporter" in hopes of attracting the attention, and ultimately the affection, of her idol, Superman.

Indeed, within a matter of days, Morna Vine has successfully employed her scientifically created super-powers to out-scoop her fellow journalists and acquire "star reporter" status on the Daily Planet, but Superman ultimately discerns the true explanation behind her journalistic successes, gives the now-remorseful Morna a well-deserved scolding for having used her super-powers selfishly, and confiscates her supply of scientific "super-equipment" (S No. 181/1: pts. I-II—"The Super-Scoops of Morna Vine!"; "The Secret of the New Supergirl!").

VINING (Professor). The inventor of an ingenious device which "can be tuned to the personal wavelength of any individual—and detect the presence of that individual a mile away!" Professor Vining's invention is stolen by the TOYMAN in Winter 1945 (WF No. 20: "The Toyman: Super-Scientist!").

VIRUS X. A deadly Kryptonian virus for which no cure has ever been discovered. Superman No. 156 describes it as "a contagion fatal in 30 days to any native of Krypton...." Because living X viruses—if, indeed, any survived the destruction of SUPERMAN's native planet—would acquire super-virulence in the alien environment of Earth in the same manner whereby Superman acquired his super-powers, Superman and all other surviving natives of KRYPTON are vulnerable to this killer virus just as they would have been had Krypton never exploded and they, and the virus, remained on Krypton.

In his experiments with Virus X prior to the death of Krypton, the Kryptonian scientist Tharb-El discovered that he could destroy the virus with "element 202," but because element 202 is fatal to human beings, Tharb-El was unsuccessful in his efforts to produce a viable cure (Oct '62: "The Last Days of Superman!" pts. I-III—"Superman's Death Sentence!"; "The Super-Comrades of All Time!"; "Superman's Last Day of Life!").

VITOR VALL. The head of a family of six—i.e., Vall and his wife, their two young children, and Vall's elderly parents—from the far-distant planet Skar who, having viewed SUPERMAN through a special scanner on their home planet, journey to Earth in March 1956 to ascertain whether Clark Kent, whom they know to be Superman, is also their long-lost cousin, a space pilot from Skar who has been missing in outer space for the past ten years.

On Earth, where Vall and his family are endowed with super-powers similar to Superman's, the Valls quickly establish that Superman is not their long-lost relative after all, but their decision to spend some time visiting with Kent anyway makes Superman apprehensive that their close association with Clark Kent, added to the fact that they possess super-powers, may pose a threat to the security of his secret identity. Rather than ask the friendly, well-meaning aliens to cut short their visit, Superman instead uses his powers to locate the Valls' missing cousin on the distant planet where he has been stranded, so that before long the Valls leave Earth voluntarily for a reunion with their long-lost relative (S No. 104/3: "The Super-Family from Outer Space").

VOHR (Professor). The inventor of a "new electronic generator," due to receive its initial testing at the opening of the World Electronics Convention, whose operation will inevitably result in the production of minute "kryptonite rays" capable of paralyzing SUPERMAN if he is in the immediate vicinity.

Because the convention committee has decided to hold a contest between BATMAN and Superman to determine which of their respective home cities, GOTHAM CITY or METROPOLIS, will receive the honor of hosting the prestigious convention—with the winner of the contest to guard the convention hall while the convention is in session—it becomes essential that Batman win the contest in order to protect Superman from possible exposure to the deadly KRYPTONITE ray-emissions from Professor Vohr's generator.

Ultimately, however, the generator suffers a complete breakdown after only a few moments of operation—thus removing the danger of any inad-

vertent harm to Superman—and the contest is declared a tie, so that half of the convention sessions will be held in Gotham City, with Batman as host guard, and half in Metropolis, under the watchful eye of Superman (WF No. 76, May/Jun '55: "When Gotham City Challenged Metropolis!").

VOL-DON. CLARK KENT's double in the Kandorian LOOK-ALIKE SQUAD (S No. 177/1, May '65: "Superman's Kryptonese Curse!"). When METROPOLIS television station WMET-TV inaugurates its new "Our American Heroes" series with a program honoring SUPERMAN, "our greatest American hero," Vol-Don and his fellow Look-Alike Squad members appear on the show along with Superman's other friends and admirers to help pay tribute to the Man of Steel (Act No. 309, Feb '64: "The Superman Super-Spectacular!").

Vol-Don and Superman

VON HENZEL (Count). A fanatical big-game hunter with a "consuming desire to hunt unusual prey" who is the inventor of a diabolical refrigeration system designed to transform a captured human being into an "imperishable statue," a ghastly trophy imprisoned for all time "in a permanent state of suspended animation." Cornered finally by SUPERMAN on his African jungle estate, Von Henzel dies when he backs fearfully away from the Man of Steel and topples into the innards of his own awesome refrigerator. "He's stiff as a board..." muses Superman grimly. "Destroyed by his own fiendish machine...!" (Act No. 45, Feb '42).

VON KAMP. The "one-time Nazi scientist" and ruthless "crime dictator," clad in a medal-bedecked officer's uniform and with a monocle over one eye, who is the mastermind behind Project X, a mysterious underworld project—carried out on a remote "uncharted island" with the aid of shipwrecked seamen forced into service as slave laborers—whose ultimate goal is the launching of a "criminal eye in the sky," an artificial satellite whose "...TV camera, equipped with a telescopic lens, will observe bank truck routes, police activities, and other information that will be sent from here to the international crime syndicate that finances 'Project X'!" Von Kamp and his henchmen are apprehended by SUPERMAN in January 1959 (Act No. 248: "The Man No Prison Could Hold!").

VON SCHULTZ (Professor). An alias employed by PERRY WHITE in November 1962 when he dons a gray wig and a monocle and poses as an archaeologist who has just unearthed Aladdin's original magic lamp as part of an elaborate and ultimately successful ruse—devised by SUPERMAN with the cooperation of the F.B.I.—to entice a notorious "international spy," never named in the chronicles, into attempting to steal the lamp so that Superman can apprehend him (S No. 157/2: "The Super-Genie of Metropolis!").

VON STORFF (Admiral). A ruthless Nazi naval officer who imprisons LOIS LANE and the crew of Captain Zeb Storme's fishing schooner with the intention of using them as slave laborers for the Third Reich, only to be defeated and apprehended by SUPERMAN in 1943. The story of Superman's battle with Admiral Von Storff unfolds in the form of a narrative told by Captain Storme's great-great-grandson to his own young grandchildren in the year 2143 A.D. (Act No. 62, Jul '43: "There'll Always Be a Superman!").

VOR. A far-distant planet whose evil rulers imprison SUPERMAN and four other super-heroes from other planets in a so-called "prison for heroes" on a barren planet—and subject BATMAN to "super-hypnotism" in order to transform him into the prison's ruthless, merciless warden—as the prelude to launching a campaign of interplanetary conquest against the captive heroes' home worlds. The scheme is ultimately thwarted by Superman and the other imprisoned heroes, who turn the tables on the hypnotized Batman, undo the effects of the super-hypnotism that have made him the Vorians' ally, and, with his help, apprehend the evil aliens and destroy the stockpile of armaments with which they had hoped to subjugate other planets (WF No. 145, Nov '64: "Prison for Heroes!" pts. I-II—no title; "The Revenge of Superman!").

VORDEN, VIC. A "Metropolis gang chief" who was arrested and sent to prison some years ago, but not before he had stolen "the only copy of a dead chemist's invaluable explosives formula," hidden it inside one of the bullets in his pistol, and then fired that bullet into the chest of METROPOLIS police officer John Kay while attempting unsuccessfully to resist arrest. In April 1954, after the bullet in Kay's chest has been removed by country doctor Henry Harris, Vorden—now at large after breaking jail—makes a series of attempts to abduct Dr. Harris and recover the extracted bullet, only to be finally apprehended, along with his henchmen, through the heroic efforts of SUPERMAN (Act No. 191: "Calling Doctor Superman!").

VORMAN, "DUDE." The leader of a gang of criminals, in league with corrupt city councilman Hugo Sleary, who use a remote-controlled guided missile in the image of SUPERMAN—the so-called "Superman-missile"—to frame Superman for a series of irresponsible acts as part of a cunning scheme to persuade the city council to banish Superman from METROPOLIS so that Vorman and his henchmen can loot the city. Exiled beyond the city limits and forbidden to reenter, Superman succeeds nevertheless in apprehending the Vorman gang, clearing himself of the charges against him, and obtaining a confession from Vorman that incriminates Councilman Sleary (WF No. 55, Dec/Jan '51-'52: "The City That Exiled Superman!").

VORN. A far-distant planetoid—in reality a "giant space ship" operated by a trio of "interplanetary criminals"—to which SUPERMAN is summoned in September 1963, ostensibly so that he can compete in the "interplanetary super-Olympic games" there, but in reality as part of an elaborate scheme by the three villains who operate the "planetoid" to trick Superman into performing a series of mighty super-deeds so that, by using "a cunning electronic device to absorb [his] super-energy" each time he competes in an event, they can accumulate sufficient super-energy inside their spacecraft's "special battery" to enable them "to crash the time-barrier into the future" and thereby "evade the Intergalactic Police" seeking to apprehend them. Realizing early on, however, that the real purpose of the bogus Olympics is to "drain [his] super-energy by trickery," Superman deliberately performs poorly in every event, thus thwarting the villains' efforts to drain away his super-power and making it possible for the Intergalactic Police to overtake and apprehend them (Act No. 304: "The Interplanetary Olympics!"). The story is in many respects similar to Action Comics No. 220 (Sep '56: "The Interplanetary Olympics"). (See THON.)

VORRELL, JAY. An underworld "sharpie," notorious for "masterminding robberies" for METROPOLIS gangsters in return for a share of their loot, who is apprehended along with his gangland allies by SUPERMAN in October 1956. Superman's efforts to apprehend Vorrell and his cohorts are at times hampered, and at times aided, by the fact that a head-on collision in outer space with "a small comet with [an] unusually powerful magnetic charge" has temporarily transformed the Man of Steel into a "colossal magnet" capable of attracting any metal in the vicinity merely by extending his hands (Act No. 221: "Superman's New Super-Power").

VUL-KOR. A ruthless water-breathing alien from a far-distant "water world"—humanoid in appearance except for his light-green hair and the large, sharklike fin protruding from his back—who, accompanied by his beautiful daughter Lya-La, arrives on Earth in September 1958 and, on an area of the ocean floor somewhere "near the Sargasso Sea," begins construction of a gigantic, diabolical "infra coil" designed to exterminate humanity so that Vul-Kor and his kind can invade and colonize the Earth. In Vul-Kor's words:

> The...coil will hurl a super heat-ray at Earth's poles! As the ice-caps melt, flood waters will deluge the continents, drowning the Earth forever! Human civilization will sink without a trace! Then my sea-breathing people can colonize this new water world!

By means of an elaborate ruse, however, SUPER-MAN sabotages the construction of the infra coil and sends Vul-Kor and Lya-La racing homeward, convinced that Earth is not habitable for beings of their species (Act No. 244: "The Super-Merman of the Sea").

VUMANIA. A barren desert island which is all that remains in modern times of a once-proud ancient kingdom. JIMMY OLSEN, the sole surviving "remote descendant" of Vumania's royal line, is Vumania's king (Act No. 231, Aug '57: "Sir Jimmy Olsen, Knight of Metropolis").

W

WAFFLE, WILMINGTON. A "famed Hollywood comic" who, clad in a SUPERMAN costume, performs a series of hilarious Superman spoofs—such as extinguishing a theater-prop bomb by dousing it with a seltzer bottle—to plug his forthcoming motion picture, unaware that warlike aliens hovering above the Earth have mistaken him for the real Superman and are intent on invading Earth unless, during the brief period they have set aside for observation, they see "Superman" display the kind of awesome power that would be necessary to thwart their invasion. Superman, who is aware of the aliens' presence, uses a ruse to persuade Waffle to abandon his comedic Superman impersonation, and then performs a feat of super-strength sufficient to cow the aliens into leaving Earth forever (S No. 93/1, Nov '54: "The Super-Joke on Superman!").

WALKER, EBENEEZER. An eccentric millionaire who, having learned of a plan by interplanetary invaders to conquer Earth by using special rays to transform various buildings and other structures into gigantic atomic bombs, moves decisively to thwart the invasion by quietly buying the affected structures and getting SUPERMAN to demolish them by offering to contribute $1,000,000 to charity in return for their destruction. Fearful that his well-known penchant for eccentricity would cause him to be branded a crackpot if he were to reveal the truth behind his bizarre demolition scheme, Walker provides Superman with no explanation whatever, but Superman soon learns of the now-thwarted alien invasion and conveys to Walker the gratitude of a grateful Earth (Act No. 214, Mar '56: "Superman, Super-Destroyer").

WALTERS, BROCK. The owner of the Walters Mine, and the secret leader of a gang of criminals who have been hijacking shipments of gold en route from the mines to the bank. SUPERMAN captures the gang in April 1941, in the process rescuing LOIS LANE from their clutches on five separate occasions (Act No. 35).

WALTERS, CYRUS. The owner of a fabulous gem collection which SUPERMAN has agreed to transport and protect when it is put on display at a charity exhibition. In an effort to prevent Superman from being entrusted with the gems, a development which would make the gems virtually impossible to steal, a gang of jewel thieves sets in motion an elaborate scheme designed to make Superman appear to be an irresponsible super-bungler unfit for duties of any kind involving the use of his super-powers. Superman ultimately sees through the scheme, however, and apprehends the criminals in February 1954 (S No. 87/2: "Superman's Super-Boners!").

WASHINGTON, GEORGE (1732-1799). The first President of the United States. SUPERMAN meets General George Washington—and facilitates his famous crossing of the Delaware River by breaking up the ice on the river—during a time-journey to the year 1776 (S No. 48/2, Sep/Oct '47: "Autograph, Please!"). Superman meets George Washington a second time, during a time-journey to the year 1779, while searching for an explanation behind a series of murder attempts on the lives of members of the Kent family (see KENT, ELY) (Act No. 132, May '49: "The Secret of the Kents!").

WASHINGTON MONUMENT, THE. A magnificent modern obelisk in Washington, D.C., which stands over 555 feet high and features an observatory at the 500-foot level which is reached by interior elevator and stairs. Completed in 1884, it is one of the

Soaring over Washington, D.C., in their "weird space-ship," the Four Galactic Thiefmasters uproot the Washington Monument from its foundations by means of a powerful "lifting-beam," 1965

world's great monuments.

In January 1943 EMIL LORING attempts to destroy the Washington Monument and other world-famous landmarks, but his mad scheme is thwarted by SUPERMAN (Act No. 56: "Design for Doom!").

In July 1954 the Washington Monument is

stolen—along with other world-famous monuments—by the Kryptonian villain MALA as part of his elaborate scheme to wreak vengeance on Superman by destroying the planet Earth (Act No. 194: "The Outlaws from Krypton!").

In February 1965 the FOUR GALACTIC THIEFMASTERS soar over Washington, D.C., in their "weird space-ship" and uproot the Washington Monument from its foundations by means of a powerful "lifting-beam." Superman recovers the stolen monument and pursues the Four Galactic Thiefmasters into outer space, unaware that the theft of the monument and the thieves' apparent flight to avoid capture are all part of the villains' heinous scheme to lure him into a diabolical "red-sun trap" (Act No. 321: "Superman--Weakest Man in the World!"). (*See also* THORONES.)

WATER SPRITE, THE. A hideous green monster—part man, part fish—that makes its appearance in March 1945, creating a potentially disastrous break in the Annisdale levee and later attempting, albeit unsuccessfully, to demolish the Annisdale dam as part of its self-proclaimed mission to wreak retribution on those who would "choke off the free flow of nature's water." In reality, however, the Water Sprite is Kenneth Darby, the most vociferous advocate of the need for a new dam and the supplier of the building materials for its construction, whose pose as the Water Sprite is part of an elaborate scheme to convince the citizens of Annisdale of the urgent need for a new dam, to reap windfall profits by providing substandard materials for its construction, and finally to destroy the dam prior to its completion in order to prevent the townspeople from discovering that the use of inferior materials would have caused the dam to crumble anyway soon after it was finished. The Water Sprite is ultimately exposed and apprehended through the heroic efforts of SUPERMAN (Act No. 82: "The Water Sprite!").

WATKINS. "A hawk-faced man of utterly ruthless features," an evil "master hypnotist" who, having hypnotized a group of innocent men into complete obedience to his will, has strapped powerful explosive devices to their waists and transformed them into "human bombs," men oblivious to death who stage one brazen robbery after another and willingly blow themselves to smithereens rather than submit to capture. "I am one of 'the human bombs,'" explains one of them to a stunned CLARK KENT and PERRY WHITE. "It is our intention to rob wherever we please. We have no fear of death. Should anyone ever attempt to stop us, we will commit suicide. . . . and innocent bystanders will also die in the resulting explosion." The weird rampage continues unabated until SUPERMAN finally apprehends Watkins and, by knocking him unconscious, releases the human bombs from his baleful hypnotic influence (S No. 17/2, Jul/Aug '42: "The Human Bomb").

WAYNE, BRUCE. The millionaire socialite who is secretly BATMAN.

WEIRTON (Professor). The inventor of a strange "cabinet-like machine" which, by means of "specially

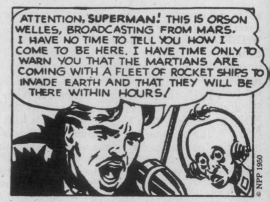

Orson Welles broadcasts a message to Superman from the planet Mars, 1950

filtered uranium rays . . . can give any person super-powers for a period of 24 hours, by speeding the evolutionary process and putting him 1,000,000 years ahead of his time!" It is Professor Weirton's invention which, in December 1951, temporarily endows SUSAN SEMPLE with "powers that the human race won't acquire for hundreds of eons!" (Act No. 163: "The Girl of Tomorrow").

WELLES, ORSON. The famous actor and director who helps SUPERMAN defeat the Martian dictator MARTLER in January-February 1950 (S No. 62/1: "Black Magic on Mars!").

WELLINS, BART. An unscrupulous seaman who, having temporarily acquired super-powers identical to SUPERMAN's as the result of having passed over a spot in the ocean where a recent "underwater earthquake forced a fragment of the old island of Atlantis to rise from the sea bottom"—a fragment somehow endowed, by virtue of "strange experiments" conducted by Atlantean scientists "centuries ago," with the ability to impart super-powers "to anyone subjected to its radiance"—brazenly proceeds to loot METROPOLIS until he is finally apprehended by SUPERMAN in July 1957. Superman's efforts to capture Wellins are severely hampered by the fact that the same undersea phenomenon that has affected Wellins has temporarily multiplied Superman's own powers "a thousandfold," to the point where they are virtually uncontrollable and where he hardly dares use them at all for fear of unleashing potentially catastrophic side effects (Act No. 230: "Superman Loses His Powers"). (*See also* ATLANTIS.)

WELLS, POINTDEXTER. The nephew of Frank Wells, the publisher of the DAILY PLANET, and an inveterate practical joker whose fondness for rubber snakes and exploding cigars causes pandemonium at the *Daily Planet* until a series of events persuade Pointdexter that his seemingly harmless pranks contain the potential for grievous harm to others. Kidnapped by members of the "Avenue Ten" gang while bravely impersonating CLARK KENT—the anticipated target of gangland vengeance—Wells courageously turns the tables and apprehends them all in February 1955 (S No. 95/2: "The Practical Joker!").

WHEELER, DAN. The secret leader of the Swindle Syndicate, a gang of criminals whose swindles include the sale of worthless real estate, bogus jewelry, and fraudulent uranium stock. Wheeler and his henchmen attempt to murder CLARK KENT in retaliation for his newspaper exposés of their various swindles, but they are apprehended by SUPERMAN in May 1955 (S No. 97/2: "The Big Game Hunt of Metropolis!").

WHEELER, LITTLE DAN. The leader of a gang of criminals whose attempts to commit a series of spectacular crimes are repeatedly thwarted by SUPERMAN in March-April 1953. Superman's efforts to foil the crimes, and indeed all of his activities during this period, are severely hampered by the presence in Earth's atmosphere of a twenty-four-hour KRYPTONITE dust shower, which forces the Man of Steel to take refuge at the bottom of Metropolis Bay, where the debilitating effects of the kryptonite cannot reach him, and to remain there until the dust shower has passed, fighting crime in METROPOLIS by fashioning an arsenal of ingenious devices—such as a gigantic periscope for keeping watch over the city and a huge trident for snaring fleeing criminals—that enable him to foil crimes while still remaining underwater (S No. 81/2: "20,000 Leagues Under the Sea with Superman").

WHIFFENSNIFF, WALTER (Professor). A bespectacled academician who stormed into the editorial office of the DAILY PLANET with the somewhat humorous accusation that "there is no Superman," that the millions who have witnessed his exploits have been indulging in "mass self-hypnotism," and that the *Daily Planet's* accounts of his adventures are contemptible efforts to "humbug the public," "sheer fabrications to sell newspapers to the gullible public…fabrications by a modern Munchausen named Kent, aided and abetted by a Miss Lois Lane."

"I've proven it over and over again on paper," insisted the indignant professor, "—and I'll stake my scientific reputation on it! There just couldn't possibly be a character who dashes about performing supernatural deeds…!"

For awhile SUPERMAN allowed the professor to maintain his delusion, only to appear sometime later at a crucial instant to capture a gang of criminals, save the professor's life, and establish beyond the slightest doubt that there is indeed a Superman (S No. 40/3, May/Jun '46: "There Is No Superman!").

WHIMPLE, OSWALD. An inept and unpopular but generally well-meaning fellow—a man who is always trying to do good deeds for others, only to have things work out badly—who causes consternation and pandemonium in the life of SUPERMAN when, through a series of coincidences, he comes into possession of a slip of paper, signed by Superman and intended originally for LOIS LANE, in which the Man of Steel agrees to carry out the bearer's every wish for a period of three full days. Fortunately for Super-

man, Whimple's requests, although frequently outlandish—as when he forces Superman to borrow three moons from the planet Jupiter to satisfy a girl's desire for "more moonlight" at a local dance—invariably involve kindnesses to others, as opposed to attempts at personal gain, and Superman emerges from his period of servitude—a period during which Whimple summons him repeatedly with blasts on a supersonic dog whistle—none the worse for wear and perhaps better off than he would have been had Lois Lane gotten the opportunity to avail herself of the same agreement (Act No. 159, Aug '51: "The Man Who Owned Superman").

WHISK, JOHN. "An unsuccessful inventor with a larcenous heart" who attempts to swindle confidence man J. WILBUR WOLFINGHAM in September-October 1952 (WF No. 60: "The Swindler Who Was Honest!").

WHITE, ALICE. The attractive white-haired woman who is the wife of DAILY PLANET editor PERRY WHITE and the mother of their three sons: WILL WHITE, PERRY WHITE, JR., and Hank White, the youngest of the three (SF No. 175, Feb/Mar '76).

WHITE, JIM. A pseudonym employed by SUPERMAN in November 1963, after exposure to red KRYPTONITE has temporarily robbed him of his superpowers and afflicted him with total amnesia, even to the point of being unable to remember his own identity. The name Jim White represents the unconscious coupling by Superman of the first name and last name, respectively, of two of his closest friends: JIMMY OLSEN and PERRY WHITE (S No. 165/2: "The Sweetheart Superman Forgot!"; *see also* S No. 169/2, May '64: "The Man Who Stole Superman's Secret Life!"). (*See* SELWYN, SALLY.)

WHITE, JOYCE. A lifelike robot which SUPERMAN pretends to marry in March 1958 as part of his plan to apprehend the "COUP" COLBY gang (S No. 120/1: "The Day That Superman Married").

WHITE, PERRY. The "gruff" (Act No. 302, Jul '63: "The Amazing Confession of Super-Perry White!"), "irascible" (S No. 49/2, Nov/Dec '47: "Clark Kent's Most Dangerous Assignment!"), "hard-boiled" (S No. 16/1, May/Jun '42: "The World's Meanest Man"; and others), "tough" (S No. 72/2, Sep/Oct '51: "The Private Life of Perry White!"), "dynamic" (S No. 73/3, Nov/Dec '51: "Perry White vs. Clark Kent!"), "sentimental" (S No. 16/1, May/Jun '42: "The World's Meanest Man"), warm-hearted (Act No. 269, Oct '60: "The Truth Mirror!"; and others), "two-fisted crusading editor" (S No. 72/2, Sep/Oct '51: "The Private Life of Perry White!") who has been the editor of the DAILY PLANET for nearly four full decades (S No. 7/1, Nov/Dec '40; and many others).

An implacable foe of censorship and defender of press freedom (S No. 11/1, Jul/Aug '41; and others) whose hard-hitting crime reporting once earned him a Pulitzer Prize, he is a giant of American journalism (S No. 72/2, Sep/Oct '51: "The Private Life of Perry White!"; *see also* Act No. 297, Feb '63: "The Man Who Betrayed Superman's Identity!"), "the best editor in the business," a man whose unique "brand of slam-

BUT, THE LAST TWO QUALITIES WILL BE OBSERVED AND JUDGED DURING THE COURSE OF YOUR EVERYDAY WORK! SO GET BACK TO YOUR JOBS, GIRLS... AND GOOD LUCK!

© NPP 1947

Perry White

bang, no-holds-barred journalism has made the **Daily Planet** the biggest paper in Metropolis!" (S No. 73/3, Nov/Dec '51: "Perry White vs. Clark Kent!").

CLARK KENT has described Perry White as a "managing editor extraordinary" who "eats, breathes and sleeps news" (WF No. 13, Spr '44: "The Freedom of the Press!"), and Action Comics No. 297 calls White "the toughest editor in the newspaper game," a man who "would sell his soul for a big story!" (Feb '63: "The Man Who Betrayed Superman's Identity!"). Although he "acts like a hardboiled editor," however, Perry White has "a heart of gold" (Act No. 269, Oct '60: "The Truth Mirror!") and a mile-wide "sentimental streak." For decades he has been the moving force behind many of the *Daily Planet*'s philanthropic activities (S No. 16/1, May/Jun '42: "The World's Meanest Man"; and others). No one has ever intimidated Perry White into suppressing a news story or editorial he felt ought to be published (S No. 16/3, May/Jun '42: "Case of the Runaway Skyscrapers"), but he has occasionally withheld stories from publication that might have wrecked the careers of innocent persons (S No. 72/2, Sep/Oct '51: "The Private Life of Perry White!") or demoralized the public (Act No. 243, Aug '58: "The Lady and the Lion").

Perry White first appears in the chronicles in November-December 1940, although, in his initial appearances, he is referred to only by his last name (S No. 7/1; and others). In May-June 1941 editor White is referred to by his full name—Perry White—for the first time in the chronicles (S No. 10/2).

However, despite the fact that Perry White has now functioned as the *Daily Planet*'s editor for nearly four full decades, the chroniclers have not been consistent regarding his precise professional title: he

has been referred to as the "editor" in numerous texts (S No. 27/1, Mar/Apr '44: "The Palace of Perilous Play!"; and many others), but he has also been described as the newspaper's "managing editor" (WF No. 13, Spr '44: "The Freedom of the Press!"; and others), its "city editor" (Act No. 133, Jun '49: "The World's Most Perfect Girl!"; Act No. 136, Sep '49: "Superman, Show-Off!"), its "chief editor" (S No. 121/3, May '58: "Jimmy Hits the Jackpot"; S No. 131/3, Aug '59: "The Unknown Super-Deeds!"), and its "editor-in-chief" (Act No. 243, Aug '58: "The Lady and the Lion"). Perry White has also been referred to as the *Daily Planet*'s "editor-publisher" (S No. 18/3, Sep/Oct '42: "The Man with the Cane") and "publisher" (S No. 117/1, Nov '57: "Clark Kent, Man of Mystery"), but these designations are contradicted by numerous texts (S No. 54/1, Sep/Oct '48: "The Wrecker"; and many others) and are certainly not accurate.

Perry White's background is treated inconsistently in the chronicles. According to Superman No. 151/1, White spent his boyhood in METROPOLIS, where he attended Public School No. 84 (Feb '62: "The Three Tough Teen-Agers!"). However, two other texts dealing with Perry White's boyhood portray him as living with his grandfather, steamboat captain Josiah White, in 1906 San Francisco (S No. 168, Apr '64: pts. I-II—"Luthor--Super-Hero!"; "Lex Luthor, Daily Planet Editor!") and as the operator of a shoeshine stand in 1920s Chicago (S No. 142/2, Jan '61: "Superman Meets Al Capone!"). All accounts agree, however, that even as a youngster, Perry White had a burning desire to pursue a career in journalism (S No. 142/2, Jan '61: "Superman Meets Al Capone!"; and others).

According to World's Finest Comics No. 13, Perry White began his career as a newsboy and gradually worked his way through the journalistic ranks to his current editorial position on the *Daily Planet* (Spr '44: "The Freedom of the Press!"). According to Superman No. 142/2, however, White graduated directly from shoeshine boy to cub reporter after Superman, on a time-journey to 1920s Chicago, provided the ambitious youngster with his first scoop story, thereby enabling the lad to land a job with the Chicago *Journal* (Jan '61: "Superman Meets Al Capone!"). At some point during the early days of his career, Perry White lived in GOTHAM CITY, where he worked as a cub reporter on the Gotham *Gazette* (WF No. 80, Jan/Feb '56: "The Super-Newspaper of Gotham City").

In time, Perry White became "the greatest news-hound of his day," "a crack reporter" whose courageous crime exposés sounded the death knell of several major underworld combines (Act No. 297, Feb '63: "The Man Who Betrayed Superman's Identity!") and won him a coveted Pulitzer Prize (S No. 72/2, Sep/Oct '51: "The Private Life of Perry White!").

By the time Clark Kent had reached high school age, Perry White had become a reporter on the *Daily Planet* (S No. 131/3, Aug '59: "The Unknown Super-

Deeds!"), and sometime prior to Clark Kent's high school graduation, White was promoted to the position of editor (Act No. 144, May '50: "Clark Kent's Career!").

Perry White lives with his attractive white-haired wife, Alice White (SF No. 175, Feb/Mar '76) in a one-story ranch-style house "in the outskirts of Metropolis" (Act No. 278, Jul '61: "The Super Powers of Perry White!"). The couple have three sons: WILL WHITE, PERRY WHITE, JR., and Hank White, the youngest of the three (SF No. 175, Feb/Mar '76).

In addition to his home in the Metropolis suburbs, Perry White also owns a home by the seashore (S No. 142/1, Jan '61: "Lois Lane's Secret Helper!"), a private yacht (S No. 121/3, May '58: "Jimmy Hits the Jackpot"), and a fishing cruiser anchored in Metropolis Harbor (Act No. 312, May '64: "King Superman versus Clark Kent, Metallo"). A confirmed workaholic who seldom takes an extended vacation (S No. 18/3, Sep/Oct '42: "The Man with the Cane"; and others), he nevertheless enjoys fishing (S No. 92/1, Sep '54: "The Impossible Headlines!"; S No. 142/1, Jan '61: "Lois Lane's Secret Helper!"), horse racing (S No. 169/2, May '64: "The Man Who Stole Superman's Secret Life!"), and relaxing in his garden (Act No. 278, Jul '61: "The Super Powers of Perry White!"). Perry White chain smokes "dollar coronas" (Act No. 297, Feb '63: "The Man Who Betrayed Superman's Identity!"). His favorite expression, usually uttered in anger or exasperation, is "Great Caesar's ghost!" (S No. 91/3, Aug '54: "Great Caesar's Ghost!"; and others).

In addition to being editor of the *Daily Planet*, Perry White is also president of the Magazine and News Association (Act No. 155, Apr '51: "The Cover Girl Mystery!"). An Indian tribe has made him an honorary chief, bestowing upon him the tribal name Chief Stony Voice (Act No. 200, Jan '55: "Tests of a Warrior!").

Perry White is one of SUPERMAN's "best friends" (Act No. 243, Aug '58: "The Lady and the Lion"; and others). The Man of Steel has dedicated a room to Perry White in his FORTRESS OF SOLITUDE (Act No. 278, Jul '61: "The Super Powers of Perry White!"; S No. 152/1, Apr '62: "The Robot Master!").

In the course of his long and colorful career, Perry White has assumed a number of alternate identities, including those of MASTERMAN (Act No. 278, Jul '61: "The Super Powers of Perry White!"), the GREAT MENTO (S No. 147/1, Aug '61: "The Great Mento!"), and PROFESSOR VON SCHULTZ (S No. 157/2, Nov '62: "The Super-Genie of Metropolis!").

Interestingly, a number of individuals in various times and places are perfect Perry White look-alikes, including the editor of the *Daily Zorian*, a so-called "telenewspaper" on the planet Zor (*see* ZOR [1952]) (Act No. 168, May '52: "The Menace of Planet Z!"); PARRI WYTE, a "remote descendant" of Perry White, who edits the *Daily Solar System* in the thirtieth century A.D. (Act No. 215, Apr '56: "The Superman of Tomorrow"); Ar-Rone, the reformed criminal who is

Perry White's double in the Kandorian LOOK-ALIKE SQUAD (Act No. 309, Feb '64: "The Superman Super-Spectacular!"; and others); and the Perry White look-alike—also named Perry White—whom Superman and BATMAN encounter during a visit to an extradimensional "parallel world" in March 1965 (WF No. 148: "Superman and Batman--Outlaw!" pts. I-II—"The Evil Superman and Batman"; "The Incredible New Super-Team!"). On the planet OCEANIA, CHESTER KING's editor at the Oceania Network bears a striking resemblance to Perry White (Act No. 265, Jun '60: "The 'Superman' from Outer Space!"). The LEGION OF SUPER-HEROES employ a lifelike Perry White robot in April 1962 as part of an elaborate hoax they play on Superman and SUPERGIRL (S No. 152/1: "The Robot Master!"), and Superman encounters a lifelike android of Perry White during a time-journey to Metropolis one million years in the future (Act No. 300, May '63: "Superman Under the Red Sun!").

In spite of the fact that Perry White appears in the chronicles more often than any other character besides Superman and LOIS LANE, the overwhelming majority of his appearances are inconsequential. Therefore, the article that follows deals only with those adventures in which Perry White plays at least a minimally significant role.

In November-December 1940 Perry White—referred to in his initial appearance only by his last name—makes his textual debut as editor of the *Daily Planet* (S No. 7/1; and others).

In May-June 1941 editor White is referred to by his full name—Perry White—for the first time in the chronicles (S No. 10/2).

In July-August 1941 Perry White punches ROLF ZIMBA in the jaw when the terrorist leader barges into the offices of the *Daily Planet* and demands the right to censor all forthcoming news stories concerning his Gold Badge Organization (S No. 11/1).

Perry White, Clark Kent, and Lois Lane, 1941

In May-June 1942, after the Daily Planet Building and all its occupants have been transported to the fourth dimension by the evil MISTER SINISTER, Perry White and Lois Lane are tied to stakes in an extradimensional valley as human sacrifices to a fearsome dinosaurlike "shadow monster." They are rescued from death, however, by the heroic intervention of Superman, who battles the monster, defeats the villain, and ultimately restores the "kidnapped" Daily Planet Building to the earthly dimension (S No. 16/3: "Case of the Runaway Skyscrapers").

In May-June 1943, after the PRANKSTER has copyrighted the English alphabet, Perry White finds himself forced to pay the villain $2,000 a week for permission to print the *Daily Planet* (S No. 22/3: "The Great ABC Panic!").

In July-August 1946, after Superman has complained aloud about being forced to "make a career of saving [Lois Lane's] life," Perry White hires PAT MALARKEY to serve as a bodyguard to both Lois Lane and Clark Kent (S No. 41/2: "Clark Kent's Bodyguard!").

In July 1949, after Perry White's old friend Norman Burwick, the editor of a weekly newspaper in the Western town of Powder Valley, has been severely injured in an explosion in his newspaper office deliberately caused by a gang of rustlers against whom Burwick had been campaigning in his newspaper, Perry White travels to Powder Valley—accompanied by Lois Lane and Clark Kent—to take over management of the paper until Burwick is well enough to return to work. Arriving in Powder Valley, White and his colleagues set to work putting out the small-town weekly and trying to track down the rustlers, but it is Superman who discovers that local blacksmith Paul Strong is secretly the leader of the rustlers and takes Strong and his cohorts into custody (Act No. 134: "Super-Cowboy!").

In September-October 1949 Superman impersonates Perry White as part of his elaborate plan for drawing Metropolis's secret petty-rackets czar (*see* SHORE, HOLLIS) into the open so that he can be easily apprehended. After the Man of Steel has abandoned his Perry White masquerade, the real Perry White helps him capture Shore and his henchmen (S No. 60/1: "The Two Identities of Superman!").

In September-October 1951 Perry White is taken captive by a gang of protection racketeers whose activities he has been investigating. Superman rescues White and apprehends his abductors, however, on a tip provided by WILL WHITE, one of Perry White's sons (S No. 72/2: "The Private Life of Perry White!"). (*See also* UNIVERSAL INSURANCE COMPANY.)

In November-December 1951, after a series of unfortunate misunderstandings with his publisher has resulted in his being fired from his job at the *Daily Planet*, Perry White obtains new employment as editor of a rival newspaper, the *Daily Dispatch*. Aided by reporter Lois Lane, who quits the *Daily Planet* to work for Perry White on the *Daily Dispatch*,

Perry White and Clark Kent, 1942

White scores a series of impressive journalistic coups, climaxed by the incredible discovery that Ray Curtis, the publisher of the *Daily Dispatch*, is secretly the mysterious underworld mastermind known as "THE INSIDER." Curtis is about to murder Perry White and Lois Lane to prevent them from printing their amazing scoop when Superman arrives on the scene in the nick of time and takes Curtis into custody. And soon afterward, after White's misunderstandings with the *Daily Planet* have been resolved, Perry White returns to his old job as the *Daily Planet*'s editor (S No. 73/3: "Perry White vs. Clark Kent!").

By March 1952 LEX LUTHOR and his henchmen have kidnapped Perry White and replaced him with a lifelike robot look-alike as part of an elaborate scheme to frame Clark Kent for Perry White's murder while at the same time keeping Superman so busy protecting Lois Lane while she carries out a series of hair-raisingly dangerous reportorial assignments that the Man of Steel will be unable to prevent the villains from committing a series of spectacular crimes. Superman ultimately thwarts the scheme, however, and apprehends Luthor and his henchmen (Act No. 166: "The Three Scoops of Death!").

In November-December 1952, after unscrupulous newspaper publisher JOHN WILTON has purchased three Metropolis newspapers and then closed down two of them, including the *Daily Planet*, so that he can operate his remaining paper virtually without competition, Perry White begins supporting himself by driving a taxicab to enable him to devote his off hours to *The Daily Metropolitan*, a fledgling newspaper launched by White and his fellow dispossessed *Daily Planet* staffers (S No. 79/2: "The End of the Planet!").

In January 1954 Perry White visits London—in the company of Lois Lane and Clark Kent—to establish an English edition of the *Daily Planet* (S No. 86/1: "The Dragon from King Arthur's Court!"); helps solve a famous jewel robbery which has remained unsolved for seven years (*see* OLSEN, JIMMY) (S No. 86/2: "Jimmy Olsen...Editor!"); and incurs the mischievous wrath of MR. MXYZPTLK by rejecting the imp's demand that he retract a *Daily Planet* news story describing Superman as "the greatest person ever to have lived!" (S No. 86/3: "The Fourth Dimension Gazette!").

Perry White and Superman, 1955

In August 1954, after learning that the *Daily Planet*'s publishers are contemplating firing Perry White and replacing him with a younger man, Superman sets in motion an elaborate ruse designed to accomplish two separate objectives: (1) inspiring Perry White to perform several outstanding journalistic feats so that the publishers will change their minds about firing him, while concealing from White the fact that his job is in jeopardy to avoid hurting his pride; and (2) improving the self-confidence of *Daily Planet* drama reporter Waldo Pippin, who is so thoroughly intimidated by White's gruff manner that he is too nervous to do a good job.

The ruse, carried out with Pippin's cooperation, involves disguising Pippin as the ghost of Julius Caesar and having him appear, as if by magic, in Perry White's office whenever White utters his favorite exclamation, "Great Caesar's ghost!" Feigning wraithly anger at his name having been used in vain so often, Pippin begins to "haunt" White's office, promising to depart into the hereafter only after White has appeased him by scoring a series of journalistic coups worthy of "great Caesar's" name.

Unnerved by the "ghost" and determined to mollify it, White courageously garners two amazing scoops, helping Superman apprehend a brutal murderer named Killer Regan and then risking his life to get exclusive coverage of Superman's rescue of the inhabitants of an island devastated by an

undersea earthquake. With White now clearly the hero of the day, the publishers quietly shelve their plans to fire him, instead granting him a raise and a new five-year contract. Waldo Pippin, for his part, has acquired new self-confidence as the result of his involvement in a situation in which, for a change, Perry White was intimidated by him. White never learns that he was on the verge of being fired, but Superman does tell him the partial truth, i.e., that "great Caesar's ghost" was actually drama reporter Pippin in disguise and that he had inspired Pippin to assume the ghostly role as a means of improving Pippin's flagging self-confidence (S No. 91/3: "Great Caesar's Ghost!").

In February 1955 Perry White is accidentally transported into the Stone Age, along with Clark Kent, Lois Lane, a bespectacled inventor named Bates, and a ruthless Metropolis mobster known as BENNY THE BRUTE (Act No. 201: "The Challenge of Stoneman!").

In July 1955 Perry White joins forces with Superman in carrying out an elaborate ruse designed to enable the Man of Steel to apprehend the "BIG GUY" (S No. 98/2: "Clark Kent Outlaw!").

In August 1955 Perry White and Lois Lane are among the prominent citizens of Metropolis who attend the city's "annual policemen's dinner," a banquet at which Clark Kent is awarded the coveted Superman Medal, a medal awarded each year by the Metropolis Police Department "to the person whose heroism...helped **Superman** the most" during the preceding year (Act No. 207: "The Four Superman Medals!").

In September 1955 MR. MXYZPTLK briefly impersonates Perry White as part of his elaborate, but unsuccessful, attempt to trick Superman into saying his name backwards so that he can temporarily banish the Man of Steel into the eighth dimension (Act No. 208: "The Magic of Mr. Mxyztplk").

In December 1955, when Superman returns to SMALLVILLE for a testimonial dinner in his honor commemorating the anniversary of his arrival on Earth as an infant from the planet KRYPTON, Perry White is on hand to present the Man of Steel with a special anniversary gift: copies of the *Daily Planet*'s French, Greek, Italian, Dutch, and Japanese editions, each with photographs of Superman performing super-feats splashed across its front page, and each with a headline wishing Superman a happy anniversary in its own native language (Act No. 211: "The Superman Spectaculars"). (*See also* DAILY PLANET.)

In February 1956 PAUL PAXTON sets in motion an elaborate scheme designed to convince Perry White and the other members of the *Daily Planet* staff that he, Paxton, is secretly Superman (Act No. 213: "Paul Paxton Alias Superman!").

In the summer of 1956 Perry White, dressed in the regalia of a Hindu mahout, rides atop an elephant held aloft by Superman in the *Daily Planet*'s annual Daily Planet Charity Show circus. Later, at Superman's request, Perry White plays the role of Santa

Perry White, Lois Lane, and Clark Kent, 1955

Perry White and Clark Kent, 1960

Claus in the elaborate tableau used to illustrate the month of December in THORNE VARDEN's spectacular Superman calendar (Act No. 212, Jan '56: "The Superman Calendar").

In August 1957 Perry White surreptitiously helps JIMMY OLSEN fulfill the last of his "three knightly deeds" by assuming the role of a reckless driver and barrelling his automobile down the street toward a female pedestrian, thereby providing Olsen with the opportunity he needs to "rescue a fair maiden in distress" (Act No. 231: "Jimmy Olsen, Knight of Metropolis"). During this same period, Perry White is kidnapped by a henchman of "MANY-FACES" FULTON, who impersonates the *Daily Planet* editor as part of an elaborate scheme to trick Jimmy Olsen into believing that Superman is dead. Superman thwarts the scheme, however, and rescues White from his abductor's clutches (S No. 115/2, Aug '57: "Jimmy Olsen's Lost Pal"). During this same period, Perry White joins forces with Superman in carrying out an elaborate, and ultimately successful, ruse designed to enable Superman to apprehend the ORGANIZER (S No. 115/3, Aug '57: "The Three Substitute Supermen!").

In November 1957 Superman carries out an elaborate, and ultimately successful, ruse designed to enable him to partially obliterate the signatures of Clark Kent and Superman on a testimonial plaque awarded to Perry White so as to prevent anyone from ever comparing the two signatures and thereby deducing that Clark Kent and Superman are actually the same man (S No. 117/1: "Clark Kent, Man of Mystery").

In March 1958 Perry White joins forces with Superman in carrying out an elaborate, and ultimately successful, ruse designed to enable the Man of Steel to apprehend crime chief "COUP" COLBY (S No. 120/1: "The Day That Superman Married").

In May 1958 Perry White joins forces with

Superman, Jimmy Olsen, and the U.S. Coast Guard to carry out an elaborate ruse that culminates in the capture of "HONEST" JOHN and a gang of "Honest" John's underworld rivals known as the Shark Gang (S No. 121/3: "Jimmy Hits the Jackpot").

In September 1958 Perry White poses as the evil Black Knight of Arthurian legend as part of an elaborate ruse devised by Superman for apprehending gang chief "BULL" MATHEWS (S No. 124/1: "The Super-Sword").

In February 1960, at a testimonial banquet in his honor, Perry White is publicly humiliated by Superman, who has been temporarily transformed into a thoughtless "super-heel" under the baleful influence of MR. MXYZPTLK's "5th dimensional hypnotism" (S No. 135/3: "The Trio of Steel!").

In April 1960, when Superman's Earthday—"the anniversary of the day [Superman] landed on Earth from the doomed planet, **Krypton**"—is celebrated in Smallville, Perry White is among those on hand to attend the festivities (S No. 136/2: "The Secret of Kryptonite!").

In January 1961 Superman journeys through the time barrier into the past, to the city of Chicago during the 1920s, where he encounters Perry White, then a youngster operating a shoeshine stand, and, by providing him with an exclusive account of his brief encounter with AL CAPONE, enables young White to land a cub reporter's job on the Chicago *Journal*. Because the Man of Steel disguises himself in civilian clothes during this sojourn in the past, however, Perry White never suspects that the man who helped him launch his newspaper career was actually Superman (S No. 142/2: "Superman Meets Al Capone!").

In February 1961 PROFESSOR OTTO JURIS sets in motion an elaborate scheme designed to convince Perry White and the other members of the *Daily Planet* staff that he, Juris, is secretly Superman (S No. 143/1: "The Great Superman Hoax!").

In July 1961, after sampling the delicious fruit of a

weird plant that he finds growing in his suburban garden, Perry White discovers, to his amazement, that the strange fruit has somehow endowed him with super-powers virtually identical to Superman's, including super-strength, X-ray vision, and the power of flight. Determined to use his newly acquired powers to aid humanity, White dons a colorful red-and-green costume and, adopting the super-heroic pseudonym of Masterman, embarks on a career as a superhero.

For a time, White uses his super-powers to do good deeds, as when he stops a runaway truck whose brakes have failed and recaptures a lion that has escaped from the zoo. Before long, however, Masterman has taken on a sinister aspect, for, as Superman soon discovers, the mind and body of Perry White have been taken over by a diabolical "plant intelligence" from the far-distant planet Zelm, the advance guard of a race of sinister "plant aliens" bent on conquering the Earth and colonizing it for themselves.

...and stares in amazement at what he has just done, as yet unaware that he has acquired super-powers as the result of his body having been taken over and inhabited by a diabolical "plant intelligence" from another world, 1961

"I landed as a spore, grew into a mature plant, and developed fruits which an earthling ate!" gloats the plant alien, Xasnu, speaking from inside the body of Perry White. "As the substance spread through his bloodstream, he first acquired super powers... and then... I finally acquired complete control of his body and mind!"

Instructed by his superiors on the planet Zelm to annihilate Superman so as to pave the way for their invasion of Earth, the "alien Perry" invades the Fortress of Solitude, clad in the costume he wears as Masterman and armed with deadly weapons made of red and green KRYPTONITE. As the super-powered adversaries lock in mortal combat, it appears that even Superman is powerless to defeat the sinister

Struggling with a stubborn safe in his office at the Daily Planet...

...Perry White rips the massive door clear off its hinges...

Perry White as Masterman, 1961

plant intelligence occupying the body of Perry White, but ultimately, at the climactic moment, Supergirl arrives on the scene and destroys the evil plant being with a chunk of white kryptonite. "Ahhh...my theory was right!" remarks Supergirl. "The alien is dying...I had a hunch white kryptonite would turn the trick! You see--the alien is a plant intelligence, and it is a known fact that white kryptonite destroys all forms of plant life!"

Perry White revives soon afterward, bereft of the super-powers he possessed while his body was inhabited by Xasnu but otherwise none the worse off for his bizarre adventure (Act No. 278: "The Super Powers of Perry White!").

In August 1961 Perry White poses as a mind reader turned criminal (*see* Great Mento, The) as part of an elaborate ruse, devised by Superman, to "round up every wanted criminal in [the] region" (S No. 147/1: "The Great Mento!").

In September 1961, while visiting the Congolese jungle to cover a native uprising for the *Daily Planet*, Perry White is reduced to "Tom Thumb size" and imprisoned inside a large glass bottle—along with Superman, Jimmy Olsen, and Lois Lane—by the space villain Brainiac (Act No. 280: "Brainiac's Super-Revenge!").

In April 1962, while in the grip of a nightmare induced by exposure to red kryptonite, Superman dreams that after having been implicated in a series of crimes and then robbed of his super-powers by a diabolical villain, he is relentlessly hounded and finally dragged off to prison by a posse led by Perry White—who appears as a sheriff in the nightmare—and Krypto the Superdog, who assume that their Superman-costumed quarry is an evil Superman impostor and steadfastly refuse to believe his impassioned claim that he is the real Superman. These events, however, are all only a nightmare, and no such incidents ever actually take place (Act No. 287: "Perry White's Manhunt for Superman!").

In July 1962, in the pressroom of the *Daily Planet*, Perry White presents Superman with an honorary plaque in gratitude for his ongoing role in "helping the Planet get many great scoops!" (S No. 154/2: "Krypton's First Superman!").

In November 1962 Perry White poses as an archaeologist who has just unearthed Aladdin's original magic lamp (*see* Von Schultz [Professor]) as part of an elaborate ruse, devised by Superman with the cooperation of the F.B.I., to enable Superman to apprehend a notorious "international spy" (S No. 157/2: "The Super-Genie of Metropolis!").

In December 1962 Perry White joins forces with Superman in carrying out an elaborate ruse designed to enable the Supermen Emergency Squad to apprehend two members of the Superman Revenge Squad (Act No. 295: "Superman Goes Wild!").

In February 1963, after a blow on the head has afflicted him with temporary amnesia, Perry White is found trudging along a highway by "underworld kingpin" Dirk Denver, who recognizes White immedi-

ately as the editor of the *Daily Planet* but who decides to capitalize on White's amnesia by duping the famed editor into using his journalistic skills to unravel the secret of Superman's dual identity, a secret for which an underworld "crime syndicate" is offering a reward of $1,000,000.

Posing as a magazine publisher, Denver convinces the amnesic Perry White that he, White, is actually Paul Webster, once "this country's top reporter" until, claims Denver, he took to drink, went on the skids, and, finally, unable to obtain employment, disappeared from the world of journalism. Feigning sympathy with "Webster's" down-and-out condition, Denver offers to give "Webster" a chance at a comeback in his old profession by hiring him as a reporter on one of his magazines. His first assignment, explains Denver, will be to solve the secret of Superman's identity.

Filled with gratitude at what he honestly believes is a heaven-sent opportunity to make a new start, the amnesic Perry White sets determinedly to work on the problem of Superman's identity, poring over the numerous books, films, and articles pertaining to Superman's career, compiling an exact physical description of the Man of Steel, finally narrowing his list of suspects down to only four individuals, including *Daily Planet* reporter Clark Kent.

Ultimately, through a clever ruse, White actually succeeds in tricking Clark Kent into betraying the fact that he is secretly Superman, but before White can relay the secret to Denver, Kent uses a ruse of his own to shock White out of his amnesic state. With his amnesia gone and his memory restored, White realizes at once that he is Perry White, editor of the *Daily Planet*, but he has lost all recollection of his brief life as reporter Paul Webster and of the knowledge he acquired of Superman's identity (Act No. 297: "The Man Who Betrayed Superman's Identity!").

In April 1963 Perry White emcees the Metropolis Daily Planet Charity Fund Benefit show, starring Superman, at the Ajax Theater (S No. 160/1: pts. I-II—"The Mortal Superman!"; "The Cage of Doom!") and poses as an ex-convict badly in need of money as part of an elaborate and ultimately successful ruse, devised by Superman and carried out with the cooperation of the Metropolis police force, designed to enable the Man of Steel to apprehend a ring of foreign spies planning to steal the blueprints for a "new type of atomic war-head" developed by the U.S. government (S No. 160/2: "The Super-Cop of Metropolis!").

In July 1963 Superman impersonates Perry White as part of his elaborate, and ultimately successful, plan for luring a ring of stock swindlers into the open so that he can easily apprehend them (Act No. 302: "The Amazing Confession of Super-Perry White!"). The story is in many respects similar to Superman No. 60/1 (Sep/Oct '49: "The Two Identities of Superman!"). (*See* Shore, Hollis.)

In August 1963, following the death of Wonder-Man, Perry White is among the throng of mourners

Lois Lane and Perry White, 1972

who gather to pay their last respects at the large stone monument that has been erected in Metropolis in Wonder-Man's honor (S No. 163/1: "Wonder-Man, the New Hero of Metropolis!").

In October 1963, while paying a call on Perry White, who is confined to the isolation ward at Metropolis General Hospital with a case of the measles, Clark Kent thwarts a holdup attempt by BENNY THE BLASTER (Act No. 305: "Why Superman Needs a Secret Identity!").

When Metropolis television station WMET-TV makes plans to inaugurate its new "Our American Heroes" series with a program honoring Superman, "our greatest American hero," Perry White cooperates with the program's producers by helping to keep the Man of Steel preoccupied with a series of assignments in order to prevent his becoming aware of the elaborate preparations being made for the surprise television tribute (Act No. 309, Feb '64: "The Superman Super-Spectacular!").

In April 1964 Superman journeys through the time barrier into the past, to the city of San Francisco in the year 1906, where he extinguishes a blaze aboard a paddle-wheeled steamboat and briefly makes the acquaintance of the vessel's captain, Josiah White, and his young grandson, Perry White (S No. 168: pts. I-II—"Luthor--Super-Hero!"; "Lex Luthor, Daily Planet Editor!").

By June 1964 Perry White and four of Superman's other good friends—Batman, Lois Lane, LORI LEMARIS, and Jimmy Olsen—have been taken captive by the Superman Revenge Squad and imprisoned in a state of suspended animation in a cave beneath

Metropolis as part of the villains' elaborate scheme to torment and demoralize Superman (Act No. 313: "The End of Clark Kent's Secret Identity!"). (*See* SUPERMAN REVENGE SQUAD, THE.)

In September 1965, when Superman Day is celebrated in Metropolis, the featured attractions in the colorful Superman Day parade include gigantic balloons in the image of Superman's closest friends—Perry White, Jimmy Olsen, and Lois Lane (Act No. 328: "Superman's Hands of Doom!").

In December 1965 Perry White is kidnapped and impersonated by "crime lord" IRON IKE as part of the villain's scheme to steal a fortune in diamonds from the penthouse showroom of a Metropolis diamond merchant. Superman rescues Perry White from his abductors and apprehends Iron Ike and his henchmen, and White single-handedly captures one of the gangsters—by clouting him over the head with a chair—when the criminal invades the offices of the *Daily Planet* determined to wreak vengeance for the capture of his fellows (Act No. 331: "Clark Kent's Masquerade as Superman!").

WHITE, PERRY, JR. The cocky young journalism-school graduate (S No. 108/2, Sep '56: "Perry White, Jr., Demon Reporter!") who is the son of DAILY PLANET editor PERRY WHITE and his wife ALICE WHITE. Perry White, Jr., has two brothers: Hank White and WILL WHITE (SF No. 175, Feb/Mar '76).

In September 1956, Perry White, Jr., a cocky young graduate "fresh out of journalism school," launches his journalistic career as a fledgling reporter for the *Daily Planet*, certain that, despite his lack of experience, he is fully capable of teaching the paper's veteran reporters some tricks of the trade. Complications arise for SUPERMAN when a series of coincidences combine to convince the overeager young reporter that Clark Kent is secretly the notorious MR. WHEELS, while at the same time preventing Kent from revealing the truth without risking the betrayal of his dual identity.

Ultimately, however, Superman's heroic efforts bring about the capture of Mr. Wheels and his henchmen by the METROPOLIS police, and Perry White, Jr., comes to realize that he misjudged Clark Kent and that he still has a great deal to learn about the profession of journalism (S No. 108/2: "Perry White, Jr., Demon Reporter!").

WHITE, WILL. The red-haired journalism-school graduate (S No. 72/2, Sep/Oct '51: "The Private Life of Perry White!") who is the son of DAILY PLANET editor PERRY WHITE and his wife ALICE WHITE. Will White has two brothers: Hank White and PERRY WHITE, JR. (SF No. 175, Feb/Mar '76).

In September-October 1951 Will White applies for a cub reporter's job on the *Daily Planet* under the alias Will Whitman, in obedience to his father's request that he demonstrate his reportorial skills on his own, without capitalizing on his father's prestige and influence. Although Perry White agrees to hire his son only if the youngster can bring in a major news story within twenty-four hours, young White fulfills the assignment—and earns his reporter's job—by uncovering the information SUPERMAN needs to enable him to apprehend a gang of protection racketeers (S No. 72/2: "The Private Life of Perry White!"). (*See also* UNIVERSAL INSURANCE COMPANY.)

WHITMAN, WILL. The alias employed by PERRY WHITE's son WILL WHITE when he applies for a job at the DAILY PLANET in September-October 1951 (S No. 72/2: "The Private Life of Perry White!").

WHITMORE, DONALD. An adventurous young man, the steward of the far-flung "Whitmore industrial empire," who outfits a nineteenth-century-style wagon train in September 1953 and attempts to retrace the precise westward route followed by the wagon train led by his ancestor Davey Whitmore, "famed pioneer scout," just one hundred years ago, only to find his own journey westward repeatedly menaced by disasters eerily identical to the ones which plagued Davey Whitmore. Donald Whitmore begins to crack under the strain of the unnerving "jinx," but SUPERMAN ultimately exposes the mastermind behind the mishaps as John Lattison, Whitmore's unscrupulous business associate, who stood to assume control of Whitmore's industrial holdings in the event Whitmore became emotionally unfit to administer them (Act No. 184: "The Covered Wagon of Doom!").

WICKSVILLE. A town in New England—founded in 1630 and noted for the witches supposed to have resided there during the seventeenth century—which LOIS LANE visits on April 27, 1959, while researching a feature article on superstitions for the DAILY PLANET. Entering a house known as "The Enchanted Cottage," the home of a witch burned at the stake in 1659 "because it was believed she had the uncanny power to read the future," Lois seats herself in the magical "witch's chair," believed to reveal the future once every hundred years to whoever sits in it, and, incredibly, begins to see and hear images from the future. Sitting spellbound in the magic chair, Lois beholds scenes, in her mind's eye, of SUPERMAN getting married, flying his bride to their marital home, celebrating his first wedding anniversary, and raising a pair of super-powered twins. Exasperatingly for Lois, however, the scenes of the future do not reveal either of the things she yearns to discover—the secret of Superman's identity or that of his bride-to-be—and soon the images of the future fade as the chair ceases to work its magic for what will be another hundred years (S No. 131/2, Aug '59: "Superman's Future Wife!").

WILDE, AJAX. An alias employed by the PRANKSTER in November-December 1945 when he poses as a wild-animal trainer as part of his scheme to rob the guests at a birthday party for LOIS LANE being given by prominent METROPOLIS practical joker Dexter Beams (S No. 37/2: "Pranks for Profit!").

WILDE, JACK. A reporter on the DAILY PLANET who, except for the fact that he does not wear eyeglasses, is a perfect look-alike for CLARK KENT (Act No. 171, Aug '52: "The Secrets of Superman!").

WILKINS, PEGGY. LOIS LANE's roommate and "closest girl-friend" (Act No. 143, Apr '50: "The Bride of Superman!"; and others). Portrayed sometimes as a brunette (S No. 61/2, Nov/Dec '49: "The Courtship of the Three Lois Lanes!") and at other times as a blonde (Act No. 143, Apr '50: "The Bride of Superman!"; S No. 65/2, Jul/Aug '50: "Superman's Sweetheart!"), Peggy has a job in a department store in November-December 1949 (S No. 61/2: "The Courtship of the Three Lois Lanes!") but has left this job for a new one by July-August 1950 (S No. 65/2: "Superman's Sweetheart!").

Superman No. 61/2 notes that Peggy Wilkins "thinks Lois [Lane] is just about tops" (Nov/Dec '49: "The Courtship of the Three Lois Lanes!"), and Superman No. 65/2 remarks that

> For years now, Lois Lane and Peggy Wilkins, her roommate, have gotten along like two peas in a pod! Their friendship has been a natural combination, like Damon and Pythias, hot dogs and mustard, or even peaches-and-cream! [Jul/Aug '50: "Superman's Sweetheart!"].

In November-December 1949 it is Peggy Wilkins who advises Lois Lane that dyeing her hair a different color may be the way to win SUPERMAN (S No. 61/2: "The Courtship of the Three Lois Lanes!"). (*See* LANE, LOIS.)

By July-August 1950 Peggy Wilkins has given up her job with a METROPOLIS department store in favor of a job as a "buyer" for a man she knows only as Mr. Martin, unaware that her new employer is actually Freddie the Fence, a notorious buyer of stolen goods. Because he knows that Peggy's new boss is a criminal, Superman begins keeping a watchful eye on her, rescuing her from death on three separate occasions, twice at the hands of rival mobsters determined to gain possession of valuable stolen merchandise entrusted to Peggy's safekeeping, and once at the hands of Freddie the Fence himself, who has decided that his new employee knows more than she should about his illegal operations.

For a time, tension develops between Peggy and Lois Lane over what Lois regards as Superman's undue attention to her attractive roommate.

Ultimately, however, Superman apprehends both Freddie the Fence and his underworld rivals, and Lois comes to realize that Superman's interest in Peggy was only professional and not romantic.

"Peggy darling!" exclaims Lois, embracing her friend. "Can you ever forgive me for doubting you? It was all Superman's fault!"

"Sure, Lois!" replies Peggy affectionately. "No mere man — not even a Superman--can break up our friendship!" (S No. 65/2: "Superman's Sweetheart!").

WILLIAMS, NICK. A wily confidence man who attempts to pass himself off as SUPERMAN's "personal manager"—with exclusive rights to the use of Superman's name for Superman products and commercial endorsements—as part of a scheme to enrich himself by capitalizing on Superman's growing reputation. Williams and the actor he has hired to impersonate Superman are apprehended by Superman in November 1938 (Act No. 6). The story is reprinted in Superman No. 3/3 (Win '40).

WILLIS, DEXTER. The nephew of Mr. Willis—"a big shot publisher" and major DAILY PLANET stockholder—and an inveterate practical joker whose fondness for rubber snakes and exploding cigars causes pandemonium at the *Daily Planet* until SUPERMAN intervenes with his super-powers to play a series of hair-raising practical jokes on Dexter that persuade the young prankster to give up practical jokes forever. Abducted by members of the "Avenue Ten" gang along with reporter CLARK KENT—whose anticrime articles have made him the target of gangland vengeance—Dexter helps Kent turn the tables and apprehend the criminals in June 1962 (Act No. 289: "The Super-Practical Joker!"). The story is in many respects similar to Superman No. 95/2 (Feb '55: "The Practical Joker!"). (*See* WELLS, POINTDEXTER.)

WILTON (Professor). An unscrupulous scientist who, having invented a machine capable of imparting super-strength, charges three honest men an extravagant sum to endow them with super-strength, while treacherously withholding the knowledge that the machine's effects are only temporary and that efforts to renew the super-strength when it fades will almost certainly prove fatal. Wilton is apprehended by SUPERMAN in March 1957 (S No. 112/3: "The Three Men of Steel!").

WILTON, JOHN. An unscrupulous newspaper publisher who purchases three METROPOLIS newspapers and then closes down two of them, including the DAILY PLANET, so that he can operate his remaining paper virtually without competition. But the dispossessed *Daily Planet* staffers respond with their own tiny newspaper, *The Daily Metropolitan*, relentlessly gathering news while supporting themselves at odd jobs and using SUPERMAN's super-powers to help them get the paper out. The furious Wilton tries to crush the fledgling paper, but by threatening to expose his chicanery to the public, Superman ultimately succeeds in forcing Wilton to unload his various Metropolis newspapers and put the *Daily Planet* back in operation under its former publisher and staff (S No. 79/2, Nov/Dec '52: "The End of the Planet!").

WILTON, WILLIS (Professor). The inventor of an extraordinary "four-dimensional projector," a device "that can send an object instantly to any place, or draw it back!" LEX LUTHOR attempts to steal the secret formula for Wilton's "four-dimensional projecting ray" in January-February 1953 (WF No. 62: "The Seven Secrets of Superman").

WIMMER, J. The publisher of the DAILY PLANET who, in December 1949, orders PERRY WHITE to fire Clark Kent and hire a more dynamic reporter in his stead on the ground that "the newspaper business is no place for shrinking violets!" Kent, however,

successfully forestalls his dismissal—and safeguards the reportorial position he sees as vital to his work as SUPERMAN—by temporarily affecting a courageous personality until the *Daily Planet* has decided to retain him, and then perpetrating an elaborate ruse to explain away his short-lived change of behavior (Act No. 139: "Clark Kent...Daredevil!").

WINKI LAMM. The mild-mannered television interviewer on the planet UUz who is secretly the "super-champion" REGOR (S No. 58/3, May/Jun '49: "The Case of the Second Superman").

WINTERS, "DOC." A "brilliant but criminal scientist" who, having recently stumbled upon a meteorite containing "a strange element unknown to Earth" which, "when properly treated," can endow an ordinary man with "super-powers for three days," makes one of his henchmen as powerful as SUPERMAN and has him pose as a surviving native of KRYPTON as part of an elaborate scheme to lure Superman away from METROPOLIS so that he and his gang can loot "a government gold supply depot" while the Man of Steel is away from the city. Winters and his cohorts are apprehended by Superman in October 1955 (Act No. 209: "The Man Who Was Mightier Than Superman").

WINTERS, HARRY. An "average American" closely resembling SUPERMAN who, thrust unexpectedly into a series of dangerous situations as the result of being clad in a Superman masquerade costume, heroically impersonates Superman in order to help the Man of Steel apprehend a gang of criminals in February 1959 (S No. 127/2: "The Make-Believe Superman!").

WINTERS, PERCIVAL. A timorous clerk, the state's key witness in the upcoming trial of racketeer "Flint" Martin, who quits his mundane job and begins to hire himself out as a death-defying daredevil after becoming convinced that he has found a magic ring guaranteed "to protect its wearer from mortal death." The so-called magic ring, however, is merely part of an elaborate scheme by the "Flint" Martin gang to trick Winters into getting himself killed prior to their leader's upcoming trial, but SUPERMAN exposes the hoax and apprehends the villains in October 1949 (Act No. 137: "The Man with the Charmed Life!").

WOKIT, WIZARD OF. An evil master of black magic and superstition who, sometime in the distant past, inhabited an enchanted castle nestled atop the highest scarp of Wokit Mountain, overlooking the "little town" of Morabia, which "still stands in the shadow of the shaggy mountains of southeastern Europe." According to Action Comics No. 86, SUPERMAN defeated the wizard, destroyed his castle, and forever broke his hold over Morabia's terror-stricken peasant populace, but the text also leaves open the possibility that the Wizard of Wokit is merely a character from ancient legend whose battle with Superman is only a fantasy in the mind of LOIS LANE (Jul '45: "The Enchanted Mountain!").

WOLFF, KARL. The consul for the nation of

Dukalia, a foreign country on "unfriendly terms" with the United States, and the mastermind behind a sinister scheme to hijack America's top-secret new "sky-sub"—an oceangoing craft capable of traveling beneath the water like a submarine or over the surface of it like a low-flying airplane—and use it to blow up the PANAMA CANAL. The scheme is thwarted by SUPERMAN in May-June 1941 (S No. 10/4).

WOLFINGHAM, J. WILBUR. The "king of old-time confidence men" (S No. 35/1, Jul/Aug '45: "Fame for Sale!"; and others), "a slick, double-talking con-man ... who would steal the teeth from a tailor's dummy" (WF No. 43, Dec/Jan '49-'50: "When Metropolis Went Mad!"). A portly man with a monocle over his right eye and an ever-present cigar clenched between his teeth, he is "the greatest con-man of all time" (WF No. 60, Sep/Oct '52: "The Swindler Who Was Honest!"), and "arch swindler" (WF No. 52, Jun/Jul '51: "The Man Who Swindled Superman!"), a "fat and florid master of flim-flam" (S No. 42/1, Sep/Oct '46: "The Men Who Wouldn't Quit!"). The exact positioning of his lone initial is uncertain, for he is referred to as J. Wilbur Wolfingham in one text (WF No. 60, Sep/Oct '52: "The Swindler Who Was Honest!"), as Wilbur J. Wolfingham in another (WF No. 52, Jun/Jul '51: "The Man Who Swindled Superman!"), and simply as Wilbur Wolfingham in all the other nine texts in which he appears (S No. 26/2, Jan/Feb '44: "Comedians' Holiday!"; and others).

J. Wilbur Wolfingham, 1944

Wolfingham proudly regards himself as the "king of confidence men" (S No. 28/1, May/Jun '44: "Lambs versus Wolfingham!"; S No. 35/1, Jul/Aug '45: "Fame for Sale!"), but the texts refer to him as a "chubby chiseler" (S No. 28/1, May/Jun '44: "Lambs versus Wolfingham!"), a "flabby flim-flam artist" (S No. 35/1, Jul/Aug '45: "Fame for Sale!"), a "fat flimflam artist" (S No. 39/3, Mar/Apr '46: "Swindle

in Sweethearts!"), an "arch-chiseler" (WF No. 43, Dec/Jan '49-'50: "When Metropolis Went Mad!"), and a "roly-poly past master of the gentle art of flimflam" (S No. 28/1, May/Jun '44: "Lambs versus Wolfingham!").

SUPERMAN has described J. Wilbur Wolfingham as "one of the most notorious flimflam artists of our century" (Act No. 79, Dec '44: "The Golden Fleece!"), and as "a notorious con-man with a long record of arrests" (WF No. 43, Dec/Jan '49-'50: "When Metropolis Went Mad!"). "Too bad Wolfingham never tried to be an honest salesman!" notes Superman No. 35/1. "He would have ranked with the best of them!" (Jul/Aug '45: "Fame for Sale!").

Ironically, however, "in spite of his crooked intentions," Wolfingham "always seems to do good to everyone but himself!" (S No. 28/1, May/Jun '44: "Lambs versus Wolfingham!"). Typically, Wolfingham's crooked schemes, intended solely for his own enrichment, end up enriching his victims instead, with the result that Wolfingham, having technically committed no crime, walks away impoverished but free to plot again. In the words of Superman No. 35/1:

> Don't buy gold bricks from strangers---but if Wilbur Wolfingham should offer you one, you might take a chance! For when that king of old-time confidence men tries to turn a dishonest penny, everyone seems to come out ahead of the game but himself! [Jul/Aug '45: "Fame for Sale!"].

By January-February 1944 Wilbur Wolfingham has formed Kum-Bak Komedy Films, a film company organized ostensibly for the purpose of enabling a group of old-time silent-movie comedians to stage a comeback, but in reality to enable Wolfingham and his henchmen to defraud the old-timers by getting them to invest their life savings in their own motion picture. After bilking the old comedians for all they are worth, the villains prepare to abscond with the funds, but Superman thwarts the nefarious scheme— and helps the old-timers realize their dream of a comeback—by getting LOIS LANE to buy up Wolfingham's stock in the insolvent film company and then by turning the company's worthless film-in-progress into a guaranteed box-office smash by agreeing to appear in it himself.

Infuriated by this unexpected turn of events, the villains attempt to sabotage the production of the film, but Superman thwarts their attempts, apprehends Wolfingham and his cohorts, and forces them to return all the money they stole (S No. 26/2: "Comedians' Holiday!").

In May-June 1944, after the town of Eden Valley has been struck by a cyclone, Wilbur Wolfingham buys up all the local property at rock-bottom prices and then, feigning generosity toward the townspeople, offers to sell them shares in an "oil well," situated on what is now his property, that is actually nothing more than a well of drinking water slicked over with a thin layer of oil.

After the gullible townsfolk have shelled out their

life savings for shares in the bogus oil well, Wolfingham prepares to abscond with the funds, but Superman arrives on the scene, apprehends Wolfingham, and then single-handedly digs a real oil well for the people of Eden Valley by burrowing deep into the Earth like a human drill.

"I feel almost sorry for him, Clark!" remarks Lois Lane to Clark Kent, as they watch a defeated and destitute Wilbur Wolfingham trudge off down the road. "In spite of his crooked intentions, he always seems to do good to everyone but himself!"

"I'd feel sorry, too," replies Kent, "--if I didn't know he'd be up to his old tricks again the first chance he gets!" (S No. 28/1: "Lambs versus Wolfingham!").

In December 1944, after fleecing a group of gullible METROPOLIS investors by persuading them to invest their money through his Rags to Riches Investment Service, a service that guarantees to increase their investments tenfold within ten days, Wilbur Wolfingham absconds with the funds he has collected and heads out west, where he buys up worthless sheep-grazing land at rock-bottom prices, salts it with bogus gold deposits, and then—after gold has supposedly been "discovered" on his property—sells it back to the local sheepmen at a price many times that which he paid for it.

It is at this point, however, that Superman intervenes, thwarting Wolfingham's efforts to cheat the sheepmen and then forcing the villain to keep his extravagant commitments to his Metropolis investors by paying them all ten times the amount they invested with him. At the end, things have turned out well for everyone but Wolfingham: having made good on all the extravagant promises he never intended to keep, he avoids going to prison, but once again he is impoverished and defeated (Act No. 79: "The Golden Fleece!").

In July-August 1945 Wilbur Wolfingham sets in motion a convoluted scheme to enrich himself by hiring himself out as a public relations expert. After signing on with the mayor of Metropolis to manage his gubernatorial campaign for a fee of $5,000, for example, Wolfingham hires a professional impersonator to impersonate the mayor and deliver an inflammatory speech calculated to destroy the mayor's chances of winning the election.

Since Wolfingham was with the real mayor while the bogus mayor was delivering the damaging speech, however, Wolfingham is in a position to clear the mayor's name and resuscitate his reputation by exposing the man who gave the speech as a "hoaxter," but the wily villain refuses to do this unless the mayor agrees to pay him an additional $10,000, noting that exposure of the so-called hoax is virtually sure to win the mayor a sympathy vote well worth Wolfingham's exorbitant public relations "fee."

The cunning scheme is thwarted by Superman, who forces Wolfingham to make good on all the extravagant public-relations promises he has made to his clients as well as to make restitution of the

J. Wilbur Wolfingham, 1945

unconscionable fees he charged them (S No. 35/1: "Fame for Sale!").

In March-April 1946 the sight of two lovers holding hands in the park inspires Wilbur Wolfingham with an idea "for the greatest swindle of my illustrious career": a lonely hearts agency headed by "Wilbur (Don Juan) Wolfingham," self-proclaimed "expert heart counsellor."

Wolfingham swindles the lovelorn who seek his help in various ways, as when he dupes young Bob Fields into agreeing to let him invest his entire life savings—promising Fields a tenfold return within a single week—as a means of persuading the wealthy father of the girl Fields loves that Fields is a prodigious young man who should be given permission to marry his daughter. Superman intervenes to thwart the various lonely-hearts swindles, however, using his super-powers and super-ingenuity to make good on the extravagant promises that Wolfingham made to his victims and forcing the villain to return the money he stole from them (S No. 39/3: "Swindle in Sweethearts!").

In September-October 1946, after overhearing three wealthy members of the Retired Executives Club complaining about how bored they are with retirement, Wilbur Wolfingham concocts an elaborate scheme to swindle the retired tycoons out of their fortunes by persuading them to finance the creation of Second Life, Incorporated, an industrial community which is ostensibly designed to enable the unhappy retirees "to go back to the happy, happy days of hard labor, and create a new industrial empire all over again!"

By pocketing the money that the retired tycoons give him for setting up the community, and by committing them to ambitious industrial contracts which require them to produce vast quantities of goods under impossible deadlines or else forfeit lavish penalties to him, Wolfingham hopes to bleed his victims white, but Superman intervenes to thwart the swindle, fulfilling the impossible contracts with his super-powers and forcing the wily villain to return to the retirees the money he stole from them (S No. 42/1: "The Men Who Wouldn't Quit!").

By April 1947 Wilbur Wolfingham has concocted an intricate scheme to bilk four wealthy victims out of $250,000 apiece by posing as the inventor of a remarkable technique for inducing suspended animation which, claims Wolfingham, makes it possible for a person to fall into a deep sleep for twenty-five years and to reawaken a quarter-century later, unaffected by the aging process, to enjoy the wealth that his investments have earned during the twenty-five years he was fast asleep.

Lured by the tempting idea of amassing even greater wealth than they already possess without any of the toil or worry normally required for financial success, Wolfingham's four intended victims eagerly pay the villain the $250,000 apiece he demands of them in return for being put in suspended animation, unaware that Wolfingham plans only to put them to sleep with a harmless anesthetic gas for about ten hours while he absconds with his ill-gotten loot.

Superman intervenes to thwart the scheme and recover the stolen $1,000,000, however, and in the process he teaches Wolfingham's four intended victims a much-needed lesson: that the "world of tomorrow" will only be the world that we ourselves create today, and that that world will be "shabby" and "poverty-stricken" if, as the four victims tried to do, "everybody leaves the work for the other fellow to do, and shirks his own share of it" (Act No. 107: "Journey into Ruin!").

In January 1948, after coming into possession of a worthless mining claim somewhere in the frozen Arctic, Wilbur Wolfingham dupes gullible but well-intentioned real-estate developer "Miracle" Jack Muldoon into paying him $10,000 for a half-interest in the claim—which comprises an entire Arctic valley—by selling Muldoon on the ludicrous notion that the ice-covered valley could be transformed into a tropical paradise by utilizing radiated heat from a nearby volcanic spring.

When Muldoon gamely attempts to fulfill this impossible dream, Superman lends a hand with his super-powers to make it come true, and when Wolfingham attempts to enrich himself by auctioning off the half-interest in the Arctic valley that he still controls, Superman intervenes to deprive him of his ill-gotten gains so that they may be used to benefit the valley's residents (Act No. 116: "The Wizard of Winter!").

In December 1949-January 1950, by posing as a fellow scientist, Wilbur Wolfingham dupes MR. HERVEY into providing him with a supply of his phenomenal new fertilizer, ostensibly so that he can use it for research, but in reality so that he can fertilize the ground around Metropolis and cause a citywide epidemic of oxygen narcosis. Then, while everyone in Metropolis is punch-drunk and slaphappy due to the overabundance of oxygen in the city's air, Wolfingham moves about the city turning the general light-headedness to his own advantage, as when he cashes a worthless check for $1,000,000 at a Metropolis bank while the bank manager is too giddy from the overoxygenated air even to inquire whether Wolfingham has $1,000,000 in his account.

Superman, however, who has remained unaffected by the oxygen narcosis, soon realizes exactly what is afoot, and before long he has thwarted Wolfingham's scheme through the simple expedient of burning up Metropolis's excess oxygen by heating up the air with a gigantic flamethrower. With the excess oxygen gone, the general giddiness vanishes, and Wolfingham is arrested by Metropolis police moments afterward for passing a bad check (WF No. 43: "When Metropolis Went Mad!").

In June-July 1951, after Wilbur Wolfingham's next-door neighbor, an elderly widow, has become a finalist in a DAILY PLANET sponsored television quiz program in which the grand prize is the fulfillment of three wishes by Superman, Wolfingham surreptitiously fixes the contest to ensure that his neighbor will win and then prevails upon the kindly widow—who does not suspect she won the contest unfairly—to make three requests of Superman which, although they seem innocuous, are actually calculated to enable Wolfingham to reap huge profits.

One request the widow makes of Superman, for example, is for flowering fruit trees to adorn her front lawn. Superman fulfills this modest request at superspeed, never suspecting that Wolfingham has capitalized on the sudden appearance of the fully grown trees in order to bilk a gullible farmer out of thousands of dollars by persuading him that the trees were produced by a new type of seed capable of producing a mature tree within only a few minutes' time. Ultimately, however, Superman becomes aware of Wolfingham's swindle, and, through an elaborate ruse of his own, he tricks the villain into relinquishing his ill-gotten gains and then unceremoniously carts him off to jail (WF No. 52: "The Man Who Swindled Superman!").

In September-October 1952, following Wilbur Wolfingham's release from prison, John Whisk, "an unsuccessful inventor with a larcenous heart," concocts an elaborate scheme to bilk the notorious con man out of $5,000 by selling him the rights to a totally worthless invention. "What a feather in my cap if I could put one over on that old swindler," thinks Whisk to himself, "...not to mention that if anything went wrong, no one would ever believe I swindled him!"

After building a worthless but nonetheless impressive-looking contraption and duping Wolfingham into believing that the device operates on a "new mechanical principle" that will enable it to revolutionize the field of engineering, Whisk sells Wolfingham the rights to it for $5,000. But when the unsuspecting Wolfingham begins to manufacture and sell the machine in an honest effort at engaging in legitimate business, the machines he manufactures turn out to be useless, and Wolfingham, the victim of his past reputation, is widely assumed to have perpetrated a swindle.

Superman, however, believes the old con man when he insists he has not deliberately swindled anyone, and ultimately, by making a few changes of his own in Whisk's worthless machine, the Man of Steel is able to convert it into a serviceable "solar heating plant," a useful invention that enables Wolfingham to recoup his losses.

"So Whisk is nothing more than a common swindler...one of that vile species who preys on his trusting fellows!" exclaims Wolfingham with ironic indignation. "Ah well, thanks to you, **Superman**, an honest man like myself has the last laugh on that crook!" (WF No. 60: "The Swindler Who Was Honest!").

WONDER-MAN. A mysterious super-hero, his true identity unknown, who appears in METROPOLIS in August 1963—clad in a light purple costume with a black belt; yellow trunks, boots, and cape; and with a yellow letter "W" emblazoned on his chest—and performs a series of stunning super-feats that soon have him eclipsing SUPERMAN as the great hero of Metropolis. Wonder-Man, who is invulnerable to KRYPTONITE and yet endowed with all the super-powers of Superman, is in reality Ajax, until recently the strongest of Superman's own Superman robots, whose super-sophisticated robot mind has been transferred out of its robot body—and into an utterly lifelike "chemically-made android body"—by members of the SUPERMAN REVENGE SQUAD as part of their elaborate plot to destroy Superman (S No. 163/1: "Wonder-Man, the New Hero of Metropolis!"). (*See* SUPERMAN REVENGE SQUAD, THE.)

WONG, RICHARD. A Chinese youngster in ME-TROPOLIS's Chinatown, forbidden by his grandfather to attend the Chinese New Year festivities until he repays a $3.00 debt to a friend, who earns the money he needs in the nick of time when CLARK KENT graciously gives him an odd job to do at the DAILY PLANET. "Golly..." beams a grateful Richard. "You're just as good as **Superman**, Mr. Kent!" (S No. 54/2, Sep/Oct '48: "The Secret of the Chinese Dragon!").

WORDENSHIRE, EARL OF. The British nobleman who is secretly the KNIGHT (BM No. 62/2, Dec/Jan '50-'51: "The Batman of England!").

WRECKER, THE. The leader of a gang of criminals and savage "dictator of destruction," so named because of the wreckage he causes when he commits his "sensational crimes." After carrying out a series of destructive escapades, however, as when they blow a hole in the Empire Dam and flood the valley beneath it in order to loot the local bank by submarine, the Wrecker and his henchmen are apprehended by SUPERMAN in September-October 1948 (S No. 54/1: "The Wrecker").

WYMAN (Superintendent). The sadistic superintendent of the Coreytown prison, a verminous hellhole where hapless chain-gang laborers endure a litany of horrors—including starvation, the sweatbox, and blood-chilling whippings inflicted by Wyman "in a murderous frenzy of sadistic hate." After deliberately allowing himself to be convicted of a crime in Coreytown, "where justice is a mockery," and sentenced to the chain gang under an alias, SUPERMAN gives the evil Wyman a taste of his own brutal medicine, drags the state's pusillanimous Governor Bixby out of bed to witness the horrors of the prison, and accumulates sufficient photographic evidence to send Wyman to prison and bring about a series of long-overdue reforms in the life at the Coreytown prison (Act No. 10, Mar '39).

WYTE, PARRI. The hard-driving editor of the *Daily Solar System*, the thirtieth-century newspaper where CRAIG KING is employed as a "telenews reporter." Wyte, a "remote descendant" of PERRY WHITE, is a perfect look-alike for his twentieth-century ancestor (Act No. 215, Apr '56: "The Superman of Tomorrow").

X

X (Count). "A much-wanted master spy"—the mastermind behind the recent theft of "the Navy's new secret air-torpedo" from a local Navy yard—whose capture by the METROPOLIS police at "an obscure waterfront warehouse" in June 1963 comes as the culmination of an elaborate ruse in which SUPERMAN pretends to have murdered CLARK KENT in a fit of jealousy over LOIS LANE so that Count X's underworld cohorts, who know that Kent has learned the scheduled date of their next secret meeting with the Count, will allow the date and place of their rendezvous to remain unchanged in the belief that Kent is dead and their secret safe (Act No. 301: "The Trial of Superman!"). The story is in many respects similar to Superman No. 62/2 (Jan/Feb '50: "The People vs. Superman!"). (*See* ACE, THE.)

XANU. An evil extradimensional scientist and would-be dictator who inhabits a bizarre world enterable from the earthly dimension by means of an antique mirror, apparently "made centuries ago" by "sorcerers from their world or ours," which serves as "a door between the two worlds." Entering the strange mirror-world with BATMAN and ROBIN in November 1961 in hopes of curing Batman of the freakish qualities he acquired during an earlier visit there, SUPERMAN defeats the evil Xanu and puts an end to his dictatorial ambitions (WF No. 121: "The Mirror Batman!").

XASNU. A diabolical "plant intelligence" from the far-distant planet Zelm, the advance guard of a race of sinister "plant aliens" bent on conquering the Earth, that seizes control of the body of PERRY WHITE in July 1961, only to be destroyed finally by a chunk of white KRYPTONITE hurled at it by SUPERGIRL (Act No. 278: "The Super Powers of Perry White!"). (*See* WHITE, PERRY.)

XENON. The so-called "twin world of Krypton," a far-distant planet—evidently the moon of the planet KRYPTON until it "spun out of its orbit and left Krypton forever"—which is smaller than Krypton in size but otherwise identical to it in virtually every respect. Xenon is the home of the scientist ZOLL ORR, who is a perfect look-alike for SUPERMAN's father JOR-EL. Zoll Orr is also the father of Kell Orr, a young man who bears an uncanny resemblance to Superman. When Xenon is menaced by earthquakes and volcanic eruptions in February 1958, heralding the onset of a chain reaction within its uranium core identical to the one that once doomed Krypton, Superman courageously pits his powers against the wave of disasters and ultimately devises a means of neutralizing the radioactivity at the planet's core so that the potentially cataclysmic chain reaction can be halted and Xenon rescued from imminent destruction (S No. 119: "The Second Superman!" chs. 1-3—"The World That Was Krypton's Twin"; "A Double for Superman"; "Superman's Mightiest Quest").

XERON. The extradimensional world—referred to also as Xeros—which is the home of the villainous VATHGAR (WF No. 118, Jun '61: "The Creature That Was Exchanged for Superman!").

XIRT-NHOJ. The magic phrase which, when spoken aloud by MR. MXYZPTLK, returns the pesky extradimensional imp to his home dimension after he has legally changed his name to John Trix in October 1961. Xirt-Nhoj is John Trix spelled backwards (S No. 148/2: "Mr. Mxyzptlk's Super-Mischief!").

XL-49. A SUPERMAN scholar of the far-distant future—endowed, apparently through scientific means, with mighty super-powers identical to Superman's—who journeys to the twentieth century via time machine for the purpose of determining whether or not Superman ever married LOIS LANE and, if not, of taking some positive action to promote a marriage between them.

After introducing himself as a super-hero from the future named Futureman, XL-49 embarks on a whirlwind "super-courtship" of Lois Lane, apparently in the hope that this will provoke Superman into offering to marry her himself. Lois eventually accepts Futureman's proposal—at first in an attempt to make Superman jealous, then out of a desire to spite the Man of Steel for failing to propose to her—but later changes her mind at the last possible moment after an elaborate ploy engineered by XL-49 has misled her into believing that Superman has intervened to express his love for her in such a way as to hold out hope of an eventual proposal.

Back in the distant future, in what may be the thirtieth century A.D., XL-49 informs a colleague that although Superman has not yet married Lois Lane, he believes he has succeeded in putting the Man of Steel "on the...path" toward matrimony (S No. 121/1, May '58: "The Bride of Futureman!").

XLYM. A "planet of another star" with a science far advanced over that of Earth. In July-August 1958, after having observed both BATMAN and SUPERMAN through their planet's "ultra-telescopes," two of Xlym's inhabitants become embroiled in a bitter quarrel over which of the two heroes would perform the most impressive feats if both were endowed with the superhuman powers of Superman. In a misguided effort to settle their wager, the two aliens teleport Batman and Superman to Xlym, endow Batman with super-powers identical to Superman's by means of a special "super-power-ray," transform both men from close friends into bitter rivals by subjecting them to a potent "hate-ray," eradicate all memory of their interplanetary visit with a special "amnesia-ray," and then teleport them back to Earth to observe which of them performs the most breathtaking feats now that they are evenly matched.

For a time, Batman and Superman astound the world with their bitter, potentially destructive, and seemingly senseless personal rivalry, but after a time Batman's super-powers suddenly vanish and the personalities of the two men return to normal, apparently because the aliens' superior on the planet Xlym became aware of his subordinates' mischief and took the appropriate superscientific steps to correct it (WF No. 95: "The Battle of the Super-Heroes!").

X-156-99F. The "red star" which is the sun of the planet LEXOR (Act No. 318, Nov '64: "The Death of Luthor!").

X-PLAM. A kindly, warm-hearted man from the mid-twenty-fourth century A.D. who journeys to the twentieth century via "time machine" and persuades LOIS LANE to marry him, firstly by showing her a future edition of the DAILY PLANET—an historical document in X-Plam's own era—in which their marriage is announced, and secondly by suggesting that she might be happier married to him than waiting interminably for SUPERMAN. Lois Lane marries X-Plam—and flies off into the future with him—out of a desire to spite Superman and to prove to herself that she can be happy without him, but when X-Plam sees how truly wretched she is in a life without Superman, he willingly sacrifices his life to return her to her own era by fatally overexposing himself to the "radioactive fuel that powers [his] time machine" (S No. 136/1, Apr '60: "The Man Who Married Lois Lane!").

Y

Y'BAR. The far-distant planet which is the home of the evil sorcerer ZERNO (WF No. 127, Aug '62: "The Sorcerer from the Stars!").

YEAST-MEN. The name used to describe the yeastlike humanoid extraterrestrial aliens—also referred to as "yeast-people"—who come upon SUPER-MAN after he has been accidentally rendered unconscious by KRYPTONITE and carry him back with them to their far-distant planet in the belief that they have captured a specimen of the average earthling. Severely weakened by the kryptonite collar around his neck—which he had placed there himself in an unsuccessful attempt to build up a kryptonite immunity—and unable to duplicate the "strange hissing speech" of his captors in order to communicate with them, Superman is studied and tested like a laboratory animal, and then patronized and coddled like a household pet, until finally he succeeds in burning off his kryptonite collar, regaining his super-strength, and persuading the "yeast-men" that he is not a lower animal at all, but rather an intelligent being like themselves entitled to his freedom and treatment as an equal (S No. 84/2, Sep/Oct '53: "A Doghouse for Superman!").

Z

ZAK-KUL. A "renegade scientist" of KANDOR, sought by the Kandorian police for crimes he committed on KRYPTON, who escapes from the bottle city in October 1958, enlarges himself to normal human size by means of an ingenious size-changing apparatus powered by the radioactive element ILLIUM-349, and then transforms himself into a SUPERMAN look-alike with the aid of an "electronic plastic surgery" machine—or "face-molding instrument"—on display in the FORTRESS OF SOLITUDE, all as part of an elaborate scheme to impersonate Superman permanently on Earth so that he can avoid being returned to Kandor to stand trial for his crimes.

With the real Superman imprisoned in the bottle city as the result of LOIS LANE's having mistaken him for the impostor and having used Zak-Kul's size-changing apparatus to reduce the Man of Steel to microscopic size, Zak-Kul—now clad in a spare Superman costume stolen from the Fortress of Solitude—literally usurps Superman's life, capturing criminals and performing super-heroic deeds, basking in the real Superman's fame and glory, even going so far as to become "an ardent suitor of Lois Lane."

Believing that she is being courted by the real Superman, Lois Lane joyously accepts Zak-Kul's proposal of marriage ("The answer is yes...yes...a million times yes!" she exclaims ecstatically; "Hurry...take me to the justice of the peace at superspeed...before you change your mind!"), and for a time the couple are actually husband and wife. "I'm the happiest girl on Earth!" thinks Lois as she and the bogus Superman share a passionate embrace. **"Superman** is my husband!"

Before long, however, Zak-Kul comes to the conclusion that he will have to kill his new bride to prevent her from learning that she has wed an impostor, and Lois is rescued from seemingly certain doom only by the heroic intervention of Superman, who escapes from Kandor in the nick of time to save Lois, apprehend his impersonator, and return the villain to the bottle city to stand trial for his crimes.

"I was married to **Superman** for a while...but the **wrong one!"** sighs Lois to Clark Kent soon afterward. "The courts, of course, annulled the marriage! Oh, Clark, will the **right Superman** ever propose to me?"

"Er...how would I know, Lois?" replies Clark Kent slyly (Act No. 245: "The Shrinking Superman!").

Zak-Kul's size-changing apparatus, confiscated by Superman, is now on display in the Fortress of Solitude (S No. 158, Jan '63: "Superman in Kandor" pts. I-III—"Invasion of the Mystery Super-Men!"; "The Dynamic Duo of Kandor!"; "The City of Super-People!").

ZAR. The far-distant planet which is the home of the playful creature GOLLO (Act No. 234, Nov '57: "The Creature of 1,000 Disguises").

ZEE (Professor). An evil scientist who, working with his colleague, Dr. Cardos, inside "a hidden [laboratory] retreat within a semi-extinct volcano somewhere in the mountains of a far-western state," has performed countless "revolting experiments" in "increasing the size of living organisms" in the hope of creating an army of zombilike human giants subject entirely to their control. When the awful work is finally completed, a horde of terrible giants, towering above the tallest trees, descends on the western United States, looting and killing, smashing trains and houses, and crushing everything in their path. Professor Zee and Dr. Cardos are ultimately trampled to death by fleeing giants when SUPERMAN demolishes their hidden laboratory, and the giants all drown in a massive flood produced by a glacier melted by Superman (S No. 8/1, Jan/Feb '41).

ZELM. The far-distant planet which is the home of the diabolical "plant alien" XASNU (Act No. 278, Jul '61: "The Super Powers of Perry White!").

ZERNO. An evil sorcerer from the far-distant planet Y'bar who is able, by means of a "strange crystal" in his possession, to summon instantaneously from distant planets awesome weapons and creatures which he can force to do his bidding. Zerno arrives on Earth in August 1962, determined to "loot and plunder" the planet and to accumulate a large supply of bronze, a metal with the power to rob all inhabitants of Y'bar "completely of [their] physical and mental strength," so that, once back on his native planet, he can "gain complete control over [his] people." Zerno and his henchman Sborg are ultimately defeated and apprehended through the heroic efforts of BATMAN, ROBIN, and SUPERMAN (WF No. 127: "The Sorcerer from the Stars!").

ZHOR. A far-distant planet with a chlorine atmosphere. In May 1963, on an uninhabited Pacific island, SUPERMAN encounters a band of Zhorian space explorers who have been stranded on the island ever since their spacecraft was severely damaged by a hurtling meteor. After learning the details of the aliens' plight, Superman repairs the damaged spacecraft and sends the Zhorian explorers safely on their way (S No. 161/2: "Superman Goes to War!").

ZIGI AND ZAGI. A pair of likable, albeit somewhat rambunctious, young brothers—Zigi has honey-blond hair, Zagi's is black—who live with their

Zagi and Zigi

father, mother, and lovely dark-haired sister Zyra (Act No. 316, Sep '64: "Zigi and Zagi's Trap for Superman!") in Centauri City, "on a planet in the Alpha Centauri system," 23,342,816,000,000 miles from Earth.

Although the texts describe them as "mischievous imps" (Act No. 315, Aug '64: "The Juvenile Delinquents from Space!") and "conniving scamps" (Act No. 316, Sep '64: "Zigi and Zagi's Trap for Superman!"), they are actually well-meaning, if fun-loving, youngsters who, arriving on Earth from their home planet—which is described as "far more scientifically advanced than Earth"—in August 1964, unintentionally wreak havoc because of their "weird scientific powers" and lack of familiarity with earthmen's ways (Act No. 315: "The Juvenile Delinquents from Space!"). Even SUPERMAN, who is driven frantic by their antics, comes to think of them fondly as "two of the nicest kids I've ever met!" (Act No. 316, Sep '64: "Zigi and Zagi's Trap for Superman!").

By August 1964 Zigi and Zagi have arrived on the planet Earth, light-years away from their native planet, as the result of having accidentally activated the controls of their father's new "space-runabout" while admiring it in front of their home in Centauri City. As the youngsters enthusiastically explore the city of METROPOLIS, their unfamiliarity with Earth customs and their command of extraterrestrial super-science combine to produce unintended mayhem, as when the brothers obligingly melt the bars of a jail cell with their "pocket blaster," thereby allowing an inmate to escape, in the naïve belief that the convict is an honest fellow who has somehow locked himself in a barred cage by mistake.

Groaning that "Those little trouble-makers create more mischief than **Mr. Mxyzptlk**" (*see* MXYZPTLK [MR.]), Superman begs the alien youngsters to go back home again, but Zigi and Zagi are having too good a time to leave, and the Man of Steel is forced to resort to an elaborate ruse—designed to make the young brothers homesick for their native planet—in order to coax the youngsters into leaving Earth.

Ultimately, Zigi and Zagi blast off for home in their father's space runabout—to Superman's everlasting relief—unaware that "psychopathic killer" "SLASH" SABRE, an escape from Metropolis Prison, has stowed away aboard their spacecraft (Act No. 315: "The Juvenile Delinquents from Space!").

When Superman learns that escaped convict "Slash" Sabre is en route to the Alpha Centauri system aboard Zigi and Zagi's spacecraft, he flashes into outer space in hot pursuit. By the time he arrives in Centauri City, however, the youngsters—who have grown quite fond of Superman—have apprehended Sabre on their own, and when they learn that Superman intends to leave their planet as soon as he has located Sabre and taken him into custody, they decide to conceal the fact that they have already captured the convict as a means of prolonging Superman's stay on their native planet.

The youngsters also concoct a scheme to make Superman their brother-in-law by marrying him off to their lovely sister Zyra, but the Man of Steel nips this scheme in the bud by successfully reuniting Zyra with the real love of her life, a "brilliant young scientist" named Zarthur, who has been erroneously believed dead ever since he failed to return from an exploratory mission in outer space. Finally, however, after having failed in his efforts to locate "Slash" Sabre, Superman returns to Metropolis empty-handed, believing the "maniacal murderer" must still be at large. But when he arrives at Metropolis Prison he finds that Sabre is already safely back in custody, having materialized earlier at the prison inside an alien "teleport bubble."

"Those mischief-makers caused me a lot of trouble," muses Superman aloud, now realizing that Zigi and Zagi must have recaptured "Slash" Sabre and whisked him back to prison on their own. "But they did it because they liked having me around. I'm flattered ... they were two of the nicest kids I've ever met!" (Act No. 316, Sep '64: "Zigi and Zagi's Trap for Superman!").

ZIMBA, ROLF. The "power-mad individual" who is the head of the Gold Badge Organization, a "secret terrorist organization" determined to "smash the government" and seize control of the United States. In July-August 1941 its members blow up the entire METROPOLIS suburb of Metrodale in retaliation for the recent arrest of some Gold Badge Organization members there, then extort tribute money from a Metropolis bank president by telling him that his bank will be "levelled to ashes in a few minutes" unless he complies with their demand. Most of the terrorists are ultimately killed or captured in a U.S. Army sweep organized by SUPERMAN, and Zimba and his few remaining henchmen perish in the crash of their getaway plane when its controls are damaged during a climactic battle with Superman (S No. 11/1).

ZOLAR. "A sinister individual," presiding over a bloodthirsty band of fanatical Arab assassins and headquartered in a secret "desert stronghold" somewhere in the Sahara, whose "thirst for radium drives